TWELFTH EDITION

OPERATIONS MANAGEMENT

Sustainability and Supply Chain Management

JAY
HEIZER

Jesse H. Jones Professor of Business Administration
Texas Lutheran University

BARRY
RENDER

Charles Harwood Professor of Operations Management
Graduate School of Business
Rollins College

CHUCK
MUNSON

Professor of Operations Management
Carson College of Business
Washington State University

PEARSON

Boston   Columbus   Indianapolis   New York   San Francisco
Amsterdam   Cape Town   Dubai   London   Madrid   Milan   Munich   Paris   Montreal   Toronto
Delhi   Mexico City   Sao Paulo   Sydney   Hong Kong   Seoul   Singapore   Taipei   Tokyo

Vice President, Business Publishing: Donna Battista
Editor-in-Chief: Stephanie Wall
Acquisitions Editor: Daniel Tylman
Editorial Assistant: Linda Albelli
Vice President, Product Marketing: Maggie Moylan
Director of Marketing, Digital Services and Products:
    Jeanette Koskinas
Field Marketing Manager: Lenny Ann Kucenski
Product Marketing Assistant: Jessica Quazza
Team Lead, Program Management: Ashley Santora
Program Manager: Claudia Fernandes
Team Lead, Project Management: Jeff Holcomb
Senior Project Manager: Jacqueline A. Martin
Operations Specialist: Carol Melville
Creative Director: Blair Brown
Art Director: Janet Slowik

Vice President, Director of Digital Strategy and Assessment:
    Paul Gentile
Manager of Learning Applications: Paul DeLuca
Director, Digital Studio: Sacha Laustsen
Digital Studio Manager: Diane Lombardo
Digital Studio Project Manager: Andra Skaalrud
Digital Studio Project Manager: Regina DaSilva
Digital Studio Project Manager: Alana Coles
Digital Studio Project Manager: Robin Lazrus
Digital Content Project Lead: Courtney Kamauf
Full-Service Project Management and Composition:
    Cenveo® Publisher Services
Interior and Cover Designer: Cenveo® Publisher Services
Cover Photos: Alaska Airlines
Printer/Binder: Manufactured in the United States by RR Donnelley
Cover Printer: Phoenix Color/Hagerstown

Microsoft and/or its respective suppliers make no representations about the suitability of the information contained in the documents and related graphics published as part of the services for any purpose. All such documents and related graphics are provided "as is" without warranty of any kind. Microsoft and/or its respective suppliers hereby disclaim all warranties and conditions with regard to this information, including all warranties and conditions of merchantability, whether express, implied or statutory, fitness for a particular purpose, title and non-infringement. In no event shall Microsoft and/or its respective suppliers be liable for any special, indirect or consequential damages or any damages whatsoever resulting from loss of use, data or profits, whether in an action of contract, negligence or other tortious action, arising out of or in connection with the use or performance of information available from the services.

The documents and related graphics contained herein could include technical inaccuracies or typographical errors. Changes are periodically added to the information herein. Microsoft and/or its respective suppliers may make improvements and/or changes in the product(s) and/or the program(s) described herein at any time. Partial screen shots may be viewed in full within the software version specified.

Microsoft® and Windows® are registered trademarks of the Microsoft Corporation in the U.S.A. and other countries. This book is not sponsored or endorsed by or affiliated with the Microsoft Corporation.

Library of Congress Cataloging-in-Publication Data

Heizer, Jay.
  [Production and operations management]
  Operations management; sustainability and supply chain management / Jay Heizer, Jesse H. Jones Professor of Business Administration, Texas Lutheran University, Barry Render, Charles Harwood Professor of Operations Management, Crummer Graduate School of Business, Rollins College, Chuck Munson, Professor of Operations Management, Carson College of Business, Washington State University. -- Twelfth edition.
    pages cm
  Original edition published under the Title: Production and operations management.
  Includes bibliographical references and index.
  ISBN 978-0-13-413042-2 -- ISBN 0-13-413042-1
1. Production management. I. Render, Barry. II. Munson, Chuck. III. Title.
  TS155.H3725 2015
  658.5--dc23
          2015036857

2 16

ISBN 10:   0-13-413042-1
ISBN 13: 978-0-13-413042-2

STUDENT VALUE EDITION

TWELFTH EDITION

OPERATIONS MANAGEMENT

Sustainability and Supply Chain Management

JAY HEIZER | **BARRY RENDER** | **CHUCK MUNSON**

ISBN-13: 978-0-13-416351-2
ISBN-10: 0-13-416351-6

Before purchasing this text, please be sure this is the correct book for your course. Once this package has been opened, you may not be able to return it to your bookstore.

ALWAYS LEARNING   **PEARSON**

To Karen Heizer Herrmann, all a sister could ever be

J.H.

To Donna, Charlie, and Jesse

B.R.

To Kim, Christopher, and Mark Munson for their unwavering support,
and to Bentonville High School teachers Velma Reed and Cheryl Gregory,
who instilled in me the importance of detail and a love of learning

C.M.

ABOUT THE AUTHORS

JAY HEIZER

Professor Emeritus, the Jesse H. Jones Chair of Business Administration, Texas Lutheran University, Seguin, Texas. He received his B.B.A. and M.B.A. from the University of North Texas and his Ph.D. in Management and Statistics from Arizona State University. He was previously a member of the faculty at the University of Memphis, the University of Oklahoma, Virginia Commonwealth University, and the University of Richmond. He has also held visiting positions at Boston University, George Mason University, the Czech Management Center, and the Otto-Von-Guericke University, Magdeburg.

Dr. Heizer's industrial experience is extensive. He learned the practical side of operations management as a machinist apprentice at Foringer and Company, as a production planner for Westinghouse Airbrake, and at General Dynamics, where he worked in engineering administration. In addition, he has been actively involved in consulting in the OM and MIS areas for a variety of organizations, including Philip Morris, Firestone, Dixie Container Corporation, Columbia Industries, and Tenneco. He holds the CPIM certification from APICS—the Association for Operations Management.

Professor Heizer has co-authored 5 books and has published more than 30 articles on a variety of management topics. His papers have appeared in the *Academy of Management Journal, Journal of Purchasing, Personnel Psychology, Production & Inventory Control Management, APICS—The Performance Advantage, Journal of Management History, IIE Solutions,* and *Engineering Management,* among others. He has taught operations management courses in undergraduate, graduate, and executive programs.

BARRY RENDER

Professor Emeritus, the Charles Harwood Professor of Operations Management, Crummer Graduate School of Business, Rollins College, Winter Park, Florida. He received his B.S. in Mathematics and Physics at Roosevelt University, and his M.S. in Operations Research and Ph.D. in Quantitative Analysis at the University of Cincinnati. He previously taught at George Washington University, University of New Orleans, Boston University, and George Mason University, where he held the Mason Foundation Professorship in Decision Sciences and was Chair of the Decision Sciences Department. Dr. Render has also worked in the aerospace industry for General Electric, McDonnell Douglas, and NASA.

Professor Render has co-authored 10 textbooks for Pearson, including *Managerial Decision Modeling with Spreadsheets, Quantitative Analysis for Management, Service Management, Introduction to Management Science,* and *Cases and Readings in Management Science. Quantitative Analysis for Management,* now in its 13th edition, is a leading text in that discipline in the United States and globally. Dr. Render's more than 100 articles on a variety of management topics have appeared in *Decision Sciences, Production and Operations Management, Interfaces, Information and Management, Journal of Management Information Systems, Socio-Economic Planning Sciences, IIE Solutions,* and *Operations Management Review,* among others.

Dr. Render has been honored as an AACSB Fellow and was twice named a Senior Fulbright Scholar. He was Vice President of the Decision Science Institute Southeast Region and served as Software Review Editor for *Decision Line* for six years and as Editor of the *New York Times* Operations Management special issues for five years. For nine years, Dr. Render was President of Management Service Associates of Virginia, Inc., whose technology clients included the FBI, NASA, the U.S. Navy, Fairfax County, Virginia, and C&P Telephone. He is currently Consulting Editor to *Pearson Press.*

Dr. Render has received Rollins College's Welsh Award as leading Professor and was selected by Roosevelt University as the recipient of the St. Claire Drake Award for Outstanding Scholarship. Dr. Render also received the Rollins College MBA Student Award for Best Overall Course, and was named Professor of the Year by full-time MBA students.

CHUCK MUNSON

Professor of Operations Management, Carson College of Business, Washington State University, Pullman, Washington. He received his BSBA *summa cum laude* in finance, along with his MSBA and Ph.D. in operations management, from Washington University in St. Louis. For two years, he served as Associate Dean for Graduate Programs in Business at Washington State. He also worked for three years as a financial analyst for Contel Telephone Corporation.

Professor Munson serves as a senior editor for *Production and Operations Management*, and he serves on the editorial review board of four other journals. He has published more than 25 articles in such journals as *Production and Operations Management, IIE Transactions, Decision Sciences, Naval Research Logistics, European Journal of Operational Research, Journal of the Operational Research Society*, and *Annals of Operations Research*. He is editor of the book *The Supply Chain Management Casebook: Comprehensive Coverage and Best Practices in SCM*, and he has co-authored the research monograph *Quantity Discounts: An Overview and Practical Guide for Buyers and Sellers*. He is also coauthor of *Managerial Decision Modeling with Spreadsheets* (4th edition), published by Pearson.

Dr. Munson has taught operations management core and elective courses at the undergraduate, MBA, and Ph.D. levels at Washington State University. He has also conducted several teaching workshops at international conferences and for Ph.D. students at Washington State University. His major awards include being a Founding Board Member of the Washington State University President's Teaching Academy (2004); winning the WSU College of Business Outstanding Teaching Award (2001 and 2015), Research Award (2004), and Service Award (2009 and 2013); and being named the WSU MBA Professor of the Year (2000 and 2008).

Brief Table of Contents

PART ONE   Introduction to Operations Management *1*

Chapter 1   **Operations and Productivity**   1

Chapter 2   **Operations Strategy in a Global Environment**   29

Chapter 3   **Project Management**   59

Chapter 4   **Forecasting**   105

PART TWO   Designing Operations *159*

Chapter 5   **Design of Goods and Services**   159

◆ Supplement 5   Sustainability in the Supply Chain   193

Chapter 6   **Managing Quality**   213

◆ Supplement 6   Statistical Process Control   245

Chapter 7   **Process Strategy**   279

◆ Supplement 7   Capacity and Constraint Management   307

Chapter 8   **Location Strategies**   337

Chapter 9   **Layout Strategies**   367

Chapter 10   **Human Resources, Job Design, and Work Measurement**   407

PART THREE   Managing Operations *441*

Chapter 11   **Supply Chain Management**   441

◆ Supplement 11   Supply Chain Management Analytics   471

Chapter 12   **Inventory Management**   487

Chapter 13   **Aggregate Planning and S&OP**   529

Chapter 14   **Material Requirements Planning (MRP) and ERP**   563

Chapter 15   **Short-Term Scheduling**   599

Chapter 16   **Lean Operations**   635

Chapter 17   **Maintenance and Reliability**   659

PART FOUR   Business Analytics Modules *677*

Module A   **Decision-Making Tools**   677

Module B   **Linear Programming**   699

Module C   **Transportation Models**   729

Module D   **Waiting-Line Models**   747

Module E   **Learning Curves**   775

Module F   **Simulation**   791

ONLINE TUTORIALS

1. **Statistical Tools for Managers**   T1-1

2. **Acceptance Sampling**   T2-1

3. **The Simplex Method of Linear Programming**   T3-1

4. **The MODI and VAM Methods of Solving Transportation Problems**   T4-1

5. **Vehicle Routing and Scheduling**   T5-1

Table of Contents

About the Authors   vi

Preface   xxiii

PART ONE   Introduction to Operations Management   *1*

Chapter 1   Operations and Productivity   1

GLOBAL COMPANY PROFILE: *HARD ROCK CAFE*   2

What Is Operations Management?   4

Organizing to Produce Goods and Services   4

The Supply Chain   6

Why Study OM?   6

What Operations Managers Do   7

The Heritage of Operations Management   8

Operations for Goods and Services   11

    Growth of Services   11

    Service Pay   12

The Productivity Challenge   13

    Productivity Measurement   14

    Productivity Variables   15

    Productivity and the Service Sector   17

Current Challenges in Operations Management   18

Ethics, Social Responsibility, and Sustainability   19

Summary   20

Key Terms   20

Ethical Dilemma   20

Discussion Questions   20

Using Software for Productivity Analysis   21

Solved Problems   21

Problems   22

CASE STUDIES   24

    Uber Technologies, Inc.   24

    Frito-Lay: Operations Management in Manufacturing Video Case   25

    Hard Rock Cafe: Operations Management in Services Video Case   25

Endnotes   26

Rapid Review   27

Self Test   28

Chapter 2   Operations Strategy in a Global Environment   29

GLOBAL COMPANY PROFILE: *BOEING*   30

A Global View of Operations and Supply Chains   32

    Cultural and Ethical Issues   35

Developing Missions and Strategies   35

    Mission   36

    Strategy   36

Achieving Competitive Advantage Through Operations   36

    Competing on Differentiation   37

    Competing on Cost   38

    Competing on Response   39

Issues in Operations Strategy   40

Strategy Development and Implementation   41

    Key Success Factors and Core Competencies   41

    Integrating OM with Other Activities   43

    Building and Staffing the Organization   43

    Implementing the 10 Strategic OM Decisions   44

Strategic Planning, Core Competencies, and Outsourcing   44

    The Theory of Comparative Advantage   46

    Risks of Outsourcing   46

    Rating Outsource Providers   47

Global Operations Strategy Options   49

Summary   50

Key Terms   50

Ethical Dilemma   51

Discussion Questions   51

Using Software to Solve Outsourcing Problems   51

Solved Problems   52

Problems   53

CASE STUDIES   55

    Rapid-Lube   55

    Strategy at Regal Marine   Video Case   55

    Hard Rock Cafe's Global Strategy   Video Case   55

    Outsourcing Offshore at Darden   Video Case   56

Endnotes   56

Rapid Review   57

Self Test   58

Chapter 3   Project Management   59

GLOBAL COMPANY PROFILE: *BECHTEL GROUP*   60

The Importance of Project Management   62

Project Planning   62
  The Project Manager   63
  Work Breakdown Structure   64
Project Scheduling   65
Project Controlling   66
Project Management Techniques: PERT and CPM   67
  The Framework of PERT and CPM   67
  Network Diagrams and Approaches   68
  Activity-on-Node Example   69
  Activity-on-Arrow Example   71
Determining the Project Schedule   71
  Forward Pass   72
  Backward Pass   74
  Calculating Slack Time and Identifying the Critical Path(s)   75
Variability in Activity Times   77
  Three Time Estimates in PERT   77
  Probability of Project Completion   79
Cost-Time Trade-Offs and Project Crashing   82
A Critique of PERT and CPM   85
Using Microsoft Project to Manage Projects   86
Summary   88
Key Terms   88
Ethical Dilemma   89
Discussion Questions   89
Using Software to Solve Project Management Problems   89
Solved Problems   90
Problems   93
CASE STUDIES   98
  Southwestern University: (A)   98
  Project Management at Arnold Palmer Hospital Video Case   99
  Managing Hard Rock's Rockfest   Video Case   100
Endnotes   102
Rapid Review   103
Self Test   104

Chapter 4   Forecasting   105

GLOBAL COMPANY PROFILE: *WALT DISNEY PARKS & RESORTS*   106
What is Forecasting?   108
  Forecasting Time Horizons   108
  Types of Forecasts   109

The Strategic Importance of Forecasting   109
  Supply-Chain Management   109
  Human Resources   110
  Capacity   110
Seven Steps in the Forecasting System   110
Forecasting Approaches   111
  Overview of Qualitative Method   111
  Overview of Quantitative Methods   112
Time-Series Forecasting   112
  Decomposition of a Time Series   112
  Naive Approach   113
  Moving Averages   114
  Exponential Smoothing   116
  Measuring Forecast Error   117
  Exponential Smoothing with Trend Adjustment   120
  Trend Projections   124
  Seasonal Variations in Data   126
  Cyclical Variations in Data   131
Associative Forecasting Methods: Regression and Correlation Analysis   131
  Using Regression Analysis for Forecasting   131
  Standard Error of the Estimate   133
  Correlation Coefficients for Regression Lines   134
  Multiple-Regression Analysis   136
Monitoring and Controlling Forecasts   138
  Adaptive Smoothing   139
  Focus Forecasting   139
Forecasting in the Service Sector   140
Summary   141
Key Terms   141
Ethical Dilemma   141
Discussion Questions   142
Using Software in Forecasting   142
Solved Problems   144
Problems   146
CASE STUDIES   153
  Southwestern University: (B)   153
  Forecasting Ticket Revenue for Orlando Magic Basketball Games   Video Case   154
  Forecasting at Hard Rock Cafe   Video Case   155
Endnotes   156
Rapid Review   157
Self Test   158

PART TWO   Designing Operations   *159*

Chapter 5   Design of Goods and Services   159

GLOBAL COMPANY PROFILE: *REGAL MARINE*   160
Goods and Services Selection   162

Product Strategy Options Support Competitive Advantage   163
Product Life Cycles   164
Life Cycle and Strategy   164

Product-by-Value Analysis 165
Generating New Products 165
Product Development 166
Product Development System 166
Quality Function Deployment (QFD) 166
Organizing for Product Development 169
Manufacturability and Value Engineering 170
Issues for Product Design 171
Robust Design 171
Modular Design 171
Computer-Aided Design (CAD) and Computer-Aided Manufacturing (CAM) 171
Virtual Reality Technology 172
Value Analysis 173
Sustainability and Life Cycle Assessment (LCA) 173
Product Development Continuum 173
Purchasing Technology by Acquiring a Firm 174
Joint Ventures 174
Alliances 175
Defining a Product 175
Make-or-Buy Decisions 176
Group Technology 177
Documents for Production 178
Product Life-Cycle Management (PLM) 178
Service Design 179
Process–Chain–Network (PCN) Analysis 179
Adding Service Efficiency 181
Documents for Services 181
Application of Decision Trees to Product Design 182
Transition to Production 184
Summary 184
Key Terms 185
Ethical Dilemma 185
Discussion Questions 185
Solved Problem 186
Problems 186
CASE STUDIES 189
De Mar's Product Strategy 189
Product Design at Regal Marine Video Case 189
Endnotes 190
Rapid Review 191
Self Test 192

Supplement 5 Sustainability in the Supply Chain 193

Corporate Social Responsibility 194
Sustainability 195
Systems View 195
Commons 195
Triple Bottom Line 195

Design and Production for Sustainability 198
Product Design 198
Production Process 200
Logistics 200
End-of-Life Phase 203
Regulations and Industry Standards 203
International Environmental Policies and Standards 204
Summary 205
Key Terms 205
Discussion Questions 205
Solved Problems 206
Problems 207
CASE STUDIES 208
Building Sustainability at the Orlando Magic's Amway Center Video Case 208
Green Manufacturing and Sustainability at Frito-Lay Video Case 209
Endnotes 210
Rapid Review 211
Self Test 212

Chapter 6 Managing Quality 213

GLOBAL COMPANY PROFILE: *ARNOLD PALMER HOSPITAL* 214
Quality and Strategy 216
Defining Quality 217
Implications of Quality 217
Malcolm Baldrige National Quality Award 218
ISO 9000 International Quality Standards 218
Cost of Quality (COQ) 218
Ethics and Quality Management 219
Total Quality Management 219
Continuous Improvement 220
Six Sigma 221
Employee Empowerment 222
Benchmarking 222
Just-in-Time (JIT) 224
Taguchi Concepts 224
Knowledge of TQM Tools 225
Tools of TQM 226
Check Sheets 226
Scatter Diagrams 227
Cause-and-Effect Diagrams 227
Pareto Charts 227
Flowcharts 228
Histograms 229
Statistical Process Control (SPC) 229
The Role of Inspection 230
When and Where to Inspect 230
Source Inspection 231

    Service Industry Inspection   232

    Inspection of Attributes versus Variables   233

TQM in Services   233

Summary   235

Key Terms   235

Ethical Dilemma   235

Discussion Questions   236

Solved Problems   236

Problems   237

CASE STUDIES   239

    Southwestern University: (C)   239

    The Culture of Quality at Arnold Palmer Hospital
    Video Case   240

    Quality Counts at Alaska Airlines   Video Case   240

    Quality at the Ritz-Carlton Hotel Company
    Video Case   242

Endnotes   242

Rapid Review   243

Self Test   244

Supplement 6   Statistical Process Control   245

Statistical Process Control (SPC)   246

    Control Charts for Variables   248

    The Central Limit Theorem   248

    Setting Mean Chart Limits ($\bar{x}$-Charts)   250

    Setting Range Chart Limits (R-Charts)   253

    Using Mean and Range Charts   254

    Control Charts for Attributes   256

    Managerial Issues and Control Charts   259

Process Capability   260

    Process Capability Ratio (C_p)   260

    Process Capability Index (C_{pk})   261

Acceptance Sampling   262

    Operating Characteristic Curve   263

    Average Outgoing Quality   264

Summary   265

Key Terms   265

Discussion Questions   265

Using Software for SPC   266

Solved Problems   267

Problems   269

CASE STUDIES   274

    Bayfield Mud Company   274

    Frito-Lay's Quality-Controlled Potato Chips
    Video Case   275

    Farm to Fork: Quality at Darden Restaurants
    Video Case   276

Endnotes   276

Rapid Review   277

Self Test   278

Chapter 7   Process Strategy   279

GLOBAL COMPANY PROFILE: *HARLEY-DAVIDSON*   280

Four Process Strategies   282

    Process Focus   282

    Repetitive Focus   283

    Product Focus   284

    Mass Customization Focus   284

    Process Comparison   286

Selection of Equipment   288

Process Analysis and Design   288

    Flowchart   289

    Time-Function Mapping   289

    Process Charts   289

    Value-Stream Mapping   290

    Service Blueprinting   292

Special Considerations for Service Process
    Design   293

Production Technology   294

    Machine Technology   294

    Automatic Identification Systems (AISs) and RFID   295

    Process Control   295

    Vision Systems   296

    Robots   296

    Automated Storage and Retrieval Systems
    (ASRSs)   296

    Automated Guided Vehicles (AGVs)   296

    Flexible Manufacturing Systems (FMSs)   297

    Computer-Integrated Manufacturing (CIM)   297

Technology in Services   298

Process Redesign   298

Summary   299

Key Terms   299

Ethical Dilemma   300

Discussion Questions   300

Solved Problem   300

Problems   301

CASE STUDIES   302

    Rochester Manufacturing's Process Decision   302

    Process Strategy at Wheeled Coach   Video Case   302

    Alaska Airlines: 20-Minute Baggage Process—
    Guaranteed!   Video Case   303

    Process Analysis at Arnold Palmer Hospital
    Video Case   304

Endnotes   304

Rapid Review   305

Self Test   306

Supplement 7   Capacity and Constraint
                Management   307

Capacity   308

    Design and Effective Capacity   309

Capacity and Strategy 311

Capacity Considerations 311

Managing Demand 312

Service-Sector Demand and Capacity Management 313

Bottleneck Analysis and the Theory of Constraints 314

Theory of Constraints 317

Bottleneck Management 317

Break-Even Analysis 318

Single-Product Case 319

Multiproduct Case 320

Reducing Risk with Incremental Changes 322

Applying Expected Monetary Value (EMV) to Capacity Decisions 323

Applying Investment Analysis to Strategy-Driven Investments 324

Investment, Variable Cost, and Cash Flow 324

Net Present Value 324

Summary 326

Key Terms 327

Discussion Questions 327

Using Software for Break-Even Analysis 327

Solved Problems 328

Problems 330

CASE STUDY 333

Capacity Planning at Arnold Palmer Hospital Video Case 333

Endnote 334

Rapid Review 335

Self Test 336

Chapter 8 Location Strategies 337

GLOBAL COMPANY PROFILE: *FEDEX* 338

The Strategic Importance of Location 340

Factors That Affect Location Decisions 341

Labor Productivity 342

Exchange Rates and Currency Risk 342

Costs 342

Political Risk, Values, and Culture 343

Proximity to Markets 343

Proximity to Suppliers 344

Proximity to Competitors (Clustering) 344

Methods of Evaluating Location Alternatives 344

The Factor-Rating Method 345

Locational Cost–Volume Analysis 346

Center-of-Gravity Method 348

Transportation Model 349

Service Location Strategy 350

Geographic Information Systems 351

Summary 353

Key Terms 353

Ethical Dilemma 354

Discussion Questions 354

Using Software to Solve Location Problems 354

Solved Problems 355

Problems 357

CASE STUDIES 362

Southern Recreational Vehicle Company 362

Locating the Next Red Lobster Restaurant Video Case 362

Where to Place the Hard Rock Cafe Video Case 363

Endnote 364

Rapid Review 365

Self Test 366

Chapter 9 Layout Strategies 367

GLOBAL COMPANY PROFILE: *McDONALD'S* 368

The Strategic Importance of Layout Decisions 370

Types of Layout 370

Office Layout 371

Retail Layout 372

Servicescapes 375

Warehouse and Storage Layouts 375

Cross-Docking 376

Random Stocking 377

Customizing 377

Fixed-Position Layout 377

Process-Oriented Layout 378

Computer Software for Process-Oriented Layouts 382

Work Cells 383

Requirements of Work Cells 383

Staffing and Balancing Work Cells 384

The Focused Work Center and the Focused Factory 386

Repetitive and Product-Oriented Layout 386

Assembly-Line Balancing 387

Summary 392

Key Terms 392

Ethical Dilemma 392

Discussion Questions 392

Using Software to Solve Layout Problems 393

Solved Problems 394

Problems 396

CASE STUDIES 402

State Automobile License Renewals 402

Laying Out Arnold Palmer Hospital's New Facility Video Case 402

Facility Layout at Wheeled Coach Video Case 404

Endnotes 404

Rapid Review 405

Self Test 406

Chapter 10 Human Resources, Job Design, and Work Measurement   407

GLOBAL COMPANY PROFILE: *RUSTY WALLACE'S NASCAR RACING TEAM*   408

Human Resource Strategy for Competitive Advantage   410

Constraints on Human Resource Strategy   410

Labor Planning   411

Employment-Stability Policies   411

Work Schedules   411

Job Classifications and Work Rules   412

Job Design   412

Labor Specialization   412

Job Expansion   413

Psychological Components of Job Design   413

Self-Directed Teams   414

Motivation and Incentive Systems   415

Ergonomics and the Work Environment   415

Methods Analysis   417

The Visual Workplace   420

Labor Standards   420

Historical Experience   421

Time Studies   421

Predetermined Time Standards   425

Work Sampling   427

Ethics   430

Summary   430

Key Terms   430

Ethical Dilemma   431

Discussion Questions   431

Solved Problems   432

Problems   434

CASE STUDIES   437

Jackson Manufacturing Company   437

The "People" Focus: Human Resources at Alaska Airlines   Video Case   437

Hard Rock's Human Resource Strategy Video Case   438

Endnotes   438

Rapid Review   439

Self Test   440

PART THREE   Managing Operations   *441*

Chapter 11 Supply Chain Management   441

GLOBAL COMPANY PROFILE: *DARDEN RESTAURANTS*   442

The Supply Chain's Strategic Importance   444

Sourcing Issues: Make-or-Buy and Outsourcing   446

Make-or-Buy Decisions   447

Outsourcing   447

Six Sourcing Strategies   447

Many Suppliers   447

Few Suppliers   447

Vertical Integration   448

Joint Ventures   448

Keiretsu Networks   448

Virtual Companies   449

Supply Chain Risk   449

Risks and Mitigation Tactics   450

Security and JIT   451

Managing the Integrated Supply Chain   451

Issues in Managing the Integrated Supply Chain   451

Opportunities in Managing the Integrated Supply Chain   452

Building the Supply Base   454

Supplier Evaluation   454

Supplier Development   454

Negotiations   455

Contracting   455

Centralized Purchasing   455

E-Procurement   456

Logistics Management   456

Shipping Systems   456

Warehousing   457

Third-Party Logistics (3PL)   458

Distribution Management   459

Ethics and Sustainable Supply Chain Management   460

Supply Chain Management Ethics   460

Establishing Sustainability in Supply Chains   460

Measuring Supply Chain Performance   461

Assets Committed to Inventory   461

Benchmarking the Supply Chain   463

The SCOR Model   463

Summary   464

Key Terms   465

Ethical Dilemma   465

Discussion Questions   465

Solved Problems   465

Problems   466

CASE STUDIES   467

Darden's Global Supply Chains   Video Case   467

Supply Chain Management at Regal Marine
Video Case 467

Arnold Palmer Hospital's Supply Chain
Video Case 468

Endnote 468

Rapid Review 469

Self Test 470

Supplement 11 Supply Chain Management Analytics 471

Techniques for Evaluating Supply Chains 472

Evaluating Disaster Risk in the Supply Chain 472

Managing the Bullwhip Effect 474

A Bullwhip Effect Measure 475

Supplier Selection Analysis 476

Transportation Mode Analysis 477

Warehouse Storage 478

Summary 479

Discussion Questions 480

Solved Problems 480

Problems 482

Rapid Review 485

Self Test 486

Chapter 12 Inventory Management 487

GLOBAL COMPANY PROFILE: *AMAZON.COM* 488

The Importance of Inventory 490

Functions of Inventory 490

Types of Inventory 490

Managing Inventory 491

ABC Analysis 491

Record Accuracy 493

Cycle Counting 493

Control of Service Inventories 494

Inventory Models 495

Independent vs. Dependent Demand 495

Holding, Ordering, and Setup Costs 495

Inventory Models for Independent Demand 496

The Basic Economic Order Quantity (EOQ) Model 496

Minimizing Costs 497

Reorder Points 501

Production Order Quantity Model 502

Quantity Discount Models 505

Probabilistic Models and Safety Stock 508

Other Probabilistic Models 511

Single-Period Model 513

Fixed-Period (*P*) Systems 514

Summary 515

Key Terms 515

Ethical Dilemma 515

Discussion Questions 515

Using Software to Solve Inventory Problems 516

Solved Problems 517

Problems 520

CASE STUDIES 524

Zhou Bicycle Company 524

Parker Hi-Fi Systems 525

Managing Inventory at Frito-Lay Video Case 525

Inventory Control at Wheeled Coach Video Case 526

Endnotes 526

Rapid Review 527

Self Test 528

Chapter 13 Aggregate Planning and S&OP 529

GLOBAL COMPANY PROFILE: *FRITO-LAY* 530

The Planning Process 532

Sales and Operations Planning 533

The Nature of Aggregate Planning 534

Aggregate Planning Strategies 535

Capacity Options 535

Demand Options 536

Mixing Options to Develop a Plan 537

Methods for Aggregate Planning 538

Graphical Methods 538

Mathematical Approaches 543

Aggregate Planning in Services 545

Restaurants 546

Hospitals 546

National Chains of Small Service Firms 546

Miscellaneous Services 546

Airline Industry 547

Revenue Management 547

Summary 550

Key Terms 550

Ethical Dilemma 551

Discussion Questions 551

Using Software for Aggregate Planning 552

Solved Problems 554

Problems 555

CASE STUDIES 559

Andrew-Carter, Inc. 559

Using Revenue Management to Set Orlando Magic Ticket Prices Video Case 560

Endnote 560

Rapid Review 561

Self Test 562

Chapter 14 Material Requirements Planning (MRP) and ERP 563

GLOBAL COMPANY PROFILE: *WHEELED COACH* 564

Dependent Demand 566

Dependent Inventory Model Requirements   566

   Master Production Schedule   567

   Bills of Material   568

   Accurate Inventory Records   570

   Purchase Orders Outstanding   570

   Lead Times for Components   570

MRP Structure   571

MRP Management   575

   MRP Dynamics   575

   MRP Limitations   575

Lot-Sizing Techniques   576

Extensions of MRP   580

   Material Requirements Planning II (MRP II)   580

   Closed-Loop MRP   581

   Capacity Planning   581

MRP in Services   583

   Distribution Resource Planning (DRP)   584

Enterprise Resource Planning (ERP)   584

   ERP in the Service Sector   587

Summary   587

Key Terms   587

Ethical Dilemma   587

Discussion Questions   588

Using Software to Solve MRP Problems   588

Solved Problems   589

Problems   592

CASE STUDIES   595

   When 18,500 Orlando Magic Fans Come to Dinner Video Case   595

   MRP at Wheeled Coach   Video Case   596

Endnotes   596

Rapid Review   597

Self Test   598

Chapter 15   Short-Term Scheduling   599

GLOBAL COMPANY PROFILE: *ALASKA AIRLINES*   600

The Importance of Short-Term Scheduling   602

Scheduling Issues   602

   Forward and Backward Scheduling   603

   Finite and Infinite Loading   604

   Scheduling Criteria   604

Scheduling Process-Focused Facilities   605

Loading Jobs   605

   Input–Output Control   606

   Gantt Charts   607

   Assignment Method   608

Sequencing Jobs   611

   Priority Rules for Sequencing Jobs   611

   Critical Ratio   614

   Sequencing N Jobs on Two Machines: Johnson's Rule   615

   Limitations of Rule-Based Sequencing Systems   616

Finite Capacity Scheduling (FCS)   617

Scheduling Services   618

   Scheduling Service Employees with Cyclical Scheduling   620

Summary   621

Key Terms   621

Ethical Dilemma   621

Discussion Questions   622

Using Software for Short-Term Scheduling   622

Solved Problems   624

Problems   627

CASE STUDIES   630

   Old Oregon Wood Store   630

   From the Eagles to the Magic: Converting the Amway Center   Video Case   631

   Scheduling at Hard Rock Cafe   Video Case   632

Endnotes   632

Rapid Review   633

Self Test   634

Chapter 16   Lean Operations   635

GLOBAL COMPANY PROFILE: *TOYOTA MOTOR CORPORATION*   636

Lean Operations   638

   Eliminate Waste   638

   Remove Variability   639

   Improve Throughput   640

Lean and Just-in-Time   640

   Supplier Partnerships   640

   Lean Layout   642

   Lean Inventory   643

   Lean Scheduling   646

   Lean Quality   649

Lean and the Toyota Production System   649

   Continuous Improvement   649

   Respect for People   649

   Processes and Standard Work Practice   650

Lean Organizations   650

   Building a Lean Organization   650

   Lean Sustainability   652

Lean in Services   652

Summary   653

Key Terms   653

Ethical Dilemma   653

Discussion Questions   653

Solved Problem   653

Problems   654

CASE STUDIES 655

Lean Operations at Alaska Airlines Video Case 655

JIT at Arnold Palmer Hospital Video Case 656

Endnote 656

Rapid Review 657

Self Test 658

Chapter 17 Maintenance and Reliability 659

GLOBAL COMPANY PROFILE: *ORLANDO UTILITIES COMMISSION* 660

The Strategic Importance of Maintenance and Reliability 662

Reliability 663

System Reliability 663

Providing Redundancy 665

Maintenance 667

Implementing Preventive Maintenance 667

Increasing Repair Capabilities 670

Autonomous Maintenance 670

Total Productive Maintenance 671

Summary 671

Key Terms 671

Ethical Dilemma 671

Discussion Questions 671

Using Software to Solve Reliability Problems 672

Solved Problems 672

Problems 672

CASE STUDY 674

Maintenance Drives Profits at Frito-Lay Video Case 674

Rapid Review 675

Self Test 676

PART FOUR Business Analytics Modules 677

Module A Decision-Making Tools 677

The Decision Process in Operations 678

Fundamentals of Decision Making 679

Decision Tables 680

Types of Decision-Making Environments 681

Decision Making Under Uncertainty 681

Decision Making Under Risk 682

Decision Making Under Certainty 683

Expected Value of Perfect Information (EVPI) 683

Decision Trees 684

A More Complex Decision Tree 686

The Poker Decision Process 688

Summary 689

Key Terms 689

Discussion Questions 689

Using Software for Decision Models 689

Solved Problems 691

Problems 692

CASE STUDY 696

Warehouse Tenting at the Port of Miami 696

Endnote 696

Rapid Review 697

Self Test 698

Module B Linear Programming 699

Why Use Linear Programming? 700

Requirements of a Linear Programming Problem 701

Formulating Linear Programming Problems 701

Glickman Electronics Example 701

Graphical Solution to a Linear Programming Problem 702

Graphical Representation of Constraints 702

Iso-Profit Line Solution Method 703

Corner-Point Solution Method 705

Sensitivity Analysis 705

Sensitivity Report 706

Changes in the Resources or Right-Hand-Side Values 706

Changes in the Objective Function Coefficient 707

Solving Minimization Problems 708

Linear Programming Applications 710

Production-Mix Example 710

Diet Problem Example 711

Labor Scheduling Example 712

The Simplex Method of LP 713

Integer and Binary Variables 713

Creating Integer and Binary Variables 713

Linear Programming Applications with Binary Variables 714

A Fixed-Charge Integer Programming Problem 715

Summary 716

Key Terms 716

Discussion Questions 716

Using Software to Solve LP Problems 716

Solved Problems 718

Problems 720

CASE STUDIES 725

Quain Lawn and Garden, Inc. 725

Scheduling Challenges at Alaska Airlines Video Case 726

Endnotes 726

Rapid Review 727

Self Test 728

Module C   Transportation Models   729

Transportation Modeling   730

Developing an Initial Solution   732

  The Northwest-Corner Rule   732

  The Intuitive Lowest-Cost Method   733

The Stepping-Stone Method   734

Special Issues in Modeling   737

  Demand Not Equal to Supply   737

  Degeneracy   737

Summary   738

Key Terms   738

Discussion Questions   738

Using Software to Solve Transportation Problems   738

Solved Problems   740

Problems   741

CASE STUDY   743

  Custom Vans, Inc.   743

Rapid Review   745

Self Test   746

Module D   Waiting-Line Models   747

Queuing Theory   748

Characteristics of a Waiting-Line System   749

  Arrival Characteristics   749

  Waiting-Line Characteristics   750

  Service Characteristics   751

  Measuring a Queue's Performance   752

Queuing Costs   753

The Variety of Queuing Models   754

  Model A (M/M/1): Single-Server Queuing Model with Poisson Arrivals and Exponential Service Times   754

  Model B (M/M/S): Multiple-Server Queuing Model   757

  Model C (M/D/1): Constant-Service-Time Model   762

  Little's Law   763

  Model D (M/M/1 with Finite Source): Finite-Population Model   763

Other Queuing Approaches   765

Summary   765

Key Terms   765

Discussion Questions   765

Using Software to Solve Queuing Problems   766

Solved Problems   766

Problems   768

CASE STUDIES   771

  New England Foundry   771

  The Winter Park Hotel   772

Endnotes   772

Rapid Review   773

Self Test   774

Module E   Learning Curves   775

What Is a Learning Curve?   776

Learning Curves in Services and Manufacturing   777

Applying the Learning Curve   778

  Doubling Approach   778

  Formula Approach   779

  Learning-Curve Table Approach   779

Strategic Implications of Learning Curves   782

Limitations of Learning Curves   783

Summary   783

Key Term   783

Discussion Questions   783

Using Software for Learning Curves   784

Solved Problems   784

Problems   785

CASE STUDY   787

  SMT's Negotiation with IBM   787

Endnote   788

Rapid Review   789

Self Test   790

Module F   Simulation   791

What Is Simulation?   792

Advantages and Disadvantages of Simulation   793

Monte Carlo Simulation   794

Simulation with Two Decision Variables: An Inventory Example   797

Summary   799

Key Terms   799

Discussion Questions   799

Using Software in Simulation   800

Solved Problems   801

Problems   802

CASE STUDY   805

  Alabama Airlines' Call Center   805

Endnote   806

Rapid Review   807

Self Test   808

Appendix   A1

Bibliography   B1

Name Index   I1

General Index   I7

ONLINE TUTORIALS

1. **Statistical Tools for Managers**   **T1-1**

    Discrete Probability Distributions   T1-2

    Expected Value of a Discrete Probability Distribution   *T1-3*

    Variance of a Discrete Probability Distribution   *T1-3*

    Continuous Probability Distributions   T1-4

    The Normal Distribution   *T1-4*

    Summary   T1-7

    Key Terms   T1-7

    Discussion Questions   T1-7

    Problems   T1-7

    Bibliography   T1-7

2. **Acceptance Sampling**   **T2-1**

    Sampling Plans   T2-2

    Single Sampling   *T2-2*

    Double Sampling   *T2-2*

    Sequential Sampling   *T2-2*

    Operating Characteristic (OC) Curves   T2-2

    Producer's and Consumer's Risk   T2-3

    Average Outgoing Quality   T2-5

    Summary   T2-6

    Key Terms   T2-6

    Solved Problem   T2-7

    Discussion Questions   T2-7

    Problems   T2-7

3. **The Simplex Method of Linear Programming**   **T3-1**

    Converting the Constraints to Equations   T3-2

    Setting Up the First Simplex Tableau   T3-2

    Simplex Solution Procedures   T3-4

    Summary of Simplex Steps for Maximization Problems   T3-6

    Artificial and Surplus Variables   T3-7

    Solving Minimization Problems   T3-7

    Summary   T3-8

    Key Terms   T3-8

    Solved Problem   T3-8

    Discussion Questions   T3-8

    Problems   T3-9

4. **The MODI and VAM Methods of Solving Transportation Problems**   **T4-1**

    MODI Method   T4-2

    How to Use the MODI Method   *T4-2*

    Solving the Arizona Plumbing Problem with MODI   *T4-2*

    Vogel's Approximation Method: Another Way to Find an Initial Solution   T4-4

    Discussion Questions   T4-8

    Problems   T4-8

5. **Vehicle Routing and Scheduling**   **T5-1**

    Introduction   T5-2

    Service Delivery Example: Meals-for-ME   *T5-2*

    Objectives of Routing and Scheduling Problems   T5-2

    Characteristics of Routing and Scheduling Problems   T5-3

    Classifying Routing and Scheduling Problems   *T5-3*

    Solving Routing and Scheduling Problems   *T5-4*

    Routing Service Vehicles   T5-5

    The Traveling Salesman Problem   *T5-5*

    Multiple Traveling Salesman Problem   *T5-8*

    The Vehicle Routing Problem   *T5-9*

    Cluster First, Route Second Approach   *T5-10*

    Scheduling Service Vehicles   T5-11

    The Concurrent Scheduler Approach   *T5-13*

    Other Routing and Scheduling Problems   T5-13

    Summary   T5-14

    Key Terms   T5-15

    Discussion Questions   T5-15

    Problems   T5-15

    Case Study: Routing and Scheduling of Phlebotomists   T5-17

    Bibliography   T5-17

Welcome to your operations management (OM) course. In this book, we present a state-of-the-art view of the operations function. Operations is an exciting area of management that has a profound effect on productivity. Indeed, few other activities have as much impact on the quality of our lives. The goal of this text is to present a broad introduction to the field of operations in a realistic, practical manner. Even if you are not planning on a career in the operations area, you will likely be working with people in operations. Therefore, having a solid understanding of the role of operations in an organization will be of substantial benefit to you. This book will also help you understand how OM affects society and your life. Certainly, you will better understand what goes on behind the scenes when you attend a concert or major sports event; purchase a bag of Frito-Lay potato chips; buy a meal at an Olive Garden or a Hard Rock Cafe; place an order through Amazon.com; board a flight on Alaska Airlines; or enter a hospital for medical care. More than one and a half million readers of our earlier editions seem to have endorsed this premise.

We welcome comments by email from our North American readers and from students using the International edition, the Indian edition, the Arabic edition, and our editions in Portuguese, Spanish, Turkish, Indonesian, and Chinese. Hopefully, you will find this material useful, interesting, and even exciting.

New to This Edition

We've made significant revisions to this edition, and want to share some of the changes with you.

Five New *Video Case Studies* Featuring Alaska Airlines

In this edition, we take you behind the scenes of Alaska Airlines, consistently rated as one of the top carriers in the country. This fascinating organization opened its doors—and planes—so we could examine leading edge OM in the airlines industry. We observe: the quality program at Alaska Air (Chapter 6); the process analysis behind the airline's 20-minute baggage retrieval guarantee (Chapter 7); how Alaska empowers its employees (Chapter 10); the airline's use of Lean, 5s, kaizen, and Gemba walks (Chapter 16); and the complexities of scheduling (Module B).

Our prior editions focused on integrated *Video Case Studies* for the Orlando Magic basketball team, Frito-Lay, Darden Restaurants, Hard Rock Cafe, Arnold Palmer Hospital, Wheeled Coach Ambulances, and Regal Marine. These *Video Case Studies* appear in this edition as well, along with the five new ones for Alaska Airlines. All of our videos are created by the authors, with the outstanding coauthorship of Beverly Amer at Northern Arizona University, to explicitly match with text content and terminology.

Alaska Airlines: 20-Minute Baggage Process—Guaranteed! **Video Case**

Alaska Airlines is unique among the nine major U.S. carriers not only for its extensive flight coverage of remote towns throughout Alaska (it also covers the U.S., Hawaii, and Mexico from its primary hub in Seattle). It is also one of the smallest independent airlines, with 10,300 employees, including 3,000 flight attendants and 1,500 pilots. What makes it really unique, though, is its ability to build state-of-the-art processes, using the latest technology, that yield high customer satisfaction. Indeed, J. D. Power and Associates has ranked Alaska Airlines highest in North America for seven years in a row for customer satisfaction.

Alaska Airlines was the first to sell tickets via the Internet, first to offer Web check-in and print boarding passes online, and first with kiosk check-in. As Wayne Newton, Director of System Operation Control, states, "We are passionate about our processes. If it's not measured, it's not managed."

One of the processes Alaska is most proud of is its baggage handling system. Passengers can check in at kiosks, tag their own bags with bar code stickers, and deliver them to a customer service agent at the carousel, which carries the bags through the vast underground system that eventually delivers the bags to a baggage handler. En route, each bag passes through TSA automated screening and is manually opened or inspected if it appears suspicious. With the help of bar code readers, conveyer belts automatically sort and transfer bags to their location (called a "pier") at the tarmac level. A baggage handler then loads the bags onto a cart and takes it to

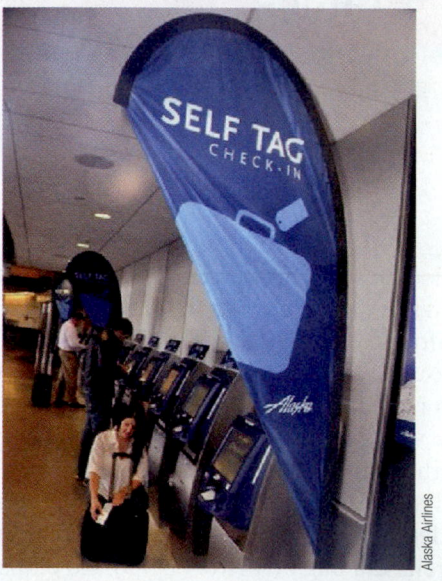

Alaska Airlines

Creating Your Own Excel Spreadsheets

We continue to provide two free decision support software programs, Excel OM for Windows and Mac and POM for Windows, to help you and your students solve homework problems and case studies. These excellent packages are found in MyOMLab and at our text's Student Download Page.

Many instructors also encourage students to develop their own Excel spreadsheet models to tackle OM issues. With this edition, we provide numerous examples at chapter end on how to do so. "Creating Your Own Excel Spreadsheets" examples now appear in Chapters 1, 2, 4, 8, 12, and 13, Supplement 6, Supplement 7, and Modules A, B, and F. We hope these eleven samples will help expand students' spreadsheet capabilities.

Using Software for Productivity Analysis

This section presents three ways to solve productivity problems with computer software. First, you can create your own Excel spreadsheets to conduct productivity analysis. Second, you can use the Excel OM software that comes with this text. Third, POM for Windows is another program that is available with this text.

CREATING YOUR OWN EXCEL SPREADSHEETS
Program 1.1 illustrates how to build an Excel spreadsheet for the data in Example 2.

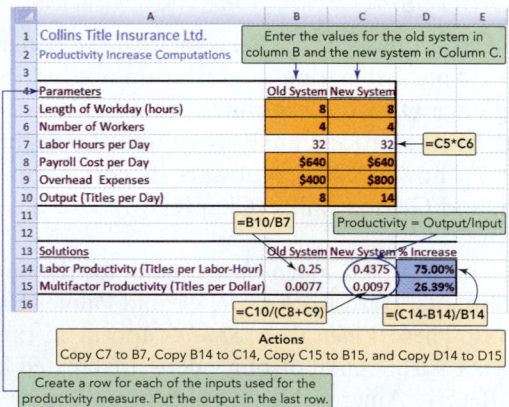

Program **1.1**

✖ **USING EXCEL OM**
Excel OM is an Excel "add-in" with 24 Operations Management decision support "Templates." To access the templates, double-click on the *Excel OM* tab at the top of the page, then in the menu bar choose the appropriate chapter (in this case Chapter 1), from either the "Chapter" or "Alphabetic" tab on the left. Each of Excel OM's 24 modules includes instructions for that particular module. The instructions can be turned on or off via the "instruction" tab in the menu bar.

P USING POM FOR WINDOWS
POM for Windows is decision support software that includes 24 Operations Management modules. The modules are accessed by double-clicking on *Module* in the menu bar, and then double-clicking on the appropriate (in this case *Productivity*) item. Instructions are provided for each module just below the menu bar.

Expanding and Reordering Our Set of Homework Problems

We believe that a vast selection of quality homework problems, ranging from easy to challenging (denoted by one to four dots), is critical for both instructors and students. Instructors need a broad selection of problems to choose from for homework, quizzes, and exams—without reusing the same set from semester to semester. We take pride in having more problems—by far, with 807—than any other OM text. We added dozens of new problems this edition. The following table illustrates the selection by chapter.

Chapter	Number of Problems	Chapter	Number of Problems	Chapter	Number of Problems
1	18	Supplement 7	45	15	27
2	12	8	34	16	12
3	33	9	27	17	24
4	59	10	46	Module A	32
5	28	11	8	Module B	42
Supplement 5	19	Supplement 11	20	Module C	18
6	21	12	53	Module D	39
Supplement 6	55	13	26	Module E	33
7	17	14	32	Module F	25

Further, with the majority of our adopters now using the MyOMLab learning system in their classes, we have reorganized all the homework problems—both those appearing in the printed text, as well as the Additional Homework Problems that are available in MyOMLab—by topic heading. We are identifying all problems by topic (see the following example).

The list of all problems by topic also appears at the end of each boxed example, as well as in the Rapid Review that closes each chapter. These handy references should make it easier to assign problems for homework, quizzes, and exams. A rich set of assignable problems and cases makes the learning experience more complete and pedagogically sound.

CHAPTER 5 | DESIGN OF GOODS AND SERVICES **187**

Problem 5.3 is available in MyOMLab.

Problems 5.4–5.8 relate to Product Development

•• **5.4**   Construct a house of quality matrix for a wristwatch. Be sure to indicate specific customer wants that you think the general public desires. Then complete the matrix to show how an operations manager might identify specific attributes that can be measured and controlled to meet those customer desires.

•• **5.5**   Using the house of quality, pick a real product (a good or service) and analyze how an existing organization satisfies customer requirements.

•• **5.6**   Prepare a house of quality for a mousetrap.

•• **5.7**   Conduct an interview with a prospective purchaser of a new bicycle and translate the customer's *wants* into the specific *hows* of the firm.

•••• **5.8**   Using the house of quality sequence, as described in Figure 5.4 on page 169, determine how you might deploy resources to achieve the desired quality for a product or service whose production process you understand.

Problems 5.9–5.17 relate to Defining a Product

•• **5.9**   Prepare a bill of material for (a) a pair of eyeglasses and its case or (b) a fast-food sandwich (visit a local sandwich

Problems 5.21–5.28 relate to the Application of Decision Trees to Product Design

•• **5.21**   The product design group of Iyengar Electric Supplies, Inc., has determined that it needs to design a new series of switches. It must decide on one of three design strategies. The market forecast is for 200,000 units. The better and more sophisticated the design strategy and the more time spent on value engineering, the less will be the variable cost. The chief of engineering design, Dr. W. L. Berry, has decided that the following costs are a good estimate of the initial and variable costs connected with each of the three strategies:
a) *Low-tech:* A low-technology, low-cost process consisting of hiring several new junior engineers. This option has a fixed cost of $45,000 and variable-cost probabilities of .3 for $.55 each, .4 for $.50, and .3 for $.45.
b) *Subcontract:* A medium-cost approach using a good outside design staff. This approach would have a fixed cost of $65,000 and variable-cost probabilities of .7 of $.45, .2 of $.40, and .1 of $.35.
c) *High-tech:* A high-technology approach using the very best of the inside staff and the latest computer-aided design technology. This approach has a fixed cost of $75,000 and variable-cost probabilities of .9 of $.40 and .1 of $.35.

What is the best decision based on an expected monetary value (EMV) criterion? (*Note:* We want the lowest EMV, as we are dealing with costs in this problem.) **Px**

•• **5.22**   MacDonald Products, Inc., of Clarkson, New York, has the option of (a) proceeding immediately with production of

Jay, Barry, and Chuck's OM Blog

As a complement to this text, we have created a companion blog, with coordinated features to help teach the OM course. There are teaching tips, highlights of OM items in the news (along with class discussion questions and links), video tips, guest posts by instructors using our text, sample OM syllabi from dozens of colleges, and much more—all arranged by chapter. To learn more about any chapter topics, visit *www.heizerrenderOM.wordpress.com*. As you prepare your lectures and syllabus, scan our blog for discussion ideas, teaching tips, and classroom exercises.

Lean Operations

In previous editions, we sought to explicitly differentiate the concepts of just-in-time, Lean, and Toyota Production System in Chapter 16. However, there is significant overlap and interchangeability among those three concepts, so we have revised Chapter 16 to incorporate the three concepts into an overall concept of "Lean." The chapter suggests that students view Lean as a comprehensive integrated operations strategy that sustains competitive advantage and results in increased returns to all stakeholders.

Chapter-by-Chapter Changes

To highlight the extent of the revisions in this edition, here are a few of the changes, on a chapter-by-chapter basis.

Chapter 1: Operations and Productivity

We updated Table 1.4 to reflect employment in various sectors and expanded our discussion of Lean operations. Our new case, Uber Technologies, introduces productivity by discussing the disruptive nature of the Uber business model. In addition, there is a new "Creating Your Own Excel Spreadsheets" example for both labor productivity and multifactor productivity.

Chapter 2: Operations Strategy in a Global Environment

We have updated Figure 2.1 to better reflect changes in the growth of world trade and Figure 2.5 to reflect product life cycle changes. The Minute Lube case has been revised as Rapid Lube. Example 1 (National Architects) has been expanded to clarify factor rating calculations and is also demonstrated with a "Creating Your Own Excel Spreadsheets" presentation.

Chapter 3: Project Management

We rewrote and updated the Bechtel Global Company Profile and added a new section on well-defined projects with the "agile" and "waterfall" approaches. There are two new OM in Action boxes: "Agile Project Management at Mastek," and "Behind the Tour de France."

Chapter 4: Forecasting

We created a new table comparing the MAD, MSE, and MAPE forecasting error measures. There is also a new OM in Action box called "NYC's Potholes and Regression Analysis."

Chapter 5: Design of Goods and Services

We expanded our treatment of *concurrent engineering* and added two new discussion questions. Solved Problem 5.1 has been revised.

Supplement 5: Sustainability in the Supply Chain

We wrote a new introductory section on Corporate Social Responsibility. There is also a new OM in Action box called "Blue Jeans and Sustainability" and 10 new homework problems.

Chapter 6: Managing Quality

We added new material to expand our discussion of Taguchi's quality loss function. There is a new section on SERVQUAL, and a new video case study, "Quality Counts at Alaska Airlines," appears here.

Supplement 6: Statistical Process Control

We added a figure on the relationship between sample size and sampling distribution. We also added raw data to Examples S2 and S3 to illustrate how ranges are computed. There is a new Excel spreadsheet to show students how to make their own *c*-chart, and we have added three new homework problems.

Chapter 7: Process Strategy

We wrote a new section on machine technology and additive manufacturing. There are two new discussion questions and three new homework problems. Our second new video case study is called "Alaska Airlines: 20-Minute Baggage Process—Guaranteed!"

Supplement 7: Capacity and Constraint Management

We added a new Table S7.1, which compares and clarifies three capacity measurements, with an example of each. There is a new treatment of expected output and actual output in Example S2. The discussion of bottleneck time versus throughput time has also been expanded. Example S3, capacity analysis with parallel processes, has been revised. We have also added a new "Creating Your Own Excel Spreadsheets" example for a break-even model. Finally, we updated the Arnold Palmer Hospital capacity planning case with recent data.

Chapter 8: Location Strategies

We added two new OM in Action boxes: "Iowa—Home of Corn and Facebook" and "Denmark's Meat Cluster." We changed the notation for the center-of-gravity model to simplify the equation and provided a new "Creating Your Own Excel Spreadsheets" presentation for the center-of-gravity example.

Chapter 9: Layout Strategies

We created a new Muther grid for office relationship charting and added a spread of five layouts showing how offices have evolved over time. There is a new OM in Action box called "Amazon Lets Loose the Robots," and there is a new graphic example of Proplanner's Flow Path Calculator. We have included a formula for idle time as a second measure of balance assignment efficiency and added new technology issues to the Arnold Palmer Hospital video case.

Chapter 10: Human Resources, Job Design, and Work Measurement

We added a new OM in Action box, "The Missing Perfect Chair," and revised the Operations Chart as a service example. Our third new video case study is "The 'People' Focus: Human Resources at Alaska Airlines."

Chapter 11: Supply Chain Management

We added "outsourcing" as a supply chain risk in Table 11.3.

Supplement 11: Supply Chain Management Analytics

We added a major section on the topic of Warehouse Storage, with a new model for allocating inventory to storage locations. There is a new discussion question and three new homework problems.

Chapter 12: Inventory Management

New Programs 12.1 and 12.2 illustrate "Creating Your Own Excel Spreadsheets" for both the production run model and the single-period inventory model. The Excel function NORMSINV is introduced throughout the chapter. The Quantity Discount Model section is totally rewritten to illustrate the *feasible solution* shortcut. Solved Problem 12.5 is likewise redone with the new approach.

Chapter 13: Aggregate Planning and S&OP

We added a new OM in Action box, "Revenue Management Makes Disney the 'King' of the Broadway Jungle." We also provided a new "Creating Your Own Excel Spreadsheets" example for the transportation method for aggregate planning, using the Solver approach.

Chapter 14: Material Requirements Planning (MRP) and ERP

The MRP II example now includes greenhouse gasses.

Chapter 15: Short-Term Scheduling

We begin this chapter with a new Global Company Profile featuring Alaska Airlines and the scheduling issues it faces in its northern climate. We have added two new graphics to help illustrate Forward and Backward Scheduling. There is also a new section called Performance Criteria, detailing how the choice of priority rule depends on four quantifiable criteria. We now explicitly define the performance criteria for sequencing jobs as separate numbered equations. Also, we provide an explicit formula for job lateness. There is a new OM in Action box called "Starbucks' Controversial Scheduling Software."

Chapter 16: Lean Operations

This chapter saw a major reorganization and rewrite with an enhanced focus on Lean operations. There is more material on supplier partnerships and building lean organizations. A new OM in Action box describes the use of kaizen at San Francisco General Hospital, and we have added a new video case study called "Lean Operations at Alaska Airlines."

Chapter 17: Maintenance and Reliability

There are no major changes in this chapter.

Module A: Decision-Making Tools

We added a discussion of "big data" and a new "Creating Your Own Excel Spreadsheets" example on how to evaluate a decision table.

Module B: Linear Programming

There is a new section on integer and binary programming, two new homework problems, and a new video case study called "Using LP to Meet Scheduling Challenges at Alaska Airlines." The corner point method is now covered *before* the iso-profit line approach.

Module C: Transportation Models

There are no major changes to Module C.

Module D: Waiting-Line Models

The limited population model (Model D) has been replaced by the finite population model, M/M/1 with finite source. This standardizes the queuing notation to match the M/M/1, M/M/s, and M/D/1. We have also expanded the coverage of Little's Law and added six new homework problems.

Module E: Learning Curves

There are no major changes to Module E.

Module F: Simulation

We added a new "Creating Your Own Excel Spreadsheets" example for a simulation problem.

Student Resources

To liven up the course and help students learn the content material, we have made available the following resources:

◆ *Forty-one exciting Video Case Studies (videos located at MyOMLab):* These *Video Case Studies* feature real companies (Alaska Airlines, The Orlando Magic, Frito-Lay, Darden Restaurants, Regal Marine, Hard Rock Cafe, Ritz-Carlton, Wheeled Coach, and Arnold Palmer Hospital) and allow students to watch short videos, read about the key topics, and answer questions. These case studies can also be assigned without using class time to show the videos. Each of them was developed and written by the text authors to specifically supplement the book's content. Instructors who wish to use these in class, and who don't have access to MyOMLab, should contact their Pearson Publishing Representative for access to the MyOMLab materials.

- *POM for Windows software (located at MyOMLab and at the Student Download Page, www.pearsonhighered.com/heizer):* POM for Windows is a powerful tool for easily solving OM problems. Its 24 modules can be used to solve most of the homework problems in the text.
- *Excel OM problem-solving software (located at MyOMLab and at the Student Download Page, www.pearsonhighered.com/heizer):* Excel OM is our exclusive user-friendly Excel add-in. Excel OM automatically creates worksheets to model and solve problems. Users select a topic from the pull-down menu and fill in the data, and then Excel will display and graph (where appropriate) the results. This software is great for student homework, what-if analysis, and classroom demonstrations. This edition includes a new version of Excel OM that is compatible with Microsoft Excel 2013 for Windows, Excel 2011 and 2016 for Mac, and earlier versions of Excel. Professor Howard Weiss, Temple University, developed both Excel OM for Windows and Mac, and POM for Windows to accompany our text and its problem set.
- *Excel OM data files (located at MyOMLab and at the Student Download Page, www.pearsonhighered.com/heizer):* These data files are prepared for specific examples and allow users to solve all the marked text examples without reentering any data.
- *Active Models (located at MyOMLab and at the Student Download Page, www.pearsonhighered.com/heizer):* These 28 Active Models are Excel-based OM simulations, designed to help students understand the quantitative methods shown in the textbook examples. Students may change the data in order to see how the changes affect the answers.
- *Virtual tours (located at MyOMLab):* These company tours provide direct links to companies—ranging from a hospital to an auto manufacturer—that practice key OM concepts. After touring each Web site, students are asked questions directly related to the concepts discussed in the chapter.
- *Online Tutorial Chapters (located at MyOMLab and at the Student Download Page, www.pearsonhighered.com/heizer):* "Statistical Tools for Managers," "Acceptance Sampling," "The Simplex Method of Linear Programming," "The MODI and VAM Methods of Solving Transportation Problems," and "Vehicle Routing and Scheduling" are provided as additional material.
- *Additional practice problems (located at MyOMLab):* These problems provide problem-solving experience. They supplement the examples and solved problems found in each chapter.
- *Additional case studies (located at MyOMLab and at the Student Download Page, www.pearsonhighered.com/heizer):* Over two dozen additional case studies supplement the ones in the text. Detailed solutions appear in the Solutions Manual.
- *Virtual office hours (located at MyOMLab):* Professors Heizer, Render, and Munson walk students through all 89 Solved Problems in a series of 5- to 20-minute explanations. These have been updated with this new edition.

Instructor Resources

At the Instructor Resource Center, *www.pearsonhighered.com/irc*, instructors can easily register to gain access to a variety of instructor resources available with this text in downloadable format. If assistance is needed, our dedicated technical support team is ready to help with the media supplements that accompany this text. Visit *http://247.pearsoned.com* for answers to frequently asked questions and toll-free user support phone numbers.

The following supplements are available with this text:

Instructor's Resource Manual

The Instructor's Resource Manual, updated by co-author Chuck Munson, contains many useful resources for instructors—PowerPoint presentations with annotated notes, course outlines, video notes, blog highlights, learning techniques, Internet exercises and sample answers, case analysis ideas, additional teaching resources, and faculty notes.

Instructor's Solutions Manual

The Instructor's Solutions Manual, written by the authors, contains the answers to all of the discussion questions, *Ethical Dilemmas*, Active Models, and cases in the text, as well as worked-out solutions to all the end-of-chapter problems, additional homework problems, and additional case studies.

PowerPoint Presentations

An extensive set of PowerPoint presentations, created by Professor Jeff Heyl of Lincoln University, is available for each chapter. With well over 2,000 slides, this set has excellent color and clarity.

Test Bank / TestGen® Computerized Test Bank

The test bank, updated by James Roh, contains a variety of true/false, multiple-choice, short-answer, and essay questions, along with a selection of written problems, for each chapter. Test questions are annotated with the following information:

- Difficulty level
- Type: multiple-choice, true/false, short-answer, essay, problem
- Learning objective
- AACSB (see the description that follows)

TestGen®, Pearson Education's test-generating software, is PC/MAC compatible and preloaded with all the test bank questions. The test program permits instructors to edit, add, and delete questions from the test bank to create customized tests.

AACSB

The Association to Advance Collegiate Schools of Business (AACSB)

The test bank has connected select questions to the general knowledge and skill guidelines found in the AACSB Assurance of Learning standards.

AACSB is a not-for-profit corporation of educational institutions, corporations, and other organizations devoted to the promotion and improvement of higher education in business administration and accounting. A collegiate institution offering degrees in business administration or accounting may volunteer for AACSB accreditation review. The AACSB makes initial accreditation decisions and conducts periodic reviews to promote continuous quality improvement in management education. Pearson Education is a proud member of the AACSB and is pleased to provide advice to help you apply AACSB assurance of learning standards.

What are AACSB assurance of learning standards? One of the criteria for AACSB accreditation is quality of the curricula. Although no specific courses are required, the AACSB expects a curriculum to include learning experiences in the following areas:

- Written and oral communication
- Ethical understanding and reasoning
- Analytical thinking
- Information technology
- Interpersonal relations and teamwork
- Diverse and multicultural work environments
- Reflective thinking
- Application of knowledge

Questions that test skills relevant to these guidelines are appropriately tagged. For example, a question regarding clothing manufactured for U.S. firms by 10-year olds in Asia would receive the Ethical understanding and reasoning tag.

Tagged questions help you measure whether students are grasping the course content that aligns with the AACSB guidelines noted. In addition, the tagged questions may help instructors identify potential applications of these skills. This in turn may suggest enrichment activities or other educational experiences to help students achieve these skills.

Video Package

Designed and created by the authors specifically for their Heizer/Render/Munson texts, the video package contains the following 41 videos:

- Frito-Lay: Operations Management in Manufacturing (Chapter 1)
- Hard Rock Cafe: Operations Management in Services (Chapter 1)
- Strategy at Regal Marine (Chapter 2)
- Hard Rock Cafc's Global Strategy (Chapter 2)
- Outsourcing Offshore at Darden (Chapter 2)
- Project Management at Arnold Palmer Hospital (Chapter 3)
- Managing Hard Rock's Rockfest (Chapter 3)
- Forecasting Ticket Revenue for Orlando Magic Basketball Games (Chapter 4)
- Forecasting at Hard Rock Cafe (Chapter 4)
- Product Design at Regal Marine (Chapter 5)
- Building Sustainability at the Orlando Magic's Amway Center (Supplement 5)
- Green Manufacturing and Sustainability at Frito-Lay (Supplement 5)
- Quality Counts at Alaska Airlines (Chapter 6)
- The Culture of Quality at Arnold Palmer Hospital (Chapter 6)
- Quality at the Ritz-Carlton Hotel Company (Chapter 6)
- Frito-Lay's Quality-Controlled Potato Chips (Supplement 6)
- Farm to Fork: Quality at Darden Restaurants (Supplement 6)
- Alaska Airlines: 20-Minute Baggage Process—Guaranteed! (Chapter 7)
- Process Strategy at Wheeled Coach (Chapter 7)
- Process Analysis at Arnold Palmer Hospital (Chapter 7)
- Capacity Planning at Arnold Palmer Hospital (Supplement 7)
- Locating the Next Red Lobster Restaurant (Chapter 8)
- Where to Place the Hard Rock Cafe (Chapter 8)
- Facility Layout at Wheeled Coach (Chapter 9)
- Laying Out Arnold Palmer Hospital's New Facility (Chapter 9)
- The "People" Focus: Human Resources at Alaska Airlines (Chapter 10)
- Hard Rock's Human Resource Strategy (Chapter 10)
- Darden's Global Supply Chains (Chapter 11)
- Supply Chain Management at Regal Marine (Chapter 11)
- Arnold Palmer Hospital's Supply Chain (Chapter 11)
- Managing Inventory at Frito-Lay (Chapter 12)
- Inventory Control at Wheeled Coach (Chapter 12)
- Using Revenue Management to Set Orlando Magic Ticket Prices (Chapter 13)
- When 18,500 Orlando Magic Fans Come to Dinner (Chapter 14)
- MRP at Wheeled Coach (Chapter 14)
- From the Eagles to the Magic: Converting the Amway Center (Chapter 15)
- Scheduling at Hard Rock Cafe (Chapter 15)
- Lean Operations at Alaska Airlines (Chapter 16)
- JIT at Arnold Palmer Hospital (Chapter 16)
- Maintenance Drives Profits at Frito-Lay (Chapter 17)
- Scheduling Challenges at Alaska Airlines (Module B)

Acknowledgments

We thank the many individuals who were kind enough to assist us in this endeavor. The following professors provided insights that guided us in this edition (their names are in bold) and in prior editions:

ALABAMA

John Mittenthal
University of Alabama

Philip F. Musa
University of Alabama at Birmingham

William Petty
University of Alabama

Doug Turner
Auburn University

ALASKA

Paul Jordan
University of Alaska

ARIZONA

Susan K. Norman
Northern Arizona University

Scott Roberts
Northern Arizona University

Vicki L. Smith-Daniels
Arizona State University

Susan K. Williams
Northern Arizona University

CALIFORNIA

Jean-Pierre Amor
University of San Diego

Moshen Attaran
California State University–Bakersfield

Ali Behnezhad
California State University–Northridge

Joe Biggs
California Polytechnic State University

Lesley Buehler
Ohlone College

Rick Hesse
Pepperdine

Ravi Kathuria
Chapman University

Richard Martin
California State University–Long Beach

Ozgur Ozluk
San Francisco State University

Zinovy Radovilsky
California State University–Hayward

Robert J. Schlesinger
San Diego State University

V. Udayabhanu
San Francisco State University

Rick Wing
San Francisco State University

COLORADO

Peter Billington
Colorado State University–Pueblo

Gregory Stock
University of Colorado at Colorado Springs

CONNECTICUT

David Cadden
Quinnipiac University

Larry A. Flick
Norwalk Community Technical College

FLORIDA

Joseph P. Geunes
University of Florida

Rita Gibson
Embry-Riddle Aeronautical University

Jim Gilbert
Rollins College

Donald Hammond
University of South Florida

Wende Huehn-Brown
St. Petersburg College

Adam Munson
University of Florida

Ronald K. Satterfield
University of South Florida

Theresa A. Shotwell
Florida A&M University

Jeff Smith
Florida State University

GEORGIA

John H. Blackstone
University of Georgia

Johnny Ho
Columbus State University

John Hoft
Columbus State University

John Miller
Mercer University

Nikolay Osadchiy
Emory University

Spyros Reveliotis
Georgia Institute of Technology

ILLINOIS

Suad Alwan
Chicago State University

Lori Cook
DePaul University

Matt Liontine
University of Illinois–Chicago

Zafar Malik
Governors State University

INDIANA

Barbara Flynn
Indiana University

B.P. Lingeraj
Indiana University

Frank Pianki
Anderson University

Stan Stockton
Indiana University

Jerry Wei
University of Notre Dame

Jianghua Wu
Purdue University

Xin Zhai
Purdue University

IOWA

Debra Bishop
Drake University

Kevin Watson
Iowa State University

Lifang Wu
University of Iowa

KANSAS

William Barnes
Emporia State University

George Heinrich
Wichita State University

Sue Helms
Wichita State University

Hugh Leach
Washburn University

M.J. Riley
Kansas State University

Teresita S. Salinas
Washburn University

Avanti P. Sethi
Wichita State University

KENTUCKY

Wade Ferguson
Western Kentucky University

Kambiz Tabibzadeh
Eastern Kentucky University

LOUISIANA

Roy Clinton
University of Louisiana at Monroe

L. Wayne Shell (retired)
Nicholls State University

MARYLAND

Eugene Hahn
Salisbury University

Samuel Y. Smith, Jr.
University of Baltimore

MASSACHUSETTS

Peter Ittig
University of Massachusetts

Jean Pierre Kuilboer
University of Massachusetts–Boston

Dave Lewis
University of Massachusetts–Lowell

Mike Maggard (retired)
Northeastern University

Peter Rourke
Wentworth Institute of Technology

Daniel Shimshak
University of Massachusetts–Boston

Ernest Silver
Curry College

Yu Amy Xia
Northeastern University

MICHIGAN

Darlene Burk
Western Michigan University

Damodar Golhar
Western Michigan University

Dana Johnson
Michigan Technological University

Doug Moodie
Michigan Technological University

MINNESOTA

Rick Carlson
Metropolitan State University

John Nicolay
University of Minnesota

Michael Pesch
St. Cloud State University

Manus Rungtusanatham
University of Minnesota

Kingshuk Sinha
University of Minnesota

Peter Southard
University of St. Thomas

MISSOURI

Shahid Ali
Rockhurst University

Stephen Allen
Truman State University

Sema Alptekin
University of Missouri–Rolla

Gregory L. Bier
University of Missouri–Columbia

James Campbell
University of Missouri–St. Louis

Wooseung Jang
University of Missouri–Columbia

Mary Marrs
University of Missouri–Columbia

A. Lawrence Summers
University of Missouri

NEBRASKA

Zialu Hug
University of Nebraska–Omaha

NEVADA

Joel D. Wisner
University of Nevada, Las Vegas

NEW JERSEY

Daniel Ball
Monmouth University

Leon Bazil
Stevens Institute of Technology

Mark Berenson
Montclair State University

Grace Greenberg
Rider University

Joao Neves
The College of New Jersey

Leonard Presby
William Paterson University

Faye Zhu
Rowan University

NEW MEXICO

William Kime
University of New Mexico

NEW YORK

Theodore Boreki
Hofstra University

John Drabouski
DeVry University

Richard E. Dulski
Daemen College

Jonatan Jelen
Baruch College

Beate Klingenberg
Marist College

Donna Mosier
SUNY Potsdam

Elizabeth Perry
SUNY Binghamton

William Reisel
St. John's University

Kaushik Sengupta
Hofstra University

Girish Shambu
Canisius College

Rajendra Tibrewala
New York Institute of Technology

NORTH CAROLINA

Coleman R. Rich
Elon University

Ray Walters
Fayetteville Technical Community College

OHIO

Victor Berardi
Kent State University

Andrew R. Thomas
University of Akron

OKLAHOMA

Wen-Chyuan Chiang
University of Tulsa

OREGON

Anne Deidrich
Warner Pacific College

Gordon Miller
Portland State University

John Sloan
Oregon State University

PENNSYLVANIA

Henry Crouch
Pittsburgh State University

Jeffrey D. Heim
Pennsylvania State University

James F. Kimpel
University of Pittsburgh

Ian M. Langella
Shippensburg University

Prafulla Oglekar
LaSalle University

David Pentico
Duquesne University

Stanford Rosenberg
LaRoche College

Edward Rosenthal
Temple University

Susan Sherer
Lehigh University

Howard Weiss
Temple University

RHODE ISLAND

Laurie E. Macdonald
Bryant College

John Swearingen
Bryant College

Susan Sweeney
Providence College

SOUTH CAROLINA

Jerry K. Bilbrey
Anderson University

Larry LaForge
Clemson University

Emma Jane Riddle
Winthrop University

TENNESSEE

Joseph Blackburn
Vanderbilt University

Hugh Daniel
Lipscomb University

Cliff Welborn
Middle Tennessee State University

TEXAS

Warren W. Fisher
Stephen F. Austin State University

Garland Hunnicutt
Texas State University

Gregg Lattier
Lee College

Henry S. Maddux III
Sam Houston State University

Arunachalam Narayanan
Texas A&M University

Ranga V. Ramasesh
Texas Christian University

Victor Sower
San Houston State University

Cecelia Temponi
Texas State University

John Visich-Disc
University of Houston

Dwayne Whitten
Texas A&M University

Bruce M. Woodworth
University of Texas–El Paso

UTAH

William Christensen
Dixie State College of Utah

Shane J. Schvaneveldt
Weber State University

Madeline Thimmes (retired)
Utah State University

VIRGINIA

Andy Litteral
University of Richmond

Arthur C. Meiners, Jr.
Marymount University

Michael Plumb
Tidewater Community College

WASHINGTON

Mark McKay
University of Washington

Chris Sandvig
Western Washington University

John Stec
Oregon Institute of Technology

WASHINGTON, DC

Narendrea K. Rustagi
Howard University

WEST VIRGINIA

Charles Englehardt
Salem International University

Daesung Ha
Marshall University

John Harpell
West Virginia University

James S. Hawkes
University of Charleston

WISCONSIN

James R. Gross
University of Wisconsin–Oshkosh

Marilyn K. Hart (retired)
University of Wisconsin–Oshkosh

Niranjan Pati
University of Wisconsin–La Crosse

X. M. Safford
Milwaukee Area Technical College

Rao J. Taikonda
University of Wisconsin–Oshkosh

WYOMING

Cliff Asay
University of Wyoming

INTERNATIONAL

Steven Harrod
Technical University of Denmark

Robert D. Klassen
University of Western Ontario

Ronald Lau
Hong Kong University of Science and Technology

In addition, we appreciate the wonderful people at Pearson Education who provided both help and advice: Stephanie Wall, our superb editor-in-chief; Lenny Ann Kucenski, our dynamo marketing manager; Linda Albelli, our editorial assistant; Courtney Kamauf and Andra Skaalrud for their fantastic and dedicated work on MyOMLab; Jeff Holcomb, our project manager team lead; Claudia Fernandes, our program manager; Jacqueline Martin, our senior project manager; and Heidi Allgair, our project manager at Cenveo® Publisher Services. We are truly blessed to have such a fantastic team of experts directing, guiding, and assisting us.

In this edition, we were thrilled to be able to include one of the country's premier airlines, Alaska Airlines, in our ongoing Video Case Study series. This was possible because of the wonderful efforts of COO/EVP-Operations Ben Minicucci, and his superb management team. This included John Ladner (Managing Director, Seattle Station Operations), Wayne Newton (Managing Director, Station Operations Control), Mike McQueen (Director, Schedule Planning), Chad Koehnke (Director, Planning and Resource Allocation), Cheryl Schulz (Executive Assistant to EVP Minicucci), Jeffrey Butler (V.P. Airport Operations & Customer Service), Dan Audette (Manager of Operations Research and Analysis), Allison Fletcher (Process Improvement Manager), Carlos Zendejas (Manager Line-Flying Operations, Pilots), Robyn Garner (Flight Attendant Trainer), and Nikki Meier and Sara Starbuck (Process Improvement Facilitators). We are grateful to all of these fine people, as well as the many others that participated in the development of the videos and cases during our trips to the Seattle headquarters.

We also appreciate the efforts of colleagues who have helped to shape the entire learning package that accompanies this text. Professor Howard Weiss (Temple University) developed the Active Models, Excel OM, and POM for Windows software; Professor Jeff Heyl (Lincoln University) created the PowerPoint presentations; and Professor James Roh (Rowan University) updated the test bank. Beverly Amer (Northern Arizona University) produced and directed the video series; Professors Keith Willoughby (Bucknell University) and Ken Klassen (Brock University) contributed the two Excel-based simulation games; and Professor Gary LaPoint (Syracuse University) developed the Microsoft Project crashing exercise and the dice game for SPC. We have been fortunate to have been able to work with all these people.

We wish you a pleasant and productive introduction to operations management.

JAY HEIZER
Texas Lutheran University
1000 W. Court Street
Seguin, TX 78155
Email: jheizer@tlu.edu

BARRY RENDER
Graduate School of Business
Rollins College
Winter Park, FL 32789
Email: brender@rollins.edu

CHUCK MUNSON
Carson College of Business
Washington State University
Pullman, WA 99164-4746
Email: munson@wsu.edu

TWO VERSIONS ARE AVAILABLE

This text is available in two versions: *Operations Management*, 12th edition, a hardcover, and *Principles of Operations Management*, 10th edition, a paperback. Both books include the identical core Chapters 1–17. However, *Operations Management*, 12th edition also includes six business analytics modules in Part IV.

OPERATIONS MANAGEMENT, 12TH EDITION
ISBN: 0-13-413042-1

PART I INTRODUCTION TO OPERATIONS MANAGEMENT
1. Operations and Productivity
2. Operations Strategy in a Global Environment
3. Project Management
4. Forecasting

PART II DESIGNING OPERATIONS
5. Design of Goods and Services
S5. Sustainability in the Supply Chain
6. Managing Quality
S6. Statistical Process Control
7. Process Strategy
S7. Capacity and Constraint Management
8. Location Strategies
9. Layout Strategies
10. Human Resources, Job Design, and Work Measurement

PART III MANAGING OPERATIONS
11. Supply Chain Management
S11. Supply Chain Management Analytics
12. Inventory Management
13. Aggregate Planning and S&OP
14. Material Requirements Planning (MRP) and ERP
15. Short-Term Scheduling
16. Lean Operations
17. Maintenance and Reliability

PART IV BUSINESS ANALYTICS MODULES
A. Decision-Making Tools
B. Linear Programming
C. Transportation Models
D. Waiting-Line Models
E. Learning Curves
F. Simulation

ONLINE TUTORIALS
1. Statistical Tools for Managers
2. Acceptance Sampling
3. The Simplex Method of Linear Programming
4. The MODI and VAM Methods of Solving Transportation Problems
5. Vehicle Routing and Scheduling

PRINCIPLES OF OPERATIONS MANAGEMENT, 10TH EDITION
ISBN: 0-13-418198-0

PART I INTRODUCTION TO OPERATIONS MANAGEMENT
1. Operations and Productivity
2. Operations Strategy in a Global Environment
3. Project Management
4. Forecasting

PART II DESIGNING OPERATIONS
5. Design of Goods and Services
S5. Sustainability in the Supply Chain
6. Managing Quality
S6. Statistical Process Control
7. Process Strategy
S7. Capacity and Constraint Management
8. Location Strategies
9. Layout Strategies
10. Human Resources, Job Design, and Work Measurement

PART III MANAGING OPERATIONS
11. Supply Chain Management
S11. Supply Chain Management Analytics
12. Inventory Management
13. Aggregate Planning and S&OP
14. Material Requirements Planning (MRP) and ERP
15. Short-Term Scheduling
16. Lean Operations
17. Maintenance and Reliability

ONLINE TUTORIALS
1. Statistical Tools for Managers
2. Acceptance Sampling
3. The Simplex Method of Linear Programming
4. The MODI and VAM Methods of Solving Transportation Problems
5. Vehicle Routing and Scheduling

OPERATIONS MANAGEMENT

Sustainability and Supply Chain Management

Name Index

A

Abernathy, Frederick H., B5
Adenso-Diaz, B., B5
Aft, Larry, B4
Aghazadeh, S. M., B3
Ait-Kadi, D., B6
Alexander, Larry, 753
Alexy, Oliver, B2
Ambec, Stefan, B2
Anand, Gopesh, B2
Anderson, Edward James, B3
Anderson, Ross, B6
Andrews, D. M., B4
Anthony, S. D., B2
Anupindi, Ravi, B3
Armstrong, A. J., B5
Arnold, J. R., B5
Ashkenas, R. N., B1
Autry, Chad W., B4

B

Babai, M. Z., B5
Babbage. Charles, 412
Bakar, N. A., B4
Baker, Kenneth A., B6
Bakir, S. T., B2
Balakrishnan, R., 713n, B1, B6, B7
Baldridge, Malcolm, 218
Ballou, Ronald H., B3
Bamford, James, B2
Banerjee, S. B., B2
Banks, Jerry, B7
Barba-Gutierrez, Y., B5
Barnes, R. M., B4
Baron, Opher, B5
Bartness, A. D., B3
Bauer, Eric, B6
Beatty, Richard W., B4
Becker, Brian E., B4
Beckman, S. L., B1
Bell, Glenn, 18
Bell, Steve, B5
Benton, W. C., B5
Berenson, Mark, B1
Berger, Paul D., B4
Berry, Leonard L., 233n
Berry, W. L., B3, B5
Besterfield, Dale H., B2
Bilginer, Özlem, B5
Birchfield, J., B3
Birchfield, J. C., B3
Black, I. T., B6
Blackburn, Joseph, B4
Blackstone, John H., B3
Blank, Ronald, B6
Blecker, Thorsten, B4

Bockstette, V., 194n
Boh, W. F., B7
Bolander, Steven, B5
Bowers, John, B3
Boyd, L. H., B3
Boyer, Kenneth K., B4
Bradley, Milton, 493
Bravard, J., B1
Bridger, R. S., B4
Broedner, P., B1
Brown, Bruce, B2
Brown, Mark G., B2
Buboltz, W.C., 413n
Buchannan, Leigh, B6
Buckley, Peter J., B2
Burch, Bill, 744
Burt, D. N., B5
Burton, Jeff, 409
Busch, Kurt, 409
Buxey, G., B5

C

Caiola, Gene, B5
Camevalli, J. A., B2
Campbell, Omar, B1
Canonaco, P., B7
Carson, J. S., B7
Cavanagh, R. R., B2
Cayirli, Tugba, B6
Chambers, Chester, B3
Chapman, S. N., B5
Chapman, Stephen, B5, B6
Chen, Bintong, B4
Chen, Fangruo., B5
Chen, Ming, B5
Chen, Wen-Chih, B3
Chen, Zhi-Long, B5
Chien, C., B3
Chopra, S., B3
Chopra, Sunil, B4, B5
Chu, K. F., B7
Chua, R. C. H., B2
Cleland, D. L., B1
Clive, L. M., B5
Cloutier, T. J., 678
Cochran, J. K., B7
Collins, Bob, 404
Combs, James G., B4
Coogan, Denise, 205
Cook, Lori, 772
Coupe, Henry, 402
Couto, J. P., B7
Crandall, Richard E., B4, B5
Criscuelo, P., B2
Crook, T. Russell, B4
Crosby, Philip B., 219, 219n, B2

Crotts, J. C., B1

D

Dahlgaard, J. J., B2
Datar, S. M., 242n
Davenport, T. H., B3
Davis, Leon, 630
Davis, Stanley B., B2
Dawande, M., B5
De Jong, A., B4
De Mathis J. J., B5
De Ruyter, K., B4
Debo, L. G., B3
DeFeo, J. A., B2
DeHoratius, N., 495n
Deimler, Mike, B2
Dellaert, N. P., B3
Dellande, S., B1
DeLong, George, 656
Deming, W. Edwards, 10, 218, 219, 220, 246n
Denton, Brian T., B6
Derman, O., B5
Deshmukh, S., B3
Devenney, George, 805
Dibbern, J., B1
Dickson, D. R., B1
Diebold, F. X., B1
Diehl Gregory W., B5
Dietrich, Brenda, B6
Dillman, Bob, 771
Disney, Stephen M., B4
Doğru, Mustafa K., B5
Dolgui, A., B5
Donnelly, P., B6
Dorso, Chris, 560
Douglas, David, 805
Drezner, Z., B3, B7
Duran, G., B6
Duray, R., B3

E

Elg, M., B2
Eppinger, S., B2
Epstein, Marc J., B2
Erhun, Feryal, B5
Ernst, David, B2
Espinosa, J. A., B7
Evans, J. R., B2

F

Farmer, Adam, B6
Fayurd, A.L., 372n
Feigenbaum, A. V., 219
Ferrari, Alex, 696
Fildes, Robert, B1
Finigen, Tim, B6

Fisher, Marshall L., 446n
Fitzsimmons, J., 351n
Fletcher, Allison, 656
Flinchbauh, Jamie, B6
Florida, R., B3
Flynn, B. B., B1
Flynn, E. J., B1
Ford, Henry, 10
Ford, R. C., B1
Fornell, C., 46n
Foster, G., 242n
Foster, Thomas, B2
Freivalds, Andris, B4

G
Galt, J., B1
Gantt, Henry L., 9, 607
Gardiner, Stanley C., B3
Gardner, Leslie, 239
Georgoff, D. M., B1
Gerstenfeld, Arthur, B4
Gerwin, Donald, B2
Gianipero, L. C., B4
Gibson, Randall R., B7
Gilbreth, Frank, 9, 420, 426
Gilbreth, Lillian, 9, 420
Gilliland, M., B1
Gitlow, Howard S., B2
Goetsch, David L., B2
Goldratt, Eliyaha, 317n, B3
Goldsby, Thomas J., B4
Gonul, M. S., B1
Gonzalez-Benito, J., B2
Gonzalez-Benito, O., B2
Goodale, John C., B3
Goodwin, Paul, B1
Gordon, Jeff, 408–409
Gordon, John Steel, B1
Graban, Mark, B6
Gray, John V., B2
Green, L. V., B7
Greenwald, Bruce, B1
Groebner, D., 134n
Gross, Donald, B7
Gross, E. E. Jr., 418
Gryna, F. M., B2
Guergachi, A., B7
Gupta, M. C., B3
Gupta, S. M., B5
Gwynne, Peter, B2

H
Hackman, J. R., 413, 413n
Hafeznezami, S., B3
Haines, Steven, B2
Hale, T., 713n, 744n
Hall, Joseph M., B3
Hall, Robert W., B6
Hammond, J. S., B6
Handfield, R. B., B4
Handfield, Robert B., B4
Hanke, J. E., B1

Hanna, M., 713n, 744n, B1, B3, B5, B6, B7
Harmon, Larry, 189
Harris, Carl M., B7
Harris, Chris, B5
Harrod, Steven, B6
Haugh, Helen M., B2
Hegde, V. G., B3
Heinzl, A., B1
Helgadottir, Hilder, B1
Helms, A. S., 427n
Heragu, S. S., B4
Heyer, N., B4
Hirschheim, R., B1
Hoffman, Ken, 632
Holweg, M., B6
Hooper, Ana, 276
Horngren, C. T., 242n
Hounshell, D. A., B1
Hu, J., B4
Huang, H. C., B7
Huang, L., B1
Huang, T., B1
Hug, Z., B3
Hult, G., B4
Humphries, Jim, B6
Huselid, Mark A., B4
Hvolby, H., B5

I
Iger, Robert, 106
Immonen, A., B2
Inderfurth, Karl, B3
Inoue, L., B6
Ireland, L. R., B1
Ireland, R. D., B6

J
Jackson, Jonathan, B5
Jackson, Wilma, 744
Jacobs, F. R., B5
Jain, Chaman L., B1
Jarrett, Dale, 409
Jayaraman, V., B4
Jennings, C. L., B3
Johns, T., B1
Johnson, Alan, B4
Johnson, M. Eric, 285n, B3
Johnson, Steven, B4
Jones, Daniel T., B6
Jonsson, Patrik, B3
Joshi, M. P., B1
Juran J. M., 219, 219n, 227

K
Kahn, Judd, B1
Kanawaty, George, 422n
Kane, H., B6
Kanet, J., B5
Kaplan, Robert S., B1
Kara, S., B4
Karlos, A., B1
Kathuria, R., B1

Kayis, B., B4
Keating, B., B1
Keefer, Donald L., B6
Kellogg, Deborah L., B6
Kelton, W. D., B7
Kennedy, M., B3
Kenney, R. L., B6
Keren, Baruch, B5
Kersten, Wolfgang, B4
Kerzner, H., B1
Keyte, Beau, B6
Kimes, S., 351n
Kimes, S. E., B5
Kin, S., B5
Kinard, Jerry, 275n
King-Metters, K., B5
Kinkel, S., B1
Kirchmier, Bill, B6
Klamroth, K., B3
Klassen, K., B7
Klassen, R., B4
Knight, Jim, 438
Koberstein, A., B5
Kohnke, E. J., B4
Koksalan, M., B7
Konz, S., B4
Konz, Stephan, 422n
Kopezak, Laura Rock, 285n
Kouvelis, Panos, B7
Kramer, M. R., 194n
Krehbiel, Tim, B1
Kreipl, Stephan, B4
Krishnan, M.S., 46n
Krishnan, V., B2
Krupp, James A. G., B5
Kuo, C., 348n

L
Ladner, John, 655
Lambrecht, Marc R., B4
Lane, Randy, 630
Langella, I. M., B3
Lanoie, Paul, B2
Larson, E. W., B1
Larson, S., B4
Laszlo, Chris, B2
Laubacher, R J., B1
Lawrence, M., B1
Lay, G., B1
Lee, Chieh, B4
Lee, Chung-Yee, B1
Lee, Eva K., B3
Lee, H., B5
Lee, Hau L., B1
Lemmink, J., B4
Leno, Jay, 172
Leon, Steve, 194
Leonard, M., B1
Leone, Charlie, 631–632
Leong, G. K., B6
Leong, G. Keong, B4
Leppa, Carol J., B6

Levine, David, B1
Lewis, Mike, B1
Lewis, William W., B1
Li, Shanling, B3
Lian, Z., B5
Liker, Jeffrey K., B6
Lin, H., B3
Lindner, C.A., 427n
Lindsay, W. M., B2
Lindsey, Todd, 155
Linton, J. D., B4
Liu, X., B5
Loch, C. H., B2
Locher, Drew, B6
Lopez, P., B6
Louly, Mohamed-Aly, B5

M
MacLean, D., B2
Maier, Anja M., B3
Malone, T. W., B1
Malone, Tom, 199
Malykhina, E., 495n
Mantel, S., B1
Maroto, A., B1
Martin, C. H., B6
Martins, Alex, 208–209
Marucheck, Ann S., B4
Mathison, George, 771–772
Matta, N. F., B1
Matthes, N., B3
Matthews, C. H., B6
Mattsson, Stig-Arne, B3
May, Jerrold H., B3
Maylor, Harvey, B1
McAlister, V. C., B7
McCormack, Angela, 275
McDonald, A., B7
McDonald, Stan C., B5
McEwan, Dr. Angus, 224
McFadden, Kathleen, 437
McGinnis, L. F., B4
McLaren, T., B7
McLaughlin, Patrick, B1
Medina-Borja, A., B6
Mehrotra, Vijay, B7
Meindl, Peter, B4
Menge, J. B., B6
Mentzer, John T., B3
Meredith, J. R., B1
Metters, Richard, B5
Midler, Paul, B1
Miguel, P. A. C., B2
Miller, C. C., B6
Miller, Luke T., B6
Milligan, G. W., B3
Mincsovics, G. Z., B3
Minicucci, Ben, 240–241, 655
Mitra, Amit, B2, B3
Monczka, R. M., B4
Mondschein, S. V., B6
Montgomery, D. C., B3

Morgan, James M., B6
Morgan, R., B1
Morrice, D., B3
Morrison, J. Bradley, B7
Morton, D., B3
Morton, Thomas E., B6
Moultrie, James, B3
Mukhopadhyay, S., B5
Munday, Oliver, 363–364
Munson, Charles L., B4, B5
Murat, A., B4
Murdick, R. G., B1
Muthusamy, S. K., B4

N
Najjar, L., B3
Narayanan, Sriram, B4
Nawler, Pete, 771
Nelson, B. L., B7
Nelson-Peterson, Dana L, B6
Neuman, R. P., B2
Neumann, Patrick W., B4
Newton, Wayne, 241, 303
Nicely, John, 595–596, 604
Nicol, D. M., B7
Niebel, B. W., 422n, B4
Nielsen, P., B5
Nielson, I., B5
Niemann, G., 426n
Norri, S., B7
Norris, G., B5
Norton, David P., B1

O
O'Sullivan, Jill, B5
O'Connell, Andrew, B6
Oates, David, B1
Oberwetter, R., 548n
Ohno, Taiichi, 636, 638, 649
Oldham, Greg R., 413, 413n
Oliver, Alexy, B2
Olson, Paul R., 402n
Olsson, J., B2
Onkal, D., B1
Özen, Ulaş, B5
Ozer, O., B5

P
Paine, Lincoln, B4
Paleologo, G. A., B6
Pande, P. S., B2
Parasuranam, A., 233n
Pareto, Vefredo, 227, 491
Parker, Thomas, B5
Parks, Charles M., B6
Parlar, M., B7
Parmigiani, G., B6
Partovi, F. Y., B3
Pasupathy, K., B6
Patterson, J. L., B4
Pentico, David W., B6
Perez, Anthony, 154, 560

Petcavage, S., B5
Peterson, A.P. G., 418
Peterson, R., B5
Peterson, Silva, 14
Petroski, Henry, B2
Pfeffer, Jeffrey, B4
Pfitzer, M., 194n
Pfund, M. E., B3
Phillippi, Brian, B6
Phillips, D. T., B6
Phillips, Paul, 678
Phyper, J. D., B2
Pinedo, M., B6
Pinedo, Michael, B4
Ping, J., B7
Pinkerton, R., B5
Pisano, Gary P., B2, B4
Plenert, Gerhard, B6
Poanski, Tom, 744
Porter, M. E., 194n
Porter, Michael, 40, 40n, B1, B3
Prabhu, N. U., B7
Prahalad, C. K., B2
Pronovost, Dr. Peter, 232
Pullman, M., B5
Pullman, Madeleine E., B3
Pyke, D. F., B5

Q
Qi, Y., B3
Quain, Bill, 725–726
Quain, Jeane, 725–726
Quillien, Jenny, B4

R
Radnor, Zoe J., B6
Rahman, Anisur, B6
Raiffa, H., B6
Raman, A., 495n
Rangaswami, M. R., B2
Rao, Tom, 674
Reeves, Martin, B2
Reich, Robert, 416
Reiner, Rob, 362–363
Reinhardt, Gilles, B5
Render, Barry, 713n, 744n, B1, B3, B5, B6, B7
Renouf, E., B7
Richardson, D. J., 409
Rizzo, Tony, 743–744
Robidoux, L., B6
Roche, K., B7
Rolewicz, Jamie, 408
Roodbergen, Kees Jan, B4
Rosenfield, D. B., B1
Rossetti, Manuel D., B7
Roth, Aleda V., B2
Roth, H. P., B3
Rothfeder, Jeffry, B1
Roubellat, F., B6
Roy, Anjan, B3
Rubalcaba, L., B1

Rubin, Paul A., B5
Rudberg, Martin, B1
Rugtusanatham, M. Johnny, B3

S

Saaksvuori, A., B2
Sadowski, R. P., B7
Sahay, B. S., B1
Salter, A., B2
Saltzman, Robert M., B7
Salvador, Fabrizio, B3
Salvendy, G., B4
Samaddar, S., B5
Sampson, Scott, 179–180, 180n
San, G., B1
Sasser, W. Earl, 402n
Sayre, Kim, B6
Schlaifer, R., B6
Schmeidler, Neil, B4
Schmenner, R. W., B7
Schonberger, Richard J., B6
Schrattenholzer, L., B7
Schroeder, R. G., B1, B2
Scudder, Gary, B4
Segerstedt, A., B5
Seider, Warren D., B2
Sethi, Suresh P., B5
Shah, Piyush, B1
Shahrokh, Shahraki, B4
Sharafali, M., B7
Shaw, B. W., 427n
Sheen, G., B3
Shewart, Walter, 10, 246
Shi, Chunming, B4
Shingo, Shiego, 644
Shortle, John F., B7
Siggelkow, Nicolaj, B1
Sillekens, Thomas, B5
Simmons, B. L., B4
Singhal, V. R., B4
Sinha, K. K., B4
Skinner, Wickham, B1
Slack, Nigel, B1
Slaughter, S. A., B7
Smith, Adam, 412
Smith, Bernard, 140, 140n
Smith, Fred, 338
Smith, Jeffrey S., B6
Smunt, T. L., B7
Snir, Eli M., B3
Snyder, L. V., B3
Sodhi, M. S., B7
Sonne, Michael, B4
Sorensen, Charles, 10
Sower, V. E., B3
Spangler, W. E., B3
Sprague, Linda G., B1
Sridharan, V., B5
Sriskandarajah, C., B5
Stair, R. M., 713n, 744n, B1, B3, B5, B6, B7

Stair, R. M. Jr., B6
Stamp, M., 194n
Stanford, D. A., B7
Stanley, L. L., B4
Stanowy, A., B4
Stark, Cathy, 630
Steger-Jensen, Kenn, B5
Stein, Andrew C., B5
Stephens, M. P., B6
Stepney, Nigel, 224
Stern, Scott, B3
Stewart, D. M., B2
Stoner, J. A., 95n
Stoner, J. A. F., B2
Strange, Roger, B2
Strum, D. P., B3
Sud, V. P., B7
Suhl, L., B5
Summer, M., B5
Summers, Donna, B2, B3
Sunny Yang, Shu-Jung, B3
Sural, H., B7
Surowski, Tom, 630
Sutera, Carla, 66
Swamidass, Paul M., B3
Swanson, Kathy, 240, 304, 333, 402
Swets, N. B., B7
Syntetos, A. A., B5

T

Taghavi, A., B4
Tallman, Stephen, B3
Talwar, A., B2
Tan, K., B4
Tang, Kwei, B2
Tangen, S., B1
Taylor, Bernard, B7
Taylor, Frederick W., 9, 10, 415, 420, 421
Taylor, G. Don Jr., B4
Taylor, S. J .E., B7
Taylor, Sam G., B5
Teixeira, J. C., B7
Terwiesch, C., B2
Teunter, Ruud H., B5
Thomas, A., 413n
Thompson, G. M., B5
Thompson, James M., B7
Tian, Feng, B5
Tian, Zhili, B7
Tibben-Lembke, Ronald S., B3
Tippet, L., 427
Toktay, L. B., B3
Tolo, B., B4
Tomas M., B4
Tompkins, James A., B4
Ton, Z., 495n
Toyoda, Eiji, 649
Trietsch, Dan, B6
Tseng, C. L., B4
Turbide, Dave, B5

Ulrich, Karl T., B2
Upton, David, B4
Urs, Rajiv, B1

V

Vaidyanathan, R., B6
van Biema, Michael, B1
van Veen-Dirks, Paula, B6
Van Wassenhove, L. N., B3
Vargas, L. G., B3
Veeraraghavan, S., B6
Veral, Emre, B6
Verganti, Roberto, B2, B4
Verma, Rohit, B3
Verzuh, Eric, B1
Village, Judy, B4
Villalta, D. L., B4
Vis, I. F. A., B4
Vollmann, T. E., B5

W

Wagner, H. M., B5
Walczak, Steven, B6
Wallace, Rusty, 408
Walsh, Ellen, B4
Walter, Janie, 189
Walton, S., B5
Wang, L., B3
Wang, Phanich P., B4
Wang, Q., B6
Wankel, C., B2
Ward, P. T., B3
Waring, J., B6
Watson, Kevin J., B3
Watts, C. A., B7
Weeks, J., 372n
Weil, Marty, B6
Weintraub, G. Y., B6
Welborn, Cliff, B3
Wells, John, 274
Wemmerlöv, U., B4
West, B. M., B1
Weston, M., B7
Whalen, Lynn, 596
Wheeler, J. V., B4
Whitaker, J., 46n
White, Catherine M., B4
White, G., B3
White, J. A., B4
White, R. E., 348n
Whitin, T. M., B5
Whitney, Eli, 9
Whybark, D. C., B5
Wichern, D. W., B1
Wilson, J. H., B1
Winkelspecht, C., 413n
Wisner, Joel, B4
Wisner, Joel D., 239
Witt, Clyde E., B5
Wolf, Martin, B1
Womack, James P., B6

Wren, Daniel A., B1
Wright, George, 630
Wright, T. P., 776, 776n
Wyckoff, D. Daryl, 402n
Wynter, L., B6
Wysocki, R. K., B1

X

Xie, Xiaolan, B7
Xin Xu, Sean, B5

Y

Yan Kovic, N., B7
Yan, Xinghao, B2
Yang, Shilei, B4
Yoo, S., B5
Yoogalingam, R., B7
Yurklewicz, Jack, B1

Z

Zeithaml, Valarie A., 233n
Zeng, Amy Z., B4

Zhang, Aheng, B7
Zhang, M., B3
Zhang, X., B6
Zhao, Hui, B2
Zhao, T., B4
Zhao, X., B3
Zhao, Yong-Pin, 524
Zhexembayeva, N., B2
Zipkin, Paul, B3

General Index

A

ABC analysis, 491–492
Acceptable quality level (AQL), 263
Acceptance sampling, 262–265, T2–1 to T2–7
  average outgoing quality (AOQ), 264–265, T2–5 to T2–6
  erroneous conclusions and, 263n
  operating characteristic (OC) curve and, 263–264
  sampling plans, T2–2
Accurate inventory records, MRP and, 570
Accurate pull data, 452
Activity charts, job design and, 418
Activity map, 43
Activity times, variability in, 77–82
Activity-on-arrow (AOA), 68, 71
Activity-on-node (AON), 68, 69–70, 90
Adaptive smoothing, forecasting and, 139
Additive manufacturing, 295
Advanced shipping notice (ASN), 454
Aggregate planning, 529–562
  capacity options, 535–536
  chase strategy and, 537
  comparison of planning methods for, 537
  demand options and, 536–537
  disaggregation and, 535
  ethical dilemma, 551
  graphical methods and, 538–543
  level strategy and, 538
  master production schedule and, 535
  mathematical approaches and, 543–545
  methods for, 538–543
  mixing options to develop a plan and, 537–538
  nature of, 534–535
  planning process and, 532–533
  revenue management and, 547–550
  sales and operating planning (S&OP) and, 533–534
  scheduling issues and, 603
  services and, 545–547
  software for, 552–553
  S&OP definition, 533
  strategies for, 535–538
  transportation method of linear programming and, 543–545
  yield management and, 547–550

Aggregate scheduling. *See* Aggregate planning
Agile project management, 67
Air Berlin, 257
Aircraft industry, 417
Airfreight, logistics management and, 457
Airline industry:
  aggregate planning and, 547
  capacity, matching to demand, 313
  inventory, 652
  organizational chart, 5
  revenue management, 551
  scheduling services in, 619
  sustainability, 194
AirTran, 257
Alabama Airlines, 805–806
Alaska, long-range economic forecasting, 111
Alaska Airlines:
  baggage process strategy, 303–304
  Global Company Profile, 600–601
  human resources, 437–438
  inspection, 232
  lean operations, 651, 655–656
  quality, 240–242
  scheduling challenges, 726
  short-term scheduling, 600–602
  sustainability, 199
Alenia Aeronautica, 30–31
Algebraic approach, break-even analysis and, 319–320
Align Technology, 285
Alliances, 175
  time-based competition and, 175
Allowable ranges for objective function coefficients, 708
Allstate Insurance, 163
All-units discount, 507
Amazon.com, 110
  Global Company Profile, 488–489
  supply chain, 445
  warehouse strategy, 376
Ambient conditions, 375
American Hardware Supply, 140
American National Can Company, 289, 290
American Society for Quality (ASQ), 8, 217
Amway Center, 208–209, 631–632
Analysis and design, process strategy and, 289
Andon, 637, 642

Anheuser-Busch, 463
AOA (Activity-on-arrow), 68, 71
AON (Activity-on-node), 68, 69–70
APEC, 34
APICS (Association for Operations Management), 8
APICS Supply Chain Council, 464
Apple, 41, 45, 109–110, 162, 195
Application of decision trees
  evaluating disaster risk, 473–474
  product design, 182–184
Appointment system, 314
Appraisal costs, quality and, 218
Approaches to forecasting, 111–112
Arby's, use of GIS system, 353
ArcGIS, 353
Arcs, routing and scheduling vehicles and, T5–3
Area under the normal curve, T1–4 to T1–5
Argentina, MERCOSUR and, 34
Arnold Palmer Hospital, 66
  building construction, 66
  capacity planning, 333–334
  flowchart, 229
  Global Company Profile, 214–215
  hospital layout, 402–404
  inspection, 232
  JIT, 656
  labor standards and, 428
  managing quality, 214–215
  mission statement, 36
  process analysis, 304
  process focus, 283
  project management, 99–100
  supply chain, 468
Arrival characteristics, waiting line systems and, 749–752
  behavior of arrivals, 750
  characteristics of, 749–750
  pattern of arrivals and, 749–750
  Poisson distribution, 737
Artifacts, servicescapes and, 375
Artificial variables, T3–8
ASRS, 296
Assembly chart, 178
Assembly drawing, 178
Assembly line
  labor specialization, 412
  product-oriented layout and, 386
  regulations, 203–204
  repetitive manufacturing, 280–281
  scheduling, 605
  sustainability, 203

Note: Page numbers beginning with a T refer to the Online Tutorial chapters that appear on our web site **www.pearsonhighered.com/heizer**.

Assembly-line balancing, product-oriented layout and, 386
Assets committed to inventory, 461–463
Assignable variations, statistical process control and, 247
Assignment method, loading and, 608–610
Association for Operations Management (APICS), 8
Associative forecasting methods, 112, 131–137
  correlation coefficient for regression lines, 134–136
  linear-regression analysis, 131–136
  multiple regression analysis, 136–137
  regression analysis, 131–137
  standard deviation of the estimate, 133–134
  standard error of the estimate, 133–134
Assumptions, break-even analysis and, 318–319
Atlas GIS, 353
AT&T, 218
Attract and retain global talent, global view of operations and, 34–35
Attribute(s):
  c-charts and, 257–259
  control charts for, 256–259
  p-charts and, 256–257, 259
  versus variables, inspection and, 233
Auctions, online, 456
Auctions, supply chain management, and, 455
Audi, 46
Australia, SEATO and, 34
Automated Storage and Retrieval Systems (ASRS), 296, 297
Automatic Guided Vehicles (AGV), 296
Automatic identification systems (AIS), 295, 377
Automation, service efficiency and, 181
Automobile manufacturing. *See also* Ford Motor Co.
  bullwhip effect in, 476
  sustainability, 203, 205
Autonomous maintenance, 670
Avendra, 456
Average observed time, 422
Average outgoing quality, 264–265, T2–5 to T2–6
Avis car rental, 730

B

Babbage, Charles, 412
Back ordering, 536–537
Backup redundancy, 665–666

Backward integration, 448
Backward pass, 74
Backward scheduling, 604
BAE Systems, 30
Balancing work cells, 384–386
Balking customers, 750
Ballard Power Systems, 175
Baltimore, Port of, 119–120
Bank of America, 643
Banks
  organizational chart, 5
  scheduling for services and, 618
Basic feasible solution, T3–3
Basic variables, T3–3
Baxter International, 642
Bay Medical Center, simulation and, 792
Bayfield Mud Company, SPC and, 274–275
Bechtel Group, Global Company Profile, 60–61
Beer, supply chain for, 444
Behavior of arrivals, 750
Bell Laboratories, 246
Benchmarking, 222–224
  supply chain, 463
Benetton, 32, 370, 453, 585
Best Buy, 375
Beta probability distribution, 77–78
Bias, forecasts and, 138
Big data, 679
Bills-of-material (BOM), 175, 568–570
Binary variables, 713–715
Blanket orders, 453
Blue Cross, 46
BMW, 34, 203
Boeing Aircraft, 173, 388–389
  Global Company Profile, 30–31
  operations strategy, 40
  product reliability, 668
  supply chain risks and tactics, 450
  sustainable product design, 199
Bose Corp., 216
Boston Medical Center, 415
Bottleneck analysis and theory of constraints, 314–318
  management of, 317–318
  time and, 315
Bottom line, triple, 195–198
BP, 204
Brazil, MERCOSUR and, 34
Break-bulk warehouse function, 457
Breakdown maintenance, 667
Break-even analysis, 318–322
  assumptions and, 318–319
  definition, 318
  fixed costs, 318
  multiproduct case and, 320–322
  revenue function, 318
  single-product case and, 319–320

Bristol-Myers Squibb, 111
British Petroleum (BP), 204
Buckets, MRP and, 576
Buffer, in bottleneck management, 317
Building the supply base, centralized purchasing, 455–456
Build-to-order (BTO), 285
Bullwhip effect, 452, 474–476
Burger King, 386, 794
Buybacks, 455

C

CAD, 171–172
Cadillac, 218
CAFTA, 34
Calculating slack time, 75–76
California drought, 197
Call center industry, location strategies and, 47
CAM, 172
Canada, NAFTA and, 34
Canon, 384
"Cap and trade" principle, 204
Capacity. *See also* Break-even analysis
  aggregate planning, 535–536
  analysis and, 314
  applying expected monetary value (EMV) to capacity decisions, 323
  applying investment analysis to strategy-driven investments, 324–326
  bottleneck analysis and theory of constraints, 314–318
  break-even analysis, 318–322
  capacity exceeds demand, 312
  considerations and, 311
  definition, 308
  demand management and, 312–313
  design and, 309–311
  effective capacity, 309–311
  forecasting and, 109, 110
  managing demand, 312–313
  net present value and, 324–326
  reducing risks with incremental changes, 322–323
  service sector demand, 313–314
  strategy and, 311
  strategy-driven investments and, 324–326
  theory of constraints, 317
  using software, 327
Capacity analysis, 314
Capacity management, service sector and, 314
Capacity planning, MRP and, 581–583
Capacity plans, scheduling issues and, 602–603
Capital, as a productivity variable, 15, 16

Car rental companies, 730
Carbon footprint, 197
Cartoon industry in Manila, 33
Carvel Ice Cream, use of GIS system, 352
Case Studies:
    Alabama Airlines' Call Center, 805–806
    Alaska Airlines:
        human resources, 437–438
        lean operations, 655–656
        process strategy, 303–304
        quality, 240–242
        scheduling challenges, 726
    Amway Center sustainability, 208–209
    Andrew Carter, Inc. aggregate planning, 559–560
    Arnold Palmer Hospital
        capacity planning, 333–334
        hospital layout, 402–404
        JIT, 656
        process analysis, 304
        project management, 99–100
        quality, 240
        supply chain, 468
    Bayfield Mud Company, SPC and, 274–275
    Custom Vans. Inc. transportation problem, 743–744
    Darden Restaurants
        outsourcing offshore, 56
        Red Lobster, location and strategies, 362–363
        statistical process control, 276
        supply chain and, 467
    De Mar's Product Strategy, 189
    Frito-Lay
        inventory management, 525–526
        maintenance, 674
        operations management, 25
        statistical process control, 275
        sustainability, 209–210
    Hard Rock Cafe
        forecasting, 155–156
        global strategy, 55–56
        human resource strategy, 438
        location strategy, 363–364
        operations management in services, 25–26
        project management, 77, 100–102
        scheduling, 632
    Jackson Manufacturing Co., work measurement, 437
    New England Foundry, waiting-line models, 771–772
    Old Oregon Wood Store, short-term scheduling and, 630
    Orlando Magic
        forecasting, 154–155

    MRP and, 595–596
    revenue management, 560
    short-term scheduling, 631–632
    sustainability, 208–209
    Parker Hi-Fi Systems, inventory management and, 525
    Phlebotomists, routing and scheduling, T5–17 to T5–18
    Port of Miami warehouse tenting, 696
    Quain Lawn and Garden, Inc., LP problem, 725–726
    Rapid-Lube, operations strategy in a global environment and, 55
    Regal Marine
        global strategy, 55
        product design, 189–190
        supply chain management, 467–468
    Ritz-Carlton Hotel company quality, 242
    Rochester Manufacturing Corp., 302
    SMT's negotiation with IBM, 787–788
    Southern Recreational Vehicle Co., location strategies and, 362
    Southwestern University:
        forecasting, 153–154
        project management, 98–99
        quality, 239–240
    State automobile license renewals, 402
    Uber Technologies, Inc., 24
    Wheeled Coach
        inventory control, 526
        layout strategy, 404
        MRP and, 596
        process strategy, 302–303
    Winter Park Hotel, waiting line models, 772
    Zhou Bicycle Co., inventory management and, 524–525
Cash flow, investment analysis and, 324
Cash for Clunkers program, 476
Caterpillar, 49, 50, 203, 474
Cause-and-effect diagrams, 226, 227
c-charts, 257–259
Center-of-gravity method, location strategies and, 348–349, 348n
Central limit theorem, 248–249
Certainty, decision making under, 683
Certification, supplier, 454
Cessna Aircraft Company, 642
Changes in objective function coefficient, 707–708
Changes in resources or right-hand-side values, LP and, 706–707

Channel assembly, supply chain management and, 457–458
Characteristics of goods and services, 11
Characteristics of vehicle routing and scheduling problems, T5–3 to T5–5
Charleston, port of, 451
Charts. See Control charts
Chase strategy, aggregate scheduling and, 537
Check sheets, TQM tools and, 226–227
Checklist, source inspection and, 231
Chengdu Aircraft, 30
Chile, SEATO and, 34
China
    ethics within supply chain, 460
    manufacturing in, 48, 51
Chinese postman problem (CPP), T5–4
CIM, 297–298
Cisco Systems, 372
Clark and Wright Savings heuristic, T5–5, T5–7 to T5–8
Classifying routing and scheduling vehicle problems, T5–3 to T5–4
Closed-loop material requirements planning, 581
Closed-loop supply chain, 203, 461
Cluster first, route second approach, T5–10 to T5–11
Clustering, 344
Cobham, 30
Coca-Cola, 198, 463
Coefficient approach, learning curve and, 779–782
Coefficient of correlation, 134–136
Coefficient of determination, 136
Collaborative planning, forecasting, and replenishment (CPFR), 110, 453
Colruyt, Franz, 38
Commodities transport, 457
Common, resources in the, 195
Company reputation, quality and, 217
Comparative advantage, theory of outsourcing, 46
Comparison of aggregate planning methods, 537
Comparison of process choices, 286–288
Competing on cost
    differentiation, operations and, 37–38
    experience differentiation, 38
    operations and, 38
    product strategy options and, 164
    response, operations, 39–40

Competitive advantage, operations and, 36–39
  Amazon.com, 488–489
  Arnold Palmer Hospital and, 214–215
  Bechtel and, 60–61
  Boeing and, 30–31
  cost and, 38
  Darden Restaurants, 442–443
  definition, 36–37
  differentiation and, 37–38
  Federal Express, 338–339
  Frito-Lay, 530–531
  human resources and, 410–411
  lean operations and, 636–637
  McDonalds, 368–369
  Orlando Utilities Commission, 660–661
  product strategy options and, 163–164
  Regal Marine and, 160–161
  Walt Disney World and, 106–107
  Wheeled Coach, 564–565
Competitive bidding, 455
Competitors, location proximity to, 344
Components, lead time for, 570–571
Computer numerical control (CNC), 295
Computer software. *See also* Excel, creating your own spreadsheets; Excel OM; POM for Windows
  for process oriented layouts, 382–383
  for simulations, 800
Computer-aided design (CAD), 161, 171, 297
Computer-aided manufacturing (CAM), 172, 297
Computer-integrated manufacturing (CIM), 297–298
Concurrent engineering, 170
Concurrent scheduler approach, T5–13
Configuration management, 178
Consignment inventory, JIT and, 642
Constant work-in-process (ConWIP), 606–607
Constant-service-time model, 762
Constraints:
  graphical representation of, LP problem and, 702–703
  human resource strategy and, 410
  linear programming and, 701
Consumer market survey, forecasting and, 111–112
Consumer Product Safety Commission, 203
Consumer's risk, 263, T2–3 to T2–4
Containers. *See* Kanban
Continuous improvement
  TPS and, 649

TQM and, 220–221
Continuous probability distributions, statistical tools and, T1–5 to T1–8
Contracting, with suppliers, 455
Contribution, break-even analysis and, 318
Contribution, defined, 165n
Control charts, 230, 241
  attributes, 256–258
  building process, 247–248
  c-charts, 257–259
  defined, 246
  managerial issues and, 259–260
  patterns on, 259
  p-charts, 256–257, 259
  R-charts, 248, 253–254
  steps to follow in using, 254–255
  variables, 248, 259
  x-bar chart, 248, 250–253, 259
Control of service inventory, 494–495
Controlling, project management and, 66–67
Controlling forecasts, 138–140
ConWIP cards, 606–607
Coors, 112
Core competencies, 42–43
Core job characteristics, 413–414
Corner-point solution method, 705
Corporate social responsibility (CSR), 194
Correlation analysis, associative forecasting methods and, 131–137
Correlation coefficients for regression lines, 134–136
Cost of goods sold, 462
Cost of quality (COQ), 218–219
Cost-based price model, 455
Costco, 495, 758
Cost(s)
  breakdown, 668–669
  competing on, 38
  globalization, 33
  intangible, 342
  intuitive lowest-cost transportation model, 733–734
  location and, 340–341
  queuing, 753–754
  reduction through value engineering, 170
  tangible, 342
Cost-time trade-offs, project management and, 82–85
Council of Supply Chain Management Professionals, 8
C_p ratio, 260–261
CPFR (collaborative planning, forecasting, and replenishment), 110
C_{pk} index, 261–262

CPM. *See* Critical path method (CPM)
Crashing, project management and, 82–85
Criteria, scheduling and, 604–605
Critical path, 67, 91–92
Critical path analysis, 71–72
Critical path method (CPM)
  activity-on-arrow example, 68, 71
  activity-on-node example, 69–70
  calculating slack time, 75–76
  critique of, 85–86
  determining the project schedule, 71–76
  framework of, 67–68
  Gantt charts *versus,* 65
  identifying the critical path, 72
  network diagrams and approaches, 68
  variability in activity time, 77–82
Critical ratio (CR), sequencing and, 614–615
Critique of PERT and CPM, 85–86
Crosby, Philip B., 219
Cross-docking, 376
Crossover charts, 286–287
Cross-sourcing, 450
CSR (corporate social responsibility), 194
Cultural issues, global view of operations and, 35
Culture, location strategy and, 343
Cumulative probability distribution, Monte Carlo Simulation and, 794
Currency risks, location strategies and, 342
Curtis-Wright Corp., 776
Custom Vans. Inc., 743–744
Customer interaction, process design and, 293–294
Customer relationship management (CRM) software, 584
Customer service, dissatisfaction from outsourcing, 46
Customers, understanding
  focus, 288
  new products and, 166, 167
  sustainability, 195–196
Customizing. *See also* Mass customization
  service efficiency, increasing, 181
  warehousing layout and, 377
Cycle counting, inventory management and, 493–494
Cycle time, focused work center and focused factory and, 389, 389n
Cycles, forecasting and, 113, 131
Cyclical scheduling, 620–621
Cyclical variations in data, forecasting and, 131

D

Daimler-BMW, joint venture and, 448
Darden Restaurants. *See also* Olive
    Garden Restaurant, Red
    Lobster Restaurant
  Global Company Profile, 442–443
  outsourcing offshore, 56
  statistical process control, 253, 276
  supply chain management, 442–
    443, 460, 467
  supply chain risks and tactics, 450
  use of GIS system, 352
Dassault, 30
Data, big, 679
De Mar, 189
Deadhead time, T5–12
Decibel (dB) levels, 418
Decision making:
  under certainty, 681–682, 683
  expected value of perfect
    information (EVPI), 683–684
  expected value with perfect
    information (EVwPI), 683–684
  under risk, 682–683
Decision making tools, 677–698. *See*
    also decision trees
  under certainty, 681–682, 683
  decision tables, 680
  decision trees, 684–688
  expected value of perfect
    information (EVPI), 683–684
  expected value with perfect
    information (EVwPI), 683–684
  fundamentals of, 679–680
  process in operations and, 678–679
  under risk, 682–683
Decision tables, 680
Decision trees, 684–688
  definition, 684
  evaluating disaster risk, 473–474
  more complex, 686–688
  poker decision process, 688
  product design and, 182–184
  using software, 689–690
Decision variables, linear
    programming and, 702
Decline phase, product life cycle and,
    165
Decomposition of a time series,
    112–113
Defects, control charts for, 258
Defining a product, 175–177
Degeneracy, transportation modeling
    and, 737–738
Delay
  allowances, 422
  waste, 289n
Delay customization, adding service
    efficiency and, 181
Dell computers
  inventory management, 463
  mass customization and, 284–285

quality, 216
Deloitte & Touche, 372
Delphi method, forecasting and, 111
Delta Airlines, 66, 257
  Gantt chart of service activities, 65
Demand exceeds capacity, 312
Demand forecasts, 109
  exponential smoothing, 116–117
  moving averages, 114–116
  regression, 131–137
  steady (naive approach), 113–114
Demand is variable and lead time is
    constant, probability models
    and, 511
Demand management in service
    sector, 313–314
Demand not equal to supply,
    transportation models and, 737
Demand options, aggregate strategies
    and, 536–537
Deming, W. Edwards, 218, 219, 246n
Deming Prize, 218
Deming's 14 points, quality and, 220
Denim production, 197
Department of Agriculture
  product definition, 175–176
Dependent demand, 495, 566
Dependent inventory model
    requirements, 566–571
  accurate inventory records and, 570
  bills-of-material and, 568–570
  lead times for components and,
    570
  low level coding, 570
  master production schedule and,
    567–568
  modular bills, 569–570
  planning bill, 570
  purchase orders outstanding and,
    570
Dependent selections, 714
Depot node, routing and scheduling
    vehicles and, T5–3
Design and production for
    sustainability, 19, 173, 198–200
Design capacity, 309
Design for manufacture and assembly
    (DFMA), 171
Design of goods and services,
    159–192. *See also* Product
    Development
  adding service efficiency and, 181
  alliances and, 175
  application of decision trees to
    product design, 182–184
  bill of material (BOM) and, 175
  computer-aided design (CAD) and,
    171–172
  computer-aided manufacturing
    (CAM) and, 172
  defining the product, 175–177
  documents for production, 178–179

documents for services, 181–182
generating new products, 165–166
goods and services selection,
    162–165
group technology and, 177
issues for product design, 171–173
joint ventures and, 174–175
life cycle and strategy and, 164–
    165
life cycle assessment (LCA), 173
make-or-buy decisions and, 176–
    177
modular design and, 171
OM decisions and, 8
process-chain-network (PCN)
    analysis, 179–181
product development, 166–170
product development continuum,
    173–175
product life cycles and, 164
product life-cycle management
    (PLC) and, 178–179
product strategy options support
    competitive advantage and,
    163–164
product-by-value analysis, 165
purchasing technology by
    acquiring a firm and, 174
robust design and, 171
service design, 179–182
sustainability, 19, 173, 198–200
time-based competition, 173–175
transition to production, 184
value analysis and, 173
virtual reality technology and,
    172–173
Determinants of service quality, 234
Determining project schedule
  backward pass, 74–75
  calculating slack time, 75–76
  forward pass, 72–74
  identifying critical paths, 75–76
Developing missions and strategies,
    35–36
DFMA, 171
DHL, supply chain and, 457, 458
Diehl, 30
Diet problem, LP and, 711
Differences between goods and
    services, 11
Differentiation, competitive
    advantage and, 37–38, 163–
    164
Direct interaction, process chain and,
    180
Disaggregation, aggregate planning
    and, 535
Disaster risk in supply chain,
    evaluating, 472–474
Discrete probability distributions,
    strategic tools and, T1–2 to
    T1–3

Diseconomies of scale, 311
Disney Parks and Resorts. *See* Walt Disney Parks and Resorts
Disney World. *See* Walt Disney Parks and Resorts
Disneyland, 375
Dispatching jobs, priority rules and, 611–612
Distance reduction, JIT layout and, 643
Distribution management, supply chain management and, 459
Distribution resource planning (DRP), 584
Distribution systems, supply-chain management, 459
Distributions, control chart, 247
DMAIC, TQM and, 221
Documents:
  for production, 178–179
  for services, 181–182
Domestic Port Radiation Initiative supply chain risks and tactics, 450
Dominican Republic, CAFTA and, 34
Double smoothing, 124
Doubling approach, learning curve, 778–779
Dow Chemical, 194
Drop shipping, 454
Drum, in bottleneck management, 317
Dual value, 707
Dubuque, Iowa, call center, 47
Dummy destinations, 737
Dummy sources, 737
DuPont, 46, 163, 222
Dutch auctions, 456
Dynamics, MRP and, 575

E

Earliest due date (EDD), 611, 614
Earliest finish time (EF), critical path analysis and, 72, 73
Earliest start time (ES), critical path analysis and, 72, 73
Earthquake damage, 472
Eco Index, 204
Economic change, generating new products, 166
Economic forecasts, 109
Economic order quantity (EOQ) models, 496–497
  lot sizing and, 577–578
  minimize costs, 497
  production order quantity model, 502–504
  quantity discount model, 505–507
  reorder points, 501–502
  robust model, 500–501
Economic sustainability, 197
Economies of scale, 311

Effective capacity, 309
Efficiency
  capacity and, 310
  of line balance, 391
Electronic data interchange (EDI), 454
Electronic ordering and funds transfer, 453–454
Eliminate waste, lean operations and, 638–639
Elliot Health System, 415
Emergency room
  process layout, 379
  queuing, 753
Emirates, 257
Employee empowerment
  job expansion and, 413
  OM and, 18
  TPS and, 649
  TQM and, 222
Employees
  lean operations and JIT, 643
  recruiting globally, 34–35
Employment stability policies, 411
EMV. *See* Expected monetary value
End-of-life phase, 203
Energy Star rating, 204
Engineering change notice (ECN), 178
Engineering drawing, 175
Enterprise Resource Planning (ERP), 566, 584–587. *See also* Material requirements planning
Environment
  supply chain ethics and, 460
  sustainability and, 196–197
Environmental Protection Agency (EPA), 204
Environmentally sensitive production, OM and, 18
EOQ (economic order quantity models), 496–497
E-procurement, 456
Equally likely, decision-making under uncertainty, 681
Equipment, selecting for process strategy, 288
Ergonomics, work environment and, 415–417
  feedback to operators, 417
  operators input to machines, 416–417
Erie Canal, 457
Errors, type 1 and type 2, 263
Ethical dilemmas:
  aggregate planning, 551
  airline revenue management, 551
  car battery recycling, 20
  design of goods and services, 185
  human resources, job design, work measurement and, 431
  inventory management, 515

layout strategy, 392
lean operations, 653
location strategies, 354
maintenance and reliability, 671
managing quality, 235
material requirements planning (MRP) and ERP, 587
operation and productivity, 20
operation strategy in a global environment, 51
process strategy, 300
project management, 64, 89
short-term scheduling, 621–622
supply-chain management, 465
test scores and forecasting, 141
Ethical issues
  global view of operations and, 35
Ethics:
  human resources, job design and work measurement, 430
  project management and, 64
  quality management and, 219
  response identification, 19
  social responsibility and, 19
  supply chain and, 460, 465
  sustainability and, 19
EU Emissions Trading System (EUETS), 204
European Union (EU), 34, 34n
  environmental regulations, 204
  standard for the exchange of product data (STEP), 172
Evaluating disaster risk in supply chain, 472–474
Even-numbered problems, solutions to, A7–A20
EVPI (expected value of perfect information), 683–684
EVwPI (expected value with perfect information), 683–684
Excel OM:
  accessing, 21
  aggregate planning and, 553
  break-even analysis and, 327
  decision models and, 689, 690
  develop x-bar charts, *p*-charts, *c*-charts, OC curves, acceptance sampling and process capability, 266
  forecasting and, 143
  inventory management and, 517
  layout problems and, 393
  learning curves and, 784
  linear programming, 718
  location problems and, 354
  MRP and ERP and, 588–589
  outsourcing problems, 51
  project scheduling and, 89, 90
  queuing problems, 766
  reliability and, 672
  short-term scheduling and, 622–624

simulation and, 801
transportation problems, 738–739, 738–7397
using and, A5
Excel Solver, 552–553, 706, 713–714
Excel spreadsheets, creating your own
  aggregate planning, 552–553
  break-even analysis, 327
  control limits for c-chart, 266
  creating your own spreadsheets, 21
  decision models, 689, 690
  factor rating analysis, 52
  forecasting, 142–143
  inventory management, 516
  linear programs, 716–717
  location strategies, 354
  outsourcing problems, 51
  simulation, 800–801
  transportation problems, 738
Exchange rates
  reducing risk through globalization, 33–34, 342
Expected monetary value (EMV), 682–683
  capacity decisions, 323
  decision tree analysis, 684–686
Expected value:
  of discrete probability distribution, statistical tools and, T1–3
  of perfect information (EVPI), 683–684
  with perfect information, (EVwPI), 683–684
Experience differentiation, 38
  Disney and, 38
Exponential smoothing
  forecasting and, 116–117
  smoothing constant, 116–117
  trend adjustment and, 120–124
Extensions of MRP, 580–583
  capacity planning, 581–583
  closed loop, 581
  material requirements planning II, 580–581
External failure costs, quality and, 218

F

Fabrication line, production-oriented layout and, 386
Factor weighting technique, 477
Factor-rating method
  location strategies and, 345–346
  outsource providers, 47
Factors affecting location decisions and, 341–344
  costs, 342
  currency risk, 342
  exchange rates, 342

labor productivity, 342
political risks, 343
proximity to markets, 343
proximity to suppliers, 344
Faro Technologies, 264
Fast Track, 66
Fast-food restaurants
  forecasting and, 140–141
  repetitive process using modules, 283
Fatigue allowances, 422
Feasible region, 703
Feasible tour, T5–3
FedEx, 141, 218
  Global Company Profile, 338–339
  customized warehouses, 377
  logistics, 458
Feedback to operators, 417
Feed-mix problem, LP and, 711
Feigenbaum, Armand V., 219
Ferrari racing team, 224
FIFS (first in, first served), 751n
Finance/accounting, OM and, 4
Finished-goods inventory, 491
Finite capacity scheduling (FCS), 597, 617–618
Finite loading, 604
Finite-population waiting model, 749, 763–765
First Simplex tableau, T3–2 to T3–4
First-come, first-served (FCFS) system, 314, 611, 614
First-in, first-out (FIFO), 751, 751n
First-in, first-served (FIFS), 751n
First-order smoothing, 124
Fish-bone chart, 227
Five forces analysis, 40
5 Ss, lean operations and, 639, 639n
Fixed costs, break-even analysis and, 318
Fixed fees, 507
Fixed-charge integer programming problem, 715
Fixed-period (P) inventory systems, 514–515
Fixed-position layout, 370, 377–378
Fixed-quantity (Q) inventory system, 514
Flexibility, process strategy and, 288
Flexibility increased, JIT layout and, 643
Flexible manufacturing system (FMS), 297
Flexible response, 39
Flexible workweek, 412
Flextronics, 45
Flow diagrams, 418, 419
Flow time, 611
Flowcharts, 226, 228–229, 289
Flowers Bakery, 246

Focus forecasting, 139–140
Focused factory, 386
Focused processes, 287–288
Focused work center, 386
Food and Drug Administration, 203
Foot Locker, 586
Ford Motor Co., 175, 198, 447, 646
Forecast error, measuring, 117–120
Forecasting, 105–166. *See also* Associative forecasting methods; Time series forecasting
  adaptive smoothing and, 139
  approaches to, 111–112
  associative methods, regression & correlation analysis and, 131–137
  bias and, 138
  capacity and, 110
  coefficient of determination and, 136
  correlation coefficients for regression lines and, 134–136
  defined, 108
  Delphi method and, 111
  demand forecast and, 109
  economic forecasts and, 109
  fast food restaurants and, 140
  focus forecasting and, 139–140
  human resources and, 110
  jury of executive opinion and, 111
  linear regression analysis and, 131–136
  market survey and, 111–112
  monitoring and controlling forecasts and, 138–140
  multiple regression analysis and, 136–137
  qualitative methods and, 111–112
  quantitative method and, 112
  regression analysis and, 131–137
  service sector and, 140–141
  seven steps in, 110–111
  software in, 142–144
  specialty retail shops and, 140
  standard error of the estimate and, 133–134
  strategic importance of, 109–110
  supply chain management and, 109–110
  technological forcasts and, 109
  time horizons and, 108–109
  types of, 109
  using software and, 142–144
Formula approach, learning curves and, 779
Formulating problems, LP and, 701–702
Forward integration, 448
Forward pass, 72–74
Forward scheduling, 603

Four process strategies, 282–288
  mass customization focus, 284–285
  process focus, 282–283
  product focus, 284
  repetitive focus, 283
Framework of PERT and CPM, 67–68
Franz Colruyt, low-cost strategy and, 38
Free slack, 75
Freezing schedule, 647
Frito-Lay
  aggregate planning and, 530–531
  Global Company Profile, 530–531
  maintenance, 662, 674
  managing inventory, 525–526
  operations management, 25
  product focus, 284
  statistical process control, 275
  sustainability, 197–198, 200, 209–210
  x-bar charts, 255
Fuji Heavy Industries, 30
Functional area, mission and, 36
Functionality, servicescapes and, 375
Functions of inventory, 490
Future time horizon, forecasting and, 108–109

G

Gantt charts, 607–608
  load chart, 607
  Microsoft Project view, 86–87
  project scheduling and, 65
  schedule chart, 607–608
Gap, 421, 460
Gemba or Gemba walk, 651, 655
General Electric, 30, 195, 219, 221, 246
General Motors (GM), 164
Generating new products, 165–166
Geographic information systems (GISs), location strategies and, 351–353
GeoMedia, 353
Giant Manufacturing Company, 447
Gillette, 162
Glidden Paints, 134
Global Aquaculture Alliance, 460
Global Company Profiles:
  Alaska Airlines, 600–601
  Amazon.com, 488–489
  Arnold Palmer Hospital, 214–215
  Bechtel Group, 60–61
  Boeing Aircraft, 30–31
  Darden Restaurants, 442–443
  FedEx, 338–339
  Frito-Lay, 530–531
  Hard Rock Cafe, 2–3
  Harley-Davidson, 280–281
  McDonald's, 368–369

NASCAR Racing Team, 408–409
  Orlando Utilities Commission, 660–661
  Regal Marine, 160–161
  Toyota Motor Corp., 636–637
  Walt Disney Parks and Resorts, 106–107
  Wheeled Coach, 564–565
Global implications
  impact of culture and ethics and, 35
  quality and, 218
Global Insights, 110
Global operations. See Operations strategy in a global environment
Global operations strategy options, 49–50
Global strategy, 49
Global view of operations, supply chains and, 32–35
  attract and retain global talent and, 34–35
  improve products and, 34
  improve supply chain and, 33
  reduce costs, 33
The Goal: A Process of Ongoing Improvement (Goldratt and Cox), 317n
"Going green." See Sustainability
GOL-Brazil, 257
Goods, differences from services, 11
Goods and services selection
  design of, 162–165
  importance of, 162
  life cycle and strategy, 164–165
  operations and, 11–13
  product decision, 163
  product life cycles, 164
  product strategy options, 163–164
  product-by-value analysis, 165
Graphic approach, break-even analysis and, 319–320
Graphical methods for aggregate scheduling, 538–543
Graphical representation of constraints, LP and, 702–705
Graphical solution to LP problem, 702–705
Graphical techniques, 538–543
Great Ormond Street Hospital, 223, 224
Greenhouse gas (GHG) emissions, 204
Greenlist classification, 196
Gross material requirements plan, MRP and, 571–572
Group technology, 177
Growth of services, OM and, 11–12
Growth phase, product life cycle and, 165

H

Hafei Aviation, 30
Haier, globalization and, 32
Hallmark, 385–386
Hansel, 651
Hard Rock Cafe
  Global Company Profile, 2–3
  experience differentiation, 38
  forecasting, 155–156
  global strategy, 55–56
  human resource strategy, 415, 438
  layout strategy, 375
  location strategy, 363–364
  operations management in services, 25–26
  Pareto charts and, 228
  portion-control standard, 176, 177
  project management, 77, 100–102
  scheduling, 632
  supply chain, 450
Hard Rock Hotel, 232
Harley-Davidson, 289
  Global Company Profile, 280–281
Hawthorne studies, 413
Heart surgery learning curve, 776, 778
Heijunka, 647, 651
Heinz, 49
Heritage of OM, 8–10
Hershey, 172
Hertz Car Rental, 730
Heuristic, assembly-line balancing and, 389
Hewlett-Packard, 39, 46, 173
  supply chain management, 453
Histogram, 226
Historical experience, labor standards and, 421
Holding costs, 495
Home Depot
  inventory management, 461, 463
  use of GIS system, 353
Honda, 42, 172
  supply chain risks and tactics, 450
Hong Kong, SEATO and, 34
Hospitals. See also Arnold Palmer Hospital
  accident avoidance, 232
  benchmarking handoffs, 224
  differentiation, 163–164
  emergency room process layout, 379
  forecasting, 129–130
  inventory management, 652
  lean operations, 651
  learning curve, 776, 778
  MRP and, 584
  operating room traffic jams, 415
  process strategy, 284
  quality management, 223, 224

scheduling services and, 618
zero-wait ER guarantee, 766
Hotels
  MRP and, 584
  site selection, location strategies and, 351
  technology changes, 298
House of quality, 166–169
HP Project, 66
Human resource, job design, work management and, 407–440. *See also* labor standards
  competitive advantage for, 410
  constraints on, 410
  employment-stability policies and, 411
  ergonomics and the work environment, 415–417
  ethics, the work measurement and, 430–431
  forecasting, 110
  job classifications, work rules and, 412
  job design and, 412–415
  labor planning and, 411–412
  labor standards, 420–430
  methods analysis, 417–419
  motivation, incentive systems and, 415
  objective of, 410
  psychological components of job design , 413–414
  self-directed teams and, 414
  visual work place, 420
  work schedules and, 411–412
Human resources, forecasting and, 109
Humidity, in work area, 417
Hyatt, 456
Hyundai Shipyard, 79

I

IBM, 46, 49
  closed-loop supply chain, 461
  reshoring, 47
  SMT's negotiation with, 787–788
Idea Works, 257
Ikea, 377
Illumination, 417–418
Impact on employees, JIT layout and, 643
Implementing 10 strategic OM decisions, 44
Importance of
  inventory, 490–491
  project management, 62
Improve operations, global view of operations and, 34
Improve products, global view of operations and, 34
Improve supply chain, global view of operations and, 33

Incentives:
  for individual or group productivity, 415
  job design and, 415
  managing the supply chain, 452
Increased flexibility, JIT layout and, 643
Independent demand, inventory models and, 495
  basic economic order quantity (EOQ) model, 496–497
  minimizing costs, 497–501
  production order quantity model, 502–504
  quantity discount models, 505–507
  reorder points, 501–502
Independent processing region, 180
India, call centers in, 47
Indonesia, manufacturing in, 51
Industrial engineering, OM and, 10
Infant mortality, 667
Infinite arrival population, 749
Infinite loading, 604
Information technology, 10
Ingall Ship Building Corporation, 378
Initial failure rate, 667
Initial solution, transportation models and, 732–734
Innovation, new products and, 163
Input-output control, loading jobs and, 606–607
Inspection:
  attributes *versus* variables, 233
  definition, 230
  quality role, 230–233
  service industry and, 232
  source and, 231
  waste, 289n
  when and where, 230–231
Institute for Supply Management (ISM), 8
Intangible costs, location strategies and, 342
Integer variables, 713
Integrated supply chain, managing and, 451–454
  issues in, 451–452
  opportunities in, 452–454
Intermittent processes, 282
Internal benchmarking, 223
Internal failure costs, quality and, 218
International business, 49
International Organization for Standardization (ISO), 204–205
International standards
  environmental, 204–205
  quality, 218, 454
International strategy, global operations and, 49
Introductory phase, product life cycle and, 165

Intuitive lowest-cost method, 733–734
Inventory
  accurate records, 570
  assets committed to, 462–463
  capacity options, 535–536
  functions of, 490
  lean operations, 643–646, 652
  maintenance/repair/operating (MRO) inventory, 490–491
  quantities and values, 462n
  raw material inventory and, 490
  types of, 490–491
  work-in-process (WIP) and, 490
Inventory analysis, simulation and, 797–799
Inventory management, 487–528. *See also* Independent demand
  classifying items through ABC analysis, 491–492
  control of service inventories, 494–495
  cycle counting, 493–494
  demand, independent *vs.* dependent, 495
  ethical dilemma, 515
  fixed-period (P) systems and, 514–515
  holding, ordering, and setup costs, 495–496
  importance of, 490–491
  independent demand, models for, 496–507
  just-in-time, 643–646
  kanban, 647–649
  managing and, 491–495
  mass customization, 285
  models, 495–514
  other probabilistic models, 511–513
  probabilistic models and safety stock, 508–513
  record accuracy, 493
  single-period model, 513–514
  using software, 516–517
Inventory turnover, 462
Inventory types, 490–491
Investment analysis, capacity planning and, 324–326
Invisalign Corp., 172
iPad menu, 289
Ishikawa diagrams, 227
ISO, 703n
ISO 9000, 218, 454
ISO 14000, 204–205, 454
ISO-cost line, 708–709
ISO-profit line solutions method, 703–705
Issues in:
  integrated supply chain, 451–452
  operations strategy, 40–41
  short-term scheduling, 602–605
Item aggregation, 507

J

J R Simplot, 179
Jackson Manufacturing Co., 437
Jagoda Wholesalers, 130–131
Japan/Japanese. *See also* Toyota
    Production System
  collegial management structure, 170
  Deming Prize, 218
  earthquake damage, 472
  5Ss, 639
  Gemba or Gemba walk, 651
  kanban, 647–649
  keiretsu networks, 448–449
  SEATO and, 34
  Takumi, 219
JC Penney, 453
Jidoka, 650, 651
JIT. *See* Just-in-time
Jo-Ann Stores, use of GIS system,
    353
Job characteristics, 413–414
Job classifications, 412
Job design, 412–415. *See also*
    Methods analysis
  core job characteristics and, 413–
    414
  definition, 412
  Hawthorne Studies and, 413
  job expansion, 413
  labor specialization, 412
  limitations of job expansion,
    414
  motivation and incentive systems
    and, 415
  psychological components of,
    413–414
  self-directed teams, 414
Job enlargement, human resource
    strategy and, 413
Job enrichment, 413
Job expansion, 413
  limitations, 414
Job lots, 379
Job rotation, 413
Job shops, facilities, 605
  scheduling, 617
Job specialization, 412
John Deere, 536
Johns Hopkins Medical Center, 232
Johnson & Johnson, 46, 219
Johnson Controls, 463
Johnson Electric Holdings, LTD.,
    39
Johnson's rule, sequencing and,
    615–616
Johnsonville Sausage Co., 415
Johnstown Foundry, Inc., 431
Joint ventures
  supply-chain management and,
    448
  time-based competition and,
    174–175

Jones Law Offices
  inspection, 232
Juran, Joseph M., 219
Jury of executive opinion, 111
Just-in-time (JIT)
  consignment inventory and, 642
  definition of, 638
  distance reduction and, 643
  impact on employees and, 643
  increased flexibility and, 643
  inventory and, 643–646
  Kanban and, 647–649
  layout and, 642–643
  MRP and, 576
  partnerships and, 640–642
  quality and, 224, 649
  reduced space and inventory and,
    643
  remove variability and, 643–644
  scheduling and, 646–649
  security, 451
  supply chain risk and, 451
  TQM and, 224
Just-in-time (JIT) inventory
  reduce setup costs, 645–646

K

Kaizen, lean production and, 649,
    651
Kaizen event, 649
Kanban, JIT and, 420, 647–649
  advantages of, 648–649
  definition, 647
  number of cards or containers and,
    648
Kawasaki Heavy Ind, 30
Keiretsu networks, 448–449
Key success factors (KSFs), 41–43,
    341
Kindle, forecasting and, 110
Kits, BOMs and, 570
Kitted material, MRP and, 570
Knowledge society, 16–17
Knowledge-based pay systems, 415
Kodak, 646
Komatsu, 50
Korean Airlines, 30
Kroger, 375

L

La Quinta hotel site selection, 351
Labinel, 30
Labor planning, human resources
    and, 411–412
  employment-stability policies and,
    411
  job classifications and, 412
  work rules and, 412
  work schedules and, 411–412
Labor productivity
  location strategies and, 342
  as productivity variable, 15, 16

Labor scheduling example, LP and,
    712–713
Labor specialization, job design and,
    412
Labor standards, 420–430
  historical experience, 421
  predetermined time standards,
    425–427
  time studies, 421–425
  work sampling, 427–430
Large lots, integrated supply chain
    and, 452
Last-in, first-out (LIFO), 751n
Last-in, first-served (LIFS), 751n
Latecoere, 30
Latest finish time (LF), 72, 74
Latest start time (LS), 72, 74
Layout, types of, 370–371
Layout design, OM decisions and, 42
Layout strategies, 367–406
  ethical dilemma, 392
  fixed-position layout, 370, 377–378
  lean operations, 642–643, 652
  lean operations and JIT, 642–643
  office layout and, 370, 371–372
  process-oriented layout and, 371,
    378–383
  product-oriented, 371
  repetitive and product-oriented
    layout and, 386–391
  retail layout and, 370, 372–375
  servicescapes, 375
  strategic importance of, 370
  types of, 370–371
  using software, 393
  warehouse and storage layouts and,
    370, 375–377
  work cells, 371, 383–386
Lead time:
  additional probabilistic models,
    511–513
  inventory model and, 501
  MRP and, 570–571
  probabilistic model, inventory
    management and, 511–513
Leaders in quality, 219
Lean operations, 19, 635–658
  definition, 638
  eliminate waste and, 638–639
  ethical dilemma, 653
  5Ss and, 639
  improve throughput and, 640
  inventory and, 643–646
  just-in-time, 640–649
  kanban, 647–649
  layout and, 642–643
  lean organizations, 650–652
  material requirements planning
    and, 576
  quality and, 649
  removing variability, 639–640
  scheduling and, 646–649

services, 652
seven wastes and, 638
supplier partnerships, 640–642
throughput, 640
Toyota production system and, 638, 649–650
waste elimination, 638–639
Learn to improve operations, global view of operations and, 34
Learning curves, 775–790
applying, 778–782
coefficients and, 779–781
definition, 776
doubling approach and, 777, 778–779
formula approach and, 779
limitations of, 783
services, manufacturing and, 777–778
strategic implication of, 782–783
table approach and, 779–782
Least-squares method, trend projections and, 124–126
Legal change, product development and, 166
Legends of Poker, 678, 688
Lekin® finite capacity scheduling software, 617–618
Level schedules, JIT and, 647
Level scheduling, 538
Level strategy, aggregate planning and, 538
Levi, 197
Lexus, 111
Life cycle, strategy and, 34, 164–165
Life cycle assessment, 173, 198
Limitations of :
job expansion, 414
learning curves, 783
MRP, 575–576
rule-based dispatching systems, 616–617
Limited arrival population, 749
Linear programming (LP), 699–728
changes in the objective function coefficient and, 707–708
changes in the resources, 706–707
corner-point method and, 705
definition of, 700
diet problem and, 711
feasible region and, 703
feed-mix problem and, 711
fixed-charge problem, 715
formulating problem and, 701–702
Glickman Electronics example, 701–702
graphical solution to, 702–705
integer and binary variables, 713–715
iso cost, 708
iso-profit line solution method and, 703–705

labor scheduling and, 712–713
minimization problems and, 708–709
objective function and, 701, 707–708
production-mix example and, 710–711
requirements of a programming problem and, 701
right-hand-side values and, 706–707
sensitivity analysis, 705–708
sensitivity report, 706
simplex method of, 713
transportation method, 543–545
using software, 716–718
validity range for shadow prices, 707
why we use LP, 707
Linear regression analysis, 131–136
Lion King revenue management, 548
Little's Law, 763
L.L. Bean, 223
Loading jobs, short term scheduling and, 604, 605
assignment method, 608–610
Gantt charts, 607–608
input-output control, 606–607
Local optimization, managing the supply chain and, 451–452
Location, costs and, 340–341
Location, importance of, 340–341
Location decisions, factors affecting, 341–344
Location strategies, 337–366
center-of-gravity method and, 348–349
costs of, 340–341, 342
exchange rates and currency risk and, 342
factors affecting location decisions, 341–344
geographic information systems (GIS), 351–353
methods of evaluating location alternatives, 344–350
objective of, 340
political risks, values and culture and, 343
proximity to competitors and, 344
proximity to markets and, 343–344
proximity to suppliers and, 344
service location strategy, 350–351
strategic importance of, 340–341
tangible costs and, 342
transportation model, 349–350
using software, 354–355
Locational cost-volume analysis, 346–347
Lockheed Martin, 172
Logan Airport, 700

Logistics management, supply chain management, and, 456–459
reverse, 203, 460–461
shipping systems and, 456–457
sustainability, 200–202
third-party logistics (3PL) and, 458–459
warehousing and, 457–458
Longest processing time (LPT), 611
Long-range forecast, 108–109
Los Angeles Airport, M/M/S model and, 761
Lot size reduction
integrated supply chain and, 452
lean operations and JIT, 644–645
Lot sizing decision, 576–580
Lot sizing summary, 579–580
Lot sizing techniques, MRP and, 576–580
economic order quantity, 577–578
lot-for-lot, 576
periodic order quantity, 578–579
Lot tolerance percent defective (LTPD), 359
Lot-for-lot, 576
Low-cost leadership, 38
Low-level coding, MRP and, 570
Lufthansa, 257, 313

M
Machine technology, 294–295
Machines, operator input to, 416–417
MAD (mean absolute deviation), 118–119, 121
Maintenance and reliability, 659–676
autonomous maintenance, 670
defined, 662
ethical dilemma, 671
increasing repair capabilities, 670
preventive maintenance, 667–670
reliability, 663–667
strategic importance of, 662–663
total productive maintenance, 671
Maintenance/repair/operating (MROs) inventories and, 490–491
Major league baseball umpires, 610
Make-or-buy decisions, 176–177, 446–447
Malcolm Baldrige National Quality Awards, 45, 218
Management, as productivity variable, 15, 16–17
Management, MRP and dynamics of, 575
JIT and, 576
Management process, OM and, 7
Manager, project, 63–64
Managerial issues, control charts and, 259–260
Managing bullwhip effect, 474–476
Managing demand, capacity and, 312–313

Managing inventory. *See* Inventory management
Managing quality, 213–244. *See also* Total quality management
  cost of, 218–219
  defining, 217–219
  ethics and, 219
  implications of, 217–218
  international quality standards, 218
  role of inspection, 230–233
  services and, 233–234
  strategy and, 216
  tools of TQM, 226–230
  total quality management, 219–226
Manila, cartoon industry in, 33
Manufacturability, product development and, 170
Manufacturing
  learning curve and, 777–778
  organizational chart, 5
  regulations, 203–204
  repetitive, 280–281
Manufacturing cycle time, 640
MAPE (Mean absolute percent error), 120, 121
MapInfo, 353
Maptitude, 353
Maquiladoras, 34
Market survey, 111–112
Market-based price model, 455
Marketing, OM and, 4
Markets
  global view of operations and, 34
  proximity to, 343–344
Marriott, 456
Mass customization
  focus in, 284–285, 286
  OM and, 19
Mastek Corp., agile project management, 67
Master production schedule, 535, 567–568
Master schedule, scheduling issues and, 575, 603
Material flow cycle, 491
Material handling costs, 375
Material requirements planning (MRP), 563–598. *See also* Dependent inventory model requirements
  buckets and, 576
  capacity planning and, 581–583
  closed loop, 581
  defined, 566
  dependent demand, 566
  dependent inventory model requirements and, 566–571
  distribution resource planning (DRP) and, 584
  dynamics, 575
  enterprise resource planning (ERP), 584–587

ethical dilemma, 587
extensions of, 580–583
gross material requirements plan and , 571–572
JIT and, 576
limitations and, 575–576
lot-sizing techniques and, 576–580
net requirements plan and, 572–575
planning bill, time-phased product structure and, 570
safety stock and, 575
services and, 583–584, 587
structure for, 571–575
using software, 588–589
Material requirements planning II (MRP II), 580–581
Mathematical approaches, aggregate planning and, 543–545
Matrix organization, 63
Mattel, 48, 204
Maturity phase, product life cycle and, 165
Maximax, decision-making under uncertainty and, 681
Maximin, decision-making under uncertainty, 681
Maximization problems, linear programming and, T3–7
McDonald's Corp., 42, 175, 235, 755
  Global Company Profile, 368–369
  hamburger assembly line, 387
  inventory management, 463, 652
  process analysis, 288
  process strategy, 298
  quality, 235
  scheduling, 652
  supply chain risks and tactics, 450
McKesson Corp., 494, 642
Mean absolute deviation (MAD), 118–119, 121
Mean absolute percent error (MAPE), 120, 121
Mean chart limits, setting of, 250–253
Mean squared error (MSE), 119–120, 121
Mean time between failures (MTBF), 664–665
Measurement, productivity and, 14–15
Measuring:
  forecast error, 117–120
  supply chain performance, 461–464
Medium-range forecast, 108–109
Meijer, 421
Mercedes-Benz, 46, 172, 175, 223, 340
  sustainability, 198, 203
Merck mission statement, 36
MERCOSUR, 34
Mercury Marine, 445
Messier-Bugatti, 30

Messier-Dowty, 30
Methods analysis, 417–419
Methods for aggregate planning, 538–545
Methods of evaluating location alternatives,
  center-of-gravity method, 348–349
  factor-rating method, 344–350
  locational cost-volume analysis, 346–347
  transportation model, 349–350
Methods time measurement (MTM), 427
Methods Time Measurement Association, 427n
Mexico, NAFTA and, 34
Micro Saint software, 792
MicroGreen Polymers, 199
Microsoft Corp., 40, 64–65, 112, 172, 174
Microsoft Project, 66
  entering data, 86
  PERT analysis, 87
  project management and, 86–88
  tracking the time status of a project, 87–88
  viewing the project schedule, 86–87
Milliken, 218
Milton Bradley, 493
Milwaukee Paper
  activity-on-arrow (AOA), 71
  activity-on-node (AON), 68–70, 71
  completion of product on time and, 79
  computing project variance, 78
  critical path, 76
  earliest finish time (EFT), 73
  earliest start time (EST), 73
  expected times and, 78
  latest finish time (LFT) and, 74–75
  latest start time, (LST) and, 74–75
  project crashing, 83–85
  project network, 87
  project schedule, 86–87, 90
  sample Gantt chart, 86
  slack time and, 75–76
  standard deviation and, 79
  time estimates, 71
  variances, 78, 79
MindView, 66
Minimal-cost-flow problem, T5–13
Minimization problems, LP and, 708–709, T3–7 to T3–8
Minimizing costs, independent demand inventory and, 497–501
Minimum cost of insertion technique, T5–10
Miscellaneous services, aggregate planning and, 546–547
Missions, global view of operations and, 35–36, 37

Mitigation tactics, supply chain risks, 450
Mitsubishi Heavy Ind, 30
Mixed strategy, aggregate planning and, 538
Mixing options, aggregate scheduling and, 537–538
MNC (Multinational corporation), 49
Models, independent demand and, 502–507
MODI method (modified distribution):
　how to use, T4–2 to T4–4
　solving a problem, T4–2 to T4–4
　transportation problems and, T4–2 to T4–4
Modular bills, MRP and, 569–570
Modular design, product development and, 171
Modularization, service efficiency and, 181
Modules, repetitive focus and, 283
Moment-of-truth, service design and, 181
Monitoring forecasts, 138–139
Monte Carlo method, 794
Monte Carlo simulation, 794–797
Monterey Jack cheese, 175–176
Most likely time, PERT and, 77
Motivation, incentive systems, 415
Motivation systems, job design and, 415
Motorola, 218, 221
Moving averages
　quantitative forecasting and, 114–116
　weighted, 115–116
MROs, 490–491
MRP., *see* Material requirements planning
Mrs. Field's Cookies, 375
MSE (mean squared error), 119–120, 121
Muda, 651
Multidomestic strategy, global operations and, 49
Multifactor productivity, 14–15
Multimodal shipping, logistics management and, 457
Multinational corporation (MNC), 49
Multiphase system, 752
Multiple regression, 136–137
Multiple regression analysis, 136–137
Multiple server queuing model, 757–761
Multiple traveling salesmen problem (MTSP), T5–4, T5–8
Multiplicative seasonal model, 127
Multiproduct case, break-even analysis and, 320–322
Muther Grid, 372

N

Nabisco, 110
NAFTA (North American Free Trade Agreement), 34
Naive approach, quantitative forecasting and, 113–114
NASCAR Racing Team, Global Company Profile, 408–409
National car rental, 730
National chains, aggregate planning and, 546
National Highway Safety Administration, 203
Natural variations, statistical process control and, 246–247
Nature of aggregate planning, 534–535
Nearest neighbor procedure, T5–5 to T5–7
Negative exponential probability distribution, 752
Negotiation strategies, vendor selection and, 455
Nestlé, 50, 455
Net material requirements plan, MRP and, 572–574
Net present value, strategy-driven investments and, 324–326
Net requirements plan, MRP and, 572–575
Networks, routing and scheduling vehicles and, T5–3
New challenges in OM, 18–19
New England Foundry, 771–772
New Guinea, SEATO and, 34
New products, generating, 165–166
New York City potholes, regression analysis of, 137
New Zealand, SEATO and, 34
Night Hawk, 314
Nike, 112, 458
Nintendo, 110
Nissan
　annual inventory turnover, 463
　level strategy, 538
　low-emission vehicles, 194
　scheduling, 577
　supply chain risks and tactics, 450
Nodel Construction Company, 132–137
Nodes, routing and scheduling vehicles and, T5–3
Noise, in work area, 417, 418
Non-basic variables, T3–3
Nordstrom Department Store inspection, 232
Normal curve areas, A2–A3, T1–4 to T1–7
Normal distribution, A2–A3
Normal time, labor standards and, 422, 423

North American Free Trade Agreement, 34
Northwest-corner rule, transportation models and, 732–733
Nucor, 216
Nurse shortage, 619
N.Y. Edison, 125–126

O

Oakwood Hospital, 766
Objective function, LP problems and, 701
Objective function coefficients, allowable ranges and, 707–708
Objectives of routing and scheduling vehicle problems, T5–2
Occupational Safety and Health Administration (OSHA), 203, 431, 431n
Office Depot, 421, 459
Office layout, 370, 371–372
Office Max, 534
Office relationships chart, 372
Official Board Markets weekly publication, 455
Old Oregon Wood Store, 630
Olive Garden Restaurant. *See also* Darden Restaurants
　forecasting, 113
　inspection, 232
　JIT, 640
OM. *See* Operations management
OM in Action
　airline capacity, matching to demand, 313
　Align Technology mass customization, 285
　Amazon robot warehouse strategy, 376
　Benetton, ERP software and, 585
　blue jeans and sustainability, 197
　car assembly lines, sustainability in, 203
　Cessna Aircraft Company lean production, 642
　Delta Airlines, project management and, 66
　Denmark's meat cluster, 345
　DHL, supply chain and, 458
　Disney musical's revenue management, 548
　frequent flyer miles, booking seat with, 257
　hospital accident avoidance, 232
　hospital benchmarks against Ferrari Racing Team, 224
　hotel industry, technology changes and, 298
　incentives to unsnarl traffic jams in the OR, 415
　Iowa data center locations, 343
　iPad menu, 289

OM in Action (*Continued*)
JC Penney, supply chain and, 453
La Quinta hotel site selection, 351
Lean Production at Cessna
Aircraft, 642
mass customization for straight
teeth, 285
Mastek Corp. agile project
management, 67
Milton Bradley inventory
management, 493
missing perfect chair, 416
New York City potholes and
regression analysis, 137
Oakwood Healthcare ER
guarantee, 753
Olive Garden, forecasting and, 113
operating room traffic jams, 415
Orlando Magic short-term
scheduling, 604
Reshoring to Small-Town U.S.A., 47
retail services, saving time, 421
retail's last 10 yards, 495
RFID tags help control bullwhip
effect, 475
Richey International's spies, 235
roses, supply-chain management
and, 446
San Francisco General Hospital
lean operations, 651
Snapper, aggregate planning and,
535
Starbucks Coffee
productivity and, 14
simulation, 797
Subaru's clean, green set of wheels,
205
Taco Bell
product development, 174
productivity and lower costs and,
18
3D printers, 172
Tour de France, 85
Toyota reworking production, 650
UPS
linear programming, 709
staffing, 426
U.S. cartoon production in Manila,
global view of operations, 33
Zero wait time guarantee in
Michigan's ER, 753
One-sided window, T5–12
Online auctions, 456
Online catalogues, 456
Online exchanges, 456
On-time delivery, 488
Operating characteristics (OC)
curves, 263–264, T2–2 to T2–3
Operations analyst, OM and, 9
Operations and productivity,
1–28. *See also* operations
management

Operations chart
job design and, 418
method analysis and, 419
Operations layout strategy. *See*
Layout strategies
Operations management
decision process in, 678–679
definition, 4
ethics and social responsibility, 19
goods and services, 11–13
growth of services, 11–12
Hard Rock Café and, 2–3
heritage of, 8–10
integrating with other activities, 43
job opportunities in, 7–8
management process, 7
new challenges, 18–19
operations for goods and services,
11–13
organizing to produce goods and
services, 4, 6
productivity, service sector and,
17–18
productivity challenge, 13–18
productivity measurement, 14–15
productivity variables, 15–17
reasons to study, 6–7
service growth, 11–12
service pay, 12–13
significant events in OM, 10
supply chain and, 6
ten strategy decisions, 7, 8
what operation managers do, 7–8
where OM jobs are, 7–8
why study?, 6–7
Operations managers jobs, 7–8
Operations strategy in a global
environment, 29–58
competitive advantage through
operations, 36–39
developing missions and strategies,
35–36
global view, 32–35
issues in, 40–41
outsourcing, 44–48
strategy development and
implementation, 41–44
strategy options, 49–50
ten strategic OM decisions, 39, 43,
44
using software, 51–52
Operator input to machines, 416–
417
Opportunities in an integrated supply
chain, 452–454
Opportunity cost, assignment
method and, 608–610, 608n
Opportunity loss, 610
Optimistic time in PERT, 77
Options, limiting for service
efficiency, 181
Oracle Primavera, 66

Ordering cost, 495–496
Organization, building and staffing,
43–44
Organization charts, 5
Organizing for product development,
169–170
Organizing to produce goods and
services, 4, 6
Origin points, transportation
modeling and, 730
Orlando Magic, 230. *See also* Amway
Center
aggregate planning, revenue
management, and, 560
control chart, 230
forecasting and, 154–155
MRP and, 595–596
short-term scheduling and, 604,
631–632
sustainability, 208–209
Orlando Utilities Commission,
Global Company Profile,
660–661
Otis Elevator, 342
Outsourcing
defined, 44–46
rating outsource providers, 47–48
risks of, 46–47
theory of comparative advantage,
46
types of, 447

P
P system, 514–515
Pacific Cycle LLC, 447
Paddy-Hopkirk Factory, 419
Paraguay, MERCOSUR and, 34
Parallel path, redundancy and,
666–667
Parameter, sensitivity analysis and,
705–706
Parametric Technology Corp., 179
Pareto charts, 226, 227–228
Pareto principle, 491
Park Plaza Hotel, 198
Parker Hi-Fi Systems, 525
Partial tour, T5–6
Partnering relationships, supply chain
strategies and, 19
Partnerships, JIT and, 640–642
Part-time employees, 412
Path, T5–6
Pattern of arrivals at the system,
749–750
Pay, service sector and, 12–13
p-charts, 256–257, 259
Pegging, 575
People, sustainability issues and,
195–196
PepsiCo
mission statement, 36
supply chain management, 462–463

sustainable production process, 200

Performance criteria, for sequencing jobs, 611

Periodic inventory systems, 493

Periodic order quantity (POQ), 578–579

Perpetual inventory system, 493, 514

Perrier, 219

Personal ethics, 460

Personal time allowances, 422

PERT (program evaluation and review technique)
  activity-on-arrow (AOA) example, 71
  activity-on-node (AON) example, 69–70
  critique, 85–86
  framework, 67–68
  Gantt charts *versus,* 65
  Microsoft Project analysis, 87
  network diagrams and approaches, 68
  probability of project completion, 79–82
  time estimates, 77–78

PERT analysis, Microsoft Project and, 87

Pessimistic time estimate, PERT and, 77

Phantom bills of material, MRP and, 570

Pharmaceutical companies, use of RFID tags, 295

Philippines, cartoon industry and, 33

Physical sciences, OM and, 10

Pig production, 300

Pilferage, 494

Ping Inc., 285

Pipelines, logistics management and, 457

Pirelli SpA, 52–53

Pivot column, T3–4

Pivot number, T3–4

Pivot row, T3–4

Pixar, 373

Plan-Do-Check-Act (PDCA), 220–221

Planned order receipt, MRP and, 574

Planned order release, MRP and, 574

Planning bills, MRP and, 570

Planning horizons, aggregate planning and, 532–533

Planning process, aggregate planning and, 532–533

Plant manager position, OM and, 9

Poisson distribution, 250n, 750

Poisson table, A4

Poka-yoke
  lean operations, 650
  service blueprinting, 292
  source inspection and, 231

Political change, generating new products and, 166

Political risk, location strategy and, 343

Polycon Industries, 646

POM for Windows, A6–A7
  accessing, 21
  aggregate planning, 553
  break-even analysis, 327
  decision table and trees, 689
  factor rating models, 51
  forecasting, 144
  inventory problems, 517
  layout strategy, 393
  learning curves, 784
  linear programming, 718
  location problems, 354–355
  material requirements planning (MRP), 588
  project scheduling, 89
  queuing problems, 766
  reliability problems, 672
  short-term scheduling, 624
  simulation and, 801
  SPC control charts, OC curves, acceptance sampling and process capability, 267
  transportation problems, 739
  use of, A6–A7

Porsche, 650

Port of Baltimore, 119–120

Port of Charleston, 451

Port of Miami warehouse tenting, 696

Portion-control standards, 176

Postponement, mass customization and, 285
  supply chain management and, 453

Potholes, New York City, 137

Pratt & Whitney, machine technology and, 295

Precedence relationship, in assembly-line balancing, 387

Predetermined time standards, 425–427

Preferred Hotels and Resorts Worldwide, 235

Prevention costs, quality and, 218

Preventive maintenance, 667–670

Priority rules, sequencing jobs and, 611–614

Probabilistic inventory models and safety stock, 508–510
  other models, 511–513

Probability distribution, Monte Carlo simulation, 794

Process analysis, design and, 288–293
  flowchart, 289
  job design and, 419
  process chart, 289–290
  service blueprinting, 292–293

time-function mapping, 289

value-stream mapping, 290–291

Process capability, SPC and, 260–262
  definition, 260
  index (C_{pk}) and, 261–262
  ratio (C_p) and, 260–261

Process charts, 289–290, 418, 419

Process choices, comparison of, 286–288

Process comparison, 286–288

Process control, 295–296

Process design
  mass customization, 285
  OM and
    customer interaction and, 293–294

Process focus
  process strategies and, 282–283, 286
  scheduling, 605

Process improvement consultants, OM positions and, 9

Process mapping, 289

Process redesign, 298–299

Process strategy, 279–305
  analysis and design, 288–293
  comparison and, 286–288
  defined, 282
  equipment and technology selection, 288
  four process strategies, 282–288
  mass customization focus and, 284–286
  process focus and, 282–283
  process redesign, 298–299
  product focus, 284
  production technology, 294–298
  repetitive focus and, 283
  service process design, special considerations for, 293–294
  technology in services, 298

Process time of a station, 314

Process-chain-network (PCN) analysis, 179–181

Process-focused facilities, 605

Process-oriented layout, 371, 378–383
  computer software for, 382–383
  focused work center and focused factory, 386
  work cells and, 371, 383–386

Procter & Gamble, 172–173, 195, 198, 474

Producer's risk, 263, T2–3 to T2–4

Product decision, 163

Product design issues, 171–173. *See also* Design of goods and services
  application of decision trees and, 182–184
  computer-aided design (CAD), 171
  computer-aided manufacturing (CAM), 172

Product design issues (*Continued*)
  life cycle assessment (LCA), 173
  mass customization, 285
  modular design, 171
  regulations, 203
  robust design, 171
  standard for the exchange of
      product data (STEP), 172
  sustainability, 173, 198–200
  3D printing and, 172
  value analysis, 173
  virtual reality technology, 172–173
Product development, 166–170
  alliances and, 175
  continuum, 173–175
  development system, 166
  global OM, 34
  house of quality and, 166–169
  issues for design and, 171–173
  joint ventures and, 174–175
  manufacturability and, 170
  OM challenges, 19
  organizing for, 169–170
  purchasing technology by
      acquiring a firm and, 174
  quality function deployment
      (QFD), 166–169
  teams and, 170
  3-D printing, 172
  value engineering and, 170
Product development continuum,
    173–175
Product failure rate (FR), reliability
    and, 664
Product focus, 284, 286, 288
Product generation, new
    opportunities, 166
Product liability, quality and, 218
Product life cycle, 164
  management and, 178–179
  strategy and, 41, 164–165
Product life-cycle management
    (PLM), 178–179
Product manager, 169–170
Product strategy options support
    competitive advantage, 163–
    164
Product-by-value analysis, 165
Product-focused facilities, 605
Production
  defined, 4
  doubling along learning curve,
      777
  transition from design to, 184
  varying capacity, 536
Production order quantity model,
    502–504
Production technology, 294–298
  automated guided vehicles (AGV),
      296
  automated storage and retrieval
      system (ASRS), 296

automatic identification system
    (AIS), 295
computer-integrated manufacturing
    (CIM), 297–298
flexible manufacturing system
    (FMS), 297
machine technology, 294–295
process control, 295–296
radio frequency identification
    (RFID), 295
robots, 296
vision systems, 296
Production-mix example, LP and,
    710–711
Production/operations, OM and, 4
Productivity
  defined, 13
  multifactor, 14–15
  single-factor, 14
Productivity, Starbucks Coffee and,
    14
Productivity challenge and OM, 13
  defined, 13
  measurement of, 14–15
  service sector and, 17–18
  variables, 15–17
Productivity variables, 15–17
Product-oriented layout, 371, 386–
    391, 387
  assembly line balancing and,
      387–391
Profit, sustainability and, 197
Program evaluation and review
    technique (PERT). *See* PERT
Project completion probability, 79–82
Project controlling, 66–67
Project crashing and cost-time trade-
    offs, 82–85
Project management, 60–104
  activity-on-arrow example, 71
  activity-on-node example, 69–70
  calculating slack time, 75–76
  cost-time trade-offs, 82–85
  critical path analysis, 71–72
  critique of PERT and CPM, 85–86
  determining the project schedule,
      71–76
  ethical dilemma, 89
  ethical issues in, 64
  framework of PERT and CPM,
      67–68
  identifying the critical path, 75–76
  importance of, 62
  Microsoft Project, 77, 86–88
  network diagrams and approaches,
      68
  non-critical paths, 81–82
  PERT/CPM in, 67–68
  probability of project completion,
      79–82
  project controlling, 66–67
  project crashing, 82–85

project planning, 62–65
project scheduling and, 65
time estimates in, 77–78
using software, 89–90
variability in activity times, 77–82
work breakdown structure, 64–65
Project Management Institute (PMI),
    8, 64
Project manager, 63–64
Project network, 69
Project organization, 62–63
Project planning, 62–65
Project scheduling, 65
  determining, 71–76
  Microsoft Project view, 86–87
Proplanner, 179, 383
Provide better goods and services,
    global view of operations and,
    34
Providing redundancy, reliability and,
    665–667
Proximity
  to competitors, location strategies
      and, 344
  to markets, location strategies and,
      343–344
  to suppliers, location strategies
      and, 344
  in workspace, 372
Psychological components, job design
    and, 413–414
Pull data, 452
Pull system, 640
  kanban, 647–649
Purchase orders outstanding, MRP
    and, 570
Purchase technology by acquiring
    firm, 174
Purchasing, centralized, 455–456
Purdue Pharma LP, 298
Push systems, 640

Q
Q systems, 514
QFD. *See* Quality Function
    Deployment (QFD)
Quain Lawn and Garden, Inc.,
    725–726
Qualitative forecasting methods, 111
  consumer market survey, 111–112
  Delphi method, 111
  jury of executive opinion, 111
  market survey, 111–112
  sales force composite, 111
Quality, 213–244. *See also* Total
    quality management (TQM)
  cost of, 218–219
  defining, 217–219
  demand, capacity and, 311–287
  ethics and, 219
  house of, 166–167
  implications of, 217–218

international quality standards, 218, 454
leaders in, 219
lean operations, 649
Malcolm Baldrige National Quality Award, 218
productivity measurement, 15
role of inspection, 230–233
services and, 233–234
strategy and, 216
tools of TQM, 226–230
total quality management, 219–226
Quality circle, 222
Quality control, 10
Quality function deployment (QFD), 166–169
Quality loss function (QLF), 225
Quality manager, 9
Quality robust, 224–225
Quantitative forecasts, 111
associative models, 112
time series models, 112
Quantity discount models, inventory management and, 505–507
Quantity discounts
contracting, 455
Queue costs, 753–754
Queuing models, variety of, 754–765
Little's Law and, 763
Model A(M/M/l): single channel with Poisson arrivals/ exponential service times, 754–757
Model B(M/M/S): multiple-channel queuing model, 757–761
Model C(M/D/l): constant-service-time model, 762
Model D: finite-population model, 763–765
use of waiting-line tables, 759–760
using software, 766
Queuing problems, simulation of, 797
Queuing theory, 748–749
Quik Lube, 260

R
Rackspace, 534
Radio frequency identification (RFID), 295, 452, 475
Railroads, logistics management and, 457
Random number
table of, 795, A4
Random number intervals, Monte Carlo simulation and, 795
Random stocking, warehouse layout and, 377
Random variations, time series forecasting and, 113
Range chart limits, setting of, 253–254

using of, 253–254
Rapid Reviews:
Chapter 1 Operations and Productivity, 27–28
Chapter 2 Operations Strategy in a Global Environment, 57–58
Chapter 3 Project Management, 103–104
Chapter 4 Forecasting, 165–166
Chapter 5 Design of Goods and Services, 191–192
Chapter 6 Managing Quality, 243–244
Chapter 7 Process Strategy and Sustainability, 305–306
Chapter 8 Location Strategies, 365–366
Chapter 9 Layout Strategies, 405–406
Chapter 10 Human Resources, Job Design, and Work Measurement, 439–440
Chapter 11 Supply-Chain Management, 469–470
Chapter 12 Inventory Management, 527–528
Chapter 13 Aggregate Planning, 561–562
Chapter 14 Material Requirement Planning (MRP) and ERP, 597–598
Chapter 15 Short-Term Scheduling, 633–634
Chapter 16 Lean Operations, 657–658
Chapter 17 Maintenance and Reliability, 675–676
Module A. Decision Making Tools, 697–698
Module B. Linear Programming, 727–728
Module C. Transportation Model, 745–746
Module D. Waiting Line Models, 773–774
Module E. Learning Curves, 789–790
Module F. Simulation, 807–808
Supplement 5 Sustainability in the Supply Chain, 211–212
Supplement 6 Statistical Process Control, 277–278
Supplement 7 Capacity and Constraint Management, 305–306
Supplement 11 Supply-Chain Management Analytics, 485–486
Rapid-Lube case study, 55
Rating outsource providers, 47–48
Raw material inventory, 490
R-chart, 248, 253–254

Record accuracy, inventory management and, 493
Red Lobster Restaurants
location studies, 362–363
time study, 423
Reduce costs, global view of operations and, 33–34
Reduce inventory, JIT and, 643–644
Reduce lot sizes, JIT and, 644–645
Reduce setup costs, JIT and, 645–646
Reduce variability, JIT inventory and, 643–644
Reduced space and inventory, JIT and, 643
Redundancy, reliability and, 665–667
Regal Marine, 55, 162
Global Company Profile, 160–161
product design, 189–190
strategy at, 55
supply chain management, 467–468
Regression and correlation analysis, forecasting and, 131–137
Relationship chart, 372
Reliability, 663–667. See also Maintenance and reliability
defined, 662
providing redundancy and, 665–667
using software to improve, 672
Reneging customers, 750
Reorder point (ROP) inventory management and, 501–502
Repair capabilities, increasing, 670
Repetitive and product-oriented layout, 386–391
Repetitive facilities, scheduling and, 605
Repetitive focus, process strategy and, 283, 286
Repetitive manufacturing, Harley Davidson and, 280–281
Reputation, quality and, 217
"Request for quotation," 447
Requirements of an LP problem, 701
Reservations systems, 314
Reshoring, 46, 47
Resource Conservation and Recovery Act, 204
Resources, linear programming and, 706–707
Resources view, operations strategy and, 40
Respect for people, TPS and, 649
Response, competitive advantage and, 39–40
Restaurants. See also Darden restaurants; Fast-food restaurants
aggregate planning and, 546
MRP and, 583–584
Retail layout, 370, 372–375

Retail stores. *See also* Specialty retail shops
  inventory management, 495
  job design, 421
  scheduling services and, 618–619
Revenue function, break-even analysis and, 318
Revenue management, aggregate planning and, 547–550
Revenue sharing, 455
Reverse auctions, 456
Reverse logistics, 203, 460–461
RFID, 295, 452, 475
RFQs (requests for quotes), 447
Richey International, 235
Ricoh Corp., 228
Right-hand/left-hand chart, 418
Right-hand-side values, LP and, 706–707
Risk
  decision making under, 682–683
  outsourcing, 46–47
  reducing with incremental changes, 322–323
  supply chain and, 449–451, 472–474
Ritz-Carlton Hotels
  quality, 218, 242
Robert Bosch, 34
Robots, 296, 297, 376
Robust design, product development and, 171
Robust model, inventory management and, 500–501
Rochester Manufacturing Corp., 302
Rolls-Royce, 30
Rope, in bottleneck management, 317
Route sheet, 178
Routing service vehicles, T5–5 to T5–11
Routing vehicles, T5–4
Rubbermaid, 162, 534
Run test, charts and, 260
Rusty Wallace's NASCAR Racing Team, Global Company Profile, 408–409

S
Saab, 30
Saber Roofing, use of GIS system, 352–353
SAE (Society of Automotive Engineers), 176–177
Safe Drinking Water Act, 204
Safe Place Infant Security Solution, 295
Safeskin Corp., 37
Safety stock
  inventory management and, 501, 508–510
  MRP and, 575

Sales and operations planning (S&OP), 533–534
Sales force composite, forecasting and, 111
Sales incentives, 452
Sample missions, 37
Samples, SPC and, 247. *See also* Acceptance sampling
Sam's Club, 495
Samsung, 34, 163
San Diego Hospital, 129–130
San Francisco General Hospital, 651
SAP AG, 586
SAP PLM, 179
SAS, 257
SAS/GIS, 353
S.C. Johnson, 196, 200
Scatter diagrams, TQM tools and, 226, 227
Scheduling
  criteria, 604–605
  decisions, 532
  forward and backward and, 603–604
  just-in-time and, 646–649
  lean operations, 646–649, 652
  linear programming example, 712–713
  mass customization, 285
  OM decisions and, 8
  project, 65, 71–76
  service vehicles and, T5–11 to T5–13
  vehicles, T5–4
Schneider National, 457
Schwinn Bicycle Co., 447
SCOR model, 463–464
Seasonal demands, capacity and, 312
  aggregate planning, 537
  airline industry, 313
Seasonal variations in data, 126–131
Seasonality, time series and, 112
SEATO, 34
Second-order smoothing, 124
Security, JIT, supply chain management and, 451
Selection of equipment and technology, process strategy and, 294–298
Self-directed teams, 414
Sensitivity analysis, LP and, 705–708
Sensitivity Report, 706
Sequencing, jobs in work centers, 611–617
  critical ratio and, 614–615
  definition, 611
  earliest due date, 611, 614
  first come, first served, 614
  Johnson's rule and, 615–616
  limitations of rule-based dispatching systems, 616–617

  priority rules for dispatching jobs, 611–614
  shortest processing time, 611, 614
Sequential sampling, T2–2
Service blueprinting, 292–293
Service industry inspection, 232
Service level, probabilistic models and, 508
Service pay, 12–13
Service recovery, 234
Service sector
  defined, 12
  demand and capacity management in, 313–314
  documents for, 181–182
  efficiency and, 181
  forecasting and, 140–141
  location strategy, 350–351
  operations in, 11–13
  organization chart, 5
  productivity, boosting, 294
  productivity and, 17–18
  TQM in, 232–234
Service vehicle scheduling, T5–11 to T5–13
Service(s). *See also* Service Sector
  aggregate planning and, 545–547
  defined, 11
  design of, goods and, 179–182
  differences from goods and, 11
  documents for, 179–182
  focus, 288
  growth of, 11–12
  inventory control, 494–495
  lean operations in, 652
  learning curves in, 777–778
  MRP and, 583–584
  pay in, 12–13
  process design, 293–294
  scheduling and, 618–621
  service blueprinting, process strategy and, 292–293
  service characteristics, waiting line system and, 751–752
  service time distribution, waiting line system and, 752
  technology, 298
  total quality management, services and, 233–234
Servicescapes, 375
SERVQUAL, 234
Setup cost, 496
  reducing in lean operations and JIT, 645–646
Setup time, 496
  steps for reducing, 646
Seven steps in forecasting, 110–111
Seven tools of TQM, 226–230
Seven wastes, lean operations and, 638
Shader Electronics, LP problem example, T3–1 to T3–7

Shadow price, 707
Shared value, 194
Shell Lubricants, 299
Sherwin Williams, 163
Shipping systems, 456–457
Shortest processing time (SPT), 611, 614
Short-range forecast, 108
Short-term scheduling, 599–634. *See also* Scheduling
  airlines, 619
  cyclical scheduling, service employees and, 620–621
  ethical dilemma, 621–622
  finite capacity (FCS) and, 617–618
  finite loading, and, 604
  importance of, 602
  infinite loading and, 604
  issues and, 602–605
  limitations of rule-based dispatching systems, 616–617
  loading jobs, 605–610
  priority rules for sequencing jobs and, 611–614
  process-focused facilities and, 605
  repetitive facilities and, 605
  scheduling criteria, 604–605
  sequencing, jobs in work centers, 611–617
  services and, 618–621
  using software, 622–624
Shouldice hospital, 163–164, 284
Shrinkage, 494
Siemens, 179, 382
Significant events in OM, 10
Signs, symbols, artifacts, 375
Simplex method of LP, 713, T3–1 to T3–10. *See also* Linear programming
  artificial and surplus variable, T3–7
  converting constants to equations, T3–2
  definition, 713, T3–2
  setting up first simplex table, T3–2 to T3–4
  simplex solution procedures, T3–4 to T3–6
  solving minimization problems, T3–7 to T3–8
  summary of simplex steps for maximization problems, T3–6
Simulation, 791–808
  advantages and disadvantages, 793
  defined, 792
  inventory example, 797–799
  Monte Carlo, 794–797
  queuing problem and, 797
  using software, 800–801
Singapore Airlines, 257
Single channel queuing model/ Poisson arrivals/ exponential service times, 754–757

Single sampling, T2–2
Single-factor productivity, 14
Single-period inventory model, 513–514
Single-phase system, 752
Single-product case, break-even analysis and, 319–320
Single-server queuing system, 751, 754–757
Single-stage control of replenishment, 452
Six Sigma, 221–222, 222n, 261
Size of arrival population, 749
SKUs, 495
Slack time, 75–76
Slack variables, simplex method and, T3–2
Slotting fees, 374, 392
Smith, Adam, 412
Smiths Aerospace, 30
Smoothing constant, 116–117
SMT's negotiation with IBM, 787–788
Snapper Lawn Mowers, 534–535
Social accounting, 197
Social responsibility, OM and, 19
Sociological and demographic change, generating new products and, 166
Software. *See* Excel OM; Excel spreadsheets, creating your own; POM for Windows
Solutions to even-numbered problems, A8–A19
Solved Problems
  aggregate planning, 554–555
  capacity and constraint management, 328–329
  decision making, 691–692
  forecasting, 144–146
  human resources, job design, and work measurement, 432–433
  inventory management, 517–519
  layout strategy, 394–396
  lean operations, 653–654
  learning curves, 784–785
  linear programming, 718–719
  location problems, 355–357
  maintenance and reliability, 672
  modem production, 53
  MRP and ERP and, 589–592
  process strategy, 300
  product design, 186
  project management, 90–93
  quality, 236
  queuing, 766–768
  short-term scheduling, 624–626
  simulation, 801–802
  statistical process control, 267–268
  supply chain management, 465–466
  supply chain management analytics, 480–481

sustainability, 206–207
  tire industry globalization, 52–53
  transportation modeling, 740–741
Solving routing and scheduling vehicle problems, T5–4
Sony, 32, 46, 225
Source inspection, 231
Sourcing issues: make-or-buy *vs.* outsourcing, 446–447
South Korea
  SEATO and, 31
South Korea, manufacturing in, 51
Southern Recreational Vehicle Co., 362
Southwest Airlines, 38, 257, 313, 414
  activity mapping, 43, 44
  activity mapping of low-cost competitive advantage, 44
Southwestern University
  forecasting, 154–155
  project management, 98–99
  quality management, 239–240
Spatial layout, 375
Special considerations for service process design, 293–294
Special packaging, 454
Specialty retail shops, forecasting and, 140
St. John's Health Center, 415
Staffing
  capacity, 536
  global talent, 34–35
  organization, 43–44
  work cells, 384–386
Stakeholders, 19
Standard deviation, calculation, 248n
Standard deviation of the regression, 133
Standard error of the estimate, 133–134
Standard for the exchange of product data (STEP), 172
Standard normal distribution, T1–5 to T1–7
Standard normal table, A2–A3, T1–5 to T1–7
Standard time, labor standards and, 422, 423
Standard work practice, TPS and, 650
Standardization, supply-chain management and, 453
Starbucks Coffee
  productivity and, 14
  scheduling software, 619
  simulation and, 797
Statistical process control (SPC), 226, 229–230, 245–278
  acceptance sampling, 262–265
  assignable variations, 247
  average outgoing quality (AOQ) and, 264–265

Statistical process control (*Continued*)
  c-charts, 257–259
  central limit theorem and, 248–249
  control charts, 230, 241, 247–248
  control charts for attributes, 256–259
  control charts for variables, 248
  definition, 246
  managerial issues and control charts, 259–260
  mean chart limits, 250–253
  natural variations, 246–247
  operating characteristic curve and, 263–264
  patterns on control charts, 259
  p-charts, 256–257, 259
  process capability, 260–262
  process capability index and, 261–262
  process capability ratio and, 260–261
  R-chart, 248, 253–254
  samples, 247
  setting mean and range charts, 254–256
  setting range chart limits and, 253–254
  using ranges and mean charts, 250–255
  using software, 266–267
  variables for, 248
  which chart to use, 259
  x-bar chart, 248, 250–253, 259
Statistical tools for managers, T1–1 to T1–8
  continuous probability distributions, T1–4 to T1–7
  discrete probability distribution, T1–2 to T1–4
  expected value of a discrete probability distribution, T1–3
  variance of a discrete probability distribution, T1–3 to T1–4
Status, viewing in Microsoft Project, 87–88
Steakhouses restaurant chain, 289
Stepping-stone method, transportation model and, 734–737
Stock-keeping units (SKUs), 377
Stop & Shop, 376
Stopwatch studies, 421–424
Storage, 289n, 478–479
Strategic importance of:
  layout decisions, 370
  learning curves, 782–783
  location, 340–341
  maintenance and reliability, 662–663
  short-term scheduling, 602
  supply-chain management, 444–446

Strategic OM decisions, 41–43
Strategy
  aggregate planning, 535–538
  capacity and, 311
  competitive advantages and, 163–164
  definition, 36
  developing missions and, 35–36
  driven investments, applying investment analysis to, 324–326
  global operation options and, 49
  human resource, 410
  international, 49
  issues in operations and, 41–44
  life cycle and, 164–165
  multidomestic, 49
  operations in a global environment, 29–58
  quality and, 216
  service locations and, 350–351
  transnational, 50
Strategy, aggregate planning development and implementation
  key success factors, 41–42
Strategy development and implementation, 41–44
  building and staffing the organization, 43–44
  core competencies and, 42–43
  implementing 10 strategic OM decisions and, 44
  integrating OM and other activities, 43
  key success factors, 41–43
Structure for MRP, 571–575
Subaru, 205
Subcontracting, 536
Sub-Saharan Africa, 460
Subtours, T5–8
Super Fast Pizza, 40
Supplier selection analysis, 476–477
Suppliers
  audits of, 195
  development, 454–455
  evaluation, 454
  lean operations in services and, 652
  location in proximity to, 344
  partnerships in lean operations and JIT, 640–642
Supply chain, 6
  partnering, 19
  risk, 449–451
Supply-chain management, 441–470
Supply chain management analytics, 471–486
  evaluation techniques, 472–474
  managing the bullwhip effect, 474–476
  supplier selection analysis and, 476–477
Supply Chain Operations Reference model (SCOR), 463–464

transportation mode analysis and, 477–478
  warehouse storage, 478–479
Supply Chain Operations Reference model (SCOR), 463–464
  benchmarking and, 463
  definition, 444
  distribution management, 459
  E-procurement and, 456
  ethics and, 460, 465
  forecasting and, 109–110
  globalization, 33
  integrated and, 451–454
  inventory assets, 461–463
  JIT and, 451
  joint ventures and, 448
  keiretsu networks and, 448–449
  logistics management, 456–459
  Manager and Planner, 9
  measuring performance and, 461–464
  mitigation tactics and, 450
  objective of, 444
  risk, 449–451
  software, 584
  sourcing issues: make-or-buy *vs.* outsourcing, 446–447
  sourcing strategies and, 447–449
  strategic importance of, 444–446
  strategies and, 447–449
  suppliers, few, many and, 447
  supply base, building, 454–456
Supply Chain Operations Reference (SCOR) model, 463–464
  sustainability and, 460–461
  vertical integration, 448
  virtual companies, 449
Surplus variables, T3–7
Surrogate (substitute) interaction, process, 180
Survey, market, 111–112
Sustainability
  commons, 195
  corporate social responsibility, 194
  end-of-life phase, 203
  lean operations, 652
  logistics, 200–202
  OM and, 19
  product design, 198–200
  product design and, 173
  production process, 200
  regulations and industry standards, 203–205
  supply-chain management, and, 460–461
  systems view, 195
  triple bottom line, 195–198
Sustainability software, 584
SWOT analysis, 41
Symbols, servicescapes, and, 375
System nervousness, 575

System reliability, 663–665
Systems view of sustainability, 195

T

Tables
control chart limits, 252
learning-curve approach, 779–782
Normal curve areas, A2–A3
Poisson distribution, A4
random numbers, 795, A4
TacoBell, 164
forecasting, 140
lowering costs with productivity
and energy savings, 18
product development, 174
Taguchi concepts, 224–225
Takt time, 384, 384n
Takumi, 219
TAL Apparel Ltd., 452, 453
Tangible costs, location strategies
and, 342
Target-oriented quality, 225
Teams, self-directed, 414
Techniques for evaluating supply
chain, 472
Technological change, generating new
products and, 166
Technological forecasts, 109
Technology. *See also* Production
technology
acquiring by purchasing firm, 174
focus, 288
group, 177
human resource constraints, 410
Teijin Ltd, 174–175
Teijin Seiki, 30
Temperature, in work area, 417
Temple University Hospital, 776, 778
Ten OM strategy decisions, 7, 8, 39,
43, 44
Tesla, 194
Test scores, forecasting success by,
141
Texas Instruments, 49, 218, 222
Thales, 30
Theory of comparative advantage, 46
Theory of constraints (TOC),
capacity and constraint
management, 317
Therbligs, 426
Third-party logistics (3PL), 458–459
Three Mile Island nuclear facility,
417
Three time estimates in PERT, 77–78
3M, 162
3-D printing, 172
Throughput, lean operations and,
640
Throughput time, 315
Time aggregation, 507
Time estimates, in PERT, 77–78
Time fences, 575

Time horizons, 108–109
Time Measurement Units (TMUs),
426
Time series forecasting, 112–131
cycles in, 113
cyclical variations in data, 131
decomposition of time series and,
112–113
exponential smoothing and,
116–117
exponential smoothing with trend
adjustment, 120–124
least-square methods, 124–126
mean absolute deviation, 118–119
measuring forecast error, 117–120
moving averages and, 114–116
naive approach to, 113–114
random variations and, 113
seasonal variations in data,
126–131
seasonality, 112–113
smoothing constant, 116–117
trend and, 112
trend projections and, 124–126
Time status, viewing in Microsoft
Project, 87–88
Time studies, labor standards and,
421–425, 430
Time-based competition, product
development and, 173–175
alliances, 175
joint ventures, 174–175
purchasing technology by buying a
firm, 174
Time-function mapping, 289
Tools of total quality management,
225–230. *See also* Control
charts
cause and effect diagrams, 227
check sheets, 226
flowcharts, 228–229
histogram, 229
knowledge of, 225
Pareto charts, 227–228
scatter diagrams, 227
statistical process control,
229–230
Toray Industries, 30
Toshiba, 497
Total productive maintenance
(TPM), 671
Total quality management (TQM),
219–230
benchmarking, 222–223
continuous improvement, 220–221
definition, 219
employee empowerment, 222
flow chart, 216
just-in-time, 224
plan-do-check-act (PDCA),
220–221
services, 232–234

Six Sigma, 221–222
Taguchi concepts, 224–225
tools of, 225–230
total productive maintenance
(TPM), 671
Total slack time, 76
Tour, T5–15
Tour de France, 85
Toy manufacturing in China, 48
Toyota Motor Corp., 34, 110, 164,
651
annual inventory turnover, 463
Global Company Profile, 636–637
level strategy, 538
low-emission vehicles, 194
reworking production line, 650
supply chain risks and tactics,
450
Toyota Production System, 636–637,
649–650
continuous improvement and, 649
defined, 638
respect for people, 649
standard work practice, 650
Toys "R" Us, 421
TQM. *See* Total quality management
(TQM)
Tracking signal, forecasts and, 138
Transition to production, 184
Transnational strategy, global
operations and, 50
Transportation
location strategies and, 349–350
waste, 289n
Transportation matrix, 731
Transportation method of linear
programming, 543–545
Transportation mode analysis,
477–478
Transportation models, 729–746
defined, 730
degenergy and, 737–738
demand not equal to supply and,
737
initial solution and, 732–734
intuitive lowest-cost method and,
733–734
location and strategies and,
349–350
northwest-corner rule and, 732–733
special issues in, 737–738
stepping-stone method and,
734–737
using software, 738–739
Transportation problems,
MODI and VAM methods and,
T4–1 to T4–10
MODI method, T4–2 to T4–4
VOGEL's approximation method
(VAM), T4–4 to T4–7
Traveling salesman problem (TSP),
T5–4, T5–5 to T5–8

Trend projections, forecasting and, 112, 124–126
Triple bottom line, 195–198
Trucking
  logistics management and, 457
  sustainability and, 201
Trust, managing the supply chain and, 453
TRW airbag plant, 222
Turkish airline, 257
24/7 operations, scheduling services and, 619
Twin Falls, Idaho, call center, 50
Two-bin system, 493
Two-sided window, T5–12
Type I error, 263
Type II error, 263
Types of forecasts, 109
Tyson, 450

U

Uber Technologies, Inc., 24
Umpires, major league baseball, 610
U.N. Framework Convention on Climate Change (UNFCCC), 204
Understand markets, global view of operations and, 34
Undirected arcs, routing and scheduling vehicles, T5–3
Unifi, 445
United Airlines, 354
United States trade agreements, 34
Unlimited arrival population, 749
UPS (United Parcel Service), 416, 426, 457, 651
  logistics, 201, 458
  maintenance and, 662
  sustainable product design, 198
Uruguay, MERCOSUR and, 34
U.S., NAFTA and, 34
U.S. Army, 792
US Airways, 257
U.S. Navy, 67
Using ExcelOM, A5
Using POM for Windows, A6–A7
Utilization, capacity and, 310

V

Validity range for the shadow price, LP and, 707
Value, shared, 194
Value analysis, 173
Value engineering, product development and, 170
Value stream mapping (VSM), 290–291
Value-chain analysis, 40
Values, location strategy and, 343
Values for use in Poisson distribution, A4
Variability, lean operations and, 639–640, 643–644
Variability in activity times, project management and, 77–82

probability of project completion, 79–82
three time estimates in PERT, 77–78
Variable costs, break-even analysis and, 318, 324
Variable data, control charts for, 259
Variable inspection, 232
Variable(s), control charts for, 248, 259
Variance of a discrete probability distribution, statistical tools and, T1–3 to T1–4
Vehicle routing and scheduling, T5–1 to T5–18
  characteristics of problems, and, T5–3 to T5–5
  introduction, T5–2
  objectives of routing and scheduling problems, T5–2
  other problems, T5–13 to T5–14
  routing service vehicles, T5–5 to T5–11
  scheduling service vehicles, T5–11 to T5–13
Vendor-managed inventory (VMI), 452–453
Vertical integration, supply-chain management and, 448
Video Case Studies:
  Alaska Airlines:
    human resources, 437–438
    lean operations, 655–656
    process strategy, 303–304
    quality, 240–242
    scheduling challenges, 726
  Amway Center sustainability, 208–209
  Arnold Palmer Hospital:
    capacity planning, 333–334
    culture of quality, 240
    hospital layout, 402–404
    JIT, 656
    process analysis, 304
    project management, 99–100
    supply chain and, 468
  Darden Restaurants:
    location strategies, 362–363
    outsourcing offshore, 56
    statistical process control, 276
    supply chain, 467
  Frito-Lay:
    maintenance, 674
    managing inventory, 525–526
    operations management, 25
    statistical process control, 275
    sustainability, 209–210
  Hard Rock Cafe:
    forecasting, 155–156
    global strategy, 55–56
    human resource strategy, 438
    location strategy, 363–364

operations management in services, 25–26
  project management, 77, 100–102
  scheduling, 632
Orlando Magic:
  forecasting and, 154–155
  MRP and, 595–596
  revenue management, 560
  short-term scheduling, 631–632
  sustainability, 208–209
Red Lobster, location and strategies, 362–363
Regal Marine:
  product design, 189–190
  strategy at, 55
  supply-chain management at, 467–468
Ritz-Carlton Hotel company, 242
Wheeled Coach:
  inventory control, 526
  layout strategy, 404
  MRP and, 596
  process strategy, 302–303
Viewing the project schedule, Microsoft Project and, 86–87
Virgin Australia, 257
Virtual companies, sourcing strategies and, 449
  supply chain strategies and, 449
Virtual reality technology, 172–173
Vision systems, production technology and, 296
Visual workplace, job design and, 420
Vizio, Inc., 449
Vogel's approximation method (VAM), transportation problems and, T4–4 to T4–7
Volkswagen, 173, 349–350
Volvo, 32

W

Waiting line models, 747–774
  arrival characteristics and, 749–750
  characteristics of waiting line system, 749–752
  measuring queue performance and, 752
  multiphase system and, 752
  multiple-server queuing system and, 752
  other queuing approaches, 765
  queuing costs, 753–754
  queuing models, varieties of, 754–765
  queuing theory, 748–749
  service characteristics and, 751–752
  single-phase system and, 752
  use of tables and, 759–761
  using software, 766
  waiting-line characteristics and, 750–751
Waiting lines, 748

Walmart, 375
   competing on cost and, 38
   cross-docking strategy, 376
   retail layout and, 375
   RFID, 475
   RFID and supply chain, 452, 475
   scheduling, 652
   supply chain management and, 110, 445, 460, 463
   supply chain risks and tactics, 450
   supply-chain review, 196
Walmart Marketplace, 454
Walt Disney Co. *See also* Walt Disney Parks and Resorts
   Lion King revenue management, 548
Walt Disney Parks and Resorts
   experience differentiation and, 38
   forecasting and, 110–111
   Global Company Profile, 106–107
   maintenance, 662
   new products, 162
   waiting lines and, 748
Warehouse
   logistics management and, 457–458
   storage, 478–479
Warehousing layout, 370, 375–377
   cross-docking, 376
   customizing, 377
   objective, 375
   random stocking, 377
Waste, 289n
Waste elimination, lean production and, 638–639

Waterfall approach to projects, 67
Waterways, logistics management and, 457
WBS (work breakdown structure), 64–65
Weeks of supply, 462–463
Weighted moving average forecasts, 115–116
Western Electric Hawthorne plant, 413
What is a learning curve?, 776–777
Wheeled Coach
   Global Company Profile, 564–565
   inventory control, 526
   layout strategy, 404
   MRP and, 564–565, 568, 596
   process strategy, 302–303
Where are OM jobs?, 7–8
Whirlpool, 35, 201, 296
Why study OM, 6–7
Why use linear programming, 700
Wilheim Karmann, 46
Windows, Microsoft's development structure, 64–65
Winter Park Hotel, 772
Work balance chart, 385
Work breakdown structure (WBS), project management and, 64–65
Work cells, layout and, 371, 383–386
   advantage of, 384
   focused work center and focused factory, 386
   requirements of, 383–384

   staffing and balancing, 384–386
Work environment
   ergonomics and, 415–417
   job design and, 417
Work measurement (labor standards)
   historical experience and, 421
   predetermined time standards and, 425–427
   time studies and, 421–425
   work sampling and, 427–430
Work order, 178
Work rules, human resources and, 412
Work sampling, labor standards and, 427–429
Work schedules, labor planning and, 411–412
Work-in-process (WIP) inventory, 490, 604–605
World Trade Organization (WTO), 34
   ethical issues, 35

X
x-bar chart, 248, 250–253, 259
Xerox, 218, 223

Y
Yield management, aggregate planning and, 547–550

Z
z values, A2–A3
   sample size for time study, 424
Zero opportunity costs, 609
Zhou Bicycle Co., 524–525

Operations and Productivity

CHAPTER OUTLINE

GLOBAL COMPANY PROFILE: *Hard Rock Cafe*

- What Is Operations Management? *4*
- Organizing to Produce Goods and Services *4*
- The Supply Chain *6*
- Why Study OM? *6*
- What Operations Managers Do *7*
- The Heritage of Operations Management *8*
- Operations for Goods and Services *11*
- The Productivity Challenge *13*
- Current Challenges in Operations Management *18*
- Ethics, Social Responsibility, and Sustainability *19*

Alaska Airlines

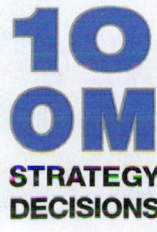

10 OM STRATEGY DECISIONS

- Design of Goods and Services
- Managing Quality
- Process Strategy
- Location Strategies
- Layout Strategies
- Human Resources
- Supply-Chain Management
- Inventory Management
- Scheduling
- Maintenance

Operations Management at Hard Rock Cafe

Operations managers throughout the world are producing products every day to provide for the well-being of society. These products take on a multitude of forms. They may be washing machines at Whirlpool, motion pictures at DreamWorks, rides at Disney World, or food at Hard Rock Cafe. These firms produce thousands of complex products every day—to be delivered as the customer ordered them, when the customer wants them, and where the customer wants them. Hard Rock does this for over 35 million guests worldwide every year. This is a challenging task, and the operations manager's job, whether at Whirlpool, DreamWorks, Disney, or Hard Rock, is demanding.

Andre Jenny/Alamy

Hard Rock Cafe in Orlando, Florida, prepares over 3,500 meals each day. Seating more than 1,500 people, it is one of the largest restaurants in the world. But Hard Rock's operations managers serve the hot food hot and the cold food cold.

Operations managers are interested in the attractiveness of the layout, but they must be sure that the facility contributes to the efficient movement of people and material with the necessary controls to ensure that proper portions are served.

Demetrio Carrasco/Rough Guides/Dorling Kindersley, Ltd.

Lots of work goes into designing, testing, and costing meals. Then suppliers deliver quality products on time, every time, for well-trained cooks to prepare quality meals. But none of that matters unless an enthusiastic waitstaff, such as the one shown here, holding guitars previously owned by members of U2, is doing its job.

Efficient kitchen layouts, motivated personnel, tight schedules, and the right ingredients at the right place at the right time are required to delight the customer.

Orlando-based Hard Rock Cafe opened its first restaurant in London in 1971, making it over 45 years old and the granddaddy of theme restaurants. Although other theme restaurants have come and gone, Hard Rock is still going strong, with 150 restaurants in more than 53 countries—and new restaurants opening each year. Hard Rock made its name with rock music memorabilia, having started when Eric Clapton, a regular customer, marked his favorite bar stool by hanging his guitar on the wall in the London cafe. Now Hard Rock has 70,000 items and millions of dollars invested in memorabilia. To keep customers coming back time and again, Hard Rock creates value in the form of good food and entertainment.

The operations managers at Hard Rock Cafe at Universal Studios in Orlando provide more than 3,500 custom products—in this case meals—every day. These products are designed, tested, and then analyzed for cost of ingredients, labor requirements, and customer satisfaction. On approval, menu items are put into production—and then only if the ingredients are available from qualified suppliers. The production process, from receiving, to cold storage, to grilling or baking or frying, and a dozen other steps, is designed and maintained to yield a quality meal. Operations managers, using the best people they can recruit and train, also prepare effective employee schedules and design efficient layouts.

Managers who successfully design and deliver goods and services throughout the world understand operations. In this text, we look not only at how Hard Rock's managers create value but also how operations managers in other services, as well as in manufacturing, do so. Operations management is demanding, challenging, and exciting. It affects our lives every day. Ultimately, operations managers determine how well we live.

LEARNING OBJECTIVES

LO 1.1 *Define* operations management 4

LO 1.2 *Explain* the distinction between goods and services 11

LO 1.3 *Explain* the difference between production and productivity 13

LO 1.4 *Compute* single-factor productivity 14

LO 1.5 *Compute* multifactor productivity 15

LO 1.6 *Identify* the critical variables in enhancing productivity 16

STUDENT TIP
Let's begin by defining what this course is about.

LO 1.1 *Define* operations management

VIDEO 1.1
Operations Management at Hard Rock

VIDEO 1.2
Operations Management at Frito-Lay

Production
The creation of goods and services.

Operations management (OM)
Activities that relate to the creation of goods and services through the transformation of inputs to outputs.

What Is Operations Management?

Operations management (OM) is a discipline that applies to restaurants like Hard Rock Cafe as well as to factories like Ford and Whirlpool. The techniques of OM apply throughout the world to virtually all productive enterprises. It doesn't matter if the application is in an office, a hospital, a restaurant, a department store, or a factory—the production of goods and services requires operations management. And the *efficient* production of goods and services requires effective applications of the concepts, tools, and techniques of OM that we introduce in this book.

As we progress through this text, we will discover how to manage operations in an economy in which both customers and suppliers are located throughout the world. An array of informative examples, charts, text discussions, and pictures illustrates concepts and provides information. We will see how operations managers create the goods and services that enrich our lives.

In this chapter, we first define *operations management*, explaining its heritage and exploring the exciting role operations managers play in a huge variety of organizations. Then we discuss production and productivity in both goods- and service-producing firms. This is followed by a discussion of operations in the service sector and the challenge of managing an effective and efficient production system.

Production is the creation of goods and services. **Operations management (OM)** is the set of activities that creates value in the form of goods and services by transforming inputs into outputs. Activities creating goods and services take place in all organizations. In manufacturing firms, the production activities that create goods are usually quite obvious. In them, we can see the creation of a tangible product such as a Sony TV or a Harley-Davidson motorcycle.

In an organization that does not create a tangible good or product, the production function may be less obvious. We often call these activities *services*. The services may be "hidden" from the public and even from the customer. The product may take such forms as the transfer of funds from a savings account to a checking account, the transplant of a liver, the filling of an empty seat on an airplane, or the education of a student. Regardless of whether the end product is a good or service, the production activities that go on in the organization are often referred to as operations, or *operations management*.

STUDENT TIP
Operations is one of the three functions that every organization performs.

Organizing to Produce Goods and Services

To create goods and services, all organizations perform three functions (see Figure 1.1). These functions are the necessary ingredients not only for production but also for an organization's survival. They are:

1. *Marketing*, which generates the demand, or at least takes the order for a product or service (nothing happens until there is a sale).
2. *Production/operations*, which creates, produces, and delivers the product.
3. *Finance/accounting*, which tracks how well the organization is doing, pays the bills, and collects the money.

Universities, churches or synagogues, and businesses all perform these functions. Even a volunteer group such as the Boy Scouts of America is organized to perform these three basic

(A)

Commercial Bank

Operations
Teller scheduling
Check clearing
Collection
Transaction processing
Facilities design/layout
Vault operations
Maintenance
Security

Finance
Investments
Securities
Real estate

Accounting

Auditing

Marketing
Loans
 Commercial
 Industrial
 Financial
 Personal
 Mortgage

Trust department

stockshoppe/Shutterstock

Figure **1.1**

Organization Charts for Two Service Organizations and One Manufacturing Organization

(A) a bank, (B) an airline, and (C) a manufacturing organization. The blue areas are OM activities.

❶ STUDENT TIP

The areas in blue indicate the significant role that OM plays in both manufacturing and service firms.

(B)

Airline

Operations
Ground support equipment
Maintenance
Ground operations
 Facility maintenance
 Catering
Flight operations
 Crew scheduling
 Flying
 Communications
 Dispatching
Management science

Finance/accounting
Accounting
 Accounts payable
 Accounts receivable
 General ledger
Finance
 Cash control
 International
  exchange

Marketing
Traffic administration
 Reservations
 Schedules
 Tariffs (pricing)
Sales
Advertising

Sergiy Serdyuk/Fotolia

(C)

Manufacturing

Operations
Facilities
 Construction; maintenance
Production and inventory control
 Scheduling; materials control
Quality assurance and control
Supply-chain management
Manufacturing
 Tooling; fabrication; assembly
Design
 Product development and design
 Detailed product specifications
Industrial engineering
 Efficient use of machines, space,
 and personnel
Process analysis
 Development and installation of
 production tools and equipment

Finance/accounting
Disbursements/credits
 Accounts receivable
 Accounts payable
 General ledger
Funds management
 Money market
 International exchange
Capital requirements
 Stock issue
 Bond issue and recall

Marketing
Sales promotion
Advertising
Sales
Market research

Alexzel/Shutterstock

Figure **1.2**

Soft Drink Supply Chain

A supply chain for a bottle of Coke requires a beet or sugar cane farmer, a syrup producer, a bottler, a distributor, and a retailer, each adding value to satisfy a customer. Only with collaborations between all members of the supply chain can efficiency and customer satisfaction be maximized. The supply chain, in general, starts with the provider of basic raw materials and continues all the way to the final customer at the retail store.

Farmer ⇒ Syrup producer ⇒ Bottler ⇒ Distributor ⇒ Retailer

Supply chain

A global network of organizations and activities that supplies a firm with goods and services.

functions. Figure 1.1 shows how a bank, an airline, and a manufacturing firm organize themselves to perform these functions. The blue-shaded areas show the operations functions in these firms.

The Supply Chain

Through the three functions—marketing, operations, and finance—value for the customer is created. However, firms seldom create this value by themselves. Instead, they rely on a variety of suppliers who provide everything from raw materials to accounting services. These suppliers, when taken together, can be thought of as a *supply chain*. A supply chain (see Figure 1.2) is a global network of organizations and activities that supply a firm with goods and services.

As our society becomes more technologically oriented, we see increasing specialization. Specialized expert knowledge, instant communication, and cheaper transportation also foster specialization and worldwide supply chains. It just does not pay for a firm to try to do everything itself. The expertise that comes with specialization exists up and down the supply chain, adding value at each step. When members of the supply chain collaborate to achieve high levels of customer satisfaction, we have a tremendous force for efficiency and competitive advantage. Competition in the 21st century is not between companies; it is between *supply chains*.

STUDENT TIP ◆

Good OM managers are scarce and, as a result, career opportunities and pay are excellent.

Why Study OM?

We study OM for four reasons:

1. OM is one of the three major functions of any organization, and it is integrally related to all the other business functions. All organizations market (sell), finance (account), and produce (operate), and it is important to know how the OM activity functions. Therefore, we study *how people organize themselves for productive enterprise*.
2. We study OM because we want to know *how goods and services are produced*. The production function is the segment of our society that creates the products and services we use.
3. We study OM to *understand what operations managers do*. Regardless of your job in an organization, you can perform better if you understand what operations managers do. In addition, understanding OM will help you explore the numerous and lucrative career opportunities in the field.
4. We study OM *because it is such a costly part of an organization*. A large percentage of the revenue of most firms is spent in the OM function. Indeed, OM provides a major opportunity for an organization to improve its profitability and enhance its service to society. Example 1 considers how a firm might increase its profitability via the production function.

Example 1	EXAMINING THE OPTIONS FOR INCREASING CONTRIBUTION

Fisher Technologies is a small firm that must double its dollar contribution to fixed cost and profit in order to be profitable enough to purchase the next generation of production equipment. Management has determined that if the firm fails to increase contribution, its bank will not make the loan and the equipment cannot be purchased. If the firm cannot purchase the equipment, the limitations of the old equipment will force Fisher to go out of business and, in doing so, put its employees out of work and discontinue producing goods and services for its customers.

APPROACH ▶ Table 1.1 shows a simple profit-and-loss statement and three strategic options (marketing, finance/accounting, and operations) for the firm. The first option is a *marketing option*, where excellent marketing management may increase sales by 50%. By increasing sales by 50%, contribution will in turn increase 71%. But increasing sales 50% may be difficult; it may even be impossible.

TABLE 1.1	Options for Increasing Contribution			
		MARKETING OPTION[a]	**FINANCE/ ACCOUNTING OPTION**[b]	**OM OPTION**[c]
	CURRENT	**INCREASE SALES REVENUE 50%**	**REDUCE FINANCE COSTS 50%**	**REDUCE PRODUCTION COSTS 20%**
Sales	$100,000	$150,000	$100,000	$100,000
Costs of goods	−80,000	−120,000	−80,000	−64,000
Gross margin	20,000	30,000	20,000	36,000
Finance costs	−6,000	−6,000	−3,000	−6,000
Subtotal	14,000	24,000	17,000	30,000
Taxes at 25%	−3,500	−6,000	−4,250	−7,500
Contribution[d]	$ 10,500	$ 18,000	$ 12,750	$ 22,500

[a]Increasing sales 50% increases contribution by $7,500, or 71% (7,500/10,500).

[b]Reducing finance costs 50% increases contribution by $2,250, or 21% (2,250/10,500).

[c]Reducing production costs 20% increases contribution by $12,000, or 114% (12,000/10,500).

[d]Contribution to fixed cost (excluding finance costs) and profit.

The second option is a *finance/accounting option*, where finance costs are cut in half through good financial management. But even a reduction of 50% is still inadequate for generating the necessary increase in contribution. Contribution is increased by only 21%.

The third option is an *OM option*, where management reduces production costs by 20% and increases contribution by 114%.

SOLUTION ▶ Given the conditions of our brief example, Fisher Technologies has increased contribution from $10,500 to $22,500. It may now have a bank willing to lend it additional funds.

INSIGHT ▶ The OM option not only yields the greatest improvement in contribution but also may be the only feasible option. Increasing sales by 50% and decreasing finance cost by 50% may both be virtually impossible. Reducing operations cost by 20% may be difficult but feasible.

LEARNING EXERCISE ▶ What is the impact of only a 15% decrease in costs in the OM option? [Answer: A $19,500 contribution; an 86% increase.]

Example 1 underscores the importance of the effective operations activity of a firm. Development of increasingly effective operations is the approach taken by many companies as they face growing global competition.

What Operations Managers Do

All good managers perform the basic functions of the management process. The management process consists of *planning*, *organizing*, *staffing*, *leading*, and *controlling*. Operations managers apply this management process to the decisions they make in the OM function. The **10 strategic OM decisions** are introduced in Table 1.2. Successfully addressing each of these decisions requires planning, organizing, staffing, leading, and controlling.

Where Are the OM Jobs? How does one get started on a career in operations? The 10 strategic OM decisions identified in Table 1.2 are made by individuals who work in the disciplines shown in the blue areas of Figure 1.1. Business students who know their accounting,

10 Strategic OM Decisions

Design of goods and services
Managing quality
Process strategy
Location strategies
Layout strategies
Human resources
Supply-chain management
Inventory management
Scheduling
Maintenance

STUDENT TIP ◆

An operations manager must successfully address the 10 decisions around which this text is organized.

TABLE 1.2	Ten Strategic Operations Management Decisions
DECISION	**CHAPTER(S)**
1. *Design of goods and services:* Defines much of what is required of operations in each of the other OM decisions. For instance, product design usually determines the lower limits of cost and the upper limits of quality, as well as major implications for sustainability and the human resources required.	5, Supplement 5
2. *Managing quality:* Determines the customer's quality expectations and establishes policies and procedures to identify and achieve that quality.	6, Supplement 6
3. *Process and capacity strategy:* Determines how a good or service is produced (i.e., the process for production) and commits management to specific technology, quality, human resources, and capital investments that determine much of the firm's basic cost structure.	7, Supplement 7
4. *Location strategy:* Requires judgments regarding nearness to customers, suppliers, and talent, while considering costs, infrastructure, logistics, and government.	8
5. *Layout strategy:* Requires integrating capacity needs, personnel levels, technology, and inventory requirements to determine the efficient flow of materials, people, and information.	9
6. *Human resources and job design:* Determines how to recruit, motivate, and retain personnel with the required talent and skills. People are an integral and expensive part of the total system design.	10
7. *Supply chain management:* Decides how to integrate the supply chain into the firm's strategy, including decisions that determine what is to be purchased, from whom, and under what conditions.	11, Supplement 11
8. *Inventory management:* Considers inventory ordering and holding decisions and how to optimize them as customer satisfaction, supplier capability, and production schedules are considered.	12, 14, 16
9. *Scheduling:* Determines and implements intermediate- and short-term schedules that effectively and efficiently utilize both personnel and facilities while meeting customer demands.	13, 15
10. *Maintenance:* Requires decisions that consider facility capacity, production demands, and personnel necessary to maintain a reliable and stable process.	17

statistics, finance, and OM have an opportunity to assume entry-level positions in all of these areas. As you read this text, identify disciplines that can assist you in making these decisions. Then take courses in those areas. The more background an OM student has in accounting, statistics, information systems, and mathematics, the more job opportunities will be available. About 40% of *all* jobs are in OM.

The following professional organizations provide various certifications that may enhance your education and be of help in your career:

- APICS, the Association for Operations Management (www.apics.org)
- American Society for Quality (ASQ) (www.asq.org)
- Institute for Supply Management (ISM) (www.ism.ws)
- Project Management Institute (PMI) (www.pmi.org)
- Council of Supply Chain Management Professionals (www.cscmp.org)

Figure 1.3 shows some recent job opportunities.

The Heritage of Operations Management

The field of OM is relatively young, but its history is rich and interesting. Our lives and the OM discipline have been enhanced by the innovations and contributions of numerous individuals. We now introduce a few of these people, and we provide a summary of significant events in operations management in Figure 1.4.

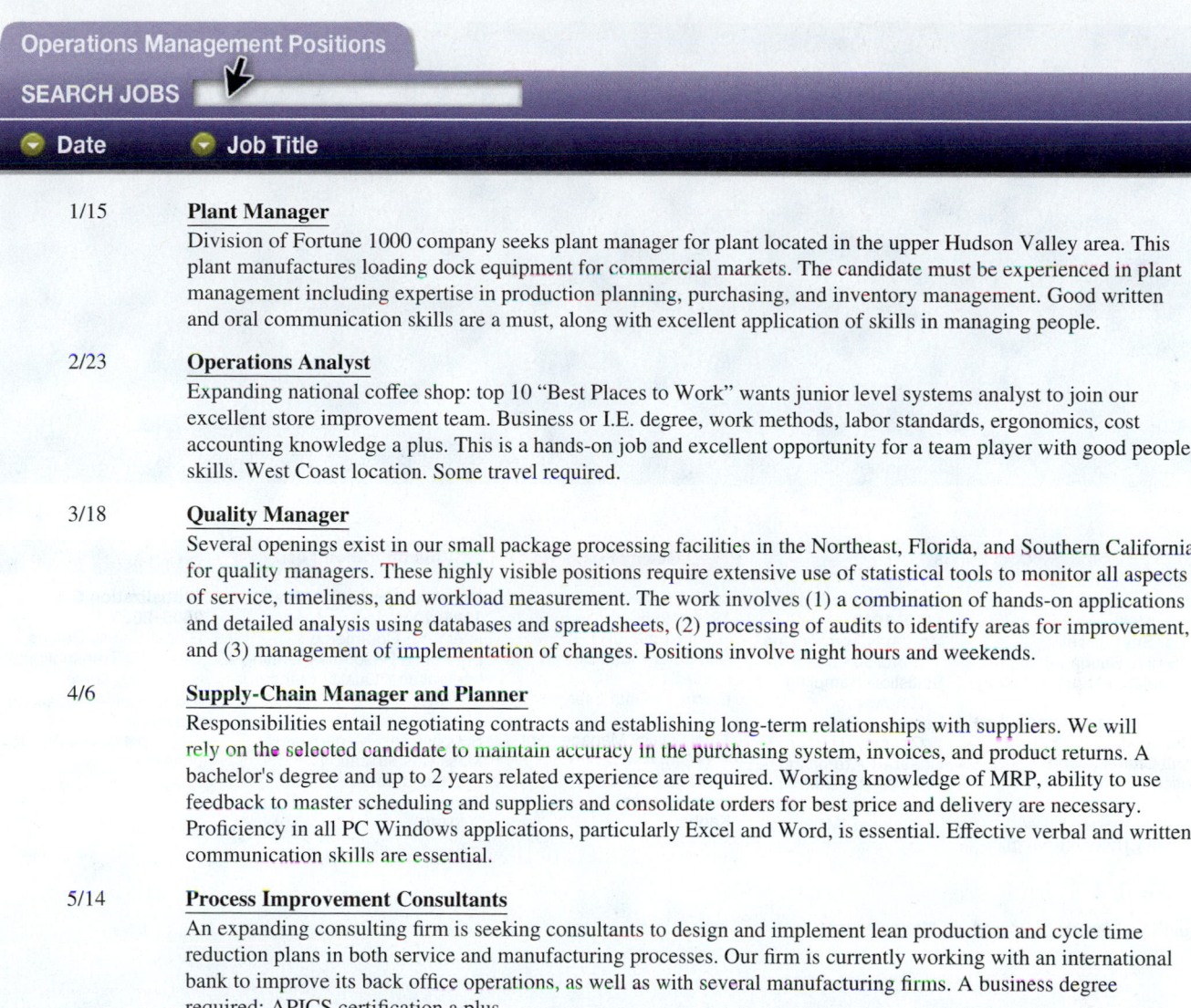

Operations Management Positions

SEARCH JOBS

Date	Job Title

1/15 **Plant Manager**

Division of Fortune 1000 company seeks plant manager for plant located in the upper Hudson Valley area. This plant manufactures loading dock equipment for commercial markets. The candidate must be experienced in plant management including expertise in production planning, purchasing, and inventory management. Good written and oral communication skills are a must, along with excellent application of skills in managing people.

2/23 **Operations Analyst**

Expanding national coffee shop: top 10 "Best Places to Work" wants junior level systems analyst to join our excellent store improvement team. Business or I.E. degree, work methods, labor standards, ergonomics, cost accounting knowledge a plus. This is a hands-on job and excellent opportunity for a team player with good people skills. West Coast location. Some travel required.

3/18 **Quality Manager**

Several openings exist in our small package processing facilities in the Northeast, Florida, and Southern California for quality managers. These highly visible positions require extensive use of statistical tools to monitor all aspects of service, timeliness, and workload measurement. The work involves (1) a combination of hands-on applications and detailed analysis using databases and spreadsheets, (2) processing of audits to identify areas for improvement, and (3) management of implementation of changes. Positions involve night hours and weekends.

4/6 **Supply-Chain Manager and Planner**

Responsibilities entail negotiating contracts and establishing long-term relationships with suppliers. We will rely on the selected candidate to maintain accuracy in the purchasing system, invoices, and product returns. A bachelor's degree and up to 2 years related experience are required. Working knowledge of MRP, ability to use feedback to master scheduling and suppliers and consolidate orders for best price and delivery are necessary. Proficiency in all PC Windows applications, particularly Excel and Word, is essential. Effective verbal and written communication skills are essential.

5/14 **Process Improvement Consultants**

An expanding consulting firm is seeking consultants to design and implement lean production and cycle time reduction plans in both service and manufacturing processes. Our firm is currently working with an international bank to improve its back office operations, as well as with several manufacturing firms. A business degree required; APICS certification a plus.

Figure **1.3**

Many Opportunities Exist for Operations Managers

Eli Whitney (1800) is credited for the early popularization of interchangeable parts, which was achieved through standardization and quality control. Through a contract he signed with the U.S. government for 10,000 muskets, he was able to command a premium price because of their interchangeable parts.

Frederick W. Taylor (1881), known as the father of scientific management, contributed to personnel selection, planning and scheduling, motion study, and the now popular field of ergonomics. One of his major contributions was his belief that management should be much more resourceful and aggressive in the improvement of work methods. Taylor and his colleagues, Henry L. Gantt and Frank and Lillian Gilbreth, were among the first to systematically seek the best way to produce.

Another of Taylor's contributions was the belief that management should assume more responsibility for:

1. Matching employees to the right job.
2. Providing the proper training.
3. Providing proper work methods and tools.
4. Establishing legitimate incentives for work to be accomplished.

Everett Collection/Newscom

Cost Focus		Quality Focus	Customization Focus	Globalization Focus
Early Concepts 1776–1880	**Mass Production Era 1910–1980**	**Lean Production Era 1980–1995**	**Mass Customization Era 1995–2005**	**Globalization Era 2005–2020**
Labor Specialization (Smith, Babbage)	Moving Assembly Line (Ford/Sorensen)	Just-in-Time (JIT)	Internet/E-Commerce	Global Supply Chains
Standardized Parts (Whitney)	Statistical Sampling (Shewhart)	Computer-Aided Design (CAD)	Enterprise Resource Planning	Growth of Transnational Organizations
	Economic Order Quantity (Harris)	Electronic Data Interchange (EDI)	International Quality Standards (ISO)	Instant Communications
Scientific Management Era 1880–1910	Linear Programming	Total Quality Management (TQM)	Finite Scheduling	Sustainability
Gantt Charts (Gantt)	PERT/CPM (DuPont)	Baldrige Award	Supply Chain Management	Ethics in a Global Workforce
Motion & Time Studies (Gilbreth)	Material Requirements Planning (MRP)	Empowerment	Mass Customization	Logistics
Process Analysis (Taylor)		Kanbans	Build-to-Order	
Queuing Theory (Erlang)			Radio Frequency Identification (RFID)	

Figure **1.4**

Significant Events in Operations Management

By 1913, Henry Ford and Charles Sorensen combined what they knew about standardized parts with the quasi-assembly lines of the meatpacking and mail-order industries and added the revolutionary concept of the assembly line, where men stood still and material moved.

Quality control is another historically significant contribution to the field of OM. Walter Shewhart (1924) combined his knowledge of statistics with the need for quality control and provided the foundations for statistical sampling in quality control. W. Edwards Deming (1950) believed, as did Frederick Taylor, that management must do more to improve the work environment and processes so that quality can be improved.

Operations management will continue to progress as contributions from other disciplines, including *industrial engineering, statistics, management,* and *economics,* improve decision making.

Innovations from the *physical sciences* (biology, anatomy, chemistry, physics) have also contributed to advances in OM. These innovations include new adhesives, faster integrated circuits, gamma rays to sanitize food products, and specialized glass for iPhones and plasma TVs. Innovation in products and processes often depends on advances in the physical sciences.

Especially important contributions to OM have come from *information technology*, which we define as the systematic processing of data to yield information. Information technology—with wireless links, Internet, and e-commerce—is reducing costs and accelerating communication.

Decisions in operations management require individuals who are well versed in analytical tools, in information technology, and often in one of the biological or physical sciences. In this textbook, we look at the diverse ways a student can prepare for a career in operations management.

Operations for Goods and Services

STUDENT TIP

Services are especially important because almost 80% of all jobs are in service firms.

Manufacturers produce a tangible product, while service products are often intangible. But many products are a combination of a good and a service, which complicates the definition of a service. Even the U.S. government has trouble generating a consistent definition. Because definitions vary, much of the data and statistics generated about the service sector are inconsistent. However, we define services as including repair and maintenance, government, food and lodging, transportation, insurance, trade, financial, real estate, education, legal, medical, entertainment, and other professional occupations.

Services

Economic activities that typically produce an intangible product (such as education, entertainment, lodging, government, financial, and health services).

The operation activities for both goods and services are often very similar. For instance, both have quality standards, are designed and produced on a schedule that meets customer demand, and are made in a facility where people are employed. However, some major differences *do* exist between goods and services. These are presented in Table 1.3.

LO 1.2 *Explain* the distinction between goods and services

We should point out that in many cases, the distinction between goods and services is not clear-cut. In reality, almost all services and almost all goods are a mixture of a service and a tangible product. Even services such as consulting may require a tangible report. Similarly, the sale of most goods includes a service. For instance, many products have the service components of financing and delivery (e.g., automobile sales). Many also require after-sale training and maintenance (e.g., office copiers and machinery). "Service" activities may also be an integral part of production. Human resource activities, logistics, accounting, training, field service, and repair are all service activities, but they take place within a manufacturing organization. Very few services are "pure," meaning they have no tangible component. Counseling may be one of the exceptions.

Growth of Services

Services constitute the largest economic sector in postindustrial societies. Until about 1900, most Americans were employed in agriculture. Increased agricultural productivity allowed people to leave the farm and seek employment in the city. Similarly, manufacturing employment has decreased for the past 60 years. The changes in agriculture, manufacturing, and service employment as a percentage of the workforce are shown in Figure 1.5. Although the *number* of people employed in manufacturing has decreased since 1950, each person is now producing almost 20 times more than in 1950. Services became the dominant

| TABLE 1.3 | Differences Between Goods and Services |

CHARACTERISTICS OF SERVICES	CHARACTERISTICS OF GOODS
Intangible: Ride in an airline seat	Tangible: The seat itself
Produced and consumed simultaneously: Beauty salon produces a haircut that is consumed as it is produced	Product can usually be kept in inventory (beauty care products)
Unique: Your investments and medical care are unique	Similar products produced (iPods)
High customer interaction: Often what the customer is paying for (consulting, education)	Limited customer involvement in production
Inconsistent product definition: Auto insurance changes with age and type of car	Product standardized (iPhone)
Often knowledge based: Legal, education, and medical services are hard to automate	Standard tangible product tends to make automation feasible
Services dispersed: Service may occur at retail store, local office, house call, or via Internet.	Product typically produced at a fixed facility
Quality may be hard to evaluate: Consulting, education, and medical services	Many aspects of quality for tangible products are easy to evaluate (strength of a bolt)
Reselling is unusual: Musical concert or medical care	Product often has some residual value

Figure **1.5**

U.S. Agriculture, Manufacturing, and Service Employment

Source: U.S. Bureau of Labor Statistics.

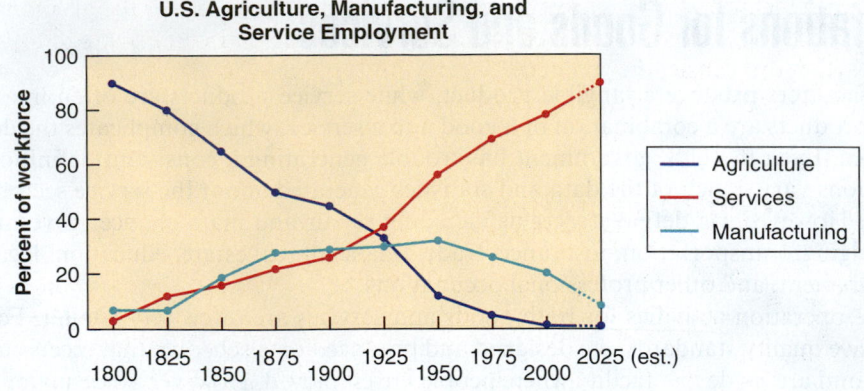

U.S. Agriculture, Manufacturing, and Service Employment

Service sector

The segment of the economy that includes trade, financial, lodging, education, legal, medical, and other professional occupations.

employer in the early 1920s, with manufacturing employment peaking at about 32% in 1950. The huge productivity increases in agriculture and manufacturing have allowed more of our economic resources to be devoted to services. Consequently, much of the world can now enjoy the pleasures of education, health services, entertainment, and myriad other things that we call services. Examples of firms and percentage of employment in the U.S. service sector are shown in Table 1.4. Table 1.4 also provides employment percentages for the nonservice sectors of manufacturing, construction, agriculture, and mining on the bottom four lines.

Service Pay

Although there is a common perception that service industries are low paying, in fact, many service jobs pay very well. Operations managers in the maintenance facility of an airline are very well paid, as are the operations managers who supervise computer services to the financial community. About 42% of all service workers receive wages above the national average. However, the service-sector average is driven down because 14 of the U.S. Department of

TABLE 1.4	Examples of Organizations in Each Sector	
SECTOR	**EXAMPLE**	**PERCENT OF ALL JOBS**
Service Sector		
Education, Medical, Other	San Diego State University, Arnold Palmer Hospital	15.3
Trade (retail, wholesale), Transportation	Walgreen's, Walmart, Nordstrom, Alaska Airlines	15.8
Information, Publishers, Broadcast	IBM, Bloomberg, Pearson, ESPN	1.9
Professional, Legal, Business Services, Associations	Snelling and Snelling, Waste Management, American Medical Association, Ernst & Young	13.6
Finance, Insurance, Real Estate	Citicorp, American Express, Prudential, Aetna	9.6
Leisure, Lodging, Entertainment	Olive Garden, Motel 6, Walt Disney	10.4
Government (Fed, State, Local)	U.S., State of Alabama, Cook County	15.6
Manufacturing Sector	General Electric, Ford, U.S. Steel, Intel	8.6
Construction Sector	Bechtel, McDermott	4.3
Agriculture	King Ranch	1.4
Mining Sector	Homestake Mining	.5
Grand Total		100.0

The Service Sector rows total 85.2.

Source: Bureau of Labor Statistics, 2015.

Commerce categories of the 33 service industries do indeed pay below the all-private industry average. Of these, retail trade, which pays only 61% of the national private industry average, is large. But even considering the retail sector, the average wage of all service workers is about 96% of the average of all private industries.

The Productivity Challenge

The creation of goods and services requires changing resources into goods and services. The more efficiently we make this change, the more productive we are and the more value is added to the good or service provided. Productivity is the ratio of outputs (goods and services) divided by the inputs (resources, such as labor and capital) (see Figure 1.6). The operations manager's job is to enhance (improve) this ratio of outputs to inputs. Improving productivity means improving efficiency.[1]

This improvement can be achieved in two ways: reducing inputs while keeping output constant or increasing output while keeping inputs constant. Both represent an improvement in productivity. In an economic sense, inputs are labor, capital, and management, which are integrated into a production system. Management creates this production system, which provides the conversion of inputs to outputs. Outputs are goods and services, including such diverse items as guns, butter, education, improved judicial systems, and ski resorts. *Production* is the making of goods and services. High production may imply only that more people are working and that employment levels are high (low unemployment), but it does not imply high *productivity*.

Measurement of productivity is an excellent way to evaluate a country's ability to provide an improving standard of living for its people. *Only through increases in productivity can the standard of living improve.* Moreover, only through increases in productivity can labor, capital, and management receive additional payments. If returns to labor, capital, or management are increased without increased productivity, prices rise. On the other hand, downward pressure is placed on prices when productivity increases because more is being produced with the same resources.

The benefits of increased productivity are illustrated in the *OM in Action* box "Improving Productivity at Starbucks."

For well over a century (from about 1869), the U.S. has been able to increase productivity at an average rate of almost 2.5% per year. Such growth has doubled U.S. wealth every 30 years. The manufacturing sector, although a decreasing portion of the U.S. economy, has on occasion seen annual productivity increases exceeding 4%, and service sector increases of almost 1%. However, U.S. annual productivity growth in the early part of the 21st century is slightly below the 2.5% range for the economy as a whole and in recent years has been trending down.[2]

In this text, we examine how to improve productivity through operations management. Productivity is a significant issue for the world and one that the operations manager is uniquely qualified to address.

⬥ **STUDENT TIP**
Why is productivity important? Because it determines our standard of living.

Productivity
The ratio of outputs (goods and services) divided by one or more inputs (such as labor, capital, or management).

LO 1.3 *Explain* the difference between production and productivity

Inputs	Transformation	Outputs
Labor, capital, management	The U.S. economic system transforms inputs to outputs at about an annual 2.5% increase in productivity per year. *The productivity increase is the result of a mix of capital (38% of 2.5%), labor (10% of 2.5%), and management (52% of 2.5%).*	Goods and services

Feedback loop

Figure **1.6**

The Economic System Adds Value by Transforming Inputs to Outputs

An effective feedback loop evaluates performance against a strategy or standard. It also evaluates customer satisfaction and sends signals to managers controlling the inputs and transformation process.

OM in Action | Improving Productivity at Starbucks

"This is a game of seconds …" says Silva Peterson, whom Starbucks has put in charge of saving seconds. Her team of 10 analysts is constantly asking themselves: "How can we shave time off this?"

Peterson's analysis suggested that there were some obvious opportunities. First, stop requiring signatures on credit-card purchases under $25. This sliced 8 seconds off the transaction time at the cash register.

Then analysts noticed that Starbucks' largest cold beverage, the Venti size, required two bending and digging motions to scoop up enough ice. The scoop was too small. Redesign of the scoop provided the proper amount in one motion and cut 14 seconds off the average time of 1 minute.

Third were new espresso machines; with the push of a button, the machines grind coffee beans and brew. This allowed the server, called a "barista" in Starbucks's vocabulary, to do other things. The savings: about 12 seconds per espresso shot.

As a result, operations improvements at Starbucks outlets have increased the average transactions per hour to 11.7—a 46% increase—and yearly volume by $250,000, to about $1 million. The result: a 27% improvement in overall productivity—about 4.5% per year. In the service industry, a 4.5% per year increase is very tasty.

Sources: BusinessWeek (August 23–30, 2012) and *The Wall Street Journal* (October 13, 2010 and August 4, 2009).

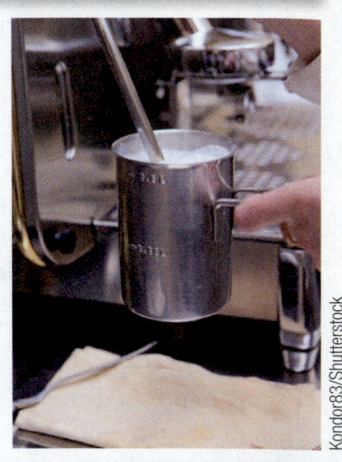

Kondor83/Shutterstock

Productivity Measurement

LO 1.4 *Compute single-factor productivity*

The measurement of productivity can be quite direct. Such is the case when productivity is measured by labor-hours per ton of a specific type of steel. Although labor-hours is a common measure of input, other measures such as capital (dollars invested), materials (tons of ore), or energy (kilowatts of electricity) can be used.[3] An example of this can be summarized in the following equation:

$$\text{Productivity} = \frac{\text{Units produced}}{\text{Input used}} \qquad (1\text{-}1)$$

For example, if units produced = 1,000 and labor-hours used is 250, then:

$$\text{Single-factor productivity} = \frac{\text{Units produced}}{\text{Labor-hours used}} = \frac{1{,}000}{250} = 4 \text{ units per labor-hour}$$

The use of just one resource input to measure productivity, as shown in Equation (1-1), is known as **single-factor productivity**. However, a broader view of productivity is **multifactor productivity**, which includes all inputs (e.g., capital, labor, material, energy). Multifactor productivity is also known as *total factor productivity*. Multifactor productivity is calculated by combining the input units as shown here:

Single-factor productivity

Indicates the ratio of goods and services produced (outputs) to one resource (input).

Multifactor productivity

Indicates the ratio of goods and services produced (outputs) to many or all resources (inputs).

$$\text{Multifactor productivity} = \frac{\text{Output}}{\text{Labor} + \text{Material} + \text{Energy} + \text{Capital} + \text{Miscellaneous}} \qquad (1\text{-}2)$$

To aid in the computation of multifactor productivity, the individual inputs (the denominator) can be expressed in dollars and summed as shown in Example 2.

Example 2 | COMPUTING SINGLE-FACTOR AND MULTIFACTOR GAINS IN PRODUCTIVITY

Collins Title Insurance Ltd. wants to evaluate its labor and multifactor productivity with a new computerized title-search system. The company has a staff of four, each working 8 hours per day (for a payroll cost of $640/day) and overhead expenses of $400 per day. Collins processes and closes on 8 titles each day. The new computerized title-search system will allow the processing of 14 titles per day. Although the staff, their work hours, and pay are the same, the overhead expenses are now $800 per day.

APPROACH ▶ Collins uses Equation (1-1) to compute labor productivity and Equation (1-2) to compute multifactor productivity.

SOLUTION ▶

Labor productivity with the old system: $\dfrac{8 \text{ titles per day}}{32 \text{ labor-hours}} = .25$ titles per labor-hour

Labor productivity with the new system: $\dfrac{14 \text{ titles per day}}{32 \text{ labor-hours}} = .4375$ titles per labor-hour

Multifactor productivity with the old system: $\dfrac{8 \text{ titles per day}}{\$640 + 400} = .0077$ titles per dollar

Multifactor productivity with the new system: $\dfrac{14 \text{ titles per day}}{\$640 + 800} = .0097$ titles per dollar

LO 1.5 *Compute multifactor productivity*

Labor productivity has increased from .25 to .4375. The change is $(.4375 - .25)/.25 = 0.75$, or a 75% increase in labor productivity. Multifactor productivity has increased from .0077 to .0097. This change is $(.0097 - .0077)/.0077 = 0.26$, or a 26% increase in multifactor productivity.

INSIGHT ▶ Both the labor (single-factor) and multifactor productivity measures show an increase in productivity. However, the multifactor measure provides a better picture of the increase because it includes all the costs connected with the increase in output.

LEARNING EXERCISE ▶ If the overhead goes to $960 (rather than $800), what is the multifactor productivity? [Answer: .00875.]

RELATED PROBLEMS ▶ 1.1, 1.2, 1.4, 1.5, 1.6, 1.7, 1.8, 1.9, 1.10, 1.11, 1.13, 1.14, 1.17

Use of productivity measures aids managers in determining how well they are doing. But results from the two measures can be expected to vary. If labor productivity growth is entirely the result of capital spending, measuring just labor distorts the results. Multifactor productivity is usually better, but more complicated. Labor productivity is the more popular measure. The multifactor-productivity measures provide better information about the trade-offs among factors, but substantial measurement problems remain. Some of these measurement problems are:

1. *Quality* may change while the quantity of inputs and outputs remains constant. Compare an HDTV of this decade with a black-and-white TV of the 1950s. Both are TVs, but few people would deny that the quality has improved. The unit of measure—a TV—is the same, but the quality has changed.
2. *External elements* may cause an increase or a decrease in productivity for which the system under study may not be directly responsible. A more reliable electric power service may greatly improve production, thereby improving the firm's productivity because of this support system rather than because of managerial decisions made within the firm.
3. *Precise units of measure* may be lacking. Not all automobiles require the same inputs: Some cars are subcompacts, others are 911 Turbo Porsches.

Productivity measurement is particularly difficult in the service sector, where the end product can be hard to define. For example, economic statistics ignore the quality of your haircut, the outcome of a court case, or the service at a retail store. In some cases, adjustments are made for the quality of the product sold but *not* the quality of the sales presentation or the advantage of a broader product selection. Productivity measurements require specific inputs and outputs, but a free economy is producing worth—what people want—which includes convenience, speed, and safety. Traditional measures of outputs may be a very poor measure of these other measures of worth. Note the quality-measurement problems in a law office, where each case is different, altering the accuracy of the measure "cases per labor-hour" or "cases per employee."

Productivity Variables

As we saw in Figure 1.6, productivity increases are dependent on three **productivity variables:**

1. *Labor,* which contributes about 10% of the annual increase.
2. *Capital,* which contributes about 38% of the annual increase.
3. *Management,* which contributes about 52% of the annual increase.

These three factors are critical to improved productivity. They represent the broad areas in which managers can take action to improve productivity.

Productivity variables
The three factors critical to productivity improvement—labor, capital, and the art and science of management.

Figure **1.7**

About Half of the 17-Year-Olds in the U.S. Cannot Correctly Answer Questions of This Type

LO 1.6 *Identify* the critical variables in enhancing productivity

Labor   Improvement in the contribution of labor to productivity is the result of a healthier, better-educated, and better-nourished labor force. Some increase may also be attributed to a shorter workweek. Historically, about 10% of the annual improvement in productivity is attributed to improvement in the quality of labor. Three key variables for improved labor productivity are:

1. Basic education appropriate for an effective labor force.
2. Diet of the labor force.
3. Social overhead that makes labor available, such as transportation and sanitation.

Illiteracy and poor diets are a major impediment to productivity, costing countries up to 20% of their productivity. Infrastructure that yields clean drinking water and sanitation is also an opportunity for improved productivity, as well as an opportunity for better health, in much of the world.

In developed nations, the challenge becomes *maintaining and enhancing the skills of labor* in the midst of rapidly expanding technology and knowledge. Recent data suggest that the average American 17-year-old knows significantly less mathematics than the average Japanese at the same age, and about half cannot answer the questions in Figure 1.7. Moreover, about one-third of American job applicants tested for basic skills were deficient in reading, writing, or math.

Overcoming shortcomings in the quality of labor while other countries have a better labor force is a major challenge. Perhaps improvements can be found not only through increasing competence of labor but also via *better utilized labor with a stronger commitment*. Training, motivation, team building, and the human resource strategies discussed in Chapter 10, as well as improved education, may be among the many techniques that will contribute to increased labor productivity. Improvements in labor productivity are possible; however, they can be expected to be increasingly difficult and expensive.

Capital   Human beings are tool-using animals. Capital investment provides those tools. Capital investment has increased in the U.S. every year except during a few very severe recession periods. Annual capital investment in the U.S. has increased at an annual rate of 1.5% after allowances for depreciation.

Inflation and taxes increase the cost of capital, making capital investment increasingly expensive. When the capital invested per employee drops, we can expect a drop in productivity. Using labor rather than capital may reduce unemployment in the short run, but it also makes economies less productive and therefore lowers wages in the long run. Capital investment is often a necessary, but seldom a sufficient, ingredient in the battle for increased productivity.

The trade-off between capital and labor is continually in flux. The higher the cost of capital or perceived risk, the more projects requiring capital are "squeezed out": they are not pursued because the potential return on investment for a given risk has been reduced. Managers adjust their investment plans to changes in capital cost and risk.

Management   Management is a factor of production and an economic resource. Management is responsible for ensuring that labor and capital are effectively used to increase productivity. Management accounts for over half of the annual increase in productivity. This increase includes improvements made through the use of knowledge and the application of technology.

Using knowledge and technology is critical in postindustrial societies. Consequently, postindustrial societies are also known as **knowledge societies**. Knowledge societies are those in which much of the labor force has migrated from manual work to technical and information-processing

Knowledge society

A society in which much of the labor force has migrated from manual work to work based on knowledge.

The effective use of capital often means finding the proper trade-off between investment in capital assets (automation, left) and human assets (a manual process, right). While there are risks connected with any investment, the cost of capital and physical investments is fairly clear-cut, but the cost of employees has many hidden costs including fringe benefits, social insurance, and legal constraints on hiring, employment, and termination.

tasks requiring ongoing education. The required education and training are important high-cost items that are the responsibility of operations managers as they build organizations and workforces. The expanding knowledge base of contemporary society requires that managers use *technology and knowledge effectively.*

More effective use of capital also contributes to productivity. It falls to the operations manager, as a productivity catalyst, to select the best new capital investments as well as to improve the productivity of existing investments.

The productivity challenge is difficult. A country cannot be a world-class competitor with second-class inputs. Poorly educated labor, inadequate capital, and dated technology are second-class inputs. High productivity and high-quality outputs require high-quality inputs, including good operations managers.

Productivity and the Service Sector

The service sector provides a special challenge to the accurate measurement of productivity and productivity improvement. The traditional analytical framework of economic theory is based primarily on goods-producing activities. Consequently, most published economic data relate to goods production. But the data do indicate that, as our contemporary service economy has increased in size, we have had slower growth in productivity.

Siemens, a multi-billion-dollar German conglomerate, has long been known for its apprentice programs in its home country. Because education is often the key to efficient operations in a technological society, Siemens has spread its apprentice-training programs to its U.S. plants. These programs are laying the foundation for the highly skilled workforce that is essential for global competitiveness.

OM in Action   Taco Bell Improves Productivity and Goes Green to Lower Costs

Founded in 1962 by Glenn Bell, Taco Bell seeks competitive advantage via low cost. Like many other services, Taco Bell relies on its operations management to improve productivity and reduce cost.

Its menu and meals are designed to be easy to prepare. Taco Bell has shifted a substantial portion of food preparation to suppliers who could perform food processing more efficiently than a stand-alone restaurant. Ground beef is precooked prior to arrival and then reheated, as are many dishes that arrive in plastic boil bags for easy sanitary reheating. Similarly, tortillas arrive already fried and onions prediced. Efficient layout and automation has cut to 8 seconds the time needed to prepare tacos and burritos and has cut time in the drive-through lines by 1 minute. These advances have been combined with training and empowerment to increase the span of management from one supervisor for 5 restaurants to one supervisor for 30 or more.

Operations managers at Taco Bell have cut in-store labor by 15 hours per day and reduced floor space by more than 50%. The result is a store that can average 164 seconds for each customer, from drive-up to pull-out.

In 2010, Taco Bell completed the rollout of its new Grill-to-Order kitchens by installing water- and energy-saving grills that conserve 300 million gallons of water and 200 million kilowatt hours of electricity each year. This "green"-inspired cooking method also saves the company's 5,800 restaurants $17 million per year.

Effective operations management has resulted in productivity increases that support Taco Bell's low-cost strategy. Taco Bell is now the fast-food low-cost leader with a 58% share of the Mexican fast-food market.

Bob Pardue-Signs/Alamy

Sources: Business Week (May 5, 2011); *Harvard Business Review* (July/August 2008); and J. Hueter and W. Swart, *Interfaces* (Vol. 28; issue 1).

Productivity of the service sector has proven difficult to improve because service-sector work is:

1. Typically labor intensive (e.g., counseling, teaching).
2. Frequently focused on unique individual attributes or desires (e.g., investment advice).
3. Often an intellectual task performed by professionals (e.g., medical diagnosis).
4. Often difficult to mechanize and automate (e.g., a haircut).
5. Often difficult to evaluate for quality (e.g., performance of a law firm).

The more intellectual and personal the task, the more difficult it is to achieve increases in productivity. Low-productivity improvement in the service sector is also attributable to the growth of low-productivity activities in the service sector. These include activities not previously a part of the measured economy, such as child care, food preparation, house cleaning, and laundry service. These activities have moved out of the home and into the measured economy as more and more women have joined the workforce. Inclusion of these activities has probably resulted in lower measured productivity for the service sector, although, in fact, actual productivity has probably increased because these activities are now more efficiently produced than previously.

However, despite the difficulty of improving productivity in the service sector, improvements are being made. And this text presents a multitude of ways to make these improvements. Indeed, what can be done when management pays attention to how work actually gets done is astonishing!

Although the evidence indicates that all industrialized countries have the same problem with service productivity, the U.S. remains the world leader in overall productivity *and* service productivity. Retailing is twice as productive in the U.S. as in Japan, where laws protect shopkeepers from discount chains. The U.S. telephone industry is at least twice as productive as Germany's. The U.S. banking system is also 33% more efficient than Germany's banking oligopolies. However, because productivity is central to the operations manager's job and because the service sector is so large, we take special note in this text of how to improve productivity in the service sector. (See, for instance, the *OM in Action* box "Taco Bell Improves Productivity and Goes Green to Lower Costs.")

Current Challenges in Operations Management

Operations managers work in an exciting and dynamic environment. This environment is the result of a variety of challenging forces, from globalization of world trade to the transfer of ideas, products, and money at electronic speeds. Let's look at some of these challenges:

◆ *Globalization:* The rapid decline in the cost of communication and transportation has made markets global. Similarly, resources in the form of capital, materials, talent, and labor are also now global. As a result, countries throughout the world are contributing to globalization as they vie for economic growth. Operations managers are rapidly seeking creative designs, efficient production, and high-quality goods via international collaboration.

◆ *Supply-chain partnering:* Shorter product life cycles, demanding customers, and fast changes in technology, materials, and processes require supply-chain partners to be in tune with the needs of end users. And because suppliers may be able to contribute unique expertise, operations managers are outsourcing and building long-term partnerships with critical players in the supply chain.

◆ *Sustainability:* Operations managers' continuing battle to improve productivity is concerned with designing products and processes that are ecologically sustainable. This means designing green products and packaging that minimize resource use, can be recycled or re-used, and are generally environmentally friendly.

◆ *Rapid product development:* Technology combined with rapid international communication of news, entertainment, and lifestyles is dramatically chopping away at the life span of products. OM is answering with new management structures, enhanced collaboration, digital technology, and creative alliances that are more responsive and effective.

◆ *Mass customization:* Once managers recognize the *world* as the marketplace, the cultural and individual differences become quite obvious. In a world where consumers are increasingly aware of innovation and options, substantial pressure is placed on firms to respond in a creative way. And OM must rapidly respond with product designs and flexible production processes that cater to the individual whims of consumers. The goal is to produce customized products, whenever and wherever needed.

◆ *Lean operations:* Lean is the management model sweeping the world and providing the standard against which operations managers must compete. Lean can be thought of as the driving force in a well-run operation, where the customer is satisfied, employees are respected, and waste does not exist. The theme of this text is to build organizations that are more efficient, where management creates enriched jobs that help employees engage in continuous improvement, and where goods and services are produced and delivered when and where the customer desires them. These ideas are also captured in the phrase *Lean*.

These challenges must be successfully addressed by today's operations managers. This text will provide you with the foundations necessary to meet those challenges.

Ethics, Social Responsibility, and Sustainability

The systems that operations managers build to convert resources into goods and services are complex. And they function in a world where the physical and social environment is evolving, as are laws and values. These dynamics present a variety of challenges that come from the conflicting perspectives of stakeholders, such as customers, distributors, suppliers, owners, lenders, employees, and community. Stakeholders, as well as government agencies at various levels, require constant monitoring and thoughtful responses.

Identifying ethical and socially responsible responses while developing sustainable processes that are also effective and efficient productive systems is not easy. Managers are also challenged to:

◆ Develop and produce safe, high-quality green products
◆ Train, retain, and motivate employees in a safe workplace
◆ Honor stakeholder commitments

Managers must do all this while meeting the demands of a very competitive and dynamic world marketplace. If operations managers have a *moral awareness and focus on increasing productivity in this system*, then many of the ethical challenges will be successfully addressed. The organization will use fewer resources, the employees will be committed, the market will be satisfied, and the ethical climate will be enhanced. Throughout this text, we note ways in which operations managers can take ethical and socially responsible actions while successfully addressing these challenges of the market. We also conclude each chapter with an *Ethical Dilemma* exercise.

Stakeholders
Those with a vested interest in an organization, including customers, distributors, suppliers, owners, lenders, employees, and community members.

Summary

Operations, marketing, and finance/accounting are the three functions basic to all organizations. The operations function creates goods and services. Much of the progress of operations management has been made in the twentieth century, but since the beginning of time, humankind has been attempting to improve its material well-being. Operations managers are key players in the battle to improve productivity.

As societies become increasingly affluent, more of their resources are devoted to services. In the U.S., more than 85% of the workforce is employed in the service sector. Productivity improvements and a sustainable environment are difficult to achieve, but operations managers are the primary vehicle for making improvements.

Key Terms

Production (p. 4)
Operations management (OM) (p. 4)
Supply chain (p. 6)
10 strategic OM decisions (p. 7)

Services (p. 11)
Service sector (p. 12)
Productivity (p. 13)
Single-factor productivity (p. 14)

Multifactor productivity (p. 14)
Productivity variables (p. 15)
Knowledge society (p. 16)
Stakeholders (p. 19)

Ethical Dilemma

The American car battery industry boasts that its recycling rate now exceeds 95%, the highest rate for any commodity. However, with changes brought about by specialization and globalization, parts of the recycling system are moving offshore. This is particularly true of automobile batteries, which contain lead. The Environmental Protection Agency (EPA) is contributing to the offshore flow with newly implemented standards that make domestic battery recycling increasingly difficult and expensive. The result is a major increase in used batteries going to Mexico, where environmental standards and control are less demanding than they are in the U.S. One in five batteries is now exported to Mexico. There is seldom difficulty finding buyers because lead is expensive and in worldwide demand. While U.S.

recyclers operate in sealed, mechanized plants, with smokestacks equipped with scrubbers and plant surroundings monitored for traces of lead, this is not the case in most Mexican plants. The harm from lead is legendary, with long-run residual effects. Health issues include high blood pressure, kidney damage, detrimental effects on fetuses during pregnancy, neurological problems, and arrested development in children.

Given the two scenarios below, what action do you take?

a) You own an independent auto repair shop and are trying to safely dispose of a few old batteries each week. (Your battery supplier is an auto parts supplier who refuses to take your old batteries.)

b) You are manager of a large retailer responsible for disposal of thousands of used batteries each day.

Discussion Questions

1. Why should one study operations management?
2. Identify four people who have contributed to the theory and techniques of operations management.
3. Briefly describe the contributions of the four individuals identified in the preceding question.
4. Figure 1.1 outlines the operations, finance/accounting, and marketing functions of three organizations. Prepare a chart similar to Figure 1.1 outlining the same functions for one of the following:
   a. a newspaper
   b. a drugstore
   c. a college library
   d. a summer camp
   e. a small costume-jewelry factory
5. Answer Question 4 for some other organization, perhaps an organization where you have worked.
6. What are the three basic functions of a firm?
7. Identify the 10 strategic operations management decisions.
8. Name four areas that are significant to improving labor productivity.
9. The U.S., and indeed much of the rest of the world, has been described as a "knowledge society." How does this affect productivity measurement and the comparison of productivity between the U.S. and other countries?
10. What are the measurement problems that occur when one attempts to measure productivity?
11. Mass customization and rapid product development were identified as challenges to modern manufacturing operations. What is the relationship, if any, between these challenges? Can you cite any examples?
12. What are the five reasons productivity is difficult to improve in the service sector?
13. Describe some of the actions taken by Taco Bell to increase productivity that have resulted in Taco Bell's ability to serve "twice the volume with half the labor."
14. As a library or Internet assignment, find the U.S. productivity rate (increase) last year for the (a) national economy, (b) manufacturing sector, and (c) service sector.

Using Software for Productivity Analysis

This section presents three ways to solve productivity problems with computer software. First, you can create your own Excel spreadsheets to conduct productivity analysis. Second, you can use the Excel OM software that comes with this text. Third, POM for Windows is another program that is available with this text.

CREATING YOUR OWN EXCEL SPREADSHEETS

Program 1.1 illustrates how to build an Excel spreadsheet for the data in Example 2.

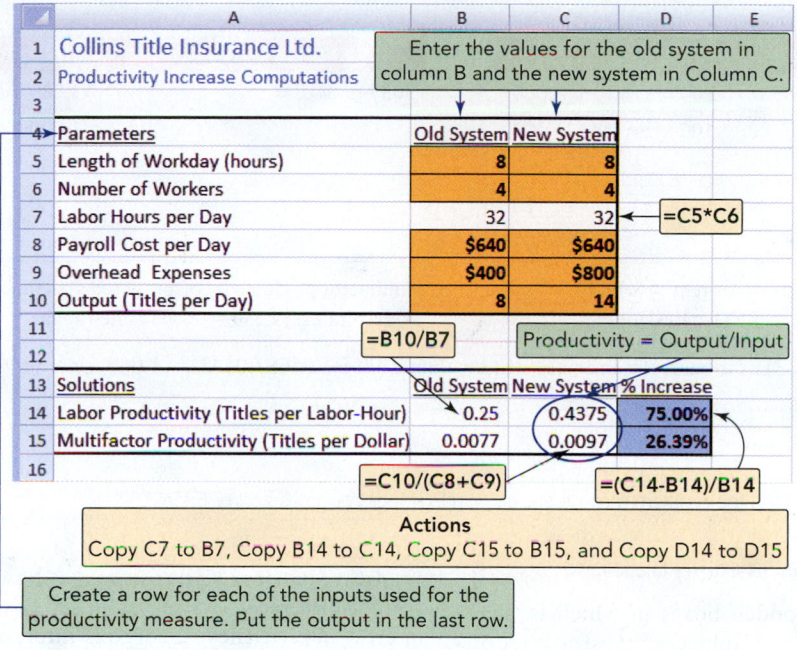

Program **1.1**

✗ USING EXCEL OM

Excel OM is an Excel "add-in" with 24 Operations Management decision support "Templates." To access the templates, double-click on the *Excel OM* tab at the top of the page, then in the menu bar choose the appropriate chapter (in this case Chapter 1), from either the "Chapter" or "Alphabetic" tab on the left. Each of Excel OM's 24 modules includes instructions for that particular module. The instructions can be turned on or off via the "instruction" tab in the menu bar.

P USING POM FOR WINDOWS

POM for Windows is decision support software that includes 24 Operations Management modules. The modules are accessed by double-clicking on *Module* in the menu bar, and then double-clicking on the appropriate (in this case *Productivity*) item. Instructions are provided for each module just below the menu bar.

Solved Problems   Virtual Office Hours help is available in MyOMLab.

SOLVED PROBLEM 1.1

Productivity can be measured in a variety of ways, such as by labor, capital, energy, material usage, and so on. At Modern Lumber, Inc., Art Binley, president and producer of apple crates sold to growers, has been able, with his current equipment, to produce 240 crates per 100 logs. He currently purchases 100 logs per day, and each log requires 3 labor-hours to process. He believes that he can hire a professional buyer who can buy a better-quality log at the same cost. If this is the case, he can increase his production to 260 crates per 100 logs. His labor-hours will increase by 8 hours per day.

What will be the impact on productivity (measured in crates per labor-hour) if the buyer is hired?

SOLUTION

(a) Current labor productivity $= \dfrac{240 \text{ crates}}{100 \text{ logs} \times 3 \text{ hours/log}}$

$= \dfrac{240}{300}$

$= .8$ crates per labor-hour

(b) Labor productivity with buyer $= \dfrac{260 \text{ crates}}{(100 \text{ logs} \times 3 \text{ hours/log}) + 8 \text{ hours}}$

$= \dfrac{260}{308}$

$= .844$ crates per labor-hour

Using current productivity (.80 from [a]) as a base, the increase will be 5.5% (.844/.8 = 1.055, or a 5.5% increase).

SOLVED PROBLEM 1.2

Art Binley has decided to look at his productivity from a multi-factor (total factor productivity) perspective (refer to Solved Problem 1.1). To do so, he has determined his labor, capital, energy, and material usage and decided to use dollars as the common denominator. His total labor-hours are now 300 per day and will increase to 308 per day. His capital and energy costs will remain constant at $350 and $150 per day, respectively. Material costs for the 100 logs per day are $1,000 and will remain the same. Because he pays an average of $10 per hour (with fringes), Binley determines his productivity increase as follows:

SOLUTION

CURRENT SYSTEM		
Labor:	300 hrs. @10 = 3,000	
Material:	100 logs/day	1,000
Capital:		350
Energy:		150
Total Cost:		$4,500

SYSTEM WITH PROFESSIONAL BUYER	
308 hrs. @10 =	$3,080
	1,000
	350
	150
	$4,580

Multifactor productivity of current system:
= 240 crates/$4,500 = .0533 crates/dollar

Multifactor productivity of proposed system:
= 260 crates/$4,580 = .0568 crates/dollar

Using current productivity (.0533) as a base, the increase will be .066. That is, .0568/.0533 = 1.066, or a 6.6% increase.

Problems   Note: **Px** means the problem may be solved with POM for Windows and/or Excel OM.

Problems 1.1 to 1.17 relate to The Productivity Challenge

• **1.1**   Chuck Sox makes wooden boxes in which to ship motorcycles. Chuck and his three employees invest a total of 40 hours per day making the 120 boxes.
a) What is their productivity?
b) Chuck and his employees have discussed redesigning the process to improve efficiency. If they can increase the rate to 125 per day, what will be their new productivity?
c) What will be their unit *increase* in productivity per hour?
d) What will be their percentage change in productivity? **Px**

• **1.2**   Carbondale Casting produces cast bronze valves on a 10-person assembly line. On a recent day, 160 valves were produced during an 8-hour shift.
a) Calculate the labor productivity of the line.
b) John Goodale, the manager at Carbondale, changed the layout and was able to increase production to 180 units per 8-hour shift. What is the new labor productivity per labor-hour?
c) What is the percentage of productivity increase? **Px**

• **1.3**   This year, Druehl, Inc., will produce 57,600 hot water heaters at its plant in Delaware, in order to meet expected global demand. To accomplish this, each laborer at the plant will work 160 hours per month. If the labor productivity at the plant is 0.15 hot water heaters per labor-hour, how many laborers are employed at the plant?

• **1.4**   Lori Cook produces "Final Exam Care Packages" for resale by her sorority. She is currently working a total of 5 hours per day to produce 100 care packages.
a) What is Lori's productivity?
b) Lori thinks that by redesigning the package, she can increase her total productivity to 133 care packages per day. What will be her new productivity?
c) What will be the percentage increase in productivity if Lori makes the change? **Px**

•• **1.5**   George Kyparisis makes bowling balls in his Miami plant. With recent increases in his costs, he has a newfound interest in efficiency. George is interested in determining the productivity of his organization. He would like to know if his organization is maintaining the manufacturing average of 3% increase in productivity per year? He has the following data representing a month from last year and an equivalent month this year:

	LAST YEAR	NOW
Units produced	1,000	1,000
Labor (hours)	300	275
Resin (pounds)	50	45
Capital invested ($)	10,000	11,000
Energy (BTU)	3,000	2,850

Show the productivity percentage change for each category and then determine the improvement for labor-hours, the typical standard for comparison. **Px**

•• **1.6**   George Kyparisis (using data from Problem 1.5) determines his costs to be as follows:

◆ *Labor:* $10 per hour
◆ *Resin:* $5 per pound
◆ *Capital expense:* 1% per month of investment
◆ *Energy:* $0.50 per BTU

Show the percent change in productivity for one month last year versus one month this year, on a multifactor basis with dollars as the common denominator. **Px**

• **1.7** Hokey Min's Kleen Karpet cleaned 65 rugs in October, consuming the following resources:

Labor:	520 hours at $13 per hour
Solvent:	100 gallons at $5 per gallon
Machine rental:	20 days at $50 per day

a) What is the labor productivity per dollar?
b) What is the multifactor productivity? **Px**

•• **1.8** Lillian Fok is president of Lakefront Manufacturing, a producer of bicycle tires. Fok makes 1,000 tires per day with the following resources:

Labor:	400 hours per day @ $12.50 per hour
Raw material:	20,000 pounds per day @ $1 per pound
Energy:	$5,000 per day
Capital costs:	$10,000 per day

a) What is the labor productivity per labor-hour for these tires at Lakefront Manufacturing?
b) What is the multifactor productivity for these tires at Lakefront Manufacturing?
c) What is the percent change in multifactor productivity if Fok can reduce the energy bill by $1,000 per day without cutting production or changing any other inputs? **Px**

••• **1.9** Brown's, a local bakery, is worried about increased costs—particularly energy. Last year's records can provide a fairly good estimate of the parameters for this year. Wende Brown, the owner, does not believe things have changed much, but she did invest an additional $3,000 for modifications to the bakery's ovens to make them more energy efficient. The modifications were supposed to make the ovens at least 15% more efficient. Brown has asked you to check the energy savings of the new ovens and also to look over other measures of the bakery's productivity to see if the modifications were beneficial. You have the following data to work with:

	LAST YEAR	NOW
Production (dozen)	1,500	1,500
Labor (hours)	350	325
Capital investment ($)	15,000	18,000
Energy (BTU)	3,000	2,750

Px

Taras Vyshnya/Shutterstock

•• **1.10** Munson Performance Auto, Inc., modifies 375 autos per year. The manager, Adam Munson, is interested in obtaining a measure of overall performance. He has asked you to provide him with a multifactor measure of last year's performance as a benchmark for future comparison. You have assembled the following data. Resource inputs were labor, 10,000 hours; 500 suspension and engine modification kits; and energy, 100,000 kilowatt-hours. Average labor cost last year was $20 per hour, kits cost $1,000 each, and energy costs were $3 per kilowatt-hour. What do you tell Mr. Munson? **Px**

•• **1.11** Lake Charles Seafood makes 500 wooden packing boxes for fresh seafood per day, working in two 10-hour shifts. Due to increased demand, plant managers have decided to operate three 8-hour shifts instead. The plant is now able to produce 650 boxes per day.
a) Calculate the company's productivity before the change in work rules and after the change.
b) What is the percentage increase in productivity?
c) If production is increased to 700 boxes per day, what is the new productivity? **Px**

••• **1.12** Charles Lackey operates a bakery in Idaho Falls, Idaho. Because of its excellent product and excellent location, demand has increased by 25% in the last year. On far too many occasions, customers have not been able to purchase the bread of their choice. Because of the size of the store, no new ovens can be added. At a staff meeting, one employee suggested ways to load the ovens differently so that more loaves of bread can be baked at one time. This new process will require that the ovens be loaded by hand, requiring additional manpower. This is the only thing to be changed. If the bakery makes 1,500 loaves per month with a labor productivity of 2.344 loaves per labor-hour, how many workers will Lackey need to *add*? (*Hint:* Each worker works 160 hours per month.)

•• **1.13** Refer to Problem 1.12. The pay will be $8 per hour for employees. Charles Lackey can also improve the yield by purchasing a new blender. The new blender will mean an increase in his investment. This added investment has a cost of $100 per month, but he will achieve the same output (an increase to 1,875) as the change in labor-hours. Which is the better decision?
a) Show the productivity change, in loaves per dollar, with an increase in labor cost (from 640 to 800 hours).
b) Show the new productivity, in loaves per dollar, with only an increase in investment ($100 per month more).
c) Show the percent productivity change for labor and investment.

••• **1.14** Refer to Problems 1.12 and 1.13. If Charles Lackey's utility costs remain constant at $500 per month, labor at $8 per hour, and cost of ingredients at $0.35 per loaf, but Charles does not purchase the blender suggested in Problem 1.13, what will the productivity of the bakery be? What will be the percent increase or decrease?

•• **1.15** In December, General Motors produced 6,600 customized vans at its plant in Detroit. The labor productivity at this plant is known to have been 0.10 vans per labor-hour during that month. 300 laborers were employed at the plant that month.
a) How many hours did the average laborer work that month?
b) If productivity can be increased to 0.11 vans per labor-hour, how many hours would the average laborer work that month?

··1.16 Susan Williams runs a small Flagstaff job shop where garments are made. The job shop employs eight workers. Each worker is paid $10 per hour. During the first week of March, each worker worked 45 hours. Together, they produced a batch of 132 garments. Of these garments, 52 were "seconds" (meaning that they were flawed). The seconds were sold for $90 each at a factory outlet store. The remaining 80 garments were sold to retail outlets at a price of $198 per garment. What was the labor productivity, in dollars per labor-hour, at this job shop during the first week of March?

···1.17 As part of a study for the Department of Labor Statistics, you are assigned the task of evaluating the improvement in productivity of small businesses. Data for one of the small businesses you are to evaluate are shown at right. The data are the monthly average of last year and the monthly average this year. Determine the multifactor productivity with dollars as the common denominator for:

a) Last year.
b) This year.
c) Then determine the percent change in productivity for the monthly average last year versus the monthly average this year on a multifactor basis.

- ◆ *Labor:* $8 per hour
- ◆ *Capital:* 0.83% per month of investment
- ◆ *Energy:* $0.60 per BTU

	LAST YEAR	THIS YEAR
Production (dozen)	1,500	1,500
Labor (hours)	350	325
Capital investment ($)	15,000	18,000
Energy (BTU)	3,000	2,700

CASE STUDIES

Uber Technologies, Inc.

The $41 billion dollar firm Uber Technology, Inc., is unsettling the traditional taxi business. In over 40 countries and 240 markets around the world, Uber and similar companies are challenging the existing taxi business model. Uber and its growing list of competitors, Lyft, Sidecar, and Flywheel in America, and fledging rivals in Europe, Asia, and India, think their smart phone apps can provide a new and improved way to call a taxi. This disruptive business model uses an app to arrange rides between riders and cars, theoretically a nearby car, which is tracked by the app. The Uber system also provides a history of rides, routes, and fees as well as automatic billing. In addition, driver and rider are also allowed to evaluate each other. The services are increasingly popular, worrying established taxi services in cities from New York to Berlin, and from Rio de Janeiro to Bangkok. In many markets, Uber has proven to be the best, fastest, and most reliable way to find a ride. Consumers worldwide are endorsing the system as a replacement for the usual taxi ride. As the most established competitor in the field, Uber is putting more cars on the road, meaning faster pickup times, which should attract even more riders, which in turn attracts even more drivers, and so on. This growth cycle may speed the demise of the existing taxi businesses as well as provide substantial competition for firms with a technology-oriented model similar to Uber's.

The Uber business model initially attempts to bypass a number of regulations and at the same time offer better service and lower fees than traditional taxis. However, the traditional taxi industry is fighting back, and regulations are mounting. The regulations vary by country and city, but increasingly special licensing, testing, and inspections are being imposed. Part of the fee charged to riders does not go to the driver, but to Uber, as there are real overhead costs. Uber's costs, depending on the locale, may include insurance, background checks for drivers, vetting of vehicles, software development and maintenance, and centralized billing. How these overhead costs compare to traditional taxi costs is yet to be determined. Therefore, improved efficiency may not be immediately obvious, and contract provisions are significant (see www.uber.com/legal/usa/terms).

In addition to growing regulations, a complicating factor in the model is finding volunteer drivers at inopportune times. A sober driver and a clean car at 1:00 a.m. New Year's Eve does cost more. Consequently, Uber has introduced "surge" pricing. Surge pricing means a higher price, sometimes much higher, than normal. Surge pricing has proven necessary to ensure that cars and drivers are available at unusual times. These higher surge prices can be a shock to riders, making the "surge price" a contentious issue.

Discussion Questions

1. The market has decided that Uber and its immediate competitors are adding efficiency to our society. How is Uber providing that added efficiency?

2. Do you think the Uber model will work in the trucking industry?

3. In what other areas/industries might the Uber model be used?

Sources: Wall Street Journal (January 2, 2015), B3, and (Dec. 18, 2014), D1; and www.bloombergview.com/articles/2014-12-11/can-uber-rule-the-world.

Frito-Lay: Operations Management in Manufacturing

Frito-Lay, the massive Dallas-based subsidiary of PepsiCo, has 38 plants and 48,000 employees in North America. Seven of Frito-Lay's 41 brands exceed $1 billion in sales: Fritos, Lay's, Cheetos, Ruffles, Tostitos, Doritos, and Walker's Potato Chips. Operations is the focus of the firm—from designing products for new markets, to meeting changing consumer preferences, to adjusting to rising commodity costs, to subtle issues involving flavors and preservatives—OM is under constant cost, time, quality, and market pressure. Here is a look at how the 10 decisions of OM are applied at this food processor.

In the food industry, product development kitchens experiment with new products, submit them to focus groups, and perform test marketing. Once the product specifications have been set, processes capable of meeting those specifications and the necessary quality standards are created. At Frito-Lay, quality begins at the farm, with onsite inspection of the potatoes used in Ruffles and the corn used in Fritos. Quality continues throughout the manufacturing process, with visual inspections and with statistical process control of product variables such as oil, moisture, seasoning, salt, thickness, and weight. Additional quality evaluations are conducted throughout shipment, receipt, production, packaging, and delivery.

The production process at Frito-Lay is designed for large volumes and small variety, using expensive special-purpose equipment, and with swift movement of material through the facility. Product-focused facilities, such as Frito-Lay's, typically have high capital costs, tight schedules, and rapid processing. Frito-Lay's facilities are located regionally to aid in the rapid delivery of products because freshness is a critical issue. Sanitary issues and necessarily fast processing of products put a premium on an efficient layout. Production lines are designed for balanced throughput and high utilization. Cross-trained workers, who handle a variety of production lines, have promotion paths identified for their particular skill set. The company rewards employees with medical, retirement, and education plans. Its turnover is very low.

The supply chain is integral to success in the food industry; vendors must be chosen with great care. Moreover, the finished food product is highly dependent on perishable raw materials. Consequently, the supply chain brings raw material (potatoes, corn, etc.) to the plant securely and rapidly to meet tight production schedules. For instance, from the time that potatoes are picked in St. Augustine, Florida, until they are unloaded at the Orlando plant, processed, packaged, and shipped from the plant is under 12 hours. The requirement for fresh product requires on-time, just-in-time deliveries combined with both low raw material and finished goods inventories. The continuous-flow nature of the specialized equipment in the production process permits little work-in-process inventory. The plants usually run 24/7. This means that there are four shifts of employees each week.

Tight scheduling to ensure the proper mix of fresh finished goods on automated equipment requires reliable systems and effective maintenance. Frito-Lay's workforce is trained to recognize problems early, and professional maintenance personnel are available on every shift. Downtime is very costly and can lead to late deliveries, making maintenance a high priority.

Discussion Questions*

1. From your knowledge of production processes and from the case and the video, identify how each of the 10 decisions of OM is applied at Frito-Lay.
2. How would you determine the productivity of the production process at Frito-Lay?
3. How are the 10 decisions of OM different when applied by the operations manager of a production process such as Frito-Lay versus a service organization such as Hard Rock Cafe (see the Hard Rock Cafe video case below)?

*You may wish to view the video that accompanies this case before addressing these questions.

Hard Rock Cafe: Operations Management in Services

In its 45 years of existence, Hard Rock has grown from a modest London pub to a global power managing 150 cafes, 13 hotels/casinos, and live music venues. This puts Hard Rock firmly in the service industry—a sector that employs over 75% of the people in the U.S. Hard Rock moved its world headquarters to Orlando, Florida, in 1988 and has expanded to more than 40 locations throughout the U.S., serving over 100,000 meals each day. Hard Rock chefs are modifying the menu from classic American—burgers and chicken wings—to include higher-end items such as stuffed veal chops and lobster tails. Just as taste in music changes over time, so does Hard Rock Cafe, with new menus, layouts, memorabilia, services, and strategies.

At Orlando's Universal Studios, a traditional tourist destination, Hard Rock Cafe serves over 3,500 meals each day. The cafe employs about 400 people. Most are employed in the restaurant, but some work in the retail shop. Retail is now a standard and increasingly prominent feature in Hard Rock Cafes (since close to 48% of revenue comes from this source).

Cafe employees include kitchen and waitstaff, hostesses, and bartenders. Hard Rock employees are not only competent in their job skills but are also passionate about music and have engaging personalities. Cafe staff is scheduled down to 15-minute intervals to meet seasonal and daily demand changes in the tourist environment of Orlando. Surveys are done on a regular basis to evaluate quality of food and service at the cafe. Scores are rated on a 1-to-7 scale, and if the score is not a 7, the food or service is a failure.

Hard Rock is adding a new emphasis on live music and is redesigning its restaurants to accommodate the changing tastes. Since Eric Clapton hung his guitar on the wall to mark his favorite bar stool, Hard Rock has become the world's leading collector and exhibitor of rock 'n' roll memorabilia, with changing exhibits at its cafes throughout the world. The collection includes 70,000 pieces, valued at $40 million. In keeping with the times, Hard Rock also maintains a Web site, www.hardrock.com, which receives over 100,000 hits per week, and a weekly cable television program on VH1. Hard Rock's brand recognition, at 92%, is one of the highest in the world.

Discussion Questions*

1. From your knowledge of restaurants, from the video, from the *Global Company Profile* that opens this chapter, and from the case itself, identify how each of the 10 OM strategy decisions is applied at Hard Rock Cafe.

2. How would you determine the productivity of the kitchen staff and waitstaff at Hard Rock?

3. How are the 10 OM strategy decisions different when applied to the operations manager of a service operation such as Hard Rock versus an automobile company such as Ford Motor Company?

*You may wish to view the video that accompanies this case before addressing these questions.

- **Additional Case Study:** Visit MyOMLab for these case studies:
  National Air Express: Introduces the issue of productivity, productivity improvement, and measuring productivity.
  Zychol Chemicals Corp.: The production manager must prepare a productivity report, which includes multifactor analysis.

Endnotes

1. *Efficiency* means doing the job well—with a minimum of resources and waste. Note the distinction between being *efficient*, which implies doing the job well, and *effective*, which means doing the right thing. A job well done—say, by applying the 10 strategic decisions of operations management—helps us be *efficient*; developing and using the correct strategy helps us be *effective*.

2. U.S. Dept. of Labor, 2015: www.bls.gov/lpc/

3. The quality and time period are assumed to remain constant.

Chapter 1 *Rapid* Review

MyOMLab

Main Heading	Review Material	MyOMLab
WHAT IS OPERATIONS MANAGEMENT? (p. 4)	■ **Production**—The creation of goods and services ■ **Operations management (OM)**—Activities that relate to the creation of goods and services through the transformation of inputs to outputs	Concept Questions: 1.1–1.4 **VIDEOS 1.1** and **1.2** OM at Hard Rock OM at Frito-Lay
ORGANIZING TO PRODUCE GOODS AND SERVICES (pp. 4–6)	All organizations perform three functions to create goods and services: 1. *Marketing*, which generates demand 2. *Production/operations*, which creates the product 3. *Finance/accounting*, which tracks how well the organization is doing, pays the bills, and collects the money	Concept Questions: 2.1–2.4
THE SUPPLY CHAIN (p. 6)	■ **Supply chain**—A global network of organizations and activities that supply a firm with goods and services	Concept Questions: 3.1–3.4
WHY STUDY OM? (pp. 6–7)	We study OM for four reasons: 1. To learn how people organize themselves for productive enterprise 2. To learn how goods and services are produced 3. To understand what operations managers do 4. Because OM is a costly part of an organization	Concept Questions: 4.1–4.2
WHAT OPERATIONS MANAGERS DO (pp. 7–8)	Ten **OM strategic decisions** are required of operations managers: 1. Design of goods and services 2. Managing quality 3. Process strategy 4. Location strategies 5. Layout strategies 6. Human resources 7. Supply chain management 8. Inventory management 9. Scheduling 10. Maintenance About 40% of *all* jobs are in OM. Operations managers possess job titles such as plant manager, quality manager, process improvement consultant, and operations analyst.	Concept Questions: 5.1–5.4
THE HERITAGE OF OPERATIONS MANAGEMENT (pp. 8–10)	Significant events in modern OM can be classified into six eras: 1. Early concepts (1776–1880)—Labor specialization (Smith, Babbage), standardized parts (Whitney) 2. Scientific management (1880–1910)—Gantt charts (Gantt), motion and time studies (Gilbreth), process analysis (Taylor), queuing theory (Erlang) 3. Mass production (1910–1980)—Assembly line (Ford/Sorensen), statistical sampling (Shewhart), economic order quantity (Harris), linear programming (Dantzig), PERT/CPM (DuPont), material requirements planning 4. Lean production (1980–1995)—Just-in-time, computer-aided design, electronic data interchange, total quality management, Baldrige Award, empowerment, kanbans 5. Mass customization (1995–2005)—Internet/e-commerce, enterprise resource planning, international quality standards, finite scheduling, supply-chain management, mass customization, build-to-order, radio frequency identification (RFID) 6. Globalization era (2005–2020)—Global supply chains, growth of transnational organizations, instant communications, sustainability, ethics in a global work force, logistics and shipping	Concept Questions: 6.1–6.4
OPERATIONS FOR GOODS AND SERVICES (pp. 11–13)	■ **Services**—Economic activities that typically produce an intangible product (such as education, entertainment, lodging, government, financial, and health services). Almost all services and almost all goods are a mixture of a service and a tangible product. ■ **Service sector**—The segment of the economy that includes trade, financial, lodging, education, legal, medical, and other professional occupations. Services now constitute the largest economic sector in postindustrial societies. The huge productivity increases in agriculture and manufacturing have allowed more of our economic resources to be devoted to services. Many service jobs pay very well.	Concept Questions: 7.1–7.4

Main Heading	Review Material	
THE PRODUCTIVITY CHALLENGE (pp. 13–18)	■ **Productivity**—The ratio of outputs (goods and services) divided by one or more inputs (such as labor, capital, or management) High production means producing many units, while high productivity means producing units efficiently. Only through increases in productivity can the standard of living of a country improve. U.S. productivity has averaged a 2.5% increase per year for over a century. $$\text{Single-factor productivity} = \frac{\text{Units produced}}{\text{Input used}} \qquad (1\text{-}1)$$ ■ **Single-factor productivity**—Indicates the ratio of goods and services produced (outputs) to one resource (input). ■ **Multifactor productivity**—Indicates the ratio of goods and services produced (outputs) to many or all resources (inputs). Multifactor productivity $$= \frac{\text{Output}}{\text{Labor} + \text{Material} + \text{Energy} + \text{Capital} + \text{Miscellaneous}} \qquad (1\text{-}2)$$ Measurement problems with productivity include: (1) the quality may change, (2) external elements may interfere, and (3) precise units of measure may be lacking. ■ **Productivity variables**—The three factors critical to productivity improvement are labor (10%), capital (38%), and management (52%). ■ **Knowledge society**—A society in which much of the labor force has migrated from manual work to work based on knowledge	Concept Questions: 8.1–8.4 Problems: 1.1–1.17 Virtual Office Hours for Solved Problems: 1.1, 1.2
CURRENT CHALLENGES IN OPERATIONS MANAGEMENT (pp. 18–19)	Some of the current challenges for operations managers include: ■ Global focus; international collaboration ■ Supply chain partnering; joint ventures; alliances ■ Sustainability; green products; recycle, reuse ■ Rapid product development; design collaboration ■ Mass customization; customized products ■ Lean operations; continuous improvement and elimination of waste	Concept Questions: 9.1–9.4
ETHICS, SOCIAL RESPONSIBILITY, AND SUSTAINABILITY (p. 19)	Among the many ethical challenges facing operations managers are (1) efficiently developing and producing safe, quality products; (2) maintaining a clean environment; (3) providing a safe workplace; and (4) honoring stakeholder commitments. ■ **Stakeholders**—Those with a vested interest in an organization	Concept Question: 10.1

Self Test

■ **Before taking the self-test,** refer to the learning objectives listed at the beginning of the chapter and the key terms listed at the end of the chapter.

LO 1.1 Productivity increases when:
a) inputs increase while outputs remain the same.
b) inputs decrease while outputs remain the same.
c) outputs decrease while inputs remain the same.
d) inputs and outputs increase proportionately.
e) inputs increase at the same rate as outputs.

LO 1.2 Services often:
a) are tangible.
b) are standardized.
c) are knowledge based.
d) are low in customer interaction.
e) have consistent product definition.

LO 1.3 Productivity:
a) can use many factors as the numerator.
b) is the same thing as production.
c) increases at about 0.5% per year.
d) is dependent upon labor, management, and capital.
e) is the same thing as effectiveness.

LO 1.4 Single-factor productivity:
a) remains constant.
b) is never constant.
c) usually uses labor as a factor.
d) seldom uses labor as a factor.
e) uses management as a factor.

LO 1.5 Multifactor productivity:
a) remains constant.
b) is never constant.
c) usually uses substitutes as common variables for the factors of production.
d) seldom uses labor as a factor.
e) always uses management as a factor.

LO 1.6 Productivity increases each year in the U.S. are a result of three factors:
a) labor, capital, management
b) engineering, labor, capital
c) engineering, capital, quality control
d) engineering, labor, data processing
e) engineering, capital, data processing

Answers: LO 1.1. b; LO 1.2. c; LO 1.3. d; LO 1.4. c; LO 1.5. c; LO 1.6. a.

Operations Strategy in a Global Environment

CHAPTER OUTLINE

GLOBAL COMPANY PROFILE: *Boeing*

◆ A Global View of Operations and Supply Chains *32*

◆ Developing Missions and Strategies *35*

◆ Achieving Competitive Advantage Through Operations *36*

◆ Issues in Operations Strategy *40*

◆ Strategy Development and Implementation *41*

◆ Strategic Planning, Core Competencies, and Outsourcing *44*

◆ Global Operations Strategy Options *49*

Alaska Airlines

Boeing's Global Supply-Chain Strategy Yields Competitive Advantage

Boeing's strategy for its 787 Dreamliner is unique for its technologically advanced product design and vast global supply chain.

The Dreamliner incorporates the latest in a wide range of aerospace technologies, from airframe and engine design to super-lightweight titanium-graphite laminate and carbon-fiber composites. The electronic monitoring system that allows the airplane to report maintenance

With the 787's state-of-the-art design, more spacious interior, and global suppliers, Boeing has garnered record sales worldwide.

Some of the International Suppliers of Boeing 787 Components

SUPPLIER	HQ COUNTRY	COMPONENT
Latecoere	France	Passenger doors
Labinel	France	Wiring
Dassault	France	Design and product life cycle management software
Messier-Bugatti	France	Electric brakes
Thales	France	Electrical power conversion system
Messier-Dowty	France	Landing gear structure
Diehl	Germany	Interior lighting
Cobham	UK	Fuel pumps and valves
Rolls-Royce	UK	Engines
Smiths Aerospace	UK	Central computer system
BAE Systems	UK	Electronics
Alenia Aeronautica	Italy	Upper center fuselage
Toray Industries	Japan	Carbon fiber for wing and tail units
Fuji Heavy Industries	Japan	Center wing box
Kawasaki Heavy Ind.	Japan	Forward fuselage, fixed sections of wing
Teijin Seiki	Japan	Hydraulic actuators
Mitsubishi Heavy Ind.	Japan	Wing box
Chengdu Aircraft	China	Rudder
Hafei Aviation	China	Parts
Korean Airlines	South Korea	Wingtips
Saab	Sweden	Cargo and access doors

requirements in real time to ground-based computer systems is another product innovation. Boeing's collaboration with General Electric and Rolls-Royce has resulted in the development of more efficient engines and an emissions reduction of 20%. The advances in engine technology contribute as much as 8% of the increased fuel/payload efficiency of the new airplane, representing a nearly two-generation jump in technology.

Boeing's design group at its Everett, Washington, facility led an international team of aerospace companies in development of this state-of-the-art plane. Technologically advanced design, new manufacturing processes, and a committed international supply chain have helped Boeing and its partners achieve unprecedented levels of performance in design and manufacture.

State-of-the-art composite sections of the 787 are built around the world and shipped to Boeing for final assembly.

Components from Boeing's worldwide supply chain come together on assembly lines in Everett, Washington, and Charleston, South Carolina. Although components come from throughout the world, about 35% of the 787 structure comes from Japanese companies.

The 787 is global not only because it has a range of 8,300 miles, but also because it is built all over the world. With a huge financial commitment of over $5 billion, Boeing needed partners. The global nature of both the technology and the aircraft market meant finding exceptional engineering talent and suppliers, wherever they might be. It also meant developing a culture of collaboration and integration with firms willing to step up to the risk associated with this revolutionary and very expensive new product.

State-of-the-art technology, multinational aircraft certifications, the cross-culture nature of the communications, and logistical challenges all added to the supply chain risk. In the end, Boeing accepted the challenge of teaming with more than 300 suppliers in over a dozen countries. Twenty of these suppliers developed technologies, design concepts, and major systems for the 787. Some of them are shown in the table. The partners brought commitment to the table. The expectation is that countries that have a stake in the Dreamliner are more likely to buy from Boeing than from its European competitor, Airbus.

Japanese companies are producing over 35% of the project, and Italy's Alenia Aeronautica is building an additional 10% of the plane.

The innovative Dreamliner, with its global range and worldwide supply chain, is setting new levels of operational efficiency. As a result, it is the fastest-selling commercial jet in history with over 1,100 planes sold. Boeing's Dreamliner reflects the global nature of business in the 21st century.

Boeing's collaborative technology enables a "virtual workspace" that allows Everett, Washington-based engineers, as well as partners in Australia, Japan, Italy, Canada, and across the United States, to make concurrent design changes to the airplane in real time. Digitally designing, building, and testing before production not only reduces design time and errors, but also improves efficiencies in component manufacturing and assembly.

LEARNING OBJECTIVES

LO 2.1 *Define* mission and strategy 36

LO 2.2 *Identify* and explain three strategic approaches to competitive advantage 36

LO 2.3 *Understand* the significance of key success factors and core competencies 42

LO 2.4 *Use* factor rating to evaluate both country and outsource providers 47

LO 2.5 *Identify* and explain four global operations strategy options 49

A Global View of Operations and Supply Chains

Today's successful operations manager has a global view of operations strategy. Since the early 1990s, nearly 3 billion people in developing countries have overcome the cultural, religious, ethnic, and political barriers that constrain productivity. And now they are all players on the global economic stage. As these barriers disappear, simultaneous advances are being made in technology, reliable shipping, and inexpensive communication. These changes mean that, increasingly, firms find their customers and suppliers located around the world. The unsurprising result is the growth of world trade (see Figure 2.1), global capital markets, and the international movement of people. This means increasing economic integration and interdependence of countries—in a word, globalization. In response, organizations are hastily extending their distribution channels and supply chains globally. The result is innovative strategies where firms compete not just with their own expertise but with the talent in their entire global supply chain. For instance:

- Boeing is competitive because both its sales and supply chain are worldwide.
- Italy's Benetton moves inventory to stores around the world faster than its competition with rapid communication and by building exceptional flexibility into design, production, and distribution.
- Sony purchases components from a supply chain that extends to Thailand, Malaysia, and elsewhere around the world for assembly of its electronic products, which in turn are distributed around the world.
- Volvo, considered a Swedish company, was purchased by a Chinese company, Geely. But the current Volvo S40 is assembled in Belgium, South Africa, Malaysia, and China, on a platform shared with the Mazda 3 (built in Japan) and the Ford Focus (built in Europe).
- China's Haier (pronounced "higher") is now producing compact refrigerators (it has one-third of the U.S. market) and refrigerated wine cabinets (it has half of the U.S. market) in South Carolina.

Figure **2.1**

Growth of World Trade as a Percent of World GDP

Sources: World Bank; World Trade Organization; and IMF.

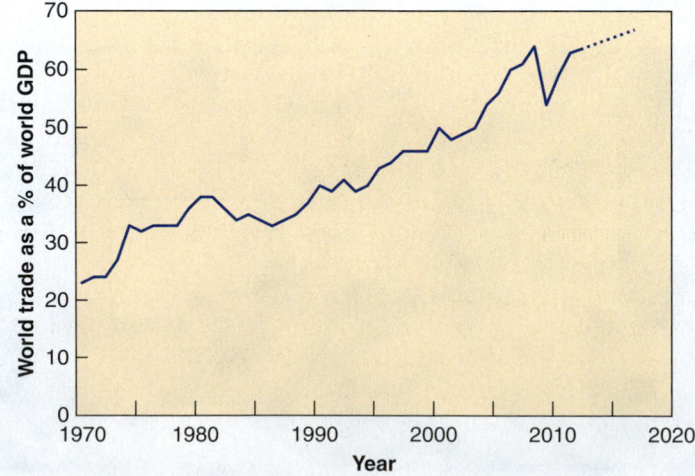

Globalization means customers, talent, and suppliers are worldwide. The new standards of global competitiveness impact quality, variety, customization, convenience, timeliness, and cost. Globalization strategies contribute efficiency, adding value to products and services, but they also complicate the operations manager's job. Complexity, risk, and competition are intensified, forcing companies to adjust for a shrinking world.

We have identified six reasons domestic business operations decide to change to some form of international operation. They are:

1. Improve the supply chain.
2. Reduce costs and exchange rate risk.
3. Improve operations.
4. Understand markets.
5. Improve products.
6. Attract and retain global talent.

Let us examine, in turn, each of the six reasons.

Improve the Supply Chain   The supply chain can often be improved by locating facilities in countries where unique resources are available. These resources may be human resource expertise, low-cost labor, or raw material. For example, auto-styling studios from throughout the world have migrated to the auto mecca of southern California to ensure the necessary expertise in contemporary auto design. Similarly, world athletic shoe production has migrated from South Korea to Guangzhou, China; this location takes advantage of the low-cost labor and production competence in a city where 40,000 people work making athletic shoes for the world. And a perfume manufacturer wants a presence in Grasse, France, where much of the world's perfume essences are prepared from the flowers of the Mediterranean.

Reduce Costs and Exchange Rate Risk   Many international operations seek to reduce risks associated with changing currency values (exchange rates) as well as take advantage of the tangible opportunities to reduce their direct costs. (See the *OM in Action* box "U.S. Cartoon Production at Home in Manila.") Less stringent government regulations on a wide variety of operations practices (e.g., environmental control, health and safety) can also reduce indirect costs.

Shifting low-skilled jobs to another country has several potential advantages. First, and most obviously, the firm may reduce costs. Second, moving the lower-skilled jobs to a lower-cost location frees higher-cost workers for more valuable tasks. Third, reducing wage costs allows the savings to be invested in improved products and facilities (and the retraining of existing workers, if necessary) at the home location. Finally, having facilities in countries with different currencies can allow firms to finesse currency risk (and related costs) as economic conditions dictate.

OM in Action   U.S. Cartoon Production at Home in Manila

Fred Flintstone is not from Bedrock. He is actually from Manila, capital of the Philippines. So are Tom and Jerry, Aladdin, and Donald Duck. More than 90% of American television cartoons are produced in Asia and India, with the Philippines leading the way. With their natural advantage of English as an official language and a strong familiarity with U.S. culture, animation companies in Manila now employ more than 1,700 people. Filipinos understand Western culture, and "you need to have a group of artists that can understand the humor that goes with it," says Bill Dennis, a Hanna-Barbera executive.

Major studios like Disney, Marvel, Warner Brothers, and Hanna-Barbera send *storyboards*—cartoon action outlines—and voice tracks to the Philippines.

Artists there draw, paint, and film about 20,000 sketches for a 30-minute episode. The cost of $130,000 to produce an episode in the Philippines compares with $160,000 in Korea and $500,000 in the United States.

Sources: Animation Insider (March 30, 2011); *The New York Times* (February 26, 2004): and *The Wall Street Journal* (August 9, 2005).

artistico/Fotolia

Maquiladoras

Mexican factories located along the U.S.–Mexico border that receive preferential tariff treatment.

World Trade Organization (WTO)

An international organization that promotes world trade by lowering barriers to the free flow of goods across borders.

North American Free Trade Agreement (NAFTA)

A free trade agreement between Canada, Mexico, and the United States.

European Union (EU)

A European trade group that has 28 member states.

The United States and Mexico have created maquiladoras (free trade zones) that allow manufacturers to cut their costs by paying only for the value added by Mexican workers. If a U.S. manufacturer, such as Caterpillar, brings a $1,000 engine to a maquiladora operation for assembly work costing $200, tariff duties will be charged only on the $200 of work performed in Mexico.

Trade agreements also help reduce tariffs and thereby reduce the cost of operating facilities in foreign countries. The World Trade Organization (WTO) has helped reduce tariffs from 40% in 1940 to less than 3% today. Another important trade agreement is the North American Free Trade Agreement (NAFTA). NAFTA seeks to phase out all trade and tariff barriers among Canada, Mexico, and the U.S. Other trade agreements that are accelerating global trade include APEC (the Pacific Rim countries), SEATO (Australia, New Zealand, Japan, Hong Kong, South Korea, New Guinea, and Chile), MERCOSUR (Argentina, Brazil, Paraguay, and Uruguay), and CAFTA (Central America, Dominican Republic, and United States).

Another trading group is the European Union (EU).[1] The European Union has reduced trade barriers among the participating European nations through standardization and a common currency, the euro. However, this major U.S. trading partner, with over 500 million people, is also placing some of the world's most restrictive conditions on products sold in the EU. Everything from recycling standards to automobile bumpers to hormone-free farm products must meet EU standards, complicating international trade.

Improve Operations   Operations learn from better understanding of management innovations in different countries. For instance, the Japanese have improved inventory management, the Germans are aggressively using robots, and the Scandinavians have contributed to improved ergonomics throughout the world.

Another reason to have international operations is to reduce response time to meet customers' changing product and service requirements. Customers who purchase goods and services from U.S. firms are increasingly located in foreign countries. Providing them with quick and adequate service is often improved by locating facilities in their home countries.

Understand Markets   Because international operations require interaction with foreign customers, suppliers, and other competitive businesses, international firms inevitably learn about opportunities for new products and services. Europe led the way with cell phone innovations, and then the Japanese and Indians led with cell phone fads. Knowledge of markets not only helps firms understand where the market is going but also helps firms diversify their customer base, add production flexibility, and smooth the business cycle.

Another reason to go into foreign markets is the opportunity to expand the *life cycle* (i.e., stages a product goes through; see Chapter 5) of an existing product. While some products in the U.S. are in a "mature" stage of their product life cycle, they may represent state-of-the-art products in less-developed countries.

Improve Products   Learning does not take place in isolation. Firms serve themselves and their customers well when they remain open to the free flow of ideas. For example, Toyota and BMW will manage joint research and share development costs on battery research for the next generation of green cars. Their relationship also provides Toyota with BMW's highly regarded diesel engines for its European market, where diesel-powered vehicles make up more than half of the market. The payoff is reduced risk in battery development for both, a state-of-the-art diesel engine for Toyota in Europe, and lower per-unit diesel engine cost for BMW. Similarly, international learning in operations is taking place as South Korea's Samsung and Germany's Robert Bosch join to produce lithium-ion batteries to the benefit of both.

Attract and Retain Global Talent   Global organizations can attract and retain better employees by offering more employment opportunities. They need people in all functional areas and areas of expertise worldwide. Global firms can recruit and retain good employees because they provide both greater growth opportunities and insulation against

A worldwide strategy places added burdens on operations management. Because of economic and lifestyle differences, designers must target products to each market. For instance, clothes washers sold in northern countries must spin-dry clothes much better than those in warmer climates, where consumers are likely to line-dry them. Similarly, as shown here, Whirlpool refrigerators sold in Bangkok are manufactured in bright colors because they are often put in living rooms.

Kraipit Phanvut/Sipa Press

unemployment during times of economic downturn. During economic downturns in one country or continent, a global firm has the means to relocate unneeded personnel to more prosperous locations.

So, to recap, successfully achieving a competitive advantage in our shrinking world means maximizing all the possible opportunities, from tangible to intangible, that international operations can offer.

Cultural and Ethical Issues

While there are great forces driving firms toward globalization, many challenges remain. One of these challenges is reconciling differences in social and cultural behavior. With issues ranging from bribery, to child labor, to the environment, managers sometimes do not know how to respond when operating in a different culture. What one country's culture deems acceptable may be considered unacceptable or illegal in another. It is not by chance that there are fewer female managers in the Middle East than in India.

In the last decade, changes in international laws, agreements, and codes of conduct have been applied to define ethical behavior among managers around the world. The WTO, for example, helps to make uniform the protection of both governments and industries from foreign firms that engage in unethical conduct. Even on issues where significant differences between cultures exist, as in the area of bribery or the protection of intellectual property, global uniformity is slowly being accepted by most nations.

Despite cultural and ethical differences, we live in a period of extraordinary mobility of capital, information, goods, and even people. We can expect this to continue. The financial sector, the telecommunications sector, and the logistics infrastructure of the world are healthy institutions that foster efficient and effective use of capital, information, and goods. Globalization, with all its opportunities and risks, is here. It must be embraced as managers develop their missions and strategies.

Developing Missions and Strategies

An effective operations management effort must have a *mission* so it knows where it is going and a *strategy* so it knows how to get there. This is the case for a small domestic organization as well as a large international organization.

♦ STUDENT TIP

Getting an education and managing an organization both require a mission and strategy.

Mission
The purpose or rationale for an organization's existence.

LO 2.1 *Define* mission and strategy

Strategy
How an organization expects to achieve its missions and goals.

LO 2.2 *Identify* and explain three strategic approaches to competitive advantage

VIDEO 2.1
Operations Strategy at Regal Marine

Competitive advantage
The creation of a unique advantage over competitors.

Mission

Economic success, indeed survival, is the result of identifying missions to satisfy a customer's needs and wants. We define the organization's **mission** as its purpose—what it will contribute to society. Mission statements provide boundaries and focus for organizations and the concept around which the firm can rally. The mission states the rationale for the organization's existence. Developing a good strategy is difficult, but it is much easier if the mission has been well defined. Figure 2.2 provides examples of mission statements.

Once an organization's mission has been decided, each functional area within the firm determines its supporting mission. By *functional area* we mean the major disciplines required by the firm, such as marketing, finance/accounting, and production/operations. Missions for each function are developed to support the firm's overall mission. Then within that function lower-level supporting missions are established for the OM functions. Figure 2.3 provides such a hierarchy of sample missions.

Strategy

With the mission established, strategy and its implementation can begin. **Strategy** is an organization's action plan to achieve the mission. Each functional area has a strategy for achieving its mission and for helping the organization reach the overall mission. These strategies exploit opportunities and strengths, neutralize threats, and avoid weaknesses. In the following sections, we will describe how strategies are developed and implemented.

Firms achieve missions in three conceptual ways: (1) differentiation, (2) cost leadership, and (3) response. This means operations managers are called on to deliver goods and services that are (1) *better*, or at least different, (2) *cheaper*, and (3) more *responsive*. Operations managers translate these *strategic concepts* into tangible tasks to be accomplished. Any one or combination of these three strategic concepts can generate a system that has a unique advantage over competitors.

Achieving Competitive Advantage Through Operations

Each of the three strategies provides an opportunity for operations managers to achieve competitive advantage. **Competitive advantage** implies the creation of a system that has a unique advantage over competitors. The idea is to create customer value in an efficient and sustainable way. Pure forms of these strategies may exist, but operations managers will more likely

Figure **2.2**

Mission Statements for Three Organizations

Source: Mission statement from Merck. Copyright © by Merck & Co., Inc. Reprinted with permission.

Merck
The mission of Merck is to provide society with superior products and services—innovations and solutions that improve the quality of life and satisfy customer needs—to provide employees with meaningful work and advancement opportunities and investors with a superior rate of return.
PepsiCo
Our mission is to be the world's premier consumer products company focused on convenient foods and beverages. We seek to produce financial rewards to investors as we provide opportunities for growth and enrichment to our employees, our business partners and the communities in which we operate. And in everything we do, we strive for honesty, fairness and integrity.
Arnold Palmer Hospital
Arnold Palmer Hospital for Children provides state of the art, family-centered healthcare focused on restoring the joy of childhood in an environment of compassion, healing, and hope.

Sample Company Mission
To manufacture and service an innovative, growing, and profitable worldwide microwave communications business that exceeds our customers' expectations.

Sample Operations Management Mission
To produce products consistent with the company's mission as the worldwide low-cost manufacturer.

Sample OM Department Missions	
Product design	To design and produce products and services with outstanding quality and inherent customer value.
Quality management	To attain the exceptional value that is consistent with our company mission and marketing objectives by close attention to design, supply chain, production, and field service opportunities.
Process design	To determine, design, and develop the production process and equipment that will be compatible with low-cost product, high quality, and a good quality of work life.
Location	To locate, design, and build efficient and economical facilities that will yield high value to the company, its employees, and the community.
Layout design	To achieve, through skill, imagination, and resourcefulness in layout and work methods, production effectiveness and efficiency while supporting a high quality of work life.
Human resources	To provide a good quality of work life, with well-designed, safe, rewarding jobs, stable employment, and equitable pay, in exchange for outstanding individual contribution from employees at all levels.
Supply-chain management	To collaborate with suppliers to develop innovative products from stable, effective, and efficient sources of supply.
Inventory	To achieve low investment in inventory consistent with high customer service levels and high facility utilization.
Scheduling	To achieve high levels of throughput and timely customer delivery through effective scheduling.
Maintenance	To achieve high utilization of facilities and equipment by effective preventive maintenance and prompt repair of facilities and equipment.

Figure **2.3**

Sample Missions for a Company, the Operations Function, and Major OM Departments

be called on to implement some combination of them. Let us briefly look at how managers achieve competitive advantage via *differentiation*, *low cost*, and *response*.

Competing on Differentiation

Safeskin Corporation is number one in latex exam gloves because it has differentiated itself and its products. It did so by producing gloves that were designed to prevent allergic reactions about which doctors were complaining. When other glove makers caught up, Safeskin developed hypoallergenic gloves. Then it added texture to its gloves. Then it developed a synthetic disposable glove for those allergic to latex—always staying ahead of the competition. Safeskin's strategy is to develop a reputation for designing and producing reliable state-of-the-art gloves, thereby differentiating itself.

Differentiation is concerned with providing *uniqueness*. A firm's opportunities for creating uniqueness are not located within a particular function or activity but can arise in virtually everything the firm does. Moreover, because most products include some service, and most services

⚠ STUDENT TIP

For many organizations, the operations function provides *the* competitive advantage.

Differentiation

Distinguishing the offerings of an organization in a way that the customer perceives as adding value.

include some product, the opportunities for creating this uniqueness are limited only by imagination. Indeed, differentiation should be thought of as going beyond both physical characteristics and service attributes to encompass everything about the product or service that influences the value that the customers derive from it. Therefore, effective operations managers assist in defining everything about a product or service that will influence the potential value to the customer. This may be the convenience of a broad product line, product features, or a service related to the product. Such services can manifest themselves through convenience (location of distribution centers, stores, or branches), training, product delivery and installation, or repair and maintenance services.

In the service sector, one option for extending product differentiation is through an *experience*. Differentiation by experience in services is a manifestation of the growing "experience economy." The idea of experience differentiation is to engage the customer—to use people's five senses so they become immersed, or even an active participant, in the product. Disney does this with the Magic Kingdom. People no longer just go on a ride; they are immersed in the Magic Kingdom—surrounded by dynamic visual and sound experiences that complement the physical ride. Some rides further engage the customer with changing air flow and smells, as well as having them steer the ride or shoot at targets or villains. Even movie theaters are moving in this direction with surround sound, moving seats, changing "smells," and mists of "rain," as well as multimedia inputs to story development.

Experience differentiation

Engaging a customer with a product through imaginative use of the five senses, so the customer "experiences" the product.

Theme restaurants, such as Hard Rock Cafe, likewise differentiate themselves by providing an "experience." Hard Rock engages the customer with classic rock music, big-screen rock videos, memorabilia, and staff who can tell stories. In many instances, a full-time guide is available to explain the displays, and there is always a convenient retail store so the guest can take home a tangible part of the experience. The result is a "dining experience" rather than just a meal. In a less dramatic way, both Starbucks and your local supermarket deliver an experience when they provide music and the aroma of fresh coffee or freshly baked bread.

VIDEO 2.2
Hard Rock's Global Strategy

Competing on Cost

Southwest Airlines has been a consistent moneymaker while other U.S. airlines have lost billions. Southwest has done this by fulfilling a need for low-cost and short-hop flights. Its operations strategy has included use of secondary airports and terminals, first-come, first-served seating, few fare options, smaller crews flying more hours, snacks-only or no-meal flights, and no downtown ticket offices.

In addition, and less obviously, Southwest has very effectively matched capacity to demand and effectively utilized this capacity. It has done this by designing a route structure that matches the capacity of its Boeing 737, the only plane in its fleet. Second, it achieves more air miles than other airlines through faster turnarounds—its planes are on the ground less.

One driver of a low-cost strategy is a facility that is effectively utilized. Southwest and others with low-cost strategies understand this and use financial resources effectively. Identifying the optimum size (and investment) allows firms to spread overhead costs, providing a cost advantage. For instance, Walmart continues to pursue its low-cost strategy with superstores, open 24 hours a day. For 20 years, it has successfully grabbed market share. Walmart has driven down store overhead costs, shrinkage, and distribution costs. Its rapid transportation of goods, reduced warehousing costs, and direct shipment from manufacturers have resulted in high inventory turnover and made it a low-cost leader.

Likewise, Franz Colruyt, a Belgian discount food retailer, is also an aggressive cost cutter. Colruyt cuts overhead by using converted factory warehouses, movie theaters, and garages as outlets. Customers find no background music, shopping bags, or bright lights: all have been eliminated to cut costs. Walmart and Colruyt are winning with a low-cost strategy.

Low-cost leadership

Achieving maximum value, as perceived by the customer.

Low-cost leadership entails achieving maximum *value* as defined by your customer. It requires examining each of the 10 OM decisions in a relentless effort to drive down costs while meeting customer expectations of value. A low-cost strategy does *not* imply low value or low quality.

Competing on Response

The third strategy option is response. Response is often thought of as *flexible* response, but it also refers to *reliable* and *quick* response. Indeed, we define response as including the entire range of values related to timely product development and delivery, as well as reliable scheduling and flexible performance.

Flexible response may be thought of as the ability to match changes in a marketplace where design innovations and volumes fluctuate substantially.

Hewlett-Packard is an exceptional example of a firm that has demonstrated flexibility in both design and volume changes in the volatile world of personal computers. HP's products often have a life cycle of months, and volume and cost changes during that brief life cycle are dramatic. However, HP has been successful at institutionalizing the ability to change products and volume to respond to dramatic changes in product design and costs—thus building a *sustainable competitive advantage*.

The second aspect of response is the *reliability* of scheduling. One way the German machine industry has maintained its competitiveness despite having the world's highest labor costs is through reliable response. This response manifests itself in reliable scheduling. German machine firms have meaningful schedules—and they perform to these schedules. Moreover, the results of these schedules are communicated to the customer, and the customer can, in turn, rely on them. Consequently, the competitive advantage generated through reliable response has value to the end customer.

The third aspect of response is *quickness*. Johnson Electric Holdings, Ltd., with headquarters in Hong Kong, makes 83 million tiny motors each month. The motors go in cordless tools, household appliances, and personal care items such as hair dryers; dozens are found in each automobile. Johnson's major competitive advantage is speed: speed in product development, speed in production, and speed in delivery.

Whether it is a production system at Johnson Electric or a pizza delivered in 5 minutes by Pizza Hut, the operations manager who develops systems that respond quickly can have a competitive advantage.

In practice, differentiation, low cost, and response can increase productivity and generate a sustainable competitive advantage. Proper implementation of the ten decisions by operations managers (see Figure 2.4) will allow these advantages to be achieved.

Response
A set of values related to rapid, flexible, and reliable performance.

Figure **2.4**

Achieving Competitive Advantage Through Operations

Response strategy wins orders at Super Fast Pizza. Using a wireless connection, orders are transmitted to $20,000 kitchens in vans. The driver, who works solo, receives a printed order, goes to the kitchen area, pulls premade pizzas from the cooler, and places them in the oven—it takes about 1 minute. The driver then delivers the pizza—sometimes even arriving before the pizza is ready.

Darren Hauck/AP Images

Issues in Operations Strategy

Whether the OM strategy is differentiation, cost, or response (as shown in Figure 2.4), OM is a critical player. Therefore, prior to establishing and attempting to implement a strategy, some alternate perspectives may be helpful. One perspective is to take a **resources view**. This means thinking in terms of the financial, physical, human, and technological resources available and ensuring that the potential strategy is compatible with those resources. Another perspective is Porter's value-chain analysis.[2] **Value-chain analysis** is used to identify activities that represent strengths, or potential strengths, and may be opportunities for developing competitive advantage. These are areas where the firm adds its unique *value* through product research, design, human resources, supply-chain management, process innovation, or quality management. Porter also suggests analysis of competitors via what he calls his **five forces model**.[3] These potential competing forces are immediate rivals, potential entrants, customers, suppliers, and substitute products.

In addition to the competitive environment, the operations manager needs to understand that the firm is operating in a system with many other external factors. These factors range from economic, to legal, to cultural. They influence strategy development and execution and require constant scanning of the environment.

The firm itself is also undergoing constant change. Everything from resources, to technology, to product life cycles is in flux. Consider the significant changes required within the firm as its products move from introduction, to growth, to maturity, and to decline (see Figure 2.5). These internal changes, combined with external changes, require strategies that are dynamic.

In this chapter's *Global Company Profile*, Boeing provides an example of how strategy must change as technology and the environment change. Boeing can now build planes from carbon fiber, using a global supply chain. Like many other OM strategies, Boeing's strategy has changed with technology and globalization. Microsoft has also had to adapt quickly to a changing environment. Faster processors, new computer languages, changing customer preferences, increased security issues, the Internet, the cloud, and Google have all driven changes at Microsoft. These forces have moved Microsoft's product strategy from operating systems to office products, to Internet service provider, and now to integrator of computers, cell phones, games, and television via the cloud.

The more thorough the analysis and understanding of both the external and internal factors, the more likely that a firm can find the optimum use of its resources. Once a firm understands itself and the environment, a SWOT analysis, which we discuss next, is in order.

Resources view

A method managers use to evaluate the resources at their disposal and manage or alter them to achieve competitive advantage.

Value-chain analysis

A way to identify those elements in the product/service chain that uniquely add value.

Five forces model

A method of analyzing the five forces in the competitive environment.

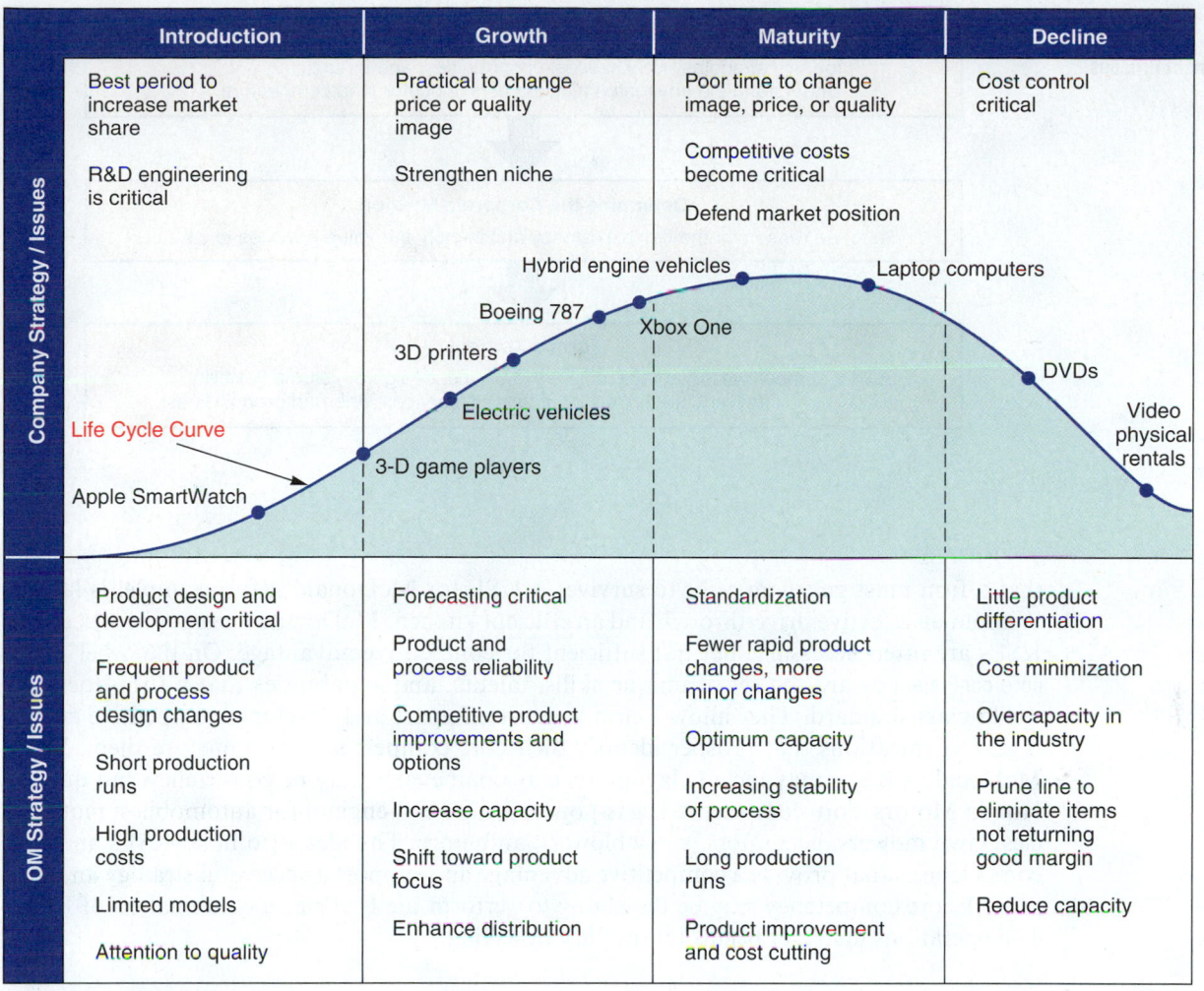

	Introduction	Growth	Maturity	Decline
Company Strategy / Issues	Best period to increase market share R&D engineering is critical	Practical to change price or quality image Strengthen niche	Poor time to change image, price, or quality Competitive costs become critical Defend market position	Cost control critical
OM Strategy / Issues	Product design and development critical Frequent product and process design changes Short production runs High production costs Limited models Attention to quality	Forecasting critical Product and process reliability Competitive product improvements and options Increase capacity Shift toward product focus Enhance distribution	Standardization Fewer rapid product changes, more minor changes Optimum capacity Increasing stability of process Long production runs Product improvement and cost cutting	Little product differentiation Cost minimization Overcapacity in the industry Prune line to eliminate items not returning good margin Reduce capacity

Curve labels: Apple SmartWatch · 3-D game players · Electric vehicles · 3D printers · Boeing 787 · Hybrid engine vehicles · Xbox One · Laptop computers · DVDs · Video physical rentals · Life Cycle Curve

Figure **2.5**

Strategy and Issues During a Product's Life

Strategy Development and Implementation

A SWOT analysis is a formal review of internal strengths and weaknesses and external opportunities and threats. Beginning with SWOT analyses, organizations position themselves, through their strategy, to have a competitive advantage. A firm may have excellent design skills or great talent at identifying outstanding locations. However, it may recognize limitations of its manufacturing process or in finding good suppliers. The idea is to maximize opportunities and minimize threats in the environment while maximizing the advantages of the organization's strengths and minimizing the weaknesses. Any preconceived ideas about mission are then reevaluated to ensure they are consistent with the SWOT analysis. Subsequently, a strategy for achieving the mission is developed. This strategy is continually evaluated against the value provided customers and competitive realities. The process is shown in Figure 2.6. From this process, key success factors are identified.

Key Success Factors and Core Competencies

Because no firm does everything exceptionally well, a successful strategy requires determining the firm's key success factors and core competencies. Key success factors (KSFs) are those activities that are necessary for a firm to achieve its goals. Key success factors can be so significant

Figure **2.6**

Strategy Development Process

Analyze the Environment
Identify strengths, weaknesses, opportunities, and threats.
Understand the environment, customers, industry, and competitors.

⬇

Determine the Corporate Mission
State the reason for the firm's existence and identify the value it wishes to create.

⬇

Form a Strategy
Build a competitive advantage, such as low price, design or volume flexibility, quality, quick delivery, dependability, after-sale services, or broad product lines.

Core competencies

A set of skills, talents, and capabilities in which a firm is particularly strong.

that a firm must get them right to survive. A KSF for McDonald's, for example, is layout. Without an effective drive-through and an efficient kitchen, McDonald's cannot be successful. KSFs are often necessary, but not sufficient for competitive advantage. On the other hand, core competencies are the set of unique skills, talents, and capabilities that a firm does at a world-class standard. They allow a firm to set itself apart and develop a competitive advantage. Organizations that prosper identify their core competencies and nurture them. While McDonald's KSFs may include layout, its core competency may be consistency and quality. Honda Motors' core competence is gas-powered engines—engines for automobiles, motorcycles, lawn mowers, generators, snow blowers, and more. The idea is to build KSFs and core competencies that provide a competitive advantage and support a successful strategy and mission. A core competency may be the ability to perform the KSFs or a combination of KSFs. The operations manager begins this inquiry by asking:

LO 2.3 *Understand* the significance of key success factors and core competencies

- "What tasks must be done particularly well for a given strategy to succeed?"
- "Which activities provide a competitive advantage?"
- "Which elements contain the highest likelihood of failure, and which require additional commitment of managerial, monetary, technological, and human resources?"

Only by identifying and strengthening key success factors and core competencies can an organization achieve sustainable competitive advantage. In this text we focus on the 10 strategic OM decisions that typically include the KSFs. These decisions, plus major decision areas for marketing and finance, are shown in Figure 2.7.

Honda's core competence is the design and manufacture of gas-powered engines. This competence has allowed Honda to become a leader in the design and manufacture of a wide range of gas-powered products. Tens of millions of these products are produced and shipped around the world.

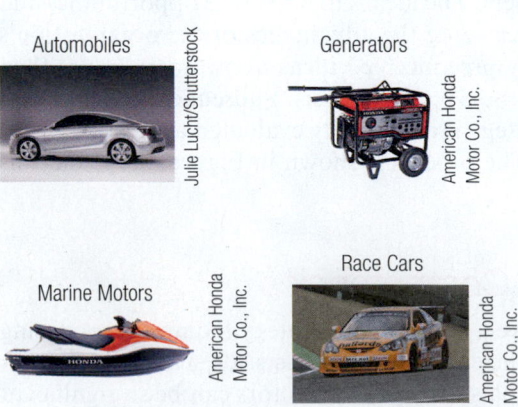

Automobiles — Julie Lucht/Shutterstock

Generators — American Honda Motor Co., Inc.

Marine Motors — American Honda Motor Co., Inc.

Race Cars — American Honda Motor Co., Inc.

Motorcycles — Courtesy of www.HondaNews.com

Water Pumps — American Honda Motor Co., Inc.

4-Wheel Scooters — American Honda Motor Co., Inc.

Snow Blowers — American Honda Motor Co., Inc.

Support a Core Competency and Implement Strategy by Identifying and Executing the Key Success Factors in the Functional Areas

Marketing	**Finance/Accounting**	**Operations**
Service Distribution Promotion Price Channels of distribution Product positioning (image, functions)	Leverage Cost of capital Working capital Receivables Payables Financial control Lines of credit	

10 OM Decisions	Sample Options	Chapter
Product	Customized or standardized; sustainability	5,S5
Quality	Define customer quality expectations and how to achieve them	6,S6
Process	Facility design, capacity, how much automation	7,S7
Location	Near supplier or near customer	8
Layout	Work cells or assembly line	9
Human resources	Specialized or enriched jobs	10
Supply chain	Single or multiple suppliers	11, S11
Inventory	When to reorder; how much to keep on hand	12,14,16
Schedule	Stable or fluctuating production rate	13,15
Maintenance	Repair as required or preventive maintenance	17

STUDENT TIP

These 10 decisions are used to implement a specific strategy and yield a competitive advantage.

Integrating OM with Other Activities

Whatever the KSFs and core competencies, they must be supported by the related activities. One approach to identifying the activities is an **activity map**, which links competitive advantage, KSFs, and supporting activities. For example, Figure 2.8 shows how Southwest Airlines, whose core competency is operations, built a set of integrated activities to support its low-cost competitive advantage. Notice how the KSFs support operations and in turn are supported by other activities. The activities fit together and reinforce each other. In this way, all of the areas support the company's objectives. For example, short-term scheduling in the airline industry is dominated by volatile customer travel patterns. Day-of-week preference, holidays, seasonality, college schedules, and so on all play roles in changing flight schedules. Consequently, airline scheduling, although an OM activity, is tied to marketing. Effective scheduling in the trucking industry is reflected in the amount of time trucks travel loaded. But maximizing the time trucks travel loaded requires the integration of information from deliveries completed, pickups pending, driver availability, truck maintenance, and customer priority. Success requires integration of all of these activities.

    The better the activities are integrated and reinforce each other, the more sustainable the competitive advantage. By focusing on enhancing its core competence and KSFs with a supporting set of activities, firms such as Southwest Airlines have built successful strategies.

Activity map

A graphical link of competitive advantage, KSFs, and supporting activities.

Building and Staffing the Organization

Once a strategy, KSFs, and the necessary integration have been identified, the second step is to group the necessary activities into an organizational structure. Then, managers must staff the organization with personnel who will get the job done. The manager works with subordinate managers to build plans, budgets, and programs that will successfully implement strategies that achieve missions. Firms tackle this organization of the operations function in a variety of

Figure **2.8**

Activity Mapping of Southwest Airlines' Low-Cost Competitive Advantage

To achieve a low-cost competitive advantage, Southwest has identified a number of key success factors (connected by red arrows) and support activities (shown by blue arrows). As this figure indicates, Southwest's low-cost strategy is highly dependent on a very well-run operations function.

ways. The organization charts shown in Chapter 1 (Figure 1.1) indicate the way some firms have organized to perform the required activities. *The operations manager's job is to implement an OM strategy, provide competitive advantage, and increase productivity.*

Implementing the 10 Strategic OM Decisions

As mentioned earlier, the implementation of the 10 strategic OM decisions is influenced by a variety of issues—from missions and strategy to key success factors and core competencies—while addressing such issues as product mix, product life cycle, and competitive environment. Because each product brings its own mix of attributes, the importance and method of implementation of the 10 strategic OM decisions will vary. Throughout this text, we discuss how these decisions are implemented in ways that provide competitive advantage. How this might be done for two drug companies, one seeking competitive advantage via differentiation and the other via low cost, is shown in Table 2.1.

Strategic Planning, Core Competencies, and Outsourcing

As organizations develop missions, goals, and strategies, they identify their strengths—what they do as well as or better than their competitors—as their *core competencies*. By contrast, *non-core activities*, which can be a sizable portion of an organization's total business, are good candidates for outsourcing. Outsourcing is transferring activities that have traditionally been internal to external suppliers.

Outsourcing is not a new concept, but it does add complexity and risk to the supply chain. Because of its potential, outsourcing continues to expand. The expansion is accelerating due to

Outsourcing

Transferring a firm's activities that have traditionally been internal to external suppliers.

TABLE 2.1	Operations Strategies of Two Drug Companies*	
COMPETITIVE ADVANTAGE	**BRAND NAME DRUGS, INC.** PRODUCT DIFFERENTIATION STRATEGY	**GENERIC DRUG CORP.** LOW-COST STRATEGY
Product selection and design	Heavy R&D investment; extensive labs; focus on development in a broad range of drug categories	Low R&D investment; focus on development of generic drugs
Quality	Quality is major priority, standards exceed regulatory requirements	Meets regulatory requirements on a country-by-country basis, as necessary
Process	Product and modular production process; tries to have long product runs in specialized facilities; builds capacity ahead of demand	Process focused; general production processes; "job shop" approach, short-run production; focus on high utilization
Location	Still located in city where it was founded	Recently moved to low-tax, low-labor-cost environment
Layout	Layout supports automated product-focused production	Layout supports process-focused "job shop" practices
Human resources	Hire the best; nationwide searches	Very experienced top executives hired to provide direction; other personnel paid below industry average
Supply chain	Long-term supplier relationships	Tends to purchase competitively to find bargains
Inventory	Maintains high finished goods inventory primarily to ensure all demands are met	Process focus drives up work-in-process inventory; finished goods inventory tends to be low
Scheduling	Centralized production planning	Many short-run products complicate scheduling
Maintenance	Highly trained staff; extensive parts inventory	Highly trained staff to meet changing demands

*Notice how the 10 decisions are altered to build two distinct strategies in the same industry.

three global trends: (1) increased technological expertise, (2) more reliable and cheaper transportation, and (3) the rapid development and deployment of advancements in telecommunications and computers. This rich combination of economic advances is contributing to both lower cost and more specialization. As a result more firms are candidates for outsourcing of non-core activities.

Outsourcing implies an agreement (typically a legally binding contract) with an external organization. The classic make-or-buy decision, concerning which products to make and which to buy, is the basis of outsourcing. When firms such as Apple find that their core competency is in creativity, innovation, and product design, they may want to outsource manufacturing.

VIDEO 2.3
Outsourcing Offshore at Darden

Contract manufacturers such as Flextronics provide outsourcing service to IBM, Cisco Systems, HP, Microsoft, Sony, Nortel, Ericsson, and Sun, among many others. Flextronics is a high-quality producer that has won over 450 awards, including the Malcolm Baldrige Award. One of the side benefits of outsourcing is that client firms such as IBM can actually improve their performance by using the competencies of an outstanding firm like Flextronics. But there are risks involved in outsourcing.

Keith Dannemiller/Alamy

Outsourcing manufacturing is an extension of the long-standing practice of *subcontracting* production activities, which when done on a continuing basis is known as *contract manufacturing*. Contract manufacturing is becoming standard practice in many industries, from computers to automobiles. For instance, Johnson & Johnson, like many other big drug companies whose core competency is research and development, often farms out manufacturing to contractors. On the other hand, Sony's core competency is electromechanical design of chips. This is its core competency, but Sony is also one of the best in the world when it comes to rapid response and specialized production of these chips. Therefore, Sony finds that it wants to be its own *manufacturer*, while specialized providers come up with major innovations in such areas as software, human resources, and distribution. These areas are the providers' business, not Sony's, and the provider may very well be better at it than Sony.

Other examples of outsourcing non-core activities include:

- DuPont's legal services routed to the Philippines
- IBM's handing of travel services and payroll and Hewlett-Packard's provision of IT services to P&G
- Production of the Audi A4 convertible and Mercedes CLK convertible by Wilheim Karmann in Osnabruck, Germany
- Blue Cross sending hip resurfacing surgery patients to India

Managers evaluate their strategies and core competencies and ask themselves how to use the assets entrusted to them. Do they want to be the company that does low-margin work at 3%–4% or the innovative firm that makes a 30%–40% margin? PC and iPad contract manufacturers in China and Taiwan earn 3%–4%, but Apple, which innovates, designs, and sells, has a margin 10 times as large.

The Theory of Comparative Advantage

Theory of comparative advantage

A theory which states that countries benefit from specializing in (and exporting) goods and services in which they have relative advantage, and they benefit from importing goods and services in which they have a relative disadvantage.

The motivation for international outsourcing comes from the **theory of comparative advantage**. This theory focuses on the economic concept of relative advantage. According to the theory, if an external provider, regardless of its geographic location, can perform activities more productively than the purchasing firm, then the external provider should do the work. This allows the purchasing firm to focus on what it does best—its core competencies. Consistent with the theory of comparative advantage, outsourcing continues to grow. But outsourcing the wrong activities can be a disaster. And even outsourcing non-core activities has risks.

STUDENT TIP ◆

The substantial risk of outsourcing requires managers to invest in the effort to make sure they do it right.

Risks of Outsourcing

Risk management starts with a realistic analysis of uncertainty and results in a strategy that minimizes the impact of these uncertainties. Indeed, outsourcing *is* risky, with roughly half of all outsourcing agreements failing because of inadequate planning and analysis. Timely delivery and quality standards can be major problems, as can underestimating increases in inventory and logistics costs. Some potential advantages and disadvantages of outsourcing are shown in Table 2.2. A survey of North American companies found that, as a group, those that outsourced customer service saw a drop in their score on the American Consumer Satisfaction Index. The declines were roughly the same whether companies outsourced domestically or overseas.[4]

However, when outsourcing is overseas, additional issues must be considered. These issues include financial attractiveness, people skills and availability, and the general business environment. Another risk of outsourcing overseas is the political backlash that results from moving jobs to foreign countries. The perceived loss of jobs has fueled anti-outsourcing rhetoric. This rhetoric is contributing to a process known as *reshoring*, the return of business activity to the originating country. (See the *OM in Action* box "Reshoring to Small-Town U.S.A.")

TABLE 2.2	Potential Advantages and Disadvantages of Outsourcing	
ADVANTAGES	**DISADVANTAGES**
Cost savings	Increased logistics and inventory costs
Gaining outside expertise that comes with specialization	Loss of control (quality, delivery, etc.)
Improving operations and service	Potential creation of future competition
Maintaining a focus on core competencies	Negative impact on employees
Accessing outside technology	Risks may not manifest themselves for years

In addition to the external risks, operations managers must deal with other issues that outsourcing brings. These include: (1) reduced employment levels, (2) changes in facility requirements, (3) potential adjustments to quality control systems and manufacturing processes, and (4) expanded logistics issues, including insurance, tariffs, customs, and timing.

To summarize, managers can find substantial efficiencies in outsourcing non-core activities, but they must be cautious in outsourcing those elements of the product or service that provide a competitive advantage. The next section provides a methodology that helps analyze the outsourcing decision process.

Rating Outsource Providers

Research indicates that the most common reason for the failure of outsourcing agreements is that the decisions are made without sufficient analysis. The *factor-rating method* provides an objective way to evaluate outsource providers. We assign points for each factor to each provider and then importance weights to each of the factors. We now apply the technique in Example 1 to compare outsourcing providers being considered by a firm.

LO 2.4 *Use* factor rating to evaluate both country and outsource providers

---

OM in Action   Reshoring to Small-Town U.S.A.

U.S. companies continue their global search for efficiency by outsourcing call centers and back-office operations, but many find they need to look no farther than a place like Dubuque, Iowa.

To U.S. firms facing quality problems with their outsourcing operations overseas and bad publicity at home, small-town America is emerging as a pleasant alternative. Dubuque (population 57,313), Nacogdoches, Texas (population 29,914), or Twin Falls, Idaho (population 34,469), may be the perfect call center location. Even though the pay is low, the jobs are some of the best available to small-town residents.

By moving out of big cities to the cheaper labor and real estate of small towns, companies can save millions and still increase productivity. A call center in a town that just lost its major manufacturing plant finds the jobs easy to fill.

IBM, which has been criticized in the past for moving jobs to India and other offshore locations, picked Dubuque for its new remote computer-services center with 1,300 jobs.

Taking advantage of even cheaper wages in other countries will not stop soon, though. Is India the unstoppable overseas call center capital

that people think it is? Not at all. Despite its population of 1.3 billion, only a small percentage of its workers have the language skills and technical education to work in Western-style industries. Already, India has been warned that if call centers can't recruit at reasonable wages, its jobs will move to the Philippines, South Africa, and Ghana. And indeed, Dell, Apple, and Britain's Powergen are reshoring from Indian call centers, claiming their costs had become too high.

Keith Dannemiller/Alamy

Sources: Industry Week (August 5, 2014) and *The Wall Street Journal*, (November 27, 2013).

Example 1

RATING PROVIDER SELECTION CRITERIA

National Architects, Inc., a San Francisco–based designer of high-rise office buildings, has decided to outsource its information technology (IT) function. Three outsourcing providers are being actively considered: one in the U.S., one in India, and one in Israel.

APPROACH ▶   National's VP–Operations, Susan Cholette, has made a list of seven criteria she considers critical. After putting together a committee of four other VPs, she has rated each firm (boldface type, on a 1–5 scale, with 5 being highest) and has also placed an importance weight on each of the factors, as shown in Table 2.3.

TABLE 2.3	Factor Ratings Applied to National Architects' Potential IT Outsourcing Providers		
		OUTSOURCE PROVIDERS		
FACTOR (CRITERION)*	**IMPORTANCE WEIGHT**	**BIM (U.S.)**	**S.P.C. (INDIA)**	**TELCO (ISRAEL)**
1. Can reduce operating costs	.2	.2 × **3** = .6	.2 × **3** = .6	.2 × **5** = 1.0
2. Can reduce capital investment	.2	.2 × **4** = .8	.2 × **3** = .6	.2 × **3** = .6
3. Skilled personnel	.2	.2 × **5** = 1.0	.2 × **4** = .8	.2 × **3** = .6
4. Can improve quality	.1	.1 × **4** = .4	.1 × **5** = .5	.1 × **2** = .2
5. Can gain access to technology not in company	.1	.1 × **5** = .5	.1 × **3** = .3	.1 × **5** = .5
6. Can create additional capacity	.1	.1 × **4** = .4	.1 × **2** = .2	.1 × **4** = .4
7. Aligns with policy/philosophy/culture	.1	.1 × **2** = .2	.1 × **3** = .3	.1 × **5** = .5
Total Weighted Score		3.9	3.3	3.8

*These seven major criteria are based on a survey of 165 procurement executives, as reported in J. Schildhouse, *Inside Supply Management* (December 2005): 22–29.

SOLUTION ▶   Susan multiplies each rating by the weight and sums the products in each column to generate a total score for each outsourcing provider. She selects BIM, which has the highest overall rating.

INSIGHT ▶   When the total scores are as close (3.9 vs. 3.8) as they are in this case, it is important to examine the sensitivity of the results to inputs. For example, if one of the importance weights or factor scores changes even marginally, the final selection may change. Management preference may also play a role here.

LEARNING EXERCISE ▶   Susan decides that "Skilled personnel" should instead get a weight of 0.1 and "Aligns with policy/philosophy/culture" should increase to 0.2. How do the total scores change? [Answer: BIM = 3.6, S.P.C. = 3.2, and Telco = 4.0, so Telco would be selected.]

RELATED PROBLEMS ▶   2.8–2.12

EXCEL OM Data File **Ch02Ex1.xls** can be found in **MyOMLab**.

Most U.S. toy companies now outsource their production to Chinese manufacturers. Cost savings are significant, but there are several downsides, including loss of control over such issues as quality. A few years ago, Mattel had to recall 10.5 million Elmos, Big Birds, and SpongeBobs. These made-in-China toys contained excessive levels of lead in their paint. More recently, quality issues have dealt with poisonous pet food, tainted milk products, and contaminated sheetrock.

A. Ramey/PhotoEdit, Inc.

Global Operations Strategy Options

As we suggested early in this chapter, many operations strategies now require an international dimension. An international business is any firm that engages in international trade or investment. A multinational corporation (MNC) is a firm with *extensive* international business involvement. MNCs buy resources, create goods or services, and sell goods or services in a variety of countries. The term *multinational corporation* applies to most of the world's large, well-known businesses. Certainly IBM is a good example of an MNC. It imports electronics components to the U.S. from over 50 countries, exports to over 130 countries, has facilities in 45 countries, and earns more than half its sales and profits abroad.

Operations managers of international and multinational firms approach global opportunities with one of four strategies: *international, multidomestic, global,* or *transnational* (see Figure 2.9). The matrix of Figure 2.9 has a vertical axis of cost reduction and a horizontal axis of local responsiveness. Local responsiveness implies quick response and/or the differentiation necessary for the local market. The operations manager must know how to position the firm in this matrix. Let us briefly examine each of the four strategies.

An international strategy uses exports and licenses to penetrate the global arena. This strategy is the least advantageous, with little local responsiveness and little cost advantage. But an international strategy is often the easiest, as exports can require little change in existing operations, and licensing agreements often leave much of the risk to the licensee.

The multidomestic strategy has decentralized authority with substantial autonomy at each business. These are typically subsidiaries, franchises, or joint ventures with substantial independence. The advantage of this strategy is maximizing a competitive response for the local market; however, the strategy has little or no cost advantage. Many food producers, such as Heinz, use a multidomestic strategy to accommodate local tastes because global integration of the production process is not critical. The concept is one of "we were successful in the home market; let's export the management talent and processes, not necessarily the product, to accommodate another market."

A global strategy has a high degree of centralization, with headquarters coordinating the organization to seek out standardization and learning between plants, thus generating economies of scale. This strategy is appropriate when the strategic focus is cost reduction but has little to recommend it when the demand for local responsiveness is high. Caterpillar, the world leader in earth-moving equipment, and Texas Instruments, a world leader in semiconductors, pursue global strategies. Caterpillar and Texas Instruments find this strategy advantageous because the end products are similar throughout the world. Earth-moving equipment is the same in Nigeria as in Iowa.

International business
A firm that engages in cross-border transactions.

Multinational corporation (MNC)
A firm that has extensive involvement in international business, owning or controlling facilities in more than one country.

International strategy
A strategy in which global markets are penetrated using exports and licenses.

Multidomestic strategy
A strategy in which operating decisions are decentralized to each country to enhance local responsiveness.

Global strategy
A strategy in which operating decisions are centralized and headquarters coordinates the standardization and learning between facilities.

LO 2.5 *Identify* and explain four global operations strategy options

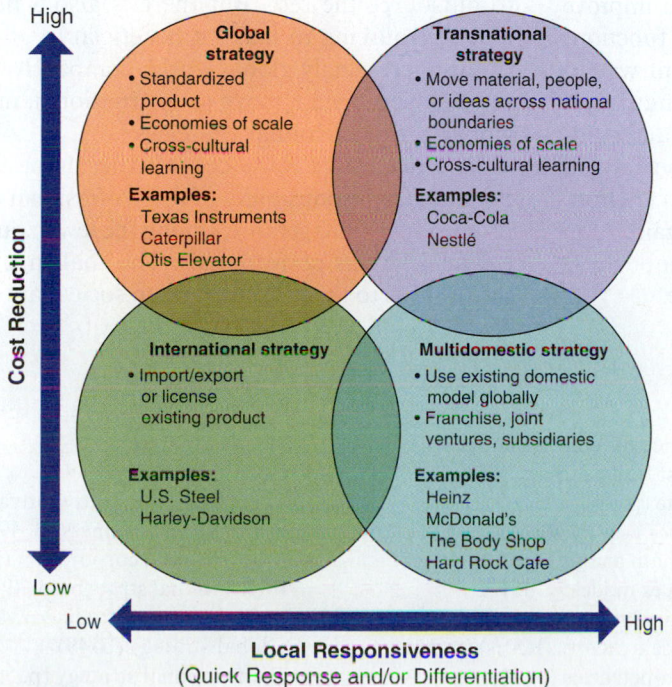

Figure **2.9**

Four International Operations Strategies

Source: See a similar presentation in M. Hitt, R. D. Ireland, and R. E. Hoskisson, *Strategic Management: Concepts, Competitiveness, and Globalization,* 8th ed. (Cincinnati: Southwestern College Publishing).

In a continuing fierce worldwide battle, both Komatsu and Caterpillar seek global advantage in the heavy equipment market. As Komatsu (left) moved west to the UK, Caterpillar (right) moved east, with 13 facilities and joint ventures in China. Both firms are building equipment throughout the world as cost and logistics dictate. Their global strategies allow production to move as markets, risk, and exchange rates suggest.

Transnational strategy

A strategy that combines the benefits of global-scale efficiencies with the benefits of local responsiveness.

A transnational strategy exploits the economies of scale and learning, as well as pressure for responsiveness, by recognizing that core competence does not reside in just the "home" country but can exist anywhere in the organization. *Transnational* describes a condition in which material, people, and ideas cross—or *transgress*—national boundaries. These firms have the potential to pursue all three operations strategies (i.e., differentiation, low cost, and response). Such firms can be thought of as "world companies" whose country identity is not as important as their interdependent network of worldwide operations. Nestlé is a good example of such a company. Although it is legally Swiss, 95% of its assets are held and 98% of its sales are made outside Switzerland. Fewer than 10% of its workers are Swiss.

Summary

Global operations provide an increase in both the challenges and opportunities for operations managers. Although the task is difficult, operations managers can and do improve productivity. They build and manage global OM functions and supply chains that contribute in a significant way to competitiveness. Organizations identify their strengths and weaknesses. They then develop effective missions and strategies that account for these strengths and weaknesses and complement the opportunities and threats in the environment. If this procedure is performed well, the organization can have competitive advantage through some combination of product differentiation, low cost, and response.

Increasing specialization provides economic pressure to build organizations that focus on core competencies and to outsource the rest. But there is also a need for planning outsourcing to make it beneficial to all participants. In this increasingly global world, competitive advantage is often achieved via a move to international, multidomestic, global, or transnational strategies.

Effective use of resources, whether domestic or international, is the responsibility of the professional manager, and professional managers are among the few in our society who *can* achieve this performance. The challenge is great, and the rewards to the manager and to society are substantial.

Key Terms

Maquiladoras (p. 34)
World Trade Organization (WTO) (p. 34)
North American Free Trade Agreement (NAFTA) (p. 34)
European Union (EU) (p. 34)
Mission (p. 36)
Strategy (p. 36)
Competitive advantage (p. 36)
Differentiation (p. 38)

Experience differentiation (p. 38)
Low-cost leadership (p. 38)
Response (p. 39)
Resources view (p. 40)
Value-chain analysis (p. 40)
Five forces model (p. 40)
SWOT analysis (p. 41)
Key success factors (KSFs) (p. 41)
Core competencies (p. 42)

Activity map (p. 43)
Outsourcing (p. 44)
Theory of comparative advantage (p. 46)
International business (p. 49)
Multinational corporation (MNC) (p. 49)
International strategy (p. 49)
Multidomestic strategy (p. 49)
Global strategy (p. 49)
Transnational strategy (p. 50)

Ethical Dilemma

As a manufacturer of athletic shoes whose image—indeed performance—is widely regarded as socially responsible, you find your costs increasing. Traditionally, your athletic shoes have been made in Indonesia and South Korea. Although the ease of doing business in those countries has been improving, wage rates have also been increasing. The labor-cost differential between your current suppliers and a contractor who will get the shoes made in China now exceeds $1 per pair. Your sales next year are projected to be 10 million pairs, and your analysis suggests that this cost differential is not offset by any other tangible costs; you face only the political risk and potential damage to your commitment to social responsibility. Thus, this $1 per pair savings should flow directly to your bottom line. There is no doubt that the Chinese government engages in censorship, remains repressive, and is a long way from a democracy. Moreover, you will have little or no control over working conditions, sexual harassment, and pollution. What do you do, and on what basis do you make your decision?

Michael S. Yamashita/Corbis

Discussion Questions

1. Based on the descriptions and analyses in this chapter, would Boeing be better described as a global firm or a transnational firm? Discuss.
2. List six reasons to internationalize operations.
3. Coca-Cola is called a global product. Does this mean that Coca-Cola is formulated in the same way throughout the world? Discuss.
4. Define *mission*.
5. Define *strategy*.
6. Describe how an organization's *mission* and *strategy* have different purposes.
7. Identify the mission and strategy of your automobile repair garage. What are the manifestations of the 10 strategic OM decisions at the garage? That is, how is each of the 10 decisions accomplished?
8. As a library or Internet assignment, identify the mission of a firm and the strategy that supports that mission.
9. How does an OM strategy change during a product's life cycle?
10. There are three primary ways to achieve competitive advantage. Provide an example, not included in the text, of each. Support your choices.
11. Given the discussion of Southwest Airlines in the text, define an *operations* strategy for that firm now that it has purchased AirTran.
12. How must an operations strategy integrate with marketing and accounting?
13. How would you summarize outsourcing trends?
14. What potential cost-saving advantages might firms experience by using outsourcing?
15. What internal issues must managers address when outsourcing?
16. How should a company select an outsourcing provider?
17. What are some of the possible consequences of poor outsourcing?
18. What global operations strategy is most descriptive of McDonald's?

Using Software to Solve Outsourcing Problems

Excel, Excel OM, and POM for Windows may be used to solve many of the problems in this chapter.

CREATING YOUR OWN EXCEL SPREADSHEETS

Program 2.1 illustrates how to build an Excel spreadsheet for the data in Example 1. In this example the factor rating method is used to compare National Architects' three potential outsourcing providers.

This program provides the data inputs for seven important factors, including their weights (0.0–1.0) and ratings (1–5 scale where 5 is the highest rating) for each country. As we see, BIM is most highly rated, with a 3.9 score, versus 3.3 for S.P.C. and 3.8 for Telco.

✗ USING EXCEL OM

Excel OM (free with your text and also found in MyOMLab) may be used to solve Example 1 (with the Factor Rating module).

ℙ USING POM FOR WINDOWS

POM for Windows also includes a factor rating module. For details, refer to Appendix IV. POM for Windows is also found in MyOMLab and can solve all problems labeled with a ℙ.

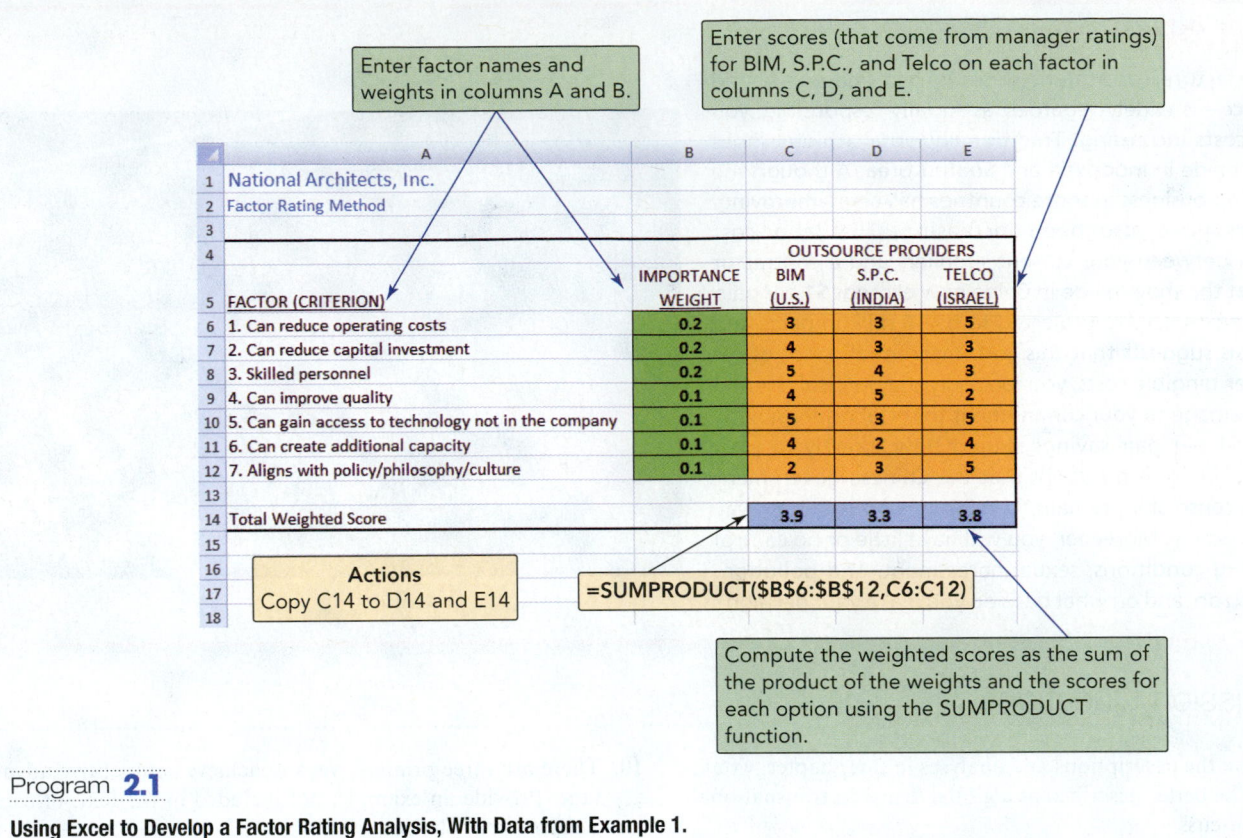

Enter factor names and weights in columns A and B.

Enter scores (that come from manager ratings) for BIM, S.P.C., and Telco on each factor in columns C, D, and E.

	A	B	C	D	E
1	National Architects, Inc.				
2	Factor Rating Method				
3					
4				OUTSOURCE PROVIDERS	
5	FACTOR (CRITERION)	IMPORTANCE WEIGHT	BIM (U.S.)	S.P.C. (INDIA)	TELCO (ISRAEL)
6	1. Can reduce operating costs	0.2	3	3	5
7	2. Can reduce capital investment	0.2	4	3	3
8	3. Skilled personnel	0.2	5	4	3
9	4. Can improve quality	0.1	4	5	2
10	5. Can gain access to technology not in the company	0.1	5	3	5
11	6. Can create additional capacity	0.1	4	2	4
12	7. Aligns with policy/philosophy/culture	0.1	2	3	5
13					
14	Total Weighted Score		3.9	3.3	3.8
15					
16	**Actions**				
17	Copy C14 to D14 and E14				
18					

=SUMPRODUCT($B$6:$B$12,C6:C12)

Compute the weighted scores as the sum of the product of the weights and the scores for each option using the SUMPRODUCT function.

Program **2.1**

Using Excel to Develop a Factor Rating Analysis, With Data from Example 1.

Solved Problems
Virtual Office Hours help is available in MyOMLab.

SOLVED PROBLEM 2.1

The global tire industry continues to consolidate. Michelin buys Goodrich and Uniroyal and builds plants throughout the world. Bridgestone buys Firestone, expands its research budget, and focuses on world markets. Goodyear spends almost 4% of its sales revenue on research. These three aggressive firms have come to dominate the world tire market, with total market share approaching 60%. And the German tire maker Continental AG has strengthened its position as fourth in the world, with a dominant presence in Germany and a research budget of 6%. Against this formidable array, the old-line Italian tire company Pirelli SpA is challenged to respond effectively. Although Pirelli still has almost 5% of the market, it is a relatively small player in a tough, competitive business.

And although the business is reliable even in recessions, as motorists still need replacement tires, the competition is getting stronger. The business rewards companies that have large market shares and long production runs. Pirelli, with its small market share and 1,200 specialty tires, has neither. However, Pirelli has some strengths: an outstanding reputation for tire research and excellent high-performance tires, including supplying specially engineered tires for performance automobiles, Ducati motorcycles, and Formula 1 racing teams. In addition, Pirelli's operations managers complement the creative engineering with world-class innovative manufacturing processes that allow rapid changeover to different models and sizes of tires.

Use a SWOT analysis to establish a feasible strategy for Pirelli.

SOLUTION

First, find an opportunity in the world tire market that avoids the threat of the mass-market onslaught by the big-three tire makers. Second, use the internal marketing strength represented by Pirelli's strong brand name supplying Formula 1 racing and a history of winning World Rally Championships. Third, maximize the innovative capabilities of an outstanding operations function. This is a classic differentiation strategy, supported by activity mapping that ties Pirelli's marketing strength to research and its innovative operations function.

To implement this strategy, Pirelli is differentiating itself with a focus on higher-margin performance tires and away from the low-margin standard tire business. Pirelli has established deals with luxury brands Jaguar, BMW, Maserati, Ferrari, Bentley, and Lotus Elise and established itself as a provider of a large share of the tires on new Porsches and S-class Mercedes. Pirelli also made a strategic decision to divest itself of other businesses. As a result, the vast majority of the company's tire production is now high-performance tires. People are willing to pay a premium for Pirellis.

The operations function continued to focus its design efforts on performance tires and developing a system of modular tire manufacture that allows much faster switching between models. This modular system, combined with billions of dollars in new manufacturing investment, has driven batch sizes down to as small as 150 to 200, making small-lot performance tires economically feasible. Manufacturing innovations at Pirelli have streamlined the production process, moving it from a 14-step process to a 3-step process.

Pirelli still faces a threat from the big three going after the performance market, but the company has bypassed its weakness of having a small market share with a substantial research budget and an innovative operations function. The firm now has 19 plants in 13 countries and a presence in more than 160 countries, with sales approaching $8 billion.

Sources: Based on *The Economist* (January 8, 2011): 65; **www.pirelli.com**; and **RubberNews.com**.

SOLVED PROBLEM 2.2

DeHoratius Electronics, Inc., is evaluating several options for sourcing a critical processor for its new modem. Three sources are being considered: Hi-Tech in Canada, Zia in Hong Kong, and Zaragoza in Spain. The owner, Nicole DeHoratius, has determined that only three criteria are critical. She has rated each firm on a 1–5 scale (with 5 being highest) and has also placed an importance weight on each of the factors, as shown below:

| FACTOR (CRITERION) | IMPORTANCE WEIGHT | OUTSOURCE PROVIDERS | | | | | |
| | | HI-TECH (CANADA) | | ZIA (HONG KONG) | | ZARAGOZA (SPAIN) | |
		Rating	Wtd. Score	Rating	Wtd.score	Rating	Wtd. Score
1. Cost	.5	3	1.5	3	1.5	5	2.5
2. Reliability	.2	4	.8	3	.6	3	.6
3. Competence	.3	5	1.5	4	1.2	3	.9
Totals	1.0		3.8		3.3		4.0

SOLUTION

Nicole multiplies each rating by the weight and sums the products in each column to generate a total score for each outsourcing provider. For example the weighted score for Hi-Tech equals $(.5 \times 3) + (.2 \times 4) + (.3 \times 5) = 1.5 + .8 + 1.5 = 3.8$. She selects Zaragoza, which has the highest overall rating.

Problems

Note: **PX** means the problem may be solved with POM for Windows and/or Excel OM.

Problems 2.1–2.3 relate to A Global View of Operations and Supply Chains

•• **2.1**   Match the product with the proper parent company and country in the table below:

PRODUCT	PARENT COMPANY	COUNTRY
Arrow Shirts	a. Volkswagen	1. France
Braun Household Appliances	b. Bidermann International	2. Great Britain
Volvo Autos	c. Bridgestone	3. Germany
Firestone Tires	d. Campbell Soup	4. Japan
Godiva Chocolate	e. Credit Lyonnais	5. U.S.
Häagen-Dazs Ice Cream (USA)	f. Tata	6. Switzerland
Jaguar Autos	g. Procter & Gamble	7. China
MGM Movies	h. Michelin	8. India
Lamborghini Autos	i. Nestlé	
Goodrich Tires	j. Geely	
Alpo Pet Foods		

•• **2.2**   Based on the corruption perception index developed by Transparency International (**www.transparency.org**), rank the following countries from most corrupt to least: Venezuela, Denmark, the U.S., Switzerland, and China.

•• **2.3**   Based on the competitiveness ranking developed by the Global Competitiveness Index (**www.weforum.org**), rank the following countries from most competitive to least: Mexico, Switzerland, the U.S., and China.

Problems 2.4 and 2.5 relate to Achieving Competitive Advantage Through Operations

• **2.4**   The text provides three primary strategic approaches (differentiation, cost, and response) for achieving competitive advantage. Provide an example of each not given in the text. Support your choices. (*Hint:* Note the examples provided in the text.)

•• **2.5**   Within the food service industry (restaurants that serve meals to customers, but not just fast food), find examples of firms that have sustained competitive advantage by competing on the basis of (1) cost leadership, (2) response, and (3) differentiation. Cite one example in each category; provide a sentence or two in support of each choice. Do not use fast-food chains for all categories. (*Hint:* A "99¢ menu" is very easily copied and is not a good source of sustained advantage.)

Problem 2.6 relates to Issues in Operations Strategy

••• **2.6**   Identify how changes within an organization affect the OM strategy for a company. For instance, discuss what impact the following internal factors might have on OM strategy:
a) Maturing of a product.
b) Technology innovation in the manufacturing process.
c) Changes in laptop computer design that builds in wireless technology.

Problem 2.7 relates to Strategy Development and Implementation

••• **2.7**   Identify how changes in the external environment affect the OM strategy for a company. For instance, discuss what impact the following external factors might have on OM strategy:
a) Major increases in oil prices.
b) Water- and air-quality legislation.

c) Fewer young prospective employees entering the labor market.

d) Inflation versus stable prices.

e) Legislation moving health insurance from a pretax benefit to taxable income.

Problems 2.8–2.12 relate to Strategic Planning, Core Competencies, and Outsourcing

•• **2.8** Claudia Pragram Technologies, Inc., has narrowed its choice of outsourcing provider to two firms located in different countries. Pragram wants to decide which one of the two countries is the better choice, based on risk-avoidance criteria. She has polled her executives and established four criteria. The resulting ratings for the two countries are presented in the table below, where 1 is a lower risk and 3 is a higher risk.

SELECTION CRITERION	ENGLAND	CANADA
Price of service from outsourcer	2	3
Nearness of facilities to client	3	1
Level of technology	1	3
History of successful outsourcing	1	2

The executives have determined four criteria weightings: Price, with a weight of 0.1; Nearness, with 0.6; Technology, with 0.2; and History, with 0.1.

a) Using the factor-rating method, which country would you select?

b) Double each of the weights used in part (a) (to 0.2, 1.2, 0.4, and 0.2, respectively). What effect does this have on your answer? Why? **P_X**

•• **2.9** Ranga Ramasesh is the operations manager for a firm that is trying to decide which one of four countries it should research for possible outsourcing providers. The first step is to select a country based on cultural risk factors, which are critical to eventual business success with the provider. Ranga has reviewed outsourcing provider directories and found that the four countries in the table that follows have an ample number of providers from which they can choose. To aid in the country selection step, he has enlisted the aid of a cultural expert, John Wang, who has provided ratings of the various criteria in the table. The resulting ratings are on a 1 to 10 scale, where 1 is a low risk and 10 is a high risk.

John has also determined six criteria weightings: Trust, with a weight of 0.4; Quality, with 0.2; Religious, with 0.1; Individualism, with 0.1; Time, with 0.1; and Uncertainty, with 0.1. Using the factor-rating method, which country should Ranga select? **P_X**

CULTURE SELECTION CRITERION	MEXICO	PANAMA	COSTA RICA	PERU
Trust	1	2	2	1
Society value of quality work	7	10	9	10
Religious attitudes	3	3	3	5
Individualism attitudes	5	2	4	8
Time orientation attitudes	4	6	7	3
Uncertainty avoidance attitudes	3	2	4	2

•• **2.10** Fernando Garza's firm wishes to use factor rating to help select an outsourcing provider of logistics services.

a) With weights from 1–5 (5 highest) and ratings 1–100 (100 highest), use the following table to help Garza make his decision:

CRITERION	WEIGHT	RATING OF LOGISTICS PROVIDERS		
		OVERNIGHT SHIPPING	WORLDWIDE DELIVERY	UNITED FREIGHT
Quality	5	90	80	75
Delivery	3	70	85	70
Cost	2	70	80	95

b) Garza decides to increase the weights for quality, delivery, and cost to 10, 6, and 4, respectively. How does this change your conclusions? Why?

c) If Overnight Shipping's ratings for each of the factors increase by 10%, what are the new results? **P_X**

••• **2.11** Walker Accounting Software is marketed to small accounting firms throughout the U.S. and Canada. Owner George Walker has decided to outsource the company's help desk and is considering three providers: Manila Call Center (Philippines), Delhi Services (India), and Moscow Bell (Russia). The following table summarizes the data Walker has assembled. Which outsourcing firm has the best rating? (Higher weights imply higher importance and higher ratings imply more desirable providers.) **P_X**

CRITERION	IMPORTANCE WEIGHT	PROVIDER RATINGS		
		MANILA	DELHI	MOSCOW
Flexibility	0.5	5	1	9
Trustworthiness	0.1	5	5	2
Price	0.2	4	3	6
Delivery	0.2	5	6	6

•••• **2.12** Rao Technologies, a California-based high-tech manufacturer, is considering outsourcing some of its electronics production. Four firms have responded to its request for bids, and CEO Mohan Rao has started to perform an analysis on the scores his OM team has entered in the table below.

FACTOR	WEIGHT	RATINGS OF OUTSOURCE PROVIDERS			
		A	B	C	D
Labor	w	5	4	3	5
Quality procedures	30	2	3	5	1
Logistics system	5	3	4	3	5
Price	25	5	3	4	4
Trustworthiness	5	3	2	3	5
Technology in place	15	2	5	4	4
Management team	15	5	4	2	1

Weights are on a scale from 1 through 30, and the outsourcing provider scores are on a scale of 1 through 5. The weight for the labor factor is shown as a w because Rao's OM team cannot agree on a value for this weight. For what range of values of w, if any, is company C a recommended outsourcing provider, according to the factor-rating method?

Problem 2.13 relates to Global Operations Strategy Options

•• **2.13** Does Boeing practice a multinational operations strategy, a global operations strategy, or a transnational operations strategy? Support your choice with specific references to Boeing's operations and the characteristics of each type of organization.

CASE STUDIES

Rapid-Lube

A huge market exists for automobile tune-ups, oil changes, and lubrication service for more than 250 million vehicles on U.S. roads. Some of this demand is filled by full-service auto dealerships, some by Walmart and Firestone, and some by other tire/service dealers. However, Rapid-Lube, Mobil-Lube, Jiffy-Lube and others have also developed strategies to accommodate this opportunity.

Rapid-Lube stations perform oil changes, lubrication, and interior cleaning in a spotless environment. The buildings are clean, usually painted white, and often surrounded by neatly trimmed landscaping. To facilitate fast service, cars can be driven through three abreast. At Rapid-Lube, the customer is greeted by service representatives who are graduates of Rapid-Lube U. The Rapid-Lube school is not unlike McDonald's Hamburger University near Chicago or Holiday Inn's training school in Memphis. The greeter takes the order, which typically includes fluid checks (oil, water, brake fluid, transmission fluid, differential grease) and the necessary lubrication, as well as filter changes for air and oil. Service personnel in neat uniforms then move into action. The standard three-person team has one person checking fluid levels under the hood, another assigned interior vacuuming and window cleaning, and the third in the garage pit, removing the oil filter, draining the oil, checking the differential and transmission, and lubricating as necessary. Precise task assignments and good training are designed to move the car into and out of the bay in 10 minutes. The business model is to charge no more, and hopefully less, than gas stations, automotive repair chains, and auto dealers, while providing better and faster service.

Discussion Questions

1. What constitutes the mission of Rapid-Lube?

2. How does the Rapid-Lube operations strategy provide competitive advantage? (*Hint:* Evaluate how Rapid-Lube's traditional competitors perform the 10 decisions of operations management vs. how Rapid-Lube performs them.)

3. Is it likely that Rapid-Lube has increased productivity over its more traditional competitors? Why? How would we measure productivity in this industry?

Strategy at Regal Marine

Video Case

Regal Marine, one of the U.S.'s 10 largest power-boat manufacturers, achieves its mission—providing luxury performance boats to customers worldwide—using the strategy of differentiation. It differentiates its products through constant innovation, unique features, and high quality. Increasing sales at the Orlando, Florida, family-owned firm suggest that the strategy is working.

As a quality boat manufacturer, Regal Marine starts with continuous innovation, as reflected in computer-aided design (CAD), high-quality molds, and close tolerances that are controlled through both defect charts and rigorous visual inspection. In-house quality is not enough, however. Because a product is only as good as the parts put into it, Regal has established close ties with a large number of its suppliers to ensure both flexibility and perfect parts. With the help of these suppliers, Regal can profitably produce a product line of 22 boats, ranging from the $14,000 19-foot boat to the $500,000 44-foot Commodore yacht.

"We build boats," says VP Tim Kuck, "but we're really in the 'fun' business. Our competition includes not only 300 other boat, canoe, and yacht manufacturers in our $17 billion industry, but home theaters, the Internet, and all kinds of alternative family entertainment." Fortunately Regal has been paying down debt and increasing market share.

Regal has also joined with scores of other independent boat makers in the American Boat Builders Association. Through economies of scale in procurement, Regal is able to navigate against billion-dollar competitor Brunswick (makers of the Sea Ray and Bayliner brands). The *Global Company Profile* featuring Regal Marine (which opens Chapter 5) provides further background on Regal and its strategy.

Discussion Questions*

1. State Regal Marine's mission in your own words.

2. Identify the strengths, weaknesses, opportunities, and threats that are relevant to the strategy of Regal Marine.

3. How would you define Regal's strategy?

4. How would each of the 10 operations management decisions apply to operations decision making at Regal Marine?

*You may wish to view the video that accompanies the case before addressing these questions.

Hard Rock Cafe's Global Strategy

Video Case

Hard Rock brings the concept of the "experience economy" to its cafe operation. The strategy incorporates a unique "experience" into its operations. This innovation is somewhat akin to mass customization in manufacturing. At Hard Rock, the experience concept is to provide not only a custom meal from the menu but a dining event that includes a unique visual and sound experience not duplicated anywhere else in the world. This strategy is succeeding. Other theme restaurants have come and gone while Hard Rock continues to grow. As Professor C. Markides of the London Business School says, "The trick is not to play the game better than the competition, but to develop and play an altogether different game."* At Hard Rock, the different game is the experience game.

From the opening of its first cafe in London in 1971, during the British rock music explosion, Hard Rock has been serving food and rock music with equal enthusiasm. Hard Rock Cafe has 40 U.S. locations, about a dozen in Europe, and the remainder

*Constantinos Markides, "Strategic Innovation," *MIT Sloan Management Review* 38, no. 3: 9.

scattered throughout the world, from Bangkok and Beijing to Beirut. New construction, leases, and investment in remodeling are long term; so a global strategy means special consideration of political risk, currency risk, and social norms in a context of a brand fit. Although Hard Rock is one of the most recognized brands in the world, this does not mean its cafe is a natural everywhere. Special consideration must be given to the supply chain for the restaurant and its accompanying retail store. About 48% of a typical cafe's sales are from merchandise.

The Hard Rock Cafe business model is well defined, but because of various risk factors and differences in business practices and employment law, Hard Rock elects to franchise about half of its cafes. Social norms and preferences often suggest some tweaking of menus for local taste. For instance, Hard Rock focuses less on hamburgers and beef and more on fish and lobster in its British cafes.

Because 70% of Hard Rock's guests are tourists, recent years have found it expanding to "destination" cities. While this has been a winning strategy for decades, allowing the firm to grow from one London cafe to 145 facilities in 60 countries, it has made Hard Rock susceptible to economic fluctuations that hit the tourist business hardest. So Hard Rock is signing a long-term lease for a new location in Nottingham, England, to join recently opened cafes in Manchester and Birmingham—cities that are not standard tourist destinations. At the same time, menus are being upgraded. Hopefully, repeat business from locals in these cities will smooth demand and make Hard Rock less dependent on tourists.

Discussion Questions*

1. Identify the strategy changes that have taken place at Hard Rock Cafe since its founding in 1971.
2. As Hard Rock Cafe has changed its strategy, how has its responses to some of the 10 decisions of OM changed?
3. Where does Hard Rock fit in the four international operations strategies outlined in Figure 2.9? Explain your answer.

*You may wish to view the video that accompanies the case before addressing these questions.

Outsourcing Offshore at Darden

Video Case

Darden Restaurants, owner of popular brands such as Olive Garden, Bahama Breeze, and Longhorn Grill, serves more than 320 million meals annually in over 1,500 restaurants across the U.S. and Canada. To achieve competitive advantage via its supply chain, Darden must achieve excellence at each step. With purchases from 35 countries, and seafood products with a shelf life as short as 4 days, this is a complex and challenging task.

Those 320 million meals annually mean 40 million pounds of shrimp and huge quantities of tilapia, swordfish, and other fresh purchases. Fresh seafood is typically flown to the U.S. and monitored each step of the way to ensure that 34°F is maintained.

Darden's purchasing agents travel the world to find competitive advantage in the supply chain. Darden personnel from supply chain and development, quality assurance, and environmental relations contribute to developing, evaluating, and checking suppliers. Darden also has seven native-speaking representatives living on other continents to provide continuing support and evaluation of suppliers. All suppliers must abide by Darden's food standards, which typically exceed FDA and other industry standards. Darden expects continuous improvement in durable relationships that increase quality and reduce cost.

Darden's aggressiveness and development of a sophisticated supply chain provide an opportunity for outsourcing. Much food preparation is labor intensive and is often more efficient when handled in bulk. This is particularly true where large volumes may justify capital investment. For instance, Tyson and Iowa Beef prepare meats to Darden's specifications much more economically than can individual restaurants. Similarly, Darden has found that it can outsource both the cutting of salmon to the proper portion size and the cracking/peeling of shrimp more cost-effectively offshore than in U.S. distribution centers or individual restaurants.

Discussion Questions*

1. What are some outsourcing opportunities in a restaurant?
2. What supply chain issues are unique to a firm sourcing from 35 countries?
3. Examine how other firms or industries develop international supply chains as compared to Darden.
4. Why does Darden outsource harvesting and preparation of much of its seafood?

*You may wish to view the video that accompanies this case study before answering these questions.

- **Additional Case Study:** Visit MyOMLab for this free case study:
  Outsourcing to Tata: The Indian outsourcing firm is hired by New Mexico.

Endnotes

1. The 28 members of the European Union (EU) as of 2015 were Austria, Belgium, Bulgaria, Cyprus, Croatia, Czech Republic, Denmark, Estonia, Finland, France, Germany, Greece, Hungary, Ireland, Italy, Latvia, Lithuania, Luxembourg, Malta, the Netherlands, Poland, Portugal, Romania, Slovakia, Slovenia, Spain, Sweden, and United Kingdom. Not all have adopted the euro. In addition, Iceland, Macedonia, Montenegro, and Turkey are candidates for entry into the European Union.

2. M. E. Porter, *Competitive Advantage: Creating and Sustaining Superior Performance.* New York: The Free Press, 1985.

3. M. E. Porter, *Competitive Strategy: Techniques for Analyzing Industries and Competitors.* New York: The Free Press, 1980, 1998.

4. J. Whitaker, M. S. Krishnan, and C. Fornell. "How Offshore Outsourcing Affects Customer Satisfaction." *The Wall Street Journal* (July 7, 2008): R4.

Chapter 2 *Rapid* Review

My**OM**Lab

Main Heading	Review Material	
A GLOBAL VIEW OF OPERATIONS AND SUPPLY CHAINS (pp. 32–35)	Domestic business operations decide to change to some form of international operations for six main reasons: 1. Improve supply chain 2. Reduce costs and exchange rate risks 3. Improve operations 4. Understand markets 5. Improve products 6. Attract and retain global talent ▪ **Maquiladoras**—Mexican factories located along the U.S.–Mexico border that receive preferential tariff treatment. ▪ **World Trade Organization (WTO)**—An international organization that promotes world trade by lowering barriers to the free flow of goods across borders. ▪ **NAFTA**—A free trade agreement between Canada, Mexico, and the United States. ▪ **European Union (EU)**—A European trade group that has 28 member states.	Concept Questions: 1.1–1.4 Problems: 2.1–2.3
DEVELOPING MISSIONS AND STRATEGIES (pp. 35–36)	An effective operations management effort must have a *mission* so it knows where it is going and a *strategy* so it knows how to get there. ▪ **Mission**—The purpose or rationale for an organization's existence. ▪ **Strategy**—How an organization expects to achieve its missions and goals. The three strategic approaches to competitive advantage are: **1.** Differentiation **2.** Cost leadership 3. Response	Concept Questions: 2.1–2.4 **VIDEO 2.1** Operations Strategy at Regal Marine
ACHIEVING COMPETITIVE ADVANTAGE THROUGH OPERATIONS (pp. 36–40)	▪ **Competitive advantage**—The creation of a unique advantage over competitors. ▪ **Differentiation**—Distinguishing the offerings of an organization in a way that the customer perceives as adding value. ▪ **Experience differentiation**—Engaging the customer with a product through imaginative use of the five senses, so the customer "experiences" the product. ▪ **Low-cost leadership**—Achieving maximum value, as perceived by the customer. ▪ **Response**—A set of values related to rapid, flexible, and reliable performance.	Concept Questions: 3.1–3.4 Problems: 2.4–2.5 **VIDEO 2.2** Hard Rock's Global Strategy
ISSUES IN OPERATIONS STRATEGY (pp. 40–41)	▪ **Resources view**—A view in which managers evaluate the resources at their disposal and manage or alter them to achieve competitive advantage. ▪ **Value-chain analysis**—A way to identify the elements in the product/service chain that uniquely add value. ▪ **Five forces model**—A way to analyze the five forces in the competitive environment. Forces in Porter's five forces model are (1) immediate rivals, (2) potential entrants, (3) customers, (4) suppliers, and (5) substitute products. Different issues are emphasized during different stages of the product life cycle: ▪ *Introduction*—Company strategy: Best period to increase market share, R&D engineering is critical. OM strategy: Product design and development critical, frequent product and process design changes, short production runs, high production costs, limited models, attention to quality. ▪ *Growth*—Company strategy: Practical to change price or quality image, strengthen niche. OM strategy: Forecasting critical, product and process reliability, competitive product improvements and options, increase capacity, shift toward product focus, enhance distribution. ▪ *Maturity*—Company strategy: Poor time to change image or price or quality, competitive costs become critical, defend market position. OM strategy: Standardization, less rapid product changes (more minor changes), optimum capacity, increasing stability of process, long production runs, product improvement and cost cutting. ▪ *Decline*—Company strategy: Cost control critical. OM strategy: Little product differentiation, cost minimization, overcapacity in the industry, prune line to eliminate items not returning good margin, reduce capacity.	Concept Questions: 4.1–4.4 Problem: 2.6

Main Heading	Review Material	
STRATEGY DEVELOPMENT AND IMPLEMENTATION (pp. 41–44)	■ **SWOT analysis**—A method of determining internal strengths and weaknesses and external opportunities and threats. ■ **Key success factors (KSFs)**—Activities or factors that are key to achieving competitive advantage. ■ **Core competencies**—A set of unique skills, talents, and activities that a firm does particularly well. A core competence may be a combination of KSFs. ■ **Activity map**—A graphical link of competitive advantage, KSFs, and supporting activities.	Concept Questions: 5.1–5.4 Problem: 2.7 Virtual Office Hours for Solved Problem: 2.1
STRATEGIC PLANNING, CORE COMPETENCIES, AND OUTSOURCING (pp. 44–48)	■ **Outsourcing**—Procuring from external sources services or products that are normally part of an organization. ■ **Theory of comparative advantage**—The theory which states that countries benefit from specializing in (and exporting) products and services in which they have relative advantage and importing goods in which they have a relative disadvantage. Perhaps half of all outsourcing agreements fail because of inappropriate planning and analysis. Potential risks of outsourcing include: ■ A drop in quality or customer service ■ Political backlash that results from outsourcing to foreign countries ■ Negative impact on employees ■ Potential future competition ■ Increased logistics and inventory costs The most common reason given for outsourcing failure is that the decision was made without sufficient understanding and analysis. The factor-rating method is an excellent tool for dealing with both country risk assessment and provider selection problems.	Concept Questions: 6.1–6.4 Problems: 2.8–2.12 Virtual Office Hours for Solved Problem: 2.2 **VIDEO 2.3** Outsourcing Offshore at Darden
GLOBAL OPERATIONS STRATEGY OPTIONS (pp. 49–50)	■ **International business**—A firm that engages in cross-border transactions. ■ **Multinational corporation (MNC)**—A firm that has extensive involvement in international business, owning or controlling facilities in more than one country. The four operations strategies for approaching global opportunities can be classified according to local responsiveness and cost reduction: ■ **International strategy**—A strategy in which global markets are penetrated using exports and licenses with little local responsiveness. ■ **Multidomestic strategy**—A strategy in which operating decisions are decentralized to each country to enhance local responsiveness. ■ **Global strategy**—A strategy in which operating decisions are centralized and headquarters coordinates the standardization and learning between facilities. ■ **Transnational strategy**—A strategy that combines the benefits of global-scale efficiencies with the benefits of local responsiveness. These firms transgress national boundaries.	Concept Questions: 7.1–7.4 Problem 2.13

Self Test

■ **Before taking the self-test,** refer to the learning objectives listed at the beginning of the chapter and the key terms listed at the end of the chapter.

LO 2.1 A mission statement is beneficial to an organization because it:
   a) is a statement of the organization's purpose.
   b) provides a basis for the organization's culture.
   c) identifies important constituencies.
   d) details specific income goals.
   e) ensures profitability.

LO 2.2 The three strategic approaches to competitive advantage are ____, ____, and _____.

LO 2.3 Core competencies are those strengths in a firm that include:
   a) specialized skills.
   b) unique production methods.
   c) proprietary information/knowledge.
   d) things a company does better than others.
   e) all of the above.

LO 2.4 Evaluating outsourcing providers by comparing their weighted average scores involves:
   a) factor-rating analysis.
   b) cost-volume analysis.
   c) transportation model analysis.
   d) linear regression analysis.
   e) crossover analysis.

LO 2.5 A company that is organized across international boundaries, with decentralized authority and substantial autonomy at each business via subsidiaries, franchises, or joint ventures, has:
   a) a global strategy.
   b) a transnational strategy.
   c) an international strategy.
   d) a multidomestic strategy.

Answers: LO 2.1. a; LO 2.2. differentiation, cost leadership, response; LO 2.3. e; LO 2.4. a; LO 2.5. c.

Project Management

CHAPTER OUTLINE

GLOBAL COMPANY PROFILE: *Bechtel Group*

◆ The Importance of Project Management *62*

◆ Project Planning *62*

◆ Project Scheduling *65*

◆ Project Controlling *66*

◆ Project Management Techniques: PERT and CPM *67*

◆ Determining the Project Schedule *71*

◆ Variability in Activity Times *77*

◆ Cost-Time Trade-Offs and Project Crashing *82*

◆ A Critique of PERT and CPM *85*

◆ Using Microsoft Project to Manage Projects *86*

Alaska Airlines

CHAPTER 3

Project Management Provides a Competitive Advantage for Bechtel

Over a century old, the San Francisco–based Bechtel Group (www.bechtel.com) is the world's premier manager of massive construction and engineering projects. Known for billion-dollar projects, Bechtel is famous for its construction feats on the Hoover Dam, the Boston Central Artery/Tunnel project, the Riyadh, Saudi Arabia Metro, and over 25,000 other projects in 160 countries. With 53,000 employees and revenues over $39 billion, Bechtel is the U.S.'s largest project manager.

Philipus/Alamy

A massive dredge hired by Bechtel removes silt from Iraq's port at Umm Qasr. This paved the way for large-scale deliveries of U.S. food and the return of commercial shipping.

Steve Hebert/Bechtel National, Inc./PRN/Newscom

In addition to major construction projects, Bechtel used its project management skills to provide emergency response to major catastrophes as it did here in the wake of Hurricane Katrina.

Conditions weren't what Bechtel expected when it won a series of billion-dollar contracts from the U.S. government to help reconstruct war-torn Iraq in the last decade. That country's defeat by Allied forces hadn't caused much war damage. Instead, what Bechtel found was a nation that had been crumbling for years. None of the sewage plants in Baghdad worked. Power flicked on and off. Towns and cities had been left to decay. And scavengers were stealing everything from museum artifacts to electric power lines. Bechtel's job was to oversee electric power, sewage, transportation, and airport repairs.

Bechtel's crews travelled under armed escort and slept in trailers surrounded by razor wire. But the company's efforts have paid off. Iraq's main seaport, Umm Qasr, has opened. Electrical generation is back to prewar levels, and Bechtel has refurbished more than 1,200 schools.

With a global procurement program, Bechtel easily tapped the company's network of suppliers and buyers worldwide to help rebuild Iraq's infrastructure.

Courtesy of Bechtel Corporation

Managing massive construction projects such as this is the strength of Bechtel. With large penalties for late completion and incentives for early completion, a good project manager is worth his or her weight in gold.

Other interesting recent Bechtel projects include:

- Constructing 30 high-security data centers worldwide for Equinix, Inc. ($1.2 billion).
- Building and running a rail line between London and the Channel Tunnel ($4.6 billion).
- Developing an oil pipeline from the Caspian Sea region to Russia ($850 million).
- Expanding the Dubai Airport in the United Arab Emirates ($600 million) and the Miami International Airport ($2 billion).
- Building liquefied natural gas plants in Trinidad, West Indies ($1 billion).

- Building a new subway for Athens, Greece ($2.6 billion).
- Constructing a natural gas pipeline in Thailand ($700 million).
- Building 30 plants for iMotors.com, a company that sells refurbished autos online ($300 million).
- Building a highway to link the north and south of Croatia ($303 million).

When companies or countries seek out firms to manage massive projects, they go to Bechtel, which, again and again, through outstanding project management, has demonstrated its competitive advantage. ◗

Thomas Hartwell/U.S. Agency for International Development (USAID)

Reconstructed terminal at Baghdad International Airport.

Joe Cavaretta/AP Images

Bechtel was the construction contractor for the Hoover Dam. This dam, on the Colorado River, is the highest in the Western Hemisphere.

LEARNING OBJECTIVES

LO 3.1 *Use* a Gantt chart for scheduling 65

LO 3.2 *Draw* AOA and AON networks 69

LO 3.3 *Complete* forward and backward passes for a project 72

LO 3.4 *Determine* a critical path 76

LO 3.5 *Calculate* the variance of activity times 78

LO 3.6 *Crash* a project 83

STUDENT TIP ◆
Wherever your career takes you, one of the most useful tools you can have, as a manager, is the ability to manage a project.

VIDEO 3.1
Project Management at Hard Rock's Rockfest

The Importance of Project Management

When Bechtel, the subject of the opening Global Company Profile, begins a project, it quickly has to mobilize substantial resources, often consisting of manual workers, construction professionals, cooks, medical personnel, and even security forces. Its project management team develops a supply chain to access materials to build everything from ports to bridges, dams, and monorails. Bechtel is just one example of a firm that faces modern phenomena: growing project complexity and collapsing product/service life cycles. This change stems from awareness of the strategic value of time-based competition and a quality mandate for continuous improvement. Each new product/service introduction is a unique event—a project. In addition, projects are a common part of our everyday life. We may be planning a wedding or a surprise birthday party, remodeling a house, or preparing a semester-long class project.

Scheduling projects can be a difficult challenge for operations managers. The stakes in project management are high. Cost overruns and unnecessary delays occur due to poor scheduling and poor controls.

Projects that take months or years to complete are usually developed outside the normal production system. Project organizations within the firm may be set up to handle such jobs and are often disbanded when the project is complete. On other occasions, managers find projects just a part of their job. The management of projects involves three phases (see Figure 3.1):

1. *Planning:* This phase includes goal setting, defining the project, and team organization.
2. *Scheduling:* This phase relates people, money, and supplies to specific activities and relates activities to each other.
3. *Controlling:* Here the firm monitors resources, costs, quality, and budgets. It also revises or changes plans and shifts resources to meet time and cost demands.

We begin this chapter with a brief overview of these functions. Three popular techniques to allow managers to plan, schedule, and control—Gantt charts, PERT, and CPM—are also described.

Project Planning

Project organization
An organization formed to ensure that programs (projects) receive the proper management and attention.

Projects can be defined as a series of related tasks directed toward a major output. In some firms a project organization is developed to make sure existing programs continue to run smoothly on a day-to-day basis while new projects are successfully completed.

For companies with multiple large projects, such as a construction firm, a project organization is an effective way of assigning the people and physical resources needed. It is a temporary organization structure designed to achieve results by using specialists from throughout the firm.

The project organization may be most helpful when:

1. Work tasks can be defined with a specific goal and deadline.
2. The job is unique or somewhat unfamiliar to the existing organization.
3. The work contains complex interrelated tasks requiring specialized skills.

Planning the Project (Before project)

Time | Cost

Performance
Set the goals | Define the project | Develop work breakdown structure | Identify team/ resources

Figure **3.1**

Project Planning, Scheduling, and Controlling

Scheduling the Project

Sequence activities | Assign people | Schedule deliverables | Schedule resources

Adams ✓
Smith ✓
Jones ✓

1.1
1.2
2.0
2.1
2.11

June
S M T W T F S
1 2 3 4 5 6
7 8 9 10 11 12 13

⬥ **STUDENT TIP**

Managers must "make the plan and then work the plan."

Controlling the Project (During project)

1.1
1.2
2.0
2.1
2.11

Monitor resources, costs, quality

Revise and change plans

Adams ✓
Smith ✓
Jones ✓

Shift resources

4. The project is temporary but critical to the organization.
5. The project cuts across organizational lines.

The Project Manager

An example of a project organization is shown in Figure 3.2. Project team members are temporarily assigned to a project and report to the project manager. The manager heading the project coordinates activities with other departments and reports directly to top management. Project managers receive high visibility in a firm and are responsible for making sure that (1) all necessary activities are finished in proper sequence and on time; (2) the project comes in within budget; (3) the project meets its quality goals; and (4) the people assigned to the project receive the motivation, direction, and information needed to do their jobs. This means that project managers should be good coaches and communicators, and be able to organize activities from a variety of disciplines.

Figure **3.2**

A Sample Project Organization

⬥ **STUDENT TIP**

Project organizations can be temporary or permanent. A permanent organization is usually called a *matrix organization*.

Ethical Issues Faced in Project Management   Project managers not only have high visibility but they also face ethical decisions on a daily basis. How they act establishes the code of conduct for the project. Project managers often deal with (1) offers of gifts from contractors, (2) pressure to alter status reports to mask the reality of delays, (3) false reports for charges of time and expenses, and (4) pressures to compromise quality to meet bonuses or avoid penalties related to schedules.

Using the Project Management Institute's (**www.pmi.org**) ethical codes is one means of trying to establish standards. These codes need to be accompanied by good leadership and a strong organizational culture, with its ingrained ethical standards and values.

Work Breakdown Structure

Work breakdown structure (WBS)

A hierarchical description of a project into more and more detailed components.

The project management team begins its task well in advance of project execution so that a plan can be developed. One of its first steps is to carefully establish the project's objectives, then break the project down into manageable parts. This work breakdown structure (WBS) defines the project by dividing it into its major subcomponents (or tasks), which are then subdivided into more detailed components, and finally into a set of activities and their related costs. The division of the project into smaller and smaller tasks can be difficult, but is critical to managing the project and to scheduling success. Gross requirements for people, supplies, and equipment are also estimated in this planning phase.

The work breakdown structure typically decreases in size from top to bottom and is indented like this:

Level
1. Project
2.   Major tasks in the project
3.   Subtasks in major tasks
4.   Activities (or "work packages") to be completed

This hierarchical framework can be illustrated with the development of Microsoft's operating system Windows 8. As we see in Figure 3.3, the project, creating a new operating system, is labeled 1.0. The first step is to identify the major tasks in the project (level 2). Three examples would be software design (1.1), cost management plan (1.2), and system testing (1.3). Two major subtasks for 1.1 are development of graphical user interfaces (GUIs) (1.1.1) and creating compatibility with previous versions of Windows (1.1.2). The major subtasks for 1.1.2 are level-4 activities, such as creating a team to handle compatibility with Windows 7 (1.1.2.1),

Figure **3.3**

Work Breakdown Structure

creating a team for Windows Vista (1.1.2.2), and creating a team for Windows XP (1.1.2.3). There are usually many level-4 activities.

Project Scheduling

Project scheduling involves sequencing and allotting time to all project activities. At this stage, managers decide how long each activity will take and compute the resources needed at each stage of production. Managers may also chart separate schedules for personnel needs by type of skill (management, engineering, or pouring concrete, for example) and material needs.

One popular project scheduling approach is the Gantt chart. Gantt charts are low-cost means of helping managers make sure that (1) activities are planned, (2) order of performance is documented, (3) activity time estimates are recorded, and (4) overall project time is developed. As Figure 3.4 shows, Gantt charts are easy to understand. Horizontal bars are drawn for each project activity along a time line. This illustration of a routine servicing of a Delta jetliner during a 40-minute layover shows that Gantt charts also can be used for scheduling repetitive operations. In this case, the chart helps point out potential delays. The *OM in Action* box on Delta provides additional insights.

On simple projects, scheduling charts such as these permit managers to observe the progress of each activity and to spot and tackle problem areas. Gantt charts, though, do not adequately illustrate the interrelationships between the activities and the resources.

PERT and CPM, the two widely used network techniques that we shall discuss shortly, *do* have the ability to consider precedence relationships and interdependency of activities. On complex projects, the scheduling of which is almost always computerized, PERT and CPM thus have an edge over the simpler Gantt charts. Even on huge projects, though, Gantt charts can be used as summaries of project status and may complement the other network approaches.

To summarize, whatever the approach taken by a project manager, project scheduling serves several purposes:

1. It shows the relationship of each activity to others and to the whole project.
2. It identifies the precedence relationships among activities.
3. It encourages the setting of realistic time and cost estimates for each activity.
4. It helps make better use of people, money, and material resources by identifying critical bottlenecks in the project.

Gantt charts
Planning charts used to schedule resources and allocate time.

⬥ **STUDENT TIP**
Gantt charts are simple and visual, making them widely used.

LO 3.1 *Use a Gantt chart for scheduling*

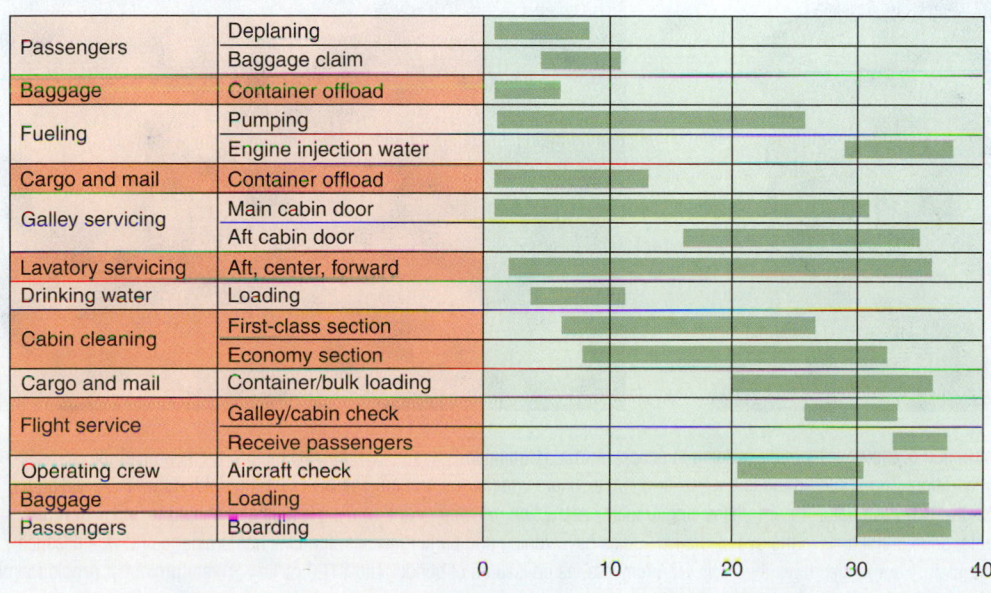

Figure **3.4**

Gantt Chart of Service Activities for a Delta Jet during a 40-Minute Layover

Delta saves $50 million a year with this turnaround time, which is a reduction from its traditional 60-minute routine.

OM in Action   Delta's Ground Crew Orchestrates a Smooth Takeoff

Flight 574's engines screech its arrival as the jet lumbers down Richmond's taxiway with 140 passengers arriving from Atlanta. In 40 minutes, the plane is to be airborne again.

However, before this jet can depart, there is business to attend to: passengers, luggage, and cargo to unload and load; thousands of gallons of jet fuel and countless drinks to restock; cabin and restrooms to clean; toilet holding tanks to drain; and engines, wings, and landing gear to inspect.

The 10-person ground crew knows that a miscue anywhere—a broken cargo loader, lost baggage, misdirected passengers—can mean a late departure and trigger a chain reaction of headaches from Richmond to Atlanta to every destination of a connecting flight.

Carla Sutera, the operations manager for Delta's Richmond International Airport, views the turnaround operation like a pit boss awaiting a race car. Trained crews are in place for Flight 574 with baggage carts and tractors, hydraulic cargo loaders, a truck to load food and drinks, another to lift the cleanup crew, another to put fuel on, and a fourth to take water off. The "pit crew" usually performs so smoothly that most passengers never suspect the proportions of the effort. Gantt charts, such as the one in Figure 3.4, aid Delta and other airlines with the staffing and scheduling that are needed for this task.

Sources: Knight Ridder Tribune Business News (July 16, 2005) and (November 21, 2002).

Jeff Topping/Getty Images

Project Controlling

VIDEO 3.2
Project Management at Arnold Palmer Hospital

The control of projects, like the control of any management system, involves close monitoring of resources, costs, quality, and budgets. Control also means using a feedback loop to revise the project plan and having the ability to shift resources to where they are needed most. Computerized PERT/CPM reports and charts are widely available today from scores of competing software firms. Some of the more popular of these programs are Oracle Primavera (by Oracle), MindView (by Match Ware), HP Project (by Hewlett-Packard), Fast Track (by AEC Software), and Microsoft Project (by Microsoft Corp.), which we illustrate in this chapter.

STUDENT TIP ◆
To use project management software, you first need to understand the next two sections in this chapter.

These programs produce a broad variety of reports, including (1) detailed cost breakdowns, (2) labor requirements, (3) cost and hour summaries, (4) raw material and expenditure forecasts, (5) variance reports, (6) time analysis reports, and (7) work status reports.

Courtesy Arnold Palmer Medical Center

Courtesy Arnold Palmer Medical Center

Construction of the new 11-story building at Arnold Palmer Hospital in Orlando, Florida, was an enormous project for the hospital administration. The photo on the left shows the first six floors under construction. The photo on the right shows the building as completed two years later. Prior to beginning actual construction, regulatory and funding issues added, as they do with most projects, substantial time to the overall project. Cities have zoning and parking issues; the EPA has drainage and waste issues; and regulatory authorities have their own requirements, as do issuers of bonds. The $100 million, 4-year project at Arnold Palmer Hospital is discussed in the Video Case Study at the end of this chapter.

OM in Action   Agile Project Management at Mastek

Agile project management has changed the way that Mastek Corp., in Mumbai, India, develops its educational software products. On a traditional well-defined project, managers are actively involved in directing work and telling their team what needs to be done—a style often referred to as a step-by-step *waterfall* style of project management.

Agile project management is different. In the early stages, the project manager creates a high-level plan, based on outline requirements and a high-level view of the solution. From that point, the end project is created iteratively and incrementally, with each increment building on the output of steps preceding it.

The principles of agile are essentially communication and transparency. Instead of waiting for something to be delivered, with limited understanding of the desired end result, there are numerous checkpoints and feedback loops to track progress.

Agile provides Mastek the ability to keep costs under control. Without agile, the cost of quality increases. "It's much harder to correct mistakes when a software product is nearing its final phase of development," says a company executive. "It's much better to develop it as you go along. I think agile project management would help any software developer."

Sources: AMPG International (2015) and **www.cprime.com** (2012).

Controlling projects can be difficult. The stakes are high; cost overruns and unnecessary delays can occur due to poor planning, scheduling, and controls. Some projects are "well-defined," whereas others may be "ill-defined." Projects typically only become well-defined after detailed extensive initial planning and careful definition of required inputs, resources, processes, and outputs. Well-established projects where constraints are known (e.g., buildings and roads) and engineered products (e.g., airplanes and cars) with well-defined specifications and drawings may fall into this category. Well-defined projects are assumed to have changes small enough to be managed without substantially revising plans. They use what is called a *waterfall* approach, where the project progresses smoothly, in a step-by-step manner, through each phase to completion.

But many projects, such as software development (e.g., 3-D games) and new technology (e.g., landing the Mars land rover) are ill-defined. These projects require what is known as an *agile* style of management with collaboration and constant feedback to adjust to the many unknowns of the evolving technology and project specifications. The *OM in Action* box "Agile Project Management at Mastek" provides such an example. Most projects fall somewhere between waterfall and agile.

Project Management Techniques: PERT and CPM

Program evaluation and review technique (PERT) and the **critical path method (CPM)** were both developed in the 1950s to help managers schedule, monitor, and control large and complex projects. CPM arrived first, as a tool developed to assist in the building and maintenance of chemical plants at duPont. Independently, PERT was developed in 1958 for the U.S. Navy.

The Framework of PERT and CPM

PERT and CPM both follow six basic steps:

1. Define the project and prepare the work breakdown structure.
2. Develop the relationships among the activities. Decide which activities must precede and which must follow others.
3. Draw the network connecting all the activities.
4. Assign time and/or cost estimates to each activity.
5. Compute the *longest* time path through the network. This is called the **critical path**.
6. Use the network to help plan, schedule, monitor, and control the project.

Step 5, finding the critical path, is a major part of controlling a project. The activities on the critical path represent tasks that will delay the entire project if they are not completed on time. Managers can gain the flexibility needed to complete critical tasks by identifying

Program evaluation and review technique (PERT)

A project management technique that employs three time estimates for each activity.

Critical path method (CPM)

A project management technique that uses only one time factor per activity.

Critical path

The computed *longest* time path(s) through a network.

noncritical activities and replanning, rescheduling, and reallocating labor and financial resources.

Although PERT and CPM differ to some extent in terminology and in the construction of the network, their objectives are the same. Furthermore, the analysis used in both techniques is very similar. The major difference is that PERT employs three time estimates for each activity. These time estimates are used to compute expected values and standard deviations for the activity. CPM makes the assumption that activity times are known with certainty and hence requires only one time factor for each activity.

For purposes of illustration, the rest of this section concentrates on a discussion of PERT. Most of the comments and procedures described, however, apply just as well to CPM.

PERT and CPM are important because they can help answer questions such as the following about projects with thousands of activities:

1. When will the entire project be completed?
2. What are the critical activities or tasks in the project—that is, which activities will delay the entire project if they are late?
3. Which are the noncritical activities—the ones that can run late without delaying the whole project's completion?
4. What is the probability that the project will be completed by a specific date?
5. At any particular date, is the project on schedule, behind schedule, or ahead of schedule?
6. On any given date, is the money spent equal to, less than, or greater than the budgeted amount?
7. Are there enough resources available to finish the project on time?
8. If the project is to be finished in a shorter amount of time, what is the best way to accomplish this goal at the least cost?

Network Diagrams and Approaches

The first step in a PERT or CPM network is to divide the entire project into significant activities in accordance with the work breakdown structure. There are two approaches for drawing a project network: activity on node (AON) and activity on arrow (AOA). Under the AON convention, *nodes* designate activities. Under AOA, *arrows* represent activities. Activities consume time and resources. The basic difference between AON and AOA is that the nodes in an AON diagram represent activities. In an AOA network, the nodes represent the starting and finishing times of an activity and are also called *events*. So nodes in AOA consume neither time nor resources.

Activity-on-node (AON)

A network diagram in which nodes designate activities.

Activity-on-arrow (AOA)

A network diagram in which arrows designate activities.

Although both AON and AOA are popular in practice, many of the project management software packages, including Microsoft Project, use AON networks. For this reason, although we illustrate both types of networks in the next examples, we focus on AON networks in subsequent discussions in this chapter.

Example 1   PREDECESSOR RELATIONSHIPS FOR POLLUTION CONTROL AT MILWAUKEE PAPER

Milwaukee Paper Manufacturing had long delayed the expense of installing advanced computerized air pollution control equipment in its facility. But when the board of directors adopted a new proactive policy on sustainability, it did not just *authorize* the budget for the state-of-the-art equipment. It directed the plant manager, Julie Ann Williams, to complete the installation in time for a major announcement of the policy, on Earth Day, exactly 16 weeks away! Under strict deadline from her bosses, Williams needs to be sure that installation of the filtering system progresses smoothly and on time.

Given the following information, develop a table showing activity precedence relationships.

APPROACH ▶ Milwaukee Paper has identified the eight activities that need to be performed in order for the project to be completed. When the project begins, two activities can be simultaneously started: building the internal components for the device (activity A) and the modifications necessary for the floor and roof (activity B). The construction of the collection stack (activity C) can begin when the internal components are completed. Pouring the concrete floor and installation of the frame (activity D) can be started as soon as the internal components are completed and the roof and floor have been modified.

After the collection stack has been constructed, two activities can begin: building the high-temperature burner (activity E) and installing the pollution control system (activity F). The air pollution device can be installed (activity G) after the concrete floor has been poured, the frame has been installed, and the high-temperature burner has been built. Finally, after the control system and pollution device have been installed, the system can be inspected and tested (activity H).

SOLUTION ▶ Activities and precedence relationships may seem rather confusing when they are presented in this descriptive form. It is therefore convenient to list all the activity information in a table, as shown in Table 3.1. We see in the table that activity A is listed as an *immediate predecessor* of activity C. Likewise, both activities D and E must be performed prior to starting activity G.

TABLE 3.1	Milwaukee Paper Manufacturing's Activities and Predecessors	
ACTIVITY	**DESCRIPTION**	**IMMEDIATE PREDECESSORS**
A	Build internal components	—
B	Modify roof and floor	—
C	Construct collection stack	A
D	Pour concrete and install frame	A, B
E	Build high-temperature burner	C
F	Install pollution control system	C
G	Install air pollution device	D, E
H	Inspect and test	F, G

INSIGHT ▶ To complete a network, all predecessors must be clearly defined.

LEARNING EXERCISE ▶ What is the impact on this sequence of activities if Environmental Protection Agency (EPA) approval is required after *Inspect and Test?* [Answer: The immediate predecessor for the new activity would be H, *Inspect and Test*, with *EPA approval* as the last activity.]

Activity-on-Node Example

Note that in Example 1, we only list the *immediate* predecessors for each activity. For instance, in Table 3.1, because activity A precedes activity C, and activity C precedes activity E, the fact that activity A precedes activity E is *implicit*. This relationship need not be explicitly shown in the activity precedence relationships.

When there are many activities in a project with fairly complicated precedence relationships, it is difficult for an individual to comprehend the complexity of the project from just the tabular information. In such cases, a visual representation of the project, using a *project network*, is convenient and useful. A project network is a diagram of all the activities and the precedence relationships that exist between these activities in a project. Example 2 illustrates how to construct an AON project network for Milwaukee Paper Manufacturing.

LO 3.2 *Draw* AOA and AON networks

It is convenient to have the project network start and finish with a unique node. In the Milwaukee Paper example, it turns out that a unique activity, H, is the last activity in the project. We therefore automatically have a unique ending node.

In situations in which a project has multiple ending activities, we include a "dummy" ending activity. We illustrate this type of situation in Solved Problem 3.1 at the end of this chapter.

Example 2

Dummy activity

An activity having no time that is inserted into a network to maintain the logic of the network.

Figure 3.5

Beginning AON Network for Milwaukee Paper

Figure 3.6

Intermediate AON Network for Milwaukee Paper

Figure 3.7

Complete AON Network for Milwaukee Paper

AON GRAPH FOR MILWAUKEE PAPER

Draw the AON network for Milwaukee Paper, using the data in Example 1.

APPROACH ▶ In the AON approach, we denote each activity by a node. The lines, or arrows, represent the precedence relationships between the activities.

SOLUTION ▶ In this example, there are two activities (A and B) that do not have any predecessors. We draw separate nodes for each of these activities, as shown in Figure 3.5. Although not required, it is usually convenient to have a unique starting activity for a project. We have therefore included a *dummy activity* called *Start* in Figure 3.5. This dummy activity does not really exist and takes up zero time and resources. Activity *Start* is an immediate predecessor for both activities A and B, and it serves as the unique starting activity for the entire project.

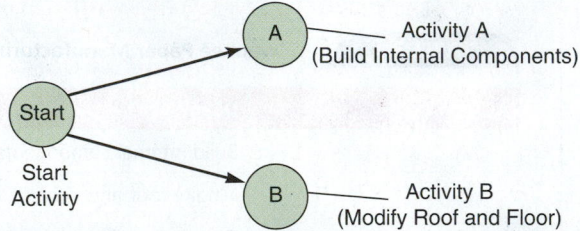

We now show the precedence relationships using lines with arrow symbols. For example, an arrow from activity Start to activity A indicates that Start is a predecessor for activity A. In a similar fashion, we draw an arrow from Start to B.

Next, we add a new node for activity C. Because activity A precedes activity C, we draw an arrow from node A to node C (see Figure 3.6). Likewise, we first draw a node to represent activity D. Then, because activities A and B both precede activity D, we draw arrows from A to D and from B to D (see Figure 3.6).

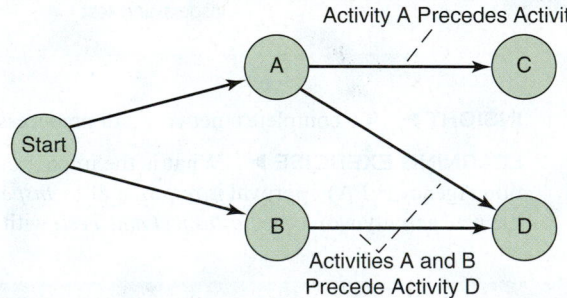

We proceed in this fashion, adding a separate node for each activity and a separate line for each precedence relationship that exists. The complete AON project network for the Milwaukee Paper Manufacturing project is shown in Figure 3.7.

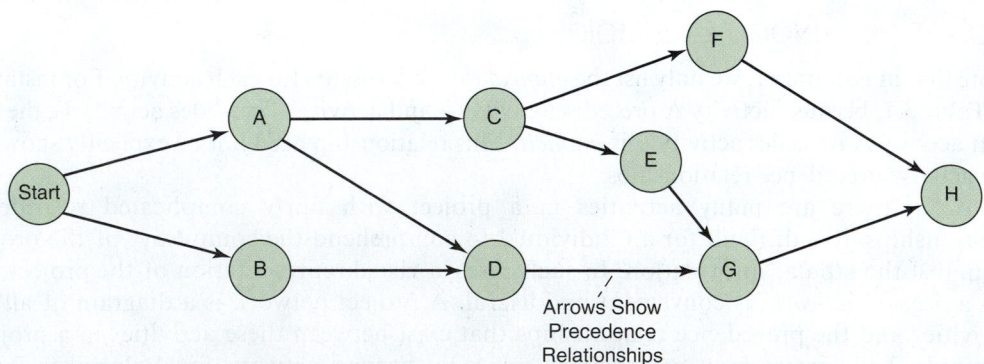

INSIGHT ▶ Drawing a project network properly takes some time and experience. We would like the lines to be straight and arrows to move to the right when possible.

LEARNING EXERCISE ▶ If *EPA Approval* occurs after *Inspect and Test*, what is the impact on the graph? [Answer: A straight line is extended to the right beyond H (with a node I added) to reflect the additional activity.]

RELATED PROBLEMS ▶ 3.4a, 3.5, 3.8, 3.9, 3.10, 3.11a, 3.12 (3.13–3.14 are available in MyOMLab)

Activity-on-Arrow Example

In an AOA project network we can represent activities by arrows. A node represents an *event*, which marks the start or completion time of an activity. We usually identify an event (node) by a number.

Example 3 | **ACTIVITY-ON-ARROW FOR MILWAUKEE PAPER**

Draw the complete AOA project network for Milwaukee Paper's problem.

APPROACH ▶ Using the data from Table 3.1 in Example 1, draw one activity at a time, starting with A.

SOLUTION ▶ We see that activity A starts at event 1 and ends at event 2. Likewise, activity B starts at event 1 and ends at event 3. Activity C, whose only immediate predecessor is activity A, starts at node 2 and ends at node 4. Activity D, however, has two predecessors (i.e., A and B). Hence, we need both activities A and B to end at event 3, so that activity D can start at that event. However, we cannot have multiple activities with common starting and ending nodes in an AOA network. To overcome this difficulty, in such cases, we may need to add a dummy line (activity) to enforce the precedence relationship. The dummy activity, shown in Figure 3.8 as a dashed line, is inserted between events 2 and 3 to make the diagram reflect the precedence between A and D. The remainder of the AOA project network for Milwaukee Paper's example is also shown.

Figure **3.8**

Complete AOA Network (with Dummy Activity) for Milwaukee Paper

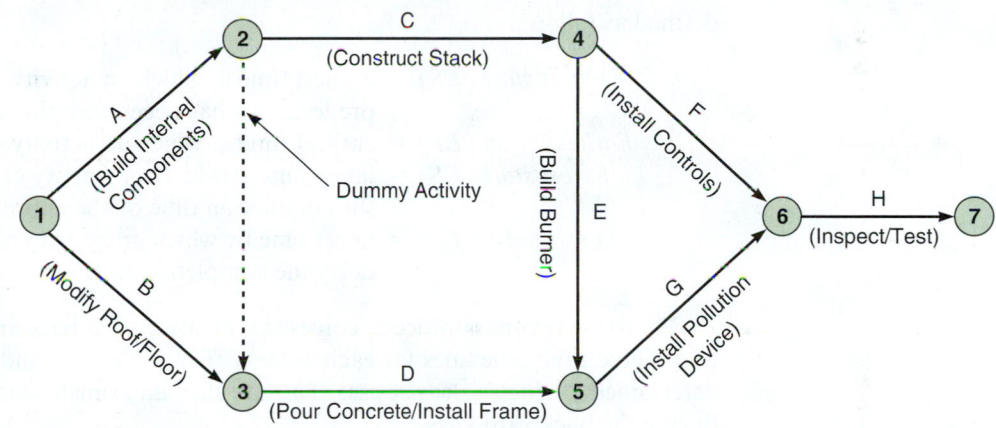

STUDENT TIP ❗

The dummy activity consumes no time, but note how it changes precedence. Now activity D cannot begin until *both* B and the dummy are complete.

INSIGHT ▶ Dummy activities are common in AOA networks. They do not really exist in the project and take zero time.

LEARNING EXERCISE ▶ A new activity, *EPA Approval*, follows activity H. Add it to Figure 3.8. [Answer: Insert an arrowed line from node 7, which ends at a new node 8, and is labeled I (EPA Approval).]

RELATED PROBLEMS ▶ 3.4b, 3.6, 3.7

Determining the Project Schedule

Look back at Figure 3.7 (in Example 2) for a moment to see Milwaukee Paper's completed AON project network. Once this project network has been drawn to show all the activities and their precedence relationships, the next step is to determine the project schedule. That is, we need to identify the planned starting and ending time for each activity.

Let us assume Milwaukee Paper estimates the time required for each activity, in weeks, as shown in Table 3.2. The table indicates that the total time for all eight of the company's activities is 25 weeks. However, because several activities can take place simultaneously, it is clear that the total project completion time may be less than 25 weeks. To find out just how long the project will take, we perform the critical path analysis for the network.

Critical path analysis

A process that helps determine a project schedule.

TABLE 3.2	Time Estimates for Milwaukee Paper Manufacturing	
ACTIVITY	**DESCRIPTION**	**TIME (WEEKS)**
A	Build internal components	2
B	Modify roof and floor	3
C	Construct collection stack	2
D	Pour concrete and install frame	4
E	Build high-temperature burner	4
F	Install pollution control system	3
G	Install air pollution device	5
H	Inspect and test	2
	Total time (weeks)	25

As mentioned earlier, the critical path is the *longest* time path through the network. To find the critical path, we calculate two distinct starting and ending times for each activity. These are defined as follows:

$$\textit{Earliest start (ES)} = \text{earliest time at which an activity can start, assuming all predecessors have been completed}$$
$$\textit{Earliest finish (EF)} = \text{earliest time at which an activity can be finished}$$
$$\textit{Latest start (LS)} = \text{latest time at which an activity can start so as to not delay the completion time of the entire project}$$
$$\textit{Latest finish (LF)} = \text{latest time by which an activity has to finish so as to not delay the completion time of the entire project}$$

We use a two-pass process, consisting of a forward pass and a backward pass, to determine these time schedules for each activity. The early start and finish times (ES and EF) are determined during the forward pass. The late start and finish times (LS and LF) are determined during the backward pass.

Forward pass

A process that identifies all the early times.

LO 3.3 *Complete* forward and backward passes for a project

Forward Pass

To clearly show the activity schedules on the project network, we use the notation shown in Figure 3.9. The ES of an activity is shown in the top left corner of the node denoting that activity. The EF is shown in the top right corner. The latest times, LS and LF, are shown in the bottom-left and bottom-right corners, respectively.

Figure **3.9**

Notation Used in Nodes for Forward and Backward Pass

Activity Name or Symbol

Earliest Start — ES   A   EF — Earliest Finish

Latest Start — LS   2   LF — Latest Finish

Activity Duration

Earliest Start Time Rule Before an activity can start, *all* its immediate predecessors must be finished:

◆ If an activity has only a single immediate predecessor, its ES equals the EF of the predecessor.

◆ If an activity has multiple immediate predecessors, its ES is the maximum of all EF values of its predecessors. That is:

$$ES = Max \{EF \text{ of all immediate predecessors}\} \qquad (3\text{-}1)$$

Earliest Finish Time Rule The earliest finish time (EF) of an activity is the sum of its earliest start time (ES) and its activity time. That is:

$$EF = ES + Activity \text{ time} \qquad (3\text{-}2)$$

Example 4

COMPUTING EARLIEST START AND FINISH TIMES FOR MILWAUKEE PAPER

Calculate the earliest start and finish times for the activities in the Milwaukee Paper Manufacturing project.

APPROACH ▶ Use Table 3.2, which contains the activity times. Complete the project network for the company's project, along with the ES and EF values for all activities.

SOLUTION ▶ With the help of Figure 3.10, we describe how these values are calculated.

Because activity Start has no predecessors, we begin by setting its ES to 0. That is, activity Start can begin at time 0, which is the same as the beginning of week 1. If activity Start has an ES of 0, its EF is also 0, since its activity time is 0.

Next, we consider activities A and B, both of which have only Start as an immediate predecessor. Using the earliest start time rule, the ES for both activities A and B equals zero, which is the EF of activity Start. Now, using the earliest finish time rule, the EF for A is 2 (= 0 + 2), and the EF for B is 3 (= 0 + 3).

Since activity A precedes activity C, the ES of C equals the EF of A (= 2). The EF of C is therefore 4 (= 2 + 2).

We now come to activity D. Both activities A and B are immediate predecessors for D. Whereas A has an EF of 2, activity B has an EF of 3. Using the earliest start time rule, we compute the ES of activity D as follows:

$$ES \text{ of } D = Max\{EF \text{ of A}, EF \text{ of B}\} = Max(2, 3) = 3$$

The EF of D equals 7 (= 3 + 4). Next, both activities E and F have activity C as their only immediate predecessor. Therefore, the ES for both E and F equals 4 (= EF of C). The EF of E is 8 (= 4 + 4), and the EF of F is 7 (= 4 + 3).

Activity G has both activities D and E as predecessors. Using the earliest start time rule, its ES is therefore the maximum of the EF of D and the EF of E. Hence, the ES of activity G equals 8 (= maximum of 7 and 8), and its EF equals 13 (= 8 + 5).

Finally, we come to activity H. Because it also has two predecessors, F and G, the ES of H is the maximum EF of these two activities. That is, the ES of H equals 13 (= maximum of 13 and 7). This implies that the EF of H is 15 (= 13 + 2). Because H is the last activity in the project, this also implies that the earliest time in which the entire project can be completed is 15 weeks.

INSIGHT ▶ The ES of an activity that has only one predecessor is simply the EF of that predecessor. For an activity with more than one predecessor, we must carefully examine the EFs of all immediate predecessors and choose the largest one.

LEARNING EXERCISE ▶ A new activity I, *EPA Approval*, takes 1 week. Its predecessor is activity H. What are I's ES and EF? [Answer: 15, 16]

RELATED PROBLEMS ▶ 3.15, 3.16, 3.19c

EXCEL **OM** Data File **Ch03Ex4.xls** can be found in MyOMLab.

Although the forward pass allows us to determine the earliest project completion time, it does not identify the critical path. To identify this path, we need to now conduct the backward pass to determine the LS and LF values for all activities.

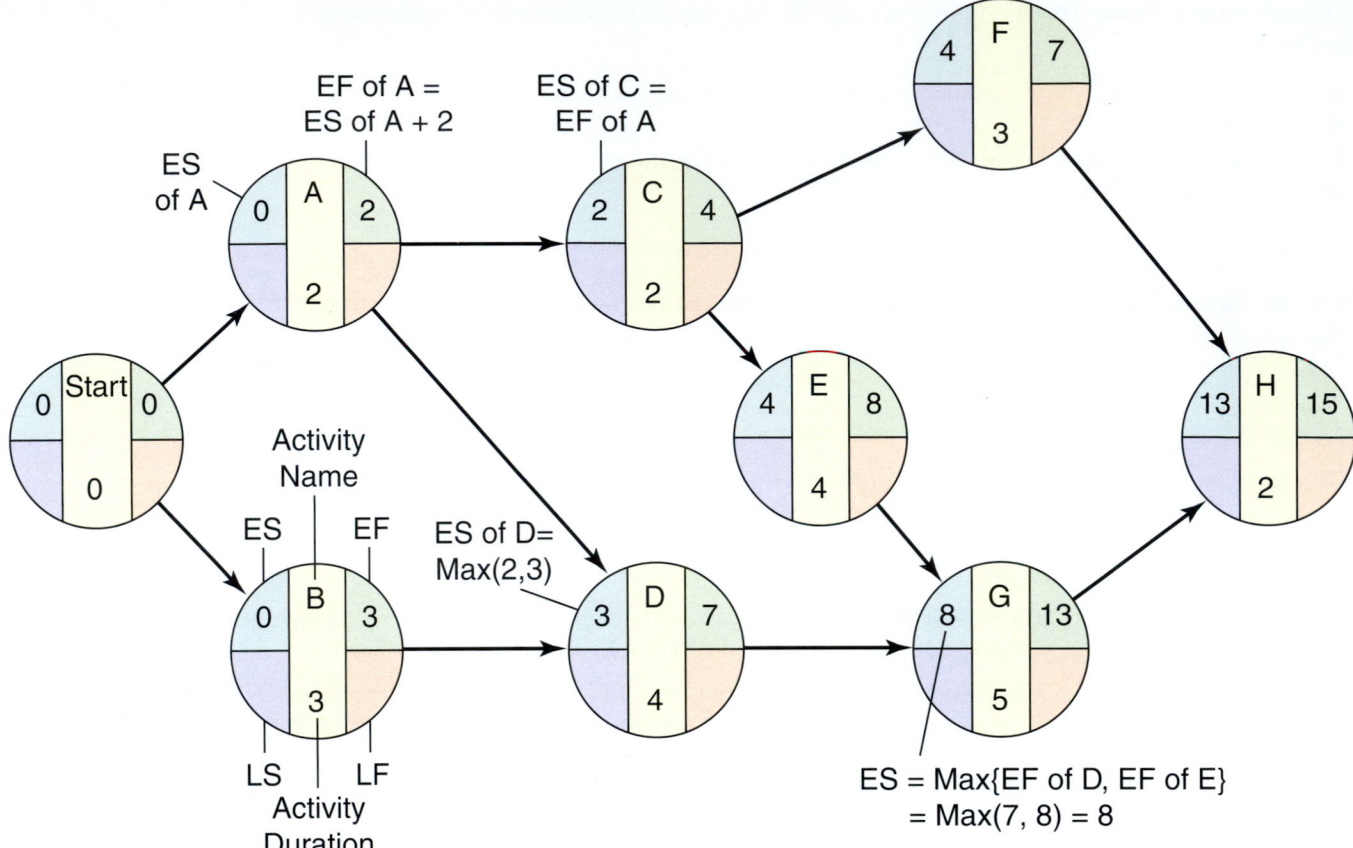

Figure **3.10** **Earliest Start and Earliest Finish Times for Milwaukee Paper**

Backward Pass

Backward pass

An activity that finds all the late start and late finish times.

Just as the forward pass began with the first activity in the project, the **backward pass** begins with the last activity in the project. For each activity, we first determine its LF value, followed by its LS value. The following two rules are used in this process.

Latest Finish Time Rule This rule is again based on the fact that before an activity can start, all its immediate predecessors must be finished:

- If an activity is an immediate predecessor for just a single activity, its LF equals the LS of the activity that immediately follows it.
- If an activity is an immediate predecessor to more than one activity, its LF is the minimum of all LS values of all activities that immediately follow it. That is:

$$LF = Min\{LS \text{ of all immediate following activities}\} \qquad (3\text{-}3)$$

Latest Start Time Rule The latest start time (LS) of an activity is the difference of its latest finish time (LF) and its activity time. That is:

$$LS = LF - \text{Activity time} \qquad (3\text{-}4)$$

Example 5 | COMPUTING LATEST START AND FINISH TIMES FOR MILWAUKEE PAPER

Calculate the latest start and finish times for each activity in Milwaukee Paper's pollution project.

APPROACH ▶ Use Figure 3.10 as a beginning point. Overlay 1 of Figure 3.10 shows the complete project network for Milwaukee Paper, along with added LS and LF values for all activities. In what follows, we see how these values were calculated.

SOLUTION ▶ We begin by assigning an LF value of 15 weeks for activity H. That is, we specify that the latest finish time for the entire project is the same as its earliest finish time. Using the latest start time rule, the LS of activity H is equal to 13 (= 15 − 2).

Because activity H is the lone succeeding activity for both activities F and G, the LF for both F and G equals 13. This implies that the LS of G is 8 (= 13 − 5), and the LS of F is 10 (= 13 − 3).

Proceeding in this fashion, we see that the LF of E is 8 (= LS of G), and its LS is 4 (= 8 − 4). Likewise, the LF of D is 8 (= LS of G), and its LS is 4 (= 8 − 4).

We now consider activity C, which is an immediate predecessor to two activities: E and F. Using the latest finish time rule, we compute the LF of activity C as follows:

$$\text{LF of C} = \text{Min}\{\text{LS of E, LS of F}\} = \text{Min}(4, 10) = 4$$

The LS of C is computed as 2 (= 4 − 2). Next, we compute the LF of B as 4 (= LS of D) and its LS as 1 (= 4 − 3).

We now consider activity A. We compute its LF as 2 (= minimum of LS of C and LS of D). Hence, the LS of activity A is 0 (= 2 − 2). Finally, both the LF and LS of activity Start are equal to 0.

INSIGHT ▶ The LF of an activity that is the predecessor of only one activity is just the LS of that following activity. If the activity is the predecessor to more than one activity, its LF is the smallest LS value of all activities that follow immediately.

LEARNING EXERCISE ▶ A new activity I, *EPA Approval*, takes 1 week. Its predecessor is activity H. What are I's LS and LF? [Answer: 15, 16]

RELATED PROBLEMS ▶ 3.15, 3.19c

Calculating Slack Time and Identifying the Critical Path(s)

After we have computed the earliest and latest times for all activities, it is a simple matter to find the amount of slack time that each activity has. Slack is the length of time an activity can be delayed without delaying the entire project. Mathematically:

$$\text{Slack} = \text{LS} - \text{ES} \quad \text{or} \quad \text{Slack} = \text{LF} - \text{EF} \qquad (3\text{-}5)$$

Slack time

Free time for an activity. Also referred to as free float or free slack.

Example 6 | **CALCULATING SLACK TIMES FOR MILWAUKEE PAPER**

Calculate the slack for the activities in the Milwaukee Paper project.

APPROACH ▶ Start with the data in Overlay 1 of Figure 3.10 in Example 5 and develop Table 3.3 one line at a time.

SOLUTION ▶ Table 3.3 summarizes the ES, EF, LS, LF, and slack time for all of the firm's activities. Activity B, for example, has 1 week of slack time because its LS is 1 and its ES is 0 (alternatively, its LF is 4 and its EF is 3). This means that activity B can be delayed by up to 1 week, and the whole project can still be finished in 15 weeks.

On the other hand, activities A, C, E, G, and H have *no* slack time. This means that none of them can be delayed without delaying the entire project. Conversely, if plant manager Julie Ann Williams wants to reduce the total project times, she will have to reduce the length of one of these activities.

Overlay 2 of Figure 3.10 shows the slack computed for each activity.

INSIGHT ▶ Slack may be computed from either early/late starts or early/late finishes. The key is to find which activities have zero slack.

| TABLE 3.3 | Milwaukee Paper's Schedule and Slack Times |

ACTIVITY	ACTIVITY TIME	EARLIEST START ES	EARLIEST FINISH EF	LATEST START LS	LATEST FINISH LF	SLACK LS – ES	ON CRITICAL PATH
A	2	0	2	0	2	0	Yes
B	3	0	3	1	4	1	No
C	2	2	4	2	4	0	Yes
D	4	3	7	4	8	1	No
E	4	4	8	4	8	0	Yes
F	3	4	7	10	13	6	No
G	5	8	13	8	13	0	Yes
H	2	13	15	13	15	0	Yes

LEARNING EXERCISE ▶ A new activity I, *EPA Approval*, follows activity H and takes 1 week. Is i on the critical path? [Answer: Yes, it's LS – ES = 0]

RELATED PROBLEMS ▶ 3.8d, 3.15d, 3.19c

ACTIVE MODEL 3.1 This example is further illustrated in Active Model 3.1 in MyOMLab.

LO 3.4 *Determine* a critical path

The activities with zero slack are called *critical activities* and are said to be on the critical path. The critical path is a continuous path through the project network that:

◆ Starts at the first activity in the project (Start in our example).
◆ Terminates at the last activity in the project (H in our example).
◆ Includes only critical activities (i.e., activities with no slack time).

Example 7

SHOWING CRITICAL PATH WITH BLUE ARROWS

Show Milwaukee Paper's critical path and find the project completion time.

APPROACH ▶ We use Table 3.3 and Overlay 3 of Figure 3.10. Overlay 3 of Figure 3.10 indicates that the total project completion time of 15 weeks corresponds to the longest path in the network. That path is Start-A-C-E-G-H in network form. It is shown with thick blue arrows.

INSIGHT ▶ The critical path follows the activities with slack = 0. This is considered the longest path through the network.

LEARNING EXERCISE ▶ Why are activities B, D, and F not on the path with the thick blue line? [Answer: They are not critical and have slack values of 1, 1, and 6 weeks, respectively.]

RELATED PROBLEMS ▶ 3.5–3.11, 3.16, 3.19b, 3.21a

Total Slack Time Look again at the project network in Overlay 3 of Figure 3.10. Consider activities B and D, which have slack of 1 week each. Does it mean that we can delay *each* activity by 1 week, and still complete the project in 15 weeks? The answer is no.

Let's assume that activity B is delayed by 1 week. It has used up its slack of 1 week and now has an EF of 4. This implies that activity D now has an ES of 4 and an EF of 8. Note that these are also its LS and LF values, respectively. That is, activity D also has no slack time now. Essentially, the slack of 1 week that activities B and D had is, for that path, *shared* between them. Delaying either activity by 1 week causes not only that activity, but also the other activity, to lose its slack. This type of a slack time is referred to as *total slack*. Typically, when two or more noncritical activities appear successively in a path, they share total slack.

To plan, monitor, and control the huge number of details involved in sponsoring a rock festival attended by more than 100,000 fans, managers use Microsoft Project and the tools discussed in this chapter. The *Video Case Study* "Managing Hard Rock's Rockfest," at the end of the chapter, provides more details of the management task.

Tim Coggin/Alamy

Variability in Activity Times

In identifying all earliest and latest times so far, and the associated critical path(s), we have adopted the CPM approach of assuming that all activity times are known and fixed constants. That is, there is no variability in activity times. However, in practice, it is likely that activity completion times vary depending on various factors.

For example, building internal components (activity A) for Milwaukee Paper Manufacturing is estimated to finish in 2 weeks. Clearly, supply-chain issues such as late arrival of materials, absence of key personnel, and so on could delay this activity. Suppose activity A actually ends up taking 3 weeks. Because A is on the critical path, the entire project will now be delayed by 1 week to 16 weeks. If we had anticipated completion of this project in 15 weeks, we would obviously miss our Earth Day deadline.

Although some activities may be relatively less prone to delays, others could be extremely susceptible to delays. For example, activity B (modify roof and floor) could be heavily dependent on weather conditions. A spell of bad weather could significantly affect its completion time.

This means that we cannot ignore the impact of variability in activity times when deciding the schedule for a project. PERT addresses this issue.

Three Time Estimates in PERT

In PERT, we employ a probability distribution based on three time estimates for each activity, as follows:

Optimistic time (a) = time an activity will take if everything goes as planned. In estimating this value, there should be only a small probability (say, 1/100) that the activity time will be $< a$.

Pessimistic time (b) = time an activity will take assuming very unfavorable conditions. In estimating this value, there should also be only a small probability (also 1/100) that the activity time will be $> b$.

Most likely time (m) = most realistic estimate of the time required to complete an activity.

When using PERT, we often assume that activity time estimates follow the beta probability distribution (see Figure 3.11). This continuous distribution is often appropriate for determining the expected value and variance for activity completion times.

⚠ STUDENT TIP

PERT's ability to handle three time estimates for each activity enables us to compute the probability that we can complete the project by a target date.

Optimistic time
The "best" activity completion time that could be obtained in a PERT network.

Pessimistic time
The "worst" activity time that could be expected in a PERT network.

Most likely time
The most probable time to complete an activity in a PERT network.

Figure **3.11**

Beta Probability Distribution with Three Time Estimates

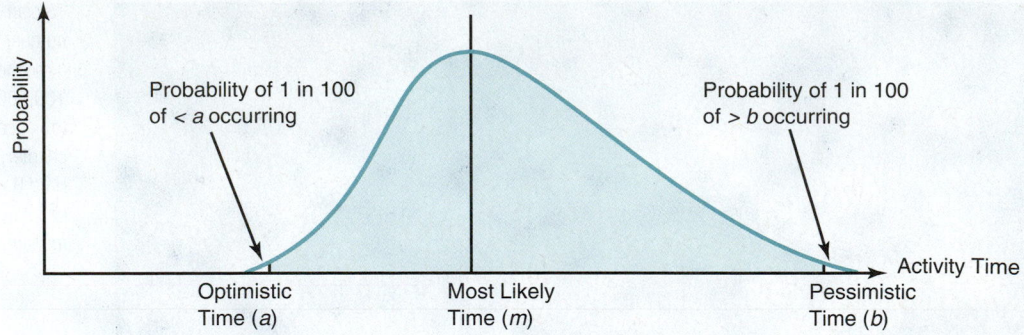

To find the *expected activity time, t*, the beta distribution weights the three time estimates as follows:

$$t = (a + 4m + b)/6 \tag{3-6}$$

That is, the most likely time (*m*) is given four times the weight as the optimistic time (*a*) and pessimistic time (*b*). The time estimate *t* computed using Equation (3-6) for each activity is used in the project network to compute all earliest and latest times.

To compute the *dispersion* or *variance of activity completion time*, we use the formula:[1]

$$\text{Variance} = [(b - a)/6]^2 \tag{3-7}$$

Example 8

EXPECTED TIMES AND VARIANCES FOR MILWAUKEE PAPER

Julie Ann Williams and the project management team at Milwaukee Paper want an expected time and variance for Activity F (Installing the Pollution Control System) where:

$$a = 1 \text{ week}, m = 2 \text{ weeks}, b = 9 \text{ weeks}$$

APPROACH ▶   Use Equations (3–6) and (3–7) to compute the expected time and variance for F.

SOLUTION ▶   The expected time for Activity F is:

$$t = \frac{a + 4m + b}{6} = \frac{1 + 4(2) + 9}{6} = \frac{18}{6} = 3 \text{ weeks}$$

LO 3.5 *Calculate* the variance of activity times

The variance for Activity F is:

$$\text{Variance} = \left[\frac{(b - a)}{6}\right]^2 = \left[\frac{(9 - 1)}{6}\right]^2 = \left(\frac{8}{6}\right)^2 = \frac{64}{36} = 1.78$$

INSIGHT ▶   Williams now has information that allows her to understand and manage Activity F. The expected time is, in fact, the activity time used in our earlier computation and identification of the critical path.

LEARNING EXERCISE ▶   Review the expected times and variances for all of the other activities in the project. These are shown in Table 3.4.

STUDENT TIP ◗

Can you see why the variance is higher in some activities than in others? Note the spread between the optimistic and pessimistic times.

TABLE 3.4	Time Estimates (in weeks) for Milwaukee Paper's Project				
ACTIVITY	**OPTIMISTIC** a	**MOST LIKELY** m	**PESSIMISTIC** b	**EXPECTED TIME** $t = (a + 4m + b)/6$	**VARIANCE** $[(b - a)/6]^2$
A	1	2	3	2	$[(3 - 1)/6]^2 = 4/36 = .11$
B	2	3	4	3	$[(4 - 2)/6]^2 = 4/36 = .11$
C	1	2	3	2	$[(3 - 1)/6]^2 = 4/36 = .11$
D	2	4	6	4	$[(6 - 2)/6]^2 = 16/36 = .44$
E	1	4	7	4	$[(7 - 1)/6]^2 = 36/36 = 1.00$
F	1	2	9	3	$[(9 - 1)/6]^2 = 64/36 = 1.78$
G	3	4	11	5	$[(11 - 3)/6]^2 = 64/36 = 1.78$
H	1	2	3	2	$[(3 - 1)/6]^2 = 4/36 = .11$

RELATED PROBLEMS ▶   3.17a, b, 3.18, 3.19a, 3.20a (3.26b, 3.27 are available in MyOMLab)

EXCEL OM Data File **Ch03Ex8.xls** can be found in MyOMLab.

Kim Hong-Ji/Reuters

Here we see a ship being built at the Hyundai shipyard, Asia's largest shipbuilder, in Korea. Managing this project uses the same techniques as managing the remodeling of a store, installing a new production line, or implementing a new computer system.

Probability of Project Completion

The critical path analysis helped us determine that Milwaukee Paper's expected project completion time is 15 weeks. Julie Ann Williams knows, however, that there is significant variation in the time estimates for several activities. Variation in activities that are on the critical path can affect the overall project completion time—possibly delaying it. This is one occurrence that worries the plant manager considerably.

PERT uses the variance of critical path activities to help determine the variance of the overall project. Project variance is computed by summing variances of *critical* activities:

$$\sigma_p^2 = \text{Project variance} = \Sigma(\text{variances of activities on critical path}) \qquad (3\text{-}8)$$

Example 9

COMPUTING PROJECT VARIANCE AND STANDARD DEVIATION FOR MILWAUKEE PAPER

Milwaukee Paper's managers now wish to know the project's variance and standard deviation.

APPROACH ▶   Because the activities are independent, we can add the variances of the activities on the critical path and then take the square root to determine the project's standard deviation.

SOLUTION ▶   From Example 8 (Table 3.4), we have the variances of all of the activities on the critical path. Specifically, we know that the variance of activity A is 0.11, variance of activity C is 0.11, variance of activity E is 1.00, variance of activity G is 1.78, and variance of activity H is 0.11.

Compute the total project variance and project standard deviation:

$$\text{Project variance}(\sigma_p^2) = 0.11 + 0.11 + 1.00 + 1.78 + 0.11 = 3.11$$

which implies:

$$\text{Project standard deviation}(\sigma_p) = \sqrt{\text{Project variance}} = \sqrt{3.11} = 1.76 \text{ weeks}$$

INSIGHT ▶   Management now has an estimate not only of expected completion time for the project but also of the standard deviation of that estimate.

LEARNING EXERCISE ▶   If the variance for activity A is actually 0.30 (instead of 0.11), what is the new project standard deviation? [Answer: 1.817.]

RELATED PROBLEMS ▶   3.17e (3.24 is available in MyOMLab)

Figure **3.12**

Probability Distribution for Project Completion Times at Milwaukee Paper

Standard Deviation = 1.76 Weeks

15 Weeks

(Expected Completion Time)

How can this information be used to help answer questions regarding the probability of finishing the project on time? PERT makes two more assumptions: (1) total project completion times follow a normal probability distribution, and (2) activity times are statistically independent. With these assumptions, the bell-shaped normal curve shown in Figure 3.12 can be used to represent project completion dates. This normal curve implies that there is a 50% chance that the manufacturer's project completion time will be less than 15 weeks and a 50% chance that it will exceed 15 weeks.

Example 10

PROBABILITY OF COMPLETING A PROJECT ON TIME

Julie Ann Williams would like to find the probability that her project will be finished on or before the 16-week Earth Day deadline.

APPROACH ▶ To do so, she needs to determine the appropriate area under the normal curve. This is the area to the left of the 16th week.

SOLUTION ▶ The standard normal equation can be applied as follows:

$$Z = (\text{Due date} - \text{Expected date of completion})/\sigma_p$$
$$= (16 \text{ weeks} - 15 \text{ weeks})/1.76 \text{ weeks} = 0.57 \qquad (3\text{-}9)$$

where Z is the number of standard deviations the due date or target date lies from the mean or expected date.

Referring to the Normal Table in Appendix I (alternatively using the Excel formula =NORMSDIST(0.57)), we find a Z-value of 0.57 to the right of the mean indicates a probability of 0.7157. Thus, there is a 71.57% chance that the pollution control equipment can be put in place in 16 weeks or less. This is shown in Figure 3.13.

STUDENT TIP ◆

Here is a chance to review your statistical skills and use of a normal distribution table (Appendix I).

Figure **3.13**

Probability That Milwaukee Paper Will Meet the 16-Week Deadline

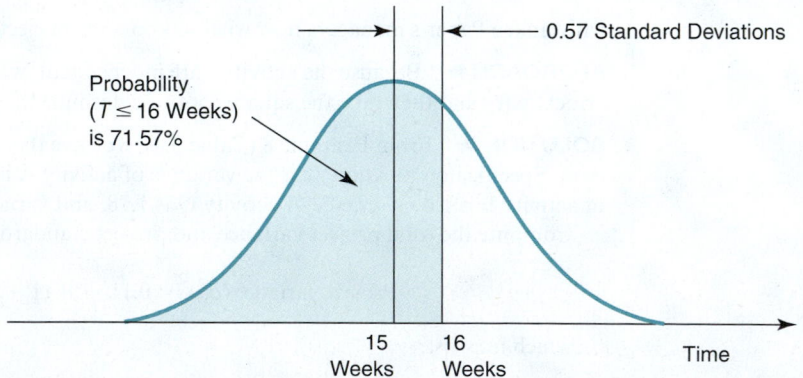

0.57 Standard Deviations

Probability
($T \leq 16$ Weeks)
is 71.57%

15 Weeks   16 Weeks   Time

INSIGHT ▶ The shaded area to the left of the 16th week (71.57%) represents the probability that the project will be completed in less than 16 weeks.

LEARNING EXERCISE ▶ What is the probability that the project will be completed on or before the 17th week? [Answer: About 87.2%.]

RELATED PROBLEMS ▶ 3.17f, 3.19d, 3.20d, 3.21b, 3.23 (3.25, 3.26e,f,g are available in MyOMLab)

Determining Project Completion Time for a Given Confidence Level   Let's say Julie Ann Williams is worried that there is only a 71.57% chance that the pollution control equipment can be put in place in 16 weeks or less. She thinks that it may be possible to plead with the board of directors for more time. However, before she approaches the board, she wants to arm herself with sufficient information about the project. Specifically, she wants to find the deadline by which she has a 99% chance of completing the project. She hopes to use her analysis to convince the board to agree to this extended deadline, even though she is aware of the public relations damage the delay will cause.

Clearly, this due date would be greater than 16 weeks. However, what is the exact value of this new due date? To answer this question, we again use the assumption that Milwaukee Paper's project completion time follows a normal probability distribution with a mean of 15 weeks and a standard deviation of 1.76 weeks.

Example 11

COMPUTING PROBABILITY FOR ANY COMPLETION DATE

Julie Ann Williams wants to find the due date that gives her company's project a 99% chance of *on-time* completion.

APPROACH ▶   She first needs to compute the Z-value corresponding to 99%, as shown in Figure 3.14. Mathematically, this is similar to Example 10, except the unknown is now the due date rather than Z.

Figure 3.14

Z-Value for 99% Probability of Project Completion at Milwaukee Paper

SOLUTION ▶   Referring again to the Normal Table in Appendix I (alternatively using the Excel formula =NORMSINV(0.99)), we identify a Z-value of 2.33 as being closest to the probability of 0.99. That is, Julie Ann Williams's due date should be 2.33 standard deviations above the mean project completion time. Starting with the standard normal equation [see Equation (3-9)], we can solve for the due date and rewrite the equation as:

$$\text{Due date} = \text{Expected completion time} + (Z \times \sigma_p)$$
$$= 15 + (2.33 \times 1.76) = 19.1 \text{ weeks} \tag{3-10}$$

INSIGHT ▶   If Williams can get the board to agree to give her a new deadline of 19.1 weeks (or more), she can be 99% sure of finishing the project by that new target date.

LEARNING EXERCISE ▶   What due date gives the project a 95% chance of on-time completion? [Answer: About 17.9 weeks.]

RELATED PROBLEMS ▶   3.21c, 3.23e

Variability in Completion Time of Noncritical Paths   In our discussion so far, we have focused exclusively on the variability in the completion times of activities on the critical path. This seems logical because these activities are, by definition, the more important activities in a project network. However, when there is variability in activity times, it is important that we also investigate the variability in the completion times of activities on *noncritical* paths.

Consider, for example, activity D in Milwaukee Paper's project. Recall from Overlay 3 in Figure 3.10 (in Example 7) that this is a noncritical activity, with a slack time of 1 week. We have therefore not considered the variability in D's time in computing the probabilities of project completion times. We observe, however, that D has a variance of 0.44 (see Table 3.4 in

Example 8). In fact, the pessimistic completion time for D is 6 weeks. This means that if D ends up taking its pessimistic time to finish, the project will not finish in 15 weeks, even though D is not a critical activity.

For this reason, when we find probabilities of project completion times, it may be necessary for us to not focus only on the critical path(s). Indeed, some research has suggested that expending project resources to reduce the variability of activities not on the critical path can be an effective element in project management. We may need also to compute these probabilities for noncritical paths, especially those that have relatively large variances. It is possible for a noncritical path to have a smaller probability of completion within a due date, when compared with the critical path. Determining the variance and probability of completion for a noncritical path is done in the same manner as Examples 9 and 10.

What Project Management Has Provided So Far Project management techniques have thus far been able to provide Julie Ann Williams with several valuable pieces of management information:

1. The project's expected completion date is 15 weeks.
2. There is a 71.57% chance that the equipment will be in place within the 16-week deadline. PERT analysis can easily find the probability of finishing by any date Williams is interested in.
3. Five activities (A, C, E, G, and H) are on the critical path. If any one of these is delayed for any reason, the entire project will be delayed.
4. Three activities (B, D, F) are not critical and have some slack time built in. This means that Williams can borrow from their resources, and, if necessary, she may be able to speed up the whole project.
5. A detailed schedule of activity starting and ending dates, slack, and critical path activities has been made available (see Table 3.3 in Example 6).

Cost-Time Trade-Offs and Project Crashing

While managing a project, it is not uncommon for a project manager to be faced with either (or both) of the following situations: (1) the project is behind schedule, and (2) the scheduled project completion time has been moved forward. In either situation, some or all of the remaining activities need to be speeded up (usually by adding resources) to finish the project by the desired due date. The process by which we shorten the duration of a project in the cheapest manner possible is called project crashing.

Crashing

Shortening activity time in a network to reduce time on the critical path so total completion time is reduced.

CPM is a technique in which each activity has a *normal* or *standard* time that we use in our computations. Associated with this normal time is the *normal* cost of the activity. However, another time in project management is the *crash time*, which is defined as the shortest duration required to complete an activity. Associated with this crash time is the *crash cost* of the activity. Usually, we can shorten an activity by adding extra resources (e.g., equipment, people) to it. Hence, it is logical for the crash cost of an activity to be higher than its normal cost.

The amount by which an activity can be shortened (i.e., the difference between its normal time and crash time) depends on the activity in question. We may not be able to shorten some activities at all. For example, if a casting needs to be heat-treated in the furnace for 48 hours, adding more resources does not help shorten the time. In contrast, we may be able to shorten some activities significantly (e.g., frame a house in 3 days instead of 10 days by using three times as many workers).

Likewise, the cost of crashing (or shortening) an activity depends on the nature of the activity. Managers are usually interested in speeding up a project at the least additional cost. Hence, when choosing which activities to crash, and by how much, we need to ensure the following:

- The amount by which an activity is crashed is, in fact, permissible
- Taken together, the shortened activity durations will enable us to finish the project by the due date
- The total cost of crashing is as small as possible

Crashing a project involves four steps:

LO 3.6 *Crash* a project

STEP 1: Compute the crash cost per week (or other time period) for each activity in the network. If crash costs are linear over time, the following formula can be used:

$$\text{Crash cost per period} = \frac{(\text{Crash cost} - \text{Normal cost})}{(\text{Normal time} - \text{Crash time})} \qquad (3\text{-}11)$$

STEP 2: Using the current activity times, find the critical path(s) in the project network. Identify the critical activities.

STEP 3: If there is only one critical path, then select the activity on this critical path that (a) can still be crashed and (b) has the smallest crash cost per period. Crash this activity by one period.

If there is more than one critical path, then select one activity from each critical path such that (a) each selected activity can still be crashed and (b) the total crash cost per period of *all* selected activities is the smallest. Crash each activity by one period. Note that the same activity may be common to more than one critical path.

STEP 4: Update all activity times. If the desired due date has been reached, stop. If not, return to Step 2.

We illustrate project crashing in Example 12.

Example 12

PROJECT CRASHING TO MEET A DEADLINE AT MILWAUKEE PAPER

Suppose the plant manager at Milwaukee Paper Manufacturing has been given only 13 weeks (instead of 16 weeks) to install the new pollution control equipment. As you recall, the length of Julie Ann Williams's critical path was 15 weeks, but she must now complete the project in 13 weeks.

APPROACH ▶ Williams needs to determine which activities to crash, and by how much, to meet this 13-week due date. Naturally, Williams is interested in speeding up the project by 2 weeks, at the least additional cost.

SOLUTION ▶ The company's normal and crash times, and normal and crash costs, are shown in Table 3.5. Note, for example, that activity B's normal time is 3 weeks (the estimate used in computing the critical path), and its crash time is 1 week. This means that activity B can be shortened by up to 2 weeks if extra resources are provided. The cost of these additional resources is $4,000 (= difference between the crash cost of $34,000 and the normal cost of $30,000). If we assume that the crashing cost is linear over time (i.e., the cost is the same each week), activity B's crash cost per week is $2,000 (= $4,000/2).

TABLE 3.5	Normal and Crash Data for Milwaukee Paper Manufacturing					
	TIME (WEEKS)		**COST ($)**		**CRASH COST PER WEEK ($)**	**CRITICAL PATH?**
ACTIVITY	**NORMAL**	**CRASH**	**NORMAL**	**CRASH**		
A	2	1	22,000	22,750	750	Yes
B	3	1	30,000	34,000	2,000	No
C	2	1	26,000	27,000	1,000	Yes
D	4	3	48,000	49,000	1,000	No
E	4	2	56,000	58,000	1,000	Yes
F	3	2	30,000	30,500	500	No
G	5	2	80,000	84,500	1,500	Yes
H	2	1	16,000	19,000	3,000	Yes

This calculation for Activity B is shown in Figure 3.15. Crash costs for all other activities can be computed in a similar fashion.

Figure **3.15**

**Crash and Normal Times and
Costs for Activity B**

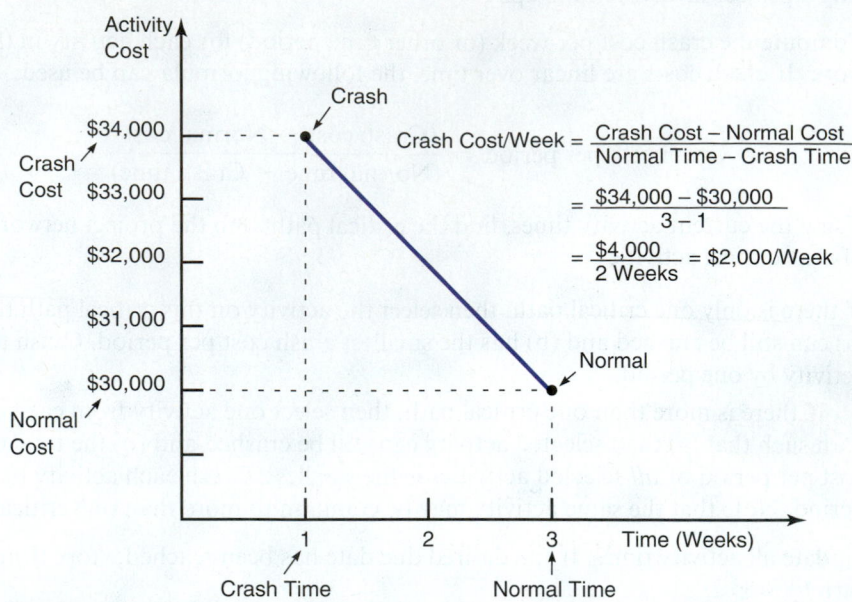

Figure **3.15**

**Crash and Normal Times and
Costs for Activity B**

Steps 2, 3, and 4 can now be applied to reduce Milwaukee Paper's project completion time at a minimum cost. We show the project network for Milwaukee Paper again in Figure 3.16.

Figure **3.16**

**Critical Path and Slack Times
for Milwaukee Paper**

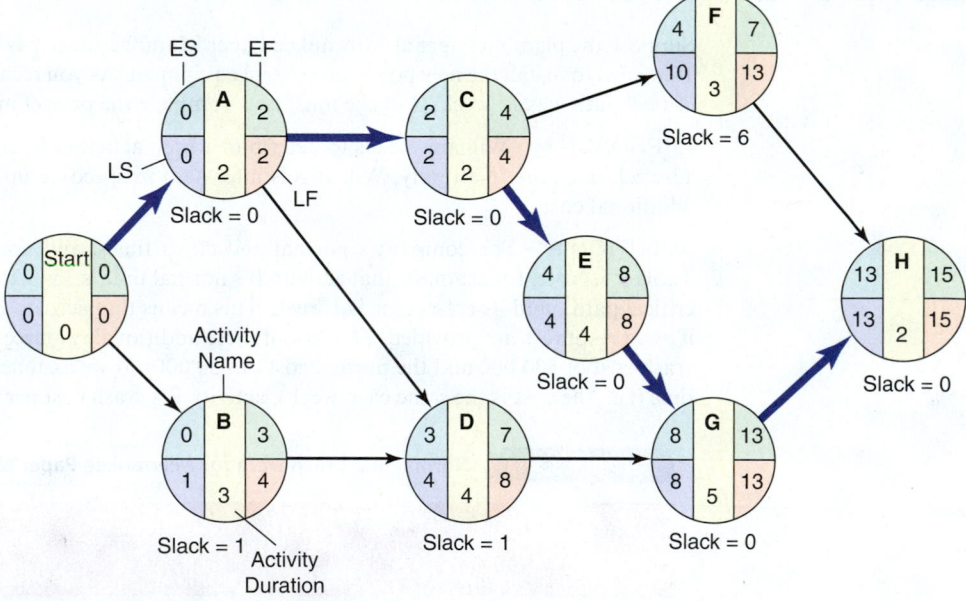

The current critical path (using normal times) is Start–A–C–E–G–H, in which Start is just a dummy starting activity. Of these critical activities, activity A has the lowest crash cost per week of $750. Julie Ann Williams should therefore crash activity A by 1 week to reduce the project completion time to 14 weeks. The cost is an additional $750. Note that activity A cannot be crashed any further, since it has reached its crash limit of 1 week.

At this stage, the original path Start–A–C–E–G–H remains critical with a completion time of 14 weeks. However, a new path Start–B–D–G–H is also critical now, with a completion time of 14 weeks. Hence, any further crashing must be done to both critical paths.

On each of these critical paths, we need to identify one activity that can still be crashed. We also want the total cost of crashing an activity on each path to be the smallest. We might be tempted to simply pick the activities with the smallest crash cost per period in each path. If we did this, we would select activity C from the first path and activity D from the second path. The total crash cost would then be $2,000 (= $1,000 + $1,000).

But we spot that activity G is common to both paths. That is, by crashing activity G, we will simultaneously reduce the completion time of both paths. Even though the $1,500 crash cost for activity G is higher than that for activities C and D, we would still prefer crashing G because the total crashing cost will now be only $1,500 (compared with the $2,000 if we crash C and D).

INSIGHT ▶ To crash the project down to 13 weeks, Williams should crash activity A by 1 week and activity G by 1 week. The total additional cost will be $2,250 (= $750 + $1,500). This is important because many contracts for projects include bonuses or penalties for early or late finishes.

LEARNING EXERCISE ▶ Say the crash cost for activity B is $31,000 instead of $34,000. How does this change the answer? [Answer: no change.]

RELATED PROBLEMS ▶ 3.28–3.32 (3.33 is available in MyOMLab)

EXCEL **OM** Data File **Ch03Ex12.xls** can be found in MyOMLab.

A Critique of PERT and CPM

As a critique of our discussions of PERT, here are some of its features about which operations managers need to be aware:

Advantages

1. Especially useful when scheduling and controlling large projects.
2. Straightforward concept and not mathematically complex.
3. Graphical networks help highlight relationships among project activities.
4. Critical path and slack time analyses help pinpoint activities that need to be closely watched.
5. Project documentation and graphs point out who is responsible for various activities.
6. Applicable to a wide variety of projects.
7. Useful in monitoring not only schedules but costs as well.

OM in Action   Behind the Tour de France

The large behind-the-scenes operations that support a football World Cup or Formula One racing team are well-known, but a Tour de France team also needs major support. "A Tour de France team is like a large traveling circus," says the coach of the Belkin team. "The public only sees the riders, but they could not function without the unseen support staff." The base to the team's cycling pyramid includes everything from osteopaths to mechanics, from logistics staff to PR people. Their project management skills require substantial know-how, as well as the ability to guarantee that riders are in peak physical, nutritional, and psychological condition. This can mean deciding which snack bars to give the cyclists before, during, and after race stages, while ensuring there are scientifically based cooling regimens in place for the riders. The team's huge truck, coach, three vans, and five cars resemble the sort of traveling convoy more associated with an international music act. Here are just some of the supplies the project management team for Belkin handles:

- 11 mattresses
- 36 aero suits, 45 bib shorts, 54 race jerseys, 250 podium caps
- 63 bikes
- 140 wheels, 220 tires
- 250 feeding bags, 3,000 water bottles
- 2,190 nutrition gels, 3,800 nutrition bars

Marc Pagani Photography/Shutterstock

- 10 jars of peanut butter, 10 boxes of chocolate sprinkles, 20 bags of wine gums, 20 jars of jam
- 80 kg of nuts, raisins, apricots, and figs, plus 50 kg of cereals

The project management behind a world-tour team is complex: These top teams often compete in two to three races simultaneously, in different countries and sometimes on different continents. Each team has 25–35 riders (9 compete in any single race), coming from different parts of the world, going to different races at different times, each with his own physique and strengths. They have customized bikes, uniforms, and food preferences. The support staff can include another 30 people.

Sources: BBC News (July 6, 2014) and *The Operations Room* (June 24, 2013).

Limitations

1. Project activities have to be clearly defined, independent, and stable in their relationships.
2. Precedence relationships must be specified and networked together.
3. Time estimates tend to be subjective and are subject to fudging by managers who fear the dangers of being overly optimistic or not pessimistic enough.
4. There is the inherent danger of placing too much emphasis on the longest, or critical, path. Near-critical paths need to be monitored closely as well.

Using Microsoft Project to Manage Projects

Milwaukee Paper Co. Activities		
ACTIVITY	**TIME (WKS)**	**PREDE-CESSORS**
A	2	—
B	3	—
C	2	A
D	4	A, B
E	4	C
F	3	C
G	5	D, E
H	2	F, G

The approaches discussed so far are effective for managing small projects. However, for large or complex projects, specialized project management software is much preferred. In this section, we provide a brief introduction to the most popular example of such specialized software, Microsoft Project. A time-limited version of Microsoft Project may be requested with this text.

Microsoft Project is extremely useful in drawing project networks, identifying the project schedule, and managing project costs and other resources.

Entering Data   Let us again consider the Milwaukee Paper Manufacturing project. Recall that this project has eight activities (repeated in the margin). The first step is to define the activities and their precedence relationships. To do so, we select **File|New** to open a blank project. We type the project start date (as July 1), then enter all activity information (see Program 3.1). For each activity (or task, as Microsoft Project calls it), we fill in the name and duration. The description of the activity is also placed in the *Task Name* column in Program 3.1. As we enter activities and durations, the software automatically inserts start and finish dates.

The next step is to define precedence relationships between these activities. To do so, we enter the relevant activity numbers (e.g., 1, 2) in the *Predecessors* column.

Viewing the Project Schedule   When all links have been defined, the complete project schedule can be viewed as a Gantt chart. We can also select **View|Network Diagram** to view the schedule as a project network (shown in Program 3.2). The critical path is shown in red on the

Click here to select different views.

View has been zoomed out to show weeks.

Gantt chart view.

Project will finish on Friday, 10/14.

Program **3.1**

Gantt Chart in Microsoft Project for Milwaukee Paper Manufacturing

Program **3.2**

Project Network in Microsoft Project for Milwaukee Paper Manufacturing

screen in the network diagram. We can click on any of the activities in the project network to view details of the activities. Likewise, we can easily add or remove activities from the project network. Each time we do so, Microsoft Project automatically updates all start dates, finish dates, and the critical path(s). If desired, we can manually change the layout of the network (e.g., reposition activities) by changing the options in **Format|Layout**.

Programs 3.1 and 3.2 show that if Milwaukee Paper's project starts July 1, it can be finished on October 14. The start and finish dates for all activities are also clearly identified. Project management software, we see, can greatly simplify the scheduling procedures discussed earlier in this chapter.

PERT Analysis Microsoft Project does not perform the PERT probability calculations discussed in Examples 10 and 11. However, by clicking **View|Toolbars|PERT Analysis**, we can get Microsoft Project to allow us to enter optimistic, most likely, and pessimistic times for each activity. We can then choose to view Gantt charts based on any of these three times for each activity.

Tracking the Time Status of a Project Perhaps the biggest advantage of using software to manage projects is that it can track the progress of the project. In this regard, Microsoft Project has many features available to track individual activities in terms of time, cost, resource usage, and so on.

An easy way to track the time progress of tasks is to enter the percent of work completed for each task. One way to do so is to double-click on any activity in the *Task Name* column in Program 3.1. A window is displayed that allows us to enter the percent of work completed for each task.

The table in the margin provides data regarding the percent of each of Milwaukee Paper's activities that are completed as of today. (Assume that today is Friday, August 12, i.e., the end of the sixth week of the project schedule.)

As shown in Program 3.3, the Gantt chart immediately reflects this updated information by drawing a thick line within each activity's bar. The length of this line is proportional to the percent of that activity's work that has been completed.

How do we know if we are on schedule? Notice that there is a vertical line shown on the Gantt chart corresponding to today's date. Microsoft Project will automatically move this line to correspond with the current date. If the project is on schedule, we should see all bars to the *left*

◆ **STUDENT TIP**

Now that you understand the workings of PERT and CPM, you are ready to master this useful program. Knowing such software gives you an edge over others in the job market.

Pollution Project Percentage Completed on Aug. 12	
ACTIVITY	**COMPLETED**
A	100
B	100
C	100
D	10
E	20
F	20
G	0
H	0

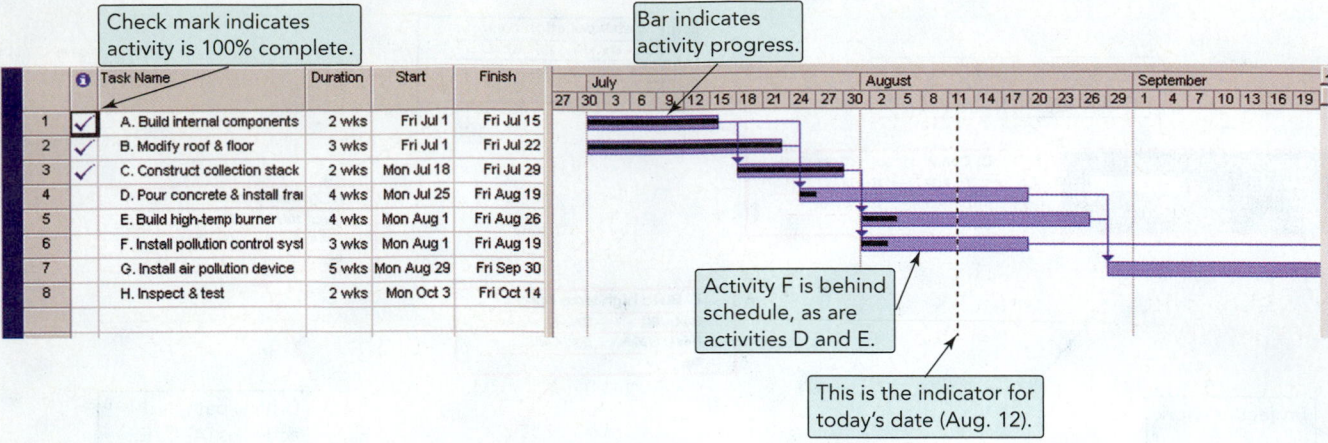

Program **3.3**

Tracking Project Progress in Microsoft Project

of today's line indicate that they have been completed. For example, Program 3.3 shows that activities A, B, and C are on schedule. In contrast, activities D, E, and F appear to be behind schedule. These activities need to be investigated further to determine the reason for the delay. This type of easy *visual* information is what makes such software so useful in practice for project management.

We encourage you to load the copy of Microsoft Project that may be ordered with your text and to create a project network for work you are currently doing.

Summary

PERT, CPM, and other scheduling techniques have proven to be valuable tools in controlling large and complex projects. Managers use such techniques to segment projects into discrete activities (work breakdown structures), indentifying specific resources and time requirements for each. With PERT and CPM, managers can understand the status of each activity, including its earliest start, latest start, earliest finish, and latest finish (ES, LS, EF, and LF) times. By controlling the trade-off between ES and LS, managers can identify the activities that have slack and can address resource allocation, perhaps by smoothing resources. Effective project management also allows managers to focus on the activities that are critical to timely project completion. By understanding the project's critical path, they know where crashing makes the most economic sense.

Good project management also allows firms to efficiently create products and services for global markets and to respond effectively to global competition. Microsoft Project, illustrated in this chapter, is one of a wide variety of software packages available to help managers handle network modeling problems.

The models described in this chapter require good management practices, detailed work breakdown structures, clear responsibilities assigned to activities, and straightforward and timely reporting systems. All are critical parts of project management.

Key Terms

Project organization (p. 62)
Work breakdown structure (WBS) (p. 64)
Gantt charts (p. 65)
Program evaluation and review technique (PERT) (p. 67)
Critical path method (CPM) (p. 67)

Critical path (p. 67)
Activity-on-node (AON) (p. 68)
Activity-on-arrow (AOA) (p. 68)
Dummy activity (p. 70)
Critical path analysis (p. 71)
Forward pass (p. 72)

Backward pass (p. 74)
Slack time (p. 75)
Optimistic time (p. 77)
Pessimistic time (p. 77)
Most likely time (p. 77)
Crashing (p. 82)

Ethical Dilemma

Two examples of massively mismanaged projects are TAURUS and the "Big Dig." The first, formally called the London Stock Exchange Automation Project, cost $575 million before it was finally abandoned. Although most IT projects have a reputation for cost overruns, delays, and underperformance, TAURUS set a new standard.

But even TAURUS paled next to the biggest, most expensive public works project in U.S. history—Boston's 15-year-long Central Artery/Tunnel Project. Called the Big Dig, this was perhaps the poorest and most felonious case of project mismanagement in decades. From a starting $2 billion budget to a final price tag of $15 billion, the Big Dig cost more than the Panama Canal, Hoover Dam, or Interstate 95, the 1,919-mile highway between Maine and Florida.

Read about one of these two projects (or another of your choice) and explain why it faced such problems. How and why do project managers allow such massive endeavors to fall into such a state? What do you think are the causes?

Discussion Questions

1. Give an example of a situation in which project management is needed.
2. Explain the purpose of project organization.
3. What are the three phases involved in the management of a large project?
4. What are some of the questions that can be answered with PERT and CPM?
5. Define *work breakdown structure*. How is it used?
6. What is the use of Gantt charts in project management?
7. What is the difference between an activity-on-arrow (AOA) network and an activity-on-node (AON) network? Which is primarily used in this chapter?
8. What is the significance of the critical path?
9. What would a project manager have to do to crash an activity?
10. Describe how expected activity times and variances can be computed in a PERT network.
11. Define *earliest start*, *earliest finish*, *latest finish*, and *latest start* times.
12. Students are sometimes confused by the concept of critical path, and want to believe that it is the *shortest* path through a network. Convincingly explain why this is not so.
13. What are dummy activities? Why are they used in activity-on-arrow (AOA) project networks?
14. What are the three time estimates used with PERT?
15. Would a project manager ever consider crashing a noncritical activity in a project network? Explain convincingly.
16. How is the variance of the total project computed in PERT?
17. Describe the meaning of slack, and discuss how it can be determined.
18. How can we determine the probability that a project will be completed by a certain date? What assumptions are made in this computation?
19. Name some of the widely used project management software programs.
20. What is the difference between the *waterfall* approach and *agile* project management?

Using Software to Solve Project Management Problems

In addition to the Microsoft Project software illustrated earlier, both Excel OM and POM for Windows are available to readers of this text as project management tools.

✗ USING EXCEL OM

Excel OM has a Project Scheduling module. Program 3.4 uses the data from the Milwaukee Paper Manufacturing example in this chapter (see Examples 4 and 5). The PERT/CPM analysis also handles activities with three time estimates.

P USING POM FOR WINDOWS

POM for Window's Project Scheduling module can also find the expected project completion time for a CPM and PERT network with either one or three time estimates. POM for Windows also performs project crashing. For further details refer to Appendix IV.

Program **3.4**

Excel OM's Use of Milwaukee Paper Manufacturing's Data from Examples 4 and 5

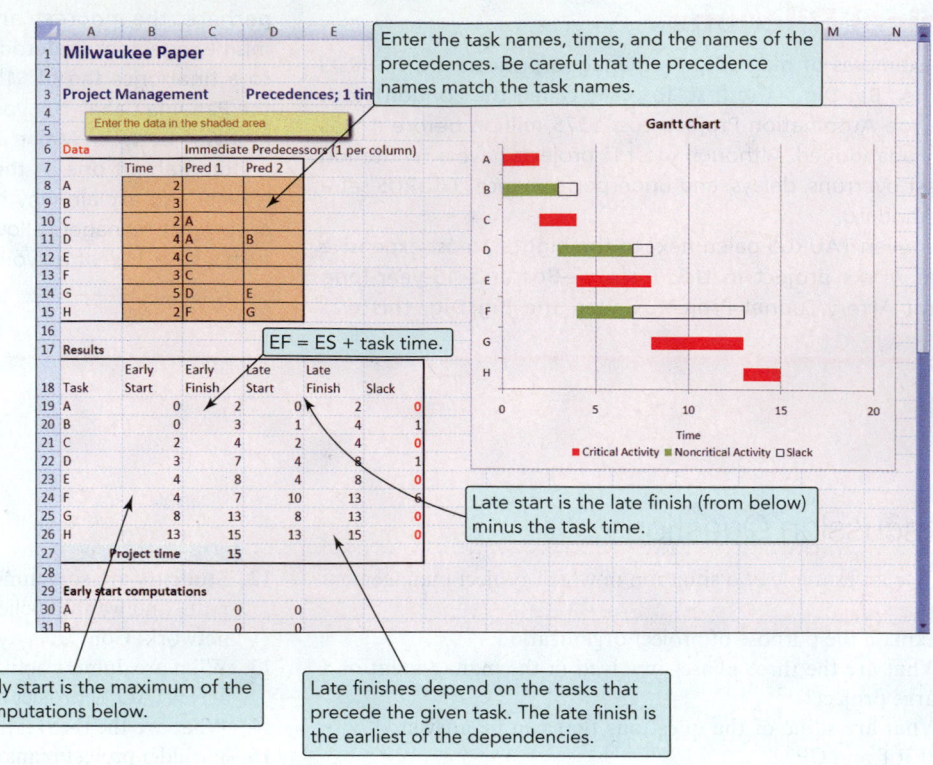

Enter the task names, times, and the names of the precedences. Be careful that the precedence names match the task names.

$EF = ES + \text{task time}$.

Late start is the late finish (from below) minus the task time.

Early start is the maximum of the computations below.

Late finishes depend on the tasks that precede the given task. The late finish is the earliest of the dependencies.

Solved Problems   Virtual Office Hours help is available in MyOMLab.

SOLVED PROBLEM 3.1

Construct an AON network based on the following:

ACTIVITY	IMMEDIATE PREDECESSOR(S)
A	—
B	—
C	—
D	A, B
E	C

SOLUTION

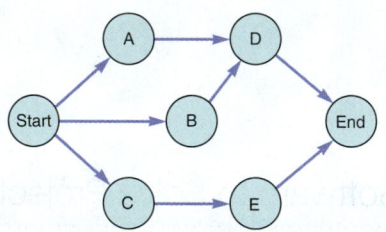

SOLVED PROBLEM 3.2

Insert a dummy activity and event to correct the following AOA network:

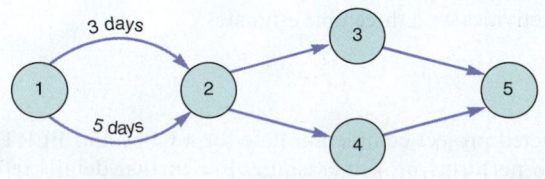

SOLUTION

Because we cannot have two activities starting and ending at the same node, we add the following dummy activity and dummy event to obtain the correct AOA network:

SOLVED PROBLEM 3.3

Calculate the critical path, project completion time T, and project variance σ_p^2, based on the following AON network information:

ACTIVITY	TIME	VARIANCE	ES	EF	LS	LF	SLACK
A	2	$\frac{2}{6}$	0	2	0	2	0
B	3	$\frac{2}{6}$	0	3	1	4	1
C	2	$\frac{4}{6}$	2	4	2	4	0
D	4	$\frac{4}{6}$	3	7	4	8	1
E	4	$\frac{2}{6}$	4	8	4	8	0
F	3	$\frac{1}{6}$	4	7	10	13	6
G	5	$\frac{1}{6}$	8	13	8	13	0

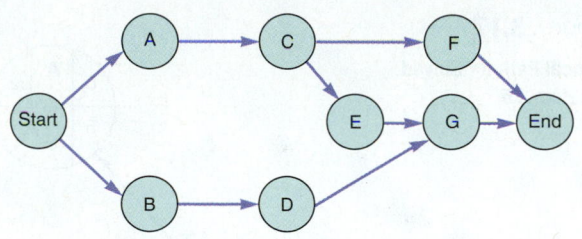

SOLUTION

We conclude that the critical path is Start–A–C–E–G–End:

$$\text{Total project time} = T = 2 + 2 + 4 + 5 = 13$$

and

$$\sigma_p^2 = \Sigma \text{ Variances on the critical path}$$

$$= \frac{2}{6} + \frac{4}{6} + \frac{2}{6} + \frac{1}{6} = \frac{9}{6} = 1.5$$

SOLVED PROBLEM 3.4

To complete the wing assembly for an experimental aircraft, Jim Gilbert has laid out the seven major activities involved. These activities have been labeled A through G in the following table, which also shows their estimated completion times (in weeks) and immediate predecessors. Determine the expected time and variance for each activity.

ACTIVITY	a	m	b	IMMEDIATE PREDECESSORS
A	1	2	3	—
B	2	3	4	—
C	4	5	6	A
D	8	9	10	B
E	2	5	8	C, D
F	4	5	6	D
G	1	2	3	E

SOLUTION

Expected times and variances can be computed using Equations (3–6) and (3–7) presented on page 78 in this chapter. The results are summarized in the following table:

ACTIVITY	EXPECTED TIME (IN WEEKS)	VARIANCE
A	2	$\frac{1}{9}$
B	3	$\frac{1}{9}$
C	5	$\frac{1}{9}$
D	9	$\frac{1}{9}$
E	5	1
F	5	$\frac{1}{9}$
G	2	$\frac{1}{9}$

SOLVED PROBLEM 3.5

Referring to Solved Problem 3.4, now Jim Gilbert would like to determine the critical path for the entire wing assembly project as well as the expected completion time for the total project. In addition, he would like to determine the earliest and latest start and finish times for all activities.

SOLUTION

The AON network for Gilbert's project is shown in Figure 3.17. Note that this project has multiple activities (A and B) with no immediate predecessors, and multiple activities (F and G) with no successors. Hence, in addition to a unique starting activity (Start), we have included a unique finishing activity (End) for the project.

Figure 3.17 shows the earliest and latest times for all activities. The results are also summarized in the following table:

ACTIVITY	ACTIVITY TIME				
	ES	EF	LS	LF	SLACK
A	0	2	5	7	5
B	0	3	0	3	0
C	2	7	7	12	5
D	3	12	3	12	0
E	12	17	12	17	0
F	12	17	14	19	2
G	17	19	17	19	0

Expected project length = 19 weeks
Variance of the critical path = 1.333
Standard deviation of the critical path = 1.155 weeks

The activities along the critical path are B, D, E, and G. These activities have zero slack as shown in the table.

Figure **3.17**

Critical Path for Solved Problem 3.5

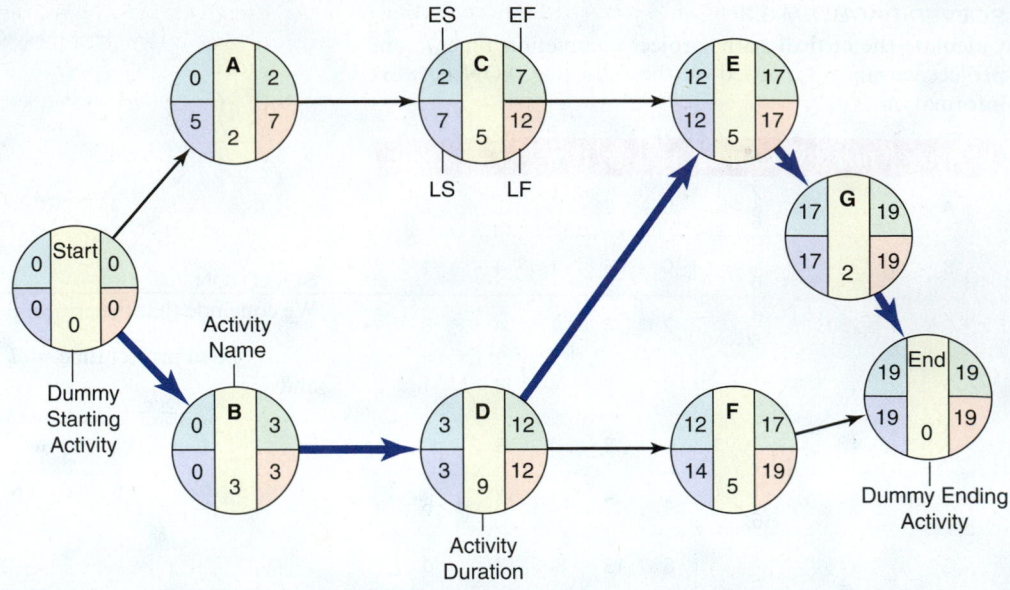

SOLVED PROBLEM 3.6

The following information has been computed from a project:

$$\text{Expected total project time} = T = 62 \text{ weeks}$$
$$\text{Project variance} (\sigma_p^2) = 81$$

What is the probability that the project will be completed 18 weeks *before* its expected completion date?

SOLUTION

The desired completion date is 18 weeks before the expected completion date, 62 weeks. The desired completion date is 44 (or 62–18) weeks:

$$\sigma_p = \sqrt{\text{Project variance}}$$

$$Z = \frac{\text{Due date} - \text{Expected completion date}}{\sigma_p}$$

$$= \frac{44 - 62}{9} = \frac{-18}{9} = -2.0$$

The normal curve appears as follows:

Because the normal curve is symmetrical and table values are calculated for positive values of Z, the area desired is equal to 1– (table value). For $Z = +2.0$ the area from the table is .97725. Thus, the area corresponding to a Z-value of −2.0 is .02275 (or 1 − .97725). Hence, the probability of completing the project 18 weeks before the expected completion date is approximately .023, or 2.3%.

SOLVED PROBLEM 3.7

Determine the least cost of reducing the project completion date by 3 months based on the following information:

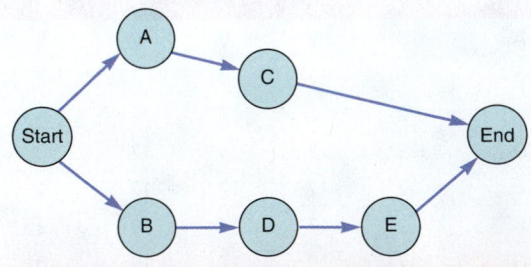

ACTIVITY	NORMAL TIME (MONTHS)	CRASH TIME (MONTHS)	NORMAL COST	CRASH COST
A	6	4	$2,000	$2,400
B	7	5	3,000	3,500
C	7	6	1,000	1,300
D	6	4	2,000	2,600
E	9	8	8,800	9,000

SOLUTION

The first step in this problem is to compute ES, EF, LS, LF, and slack for each activity.

ACTIVITY	ES	EF	LS	LF	SLACK
A	0	6	9	15	9
B	0	7	0	7	0
C	6	13	15	22	9
D	7	13	7	13	0
E	13	22	13	22	0

The critical path consists of activities B, D, and E.

Next, crash cost/month must be computed for each activity:

ACTIVITY	NORMAL TIME–CRASH TIME	CRASH COST– NORMAL COST	CRASH COST/ MONTH	CRITICAL PATH?
A	2	$400	$200/month	No
B	2	500	250/month	Yes
C	1	300	300/month	No
D	2	600	300/month	Yes
E	1	200	200/month	Yes

Finally, we will select that activity on the critical path with the smallest crash cost/month. This is activity E. Thus, we can reduce the total project completion date by 1 month for an

additional cost of $200. We still need to reduce the project completion date by 2 more months. This reduction can be achieved at least cost along the critical path by reducing activity B by 2 months for an additional cost of $500. Neither reduction has an effect on noncritical activities. This solution is summarized in the following table:

ACTIVITY	MONTHS REDUCED	COST
E	1	$200
B	2	500
		Total: $700

Problems

Note: **Px** means the problem may be solved with POM for Windows and/or Excel OM.

Problems 3.1–3.2 relate to Project Planning

• **3.1** The work breakdown structure (WBS) for building a house (levels 1 and 2) is shown below:

a) Add two level-3 activities to each of the level-2 activities to provide more detail to the WBS.
b) Select one of your level-3 activities and add two level-4 activities below it.

•• **3.2** James Lawson has decided to run for a seat as Congressman from the House of Representatives, District 34, in Florida. He views his 8-month campaign for office as a major project and wishes to create a work breakdown structure (WBS) to help control the detailed scheduling. So far, he has developed the following pieces of the WBS:

LEVEL	LEVEL ID NO.	ACTIVITY
1	1.0	Develop political campaign
2	1.1	Fund-raising plan
3	1.1.1	_____
3	1.1.2	_____
3	1.1.3	_____
2	1.2	Develop a position on major issues
3	1.2.1	_____
3	1.2.2	_____
3	1.2.3	_____
2	1.3	Staffing for campaign
3	1.3.1	_____
3	1.3.2	_____
3	1.3.3	_____
3	1.3.4	_____
2	1.4	Paperwork compliance for candidacy
3	1.4.1	_____
3	1.4.2	_____
2	1.5	Ethical plan/issues
3	1.5.1	_____

Help Lawson by providing details where the blank lines appear. Are there any other major (level-2) activities to create? If so, add an ID no. 1.6 and insert them.

Problem 3.3 relates to Project Scheduling

•• **3.3** The City Commission of Nashville has decided to build a botanical garden and picnic area in the heart of the city for the recreation of its citizens. The precedence table for all the activities required to construct this area successfully is given. Draw the Gantt chart for the whole construction activity.

CODE	ACTIVITY	DESCRIPTION	TIME (IN HOURS)	IMMEDIATE PREDECESSOR(S)
A	Planning	Find location; determine resource requirements	20	None
B	Purchasing	Requisition of lumber and sand	60	Planning
C	Excavation	Dig and grade	100	Planning
D	Sawing	Saw lumber into appropriate sizes	30	Purchasing
E	Placement	Position lumber in correct locations	20	Sawing, excavation
F	Assembly	Nail lumber together	10	Placement
G	Infill	Put sand in and under the equipment	20	Assembly
H	Outfill	Put dirt around the equipment	10	Assembly
I	Decoration	Put grass all over the garden, landscape, paint	30	Infill, outfill

Problems 3.4–3.14 relate to Project Management Techniques

•• **3.4** Refer to the table in Problem 3.3.
a) Draw the AON network for the construction activity.
b) Draw the AOA network for the construction activity.

• **3.5** Draw the activity-on-node (AON) project network associated with the following activities for Carl Betterton's construction project. How long should it take Carl and his team to complete this project? What are the critical path activities?

ACTIVITY	IMMEDIATE PREDECESSOR(S)	TIME (DAYS)
A	—	3
B	A	4
C	A	6
D	B	6
E	B	4
F	C	4
G	D	6
H	E, F	8

• **3.6** Given the activities whose sequence is described by the following table, draw the appropriate activity-on-arrow (AOA) network diagram.
a) Which activities are on the critical path?
b) What is the length of the critical path?

ACTIVITY	IMMEDIATE PREDECESSOR(S)	TIME (DAYS)
A	—	5
B	A	2
C	A	4
D	B	5
E	B	5
F	C	5
G	E, F	2
H	D	3
I	G, H	5

• **3.7** Using AOA, diagram the network described below for Lillian Fok's construction project. Calculate its critical path. How long is the minimum duration of this network?

ACTIVITY	NODES	TIME (WEEKS)	ACTIVITY	NODES	TIME (WEEKS)
J	1–2	10	N	3–4	2
K	1–3	8	O	4–5	7
L	2–4	6	P	3–5	5
M	2–3	3			

•• **3.8** Roger Ginde is developing a program in supply chain management certification for managers. Ginde has listed a number of activities that must be completed before a training program of this nature could be conducted. The activities, immediate predecessors, and times appear in the accompanying table:

ACTIVITY	IMMEDIATE PREDECESSOR(S)	TIME (DAYS)
A	—	2
B	—	5
C	—	1
D	B	10
E	A, D	3
F	C	6
G	E, F	8

a) Develop an AON network for this problem.
b) What is the critical path?
c) What is the total project completion time?
d) What is the slack time for each individual activity? **Px**

•• **3.9** Task time estimates for the modification of an assembly line at Jim Goodale's Carbondale, Illinois, factory are as follows:

ACTIVITY	TIME (IN HOURS)	IMMEDIATE PREDECESSORS
A	6.0	—
B	7.2	—
C	5.0	A
D	6.0	B, C
E	4.5	B, C
F	7.7	D
G	4.0	E, F

a) Draw the project network using AON.
b) Identify the critical path.
c) What is the expected project length?
d) Draw a Gantt chart for the project. **Px**

• **3.10** The activities described by the following table are given for the Howard Corporation in Kansas:

ACTIVITY	IMMEDIATE PREDECESSOR(S)	TIME
A	—	9
B	A	7
C	A	3
D	B	6
E	B	9
F	C	4
G	E, F	6
H	D	5
I	G, H	3

a) Draw the appropriate AON PERT diagram for J.C. Howard's management team.
b) Find the critical path.
c) What is the project completion time? **Px**

•• **3.11** The following is a table of activities associated with a project at Rafay Ishfaq's software firm in Chicago, their durations, and what activities each must precede:

ACTIVITY	DURATION (WEEKS)	PRECEDES
A (start)	1	B, C
B	1	E
C	4	F
E	2	F
F (end)	2	—

a) Draw an AON diagram of the project, including activity durations.
b) Define the critical path, listing all critical activities in chronological order.
c) What is the project duration (in weeks)?
d) What is the slack (in weeks) associated with any and all non-critical paths through the project?

• **3.12** The activities needed to build a prototype laser scanning machine at Dave Fletcher Corp. are listed in the following table. Construct an AON network for these activities.

ACTIVITY	IMMEDIATE PREDECESSOR(S)	ACTIVITY	IMMEDIATE PREDECESSOR(S)
A	—	E	B
B	—	F	B
C	A	G	C, E
D	A	H	D, F

Additional problems **3.13–3.14** are available in MyOMLab.

Problems 3.15–3.16 relate to Determining the Project Schedule

• **3.15** Dave Fletcher (see Problem 3.12) was able to determine the activity times for constructing his laser scanning machine. Fletcher would like to determine ES, EF, LS, LF, and slack for each activity. The total project completion time and the critical path should also be determined. Here are the activity times:

ACTIVITY	TIME (WEEKS)	ACTIVITY	TIME (WEEKS)
A	6	E	4
B	7	F	6
C	3	G	10
D	2	H	7

••• **3.16** The Rover 6 is a new custom-designed sports car. An analysis of the task of building the Rover 6 reveals the following list of relevant activities, their immediate predecessors, and their duration:[2]

JOB LETTER	DESCRIPTION	IMMEDIATE PREDECESSOR(S)	NORMAL TIME (DAYS)
A	Start	—	0
B	Design	A	8
C	Order special accessories	B	0.1
D	Build frame	B	1
E	Build doors	B	1
F	Attach axles, wheels, gas tank	D	1
G	Build body shell	B	2
H	Build transmission and drivetrain	B	3
I	Fit doors to body shell	G, E	1
J	Build engine	B	4
K	Bench-test engine	J	2
L	Assemble chassis	F, H, K	1
M	Road-test chassis	L	0.5
N	Paint body	I	2
O	Install wiring	N	1
P	Install interior	N	1.5
Q	Accept delivery of special accessories	C	5
R	Mount body and accessories on chassis	M, O, P, Q	1
S	Road test car	R	0.5
T	Attach exterior trim	S	1
U	Finish	T	0

a) Draw a network diagram for the project.
b) Mark the critical path and state its length.
c) If the Rover 6 had to be completed 2 days earlier, would it help to:
   i) Buy preassembled transmissions and drivetrains?
   ii) Install robots to halve engine-building time?
   iii) Speed delivery of special accessories by 3 days?
d) How might resources be borrowed from activities on the non-critical path to speed activities on the critical path? **Px**

• • • **3.17** Ross Hopkins, president of Hopkins Hospitality, has developed the tasks, durations, and predecessor relationships in the following table for building new motels. Draw the AON network and answer the questions that follow.

ACTIVITY	IMMEDIATE PREDECESSOR(S)	TIME ESTIMATES (IN WEEKS)		
		OPTIMISTIC	MOST LIKELY	PESSIMISTIC
A	—	4	8	10
B	A	2	8	24
C	A	8	12	16
D	A	4	6	10
E	B	1	2	3
F	E, C	6	8	20
G	E, C	2	3	4
H	F	2	2	2
I	F	6	6	6
J	D, G, H	4	6	12
K	I, J	2	2	3

a) What is the expected (estimated) time for activity C?
b) What is the variance for activity C?
c) Based on the calculation of estimated times, what is the critical path?
d) What is the estimated time of the critical path?
e) What is the activity variance along the critical path?
f) What is the probability of completion of the project before week 36? **Px**

• **3.18** A renovation of the gift shop at Orlando Amway Center has six activities (in hours). For the following estimates of *a*, *m*, and *b*, calculate the expected time and the standard deviation for each activity:

ACTIVITY	a	m	b
A	11	15	19
B	27	31	41
C	18	18	18
D	8	13	19
E	17	18	20
F	16	19	22	**Px**

• • **3.19** Kelle Carpet and Trim installs carpet in commercial offices. Peter Kelle has been very concerned with the amount of time it took to complete several recent jobs. Some of his workers are very unreliable. A list of activities and their optimistic completion time, the most likely completion time, and the pessimistic completion time (all in days) for a new contract are given in the following table:

ACTIVITY	TIME (DAYS)			IMMEDIATE PREDECESSOR(S)
	a	m	b	
A	3	6	8	—
B	2	4	4	—
C	1	2	3	—
D	6	7	8	C
E	2	4	6	B, D
F	6	10	14	A, E
G	1	2	4	A, E
H	3	6	9	F
I	10	11	12	G
J	14	16	20	C
K	2	8	10	H, I

a) Determine the expected completion time and variance for each activity.
b) Determine the total project completion time and the critical path for the project.
c) Determine ES, EF, LS, LF, and slack for each activity.
d) What is the probability that Kelle Carpet and Trim will finish the project in 40 days or less? **Px**

• • • **3.20** The estimated times and immediate predecessors for the activities in a project at George Kyparis's retinal scanning company are given in the following table. Assume that the activity times are independent.

ACTIVITY	IMMEDIATE PREDECESSOR	TIME (WEEKS)		
		a	m	b
A	—	9	10	11
B	—	4	10	16
C	A	9	10	11
D	B	5	8	11

jamstockfoto/Fotolia

a) Calculate the expected time and variance for each activity.
b) What is the expected completion time of the critical path? What is the expected completion time of the other path in the network?
c) What is the variance of the critical path? What is the variance of the other path in the network?
d) If the time to complete path A–C is normally distributed, what is the probability that this path will be finished in 22 weeks or less?
e) If the time to complete path B–D is normally distributed, what is the probability that this path will be finished in 22 weeks or less?
f) Explain why the probability that the *critical path* will be finished in 22 weeks or less is not necessarily the probability that the *project* will be finished in 22 weeks or less. **Px**

•••**3.21** Rich Cole Control Devices, Inc., produces custom-built relay devices for auto makers. The most recent project undertaken by Cole requires 14 different activities. Cole's managers would like to determine the total project completion time (in days) and those activities that lie along the critical path. The appropriate data are shown in the following table.

a) What is the probability of being done in 53 days?
b) What date results in a 99% probability of completion?

ACTIVITY	IMMEDIATE PREDECESSOR(S)	OPTIMISTIC TIME	MOST LIKELY TIME	PESSIMISTIC TIME
A	—	4	6	7
B	—	1	2	3
C	A	6	6	6
D	A	5	8	11
E	B, C	1	9	18
F	D	2	3	6
G	D	1	7	8
H	E, F	4	4	6
I	G, H	1	6	8
J	I	2	5	7
K	I	8	9	11
L	J	2	4	6
M	K	1	2	3
N	L, M	6	8	10

Px

•••**3.22** Four Squares Productions, a firm hired to coordinate the release of the movie *Pirates of the Caribbean: On Stranger Tides* (starring Johnny Depp), identified 16 activities to be completed before the release of the film.

a) How many weeks in advance of the film release should Four Squares have started its marketing campaign? What is the critical path? The tasks (in time units of weeks) are as follows:

ACTIVITY	IMMEDIATE PREDECESSOR(S)	OPTIMISTIC TIME	MOST LIKELY TIME	PESSIMISTIC TIME
A	—	1	2	4
B	—	3	3.5	4
C	—	10	12	13
D	—	4	5	7
E	—	2	4	5
F	A	6	7	8
G	B	2	4	5.5
H	C	5	7.7	9
I	C	9.9	10	12
J	C	2	4	5
K	D	2	4	6
L	E	2	4	6
M	F, G, H	5	6	6.5
N	J, K, L	1	1.1	2
O	I, M	5	7	8
P	N	5	7	9

b) What is the probability of completing the marketing campaign in the time (in weeks) noted in part a?
c) If activities I and J were not necessary, what impact would this have on the critical path and the number of weeks needed to complete the marketing campaign? **Px**

Tracy Whiteside/Shutterstock

••**3.23** Using PERT, Adam Munson was able to determine that the expected project completion time for the construction of a pleasure yacht is 21 months, and the project variance is 4.

a) What is the probability that the project will be completed in 17 months?
b) What is the probability that the project will be completed in 20 months?
c) What is the probability that the project will be completed in 23 months?
d) What is the probability that the project will be completed in 25 months?
e) What is the due date that yields a 95% chance of completion? **Px**

> *Additional problems* **3.24–3.27** *are available in* MyOMLab.

Problems 3.28–3.33 relate to Cost-Time Trade-Offs and Project Crashing

•• **3.28** Assume that the activities in Problem 3.11 have the following costs to shorten: A, $300/week; B, $100/week; C, $200/week; E, $100/week; and F, $400/week. Assume also that you can crash an activity down to 0 weeks in duration and that every week you can shorten the project is worth $250 to you. What activities would you crash? What is the total crashing cost?

••• **3.29** What is the minimum cost of crashing the following project that Roger Solano manages at Slippery Rock University by 4 days?

ACTIVITY	NORMAL TIME (DAYS)	CRASH TIME (DAYS)	NORMAL COST	CRASH COST	IMMEDIATE PREDECESSOR(S)
A	6	5	$ 900	$1,000	—
B	8	6	300	400	—
C	4	3	500	600	—
D	5	3	900	1,200	A
E	8	5	1,000	1,600	C

Px

•• **3.30** Three activities are candidates for crashing on a project network for a large computer installation (all are, of course, critical). Activity details are in the following table:

ACTIVITY	PREDE-CESSOR	NORMAL TIME	NORMAL COST	CRASH TIME	CRASH COST
A	—	7 days	$6,000	6 days	$6,600
B	A	4 days	1,200	2 days	3,000
C	B	11 days	4,000	9 days	6,000

a) What action would you take to reduce the critical path by 1 day?
b) Assuming no other paths become critical, what action would you take to reduce the critical path one additional day?
c) What is the total cost of the 2-day reduction? **Px**

••• **3.31** Development of Version 2.0 of a particular accounting software product is being considered by Jose Noguera's technology firm in Baton Rouge. The activities necessary for the completion of this project are listed in the following table:

ACTIVITY	NORMAL TIME (WEEKS)	CRASH TIME (WEEKS)	NORMAL COST	CRASH COST	IMMEDIATE PREDECESSOR(S)
A	4	3	$2,000	$2,600	—
B	2	1	2,200	2,800	—
C	3	3	500	500	—
D	8	4	2,300	2,600	A
E	6	3	900	1,200	B
F	3	2	3,000	4,200	C
G	4	2	1,400	2,000	D, E

a) What is the project completion date?
b) What is the total cost required for completing this project on normal time?
c) If you wish to reduce the time required to complete this project by 1 week, which activity should be crashed, and how much will this increase the total cost?
d) What is the maximum time that can be crashed? How much would costs increase? **Px**

••• **3.32** Kimpel Products makes pizza ovens for commercial use. James Kimpel, CEO, is contemplating producing smaller ovens for use in high school and college kitchens. The activities necessary to build an experimental model and related data are given in the following table:

ACTIVITY	NORMAL TIME (WEEKS)	CRASH TIME (WEEKS)	NORMAL COST ($)	CRASH COST ($)	IMMEDIATE PREDECESSOR(S)
A	3	2	1,000	1,600	—
B	2	1	2,000	2,700	—
C	1	1	300	300	—
D	7	3	1,300	1,600	A
E	6	3	850	1,000	B
F	2	1	4,000	5,000	C
G	4	2	1,500	2,000	D, E

a) What is the project completion date?
b) Crash this project to 10 weeks at the least cost.
c) Crash this project to 7 weeks (which is the maximum it can be crashed) at the least cost. **Px**

> *Additional problem* **3.33** *is available in* MyOMLab.

CASE STUDIES

Southwestern University: (A)*

Southwestern University (SWU), a large state college in Stephenville, Texas, 30 miles southwest of the Dallas/Fort Worth metroplex, enrolls close to 20,000 students. In a typical town–gown relationship, the school is a dominant force in the small city, with more students during fall and spring than permanent residents.

A longtime football powerhouse, SWU is a member of the Big Eleven conference and is usually in the top 20 in college football rankings. To bolster its chances of reaching the elusive and long-desired number-one ranking, in 2009, SWU hired the legendary Phil Flamm as its head coach.

*This integrated study runs throughout the text. Other issues facing Southwestern's football expansion include (B) forecasting game attendance (Chapter 4); (C) quality of facilities (Chapter 6); (D) break-even analysis for food services (Supplement 7); (E) location of the new stadium (Chapter 8); (F) inventory planning of football programs (Chapter 12); and (G) scheduling of campus security officers/staff for game days (Chapter 13).

| TABLE 3.6 | Southwestern University Project |

			TIME ESTIMATES (DAYS)			
ACTIVITY	DESCRIPTION	PREDECESSOR(S)	OPTIMISTIC	MOST LIKELY	PESSIMISTIC	CRASH COST/DAY
A	Bonding, insurance, tax structuring	—	20	30	40	$1,500
B	Foundation, concrete footings for boxes	A	20	65	80	3,500
C	Upgrading skybox stadium seating	A	50	60	100	4,000
D	Upgrading walkways, stairwells, elevators	C	30	50	100	1,900
E	Interior wiring, lathes	B	25	30	35	9,500
F	Inspection approvals	E	0.1	0.1	0.1	0
G	Plumbing	D, F	25	30	35	2,500
H	Painting	G	10	20	30	2,000
I	Hardware/AC/metal workings	H	20	25	60	2,000
J	Tile/carpet/windows	H	8	10	12	6,000
K	Inspection	J	0.1	0.1	0.1	0
L	Final detail work/cleanup	I, K	20	25	60	4,500

One of Flamm's demands on joining SWU had been a new stadium. With attendance increasing, SWU administrators began to face the issue head-on. After 6 months of study, much political arm wrestling, and some serious financial analysis, Dr. Joel Wisner, president of Southwestern University, had reached a decision to expand the capacity at its on-campus stadium.

Adding thousands of seats, including dozens of luxury skyboxes, would not please everyone. The influential Flamm had argued the need for a first-class stadium, one with built-in dormitory rooms for his players and a palatial office appropriate for the coach of a future NCAA champion team. But the decision was made, and *everyone*, including the coach, would learn to live with it.

The job now was to get construction going immediately after the 2015 season ended. This would allow exactly 270 days until the 2016 season opening game. The contractor, Hill Construction (Bob Hill being an alumnus, of course), signed his contract. Bob Hill looked at the tasks his engineers had outlined and looked President Wisner in the eye. "I guarantee the team will be able to take the field on schedule next year," he said with a sense of confidence. "I sure hope so," replied Wisner. "The contract penalty of $10,000 per day for running late is nothing compared to what Coach Flamm will do to you if our opening game with Penn State is delayed or canceled." Hill, sweating slightly, did not need to respond. In football-crazy Texas, Hill Construction would be *mud* if the 270-day target was missed.

Back in his office, Hill again reviewed the data (see Table 3.6) and noted that optimistic time estimates can be used as crash times. He then gathered his foremen. "Folks, if we're not 75% sure we'll finish this stadium in less than 270 days, I want this project crashed! Give me the cost figures for a target date of 250 days—also for 240 days. I want to be *early*, not just on time!"

Discussion Questions

1. Develop a network drawing for Hill Construction and determine the critical path. How long is the project expected to take?

2. What is the probability of finishing in 270 days?

3. If it is necessary to crash to 250 or 240 days, how would Hill do so, and at what costs? As noted in the case, assume that optimistic time estimates can be used as crash times.

Project Management at Arnold Palmer Hospital

Video Case

The equivalent of a new kindergarten class is born every day at Orlando's Arnold Palmer Hospital. With more than 13,000 births in the mid-2000s in a hospital that was designed 15 years earlier for a capacity of 6,500 births a year, the newborn intensive care unit was stretched to the limit. Moreover, with continuing strong population growth in central Florida, the hospital was often full. It was clear that new facilities were needed. After much analysis, forecasting, and discussion, the management team decided to build a new 273-bed building across the street from the existing hospital. But the facility had to be built in accordance with the hospital's Guiding Principles and its uniqueness as a health center dedicated to the specialized needs of women and infants. Those Guiding Principles are: *Family-centered focus, a healing environment where privacy and dignity are respected, sanctuary of caring that includes warm, serene surroundings with natural lighting, sincere and dedicated staff providing the highest quality care, and patient-centered flow and function.*

The vice president of business development, Karl Hodges, wanted a hospital that was designed from the inside out by the people who understood the Guiding Principles, who knew most about the current system, and who were going to use the new system, namely, the doctors and nurses. Hodges and his staff spent 13 months discussing expansion needs with this group, as well as with patients and the community, before developing a proposal

TABLE 3.7	Expansion Planning and Arnold Palmer Hospital Construction Activities and Times[a]	

ACTIVITY	SCHEDULED TIME	PRECEDENCE ACTIVITY(IES)
1. Proposal and review	1 month	—
2. Establish master schedule	2 weeks	1
3. Architect selection process	5 weeks	1
4. Survey whole campus and its needs	1 month	1
5. Conceptual architect's plans	6 weeks	3
6. Cost estimating	2 months	2, 4, 5
7. Deliver plans to board for consideration/decision	1 month	6
8. Surveys/regulatory review	6 weeks	6
9. Construction manager selection	9 weeks	6
10. State review of need for more hospital beds ("Certificate of Need")	3.5 months	7, 8
11. Design drawings	4 months	10
12. Construction documents	5 months	9, 11
13. Site preparation/demolish existing building	9 weeks	11
14. Construction start/building pad	2 months	12, 13
15. Relocate utilities	6 weeks	12
16. Deep foundations	2 months	14
17. Building structure in place	9 months	16
18. Exterior skin/roofing	4 months	17
19. Interior buildout	12 months	17
20. Building inspections	5 weeks	15, 19
21. Occupancy	1 month	20

[a]This list of activities is abbreviated for purposes of this case study. For simplification, assume each week = .25 months (i.e., 2 weeks = .5 month, 6 weeks = 1.5 months, etc.).

for the new facility. An administrative team created 35 user groups, which held over 1,000 planning meetings (lasting from 45 minutes to a whole day). They even created a "Supreme Court" to deal with conflicting views on the multifaceted issues facing the new hospital.

Funding and regulatory issues added substantial complexity to this major expansion, and Hodges was very concerned that the project stay on time and within budget. Tom Hyatt, director of facility development, was given the task of onsite manager of the $100 million project, in addition to overseeing ongoing renovations, expansions, and other projects. The activities in the multiyear project for the new building at Arnold Palmer are shown in Table 3.7.

Discussion Questions*

1. Develop the network for planning and construction of the new hospital at Arnold Palmer.
2. What is the critical path, and how long is the project expected to take?
3. Why is the construction of this 11-story building any more complex than construction of an equivalent office building?
4. What percent of the whole project duration was spent in planning that occurred prior to the proposal and reviews? Prior to the actual building construction? Why?

*You may wish to view the video accompanying this case before addressing these questions.

Managing Hard Rock's Rockfest

Video Case

At the Hard Rock Cafe, like many organizations, project management is a key planning tool. With Hard Rock's constant growth in hotels and cafes, remodeling of existing cafes, scheduling for Hard Rock Live concert and event venues, and planning the annual Rockfest, managers rely on project management techniques and software to maintain schedule and budget performance.

"Without Microsoft Project," says Hard Rock Vice-President Chris Tomasso, "there is no way to keep so many people on the same page." Tomasso is in charge of the Rockfest event, which is attended by well over 100,000 enthusiastic fans. The challenge is pulling it off within a tight 9-month planning horizon. As the event approaches, Tomasso devotes greater energy to its activities. For the first 3 months, Tomasso updates his Microsoft Project charts monthly. Then at the 6-month mark, he updates his progress weekly. At the 9-month mark, he checks and corrects his schedule twice a week.

Early in the project management process, Tomasso identifies 10 major tasks (called level-2 activities in a work breakdown structure, or WBS):[†] talent booking, ticketing, marketing/PR, online promotion, television, show production, travel, sponsorships, operations, and merchandising. Using a WBS, each of these is further divided into a series of subtasks. Table 3.8 identifies 26 of the major activities and subactivities, their immediate predecessors, and time estimates. Tomasso enters all these into the Microsoft Project software.[‡] Tomasso alters the Microsoft Project document and the time line as the

project progresses. "It's okay to change it as long as you keep on track," he states.

The day of the rock concert itself is not the end of the project planning. "It's nothing but surprises. A band not being able to get to the venue because of traffic jams is a surprise, but an 'anticipated' surprise. We had a helicopter on stand-by ready to fly the band in," says Tomasso.

On completion of Rockfest in July, Tomasso and his team have a 3-month reprieve before starting the project planning process again.

[†]The level-1 activity is the Rockfest concert itself.

[‡]There are actually 127 activities used by Tomasso; the list is abbreviated for this case study.

TABLE 3.8	Some of the Major Activities and Subactivities in the Rockfest Plan		
ACTIVITY	**DESCRIPTION**	**PREDECESSOR(S)**	**TIME (WEEKS)**
A	Finalize site and building contracts	—	7
B	Select local promoter	A	3
C	Hire production manager	A	3
D	Design promotional Web site	B	5
E	Set TV deal	D	6
F	Hire director	E	4
G	Plan for TV camera placement	F	2
H	Target headline entertainers	B	4
I	Target support entertainers	H	4
J	Travel accommodations for talent	I	10
K	Set venue capacity	C	2
L	Ticketmaster contract	D, K	3
M	On-site ticketing	L	8
N	Sound and staging	C	6
O	Passes and stage credentials	G, R	7
P	Travel accommodations for staff	B	20
Q	Hire sponsor coordinator	B	4
R	Finalize sponsors	Q	4
S	Define/place signage for sponsors	R, X	3
T	Hire operations manager	A	4
U	Develop site plan	T	6
V	Hire security director	T	7
W	Set police/fire security plan	V	4
X	Power, plumbing, AC, toilet services	U	8
Y	Secure merchandise deals	B	6
Z	Online merchandise sales	Y	6

Discussion Questions[§]

1. Identify the critical path and its activities for Rockfest. How long does the project take?

2. Which activities have a slack time of 8 weeks or more?

3. Identify five major challenges a project manager faces in events such as this one.

4. Why is a work breakdown structure useful in a project such as this? Take the 26 activities and break them into what you think should be level-2, level-3, and level-4 tasks.

[§]You may wish to view the video accompanying this case before addressing these questions.

- **Additional Case Study:** Visit MyOMLab for this free case study:
  Shale Oil Company: This oil refinery must shut down for maintenance of a major piece of equipment.

Endnotes

1. This formula is based on the statistical concept that from one end of the beta distribution to the other is 6 standard deviations (± 3 standard deviations from the mean). Because $(b - a)$ is 6 standard deviations, the variance is $[(b - a)/6]^2$.

2. *Source:* Adapted from James A. D. Stoner, *Management*, 6th ed. (Upper Saddle River, NJ: Pearson).

Main Heading	Review Material	MyOMLab
THE IMPORTANCE OF PROJECT MANAGEMENT (p. 62)	The management of projects involves three phases: 1. *Planning*—This phase includes goal setting, defining the project, and team organization. 2. *Scheduling*—This phase relates people, money, and supplies to specific activities and relates activities to each other. 3. *Controlling*—Here the firm monitors resources, costs, quality, and budgets. It also revises or changes plans and shifts resources to meet time and cost demands.	Concept Questions: 1.1–1.4 **VIDEO 3.1** Project Management at Hard Rock's Rockfest
PROJECT PLANNING (pp. 62–65)	Projects can be defined as a series of related tasks directed toward a major output. ■ **Project organization**—An organization formed to ensure that programs (projects) receive the proper management and attention. ■ **Work breakdown structure (WBS)**—Defines a project by dividing it into more and more detailed components.	Concept Questions: 2.1–2.4 Problems: 3.1–3.2
PROJECT SCHEDULING (pp. 65–66)	■ **Gantt charts**—Planning charts used to schedule resources and allocate time. Project scheduling serves several purposes: 1. It shows the relationship of each activity to others and to the whole project. 2. It identifies the precedence relationships among activities. 3. It encourages the setting of realistic time and cost estimates for each activity. 4. It helps make better use of people, money, and material resources by identifying critical bottlenecks in the project.	Concept Questions: 3.1–3.4 Problem: 3.3
PROJECT CONTROLLING (pp. 66–67)	Computerized programs produce a broad variety of PERT/CPM reports, including (1) detailed cost breakdowns for each task, (2) total program labor curves, (3) cost distribution tables, (4) functional cost and hour summaries, (5) raw material and expenditure forecasts, (6) variance reports, (7) time analysis reports, and (8) work status reports.	Concept Questions: 4.1–4.2 **VIDEO 3.2** Project Management at Arnold Palmer Hospital
PROJECT MANAGEMENT TECHNIQUES: PERT AND CPM (pp. 67–71)	■ **Program evaluation and review technique (PERT)**—A project management technique that employs three time estimates for each activity. ■ **Critical path method (CPM)**—A project management technique that uses only one estimate per activity. ■ **Critical path**—The computed *longest* time path(s) through a network. PERT and CPM both follow six basic steps. The activities on the critical path will delay the entire project if they are not completed on time. ■ **Activity-on-node (AON)**—A network diagram in which nodes designate activities. ■ **Activity-on-arrow (AOA)**—A network diagram in which arrows designate activities. In an AOA network, the nodes represent the starting and finishing times of an activity and are also called *events*. ■ **Dummy activity**—An activity having no time that is inserted into a network to maintain the logic of the network. A dummy ending activity can be added to the end of an AON diagram for a project that has multiple ending activities.	Concept Questions: 5.1–5.4 Problems: 3.4–3.14 Virtual Office Hours for Solved Problems: 3.1, 3.2
DETERMINING THE PROJECT SCHEDULE (pp. 71–77)	■ **Critical path analysis**—A process that helps determine a project schedule. To find the critical path, we calculate two distinct starting and ending times for each activity: ■ *Earliest start (ES)* = Earliest time at which an activity can start, assuming that all predecessors have been completed ■ *Earliest finish (EF)* = Earliest time at which an activity can be finished ■ *Latest start (LS)* = Latest time at which an activity can start, without delaying the completion time of the entire project ■ *Latest finish (LF)* = Latest time by which an activity has to finish so as to not delay the completion time of the entire project ■ **Forward pass**—A process that identifies all the early start and early finish times.	Concept Questions: 6.1–6.4 Problems: 3.15, 3.16

$$ES = \text{Max \{EF of all immediate predecessors\}} \qquad (3\text{-}1)$$

$$EF = ES + \text{Activity time} \qquad (3\text{-}2)$$

■ **Backward pass**—A process that identifies all the late start and late finish times.

$$LF = \text{Min \{LS of all immediate following activities\}} \qquad (3\text{-}3)$$

$$LS = LF - \text{Activity time} \qquad (3\text{-}4)$$

Main Heading	Review Material	MyOMLab
	■ **Slack time**—Free time for an activity. $$\text{Slack} = \text{LS} - \text{ES} \quad \text{or} \quad \text{Slack} = \text{LF} - \text{EF} \qquad (3\text{-}5)$$ The activities with zero slack are called *critical activities* and are said to be on the critical path. The critical path is a continuous path through the project network that starts at the first activity in the project, terminates at the last activity in the project, and includes only critical activities.	Virtual Office Hours for Solved Problem: 3.3 **ACTIVE** MODEL **3.1**
VARIABILITY IN ACTIVITY TIMES (pp. 77–82)	■ **Optimistic time** (*a*)—The "best" activity completion time that could be obtained in a PERT network. ■ **Pessimistic time** (*b*)—The "worst" activity time that could be expected in a PERT network. ■ **Most likely time** (*m*)—The most probable time to complete an activity in a PERT network. When using PERT, we often assume that activity time estimates follow the beta distribution. $$\text{Expected activity time } t = (a + 4m + b)/6 \qquad (3\text{-}6)$$ $$\text{Variance of activity completion time} = [(b - a)/6]^2 \qquad (3\text{-}7)$$ $$\sigma_p^2 = \text{Project variance} = \Sigma \text{ (variances of activities on critical path)} \qquad (3\text{-}8)$$ $$Z = (\text{Due date} - \text{Expected date of completion})/\sigma_p \qquad (3\text{-}9)$$ $$\text{Due date} = \text{Expected completion time} + (Z \times \sigma_p) \qquad (3\text{-}10)$$	Concept Questions: 7.1–7.4 Problems: 3.17–3.27 Virtual Office Hours for Solved Problems: 3.4, 3.5, 3.6
COST-TIME TRADE-OFFS AND PROJECT CRASHING (pp. 82–85)	■ **Crashing**—Shortening activity time in a network to reduce time on the critical path so total completion time is reduced. $$\text{Crash cost per period} = \frac{(\text{Crash cost} - \text{Normal cost})}{(\text{Normal time} - \text{Crash time})} \qquad (3\text{-}11)$$	Concept Questions: 8.1–8.4 Problems: 3.28–3.33 Virtual Office Hours for Solved Problem: 3.7
A CRITIQUE OF PERT AND CPM (pp. 85–86)	As with every technique for problem solving, PERT and CPM have a number of advantages as well as several limitations.	Concept Questions: 9.1–9.4
USING MICROSOFT PROJECT TO MANAGE PROJECTS (pp. 86–88)	Microsoft Project, the most popular example of specialized project management software, is extremely useful in drawing project networks, identifying the project schedule, and managing project costs and other resources.	Concept Questions: 10.1–10.4

Self Test

■ **Before taking the self-test,** refer to the learning objectives listed at the beginning of the chapter and the key terms listed at the end of the chapter.

LO 3.1 Which of the following statements regarding Gantt charts is true?
a) Gantt charts give a timeline and precedence relationships for each activity of a project.
b) Gantt charts use the four standard spines: Methods, Materials, Manpower, and Machinery.
c) Gantt charts are visual devices that show the duration of activities in a project.
d) Gantt charts are expensive.
e) All of the above are true.

LO 3.2 Which of the following is true about AOA and AON networks?
a) In AOA, arrows represent activities.
b) In AON, nodes represent activities.
c) Activities consume time and resources.
d) Nodes are also called *events* in AOA.
e) All of the above.

LO 3.3 Slack time equals:
a) ES + *t*.
b) LS − ES.
c) zero.
d) EF − ES.

LO 3.4 The critical path of a network is the:
a) shortest-time path through the network.
b) path with the fewest activities.
c) path with the most activities.
d) longest-time path through the network.

LO 3.5 PERT analysis computes the variance of the total project completion time as:
a) the sum of the variances of all activities in the project.
b) the sum of the variances of all activities on the critical path.
c) the sum of the variances of all activities not on the critical path.
d) the variance of the final activity of the project.

LO 3.6 The crash cost per period:
a) is the difference in costs divided by the difference in times (crash and normal).
b) is considered to be linear in the range between normal and crash.
c) needs to be determined so that the smallest cost values on the critical path can be considered for time reduction first.
d) all of the above.

Answers: LO 3.1. c; LO 3.2. e; LO 3.3. b; LO 3.4. d; LO 3.5. b; LO 3.6. d.

Forecasting

CHAPTER OUTLINE

GLOBAL COMPANY PROFILE: *Walt Disney Parks & Resorts*

◆ What Is Forecasting? *108*

◆ The Strategic Importance of Forecasting *109*

◆ Seven Steps in the Forecasting System *110*

◆ Forecasting Approaches *111*

◆ Time-Series Forecasting *112*

◆ Associative Forecasting Methods: Regression and Correlation Analysis *131*

◆ Monitoring and Controlling Forecasts *138*

◆ Forecasting in the Service Sector *140*

Alaska Airlines

Forecasting Provides a Competitive Advantage for Disney

W hen it comes to the world's most respected global brands, Walt Disney Parks & Resorts is a visible leader. Although the monarch of this magic kingdom is no man but a mouse—Mickey Mouse—it's CEO Robert Iger who daily manages the entertainment giant. Disney's global portfolio includes Shanghai Disney (2016), Hong Kong Disneyland (2005), Disneyland Paris (1992), and Tokyo Disneyland (1983). But it is Walt Disney World Resort (in Florida) and Disneyland Resort (in California) that drive profits in this $50 billion corporation, which is ranked in the top 100 in both the *Fortune* 500 and *Financial Times* Global 500.

Donald Duck, Goofy, and Mickey Mouse provide the public image of Disney to the world. Forecasts drive the work schedules of 72,000 cast members working at Walt Disney World Resort near Orlando.

Revenues at Disney are all about people—how many visit the parks and how they spend money while there. When Iger receives a daily report from his four theme parks and two water parks near Orlando, the report contains only two numbers: the *forecast* of yesterday's attendance at the parks (Magic Kingdom, Epcot, Disney's Animal Kingdom, Disney-Hollywood Studios, Typhoon Lagoon, and Blizzard Beach) and the *actual* attendance. An error close to zero is expected. Iger takes his forecasts very seriously.

The forecasting team at Walt Disney World Resort doesn't just do a daily prediction, however, and Iger is not its only customer. The team also provides daily, weekly, monthly, annual, and 5-year forecasts to the labor management, maintenance, operations, finance, and park scheduling departments. Forecasters use judgmental models, econometric models, moving-average models, and regression analysis.

The giant sphere is the symbol of Epcot, one of Disney's four Orlando parks, for which forecasts of meals, lodging, entertainment, and transportation must be made. This Disney monorail moves guests among parks and the 28 hotels on the massive 47-square-mile property (about the size of San Francisco and twice the size of Manhattan).

Kevin Fleming/Corbis

A daily forecast of attendance is made by adjusting Disney's annual operating plan for weather forecasts, the previous day's crowds, conventions, and seasonal variations. One of the two water parks at Walt Disney World Resort, Typhoon Lagoon, is shown here.

Melvyn Longhurst/Corbis

Cinderella's iconic castle is a focal point for meeting up with family and friends in the massive park. The statue of Walt Disney greets visitors to the open plaza.

With 20% of Walt Disney World Resort's customers coming from outside the United States, its economic model includes such variables as gross domestic product (GDP), cross-exchange rates, and arrivals into the U.S. Disney also uses 35 analysts and 70 field people to survey 1 million people each year. The surveys, administered to guests at the parks and its 20 hotels, to employees, and to travel industry professionals, examine future travel plans and experiences at the parks. This helps forecast not only attendance but also behavior at each ride (e.g., how long people will wait, how many times they will ride). Inputs to the monthly forecasting model include airline specials, speeches by the chair of the Federal Reserve, and Wall Street trends. Disney even monitors 3,000 school districts inside and outside the U.S. for holiday/vacation schedules. With this approach, Disney's 5-year attendance forecast yields just a 5% error on average. Its annual forecasts have a 0% to 3% error.

Attendance forecasts for the parks drive a whole slew of management decisions. For example, capacity on any day can be increased by opening at 8 A.M. instead of the usual 9 A.M., by opening more shows or rides, by adding more food/beverage carts (9 million hamburgers and 50 million Cokes are sold per year!), and by bringing in more employees (called "cast members"). Cast members are scheduled in 15-minute intervals throughout the parks for flexibility. Demand can be managed by limiting the number of guests admitted to the

dmac/Alamy

Forecasts are critical to making sure rides are not overcrowded. Disney is good at "managing demand" with techniques such as adding more street activities to reduce long lines for rides. On slow days, Disney calls fewer cast members to work.

parks, with the "FAST PASS" reservation system, and by shifting crowds from rides to more street parades.

At Disney, forecasting is a key driver in the company's success and competitive advantage. ◄

LEARNING OBJECTIVES

LO 4.1 *Understand* the three time horizons and which models apply for each 108

LO 4.2 *Explain* when to use each of the four qualitative models 111

LO 4.3 *Apply* the naive, moving-average, exponential smoothing, and trend methods 113

LO 4.4 *Compute* three measures of forecast accuracy 118

LO 4.5 *Develop* seasonal indices 127

LO 4.6 *Conduct* a regression and correlation analysis 131

LO 4.7 *Use* a tracking signal 138

What Is Forecasting?

Every day, managers like those at Disney make decisions without knowing what will happen in the future. They order inventory without knowing what sales will be, purchase new equipment despite uncertainty about demand for products, and make investments without knowing what profits will be. Managers are always trying to make better estimates of what will happen in the future in the face of uncertainty. Making good estimates is the main purpose of forecasting.

In this chapter, we examine different types of forecasts and present a variety of forecasting models. Our purpose is to show that there are many ways for managers to forecast. We also provide an overview of business sales forecasting and describe how to prepare, monitor, and judge the accuracy of a forecast. Good forecasts are an *essential* part of efficient service and manufacturing operations.

Forecasting

The art and science of predicting future events.

Forecasting is the art and science of predicting future events. Forecasting may involve taking historical data (such as past sales) and projecting them into the future with a mathematical model. It may be a subjective or an intuitive prediction (e.g., "this is a great new product and will sell 20% more than the old one"). It may be based on demand-driven data, such as customer plans to purchase, and projecting them into the future. Or the forecast may involve a combination of these, that is, a mathematical model adjusted by a manager's good judgment.

As we introduce different forecasting techniques in this chapter, you will see that there is seldom one superior method. Forecasts may be influenced by a product's position in its life cycle—whether sales are in an introduction, growth, maturity, or decline stage. Other products can be influenced by the demand for a related product—for example, navigation systems may track with new car sales. Because there are limits to what can be expected from forecasts, we develop error measures. Preparing and monitoring forecasts can also be costly and time consuming.

Few businesses, however, can afford to avoid the process of forecasting by just waiting to see what happens and then taking their chances. Effective planning in both the short run and long run depends on a forecast of demand for the company's products.

Forecasting Time Horizons

LO 4.1 *Understand* the three time horizons and which models apply for each

A forecast is usually classified by the *future time horizon* that it covers. Time horizons fall into three categories:

1. *Short-range forecast:* This forecast has a time span of up to 1 year but is generally less than 3 months. It is used for planning purchasing, job scheduling, workforce levels, job assignments, and production levels.
2. *Medium-range forecast:* A medium-range, or intermediate, forecast generally spans from 3 months to 3 years. It is useful in sales planning, production planning and budgeting, cash budgeting, and analysis of various operating plans.
3. *Long-range forecast:* Generally 3 years or more in time span, long-range forecasts are used in planning for new products, capital expenditures, facility location or expansion, and research and development.

Medium- and long-range forecasts are distinguished from short-range forecasts by three features:

1. First, intermediate and long-range forecasts *deal with more comprehensive issues* supporting management decisions regarding planning and products, plants, and processes. Implementing some facility decisions, such as GM's decision to open a new Brazilian manufacturing plant, can take 5 to 8 years from inception to completion.
2. Second, short-term forecasting usually *employs different methodologies* than longer-term forecasting. Mathematical techniques, such as moving averages, exponential smoothing, and trend extrapolation (all of which we shall examine shortly), are common to short-run projections. Broader, *less* quantitative methods are useful in predicting such issues as whether a new product, like the optical disk recorder, should be introduced into a company's product line.
3. Finally, as you would expect, short-range forecasts *tend to be more accurate* than longer-range forecasts. Factors that influence demand change every day. Thus, as the time horizon lengthens, it is likely that forecast accuracy will diminish. It almost goes without saying, then, that sales forecasts must be updated regularly to maintain their value and integrity. After each sales period, forecasts should be reviewed and revised.

Types of Forecasts

Organizations use three major types of forecasts in planning future operations:

1. **Economic forecasts** address the business cycle by predicting inflation rates, money supplies, housing starts, and other planning indicators.
2. **Technological forecasts** are concerned with rates of technological progress, which can result in the birth of exciting new products, requiring new plants and equipment.
3. **Demand forecasts** are projections of demand for a company's products or services. Forecasts drive decisions, so managers need immediate and accurate information about real demand. They need *demand-driven forecasts*, where the focus is on rapidly identifying and tracking customer desires. These forecasts may use recent point-of-sale (POS) data, retailer-generated reports of customer preferences, and any other information that will help to forecast with the most current data possible. Demand-driven forecasts drive a company's production, capacity, and scheduling systems and serve as inputs to financial, marketing, and personnel planning. In addition, the payoff in reduced inventory and obsolescence can be huge.

Economic and technological forecasting are specialized techniques that may fall outside the role of the operations manager. The emphasis in this chapter will therefore be on demand forecasting.

Economic forecasts
Planning indicators that are valuable in helping organizations prepare medium- to long-range forecasts.

Technological forecasts
Long-term forecasts concerned with the rates of technological progress.

Demand forecasts
Projections of a company's sales for each time period in the planning horizon.

The Strategic Importance of Forecasting

Good forecasts are of critical importance in all aspects of a business: *The forecast is the only estimate of demand until actual demand becomes known.* Forecasts of demand therefore drive decisions in many areas. Let's look at the impact of product demand forecast on three activities: (1) supply-chain management, (2) human resources, and (3) capacity.

Supply-Chain Management

Good supplier relations and the ensuing advantages in product innovation, cost, and speed to market depend on accurate forecasts. Here are just three examples:

♦ Apple has built an effective global system where it controls nearly every piece of the supply chain, from product design to retail store. With rapid communication and accurate data shared up and down the supply chain, innovation is enhanced, inventory costs are reduced, and speed to market is improved. Once a product goes on sale, Apple tracks demand by the hour for each store and adjusts production forecasts daily. At Apple, forecasts for its supply chain are a strategic weapon.

◆ Toyota develops sophisticated car forecasts with input from a variety of sources, including dealers. But forecasting the demand for accessories such as navigation systems, custom wheels, spoilers, and so on is particularly difficult. And there are over 1,000 items that vary by model and color. As a result, Toyota not only reviews reams of data with regard to vehicles that have been built and wholesaled but also looks in detail at vehicle forecasts before it makes judgments about the future accessory demand. When this is done correctly, the result is an efficient supply chain and satisfied customers.

◆ Walmart collaborates with suppliers such as Sara Lee and Procter & Gamble to make sure the right item is available at the right time in the right place and at the right price. For instance, in hurricane season, Walmart's ability to analyze 700 million store–item combinations means it can forecast that not only flashlights but also Pop-Tarts and beer sell at seven times the normal demand rate. These forecasting systems are known as *collaborative planning, forecasting, and replenishment* (CPFR). They combine the intelligence of multiple supply-chain partners. The goal of CPFR is to create significantly more accurate information that can power the supply chain to greater sales and profits.

Human Resources

Hiring, training, and laying off workers all depend on anticipated demand. If the human resources department must hire additional workers without warning, the amount of training declines, and the quality of the workforce suffers. A large Louisiana chemical firm almost lost its biggest customer when a quick expansion to around-the-clock shifts led to a total breakdown in quality control on the second and third shifts.

Capacity

When capacity is inadequate, the resulting shortages can lead to loss of customers and market share. This is exactly what happened to Nabisco when it underestimated the huge demand for its new Snackwell Devil's Food Cookies. Even with production lines working overtime, Nabisco could not keep up with demand, and it lost customers. Nintendo faced this problem when its Wii was introduced and exceeded all forecasts for demand. Amazon made the same error with its Kindle. On the other hand, when excess capacity exists, costs can skyrocket.

Seven Steps in the Forecasting System

Forecasting follows seven basic steps. We use Disney World, the focus of this chapter's *Global Company Profile*, as an example of each step:

1. *Determine the use of the forecast:* Disney uses park attendance forecasts to drive decisions about staffing, opening times, ride availability, and food supplies.
2. *Select the items to be forecasted:* For Disney World, there are six main parks. A forecast of daily attendance at each is the main number that determines labor, maintenance, and scheduling.
3. *Determine the time horizon of the forecast:* Is it short, medium, or long term? Disney develops daily, weekly, monthly, annual, and 5-year forecasts.
4. *Select the forecasting model(s):* Disney uses a variety of statistical models that we shall discuss, including moving averages, econometrics, and regression analysis. It also employs judgmental, or nonquantitative, models.
5. *Gather the data needed to make the forecast:* Disney's forecasting team employs 35 analysts and 70 field personnel to survey 1 million people/businesses every year. Disney also uses a firm called Global Insights for travel industry forecasts and gathers data on exchange rates, arrivals into the U.S., airline specials, Wall Street trends, and school vacation schedules.

6. *Make the forecast.*
7. *Validate and implement the results:* At Disney, forecasts are reviewed daily at the highest levels to make sure that the model, assumptions, and data are valid. Error measures are applied; then the forecasts are used to schedule personnel down to 15-minute intervals.

These seven steps present a systematic way of initiating, designing, and implementing a forecasting system. When the system is to be used to generate forecasts regularly over time, data must be routinely collected. Then actual computations are usually made by computer.

Regardless of the system that firms like Disney use, each company faces several realities:

♦ Outside factors that we cannot predict or control often impact the forecast.

♦ Most forecasting techniques assume that there is some underlying stability in the system. Consequently, some firms automate their predictions using computerized forecasting software, then closely monitor only the product items whose demand is erratic.

♦ Both product family and aggregated forecasts are more accurate than individual product forecasts. Disney, for example, aggregates daily attendance forecasts by park. This approach helps balance the over- and underpredictions for each of the six attractions.

Forecasting Approaches

There are two general approaches to forecasting, just as there are two ways to tackle all decision modeling. One is a quantitative analysis; the other is a qualitative approach. Quantitative forecasts use a variety of mathematical models that rely on historical data and/or associative variables to forecast demand. Subjective or qualitative forecasts incorporate such factors as the decision maker's intuition, emotions, personal experiences, and value system in reaching a forecast. Some firms use one approach and some use the other. In practice, a combination of the two is usually most effective.

Quantitative forecasts
Forecasts that employ mathematical modeling to forecast demand.

Qualitative forecasts
Forecasts that incorporate such factors as the decision maker's intuition, emotions, personal experiences, and value system.

Overview of Qualitative Methods

In this section, we consider four different *qualitative* forecasting techniques:

1. **Jury of executive opinion:** Under this method, the opinions of a group of high-level experts or managers, often in combination with statistical models, are pooled to arrive at a group estimate of demand. Bristol-Myers Squibb Company, for example, uses 220 well-known research scientists as its jury of executive opinion to get a grasp on future trends in the world of medical research.

2. **Delphi method:** There are three different types of participants in the Delphi method: decision makers, staff personnel, and respondents. Decision makers usually consist of a group of 5 to 10 experts who will be making the actual forecast. Staff personnel assist decision makers by preparing, distributing, collecting, and summarizing a series of questionnaires and survey results. The respondents are a group of people, often located in different places, whose judgments are valued. This group provides inputs to the decision makers before the forecast is made.

    The state of Alaska, for example, has used the Delphi method to develop its long-range economic forecast. A large part of the state's budget is derived from the million-plus barrels of oil pumped daily through a pipeline at Prudhoe Bay. The large Delphi panel of experts had to represent all groups and opinions in the state and all geographic areas.

3. **Sales force composite:** In this approach, each salesperson estimates what sales will be in his or her region. These forecasts are then reviewed to ensure that they are realistic. Then they are combined at the district and national levels to reach an overall forecast. A variation of this approach occurs at Lexus, where every quarter Lexus dealers have a "make meeting." At this meeting, they talk about what is selling, in what colors, and with what options, so the factory knows what to build.

4. **Market survey:** This method solicits input from customers or potential customers regarding future purchasing plans. It can help not only in preparing a forecast but also in improving

Jury of executive opinion
A forecasting technique that uses the opinion of a small group of high-level managers to form a group estimate of demand.

Delphi method
A forecasting technique using a group process that allows experts to make forecasts.

LO 4.2 *Explain* when to use each of the four qualitative models

Sales force composite
A forecasting technique based on salespersons' estimates of expected sales.

Market survey
A forecasting method that solicits input from customers or potential customers regarding future purchasing plans.

product design and planning for new products. The consumer market survey and sales force composite methods can, however, suffer from overly optimistic forecasts that arise from customer input.

Overview of Quantitative Methods[1]

Five quantitative forecasting methods, all of which use historical data, are described in this chapter. They fall into two categories:

1. Naive approach
2. Moving averages   **Time-series models**
3. Exponential smoothing
4. Trend projection
5. Linear regression   **Associative model**

Time series

A forecasting technique that uses a series of past data points to make a forecast.

Time-Series Models   Time-series models predict on the assumption that the future is a function of the past. In other words, they look at what has happened over a period of time and use a series of past data to make a forecast. If we are predicting sales of lawn mowers, we use the past sales for lawn mowers to make the forecasts.

Associative Models   Associative models, such as linear regression, incorporate the variables or factors that might influence the quantity being forecast. For example, an associative model for lawn mower sales might use factors such as new housing starts, advertising budget, and competitors' prices.

STUDENT TIP

Here is the meat of this chapter. We now show you a wide variety of models that use time-series data.

Time-Series Forecasting

A time series is based on a sequence of evenly spaced (weekly, monthly, quarterly, and so on) data points. Examples include weekly sales of Nike Air Jordans, quarterly earnings reports of Microsoft stock, daily shipments of Coors beer, and annual consumer price indices. Forecasting time-series data implies that future values are predicted *only* from past values and that other variables, no matter how potentially valuable, may be ignored.

Decomposition of a Time Series

Analyzing time series means breaking down past data into components and then projecting them forward. A time series has four components:

1. *Trend* is the gradual upward or downward movement of the data over time. Changes in income, population, age distribution, or cultural views may account for movement in trend.

STUDENT TIP

The peak "seasons" for sales of Frito-Lay chips are the Super Bowl, Memorial Day, Labor Day, and the Fourth of July.

2. *Seasonality* is a data pattern that repeats itself after a period of days, weeks, months, or quarters. There are six common seasonality patterns:

PERIOD LENGTH	"SEASON" LENGTH	NUMBER OF "SEASONS" IN PATTERN
Week	Day	7
Month	Week	$4-4\frac{1}{2}$
Month	Day	28–31
Year	Quarter	4
Year	Month	12
Year	Week	52

Restaurants and barber shops, for example, experience weekly seasons, with Saturday being the peak of business. See the *OM in Action* box "Forecasting at Olive Garden." Beer distributors forecast yearly patterns, with monthly seasons. Three "seasons"—May, July, and September—each contain a big beer-drinking holiday.

OM in Action | Forecasting at Olive Garden

It's Friday night in the college town of Gainesville, Florida, and the local Olive Garden restaurant is humming. Customers may wait an average of 30 minutes for a table, but they can sample new wines and cheeses and admire scenic paintings of Italian villages on the Tuscan-style restaurant's walls. Then comes dinner with portions so huge that many people take home a doggie bag. The typical bill: under $15 per person.

Crowds flock to the Darden restaurant chain's Olive Garden, Seasons 52, and Bahama Breeze for value and consistency—*and* they get it.

Every night, Darden's computers crank out forecasts that tell store managers what demand to anticipate the next day. The forecasting software generates a total meal forecast and breaks that down into specific menu items. The system tells a manager, for instance, that if 625 meals will be served the next day, "you will serve these items in these quantities. So before you go home, pull 25 pounds of shrimp and 30 pounds of crab out, and tell your operations people to prepare 42 portion packs of chicken, 75 scampi dishes, 8 stuffed flounders, and so on." Managers often fine-tune the quantities based on local conditions, such as weather or a convention, but they know what their customers are going to order.

Bob Pardue - Signs/Alamy

By relying on demand history, the forecasting system has cut millions of dollars of waste out of the system. The forecast also reduces labor costs by providing the necessary information for improved scheduling. Labor costs decreased almost a full percent in the first year, translating into additional millions in savings for the Darden chain. In the low-margin restaurant business, every dollar counts.

Sources: InformationWeek (April 1, 2014); *USA Today* (Oct. 13, 2014); and *FastCompany* (July-August 2009).

---

3. *Cycles* are patterns in the data that occur every several years. They are usually tied into the business cycle and are of major importance in short-term business analysis and planning. Predicting business cycles is difficult because they may be affected by political events or by international turmoil.

4. *Random variations* are "blips" in the data caused by chance and unusual situations. They follow no discernible pattern, so they cannot be predicted.

Figure 4.1 illustrates a demand over a 4-year period. It shows the average, trend, seasonal components, and random variations around the demand curve. The average demand is the sum of the demand for each period divided by the number of data periods.

LO 4.3 *Apply* the naive, moving-average, exponential smoothing, and trend methods

Naive Approach

The simplest way to forecast is to assume that demand in the next period will be equal to demand in the most recent period. In other words, if sales of a product—say, Nokia cell phones—were 68 units in January, we can forecast that February's sales will also be 68 phones.

Figure **4.1**

Demand Charted over 4 Years, with a Growth Trend and Seasonality Indicated

⬥ **STUDENT TIP**

Forecasting is easy when demand is stable. But with trend, seasonality, and cycles considered, the job is a lot more interesting

Naive approach

A forecasting technique that assumes that demand in the next period is equal to demand in the most recent period.

Does this make any sense? It turns out that for some product lines, this naive approach is the most cost-effective and efficient objective forecasting model. At least it provides a starting point against which more sophisticated models that follow can be compared.

Moving Averages

Moving averages

A forecasting method that uses an average of the *n* most recent periods of data to forecast the next period.

A moving-average forecast uses a number of historical actual data values to generate a forecast. Moving averages are useful *if we can assume that market demands will stay fairly steady over time*. A 4-month moving average is found by simply summing the demand during the past 4 months and dividing by 4. With each passing month, the most recent month's data are added to the sum of the previous 3 months' data, and the earliest month is dropped. This practice tends to smooth out short-term irregularities in the data series.

Mathematically, the simple moving average (which serves as an estimate of the next period's demand) is expressed as:

$$\text{Moving average} = \frac{\sum \text{demand in previous } n \text{ periods}}{n} \qquad (4\text{-}1)$$

where *n* is the number of periods in the moving average—for example, 4, 5, or 6 months, respectively, for a 4-, 5-, or 6-period moving average.

Example 1 shows how moving averages are calculated.

Example 1

DETERMINING THE MOVING AVERAGE

Donna's Garden Supply wants a 3-month moving-average forecast, including a forecast for next January, for shed sales.

APPROACH ▶ Storage shed sales are shown in the middle column of the following table. A 3-month moving average appears on the right.

MONTH	ACTUAL SHED SALES	3-MONTH MOVING AVERAGE
January	10	
February	12	
March	13	
April	16	$(10 + 12 + 13)/3 = 11\frac{2}{3}$
May	19	$(12 + 13 + 16)/3 = 13\frac{2}{3}$
June	23	$(13 + 16 + 19)/3 = 16$
July	26	$(16 + 19 + 23)/3 = 19\frac{1}{3}$
August	30	$(19 + 23 + 26)/3 = 22\frac{2}{3}$
September	28	$(23 + 26 + 30)/3 = 26\frac{1}{3}$
October	18	$(26 + 30 + 28)/3 = 28$
November	16	$(30 + 28 + 18)/3 = 25\frac{1}{3}$
December	14	$(28 + 18 + 16)/3 = 20\frac{2}{3}$

SOLUTION ▶ The forecast for December is $20\frac{2}{3}$. To project the demand for sheds in the coming January, we sum the October, November, and December sales and divide by 3: January forecast $= (18 + 16 + 14)/3 = 16$.

INSIGHT ▶ Management now has a forecast that averages sales for the last 3 months. It is easy to use and understand.

LEARNING EXERCISE ▶ If actual sales in December were 18 (rather than 14), what is the new January forecast? [Answer: $17\frac{1}{3}$.]

RELATED PROBLEMS ▶ 4.1a, 4.2b, 4.5a, 4.6, 4.8a, b, 4.10a, 4.13b, 4.15, 4.33 (4.35, 4.38 are available in MyOMLab)

EXCEL OM Data File Ch04Ex1.xls can be found in MyOMLab.

ACTIVE MODEL 4.1 This example is further illustrated in Active Model 4.1 in MyOMLab.

When a detectable trend or pattern is present, *weights* can be used to place more emphasis on recent values. This practice makes forecasting techniques more responsive to changes because more recent periods may be more heavily weighted. Choice of weights is somewhat arbitrary because there is no set formula to determine them. Therefore, deciding which weights to use requires some experience. For example, if the latest month or period is weighted too heavily, the forecast may reflect a large unusual change in the demand or sales pattern too quickly.

A weighted moving average may be expressed mathematically as:

$$\text{Weighted moving average} = \frac{\sum((\text{Weight for period } n)(\text{Demand in period } n))}{\sum \text{Weights}} \quad (4\text{-}2)$$

Example 2 shows how to calculate a weighted moving average.

Example 2

DETERMINING THE WEIGHTED MOVING AVERAGE

Donna's Garden Supply (see Example 1) wants to forecast storage shed sales by weighting the past 3 months, with more weight given to recent data to make them more significant.

APPROACH ▶ Assign more weight to recent data, as follows:

WEIGHTS APPLIED	PERIOD
3	Last month
2	Two months ago
1	Three months ago
6	Sum of weights

$$\text{Forecast for this month} = \frac{3 \times \text{Sales last mo.} + 2 \times \text{Sales 2 mos. ago} + 1 \times \text{Sales 3 mos. ago}}{\text{Sum of the weights}}$$

SOLUTION ▶ The results of this weighted-average forecast are as follows:

MONTH	ACTUAL SHED SALES	3-MONTH WEIGHTED MOVING AVERAGE
January	10	
February	12	
March	13	
April	16	$[(3 \times 13) + (2 \times 12) + (10)]/6 = 12\frac{1}{6}$
May	19	$[(3 \times 16) + (2 \times 13) + (12)]/6 = 14\frac{1}{3}$
June	23	$[(3 \times 19) + (2 \times 16) + (13)]/6 = 17$
July	26	$[(3 \times 23) + (2 \times 19) + (16)]/6 = 20\frac{1}{2}$
August	30	$[(3 \times 26) + (2 \times 23) + (19)]/6 = 23\frac{5}{6}$
September	28	$[(3 \times 30) + (2 \times 26) + (23)]/6 = 27\frac{1}{2}$
October	18	$[(3 \times 28) + (2 \times 30) + (26)]/6 = 28\frac{1}{3}$
November	16	$[(3 \times 18) + (2 \times 28) + (30)]/6 = 23\frac{1}{3}$
December	14	$[(3 \times 16) + (2 \times 18) + (28)]/6 = 18\frac{2}{3}$

The forecast for January is $15\frac{1}{3}$. Do you see how this number is computed?

INSIGHT ▶ In this particular forecasting situation, you can see that more heavily weighting the latest month provides a more accurate projection.

LEARNING EXERCISE ▶ If the assigned weights were 0.50, 0.33, and 0.17 (instead of 3, 2, and 1), what is the forecast for January's weighted moving average? Why? [Answer: There is no change. These are the same *relative* weights. Note that $\sum$ weights = 1 now, so there is no need for a denominator. When the weights sum to 1, calculations tend to be simpler.]

RELATED PROBLEMS ▶ 4.1b, 4.2c, 4.5c, 4.6, 4.7, 4.10b (4.38 is available in MyOMLab)

EXCEL OM Data File **Ch04Ex2.xls** can be found in MyOMLab.

Figure **4.2**

Actual Demand vs. Moving-Average and Weighted-Moving-Average Methods for Donna's Garden Supply

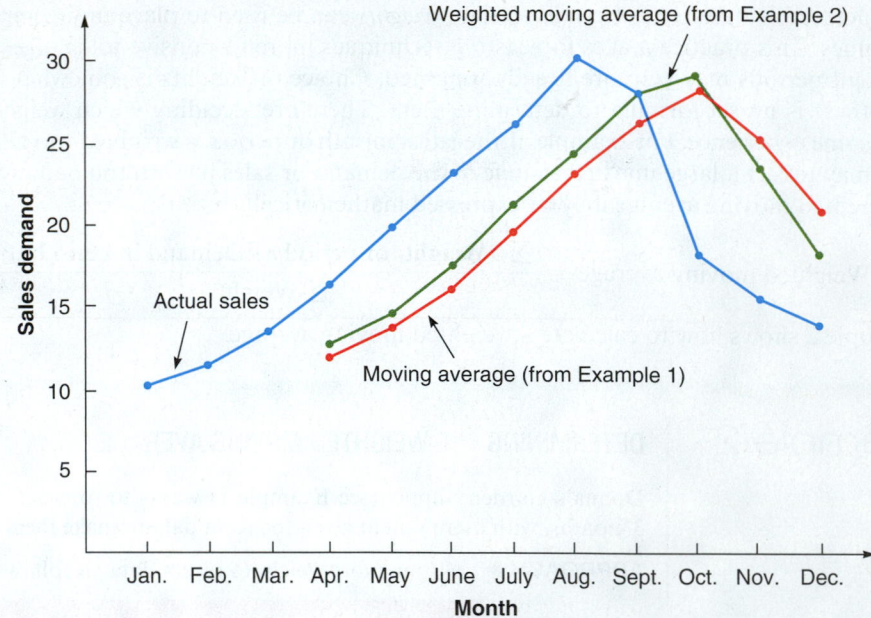

Both simple and weighted moving averages are effective in smoothing out sudden fluctuations in the demand pattern to provide stable estimates. Moving averages do, however, present three problems:

1. Increasing the size of *n* (the number of periods averaged) does smooth out fluctuations better, but it makes the method less sensitive to changes in the data.
2. Moving averages cannot pick up trends very well. Because they are averages, they will always stay within past levels and will not predict changes to either higher or lower levels. That is, they *lag* the actual values.
3. Moving averages require extensive records of past data.

Figure 4.2, a plot of the data in Examples 1 and 2, illustrates the lag effect of the moving-average models. Note that both the moving-average and weighted-moving-average lines lag the actual demand. The weighted moving average, however, usually reacts more quickly to demand changes. Even in periods of downturn (see November and December), it more closely tracks the demand.

Exponential Smoothing

Exponential smoothing

A weighted-moving-average forecasting technique in which data points are weighted by an exponential function.

Exponential smoothing is another weighted-moving-average forecasting method. It involves very *little* record keeping of past data and is fairly easy to use. The basic exponential smoothing formula can be shown as follows:

New forecast = Last period's forecast

+ α (Last period's actual demand − Last period's forecast)   (4-3)

Smoothing constant

The weighting factor used in an exponential smoothing forecast, a number greater than or equal to 0 and less than or equal to 1.

where α is a weight, or **smoothing constant**, chosen by the forecaster, that has a value greater than or equal to 0 and less than or equal to 1. Equation (4-3) can also be written mathematically as:

$$F_t = F_{t-1} + \alpha(A_{t-1} - F_{t-1})$$ (4-4)

where F_t = new forecast

F_{t-1} = previous period's forecast

α = smoothing (or weighting) constant ($0 \leq \alpha \leq 1$)

A_{t-1} = previous period's actual demand

The concept is not complex. The latest estimate of demand is equal to the old forecast adjusted by a fraction of the difference between the last period's actual demand and last period's forecast. Example 3 shows how to use exponential smoothing to derive a forecast.

Example 3

DETERMINING A FORECAST VIA EXPONENTIAL SMOOTHING

In January, a car dealer predicted February demand for 142 Ford Mustangs. Actual February demand was 153 autos. Using a smoothing constant chosen by management of $\alpha = .20$, the dealer wants to forecast March demand using the exponential smoothing model.

APPROACH ▶ The exponential smoothing model in Equations (4-3) and (4-4) can be applied.

SOLUTION ▶ Substituting the sample data into the formula, we obtain:

$$\text{New forecast (for March demand)} = 142 + .2(153 - 142) = 142 + 2.2$$
$$= 144.2$$

Thus, the March demand forecast for Ford Mustangs is rounded to 144.

INSIGHT ▶ Using just two pieces of data, the forecast and the actual demand, plus a smoothing constant, we developed a forecast of 144 Ford Mustangs for March.

LEARNING EXERCISE ▶ If the smoothing constant is changed to .30, what is the new forecast? [Answer: 145.3]

RELATED PROBLEMS ▶ 4.1c, 4.3, 4.4, 4.5d, 4.6, 4.9d, 4.11, 4.12, 4.13a, 4.17, 4.18, 4.31, 4.33, 4.34 (4.36, 4.61a are available in MyOMLab)

The *smoothing constant*, α, is generally in the range from .05 to .50 for business applications. It can be changed to give more weight to recent data (when α is high) or more weight to past data (when α is low). When α reaches the extreme of 1.0, then in Equation (4-4), $F_t = 1.0A_{t-1}$. All the older values drop out, and the forecast becomes identical to the naive model mentioned earlier in this chapter. That is, the forecast for the next period is just the same as this period's demand.

The following table helps illustrate this concept. For example, when $\alpha = .5$, we can see that the new forecast is based almost entirely on demand in the last three or four periods. When $\alpha = .1$, the forecast places little weight on recent demand and takes many periods (about 19) of historical values into account.

	WEIGHT ASSIGNED TO				
SMOOTHING CONSTANT	MOST RECENT PERIOD (α)	2ND MOST RECENT PERIOD $\alpha(1-\alpha)$	3RD MOST RECENT PERIOD $\alpha(1-\alpha)^2$	4TH MOST RECENT PERIOD $\alpha(1-\alpha)^3$	5TH MOST RECENT PERIOD $\alpha(1-\alpha)^4$
$\alpha = .1$	.1	.09	.081	.073	.066
$\alpha = .5$	.5	.25	.125	.063	.031

Selecting the Smoothing Constant Exponential smoothing has been successfully applied in virtually every type of business. However, the appropriate value of the smoothing constant, α, can make the difference between an accurate forecast and an inaccurate forecast. High values of α are chosen when the underlying average is likely to change. Low values of α are used when the underlying average is fairly stable. In picking a value for the smoothing constant, the objective is to obtain the most accurate forecast.

Measuring Forecast Error

The overall accuracy of any forecasting model—moving average, exponential smoothing, or other—can be determined by comparing the forecasted values with the actual or observed

⚠ STUDENT TIP

Forecasts tend to be more accurate as they become shorter. Therefore, forecast error also tends to drop with shorter forecasts.

values. If F_t denotes the forecast in period t, and A_t denotes the actual demand in period t, the *forecast error* (or deviation) is defined as:

$$\text{Forecast error} = \text{Actual demand} - \text{Forecast value}$$
$$= A_t - F_t$$

LO 4.4 *Compute* three measures of forecast accuracy

Several measures are used in practice to calculate the overall forecast error. These measures can be used to compare different forecasting models, as well as to monitor forecasts to ensure they are performing well. Three of the most popular measures are mean absolute deviation (MAD), mean squared error (MSE), and mean absolute percent error (MAPE). We now describe and give an example of each.

Mean Absolute Deviation   The first measure of the overall forecast error for a model is the mean absolute deviation (MAD). This value is computed by taking the sum of the absolute values of the individual forecast errors (deviations) and dividing by the number of periods of data (n):

Mean absolute deviation (MAD)

A measure of the overall forecast error for a model.

$$\text{MAD} = \frac{\sum |\text{Actual} - \text{Forecast}|}{n} \tag{4-5}$$

Example 4 applies MAD, as a measure of overall forecast error, by testing two values of α.

Example 4

DETERMINING THE MEAN ABSOLUTE DEVIATION (MAD)

During the past 8 quarters, the Port of Baltimore has unloaded large quantities of grain from ships. The port's operations manager wants to test the use of exponential smoothing to see how well the technique works in predicting tonnage unloaded. He guesses that the forecast of grain unloaded in the first quarter was 175 tons. Two values of α are to be examined: $\alpha = .10$ and $\alpha = .50$.

APPROACH ▶   Compare the actual data with the data we forecast (using each of the two α values) and then find the absolute deviation and MADs.

SOLUTION ▶   The following table shows the *detailed* calculations for $\alpha = .10$ only:

QUARTER	ACTUAL TONNAGE UNLOADED	FORECAST WITH $\alpha = .10$	FORECAST WITH $\alpha = .50$
1	180	175	175
2	168	$175.50 = 175.00 + .10(180 - 175)$	177.50
3	159	$174.75 = 175.50 + .10(168 - 175.50)$	172.75
4	175	$173.18 = 174.75 + .10(159 - 174.75)$	165.88
5	190	$173.36 = 173.18 + .10(175 - 173.18)$	170.44
6	205	$175.02 = 173.36 + .10(190 - 173.36)$	180.22
7	180	$178.02 = 175.02 + .10(205 - 175.02)$	192.61
8	182	$178.22 = 178.02 + .10(180 - 178.02)$	186.30
9	?	$178.59 = 178.22 + .10(182 - 178.22)$	184.15

To evaluate the accuracy of each smoothing constant, we can compute forecast errors in terms of absolute deviations and MADs:

QUARTER	ACTUAL TONNAGE UNLOADED	FORECAST WITH $\alpha = .10$	ABSOLUTE DEVIATION FOR $\alpha = .10$	FORECAST WITH $\alpha = .50$	ABSOLUTE DEVIATION FOR $\alpha = .50$
1	180	175	5.00	175	5.00
2	168	175.50	7.50	177.50	9.50
3	159	174.75	15.75	172.75	13.75
4	175	173.18	1.82	165.88	9.12
5	190	173.36	16.64	170.44	19.56
6	205	175.02	29.98	180.22	24.78
7	180	178.02	1.98	192.61	12.61
8	182	178.22	3.78	186.30	4.30
	Sum of absolute deviations:		82.45		98.62
	$\text{MAD} = \dfrac{\sum |\text{Deviations}|}{n}$		10.31		12.33

INSIGHT ▶ On the basis of this comparison of the two MADs, a smoothing constant of $\alpha = .10$ is preferred to $\alpha = .50$ because its MAD is smaller.

LEARNING EXERCISE ▶ If the smoothing constant is changed from $\alpha = .10$ to $\alpha = .20$, what is the new MAD? [Answer: 10.21.]

RELATED PROBLEMS ▶ 4.5b, 4.8c, 4.9c, 4.14, 4.23, 4.59b (4.35d, 4.37a, 4.38c, 4.61b are available in MyOMLab)

EXCEL OM Data File **Ch04Ex4a.xls** and **Ch04Ex4b.xls** can be found in MyOMLab.

ACTIVE MODEL 4.2 This example is further illustrated in Active Model 4.2 in MyOMLab.

Most computerized forecasting software includes a feature that automatically finds the smoothing constant with the lowest forecast error. Some software modifies the α value if errors become larger than acceptable.

Mean Squared Error The mean squared error (MSE) is a second way of measuring overall forecast error. MSE is the average of the squared differences between the forecasted and observed values. Its formula is:

Mean squared error (MSE)
The average of the squared differences between the forecasted and observed values.

$$\text{MSE} = \frac{\Sigma(\text{Forecast errors})^2}{n} \qquad (4\text{-}6)$$

Example 5 finds the MSE for the Port of Baltimore problem introduced in Example 4.

Example 5

DETERMINING THE MEAN SQUARED ERROR (MSE)

The operations manager for the Port of Baltimore now wants to compute MSE for $\alpha = .10$.

APPROACH ▶ Using the same forecast data for $\alpha = .10$ from Example 4, compute the MSE with Equation (4-6).

SOLUTION ▶

QUARTER	ACTUAL TONNAGE UNLOADED	FORECAST FOR $\alpha = .10$	(ERROR)^2
1	180	175	$5^2 = 25$
2	168	175.50	$(-7.5)^2 = 56.25$
3	159	174.75	$(-15.75)^2 = 248.06$
4	175	173.18	$(1.82)^2 = 3.31$
5	190	173.36	$(16.64)^2 = 276.89$
6	205	175.02	$(29.98)^2 = 898.80$
7	180	178.02	$(1.98)^2 = 3.92$
8	182	178.22	$(3.78)^2 = 14.29$
			Sum of errors squared $= 1{,}526.52$

$$\text{MSE} = \frac{\Sigma(\text{Forecast errors})^2}{n} = 1{,}526.52/8 = 190.8$$

INSIGHT ▶ Is this MSE = 190.8 good or bad? It all depends on the MSEs for other forecasting approaches. A low MSE is better because we want to minimize MSE. MSE exaggerates errors because it squares them.

LEARNING EXERCISE ▶ Find the MSE for $\alpha = .50$. [Answer: MSE = 195.24. The result indicates that $\alpha = .10$ is a better choice because we seek a lower MSE. Coincidentally, this is the same conclusion we reached using MAD in Example 4.]

RELATED PROBLEMS ▶ 4.8d, 4.11c, 4.14, 4.15c, 4.16c, 4.20 (4.35d, 4.37b are available in MyOMLab)

The MSE tends to accentuate large deviations due to the squared term. For example, if the forecast error for period 1 is twice as large as the error for period 2, the squared error in period 1 is four times as large as that for period 2. Hence, using MSE as the measure of forecast error typically indicates that we prefer to have several smaller deviations rather than even one large deviation.

Mean Absolute Percent Error   A problem with both the MAD and MSE is that their values depend on the magnitude of the item being forecast. If the forecast item is measured in thousands, the MAD and MSE values can be very large. To avoid this problem, we can use the mean absolute percent error (MAPE). This is computed as the average of the absolute difference between the forecasted and actual values, expressed as a percentage of the actual values. That is, if we have forecasted and actual values for n periods, the MAPE is calculated as:

Mean absolute percent error (MAPE)

The average of the absolute differences between the forecast and actual values, expressed as a percent of actual values.

$$\text{MAPE} = \frac{\sum_{i=1}^{n} 100 \, |\text{Actual}_i - \text{Forecast}_i| / \text{Actual}_i}{n} \tag{4-7}$$

Example 6 illustrates the calculations using the data from Examples 4 and 5.

Example 6

DETERMINING THE MEAN ABSOLUTE PERCENT ERROR (MAPE)

The Port of Baltimore wants to now calculate the MAPE when $\alpha = .10$.

APPROACH ▶   Equation (4-7) is applied to the forecast data computed in Example 4.

SOLUTION ▶

QUARTER	ACTUAL TONNAGE UNLOADED	FORECAST FOR $\alpha = .10$	ABSOLUTE PERCENT ERROR 100 (|ERROR|/ACTUAL)
1	180	175.00	100(5/180) = 2.78%
2	168	175.50	100(7.5/168) = 4.46%
3	159	174.75	100(15.75/159) = 9.90%
4	175	173.18	100(1.82/175) = 1.05%
5	190	173.36	100(16.64/190) = 8.76%
6	205	175.02	100(29.98/205) = 14.62%
7	180	178.02	100(1.98/180) = 1.10%
8	182	178.22	100(3.78/182) = 2.08%
			Sum of % errors = 44.75%

$$\text{MAPE} = \frac{\sum \text{absolute percent error}}{n} = \frac{44.75\%}{8} = 5.59\%$$

INSIGHT ▶   MAPE expresses the error as a percent of the actual values, undistorted by a single large value.

LEARNING EXERCISE ▶   What is MAPE when α is .50? [Answer: MAPE = 6.75%. As was the case with MAD and MSE, the $\alpha = .1$ was preferable for this series of data.]

RELATED PROBLEMS ▶   4.8e, 4.29c

The MAPE is perhaps the easiest measure to interpret. For example, a result that the MAPE is 6% is a clear statement that is not dependent on issues such as the magnitude of the input data. Table 4.1 summarizes how MAD, MSE, and MAPE differ.

Exponential Smoothing with Trend Adjustment

Simple exponential smoothing, the technique we just illustrated in Examples 3 to 6, is like any other moving-average technique: It fails to respond to trends. Other forecasting techniques that can deal with trends are certainly available. However, because exponential smoothing is such a popular modeling approach in business, let us look at it in more detail.

| TABLE 4.1 | Comparison of Measures of Forecast Error |

MEASURE	MEANING	EQUATION		APPLICATION TO CHAPTER EXAMPLE
Mean absolute deviation (MAD)	How much the forecast missed the target	$MAD = \dfrac{\Sigma \lvert Actual - Forecast \rvert}{n}$	(4-5)	For $\alpha = .10$ in Example 4, the forecast for grain unloaded was off by an average of 10.31 tons.
Mean squared error (MSE)	The square of how much the forecast missed the target	$MSE = \dfrac{\Sigma(Forecast\ errors)^2}{n}$	(4-6)	For $\alpha = .10$ in Example 5, the square of the forecast error was 190.8. This number does not have a physical meaning but is useful when compared to the MSE of another forecast.
Mean absolute percent error (MAPE)	The average percent error	$MAPE = \dfrac{\sum\limits_{i=1}^{n} 100 \lvert Actual_i - Forecast_i \rvert / Actual_i}{n}$	(4-7)	For $\alpha = .10$ in Example 6, the forecast is off by 5.59% on average. As in Examples 4 and 5, some forecasts were too high, and some were low.

Here is why exponential smoothing must be modified when a trend is present. Assume that demand for our product or service has been increasing by 100 units per month and that we have been forecasting with $\alpha = 0.4$ in our exponential smoothing model. The following table shows a severe lag in the second, third, fourth, and fifth months, even when our initial estimate for month 1 is perfect:

MONTH	ACTUAL DEMAND	FORECAST (F_t) FOR MONTHS 1–5
1	100	$F_1 = 100$ (given)
2	200	$F_2 = F_1 + \alpha(A_1 - F_1) = 100 + .4(100 - 100) = 100$
3	300	$F_3 = F_2 + \alpha(A_2 - F_2) = 100 + .4(200 - 100) = 140$
4	400	$F_4 = F_3 + \alpha(A_3 - F_3) = 140 + .4(300 - 140) = 204$
5	500	$F_5 = F_4 + \alpha(A_4 - F_4) = 204 + .4(400 - 204) = 282$

To improve our forecast, let us illustrate a more complex exponential smoothing model, one that adjusts for trend. The idea is to compute an exponentially smoothed average of the data and then adjust for positive or negative lag in trend. The new formula is:

Forecast including trend (FIT_t) = Exponentially smoothed forecast average (F_t)

$$+ \text{ Exponentially smoothed trend } (T_t) \qquad (4\text{-}8)$$

With trend-adjusted exponential smoothing, estimates for both the average and the trend are smoothed. This procedure requires two smoothing constants: α for the average and β for the trend. We then compute the average and trend each period:

$F_t = \alpha(\text{Actual demand last period}) + (1 - \alpha)(\text{Forecast last period} + \text{Trend estimate last period})$

or:

$$F_t = \alpha(A_{t-1}) + (1 - \alpha)(F_{t-1} + T_{t-1}) \qquad (4\text{-}9)$$

$T_t = \beta(\text{Forecast this period} - \text{Forecast last period}) + (1 - \beta)(\text{Trend estimate last period})$

or:

$$T_t = \beta(F_t - F_{t-1}) + (1 - \beta)T_{t-1} \qquad (4\text{-}10)$$

where F_t = exponentially smoothed forecast average of the data series in period t
  T_t = exponentially smoothed trend in period t
  A_t = actual demand in period t
  α = smoothing constant for the average $(0 \le \alpha \le 1)$
  β = smoothing constant for the trend $(0 \le \beta \le 1)$

So the three steps to compute a trend-adjusted forecast are:

STEP 1: Compute F_t, the exponentially smoothed forecast average for period t, using Equation (4-9).

STEP 2: Compute the smoothed trend, T_t, using Equation (4-10).

STEP 3: Calculate the forecast including trend, FIT_t, by the formula $FIT_t = F_t + T_t$ [from Equation (4-8)].

Example 7 shows how to use trend-adjusted exponential smoothing.

Example 7

COMPUTING A TREND-ADJUSTED EXPONENTIAL SMOOTHING FORECAST

A large Portland manufacturer wants to forecast demand for a piece of pollution-control equipment. A review of past sales, as shown below, indicates that an increasing trend is present:

MONTH (t)	ACTUAL DEMAND (A_t)	MONTH (t)	ACTUAL DEMAND (A_t)
1	12	6	21
2	17	7	31
3	20	8	28
4	19	9	36
5	24	10	?

Smoothing constants are assigned the values of $\alpha = .2$ and $\beta = .4$. The firm assumes the initial forecast average for month 1 (F_1) was 11 units and the trend over that period (T_1) was 2 units.

APPROACH ▶ A trend-adjusted exponential smoothing model, using Equations (4-9), (4-10), and (4-8) and the three steps above, is employed.

SOLUTION ▶

Step 1: Forecast average for month 2:

$$F_2 = \alpha A_1 + (1 - \alpha)(F_1 + T_1)$$
$$F_2 = (.2)(12) + (1 - .2)(11 + 2)$$
$$= 2.4 + (.8)(13) = 2.4 + 10.4 = 12.8 \text{ units}$$

Step 2: Compute the trend in period 2:

$$T_2 = \beta(F_2 - F_1) + (1 - \beta)T_1$$
$$= .4(12.8 - 11) + (1 - .4)(2)$$
$$= (.4)(1.8) + (.6)(2) = .72 + 1.2 = 1.92$$

Step 3: Compute the forecast including trend (FIT_t):

$$FIT_2 = F_2 + T_2$$
$$= 12.8 + 1.92$$
$$= 14.72 \text{ units}$$

We will also do the same calculations for the third month:

Step 1: $F_3 = \alpha A_2 + (1 - \alpha)(F_2 + T_2) = (.2)(17) + (1 - .2)(12.8 + 1.92)$
$$= 3.4 + (.8)(14.72) = 3.4 + 11.78 = 15.18$$

Step 2: $T_3 = \beta(F_3 - F_2) + (1 - \beta)T_2 = (.4)(15.18 - 12.8) + (1 - .4)(1.92)$
$$= (.4)(2.38) + (.6)(1.92) = .952 + 1.152 = 2.10$$

Step 3: $FIT_3 = F_3 + T_3$
$$= 15.18 + 2.10 = 17.28.$$

Table 4.2 completes the forecasts for the 10-month period.

TABLE 4.2	Forecast with $\alpha = .2$ and $\beta = .4$			
MONTH	**ACTUAL DEMAND**	**SMOOTHED FORECAST AVERAGE, F_t**	**SMOOTHED TREND, T_t**	**FORECAST INCLUDING TREND, FIT_t**
1	12	11	2	13.00
2	17	12.80	1.92	14.72
3	20	15.18	2.10	17.28
4	19	17.82	2.32	20.14
5	24	19.91	2.23	22.14
6	21	22.51	2.38	24.89
7	31	24.11	2.07	26.18
8	28	27.14	2.45	29.59
9	36	29.28	2.32	31.60
10	—	32.48	2.68	35.16

INSIGHT ▶ Figure 4.3 compares actual demand (A_t) to an exponential smoothing forecast that includes trend (FIT_t). *FIT* picks up the trend in actual demand. A simple exponential smoothing model (as we saw in Examples 3 and 4) trails far behind.

LEARNING EXERCISE ▶ Using the data for actual demand for the 9 months, compute the exponentially smoothed forecast average *without* trend [using Equation (4-4) as we did earlier in Examples 3 and 4]. Apply $\alpha = .2$, and assume an initial forecast average for month 1 of 11 units. Then plot the months 2–10 forecast values on Figure 4.3. What do you notice? [Answer: Month 10 forecast = 24.65. All the points are below and lag the trend-adjusted forecast.]

RELATED PROBLEMS ▶ 4.19, 4.20, 4.21, 4.22, 4.32

ACTIVE MODEL 4.3 This example is further illustrated in Active Model 4.3 in MyOMLab.

EXCEL OM Data File **Ch04Ex7.xis** can be found in MyOMLab.

Figure **4.3**

Exponential Smoothing with Trend-Adjustment Forecasts Compared to Actual Demand Data

The value of the trend-smoothing constant, β, resembles the α constant because a high β is more responsive to recent changes in trend. A low β gives less weight to the most recent trends and tends to smooth out the present trend. Values of β can be found by the trial-and-error approach or by using sophisticated commercial forecasting software, with the MAD used as a measure of comparison.

Simple exponential smoothing is often referred to as *first-order smoothing*, and trend-adjusted smoothing is called *second-order smoothing* or *double smoothing*. Other advanced exponential-smoothing models are also used, including seasonal-adjusted and triple smoothing.

Trend Projections

Trend projection

A time-series forecasting method that fits a trend line to a series of historical data points and then projects the line into the future for forecasts.

The last time-series forecasting method we will discuss is trend projection. This technique fits a trend line to a series of historical data points and then projects the slope of the line into the future for medium- to long-range forecasts. Several mathematical trend equations can be developed (for example, exponential and quadratic), but in this section, we will look at *linear* (straight-line) trends only.

If we decide to develop a linear trend line by a precise statistical method, we can apply the *least-squares method*. This approach results in a straight line that minimizes the sum of the squares of the vertical differences or deviations from the line to each of the actual observations. Figure 4.4 illustrates the least-squares approach.

A least-squares line is described in terms of its y-intercept (the height at which it intercepts the y-axis) and its expected change (slope). If we can compute the y-intercept and slope, we can express the line with the following equation:

$$\hat{y} = a + bx \tag{4-11}$$

where $\hat{y}$ (called "y hat") = computed value of the variable to be predicted (called the *dependent variable*)

a = y-axis intercept

b = slope of the regression line (or the rate of change in y for given changes in x)

x = the independent variable (which in this case is *time*)

Statisticians have developed equations that we can use to find the values of a and b for any regression line. The slope b is found by:

$$b = \frac{\sum xy - n\bar{x}\bar{y}}{\sum x^2 - n\bar{x}^2} \tag{4-12}$$

Figure 4.4

The Least-Squares Method for Finding the Best-Fitting Straight Line, Where the Asterisks Are the Locations of the Seven Actual Observations or Data Points

where
b = slope of the regression line
Σ = summation sign
x = known values of the independent variable
y = known values of the dependent variable
$\bar{x}$ = average of the x-values
$\bar{y}$ = average of the y-values
n = number of data points or observations

We can compute the y-intercept a as follows:

$$a = \bar{y} - b\bar{x} \qquad\qquad (4\text{-}13)$$

Example 8 shows how to apply these concepts.

Example 8

FORECASTING WITH LEAST SQUARES

The demand for electric power at N.Y. Edison over the past 7 years is shown in the following table, in megawatts. The firm wants to forecast next year's demand by fitting a straight-line trend to these data.

YEAR	ELECTRICAL POWER DEMAND	YEAR	ELECTRICAL POWER DEMAND
1	74	5	105
2	79	6	142
3	80	7	122
4	90		

APPROACH ▶ Equations (4-12) and (4-13) can be used to create the trend projection model.

SOLUTION ▶

YEAR (x)	ELECTRIC POWER DEMAND (y)	x^2	xy
1	74	1	74
2	79	4	158
3	80	9	240
4	90	16	360
5	105	25	525
6	142	36	852
7	122	49	854
$\Sigma x = 28$	$\Sigma y = 692$	$\Sigma x^2 = 140$	$\Sigma xy = 3,063$

$$\bar{x} = \frac{\Sigma x}{n} = \frac{28}{7} = 4 \quad \bar{y} = \frac{\Sigma y}{n} = \frac{692}{7} = 98.86$$

$$b = \frac{\Sigma xy - n\bar{x}\bar{y}}{\Sigma x^2 - n\bar{x}^2} = \frac{3,063 - (7)(4)(98.86)}{140 - (7)(4^2)} = \frac{295}{28} = 10.54$$

$$a = \bar{y} - b\bar{x} = 98.86 - 10.54(4) = 56.70$$

Thus, the least-squares trend equation is $\hat{y} = 56.70 + 10.54x$. To project demand next year, $x = 8$:

$$\text{Demand in year 8} = 56.70 + 10.54(8)$$

$$= 141.02, \text{ or } 141 \text{ megawatts}$$

INSIGHT ▶ To evaluate the model, we plot both the historical demand and the trend line in Figure 4.5. In this case, we may wish to be cautious and try to understand the year 6 to year 7 swing in demand.

Notes on the Use of the Least-Squares Method   Using the least-squares method implies that we have met three requirements:

1. We always plot the data because least-squares data assume a linear relationship. If a curve appears to be present, curvilinear analysis is probably needed.
2. We do not predict time periods far beyond our given database. For example, if we have 20 months' worth of average prices of Microsoft stock, we can forecast only 3 or 4 months into the future. Forecasts beyond that have little statistical validity. Thus, you cannot take 5 years' worth of sales data and project 10 years into the future. The world is too uncertain.
3. Deviations around the least-squares line (see Figure 4.4) are assumed to be random and normally distributed, with most observations close to the line and only a smaller number farther out.

Seasonal Variations in Data

Seasonal variations

Regular upward or downward movements in a time series that tie to recurring events.

Seasonal variations in data are regular movements in a time series that relate to recurring events such as weather or holidays. Demand for coal and fuel oil, for example, peaks during cold winter months. Demand for golf clubs or sunscreen may be highest in summer.

Seasonality may be applied to hourly, daily, weekly, monthly, or other recurring patterns. Fast-food restaurants experience *daily* surges at noon and again at 5 P.M. Movie theaters see higher demand on Friday and Saturday evenings. The post office, Toys "Я" Us, The Christmas Store, and Hallmark Card Shops also exhibit seasonal variation in customer traffic and sales.

STUDENT TIP ◆

John Deere understands seasonal variations: It has been able to obtain 70% of its orders in advance of seasonal use so it can smooth production.

Similarly, understanding seasonal variations is important for capacity planning in organizations that handle peak loads. These include electric power companies during extreme cold and warm periods, banks on Friday afternoons, and buses and subways during the morning and evening rush hours.

Demand for many products is seasonal. Yamaha, the manufacturer of this jet ski and snowmobile, produces products with complementary demands to address seasonal fluctuations.

Time-series forecasts like those in Example 8 involve reviewing the trend of data over a series of time periods. The presence of seasonality makes adjustments in trend-line forecasts necessary. Seasonality is expressed in terms of the amount that actual values differ from average values in the time series. Analyzing data in monthly or quarterly terms usually makes it easy for a statistician to spot seasonal patterns. Seasonal indices can then be developed by several common methods.

In what is called a *multiplicative seasonal model*, seasonal factors are multiplied by an estimate of average demand to produce a seasonal forecast. Our assumption in this section is that trend has been removed from the data. Otherwise, the magnitude of the seasonal data will be distorted by the trend.

Here are the steps we will follow for a company that has "seasons" of 1 month:

1. Find the *average historical demand each season* (or month in this case) by summing the demand for that month in each year and dividing by the number of years of data available. For example, if, in January, we have seen sales of 8, 6, and 10 over the past 3 years, average January demand equals (8 + 6 + 10)/3 = 8 units.
2. Compute the *average demand over all months* by dividing the total average annual demand by the number of seasons. For example, if the total average demand for a year is 120 units and there are 12 seasons (each month), the average monthly demand is 120/12 = 10 units.
3. Compute a *seasonal index* for each season by dividing that *month's* historical average demand (from Step 1) by the average demand over all months (from Step 2). For example, if the average historical January demand over the past 3 years is 8 units and the average demand over all months is 10 units, the seasonal index for January is 8/10 = .80. Likewise, a seasonal index of 1.20 for February would mean that February's demand is 20% larger than the average demand over all months.
4. Estimate next year's total annual demand.
5. Divide this estimate of total annual demand by the number of seasons, then multiply it by the seasonal index for each month. This provides the *seasonal forecast*.

LO 4.5 *Develop seasonal indices*

Example 9 illustrates this procedure as it computes seasonal indices from historical data.

Example 9 | DETERMINING SEASONAL INDICES

A Des Moines distributor of Sony laptop computers wants to develop monthly indices for sales. Data from the past 3 years, by month, are available.

APPROACH ▶ Follow the five steps listed above.

SOLUTION ▶

MONTH	DEMAND			AVERAGE PERIOD DEMAND	AVERAGE MONTHLY DEMAND[a]	SEASONAL INDEX[b]
	YEAR 1	YEAR 2	YEAR 3			
Jan.	80	85	105	90	94	.957 (= 90/94)
Feb.	70	85	85	80	94	.851 (= 80/94)
Mar.	80	93	82	85	94	.904 (= 85/94)
Apr.	90	95	115	100	94	1.064 (= 100/94)
May	113	125	131	123	94	1.309 (= 123/94)
June	110	115	120	115	94	1.223 (= 115/94)
July	100	102	113	105	94	1.117 (= 105/94)
Aug.	88	102	110	100	94	1.064 (= 100/94)
Sept.	85	90	95	90	94	.957 (= 90/94)
Oct.	77	78	85	80	94	.851 (= 80/94)
Nov.	75	82	83	80	94	.851 (= 80/94)
Dec.	82	78	80	80	94	.851 (= 80/94)

Total average annual demand = 1,128

[a]Average monthly demand = $\dfrac{1,128}{12 \text{ months}}$ = 94.   [b]Seasonal index = $\dfrac{\text{Average monthly demand for past 3 years}}{\text{Average monthly demand}}$

If we expect the annual demand for computers to be 1,200 units next year, we would use these seasonal indices to forecast the monthly demand as follows:

MONTH	DEMAND	MONTH	DEMAND
Jan.	$\dfrac{1,200}{12} \times .957 = 96$	July	$\dfrac{1,200}{12} \times 1.117 = 112$
Feb.	$\dfrac{1,200}{12} \times .851 = 85$	Aug.	$\dfrac{1,200}{12} \times 1.064 = 106$
Mar.	$\dfrac{1,200}{12} \times .904 = 90$	Sept.	$\dfrac{1,200}{12} \times .957 = 96$
Apr.	$\dfrac{1,200}{12} \times 1.064 = 106$	Oct.	$\dfrac{1,200}{12} \times .851 = 85$
May	$\dfrac{1,200}{12} \times 1.309 = 131$	Nov.	$\dfrac{1,200}{12} \times .851 = 85$
June	$\dfrac{1,200}{12} \times 1.223 = 122$	Dec.	$\dfrac{1,200}{12} \times .851 = 85$

INSIGHT ▶   Think of these indices as percentages of average sales. The average sales (without seasonality) would be 94, but with seasonality, sales fluctuate from 85% to 131% of average.

LEARNING EXERCISE ▶   If next year's annual demand is 1,150 laptops (instead of 1,200), what will the January, February, and March forecasts be? [Answer: 91.7, 81.5, and 86.6, which can be rounded to 92, 82, and 87.]

RELATED PROBLEMS ▶   4.26, 4.27 (4.40, 4.41a are available in MyOMLab)

EXCEL **OM** Data File **Ch04Ex9.xls** can be found in MyOMLab.

For simplicity, only 3 periods (years) are used for each monthly index in the preceding example. Example 10 illustrates how indices that have already been prepared can be applied to adjust trend-line forecasts for seasonality.

Example 10

APPLYING BOTH TREND AND SEASONAL INDICES

San Diego Hospital wants to improve its forecasting by applying both trend and seasonal indices to 66 months of data it has collected. It will then forecast "patient-days" over the coming year.

APPROACH ▶ A trend line is created; then monthly seasonal indices are computed. Finally, a multiplicative seasonal model is used to forecast months 67 to 78.

SOLUTION ▶ Using 66 months of adult inpatient hospital days, the following equation was computed:

$$\hat{y} = 8,090 + 21.5x$$

where

$$\hat{y} = \text{patient days}$$
$$x = \text{time, in months}$$

Based on this model, which reflects only trend data, the hospital forecasts patient days for the next month (period 67) to be:

$$\text{Patient days} = 8,090 + (21.5)(67) = 9,530 \text{ (trend only)}$$

While this model, as plotted in Figure 4.6, recognized the upward trend line in the demand for inpatient services, it ignored the seasonality that the administration knew to be present.

Figure 4.6

Trend Data for San Diego Hospital

Source: From "Modern Methods Improve Hospital Forecasting" by W. E. Sterk and E. G. Shryock from *Healthcare Financial Management* 41, no. 3, p. 97. Reprinted by permission of Healthcare Financial Management Association.

The following table provides seasonal indices based on the same 66 months. Such seasonal data, by the way, were found to be typical of hospitals nationwide.

Seasonality Indices for Adult Inpatient Days at San Diego Hospital

MONTH	SEASONALITY INDEX	MONTH	SEASONALITY INDEX
January	1.04	July	1.03
February	0.97	August	1.04
March	1.02	September	0.97
April	1.01	October	1.00
May	0.99	November	0.96
June	0.99	December	0.98

These seasonal indices are graphed in Figure 4.7. Note that January, March, July, and August seem to exhibit significantly higher patient days on average, while February, September, November, and December experience lower patient days.

However, neither the trend data nor the seasonal data alone provide a reasonable forecast for the hospital. Only when the hospital multiplied the trend-adjusted data by the appropriate seasonal index did it obtain good forecasts. Thus, for period 67 (January):

$$\text{Patient days} = (\text{Trend-adjusted forecast})(\text{Monthly seasonal index}) = (9,530)(1.04) = 9,911$$

Figure **4.7**

Seasonal Index for San Diego
Hospital

The patient-days for each month are:

Period	67	68	69	70	71	72	73	74	75	76	77	78
Month	Jan.	Feb.	March	April	May	June	July	Aug.	Sept.	Oct.	Nov.	Dec.
Forecast with Trend & Seasonality	9,911	9,265	9,764	9,691	9,520	9,542	9,949	10,068	9,411	9,724	9,355	9,572

A graph showing the forecast that combines both trend and seasonality appears in Figure 4.8.

Figure **4.8**

Combined Trend and Seasonal
Forecast

INSIGHT ▶ Notice that with trend only, the September forecast is 9,702, but with both trend and seasonal adjustments, the forecast is 9,411. By combining trend and seasonal data, the hospital was better able to forecast inpatient days and the related staffing and budgeting vital to effective operations.

LEARNING EXERCISE ▶ If the slope of the trend line for patient-days is 22.0 (rather than 21.5) and the index for December is .99 (instead of .98), what is the new forecast for December inpatient days? [Answer: 9,708.]

RELATED PROBLEMS ▶ 4.25, 4.28

Example 11 further illustrates seasonality for quarterly data at a wholesaler.

Example 11 | ADJUSTING TREND DATA WITH SEASONAL INDICES

Management at Jagoda Wholesalers, in Calgary, Canada, has used time-series regression based on point-of-sale data to forecast sales for the next 4 quarters. Sales estimates are $100,000, $120,000, $140,000, and $160,000 for the respective quarters. Seasonal indices for the four quarters have been found to be 1.30, .90, .70, and 1.10, respectively.

APPROACH ▶ To compute a seasonalized or adjusted sales forecast, we just multiply each seasonal index by the appropriate trend forecast:

$$\hat{y}_{seasonal} = Index \times \hat{y}_{trend\ forecast}$$

SOLUTION ▶
Quarter I: $\hat{y}_I = (1.30)(\$100,000) = \$130,000$
Quarter II: $\hat{y}_{II} = (.90)(\$120,000) = \$108,000$
Quarter III: $\hat{y}_{III} = (.70)(\$140,000) = \$98,000$
Quarter IV: $\hat{y}_{IV} = (1.10)(\$160,000) = \$176,000$

INSIGHT ▶ The straight-line trend forecast is now adjusted to reflect the seasonal changes.

LEARNING EXERCISE ▶ If the sales forecast for Quarter IV was $180,000 (rather than $160,000), what would be the seasonally adjusted forecast? [Answer: $198,000.]

RELATED PROBLEMS ▶ 4.25, 4.28 (4.41b is available in MyOMLab)

Cyclical Variations in Data

Cycles are like seasonal variations in data but occur every several *years*, not weeks, months, or quarters. Forecasting cyclical variations in a time series is difficult. This is because cycles include a wide variety of factors that cause the economy to go from recession to expansion to recession over a period of years. These factors include national or industrywide overexpansion in times of euphoria and contraction in times of concern. Forecasting demand for individual products can also be driven by product life cycles—the stages products go through from introduction through decline. Life cycles exist for virtually all products; striking examples include floppy disks, video recorders, and the original Game Boy. We leave cyclical analysis to forecasting texts.

Developing associative techniques of variables that affect one another is our next topic.

Cycles
Patterns in the data that occur every several years.

Associative Forecasting Methods: Regression and Correlation Analysis

Unlike time-series forecasting, *associative forecasting* models usually consider *several* variables that are related to the quantity being predicted. Once these related variables have been found, a statistical model is built and used to forecast the item of interest. This approach is more powerful than the time-series methods that use only the historical values for the forecast variable.

Many factors can be considered in an associative analysis. For example, the sales of Dell PCs may be related to Dell's advertising budget, the company's prices, competitors' prices and promotional strategies, and even the nation's economy and unemployment rates. In this case, PC sales would be called the *dependent variable*, and the other variables would be called *independent variables*. The manager's job is to develop *the best statistical relationship between PC sales and the independent variables*. The most common quantitative associative forecasting model is linear-regression analysis.

⚠ STUDENT TIP
We now deal with the same mathematical model that we saw earlier, the least-squares method. But we use any potential "cause-and-effect" variable as *x*.

Using Regression Analysis for Forecasting

We can use the same mathematical model that we employed in the least-squares method of trend projection to perform a linear-regression analysis. The dependent variables that we want to forecast will still be $\hat{y}$. But now the independent variable, x, need no longer be time. We use the equation:

$$\hat{y} = a + bx$$

where
$\hat{y}$ = value of the dependent variable (in our example, sales)
a = y-axis intercept
b = slope of the regression line
x = independent variable

Example 12 shows how to use linear regression.

Linear-regression analysis
A straight-line mathematical model to describe the functional relationships between independent and dependent variables.

LO 4.6 *Conduct* a regression and correlation analysis

Example 12

COMPUTING A LINEAR REGRESSION EQUATION

Nodel Construction Company renovates old homes in West Bloomfield, Michigan. Over time, the company has found that its dollar volume of renovation work is dependent on the West Bloomfield area payroll. Management wants to establish a mathematical relationship to help predict sales.

APPROACH ▶ Nodel's VP of operations has prepared the following table, which lists company revenues and the amount of money earned by wage earners in West Bloomfield during the past 6 years:

NODEL'S SALES (IN $ MILLIONS), y	AREA PAYROLL (IN $ BILLIONS), x	NODEL'S SALES (IN $ MILLIONS), y	AREA PAYROLL (IN $ BILLIONS), x
2.0	1	2.0	2
3.0	3	2.0	1
2.5	4	3.5	7

The VP needs to determine whether there is a straight-line (linear) relationship between area payroll and sales. He plots the known data on a scatter diagram:

From the six data points, there appears to be a slight positive relationship between the independent variable (payroll) and the dependent variable (sales): As payroll increases, Nodel's sales tend to be higher.

SOLUTION ▶ We can find a mathematical equation by using the least-squares regression approach:

SALES, y	PAYROLL, x	x^2	xy
2.0	1	1	2.0
3.0	3	9	9.0
2.5	4	16	10.0
2.0	2	4	4.0
2.0	1	1	2.0
3.5	7	49	24.5
$\Sigma y = 15.0$	$\Sigma x = 18$	$\Sigma x^2 = 80$	$\Sigma xy = 51.5$

$$\bar{x} = \frac{\Sigma x}{6} = \frac{18}{6} = 3$$

$$\bar{y} = \frac{\Sigma y}{6} = \frac{15}{6} = 2.5$$

$$b = \frac{\Sigma xy - n\bar{x}\bar{y}}{\Sigma x^2 - n\bar{x}^2} = \frac{51.5 - (6)(3)(2.5)}{80 - (6)(3^2)} = .25$$

$$a = \bar{y} - b\bar{x} = 2.5 - (.25)(3) = 1.75$$

The estimated regression equation, therefore, is:

$$\hat{y} = 1.75 + .25x$$

or:

$$\text{Sales} = 1.75 + .25 \text{ (payroll)}$$

If the local chamber of commerce predicts that the West Bloomfield area payroll will be $6 billion next year, we can estimate sales for Nodel with the regression equation:

$$\text{Sales (in \$ millions)} = 1.75 + .25(6)$$
$$= 1.75 + 1.50 = 3.25$$

or:

$$\text{Sales} = \$3,250,000$$

INSIGHT ▶ Given our assumptions of a straight-line relationship between payroll and sales, we now have an indication of the slope of that relationship: on average, sales increase at the rate of $\frac{1}{4}$ million dollars for every billion dollars in the local area payroll. This is because $b = .25$.

LEARNING EXERCISE ▶ What are Nodel's sales when the local payroll is $8 billion? [Answer: $3.75 million.]

RELATED PROBLEMS ▶ 4.34, 4.43–4.48, 4.50–4.54 (4.56a, 4.57, 4.58 are available in MyOMLab)

EXCEL OM Data File **Ch04Ex12.xls** can be found in MyOMLab.

The final part of Example 12 shows a central weakness of associative forecasting methods like regression. Even when we have computed a regression equation, we must provide a forecast of the independent variable x—in this case, payroll—before estimating the dependent variable y for the next time period. Although this is not a problem for all forecasts, you can imagine the difficulty of determining future values of *some* common independent variables (e.g., unemployment rates, gross national product, price indices, and so on).

Standard Error of the Estimate

The forecast of $3,250,000 for Nodel's sales in Example 12 is called a *point estimate* of y. The point estimate is really the *mean*, or *expected value*, of a distribution of possible values of sales. Figure 4.9 illustrates this concept.

To measure the accuracy of the regression estimates, we must compute the **standard error of the estimate**, $S_{y,x}$. This computation is called the *standard deviation of the regression:* It measures the error from the dependent variable, y, to the regression line, rather than to the mean. Equation (4-14) is a similar expression to that found in most statistics books for computing the standard deviation of an arithmetic mean:

Standard error of the estimate
A measure of variability around the regression line—its standard deviation.

$$S_{y,x} = \sqrt{\frac{\Sigma(y - y_c)^2}{n - 2}} \qquad (4\text{-}14)$$

where
$y = y$-value of each data point
$y_c =$ computed value of the dependent variable, from the regression equation
$n =$ number of data points

Figure 4.9

Distribution about the Point Estimate of $3.25 Million Sales

Glidden Paints' assembly lines require thousands of gallons every hour. To predict demand, the firm uses associative forecasting methods such as linear regression, with independent variables such as disposable personal income and GNP. Although housing starts would be a natural variable, Glidden found that it correlated poorly with past sales. It turns out that most Glidden paint is sold through retailers to customers who already own homes or businesses.

Michael Rosenfeld/Maximilian S/RGB Ventures/ SuperStock/Alamy

Equation (4-15) may look more complex, but it is actually an easier-to-use version of Equation (4-14). Both formulas provide the same answer and can be used in setting up prediction intervals around the point estimate:[2]

$$S_{y,x} = \sqrt{\frac{\sum y^2 - a\sum y - b\sum xy}{n - 2}} \qquad (4\text{-}15)$$

Example 13 shows how we would calculate the standard error of the estimate in Example 12.

Example 13

COMPUTING THE STANDARD ERROR OF THE ESTIMATE

Nodel's VP of operations now wants to know the error associated with the regression line computed in Example 12.

APPROACH ▶ Compute the standard error of the estimate, $S_{y,x}$, using Equation (4-15).

SOLUTION ▶ The only number we need that is not available to solve for $S_{y,x}$ is $\sum y^2$. Some quick addition reveals $\sum y^2 = 39.5$. Therefore:

$$S_{y,x} = \sqrt{\frac{\sum y^2 - a\sum y - b\sum xy}{n - 2}}$$

$$= \sqrt{\frac{39.5 - 1.75(15.0) - .25(51.5)}{6 - 2}}$$

$$= \sqrt{.09375} = .306 \text{ (in \$ millions)}$$

The standard error of the estimate is then $306,000 in sales.

INSIGHT ▶ The interpretation of the standard error of the estimate is similar to the standard deviation; namely, ± 1 standard deviation = .6827. So there is a 68.27% chance of sales being $\pm$ \$306,000 from the point estimate of \$3,250,000.

LEARNING EXERCISE ▶ What is the probability sales will exceed \$3,556,000? [Answer: About 16%.]

RELATED PROBLEMS ▶ 4.52e, 4.54b (4.56c, 4.57 are available in MyOMLab)

Correlation Coefficients for Regression Lines

The regression equation is one way of expressing the nature of the relationship between two variables. Regression lines are not "cause-and-effect" relationships. They merely describe the relationships among variables. The regression equation shows how one variable relates to the value and changes in another variable.

Another way to evaluate the relationship between two variables is to compute the coefficient of correlation. This measure expresses the degree or strength of the linear relationship (but note

Coefficient of correlation

A measure of the strength of the relationship between two variables.

Figure **4.10**

Five Values of the Correlation Coefficient

(a) Perfect negative correlation: $r = -1$

(b) Negative correlation

(c) No correlation: $r = 0$

(d) Positive correlation

(e) Perfect positive correlation: $r = 1$

| High | Moderate | Low | Low | Moderate | High |

| −1.0 | −0.8 | −0.6 | −0.4 | −0.2 | 0 | 0.2 | 0.4 | 0.6 | 0.8 | 1.0 |

Correlation coefficient values

that correlation does not necessarily imply causality). Usually identified as r, the coefficient of correlation can be any number between $+1$ and -1. Figure 4.10 illustrates what different values of r might look like.

To compute r, we use much of the same data needed earlier to calculate a and b for the regression line. The rather lengthy equation for r is:

$$r = \frac{n\sum xy - \sum x \sum y}{\sqrt{[n\sum x^2 - (\sum x)^2][n\sum y^2 - (\sum y)^2]}} \qquad (4\text{-}16)$$

Example 14 shows how to calculate the coefficient of correlation for the data given in Examples 12 and 13.

Example 14

DETERMINING THE COEFFICIENT OF CORRELATION

In Example 12, we looked at the relationship between Nodel Construction Company's renovation sales and payroll in its hometown of West Bloomfield. The VP now wants to know the strength of the association between area payroll and sales.

APPROACH ▶ We compute the r value using Equation (4-16). We need to first add one more column of calculations—for y^2.

SOLUTION ▶ The data, including the column for y^2 and the calculations, are shown here:

y	x	x^2	xy	y^2
2.0	1	1	2.0	4.0
3.0	3	9	9.0	9.0
2.5	4	16	10.0	6.25
2.0	2	4	4.0	4.0
2.0	1	1	2.0	4.0
3.5	7	49	24.5	12.25
$\sum y = 15.0$	$\sum x = 18$	$\sum x^2 = 80$	$\sum xy = 51.5$	$\sum y^2 = 39.5$

$$r = \frac{(6)(51.5) - (18)(15.0)}{\sqrt{[(6)(80) - (18)^2][(6)(39.5) - (15.0)^2]}}$$

$$= \frac{309 - 270}{\sqrt{(156)(12)}} = \frac{39}{\sqrt{1{,}872}}$$

$$= \frac{39}{43.3} = .901$$

INSIGHT ▶ This r of .901 appears to be a significant correlation and helps confirm the closeness of the relationship between the two variables.

LEARNING EXERCISE ▶ If the coefficient of correlation was $-.901$ rather than $+.901$, what would this tell you? [Answer: The negative correlation would tell you that as payroll went up, Nodel's sales went down—a rather unlikely occurrence that would suggest you recheck your math.]

RELATED PROBLEMS ▶ 4.43d, 4.48d, 4.50c, 4.52f, 4.54b (4.56b, 4.57 are available in MyOMLab)

Coefficient of determination

A measure of the amount of variation in the dependent variable about its mean that is explained by the regression equation.

Although the coefficient of correlation is the measure most commonly used to describe the relationship between two variables, another measure does exist. It is called the **coefficient of determination** and is simply the square of the coefficient of correlation—namely, r^2. The value of r^2 will always be a positive number in the range $0 \le r^2 \le 1$. The coefficient of determination is the percent of variation in the dependent variable (y) that is explained by the regression equation. In Nodel's case, the value of r^2 is .81, indicating that 81% of the total variation is explained by the regression equation.

Multiple-Regression Analysis

Multiple regression

An associative forecasting method with more than one independent variable.

Multiple regression is a practical extension of the simple regression model we just explored. It allows us to build a model with several independent variables instead of just one variable. For example, if Nodel Construction wanted to include average annual interest rates in its model for forecasting renovation sales, the proper equation would be:

$$\hat{y} = a + b_1 x_1 + b_2 x_2 \tag{4-17}$$

where
$$y = \text{dependent variable, sales}$$
$$a = \text{a constant, the } y \text{ intercept}$$
$$x_1 \text{ and } x_2 = \text{values of the two independent variables, area payroll and interest rates, respectively}$$
$$b_1 \text{ and } b_2 = \text{coefficients for the two independent variables}$$

The mathematics of multiple regression becomes quite complex (and is usually tackled by computer), so we leave the formulas for a, b_1, and b_2 to statistics textbooks. However, Example 15 shows how to interpret Equation (4-17) in forecasting Nodel's sales.

Example 15

USING A MULTIPLE-REGRESSION EQUATION

Nodel Construction wants to see the impact of a second independent variable, interest rates, on its sales.

APPROACH ▶ The new multiple-regression line for Nodel Construction, calculated by computer software, is:

$$\hat{y} = 1.80 + .30x_1 - 5.0x_2$$

We also find that the new coefficient of correlation is .96, implying the inclusion of the variable x_2, interest rates, adds even more strength to the linear relationship.

SOLUTION ▶ We can now estimate Nodel's sales if we substitute values for next year's payroll and interest rate. If West Bloomfield's payroll will be $6 billion and the interest rate will be .12 (12%), sales will be forecast as:

$$\text{Sales(\$ millions)} = 1.80 + .30(6) - 5.0(.12)$$
$$= 1.8 + 1.8 - .6$$
$$= 3.00$$

or:

$$\text{Sales} = \$3,000,000$$

INSIGHT ▶ By using both variables, payroll and interest rates, Nodel now has a sales forecast of $3 million and a higher coefficient of correlation. This suggests a stronger relationship between the two variables and a more accurate estimate of sales.

LEARNING EXERCISE ▶ If interest rates were only 6%, what would be the sales forecast? [Answer: $1.8 + 1.8 - 5.0(.06) = 3.3$, or $3,300,000.]

RELATED PROBLEMS ▶ 4.47, 4.49 (4.59 is available in MyOMLab)

The *OM in Action* box, "NYC's Potholes and Regression Analysis," provides an interesting example of one city's use of regression and multiple regression.

OM in Action   NYC's Potholes and Regression Analysis

New York is famous for many things, but one it does not like to be known for is its large and numerous potholes. David Letterman used to joke: "There is a pothole so big on 8th Avenue, it has its own Starbucks in it." When it comes to potholes, some years seem to be worse than others. The winter of 2014 was an exceptionally bad year. City workers filled a record 300,000 potholes during the first 4 months of the year. That's an astounding accomplishment.

But potholes are to some extent a measure of municipal competence—and they are costly. NYC's poor streets cost the average motorist an estimated $800 per year in repair work and new tires. There has been a steady and dramatic increase in potholes from around 70,000–80,000 in the 1990s to the devastatingly high 200,000–300,000 range in recent years. One theory is that bad weather causes the potholes. Using inches of snowfall as a measure of the severity of the winter, the graph below shows a plot of the number of potholes versus the inches of snow each winter.

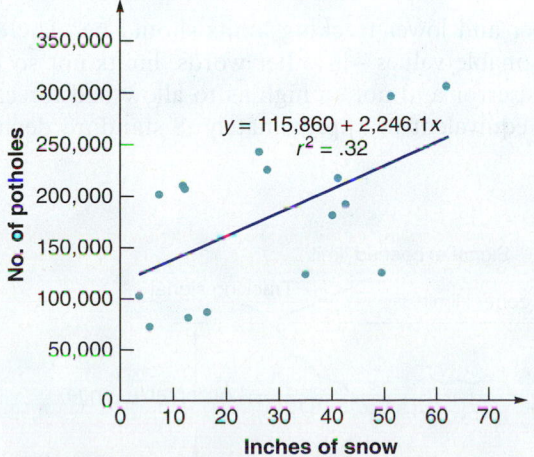

Research showed that the city would need to resurface at least 1,000 miles of roads per year just to stay even with road deterioration.

Any amount below that would contribute to a "gap" or backlog of streets needing repair. The graph below shows the plot of potholes versus the gap. With an r^2 of .81, there is a very strong relationship between the increase in the "gap" and the number of potholes. It is obvious that the real reason for the steady and substantial increase in the number of potholes is due to the increasing gap in road resurfacing.

A third model performs a regression analysis using the resurfacing gap and inches of snow as two independent variables and number of potholes as the dependent variable. That regression model's r^2 is .91.

$$\text{Potholes} = 7,801.5 + 80.6 \times \text{Resurfacing gap}$$
$$+ 930.1 \times \text{Inches of snow}$$

Sources: OR/MS Today (June, 2014) and New York Daily News (March 5, 2014).

Monitoring and Controlling Forecasts

Once a forecast has been completed, it should not be forgotten. No manager wants to be reminded that his or her forecast is horribly inaccurate, but a firm needs to determine why actual demand (or whatever variable is being examined) differed significantly from that projected. If the forecaster is accurate, that individual usually makes sure that everyone is aware of his or her talents. Very seldom does one read articles in *Fortune, Forbes,* or *The Wall Street Journal,* however, about money managers who are consistently off by 25% in their stock market forecasts.

One way to monitor forecasts to ensure that they are performing well is to use a tracking signal. A tracking signal is a measurement of how well a forecast is predicting actual values. As forecasts are updated every week, month, or quarter, the newly available demand data are compared to the forecast values.

The tracking signal is computed as the cumulative error divided by the *mean absolute deviation (MAD)*:

$$\text{Tracking signal} = \frac{\text{Cumulative error}}{\text{MAD}} \tag{4-18}$$

$$= \frac{\sum(\text{Actual demand in period } i - \text{Forecast demand in period } i)}{\text{MAD}}$$

where

$$\text{MAD} = \frac{\sum|\text{Actual} - \text{Forecast}|}{n}$$

as seen earlier, in Equation (4-5).

Positive tracking signals indicate that demand is *greater* than forecast. *Negative* signals mean that demand is *less* than forecast. A good tracking signal—that is, one with a low cumulative error—has about as much positive error as it has negative error. In other words, small deviations are okay, but positive and negative errors should balance one another so that the tracking signal centers closely around zero. A consistent tendency for forecasts to be greater or less than the actual values (that is, for a high absolute cumulative error) is called a bias error. Bias can occur if, for example, the wrong variables or trend line are used or if a seasonal index is misapplied.

Once tracking signals are calculated, they are compared with predetermined control limits. When a tracking signal exceeds an upper or lower limit, there is a problem with the forecasting method, and management may want to reevaluate the way it forecasts demand. Figure 4.11 shows the graph of a tracking signal that is exceeding the range of acceptable variation. If the model being used is exponential smoothing, perhaps the smoothing constant needs to be readjusted.

How do firms decide what the upper and lower tracking limits should be? There is no single answer, but they try to find reasonable values—in other words, limits not so low as to be triggered with every small forecast error and not so high as to allow bad forecasts to be regularly overlooked. One MAD is equivalent to approximately .8 standard deviations,

Tracking signal

A measurement of how well a forecast is predicting actual values.

Bias

A forecast that is consistently higher or consistently lower than actual values of a time series.

LO 4.7 *Use* a tracking signal

Figure **4.11**

A Plot of Tracking Signals

± 2 MADs $= \pm 1.6$ standard deviations, ± 3 MADs $= \pm 2.4$ standard deviations, and ± 4 MADs $= \pm 3.2$ standard deviations. This fact suggests that for a forecast to be "in control," 89% of the errors are expected to fall within ± 2 MADs, 98% within ± 3 MADs, or 99.9% within ± 4 MADs.[3]

Example 16 shows how the tracking signal and cumulative error can be computed.

Example 16

COMPUTING THE TRACKING SIGNAL AT CARLSON'S BAKERY

Carlson's Bakery wants to evaluate performance of its croissant forecast.

APPROACH ▶ Develop a tracking signal for the forecast, and see if it stays within acceptable limits, which we define as ± 4 MADs.

SOLUTION ▶ Using the forecast and demand data for the past 6 quarters for croissant sales, we develop a tracking signal in the following table:

QUARTER	ACTUAL DEMAND	FORECAST DEMAND	ERROR	CUMULATIVE ERROR	ABSOLUTE FORECAST ERROR	CUMULATIVE ABSOLUTE FORECAST ERROR	MAD	TRACKING SIGNAL (CUMULATIVE ERROR/MAD)
1	90	100	−10	−10	10	10	10.0	−10/10 = −1
2	95	100	−5	−15	5	15	7.5	−15/7.5 = −2
3	115	100	+15	0	15	30	10.0	0/10 = 0
4	100	110	−10	−10	10	40	10.0	−10/10 = −1
5	125	110	+15	+5	15	55	11.0	+5/11 = +0.5
6	140	110	+30	+35	30	85	14.2	+35/14.2 = +2.5

$$\text{At the end of quarter 6, MAD} = \frac{\sum |\text{Forecast errors}|}{n} = \frac{85}{6} = 14.2$$

$$\text{and Tracking signal} = \frac{\text{Cumulative error}}{\text{MAD}} = \frac{35}{14.2} = 2.5 \text{ MADs}$$

INSIGHT ▶ Because the tracking signal drifted from −2 MAD to +2.5 MAD (between 1.6 and 2.0 standard deviations), we can conclude that it is within acceptable limits.

LEARNING EXERCISE ▶ If actual demand in quarter 6 was 130 (rather than 140), what would be the MAD and resulting tracking signal? [Answer: MAD for quarter 6 would be 12.5, and the tracking signal for period 6 would be 2 MADs.]

RELATED PROBLEMS ▶ 4.59, 4.60 (4.61c is available in MyOMLab)

Adaptive Smoothing

Adaptive forecasting refers to computer monitoring of tracking signals and self-adjustment if a signal passes a preset limit. For example, when applied to exponential smoothing, the α and β coefficients are first selected on the basis of values that minimize error forecasts and then adjusted accordingly whenever the computer notes an errant tracking signal. This process is called adaptive smoothing.

Adaptive smoothing

An approach to exponential smoothing forecasting in which the smoothing constant is automatically changed to keep errors to a minimum.

Focus Forecasting

Rather than adapt by choosing a smoothing constant, computers allow us to try a variety of forecasting models. Such an approach is called focus forecasting. Focus forecasting is based on two principles:

1. Sophisticated forecasting models are not always better than simple ones.
2. There is no single technique that should be used for all products or services.

Focus forecasting

Forecasting that tries a variety of computer models and selects the best one for a particular application.

Bernard Smith, inventory manager for American Hardware Supply, coined the term *focus forecasting*. Smith's job was to forecast quantities for 100,000 hardware products purchased by American's 21 buyers.[4] He found that buyers neither trusted nor understood the exponential smoothing model then in use. Instead, they used very simple approaches of their own. So Smith developed his new computerized system for selecting forecasting methods.

Smith chose to test seven forecasting methods. They ranged from the simple ones that buyers used (such as the naive approach) to statistical models. Every month, Smith applied the forecasts of all seven models to each item in stock. In these simulated trials, the forecast values were subtracted from the most recent actual demands, giving a simulated forecast error. The forecast method yielding the least error is selected by the computer, which then uses it to make next month's forecast. Although buyers still have an override capability, American Hardware finds that focus forecasting provides excellent results.

Forecasting in the Service Sector

Forecasting in the service sector presents some unusual challenges. A major technique in the retail sector is tracking demand by maintaining good short-term records. For instance, a barbershop catering to men expects peak flows on Fridays and Saturdays. Indeed, most barbershops are closed on Sunday and Monday, and many call in extra help on Friday and Saturday. A downtown restaurant, on the other hand, may need to track conventions and holidays for effective short-term forecasting.

Specialty Retail Shops   Specialty retail facilities, such as flower shops, may have other unusual demand patterns, and those patterns will differ depending on the holiday. When Valentine's Day falls on a weekend, for example, flowers can't be delivered to offices, and those romantically inclined are likely to celebrate with outings rather than flowers. If a holiday falls on a Monday, some of the celebration may also take place on the weekend, reducing flower sales. However, when Valentine's Day falls in midweek, busy midweek schedules often make flowers the optimal way to celebrate. Because flowers for Mother's Day are to be delivered on Saturday or Sunday, this holiday forecast varies less. Due to special demand patterns, many service firms maintain records of sales, noting not only the day of the week but also unusual events, including the weather, so that patterns and correlations that influence demand can be developed.

Fast-Food Restaurants   Fast-food restaurants are well aware not only of weekly, daily, and hourly but even 15-minute variations in demands that influence sales. Therefore, detailed forecasts of demand are needed. Figure 4.12(a) shows the hourly forecast for a typical fast-food restaurant. Note the lunchtime and dinnertime peaks. This contrasts to the mid-morning and mid-afternoon peaks at FedEx's call center in Figure 4.12(b).

Firms like Taco Bell now use point-of-sale computers that track sales every quarter hour. Taco Bell found that a 6-week moving average was the forecasting technique that minimized its mean squared error (MSE) of these quarter-hour forecasts. Building this forecasting methodology into each of Taco Bell's 6,500 U.S. stores' computers, the model makes weekly projections of customer transactions. These in turn are used by store managers to schedule staff, who begin in 15-minute increments, not 1-hour blocks as in other industries. The forecasting model has been so successful that Taco Bell has increased customer service while documenting more than $50 million in labor cost savings in 4 years of use.

(a)
Hourly sales at a fast-food restaurant

(b)
Monday calls at a FedEx call center*

Figure **4.12**

Forecasts Are Unique: Note the Variations between (a) Hourly Sales at a Fast-Food Restaurant and (b) Hourly Call Volume at FedEx

*Based on historical data: see *Journal of Business Forecasting* (Winter 1999–2000): 6–11.

Summary

Forecasts are a critical part of the operations manager's function. Demand forecasts drive a firm's production, capacity, and scheduling systems and affect the financial, marketing, and personnel planning functions.

There are a variety of qualitative and quantitative forecasting techniques. Qualitative approaches employ judgment, experience, intuition, and a host of other factors that are difficult to quantify. Quantitative forecasting uses historical data and causal, or associative, relations to project future demands. The Rapid Review for this chapter

summarizes the formulas we introduced in quantitative forecasting. Forecast calculations are seldom performed by hand. Most operations managers turn to software packages such as Forecast PRO, NCSS, Minitab, Systat, Statgraphics, SAS, or SPSS.

No forecasting method is perfect under all conditions. And even once management has found a satisfactory approach, it must still monitor and control forecasts to make sure errors do not get out of hand. Forecasting can often be a very challenging, but rewarding, part of managing.

Key Terms

Forecasting (p. 108)
Economic forecasts (p. 109)
Technological forecasts (p. 109)
Demand forecasts (p. 109)
Quantitative forecasts (p. 111)
Qualitative forecasts (p. 111)
Jury of executive opinion (p. 111)
Delphi method (p. 111)
Sales force composite (p. 111)
Market survey (p. 111)

Time series (p. 112)
Naive approach (p. 114)
Moving averages (p. 114)
Exponential smoothing (p. 116)
Smoothing constant (p. 116)
Mean absolute deviation (MAD) (p. 118)
Mean squared error (MSE) (p. 119)
Mean absolute percent error (MAPE) (p. 120)
Trend projection (p. 124)
Seasonal variations (p. 126)

Cycles (p. 131)
Linear-regression analysis (p. 131)
Standard error of the estimate (p. 133)
Coefficient of correlation (p. 134)
Coefficient of determination (p. 136)
Multiple regression (p. 136)
Tracking signal (p. 138)
Bias (p. 138)
Adaptive smoothing (p. 139)
Focus forecasting (p. 139)

Ethical Dilemma

We live in a society obsessed with test scores and maximum performance. Think of the SAT, ACT, GRE, GMAT, and LSAT. Though they take only a few hours, they are supposed to give schools and companies a snapshot of a student's abiding talents.

But these tests are often spectacularly bad at forecasting performance in the real world. The SAT does a decent job (r^2 = .12) of predicting the grades of a college freshman. It is, however, less effective at predicting achievement *after* graduation.

LSAT scores bear virtually no correlation to career success as measured by income, life satisfaction, or public service.

What does the r^2 mean in this context? Is it ethical for colleges to base admissions and financial aid decisions on scores alone? What role do these tests take at your own school?

Discussion Questions

1. What is a qualitative forecasting model, and when is its use appropriate?
2. Identify and briefly describe the two general forecasting approaches.
3. Identify the three forecasting time horizons. State an approximate duration for each.
4. Briefly describe the steps that are used to develop a forecasting system.
5. A skeptical manager asks what medium-range forecasts can be used for. Give the manager three possible uses/purposes.
6. Explain why such forecasting devices as moving averages, weighted moving averages, and exponential smoothing are not well suited for data series that have trends.
7. What is the basic difference between a weighted moving average and exponential smoothing?
8. What three methods are used to determine the accuracy of any given forecasting method? How would you determine whether time-series regression or exponential smoothing is better in a specific application?
9. Research and briefly describe the Delphi technique. How would it be used by an employer you have worked for?
10. What is the primary difference between a time-series model and an associative model?
11. Define *time series*.
12. What effect does the value of the smoothing constant have on the weight given to the recent values?
13. Explain the value of seasonal indices in forecasting. How are seasonal patterns different from cyclical patterns?
14. Which forecasting technique can place the most emphasis on recent values? How does it do this?
15. In your own words, explain adaptive forecasting.
16. What is the purpose of a tracking signal?
17. Explain, in your own words, the meaning of the correlation coefficient. Discuss the meaning of a negative value of the correlation coefficient.
18. What is the difference between a dependent and an independent variable?
19. Give examples of industries that are affected by seasonality. Why would these businesses want to filter out seasonality?
20. Give examples of industries in which demand forecasting is dependent on the demand for other products.
21. What happens to the ability to forecast for periods farther into the future?
22. CEO John Goodale, at Southern Illinois Power and Light, has been collecting data on demand for electric power in its western subregion for only the past 2 years. Those data are shown in the table below.

    To plan for expansion and to arrange to borrow power from neighboring utilities during peak periods, Goodale needs to be able to forecast demand for each month next year. However, the standard forecasting models discussed in this chapter will not fit the data observed for the 2 years.
    a) What are the weaknesses of the standard forecasting techniques as applied to this set of data?
    b) Because known models are not appropriate here, propose your own approach to forecasting. Although there is no perfect solution to tackling data such as these (in other words, there are no 100% right or wrong answers), justify your model.
    c) Forecast demand for each month next year using the model you propose.

DEMAND IN MEGAWATTS		
MONTH	LAST YEAR	THIS YEAR
January	5	17
February	6	14
March	10	20
April	13	23
May	18	30
June	15	38
July	23	44
August	26	41
September	21	33
October	15	23
November	12	26
December	14	17

Using Software in Forecasting

This section presents three ways to solve forecasting problems with computer software. First, you can create your own Excel spreadsheets to develop forecasts. Second, you can use the Excel OM software that comes with the text. Third, POM for Windows is another program that is located in MyOMLab.

CREATING YOUR OWN EXCEL SPREADSHEETS

Excel spreadsheets (and spreadsheets in general) are frequently used in forecasting. Exponential smoothing, trend analysis, and regression analysis (simple and multiple) are supported by built-in Excel functions.

Program 4.1 illustrates how to build an Excel forecast for the data in Example 8. The goal for N.Y. Edison is to create a trend analysis of the year 1 to year 7 data.

As an alternative, you may want to experiment with Excel's built-in regression analysis. To do so, under the **Data** menu bar selection choose **Data Analysis**, then **Regression**. Enter your *Y* and *X* data into two columns (say A and B). When the regression window appears, enter the *Y* and *X* ranges, then select **OK**. Excel offers several plots and tables to those interested in more rigorous analysis of regression problems.

Program **4.1**

Using Excel to Develop Your Own Forecast, with Data from Example 8

✖ USING EXCEL OM

Excel OM's forecasting module has five components: (1) moving averages, (2) weighted moving averages, (3) exponential smoothing, (4) regression (with one variable only), and (5) decomposition. Excel OM's error analysis is much more complete than that available with the Excel add-in.

Program 4.2 illustrates Excel OM's input and output, using Example 2's weighted-moving-average data.

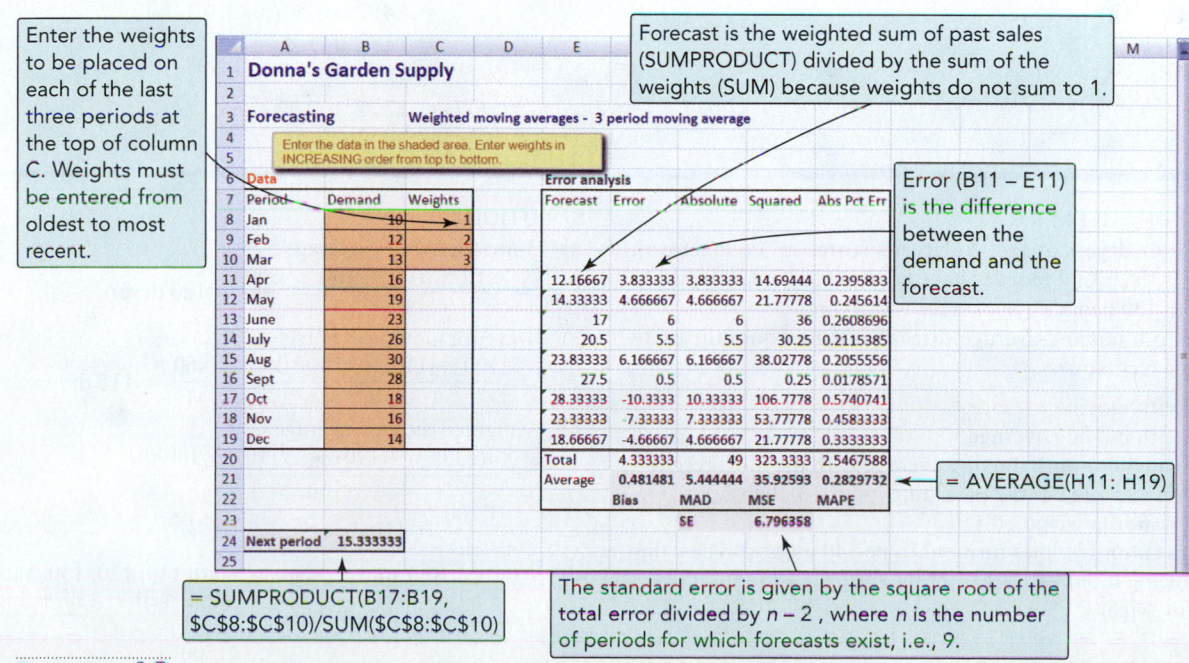

Program **4.2**

Analysis of Excel OM's Weighted-Moving-Average Program, Using Data from Example 2 as Input

Solved Problems   Virtual Office Hours help is available in MyOMLab.

SOLVED PROBLEM 4.1

Sales of Volkswagen's popular Beetle have grown steadily at auto dealerships in Nevada during the past 5 years (see table below). The sales manager had predicted before the new model was introduced that first year sales would be 410 VWs. Using exponential smoothing with a weight of $\alpha = .30$, develop forecasts for years 2 through 6.

YEAR	SALES	FORECAST
1	450	410
2	495	
3	518	
4	563	
5	584	
6	?	

SOLUTION

YEAR	FORECAST
1	410.0
2	$422.0 = 410 + .3\,(450 - 410)$
3	$443.9 = 422 + .3\,(495 - 422)$
4	$466.1 = 443.9 + .3\,(518 - 443.9)$
5	$495.2 = 466.1 + .3\,(563 - 466.1)$
6	$521.8 = 495.2 + .3\,(584 - 495.2)$

SOLVED PROBLEM 4.2

In Example 7, we applied trend-adjusted exponential smoothing to forecast demand for a piece of pollution-control equipment for months 2 and 3 (out of 9 months of data provided). Let us now continue this process for month 4. We want to confirm the forecast for month 4 shown in Table 4.2 (p. 123) and Figure 4.3 (p. 123).

   For month 4, $A_4 = 19$, with $\alpha = .2$, and $\beta = .4$.

SOLUTION

$$
\begin{aligned}
F_4 &= \alpha A_3 + (1 - \alpha)(F_3 + T_3) \\
&= (.2)(20) + (1 - .2)(15.18 + 2.10) \\
&= 4.0 + (.8)(17.28) \\
&= 4.0 + 13.82 \\
&= 17.82 \\
T_4 &= \beta(F_4 - F_3) + (1 - \beta)T_3 \\
&= (.4)(17.82 - 15.18) + (1 - .4)(2.10) \\
&= (.4)(2.64) + (.6)(2.10) \\
&= 1.056 + 1.26 \\
&= 2.32 \\
FIT_4 &= 17.82 + 2.32 \\
&= 20.14
\end{aligned}
$$

SOLVED PROBLEM 4.3

Sales of hair dryers at the Walgreens stores in Youngstown, Ohio, over the past 4 months have been 100, 110, 120, and 130 units (with 130 being the most recent sales).

   Develop a moving-average forecast for next month, using these three techniques:

a)   3-month moving average.
b)   4-month moving average.
c)   Weighted 4-month moving average with the most recent month weighted 4, the preceding month 3, then 2, and the oldest month weighted 1.
d)   If next month's sales turn out to be 140 units, forecast the following month's sales (months) using a 4-month moving average.

SOLUTION

a)   3-month moving average
$$= \frac{110 + 120 + 130}{3} = \frac{360}{3} = 120 \text{ dryers}$$

b)   4-month moving average
$$= \frac{100 + 110 + 120 + 130}{4} = \frac{460}{4} = 115 \text{ dryers}$$

c)   Weighted moving average
$$= \frac{4(130) + 3(120) + 2(110) + 1(100)}{10}$$
$$= \frac{1,200}{10} = 120 \text{ dryers}$$

d)   *Now* the four most recent sales are 110, 120, 130, and 140.
$$4\text{-month moving average} = \frac{110 + 120 + 130 + 140}{4}$$
$$= \frac{500}{4} = 125 \text{ dryers}$$

We note, of course, the lag in the forecasts, as the moving-average method does not immediately recognize trends.

SOLVED PROBLEM 4.4

The following data come from regression line projections:

PERIOD	FORECAST VALUES	ACTUAL VALUES
1	410	406
2	419	423
3	428	423
4	435	440

Compute the MAD and MSE.

SOLUTION

$$MAD = \frac{\sum |Actual - Forecast|}{n}$$

$$= \frac{|406 - 410| + |423 - 419| + |423 - 428| + |440 - 435|}{4}$$

$$= \frac{4 + 4 + 5 + 5}{4} = \frac{18}{4} = 4.5$$

$$MSE = \frac{\sum(Forecast\ errors)^2}{n}$$

$$= \frac{(406 - 410)^2 + (423 - 419)^2 + (423 - 428)^2 + (440 - 435)^2}{4}$$

$$= \frac{4^2 + 4^2 + 5^2 + 5^2}{4} = \frac{16 + 16 + 25 + 25}{4} = 20.5$$

SOLVED PROBLEM 4.5

Room registrations in the Toronto Towers Plaza Hotel have been recorded for the past 9 years. To project future occupancy, management would like to determine the mathematical trend of guest registration. This estimate will help the hotel determine whether future expansion will be needed. Given the following time-series data, develop a regression equation relating registrations to time (e.g., a trend equation). Then forecast year 11 registrations. Room registrations are in the thousands:

Year 1: 17	Year 2: 16	Year 3: 16	Year 4: 21	Year 5: 20
Year 6: 20	Year 7: 23	Year 8: 25	Year 9: 24	

SOLUTION

YEAR	REGISTRANTS, y (IN THOUSANDS)	x^2	xy
1	17	1	17
2	16	4	32
3	16	9	48
4	21	16	84
5	20	25	100
6	20	36	120
7	23	49	161
8	25	64	200
9	24	81	216
$\sum x = 45$	$\sum y = 182$	$\sum x^2 = 285$	$\sum xy = 978$

$$b = \frac{\sum xy - n\bar{x}\bar{y}}{\sum x^2 - n\bar{x}^2} = \frac{978 - (9)(5)(20.22)}{285 - (9)(25)}$$

$$= \frac{978 - 909.9}{285 - 225} = \frac{68.1}{60} = 1.135$$

$a = \bar{y} - b\bar{x} = 20.22 - (1.135)(5) = 20.22 - 5.675 = 14.545$
$\hat{y} = (registrations) = 14.545 + 1.135x$
The projection of registrations in year 11 is:
$\hat{y} = 14.545 + (1.135)(11) = 27.03$ or 27,030 guests in year 11.

SOLVED PROBLEM 4.6

Quarterly demand for Ford F150 pickups at a New York auto dealer is forecast with the equation:

$$\hat{y} = 10 + 3x$$

where x = quarters, and:

Quarter I of year 1 = 0
Quarter II of year 1 = 1
Quarter III of year 1 = 2
Quarter IV of year 1 = 3
Quarter I of year 2 = 4
and so on

and:

$\hat{y}$ = quarterly demand

The demand for trucks is seasonal, and the indices for Quarters I, II, III, and IV are 0.80, 1.00, 1.30, and 0.90, respectively. Forecast demand for each quarter of year 3. Then, seasonalize each forecast to adjust for quarterly variations.

SOLUTION

Quarter II of year 2 is coded $x = 5$; Quarter III of year 2, $x = 6$; and Quarter IV of year 2, $x = 7$. Hence, Quarter I of year 3 is coded $x = 8$; Quarter II, $x = 9$; and so on.

$\hat{y}$ (Year 3 Quarter I) = 10 + 3(8) = 34
$\hat{y}$ (Year 3 Quarter II) = 10 + 3(9) = 37
$\hat{y}$ (Year 3 Quarter III) = 10 + 3(10) = 40
$\hat{y}$ (Year 3 Quarter IV) = 10 + 3(11) = 43

Adjusted forecast = (.80)(34) = 27.2
Adjusted forecast = (1.00)(37) = 37
Adjusted forecast = (1.30)(40) = 52
Adjusted forecast = (.90)(43) = 38.7

SOLVED PROBLEM 4.7

Cengiz Haksever runs an Istanbul high-end jewelry shop. He advertises weekly in local Turkish newspapers and is thinking of increasing his ad budget. Before doing so, he decides to evaluate the past effectiveness of these ads. Five weeks are sampled, and the data are shown in the table below:

SALES ($1,000s)	AD BUDGET THAT WEEK ($100s)
11	5
6	3
10	7
6	2
12	8

Develop a regression model to help Cengiz evaluate his advertising.

SOLUTION

We apply the least-squares regression model as we did in Example 12.

SALES, y	ADVERTISING, x	x^2	xy
11	5	25	55
6	3	9	18
10	7	49	70
6	2	4	12
12	8	64	96
$\Sigma y = 45$	$\Sigma x = 25$	$\Sigma x^2 = 151$	$\Sigma xy = 251$

$$\bar{y} = \frac{45}{5} = 9 \qquad \bar{x} = \frac{25}{5} = 5$$

$$b = \frac{\Sigma xy - n\bar{x}\bar{y}}{\Sigma x^2 - n\bar{x}^2} = \frac{251 - (5)(5)(9)}{151 - (5)(5^2)}$$

$$= \frac{251 - 225}{151 - 125} = \frac{26}{26} = 1$$

$$a = \bar{y} - b\bar{x} = 9 - (1)(5) = 4$$

So the regression model is $\hat{y} = 4 + 1x$, or

Sales (in $1,000s) $= 4 + 1$ (Ad budget in $100s)

This means that for each 1-unit increase in x (or $100 in ads), sales increase by 1 unit (or $1,000).

SOLVED PROBLEM 4.8

Using the data in Solved Problem 4.7, find the coefficient of determination, r^2, for the model.

SOLUTION

To find r^2, we need to also compute Σy^2.

$$\Sigma y^2 = 11^2 + 6^2 + 10^2 + 6^2 + 12^2$$

$$= 121 + 36 + 100 + 36 + 144 = 437$$

The next step is to find the coefficient of correlation, r:

$$r = \frac{n\Sigma xy - \Sigma x\Sigma y}{\sqrt{[n\Sigma x^2 - (\Sigma x)^2][n\Sigma y^2 - (\Sigma y)^2]}}$$

$$= \frac{5(251) - (25)(45)}{\sqrt{[5(151) - (25)^2][5(437) - (45)^2]}}$$

$$= \frac{1{,}255 - 1{,}125}{\sqrt{(130)(160)}} = \frac{130}{\sqrt{20{,}800}} = \frac{130}{144.22}$$

$$= .9014$$

Thus, $r^2 = (.9014)^2 = .8125$, meaning that about 81% of the variability in sales can be explained by the regression model with advertising as the independent variable.

Problems

Note: **Px** means the problem may be solved with POM for Windows and/or Excel OM.

Problems 4.1–4.42 relate to Time-Series Forecasting

• **4.1** The following gives the number of pints of type B blood used at Woodlawn Hospital in the past 6 weeks:

WEEK OF	PINTS USED
August 31	360
September 7	389
September 14	410
September 21	381
September 28	368
October 5	374

a) Forecast the demand for the week of October 12 using a 3-week moving average.

b) Use a 3-week weighted moving average, with weights of .1, .3, and .6, using .6 for the most recent week. Forecast demand for the week of October 12.

c) Compute the forecast for the week of October 12 using exponential smoothing with a forecast for August 31 of 360 and $\alpha = .2$. **Px**

•• **4.2**

YEAR	1	2	3	4	5	6	7	8	9	10	11
DEMAND	7	9	5	9	13	8	12	13	9	11	7

a) Plot the above data on a graph. Do you observe any trend, cycles, or random variations?

b) Starting in year 4 and going to year 12, forecast demand using a 3-year moving average. Plot your forecast on the same graph as the original data.

c) Starting in year 4 and going to year 12, forecast demand using a 3-year moving average with weights of .1, .3, and .6, using .6 for the most recent year. Plot this forecast on the same graph.

d) As you compare forecasts with the original data, which seems to give the better results? **Px**

•• **4.3** Refer to Problem 4.2. Develop a forecast for years 2 through 12 using exponential smoothing with α = .4 and a forecast for year 1 of 6. Plot your new forecast on a graph with the actual data and the naive forecast. Based on a visual inspection, which forecast is better? **Px**

• **4.4** A check-processing center uses exponential smoothing to forecast the number of incoming checks each month. The number of checks received in June was 40 million, while the forecast was 42 million. A smoothing constant of .2 is used.

a) What is the forecast for July?

b) If the center received 45 million checks in July, what would be the forecast for August?

c) Why might this be an inappropriate forecasting method for this situation? **Px**

•• **4.5** The Carbondale Hospital is considering the purchase of a new ambulance. The decision will rest partly on the anticipated mileage to be driven next year. The miles driven during the past 5 years are as follows:

YEAR	MILEAGE
1	3,000
2	4,000
3	3,400
4	3,800
5	3,700

a) Forecast the mileage for next year (6th year) using a 2-year moving average.

b) Find the MAD based on the 2-year moving average. (*Hint:* You will have only 3 years of matched data.)

c) Use a weighted 2-year moving average with weights of .4 and .6 to forecast next year's mileage. (The weight of .6 is for the most recent year.) What MAD results from using this approach to forecasting? (*Hint:* You will have only 3 years of matched data.)

d) Compute the forecast for year 6 using exponential smoothing, an initial forecast for year 1 of 3,000 miles, and α = .5. **Px**

•• **4.6** The monthly sales for Yazici Batteries, Inc., were as follows:

MONTH	SALES
January	20
February	21
March	15
April	14
May	13
June	16
July	17
August	18
September	20
October	20
November	21
December	23

a) Plot the monthly sales data.

b) Forecast January sales using each of the following:
   i) Naive method.
   ii) A 3-month moving average.
   iii) A 6-month weighted average using .1, .1, .1, .2, .2, and .3, with the heaviest weights applied to the most recent months.
   iv) Exponential smoothing using an α = .3 and a September forecast of 18.
   v) A trend projection.

c) With the data given, which method would allow you to forecast next March's sales? **Px**

•• **4.7** The actual demand for the patients at Omaha Emergency Medical Clinic for the first 6 weeks of this year follows:

WEEK	ACTUAL NO. OF PATIENTS
1	65
2	62
3	70
4	48
5	63
6	52

Clinic administrator Marc Schniederjans wants you to forecast patient demand at the clinic for week 7 by using this data. You decide to use a weighted moving average method to find this forecast. Your method uses four actual demand levels, with weights of 0.333 on the present period, 0.25 one period ago, 0.25 two periods ago, and 0.167 three periods ago.

a) What is the value of your forecast? **Px**

b) If instead the weights were 20, 15, 15, and 10, respectively, how would the forecast change? Explain why.

c) What if the weights were 0.40, 0.30, 0.20, and 0.10, respectively? Now what is the forecast for week 7?

• **4.8** Daily high temperatures in St. Louis for the last week were as follows: 93, 94, 93, 95, 96, 88, 90 (yesterday).

a) Forecast the high temperature today, using a 3-day moving average.

b) Forecast the high temperature today, using a 2-day moving average.

c) Calculate the mean absolute deviation based on a 2-day moving average.

d) Compute the mean squared error for the 2-day moving average.

e) Calculate the mean absolute percent error for the 2-day moving average. **Px**

•••**4.9** Lenovo uses the ZX-81 chip in some of its laptop computers. The prices for the chip during the past 12 months were as follows:

MONTH	PRICE PER CHIP	MONTH	PRICE PER CHIP
January	$1.80	July	1.80
February	1.67	August	1.83
March	1.70	September	1.70
April	1.85	October	1.65
May	1.90	November	1.70
June	1.87	December	1.75

a) Use a 2-month moving average on all the data and plot the averages and the prices.

b) Use a 3-month moving average and add the 3-month plot to the graph created in part (a).

c) Which is better (using the mean absolute deviation): the 2-month average or the 3-month average?

d) Compute the forecasts for each month using exponential smoothing, with an initial forecast for January of $1.80. Use $\alpha = .1$, then $\alpha = .3$, and finally $\alpha = .5$. Using MAD, which α is the best? **PX**

•• **4.10** Data collected on the yearly registrations for a Six Sigma seminar at the Quality College are shown in the following table:

YEAR	1	2	3	4	5	6	7	8	9	10	11
REGISTRATIONS (000)	4	6	4	5	10	8	7	9	12	14	15

a) Develop a 3-year moving average to forecast registrations from year 4 to year 12.

b) Estimate demand again for years 4 to 12 with a 3-year weighted moving average in which registrations in the most recent year are given a weight of 2, and registrations in the other 2 years are each given a weight of 1.

c) Graph the original data and the two forecasts. Which of the two forecasting methods seems better? **PX**

• **4.11** Use exponential smoothing with a smoothing constant of 0.3 to forecast the registrations at the seminar given in Problem 4.10. To begin the procedure, assume that the forecast for year 1 was 5,000 people signing up.

a) What is the MAD? **PX**

b) What is the MSE?

•• **4.12** Consider the following actual and forecast demand levels for Big Mac hamburgers at a local McDonald's restaurant:

DAY	ACTUAL DEMAND	FORECAST DEMAND
Monday	88	88
Tuesday	72	88
Wednesday	68	84
Thursday	48	80
Friday		

The forecast for Monday was derived by observing Monday's demand level and setting Monday's forecast level equal to this demand level. Subsequent forecasts were derived by using exponential smoothing with a smoothing constant of 0.25. Using this exponential smoothing method, what is the forecast for Big Mac demand for Friday? **PX**

••• **4.13** As you can see in the following table, demand for heart transplant surgery at Washington General Hospital has increased steadily in the past few years:

YEAR	1	2	3	4	5	6
HEART TRANSPLANTS	45	50	52	56	58	?

The director of medical services predicted 6 years ago that demand in year 1 would be 41 surgeries.

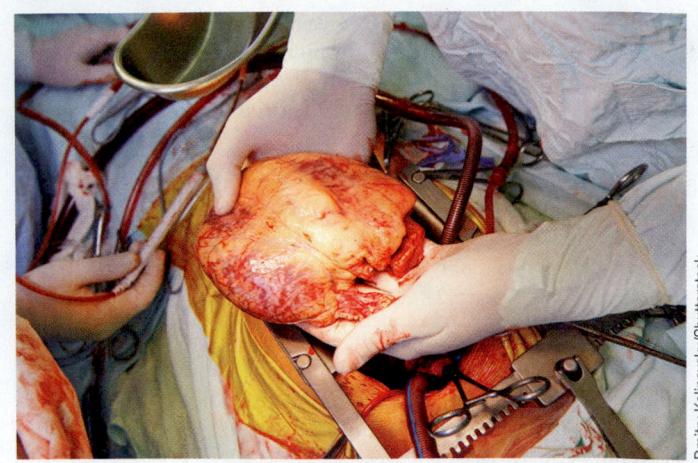

Dmitry Kalinovsky/Shutterstock

a) Use exponential smoothing, first with a smoothing constant of .6 and then with one of .9, to develop forecasts for years 2 through 6.

b) Use a 3-year moving average to forecast demand in years 4, 5, and 6.

c) Use the trend-projection method to forecast demand in years 1 through 6.

d) With MAD as the criterion, which of the four forecasting methods is best? **PX**

•• **4.14** Following are two weekly forecasts made by two different methods for the number of gallons of gasoline, in thousands, demanded at a local gasoline station. Also shown are actual demand levels, in thousands of gallons.

	FORECASTS		
WEEK	METHOD 1	METHOD 2	ACTUAL DEMAND
1	0.90	0.80	0.70
2	1.05	1.20	1.00
3	0.95	0.90	1.00
4	1.20	1.11	1.00

What are the MAD and MSE for each method?

• **4.15** Refer to Solved Problem 4.1 on page 144.

a) Use a 3-year moving average to forecast the sales of Volkswagen Beetles in Nevada through year 6.

b) What is the MAD? **PX**

c) What is the MSE?

• **4.16** Refer to Solved Problem 4.1 on page 144.

a) Using the trend projection (regression) method, develop a forecast for the sales of Volkswagen Beetles in Nevada through year 6.

b) What is the MAD? **PX**

c) What is the MSE?

• **4.17** Refer to Solved Problem 4.1 on page 144. Using smoothing constants of .6 and .9, develop forecasts for the sales of VW Beetles. What effect did the smoothing constant have on the forecast? Use MAD to determine which of the three smoothing constants (.3, .6, or .9) gives the most accurate forecast. **PX**

•••• **4.18** Consider the following actual (A_t) and forecast (F_t) demand levels for a commercial multiline telephone at Office Max:

TIME PERIOD, t	ACTUAL DEMAND, A_t	FORECAST DEMAND, F_t
1	50	50
2	42	50
3	56	48
4	46	50
5		

The first forecast, F_1, was derived by observing A_1 and setting F_1 equal to A_1. Subsequent forecast averages were derived by exponential smoothing. Using the exponential smoothing method, find the forecast for time period 5. (*Hint:* You need to first find the smoothing constant, α.)

••• **4.19** Income at the architectural firm Spraggins and Yunes for the period February to July was as follows:

MONTH	FEBRUARY	MARCH	APRIL	MAY	JUNE	JULY
Income (in $ thousand)	70.0	68.5	64.8	71.7	71.3	72.8

Use trend-adjusted exponential smoothing to forecast the firm's August income. Assume that the initial forecast average for February is $65,000 and the initial trend adjustment is 0. The smoothing constants selected are $\alpha = .1$ and $\beta = .2$. **Px**

••• **4.20** Resolve Problem 4.19 with $\alpha = .1$ and $\beta = .8$. Using MSE, determine which smoothing constants provide a better forecast. **Px**

• **4.21** Refer to the trend-adjusted exponential smoothing illustration in Example 7 on pages 122–123. Using $\alpha = .2$ and $\beta = .4$, we forecast sales for 9 months, showing the detailed calculations for months 2 and 3. In Solved Problem 4.2, we continued the process for month 4.

In this problem, show your calculations for months 5 and 6 for F_t, T_t, and FIT_t. **Px**

• **4.22** Refer to Problem 4.21. Complete the trend-adjusted exponential-smoothing forecast computations for periods 7, 8, and 9. Confirm that your numbers for F_t, T_t, and FIT_t match those in Table 4.2 (p. 123). **Px**

•• **4.23** Sales of quilt covers at Bud Banis's department store in Carbondale over the past year are shown below. Management prepared a forecast using a combination of exponential smoothing and its collective judgment for the 4 months (March, April, May, and June):

MONTH	UNIT SALES	MANAGEMENT'S FORECAST
July	100	
August	93	
September	96	
October	110	
November	124	
December	119	
January	92	
February	83	
March	101	120
April	96	114
May	89	110
June	108	108

a) Compute MAD and MAPE for management's technique.
b) Do management's results outperform (i.e., have smaller MAD and MAPE than) a naive forecast?
c) Which forecast do you recommend, based on lower forecast error? **Px**

• **4.24** The following gives the number of accidents that occurred on Florida State Highway 101 during the past 4 months:

MONTH	NUMBER OF ACCIDENTS
January	30
February	40
March	60
April	90

Forecast the number of accidents that will occur in May, using least-squares regression to derive a trend equation. **Px**

• **4.25** In the past, Peter Kelle's tire dealership in Baton Rouge sold an average of 1,000 radials each year. In the past 2 years, 200 and 250, respectively, were sold in fall, 350 and 300 in winter, 150 and 165 in spring, and 300 and 285 in summer. With a major expansion planned, Kelle projects sales next year to increase to 1,200 radials. What will be the demand during each season?

•• **4.26** George Kyparisis owns a company that manufactures sailboats. Actual demand for George's sailboats during each of the past four seasons was as follows:

SEASON	YEAR 1	YEAR 2	YEAR 3	YEAR 4
Winter	1,400	1,200	1,000	900
Spring	1,500	1,400	1,600	1,500
Summer	1,000	2,100	2,000	1,900
Fall	600	750	650	500

George has forecasted that annual demand for his sailboats in year 5 will equal 5,600 sailboats. Based on this data and the multiplicative seasonal model, what will the demand level be for George's sailboats in the spring of year 5?

•• **4.27** Attendance at Orlando's newest Disneylike attraction, Lego World, has been as follows:

QUARTER	GUESTS (IN THOUSANDS)	QUARTER	GUESTS (IN THOUSANDS)
Winter Year 1	73	Summer Year 2	124
Spring Year 1	104	Fall Year 2	52
Summer Year 1	168	Winter Year 3	89
Fall Year 1	74	Spring Year 3	146
Winter Year 2	65	Summer Year 3	205
Spring Year 2	82	Fall Year 3	98

Compute seasonal indices using all of the data. **Px**

• **4.28** North Dakota Electric Company estimates its demand trend line (in millions of kilowatt hours) to be:

$$D = 77 + 0.43Q$$

where Q refers to the sequential quarter number and $Q = 1$ for winter of Year 1. In addition, the multiplicative seasonal factors are as follows:

QUARTER	FACTOR (INDEX)
Winter	.8
Spring	1.1
Summer	1.4
Fall	.7

Forecast energy use for the four quarters of year 26 (namely quarters 101 to 104), beginning with winter.

· 4.29 The number of disk drives (in millions) made at a plant in Taiwan during the past 5 years follows:

YEAR	DISK DRIVES
1	140
2	160
3	190
4	200
5	210

a) Forecast the number of disk drives to be made next year, using linear regression.
b) Compute the mean squared error (MSE) when using linear regression.
c) Compute the mean absolute percent error (MAPE). **Px**

·· 4.30 Dr. Lillian Fok, a New Orleans psychologist, specializes in treating patients who are agoraphobic (i.e., afraid to leave their homes). The following table indicates how many patients Dr. Fok has seen each year for the past 10 years. It also indicates what the robbery rate was in New Orleans during the same year:

YEAR	1	2	3	4	5	6	7	8	9	10
NUMBER OF PATIENTS	36	33	40	41	40	55	60	54	58	61
ROBBERY RATE PER 1,000 POPULATION	58.3	61.1	73.4	75.7	81.1	89.0	101.1	94.8	103.3	116.2

Using trend (linear regression) analysis, predict the number of patients Dr. Fok will see in years 11 and 12 as a function of time. How well does the model fit the data? **Px**

··· 4.31 Emergency calls to the 911 system of Durham, North Carolina, for the past 24 weeks are shown in the following table:

WEEK	1	2	3	4	5	6	7	8	9	10	11	12
CALLS	50	35	25	40	45	35	20	30	35	20	15	40
WEEK	13	14	15	16	17	18	19	20	21	22	23	24
CALLS	55	35	25	55	55	40	35	60	75	50	40	65

a) Compute the exponentially smoothed forecast of calls for each week. Assume an initial forecast of 50 calls in the first week, and use $\alpha = .2$. What is the forecast for week 25?
b) Reforecast each period using $\alpha = .6$.
c) Actual calls during week 25 were 85. Which smoothing constant provides a superior forecast? Explain and justify the measure of error you used. **Px**

··· 4.32 Using the 911 call data in Problem 4.31, forecast calls for weeks 2 through 25 with a trend-adjusted exponential smoothing model. Assume an initial forecast for 50 calls for week 1 and an initial trend of zero. Use smoothing constants of $\alpha = .3$ and $\beta = .2$. Is this model better than that of Problem 4.31? What adjustment might be useful for further improvement? (Again, assume that actual calls in week 25 were 85.) **Px**

··· 4.33 Storrs Cycles has just started selling the new Cyclone mountain bike, with monthly sales as shown in the table. First, co-owner Bob Day wants to forecast by exponential smoothing by initially setting February's forecast equal to January's sales with $\alpha = .1$. Co-owner Sherry Snyder wants to use a three-period moving average.

	SALES	BOB	SHERRY	BOB'S ERROR	SHERRY'S ERROR
JANUARY	400	—			
FEBRUARY	380	400			
MARCH	410				
APRIL	375				
MAY					

a) Is there a strong linear trend in sales over time?
b) Fill in the table with what Bob and Sherry each forecast for May and the earlier months, as relevant.
c) Assume that May's actual sales figure turns out to be 405. Complete the table's columns and then calculate the mean absolute deviation for both Bob's and Sherry's methods.
d) Based on these calculations, which method seems more accurate? **Px**

···· 4.34 Boulanger Savings and Loan is proud of its long tradition in Winter Park, Florida. Begun by Michelle Boulanger 22 years after World War II, the S&L has bucked the trend of financial and liquidity problems that has repeatedly plagued the industry. Deposits have increased slowly but surely over the years, despite recessions in 1983, 1988, 1991, 2001, and 2010. Ms. Boulanger believes it is necessary to have a long-range strategic plan for her firm, including a 1-year forecast and preferably even a 5-year forecast of deposits. She examines the past deposit data and also peruses Florida's gross state product (GSP) over the same 44 years. (GSP is analogous to gross national product [GNP] but on the state level.) The resulting data are in the following table.

YEAR	DEPOSITS[a]	GSP[b]	YEAR	DEPOSITS[a]	GSP[b]
1	.25	.4	13	.50	1.2
2	.24	.4	14	.95	1.2
3	.24	.5	15	1.70	1.2
4	.26	.7	16	2.3	1.6
5	.25	.9	17	2.8	1.5
6	.30	1.0	18	2.8	1.6
7	.31	1.4	19	2.7	1.7
8	.32	1.7	20	3.9	1.9
9	.24	1.3	21	4.9	1.9
10	.26	1.2	22	5.3	2.3
11	.25	1.1	23	6.2	2.5
12	.33	.9	24	4.1	2.8

(continued)

YEAR	DEPOSITS[a]	GSP[b]	YEAR	DEPOSITS[a]	GSP[b]
25	4.5	2.9	35	31.1	4.1
26	6.1	3.4	36	31.7	4.1
27	7.7	3.8	37	38.5	4.0
28	10.1	4.1	38	47.9	4.5
29	15.2	4.0	39	49.1	4.6
30	18.1	4.0	40	55.8	4.5
31	24.1	3.9	41	70.1	4.6
32	25.6	3.8	42	70.9	4.6
33	30.3	3.8	43	79.1	4.7
34	36.0	3.7	44	94.0	5.0

[a] In $ millions.
[b] In $ billions.

a) Using exponential smoothing, with $\alpha = .6$, then trend analysis, and finally linear regression, discuss which forecasting model fits best for Boulanger's strategic plan. Justify the selection of one model over another.

b) Carefully examine the data. Can you make a case for excluding a portion of the information? Why? Would that change your choice of model? **Px**

Additional problems **4.35–4.42** *are available in* MyOMLab.

Problems 4.43–4.58 relate to Associative Forecasting Methods

•• **4.43** Mark Gershon, owner of a musical instrument distributorship, thinks that demand for guitars may be related to the number of television appearances by the popular group Maroon 5 during the previous month. Mark has collected the data shown in the following table:

DEMAND FOR GUITARS	3	6	7	5	10	7
MAROON 5 TV APPEARANCES	3	4	7	6	8	5

a) Graph these data to see whether a linear equation might describe the relationship between the group's television shows and guitar sales.

b) Use the least-squares regression method to derive a forecasting equation.

c) What is your estimate for guitar sales if Maroon 5 performed on TV nine times last month?

d) What are the correlation coefficient (r) and the coefficient of determination (r^2) for this model, and what do they mean? **Px**

• **4.44** Lori Cook has developed the following forecasting model:

$$\hat{y} = 36 + 4.3x$$

where $\hat{y}$ = demand for Kool Air conditioners and x = the outside temperature (°F) **Px**

a) Forecast demand for the Kool Air when the temperature is 70°F.
b) What is demand when the temperature is 80°F?
c) What is demand when the temperature is 90°F? **Px**

•• **4.45** Café Michigan's manager, Gary Stark, suspects that demand for mocha latte coffees depends on the price being charged. Based on historical observations, Gary has gathered the following data, which show the numbers of these coffees sold over six different price values:

PRICE	NUMBER SOLD
$2.70	760
$3.50	510
$2.00	980
$4.20	250
$3.10	320
$4.05	480

Using these data, how many mocha latte coffees would be forecast to be sold according to simple linear regression if the price per cup were $2.80? **Px**

• **4.46** The following data relate the sales figures of the bar in Mark Kaltenbach's small bed-and-breakfast inn in Portland, to the number of guests registered that week:

WEEK	GUESTS	BAR SALES
1	16	$330
2	12	270
3	18	380
4	14	300

a) Perform a linear regression that relates bar sales to guests (not to time).

b) If the forecast is for 20 guests next week, what are the sales expected to be? **Px**

• **4.47** The number of auto accidents in Athens, Ohio, is related to the regional number of registered automobiles in thousands (X_1), alcoholic beverage sales in $10,000s ($X_2$), and rainfall in inches (X_3). Furthermore, the regression formula has been calculated as:

$$Y = a + b_1X_1 + b_2X_2 + b_3X_3$$

where

Y = number of automobile accidents
$a = 7.5$
$b_1 = 3.5$
$b_2 = 4.5$
$b_3 = 2.5$

Calculate the expected number of automobile accidents under conditions a, b, and c:

	X_1	X_2	X_3
(a)	2	3	0
(b)	3	5	1
(c)	4	7	2

•• **4.48** Rhonda Clark, a Slippery Rock, Pennsylvania, real estate developer, has devised a regression model to help determine residential housing prices in northwestern Pennsylvania. The model was developed using recent sales in a particular neighborhood. The price (Y) of the house is based on the size (square footage = X) of the house. The model is:

$$Y = 13,473 + 37.65X$$

The coefficient of correlation for the model is 0.63.

a) Use the model to predict the selling price of a house that is 1,860 square feet.

b) An 1,860-square-foot house recently sold for $95,000. Explain why this is not what the model predicted.

c) If you were going to use multiple regression to develop such a model, what other quantitative variables might you include?

d) What is the value of the coefficient of determination in this problem? **Px**

• **4.49** Accountants at the Tucson firm, Larry Youdelman, CPAs, believed that several traveling executives were submitting unusually high travel vouchers when they returned from business trips. First, they took a sample of 200 vouchers submitted from the past year. Then they developed the following multiple-regression equation relating expected travel cost to number of days on the road (x_1) and distance traveled (x_2) in miles:

$$\hat{y} = \$90.00 + \$48.50x_1 + \$.40x_2$$

The coefficient of correlation computed was .68.

a) If Barbara Downey returns from a 300-mile trip that took her out of town for 5 days, what is the expected amount she should claim as expenses?

b) Downey submitted a reimbursement request for $685. What should the accountant do?

c) Should any other variables be included? Which ones? Why? **Px**

•• **4.50** City government has collected the following data on annual sales tax collections and new car registrations:

ANNUAL SALES TAX COLLECTIONS (IN MILLIONS)	1.0	1.4	1.9	2.0	1.8	2.1	2.3
NEW CAR REGISTRATIONS (IN THOUSANDS)	10	12	15	16	14	17	20

Determine the following:

a) The least-squares regression equation.

b) Using the results of part (a), find the estimated sales tax collections if new car registrations total 22,000.

c) The coefficients of correlation and determination. **Px**

•• **4.51** Using the data in Problem 4.30, apply linear regression to study the relationship between the robbery rate and Dr. Fok's patient load. If the robbery rate increases to 131.2 in year 11, how many phobic patients will Dr. Fok treat? If the robbery rate drops to 90.6, what is the patient projection? **Px**

••• **4.52** Bus and subway ridership for the summer months in London, England, is believed to be tied heavily to the number of tourists visiting the city. During the past 12 years, the data on the next page have been obtained:

Light Thru My Lens Photography/Getty Images

YEAR (SUMMER MONTHS)	NUMBER OF TOURISTS (IN MILLIONS)	RIDERSHIP (IN MILLIONS)
1	7	1.5
2	2	1.0
3	6	1.3
4	4	1.5
5	14	2.5
6	15	2.7
7	16	2.4
8	12	2.0
9	14	2.7
10	20	4.4
11	15	3.4
12	7	1.7

a) Plot these data and decide if a linear model is reasonable.

b) Develop a regression relationship.

c) What is expected ridership if 10 million tourists visit London in a year?

d) Explain the predicted ridership if there are no tourists at all.

e) What is the standard error of the estimate?

f) What is the model's correlation coefficient and coefficient of determination? **Px**

•• **4.53** Thirteen students entered the business program at Sante Fe College 2 years ago. The following table indicates what each student scored on the high school SAT math exam and their grade-point averages (GPAs) after students were in the Sante Fe program for 2 years:

STUDENT	A	B	C	D	E	F	G
SAT SCORE	421	377	585	690	608	390	415
GPA	2.90	2.93	3.00	3.45	3.66	2.88	2.15
STUDENT	H	I	J	K	L	M	
SAT SCORE	481	729	501	613	709	366	
GPA	2.53	3.22	1.99	2.75	3.90	1.60	

a) Is there a meaningful relationship between SAT math scores and grades?

b) If a student scores a 350, what do you think his or her GPA will be?

c) What about a student who scores 800?

•• **4.54** Dave Fletcher, the general manager of North Carolina Engineering Corporation (NCEC), thinks that his firm's engineering services contracted to highway construction firms are directly related to the volume of highway construction business contracted with companies in his geographic area. He wonders if this is really so, and if it is, can this information help him plan his operations better by forecasting the quantity of his engineering services required by construction firms in each quarter of the year? The following table presents the sales of his services and total amounts of contracts for highway construction over the past eight quarters:

QUARTER	1	2	3	4	5	6	7	8
Sales of NCEC Services (in $ thousands)	8	10	15	9	12	13	12	16
Contracts Released (in $ thousands)	153	172	197	178	185	199	205	226

a) Using this data, develop a regression equation for predicting the level of demand of NCEC's services.

b) Determine the coefficient of correlation and the standard error of the estimate. **Px**

Additional problems **4.55–4.58** are available in MyOMLab.

Problems 4.59–4.61 relate to Monitoring and Controlling Forecasts

•• **4.59** Sales of tablet computers at Ted Glickman's electronics store in Washington, D.C., over the past 10 weeks are shown in the table below:

WEEK	DEMAND	WEEK	DEMAND
1	20	6	29
2	21	7	36
3	28	8	22
4	37	9	25
5	25	10	28

a) Forecast demand for each week, including week 10, using exponential smoothing with $\alpha = .5$ (initial forecast = 20).

b) Compute the MAD.
c) Compute the tracking signal. **Px**

••• **4.60** The following are monthly actual and forecast demand levels for May through December for units of a product manufactured by the D. Bishop Company in Des Moines:

MONTH	ACTUAL DEMAND	FORECAST DEMAND
May	100	100
June	80	104
July	110	99
August	115	101
September	105	104
October	110	104
November	125	105
December	120	109

What is the value of the tracking signal as of the end of December?

Additional problem **4.61** is available in MyOMLab.

CASE STUDIES

Southwestern University: (B)*

Southwestern University (SWU), a large state college in Stephenville, Texas, enrolls close to 20,000 students. The school is a dominant force in the small city, with more students during fall and spring than permanent residents.

Always a football powerhouse, SWU is usually in the top 20 in college football rankings. Since the legendary Phil Flamm was hired as its head coach in 2009 (in hopes of reaching the elusive number 1 ranking), attendance at the five Saturday home games each year increased. Prior to Flamm's arrival, attendance generally averaged 25,000 to 29,000 per game. Season ticket sales bumped up by 10,000 just with the announcement of the new coach's arrival. Stephenville and SWU were ready to move to the big time!

Southwestern University Football Game Attendance, 2010–2015

	2010		2011		2012	
GAME	ATTENDEES	OPPONENT	ATTENDEES	OPPONENT	ATTENDEES	OPPONENT
1	34,200	Rice	36,100	Miami	35,900	USC
2[a]	39,800	Texas	40,200	Nebraska	46,500	Texas Tech
3	38,200	Duke	39,100	Ohio State	43,100	Alaska
4[b]	26,900	Arkansas	25,300	Nevada	27,900	Arizona
5	35,100	TCU	36,200	Boise State	39,200	Baylor

	2013		2014		2015	
GAME	ATTENDEES	OPPONENT	ATTENDEES	OPPONENT	ATTENDEES	OPPONENT
1	41,900	Arkansas	42,500	Indiana	46,900	LSU
2[a]	46,100	Missouri	48,200	North Texas	50,100	Texas
3	43,900	Florida	44,200	Texas A&M	45,900	South Florida
4[b]	30,100	Central Florida	33,900	Southern	36,300	Montana
5	40,500	LSU	47,800	Oklahoma	49,900	Arizona State

[a] Homecoming games.

[b] During the fourth week of each season, Stephenville hosted a hugely popular southwestern crafts festival. This event brought tens of thousands of tourists to the town, especially on weekends, and had an obvious negative impact on game attendance.

The immediate issue facing SWU, however, was not NCAA ranking. It was capacity. The existing SWU stadium, built in 1953, has seating for 54,000 fans. The following table indicates attendance at each game for the past 6 years.

One of Flamm's demands upon joining SWU had been a stadium expansion, or possibly even a new stadium. With attendance increasing, SWU administrators began to face the issue head-on. Flamm had wanted dormitories solely for his athletes in the stadium as an additional feature of any expansion.

SWU's president, Dr. Joel Wisner, decided it was time for his vice president of development to forecast when the existing stadium would "max out." The expansion was, in his mind, a given. But Wisner needed to know how long he could wait. He also sought a revenue projection, assuming an average ticket price of $50 in 2016 and a 5% increase each year in future prices.

Discussion Questions

1. Develop a forecasting model, justifying its selection over other techniques, and project attendance through 2017.

2. What revenues are to be expected in 2016 and 2017?

3. Discuss the school's options.

*This integrated case study runs throughout the text. Other issues facing Southwestern's football stadium include (A) managing the stadium project (Chapter 3); (C) quality of facilities (Chapter 6); (D) break-even analysis of food services (Supplement 7 Web site); (E) locating the new stadium (Chapter 8 Web site); (F) inventory planning of football programs (Chapter 12 Web site); and (G) scheduling of campus security officers/staff for game days (Chapter 13 Web site).

Forecasting Ticket Revenue for Orlando Magic Basketball Games

 Video Case

For its first 2 decades of existence, the NBA's Orlando Magic basketball team set seat prices for its 41-game home schedule the same for each game. If a lower-deck seat sold for $150, that was the price charged, regardless of the opponent, day of the week, or time of the season. If an upper-deck seat sold for $10 in the first game of the year, it likewise sold for $10 for every game.

But when Anthony Perez, director of business strategy, finished his MBA at the University of Florida, he developed a valuable database of ticket sales. Analysis of the data led him to build a forecasting model he hoped would increase ticket revenue. Perez hypothesized that selling a ticket for similar seats should differ based on demand.

Studying individual sales of Magic tickets on the open Stub Hub marketplace during the prior season, Perez determined the additional potential sales revenue the Magic could have made had they charged prices the fans had proven they were willing to pay on Stub Hub. This became his dependent variable, y, in a multiple-regression model.

He also found that three variables would help him build the "true market" seat price for every game. With his model, it was possible that the same seat in the arena would have as many as seven different prices created at season onset—sometimes higher than expected on average and sometimes lower.

The major factors he found to be statistically significant in determining how high the demand for a game ticket, and hence, its price, would be were:

◆ The day of the week (x_1)
◆ A rating of how popular the opponent was (x_2)
◆ The time of the year (x_3)

For the day of the week, Perez found that Mondays were the least-favored game days (and he assigned them a value of 1). The rest of the weekdays increased in popularity, up to a Saturday game, which he rated a 6. Sundays and Fridays received 5 ratings, and holidays a 3 (refer to the footnote in Table 4.3).

His ratings of opponents, done just before the start of the season, were subjective and range from a low of 0 to a high of 8. A very high-rated team in that particular season may have had one or more superstars on its roster, or have won the NBA finals the prior season, making it a popular fan draw.

Fernando Medina

Finally, Perez believed that the NBA season could be divided into four periods in popularity:

◆ Early games (which he assigned 0 scores)
◆ Games during the Christmas season (assigned a 3)
◆ Games until the All-Star break (given a 2)
◆ Games leading into the play-offs (scored with a 3)

The first year Perez built his multiple-regression model, the dependent variable y, which was a "potential premium revenue score," yielded an $r^2 = .86$ with this equation:

$$y = 14{,}996 + 10{,}801x_1 + 23{,}397x_2 + 10{,}784x_3$$

Table 4.3 illustrates, for brevity in this case study, a sample of 12 games that year (out of the total 41 home game regular season), including the potential extra revenue per game (y) to be expected using the variable pricing model.

A leader in NBA variable pricing, the Orlando Magic have learned that regression analysis is indeed a profitable forecasting tool.

Discussion Questions*

1. Use the data in Table 4.3 to build a regression model with day of the week as the only independent variable.

TABLE 4.3	Data for Last Year's Magic Ticket Sales Pricing Model				
TEAM	**DATE***	**DAY OF WEEK***	**TIME OF YEAR**	**RATING OF OPPONENT**	**ADDITIONAL SALES POTENTIAL**
Phoenix Suns	November 4	Wednesday	0	0	$12,331
Detroit Pistons	November 6	Friday	0	1	$29,004
Cleveland Cavaliers	November 11	Wednesday	0	6	$109,412
Miami Heat	November 25	Wednesday	0	3	$75,783
Houston Rockets	December 23	Wednesday	3	2	$42,557
Boston Celtics	January 28	Thursday	1	4	$120,212
New Orleans Pelicans	February 3	Monday	1	1	$20,459
L. A. Lakers	March 7	Sunday	2	8	$231,020
San Antonio Spurs	March 17	Wednesday	2	1	$28,455
Denver Nuggets	March 23	Sunday	2	1	$110,561
NY Knicks	April 9	Friday	3	0	$44,971
Philadelphia 76ers	April 14	Wednesday	3	1	$30,257

*Day of week rated as 1 = Monday, 2 = Tuesday, 3 = Wednesday, 4 = Thursday, 5 = Friday, 6 = Saturday, 5 = Sunday, 3 = holiday.

2. Use the data to build a model with rating of the opponent as the sole independent variable.
3. Using Perez's multiple-regression model, what would be the additional sales potential of a Thursday Miami Heat game played during the Christmas holiday?
4. What additional independent variables might you suggest to include in Perez's model?

*You may wish to view the video that accompanies this case before answering these questions.

Forecasting at Hard Rock Cafe

Video Case

With the growth of Hard Rock Cafe—from one pub in London in 1971 to more than 145 restaurants in 60 countries today—came a corporatewide demand for better forecasting. Hard Rock uses long-range forecasting in setting a capacity plan and intermediate-term forecasting for locking in contracts for leather goods (used in jackets) and for such food items as beef, chicken, and pork. Its short-term sales forecasts are conducted each month, by cafe, and then aggregated for a headquarters view.

The heart of the sales forecasting system is the point-of-sale (POS) system, which, in effect, captures transaction data on nearly every person who walks through a cafe's door. The sale of each entrée represents one customer; the entrée sales data are transmitted daily to the Orlando corporate headquarters' database. There, the financial team, headed by Todd Lindsey, begins the forecast process. Lindsey forecasts monthly guest counts, retail sales, banquet sales, and concert sales (if applicable) at each cafe. The general managers of individual cafes tap into the same database to prepare a daily forecast for their sites. A cafe manager pulls up prior years' sales for that day, adding information from the local Chamber of Commerce or Tourist Board on upcoming events such as a major convention, sporting event, or concert in the city where the cafe is located. The daily forecast is further broken into hourly sales, which drives employee scheduling. An hourly forecast of $5,500 in sales translates into 19 workstations, which are further broken down into a specific number of waitstaff, hosts, bartenders, and kitchen staff. Computerized scheduling software plugs in people based on their availability. Variances between forecast and actual sales are then examined to see why errors occurred.

Hard Rock doesn't limit its use of forecasting tools to sales. To evaluate managers and set bonuses, a 3-year weighted moving average is applied to cafe sales. If cafe general managers exceed their targets, a bonus is computed. Todd Lindsey, at corporate headquarters, applies weights of 40% to the most recent year's sales, 40% to the year before, and 20% to sales 2 years ago in reaching his moving average.

An even more sophisticated application of statistics is found in Hard Rock's menu planning. Using multiple regression, managers can compute the impact on demand of other menu items if the price of one item is changed. For example, if the price of a cheeseburger increases from $7.99 to $8.99, Hard Rock can predict the effect this will have on sales of chicken sandwiches, pork sandwiches, and salads. Managers do the same analysis on menu placement, with the center section driving higher sales volumes. When an item such as a hamburger is moved off the center to one of the side flaps, the corresponding effect on related items, say french fries, is determined.

HARD ROCK'S MOSCOW CAFE[a]										
MONTH	**1**	**2**	**3**	**4**	**5**	**6**	**7**	**8**	**9**	**10**
Guest count (in thousands)	21	24	27	32	29	37	43	43	54	66
Advertising (in $ thousand)	14	17	25	25	35	35	45	50	60	60

[a] These figures are used for purposes of this case study.

Discussion Questions*

1. Describe three different forecasting applications at Hard Rock. Name three other areas in which you think Hard Rock could use forecasting models.
2. What is the role of the POS system in forecasting at Hard Rock?
3. Justify the use of the weighting system used for evaluating managers for annual bonuses.
4. Name several variables besides those mentioned in the case that could be used as good predictors of daily sales in each cafe.

5. At Hard Rock's Moscow restaurant, the manager is trying to evaluate how a new advertising campaign affects guest counts. Using data for the past 10 months (see the table), develop a least-squares regression relationship and then forecast the expected guest count when advertising is $65,000.

*You may wish to view the video that accompanies this case before answering these questions.

- **Additional Case Studies:** Visit MyOMLab for these free case studies:
  North-South Airlines: Reflects the merger of two airlines and addresses their maintenance costs.
  Digital Cell Phone, Inc.: Uses regression analysis and seasonality to forecast demand at a cell phone manufacturer.

Endnotes

1. For a good review of statistical terms, refer to Tutorial 1, "Statistical Review for Managers," in MyOMLab.
2. When the sample size is large ($n > 30$), the prediction interval value of y can be computed using normal tables. When the number of observations is small, the t-distribution is appropriate. See D. Groebner et al., *Business Statistics*, 9th ed. (Upper Saddle River, NJ: Prentice Hall, 2014).

3. To prove these three percentages to yourself, just set up a normal curve for ± 1.6 standard deviations (z-values). Using the normal table in Appendix I, you find that the area under the curve is .89. This represents ± 2 MADs. Likewise, ± 3 MADs = ± 2.4 standard deviations encompass 98% of the area, and so on for ± 4 MADs.
4. Bernard T. Smith, *Focus Forecasting: Computer Techniques for Inventory Control* (Boston: CBI Publishing, 1978).

Chapter 4 *Rapid* Review

Main Heading	Review Material	MyOMLab
WHAT IS FORECASTING? (pp. 108–109)	■ **Forecasting**—The art and science of predicting future events. ■ **Economic forecasts**—Planning indicators that are valuable in helping organizations prepare medium- to long-range forecasts. ■ **Technological forecasts**—Long-term forecasts concerned with the rates of technological progress. ■ **Demand forecasts**—Projections of a company's sales for each time period in the planning horizon.	Concept Questions: 1.1–1.4
THE STRATEGIC IMPORTANCE OF FORECASTING (pp. 109–110)	*The forecast is the only estimate of demand until actual demand becomes known.* Forecasts of demand drive decisions in many areas, including: human resources, capacity, and supply chain management.	Concept Questions: 2.1–2.3
SEVEN STEPS IN THE FORECASTING SYSTEM (pp. 110–111)	■ Forecasting follows seven basic steps: (1) Determine the use of the forecast; (2) Select the items to be forecasted; (3) Determine the time horizon of the forecast; (4) Select the forecasting model(s); (5) Gather the data needed to make the forecast; (6) Make the forecast; (7) Validate and implement the results.	Concept Questions: 3.1–3.4
FORECASTING APPROACHES (pp. 111–112)	■ **Quantitative forecasts**—Forecasts that employ mathematical modeling to forecast demand. ■ **Qualitative forecast**—Forecasts that incorporate such factors as the decision maker's intuition, emotions, personal experiences, and value system. ■ **Jury of executive opinion**—Takes the opinion of a small group of high-level managers and results in a group estimate of demand. ■ **Delphi method**—Uses an interactive group process that allows experts to make forecasts. ■ **Sales force composite**—Based on salespersons' estimates of expected sales. ■ **Market survey**—Solicits input from customers or potential customers regarding future purchasing plans. ■ **Time series**—Uses a series of past data points to make a forecast.	Concept Questions: 4.1–4.4
TIME-SERIES FORECASTING (pp. 112–131)	■ **Naive approach**—Assumes that demand in the next period is equal to demand in the most recent period. ■ **Moving average**—Uses an average of the n most recent periods of data to forecast the next period. $$\text{Moving average} = \frac{\sum \text{demand in previous } n \text{ periods}}{n} \quad (4\text{-}1)$$ $$\text{Weighted moving average} = \frac{\sum((\text{Weight for period } n)(\text{Demand in period } n))}{\sum \text{Weights}} \quad (4\text{-}2)$$ ■ **Exponential smoothing**—A weighted-moving-average forecasting technique in which data points are weighted by an exponential function. ■ **Smoothing constant**—The weighting factor, α, used in an exponential smoothing forecast, a number between 0 and 1. Exponential smoothing formula: $$F_t = F_{t-1} + \alpha(A_{t-1} - F_{t-1}) \quad (4\text{-}4)$$ ■ **Mean absolute deviation (MAD)**—A measure of the overall forecast error for a model. $$\text{MAD} = \frac{\sum|\text{Actual} - \text{Forecast}|}{n} \quad (4\text{-}5)$$ ■ **Mean squared error (MSE)**—The average of the squared differences between the forecast and observed values. $$\text{MSE} = \frac{\sum(\text{Forecast errors})^2}{n} \quad (4\text{-}6)$$ ■ **Mean absolute percent error (MAPE)**—The average of the absolute differences between the forecast and actual values, expressed as a percentage of actual values. $$\text{MAPE} = \frac{\sum_{i=1}^{n} 100|\text{Actual}_i - \text{Forecast}_i|/\text{Actual}_i}{n} \quad (4\text{-}7)$$	Concept Questions: 5.1–5.4 Problems: 4.1–4.42 Virtual Office Hours for Solved Problems: 4.1–4.4 **ACTIVE MODELS 4.1–4.4**

Main Heading	Review Material	MyOMLab
	Exponential smoothing with trend adjustment Forecast including trend (FIT_t) = Exponentially smoothed forecast average (F_t) + Exponentially smoothed trend (T_t) (4-8) ■ **Trend projection**—A time-series forecasting method that fits a trend line to a series of historical data points and then projects the line into the future for forecasts. Trend projection and regression analysis $\hat{y} = a + bx$, where $b = \dfrac{\sum xy - n\bar{x}\bar{y}}{\sum x^2 - n\bar{x}^2}$ and $a = \bar{y} - b\bar{x}$ (4-11), (4-12), (4-13) ■ **Seasonal variations**—Regular upward or downward movements in a time series that tie to recurring events. ■ **Cycles**—Patterns in the data that occur every several years.	Virtual Office Hours for Solved Problems: 4.5–4.6
ASSOCIATIVE FORECASTING METHODS: REGRESSION AND CORRELATION ANALYSIS (pp. 131–137)	■ **Linear-regression analysis**—A straight-line mathematical model to describe the functional relationships between independent and dependent variables. ■ **Standard error of the estimate**—A measure of variability around the regression line. ■ **Coefficient of correlation**—A measure of the strength of the relationship between two variables. ■ **Coefficient of determination**—A measure of the amount of variation in the dependent variable about its mean that is explained by the regression equation. ■ **Multiple regression**—An associative forecasting method with > 1 independent variable. Multiple regression forecast: $\hat{y} = a + b_1x_1 + b_2x_2$ (4-17)	Concept Questions: 6.1–6.4 Problems: 4.43-4.58 **VIDEO 4.1** Forecasting Ticket Revenue for Orlando Magic Basketball Games Virtual Office Hours for Solved Problems: 4.7–4.8
MONITORING AND CONTROLLING FORE-CASTS (pp. 138–140)	■ **Tracking signal**—A measurement of how well the forecast is predicting actual values. Tracking signal $= \dfrac{\sum(\text{Actual demand in period } i - \text{Forecast demand in period } i)}{\text{MAD}}$ (4-18) ■ **Bias**—A forecast that is consistently higher or lower than actual values of a time series. ■ **Adaptive smoothing**—An approach to exponential smoothing forecasting in which the smoothing constant is automatically changed to keep errors to a minimum. ■ **Focus forecasting**—Forecasting that tries a variety of computer models and selects the best one for a particular application.	Concept Questions: 7.1–7.4 Problems: 4.59–4.61
FORECASTING IN THE SERVICE SECTOR (pp. 140–141)	Service-sector forecasting may require good short-term demand records, even per 15-minute intervals. Demand during holidays or specific weather events may also need to be tracked.	Concept Question: 8.1 **VIDEO 4.2** Forecasting at Hard Rock Cafe

Self Test

- **Before taking the self-test,** refer to the learning objectives listed at the beginning of the chapter and the key terms listed at the end of the chapter.

LO 4.1 Forecasting time horizons include:
  a) long range.
  b) medium range.
  c) short range.
  d) all of the above.

LO 4.2 Qualitative methods of forecasting include:
  a) sales force composite.
  b) jury of executive opinion.
  c) consumer market survey.
  d) exponential smoothing.
  e) all except (d).

LO 4.3 The difference between a *moving-average* model and an *exponential smoothing* model is that _____.

LO 4.4 Three popular measures of forecast accuracy are:
  a) total error, average error, and mean error.
  b) average error, median error, and maximum error.
  c) median error, minimum error, and maximum absolute error.
  d) mean absolute deviation, mean squared error, and mean absolute percent error.

LO 4.5 Average demand for iPods in the Rome, Italy, Apple store is 800 units per month. The May monthly index is 1.25. What is the seasonally adjusted sales forecast for May?
  a) 640 units
  b) 798.75 units
  c) 800 units
  d) 1,000 units
  e) cannot be calculated with the information given

LO 4.6 The main difference between simple and multiple regression is _____.

LO 4.7 The tracking signal is the:
  a) standard error of the estimate.
  b) cumulative error.
  c) mean absolute deviation (MAD).
  d) ratio of the cumulative error to MAD.
  e) mean absolute percent error (MAPE).

Answers: LO 4.1. d; LO 4.2. e; LO 4.3. exponential smoothing is a weighted moving-average model in which all prior values are weighted with a set of exponentially declining weights; LO 4.4. d; LO 4.5. d; LO 4.6. simple regression has only one independent variable; LO 4.7. d.

Design of Goods and Services

CHAPTER OUTLINE

GLOBAL COMPANY PROFILE: *Regal Marine*

- Goods and Services Selection *162*
- Generating New Products *165*
- Product Development *166*
- Issues for Product Design *171*
- Product Development Continuum *173*
- Defining a Product *175*
- Documents for Production *178*
- Service Design *179*
- Application of Decision Trees to Product Design *182*
- Transition to Production *184*

Alaska Airlines

Alaska Airlines

10 OM STRATEGY DECISIONS

- Design of Goods and Services
- Managing Quality
- Process Strategy
- Location Strategies
- Layout Strategies
- Human Resources
- Supply-Chain Management
- Inventory Management
- Scheduling
- Maintenance

Product Strategy Provides Competitive Advantage at Regal Marine

Forty years after its founding by potato farmer Paul Kuck, Regal Marine has become a powerful force on the waters of the world. The world's third-largest boat manufacturer (by global sales), Regal exports to 30 countries, including Russia and China. Almost one-third of its sales are overseas.

Product design is critical in the highly competitive pleasure boat business: "We keep in touch with our customers and we respond to the marketplace," says Kuck. "We're introducing six new models this year alone. I'd say we're definitely on the aggressive end of the spectrum."

With changing consumer tastes, compounded by material changes and ever–improving marine engineering, the design function is under constant pressure. Added to these pressures

CAD/CAM is used to design the rain cover of a new product. This process results in faster and more efficient design and production.

Here the deck, suspended from ceiling cranes, is being finished prior to being moved to join the hull. Regal is one of the first boat builders in the world to earn the ISO 9001 quality certification.

Here the finishing touches are being put on a mold used for forming the hull.

is the constant issue of cost competitiveness combined with the need to provide good value for customers.

Consequently, Regal Marine is a frequent user of computer-aided design (CAD). New designs come to life via Regal's three-dimensional CAD system, borrowed from automotive technology. Regal's naval architect's goal is to continue to reduce the time from concept to prototype to production. The sophisticated CAD system not only has reduced product development time and cost, but also has reduced problems with tooling and production, resulting in a superior product.

All of Regal's products, from its $14,000 19-foot boat to the $500,000 52-foot Sports yacht, follow a similar production process. Hulls and decks are separately hand-produced by spraying preformed molds with three to five layers of a fiberglass laminate. The hulls and decks harden and are removed to become the lower and upper structure of the boat. As they move to the assembly line, they are joined and components added at each workstation.

Wooden components, precut in-house by computer-driven routers, are delivered on a just-in-time basis for installation at one station. Engines—one of the few purchased

Once a hull has been pulled from the mold, it travels down a monorail assembly path. JIT inventory delivers engines, wiring, seats, flooring, and interiors when needed.

components—are installed at another. Racks of electrical wiring harnesses, engineered and rigged in-house, are then installed. An in-house upholstery department delivers customized seats, beds, dashboards, or other cushioned components. Finally, chrome fixtures are put in place, and the boat is sent to Regal's test tank for watertight, gauge, and system inspection.

At the final stage, smaller boats, such as this one, are placed in this test tank, where a rain machine ensures watertight fits.

LEARNING OBJECTIVES

LO 5.1 *Define* product life cycle 164

LO 5.2 *Describe* a product development system 166

LO 5.3 *Build* a house of quality 167

LO 5.4 *Explain* how time-based competition is implemented by OM 173

LO 5.5 *Describe* how goods and services are defined by OM 175

LO 5.6 *Describe* the documents needed for production 179

LO 5.7 *Explain* how the customer participates in the design and delivery of services 180

LO 5.8 *Apply* decision trees to product issues 182

Goods and Services Selection

Global firms like Regal Marine know that the basis for an organization's existence is the good or service it provides society. Great products are the keys to success. Anything less than an excellent product strategy can be devastating to a firm. To maximize the potential for success, many companies focus on only a few products and then concentrate on those products. For instance, Honda's focus, its core competency, is engines. Virtually all of Honda's sales (autos, motorcycles, generators, lawn mowers) are based on its outstanding engine technology. Likewise, Intel's focus is on microprocessors, and Michelin's is on tires.

However, because most products have a limited and even predictable life cycle, companies must constantly be looking for new products to design, develop, and take to market. Operations managers insist on strong communication among customer, product, processes, and suppliers that results in a high success rate for their new products. 3M's goal is to produce 30% of its profit from products introduced in the past 4 years. Apple generates almost 60% of its revenue from products launched in the past 4 years. Benchmarks, of course, vary by industry; Regal introduces six new boats a year, and Rubbermaid introduces a new product each day!

VIDEO 5.1
Product Strategy at Regal Marine

The importance of new products cannot be overestimated. As Figure 5.1 shows, leading companies generate a substantial portion of their sales from products less than 5 years old. The need for new products is why Gillette developed its multiblade razors, in spite of continuing high sales of its phenomenally successful Sensor razor, and why Disney continues to innovate with new rides and new parks even though it is already the world's leading family entertainment company.

Despite constant efforts to introduce viable new products, many new products do not succeed. Product selection, definition, and design occur frequently—perhaps hundreds of times

Figure 5.1

Innovation and New Products

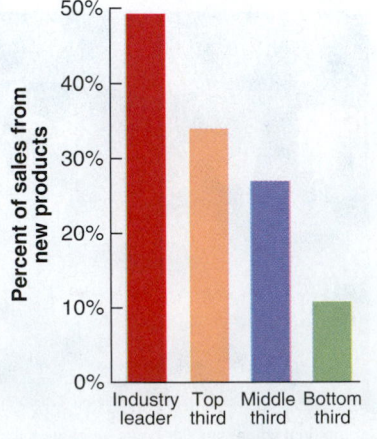

The higher the percentage of sales from the last 5 years, the more likely the firm is to be a leader.

for each financially successful product. DuPont estimates that it takes 250 ideas to yield one *marketable* product. Operations managers and their organizations build cultures that accept this risk and tolerate failure. They learn to accommodate a high volume of new product ideas while maintaining the production activities to which they are already committed.

Although the term *products* often refers to tangible goods, it also refers to offerings by service organizations. For instance, when Allstate Insurance offers a new homeowner's policy, it is referred to as a new "product." Similarly, when Citicorp opens a mortgage department, it offers a number of new mortgage "products."

An effective product strategy links product decisions with investment, market share, and product life cycle, and defines the breadth of the product line. The *objective of the* **product decision** *is to develop and implement a product strategy that meets the demands of the marketplace with a competitive advantage*. As one of the 10 decisions of OM, product strategy may focus on developing a competitive advantage via differentiation, low cost, rapid response, or a combination of these.

STUDENT TIP

Motorola went through 3,000 working models before it developed its first pocket cell phone.

Product decision

The selection, definition, and design of products.

Product Strategy Options Support Competitive Advantage

A world of options exists in the selection, definition, and design of products. Product selection is choosing the good or service to provide customers or clients. For instance, hospitals specialize in various types of patients and medical procedures. A hospital's management may decide to operate a general-purpose hospital or a maternity hospital or, as in the case of the Canadian hospital Shouldice, to specialize in hernias. Hospitals select their products when they decide what kind of hospital to be. Numerous other options exist for hospitals, just as they exist for Taco Bell and Toyota.

Service organizations like Shouldice Hospital *differentiate* themselves through their product. Shouldice differentiates itself by offering a distinctly unique and high-quality product. Its world-renowned specialization in hernia-repair service is so effective it allows patients to return

(a) Markets: In its creative way, the market has moved athletic shoes from utilitarian footwear into fashionable accessories.

(b) Technology: Samsung's latest technology: radical new smart phones that are bendable.

(c) Packaging: Sherwin-Williams' Dutch Boy has revolutionized the paint industry with its square Twist & Pour paint container.

Product Innovation Can Be Driven By Markets, Technology, and Packaging. Whether it is design focused on changes in the market (a), the application of technology at Samsung (b), or a new container at Sherwin-Williams (c), operations managers need to remind themselves that the creative process is ongoing with major production implications.

to normal living in 8 days as opposed to the average 2 weeks—and with very few complications. The entire production system is designed for this one product. Local anesthetics are used; patients enter and leave the operating room on their own; meals are served in a common dining room, encouraging patients to get out of bed for meals and join fellow patients in the lounge. As Shouldice demonstrates, product selection affects the entire production system.

Taco Bell has developed and executed a *low-cost* strategy through product design. By designing a product (its menu) that can be produced with a minimum of labor in small kitchens, Taco Bell has developed a product line that is both low cost and high value. Successful product design has allowed Taco Bell to increase the food content of its products from 27¢ to 45¢ of each sales dollar.

Toyota's strategy is *rapid response* to changing consumer demand. By executing the fastest automobile design in the industry, Toyota has driven the speed of product development down to well under 2 years in an industry whose standard is still over 2 years. The shorter design time allows Toyota to get a car to market before consumer tastes change and to do so with the latest technology and innovations.

Product decisions are fundamental to an organization's strategy and have major implications throughout the operations function. For instance, GM's steering columns are a good example of the strong role product design plays in both quality and efficiency. The redesigned steering column is simpler, with about 30% fewer parts than its predecessor. The result: Assembly time is one-third that of the older column, and the new column's quality is about seven times higher. As an added bonus, machinery on the new line costs a third less than that on the old line.

Product Life Cycles

Products are born. They live and they die. They are cast aside by a changing society. It may be helpful to think of a product's life as divided into four phases. Those phases are introduction, growth, maturity, and decline.

Product life cycles may be a matter of a few days (a concert t-shirt), months (seasonal fashions), years (Madden NFL football video game), or decades (Boeing 737). Regardless of the length of the cycle, the task for the operations manager is the same: to design a system that helps introduce new products successfully. If the operations function cannot perform effectively at this stage, the firm may be saddled with losers—products that cannot be produced efficiently and perhaps not at all.

LO 5.1 *Define* product life cycle

Figure 5.2 shows the four life cycle stages and the relationship of product sales, cash flow, and profit over the life cycle of a product. Note that typically a firm has a negative cash flow while it develops a product. When the product is successful, those losses may be recovered. Eventually, the successful product may yield a profit prior to its decline. However, the profit is fleeting—hence, the constant demand for new products.

Life Cycle and Strategy

Just as operations managers must be prepared to develop new products, they must also be prepared to develop *strategies* for new and *existing* products. Periodic examination of

Figure **5.2**

Product Life Cycle, Sales, Cost, Profit, and Loss

products is appropriate because *strategies change as products move through their life cycle*. Successful product strategies require determining the best strategy for each product based on its position in its life cycle. A firm, therefore, identifies products or families of products and their position in the life cycle. Let us review some strategy options as products move through their life cycles.

Introductory Phase   Because products in the introductory phase are still being "fine-tuned" for the market, as are their production techniques, they may warrant unusual expenditures for (1) research, (2) product development, (3) process modification and enhancement, and (4) supplier development. For example, when the iPhone was first introduced, the features desired by the public were still being determined. At the same time, operations managers were still groping for the best manufacturing techniques.

Growth Phase   In the growth phase, product design has begun to stabilize, and effective forecasting of capacity requirements is necessary. Adding capacity or enhancing existing capacity to accommodate the increase in product demand may be necessary.

Maturity Phase   By the time a product is mature, competitors are established. So high-volume, innovative production may be appropriate. Improved cost control, reduction in options, and a paring down of the product line may be effective or necessary for profitability and market share.

Decline Phase   Management may need to be ruthless with those products whose life cycle is at an end. Dying products are typically poor products in which to invest resources and managerial talent. Unless dying products make some unique contribution to the firm's reputation or its product line or can be sold with an unusually high contribution, their production should be terminated.[1]

Product-by-Value Analysis

The effective operations manager selects items that show the greatest promise. This is the Pareto principle applied to product mix: Resources are to be invested in the critical few and not the trivial many. Product-by-value analysis lists products in descending order of their *individual dollar contribution* to the firm. It also lists the *total annual dollar contribution* of the product. Low contribution on a per-unit basis by a particular product may look substantially different if it represents a large portion of the company's sales.

   A product-by-value report allows management to evaluate possible strategies for each product. These may include increasing cash flow (e.g., increasing contribution by raising selling price or lowering cost), increasing market penetration (improving quality and/or reducing cost or price), or reducing costs (improving the production process). The report may also tell management which product offerings should be eliminated and which fail to justify further investment in research and development or capital equipment. Product-by-value analysis focuses attention on the strategic direction for each product.

Product-by-value analysis

A list of products, in descending order of their individual dollar contribution to the firm, as well as the *total annual dollar contribution* of the product.

Generating New Products

Because products die; because products must be weeded out and replaced; because firms generate most of their revenue and profit from new products—product selection, definition, and design take place on a continuing basis. Consider recent product changes: DVDs to video streaming, coffee shops to Starbucks lifestyle coffee, traveling circuses to Cirque du Soleil, landlines to cell phones, cell phone to smart phones, and an Internet of digital information to an Internet of "things" that connects you and your smart phone to your home, car, and doctor. And the list goes on. Knowing how to successfully find and develop new products is a requirement.

Aggressive new product development requires that organizations build structures internally that have open communication with customers, innovative product development cultures, aggressive R&D, strong leadership, formal incentives, and training. Only then can a firm profitably and energetically focus on specific opportunities such as the following:

1. *Understanding the customer* is the premier issue in new-product development. Many commercially important products are initially thought of and even prototyped by users rather than producers. Such products tend to be developed by "lead users"—companies, organizations, or individuals that are well ahead of market trends and have needs that go far beyond those of average users. The operations manager must be "tuned in" to the market and particularly these innovative lead users.

2. *Economic change* brings increasing levels of affluence in the long run but economic cycles and price changes in the short run. In the long run, for instance, more and more people can afford automobiles, but in the short run, a recession may weaken the demand for automobiles.

3. *Sociological and demographic change* may appear in such factors as decreasing family size. This trend alters the size preference for homes, apartments, and automobiles.

4. *Technological change* makes possible everything from smart phones to iPads to artificial hearts.

5. *Political and legal change* brings about new trade agreements, tariffs, and government requirements.

6. Other changes may be brought about through *market practice, professional standards, suppliers*, and *distributors*.

Operations managers must be aware of these dynamics and be able to anticipate changes in product opportunities, the products themselves, product volume, and product mix.

Product Development

Product Development System

LO 5.2 *Describe* a product development system

An effective product strategy links product decisions with other business functions, such as R&D, engineering, marketing, and finance. A firm requires cash for product development, an understanding of the marketplace, and the necessary human talents. The product development system may well determine not only product success but also the firm's future. Figure 5.3 shows the stages of product development. In this system, product options go through a series of steps, each having its own screening and evaluation criteria, but providing a continuing flow of information to prior steps.

Optimum product development depends not only on support from other parts of the firm but also on the successful integration of all 10 of the OM decisions, from product design to maintenance. Identifying products that appear likely to capture market share, be cost-effective, and be profitable but are, in fact, very difficult to produce may lead to failure rather than success.

Quality function deployment (QFD)

A process for determining customer requirements (customer "wants") and translating them into the attributes (the "hows") that each functional area can understand and act on.

House of quality

A part of the quality function deployment process that utilizes a planning matrix to relate customer "wants" to "how" the firm is going to meet those "wants."

Quality Function Deployment (QFD)

Quality function deployment (QFD) refers to both (1) determining what will satisfy the customer and (2) translating those customer desires into the target design. The idea is to capture a rich understanding of customer wants and to identify alternative process solutions. This information is then integrated into the evolving product design. QFD is used early in the design process to help determine *what will satisfy the customer* and *where to deploy quality efforts*.

One of the tools of QFD is the **house of quality**, a graphic technique for defining the relationship between customer desires and product (or service). Only by defining this relationship in a rigorous way can managers design products and processes with features desired by customers.

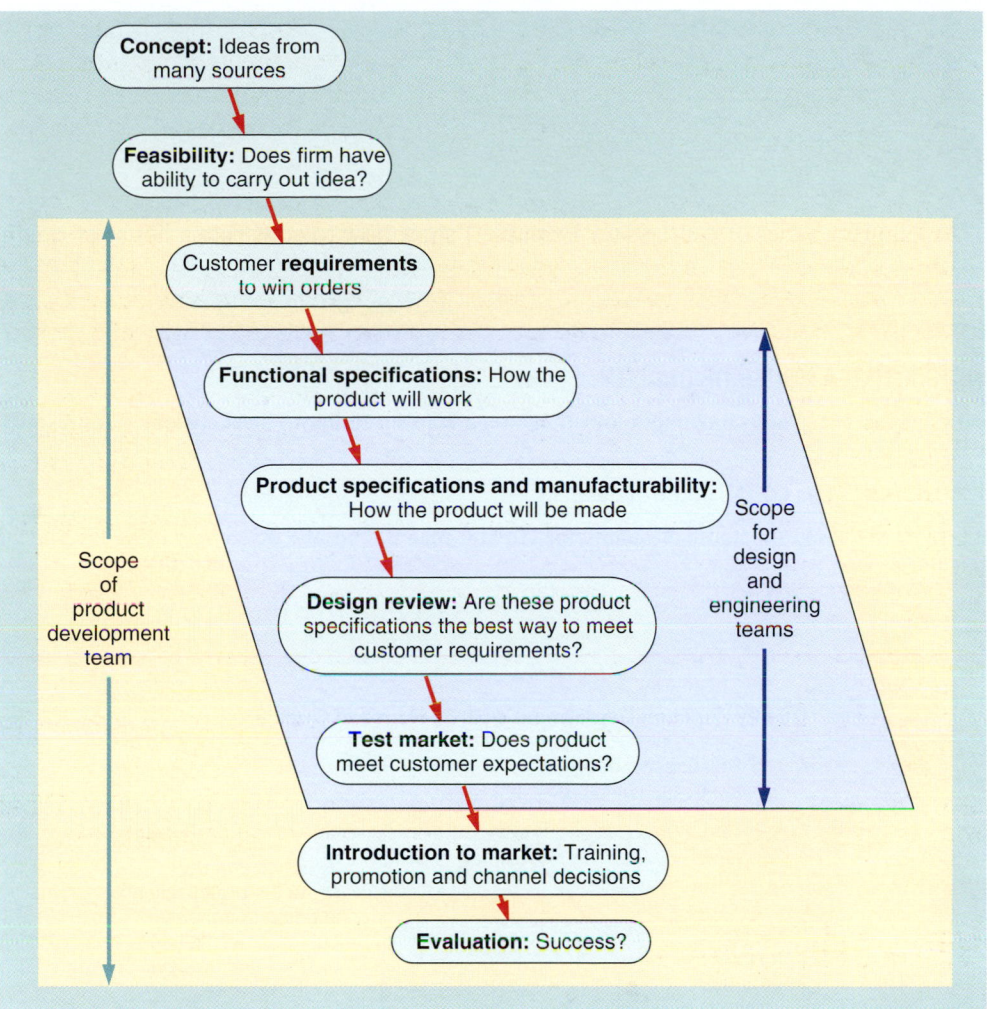

Figure **5.3**

Product Development Stages
Product concepts are developed from a variety of sources, both external and internal to the firm. Concepts that survive the product idea stage progress through various stages, with nearly constant review, feedback, and evaluation in a highly participative environment to minimize failure.

Defining this relationship is the first step in building a world-class production system. To build the house of quality, we perform seven basic steps:

1. Identify customer *wants*. (What do customers want in this product?)
2. Identify *how* the good/service will satisfy customer wants. (Identify specific product characteristics, features, or attributes and show how they will satisfy customer *wants*.)
3. Relate customer *wants* to product *hows*. (Build a matrix, as in Example 1, that shows this relationship.)
4. Identify relationships between the firm's *hows*. (How do our *hows* tie together? For instance, in the following example, there is a high relationship between low electricity requirements and auto focus, auto exposure, and number of pixels because they all require electricity. This relationship is shown in the "roof" of the house in Example 1.)
5. Develop importance ratings. (Using the *customer's* importance ratings and weights for the relationships shown in the matrix, compute *our* importance ratings, as in Example 1.)
6. Evaluate competing products. (How well do competing products meet customer wants? Such an evaluation, as shown in the two columns on the right of the figure in Example 1, would be based on market research.)
7. Determine the desirable technical attributes, your performance, and the competitor's performance against these attributes. (This is done at the bottom of the figure in Example 1.)

LO 5.3 *Build* a house of quality

The following series of overlays for Example 1 show how to construct a house of quality.

Example 1   CONSTRUCTING A HOUSE OF QUALITY

Great Cameras, Inc., wants a methodology that strengthens its ability to meet customer desires with its new digital camera.

APPROACH ▶   Use QFD's house of quality.

SOLUTION ▶   Build the house of quality for Great Cameras, Inc. We do so here using Overlays 1, 2, 3, and 4.

Quality Function Deployment's (QFD) House of Quality

Relationship between the things **we** can do

What we can **do**
(**how** the organization is going to translate customer wants into product and process attributes and design targets)

Customer importance ratings (5 = highest)

G = good
F = fair
P = poor

What the customer **wants**

Competitive assessment

How well what we do meets the customer's wants (relationship matrix)

Weighted rating

Target values (technical attributes)

Technical evaluation

INSIGHT ▶ QFD provides an analytical tool that structures design features and technical issues, as well as providing importance rankings and competitor comparison.

LEARNING EXERCISE ▶ If the market research for another country indicates that "lightweight" has the most important customer ranking (5), and reliability a 3, what is the new total importance ranking for low electricity requirements, aluminum components, and ergonomic design? [Answer: 18, 15, 27, respectively.]

RELATED PROBLEMS ▶ 5.4, 5.5, 5.6, 5.7, 5.8

Another use of quality function deployment (QFD) is to show how the quality effort will be *deployed*. As Figure 5.4 shows, *design characteristics* of House 1 become the inputs to House 2, which are satisfied by *specific components* of the product. Similarly, the concept is carried to House 3, where the specific components are to be satisfied through particular *production processes*. Once those production processes are defined, they become requirements of House 4 to be satisfied by a *quality plan* that will ensure conformance of those processes. The quality plan is a set of specific tolerances, procedures, methods, and sampling techniques that will ensure that the production process meets the customer requirements.

The QFD effort is devoted to meeting customer requirements. The *sequence* of houses is a very effective way of identifying, communicating, and deploying production resources. In this way we produce quality products, meet customer requirements, and win orders.

Organizing for Product Development

Let's look at four approaches to organizing for product development. *First*, the traditional U.S. approach to product development is an organization with distinct departments: a research and development department to do the necessary research; an engineering department to design the product; a manufacturing engineering department to design a product that can be produced; and a production department that produces the product. The distinct advantage of this approach is that fixed duties and responsibilities exist. The distinct disadvantage is lack of forward thinking: How will downstream departments in the process deal with the concepts, ideas, and designs presented to them, and ultimately what will the customer think of the product?

A *second* and popular approach is to assign a product manager to "champion" the product through the product development system and related organizations. However, a *third*, and perhaps the best, product development approach used in the U.S. seems to be the use of teams.

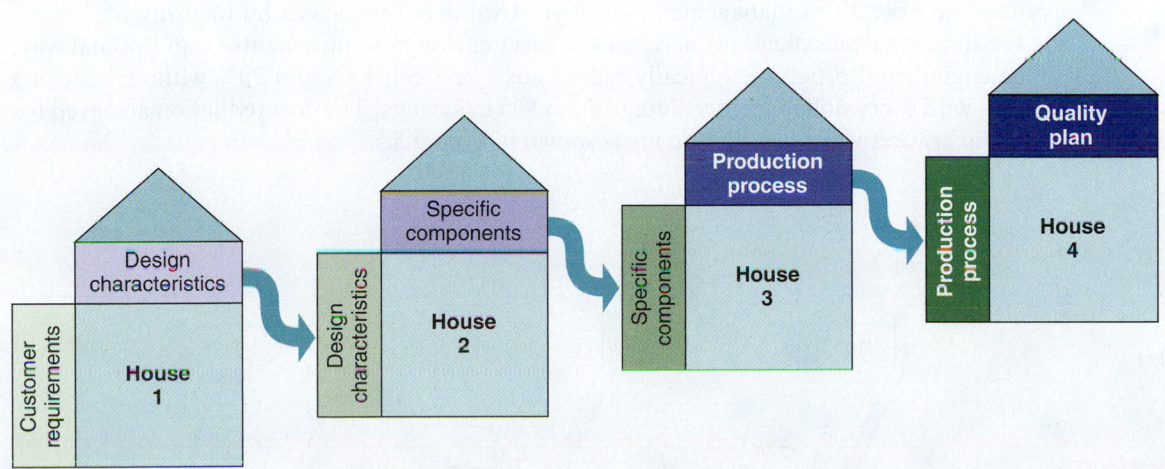

Figure **5.4**

House of Quality Sequence Indicates How to Deploy Resources to Achieve Customer Requirements

Such teams are known variously as *product development teams, design for manufacturability teams*, and *value engineering teams*.

The Japanese use a *fourth* approach. They bypass the team issue by not subdividing organizations into research and development, engineering, production, and so forth. Consistent with the Japanese style of group effort and teamwork, these activities are all in one organization. Japanese culture and management style are more collegial and the organization less structured than in most Western countries. Therefore, the Japanese find it unnecessary to have "teams" provide the necessary communication and coordination. However, the typical Western style, and the conventional wisdom, is to use teams.

Product development teams

Teams charged with moving from market requirements for a product to achieving product success.

Product development teams are charged with the responsibility of moving from market requirements for a product to achieving a product success (refer to Figure 5.3 on page 167). Such teams often include representatives from marketing, manufacturing, purchasing, quality assurance, and field service personnel. Many teams also include representatives from vendors. Regardless of the formal nature of the product development effort, research suggests that success is more likely in an open, highly participative environment where those with potential contributions are allowed to make them. The objective of a product development team is to make the good or service a success. This includes marketability, manufacturability, and serviceability.

Concurrent engineering

Simultaneous performance of the various stages of product development.

Concurrent engineering implies speedier product development through simultaneous performance of the various stages of product development (as we saw earlier in Figure 5.3). Often the concept is expanded to include all elements of a product's life cycle, from customer requirements to disposal and recycling. Concurrent engineering is facilitated by teams representing all affected areas (known as *cross-functional* teams).

Manufacturability and Value Engineering

Manufacturability and value engineering

Activities that help improve a product's design, production, maintainability, and use.

Manufacturability and value engineering activities are concerned with improvement of design and specifications at the research, development, design, and preproduction stages of product development. In addition to immediate, obvious cost reduction, design for manufacturability and value engineering may produce other benefits. These include:

1. Reduced complexity of the product.
2. Reduction of environmental impact.
3. Additional standardization of components.
4. Improvement of functional aspects of the product.
5. Improved job design and job safety.
6. Improved maintainability (serviceability) of the product.
7. Robust design.

Manufacturability and value engineering activities may be the best cost-avoidance technique available to operations management. They yield value improvement by focusing on achieving the functional specifications necessary to meet customer requirements in an optimal way. Value engineering programs typically reduce costs between 15% and 70% without reducing quality, with every dollar spent yielding $10 to $25 in savings. The cost reduction achieved for a specific bracket via value engineering is shown in Figure 5.5.

Figure **5.5**

Cost Reduction of a Bracket via Value Engineering

STUDENT TIP ◆

Each time the bracket is redesigned and simplified, we are able to produce it for less.

Issues for Product Design

In addition to developing an effective system and organization structure for product development, several considerations are important to the design of a product. We will now review six of these: (1) robust design, (2) modular design, (3) computer-aided design/computer-aided manufacturing (CAD/CAM), (4) virtual reality technology, (5) value analysis, and (6) sustainability/life cycle assessment (LCA).

Robust Design

Robust design means that the product is designed so that small variations in production or assembly do not adversely affect the product. For instance, Lucent developed an integrated circuit that could be used in many products to amplify voice signals. As originally designed, the circuit had to be manufactured very expensively to avoid variations in the strength of the signal. But after testing and analyzing the design, Lucent engineers realized that if the resistance of the circuit was reduced—a minor change with no associated costs—the circuit would be far less sensitive to manufacturing variations. The result was a 40% improvement in quality.

Robust design
A design that can be produced to requirements even with unfavorable conditions in the production process.

Modular Design

Products designed in easily segmented components are known as **modular designs**. Modular designs offer flexibility to both production and marketing. Operations managers find modularity helpful because it makes product development, production, and subsequent changes easier. Marketing may like modularity because it adds flexibility to the ways customers can be satisfied. For instance, virtually all premium high-fidelity sound systems are produced and sold this way. The customization provided by modularity allows customers to mix and match to their own taste. This is also the approach taken by Harley-Davidson, where relatively few different engines, chassis, gas tanks, and suspension systems are mixed to produce a huge variety of motorcycles. It has been estimated that many automobile manufacturers can, by mixing the available modules, never make two cars alike. This same concept of modularity is carried over to many industries, from airframe manufacturers to fast-food restaurants. Airbus uses the same wing modules on several planes, just as McDonald's and Burger King use relatively few modules (cheese, lettuce, buns, sauces, pickles, meat patties, french fries, etc.) to make a variety of meals.

Modular design
A design in which parts or components of a product are subdivided into modules that are easily interchanged or replaced.

Computer-Aided Design (CAD) and Computer-Aided Manufacturing (CAM)

Computer-aided design (CAD) is the use of computers to interactively design products and prepare engineering documentation. CAD uses three-dimensional drawing to save time and money by shortening development cycles for virtually all products (see the 3-D design photo in the Regal Marine Global Company Profile that opens this chapter). The speed and ease with which sophisticated designs can be manipulated, analyzed, and modified with CAD makes review of numerous options possible before final commitments are made. Faster development, better products, and accurate flow of information to other departments all contribute to a tremendous payoff for CAD. The payoff is particularly significant because most product costs are determined at the design stage.

Computer-aided design (CAD)
Interactive use of a computer to develop and document a product.

One extension of CAD is **design for manufacture and assembly (DFMA)** software, which focuses on the effect of design on assembly. For instance, DFMA allows Ford to build new vehicles in a virtual factory where designers examine how to put a transmission in a car on the production line, even while both the transmission and the car are still in the design stage.

Design for manufacture and assembly (DFMA)
Software that allows designers to look at the effect of design on manufacturing of the product.

CAD systems have moved to the Internet through e-commerce, where they link computerized design with purchasing, outsourcing, manufacturing, and long-term maintenance. This move also speeds up design efforts, as staff around the world can work on their unique work schedules. Rapid product change also supports the trend toward "mass customization" and,

For prototypes, spares, and in the case of Jay Leno's classic car collection, difficult-to-replace parts, 3D printing is often the answer. By scanning the original part, creating a digital file, making the necessary modifications, and feeding that data into a 3D printer, Jay's shop can make parts not otherwise available for his 1906 Stanley Steamer.

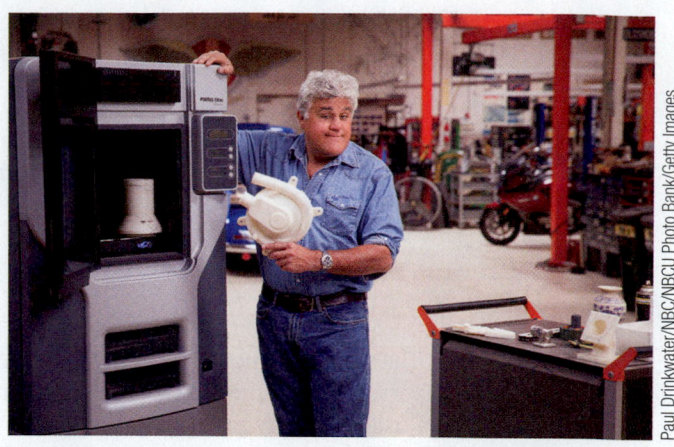

Paul Drinkwater/NBC/NBCU Photo Bank/Getty Images

Standard for the exchange of product data (STEP)

A standard that provides a format allowing the electronic transmission of three-dimensional data.

Computer-aided manufacturing (CAM)

The use of information technology to control machinery.

3-D printing

An extension of CAD that builds prototypes and small lots.

when carried to an extreme, allows customers to enter a supplier's design libraries and make changes. The result is faster and less expensive customized products. As product life cycles shorten, designs become more complex, and global collaboration has grown, the European Community (EU) has developed a standard for the exchange of product data (STEP; ISO 10303). STEP permits 3-D product information to be expressed in a standard format so it can be exchanged internationally.

Computer-aided manufacturing (CAM) refers to the use of specialized computer programs to direct and control manufacturing equipment. When CAD information is translated into instructions for CAM, the result of these two technologies is CAD/CAM. The combination is a powerful tool for manufacturing efficiency. Fewer defective units are produced, translating into less re-work and lower inventory. More precise scheduling also contributes to less inventory and more efficient use of personnel.

A related extension of CAD is 3-D printing. This technology is particularly useful for proto-type development and small lot production (as shown in the photo above). 3-D printing speeds development by avoiding a more lengthy and formal manufacturing process, as we see in the *OM in Action* box "3-D Printers Hit the Mainstream."

Virtual Reality Technology

Virtual reality

A visual form of communication in which images substitute for reality and typically allow the user to respond interactively.

Virtual reality is a visual form of communication in which images substitute for the real thing but still allow the user to respond interactively. The roots of virtual reality technology in opera-tions are in CAD. Once design information is in a CAD system, it is also in electronic digital form for other uses, such as developing 3-D layouts of everything from retail stores and res-taurant layouts to amusement parks. Procter & Gamble, for instance, builds walk-in virtual

---

OM in Action   3-D Printers Hit the Mainstream

3-D printers are revolutionizing the product design process. With instructions from 3-D CAD models, these printers "build" products by laying down succes-sive thin layers of plastic, metal, glass, or ceramics. Indeed, for many firms, 3-D printers have become indispensable.

The medical field uses the machines to make custom hearing aids. Invisalign Corp. produces individualized braces for teeth. Architects use the technology to produce models of buildings, and consumer electronics com-panies build prototypes of their latest gadgets. Microsoft uses 3-D printers to help design computer mouse devices and keyboards, while Mercedes, Honda, Boeing, and Lockheed Martin use them to fashion prototypes and to make parts that go into final products. Eventually, "a person who buys a BMW will want a part of the car with their name on it or to customize the seats to the

contours of their bodies," says 3-D Systems's CEO. And currently 3-D printing at Hershey's Chocolate World attraction means customers can order their likeness or wedding cake decoration in chocolate.

The cost of 3-D printing continues to drop. Now anyone can buy a 3-D printer, hook it up to a Wi-Fi network, and begin downloading files that will turn into real objects. Another beauty and value of 3-D printing is that it has the power to unleash a world of creative energy: People who previously only thought about an invention or improved product can now quickly make it real.

Sources: Advertising Age (January 28, 2015); BusinessWeek (April 30, 2012); and The Wall Street Journal (July 16, 2011).

stores to rapidly generate and test ideas. Changes to mechanical design, layouts, and even amusement park rides are much less expensive at the design stage than they are later.

Value Analysis

Although value engineering (discussed on page 170) focuses on *preproduction* design and manufacturing issues, value analysis, a related technique, takes place *during* the production process, when it is clear that a new product is a success. Value analysis seeks improvements that lead to either a better product, or a product made more economically, or a product with less environmental impact. The techniques and advantages for value analysis are the same as for value engineering, although minor changes in implementation may be necessary because value analysis is taking place while the product is being produced.

Value analysis

A review of successful products that takes place during the production process.

Sustainability and Life Cycle Assessment (LCA)

Product design requires that managers evaluate product options. Addressing sustainability and life cycle assessment (LCA) are two ways of doing this. *Sustainability* means meeting the needs of the present without compromising the ability of future generations to meet their needs. An LCA is a formal evaluation of the environmental impact of a product. Both sustainability and LCA are discussed in depth in the supplement to this chapter.

Product Development Continuum

As product life cycles shorten, the need for faster product development increases. And as technological sophistication of new products increases, so do the expense and risk. For instance, drug firms invest an average of 12 to 15 years and $1 billion before receiving regulatory approval for a new drug. And even then, only 1 of 5 will actually be a success. Those operations managers who master this art of product development continually gain on slower product developers. To the swift goes the competitive advantage. This concept is called time-based competition.

Often, the first company into production may have its product adopted for use in a variety of applications that will generate sales for years. It may become the "standard." Consequently, there is often more concern with getting the product to market than with optimum product design or process efficiency. Even so, rapid introduction to the market may be good management because until competition begins to introduce copies or improved versions, the product can sometimes be priced high enough to justify somewhat inefficient production design and methods.

Because time-based competition is so important, instead of developing new products from scratch (which has been the focus thus far in this chapter), a number of other strategies can be used. Figure 5.6 shows a continuum that goes from new, internally developed products (on the lower left) to "alliances." *Enhancements* and *migrations* use the organization's existing product strengths for innovation and therefore are typically faster while at the same time being less risky than developing entirely new products.

Enhancements may be changes in color, size, weight, taste, or features, such as are taking place in fast-food menu items (see the *OM in Action* box "Product Development at Taco Bell" on the next page), or even changes in commercial aircraft. Boeing's enhancements of the 737 since its introduction in 1967 has made the 737 the largest-selling commercial aircraft in history.

Boeing also uses its engineering prowess in air frames to *migrate* from one model to the next. This allows Boeing to speed development while reducing both cost and risk for new designs. This approach is also referred to as building on *product platforms*. Similarly, Volkswagen is using a versatile automobile platform (the MQB chassis) for small to midsize front-wheel-drive cars. This includes VW's Polo, Golf, Passat, Tiguan, and Skoda Octavia, and it may eventually include 44 different vehicles. The advantages are downward pressure on cost as well as faster development. Hewlett-Packard has done the same in the printer business. Enhancements and platform migrations are a way of building on existing expertise, speeding product development, and extending a product's life cycle.

The product development strategies on the lower left of Figure 5.6 are *internal* development strategies, while the three approaches we now introduce can be thought of as *external*

◆ STUDENT TIP

Fast communication, rapid technological change, and short product life cycles push product development.

Time-based competition

Competition based on time; rapidly developing products and moving them to market.

LO 5.4 *Explain* how time-based competition is implemented by OM

Figure **5.6**

Product Development
Continuum

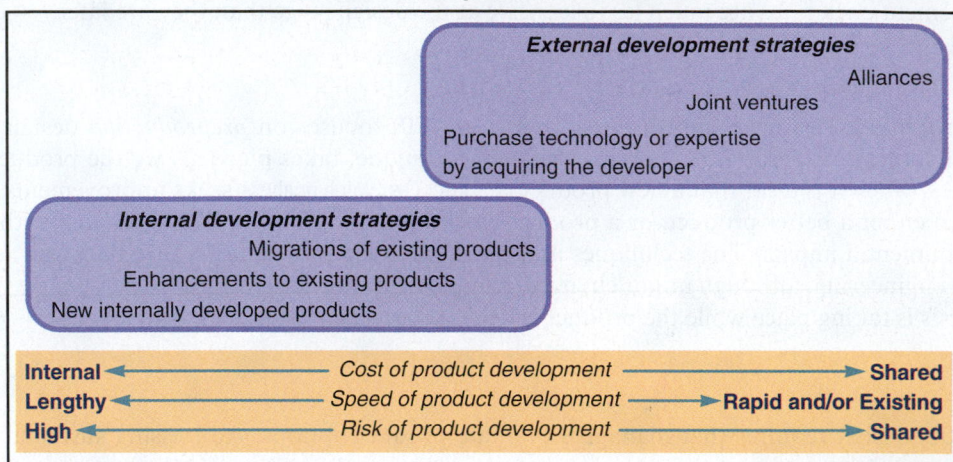

Product Development Continuum

External development strategies

Alliances

Joint ventures

Purchase technology or expertise
by acquiring the developer

Internal development strategies

Migrations of existing products

Enhancements to existing products

New internally developed products

Internal	Cost of product development	Shared
Lengthy	Speed of product development	Rapid and/or Existing
High	Risk of product development	Shared

STUDENT TIP ◆

Managers seek a variety of
approaches to obtain speed to
market. As the president of one
U.S. firm said: "If I miss one
product cycle, I'm dead."

development strategies. Firms use both. The external strategies are (1) purchase the technology, (2) establish joint ventures, and (3) develop alliances.

Purchasing Technology by Acquiring a Firm

Microsoft and Cisco Systems are examples of companies on the cutting edge of technology that often speed development by *acquiring entrepreneurial firms* that have already developed the technology that fits their mission. The issue then becomes fitting the purchased organization, its technology, its product lines, and its culture into the buying firm, rather than a product development issue.

Joint ventures

Firms establishing joint ownership to pursue new products or
markets.

Joint Ventures

In an effort to reduce the weight of new cars, GM is in a joint venture with Tokyo-based Teijin Ltd. to bring lightweight carbon fiber to GM's customers. Joint ventures such as this are

---

OM in Action | **Product Development at Taco Bell**

Chains such as Chipotle, Carl's Jr., and In-N-Out Burger may rely on a stable menu of popular items, but Taco Bell creates a constant rotation of products in hopes of not only keeping consumers coming back, but also uncovering the next big seller. Taco Bell seeks to be the leader in fast-food innovation and believes there is no finish line when it comes to being first and staying relevant. Breakfast is the fastest-growing part of the fast-food market—with dinner sales declining and lunch sales flat. Moreover, breakfast items tend to have good margins, making the crafting of breakfast hits, such as Taco Bell's new A.M. Crunchwrap and Waffle Taco, lucrative additions.

In search of ideas, the product developers mine social media, consider new ingredients, and track rivals. Some Fridays, the team does what they've dubbed a "grocery store hustle" to see what's new in retail. But the basic pillars of anything they develop remain taste, value, and speed—all of which must be attainable within the constraints and operations capability of the Taco Bell kitchen. The less a restaurant has to change its kitchen operations, ingredients, or equipment, the better.

Taco Bell's 40-person product innovation team looks at 4,000 to 4,500 ideas every year. From there developers come up with 300 to 500 prototypes, which

they then test on consumers in the lab and in test restaurants. From this huge array, Taco Bell selects dozens of items in various permutations for further review. Usually, only 8 to 10 of the new product ideas make the Taco Bell menu.

The typical product goes through about 100 iterations by the time it is launched. The Waffle Taco, for instance, was changed 80 times through various characteristics such as shape, weight, thickness, intensity of vanilla flavor in the shell, and fillings.

Taco Bell's New Waffle Taco

Sources: BusinessWeek (June 2–9, 2014); *The Wall Street Journal* (Dec. 4, 2014); www.grubgrade.com; investorplace.com/2014/03.

combined ownership, usually between just two firms, to form a new entity. Ownership can be 50–50, or one owner can assume a larger portion to ensure tighter control. Joint ventures are often appropriate for exploiting specific product opportunities that may not be central to the firm's mission. Such ventures are more likely to work when the risks are known and can be equitably shared.

Alliances

When new products are central to the mission, but substantial resources are required and sizable risk is present, then alliances may be a good strategy for product development. Alliances are cooperative agreements that allow firms to remain independent but use complementing strengths to pursue strategies consistent with their individual missions. Alliances are particularly beneficial when the products to be developed also have technologies that are in ferment. For example, Microsoft is pursuing alliances with a variety of companies to deal with the convergence of computing, the Internet, and television broadcasting. Alliances in this case are appropriate because the technological unknowns, capital demands, and risks are significant. Similarly, three firms, Mercedes-Benz, Ford Motor, and Ballard Power Systems, have formed an alliance to develop "green" cars powered by fuel cells. Alliances are much more difficult to achieve and maintain than joint ventures because of the ambiguities associated with them. It may be helpful to think of an alliance as an incomplete contract between the firms. The firms remain separate.

Enhancements, migration, acquisitions, joint ventures, and alliances are all strategies for speeding product development. Moreover, they typically reduce the risk associated with product development while enhancing the human and capital resources available.

Alliances

Cooperative agreements that allow firms to remain independent, but pursue strategies consistent with their individual missions.

Defining a Product

Once new goods or services are selected for introduction, they must be defined. First, a good or service is defined in terms of its *functions*—that is, what it is to *do*. The product is then designed, and the firm determines how the functions are to be achieved. Management typically has a variety of options as to how a product should achieve its functional purpose. For instance, when an alarm clock is produced, aspects of design such as the color, size, or location of buttons may make substantial differences in ease of manufacture, quality, and market acceptance.

Rigorous specifications of a product are necessary to ensure efficient production. Equipment, layout, and human resources cannot be determined until the product is defined, designed, and documented. Therefore, every organization needs documents to define its products. This is true of everything from meat patties, to cheese, to computers, to a medical procedure. In the case of cheese, a written specification is typical. Indeed, written specifications or standard grades exist and provide the definition for many products. For instance, Monterey Jack cheese has a written description that specifies the characteristics necessary for each Department of Agriculture grade. A portion of the Department of Agriculture grade for Monterey Jack Grade AA is shown in Figure 5.7. Similarly, McDonald's Corp. has 60 specifications for potatoes that are to be made into french fries.

Most manufactured items, as well as their components, are defined by a drawing, usually referred to as an engineering drawing. An engineering drawing shows the dimensions, tolerances, materials, and finishes of a component. The engineering drawing will be an item on a bill of material. An engineering drawing is shown in Figure 5.8. The bill of material (BOM) lists the hierarchy of components, their description, and the quantity of each required to make one unit of a product. A bill of material for a manufactured item is shown in Figure 5.9(a). Note that subassemblies and components (lower-level items) are indented at each level to indicate their subordinate position. An engineering drawing shows how to make one item on the bill of material.

STUDENT TIP
Before anything can be produced, a product's functions and attributes must be defined.

LO 5.5 *Describe* how products and services are defined by OM

Engineering drawing

A drawing that shows the dimensions, tolerances, materials, and finishes of a component.

Bill of material (BOM)

A list of the hierarchy of components, their description, and the quantity of each required to make one unit of a product.

Figure **5.7**

Monterey Jack

A portion of the general requirements for the U.S. grades of Monterey Jack cheese is shown here.

Source: Based on 58.2469 Specifications for U.S. grades of Monterey (Monterey Jack) cheese, (May 10, 1996).

§ 58.2469 Specifications for U.S. grades of Monterey (Monterey Jack) cheese

(a) *U.S. grade AA.* Monterey Cheese shall conform to the following requirements:

(1) *Flavor.* Is fine and highly pleasing, free from undesirable flavors and odors. May possess a very slight acid or feed flavor.

(2) *Body and texture.* A plug drawn from the cheese shall be reasonably firm. It shall have numerous small mechanical openings evenly distributed throughout the plug. It shall not possess sweet holes, yeast holes, or other gas holes.

(3) *Color.* Shall have a natural, uniform, bright, attractive appearance.

(4) *Finish and appearance—bandaged and paraffin-dipped.* The rind shall be sound, firm, and smooth, providing a good protection to the cheese.

Code of Federal Regulation, Parts 53 to 109, General Service Administration.

David Murray/Dorling Kindersley, Ltd.

In the food-service industry, bills of material manifest themselves in *portion-control standards.* The portion-control standard for Hard Rock Cafe's hickory BBQ bacon cheeseburger is shown in Figure 5.9(b). In a more complex product, a bill of material is referenced on other bills of material of which they are a part. In this manner, subunits (subassemblies) are part of the next higher unit (their parent bill of material) that ultimately makes a final product. In addition to being defined by written specifications, portion-control documents, or bills of material, products can be defined in other ways. For example, products such as chemicals, paints, and petroleums may be defined by formulas or proportions that describe how they are to be made. Movies are defined by scripts, and insurance coverage by legal documents known as policies.

Make-or-Buy Decisions

Make-or-buy decision

The choice between producing a component or a service and purchasing it from an outside source.

For many components of products, firms have the option of producing the components themselves or purchasing them from outside sources. Choosing between these options is known as the make-or-buy decision. The make-or-buy decision distinguishes between what the firm wants to *produce* and what it wants to *purchase.* Because of variations in quality, cost, and delivery schedules, the make-or-buy decision is critical to product definition. Many items can be purchased as a "standard item" produced by someone else. Examples are the standard bolts listed twice on the bill of material shown in Figure 5.9(a), for which there will be SAE (Society

Figure **5.8**

Engineering Drawings Such as This One Show Dimensions, Tolerances, Materials, and Finishes

(a) **Bill of Material for a Panel Weldment**

NUMBER	DESCRIPTION	QTY
A 60-71	PANEL WELDM'T	1
A 60-7	LOWER ROLLER ASSM.	1
R 60-17	ROLLER	1
R 60-428	PIN	1
P 60-2	LOCKNUT	1
A 60-72	GUIDE ASSM. REAR	1
R 60-57-1	SUPPORT ANGLE	1
A 60-4	ROLLER ASSEM.	1
02-50-1150	BOLT	1
A 60-73	GUIDE ASSM. FRONT	1
A 60-74	SUPPORT WELDM'T	1
R 60-99	WEAR PLATE	1
02-50-1150	BOLT	1

(b) **Hard Rock Cafe's Hickory BBQ Bacon Cheeseburger**

DESCRIPTION	QTY
Bun	1
Hamburger patty	8 oz.
Cheddar cheese	2 slices
Bacon	2 strips
BBQ onions	1/2 cup
Hickory BBQ sauce	1 oz.
Burger set	
Lettuce	1 leaf
Tomato	1 slice
Red onion	4 rings
Pickle	1 slice
French fries	5 oz.
Seasoned salt	1 tsp.
11-inch plate	1
HRC flag	1

Figure **5.9**

Bills of Material Take Different Forms in a (a) Manufacturing Plant and (b) Restaurant, but in Both Cases, the Product Must Be Defined

⚠ STUDENT TIP

Hard Rock's recipe here serves the same purpose as a bill of material in a factory: It defines the product for production.

of Automotive Engineers) specifications. Therefore, there typically is no need for the firm to duplicate this specification in another document.

Group Technology

Engineering drawings may also include codes to facilitate group technology. **Group technology** identifies components by a coding scheme that specifies size, shape, and the type of processing (such as drilling). This facilitates standardization of materials, components, and processes as well as the identification of families of parts. As families of parts are identified, activities and machines can be grouped to minimize setups, routings, and material handling. An example of how families of parts may be grouped is shown in Figure 5.10. Group technology provides a systematic way to review a family of components to see if an existing component might suffice on a new project. Using existing or standard components eliminates all the costs connected with the design and development of the new part, which is a major cost reduction.

Group technology

A product and component coding system that specifies the size, shape, and type of processing; it allows similar products to be grouped.

Figure **5.10**

A Variety of Group Technology Coding Schemes Move Manufactured Components from (a) Ungrouped to (b) Grouped (families of parts)

(a) Ungrouped Parts	(b) Grouped Cylindrical Parts (families of parts)				
	Grooved	Slotted	Threaded	Drilled	Machined

STUDENT TIP ●
Production personnel need clear, specific documents to help them make the product.

Documents for Production

Once a product is selected, designed, and ready for production, production is assisted by a variety of documents. We will briefly review some of these.

An **assembly drawing** simply shows an exploded view of the product. An assembly drawing is usually a three-dimensional drawing, known as an *isometric drawing*; the relative locations of components are drawn in relation to each other to show how to assemble the unit [see Figure 5.11(a)].

The **assembly chart** shows in schematic form how a product is assembled. Manufactured components, purchased components, or a combination of both may be shown on an assembly chart. The assembly chart identifies the point of production at which components flow into subassemblies and ultimately into a final product. An example of an assembly chart is shown in Figure 5.11(b).

The **route sheet** lists the operations necessary to produce the component with the material specified in the bill of material. The route sheet for an item will have one entry for each operation to be performed on the item. When route sheets include specific methods of operation and labor standards, they are often known as *process sheets*.

The **work order** is an instruction to make a given quantity of a particular item, usually to a given schedule. The ticket that a waiter writes in your favorite restaurant is a work order. In a hospital or factory, the work order is a more formal document that provides authorization to draw items from inventory, to perform various functions, and to assign personnel to perform those functions.

Engineering change notices (ECNs) change some aspect of the product's definition or documentation, such as an engineering drawing or a bill of material. For a complex product that has a long manufacturing cycle, such as a Boeing 777, the changes may be so numerous that no two 777s are built exactly alike—which is indeed the case. Such dynamic design change has fostered the development of a discipline known as configuration management, which is concerned with product identification, control, and documentation. **Configuration management** is the system by which a product's planned and changing configurations are accurately identified and for which control and accountability of change are maintained.

Product Life-Cycle Management (PLM)

Product life-cycle management (PLM) is an umbrella of software programs that attempts to bring together phases of product design and manufacture—including tying together many of

Assembly drawing
An exploded view of the product.

Assembly chart
A graphic means of identifying how components flow into subassemblies and final products.

Route sheet
A listing of the operations necessary to produce a component with the material specified in the bill of material.

Work order
An instruction to make a given quantity of a particular item.

Engineering change notice (ECN)
A correction or modification of an engineering drawing or bill of material.

Configuration management
A system by which a product's planned and changing components are accurately identified.

Product life-cycle management (PLM)
Software programs that tie together many phases of product design and manufacture.

Figure 5.11

Assembly Drawing and Assembly Chart

Source: Assembly drawing and assembly chart produced by author.

(a) Assembly Drawing

(b) Assembly Chart

J.R. Simplot Company

J.R. Simplot Company

Each year the JR Simplot potato-processing facility in Caldwell, Idaho, produces billions of french fries for quick-service restaurant chains and many other customers, both domestically and overseas (left photo). Sixty specifications (including a special blend of frying oil, a unique steaming process, and exact time and temperature for prefrying and drying) define how these potatoes become french fries. Further, 40% of all french fries must be 2 to 3 inches long, 40% must be over 3 inches long, and a few stubby ones constitute the final 20%. Quality control personnel use a micrometer to measure the fries (right photo).

the techniques discussed in the prior two sections, *Defining a Product* and *Documents for Production*. The idea behind PLM software is that product design and manufacture decisions can be performed more creatively, faster, and more economically when the data are integrated and consistent.

Although there is not one standard, PLM products often start with product design (CAD/CAM); move on to design for manufacture and assembly (DFMA); and then into product routing, materials, layout, assembly, maintenance, and even environmental issues. Integration of these tasks makes sense because many of these decision areas require overlapping pieces of data. PLM software is now a tool of many large organizations, including Lockheed Martin, GE, Procter & Gamble, Toyota, and Boeing. Boeing estimates that PLM will cut final assembly of its 787 jet from 2 weeks to 3 days. PLM is now finding its way into medium and small manufacture as well.

Shorter life cycles, more technologically challenging products, more regulations regarding materials and manufacturing processes, and more environmental issues all make PLM an appealing tool for operations managers. Major vendors of PLM software include SAP PLM (www.mySAP.com), Parametric Technology Corp. (www.ptc.com), Siemens (www.plm.automation.siemens.com), and Proplanner (www.proplanner.com).

Service Design

Much of our discussion so far has focused on what we can call tangible products—that is, goods. On the other side of the product coin are, of course, services. Service industries include banking, finance, insurance, transportation, and communications. The products offered by service firms range from a medical procedure that leaves only the tiniest scar after an appendectomy, to a shampoo and cut at a hair salon, to a great sandwich. Designing services is challenging because they have a unique characteristic—customer interaction.

Process–Chain–Network (PCN) Analysis

Process–chain–network (PCN) analysis, developed by Professor Scott Sampson, focuses on the ways in which processes can be designed to optimize interaction between firms and

Figure **5.12**

Customer Interaction Is a Strategic Choice

Process chain

A sequence of steps that accomplishes an identifiable purpose (of providing value to process participants).

their customers.[2] A **process chain** is a sequence of steps that accomplishes an activity, such as building a home, completing a tax return, or preparing a sandwich. A process participant can be a manufacturer, a service provider, or a customer. A network is a set of participants.

Each participant has a *process domain* that includes the set of activities over which it has control. The domain and interactions between two participants for sandwich preparation are shown in the PCN diagram (Figure 5.12). The activities are organized into three *process regions* for each participant:

1. The *direct interaction* region includes process steps that involve interaction between participants. For example, a sandwich buyer directly interacts with employees of a sandwich store (e.g., Subway, in the middle of Figure 5.12).
2. The *surrogate (substitute) interaction* region includes process steps in which one participant is acting on another participant's resources, such as their information, materials, or technologies. This occurs when the sandwich *supplier* is making sandwiches in the restaurant kitchen (left side of Figure 5.12) or, alternately, when the *customer* has access to buffet ingredients and assembles the sandwich himself (right side of the figure). Under surrogate interaction, *direct* interaction is limited.
3. The *independent processing* region includes steps in which the sandwich supplier and/or the sandwich customer is acting on resources where each has maximum control. Most make-to-stock production fits in this region (left side of Figure 5.12; think of the firm that assembles all those prepackaged sandwiches available in vending machines and convenience stores). Similarly, those sandwiches built at home occur to the right, in the customer's independent processing domain.

LO 5.7 *Explain* how the customer participates in the design and delivery of services

All three process regions have similar operating issues—quality control, facility location and layout, job design, inventory, and so on—but the appropriate way of handling the issues differs across regions. Service operations exist only within the area of *direct* and *surrogate interaction*.

From the operations manager's perspective, the valuable aspect of PCN analysis is insight to aid in positioning and designing processes that can achieve strategic objectives. A firm's operations are strategic in that they can define what type of business the firm is in and what value proposition it desires to provide to customers. For example, a firm may assume a low-cost strategy, operating on the left of Figure 5.12 as a manufacturer of premade sandwiches. Other firms (e.g., Subway) adopt a differentiation strategy with high customer interaction. Each of the process regions depicts a unique operational strategy.

Firms wanting to achieve high economies of scale or more control in their operations should probably position toward the independent processing region of their process domain. Firms intending to provide a value offering that focuses on customization should be positioned more toward the consumer's process domain. PCN analysis can be applied in a wide variety of business settings.

Adding Service Efficiency

Service productivity is notoriously low, in part because of customer involvement in the *design* or *delivery* of the service, or both. This complicates the product design challenge. We will now discuss a number of ways to increase service efficiency and, among these, several ways to limit this interaction.

Limit the Options   Because customers may participate in the *design* of the service (e.g., for a funeral or a hairstyle), design specifications may take the form of everything from a menu (in a restaurant), to a list of options (for a funeral), to a verbal description (a hairstyle). However, by providing a list of options (in the case of the funeral) or a series of photographs (in the case of the hairstyle), ambiguity may be reduced. An early resolution of the product's definition can aid efficiency as well as aid in meeting customer expectations.

Delay Customization   Design the product so that *customization is delayed* as late in the process as possible. This is the way a hair salon operates. Although shampoo and condition are done in a standard way with lower-cost labor, the color and styling (customizing) are done last. It is also the way most restaurants operate: How would you like that cooked? Which dressing would you prefer with your salad?

Modularization   *Modularize* the service so that customization takes the form of changing modules. This strategy allows for "custom" services to be designed as standard modular entities. Just as modular design allows you to buy a high-fidelity sound system with just the features you want, modular flexibility also lets you buy meals, clothes, and insurance on a mix-and-match (modular) basis. Investments (portfolios of stocks and bonds) and education (college curricula) are examples of how the modular approach can be used to customize a service.

Automation   Divide the service into small parts, and identify those parts that lend themselves to automation. For instance, by isolating check-cashing activity via ATM, banks have been very effective at designing a product that both increases customer service and reduces costs. Similarly, airlines have moved to ticketless service via kiosks. A technique such as kiosks reduces both costs and lines at airports—thereby increasing customer satisfaction—and providing a win–win "product" design.

Moment of Truth   High customer interaction means that in the service industry there is a *moment of truth* when the relationship between the provider and the customer is crucial. At that moment, the customer's satisfaction with the service is defined. The moment of truth is the moment that exemplifies, enhances, or detracts from the customer's expectations. That moment may be as simple as a smile from a Starbucks barista or having the checkout clerk focus on you rather than talking over his shoulder to the clerk at the next counter. Moments of truth can occur when you order at McDonald's, get a haircut, or register for college courses. The operations manager's task is to identify moments of truth and design operations that meet or exceed the customer's expectations.

Documents for Services

Because of the high customer interaction of most services, the documents for moving the product to production often take the form of explicit *job instructions* or *script*. For instance, regardless of how good a bank's products may be in terms of checking, savings, trusts, loans, mortgages, and so forth, if the interaction between participants is not done well, the product may be poorly received. Example 2 shows the kind of documentation a bank may use to move a product (drive-up window banking) to "production." Similarly, a telemarketing service has the product design communicated to production personnel in the form of a *telephone script*, while a *manuscript* is used for books, and a *storyboard* is used for movie and TV production.

Example 2

SERVICE DOCUMENTATION FOR PRODUCTION

First Bank Corp. wants to ensure effective delivery of service to its drive-up customers.

APPROACH ▶ Develop a "production" document for the tellers at the drive-up window that provides the information necessary to do an effective job.

SOLUTION ▶

Documentation for Tellers at Drive-up Windows

Customers who use the drive-up teller windows rather than walk-in lobbies require a different customer relations technique. The distance and machinery between the teller and the customer raises communication barriers. Guidelines to ensure good customer relations at the drive-up window are:

- Be especially discreet when talking to the customer through the microphone.
- Provide written instructions for customers who must fill out forms you provide.
- Mark lines to be completed or attach a note with instructions.
- Always say "please" and "thank you" when speaking through the microphone.
- Establish eye contact with the customer if the distance allows it.
- If a transaction requires that the customer park the car and come into the lobby, apologize for the inconvenience.

Source: Adapted with permission from *Teller Operations* (Chicago, IL: The Institute of Financial Education, 1999): 32.

INSIGHT ▶ By providing documentation in the form of a script/guideline for tellers, the likelihood of effective communication and a good product/service is improved.

LEARNING EXERCISE ▶ Modify the guidelines above to show how they would be different for a drive-through restaurant. [Answer: Written instructions, marking lines to be completed, or coming into the store are seldom necessary, but techniques for making change and proper transfer of the order should be included.]

RELATED PROBLEM ▶ 5.11

Application of Decision Trees to Product Design

STUDENT TIP ◆
A decision tree is a great tool for thinking through a problem.

Decision trees can be used for new-product decisions as well as for a wide variety of other management problems when uncertainty is present. They are particularly helpful when there are a series of decisions and various outcomes that lead to *subsequent* decisions followed by other outcomes. To form a decision tree, we use the following procedure:

1. Be sure that all possible alternatives and states of nature (beginning on the left and moving right) are included in the tree. This includes an alternative of "doing nothing."
2. Payoffs are entered at the end of the appropriate branch. This is the place to develop the payoff of achieving this branch.

LO 5.8 *Apply* decision trees to product issues

3. The objective is to determine the expected monetary value (EMV) of each course of action. We accomplish this by starting at the end of the tree (the right-hand side) and working toward the beginning of the tree (the left), calculating values at each step and "pruning" alternatives that are not as good as others from the same node.

Example 3 shows the use of a decision tree applied to product design.

Example 3

DECISION TREE APPLIED TO PRODUCT DESIGN

Silicon, Inc., a semiconductor manufacturer, is investigating the possibility of producing and marketing a microprocessor. Undertaking this project will require either purchasing a sophisticated CAD system or hiring and training several additional engineers. The market for the product could be either favorable or unfavorable. Silicon, Inc., of course, has the option of not developing the new product at all.

With favorable acceptance by the market, sales would be 25,000 processors selling for $100 each. With unfavorable acceptance, sales would be only 8,000 processors selling for $100 each. The cost of CAD equipment is $500,000, but that of hiring and training three new engineers is only $375,000. However, manufacturing costs should drop from $50 each when manufacturing without CAD to $40 each when manufacturing with CAD.

The probability of favorable acceptance of the new microprocessor is .40; the probability of unfavorable acceptance is .60.

APPROACH ▶ Use of a decision tree seems appropriate as Silicon, Inc., has the basic ingredients: a choice of decisions, probabilities, and payoffs.

SOLUTION ▶ In Figure 5.13 we draw a decision tree with a branch for each of the three decisions, assign the respective probabilities and payoff for each branch, and then compute the respective EMVs. The expected monetary values (EMVs) have been circled at each step of the decision tree. For the top branch:

$$\text{EMV (Purchase CAD system)} = (.4)(\$1,000,000) + (.6)(-\$20,000)$$
$$= \$388,000$$

This figure represents the results that will occur if Silicon, Inc., purchases CAD.

The expected value of hiring and training engineers is the second series of branches:

$$\text{EMV (Hire/train engineers)} = (.4)(\$875,000) + (.6)(\$25,000)$$
$$= \$365,000$$

Figure **5.13**

Decision Tree for Development of a New Product

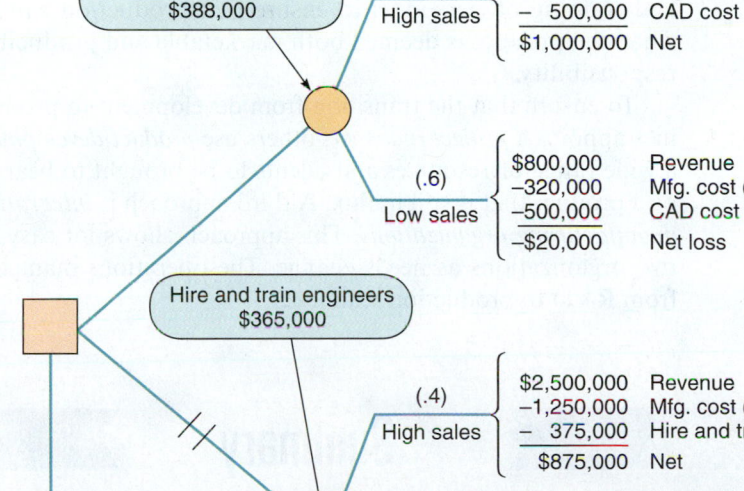

The EMV of doing nothing is $0.

Because the top branch has the highest expected monetary value (an EMV of $388,000 vs. $365,000 vs. $0), it represents the best decision. Management should purchase the CAD system.

INSIGHT ▶ Use of the decision tree provides both objectivity and structure to our analysis of the Silicon, Inc., decision.

LEARNING EXERCISE ▶ If Silicon, Inc., thinks the probabilities of high sales and low sales may be equal, at .5 each, what is the best decision? [Answer: Purchase CAD remains the best decision, but with an EMV of $490,000.]

RELATED PROBLEMS ▶ 5.21–5.27 (5.28 is available in MyOMLab)

ACTIVE MODEL 5.1 This example is further illustrated in Active Model 5.1 in MyOMLab.

STUDENT TIP ❶
One of the arts of management is knowing when a product should move from development to production.

Transition to Production

Eventually, a product, whether a good or service, has been selected, designed, and defined. It has progressed from an idea to a functional definition, and then perhaps to a design. Now, management must make a decision as to further development and production or termination of the product idea. One of the arts of management is knowing when to move a product from development to production; this move is known as *transition to production*. The product development staff is always interested in making improvements in a product. Because this staff tends to see product development as evolutionary, they may never have a completed product, but as we noted earlier, the cost of late product introduction is high. Although these conflicting pressures exist, management must make a decision—more development or production.

Once this decision is made, there is usually a period of trial production to ensure that the design is indeed producible. This is the manufacturability test. This trial also gives the operations staff the opportunity to develop proper tooling, quality control procedures, and training of personnel to ensure that production can be initiated successfully. Finally, when the product is deemed both marketable and producible, line management will assume responsibility.

To ensure that the transition from development to production is successful, some companies appoint a *project manager*; others use *product development teams*. Both approaches allow a wide range of resources and talents to be brought to bear to ensure satisfactory production of a product that is still in flux. A third approach is *integration of the product development and manufacturing organizations*. This approach allows for easy shifting of resources between the two organizations as needs change. The operations manager's job is to make the transition from R&D to production seamless.

Summary

Effective product strategy requires selecting, designing, and defining a product and then transitioning that product to production. Only when this strategy is carried out effectively can the production function contribute its maximum to the organization. The operations manager must build a product development system that has the ability to conceive, design, and produce products that will yield a competitive advantage for the firm. As products move through their life cycle (introduction, growth, maturity, and decline), the options that the operations manager should pursue change.

Both manufactured and service products have a variety of techniques available to aid in performing this activity efficiently.

Written specifications, bills of material, and engineering drawings aid in defining products. Similarly, assembly drawings, assembly charts, route sheets, and work orders are often used to assist in the actual production of the product. Once a product is in production, value analysis is appropriate to ensure maximum product value. Engineering change notices and configuration management provide product documentation.

Key Terms

Product decision (p. 163)
Product-by-value analysis (p. 165)
Quality function deployment (QFD) (p. 166)
House of quality (p. 166)
Product development teams (p. 170)
Concurrent engineering (p. 170)
Manufacturability and value engineering (p. 170)
Robust design (p. 171)
Modular design (p. 171)
Computer-aided design (CAD) (p. 171)
Design for manufacture and assembly (DFMA) (p. 171)

Standard for the exchange of product data (STEP) (p. 172)
Computer-aided manufacturing (CAM) (p. 172)
3-D printing (p. 172)
Virtual reality (p. 172)
Value analysis (p. 173)
Time-based competition (p. 173)
Joint ventures (p. 174)
Alliances (p. 175)
Engineering drawing (p. 175)
Bill of material (BOM) (p. 175)
Make-or-buy decision (p. 176)

Group technology (p. 177)
Assembly drawing (p. 178)
Assembly chart (p. 178)
Route sheet (p. 178)
Work order (p. 178)
Engineering change notice (ECN) (p. 178)
Configuration management (p. 178)
Product life-cycle management (PLM) (p. 178)
Process–chain–network (PCN) analysis (p. 179)
Process chain (p. 179)

Ethical Dilemma

John Sloan, president of Sloan Toy Company, Inc., in Oregon, has just reviewed the design of a new pull-toy locomotive for 1- to 3-year-olds. John's design and marketing staff are very enthusiastic about the market for the product and the potential of follow-on circus train cars. The sales manager is looking forward to a very good reception at the annual toy show in Dallas next month. John, too, is delighted, as he is faced with a layoff if orders do not improve.

John's production people have worked out the manufacturing issues and produced a successful pilot run. However, the quality assessment staff suggests that under certain conditions, a hook to attach cars to the locomotive and the crank for the bell can be broken off. This is an issue because children can choke on small parts such as these. In the quality test, 1- to 3-year-olds were unable to break off these parts; there were *no* failures. But when the test simulated the force of an adult tossing the locomotive into a toy box or a 5-year-old throwing it on the floor, there were failures. The estimate is that one of the two parts can be broken off 4 times out of 100,000 throws. Neither the design

nor the material people know how to make the toy safer and still perform as designed. The failure rate is low and certainly normal for this type of toy, but not at the Six Sigma level that John's firm strives for. And, of course, someone, someday may sue. A child choking on the broken part is a serious matter. Also, John was recently reminded in a discussion with legal counsel that U.S. case law suggests that new products may not be produced if there is "actual or foreseeable knowledge of a problem" with the product.

The design of successful, ethically produced new products, as suggested in this chapter, is a complex task. What should John do?

Nikolay Stefanov Dimitrov/ Shutterstock

Discussion Questions

1. Why is it necessary to document a product explicitly?
2. What techniques do we use to define a product?
3. In what ways is product strategy linked to product decisions?
4. Once a product is defined, what documents are used to assist production personnel in its manufacture?
5. What is time-based competition?
6. Describe the differences between joint ventures and alliances.
7. Describe four organizational approaches to product development. Which of these is generally thought to be best?
8. Explain what is meant by robust design.
9. What are three specific ways in which computer-aided design (CAD) benefits the design engineer?
10. What information is contained in a bill of material?
11. What information is contained in an engineering drawing?
12. What information is contained in an assembly chart? In a process sheet?
13. Explain what is meant in service design by the "moment of truth."
14. Explain how the house of quality translates customer desires into product/service attributes.
15. What strategic advantages does computer-aided design provide?
16. What is a process chain?
17. Why are the direct interaction and surrogate interaction regions in a PCN diagram important in service design?
18. Why are documents for service useful? Provide examples of four types.

Solved Problem   Virtual Office Hours help is available in MyOMLab.

SOLVED PROBLEM 5.1

Sarah King, president of King Electronics, Inc., has two design options for her new line of high-resolution monitors for CAD workstations. The production run is for 100,000 units.

Design option A has a .90 probability of yielding 60 good monitors per 100 and a .10 probability of yielding 65 good monitors per 100. This design will cost $1,000,000.

Design option B has a .80 probability of yielding 64 good units per 100 and a .20 probability of yielding 59 good units per 100. This design will cost $1,350,000.

Good or bad, each monitor will cost $75. Each good monitor will sell for $150. Bad monitors are destroyed and have no salvage value. We ignore any disposal costs in this problem.

SOLUTION

We draw the decision tree to reflect the two decisions and the probabilities associated with each decision. We then determine the payoff associated with each branch. The resulting tree is shown in Figure 5.14.

For design A:
$$EMV(\text{design A}) = (.9)(\$500,000) + (.1)(\$1,250,000)$$
$$= \$575,000$$

For design B:
$$EMV(\text{design B}) = (.8)(\$750,000) + (.2)(\$0)$$
$$= \$600,000$$

The highest payoff is design option B, at $600,000.

Figure **5.14**

Decision Tree for Solved Problem 5.1

Problems   *Note:* **Px** means the problem may be solved with POM for Windows and/or Excel OM.

Problems 5.1–5.3 relate to Goods and Services Selection

•••**5.1**   Prepare a product-by-value analysis for the following products, and given the position in its life cycle, identify the issues likely to confront the operations manager and his or her possible actions. Product Alpha has annual sales of 1,000 units and a contribution of $2,500; it is in the introductory stage. Product Bravo has annual sales of 1,500 units and a contribution of $3,000; it is in the growth stage. Product Charlie has annual sales of 3,500 units and a contribution of $1,750; it is in the decline stage.

••**5.2**   Given the contribution made on each of the three products in the following table and their position in

the life cycle, identify a reasonable operations strategy for each:

PRODUCT	PRODUCT CONTRIBUTION (% OF SELLING PRICE)	COMPANY CONTRIBUTION (%: TOTAL ANNUAL CONTRIBUTION DIVIDED BY TOTAL ANNUAL SALES)	POSITION IN LIFE CYCLE
Smart watch	30	40	Introduction
Tablet	30	50	Growth
Hand calculator	50	10	Decline

Problem 5.3 is available in MyOMLab.

Problems 5.4–5.8 relate to Product Development

•• **5.4**   Construct a house of quality matrix for a wristwatch. Be sure to indicate specific customer wants that you think the general public desires. Then complete the matrix to show how an operations manager might identify specific attributes that can be measured and controlled to meet those customer desires.

•• **5.5**   Using the house of quality, pick a real product (a good or service) and analyze how an existing organization satisfies customer requirements.

•• **5.6**   Prepare a house of quality for a mousetrap.

•• **5.7**   Conduct an interview with a prospective purchaser of a new bicycle and translate the customer's *wants* into the specific *hows* of the firm.

•••• **5.8**   Using the house of quality sequence, as described in Figure 5.4 on page 169, determine how you might deploy resources to achieve the desired quality for a product or service whose production process you understand.

Problems 5.9–5.17 relate to Defining a Product

•• **5.9**   Prepare a bill of material for (a) a pair of eyeglasses and its case or (b) a fast-food sandwich (visit a local sandwich shop like Subway, McDonald's, Blimpie, Quizno's; perhaps a clerk or the manager will provide you with details on the quantity or weight of various ingredients—otherwise, estimate the quantities).

•• **5.10**   Draw an assembly chart for a pair of eyeglasses and its case.

•• **5.11**   Prepare a script for telephone callers at the university's annual "phone-a-thon" fund raiser.

•• **5.12**   Prepare an assembly chart for a table lamp.

Problems 5.13–5.17 are available in MyOMLab.

Problems 5.18–5.20 relate to Service Design

•• **5.18**   Draw a two-participant PCN diagram (similar to Figure 5.12) for one of the following processes:
a) The process of having your computer repaired.
b) The process of pizza preparation.
c) The process of procuring tickets for a concert.

•• **5.19**   Review strategic process positioning options for the regions in Figure 5.12, discussing the operational impact (in terms of the 10 strategic OM decisions) for:
a) Manufacturing the sandwiches.
b) Direct interaction.
c) Establishing a sandwich buffet.

••• **5.20**   Select a service business that involves interaction between customers and service providers, and create a PCN diagram similar to Figure 5.12. Pick a key step that could be performed either by the service provider or by the customers. Show process positioning options for the step. Describe how the options compare in terms of efficiency, economies of scale, and opportunity for customization.

Problems 5.21–5.28 relate to the Application of Decision Trees to Product Design

•• **5.21**   The product design group of Iyengar Electric Supplies, Inc., has determined that it needs to design a new series of switches. It must decide on one of three design strategies. The market forecast is for 200,000 units. The better and more sophisticated the design strategy and the more time spent on value engineering, the less will be the variable cost. The chief of engineering design, Dr. W. L. Berry, has decided that the following costs are a good estimate of the initial and variable costs connected with each of the three strategies:
a) *Low-tech:* A low-technology, low-cost process consisting of hiring several new junior engineers. This option has a fixed cost of $45,000 and variable-cost probabilities of .3 for $.55 each, .4 for $.50, and .3 for $.45.
b) *Subcontract:* A medium-cost approach using a good outside design staff. This approach would have a fixed cost of $65,000 and variable-cost probabilities of .7 of $.45, .2 of $.40, and .1 of $.35.
c) *High-tech:* A high-technology approach using the very best of the inside staff and the latest computer-aided design technology. This approach has a fixed cost of $75,000 and variable-cost probabilities of .9 of $.40 and .1 of $.35.

What is the best decision based on an expected monetary value (EMV) criterion? (*Note:* We want the lowest EMV, as we are dealing with costs in this problem.) **Px**

•• **5.22**   MacDonald Products, Inc., of Clarkson, New York, has the option of (a) proceeding immediately with production of a new top-of-the-line stereo TV that has just completed prototype testing or (b) having the value analysis team complete a study. If Ed Lusk, VP for operations, proceeds with the existing prototype (option a), the firm can expect sales to be 100,000 units at $550 each, with a probability of .6, and a .4 probability of 75,000 at $550. If, however, he uses the value analysis team (option b), the firm expects sales of 75,000 units at $750, with a probability of .7, and a .3 probability of 70,000 units at $750. Value analysis, at a cost of $100,000, is only used in option b. Which option has the highest expected monetary value (EMV)? **Px**

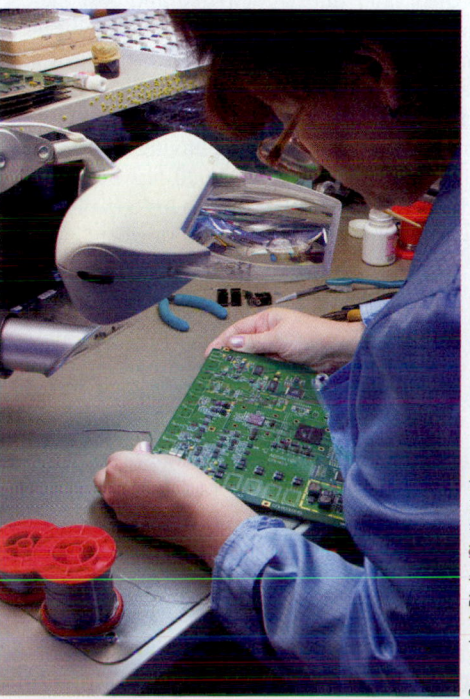

•• **5.23** Residents of Mill River have fond memories of ice skating at a local park. An artist has captured the experience in a drawing and is hoping to reproduce it and sell framed copies to current and former residents. He thinks that if the market is good he can sell 400 copies of the elegant version at $125 each. If the market is not good, he will sell only 300 at $90 each. He can make a deluxe version of the same drawing instead. He feels that if the market is good he can sell 500 copies of the deluxe version at $100 each. If the market is not good, he will sell only 400 copies at $70 each. In either case, production costs will be approximately $35,000. He can also choose to do nothing. If he believes there is a 50% probability of a good market, what should he do? Why? **Px**

•• **5.24** Ritz Products's materials manager, Tej Dhakar, must determine whether to make or buy a new semiconductor for the wrist TV that the firm is about to produce. One million units are expected to be produced over the life cycle. If the product is made, start-up and production costs of the *make* decision total $1 million, with a probability of .4 that the product will be satisfactory and a .6 probability that it will not. If the product is not satisfactory, the firm will have to reevaluate the decision. If the decision is reevaluated, the choice will be whether to spend another $1 million to redesign the semiconductor or to purchase. Likelihood of success the second time that the make decision is made is .9. If the second *make* decision also fails, the firm must purchase. Regardless of when the purchase takes place, Dhakar's best judgment of cost is that Ritz will pay $.50 for each purchased semiconductor plus $1 million in vendor development cost.
a) Assuming that Ritz must have the semiconductor (stopping or doing without is not a viable option), what is the best decision?
b) What criteria did you use to make this decision?
c) What is the worst that can happen to Ritz as a result of this particular decision? What is the best that can happen? **Px**

•• **5.25** Sox Engineering designs and constructs air conditioning and heating systems for hospitals and clinics. Currently, the company's staff is overloaded with design work. There is a major design project due in 8 weeks. The penalty for completing the design late is $14,000 per week, since any delay will cause the facility to open later than anticipated and cost the client significant revenue. If the company uses its inside engineers to complete the design, it will have to pay them overtime for all work. Sox has estimated that it will cost $12,000 per week (wages and overhead), including late weeks, to have company engineers complete the design. Sox is also considering having an outside engineering firm do the design. A bid of $92,000 has been received for the completed design. Yet another option for completing the design is to conduct a joint design by having a third engineering company complete all electromechanical components of the design at a cost of $56,000. Sox would then complete the rest of the design and control systems at an estimated cost of $30,000.

Sox has estimated the following probabilities of completing the project within various time frames when using each of the three options. Those estimates are shown in the following table:

| OPTION | PROBABILITY OF COMPLETING THE DESIGN | | | |
	ON TIME	1 WEEK LATE	2 WEEKS LATE	3 WEEKS LATE
Internal Engineers	.4	.5	.1	—
External Engineers	.2	.4	.3	.1
Joint Design	.1	.3	.4	.2

What is the best decision based on an expected monetary value criterion? (*Note:* You want the lowest EMV because we are dealing with costs in this problem.) **Px**

••• **5.26** Use the data in Solved Problem 5.1 to examine what happens to the decision if Sarah King can increase all of Design B yields from 59,000 to 64,000 by applying an expensive phosphorus to the screen at an added manufacturing cost of $250,000. Prepare the modified decision tree. What are the payoffs, and which branch has the greatest EMV?

•••• **5.27** McBurger, Inc., wants to redesign its kitchens to improve productivity and quality. Three designs, called designs K1, K2, and K3, are under consideration. No matter which design is used, daily production of sandwiches at a typical McBurger restaurant is for 500 sandwiches. A sandwich costs $1.30 to produce. Non-defective sandwiches sell, on the average, for $2.50 per sandwich. Defective sandwiches cannot be sold and are scrapped. The goal is to choose a design that maximizes the expected profit at a typical restaurant over a 300-day period. Designs K1, K2, and K3 cost $100,000, $130,000, and $180,000, respectively. Under design K1, there is a .80 chance that 90 out of each 100 sandwiches are non-defective and a .20 chance that 70 out of each 100 sandwiches are non-defective. Under design K2, there is a .85 chance that 90 out of each 100 sandwiches are non-defective and a .15 chance that 75 out of each 100 sandwiches are non-defective. Under design K3, there is a .90 chance that 95 out of each 100 sandwiches are non-defective and a .10 chance that 80 out of each 100 sandwiches are non-defective. What is the expected profit level of the design that achieves the maximum expected 300-day profit level?

Problem **5.28** is available in MyOMLab.

CASE STUDIES

De Mar's Product Strategy

De Mar, a plumbing, heating, and air-conditioning company located in Fresno, California, has a simple but powerful product strategy: *Solve the customer's problem no matter what, solve the problem when the customer needs it solved, and make sure the customer feels good when you leave.* De Mar offers guaranteed, same-day service for customers requiring it. The company provides 24-hour-a-day, 7-day-a-week service at no extra charge for customers whose air conditioning dies on a hot summer Sunday or whose toilet overflows at 2:30 A.M. As assistant service coordinator Janie Walter puts it: "We will be there to fix your A/C on the fourth of July, and it's not a penny extra. When our competitors won't get out of bed, we'll be there!"

De Mar guarantees the price of a job to the penny before the work begins. Whereas most competitors guarantee their work for 30 days, De Mar guarantees all parts and labor for one year. The company assesses no travel charge because "it's not fair to charge customers for driving out." Owner Larry Harmon says: "We are in an industry that doesn't have the best reputation. If we start making money our main goal, we are in trouble. So I stress customer satisfaction; money is the by-product."

De Mar uses selective hiring, ongoing training and education, performance measures, and compensation that incorporate customer satisfaction, strong teamwork, peer pressure, empowerment, and aggressive promotion to implement its strategy. Says credit manager Anne Semrick: "The person who wants a nine-to-five job needs to go somewhere else."

De Mar is a premium pricer. Yet customers respond because De Mar delivers value—that is, benefits for costs. In 8 years, annual sales increased from about $200,000 to more than $3.3 million.

Discussion Questions

1. What is De Mar's product? Identify the tangible parts of this product and its service components.

2. How should other areas of De Mar (marketing, finance, personnel) support its product strategy?

3. Even though De Mar's product is primarily a service product, how should each of the 10 strategic OM decisions in the text be managed to ensure that the product is successful?

Source: Reprinted with the permission of The Free Press, from *On Great Service: A Framework for Action* by Leonard L. Berry.

Product Design at Regal Marine

Video Case 📷📹

With hundreds of competitors in the boat business, Regal Marine must work to differentiate itself from the flock. As we saw in the *Global Company Profile* that opened this chapter, Regal continuously introduces innovative, high-quality new boats. Its differentiation strategy is reflected in a product line consisting of 22 models.

To maintain this stream of innovation, and with so many boats at varying stages of their life cycles, Regal constantly seeks design input from customers, dealers, and consultants. Design ideas rapidly find themselves in the styling studio, where they are placed onto CAD machines in order to speed the development process. Existing boat designs are always evolving as the company tries to stay stylish and competitive. Moreover, with life cycles as short as 3 years, a steady stream of new products is required. A few years ago, the new product was the three-passenger $11,000 Rush, a small but powerful boat capable of pulling a water-skier. This was followed with a 20-foot inboard–outboard performance boat with so many innovations that it won prize after prize in the industry. Another new boat is a redesigned 52-foot sports yacht that sleeps six in luxury staterooms. With all these models and innovations, Regal designers and production personnel are under pressure to respond quickly.

By getting key suppliers on board early and urging them to participate at the design stage, Regal improves both innovations and quality while speeding product development. Regal finds that

the sooner it brings suppliers on board, the faster it can bring new boats to the market. After a development stage that constitutes concept and styling, CAD designs yield product specifications. The first stage in actual production is the creation of the "plug," a foam-based carving used to make the molds for fiberglass hulls and decks. Specifications from the CAD system drive the carving process. Once the plug is carved, the permanent molds for each new hull and deck design are formed. Molds take about 4 to 8 weeks to make and are all handmade. Similar molds are made for many of the other features in Regal boats—from galley and

Barry Render

stateroom components to lavatories and steps. Finished molds can be joined and used to make thousands of boats.

Discussion Questions*

1. How does the concept of product life cycle apply to Regal Marine products?
2. What strategy does Regal use to stay competitive?

3. What kind of engineering savings is Regal achieving by using CAD technology rather than traditional drafting techniques?
4. What are the likely benefits of the CAD design technology?

*You may wish to view the video accompanying this case before addressing these questions.

Endnotes

1. *Contribution* is defined as the difference between direct cost and selling price. Direct costs are directly attributable to the product, namely labor and material that go into the product.

2. See Scott Sampson, "Visualizing Service Operations," *Journal of Service Research* (May 2012). More details about PCN analysis are available at **services.byu.edu.**

Chapter 5 *Rapid Review*

Main Heading	Review Material	MyOMLab
GOODS AND SERVICES SELECTION (pp. 162–165)	Although the term *products* may often refer to tangible goods, it also refers to offerings by service organizations. *The objective of the product decision is to develop and implement a product strategy that meets the demands of the marketplace with a competitive advantage.* ■ **Product Decision**—The selection, definition, and design of products. The four phases of the product life cycle are introduction, growth, maturity, and decline. ■ **Product-by-value analysis**—A list of products, in descending order of their individual dollar contribution to the firm, as well as the *total annual dollar* contribution of the product.	Concept Questions: 1.1–1.4 Problems: 5.1–5.3 **VIDEO 5.1** Product Strategy at Regal Marine
GENERATING NEW PRODUCTS (pp. 165–166)	Product selection, definition, and design take place on a continuing basis. Changes in product opportunities, the products themselves, product volume, and product mix may arise due to understanding the customer, economic change, sociological and demographic change, technological change, political/legal change, market practice, professional standards, suppliers, or distributors.	Concept Question: 2.1
PRODUCT DEVELOPMENT (pp. 166–170)	■ **Quality function deployment (QFD)**—A process for determining customer requirements (customer "wants") and translating them into attributes (the "hows") that each functional area can understand and act on. ■ **House of quality**—A part of the quality function deployment process that utilizes a planning matrix to relate customer wants to how the firm is going to meet those wants. ■ **Product development teams**—Teams charged with moving from market requirements for a product to achieving product success. ■ **Concurrent engineering**—Simultaneous performance of the various stages of product development. ■ **Manufacturability and value engineering**—Activities that help improve a product's design, production, maintainability, and use.	Concept Questions: 3.1–3.4
ISSUES FOR PRODUCT DESIGN (pp. 171–173)	■ **Robust design**—A design that can be produced to requirements even with unfavorable conditions in the production process. ■ **Modular design**—A design in which parts or components of a product are subdivided into modules that are easily interchanged or replaced. ■ **Computer-aided design (CAD)**—Interactive use of a computer to develop and document a product. ■ **Design for manufacture and assembly (DFMA)**—Software that allows designers to look at the effect of design on manufacturing of a product. ■ **Standard for the exchange of product data (STEP)**—A standard that provides a format allowing the electronic transmission of three-dimensional data. ■ **Computer-aided manufacturing (CAM)**—The use of information technology to control machinery. ■ **3-D printing**—An extension of CAD that builds prototypes and small lots. ■ **Virtual reality**—A visual form of communication in which images substitute for reality and typically allow the user to respond interactively. ■ **Value analysis**—A review of successful products that takes place during the production process. Sustainability is meeting the needs of the present without compromising the ability of future generations to meet their needs. Life cycle assessment (LCA) is part of ISO 14000; it assesses the environmental impact of a product from material and energy inputs to disposal and environmental releases. Both sustainability and LCA are discussed in depth in Supplement 5.	Concept Questions: 4.1–4.4
PRODUCT DEVELOPMENT CONTINUUM (pp. 173–175)	■ **Time-based competition**—Competition based on time; rapidly developing products and moving them to market. *Internal development strategies* include (1) new internally developed products, (2) enhancements to existing products, and (3) migrations of existing products. *External development strategies* include (1) purchase the technology or expertise by acquiring the developer, (2) establish joint ventures, and (3) develop alliances. ■ **Joint ventures**—Firms establishing joint ownership to pursue new products or markets. ■ **Alliances**—Cooperative agreements that allow firms to remain independent but pursue strategies consistent with their individual missions.	Concept Questions: 5.1–5.4

Chapter 5 *Rapid* **Review** continued

Main Heading	Review Material	MyOMLab
DEFINING A PRODUCT (pp. 175–177)	■ **Engineering drawing**—A drawing that shows the dimensions, tolerances, materials, and finishes of a component. ■ **Bill of material (BOM)**—A list of the components, their description, and the quantity of each required to make one unit of a product. ■ **Make-or-buy decision**—The choice between producing a component or a service and purchasing it from an outside source. ■ **Group technology**—A product and component coding system that specifies the size, shape, and type of processing; it allows similar products to be grouped.	Concept Questions: 6.1–6.4 Problems: 5.9, 5.10, 5.12–5.17
DOCUMENTS FOR PRODUCTION (pp. 178–179)	■ **Assembly drawing**—An exploded view of a product. ■ **Assembly chart**—A graphic means of identifying how components flow into subassemblies and final products. ■ **Route sheet**—A list of the operations necessary to produce a component with the material specified in the bill of material. ■ **Work order**—An instruction to make a given quantity of a particular item. ■ **Engineering change notice (ECN)**—A correction or modification of an engineering drawing or bill of material. ■ **Configuration management**—A system by which a product's planned and changing components are accurately identified. ■ **Product life cycle management (PLM)**—Software programs that tie together many phases of product design and manufacture.	Concept Questions: 7.1–7.4
SERVICE DESIGN (pp. 179–182)	■ **Process-chain-network (PCN) analysis**—A way to design processes to optimize interaction between firms and their customers. ■ **Process chain**—A sequence of steps that provide value to process participants. To enhance service efficiency, companies: (1) limit options, (2) delay customization, (3) modularize, (4) automate, and (5) design for the "moment of truth."	Concept Questions: 8.1–8.4
APPLICATION OF DECISION TREES TO PRODUCT DESIGN (pp. 182–184)	To form a decision tree, (1) include all possible alternatives (including "do nothing") and states of nature; (2) enter payoffs at the end of the appropriate branch; and (3) determine the expected value of each course of action by starting at the end of the tree and working toward the beginning, calculating values at each step and "pruning" inferior alternatives.	Concept Questions: 9.1–9.2 Problems: 5.21–5.25, 5.27–5.28 Virtual Office Hours for Solved Problem: 5.1 **ACTIVE** MODEL **5.1**
TRANSITION TO PRODUCTION (p. 184)	One of the arts of management is knowing when to move a product from development to production; this move is known as *transition to production*.	Concept Questions: 10.1–10.2

Self **Test**

■ **Before taking the self-test,** refer to the learning objectives listed at the beginning of the chapter and the key terms listed at the end of the chapter.

LO 5.1 A product's life cycle is divided into four stages, including:
 a) introduction.
 b) growth.
 c) maturity.
 d) all of the above.

LO 5.2 Product development systems include:
 a) bills of material.
 b) routing charts.
 c) functional specifications.
 d) product-by-values analysis.
 e) configuration management.

LO 5.3 A house of quality is:
 a) a matrix relating customer "wants" to the firm's "hows."
 b) a schematic showing how a product is put together.
 c) a list of the operations necessary to produce a component.
 d) an instruction to make a given quantity of a particular item.
 e) a set of detailed instructions about how to perform a task.

LO 5.4 Time-based competition focuses on:
 a) moving new products to market more quickly.
 b) reducing the life cycle of a product.
 c) linking QFD to PLM.
 d) design database availability.
 e) value engineering.

LO 5.5 Products are defined by:
 a) value analysis.
 b) value engineering.
 c) routing sheets.
 d) assembly charts.
 e) engineering drawings.

LO 5.6 A route sheet:
 a) lists the operations necessary to produce a component.
 b) is an instruction to make a given quantity of a particular item.
 c) is a schematic showing how a product is assembled.
 d) is a document showing the flow of product components.
 e) all of the above.

LO 5.7 The three process regions in a process–chain–network diagram are:
 a) manufacture, supplier, customer
 b) direct and surrogate, customer, provider
 c) independent, dependent, customer interaction
 d) direct interaction, surrogate interaction, independent processing

LO 5.8 Decision trees use:
 a) probabilities.
 b) payoffs.
 c) logic.
 d) options.
 e) all of the above.

Answers: LO 5.1. d; LO 5.2. c; LO 5.3. a; LO 5.4. a; LO 5.5. e; LO 5.6. a; LO 5.7. d; LO 5.8. e.

Sustainability in the Supply Chain

SUPPLEMENT OUTLINE

◆ Corporate Social Responsibility *194*
◆ Sustainability *195*

◆ Design and Production for Sustainability *198*
◆ Regulations and Industry Standards *203*

Alaska Airlines

Alaska Airlines

LEARNING OBJECTIVES

LO S5.1   **Describe** corporate social responsibility 194

LO S5.2   **Describe** sustainability 195

LO S5.3   **Explain** the 3Rs for sustainability 198

LO S5.4   **Calculate** design for disassembly 199

LO S5.5   **Explain** the impact of sustainable regulations on operations 203

Airlines from around the world, including Air China, Virgin Atlantic Airways, KLM, Alaska, Air New Zealand, and Japan Airlines, are experimenting with alternative fuels to power their jets in an effort to reduce greenhouse gas emissions and to reduce their dependence on traditional petroleum-based jet fuel. Alternative biofuels are being developed from recycled cooking oil, sewage sludge, municipal waste, coconuts, sugar cane, and genetically modified algae that feed on plant waste.

Lex Van Lieshout/EPA/Newscom

Corporate Social Responsibility[1]

LO S5.1 *Describe* corporate social responsibility

Managers must consider how the products and services they provide affect both people and the environment. Certainly, firms must provide products and services that are innovative and attractive to buyers. But today's technologies allow consumers, communities, public interest groups, and regulators to be well informed about all aspects of an organization's performance. As a result, stakeholders can have strong views about firms that fail to respect the environment or that engage in unethical conduct. Firms need to consider all the implications of a product—from design to disposal.

Many companies now realize that "doing what's right" and doing it properly can be beneficial to all stakeholders. Companies that practice **corporate social responsibility (CSR)** introduce policies that consider environmental, societal, and financial impacts in their decision making. As managers consider approaches to CSR, they find it helpful to consider the concept of creating **shared value**. *Shared value* suggests finding policies and practices that enhance the organization's competitiveness while simultaneously advancing the economic and social conditions in the communities in which it operates. For instance, note how automakers Tesla, Toyota, and Nissan find shared value in low-emission vehicles . . . vehicles that enhance their competiveness in a global market while meeting society's interest in low-emission vehicles. Similarly, Dow Chemical finds social benefits and profit in Nexera canola and sunflower seeds. These seeds yield twice as much cooking oil as soybeans, enhancing profitability to the grower. They also have a longer shelf life, which reduces operating costs throughout the supply chain. As an added bonus, the oils have lower levels of saturated fat than traditional products and contain no trans fats. A win–win for Dow and society.

Operations functions—from supply chain management to product design to production to packaging and logistics—provide an opportunity for finding shared value and meeting CSR goals.[2]

Corporate social responsibility (CSR)

Managerial decision making that considers environmental, societal, and financial impacts.

Shared value

Developing policies and practices that enhance the competitiveness of an organization while advancing the economic and social conditions in the communities in which it operates.

194

Sustainability

Sustainability is often associated with corporate social responsibility. The term sustainability refers to meeting the needs of the present without compromising the ability of future generations to meet their needs. Many people who hear of sustainability for the first time think of green products or "going green"—recycling, global warming, and saving rainforests. This is certainly part of it. However, it is more than this. True sustainability involves thinking not only about environmental resources but also about employees, customers, community, and the company's reputation. Three concepts may be helpful as managers consider sustainability decisions: a *systems* view, the *commons*, and the *triple bottom line*.

Systems View

Managers may find that their decisions regarding sustainability improve when they take a *systems* view. This means looking at a product's life from design to disposal, including all the resources required. Recognizing that both raw materials and human resources are sub-systems of any production process may provide a helpful perspective. Similarly, the product or service itself is a small part of much larger social, economic, and environmental systems. Indeed, managers need to understand the inputs and interfaces between the interacting systems and identify how changes in one system affect others. For example, hiring or laying off employees can be expected to have morale implications for internal systems (within an organization), as well as socioeconomic implications for external systems. Similarly, dumping chemicals down the drain has implications on systems beyond the firm. Once managers understand that the systems immediately under their control have interactions with systems below them and above them, more informed judgments regarding sustainability can be made.

LO S5.2 *Describe* sustainability

VIDEO S5.1
Building Sustainability at the Orlando Magic's Amway Center

Commons

Many inputs to a production system have market prices, but others do not. Those that do not are those held by the public, or in the *common*. Resources held in the *common* are often misallocated. Examples include depletion of fish in international waters and polluted air and waterways. The attitude seems to be that just a little more fishing or a little more pollution will not matter, or the adverse results may be perceived as someone else's problem. Society is still groping for solutions for use of those resources in the *common*. The answer is slowly being found in a number of ways: (1) moving some of the *common* to private property (e.g., selling radio frequency spectrum), (2) allocation of rights (e.g., establishing fishing boundaries), and (3) allocation of yield (e.g., only a given quantity of fish can be harvested). As managers understand the issues of the *commons*, they have further insight about sustainability and the obligation of caring for the *commons*.

Triple Bottom Line

Firms that do not consider the impact of their decisions on all their stakeholders see reduced sales and profits. Profit maximization is not the only measure of success. A one-dimensional bottom line, profit, will not suffice; the larger socioeconomic systems beyond the firm demand more. One way to think of sustainability is to consider the systems necessary to support the triple bottom line of the three *P*s: *people, planet*, and *profit* (see Figure S5.1), which we will now discuss.

⚠ STUDENT TIP

Profit is now just one of the three *P*s: people, planet, and profit.

People   Companies are becoming more aware of how their decisions affect people—not only their employees and customers but also those who live in the communities in which they operate. Most employers want to pay fair wages, offer educational opportunities, and provide a safe and healthy workplace. So do their suppliers. But globalization and the reliance on outsourcing to suppliers around the world complicate the task. This means companies must create policies that guide supplier selection and performance. Sustainability suggests that supplier selection and performance criteria evaluate safety in the work environment, whether living wages are paid, if child labor is used, and whether work hours are excessive. Apple, GE, Procter & Gamble, and Walmart are examples of companies that conduct supplier audits to uncover any harmful or exploitative business practices that are counter to their sustainability goals and objectives.

Figure **S5.1**

Improving the Triple Bottom Line with Sustainability

Recognizing that customers increasingly want to know that the materials in the products they buy are safe and produced in a responsible way, Walmart initiated the development of the worldwide sustainable product index for evaluating the sustainability of products. The goals of that initiative are to create a more transparent supply chain, accelerate the adoption of best practices, and drive product innovation.

Walmart found a correlation between supply-chain transparency, positive labor practices, community involvement, *and* quality, efficiency, and cost. Walmart is committed to working with its suppliers to sell quality products that are safe, that create value for customers, and that are produced in a sustainable way. The firm is accomplishing this in four ways:

1. Improving livelihoods through the creation of productive, healthy, and safe workplaces and promoting quality of life
2. Building strong communities through access to affordable, high-quality services such as education and job training that support workers and their families
3. Preventing exposure to substances that are considered harmful or toxic to human health
4. Promoting health and wellness by increasing access to nutritious products, encouraging healthy lifestyles, and promoting access to health care

Walmart's CEO has said that companies that are unfair to their people are also likely to skimp on quality and that he will not continue to do business with those suppliers. Accordingly, operations managers must consider the working conditions in which they place their employees. This includes training and safety orientations, before-shift exercises, earplugs, safety goggles, and rest breaks to reduce the possibility of worker fatigue and injury. Operations managers must also make decisions regarding the disposal of material and chemical waste, including hazardous materials, so they don't harm employees or the community.

Planet When discussing the subject of sustainability, our planet's environment is the first thing that comes to mind, so it understandably gets the most attention from managers. Operations managers look for ways to reduce the environmental impact of their operations, whether from raw material selection, process innovation, alternative product delivery methods, or disposal of products at their end-of-life. The overarching objective for operations managers is to conserve scarce resources, thereby reducing the negative impact on the environment. Here are a few examples of how organizations creatively make their operations more environmentally friendly:

◆ S.C. Johnson, the company that makes Windex, Saran Wrap, Pledge, Ziploc bags, and Raid, developed *Greenlist*, a classification system that evaluates the impact of raw materials on human and environmental health. By using *Greenlist*, S.C. Johnson has eliminated millions of pounds of pollutants from its products.

◆ Thirty-one public school districts across the state of Kentucky operate hybrid electric school buses. They estimate fuel savings as high as 40%, with fuel mileage of 7.5 mpg increasing to 12 miles per gallon, relative to standard diesel buses.

◆ Levi has started a campaign to save water in the creation of jeans, as seen in the *OM in Action* box "Blue Jeans and Sustainability."

To gauge their environmental impact on the planet, many companies are measuring their carbon footprint. Carbon footprint is a measure of the total greenhouse gas (GHG) emissions caused directly and indirectly by an organization, a product, an event, or a person. A substantial portion of greenhouse gases are released naturally by farming, cattle, and decaying forests and, to a lesser degree, by manufacturing and services. The most common greenhouse gas produced by human activities is carbon dioxide, primarily from burning fossil fuels for electricity generation, heating, and transport. Operations managers are being asked to do their part to reduce GHG emissions.

Industry leaders such as Frito-Lay have been able to break down the carbon emissions from various stages in the production process. For instance, in potato chip production, a 34.5-gram (1.2-ounce) bag of chips is responsible for about twice its weight in emissions—75 grams per bag (see Figure S5.2).

Carbon footprint

A measure of total greenhouse gas emissions caused directly or indirectly by an organization, a product, an event, or a person.

VIDEO S5.2
Green Manufacturing and Sustainability at Frito-Lay

Profit   Social and environmental sustainability do not exist without economic sustainability. Economic sustainability refers to how companies remain in business. Staying in business requires making investments, and investments require making profits. Though profits may be relatively easy to determine, other measures can also be used to gauge economic sustainability. The alternative measures that point to a successful business include risk profile, intellectual property, employee morale, and company valuation. To support economic sustainability, firms may supplement standard financial accounting and reporting with some version of *social accounting*. Social accounting can include brand equity, management talent, human capital development and benefits, research and development, productivity, philanthropy, and taxes paid.

Economic sustainability

Appropriately allocating scarce resources to make a profit.

OM in Action   Blue Jeans and Sustainability

The recent drought in California is hurting more than just farmers. It is also having a significant impact on the fashion industry and spurring changes in how jeans are made and how they should be laundered. Southern California is estimated to be the world's largest supplier of so-called premium denim, the $100 to $200-plus-a-pair of designer jeans. Water is a key component in the various steps of the processing and repeated washing with stones, or bleaching and dyeing that create that "distressed" vintage look. Southern California produces 75% of the high-end denim in the U.S. that is sold worldwide. The area employs about 200,000 people, making it the largest U.S. fashion manufacturing hub.

Now that water conservation is a global priority, major denim brands are working to cut water use. Levi, with sales of $5 billion, is using ozone machines to replace the bleach traditionally used to lighten denim. It is also reducing the number of times it washes jeans. The company has saved more than a billion liters of water since 2011 with its Levi's Water Less campaign. By 2020, the company plans to have 80% of Levi's brand products made using the Water Less process, up from about 25% currently.

Traditionally, about 34 liters of water are used in the cutting, sewing, and finishing process to make a pair of Levi's signature 501 jeans. Nearly 3,800 liters of water are used throughout the lifetime of a pair of Levi's 501. A study found cotton cultivation represents 68% of that and consumer washing another 23%. So Levi is promoting the idea that jeans only need washing

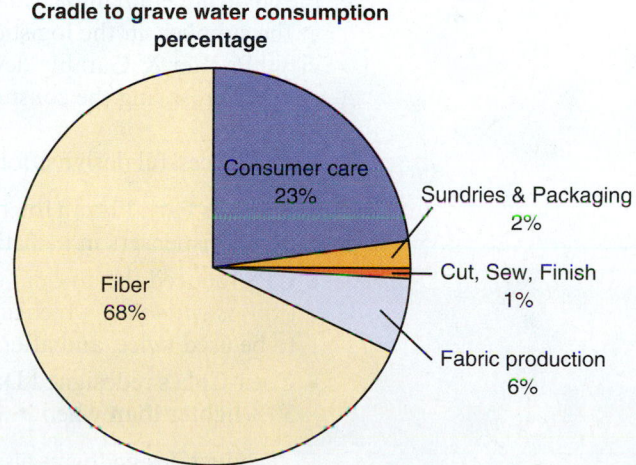

Cradle to grave water consumption percentage

- Consumer care 23%
- Sundries & Packaging 2%
- Cut, Sew, Finish 1%
- Fabric production 6%
- Fiber 68%

after 10 *wears*. (The average American consumer washes after 2 *wears*.) Levi's CEO recently urged people to stop washing their jeans, saying he hadn't washed his one-year-old jeans at the time. "You can air dry and spot clean instead," he said.

Sources: The Wall Street Journal (April 10, 2015) and *New York Times* (March 31, 2015).

Figure **S5.2**

**Carbon Footprint of a
34.5-gram Bag of Frito-Lay
Chips**

	Total carbon footprint	75 g
	Farming	44%
	Manufacture	30%
	Packaging	15%
	Shipping	9%
	Disposal	2%

Design and Production for Sustainability

The operations manager's greatest opportunity to make substantial contributions to the company's environmental objectives occurs during product life cycle assessment. **Life cycle assessment** evaluates the environmental impact of a product, from raw material and energy inputs all the way to the disposal of the product at its end-of-life. The goal is to make decisions that help reduce the environmental impact of a product throughout its entire life. Focusing on the 3*Rs*—*reduce, reuse,* and *recycle*— can help accomplish this goal. By incorporating the 3*Rs*, product design teams, process managers, and supply-chain personnel can make great strides toward reducing the environmental impact of products—to the benefit of all stakeholders.

Life cycle assessment

Analysis of environmental impacts of products from the design stage through end-of-life.

Product Design

LO S5.3 *Explain* the 3*R*s for sustainability

Product design is the most critical phase in product life cycle assessment. The decisions that are made during this phase greatly affect materials, quality, cost, processes, related packaging and logistics, and ultimately how the product will be processed when discarded. During design, one of the goals is to incorporate a systems view in the product or service design that lowers the environmental impact. This is the first *R*. Such an approach reduces waste and energy costs at the supplier, in the logistics system, and for the end user. For instance, by taking a systems view, Procter & Gamble developed *Tide Coldwater*, a detergent that gets clothes clean with cold water, saving the consumer about three-fourths of the energy used in a typical wash.

Other successful design efforts include:

- Boston's Park Plaza Hotel eliminated bars of soap and bottles of shampoo by installing pump dispensers in its bathrooms, saving the need for 1 million plastic containers a year.
- UPS reduced the amount of materials it needs for its envelopes by developing its *reusable express envelopes,* which are made from 100% recycled fiber. These envelopes are designed to be used twice, and after the second use, the envelope can be recycled.
- Coca-Cola's redesigned Dasani bottle reduced the amount of plastic needed and is now 30% lighter than when it was introduced.

Product design teams also look for *alternative* materials from which to make their products. Innovating with alternative materials can be expensive, but it may make autos, trucks, and aircraft more environmentally friendly while improving payload and fuel efficiency. Aircraft and auto makers, for example, constantly seek lighter materials to use in their products. Lighter materials translate into better fuel economy, fewer carbon emissions, and reduced operating cost. For instance:

- Mercedes is building some car exteriors from a banana fiber that is both biodegradable and lightweight.
- Some Fords have seat upholstery made from recycled plastic soda bottles and old clothing.

An excellent place for operations managers to begin the sustainability challenge is with good product design. Here Tom Malone, CEO, of MicroGreen Polymers, discusses the company's new ultra light cup with production personnel (left). The cup can be recycled over and over and never go to a landfill. Another new design is the "winglet" (right). These wing tip extensions increase climb speed, reduce noise by 6.5%, cut CO_2 emissions by 5%, and save 6% in fuel costs. Alaska Air has retrofitted its entire 737 fleet with winglets, saving $20 million annually.

◆ Boeing is using carbon fiber, epoxy composites, and titanium graphite laminate to reduce weight in its new 787 Dreamliner.

   Product designers often must decide between two or more environmentally friendly design alternatives. Example S1 deals with a *design for disassembly* cost–benefit analysis. This process focuses on the second and third *R*s: reuse and recycle. The design team analyzes the amount of revenue that might be reclaimed against the cost of disposing of the product at its end-of-life.

◆ STUDENT TIP

A fourth *R*, *improved reputation*, follows the success of reduce, reuse, and recycle.

Example S1 | DESIGN FOR DISASSEMBLY

Sound Barrier, Inc., needs to decide which of two speaker designs is better environmentally.

APPROACH ▶   The design team collected the following information for two audio speaker designs, the *Harmonizer* and the *Rocker:*

1. Resale value of the components minus the cost of transportation to the disassembly facility
2. Revenue collected from recycling
3. Processing costs, which include disassembly, sorting, cleaning, and packaging
4. Disposal costs, including transportation, fees, taxes, and processing time

SOLUTION ▶   The design team developed the following revenue and cost information for the two speaker design alternatives:

LO S5.4 *Calculate* design for disassembly

Harmonizer

PART	RESALE REVENUE PER UNIT	RECYCLING REVENUE PER UNIT	PROCESSING COST PER UNIT	DISPOSAL COST PER UNIT
Printed circuit board	$5.93	$1.54	$3.46	$0.00
Laminate back	0.00	0.00	4.53	1.74
Coil	8.56	5.65	6.22	0.00
Processor	9.17	2.65	3.12	0.00
Frame	0.00	0.00	2.02	1.23
Aluminum case	11.83	2.10	2.98	0.00
Total	$35.49	$11.94	$22.33	$2.97

Rocker

PART	RESALE REVENUE PER UNIT	RECYCLING REVENUE PER UNIT	PROCESSING COST PER UNIT	DISPOSAL COST PER UNIT
Printed circuit board	$7.88	$3.54	$2.12	$0.00
Coil	6.67	4.56	3.32	0.00
Frame	0.00	0.00	4.87	1.97
Processor	8.45	4.65	3.43	0.00
Plastic case	0.00	0.00	4.65	3.98
Total	$23.00	$12.75	$18.39	$5.95

Using the Equation (S5-1), the design team can compare the two design alternatives:

Revenue retrieval =
Total resale revenue + Total recycling revenue − Total processing cost − Total disposal cost (S5-1)

Revenue retrieval for Harmonizer = $35.49 + $11.94 − $22.33 − $2.97 = $22.13

Revenue retrieval for Rocker = $23.00 + $12.75 − $18.39 − $5.95 = $11.41

INSIGHT ▶ After analyzing both environmental revenue and cost components of each speaker design, the design team finds that the Harmonizer is the better environmental design alternative as it achieves a higher revenue retrieval opportunity. Note that the team is assuming that both products have the same market acceptance, profitability, and environmental impact.

LEARNING EXERCISE ▶ What would happen if there was a change in the supply chain that caused the processing and disposal costs to triple for the laminate back part of the Harmonizer? [Answer: The revenue retrieval from the Harmonizer is $35.49 + $11.94 − $31.39 − $6.45 = $9.59. This is less than the Rocker's revenue retrieval of $11.41, so the Rocker becomes the better environmental design alternative, as it achieves a higher revenue retrieval opportunity.]

RELATED PROBLEMS ▶ S5.1, S5.2, S5.3, S5.9, S5.12, S5.13, S5.14

Production Process

Manufacturers look for ways to reduce the amount of resources in the production process. Opportunities to reduce environmental impact during production typically revolve around the themes of energy, water, and environmental contamination. Conservation of energy and improving energy efficiency come from the use of alternative energy and more energy-efficient machinery. For example:

◆ S.C. Johnson built its own power plant that runs on natural gas and methane piped in from a nearby landfill, cutting back its reliance on coal-fired power.

◆ PepsiCo developed *Resource Conservation (ReCon)*, a diagnostic tool for understanding and reducing in-plant water and energy usage. In its first 2 years, *ReCon* helped sites across the world identify 2.2 billion liters of water savings, with a corresponding cost savings of nearly $2.7 million.

STUDENT TIP ◆
Las Vegas, always facing a water shortage, pays residents $40,000 an acre to take out lawns and replace them with rocks and native plants.

◆ Frito-Lay decided to extract water from potatoes, which are 80% water. Each year, a single factory processes 350,000 tons of potatoes, and as those potatoes are processed, the company reuses the extracted water for that factory's daily production.

These and similar successes in the production process reduce both costs and environmental concerns. Less energy is consumed, and less material is going to landfills.

Logistics

As products move along in the supply chain, managers strive to achieve efficient route and delivery networks, just as they seek to drive down operating cost. Doing so reduces environmental impact. Management analytics (such as linear programming, queuing, and vehicle routing software) help firms worldwide optimize elaborate supply-chain and distribution networks. Networks of container ships, airplanes, trains, and trucks are being analyzed to

Three key success factors in the trucking industry are (1) getting shipments to customers promptly (rapid response), (2) keeping trucks busy (capacity utilization), and (3) buying inexpensive fuel (driving down costs). Many firms have now developed devices like the one shown on the right to track location of trucks and facilitate communication between drivers and dispatchers. Some systems use global positioning satellites (shown on the left), to speed shipment response, maximize utilization of the truck, and ensure purchase of fuel at the most economical location. Sensors are also being added inside trailers. These sensors communicate whether the trailer is empty or full and detect if the trailer is connected to a truck or riding on a railroad car.

reduce the number of miles traveled or the number of hours required to make deliveries. For example:

- UPS has found that making left turns increases the time it takes to make deliveries. This in turn increases fuel usage and carbon emissions. So UPS plans its delivery truck routes with the fewest possible left turns. Likewise, airplanes fly at different altitudes and routes to take advantage of favorable wind conditions in an effort to reduce fuel use and carbon emissions.
- Food distribution companies now have trucks with three temperature zones (frozen, cool, and nonrefrigerated) instead of using three different types of trucks.
- Whirlpool radically revised its packaging to reduce "dings and dents" of appliances during delivery, generating huge savings in transportation and warranty costs.

To further enhance logistic efficiency, operations managers also evaluate equipment alternatives, taking into account cost, payback period, and the firm's stated environmental objectives. Example S2 deals with decision making that takes into account life cycle ownership costs. A firm must decide whether to pay *more* up front for vehicles to further its sustainability goals or to pay *less* up front for vehicles that do not.

Example S2 | LIFE CYCLE OWNERSHIP AND CROSSOVER ANALYSIS

Blue Star is starting a new distribution service that delivers auto parts to the service departments of auto dealerships in the local area. Blue Star has found two light-duty trucks that would do the job well, so now it needs to pick one to perform this new service. The Ford TriVan costs $28,000 to buy and uses regular unleaded gasoline, with an average fuel efficiency of 24 miles per gallon. The TriVan has an operating cost of $.20 per mile. The Honda CityVan, a hybrid truck, costs $32,000 to buy and uses regular unleaded gasoline and battery power; it gets an average of 37 miles per gallon. The CityVan has an operating cost of $.22 per mile. The distance traveled annually is estimated to be 22,000 miles, with the life of either truck expected to be 8 years. The average gas price is $4.25 per gallon.

APPROACH ▶ Blue Star applies Equation (S5-2) to evaluate total life cycle cost for each vehicle:

$$\text{Total life cycle cost} = \text{Cost of vehicle} + \text{Life cycle cost of fuel} + \text{Life cycle operating cost} \quad \text{(S5-2)}$$

a) Based on life cycle cost, which model truck is the best choice?
b) How many miles does Blue Star need to put on a truck for the costs to be equal?
c) What is the crossover point in years?

SOLUTION ▶

a) Ford TriVan:

$$\text{Total life-cycle cost} = \$28{,}000 + \left[\frac{22{,}000\frac{miles}{year}}{24\frac{miles}{gallon}}\right](\$4.25/gallon)(8\ years) + \left(22{,}000\frac{miles}{year}\right)(\$.20/mile)(8\ years)$$

$$= \$28{,}000 + \$31{,}167 + \$35{,}200 = \$94{,}367$$

Honda CityVan:

$$\text{Total life-cycle cost} = \$32{,}000 + \left[\frac{22{,}000\frac{miles}{year}}{37\frac{miles}{gallon}}\right](\$4.25/gallon)(8\ years) + \left(22{,}000\frac{miles}{year}\right)(\$.22/mile)(8\ years)$$

$$= \$32{,}000 + \$20{,}216 + \$38{,}720 = \$90{,}936$$

b) Blue Star lets M be the crossover (break-even) point in miles, sets the two life cycle cost equations equal to each other, and solves for M:

$$\text{Total cost for Ford TriVan} = \text{Total cost for Honda CityVan}$$

$$\$28{,}000 + \left[\frac{4.25\frac{\$}{gallon}}{24\frac{miles}{gallon}} + .20\frac{\$}{mile}\right](M\ miles) = \$32{,}000 + \left[\frac{4.25\frac{\$}{gallon}}{37\frac{miles}{gallon}} + .22\frac{\$}{mile}\right](M\ miles)$$

or,

$$\$28{,}000 + \left(.3770\frac{\$}{mile}\right)(M) = \$32{,}000 + \left(.3349\frac{\$}{mile}\right)(M)$$

or,

$$\left(.0421\frac{\$}{mile}\right)(M) = \$4{,}000$$

$$M = \frac{\$4{,}000}{.0421\frac{\$}{mile}} = 95{,}012\ miles$$

c) The crossover point in years is:

$$\text{Crossover point} = \frac{95{,}012\ miles}{22{,}000\frac{miles}{year}} = 4.32\ years$$

INSIGHTS ▶

a) Honda CityVan is the best choice, even though the initial fixed cost and variable operating cost per mile are higher. The savings comes from the better fuel mileage (more miles per gallon) for the Honda CityVan.

b) The crossover (break-even) point is at 95,012 miles, which indicates that at this mileage point, the cost for either truck is the same.

c) It will take 4.32 years to recoup the cost of purchasing and operating either vehicle. It will cost Blue Star approximately $.03 per mile less to operate the Honda CityVan than the Ford TriVan over the 8-year expected life.

LEARNING EXERCISE ▶ If the cost of gasoline drops to $3.25, what will be the total life-cycle cost of each van, the break-even point in miles, and the crossover point in years? [Answer: The cost of the Ford TriVan is $87,033; the Honda CityVan costs $86,179; the break-even is 144,927 miles; and the crossover point is 6.59 years.]

RELATED PROBLEMS ▶ S5.4, S5.5, S5.6, S5.10, S5.11, S5.15, S5.16, S5.17, S5.18, S5.19

End-of-Life Phase

We noted earlier that during product design, managers need to consider what happens to a product or its materials after the product reaches its end-of-life stage. Products with less material, with recycled material, or with recyclable materials all contribute to sustainability efforts, reducing the need for the "burn or bury" decision and conserving scarce natural resources.

Innovative and sustainability-conscious companies are now designing **closed-loop supply chains**, also called *reverse logistics*. Firms can no longer sell a product and then forget about it. They need to design and implement end-of-life systems for the physical return of products that facilitate recycling or reuse.

Caterpillar, through its expertise in remanufacturing technology and processes, has devised *Cat Reman,* a remanufacturing initiative, in an effort to show its commitment to sustainability. Caterpillar remanufactures parts and components that provide same-as-new performance and reliability at a fraction of new cost, while reducing the impact on the environment. The remanufacturing program is based on an exchange system where customers return a used component in exchange for a remanufactured product. The result is lower operating costs for the customer, reduced material waste, and less need for raw material to make new products. In a 1-year period, Caterpillar took back 2.1 million end-of-life units and remanufactured over 130 million pounds of material from recycled iron.

The *OM in Action* box "From Assembly Lines to Green Disassembly Lines" describes one automaker's car design philosophy to facilitate the disassembly, recycling, and reuse of its autos that have reached their end-of-life.

> **Closed-loop supply chains**
> Supply chains that consider forward and reverse product flows over the entire life cycle.

Regulations and Industry Standards

Government, industry standards, and company policies are all important factors in operational decisions. Failure to recognize these constraints can be costly. Over the last 100 years, we have seen development of regulations, standards, and policies to guide managers in product design, manufacturing/assembly, and disassembly/disposal.

To guide decisions in *product design*, U.S. laws and regulations, such as those of the Food and Drug Administration, Consumer Product Safety Commission, and National Highway Safety Administration, provide guidance and often explicit regulations.

Manufacturing and assembly activities have their own set of regulatory agencies providing guidance and standards of operations. These include the Occupational Safety and Health

> **LO S5.5** *Explain* the impact of sustainable regulations on operations

---

OM in Action | From Assembly Lines to Green Disassembly Lines

A century has passed since assembly lines were developed to make automobiles—and now we're developing *disassembly* lines to take them apart. So many automobiles are disassembled that recycling is the 16th-largest industry in the U.S. The motivation for this comes from many sources, including mandated industry recycling standards and a growing consumer interest in purchasing cars based on how "green" they are.

New car designs have traditionally been unfriendly to recyclers, with little thought given to disassembly. Some components, such as air bags, are hard to handle and dangerous, and they take time to disassemble. However, manufacturers now design in such a way that materials can be easily reused in the next generation of cars. The 2015 Mercedes S-class is 95% recyclable. BMW has disassembly plants in Europe, Japan, New York, Los Angeles, and Orlando.

A giant 200,000-square-foot facility in Baltimore (called CARS) can disassemble up to 30,000 vehicles per year. At CARS's initial "greening station," special tools puncture tanks and drain fluids and remove the battery and gas tank. Then wheels, doors, hood, and trunk are removed; next come the interior items; plastic parts are removed and sorted for recycling; then glass and interior and trunk materials. Eventually the chassis is a bale and sold as a commodity to

minimills that use scrap steel. Reusable parts are bar-coded and entered into a database. The photo shows an operator controlling the car recycling plant.

Sources: Wall Street Journal (April 29, 2008) and *Time* (February 4, 2010).

Ton Koene/Alamy

STUDENT TIP ◆

A group of 100 apparel brands and retailers have created the Eco Index to display an eco-value on a tag, like the Energy Star rating does for appliances.

Administration (OSHA), Environmental Protection Agency (EPA), and many state and local agencies that regulate workers' rights and employment standards.

U.S. agencies that govern the *disassembly and disposal of hazardous products* include the EPA and the Department of Transportation. As product life spans shorten due to ever-changing trends and innovation, product designers are under added pressure to *design for disassembly*. This encourages designers to create products that can be disassembled and whose components can be recovered, minimizing impact on the environment.

Organizations are obliged by society and regulators to reduce harm to consumers, employees, and the environment. The result is a proliferation of community, state, federal, and even international laws that often complicate compliance. The lack of coordination of regulations and reporting requirements between jurisdictions adds not just complexity but cost.

From the following examples it is apparent that nearly all industries must abide by regulations in some form or another:

◆ Commercial homebuilders are required not just to manage water runoff but to have a pollution prevention plan for each site.

◆ Public drinking water systems must comply with the Federal Safe Drinking Water Act's arsenic standard, even for existing facilities.

◆ Hospitals are required to meet the terms of the Resource Conservation and Recovery Act, which governs the storage and handling of hazardous material.

The consequences of ignoring regulations can be disastrous and even criminal. The EPA investigates environmental crimes in which companies and individuals are held accountable. Prison time and expensive fines can be handed down. (British Petroleum paid billions of dollars in fines in the past few years for breaking U.S. environmental and safety laws.) Even if a crime has not been committed, the financial impacts and customer upheaval can be disastrous to companies that do not comply with regulations. Due to lack of supplier oversight, Mattel, Inc., the largest U.S. toymaker, has recalled over 10 million toys in recent years because of consumer health hazards such as lead paint.

International Environmental Policies and Standards

Organizations such as the U.N. Framework Convention on Climate Change (UNFCCC), International Organization for Standardization (ISO), and governments around the globe are guiding businesses to reduce environmental impacts from disposal of materials to reductions in greenhouse gas (GHG) emissions. Some governments are implementing laws that mandate the outright reduction of GHG emissions by forcing companies to pay taxes based on the amount of GHG emissions that are emitted. We now provide an overview of some of the international standards that apply to how businesses operate, manufacture, and distribute goods and services.

European Union Emissions Trading System   The European Union has developed and implemented the EU Emissions Trading System (EUETS) to combat climate change. This is the key tool for reducing industrial greenhouse gas emissions in the EU. The EUETS works on the "cap-and-trade" principle. This means there is a cap, or limit, on the total amount of certain greenhouse gases that can be emitted by factories, power plants, and airlines in EU airspace. Within this cap, companies receive emission allowances, which they can sell to, or buy from, one another as needed.

ISO 14000   The International Organization for Standardization (ISO) is widely known for its contributions in ISO 9000 quality assurance standards (discussed in Chapter 6). The **ISO 14000** family grew out of the ISO's commitment to support the 1992 U.N. objective of sustainable development. ISO 14000 is a series of environmental management standards that contain five core elements: (1) environmental management, (2) auditing, (3) performance evaluation, (4) labeling, and (5) life cycle assessment. Companies that demonstrate these elements may apply for certification. ISO 14000 has several advantages:

◆ Positive public image and reduced exposure to liability

◆ Good systematic approach to pollution prevention through minimization of ecological impact of products and activities

ISO 14000

A series of environmental management standards established by the International Organization for Standardization (ISO).

OM in Action | Subaru's Clean, Green Set of Wheels with ISO 14001

"Going green" had humble beginnings. First, it was newspapers, soda cans and bottles, and corrugated packaging—the things you typically throw into your own recycling bins. Similarly, at Subaru's Lafayette, Indiana, plant, the process of becoming the first completely waste-free auto plant in North America began with employees dropping these items in containers throughout the plant. Then came employee empowerment. "We had 268 suggestions for different things to improve our recycling efforts," said Denise Coogan, plant ISO 14001 environmental compliance leader.

Some ideas were easy to handle. "With plastic shrink wrap, we found some (recyclers) wouldn't take colored shrink wrap. So we went back to our vendors and asked for only clear shrink wrap," Coogan said. Some suggestions were a lot dirtier. "We went dumpster diving to see what we were throwing away and see what we could do with it."

The last load of waste generated by Subaru made its way to a landfill 7 years ago. Since then, everything that enters the plant eventually exits as a usable product. Coogan adds, "We didn't redefine 'zero.' Zero means zero. Nothing from our manufacturing process goes to the landfill."

Last year alone, the Subaru plant recycled 13,142 tons of steel, 1,448 tons of paper products, 194 tons of plastics, 10 tons of solvent-soaked rags,

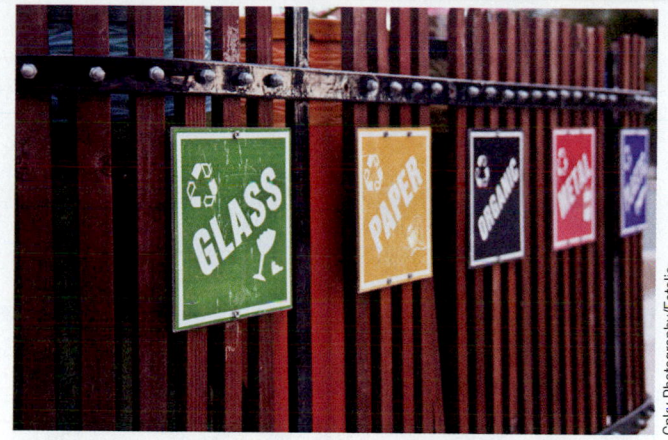

Cnky Photography/Fotolia

and 4 tons of light bulbs. Doing so conserved 29,200 trees, 670,000 gallons of oil, 34,700 gallons of gas, 10 million gallons of water, and 53,000 million watts of electricity. "Going green" isn't easy, but it can be done!

Sources: IndyStar (May 10, 2014) and *BusinessWeek* (June 6, 2011).

- ◆ Compliance with regulatory requirements and opportunities for competitive advantage
- ◆ Reduction in the need for multiple audits

ISO 14000 standards have been implemented by more than 200,000 organizations in 155 countries. Companies that have implemented ISO 14000 standards report environmental and economic benefits such as reduced raw material/resource use, reduced energy consumption, lower distribution costs, improved corporate image, improved process efficiency, reduced waste generation and disposal costs, and better utilization of recoverable resources.

ISO 14001, which addresses environmental management systems, gives guidance to companies to minimize harmful effects on the environment caused by their activities. The *OM in Action* box "Subaru's Clean, Green Set of Wheels with ISO 14001" illustrates the growing application of the ISO 14000 standards.

Summary

If a firm wants to be viable and competitive, it must have a strategy for corporate social responsibility and sustainability. Operations and supply-chain managers understand that they have a critical role in a firm's sustainability objectives. Their actions impact all the stakeholders. They must continually seek new and innovative ways to design, produce, deliver, and dispose of profitable, customer-satisfying products while adhering to many environmental regulations. Without the expertise and commitment of operations and supply-chain managers, firms are unable to meet their sustainability obligations.

Key Terms

Corporate social responsibility (CSR) (p. 194)
Shared value (p. 194)
Sustainability (p. 195)
Carbon footprint (p. 197)
Economic sustainability (p. 197)
Life cycle assessment (p. 198)
Closed-loop supply chains (p. 203)
ISO 14000 (p. 204)

Discussion Questions

1. Why must companies practice corporate social responsibility?
2. Find statements of sustainability for a well-known company online and analyze that firm's policy.
3. Explain sustainability.
4. Discuss the 3 *R*s.
5. Explain closed-loop supply chains.
6. How would you classify a company as green?
7. Why are sustainable business practices important?

Solved Problems   Virtual Office Hours help is available in MyOMLab.

SOLVED PROBLEM S5.1

The design team for Superior Electronics is creating a mobile audio player and must choose between two design alternatives. Which is the better environmental design alternative, based on achieving a higher revenue retrieval opportunity?

SOLUTION

Collecting the resale revenue per unit, recycling revenue per unit, processing cost per unit, and the disposal cost per unit, the design team computes the revenue retrieval for each design:

Design 1

PART	RESALE REVENUE PER UNIT	RECYCLING REVENUE PER UNIT	PROCESSING COST PER UNIT	DISPOSAL COST PER UNIT
Tuner	$4.93	$2.08	$2.98	$0.56
Speaker	0.00	0.00	4.12	1.23
Case	6.43	7.87	4.73	0.00
Total	$11.36	$9.95	$11.83	$1.79

Design 2

PART	RESALE REVENUE PER UNIT	RECYCLING REVENUE PER UNIT	PROCESSING COST PER UNIT	DISPOSAL COST PER UNIT
Tuner	$6.91	$4.92	$3.41	$2.13
Case	5.83	3.23	2.32	1.57
Amplifier	1.67	2.34	4.87	0.00
Speaker	0.00	0.00	3.43	1.97
Total	$14.41	$10.49	$14.03	$5.67

Using the following formula [Equation (S5-1)], compare the two design alternatives:

Revenue retrieval = Total resale revenue + Total recycling revenue − Total processing cost − Total disposal cost

Revenue retrieval Design 1 = $11.36 + $9.95
　　　　　　− $11.83 − $1.79 = $7.69

Revenue retrieval Design 2 = $14.41 + $10.49
　　　　　　− $14.03 − $5.67 = $5.20

Design 1 brings in the most revenue from its design when the product has reached its end-of-life.

SOLVED PROBLEM S5.2

The City of High Point is buying new school buses for the local school system. High Point has found two models of school buses that it is interested in. Eagle Mover costs $80,000 to buy and uses diesel fuel, with an average fuel efficiency of 10 miles per gallon. Eagle Mover has an operating cost of $.28 per mile. Yellow Transport, a hybrid bus, costs $105,000 to buy and uses diesel fuel and battery power, getting an average of 22 miles per gallon. Yellow Transport has an operating cost of $.32 per mile. The distance traveled annually is determined to be 25,000 miles, with the expected life of either bus to be 10 years. The average diesel price is $3.50 per gallon.

SOLUTION

a) Based on life cycle cost, which bus is the better choice?

Eagle Mover:

$$\$80,000 + \left[\frac{25,000\frac{miles}{year}}{10\frac{miles}{gallon}}\right](\$3.50/gallon)(10\ years) + \left(25,000\frac{miles}{year}\right)(\$.28/mile)(10\ years)$$

$$= \$80,000 + \$87,500 + \$70,000 = \$237,500$$

Yellow Transport:

$$\$105,000 + \left[\frac{25,000\frac{miles}{year}}{22\frac{miles}{gallon}}\right](\$3.50/gallon)(10\ years) + \left(25,000\frac{miles}{year}\right)(\$.32/mile)(10\ years)$$

$$= \$105,000 + \$39,773 + \$80,000 = \$224,773$$

Yellow Transport is the better choice.

b) How many miles does the school district need to put on a bus for costs to be equal?

Let M be the break-even point in miles, set the equations equal to each other, and solve for M:

Total cost for Eagle Mover = Total cost for Yellow Transport

$$\$80,000 + \left[\frac{3.50\frac{\$}{gallon}}{10\frac{miles}{gallon}} + .28\frac{\$}{mile}\right](M\ miles) = \$105,000 + \left[\frac{3.50\frac{\$}{gallon}}{22\frac{miles}{gallon}} + .32\frac{\$}{mile}\right](M\ miles)$$

$$\$80,000 + \left(.630\frac{\$}{mile}\right)(M) = \$105,000 + \left(.479\frac{\$}{mile}\right)(M)$$

$$\left(.151\frac{\$}{mile}\right)(M) = \$25,000$$

$$M = \frac{\$25,000}{.151\frac{\$}{mile}} = 165,563\ miles$$

c) What is the crossover point in years?

$$\text{Crossover point} = \frac{165,563\,miles}{25,000\dfrac{miles}{year}} = 6.62\,years$$

Problems

Problems S5.1–S5.19 relate to Design and Production for Sustainability

•• **S5.1**   The Brew House needs to decide which of two coffee maker designs is better environmentally. Using the following tables, determine which model is the better design alternative.

Brew Master

PART	RESALE REVENUE PER UNIT	RECYCLING REVENUE PER UNIT	PROCESSING COST PER UNIT	DISPOSAL COST PER UNIT
Metal frame	$1.65	$2.87	$1.25	$0.75
Timer	0.50	0.00	1.53	1.45
Plug/cord	4.25	5.65	6.22	0.00
Coffee pot	2.50	2.54	2.10	1.35

Brew Mini

PART	RESALE REVENUE PER UNIT	RECYCLING REVENUE PER UNIT	PROCESSING COST PER UNIT	DISPOSAL COST PER UNIT
Plastic frame	$1.32	$3.23	$0.95	$0.95
Plug/cord	3.95	4.35	5.22	0.00
Coffee pot	2.25	2.85	2.05	1.25

•• **S5.2**   Using the information in Problem S5.1, which design alternative is the better environmental choice if the Brew House decided to add a timer to the Brew Mini model? The timer revenue and costs are identical to those of the Brew Master.

•• **S5.3**   Using the information in Problem S5.1, which design alternative is the better environmental choice if the Brew House decided to remove the timer from the Brew Master model?

•• **S5.4**   What is the total vehicle life cycle cost of this hybrid car, given the information provided in the following table?

VEHICLE PURCHASE COST	$17,000
VEHICLE OPERATING COST PER MILE	$0.12
USEFUL LIFE OF VEHICLE	15 years
MILES PER YEAR	14,000
MILES PER GALLON	32
AVERAGE FUEL PRICE PER GALLON	$3.75

•• **S5.5**   What is the crossover point in miles between the hybrid vehicle in Problem S5.4 and this alternative vehicle from a competing auto manufacturer?

VEHICLE PURCHASE COST	$19,000
VEHICLE OPERATING COST PER MILE	$0.09
USEFUL LIFE OF VEHICLE	15 years
MILES PER YEAR	14,000
MILES PER GALLON	35
AVERAGE FUEL PRICE PER GALLON	$3.75

•• **S5.6**   Given the crossover mileage in Problem S5.5, what is the crossover point in years?

•• **S5.7**   In Problem S5.5, if gas prices rose to $4.00 per gallon, what would be the new crossover point in miles?

•• **S5.8**   Using the new crossover mileage in Problem S5.7, what is the crossover point in years?

•• **S5.9**   Mercedes is assessing which of two windshield suppliers provides a better environmental design for disassembly. Using the tables below, select between PG Glass and Glass Unlimited.

PG Glass

PART	RESALE REVENUE PER UNIT	RECYCLING REVENUE PER UNIT	PROCESSING COST PER UNIT	DISPOSAL COST PER UNIT
Glass	$12	$10	$6	$2
Steel frame	2	1	1	1
Rubber insulation	1	2	1	1

Glass Unlimited

PART	RESALE REVENUE PER UNIT	RECYCLING REVENUE PER UNIT	PROCESSING COST PER UNIT	DISPOSAL COST PER UNIT
Reflective glass	$15	$12	$7	$3
Aluminium frame	4	3	2	2
Rubber insulation	2	2	1	1

•• **S5.10**   Environmentally conscious Susan has been told that a new electric car will only generate 6 ounces of greenhouse gases (GHG) per mile, but that a standard internal combustion car is double that at 12 ounces per mile. However, the nature of electric cars is such that the new technology and electric batteries generate 30,000 lbs. of GHG to manufacture and another 10,000 lbs. to recycle. A standard car generates only 14,000 lbs. of GHG to manufacture, and recycling with established technology is only 1,000 lbs. Susan is interested in taking a systems approach that considers the life-cycle impact of her decision. How many miles must she drive the electric car for it to be the preferable decision in terms of reducing greenhouse gases?

••• **S5.11**   A Southern Georgia school district is considering ordering 53 propane-fueled school buses. "They're healthier, they're cleaner burning, and they're much quieter than the diesel option," said a school administrator. Propane-powered buses also reduce greenhouse gasses by 22% compared to gasoline-powered buses and 6% compared to diesel ones. But they come at a premium—$103,000 for a propane model, $15,000 more than the diesel equivalent.

The propane bus operating cost (above and beyond fuel cost) is 30 cents/mile, compared to 40 cents for the diesel. Diesel fuel costs about $2/gallon in Georgia, about $1 more than propane.

Bus mileage is 12 mpg for the propane model vs. 10 mpg for diesel. The life of a school bus in the district averages 9 years, and each bus travels an average of 30,000 miles per year because the district is so large and rural.

Which bus is the better choice based on a life-cycle analysis?

•• **S5.12** Green Forever, a manufacturer of lawn equipment, has preliminary drawings for two grass trimmer designs. Charla Fraley's job is to determine which is better environmentally. Specifically, she is to use the following data to help the company determine:

a) The revenue retrieval for the GF Deluxe
b) The revenue retrieval for the Premium Mate
c) Which model is the better design alternative based on revenue retrieval

GF Deluxe

PART	RESALE REVENUE PER UNIT	RECYCLING REVENUE PER UNIT	PROCESSING COST PER UNIT	DISPOSAL COST PER UNIT
Metal drive	$3.27	$4.78	$1.05	$0.85
Battery	0.00	3.68	6.18	3.05
Motor housing	3.93	2.95	2.05	1.25
Trimmer head	1.25	0.75	1.00	0.65

Premium Mate

PART	RESALE REVENUE PER UNIT	RECYCLING REVENUE PER UNIT	PROCESSING COST PER UNIT	DISPOSAL COST PER UNIT
Metal drive	$3.18	$3.95	$1.15	$0.65
Battery	0.00	2.58	4.98	2.90
Motor housing	4.05	3.45	2.45	1.90
Trimmer head	1.05	0.85	1.10	0.75

•• **S5.13** Green Forever (see Problem S5.12) has decided to add an automatic string feeder system with cost and revenue estimates as shown below to the GF Deluxe model.

a) What is the new revenue retrieval value for each model?
b) Which model is the better environmental design alternative?

PART	RESALE REVENUE PER UNIT	RECYCLING REVENUE PER UNIT	PROCESSING COST PER UNIT	DISPOSAL COST PER UNIT
String feeder system	$1.05	$1.25	$1.50	$1.40

•• **S5.14** Green Forever's challenge (see Problem S5.12) is to determine which design alternative is the better environmental choice if it uses a different battery for the Premium Mate. The alternate battery revenue and costs are as follows:

PART	RESALE REVENUE PER UNIT	RECYCLING REVENUE PER UNIT	PROCESSING COST PER UNIT	DISPOSAL COST PER UNIT
Battery	$0.00	$3.68	$4.15	$3.00

a) What is the revenue retrieval for the GF Deluxe?
b) What is the revenue retrieval for the Premium Mate?
c) Which is the better environmental design alternative?

•• **S5.15** Hartley Auto Supply delivers parts to area auto service centers and is replacing its fleet of delivery vehicles. What is the total vehicle life-cycle cost of this gasoline engine truck given the information provided in the following table?

VEHICLE PURCHASE COST	$25,000
VEHICLE OPERATING COST PER MILE	$0.13
USEFUL LIFE OF VEHICLE	10 years
MILES PER YEAR	18,000
MILES PER GALLON	25
AVERAGE FUEL PRICE PER GALLON	$2.55

•• **S5.16** Given the data in Problem S5.15 and an alternative hybrid vehicle with the specifications shown below:

a) What is the crossover point in miles?
b) Which vehicle is has the lowest cost until the crossover point is reached?

VEHICLE PURCHASE COST	$29,000
VEHICLE OPERATING COST PER MILE	$0.08
USEFUL LIFE OF VEHICLE	10 years
MILES PER YEAR	18,000
MILES PER GALLON	40
AVERAGE FUEL PRICE PER GALLON	$2.55

• **S5.17** Based the crossover point in miles found in Problem S5.16, what is this point in years?

•• **S5.18** Using the data from Problem S5.16, if gas prices rose to $3.00 per gallon, what would be the new crossover point in miles?

• **S5.19** Using the new crossover point in Problem S5.18, how many years does it take to reach that point?

CASE STUDIES

Building Sustainability at the Orlando Magic's Amway Center

Video Case

When the Amway Center opened in Orlando in 2011, it became the first LEED (Leadership in Energy and Environmental Design) gold–certified professional basketball arena in the country. It took 10 years for Orlando Magic's management to develop a plan for the new state-of-the-art sports and entertainment center. The community received not only an entertainment center but an environmentally sustainable building to showcase in its revitalized downtown location. "We wanted to make sure we brought the most sustainable measures to the construction, so in operation we can be a good partner to our community and our environment," states CEO Alex Martins. The new 875,000-square foot facility—almost triple the size of the Amway Arena it replaced—is now the benchmark for other sports facilities.

Here are a few of the elements in the Amway Center project that helped earn the LEED certification:

- The roof of the building is designed to minimize daytime heat gain by using reflective and insulated materials.
- Rainwater and air-conditioning condensation are captured and used for irrigation.
- There is 40% less water usage than in similar arenas (saving 800,000 gallons per year), mostly through use of high-efficiency restrooms, including low-flow, dual-flush toilets.
- There is 20% energy savings (about $750,000 per year) with the use of high-efficiency heating and cooling systems.
- The center used environmentally friendly building materials and recycled 83% of the wood, steel, and concrete construction waste that would have ended up in a landfill.
- There is preferred parking for hybrids and other energy-efficient cars.
- The center is maintained using green-friendly cleaning products.

LEED certification means five environmental measures and one design measure must be met when a facility is graded by the U.S. Green Building Council, which is a nationally accepted benchmark program. The categories are sustainability of site, water efficiency, energy, materials/resources, indoor environmental quality, and design innovation.

Other Amway Center design features include efficient receiving docks, food storage layouts, and venue change-over systems. Massive LED electronic signage controlled from a central control room also contributes to lower operating costs. From an operations management perspective, combining these savings with the

Fernando Medina

significant ongoing savings from reduced water and energy usage will yield a major reduction in annual operating expenses. "We think the LEED certification is not only great for the environment but good business overall," says Martins.

Discussion Questions*

1. Find a LEED-certified building in your area and compare its features to those of the Amway Center.
2. What does a facility need to do to earn the gold LEED rating? What other ratings exist?
3. Why did the Orlando Magic decide to "go green" in its new building?

*You may wish to view the video that accompanies this case before addressing these questions.

Green Manufacturing and Sustainability at Frito-Lay

Video Case 📷

Frito-Lay, the multi-billion-dollar snack food giant, requires vast amounts of water, electricity, natural gas, and fuel to produce its 41 well-known brands. In keeping with growing environmental concerns, Frito-Lay has initiated ambitious plans to produce environmentally friendly snacks. But even environmentally friendly snacks require resources. Recognizing the environmental impact, the firm is an aggressive "green manufacturer," with major initiatives in resource reduction and sustainability.

For instance, the company's energy management program includes a variety of elements designed to engage employees in reducing energy consumption. These elements include scorecards and customized action plans that empower employees and recognize their achievements.

At Frito-Lay's factory in Casa Grande, Arizona, more than 500,000 pounds of potatoes arrive every day to be washed, sliced, fried, seasoned, and portioned into bags of Lay's and Ruffles chips. The process consumes enormous amounts of energy and creates vast amounts of wastewater, starch, and potato peelings. Frito-Lay plans to take the plant off the power grid and run it almost entirely on renewable fuels and recycled water. The managers at the Casa Grande plant have also installed skylights in conference rooms, offices, and a finished goods warehouse to reduce the need for artificial light. More fuel-efficient ovens recapture heat from exhaust stacks. Vacuum hoses that pull

moisture from potato slices to recapture the water and to reduce the amount of heat needed to cook the potato chips are also being used.

Frito-Lay has also built over 50 acres of solar concentrators behind its Modesto, California, plant to generate solar power. The solar power is being converted into heat and used to cook Sun Chips. A biomass boiler, which will burn agricultural waste, is also planned to provide additional renewable fuel.

Frito-Lay is installing high-tech filters that recycle most of the water used to rinse and wash potatoes. It also recycles corn by-products to make Doritos and other snacks; starch is reclaimed and sold, primarily as animal feed, and leftover sludge is burned to create methane gas to run the plant boiler.

There are benefits besides the potential energy savings. Like many other large corporations, Frito-Lay is striving to establish its green credentials as consumers become more focused on environmental issues. There are marketing opportunities, too. The company, for example, advertises that its popular Sun Chips snacks are made using solar energy.

At Frito-Lay's Florida plant, only 3.5% of the waste goes to landfills, but that is still 1.5 million pounds annually. The goal is zero waste to landfills. The snack food maker earned its spot in the National Environmental Performance Task Program by maintaining a sustained environmental compliance record and making new commitments to reduce, reuse, and recycle at this facility.

Substantial resource reductions have been made in the production process, with an energy reduction of 21% across Frito-Lay's 34 U.S. plants. But the continuing battle for resource reduction continues. The company is also moving toward biodegradable packaging and seasoning bags and cans and bottles. While these multiyear initiatives are expensive, they have the backing at the highest levels of Frito-Lay as well as corporate executives at PepsiCo, the parent company.

Discussion Questions*

1. What are the sources of pressure on firms such as Frito-Lay to reduce their environmental footprint?
2. Identify the specific techniques that Frito-Lay is using to become a "green manufacturer."
3. Select another company and compare its green policies to those of Frito-Lay.

*You may wish to view the video that accompanies this case before answering these questions.

- **Additional Case Study:** Visit MyOMLab for this free case study:
  Environmental Sustainability at Walmart: Walmart's experiment with global sustainability.

Endnotes

1. The authors wish to thank Dr. Steve Leon, University of Central Florida, for his contributions to this supplement.
2. See related discussions in M. E. Porter and M. R. Kramer, "Creating Shared Value," *Harvard Business Review* (Jan.–Feb. 2011) and M. Pfitzer, V. Bockstette, and M. Stamp, "Innovating for Shared Values," *Harvard Business Review* (Sept. 2013).

Supplement 5 *Rapid* Review

Main Heading	Review Material	MyOMLab
CORPORATE SOCIAL RESPONSIBILITY (p. 194)	Managers must consider how the products and services they make affect people and the environment in which they operate. ■ **Corporate social responsibility (CSR)**—Managerial decision making that considers environmental, societal, and financial impacts. ■ **Shared value**—Developing policies and practices that enhance the competitiveness of an organization, while advancing the economic and social conditions in the communities in which it operates.	Concept Question: 1.1
SUSTAINABILITY (pp. 195–197)	■ **Sustainability**—Meeting the needs of the present without compromising the ability of future generations to meet their needs. Systems view—Looking at a product's life from design to disposal, including all of the resources required. The commons—Inputs or resources for a production system that are held by the public. Triple bottom line—Systems needed to support the three *Ps: people, planet*, and *profit*. To support their *people,* many companies evaluate safety in the work environment, the wages paid, work hours/week. Apple, GE, P&G, and Walmart conduct audits of their suppliers to make sure sustainability goals are met. To support the *planet,* operation managers look for ways to reduce the environmental impact of their operations. ■ **Carbon footprint**—A measure of the total GHG emissions caused directly and indirectly by an organization, product, event or person. To support their *profits,* company investments must be sustainable economically. Firms may supplement standard accounting with social accounting.	Concept Questions: 2.1–2.4 **VIDEO S5.1** Building Sustainability at the Orlando Magic's Amway Center **VIDEO S5.2** Green Manufacturing and Sustainability at Frito-Lay
DESIGN AND PRODUCTION FOR SUSTAINABILITY (pp. 198–203)	■ **Life cycle assessment**—Analysis of environmental impacts of products from the design stage through end-of-life. The 3*Rs: reduce, reuse,* and *recycle.* These must be incorporated by design teams, process managers, and supply-chain personnel. Product design is the most critical phase in the product life cycle assessment. Design for disassembly focuses on reuse and recycle. Revenue retrieval = 　　Total resale revenue + Total recycling revenue 　　　　　− Total processing cost − Total disposal cost　(S5-1) Manufacturers also look for ways to reduce the amount of scarce resources in the production process. As products move along the supply chain, logistics managers strive to achieve efficient route and delivery networks, which reduce environmental impact. Vehicles are also evaluated on a life cycle ownership cost basis. A firm must decide whether to pay more up front for sustainable vehicles or pay less up front for vehicles that may be less sustainable. Total life cycle cost = 　　Cost of vehicle + Life cycle cost of fuel + Life cycle operating cost　(S5-2) ■ **Closed-loop supply chains,** also called *reverse logistics*—Supply chains that consider the product or its materials after the product reaches its end-of-life stage. This includes forward and reverse product flows. Green disassembly lines help take cars apart so that parts can be recycled. Recycling is the 16th-largest industry in the U.S.	Concept Questions: 3.1–3.4 Problems: S5.1–S5.19 Virtual Office Hours for Solved Problems S5.1–S5.2
REGULATIONS AND INDUSTRY STANDARDS (pp. 203–205)	To guide *product design* decisions, U.S. laws and regulations often provide explicit regulations. *Manufacturing and assembly activities* are guided by OSHA, EPA, and many state and local agencies. There are also U.S. agencies that govern the *disassembly and disposal of hazardous products.* International environmental policies and standards come from the U.N., ISO, the EU, and governments around the globe. The EU has implemented the Emissions Trading System to help reduce greenhouse gas emissions. It works on a "cap-and-trade" principle. ■ **ISO 14000**—The International Organization of Standardization family of guidelines for sustainable development. ISO 14000 has been implemented by more than 200,000 organizations in 155 countries. ISO 14001 addresses environmental management systems.	Concept Questions: 4.1–4.4

Self Test

▪ **Before taking the self-test,** refer to the learning objectives listed at the beginning of the supplement and the key terms listed at the end of the supplement.

LO S5.1 Corporate social responsibility includes:
a) doing what's right.
b) having policies that consider environmental, societal, and financial impact.
c) considering a product from design to disposal.
d) all of the above.
e) a and b only.

LO S5.2 Sustainability deals:
a) solely with green products, recycling, global warming, and rain forests.
b) with keeping products that are not recyclable.
c) with meeting the needs of present and future generations.
d) with three views—systems, commons, and defects.
e) with not laying off older workers.

LO S5.3 The 3*R*s of sustainability are:
a) reputation, reuse, reduce.
b) reputation, recycle, reuse.
c) reputation, reverse logistics, renewal.
d) reuse, reduce, recycle.
e) recycle, review, reuse.

LO S5.4 Design for disassembly is:
a) cost–benefit analysis for old parts.
b) analysis of the amount of revenue that might be reclaimed versus the cost of disposing of a product.
c) a means of recycling plastic parts in autos.
d) the use of lightweight materials in products.

LO S5.5 U.S. and international agencies provide policies and regulations to guide managers in product design, manufacturing/assembly, and disassembly/disposal. They include:
a) U.N. Commission on Resettlement.
b) World Health Organization (WHO).
c) OSHA, FDA, EPA, and NHSA.
d) EPA, ISO, and British High Commission.
e) GHG Commission, UN, and ISO.

Answers: LO S5.1. d; LO S5.2. c; LO S5.3. d; LO S5.4. b; LO S5.5. c.

Managing Quality

CHAPTER OUTLINE

GLOBAL COMPANY PROFILE: *Arnold Palmer Hospital*

- Quality and Strategy *216*
- Defining Quality *217*
- Total Quality Management *219*
- Tools of TQM *226*
- The Role of Inspection *230*
- TQM in Services *233*

Alaska Air lines

Alaska Air lines

10 OM STRATEGY DECISIONS

- Design of Goods and Services
- *Managing Quality*
- Process Strategy
- Location Strategies
- Layout Strategies
- Human Resources
- Supply-Chain Management
- Inventory Management
- Scheduling
- Maintenance

Managing Quality Provides a Competitive Advantage at Arnold Palmer Hospital

Since 1989, Arnold Palmer Hospital, named after its famous golfing benefactor, has touched the lives of over 7 million children and women and their families. Its patients come not only from its Orlando location but from all 50 states and around the world. More than 12,000 babies are delivered every year at Arnold Palmer, and its huge neonatal intensive care unit boasts one of the highest survival rates in the U.S.

Every hospital professes quality health care, but at Arnold Palmer quality is the mantra—practiced in a fashion like the Ritz-Carlton practices it in the hotel industry. The hospital typically scores in the top 10% of national benchmark studies in terms of patient satisfaction. And its managers follow patient questionnaire results daily. If anything is amiss, corrective action takes place immediately.

Virtually every quality management technique we present in this chapter is employed at Arnold Palmer Hospital:

◆ *Continuous improvement:* The hospital constantly seeks new ways to lower infection rates, readmission rates, deaths, costs, and hospital stay times.

The lobby of Arnold Palmer Hospital, with its 20-foot-high Genie, is clearly intended as a warm and friendly place for children.

Courtesy Arnold Palmer Medical Center

The Storkboard is a visible chart of the status of each baby about to be delivered, so all nurses and doctors are kept up to date at a glance.

Courtesy Arnold Palmer Medical Center

This PYXIS inventory station gives nurses quick access to medicines and supplies needed in their departments. When the nurse removes an item for patient use, the item is automatically billed to that account, and usage is noted at the main supply area.

The hospital has redesigned its neonatal rooms. In the old system, there were 16 neonatal beds in an often noisy and large room. The new rooms are semiprivate, with a quiet simulated-night atmosphere. These rooms have proven to help babies develop and improve more quickly.

◆ *Employee empowerment:* When employees see a problem, they are trained to take care of it; staff are empowered to give gifts to patients displeased with some aspect of service.

◆ *Benchmarking:* The hospital belongs to a 2,000-member organization that monitors standards in many areas and provides monthly feedback to the hospital.

When Arnold Palmer Hospital began planning for a new 11-story hospital across the street from its existing building, it decided on a circular pod design, creating a patient-centered environment. Rooms use warm colors, have pull-down Murphy beds for family members, 14-foot ceilings, and natural lighting with oversized windows. The pod concept also means there is a nursing station within a few feet of each 10-bed pod, saving much wasted walking time by nurses to reach the patient. The Video Case Study in Chapter 9 examines this layout in detail.

◆ *Just-in-time:* Supplies are delivered to Arnold Palmer on a JIT basis. This keeps inventory costs low and keeps quality problems from hiding.

◆ *Tools such as Pareto charts and flowcharts:* These tools monitor processes and help the staff graphically spot problem areas and suggest ways they can be improved.

From their first day of orientation, employees from janitors to nurses learn that the patient comes first. Staff standing in hallways will never be heard discussing their personal lives or commenting on confidential issues of health care. This culture of quality at Arnold Palmer Hospital makes a hospital visit, often traumatic to children and their parents, a warmer and more comforting experience. ◀

LEARNING OBJECTIVES

LO 6.1 *Define* quality and TQM 217

LO 6.2 *Describe* the ISO international quality standards 218

LO 6.3 *Explain* Six Sigma 221

LO 6.4 *Explain* how benchmarking is used in TQM 223

LO 6.5 *Explain* quality robust products and Taguchi concepts 225

LO 6.6 *Use* the seven tools of TQM 226

VIDEO 6.1
The Culture of Quality at Arnold Palmer Hospital

STUDENT TIP ◖
High-quality products and services are the most profitable.

Quality and Strategy

As Arnold Palmer Hospital and many other organizations have found, quality is a wonderful tonic for improving operations. Managing quality helps build successful strategies of *differentiation*, *low cost*, and *response*. For instance, defining customer quality expectations has helped Bose Corp. successfully *differentiate* its stereo speakers as among the best in the world. Nucor has learned to produce quality steel at *low cost* by developing efficient processes that produce consistent quality. And Dell Computers rapidly *responds* to customer orders because quality systems, with little rework, have allowed it to achieve rapid throughput in its plants. Indeed, quality may be the key success factor for these firms, just as it is at Arnold Palmer Hospital.

As Figure 6.1 suggests, improvements in quality help firms increase sales and reduce costs, both of which can increase profitability. Increases in sales often occur as firms speed response, increase or lower selling prices, and improve their reputation for quality products. Similarly, improved quality allows costs to drop as firms increase productivity and lower rework, scrap, and warranty costs. One study found that companies with the highest quality were five times as productive (as measured by units produced per labor-hour) as companies with the poorest quality. Indeed, when the implications of an organization's long-term costs and the potential for increased sales are considered, total costs may well be at a minimum when 100% of the goods or services are perfect and defect free.

Quality, or the lack of quality, affects the entire organization from supplier to customer and from product design to maintenance. Perhaps more important, *building* an organization that can achieve quality is a demanding task. Figure 6.2 lays out the flow of activities for an organization to use to achieve total quality management (TQM). A successful quality strategy begins with an organizational culture that fosters quality, followed by an understanding of the principles of quality, and then engaging employees in the necessary activities to implement quality. When these things are done well, the organization typically satisfies its customers and obtains a competitive advantage. The ultimate goal is to win customers. Because quality causes so many other good things to happen, it is a great place to start.

Figure **6.1**

Ways Quality Improves Profitability

Two Ways Quality Improves Profitability

Improved Quality

Sales Gains via
- Improved response
- Flexible pricing
- Improved reputation

Reduced Costs via
- Increased productivity
- Lower rework and scrap costs
- Lower warranty costs

Increased Profits

Organizational practices
Leadership, Mission statement, Effective operating procedures,
Staff support, Training
Yields: What is important and what is to be accomplished.

Quality principles
Customer focus, Continuous improvement, Benchmarking,
Just-in-time, Tools of TQM
Yields: How to do what is important and to be accomplished.

Employee fulfillment
Empowerment, Organizational commitment
*Yields: Employee attitudes that can accomplish
what is important.*

Customer satisfaction
Winning orders, Repeat customers
*Yields: An effective organization with
a competitive advantage.*

Figure **6.2**

The Flow of Activities Necessary to Achieve Total Quality Management

Defining Quality

The operations manager's objective is to build a total quality management system that identifies and satisfies customer needs. Total quality management takes care of the customer. Consequently, we accept the definition of quality as adopted by the American Society for Quality (ASQ; **www.asq.org**): "The totality of features and characteristics of a product or service that bears on its ability to satisfy stated or implied needs."

Others, however, believe that definitions of quality fall into several categories. Some definitions are *user based*. They propose that quality "lies in the eyes of the beholder." Marketing people like this approach and so do customers. To them, higher quality means better performance, nicer features, and other (sometimes costly) improvements. To production managers, quality is *manufacturing based*. They believe that quality means conforming to standards and "making it right the first time." Yet a third approach is *product based*, which views quality as a precise and measurable variable. In this view, for example, really good ice cream has high butterfat levels.

This text develops approaches and techniques to address all three categories of quality. The characteristics that connote quality must first be identified through research (a user-based approach to quality). These characteristics are then translated into specific product attributes (a product-based approach to quality). Then, the manufacturing process is organized to ensure that products are made precisely to specifications (a manufacturing-based approach to quality). A process that ignores any one of these steps will not result in a quality product.

Implications of Quality

In addition to being a critical element in operations, quality has other implications. Here are three other reasons why quality is important:

1. *Company reputation:* An organization can expect its reputation for quality—be it good or bad—to follow it. Quality will show up in perceptions about the firm's new products, employment practices, and supplier relations. Self-promotion is not a substitute for quality products.

Quality
The ability of a product or service to meet customer needs.

LO 6.1 *Define* quality and TQM

STUDENT TIP
To create a quality good or service, operations managers need to know what the customer expects.

2. *Product liability:* The courts increasingly hold organizations that design, produce, or distribute faulty products or services liable for damages or injuries resulting from their use. Legislation such as the Consumer Product Safety Act sets and enforces product standards by banning products that do not reach those standards. Impure foods that cause illness, nightgowns that burn, tires that fall apart, or auto fuel tanks that explode on impact can all lead to huge legal expenses, large settlements or losses, and terrible publicity.

3. *Global implications:* In this technological age, quality is an international, as well as OM, concern. For both a company and a country to compete effectively in the global economy, products must meet global quality, design, and price expectations. Inferior products harm a firm's profitability and a nation's balance of payments.

Malcolm Baldrige National Quality Award

The global implications of quality are so important that the U.S. has established the *Malcolm Baldrige National Quality Award* for quality achievement. The award is named for former Secretary of Commerce Malcolm Baldrige. Winners include such firms as Motorola, Milliken, Xerox, FedEx, Ritz-Carlton Hotels, AT&T, Cadillac, and Texas Instruments. (For details about the Baldrige Award and its 1,000-point scoring system, visit **www.nist.gov/baldrige/**.)

The Japanese have a similar award, the Deming Prize, named after an American, Dr. W. Edwards Deming.

ISO 9000 International Quality Standards

ISO 9000

A set of quality standards developed by the International Organization for Standardization (ISO).

The move toward global supply chains has placed so much emphasis on quality that the world has united around a single quality standard, ISO 9000. ISO 9000 is *the* quality standard with international recognition. Its focus is to enhance success through eight quality management principles: (1) top management leadership, (2) customer satisfaction, (3) continual improvement, (4) involvement of people, (5) process analysis, (6) use of data-driven decision making, (7) a systems approach to management, and (8) mutually beneficial supplier relationships.

LO 6.2 *Describe* the ISO international quality standards

The ISO standard encourages establishment of quality management procedures, detailed documentation, work instructions, and recordkeeping. Like the Baldrige Awards, the assessment includes self-appraisal and problem identification. Unlike the Baldrige, ISO certified organizations must be reaudited every three years.

The latest modification of the standard, ISO 9001: 2015, follows a structure that makes it more compatible with other management systems. This version gives greater emphasis to risk-based thinking, attempting to prevent undesirable outcomes.

STUDENT TIP

International quality standards grow in prominence every year. See **www.iso.ch**.

Over one million certifications have been awarded to firms in 206 countries, including about 30,000 in the U.S. To do business globally, it is critical for a firm to be certified and listed in the ISO directory.

Cost of Quality (COQ)

Cost of quality (COQ)

The cost of doing things wrong—that is, the price of nonconformance.

Four major categories of costs are associated with quality. Called the cost of quality (COQ), they are:

- *Prevention costs:* costs associated with reducing the potential for defective parts or services (e.g., training, quality improvement programs).
- *Appraisal costs:* costs related to evaluating products, processes, parts, and services (e.g., testing, labs, inspectors).
- *Internal failure costs:* costs that result from production of defective parts or services before delivery to customers (e.g., rework, scrap, downtime).
- *External failure costs:* costs that occur after delivery of defective parts or services (e.g., rework, returned goods, liabilities, lost goodwill, costs to society).

| TABLE 6.1 | Leaders in the Field of Quality Management |

LEADER	PHILOSOPHY/CONTRIBUTION
W. Edwards Deming	Deming insisted management accept responsibility for building good systems. The employee cannot produce products that on average exceed the quality of what the process is capable of producing. His 14 points for implementing quality improvement are presented in this chapter.
Joseph M. Juran	A pioneer in teaching the Japanese how to improve quality, Juran believed strongly in top-management commitment, support, and involvement in the quality effort. He was also a believer in teams that continually seek to raise quality standards. Juran varies from Deming somewhat in focusing on the customer and defining quality as fitness for use, not necessarily the written specifications.
Armand Feigenbaum	His 1961 book *Total Quality Control* laid out 40 steps to quality improvement processes. He viewed quality not as a set of tools but as a total field that integrated the processes of a company. His work in how people learn from each other's successes led to the field of cross-functional teamwork.
Philip B. Crosby	*Quality Is Free* was Crosby's attention-getting book published in 1979. Crosby believed that in the traditional trade-off between the cost of improving quality and the cost of poor quality, the cost of poor quality is understated. The cost of poor quality should include all of the things that are involved in not doing the job right the first time. Crosby coined the term *zero defects* and stated, "There is absolutely no reason for having errors or defects in any product or service."

Source: Based on *Quality Is Free* by Philip B. Crosby (New York, McGraw-Hill, 1979) p. 58.

The first three costs can be reasonably estimated, but external costs are very hard to quantify. When GE had to recall 3.1 million dishwashers (because of a defective switch alleged to have started seven fires), the cost of repairs exceeded the value of all the machines. This leads to the belief by many experts that the cost of poor quality is consistently underestimated.

Observers of quality management believe that, on balance, the cost of quality products is only a fraction of the benefits. They think the real losers are organizations that fail to work aggressively at quality. For instance, Philip Crosby stated that quality is free. "What costs money are the unquality things—all the actions that involve not doing it right the first time."[1]

Leaders in Quality   Besides Crosby there are several other giants in the field of quality management, including Deming, Feigenbaum, and Juran. Table 6.1 summarizes their philosophies and contributions.

Takumi is a Japanese character that symbolizes a broader dimension than quality, a deeper process than education, and a more perfect method than persistence.

Ethics and Quality Management

For operations managers, one of the most important jobs is to deliver healthy, safe, and quality products and services to customers. The development of poor-quality products, because of inadequate design and production processes, not only results in higher production costs but also leads to injuries, lawsuits, and increased government regulation.

If a firm believes that it has introduced a questionable product, ethical conduct must dictate the responsible action. This may be a worldwide recall, as conducted by both Johnson & Johnson (for Tylenol) and Perrier (for sparkling water), when each of these products was found to be contaminated. A manufacturer must accept responsibility for any poor-quality product released to the public.

There are many stakeholders involved in the production and marketing of poor-quality products, including stockholders, employees, customers, suppliers, distributors, and creditors. As a matter of ethics, management must ask if any of these stakeholders are being wronged. Every company needs to develop core values that become day-to-day guidelines for everyone from the CEO to production-line employees.

Total Quality Management

Total quality management (TQM) refers to a quality emphasis that encompasses the entire organization, from supplier to customer. TQM stresses a commitment by management to have a continuing companywide drive toward excellence in all aspects of products and services that are

Total quality management (TQM)

Management of an entire organization so that it excels in all aspects of products and services that are important to the customer.

TABLE 6.2	**Deming's 14 Points for Implementing Quality Improvement**

1. Create consistency of purpose.
2. Lead to promote change.
3. Build quality into the product; stop depending on inspections to catch problems.
4. Build long-term relationships based on performance instead of awarding business on the basis of price.
5. Continuously improve product, quality, and service.
6. Start training.
7. Emphasize leadership.
8. Drive out fear.
9. Break down barriers between departments.
10. Stop haranguing workers.
11. Support, help, and improve.
12. Remove barriers to pride in work.
13. Institute a vigorous program of education and self-improvement.
14. Put everybody in the company to work on the transformation.

Source: Deming, W. Edwards. *Out of the Crisis,* pp. 23–24, © 2000 W. Edwards Deming Institute, published by The MIT Press. Reprinted by permission.

important to the customer. Each of the 10 decisions made by operations managers deals with some aspect of identifying and meeting customer expectations. Meeting those expectations requires an emphasis on TQM if a firm is to compete as a leader in world markets.

Quality expert W. Edwards Deming used 14 points (see Table 6.2) to indicate how he implemented TQM. We develop these into seven concepts for an effective TQM program: (1) continuous improvement, (2) Six Sigma, (3) employee empowerment, (4) benchmarking, (5) just-in-time (JIT), (6) Taguchi concepts, and (7) knowledge of TQM tools.

Continuous Improvement

Total quality management requires a never-ending process of continuous improvement that covers people, equipment, suppliers, materials, and procedures. The basis of the philosophy is that every aspect of an operation can be improved. The end goal is perfection, which is never achieved but always sought.

Plan-Do-Check-Act   Walter Shewhart, another pioneer in quality management, developed a circular model known as PDCA (plan, do, check, act) as his version of continuous improvement. Deming later took this concept to Japan during his work there after World War II. The PDCA cycle (also called a Deming circle or a Shewhart circle) is shown in Figure 6.3 as a circle to stress the continuous nature of the improvement process.

PDCA

A continuous improvement model of plan, do, check. act.

Figure **6.3**

PDCA Cycle

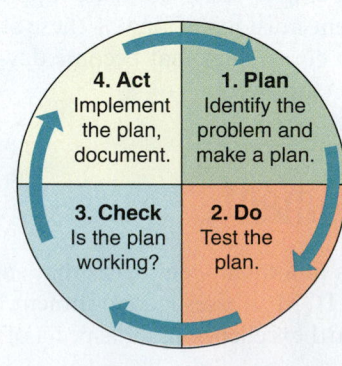

The Japanese use the word *kaizen* to describe this ongoing process of unending improvement—the setting and achieving of ever-higher goals. In the U.S., *TQM* and *zero defects* are also used to describe continuous improvement efforts. But whether it's PDCA, kaizen, TQM, or zero defects, the operations manager is a key player in building a work culture that endorses continuous improvement.

Six Sigma

The term Six Sigma, popularized by Motorola, Honeywell, and General Electric, has two meanings in TQM. In a *statistical* sense, it describes a process, product, or service with an extremely high capability (99.9997% accuracy). For example, if 1 million passengers pass through the St. Louis Airport with checked baggage each month, a Six Sigma program for baggage handling will result in only 3.4 passengers with misplaced luggage. The more common *three-sigma* program (which we address in the supplement to this chapter) would result in 2,700 passengers with misplaced bags every month. See Figure 6.4.

The second TQM definition of Six Sigma is a *program* designed to reduce defects to help lower costs, save time, and improve customer satisfaction. Six Sigma is a comprehensive system— a strategy, a discipline, and a set of tools—for achieving and sustaining business success:

- It is a *strategy* because it focuses on total customer satisfaction.
- It is a *discipline* because it follows the formal Six Sigma Improvement Model known as **DMAIC**. This five-step process improvement model (1) **Defines** the project's purpose, scope, and outputs and then identifies the required process information, keeping in mind the customer's definition of quality; (2) **Measures** the process and collects data; (3) **Analyzes** the data, ensuring repeatability (the results can be duplicated) and reproducibility (others get the same result); (4) **Improves**, by modifying or redesigning, existing processes and procedures; and (5) **Controls** the new process to make sure performance levels are maintained.
- It is a *set of seven tools* that we introduce shortly in this chapter: check sheets, scatter diagrams, cause-and-effect diagrams, Pareto charts, flowcharts, histograms, and statistical process control.

Motorola developed Six Sigma in the 1980s, in response to customer complaints about its products and in response to stiff competition. The company first set a goal of reducing defects by 90%. Within one year, it had achieved such impressive results—through benchmarking competitors, soliciting new ideas from employees, changing reward plans, adding training, and revamping critical processes—that it documented the procedures into what it called Six Sigma. Although the concept was rooted in manufacturing, GE later expanded Six Sigma into services, including human resources, sales, customer services, and financial/credit services. The concept of wiping out defects turns out to be the same in both manufacturing and services.

Six Sigma
A program to save time, improve quality, and lower costs.

LO 6.3 *Explain* Six Sigma

Lower limits / Upper limits

2,700 defects/million

3.4 defects/million

Mean

$\pm 3\sigma$

$\pm 6\sigma$

Figure **6.4**

Defects per Million for $\pm 3\sigma$ vs. $\pm 6\sigma$

◆ **STUDENT TIP**
Recall that $\pm 3\sigma$ provides 99.73% accuracy, while $\pm 6\sigma$ is 99.9997%.

Implementing Six Sigma Implementing Six Sigma is a big commitment. Indeed, successful Six Sigma programs in every firm, from GE to Motorola to DuPont to Texas Instruments, require a major time commitment, especially from top management. These leaders have to formulate the plan, communicate their buy-in and the firm's objectives, and take a visible role in setting the example for others.

Successful Six Sigma projects are clearly related to the strategic direction of a company. It is a management-directed, team-based, and expert-led approach.[2]

Employee Empowerment

Employee empowerment

Enlarging employee jobs so that the added responsibility and authority is moved to the lowest level possible in the organization.

Employee empowerment means involving employees in every step of the production process. Consistently, research suggests that some 85% of quality problems have to do with materials and processes, not with employee performance. Therefore, the task is to design equipment and processes that produce the desired quality. This is best done with a high degree of involvement by those who understand the shortcomings of the system. Those dealing with the system on a daily basis understand it better than anyone else. One study indicated that TQM programs that delegate responsibility for quality to shop-floor employees tend to be twice as likely to succeed as those implemented with "top-down" directives.[3]

When nonconformance occurs, the worker is seldom at fault. Either the product was designed wrong, the process that makes the product was designed wrong, or the employee was improperly trained. Although the employee may be able to help solve the problem, the employee rarely causes it.

Techniques for building employee empowerment include (1) building communication networks that include employees; (2) developing open, supportive supervisors; (3) moving responsibility from both managers and staff to production employees; (4) building high-morale organizations; and (5) creating such formal organization structures as teams and quality circles.

Quality circle

A group of employees meeting regularly with a facilitator to solve work-related problems in their work area.

Teams can be built to address a variety of issues. One popular focus of teams is quality. Such teams are often known as quality circles. A **quality circle** is a group of employees who meet regularly to solve work-related problems. The members receive training in group planning, problem solving, and statistical quality control. They generally meet once a week (usually after work but sometimes on company time). Although the members are not rewarded financially, they do receive recognition from the firm. A specially trained team member, called the *facilitator*, usually helps train the members and keeps the meetings running smoothly. Teams with a quality focus have proven to be a cost-effective way to increase productivity as well as quality.

Benchmarking

Benchmarking

Selecting a demonstrated standard of performance that represents the very best performance for a process or an activity.

Benchmarking is another ingredient in an organization's TQM program. **Benchmarking** involves selecting a demonstrated standard of products, services, costs, or practices that represent

Workers at this TRW airbag manufacturing plant in Marshall, Illinois, are their own inspectors. Empowerment is an essential part of TQM. This man is checking the quality of a crash sensor he built.

TRW Automotive/General Manley Ford

TABLE 6.3	Best Practices for Resolving Customer Complaints
BEST PRACTICE	**JUSTIFICATION**
Make it easy for clients to complain.	It is free market research.
Respond quickly to complaints.	It adds customers and loyalty.
Resolve complaints on the first contact.	It reduces cost.
Use computers to manage complaints.	Discover trends, share them, and align your services.
Recruit the best for customer service jobs.	It should be part of formal training and career advancement.

Source: Based on Canadian Government Guide on Complaint Mechanism.

the very best performance for processes or activities very similar to your own. The idea is to develop a target at which to shoot and then to develop a standard or benchmark against which to compare your performance. The steps for developing benchmarks are:

1. Determine what to benchmark.
2. Form a benchmark team.
3. Identify benchmarking partners.
4. Collect and analyze benchmarking information.
5. Take action to match or exceed the benchmark.

Typical performance measures used in benchmarking include percentage of defects, cost per unit or per order, processing time per unit, service response time, return on investment, customer satisfaction rates, and customer retention rates.

In the ideal situation, you find one or more similar organizations that are leaders in the particular areas you want to study. Then you compare yourself (benchmark yourself) against them. The company need not be in your industry. Indeed, to establish world-class standards, it may be best to look outside your industry. If one industry has learned how to compete via rapid product development while yours has not, it does no good to study your industry.

This is exactly what Xerox and Mercedes-Benz did when they went to L.L. Bean for order-filling and warehousing benchmarks. Xerox noticed that L.L. Bean was able to "pick" orders three times faster. After benchmarking, Xerox was immediately able to pare warehouse costs by 10%. Mercedes-Benz observed that L.L. Bean warehouse employees used flowcharts to spot wasted motions. The auto giant followed suit and now relies more on problem solving at the worker level.

Benchmarks often take the form of "best practices" found in other firms or in other divisions. Table 6.3 illustrates best practices for resolving customer complaints.

Likewise, Britain's Great Ormond Street Hospital benchmarked the Ferrari Racing Team's pit stops to improve one aspect of medical care. (See the *OM in Action* box "A Hospital Benchmarks Against the Ferrari Racing Team?")

Internal Benchmarking When an organization is large enough to have many divisions or business units, a natural approach is the internal benchmark. Data are usually much more accessible than from outside firms. Typically, one internal unit has superior performance worth learning from.

Xerox's almost religious belief in benchmarking has paid off not only by looking outward to L.L. Bean but by examining the operations of its various country divisions. For example, Xerox Europe, a $6 billion subsidiary of Xerox Corp., formed teams to see how better sales could result through internal benchmarking. Somehow, France sold five times as many color copiers as did other divisions in Europe. By copying France's approach, namely, better sales training and use of dealer channels to supplement direct sales, Norway increased sales by 152%, Holland by 300%, and Switzerland by 328%!

Benchmarks can and should be established in a variety of areas. Total quality management requires no less.

LO 6.4 *Explain* how benchmarking is used in TQM

OM in Action | A Hospital Benchmarks Against the Ferrari Racing Team?

After surgeons successfully completed a 6-hour operation to fix a hole in a 3-year-old boy's heart, Dr. Angus McEwan supervised one of the most dangerous phases of the procedure: the boy's transfer from surgery to the intensive care unit.

Thousands of such "handoffs" occur in hospitals every day, and devastating mistakes can happen during them. In fact, at least 35% of preventable hospital mishaps take place because of handoff problems. Risks come from many sources: using temporary nursing staff, frequent shift changes for interns, surgeons working in larger teams, and an ever-growing tangle of wires and tubes connected to patients.

Using an unlikely benchmark, Britain's largest children's hospital turned to Italy's Formula One Ferrari racing team for help in revamping patient handoff techniques. Armed with videos and slides, the racing team described how they analyze pit crew performance. It also explained how its system for recording errors stressed the small ones that go unnoticed in pit-stop handoffs.

To move forward, Ferrari invited a team of doctors to attend practice sessions at the British Grand Prix in order to get closer looks at pit stops. Ferrari's technical director, Nigel Stepney, then watched a video of a hospital handoff. Stepney was not impressed. "In fact, he was amazed at how clumsy, chaotic, and informal the process appeared," said one hospital official. At that meeting, Stepney described how each Ferrari crew member is required to do a specific job, in a specific sequence, and in silence.

Oliver Multhaup/AP Images

The hospital handoff, in contrast, had several conversations going on at once, while different members of its team disconnected or reconnected patient equipment, but in no particular order.

Results of the benchmarking process: handoff errors fell over 40%, with a bonus of faster handoff time.

Sources: The Wall Street Journal (December 3, 2007) and (November 14, 2006).

Just-in-Time (JIT)

The philosophy behind just-in-time (JIT) is one of continuing improvement and enforced problem solving. JIT systems are designed to produce or deliver goods just as they are needed. JIT is related to quality in three ways:

- ◆ *JIT cuts the cost of quality:* This occurs because scrap, rework, inventory investment, and damage costs are directly related to inventory on hand. Because there is less inventory on hand with JIT, costs are lower. In addition, inventory hides bad quality, whereas JIT immediately *exposes* bad quality.
- ◆ *JIT improves quality:* As JIT shrinks lead time, it keeps evidence of errors fresh and limits the number of potential sources of error. JIT creates, in effect, an early warning system for quality problems, both within the firm and with vendors.
- ◆ *Better quality means less inventory and a better, easier-to-employ JIT system:* Often the purpose of keeping inventory is to protect against poor production performance resulting from unreliable quality. If consistent quality exists, JIT allows firms to reduce all the costs associated with inventory.

Taguchi Concepts

Most quality problems are the result of poor product and process design. Genichi Taguchi has provided us with three concepts aimed at improving both product and process quality: *quality robustness*, *target-oriented quality,* and the *quality loss function*.

Quality robust

Products that are consistently built to meet customer needs despite adverse conditions in the production process.

Quality robust products are products that can be produced uniformly and consistently in adverse manufacturing and environmental conditions. Taguchi's idea is to remove the *effects* of adverse conditions instead of removing the causes. Taguchi suggests that removing the effects

Quality Loss Function (b)

- Target-oriented quality yields more product in the "best" category.
- Target-oriented quality brings products toward the target value.
- Conformance-oriented quality keeps products within 3 standard deviations.

Distribution of Specifications for Products Produced (a)

Figure **6.5**

(a) Distribution of Products Produced and (b) Quality Loss Function

Taguchi aims for the target because products produced near the upper and lower acceptable specifications result in a higher quality loss.

is often cheaper than removing the causes and more effective in producing a robust product. In this way, small variations in materials and process do not destroy product quality.

A study found that U.S. consumers preferred Sony TVs made in Japan to Sony TVs made in the U.S., even though both factories used the exact same designs and specifications. The difference in approaches to quality generated the difference in consumer preferences. In particular, the U.S. factory was *conformance-oriented*, accepting all components that were produced within specification limits. On the other hand, the Japanese factory strove to produce as many components as close to the actual target as possible (see Figure 6.5(a)).

This suggests that even though components made close to the boundaries of the specification limits may technically be acceptable, they may still create problems. For example, TV screens produced near their diameter's lower spec limit may provide a loose fit with screen frames produced near their upper spec limit, and vice versa. This implies that a final product containing many parts produced near their specification boundaries may contain numerous loose and tight fits, which could cause assembly, performance, or aesthetic concerns. Customers may be dissatisfied, resulting in possible returns, service work, or decreased future demand.

Taguchi introduced the concept of target-oriented quality as a philosophy of continuous improvement to bring the product exactly on target. As a measure, Taguchi's quality loss function (QLF) attempts to estimate the cost of deviating from the target value. Even though the item is produced within specification limits, the variation in quality can be expected to increase costs as the item output moves away from its target value. (These quality-related costs are estimates of the average cost over many such units produced.)

The QLF is an excellent way to estimate quality costs of different processes. A process that produces closer to the actual target value may be more expensive, but it may yield a more valuable product. The QLF is the tool that helps the manager determine if this added cost is worthwhile. The QLF takes the general form of a simple quadratic equation (see Figure 6.5(b)).

LO 6.5 *Explain* quality robust products and Taguchi concepts

Target-oriented quality

A philosophy of continuous improvement to bring a product exactly on target.

Quality loss function (QLF)

A mathematical function that identifies all costs connected with poor quality and shows how these costs increase as output moves away from the target value.

Knowledge of TQM Tools

To empower employees and implement TQM as a continuing effort, everyone in the organization must be trained in the techniques of TQM. In the following section, we focus on some of the diverse and expanding tools that are used in the TQM crusade.

Tools for Generating Ideas

(a) *Check Sheet:* An organized method of recording data

Defect	Hour							
	1	2	3	4	5	6	7	8
A	///	/		/	/	/	///	/
B	//	/	/	/			//	///
C	/	//					//	////

(b) *Scatter Diagram:* A graph of the value of one variable vs. another variable

(c) *Cause-and-Effect Diagram:* A tool that identifies process elements (causes) that may affect an outcome

Tools for Organizing the Data

(d) *Pareto Chart:* A graph that identifies and plots problems or defects in descending order of frequency

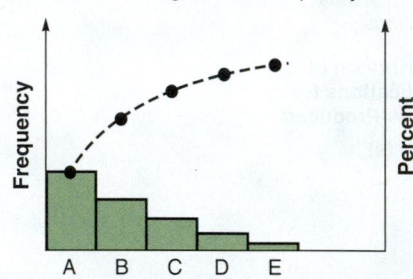

(e) *Flowchart (Process Diagram):* A chart that describes the steps in a process

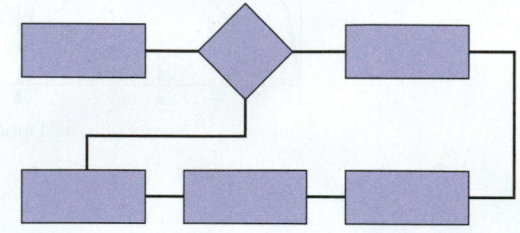

Tools for Identifying Problems

(f) *Histogram:* A distribution that shows the frequency of occurrences of a variable

(g) *Statistical Process Control Chart:* A chart with time on the horizontal axis for plotting values of a statistic

Figure 6.6

Seven Tools of TQM

STUDENT TIP ◆

These tools will prove useful in many of your courses and throughout your career.

Tools of TQM

Seven tools that are particularly helpful in the TQM effort are shown in Figure 6.6. We will now introduce these tools.

Check Sheets

LO 6.6 *Use* the seven tools of TQM

A check sheet is any kind of a form that is designed for recording data. In many cases, the recording is done so the patterns are easily seen while the data are being taken [see Figure 6.6(a)]. Check sheets help analysts find the facts or patterns that may aid subsequent analysis. An example might be a drawing that shows a tally of the areas where defects are occurring or a check sheet showing the type of customer complaints.

Figure **6.7**

Fish-Bone Chart (or Cause-and-Effect Diagram) for Problems with Missed Free-Throws
Source: Adapted from MoreSteam.com, 2007.

Scatter Diagrams

Scatter diagrams show the relationship between two measurements. An example is the positive relationship between length of a service call and the number of trips a repair person makes back to the truck for parts. Another example might be a plot of productivity and absenteeism, as shown in Figure 6.6(b). If the two items are closely related, the data points will form a tight band. If a random pattern results, the items are unrelated.

Cause-and-Effect Diagrams

Another tool for identifying quality issues and inspection points is the cause-and-effect diagram, also known as an Ishikawa diagram or a fish-bone chart. Figure 6.7 illustrates a chart (note the shape resembling the bones of a fish) for a basketball quality control problem—missed free-throws. Each "bone" represents a possible source of error.

The operations manager starts with four categories: material, machinery/equipment, manpower, and methods. These four *M*s are the "causes." They provide a good checklist for initial analysis. Individual causes associated with each category are tied in as separate bones along that branch, often through a brainstorming process. For example, the method branch in Figure 6.7 has problems caused by hand position, follow-through, aiming point, bent knees, and balance. When a fish-bone chart is systematically developed, possible quality problems and inspection points are highlighted.

Cause-and-effect diagram

A schematic technique used to discover possible locations of quality problems.

Pareto Charts

Pareto charts are a method of organizing errors, problems, or defects to help focus on problem-solving efforts. They are based on the work of Vilfredo Pareto, a 19th-century economist. Joseph M. Juran popularized Pareto's work when he suggested that 80% of a firm's problems are a result of only 20% of the causes.

Example 1 indicates that of the five types of complaints identified, the vast majority were of one type—poor room service.

Pareto charts

A graphic way of classifying problems by their level of importance, often referred to as the 80–20 rule.

Example 1

A PARETO CHART AT THE HARD ROCK HOTEL

The Hard Rock Hotel in Bali has just collected the data from 75 complaint calls to the general manager during the month of October. The manager wants to prepare an analysis of the complaints. The data provided are room service, 54; check-in delays, 12; hours the pool is open, 4; minibar prices, 3; and miscellaneous, 2.

APPROACH ▶ A Pareto chart is an excellent choice for this analysis.

SOLUTION ▶ The Pareto chart shown below indicates that 72% of the calls were the result of one cause: room service. The majority of complaints will be eliminated when this one cause is corrected.

INSIGHT ▶ This visual means of summarizing data is very helpful—particularly with large amounts of data, as in the Southwestern University case study at the end of this chapter. We can immediately spot the top problems and prepare a plan to address them.

LEARNING EXERCISE ▶ Hard Rock's bar manager decides to do a similar analysis on complaints she has collected over the past year: too expensive, 22; weak drinks, 15; slow service, 65; short hours, 8; unfriendly bartender, 12. Prepare a Pareto chart. [Answer: slow service, 53%; expensive, 18%; drinks, 12%; bartender, 10%; hours, 7%.]

RELATED PROBLEMS ▶ 6.1, 6.3, 6.7b, 6.12, 6.13, 6.16c, 6.17b

ACTIVE MODEL 6.1 This example is further illustrated in Active Model 6.1 in MyOMLab.

Pareto analysis indicates which problems may yield the greatest payoff. Pacific Bell discovered this when it tried to find a way to reduce damage to buried phone cable, the number-one cause of phone outages. Pareto analysis showed that 41% of cable damage was caused by construction work. Armed with this information, Pacific Bell was able to devise a plan to reduce cable cuts by 24% in one year, saving $6 million.

Likewise, Japan's Ricoh Corp., a copier maker, used the Pareto principle to tackle the "call-back" problem. Callbacks meant the job was not done right the first time and that a second visit, at Ricoh's expense, was needed. Identifying and retraining only the 11% of the customer engineers with the most callbacks resulted in a 19% drop in return visits.

Flowcharts

Flowcharts

Block diagrams that graphically describe a process or system.

Flowcharts graphically present a process or system using annotated boxes and interconnected lines [see Figure 6.6(e)]. They are a simple but great tool for trying to make sense of a process or explain a process. Example 2 uses a flowchart to show the process of completing an MRI at a hospital.

| Example 2 | **A FLOWCHART FOR HOSPITAL MRI SERVICE** |

Arnold Palmer Hospital has undertaken a series of process improvement initiatives. One of these is to make the MRI service efficient for patient, doctor, and hospital. The first step, the administrator believes, is to develop a flowchart for this process.

APPROACH ▶ A process improvement staffer observed a number of patients and followed them (and information flow) from start to end. Here are the 11 steps:

1. Physician schedules MRI after examining patient (START).
2. Patient taken from the examination room to the MRI lab with test order and copy of medical records.
3. Patient signs in, completes required paperwork.
4. Patient is prepped by technician for scan.
5. Technician carries out the MRI scan.
6. Technician inspects film for clarity.
7. If MRI not satisfactory (20% of time), Steps 5 and 6 are repeated.
8. Patient taken back to hospital room.
9. MRI is read by radiologist and report is prepared.
10. MRI and report are transferred electronically to physician.
11. Patient and physician discuss report (END).

SOLUTION ▶ Here is the flowchart:

INSIGHT ▶ With the flowchart in hand, the hospital can analyze each step and identify value-added activities and activities that can be improved or eliminated.

LEARNING EXERCISE ▶ A new procedure requires that if the patient's blood pressure is over 200/120 when being prepped for the MRI, she is taken back to her room for 2 hours and the process returns to Step 2. How does the flowchart change? Answer:

RELATED PROBLEMS ▶ 6.6, 6.15

Histograms

Histograms show the range of values of a measurement and the frequency with which each value occurs [see Figure 6.6(f)]. They show the most frequently occurring readings as well as the variations in the measurements. Descriptive statistics, such as the average and standard deviation, may be calculated to describe the distribution. However, the data should always be plotted so the shape of the distribution can be "seen." A visual presentation of the distribution may also provide insight into the cause of the variation.

Statistical Process Control (SPC)

Statistical process control (SPC) monitors standards, makes measurements, and takes corrective action as a product or service is being produced. Samples of process outputs are examined; if they are within acceptable limits, the process is permitted to continue. If they fall outside certain specific ranges, the process is stopped and, typically, the assignable cause located and removed.

Statistical process control (SPC)
A process used to monitor standards, make measurements, and take corrective action as a product or service is being produced.

Figure **6.8**

Control Chart for Percentage of Free-throws Missed by the Orlando Magic in Their First Nine Games of the New Season

Control charts

Graphic presentations of process data over time, with predetermined control limits.

Control charts are graphic presentations of data over time that show upper and lower limits for the process we want to control [see Figure 6.6(g)]. Control charts are constructed in such a way that new data can be quickly compared with past performance data. We take samples of the process output and plot the average of each of these samples on a chart that has the limits on it. The upper and lower limits in a control chart can be in units of temperature, pressure, weight, length, and so on.

Figure 6.8 shows the plot of sample averages in a control chart. When the samples fall within the upper and lower control limits and no discernible pattern is present, the process is said to be in control with only natural variation present. Otherwise, the process is out of control or out of adjustment.

The supplement to this chapter details how control charts of different types are developed. It also deals with the statistical foundation underlying the use of this important tool.

The Role of Inspection

Inspection

A means of ensuring that an operation is producing at the quality level expected.

To make sure a system is producing as expected, control of the process is needed. The best processes have little variation from the standard expected. In fact, if variation were completely eliminated, there would be no need for inspection because there would be no defects. The operations manager's challenge is to build such systems. However, inspection must often be performed to ensure that processes are performing to standard. This **inspection** can involve measurement, tasting, touching, weighing, or testing of the product (sometimes even destroying it when doing so). Its goal is to detect a bad process immediately. Inspection does not correct deficiencies in the system or defects in the products, nor does it change a product or increase its value. Inspection only finds deficiencies and defects. Moreover, inspections are expensive and do not add value to the product.

Inspection should be thought of as a vehicle for improving the system. Operations managers need to know critical points in the system: (1) *when to inspect* and (2) *where to inspect*.

When and Where to Inspect

Deciding when and where to inspect depends on the type of process and the value added at each stage. Inspections can take place at any of the following points:

1. At your supplier's plant while the supplier is producing.
2. At your facility upon receipt of goods from your supplier.
3. Before costly or irreversible processes.
4. During the step-by-step production process.
5. When production or service is complete.
6. Before delivery to your customer.
7. At the point of customer contact.

Good methods analysis and the proper tools can result in poka-yokes that improve both quality and speed. Here, two poka-yokes are demonstrated. First, the aluminum scoop automatically positions the french fries vertically, and second, the properly sized container ensures that the portion served is correct. McDonald's thrives by bringing rigor and consistency to the restaurant business.

Matthias Schrader/dpa picture alliance archive/Alamy

The seven tools of TQM discussed in the previous section aid in this "when and where to inspect" decision. However, inspection is not a substitute for a robust product produced by well-trained employees in a good process. In one well-known experiment conducted by an independent research firm, 100 defective pieces were added to a "perfect" lot of items and then subjected to 100% inspection. The inspectors found only 68 of the defective pieces in their first inspection. It took another three passes by the inspectors to find the next 30 defects. The last two defects were never found. So the bottom line is that there is variability in the inspection process. In addition, inspectors are only human: They become bored, they become tired, and the inspection equipment itself has variability. Even with 100% inspection, inspectors cannot guarantee perfection. Therefore, good processes, employee empowerment, and source control are a better solution than trying to find defects by inspection. You cannot inspect quality into the product.

For example, at Velcro Industries, as in many other organizations, quality was viewed by machine operators as the job of "those quality people." Inspections were based on random sampling, and if a part showed up bad, it was thrown out. The company decided to pay more attention to the system (operators, machine repair and design, measurement methods, communications, and responsibilities) and to invest more money in training. Over time as defects declined, Velcro was able to pull half its quality control people out of the process.

Source Inspection

The best inspection can be thought of as no inspection at all; this "inspection" is always done at the source—it is just doing the job properly with the operator ensuring that this is so. This may be called source inspection (or source control) and is consistent with the concept of employee empowerment, where individual employees self-check their own work. The idea is that each supplier, process, and employee *treats the next step in the process as the customer*, ensuring perfect product to the next "customer." This inspection may be assisted by the use of checklists and controls such as a fail-safe device called a *poka-yoke*, a name borrowed from the Japanese.

A poka-yoke is a foolproof device or technique that ensures production of good units every time. These special devices avoid errors and provide quick feedback of problems. A simple example of a poka-yoke device is the diesel gas pump nozzle that will not fit into the "unleaded" gas tank opening on your car. In McDonald's, the french fry scoop and standard-size container used to measure the correct quantity are poka-yokes. Similarly, in a hospital, the prepackaged surgical coverings that contain exactly the items needed for a medical procedure are poka-yokes.

Checklists are a type of poka-yoke to help ensure consistency and completeness in carrying out a task. A basic example is a to-do list. This tool may take the form of preflight checklists used by airplane pilots, surgical safety checklists used by doctors, or software quality assurance lists used by programmers. The *OM in Action* box "Safe Patients, Smart Hospitals" illustrates the important role checklists have in hospital quality.

The idea of source inspection, poka-yokes, and checklists is to guarantee 100% good product or service at each step of a process.

Source inspection
Controlling or monitoring at the point of production or purchase—at the source.

Poka-yoke
Literally translated, "mistake proofing"; it has come to mean a device or technique that ensures the production of a good unit every time.

Checklist
A type of poka-yoke that lists the steps needed to ensure consistency and completeness in a task.

OM in Action   Safe Patients, Smart Hospitals

Simple and avoidable errors are made in hospitals each day, causing patients to die. Inspired by two tragic medical mistakes—his father's misdiagnosed cancer and sloppiness that killed an 18-month-old child at Johns Hopkins—Dr. Peter Pronovost has made it his mission, often swimming upstream against the medical culture, to improve patient safety and prevent deaths.

He began by developing a basic 5-step checklist to reduce catheter infections. Inserted into veins in the groin, neck, or chest to administer fluids and medicines, catheters can save lives. But every year, 80,000 Americans get infections from *central venous catheters* (or lines), and over 30,000 of these patients die. Pronovost's checklist has dropped infection rates at hospitals that use it down to zero, saving thousands of lives and tens of millions of dollars.

His steps for doctors and nurses are simple: (1) wash your hands; (2) use sterile gloves, masks, and drapes; (3) use antiseptic on the area being opened for the catheter; (4) avoid veins in the arms and legs; and (5) take the catheter out as soon as possible. He also created a special cart, where all supplies needed are stored.

Dr. Provonost believes that many hospital errors are due to lack of standardization, poor communications, and a noncollaborative culture that is "antiquated

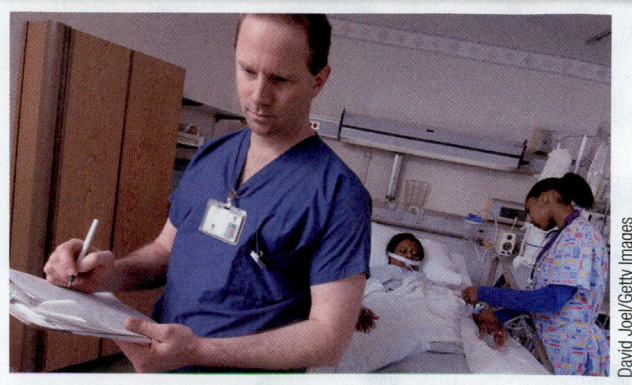

David Joel/Getty Images

and toxic." He points out that checklists in the airline industry are a science, and *every* crew member works as part of the safety team. Provonost's book has shown that one person, with small changes, can make a huge difference.

Sources: Safe Patients, Smart Hospitals (Penguin Publishers, 2011); and *The Wall Street Journal* (December 13, 2014).

Service Industry Inspection

VIDEO 6.2
Quality Counts at Alaska Airlines

In *service*-oriented organizations, inspection points can be assigned at a wide range of locations, as illustrated in Table 6.4. Again, the operations manager must decide where inspections are justified and may find the seven tools of TQM useful when making these judgments.

TABLE 6.4	Examples of Inspection in Services	
ORGANIZATION	**WHAT IS INSPECTED**	**STANDARD**
Alaska Airlines	Last bag on carousel	Less than 20 minutes after arrival at the gate
	Airplane door opened	Less than 2 minutes after arrival at the gate
Jones Law Offices	Receptionist performance	Phone answered by the second ring
	Billing	Accurate, timely, and correct format
	Attorney	Promptness in returning calls
Hard Rock Hotel	Reception desk	Use customer's name
	Doorman	Greet guest in less than 30 seconds
	Room	All lights working, spotless bathroom
	Minibar	Restocked and charges accurately posted to bill
Arnold Palmer Hospital	Billing	Accurate, timely, and correct format
	Pharmacy	Prescription accuracy, inventory accuracy
	Lab	Audit for lab-test accuracy
	Nurses	Charts immediately updated
	Admissions	Data entered correctly and completely
Olive Garden Restaurant	Busboy	Serves water and bread within one minute
	Busboy	Clears all entrèe items and crumbs prior to dessert
	Waiter	Knows and suggests specials, desserts
Nordstrom Department Store	Display areas	Attractive, well organized, stocked, good lighting
	Stockrooms	Rotation of goods, organized, clean
	Salesclerks	Neat, courteous, very knowledgeable

Inspection of Attributes versus Variables

When inspections take place, quality characteristics may be measured as either *attributes* or *variables*. Attribute inspection classifies items as being either good or defective. It does not address the *degree* of failure. For example, the lightbulb burns or it does not. Variable inspection measures such dimensions as weight, speed, size, or strength to see if an item falls within an acceptable range. If a piece of electrical wire is supposed to be 0.01 inch in diameter, a micrometer can be used to see if the product is close enough to pass inspection.

Knowing whether attributes or variables are being inspected helps us decide which statistical quality control approach to take, as we will see in the supplement to this chapter.

Attribute inspection

An inspection that classifies items as being either good or defective.

Variable inspection

Classifications of inspected items as falling on a continuum scale, such as dimension or strength.

TQM in Services

The personal component of services is more difficult to measure than the quality of the tangible component. Generally, the user of a service, like the user of a good, has features in mind that form a basis for comparison among alternatives. Lack of any one feature may eliminate the service from further consideration. Quality also may be perceived as a bundle of attributes in which many lesser characteristics are superior to those of competitors. This approach to product comparison differs little between goods and services. However, what is very different about the selection of services is the poor definition of the (1) *intangible differences between products* and (2) *the intangible expectations customers have of those products*. Indeed, the intangible attributes may not be defined at all. They are often unspoken images in the purchaser's mind. This is why all of those marketing issues such as advertising, image, and promotion can make a difference.

The operations manager plays a significant role in addressing several major aspects of service quality. First, the *tangible component of many services is important*. How well the service is designed and produced does make a difference. This might be how accurate, clear, and complete your checkout bill at the hotel is, how warm the food is at Taco Bell, or how well your car runs after you pick it up at the repair shop.

Second, another aspect of service and service quality is the process. Notice in Table 6.5 that 9 out of 10 of the determinants of service quality are related to *the service process*. Such things as reliability and courtesy are part of the process. An operations manager can

TABLE 6.5	Determinants of Service Quality

Reliability involves consistency of performance and dependability. It means that the firm performs the service right the first time and that the firm honors its promises.

Responsiveness concerns the willingness or readiness of employees to provide service. It involves timeliness of service.

Competence means possession of the required skills and knowledge to perform the service.

Access involves approachability and ease of contact.

Courtesy involves politeness, respect, consideration, and friendliness of contact personnel (including receptionists, telephone operators, etc.).

Communication means keeping customers informed in language they can understand and listening to them. It may mean that the company has to adjust its language for different consumers—increasing the level of sophistication with a well-educated customer and speaking simply and plainly with a novice.

Credibility involves trustworthiness, believability, and honesty. It involves having the customer's best interests at heart.

Security is the freedom from danger, risk, or doubt.

Understanding/knowing the customer involves making the effort to understand the customer's needs.

Tangibles include the physical evidence of the service.

Sources: Adapted from A. Parasuranam, Valarie A, Zeithaml, and Leonard L. Berry, "A Conceptual Model of Service Quality and Its Implications for Future Research," *Journal of Marketing* (1985): 49. Copyright © 1985 by the American Marketing Association. Reprinted with permission.

First passenger boarded
40 min. before departure

Flight attendants on-board
45 min. before departure

Final load
closeout
2 min. before
departure

Aircraft 97%
boarded 10 min.
before departure
time

First bag to
conveyor belt
15 min. after
arrival

Cargo door opened
1 min. after arrival

On board
check-in count
5 min. before
departure

All doors closed
2 min. before
departure

Alaska Airlines

Like many service organizations, Alaska Airlines sets quality standards in areas such as courtesy, appearance, and time. Shown here are some of Alaska Airlines 50 quality checkpoints, based on a timeline for each departure.

design processes that have these attributes and can ensure their quality through the TQM techniques discussed in this chapter. (See the Alaska Airlines photo.)

Third, the operations manager should realize that the customer's expectations are the standard against which the service is judged. Customers' perceptions of service quality result from a comparison of their "before-service expectations" with their "actual-service experience." In other words, service quality is judged on the basis of whether it meets expectations. *The manager may be able to influence both the quality of the service and the expectation.* Don't promise more than you can deliver.

Fourth, the manager must expect exceptions. There is a standard quality level at which the regular service is delivered, such as the bank teller's handling of a transaction. However, there are "exceptions" or "problems" initiated by the customer or by less-than-optimal operating conditions (e.g., the computer "crashed"). This implies that the quality control system must recognize and *have a set of alternative plans for less-than-optimal operating conditions.*

Service recovery

Training and empowering frontline workers to solve a problem immediately.

Well-run companies have **service recovery** strategies. This means they train and empower frontline employees to immediately solve a problem. For instance, staff at Marriott Hotels are drilled in the **LEARN** routine—Listen, Empathize, Apologize, React, Notify—with the final step ensuring that the complaint is fed back into the system. And at the Ritz-Carlton, staff members are trained not to say merely "sorry" but "please accept my apology." The Ritz gives them a budget for reimbursing upset guests. Similarly, employees at Alaska Airlines are empowered to soothe irritated travelers by drawing from a "toolkit" of options at their disposal.

SERVQUAL

A popular measurement scale for service quality that compares service expectations with service performance.

Managers of service firms may find **SERVQUAL** useful when evaluating performance. SERVQUAL is a widely used instrument that provides direct comparisons between customer service expectations and the actual service provided. SERVQUAL focuses on the *gaps* between the customer service expectations and the service provided on 10 service quality determinants. The most common version of the scale collapses the 10 service quality determinants shown in Table 6.5 into five factors for measurement: reliability, assurance, tangibles, empathy, and responsiveness.

Designing the product, managing the service process, matching customer expectations to the product, and preparing for the exceptions are keys to quality services. The *OM in Action* box "Richey International's Spies" provides another glimpse of how OM managers improve quality in services.

VIDEO 6.3
TQM at Ritz-Carlton Hotels

OM in Action   Richey International's Spies

How do luxury hotels maintain quality? They inspect. But when the product is one-on-one service, largely dependent on personal behavior, how do you inspect? You hire spies!

Richey International is the spy. Preferred Hotels and Resorts Worldwide and Intercontinental Hotels have both hired Richey to do quality evaluations via spying. Richey employees posing as customers perform the inspections. However, even then management must have established what the customer expects and specific services that yield customer satisfaction. Only then do managers know where and how to inspect. Aggressive training and objective inspections reinforce behavior that will meet those customer expectations.

The hotels use Richey's undercover inspectors to ensure performance to exacting standards. The hotels do not know when the evaluators will arrive. Nor what aliases they will use. Over 50 different standards are evaluated before the inspectors even check in at a luxury hotel. Over the next 24 hours, using checklists, tape recordings, and photos, written reports are prepared. The reports include evaluation of standards such as:

- Does the doorman greet each guest in less than 30 seconds?
- Does the front-desk clerk use the guest's name during check-in?
- Are the bathroom tub and shower spotlessly clean?
- How many minutes does it take to get coffee after the guest sits down for breakfast?
- Did the waiter make eye contact?
- Were minibar charges posted correctly on the bill?

Established standards, aggressive training, and inspections are part of the TQM effort at these hotels. Quality does not happen by accident.

Sources: Hotelier (Feb. 6, 2010); *Hotel and Motel Management* (August 2002); and *The Wall Street Journal* (May 12, 1999).

Summary

Quality is a term that means different things to different people. We define quality as "the totality of features and characteristics of a product or service that bears on its ability to satisfy stated or implied needs." Defining quality expectations is critical to effective and efficient operations.

Quality requires building a total quality management (TQM) environment because quality cannot be inspected into a product. The chapter also addresses seven TQM *concepts*: continuous improvement, Six Sigma, employee empowerment, benchmarking, just-in-time, Taguchi concepts, and knowledge of TQM tools. The seven TQM *tools* introduced in this chapter are check sheets, scatter diagrams, cause-and-effect diagrams, Pareto charts, flowcharts, histograms, and statistical process control (SPC).

Key Terms

Quality (p. 217)
ISO 9000 (p. 218)
Cost of quality (COQ) (p. 218)
Total quality management (TQM) (p. 219)
PDCA (p. 220)
Six Sigma (p. 221)
Employee empowerment (p. 222)
Quality circle (p. 222)
Benchmarking (p. 222)

Quality robust (p. 224)
Target-oriented quality (p. 225)
Quality loss function (QLF) (p. 225)
Cause-and-effect diagram, Ishikawa
    diagram, or fish-bone chart (p. 227)
Pareto charts (p. 227)
Flowcharts (p. 228)
Statistical process control (SPC) (p. 229)
Control charts (p. 230)

Inspection (p. 230)
Source inspection (p. 231)
Poka-yoke (p. 231)
Checklist (p. 231)
Attribute inspection (p. 233)
Variable inspection (p. 233)
Service recovery (p. 234)
SERVQUAL (p. 234)

Ethical Dilemma

A lawsuit a few years ago made headlines worldwide when a McDonald's drive-through customer spilled a cup of scalding hot coffee on herself. Claiming the coffee was too hot to be safely consumed in a car, the badly burned 80-year-old woman won $2.9 million in court. (The judge later reduced the award to $640,000.) McDonald's claimed the product was served to the correct specifications and was of proper quality. Further, the cup read "Caution—Contents May Be Hot." McDonald's coffee, at 180°, is substantially hotter (by corporate rule) than typical restaurant coffee, despite hundreds of coffee-scalding complaints in the past 10 years. Similar court cases, incidentally, resulted in smaller verdicts, but again in favor of the plaintiffs. For example, Motor City Bagel Shop was sued for a spilled cup of coffee by a drive-through patron, and Starbucks by a customer who spilled coffee on her own ankle.

Are McDonald's, Motor City, and Starbucks at fault in situations such as these? How do quality and ethics enter into these cases?

Discussion Questions

1. Explain how improving quality can lead to reduced costs.
2. As an Internet exercise, determine the Baldrige Award criteria. See the Web site **www.nist.gov/baldrige/**.
3. Which 3 of Deming's 14 points do you think are most critical to the success of a TQM program? Why?
4. List the seven concepts that are necessary for an effective TQM program. How are these related to Deming's 14 points?
5. Name three of the important people associated with the quality concepts of this chapter. In each case, write a sentence about each one summarizing his primary contribution to the field of quality management.
6. What are seven tools of TQM?
7. How does fear in the workplace (and in the classroom) inhibit learning?
8. How can a university control the quality of its output (that is, its graduates)?
9. Philip Crosby said that quality is free. Why?
10. List the three concepts central to Taguchi's approach.
11. What is the purpose of using a Pareto chart for a given problem?
12. What are the four broad categories of "causes" to help initially structure an Ishikawa diagram or cause-and-effect diagram?
13. Of the several points where inspection may be necessary, which apply especially well to manufacturing?
14. What roles do operations managers play in addressing the major aspects of service quality?
15. Explain, in your own words, what is meant by *source inspection*.
16. What are 10 determinants of service quality?
17. Name several products that do not require high quality.
18. In this chapter, we have suggested that building quality into a process and its people is difficult. Inspections are also difficult. To indicate just how difficult inspections are, count the number of *E*s (both capital *E* and lowercase *e*) in the *OM in Action* box "Richey International's Spies" on page 235 (include the title but not the source note). How many did you find? If each student does this individually, you are very likely to find a distribution rather than a single number!

Solved Problems   Virtual Office Hours help is available in MyOMLab.

SOLVED PROBLEM 6.1

Northern Airlines's frequent flyer complaints about redeeming miles for free, discounted, and upgraded travel are summarized below, in five categories, from 600 letters received this year.

COMPLAINT	FREQUENCY
Could not get through to customer service to make requests	125
Seats not available on date requested	270
Had to pay fees to get "free" seats	62
Seats were available but only on flights at odd hours	110
Rules kept changing whenever customer called	33

Develop a Pareto chart for the data.

SOLUTION

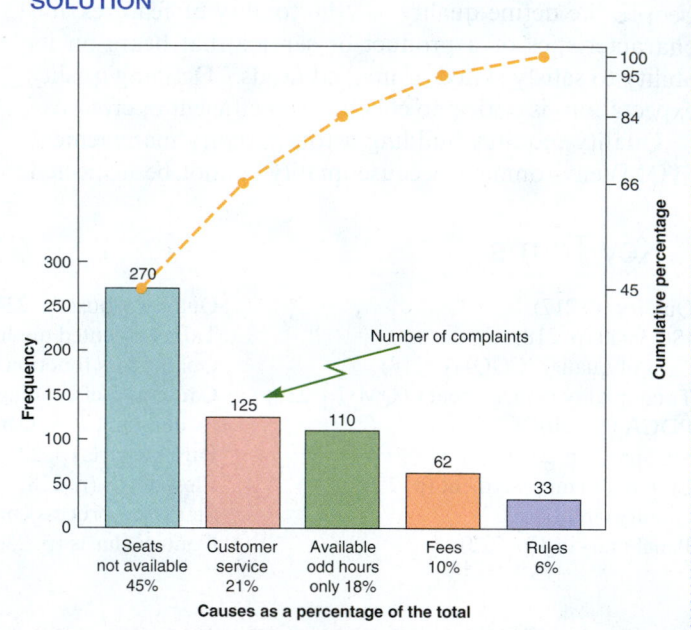

Problems

• **6.1** An avant-garde clothing manufacturer runs a series of high-profile, risqué ads on a billboard on Highway 101 and regularly collects protest calls from people who are offended by them. The company has no idea how many people in total see the ads, but it has been collecting statistics on the number of phone calls from irate viewers:

TYPE	DESCRIPTION	NUMBER OF COMPLAINTS
R	Offensive racially/ethnically	10
M	Demeaning to men	4
W	Demeaning to women	14
I	Ad is incomprehensible	6
O	Other	2

a) Depict this data with a Pareto chart. Also depict the cumulative complaint line.
b) What percent of the total complaints can be attributed to the most prevalent complaint?

• **6.2** Develop a scatter diagram for two variables of interest [say pages in the newspaper by day of the week; see the example in Figure 6.6(b)].

• **6.3** Develop a Pareto chart of the following causes of poor grades on an exam:

REASON FOR POOR GRADE	FREQUENCY
Insufficient time to complete	15
Late arrival to exam	7
Difficulty understanding material	25
Insufficient preparation time	2
Studied wrong material	2
Distractions in exam room	9
Calculator batteries died during exam	1
Forgot exam was scheduled	3
Felt ill during exam	4

• **6.4** Develop a histogram of the time it took for you or your friends to receive six recent orders at a fast-food restaurant.

•• **6.5** Kathleen McFadden's restaurant in Boston has recorded the following data for eight recent customers:

CUSTOMER NUMBER, i	MINUTES FROM TIME FOOD ORDERED UNTIL FOOD ARRIVED (y_i)	NO. OF TRIPS TO KITCHEN BY WAITRESS (x_i)
1	10.50	4
2	12.75	5
3	9.25	3
4	8.00	2
5	9.75	3
6	11.00	4
7	14.00	6
8	10.75	5

a) McFadden wants you to graph the eight points (x_i, y_i), $i = 1$, 2, … 8. She has been concerned because customers have been waiting too long for their food, and this graph is intended to help her find possible causes of the problem.
b) This is an example of what type of graph?

•• **6.6** Develop a flowchart [as in Figure 6.6(e) and Example 2] showing all the steps involved in planning a party.

•• **6.7** Consider the types of poor driving habits that might occur at a traffic light. Make a list of the 10 you consider most likely to happen. Add the category of "other" to that list.
a) Compose a check sheet [like that in Figure 6.6(a)] to collect the frequency of occurrence of these habits. Using your check sheet, visit a busy traffic light intersection at four different times of the day, with two of these times being during high-traffic periods (rush hour, lunch hour). For 15 to 20 minutes each visit, observe the frequency with which the habits you listed occurred.
b) Construct a Pareto chart showing the relative frequency of occurrence of each habit.

•• **6.8** Draw a fish-bone chart detailing reasons why an airline customer might be dissatisfied.

•• **6.9** Consider the everyday task of getting to work on time or arriving at your first class on time in the morning. Draw a fish-bone chart showing reasons why you might arrive late in the morning.

••**6.10** Construct a cause-and-effect diagram to reflect "student dissatisfied with university registration process." Use the "four *M*s" or create your own organizing scheme. Include at least 12 causes.

••**6.11** Draw a fish-bone chart depicting the reasons that might give rise to an incorrect fee statement at the time you go to pay for your registration at school.

•••**6.12** Mary Beth Marrs, the manager of an apartment complex, feels overwhelmed by the number of complaints she is receiving. Below is the check sheet she has kept for the past 12 weeks. Develop a Pareto chart using this information. What recommendations would you make?

WEEK	GROUNDS	PARKING/ DRIVES	POOL	TENANT ISSUES	ELECTRICAL/ PLUMBING
1	✓✓✓	✓✓	✓	✓✓✓	
2	✓	✓✓✓	✓✓	✓✓	✓
3	✓✓✓	✓✓✓	✓✓	✓	
4	✓	✓✓✓✓	✓	✓	✓✓
5	✓✓	✓✓✓	✓✓✓✓	✓✓	
6	✓	✓✓✓✓	✓✓		
7		✓✓✓	✓✓	✓✓	
8	✓	✓✓✓✓	✓✓	✓✓✓	✓
9	✓	✓✓	✓		
10	✓	✓✓✓✓	✓✓	✓✓	
11		✓✓✓	✓✓	✓	
12	✓✓	✓✓✓	✓✓✓	✓	

• **6.13**   Use Pareto analysis to investigate the following data collected on a printed-circuit-board assembly line:

DEFECT	NUMBER OF DEFECT OCCURRENCES
Components not adhering	143
Excess adhesive	71
Misplaced transistors	601
Defective board dimension	146
Mounting holes improperly positioned	12
Circuitry problems on final test	90
Wrong component	212

a) Prepare a graph of the data.
b) What conclusions do you reach?

•• **6.14**   A list of 16 issues that led to incorrect formulations in Tuncey Bayrak's jam manufacturing unit in New England is provided below:

List of Issues

1. Incorrect measurement	9. Variability in scale accuracy
2. Antiquated scales	10. Equipment in disrepair
3. Lack of clear instructions	11. Technician calculation off
4. Damaged raw material	12. Jars mislabeled
5. Operator misreads display	13. Temperature controls off
6. Inadequate cleanup	14. Incorrect weights
7. Incorrect maintenance	15. Priority miscommunication
8. Inadequate flow controls	16. Inadequate instructions

Create a fish-bone diagram and categorize each of these issues correctly, using the "four Ms" method.

•• **6.15**   Develop a flowchart for one of the following:
a) Filling up with gasoline at a self-serve station.
b) Determining your account balance and making a withdrawal at an ATM.
c) Getting a cone of yogurt or ice cream from an ice cream store.

•••• **6.16**   Boston Electric Generators has been getting many complaints from its major customer, Home Station, about the quality of its shipments of home generators. Daniel Shimshak, the plant manager, is alarmed that a customer is providing him with the only information the company has on shipment quality. He decides to collect information on defective shipments through a form he has asked his drivers to complete on arrival at customers' stores. The forms for the first 279 shipments have been turned in. They show the following over the past 8 weeks:

WEEK	NO. OF SHIP-MENTS	NO. OF SHIP-MENTS WITH DEFECTS	REASON FOR DEFECTIVE SHIPMENT			
			INCORRECT BILL OF LADING	INCORRECT TRUCK-LOAD	DAMAGED PRODUCT	TRUCKS LATE
1	23	5	2	2	1	
2	31	8	1	4	1	2
3	28	6	2	3	1	
4	37	11	4	4	1	2
5	35	10	3	4	2	1
6	40	14	5	6	3	
7	41	12	3	5	3	1
8	44	15	4	7	2	2

Even though Daniel increased his capacity by adding more workers to his normal contingent of 30, he knew that for many weeks he exceeded his regular output of 30 shipments per week. A review of his turnover over the past 8 weeks shows the following:

WEEK	NO. OF NEW HIRES	NO. OF TERMINATIONS	TOTAL NO. OF WORKERS
1	1	0	30
2	2	1	31
3	3	2	32
4	2	0	34
5	2	2	34
6	2	4	32
7	4	1	35
8	3	2	36

a) Develop a scatter diagram using total number of shipments and number of defective shipments. Does there appear to be any relationship?
b) Develop a scatter diagram using the variable "turnover" (number of new hires plus number of terminations) and the number of defective shipments. Does the diagram depict a relationship between the two variables?
c) Develop a Pareto chart for the type of defects that have occurred.
d) Draw a fish-bone chart showing the possible causes of the defective shipments.

••• **6.17**   A recent Gallup poll of 519 adults who flew in the past year found the following number of complaints about flying: cramped seats (45), cost (16), dislike or fear of flying (57), security measures (119), poor service (12), connecting flight problems (8), overcrowded planes (42), late planes/waits (57), food (7), lost luggage (7), and other (51).
a) What percentage of those surveyed found nothing they disliked?
b) Draw a Pareto chart summarizing these responses. Include the "no complaints" group.
c) Use the "four Ms" method to create a fish-bone diagram for the 10 specific categories of dislikes (exclude "other" and "no complaints").
d) If you were managing an airline, what two or three specific issues would you tackle to improve customer service? Why?

Christophe Testi/Shutterstock

Problems **6.18–6.20** *are available in* MyOMLab.

Problem 6.21 (available in MyOMLab**) relates to** TQM in Services

CASE STUDIES

Southwestern University: (C)*

The popularity of Southwestern University's football program under its new coach Phil Flamm surged in each of the 5 years since his arrival at the Stephenville, Texas, college. (See Southwestern University: (A) in Chapter 3 and (B) in Chapter 4.) With a football stadium close to maxing out at 54,000 seats and a vocal coach pushing for a new stadium, SWU president Joel Wisner faced some difficult decisions. After a phenomenal upset victory over its archrival, the University of Texas, at the homecoming game in the fall, Dr. Wisner was not as happy as one would think. Instead of ecstatic alumni, students, and faculty, all Wisner heard were complaints. "The lines at the concession stands were too long"; "Parking was harder to find and farther away than in the old days" (that is, before the team won regularly); "Seats weren't comfortable"; "Traffic was backed up halfway to Dallas"; and

on and on. "A college president just can't win," muttered Wisner to himself.

At his staff meeting the following Monday, Wisner turned to his VP of administration, Leslie Gardner. "I wish you would take care of these football complaints, Leslie," he said. "See what the *real* problems are and let me know how you've resolved them." Gardner wasn't surprised at the request. "I've already got a handle on it, Joel," she replied. "We've been randomly surveying 50 fans per game for the past year to see what's on their minds. It's all part of my campuswide TQM effort. Let me tally things up and I'll get back to you in a week."

When she returned to her office, Gardner pulled out the file her assistant had compiled (see Table 6.6). "There's a lot of information here," she thought.

| **TABLE 6.6** | Fan Satisfaction Survey Results (*N* = 250) |

		OVERALL GRADE				
		A	B	C	D	F
Game Day	A. Parking	90	105	45	5	5
	B. Traffic	50	85	48	52	15
	C. Seating	45	30	115	35	25
	D. Entertainment	160	35	26	10	19
	E. Printed Program	66	34	98	22	30
Tickets	A. Pricing	105	104	16	15	10
	B. Season Ticket Plans	75	80	54	41	0
Concessions	A. Prices	16	116	58	58	2
	B. Selection of Foods	155	60	24	11	0
	C. Speed of Service	35	45	46	48	76
Respondents						
Alumnus	113					
Student	83					
Faculty/Staff	16					
None of the above	38					

Open-Ended Comments on Survey Cards:

Parking a mess	More hot dog stands	Put in bigger seats	My company will buy a skybox—
Add a skybox	Seats are all metal	Friendly ushers	build it!
Get better cheerleaders	Need skyboxes	Need better seats	Programs overpriced
Double the parking attendants	Seats stink	Expand parking lots	Want softer seats
Everything is okay	Go SWU!	Hate the bleacher seats	Beat those Longhorns!
Too crowded	Lines are awful	Hot dogs cold	I'll pay for a skybox
Seats too narrow	Seats are uncomfortable	$3 for a coffee? No way!	Seats too small
Great food	I will pay more for better view	Get some skyboxes	Band was terrific
Phil F. for President!	Get a new stadium	Love the new uniforms	Love Phil Flamm
I smelled drugs being smoked	Student dress code needed	Took an hour to park	Everything is great
Stadium is ancient	I want cushioned seats	Coach is terrific	Build new stadium
Seats are like rocks	Not enough police	More water fountains	Move games to Dallas
Not enough cops for traffic	Students too rowdy	Better seats	No complaints
Game starts too late	Parking terrible	Seats not comfy	Dirty bathroom
Hire more traffic cops	Toilets weren't clean	Bigger parking lot	
Need new band	Not enough handicap spots in lot	I'm too old for bench seats	
Great!	Well done, SWU	Cold coffee served at game	

Discussion Questions

1. Using at least two different quality tools, analyze the data and present your conclusions.
2. How could the survey have been more useful?
3. What is the next step?

*This integrated case study runs throughout the text. Other issues facing Southwestern's football stadium include: (A) Managing the renovation project (Chapter 3); (B) Forecasting game attendance (Chapter 4); (D) Break-even analysis of food services (Supplement 7 Web site); (E) Locating the new stadium (Chapter 8 Web site); (F) Inventory planning of football programs (Chapter 12 Web site); and (G) Scheduling of campus security officers/staff for game days (Chapter 13 Web site).

The Culture of Quality at Arnold Palmer Hospital

Video Case

Founded in 1989, Arnold Palmer Hospital is one of the largest hospitals for women and children in the U.S., with 431 beds in two facilities totaling 676,000 square feet. Located in downtown Orlando, Florida, and named after its famed golf benefactor, the hospital, with more than 2,000 employees, serves an 18-county area in central Florida and is the only Level 1 trauma center for children in that region. Arnold Palmer Hospital provides a broad range of medical services including neonatal and pediatric intensive care, pediatric oncology and cardiology, care for high-risk pregnancies, and maternal intensive care.

The Issue of Assessing Quality Health Care

Quality health care is a goal all hospitals profess, but Arnold Palmer Hospital has actually developed comprehensive and scientific means of asking customers to judge the quality of care they receive. Participating in a national benchmark comparison against other hospitals, Arnold Palmer Hospital consistently scores in the top 10% in overall patient satisfaction. Executive Director Kathy Swanson states, "Hospitals in this area will be distinguished largely on the basis of their customer satisfaction. We must have accurate information about how our patients and their families judge the quality of our care, so I follow the questionnaire results daily. The in-depth survey helps me and others on my team to gain quick knowledge from patient feedback." Arnold Palmer Hospital employees are empowered to provide gifts in value up to $200 to patients who find reason to complain about any hospital service such as food, courtesy, responsiveness, or cleanliness.

Swanson doesn't focus just on the customer surveys, which are mailed to patients one week after discharge, but also on a variety of internal measures. These measures usually start at the grassroots level, where the staff sees a problem and develops ways to track performance. The hospital's longstanding philosophy supports the concept that each patient is important and respected as a person. That patient has the right to comprehensive, compassionate family-centered health care provided by a knowledgeable physician-directed team.

Some of the measures Swanson carefully monitors for continuous improvement are morbidity, infection rates, readmission rates, costs per case, and length of stays. The tools she uses daily include Pareto charts, flowcharts, and process charts, in addition to benchmarking against hospitals both nationally and in the southeast region.

The result of all of these efforts has been a quality culture as manifested in Arnold Palmer's high ranking in patient satisfaction and one of the highest survival rates of critically ill babies.

Discussion Questions*

1. Why is it important for Arnold Palmer Hospital to get a patient's assessment of health care quality? Does the patient have the expertise to judge the health care she receives?
2. How would you build a culture of quality in an organization such as Arnold Palmer Hospital?
3. What techniques does Arnold Palmer Hospital practice in its drive for quality and continuous improvement?
4. Develop a fish-bone diagram illustrating the quality variables for a patient who just gave birth at Arnold Palmer Hospital (or any other hospital).

*You may wish to view the video that accompanies this case before answering these questions.

Quality Counts at Alaska Airlines

Video Case

Alaska Airlines, with nearly 100 destinations, including regular service to Alaska, Hawaii, Canada, and Mexico, is the seventh-largest U.S. carrier. Alaska Airlines has won the J.D. Power and Associates Award for highest customer satisfaction in the industry for eight years in a row while being the number one on-time airline for five years in a row.

Management's unwavering commitment to quality has driven much of the firm's success and generated an extremely loyal customer base. Executive V.P. Ben Minicucci exclaims, "We have rewritten our DNA." Building an organization that can achieve quality is a demanding task, and the management at Alaska Airlines accepted the challenge. This is a highly participative quality culture, reinforced by leadership training, constant process improvement, comprehensive metrics, and frequent review of those metrics. The usual training of flight crews and pilots is supplemented with

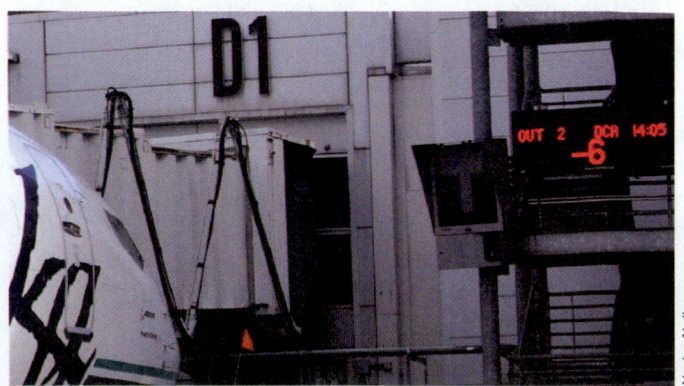

ELEMENTS	WEIGHTING	PERFORMANCE	SCORE	BONUS POINTS	TOTAL	GRADE
Process Compliance	20		15		15	B
Staffing	15		15	5	20	A+
MAP Rate (for bags)	20		15		15	B
Delays	10		9		9	A
Time to Carousel (total weight = 10)			10		10	A
Percentage of flights scanned	2	98.7%				
Percentage of bags scanned	2	70.9%				
20 Minutes all bags dropped (% compliance)	4	92.5%				
Outliers (>25mins)	2	2				
Safety Compliance	15		15	5	20	A+
Quality Compliance	10		10		10	A
Total - 100%	**100**		**89**	**10**	**99**	**A+**

Time to Carousel

Points	2	1.5	1	0
Percentage of flights scanned	95%–100%	90%–94.9%	89.9%–85%	< 84.9%

Points	2	0
Percentage of bags scanned	60% or above	≤ 59.9%

Points	0	4
Last bag percent compliance	Below 89.9%	90%–100%

Points	0	1	1.5	2
Last Bag >25 min. (Outliers)	20	15	10	5

classroom training in areas such as Six Sigma. Over 200 managers have obtained Six Sigma Green Belt certification.

Alaska collects more than 100 quality and performance metrics every day. For example, the accompanying picture tells the crew that it has 6 minutes to close the door and back away from the gate to meet the "time to pushback" target. Operations personnel review each airport hub's performance scorecard daily and the overall operations scorecard weekly. As Director of System Operations Control, Wayne Newton proclaims, "If it is not measured, it is not managed." The focus is on identifying problem areas or trends, determining causes, and working on preventive measures.

Within the operations function there are numerous detailed input metrics for station operations (such as the percentage of time that hoses are free of twists, the ground power cord is stowed, and no vehicles are parked in prohibited zones). Management operates under the assumption that if all the detailed input metrics are acceptable, the major key performance indicators, such as Alaska's on-time performance and 20-minute luggage guarantee, will automatically score well.

The accompanying table displays a sample monthly scorecard for Alaska's ground crew provider in Seattle. The major evaluation categories include process compliance, staffing (degree that crew members are available when needed), MAP rate (minimum acceptable performance for mishandled bags), delays, time to carousel, safety compliance, and quality compliance. The quality compliance category alone tracks 64 detailed input metrics using approximately 30,000 monthly observations. Each of the major categories on the scorecard has an importance weight, and the provider is assigned a weighted average score at the end of each month. The contract with the supplier provides for up to a 3.7% bonus for outstanding performance and as much as a 5.0%

penalty for poor performance. The provider's line workers receive a portion of the bonus when top scores are achieved.

As a company known for outstanding customer service, service recovery efforts represent a necessary area of emphasis. When things go wrong, employees mobilize to first communicate with, and in many cases compensate, affected customers. "It doesn't matter if it's not our fault," says Minicucci. Front-line workers are empowered with a "toolkit" of options to offer to inconvenienced customers, including the ability to provide up to 5,000 frequent flyer miles and/or vouchers for meals, hotels, luggage, and tickets. When an Alaska flight had to make an emergency landing in Eugene, Oregon, due to a malfunctioning oven, passengers were immediately texted with information about what happened and why, and they were told that a replacement plane would be arriving within one hour. Within that hour, an apology letter along with a $450 ticket voucher were already in the mail to each passenger's home. No customer complaints subsequently appeared on Twitter or Facebook. It's no wonder why Alaska's customers return again and again.

Discussion Questions*

1. What are some ways that Alaska can ensure that quality and performance metric standards are met when the company outsources its ground operations to a contract provider?
2. Identify several quality metrics, in addition to those identified earlier, that you think Alaska tracks or should be tracking.
3. Think about a previous problem that you had when flying, for example, a late flight, a missed connection, or lost luggage. How, if at all, did the airline respond? Did the airline adequately address your situation? If not, what else should they

have done? Did your experience affect your desire (positively or negative) to fly with that airline in the future?

4. See the accompanying table. The contractor received a perfect Time to Carousel score of 10 total points, even though its performance was not "perfect." How many total points would the contractor have received with the following performance

scores: 93.2% of flights scanned, 63.5% of bags scanned, 89.6% of all bags dropped within 20 minutes, and 15 bags arriving longer than 25 minutes?

*You may wish to view the video that accompanies this case before addressing these questions.

Quality at the Ritz-Carlton Hotel Company

Video Case

Ritz-Carlton. The name alone evokes images of luxury and quality. As the first hotel company to win the Malcolm Baldrige National Quality Award, the Ritz treats quality as if it is the heartbeat of the company. This means a daily commitment to meeting customer expectations and making sure that each hotel is free of any deficiency.

In the hotel industry, quality can be hard to quantify. Guests do not purchase a product when they stay at the Ritz: They buy an experience. Thus, creating the right combination of elements to make the experience stand out is the challenge and goal of every employee, from maintenance to management.

Before applying for the Baldrige Award, company management undertook a rigorous self-examination of its operations in an attempt to measure and quantify quality. Nineteen processes were studied, including room service delivery, guest reservation and registration, message delivery, and breakfast service. This period of self-study included statistical measurement of process work flows and cycle times for areas ranging from room service delivery times and reservations to valet parking and housekeeping efficiency. The results were used to develop performance benchmarks against which future activity could be measured.

With specific, quantifiable targets in place, Ritz-Carlton managers and employees now focus on continuous improvement. The goal is 100% customer satisfaction: If a guest's experience does not meet expectations, the Ritz-Carlton risks losing that guest to competition.

One way the company has put more meaning behind its quality efforts is to organize its employees into "self-directed" work teams. Employee teams determine work scheduling, what work needs to be done, and what to do about quality problems in their own areas. In order to see the relationship of their specific area to the overall goals, employees are also given the opportunity to take additional training in hotel operations. Ritz-Carlton believes that a more educated and informed employee is in a better position to make decisions in the best interest of the organization.

Discussion Questions*

1. In what ways could the Ritz-Carlton monitor its success in achieving quality?
2. Many companies say that their goal is to provide quality products or services. What actions might you expect from a company that intends quality to be more than a slogan or buzzword?
3. Why might it cost the Ritz-Carlton less to "do things right" the first time?
4. How could control charts, Pareto diagrams, and cause-and-effect diagrams be used to identify quality problems at a hotel?
5. What are some nonfinancial measures of customer satisfaction that might be used by the Ritz-Carlton?

*You may wish to view the video that accompanies this case before addressing these questions.

Source: Adapted from C. T. Horngren, S. M. Datar, and G. Foster, *Cost Accounting*, 15th ed. (Upper Saddle River, NJ: Prentice Hall, 2014).

• **Additional Case Study:** Visit MyOMLab for this free case study:
Westover Electrical, Inc.: This electric motor manufacturer has a large log of defects in its wiring process.

Endnotes

1. Philip B. Crosby, *Quality Is Free* (New York: McGraw-Hill, 1979). Further, J. M. Juran states, in his book *Juran on Quality by Design* (The Free Press 1992, p. 119), that costs of poor quality "are huge, but the amounts are not known with precision. In most companies the accounting system provides only a minority of the information needed to quantify this cost of poor quality. It takes a great deal of time and effort to extend the accounting system so as to provide full coverage."

2. To train employees in how to improve quality and its relationship to customers, there are three other key players in the Six Sigma program: Master Black Belts, Black Belts, and Green Belts.

3. "The Straining of Quality," *The Economist* (January 14, 1995): 55. We also see that this is one of the strengths of Southwest Airlines, which offers bare-bones domestic service but whose friendly and humorous employees help it obtain number-one ranking for quality. (See *Fortune* [March 6, 2006]: 65–69.)

Chapter 6 *Rapid* **Review**

Main Heading	Review Material	MyOMLab
QUALITY AND STRATEGY (pp. 216–217)	Managing quality helps build successful strategies of differentiation, low cost, and *response*. Two ways that quality improves profitability are: ■ *Sales gains* via improved response, price flexibility, increased market share, and/or improved reputation ■ *Reduced costs* via increased productivity, lower rework and scrap costs, and/or lower warranty costs	Concept Questions: 1.1–1.4 **VIDEO 6.1** The Culture and Quality at Arnold Palmer Hospital
DEFINING QUALITY (pp. 217–219)	An operations manager's objective is to build a total quality management system that identifies and satisfies customer needs. ■ **Quality**—The ability of a product or service to meet customer needs. The American Society for Quality (ASQ) defines quality as "the totality of features and characteristics of a product or service that bears on its ability to satisfy stated or implied needs." The two most well-known quality awards are: ■ *U.S.*: Malcolm Baldrige National Quality Award, named after a former secretary of commerce ■ *Japan*: Deming Prize, named after an American, Dr. W. Edwards Deming ■ **ISO 9000**—A set of quality standards developed by the International Organization for Standardization (ISO). ISO 9000 is the only quality standard with international recognition. To do business globally, being listed in the ISO directory is critical. ■ **Cost of quality (COQ)**—The cost of doing things wrong; that is, the price of nonconformance. The four major categories of costs associated with quality are *prevention costs, appraisal costs, internal failure costs,* and *external failure costs.* Four leaders in the field of quality management are W. Edwards Deming, Joseph M. Juran, Armand Feigenbaum, and Philip B. Crosby.	Concept Questions: 2.1–2.4
TOTAL QUALITY MANAGEMENT (pp. 219–226)	■ **Total quality management (TQM)**—Management of an entire organization so that it excels in all aspects of products and services that are important to the customer. Seven concepts for an effective TQM program are (1) continuous improvement, (2) Six Sigma, (3) employee empowerment, (4) benchmarking, (5) just-in-time (JIT), (6) Taguchi concepts, and (7) knowledge of TQM tools. ■ **PDCA**—A continuous improvement model that involves four stages: plan, do, check, and act. The Japanese use the word *kaizen* to describe the ongoing process of unending improvement—the setting and achieving of ever-higher goals. ■ **Six Sigma**—A program to save time, improve quality, and lower costs. In a statistical sense, Six Sigma describes a process, product, or service with an extremely high capability—99.9997% accuracy, or 3.4 defects per million. ■ **Employee empowerment**—Enlarging employee jobs so that the added responsibility and authority are moved to the lowest level possible in the organization. Business literature suggests that some 85% of quality problems have to do with materials and processes, not with employee performance. ■ **Quality circle**—A group of employees meeting regularly with a facilitator to solve work-related problems in their work area. ■ **Benchmarking**—Selecting a demonstrated standard of performance that represents the very best performance for a process or an activity. The philosophy behind just-in-time (JIT) involves continuing improvement and enforced problem solving. JIT systems are designed to produce or deliver goods just as they are needed. ■ **Quality robust**—Products that are consistently built to meet customer needs, despite adverse conditions in the production process. ■ **Target-oriented quality**—A philosophy of continuous improvement to bring the product exactly on target. ■ **Quality loss function (QLF)**—A mathematical function that identifies all costs connected with poor quality and shows how these costs increase as output moves away from the target value.	Concept Questions: 3.1–3.4

Main Heading	Review Material	MyOMLab
TOOLS OF TQM (pp. 226–230)	TQM tools that generate ideas include the *check sheet* (organized method of recording data), *scatter diagram* (graph of the value of one variable vs. another variable), and *cause-and-effect diagram*. Tools for organizing the data are the *Pareto chart* and *flowchart*. Tools for identifying problems are the *histogram* (distribution showing the frequency of occurrences of a variable) and *statistical process control chart*. ■ **Cause-and-effect diagram**—A schematic technique used to discover possible locations of quality problems. (Also called an Ishikawa diagram or a fish-bone chart.) The 4 *M*s (material, machinery/equipment, manpower, and methods) may be broad "causes." ■ **Pareto chart**—A graphic that identifies the few critical items as opposed to many less important ones. ■ **Flowchart**—A block diagram that graphically describes a process or system. ■ **Statistical process control (SPC)**—A process used to monitor standards, make measurements, and take corrective action as a product or service is being produced. ■ **Control chart**—A graphic presentation of process data over time, with predetermined control limits.	Concept Questions: 4.1–4.4 Problems: 6.1, 6.3, 6.5, 6.8–6.14, 6.16–6.20 **ACTIVE MODEL 6.1** Virtual Office Hours for Solved Problem: 6.1
THE ROLE OF INSPECTION (pp. 230–233)	■ **Inspection**—A means of ensuring that an operation is producing at the quality level expected. ■ **Source inspection**—Controlling or monitoring at the point of production or purchase: at the source. ■ **Poka-yoke**—Literally translated, "mistake proofing"; it has come to mean a device or technique that ensures the production of a good unit every time. ■ **Checklist**—A type of poka-yoke that lists the steps needed to ensure consistency and completeness in a task. ■ **Attribute inspection**—An inspection that classifies items as being either good or defective. ■ **Variable inspection**—Classifications of inspected items as falling on a continuum scale, such as dimension, size, or strength.	Concept Questions: 5.1–5.4 **VIDEO 6.2** Quality Counts at Alaska Airlines
TQM IN SERVICES (pp. 233–235)	Determinants of service quality: reliability, responsiveness, competence, access, courtesy, communication, credibility, security, understanding/knowing the customer, and tangibles. ■ **Service recovery**—Training and empowering frontline workers to solve a problem immediately. ■ **SERVQUAL**—A popular measurement scale for service quality that compares service expectations with service performance.	Concept Questions: 6.1–6.4 Problem: 6.21 **VIDEO 6.3** TQM at Ritz-Carlton Hotels

Self Test

■ **Before taking the self-test,** refer to the learning objectives listed at the beginning of the chapter and the key terms listed at the end of the chapter.

LO 6.1 In this chapter, *quality* is defined as:
a) the degree of excellence at an acceptable price and the control of variability at an acceptable cost.
b) how well a product fits patterns of consumer preferences.
c) the totality of features and characteristics of a product or service that bears on its ability to satisfy stated or implied needs.
d) being impossible to define, but you know what it is.

LO 6.2 ISO 9000 is an international standard that addresses _____.

LO 6.3 If 1 million passengers pass through the Jacksonville Airport with checked baggage each year, a successful Six Sigma program for baggage handling would result in how many passengers with misplaced luggage?
a) 3.4
b) 6.0
c) 34
d) 2,700
e) 6 times the monthly standard deviation of passengers

LO 6.4 The process of identifying other organizations that are best at some facet of your operations and then modeling your organization after them is known as:
a) continuous improvement.
b) employee empowerment.
c) benchmarking.
d) copycatting.
e) patent infringement.

LO 6.5 The Taguchi method includes all except which of the following major concepts?
a) Employee involvement
b) Remove the effects of adverse conditions
c) Quality loss function
d) Target specifications

LO 6.6 The seven tools of total quality management are _____, _____, _____, _____, _____, _____, and _____.

Answers: LO 6.1. c; LO 6.2. quality management systems; LO 6.3. a; LO 6.4. c; LO 6.5. a; LO 6.6. check sheets, scatter diagrams, cause-and-effect diagrams, Pareto charts, flowcharts, histograms, SPC charts.

Statistical Process Control

SUPPLEMENT OUTLINE

◆ Statistical Process Control (SPC) *246* ◆ Process Capability *260*
◆ Acceptance Sampling *262*

Alaska Airlines

Alaska Airlines

LEARNING OBJECTIVES

LO S6.1 *Explain* the purpose of a control chart 247

LO S6.2 *Explain* the role of the central limit theorem in SPC 248

LO S6.3 *Build* $\bar{x}$-charts and *R*-charts 250

LO S6.4 *List* the five steps involved in building control charts 254

LO S6.5 *Build* *p*-charts and *c*-charts 256

LO S6.6 *Explain* process capability and compute C_p and C_{pk} 260

LO S6.7 *Explain* acceptance sampling 262

As part of its statistical process control system, Flowers Bakery, in Georgia, uses a digital camera to inspect just-baked sandwich buns as they move along the production line. Items that don't measure up in terms of color, shape, seed distribution, or size are identified and removed automatically from the conveyor.

Georgia Tech

Statistical Process Control (SPC)

In this supplement, we address statistical process control—the same techniques used at BetzDearborn, at Arnold Palmer Hospital, at GE, and at Southwest Airlines to achieve quality standards. Statistical process control (SPC) is the application of statistical techniques to ensure that processes meet standards. All processes are subject to a certain degree of variability. While studying process data in the 1920s, Walter Shewhart of Bell Laboratories made the distinction between the common (natural) and special (assignable) causes of variation. He developed a simple but powerful tool to separate the two—the control chart.

A process is said to be operating *in statistical control* when the only source of variation is common (natural) causes. The process must first be brought into statistical control by detecting and eliminating special (assignable) causes of variation.[1] Then its performance is predictable, and its ability to meet customer expectations can be assessed. The *objective* of a process control system is to *provide a statistical signal when assignable causes of variation are present*. Such a signal can quicken appropriate action to eliminate assignable causes.

Natural Variations   Natural variations affect almost every process and are to be expected. Natural variations are the many sources of variation that occur within a process, even one that is in statistical control. Natural variations form a pattern that can be described as a *distribution*.

As long as the distribution (output measurements) remains within specified limits, the process is said to be "in control," and natural variations are tolerated.

Statistical process control (SPC)

A process used to monitor standards by taking measurements and corrective action as a product or service is being produced.

Control chart

A graphical presentation of process data over time.

Natural variations

Variability that affects every production process to some degree and is to be expected; also known as common cause.

(a) Samples of the product, say five boxes of cereal taken off the filling machine line, vary from one another in weight.

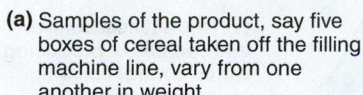

Each of these represents one sample of five boxes of cereal.

(b) After enough sample means are taken from a stable process, they form a pattern called a *distribution*.

The solid line represents the distribution.

(c) There are many types of distributions, including the normal (bell-shaped) distribution, but distributions do differ in terms of central tendency (mean), standard deviation or variance, and shape.

(d) If only natural causes of variation are present, the output of a process forms a distribution that is stable over time and is predictable.

(e) If assignable causes of variation are present, the process output is not stable over time and is not predictable. That is, when causes that are not an expected part of the process occur, the samples will yield unexpected distributions that vary by central tendency, standard deviation, and shape.

Figure **S6.1**

Natural and Assignable Variation

Assignable Variations   Assignable variation in a process can be traced to a specific reason. Factors such as machine wear, misadjusted equipment, fatigued or untrained workers, or new batches of raw material are all potential sources of assignable variations.

Natural and assignable variations distinguish two tasks for the operations manager. The first is to *ensure that the process is capable* of operating under control with only natural variation. The second is, of course, to *identify and eliminate assignable variations* so that the processes will remain under control.

Assignable variation
Variation in a production process that can be traced to specific causes.

Samples   Because of natural and assignable variation, statistical process control uses averages of small samples (often of four to eight items) as opposed to data on individual parts. Individual pieces tend to be too erratic to make trends quickly visible.

Figure S6.1 provides a detailed look at the important steps in determining process variation. The horizontal scale can be weight (as in the number of ounces in boxes of cereal) or length (as in fence posts) or any physical measure. The vertical scale is frequency. The samples of five boxes of cereal in Figure S6.1 **(a)** are weighed, **(b)** form a distribution, and **(c)** can vary. The distributions formed in **(b)** and **(c)** will fall in a predictable pattern **(d)** if only natural variation is present. If assignable causes of variation are present, then we can expect either the mean to vary or the dispersion to vary, as is the case in **(e)**.

Control Charts   The process of building control charts is based on the concepts presented in Figure S6.2. This figure shows three distributions that are the result of outputs from three types of processes. We plot small samples and then examine characteristics of the resulting data to see if the process is within "control limits." The purpose of control charts is to help distinguish between natural variations and variations due to assignable causes. As seen in Figure S6.2, a process is **(a)** in control *and the process is capable of producing within established control limits,* **(b)** in control *but the process is not capable of producing within established*

LO S6.1 *Explain* the purpose of a control chart

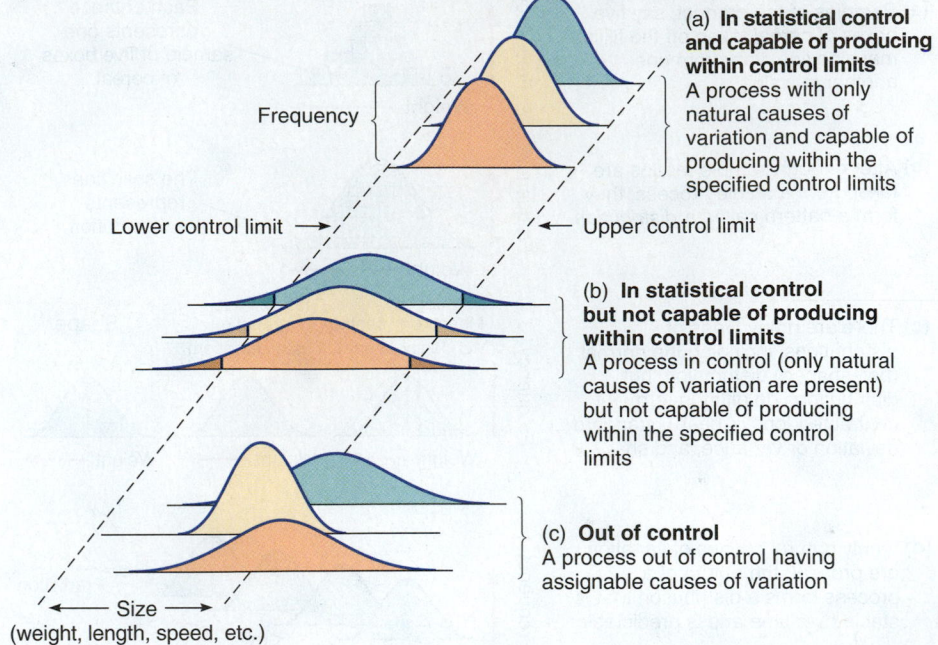

(a) **In statistical control and capable of producing within control limits**
A process with only natural causes of variation and capable of producing within the specified control limits

Frequency

Lower control limit →   ← Upper control limit

(b) **In statistical control but not capable of producing within control limits**
A process in control (only natural causes of variation are present) but not capable of producing within the specified control limits

(c) **Out of control**
A process out of control having assignable causes of variation

← Size →
(weight, length, speed, etc.)

limits, or **(c)** out of control. We now look at ways to build control charts that help the operations manager keep a process under control.

Control Charts for Variables

The variables of interest here are those that have continuous dimensions. They have an infinite number of possibilities. Examples are weight, speed, length, or strength. Control charts for the mean, $\bar{x}$ or x-bar, and the range, R, are used to monitor processes that have continuous dimensions. The $\bar{x}$-chart tells us whether changes have occurred in the central tendency (the mean, in this case) of a process. These changes might be due to such factors as tool wear, a gradual increase in temperature, a different method used on the second shift, or new and stronger materials. The *R-chart* values indicate that a gain or loss in dispersion has occurred. Such a change may be due to worn bearings, a loose tool, an erratic flow of lubricants to a machine, or to sloppiness on the part of a machine operator. The two types of charts go hand in hand when monitoring variables because they measure the two critical parameters: central tendency and dispersion.

The Central Limit Theorem

The theoretical foundation for $\bar{x}$-charts is the central limit theorem. This theorem states that regardless of the distribution of the population, the distribution of $\bar{x}$s (each of which is a mean of a sample drawn from the population) will tend to follow a normal curve as the number of samples increases. Fortunately, even if each sample (n) is fairly small (say, 4 or 5), the distributions of the averages will still roughly follow a normal curve. The theorem also states that: (1) the mean of the distribution of the $\bar{x}$s (called $\bar{\bar{x}}$) will equal the mean of the overall population (called μ); and (2) the standard deviation of the *sampling distribution*, $\sigma_{\bar{x}}$, will be the *population (process) standard deviation*, divided by the square root of the sample size, n. In other words:[2]

$$\bar{\bar{x}} = \mu \tag{S6-1}$$

and

$$\sigma_{\bar{x}} = \frac{\sigma}{\sqrt{n}} \tag{S6-2}$$

$\bar{x}$-chart

A quality control chart for variables that indicates when changes occur in the central tendency of a production process.

R-chart

A control chart that tracks the "range" within a sample; it indicates that a gain or loss in uniformity has occurred in dispersion of a production process.

Central limit theorem

The theoretical foundation for $\bar{x}$-charts, which states that regardless of the distribution of the population of all parts or services, the distribution of $\bar{x}$s tends to follow a normal curve as the number of samples increases.

LO S6.2 *Explain* the role of the central limit theorem in SPC

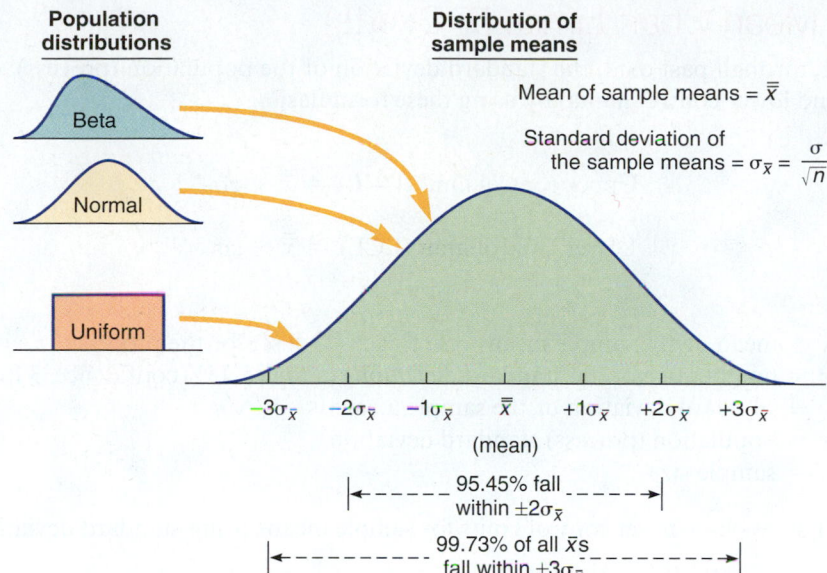

Figure **S6.3**

The Relationship Between Population and Sampling Distributions

Even though the population distributions will differ (e.g., normal, beta, uniform), each with its own mean (μ) and standard deviation (σ), the distribution of sample means always approaches a normal distribution.

Figure S6.3 shows three possible population distributions, each with its own mean, μ, and standard deviation, σ. If a series of random samples ($\bar{x}_1$, $\bar{x}_2$, $\bar{x}_3$, $\bar{x}_4$, and so on), each of size n, is drawn from any population distribution (which could be normal, beta, uniform, and so on), the resulting distribution of $\bar{x}_i$s will approximate a normal distribution (see Figure S6.3).

Moreover, the sampling distribution, as is shown in Figure S6.4(a), will have less variability than the process distribution. Because the sampling distribution is normal, we can state that:

- 95.45% of the time, the sample averages will fall within $\pm 2\sigma_{\bar{x}}$ if the process has only natural variations.
- 99.73% of the time, the sample averages will fall within $\pm 3\sigma_{\bar{x}}$ if the process has only natural variations.

If a point on the control chart falls outside of the $\pm 3\sigma_{\bar{x}}$ control limits, then we are 99.73% sure the process has changed. Figure S6.4(b) shows that as the sample size increases, the sampling distribution becomes narrower. So the sample statistic is closer to the true value of the population for larger sample sizes. This is the theory behind control charts.

Figure **S6.4**

The Sampling Distribution of Means Is Normal

The process distribution from which the sample was drawn was also normal, but it could have been any distribution.

Setting Mean Chart Limits ($\bar{x}$-Charts)

If we know, through past data, the standard deviation of the population (process), σ, we can set upper and lower control limits[3] by using these formulas:

$$\text{Upper control limit (UCL)} = \bar{\bar{x}} + z\sigma_{\bar{x}} \qquad \text{(S6-3)}$$

$$\text{Lower control limit (LCL)} = \bar{\bar{x}} - z\sigma_{\bar{x}} \qquad \text{(S6-4)}$$

LO S6.3 *Build $\bar{x}$-charts and R-charts*

where

$\bar{\bar{x}}$ = mean of the sample means or a target value set for the process
z = number of normal standard deviations (2 for 95.45% confidence, 3 for 99.73%)
$\sigma_{\bar{x}}$ = standard deviation of the sample means = $\sigma/\sqrt{n}$
σ = population (process) standard deviation
n = sample size

Example S1 shows how to set control limits for sample means using standard deviations.

Example S1

SETTING CONTROL LIMITS USING SAMPLES

The weights of boxes of Oat Flakes within a large production lot are sampled each hour. Managers want to set control limits that include 99.73% of the sample means.

APPROACH ▶ Randomly select and weigh nine ($n = 9$) boxes each hour. Then find the overall mean and use Equations (S6-3) and (S6-4) to compute the control limits. Here are the nine boxes chosen for Hour 1:

| Oat Flakes 17 oz. | Oat Flakes 13 oz. | Oat Flakes 16 oz. | Oat Flakes 18 oz. | Oat Flakes 17 oz. | Oat Flakes 16 oz. | Oat Flakes 15 oz. | Oat Flakes 17 oz. | Oat Flakes 16 oz. |

SOLUTION ▶

$$\text{The average weight in the first hourly sample} = \frac{17 + 13 + 16 + 18 + 17 + 16 + 15 + 17 + 16}{9}$$

$$= 16.1 \text{ ounces.}$$

Also, the *population (process)* standard deviation (σ) is known to be 1 ounce. We do not show each of the boxes randomly selected in hours 2 through 12, but here are all 12 hourly samples:

WEIGHT OF SAMPLE		WEIGHT OF SAMPLE		WEIGHT OF SAMPLE	
HOUR	(AVG. OF 9 BOXES)	HOUR	(AVG. OF 9 BOXES)	HOUR	(AVG. OF 9 BOXES)
1	16.1	5	16.5	9	16.3
2	16.8	6	16.4	10	14.8
3	15.5	7	15.2	11	14.2
4	16.5	8	16.4	12	17.3

The average mean $\bar{\bar{x}}$ of the 12 samples is calculated to be exactly 16 ounces $\left[\bar{\bar{x}} = \dfrac{\sum\limits_{i=1}^{12} (\text{Avg. of 9 Boxes})}{12} \right]$.

We therefore have $\bar{\bar{x}} = 16$ ounces, $\sigma = 1$ ounce, $n = 9$, and $z = 3$. The control limits are:

$$\text{UCL}_{\bar{x}} = \bar{\bar{x}} + z\sigma_{\bar{x}} = 16 + 3\left(\frac{1}{\sqrt{9}}\right) = 16 + 3\left(\frac{1}{3}\right) = 17 \text{ ounces}$$

$$\text{LCL}_{\bar{x}} = \bar{\bar{x}} - z\sigma_{\bar{x}} = 16 - 3\left(\frac{1}{\sqrt{9}}\right) = 16 - 3\left(\frac{1}{3}\right) = 15 \text{ ounces}$$

The 12 samples are then plotted on the following control chart:

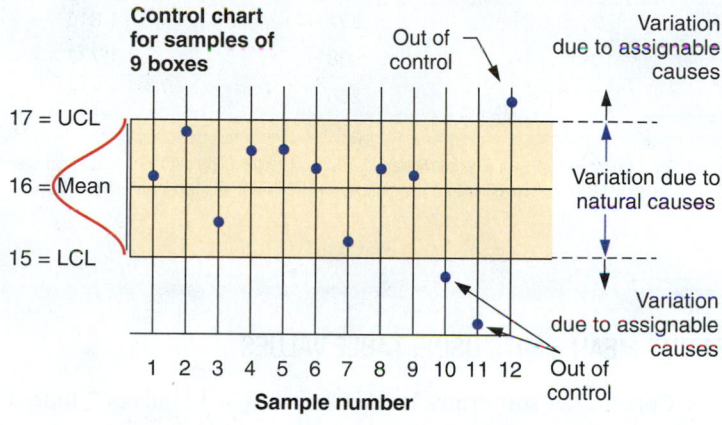

INSIGHT ▶ Because the means of recent sample averages fall outside the upper and lower control limits of 17 and 15, we can conclude that the process is becoming erratic and is *not* in control.

LEARNING EXERCISE ▶ If Oat Flakes's population standard deviation (σ) is 2 (instead of 1), what is your conclusion? [Answer: LCL = 14, UCL = 18; the process would be in control.]

RELATED PROBLEMS ▶ S6.1, S6.2, S6.4, S6.8, S6.10a,b (S6.28 is available in MyOMLab)

ACTIVE MODEL S6.1 This example is further illustrated in Active Model S6.1 in MyOMLab.

EXCEL OM Data File **CH06ExS1.XLS** can be found in MyOMLab.

Because process standard deviations are often not available, we usually calculate control limits based on the average *range* values rather than on standard deviations. Table S6.1 provides the necessary conversion for us to do so. The *range* (R_i) is defined as the difference between the largest and smallest items in one sample. For example, the heaviest box of Oat Flakes in Hour 1 of Example S1 was 18 ounces and the lightest was 13 ounces, so the range for that hour is 5 ounces. We use Table S6.1 and the equations:

$$\text{UCL}_{\bar{x}} = \bar{\bar{x}} + A_2\overline{R} \tag{S6-5}$$

and:

$$\text{LCL}_{\bar{x}} = \bar{\bar{x}} - A_2\overline{R} \tag{S6-6}$$

where $\overline{R} = \dfrac{\displaystyle\sum_{i=1}^{k} R_i}{k}$ = average range of all the samples; R_i = range for sample i

A_2 = value found in Table S6.1 k = total number of samples

$\bar{\bar{x}}$ = mean of the sample means

Example S2 shows how to set control limits for sample means by using Table S6.1 and the average range.

TABLE S6.1	Factors for Computing Control Chart Limits (3 sigma)		
SAMPLE SIZE, n	MEAN FACTOR, A_2	UPPER RANGE, D_4	LOWER RANGE, D_3
2	1.880	3.268	0
3	1.023	2.574	0
4	.729	2.282	0
5	.577	2.115	0
6	.483	2.004	0
7	.419	1.924	0.076
8	.373	1.864	0.136
9	.337	1.816	0.184
10	.308	1.777	0.223
12	.266	1.716	0.284

Source: Reprinted by permission of American Society for Testing Materials. Copyright 1951. Taken from Special Technical Publication 15–C, "Quality Control of Materials," pp. 63 and 72. Copyright ASTM INTERNATIONAL. Reprinted with permission.

Example S2

SETTING MEAN LIMITS USING TABLE VALUES

Super Cola bottles soft drinks labeled "net weight 12 ounces." Indeed, an overall process average of 12 ounces has been found by taking 10 samples, in which each sample contained 5 bottles. The OM team wants to determine the upper and lower control limits for averages in this process.

APPROACH ▶ Super Cola first examines the 10 samples to compute the average range of the process. Here are the data and calculations:

SAMPLE	WEIGHT OF LIGHTEST BOTTLE IN SAMPLE OF $n = 5$	WEIGHT OF HEAVIEST BOTTLE IN SAMPLE OF $n = 5$	RANGE (R_i) = DIFFERENCE BETWEEN THESE TWO
1	11.50	11.72	.22
2	11.97	12.00	.03
3	11.55	12.05	.50
4	12.00	12.20	.20
5	11.95	12.00	.05
6	10.55	10.75	.20
7	12.50	12.75	.25
8	11.00	11.25	.25
9	10.60	11.00	.40
10	11.70	12.10	.40
			$\sum R_i = 2.50$

$$\text{Average Range} = \frac{2.50}{10 \text{ samples}} = .25 \text{ ounces}$$

Now Super Cola applies Equations (S6-5) and (S6-6) and uses the A_2 column of Table S6.1.

SOLUTION ▶ Looking in Table S6.1 for a sample size of 5 in the mean factor A_2 column, we find the value .577. Thus, the upper and lower control chart limits are:

$$\text{UCL}_{\bar{x}} = \bar{\bar{x}} + A_2 \bar{R}$$
$$= 12 + (.577)(.25)$$
$$= 12 + .144$$
$$= 12.144 \text{ ounces}$$

$$LCL_{\bar{x}} = \bar{\bar{x}} - A_2\overline{R}$$

$$= 12 - .144$$

$$= 11.856 \text{ ounces}$$

INSIGHT ▶ The advantage of using this range approach, instead of the standard deviation, is that it is easy to apply and may be less confusing.

LEARNING EXERCISE ▶ If the sample size was $n = 4$ and the average range $= .20$ ounces, what are the revised $UCL_{\bar{x}}$ and $LCL_{\bar{x}}$? [Answer: 12.146, 11.854.]

RELATED PROBLEMS ▶ S6.3a, S6.5, S6.6, S6.7, S6.9, S6.10b,c,d, S6.11, S6.26 (S6.29a, S6.30a, S6.31a, S6.32a, S6.33a are available in MyOMLab)

EXCEL OM Data File **CH06ExS2.xls** can be found in MyOMLab.

Setting Range Chart Limits (*R*-Charts)

In Examples S1 and S2, we determined the upper and lower control limits for the process *average*. In addition to being concerned with the process average, operations managers are interested in the process *dispersion*, or *range*. Even though the process average is under control, the dispersion of the process may not be. For example, something may have worked itself loose in a piece of equipment that fills boxes of Oat Flakes. As a result, the average of the samples may remain the same, but the variation within the samples could be entirely too large. For this reason, operations managers use control charts for ranges to monitor the process variability, as well as control charts for averages, which monitor the process central tendency. The theory behind the control charts for ranges is the same as that for process average control charts. Limits are established that contain ± 3 standard deviations of the distribution for the average range $\overline{R}$. We can use the following equations to set the upper and lower control limits for ranges:

$$UCL_R = D_4\overline{R} \tag{S6-7}$$

$$LCL_R = D_3\overline{R} \tag{S6-8}$$

where

$$UCL_R = \text{upper control chart limit for the range}$$
$$LCL_R = \text{lower control chart limit for the range}$$
$$D_4 \text{ and } D_3 = \text{values from Table S6.1}$$

$\bar{x}$ (mean) Chart

UCL=11.524
$\bar{\bar{x}}$=10.959
LCL=10.394

R (Range) Chart

UCL=0.6943
$\overline{R}$=0.2125
LCL=0

Salmon filets are monitored by Darden Restaurant's SPC software, which includes $\bar{x}$-(mean) charts and *R*-(range) charts. Darden uses average weight as a measure of central tendency for salmon filets. The range is the difference between the heaviest and the lightest filets in each sample. The video case study "Farm to Fork," at the end of this supplement, asks you to interpret these figures.

VIDEO S6.1
Farm to Fork: Quality of Darden Restaurants

Example S3 shows how to set control limits for sample ranges using Table S6.1 and the average range.

Example S3

SETTING RANGE LIMITS USING TABLE VALUES

Roy Clinton's mail-ordering business wants to measure the response time of its operators in taking customer orders over the phone. Clinton lists below the time recorded (in minutes) from five different samples of the ordering process with four customer orders per sample. He wants to determine the upper and lower range control chart limits.

APPROACH ▶ Looking in Table S6.1 for a sample size of 4, he finds that $D_4 = 2.282$ and $D_3 = 0$.

SOLUTION ▶

SAMPLE	OBSERVATIONS (MINUTES)	SAMPLE RANGE (R_i)
1	5, 3, 6, 10	$10 - 3 = 7$
2	7, 5, 3, 5	$7 - 3 = 4$
3	1, 8, 3, 12	$12 - 1 = 11$
4	7, 6, 2, 1	$7 - 1 = 6$
5	3, 15, 6, 12	$15 - 3 = 12$
		$\Sigma R_i = 40$

$$\overline{R} = \frac{40}{5} = 8$$

$$\text{UCL}_R = 2.282(8) = 18.256 \text{ minutes}$$

$$\text{LCL}_R = 0(8) = 0 \text{ minutes}$$

INSIGHT ▶ Computing ranges with Table S6.1 is straightforward and an easy way to evaluate dispersion. No sample ranges are out of control.

LEARNING EXERCISE ▶ Clinton decides to increase the sample size to $n = 6$ (with no change in average range, $\overline{R}$). What are the new UCL_R and LCL_R values? [Answer: 16.032, 0.]

RELATED PROBLEMS ▶ S6.3b, S6.5, S6.6, S6.7, S6.9, S6.10c, S6.11, S6.12, S6.26 (S6.29b, S6.30b, S6.31b, S6.32b, S6.33b are available in MyOMLab)

Using Mean and Range Charts

The normal distribution is defined by two parameters, the *mean* and *standard deviation*. The $\overline{x}$ (mean)-chart and the R-chart mimic these two parameters. The $\overline{x}$-chart is sensitive to shifts in the process mean, whereas the R-chart is sensitive to shifts in the process standard deviation. Consequently, by using both charts we can track changes in the process distribution.

For instance, the samples and the resulting $\overline{x}$-chart in Figure S6.5(a) show the shift in the process mean, but because the dispersion is constant, no change is detected by the R-chart. Conversely, the samples and the $\overline{x}$-chart in Figure S6.5(b) detect no shift (because none is present), but the R-chart does detect the shift in the dispersion. Both charts are required to track the process accurately.

LO S6.4 *List the five steps involved in building control charts*

Steps to Follow When Building Control Charts There are five steps that are generally followed in building $\overline{x}$- and R-charts:

1. Collect 20 to 25 samples, often of $n = 4$ or $n = 5$ observations each, from a stable process, and compute the mean and range of each.
2. Compute the overall means ($\overline{\overline{x}}$ and $\overline{R}$), set appropriate control limits, usually at the 99.73% level, and calculate the preliminary upper and lower control limits. Refer to Table S6.2 for other control limits. *If the process is not currently stable and in control*, use the desired mean, μ, instead of $\overline{\overline{x}}$ to calculate limits.

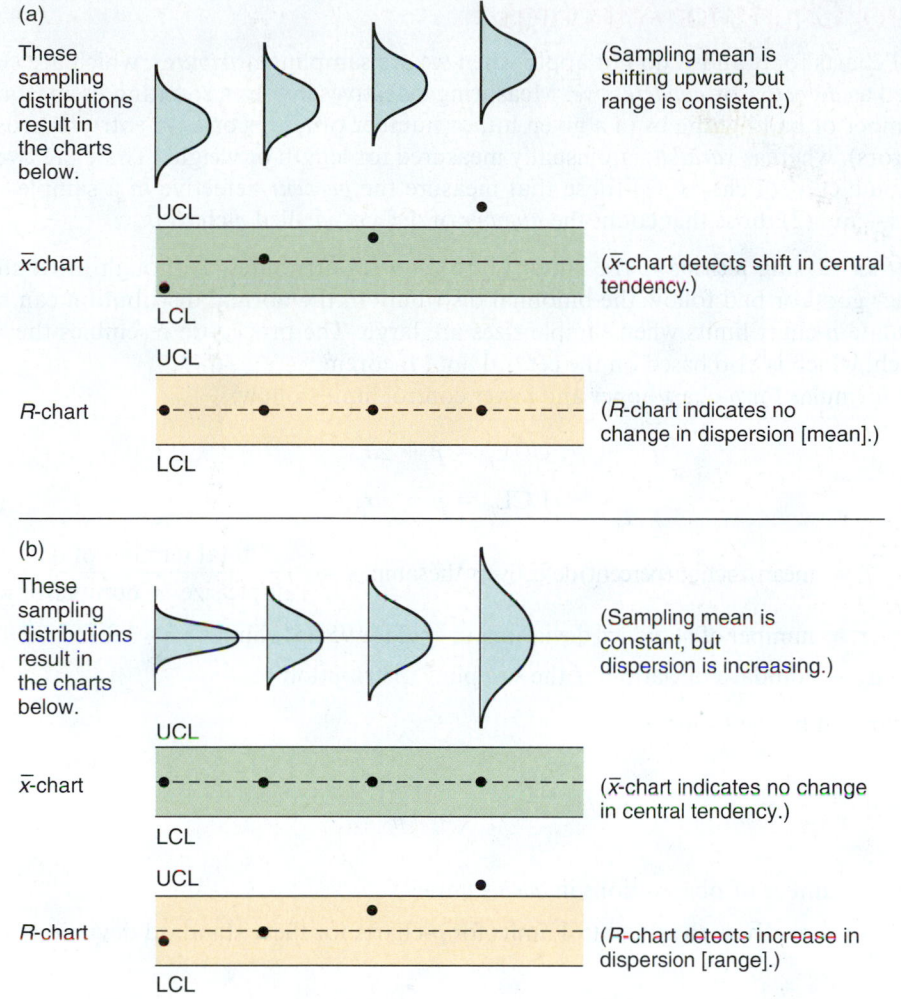

(a)

These sampling distributions result in the charts below.

(Sampling mean is shifting upward, but range is consistent.)

UCL

$\bar{x}$-chart

($\bar{x}$-chart detects shift in central tendency.)

LCL

UCL

R-chart

(R-chart indicates no change in dispersion [mean].)

LCL

(b)

These sampling distributions result in the charts below.

(Sampling mean is constant, but dispersion is increasing.)

UCL

$\bar{x}$-chart

($\bar{x}$-chart indicates no change in central tendency.)

LCL

UCL

R-chart

(R-chart detects increase in dispersion [range].)

LCL

Figure **S6.5**

Mean and Range Charts Complement Each Other by Showing the Mean and Dispersion of the Normal Distribution

♦ STUDENT TIP

Mean ($\bar{x}$) charts are a measure of *central tendency*, while range (R) charts are a measure of *dispersion*. SPC requires both charts for a complete assessment because a sample mean could be out of control while the range is in control and vice versa.

3. Graph the sample means and ranges on their respective control charts, and determine whether they fall outside the acceptable limits.

4. Investigate points or patterns that indicate the process is out of control. Try to assign causes for the variation, address the causes, and then resume the process.

5. Collect additional samples and, if necessary, revalidate the control limits using the new data.

TABLE S6.2

Common z Values

DESIRED CONTROL LIMIT (%)	Z-VALUE (STANDARD DEVIATION REQUIRED FOR DESIRED LEVEL OF CONFIDENCE)
90.0	1.65
95.0	1.96
95.45	2.00
99.0	2.58
99.73	3.00

Donna McWilliam/AP Images

Frito-Lay uses $\bar{x}$ charts to control production quality at critical points in the process. About every 40 minutes, three batches of chips are taken from the conveyor (on the left) and analyzed electronically to get an average salt content, which is plotted on an $\bar{x}$-chart (on the right). Points plotted in the green zone are "in control," while those in the yellow zone are "out of control." The SPC chart is displayed where all production employees can monitor process stability.

Control Charts for Attributes

LO S6.5 *Build p-charts and c-charts*

Control charts for $\bar{x}$ and R do not apply when we are sampling *attributes*, which are typically classified as *defective* or *nondefective*. Measuring defectives involves counting them (for example, number of bad lightbulbs in a given lot, or number of letters or data entry records typed with errors), whereas *variables* are usually measured for length or weight. There are two kinds of attribute control charts: (1) those that measure the *percent* defective in a sample—called *p*-charts—and (2) those that count the *number* of defects—called *c*-charts.

p-chart

A quality control chart that is used to control attributes.

p-Charts Using *p*-charts is the chief way to control attributes. Although attributes that are either good or bad follow the binomial distribution, the normal distribution can be used to calculate *p*-chart limits when sample sizes are large. The procedure resembles the $\bar{x}$-chart approach, which is also based on the central limit theorem.

The formulas for *p*-chart upper and lower control limits follow:

VIDEO S6.2
Frito-Lay's Quality-Controlled Potato Chips

$$UCL_p = \bar{p} + z\sigma_p \tag{S6-9}$$

$$LCL_p = \bar{p} - z\sigma_p \tag{S6-10}$$

where $\bar{p}$ = mean fraction (percent) defective in the samples = $\dfrac{\text{total number of defects}}{\text{sample size} \times \text{number of samples}}$

  z = number of standard deviations ($z = 2$ for 95.45% limits; $z = 3$ for 99.73% limits)

  σ_p = standard deviation of the sampling distribution

σ_p is estimated by the formula:

$$\hat{\sigma}_p = \sqrt{\frac{\bar{p}(1 - \bar{p})}{n}} \tag{S6-11}$$

where n = number of observations in *each* sample[4]

Example S4 shows how to set control limits for *p*-charts for these standard deviations.

Example S4

SETTING CONTROL LIMITS FOR PERCENT DEFECTIVE

Clerks at Mosier Data Systems key in thousands of insurance records each day for a variety of client firms. CEO Donna Mosier wants to set control limits to include 99.73% of the random variation in the data entry process when it is in control.

APPROACH ▶ Samples of the work of 20 clerks are gathered (and shown in the table). Mosier carefully examines 100 records entered by each clerk and counts the number of errors. She also computes the fraction defective in each sample. Equations (S6-9), (S6-10), and (S6-11) are then used to set the control limits.

SAMPLE NUMBER	NUMBER OF ERRORS	FRACTION DEFECTIVE	SAMPLE NUMBER	NUMBER OF ERRORS	FRACTION DEFECTIVE
1	6	.06	11	6	.06
2	5	.05	12	1	.01
3	0	.00	13	8	.08
4	1	.01	14	7	.07
5	4	.04	15	5	.05
6	2	.02	16	4	.04
7	5	.05	17	11	.11
8	3	.03	18	3	.03
9	3	.03	19	0	.00
10	2	.02	20	4	.04
				80	

SOLUTION ▶

$$\bar{p} = \frac{\text{Total number of errors}}{\text{Total number of records examined}} = \frac{80}{(100)(20)} = .04$$

$$\hat{\sigma}_p = \sqrt{\frac{(.04)(1 - .04)}{100}} = .02 \text{ (rounded up from .0196)}$$

(*Note:* 100 is the size of *each* sample = *n*.)

$$\text{UCL}_p = \bar{p} + z\hat{\sigma}_p = .04 + 3(.02) = .10$$

$$\text{LCL}_p = \bar{p} - z\hat{\sigma}_p = .04 - 3(.02) = 0$$

(because we cannot have a negative percentage defective)

INSIGHT ▶ When we plot the control limits and the sample fraction defectives, we find that only one data-entry clerk (number 17) is out of control. The firm may wish to examine that individual's work a bit more closely to see if a serious problem exists (see Figure S6.6).

Figure **S6.6**

***p*-Chart for Data Entry for Example S4**

STUDENT TIP ◆

We are always pleased to be at zero or below the center line in a *p*-chart.

LEARNING EXERCISE ▶ Mosier decides to set control limits at 95.45% instead. What are the new UCL_p and LCL_p? [Answer: 0.08, 0]

RELATED PROBLEMS ▶ S6.13–S6.20, S6.25, S6.27 (S6.35–S6.39 are available in MyOMLab)

ACTIVE MODEL **S6.2** This example is further illustrated in Active Model S6.2 in MyOMLab.

EXCEL OM Data File **Ch06ExS4.xls** can be found in MyOMLab.

The *OM in Action* box "Trying to Land a Seat with Frequent Flyer Miles" provides a real-world follow-up to Example S4.

***c*-Charts** In Example S4, we counted the number of defective records entered. A defective record was one that was not exactly correct because it contained at least one defect. However, a bad record may contain more than one defect. We use *c*-charts to control the *number* of defects per unit of output (or per insurance record, in the preceding case).

***c*-chart**

A quality control chart used to control the number of defects per unit of output.

OM in Action | Trying to Land a Seat with Frequent Flyer Miles

How hard is it to redeem your 25,000 frequent flyer points for airline tickets? That depends on the airline. (It also depends on the city. Don't try to get into or out of San Francisco!) When the consulting firm Idea Works made 280 requests for a standard mileage award to each of 24 airlines' Web sites (a total of 6,720 requests), the success rates ranged from a low of 25.7% and 27.1% (at US Airways and Delta, respectively) to a high of 100% at GOL-Brazil and 99.3% at Southwest.

The overall average of 68.6% for the two dozen carriers provides the center line in a *p*-chart. With 3-sigma upper and lower control limits of 82.5% and 54.7%, the other top and bottom performers are easily spotted. "Out of control" (but in a positive *outperforming* way) are GOL and Southwest,

Lufthansa (85.0%), Singapore (90.7%), Virgin Australia (91.4%), and Air Berlin (96.4%).

Out of control *on the negative side* are US Airways and Delta, plus Emirates (35.7%), AirTran (47.1%), Turkish (49.3%), and SAS (52.9%).

Control charts can help airlines see where they stand relative to competitors in such customer service activities as lost bags, on-time rates, and ease of redeeming mileage points. "I think airlines are getting the message that availability is important. Are airlines where they need to be? I don't think so," says the president of Idea Works.

Sources: Wall Street Journal (May 26, 2011); and *Consumer Reports* (November 2014).

Sampling wine from these wooden barrels, to make sure it is aging properly, uses both SPC (for alcohol content and acidity) and subjective measures (for taste).

Charles O'Rear/Corbis

Control charts for defects are helpful for monitoring processes in which a large number of potential errors can occur, but the actual number that do occur is relatively small. Defects may be errors in newspaper words, bad circuits in a microchip, blemishes on a table, or missing pickles on a fast-food hamburger.

The Poisson probability distribution,[5] which has a variance equal to its mean, is the basis for c-charts. Because $\bar{c}$ is the mean number of defects per unit, the standard deviation is equal to $\sqrt{\bar{c}}$. To compute 99.73% control limits for $\bar{c}$, we use the formula:

$$\text{Control limits} = \bar{c} \pm 3\sqrt{\bar{c}} \tag{S6-12}$$

Example S5 shows how to set control limits for a $\bar{c}$-chart.

Example S5

SETTING CONTROL LIMITS FOR NUMBER OF DEFECTS

Red Top Cab Company receives several complaints per day about the behavior of its drivers. Over a 9-day period (where days are the units of measure), the owner, Gordon Hoft, received the following numbers of calls from irate passengers: 3, 0, 8, 9, 6, 7, 4, 9, 8, for a total of 54 complaints. Hoft wants to compute 99.73% control limits.

APPROACH ▶ He applies Equation (S6–12).

SOLUTION ▶ $\bar{c} = \dfrac{54}{9} = 6$ complaints per day

Thus:

$$\text{UCL}_c = \bar{c} + 3\sqrt{\bar{c}} = 6 + 3\sqrt{6} = 6 + 3(2.45) = 13.35, \text{ or } 13$$

$$\text{LCL}_c = \bar{c} - 3\sqrt{\bar{c}} = 6 - 3\sqrt{6} = 6 - 3(2.45) = 0 \leftarrow \text{(since it cannot be negative)}$$

INSIGHT ▶ After Hoft plotted a control chart summarizing these data and posted it prominently in the drivers' locker room, the number of calls received dropped to an average of three per day. Can you explain why this occurred?

LEARNING EXERCISE ▶ Hoft collects 3 more days' worth of complaints (10, 12, and 8 complaints) and wants to combine them with the original 9 days to compute updated control limits. What are the revised UCL_c and LCL_c? [Answer: 14.94, 0.]

RELATED PROBLEMS ▶ S6.21, S6.22, S6.23, S6.24

EXCEL OM Data File Ch06SExS5.xls can be found in MyOMLab.

TABLE S6.3	**Helping You Decide Which Control Chart to Use**

VARIABLE DATA
USING AN $\bar{x}$-CHART AND AN R-CHART

1. Observations are *variables*, which are usually products measured for size or weight. Examples are the width or length of a wire and the weight of a can of Campbell's soup.
2. Collect 20 to 25 samples, usually of $n = 4$, $n = 5$, or more, each from a stable process, and compute the means for an $\bar{x}$-chart and the ranges for an R-chart.
3. We track samples of n observations each, as in Example S1.

ATTRIBUTE DATA
USING A p-CHART

1. Observations are *attributes* that can be categorized as good or bad (or pass–fail, or functional–broken); that is, in two states.
2. We deal with fraction, proportion, or percent defectives.
3. There are several samples, with many observations in each. For example, 20 samples of $n = 100$ observations in each, as in Example S4.

ATTRIBUTE DATA
USING A c-CHART

1. Observations are *attributes* whose defects per unit of output can be counted.
2. We deal with the number counted, which is a small part of the possible occurrences.
3. Defects may be: number of blemishes on a desk; flaws in a bolt of cloth; crimes in a year; broken seats in a stadium; typos in a chapter of this text; or complaints in a day, as is shown in Example S5.

STUDENT TIP

This is a really useful table. When you are not sure which control chart to use, turn here for clarification.

Managerial Issues and Control Charts

In an ideal world, there is no need for control charts. Quality is uniform and so high that employees need not waste time and money sampling and monitoring variables and attributes. But because most processes have not reached perfection, managers must make three major decisions regarding control charts.

First, managers must select the points in their process that need SPC. They may ask "Which parts of the job are critical to success?" or "Which parts of the job have a tendency to become out of control?"

Second, managers need to decide if variable charts (i.e., $\bar{x}$ and R) or attribute charts (i.e., p and c) are appropriate. Variable charts monitor weights or dimensions. Attribute charts are more of a "yes–no" or "go–no go" gauge and tend to be less costly to implement. Table S6.3 can help you understand when to use each of these types of control charts.

Third, the company must set clear and specific SPC policies for employees to follow. For example, should the data-entry process be halted if a trend is appearing in percent defective records being keyed? Should an assembly line be stopped if the average length of five successive samples is above the centerline? Figure S6.7 illustrates some of the patterns to look for over time in a process.

Normal behavior. Process is "in control."

One point out above (or below). Investigate for cause. Process is "out of control."

Trends in either direction, 5 points. Investigate for cause of progressive change. This could be the result of gradual tool wear.

Two points very near lower (or upper) control. Investigate for cause.

Run of 5 points above (or below) central line. Investigate for cause.

Erratic behavior. Investigate.

Figure S6.7

Patterns to Look for on Control Charts

Source: Adapted from Bertrand L. Hansen, *Quality Control: Theory and Applications* (1991): 65. Reprinted by permission of Prentice Hall, Upper Saddle River, NJ.

STUDENT TIP

Workers in companies such as Frito-Lay are trained to follow rules like these.

Run test

A test used to examine the points in a control chart to see if nonrandom variation is present.

A tool called a run test is available to help identify the kind of abnormalities in a process that we see in Figure S6.7. In general, a run of 5 points above or below the target or centerline may suggest that an assignable, or nonrandom, variation is present. When this occurs, even though all the points may fall inside the control limits, a flag has been raised. This means the process may not be statistically in control. A variety of run tests are described in books on the subject of quality methods.

STUDENT TIP ⬦

Here we deal with whether a process meets the specification it was *designed* to yield.

Process Capability

Statistical process control means keeping a process in control. This means that the natural variation of the process must be stable. However, a process that is in statistical control may not yield goods or services that meet their *design specifications* (tolerances). In other words, the variation should be small enough to produce consistent output within specifications. The ability of a process to meet design specifications, which are set by engineering design or customer requirements, is called process capability. Even though that process may be statistically in control (stable), the output of that process may not conform to specifications.

Process capability

The ability to meet design specifications.

For example, let's say the time a customer expects to wait for the completion of a lube job at Quik Lube is 12 minutes, with an acceptable tolerance of ± 2 minutes. This tolerance gives an upper specification of 14 minutes and a lower specification of 10 minutes. The lube process has to be capable of operating within these design specifications—if not, some customers will not have their requirements met. As a manufacturing example, the tolerances for Harley-Davidson cam gears are extremely low, only 0.0005 inch—and a process must be designed that is capable of achieving this tolerance.

There are two popular measures for quantitatively determining if a process is capable: process capability ratio (C_p) and process capability index (C_{pk}).

LO S6.6 *Explain* process capability and compute C_p and C_{pk}

Process Capability Ratio (C_p)

For a process to be capable, its values must fall within upper and lower specifications. This typically means the process capability is within ± 3 standard deviations from the process mean. Because this range of values is 6 standard deviations, a capable process tolerance, which is the difference between the upper and lower specifications, must be greater than or equal to 6.

C_p

A ratio for determining whether a process meets design specifications; a ratio of the specification to the process variation.

The process capability ratio, C_p, is computed as:

$$C_p = \frac{\text{Upper specification} - \text{Lower specification}}{6\sigma} \quad \text{(S6-13)}$$

Example S6 shows the computation of C_p.

Example S6

PROCESS CAPABILITY RATIO (C_p)

In a GE insurance claims process, $\bar{x} = 210.0$ minutes, and $\sigma = .516$ minutes.

The design specification to meet customer expectations is 210 ± 3 minutes. So the Upper Specification is 213 minutes and the lower specification is 207 minutes. The OM manager wants to compute the process capability ratio.

APPROACH ▶ GE applies Equation (S6-13).

SOLUTION ▶ $C_p = \dfrac{\text{Upper specification} - \text{Lower specification}}{6\sigma} = \dfrac{213 - 207}{6(.516)} = 1.938$

INSIGHT ▶ Because a ratio of 1.00 means that 99.73% of a process's outputs are within specifications, this ratio suggests a very capable process, with nonconformance of less than 4 claims per million.

LEARNING EXERCISE ▶ If $\sigma = .60$ (instead of .516), what is the new C_p? [Answer: 1.667, a very capable process still.]

RELATED PROBLEMS ▶ S6.40, S6.41 (S6.50 is available in MyOMLab)

ACTIVE MODEL S6.3 This example is further illustrated in Active Model S6.3 in MyOMLab.

EXCEL OM Data File Ch06SExS6.xls can be found in MyOMLab.

A capable process has a C_p of at least 1.0. If the C_p is less than 1.0, the process yields products or services that are outside their allowable tolerance. With a C_p of 1.0, 2.7 parts in 1,000 can be expected to be "out of spec."[6] The higher the process capability ratio, the greater the likelihood the process will be within design specifications. Many firms have chosen a C_p of 1.33 (a 4-sigma standard) as a target for reducing process variability. This means that only 64 parts per million can be expected to be out of specification.

Recall that in Chapter 6 we mentioned the concept of *Six Sigma* quality, championed by GE and Motorola. This standard equates to a C_p of 2.0, with only 3.4 defective parts per million (very close to zero defects) instead of the 2.7 parts per 1,000 with 3-sigma limits.

Although C_p relates to the spread (dispersion) of the process output relative to its tolerance, it does not look at how well the process average is centered on the target value.

Process Capability Index (C_{pk})

The process capability index, C_{pk}, measures the difference between the desired and actual dimensions of goods or services produced.

The formula for C_{pk} is:

$$C_{pk} = \text{Minimum of} \left[\frac{\text{Upper specification limit} - \overline{X}}{3\sigma}, \frac{\overline{X} - \text{Lower specification limit}}{3\sigma} \right]$$

(S6-14)

where $\overline{X}$ = process mean

σ = standard deviation of the process population

When the C_{pk} index for both the upper and lower specification limits equals 1.0, the process variation is centered and the process is capable of producing within ± 3 standard deviations (fewer than 2,700 defects per million). A C_{pk} of 2.0 means the process is capable of producing fewer than 3.4 defects per million. For C_{pk} to exceed 1, σ must be less than $\frac{1}{3}$ of the difference between the specification and the process mean ($\overline{X}$). Figure S6.8 shows the meaning of various measures of C_{pk}, and Example S7 shows an application of C_{pk}.

C_{pk}
A proportion of variation (3σ) between the center of the process and the nearest specification limit.

Example S7 | PROCESS CAPABILITY INDEX (C_{pk})

You are the process improvement manager and have developed a new machine to cut insoles for the company's top-of-the-line running shoes. You are excited because the company's goal is no more than 3.4 defects per million, and this machine may be the innovation you need. The insoles cannot be more than $\pm .001$ of an inch from the required thickness of .250". You want to know if you should replace the existing machine, which has a C_{pk} of 1.0.

Mean of the new process $\overline{X} = .250$ inches.
Standard deviation of the new process $= \sigma = .0005$ inches.

APPROACH ▶ You decide to determine the C_{pk}, using Equation (S6-14), for the new machine and make a decision on that basis.

SOLUTION ▶   Upper specification limit $= .251$ inches

Lower specification limit $= .249$ inches

$$C_{pk} = \text{Minimum of} \left[\frac{\text{Upper specification limit} - \overline{X}}{3\sigma}, \frac{\overline{X} - \text{Lower specification limit}}{3\sigma} \right]$$

$$C_{pk} = \text{Minimum of} \left[\frac{.251 - .250}{(3).0005}, \frac{.250 - .249}{(3).0005} \right]$$

Both calculations result in: $\dfrac{.001}{.0015} = .67$.

INSIGHT ▶ Because the new machine has a C_{pk} of only 0.67, the new machine should *not* replace the existing machine.

LEARNING EXERCISE ▶ If the insoles can be $\pm.002''$ (instead of $.001''$) from the required $.250''$, what is the new C_{pk}? [Answer: 1.33 and the new machine *should* replace the existing one.]

RELATED PROBLEMS ▶ S6.41–S6.45 (S6.46–S6.49 are available in MyOMLab)

ACTIVE MODEL S6.2 This example is further illustrated in Active Model S6.2 in MyOMLab.

EXCEL OM Data File **Ch06SExS7.xls** can be found in MyOMLab.

Note that C_p and C_{pk} will be the same when the process is centered. However, if the mean of the process is not centered on the desired (specified) mean, then the smaller numerator in Equation (S6-14) is used (the minimum of the difference between the upper specification limit and the mean or the lower specification limit and the mean). This application of C_{pk} is shown in Solved Problem S6.4. C_{pk} is the standard criterion used to express process performance.

Acceptance Sampling[7]

Acceptance sampling

A method of measuring random samples of lots or batches of products against predetermined standards.

LO S6.7 *Explain acceptance sampling*

Acceptance sampling is a form of testing that involves taking random samples of "lots," or batches, of finished products and measuring them against predetermined standards. Sampling is more economical than 100% inspection. The quality of the sample is used to judge the quality of all items in the lot. Although both attributes and variables can be inspected by acceptance sampling, attribute inspection is more commonly used, as illustrated in this section.

Acceptance sampling can be applied either when materials arrive at a plant or at final inspection, but it is usually used to control incoming lots of purchased products. A lot of items rejected, based on an unacceptable level of defects found in the sample, can (1) be returned to the supplier or (2) be 100% inspected to cull out all defects, with the cost of this screening usually billed to the supplier. However, acceptance sampling is not a substitute for adequate process controls. In fact, the current approach is to build statistical quality controls at suppliers so that acceptance sampling can be eliminated.

Figure S6.8

Meanings of C_{pk} Measures

A C_{pk} index of 1.0 for both the upper and lower specification limits indicates that the process variation is within the upper and lower specification limits. As the C_{pk} index goes above 1.0, the process becomes increasingly target oriented, with fewer defects. If the C_{pk} is less than 1.0, the process will not produce within the specified tolerance. Because a process may not be centered, or may "drift," a C_{pk} above 1 is desired.

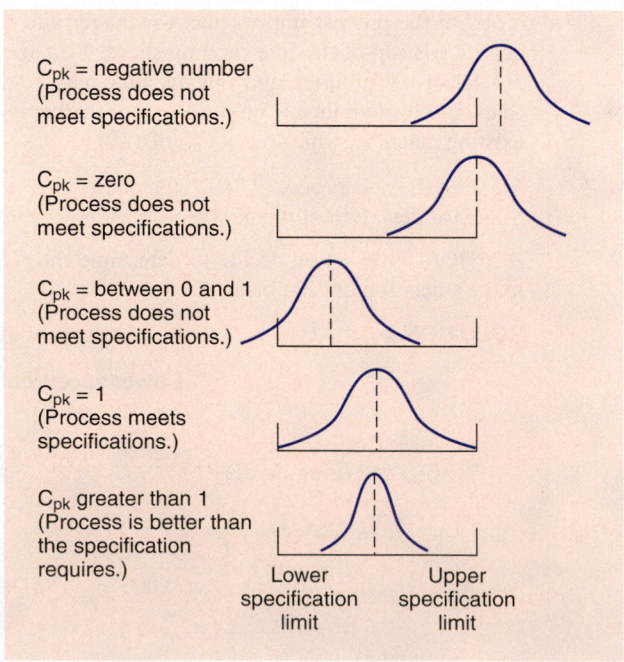

C_{pk} = negative number (Process does not meet specifications.)

C_{pk} = zero (Process does not meet specifications.)

C_{pk} = between 0 and 1 (Process does not meet specifications.)

C_{pk} = 1 (Process meets specifications.)

C_{pk} greater than 1 (Process is better than the specification requires.)

Lower specification limit   Upper specification limit

Raw data for Statistical Process Control is collected in a wide variety of ways. Here physical measures using a micrometer (on the left) and a microscope (on the right) are being made.

Operating Characteristic Curve

The operating characteristic (OC) curve describes how well an acceptance plan discriminates between good and bad lots. A curve pertains to a specific plan—that is, to a combination of n (sample size) and c (acceptance level). It is intended to show the probability that the plan will accept lots of various quality levels.

With acceptance sampling, two parties are usually involved: the producer of the product and the consumer of the product. In specifying a sampling plan, each party wants to avoid costly mistakes in accepting or rejecting a lot. The producer usually has the responsibility of replacing all defects in the rejected lot or of paying for a new lot to be shipped to the customer. The producer, therefore, wants to avoid the mistake of having a good lot rejected (producer's risk). On the other hand, the customer or consumer wants to avoid the mistake of accepting a bad lot because defects found in a lot that has already been accepted are usually the responsibility of the customer (consumer's risk). The OC curve shows the features of a particular sampling plan, including the risks of making a wrong decision. The steeper the curve, the better the plan distinguishes between good and bad lots.[8]

Figure S6.9 can be used to illustrate one sampling plan in more detail. Four concepts are illustrated in this figure.

The acceptable quality level (AQL) is the poorest level of quality that we are willing to accept. In other words, we wish to accept lots that have this or a better level of quality, but no worse. If an acceptable quality level is 20 defects in a lot of 1,000 items or parts, then AQL is $20/1{,}000 = 2\%$ defectives.

The lot tolerance percentage defective (LTPD) is the quality level of a lot that we consider bad. We wish to reject lots that have this or a poorer level of quality. If it is agreed that an unacceptable quality level is 70 defects in a lot of 1,000, then the LTPD is $70/1{,}000 = 7\%$ defective.

To derive a sampling plan, producer and consumer must define not only "good lots" and "bad lots" through the AQL and LTPD, but they must also specify risk levels.

Producer's risk (α) is the probability that a "good" lot will be rejected. This is the risk that a random sample might result in a much higher proportion of defects than the population of all items. A lot with an acceptable quality level of AQL still has an α chance of being rejected. Sampling plans are often designed to have the producer's risk set at $\alpha = .05$, or 5%.

Consumer's risk (β) is the probability that a "bad" lot will be accepted. This is the risk that a random sample may result in a lower proportion of defects than the overall population of items. A common value for consumer's risk in sampling plans is $\beta = .10$, or 10%.

The probability of rejecting a good lot is called a type I error. The probability of accepting a bad lot is a type II error.

Sampling plans and OC curves may be developed by computer (as seen in the software available with this text), by published tables, or by calculation, using binomial or Poisson distributions.

Operating characteristic (OC) curve
A graph that describes how well an acceptance plan discriminates between good and bad lots.

Producer's risk
The mistake of having a producer's good lot rejected through sampling.

Consumer's risk
The mistake of a customer's acceptance of a bad lot overlooked through sampling.

Acceptable quality level (AQL)
The quality level of a lot considered good.

Lot tolerance percentage defective (LTPD)
The quality level of a lot considered bad.

Type I error
Statistically, the probability of rejecting a good lot.

Type II error
Statistically, the probability of accepting a bad lot.

An Operating Characteristic (OC) Curve Showing Producer's and Consumer's Risks

A good lot for this particular acceptance plan has less than or equal to 2% defectives. A bad lot has 7% or more defectives.

Average Outgoing Quality

In most sampling plans, when a lot is rejected, the entire lot is inspected and all defective items replaced. Use of this replacement technique improves the average outgoing quality in terms of percent defective. In fact, given (1) any sampling plan that replaces all defective items encountered and (2) the true incoming percent defective for the lot, it is possible to determine the **average outgoing quality (AOQ)** in percentage defective. The equation for AOQ is:

Average outgoing quality (AOQ)

The percentage defective in an average lot of goods inspected through acceptance sampling.

$$\text{AOQ} = \frac{(P_d)(P_a)(N - n)}{N} \tag{S6-15}$$

where

P_d = true percentage defective of the lot
P_a = probability of accepting the lot for a given sample size and quantity defective
N = number of items in the lot
n = number of items in the sample

The maximum value of AOQ corresponds to the highest average percentage defective or the lowest average quality for the sampling plan. It is called the *average outgoing quality limit (AOQL)*.

This laser tracking device, by Faro Technologies, enables quality control personnel to measure and inspect parts and tools during production. The portable tracker can measure objects from 262 feet away and takes to up 1,000 accurate readings per second.

Faro Technologies

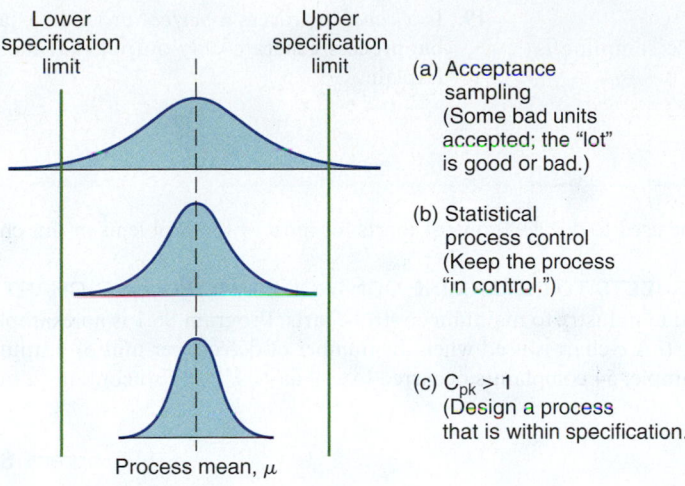

Lower specification limit

Upper specification limit

(a) Acceptance sampling (Some bad units accepted; the "lot" is good or bad.)

(b) Statistical process control (Keep the process "in control.")

(c) $C_{pk} > 1$ (Design a process that is within specification.)

Process mean, μ

Figure **S6.10**

The Application of Statistical Process Control Techniques Contributes to the Identification and Systematic Reduction of Process Variability

Acceptance sampling is useful for screening incoming lots. When the defective parts are replaced with good parts, acceptance sampling helps to increase the quality of the lots by reducing the outgoing percent defective.

Figure S6.10 compares acceptance sampling, SPC, and C_{pk}. As the figure shows, (a) acceptance sampling by definition accepts some bad units, (b) control charts try to keep the process in control, but (c) the C_{pk} index places the focus on improving the process. As operations managers, that is what we want to do—improve the process.

Summary

Statistical process control is a major statistical tool of quality control. Control charts for SPC help operations managers distinguish between natural and assignable variations. The $\bar{x}$-chart and the R-chart are used for variable sampling, and the p-chart and the c-chart for attribute sampling.

The C_{pk} index is a way to express process capability. Operating characteristic (OC) curves facilitate acceptance sampling and provide the manager with tools to evaluate the quality of a production run or shipment.

Key Terms

Statistical process control (SPC) (p. 246)
Control chart (p. 246)
Natural variations (p. 246)
Assignable variation (p. 247)
$\bar{x}$-chart (p. 248)
R-chart (p. 248)
Central limit theorem (p. 248)
p-chart (p. 255)

c-chart (p. 257)
Run test (p. 260)
Process capability (p. 260)
C_p (p. 260)
C_{pk} (p. 261)
Acceptance sampling (p. 262)
Operating characteristic (OC) curve (p. 263)
Producer's risk (p. 263)
Consumer's risk (p. 263)

Acceptable quality level (AQL) (p. 263)
Lot tolerance percentage defective (LTPD) (p. 263)
Type I error (p. 263)
Type II error (p. 263)
Average outgoing quality (AOQ) (p. 264)

Discussion Questions

1. List Shewhart's two types of variation. What are they also called?
2. Define "in statistical control."
3. Explain briefly what an $\bar{x}$-chart and an R-chart do.
4. What might cause a process to be out of control?
5. List five steps in developing and using $\bar{x}$-charts and R-charts.
6. List some possible causes of assignable variation.
7. Explain how a person using 2-sigma control charts will more easily find samples "out of bounds" than 3-sigma control charts. What are some possible consequences of this fact?
8. When is the desired mean, μ, used in establishing the centerline of a control chart instead of $\bar{\bar{x}}$?

9. Can a production process be labeled as "out of control" because it is too good? Explain.
10. In a control chart, what would be the effect on the control limits if the sample size varied from one sample to the next?
11. Define C_{pk} and explain what a C_{pk} of 1.0 means. What is C_p?
12. What does a run of 5 points above or below the centerline in a control chart imply?
13. What are the acceptable quality level (AQL) and the lot tolerance percentage defective (LTPD)? How are they used?
14. What is a run test, and when is it used?
15. Discuss the managerial issues regarding the use of control charts.
16. What is an OC curve?

17. What is the purpose of acceptance sampling?

18. What two risks are present when acceptance sampling is used?

19. Is a *capable* process a *perfect* process? That is, does a capable process generate only output that meets specifications? Explain.

Using Software for SPC

Excel, Excel OM, and POM for Windows may be used to develop control charts for most of the problems in this chapter.

✘ CREATING YOUR OWN EXCEL SPREADSHEETS TO DETERMINE CONTROL LIMITS FOR A C-CHART

Excel and other spreadsheets are extensively used in industry to maintain control charts. Program S6.1 is an example of how to use Excel to determine the control limits for a *c*-chart. A *c*-chart is used when the number of defects per unit of output is known. The data from Example S5 are used here. In this example, 54 complaints occurred over 9 days. Excel also contains a built-in graphing ability with Chart Wizard.

Program S6.1

An Excel Spreadsheet for Creating a *c*-Chart for Example S5

✘ USING EXCEL OM

Excel OM's Quality Control module has the ability to develop $\bar{x}$-charts, *p*-charts, and *c*-charts. It also handles OC curves, acceptance sampling, and process capability. Program S6.2 illustrates Excel OM's spreadsheet approach to computing the $\bar{x}$ control limits for the Oat Flakes company in Example S1.

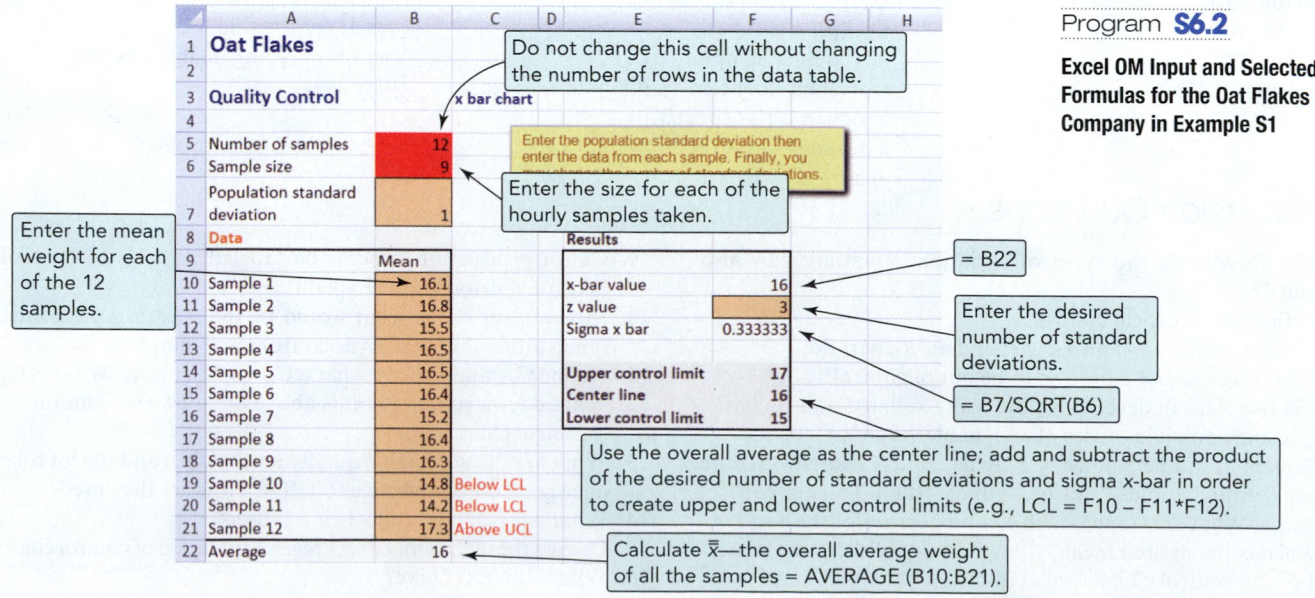

Program S6.2

Excel OM Input and Selected Formulas for the Oat Flakes Company in Example S1

P **USING POM FOR WINDOWS**
The POM for Windows Quality Control module has the ability to compute all the SPC control charts we introduced in this supplement, as well as OC curves, acceptance sampling, and process capability. See Appendix IV for further details.

Solved Problems   Virtual Office Hours help is available in MyOMLab.

SOLVED PROBLEM S6.1

A manufacturer of precision machine parts produces round shafts for use in the construction of drill presses. The average diameter of a shaft is .56 inch. Inspection samples contain 6 shafts each. The average range of these samples is .006 inch. Determine the upper and lower $\bar{x}$ control chart limits.

SOLUTION

The mean factor A_2 from Table S6.1, where the sample size is 6, is seen to be .483. With this factor, you can obtain the upper and lower control limits:

$$UCL_{\bar{x}} = .56 + (.483)(.006)$$
$$= .56 + .0029$$
$$= .5629 \text{ inch}$$
$$LCL_{\bar{x}} = .56 - .0029$$
$$= .5571 \text{ inch}$$

SOLVED PROBLEM S6.2

Nocaf Drinks, Inc., a producer of decaffeinated coffee, bottles Nocaf. Each bottle should have a net weight of 4 ounces. The machine that fills the bottles with coffee is new, and the operations manager wants to make sure that it is properly adjusted. Bonnie Crutcher, the operations manager, randomly selects and weighs $n = 8$ bottles and records the average and range in ounces for each sample. The data for several samples is given in the following table. Note that every sample consists of 8 bottles.

SAMPLE	SAMPLE RANGE	SAMPLE AVERAGE	SAMPLE	SAMPLE RANGE	SAMPLE AVERAGE
A	.41	4.00	E	.56	4.17
B	.55	4.16	F	.62	3.93
C	.44	3.99	G	.54	3.98
D	.48	4.00	H	.44	4.01

Is the machine properly adjusted and in control?

SOLUTION

We first find that $\bar{\bar{x}} = 4.03$ and $\bar{R} = .505$. Then, using Table S6.1, we find:

$$UCL_{\bar{x}} = \bar{\bar{x}} + A_2\bar{R} = 4.03 + (.373)(.505) = 4.22$$
$$LCL_{\bar{x}} = \bar{\bar{x}} - A_2\bar{R} = 4.03 - (.373)(.505) = 3.84$$
$$UCL_R = D_4\bar{R} = (1.864)(.505) = .94$$
$$LCL_R = D_3\bar{R} = (.136)(.505) = .07$$

It appears that the process average and range are both in statistical control.

The operations manager needs to determine if a process with a mean (4.03) slightly above the desired mean of 4.00 is satisfactory; if it is not, the process will need to be changed.

SOLVED PROBLEM S6.3

Altman Distributors, Inc., fills catalog orders. Samples of size $n = 100$ orders have been taken each day over the past 6 weeks. The average defect rate was .05. Determine the upper and lower limits for this process for 99.73% confidence.

SOLUTION

$z = 3, \bar{p} = .05$. Using Equations (S6-9), (S6-10), and (S6-11):

$$UCL_p = \bar{p} + 3\sqrt{\frac{\bar{p}(1 - \bar{p})}{n}} = .05 + 3\sqrt{\frac{(.05)(1 - .05)}{100}}$$
$$= .05 + 3(0.0218) = .1154$$

$$LCL_p = \bar{p} - 3\sqrt{\frac{\bar{p}(1 - \bar{p})}{n}} = .05 - 3(0.0218)$$
$$= .05 - .0654 = 0 \quad \text{(because percentage defective cannot be negative)}$$

SOLVED PROBLEM S6.4

Ettlie Engineering has a new catalyst injection system for your countertop production line. Your process engineering department has conducted experiments and determined that the mean is 8.01 grams with a standard deviation of .03. Your specifications are: $\mu = 8.0$ and $\sigma = .04$, which means an upper specification limit of 8.12 [$= 8.0 + 3(.04)$] and a lower specification limit of 7.88 [$= 8.0 - 3(.04)$].

What is the C_{pk} performance of the injection system?

SOLUTION

Using Equation (S6-14):

$$C_{pk} = \text{Minimum of} \left[\frac{\text{Upper specification limit} - \overline{X}}{3\sigma}, \frac{\overline{X} - \text{Lower specification limit}}{3\sigma} \right]$$

where

$\overline{X} = $ process mean
$\sigma = $ standard deviation of the process population

$$C_{pk} = \text{Minimum of} \left[\frac{8.12 - 8.01}{(3)(.03)}, \frac{8.01 - 7.88}{(3)(.03)} \right]$$

$$\left[\frac{.11}{.09} = 1.22, \frac{.13}{.09} = 1.44 \right]$$

The minimum is 1.22, so the C_{pk} is within specifications and has an implied error rate of less than 2,700 defects per million.

SOLVED PROBLEM S6.5

Airlines lose thousands of checked bags every day, and America South Airlines is no exception to the industry rule. Over the past 6 weeks, the number of bags "misplaced" on America South flights has been 18, 10, 4, 6, 12, and 10. The head of customer service wants to develop a c-chart at 99.73% levels.

SOLUTION

She first computes $\bar{c} = \dfrac{18 + 10 + 4 + 6 + 12 + 10}{6} = \dfrac{60}{6} = 10$ bags/week

Then, using Equation (S6-12):

$$UCL_c = \bar{c} + 3\sqrt{\bar{c}} = 10 + 3\sqrt{10} = 10 + 3(3.16) = 19.48 \text{ bags}$$

$$LCL_C = \bar{c} - 3\sqrt{\bar{c}} = 10 - 3\sqrt{10} = 10 - 3(3.16) = .52 \text{ bag}$$

Problems

Note: **Px** *means the problem may be solved with POM for Windows and/or Excel OM/Excel.*

Problems S6.1–S6.39 relate to Statistical Process Control (SPC)

• **S6.1** Boxes of Honey-Nut Oatmeal are produced to contain 14 ounces, with a standard deviation of .1 ounce. Set up the 3-sigma $\bar{x}$-chart for a sample size of 36 boxes. **Px**

• **S6.2** The overall average on a process you are attempting to monitor is 50 units. The process population standard deviation is 1.72. Determine the upper and lower control limits for a mean chart, if you choose to use a sample size of 5. **Px**
a) Set $z = 3$.
b) Now set $z = 2$. How do the control limits change?

• **S6.3** Thirty-five samples of size 7 each were taken from a fertilizer-bag-filling machine. The results were overall mean = 57.75 lb; average range = 1.78 lb.
a) Determine the upper and lower control limits of the $\bar{x}$-chart, where $\sigma = 3$.
b) Determine the upper and lower control limits of the R-chart, where $\sigma = 3$. **Px**

• **S6.4** Rosters Chicken advertises "lite" chicken with 30% fewer calories than standard chicken. When the process for "lite" chicken breast production is in control, the average chicken breast contains 420 calories, and the standard deviation in caloric content of the chicken breast population is 25 calories.

Rosters wants to design an $\bar{x}$-chart to monitor the caloric content of chicken breasts, where 25 chicken breasts would be chosen at random to form each sample.
a) What are the lower and upper control limits for this chart if these limits are chosen to be *four* standard deviations from the target?
b) What are the limits with three standard deviations from the target? **Px**

• **S6.5** Ross Hopkins is attempting to monitor a filling process that has an overall average of 705 cc. The average range is 6 cc. If you use a sample size of 10, what are the upper and lower control limits for the mean and range?

•• **S6.6** Sampling four pieces of precision-cut wire (to be used in computer assembly) every hour for the past 24 hours has produced the following results:

HOUR	$\bar{X}$	R	HOUR	$\bar{X}$	R
1	3.25″	.71″	13	3.11″	.85″
2	3.10	1.18	14	2.83	1.31
3	3.22	1.43	15	3.12	1.06
4	3.39	1.26	16	2.84	.50
5	3.07	1.17	17	2.86	1.43
6	2.86	.32	18	2.74	1.29
7	3.05	.53	19	3.41	1.61
8	2.65	1.13	20	2.89	1.09
9	3.02	.71	21	2.65	1.08
10	2.85	1.33	22	3.28	.46
11	2.83	1.17	23	2.94	1.58
12	2.97	.40	24	2.64	.97

Develop appropriate control charts and determine whether there is any cause for concern in the cutting process. Plot the information and look for patterns. **Px**

•• **S6.7** Auto pistons at Wemming Chung's plant in Shanghai are produced in a forging process, and the diameter is a critical factor that must be controlled. From sample sizes of 10 pistons produced each day, the mean and the range of this diameter have been as follows:

DAY	MEAN (MM)	RANGE (MM)
1	156.9	4.2
2	153.2	4.6
3	153.6	4.1
4	155.5	5.0
5	156.6	4.5

a) What is the value of $\bar{\bar{x}}$?
b) What is the value of $\bar{R}$?
c) What are the $UCL_{\bar{x}}$ and $LCL_{\bar{x}}$, using 3σ? Plot the data.
d) What are the UCL_R and LCL_R, using 3σ? Plot the data.
e) If the true diameter mean should be 155 mm and you want this as your center (nominal) line, what are the new $UCL_{\bar{x}}$ and $LCL_{\bar{x}}$? **Px**

•• **S6.8** A. Choudhury's bowling ball factory in Illinois makes bowling balls of adult size and weight only. The standard deviation in the weight of a bowling ball produced at the factory is known to be 0.12 pounds. Each day for 24 days, the average weight, in pounds, of nine of the bowling balls produced that day has been assessed as follows:

DAY	AVERAGE (lb)	DAY	AVERAGE (lb)
1	16.3	13	16.3
2	15.9	14	15.9
3	15.8	15	16.3
4	15.5	16	16.2
5	16.3	17	16.1
6	16.2	18	15.9
7	16.0	19	16.2
8	16.1	20	15.9
9	15.9	21	15.9
10	16.2	22	16.0
11	15.9	23	15.5
12	15.9	24	15.8

a) Establish a control chart for monitoring the average weights of the bowling balls in which the upper and lower control limits are each two standard deviations from the mean. What are the values of the control limits?
b) If three standard deviations are used in the chart, how do these values change? Why? **Px**

•• **S6.9** Organic Grains LLC uses statistical process control to ensure that its health-conscious, low-fat, multigrain sandwich loaves have the proper weight. Based on a previously stable and in-control process, the control limits of the $\bar{x}$- and R-charts are $UCL_{\bar{x}} = 6.56$. $LCL_{\bar{x}} = 5.84$, $UCL_R = 1.141$, $LCL_R = 0$. Over the past few days, they have taken five random samples of four loaves each and have found the following:

	NET WEIGHT			
SAMPLE	LOAF #1	LOAF #2	LOAF #3	LOAF #4
1	6.3	6.0	5.9	5.9
2	6.0	6.0	6.3	5.9
3	6.3	4.8	5.6	5.2
4	6.2	6.0	6.2	5.9
5	6.5	6.6	6.5	6.9

Is the process still in control? Explain why or why not. **Px**

••• **S6.10** A process that is considered to be in control measures an ingredient in ounces. Below are the last 10 samples (each of size $n = 5$) taken. The population process standard deviation, σ, is 1.36.

				SAMPLES					
1	2	3	4	5	6	7	8	9	10
10	9	13	10	12	10	10	13	8	10
9	9	9	10	10	10	11	10	8	12
10	11	10	11	9	8	10	8	12	9
9	11	10	10	11	12	8	10	12	8
12	10	9	10	10	9	9	8	9	12

a) What is $\sigma_{\bar{x}}$?
b) If $z = 3$, what are the control limits for the mean chart?
c) What are the control limits for the range chart?
d) Is the process in control? **Px**

••• **S6.11** Twelve samples, each containing five parts, were taken from a process that produces steel rods at Emmanuel Kodzi's factory. The length of each rod in the samples was determined. The results were tabulated and sample means and ranges were computed. The results were:

SAMPLE	SAMPLE MEAN (in.)	RANGE (in.)
1	10.002	0.011
2	10.002	0.014
3	9.991	0.007
4	10.006	0.022
5	9.997	0.013
6	9.999	0.012
7	10.001	0.008
8	10.005	0.013
9	9.995	0.004
10	10.001	0.011
11	10.001	0.014
12	10.006	0.009

a) Determine the upper and lower control limits and the overall means for $\bar{x}$-charts and R-charts.
b) Draw the charts and plot the values of the sample means and ranges.
c) Do the data indicate a process that is in control?
d) Why or why not? **Px**

•• **S6.12** Eagletrons are all-electric automobiles produced by Mogul Motors, Inc. One of the concerns of Mogul Motors is that the Eagletrons be capable of achieving appropriate maximum speeds. To monitor this, Mogul executives take samples of eight Eagletrons at a time. For each sample, they determine the average maximum speed and the range of the maximum speeds within the sample. They repeat this with 35 samples to obtain 35 sample means and 35 ranges. They find that the average sample mean is 88.50 miles per hour, and the average range is 3.25 miles per hour. Using these results, the executives decide to establish an R chart. They would like this chart to be established so that when it shows that the range of a sample is not within the control limits, there is only approximately a 0.0027 probability that this is due to natural variation. What will be the upper control limit (UCL) and the lower control limit (LCL) in this chart? **Px**

•• **S6.13** The defect rate for data entry of insurance claims has historically been about 1.5%.
a) What are the upper and lower control chart limits if you wish to use a sample size of 100 and 3-sigma limits?
b) What if the sample size used were 50, with 3σ?
c) What if the sample size used were 100, with 2σ?
d) What if the sample size used were 50, with 2σ?
e) What happens to $\hat{\sigma}_p$ when the sample size is larger?
f) Explain why the lower control limit cannot be less than 0. **Px**

•• **S6.14** You are attempting to develop a quality monitoring system for some parts purchased from Charles Sox Manufacturing Co. These parts are either good or defective. You have decided to take a sample of 100 units. Develop a table of the appropriate upper and lower control chart limits for various values of the average fraction defective in the samples taken. The values for $\bar{p}$ in this table should range from 0.02 to 0.10 in increments of 0.02. Develop the upper and lower control limits for a 99.73% confidence level.

	N = 100	
$\bar{P}$	UCL	LCL
0.02		
0.04		
0.06		
0.08		
0.10		

Px

•• **S6.15** The results of an inspection of DNA samples taken over the past 10 days are given below. Sample size is 100.

DAY	1	2	3	4	5	6	7	8	9	10
DEFECTIVES	7	6	6	9	5	6	0	8	9	1

a) Construct a 3-sigma p-chart using this information.
b) Using the control chart in part (a), and finding that the number of defectives on the next three days are 12, 5, and 13, is the process in control? **Px**

• **S6.16** In the past, the defective rate for your product has been 1.5%. What are the upper and lower control chart limits if you wish to use a sample size of 500 and $z = 3$? **Px**

• **S6.17** Refer to Problem S6.16. If the defective rate was 3.5% instead of 1.5%, what would be the control limits ($z = 3$)? **Px**

•• **S6.18** Five data entry operators work at the data processing department of the Birmingham Bank. Each day for 30 days, the number of defective records in a sample of 250 records typed by these operators has been noted, as follows:

SAMPLE NO.	NO. DEFECTIVE	SAMPLE NO.	NO. DEFECTIVE	SAMPLE NO.	NO. DEFECTIVE
1	7	11	18	21	17
2	5	12	5	22	12
3	19	13	16	23	6
4	10	14	4	24	7
5	11	15	11	25	13
6	8	16	8	26	10
7	12	17	12	27	14
8	9	18	4	28	6
9	6	19	6	29	12
10	13	20	16	30	3

a) Establish 3σ upper and lower control limits.
b) Why can the lower control limit not be a negative number?
c) The industry standards for the upper and lower control limits are 0.10 and 0.01, respectively. What does this imply about Birmingham Bank's own standards? **Px**

•• **S6.19** Houston North Hospital is trying to improve its image by providing a positive experience for its patients and their relatives. Part of the "image" program involves providing tasty, inviting patient meals that are also healthful. A questionnaire accompanies each meal served, asking the patient, among other things, whether he or she is satisfied or unsatisfied with the meal. A 100-patient sample of the survey results over the past 7 days yielded the following data:

DAY	NO. OF UNSATISFIED PATIENTS	SAMPLE SIZE
1	24	100
2	22	100
3	8	100
4	15	100
5	10	100
6	26	100
7	17	100

Construct a *p*-chart that plots the percentage of patients unsatisfied with their meals. Set the control limits to include 99.73% of the random variation in meal satisfaction. Comment on your results. **Px**

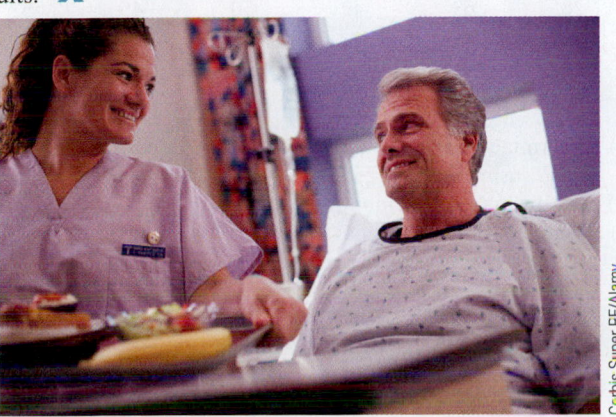

Corbis Super RF/Alamy

•• **S6.20** Jamison Kovach Supply Company manufactures paper clips and other office products. Although inexpensive, paper clips have provided the firm with a high margin of profitability. Sample size is 200. Results are given for the last 10 samples:

SAMPLE	1	2	3	4	5	6	7	8	9	10
DEFECTIVES	5	7	4	4	6	3	5	6	2	8

a) Establish upper and lower control limits for the control chart and graph the data.
b) Has the process been in control?
c) If the sample size were 100 instead, how would your limits and conclusions change? **Px**

• **S6.21** Peter Ittig's department store, Ittig Brothers, is Amherst's largest independent clothier. The store receives an average of six returns per day. Using $z = 3$, would nine returns in a day warrant action? **Px**

•• **S6.22** An ad agency tracks the complaints, by week received, about the billboards in its city:

WEEK	NO. OF COMPLAINTS
1	4
2	5
3	4
4	11
5	3
6	9

a) What type of control chart would you use to monitor this process? Why?
b) What are the 3-sigma control limits for this process? Assume that the historical complaint rate is unknown.
c) Is the process in control, according to the control limits? Why or why not?
d) Assume now that the historical complaint rate has been four calls a week. What would the 3-sigma control limits for this process be now? Has the process been in control according to the control limits? **Px**

•• **S6.23** The school board is trying to evaluate a new math program introduced to second-graders in five elementary schools across the county this year. A sample of the student scores on standardized math tests in each elementary school yielded the following data:

SCHOOL	NO. OF TEST ERRORS
A	52
B	27
C	35
D	44
E	55

Construct a *c*-chart for test errors, and set the control limits to contain 99.73% of the random variation in test scores. What does the chart tell you? Has the new math program been effective? **Px**

•• **S6.24** Telephone inquiries of 100 IRS "customers" are monitored daily at random. Incidents of incorrect information or other nonconformities (such as impoliteness to customers) are recorded. The data for last week follow:

DAY	NO. OF NONCONFORMITIES
1	5
2	10
3	23
4	20
5	15

a) Construct a 3-standard deviation c-chart of nonconformities.
b) What does the control chart tell you about the IRS telephone operators? **Px**

••• **S6.25** The accounts receivable department at Rick Wing Manufacturing has been having difficulty getting customers to pay the full amount of their bills. Many customers complain that the bills are not correct and do not reflect the materials that arrived at their receiving docks. The department has decided to implement SPC in its billing process. To set up control charts, 10 samples of 50 bills each were taken over a month's time and the items on the bills checked against the bill of lading sent by the company's shipping department to determine the number of bills that were not correct. The results were:

SAMPLE NO.	NO. OF INCORRECT BILLS	SAMPLE NO.	NO. OF INCORRECT BILLS
1	6	6	5
2	5	7	3
3	11	8	4
4	4	9	7
5	0	10	2

a) Determine the value of p-bar, the mean fraction defective. Then determine the control limits for the p-chart using a 99.73% confidence level (3 standard deviations). Has this process been in control? If not, which samples were out of control?
b) How might you use the quality tools discussed in Chapter 6 to determine the source of the billing defects and where you might start your improvement efforts to eliminate the causes? **Px**

••• **S6.26** West Battery Corp. has recently been receiving complaints from retailers that its 9-volt batteries are not lasting as long as other name brands. James West, head of the TQM program at West's Austin plant, believes there is no problem because his batteries have had an average life of 50 hours, about 10% longer than competitors' models. To raise the lifetime above this level would require a new level of technology not available to West. Nevertheless, he is concerned enough to set up hourly assembly line checks. Previously, after ensuring that the process was running properly, West took size $n = 5$ samples of 9-volt batteries for each of 25 hours to establish the standards for control chart limits. Those samples are shown in the following table:

West Battery Data—Battery Lifetimes (in hours)

HOUR SAMPLE TAKEN	1	2	3	4	5	$\overline{X}$	R
1	51	50	49	50	50	50.0	2
2	45	47	70	46	36	48.8	34
3	50	35	48	39	47	43.8	15
4	55	70	50	30	51	51.2	40
5	49	38	64	36	47	46.8	28
6	59	62	40	54	64	55.8	24
7	36	33	49	48	56	44.4	23
8	50	67	53	43	40	50.6	27
9	44	52	46	47	44	46.6	8
10	70	45	50	47	41	50.6	29
11	57	54	62	45	36	50.8	26
12	56	54	47	42	62	52.2	20
13	40	70	58	45	44	51.4	30
14	52	58	40	52	46	49.6	18
15	57	42	52	58	59	53.6	17
16	62	49	42	33	55	48.2	29
17	40	39	49	59	48	47.0	20
18	64	50	42	57	50	52.6	22
19	58	53	52	48	50	52.2	10
20	60	50	41	41	50	48.4	19
21	52	47	48	58	40	49.0	18
22	55	40	56	49	45	49.0	16
23	47	48	50	50	48	48.6	3
24	50	50	49	51	51	50.2	2
25	51	50	51	51	62	53.0	12

With these limits established, West now takes 5 more hours of data, which are shown in the following table:

HOUR	1	2	3	4	5
26	48	52	39	57	61
27	45	53	48	46	66
28	63	49	50	45	53
29	57	70	45	52	61
30	45	38	46	54	52

a) Determine means and the upper and lower control limits for $\overline{x}$ and R (using the first 25 hours only).
b) Has the manufacturing process been in control?
c) Comment on the lifetimes observed. **Px**

• • • • S6.27 One of New England Air's top competitive priorities is on-time arrivals. Quality VP Clair Bond decided to personally monitor New England Air's performance. Each week for the past 30 weeks, Bond checked a random sample of 100 flight arrivals for on-time performance. The table that follows contains the number of flights that did not meet New England Air's definition of "on time":

SAMPLE (WEEK)	LATE FLIGHTS	SAMPLE (WEEK)	LATE FLIGHTS
1	2	16	2
2	4	17	3
3	10	18	7
4	4	19	3
5	1	20	2
6	1	21	3
7	13	22	7
8	9	23	4
9	11	24	3
10	0	25	2
11	3	26	2
12	4	27	0
13	2	28	1
14	2	29	3
15	8	30	4

a) Using a 95% confidence level, plot the overall percentage of late flights ($\bar{p}$) and the upper and lower control limits on a control chart.
b) Assume that the airline industry's upper and lower control limits for flights that are not on time are .1000 and .0400, respectively. Draw them on your control chart.
c) Plot the percentage of late flights in each sample. Do all samples fall within New England Air's control limits? When one falls outside the control limits, what should be done?
d) What can Clair Bond report about the quality of service? **Px**

Additional problems S6.28–S6.39 are available in MyOMLab.

Problems S6.40–S6.50 relate to Process Capability

• S6.40 The difference between the upper specification and the lower specification for a process is 0.6". The standard deviation is 0.1". What is the process capability ratio, C_p? Interpret this number. **Px**

• • S6.41 Meena Chavan Corp.'s computer chip production process yields DRAM chips with an average life of 1,800 hours and $\sigma = 100$ hours. The tolerance upper and lower specification limits are 2,400 hours and 1,600 hours, respectively. Is this process capable of producing DRAM chips to specification? **Px**

• • S6.42 Linda Boardman, Inc., an equipment manufacturer in Boston, has submitted a sample cutoff valve to improve your manufacturing process. Your process engineering department has conducted experiments and found that the valve has a mean (μ) of 8.00 and a standard deviation (σ) of .04. Your desired performance is $\mu = 8.0 \pm 3\sigma$, where $\sigma = .045$. What is the C_{pk} of the Boardman valve? **Px**

• • S6.43 The specifications for a plastic liner for concrete highway projects calls for a thickness of 3.0 mm $\pm$.1 mm. The standard deviation of the process is estimated to be .02 mm. What are the upper and lower specification limits for this product? The process is known to operate at a mean thickness of 3.0 mm. What is the C_{pk} for this process? About what percentage of all units of this liner will meet specifications? **Px**

• • S6.44 Frank Pianki, the manager of an organic yogurt processing plant, desires a quality specification with a mean of 16 ounces, an upper specification limit of 16.5, and a lower specification limit of 15.5. The process has a mean of 16 ounces and a standard deviation of 1 ounce. Determine the C_{pk} of the process. **Px**

• • S6.45 A process filling small bottles with baby formula has a target of 3 ounces ± 0.150 ounce. Two hundred bottles from the process were sampled. The results showed the average amount of formula placed in the bottles to be 3.042 ounces. The standard deviation of the amounts was 0.034 ounce. Determine the value of C_{pk}. Roughly what proportion of bottles meet the specifications? **Px**

Additional problems S6.46–S6.50 are available in MyOMLab.

Problems S6.51–S6.55 relate to Acceptance Sampling

• • S6.51 As the supervisor in charge of shipping and receiving, you need to determine *the average outgoing quality* in a plant where the known incoming lots from your assembly line have an average defective rate of 3%. Your plan is to sample 80 units of every 1,000 in a lot. The number of defects in the sample is not to exceed 3. Such a plan provides you with a probability of acceptance of each lot of .79 (79%). What is your average outgoing quality? **Px**

• • S6.52 An acceptance sampling plan has lots of 500 pieces and a sample size of 60. The number of defects in the sample may not exceed 2. This plan, based on an OC curve, has a probability of .57 of accepting lots when the incoming lots have a defective rate of 4%, which is the historical average for this process. What do you tell your customer the average outgoing quality is? **Px**

• • S6.53 The percent defective from an incoming lot is 3%. An OC curve showed the probability of acceptance to be 0.55. Given a lot size of 2,000 and a sample of 100, determine the average outgoing quality in percent defective.

• • S6.54 In an acceptance sampling plan developed for lots containing 1,000 units, the sample size n is 85. The percent defective of the incoming lots is 2%, and the probability of acceptance is 0.64. What is the average outgoing quality?

• • S6.55 We want to determine the AOQ for an acceptance sampling plan when the quality of the incoming lots in percent defective is 1.5%, and then again when the incoming percent defective is 5%. The sample size is 80 units for a lot size of 550 units. Furthermore, P_a at 1.5% defective levels is 0.95. At 5% incoming defective levels, the P_a is found to be 0.5. Determine the average outgoing quality for both incoming percent defective levels.

CASE STUDIES

Bayfield Mud Company

In November 2015, John Wells, a customer service representative of Bayfield Mud Company, was summoned to the Houston warehouse of Wet-Land Drilling, Inc., to inspect three boxcars of mudtreating agents that Bayfield had shipped to the Houston firm. (Bayfield's corporate offices and its largest plant are located in Orange, Texas, which is just west of the Louisiana–Texas border.) Wet-Land had filed a complaint that the 50-pound bags of treating agents just received from Bayfield were short-weight by approximately 5%.

The short-weight bags were initially detected by one of Wet-Land's receiving clerks, who noticed that the railroad scale tickets indicated that net weights were significantly less on all three boxcars than those of identical shipments received on October 25, 2015. Bayfield's traffic department was called to determine if lighter-weight pallets were used on the shipments. (This might explain the lighter net weights.) Bayfield indicated, however, that no changes had been made in loading or palletizing procedures. Thus, Wet-Land engineers randomly checked 50 bags and discovered that the average net weight was 47.51 pounds. They noted from past shipments that the process yielded bag net weights averaging exactly 50.0 pounds, with an acceptable standard deviation σ of 1.2 pounds. Consequently, they concluded that the sample indicated a significant short-weight. (The reader may wish to verify this conclusion.) Bayfield was then contacted, and Wells was sent to investigate the complaint. Upon arrival, Wells verified the complaint and issued a 5% credit to Wet-Land.

Wet-Land management, however, was not completely satisfied with the issuance of credit. The charts followed by their mud engineers on the drilling platforms were based on 50-pound bags of treating agents. Lighter-weight bags might result in poor chemical control during the drilling operation and thus adversely affect drilling efficiency. (Mud-treating agents are used to control the pH and other chemical properties of the core during drilling operation.) This defect could cause severe economic consequences because of the extremely high cost of oil and natural gas well-drilling operations. Consequently, special-use instructions had to accompany the delivery of these shipments to the drilling platforms. Moreover, the short-weight shipments had to be isolated in Wet-Land's warehouse, causing extra handling and poor space utilization. Thus, Wells was informed that Wet-Land might seek a new supplier of mud-treating agents if, in the future, it received bags that deviated significantly from 50 pounds.

The quality control department at Bayfield suspected that the lightweight bags might have resulted from "growing pains" at the Orange plant. Because of the earlier energy crisis, oil and natural gas exploration activity had greatly increased. In turn, this increased activity created increased demand for products produced by related industries, including drilling muds. Consequently, Bayfield had to expand from a one-shift (6:00 A.M. to 2:00 P.M.) to a two-shift (2:00 P.M. to 10:00 P.M.) operation in mid-2010, and finally to a three-shift operation (24 hours per day) in the fall of 2015.

TIME	AVERAGE WEIGHT (POUNDS)	RANGE		TIME	AVERAGE WEIGHT (POUNDS)	RANGE	
		SMALLEST	LARGEST			SMALLEST	LARGEST
6:00 A.M.	49.6	48.7	50.7	6:00 P.M.	46.8	41.0	51.2
7:00	50.2	49.1	51.2	7:00	50.0	46.2	51.7
8:00	50.6	49.6	51.4	8:00	47.4	44.0	48.7
9:00	50.8	50.2	51.8	9:00	47.0	44.2	48.9
10:00	49.9	49.2	52.3	10:00	47.2	46.6	50.2
11:00	50.3	48.6	51.7	11:00	48.6	47.0	50.0
12 noon	48.6	46.2	50.4	12 midnight	49.8	48.2	50.4
1:00 P.M.	49.0	46.4	50.0	1:00 A.M.	49.6	48.4	51.7
2:00	49.0	46.0	50.6	2:00	50.0	49.0	52.2
3:00	49.8	48.2	50.8	3:00	50.0	49.2	50.0
4:00	50.3	49.2	52.7	4:00	47.2	46.3	50.5
5:00	51.4	50.0	55.3	5:00	47.0	44.1	49.7
6:00	51.6	49.2	54.7	6:00	48.4	45.0	49.0
7:00	51.8	50.0	55.6	7:00	48.8	44.8	49.7
8:00	51.0	48.6	53.2	8:00	49.6	48.0	51.8
9:00	50.5	49.4	52.4	9:00	50.0	48.1	52.7
10:00	49.2	46.1	50.7	10:00	51.0	48.1	55.2
11:00	49.0	46.3	50.8	11:00	50.4	49.5	54.1
12 midnight	48.4	45.4	50.2	12 noon	50.0	48.7	50.9
1:00 A.M.	47.6	44.3	49.7	1:00 P.M.	48.9	47.6	51.2
2:00	47.4	44.1	49.6	2:00	49.8	48.4	51.0
3:00	48.2	45.2	49.0	3:00	49.8	48.8	50.8
4:00	48.0	45.5	49.1	4:00	50.0	49.1	50.6
5:00	48.4	47.1	49.6	5:00	47.8	45.2	51.2

(cont'd)

| TIME | AVERAGE WEIGHT (POUNDS) | RANGE | | TIME | AVERAGE WEIGHT (POUNDS) | RANGE | |
		SMALLEST	LARGEST			SMALLEST	LARGEST
6:00 A.M.	48.6	47.4	52.0	6:00 P.M.	46.4	44.0	49.7
7:00	50.0	49.2	52.2	7:00	46.4	44.4	50.0
8:00	49.8	49.0	52.4	8:00	47.2	46.6	48.9
9:00	50.3	49.4	51.7	9:00	48.4	47.2	49.5
10:00	50.2	49.6	51.8	10:00	49.2	48.1	50.7
11:00	50.0	49.0	52.3	11:00	48.4	47.0	50.8
12 noon	50.0	48.8	52.4	12 midnight	47.2	46.4	49.2
1:00 P.M.	50.1	49.4	53.6	1:00 A.M.	47.4	46.8	49.0
2:00	49.7	48.6	51.0	2:00	48.8	47.2	51.4
3:00	48.4	47.2	51.7	3:00	49.6	49.0	50.6
4:00	47.2	45.3	50.9	4:00	51.0	50.5	51.5
5:00	46.8	44.1	49.0	5:00	50.5	50.0	51.9

The additional night-shift bagging crew was staffed entirely by new employees. The most experienced foremen were temporarily assigned to supervise the night-shift employees. Most emphasis was placed on increasing the output of bags to meet ever-increasing demand. It was suspected that only occasional reminders were made to double-check the bag weight-feeder. (A double-check is performed by systematically weighing a bag on a scale to determine if the proper weight is being loaded by the weight-feeder. If there is significant deviation from 50 pounds, corrective adjustments are made to the weight-release mechanism.)

To verify this expectation, the quality control staff randomly sampled the bag output and prepared the chart on the previous page. Six bags were sampled and weighed each hour.

Discussion Questions

1. What is your analysis of the bag-weight problem?

2. What procedures would you recommend to maintain proper quality control?

Source: Professor Jerry Kinard, Western Carolina University. Reprinted with permission.

Frito-Lay's Quality-Controlled Potato Chips

Video Case

Frito-Lay, the multi-billion-dollar snack food giant, produces billions of pounds of product every year at its dozens of U.S. and Canadian plants. From the farming of potatoes—in Florida, North Carolina, and Michigan—to factory and to retail stores, the ingredients and final product of Lay's chips, for example, are inspected at least 11 times: in the field, before unloading at the plant, after washing and peeling, at the sizing station, at the fryer, after seasoning, when bagged (for weight), at carton filling, in the warehouse, and as they are placed on the store shelf by Frito-Lay personnel. Similar inspections take place for its other famous products, including Cheetos, Fritos, Ruffles, and Tostitos.

In addition to these employee inspections, the firm uses proprietary vision systems to look for defective potato chips. Chips are pulled off the high-speed line and checked twice if the vision system senses them to be too brown.

The company follows the very strict standards of the American Institute of Baking (AIB), standards that are much tougher than those of the U.S. Food and Drug Administration. Two unannounced AIB site visits per year keep Frito-Lay's plants on their toes. Scores, consistently in the "excellent" range, are posted, and every employee knows exactly how the plant is doing.

There are two key metrics in Frito-Lay's continuous improvement quality program: (1) total customer complaints (measured on a complaints per million bag basis) and (2) hourly or daily statistical process control scores (for oil, moisture, seasoning, and salt content, for chip thickness, for fryer temperature, and for weight).

In the Florida plant, Angela McCormack, who holds engineering and MBA degrees, oversees a 15-member quality assurance staff. They watch all aspects of quality, including training employees on the factory floor, monitoring automated processing equipment, and developing and updating statistical process control (SPC) charts. The upper and lower control limits for one checkpoint, salt content in Lay's chips, are 2.22% and 1.98%, respectively. To see exactly how these limits are created using SPC, watch the video that accompanies this case.

Discussion Questions*

1. Angela is now going to evaluate a new salt process delivery system and wants to know if the upper and lower control limits at 3 standard deviations for the new system will meet the upper and lower control specifications noted earlier.

    The data (in percents) from the initial trial samples are:

    Sample 1: 1.98, 2.11, 2.15, 2.06
    Sample 2: 1.99, 2.0, 2.08, 1.99
    Sample 3: 2.20, 2.10. 2.20, 2.05
    Sample 4: 2.18, 2.01, 2.23, 1.98
    Sample 5: 2.01, 2.08, 2.14, 2.16

    Provide the report to Angela.

2. What are the advantages and disadvantages of Frito-Lay drivers stocking their customers' shelves?

3. Why is quality a critical function at Frito-Lay?

*You may wish to view the video that accompanies this case before answering these questions.

Farm to Fork: Quality at Darden Restaurants

Video Case

Darden Restaurants, the $6.3 billion owner of such popular brands as Olive Garden, Seasons 52, and Bahama Breeze, serves more than 320 million meals annually in its 1,500 restaurants across the U.S. and Canada. Before any one of these meals is placed before a guest, the ingredients for each recipe must pass quality control inspections at the source, ranging from measurement and weighing to tasting, touching, or lab testing. Darden has differentiated itself from its restaurant peers by developing the gold standard in continuous improvement.

To assure both customers and the company that quality expectations are met, Darden uses a rigorous inspection process, employing statistical process control (SPC) as part of its "Farm to Fork" program. More than 50 food scientists, microbiologists, and public health professionals report to Ana Hooper, vice president of quality assurance.

As part of Darden's Point Source program, Hooper's team, based in Southeast Asia (in China, Thailand, and Singapore) and Latin America (in Equador, Honduras, and Chile), approves and inspects—and works with Darden buyers to purchase—more than 50 million pounds of seafood each year for restaurant use. Darden used to build quality in at the end by inspecting shipments as they reached U.S. distribution centers. Now, thanks to coaching and partnering with vendors abroad, Darden needs but a few domestic inspection labs to verify compliance to its exacting standards. Food vendors in source countries know that when supplying Darden, they are subject to regular audits that are stricter than U.S. Food and Drug Administration (FDA) standards.

Two Quality Success Stories

Quality specialists' jobs include raising the bar and improving quality and safety at all plants in their geographic area. The Thai quality representative, for example, worked closely with several of Darden's largest shrimp vendors to convert them to a production-line-integrated quality assurance program. The vendors were able to improve the quality of shrimp supplied and reduce the percentage of defects by 19%.

Likewise, when the Darden quality teams visited fields of growers/shippers in Mexico recently, it identified challenges such as low employee hygiene standards, field food safety problems, lack of portable toilets, child labor, and poor working conditions. Darden addressed these concerns and hired third-party independent food safety verification firms to ensure continued compliance to standards.

SPC Charts

SPC charts, such as the one shown on page 253 in this supplement, are particularly important. These charts document precooked food weights; meat, seafood and poultry temperatures; blemishes on produce; and bacteria counts on shrimp—just to name a few. Quality assurance is part of a much bigger process that is key to Darden's success—its supply chain (see Chapters 2 and 11 for discussion and case studies on this topic). That's because quality comes from the source and flows through distribution to the restaurant and guests.

Discussion Questions*

1. How does Darden build quality into the supply chain?
2. Select two potential problems—one in the Darden supply chain and one in a restaurant—that can be analyzed with a fish-bone chart. Draw a complete chart to deal with each problem.
3. Darden applies SPC in many product attributes. Identify where these are probably used.
4. The SPC chart on page 253 illustrates Darden's use of control charts to monitor the weight of salmon filets. Given these data, what conclusion do you, as a Darden quality control inspector, draw? What report do you issue to your supervisor? How do you respond to the salmon vendor?

*You might want to view the video that accompanies this case before answering these questions.

- **Additional Case Study:** Visit MyOMLab for this free case study:
  Green River Chemical Company: Involves a company that needs to set up a control chart to monitor sulfate content because of customer complaints.

Endnotes

1. Removing assignable causes is work. Quality expert W. Edwards Deming observed that a state of statistical control is not a natural state for a manufacturing process. Deming instead viewed it as an achievement, arrived at by elimination, one by one, by determined effort, of special causes of excessive variation.
2. The standard deviation is easily calculated as

$$\sigma = \sqrt{\frac{\sum_{i=1}^{n}(x_i - \bar{x})^2}{n - 1}}.$$ For a good review of this and other statistical terms, refer to Tutorial 1, "Statistical Review for Managers," in MyOMLab.

3. Lower control limits cannot take negative values in control charts. So the LCL = max $(0, \bar{\bar{x}} - z\sigma_{\bar{x}})$.
4. If the sample sizes are not the same, other techniques must be used.
5. A Poisson probability distribution is a discrete distribution commonly used when the items of interest (in this case, defects) are infrequent or occur in time or space.

6. This is because a C_p of 1.0 has 99.73% of outputs within specifications. So $1.00 - .9973 = .0027$; with 1,000 parts, there are $.0027 = 1,000 = 2.7$ defects.

   For a C_p of 2.0, 99.99966% of outputs are "within spec." So $1.00 - .9999966 = .0000034$; with 1 million parts, there are 3.4 defects.
7. Refer to Tutorial 2 in MyOMLab for an extended discussion of acceptance sampling.
8. Note that sampling always runs the danger of leading to an erroneous conclusion. Let us say that in one company the total population under scrutiny is a load of 1,000 computer chips, of which in reality only 30 (or 3%) are defective. This means that we would want to accept the shipment of chips, because for this particular firm 4% is the allowable defect rate. However, if a random sample of $n = 50$ chips was drawn, we could conceivably end up with 0 defects and accept that shipment (that is, it is okay), or we could find all 30 defects in the sample. If the latter happened, we could wrongly conclude that the whole population was 60% defective and reject them all.

Supplement 6 *Rapid Review*

Main Heading	Review Material	MyOMLab

STATISTICAL PROCESS CONTROL (SPC)
(pp. 246–260)

- **Statistical process control (SPC)**—A process used to monitor standards by taking measurements and corrective action as a product or service is being produced.
- **Control chart**—A graphical presentation of process data over time.

A process is said to be operating *in statistical control* when the only source of variation is common (natural) causes. The process must first be brought into statistical control by detecting and eliminating special (assignable) causes of variation. *The objective of a process control system is to provide a statistical signal when assignable causes of variation are present.*

- **Natural variations**—The variability that affects every production process to some degree and is to be expected; also known as common cause.

When natural variations form a *normal distribution,* they are characterized by two parameters:

- Mean, μ (the measure of central tendency—in this case, the average value)
- Standard deviation, σ (the measure of dispersion)

As long as the distribution (output measurements) remains within specified limits, the process is said to be "in control," and natural variations are tolerated.

- **Assignable variation**—Variation in a production process that can be traced to specific causes.

Control charts for the mean, $\bar{x}$, and the range, R, are used to monitor *variables* (outputs with continuous dimensions), such as weight, speed, length, or strength.

- **$\bar{x}$-chart**—A quality control chart for variables that indicates when changes occur in the central tendency of a production process.
- **R-chart**—A control chart that tracks the range within a sample; it indicates that a gain or loss in uniformity has occurred in dispersion of a production process.
- **Central limit theorem**—The theoretical foundation for $\bar{x}$-charts, which states that regardless of the distribution of the population of all parts or services, the $\bar{x}$ distribution will tend to follow a normal curve as the number of samples increases:

$$\bar{\bar{x}} = \mu \qquad \text{(S6-1)}$$

$$\sigma_{\bar{x}} = \frac{\sigma}{\sqrt{n}} \qquad \text{(S6-2)}$$

The $\bar{x}$-chart limits, if we know the true standard deviation σ of the process population, are:

$$\text{Upper control limit (UCL)} = \bar{\bar{x}} + z\sigma_{\bar{x}} \qquad \text{(S6-3)}$$

$$\text{Lower control limit (LCL)} = \bar{\bar{x}} - z\sigma_{\bar{x}} \qquad \text{(S6-4)}$$

where z = confidence level selected (e.g., $z = 3$ is 99.73% confidence).

The *range*, R, of a sample is defined as the difference between the largest and smallest items. If we do not know the true standard deviation, σ, of the population, the $\bar{x}$-chart limits are:

$$\text{UCL}_{\bar{x}} = \bar{\bar{x}} + A_2\bar{R} \qquad \text{(S6-5)}$$

$$\text{LCL}_{\bar{x}} = \bar{\bar{x}} - A_2\bar{R} \qquad \text{(S6-6)}$$

In addition to being concerned with the process average, operations managers are interested in the process dispersion, or range. The R-chart control limits for the range of a process are:

$$\text{UCL}_R = D_4\bar{R} \qquad \text{(S6-7)}$$

$$\text{LCL}_R = D_3\bar{R} \qquad \text{(S6-8)}$$

Attributes are typically classified as *defective* or *nondefective.* The two attribute charts are (1) *p*-charts (which measure the *percent* defective in a sample), and (2) *c*-charts (which *count* the number of defects in a sample).

- **p-chart**—A quality control chart that is used to control attributes:

$$\text{UCL}_p = \bar{p} + z\sigma_p \qquad \text{(S6-9)}$$
$$\text{LCL}_p = \bar{p} - z\sigma_p \qquad \text{(S6-10)}$$

$$\hat{\sigma}_p = \sqrt{\frac{\bar{p}(1 - \bar{p})}{n}} \qquad \text{(S6-11)}$$

- **c-chart**—A quality control chart used to control the number of defects per unit of output. The Poisson distribution is the basis for *c*-charts, whose 99.73% limits are computed as:

$$\text{Control limits} = \bar{c} \pm 3\sqrt{\bar{c}} \qquad \text{(S6-12)}$$

- **Run test**—A test used to examine the points in a control chart to determine whether nonrandom variation is present.

Concept Questions: 1.1–1.4

Problems: S6.1–S6.39

VIDEO S6.1
Farm to Fork: Quality at Darden Restaurants

Virtual Office Hours for Solved Problems: S6.1–S6.3

ACTIVE MODELS S6.1 and S6.2

VIDEO S6.2
Frito-Lay's Quality-Controlled Potato Chips

Virtual Office Hours for Solved Problem: S6.5

Main Heading	Review Material	MyOMLab
PROCESS CAPABILITY (pp. 260–262)	■ **Process capability**—The ability to meet design specifications. ■ **C_p**—A ratio for determining whether a process meets design specifications. $$C_p = \frac{(\text{Upper specification} - \text{Lower specification})}{6\sigma} \quad \text{(S6-13)}$$ ■ **C_{pk}**—A proportion of variation (3σ) between the center of the process and the nearest specification limit: $$C_{pk} = \text{Minimum of} \left[\frac{\text{Upper spec limit} - \overline{X}}{3\sigma}, \frac{\overline{X} - \text{Lower spec limit}}{3\sigma} \right] \quad \text{(S6-14)}$$	Concept Questions: 2.1–2.4 Problems: S6.40-S6.50 Virtual Office Hours for Solved Problems: S6.4 **ACTIVE MODEL S6.3**
ACCEPTANCE SAMPLING (pp. 262–265)	■ **Acceptance sampling**—A method of measuring random samples of lots or batches of products against predetermined standards. ■ **Operating characteristic (OC) curve**—A graph that describes how well an acceptance plan discriminates between good and bad lots. ■ **Producer's risk**—The mistake of having a producer's good lot rejected through sampling. ■ **Consumer's risk**—The mistake of a customer's acceptance of a bad lot overlooked through sampling. ■ **Acceptable quality level (AQL)**—The quality level of a lot considered good. ■ **Lot tolerance percent defective (LTPD)**—The quality level of a lot considered bad. ■ **Type I error**—Statistically, the probability of rejecting a good lot. ■ **Type II error**—Statistically, the probability of accepting a bad lot. ■ **Average outgoing quality (AOQ)**—The percent defective in an average lot of goods inspected through acceptance sampling: $$AOQ = \frac{(P_d)(P_a)(N - n)}{N} \quad \text{(S6-15)}$$	Concept Questions: 3.1–3.4 Problems: S6.51–S6.55

Self Test

■ **Before taking the self-test,** refer to the learning objectives listed at the beginning of the supplement and the key terms listed at the end of the supplement.

LO S6.1 If the mean of a particular sample is within control limits and the range of that sample is not within control limits:
 a) the process is in control, with only assignable causes of variation.
 b) the process is not producing within the established control limits.
 c) the process is producing within the established control limits, with only natural causes of variation.
 d) the process has both natural and assignable causes of variation.

LO S6.2 The central limit theorem:
 a) is the theoretical foundation of the *c*-chart.
 b) states that the average of assignable variations is zero.
 c) allows managers to use the normal distribution as the basis for building some control charts.
 d) states that the average range can be used as a proxy for the standard deviation.
 e) controls the steepness of an operating characteristic curve.

LO S6.3 The type of chart used to control the central tendency of variables with continuous dimensions is:
 a) $\overline{x}$-chart.
 b) *R*-chart.
 c) *p*-chart.
 d) *c*-chart.
 e) none of the above.

LO S6.4 If parts in a sample are measured and the mean of the sample measurement is outside the control limits:
 a) the process is out of control, and the cause should be established.
 b) the process is in control but not capable of producing within the established control limits.
 c) the process is within the established control limits, with only natural causes of variation.
 d) all of the above are true.

LO S6.5 Control charts for attributes are:
 a) *p*-charts.
 b) *c*-charts.
 c) *R*-charts.
 d) $\overline{x}$-charts.
 e) both a and b.

LO S6.6 The ability of a process to meet design specifications is called:
 a) Taguchi.
 b) process capability.
 c) capability index.
 d) acceptance sampling.
 e) average outgoing quality.

LO S6.7 The _____ risk is the probability that a lot will be rejected despite the quality level exceeding or meeting the _____.

Answers: LO S6.1. b; LO S6.2. c; LO S6.3. a; LO S6.4. a; LO S6.5. e; LO S6.6. b; LO S6.7. producer's, AQL

Process Strategy

CHAPTER OUTLINE

GLOBAL COMPANY PROFILE: *Harley-Davidson*

◆ Four Process Strategies *282*

◆ Selection of Equipment *288*

◆ Process Analysis and Design *288*

◆ Special Considerations for Service Process Design *293*

◆ Production Technology *294*

◆ Technology in Services *298*

◆ Process Redesign *298*

Alaska Airlines

Alaska Airlines

10 OM STRATEGY DECISIONS

- Design of Goods and Services
- Managing Quality
- *Process Strategy*
- Location Strategies
- Layout Strategies
- Human Resources
- Supply-Chain Management
- Inventory Management
- Scheduling
- Maintenance

Repetitive Manufacturing Works at Harley-Davidson

Since Harley-Davidson's founding in Milwaukee in 1903, it has competed with hundreds of manufacturers, foreign and domestic. The competition has been tough. Recent competitive battles have been with the Japanese, and earlier battles were with the German, English, and Italian manufacturers. But after over 110 years, Harley is the only major U.S. motorcycle company. The company now has five U.S. facilities and an assembly plant in Brazil. The Sportster powertrain is manufactured in Wauwatosa, Wisconsin, and the sidecars, saddlebags, windshields, and other specialty items are produced in Tomahawk, Wisconsin. The Touring and Softail bikes are assembled in York, Pennsylvania, while the Sportster models, Dyna models, and VRSC models of motorcycles are produced in Kansas City, Missouri.

As a part of management's lean manufacturing effort, Harley groups production of parts that require similar processes together. The result is work cells. Using the latest technology, work cells perform in one location all the operations necessary for production of a specific module. Raw materials are moved to the work cells for module production. The modules then proceed

Flowchart Showing the Production Process at Harley-Davidson's York Assembly Plant

| Frame tube bending | Frame-building work cells | Frame machining | Hot-paint frame painting |

THE ASSEMBLY LINE

Incoming parts

Engines and transmissions

Engines arrive on a JIT schedule from a 10-station work cell in Milwaukee.

TESTING 28 tests

Air cleaners	Oil tank work cell
Fluids and mufflers	Shocks and forks
Fuel tank work cell	Handlebars
Wheel work cell	Fender work cell

In less than 3 hours, 450 parts and subassemblies go into a Harley motorcycle.

Roller testing

Crating

fckncg/Alamy

Rick Friedman/Corbis

Wheel assembly modules are prepared in a work cell for JIT delivery to the assembly line.

Rick Friedman/Corbis

For manufacturers like Harley-Davidson, which produces a large number of end products from a relatively small number of options, modular bills of material provide an effective solution.

to the assembly line. As a double check on quality, Harley has also installed "light curtain" technology, which uses an infrared sensor to verify the bin from which an operator is taking parts. Materials go to the assembly line on a just-in-time basis, or as Harley calls it, using a Materials as Needed (MAN) system.

The 12.5-million-square-foot York facility includes manufacturing cells that perform tube bending, frame-building, machining, painting, and polishing. Innovative manufacturing techniques use robots to load machines and highly automated production to reduce machining time. Automation and precision sensors play a key role in maintaining tolerances and producing a quality product. Each day the York facility produces up to 600 heavy-duty factory-custom motorcycles. Bikes are assembled with different engine displacements, multiple wheel options, colors, and accessories. The result is a huge number of variations in the motorcycles available, which allows customers to individualize their purchase. (See **www.Harley-Davidson.com** for an example of modular customization.) The Harley-Davidson production system works because high-quality modules are brought together on a tightly scheduled repetitive production line. ◀

Nuccio DiNuzzo/KRT/Newscom

Engines are assembled in Memomonee Falls, Wisconsin, and placed in their own protective containers for shipment to the York facility. Upon arrival in York, engines are placed on an overhead conveyor for movement directly to the assembly line.

Rick Friedman/Corbis

It all comes together on the line. Any employee who spots a problem has the authority to stop the line until the problem in corrected. The multicolored "andon" light above the line signals the severity of the problem.

LEARNING OBJECTIVES

LO 7.1 *Describe* four process strategies 282

LO 7.2 *Compute* crossover points for different processes 286

LO 7.3 *Use* the tools of process analysis 289

LO 7.4 *Describe* customer interaction in service processes 293

LO 7.5 *Identify* recent advances in production technology 294

Four Process Strategies

In Chapter 5, we examined the need for the selection, definition, and design of goods and services. Our purpose was to create environmentally friendly goods and services that could be delivered in an ethical, sustainable manner. We now turn to their production. A major decision for an operations manager is finding the best way to produce so as not to waste our planet's resources. Let's look at ways to help managers design a process for achieving this goal.

A process strategy is an organization's approach to transforming resources into goods and services. *The objective is to create a process that can produce offerings that meet customer requirements within cost and other managerial constraints.* The process selected will have a long-term effect on efficiency and flexibility of production, as well as on cost and quality of the goods produced.

Virtually every good or service is made by using some variation of one of four process strategies: (1) process focus, (2) repetitive focus, (3) product focus, and (4) mass customization. The relationship of these four strategies to volume and variety is shown in Figure 7.1. We examine *Arnold Palmer Hospital* as an example of a process-focused firm, *Harley-Davidson* as a repetitive producer, *Frito-Lay* as a product-focused operation, and *Dell* as a mass customizer.

Process strategy
An organization's approach to transforming resources into goods and services.

LO 7.1 *Describe* four process strategies

Process Focus

The vast majority of global production is devoted to making *low-volume*, *high-variety* products in places called "job shops." Such facilities are organized around specific activities or processes. In a factory, these processes might be departments devoted to welding, grinding, and painting. In an office, the processes might be accounts payable, sales, and payroll. In a restaurant, they might be bar, grill, and bakery. Such facilities are process focused in terms of equipment, layout, and supervision. They provide a high degree of product flexibility as products move between the specialized processes. Each process is designed to perform a variety of activities and handle frequent changes. Consequently, they are also called *intermittent processes*.

Process focus
A production facility organized around processes to facilitate low-volume, high-variety production.

Figure 7.1

Process Selected Must Fit with Volume and Variety

Volume

| Low Volume | Repetitive Process | High Volume |

High Variety
one or few units per run
(allows customization)

Process Focus
projects, job shops
(machine, print,
hospitals, restaurants)
Arnold Palmer Hospital

Mass Customization
(difficult to achieve but huge rewards)
Dell Computer

Variety (flexibility)

Changes in Modules
modest runs,
standardized modules

Repetitive
(autos, motorcycles,
home appliances)
Harley-Davidson

Changes in Attributes
(such as grade, quality,
size, thickness, etc.)
long runs only

Poor Strategy
(Both fixed and variable costs are high.)

Product Focus
(commercial baked goods,
steel, glass, beer)
Frito-Lay

(a)	(b)	(c)	(d)
Process Focus (low-volume, high-variety, intermittent process) Arnold Palmer Hospital	**Repetitive Focus** (modular) Harley-Davidson	**Product Focus** (high-volume, low-variety, continuous process) Frito-Lay	**Mass Customization** (high-volume, high-variety) Dell Computer
Many inputs	**Raw material and module inputs**	**Few inputs**	**Many part and component inputs**
(surgeries, sick patients, baby deliveries, emergencies)	(multiple engines and wheel modules)	(corn, potatoes, water, seasoning)	(chips, hard drives, software, cases)
Many departments and many routings	Few modules		Many modules
Many different outputs (uniquely treated patients)	Modules combined for many outputs (many combinations of motorcycles)	Output variations in size, shape, and packaging (3-oz, 5-oz, 24-oz packages labeled for each market)	Many output versions (custom PCs and notebooks)

Brasiliao/Shutterstock · 300dpi/Shutterstock · Tund/Shutterstock · Archman/Shutterstock

Figure 7.2

Four Process Options with an Example of Each

Referring to Figure 7.2(a), imagine a diverse group of patients entering Arnold Palmer Hospital, a process-focused facility, to be routed to specialized departments, treated in a distinct way, and then exiting as uniquely cared-for individuals.

Process-focused facilities have high variable costs with extremely low utilization of facilities, as low as 5%. This is the case for many restaurants, hospitals, and machine shops. However, facilities that lend themselves to electronic controls can do somewhat better.

Repetitive Focus

Repetitive processes, as we saw in the Global Company Profile on Harley-Davidson, use modules (see Figure 7.2b). Modules are parts or components previously prepared, often in a product-focused (continuous) process.

The repetitive process is the classic assembly line. Widely used in the assembly of virtually all automobiles and household appliances, it has more structure and consequently less flexibility than a process-focused facility.

Fast-food firms are another example of a repetitive process using modules. This type of production allows more customizing than a product-focused facility; modules (for example, meat, cheese, sauce, tomatoes, onions) are assembled to get a quasi-custom product, a cheeseburger. In this manner, the firm obtains both the economic advantages of the product-focused model (where many of the modules are prepared) and the custom advantage of the low-volume, high-variety model.

VIDEO 7.1
Process Strategy at Wheeled Coach Ambulance

Modules
Parts or components of a product previously prepared, often in a continuous process.

Repetitive process
A product-oriented production process that uses modules.

Product Focus

Product focus

A facility organized around products; a product-oriented, high-volume, low-variety process.

High-volume, low-variety processes are product focused. The facilities are organized around *products*. They are also called *continuous processes* because they have very long, continuous production runs. Products such as glass, paper, tin sheets, lightbulbs, beer, and potato chips are made via a continuous process. Some products, such as lightbulbs, are discrete; others, such as rolls of paper, are made in a continuous flow. Still others, such as repaired hernias at Canada's famous Shouldice Hospital, are services. It is only with standardization and effective quality control that firms have established product-focused facilities. An organization producing the same lightbulb or hot dog bun day after day can organize around a product. Such an organization has an inherent ability to set standards and maintain a given quality, as opposed to an organization that is producing unique products every day, such as a print shop or general-purpose hospital. For example, Frito-Lay's family of products is also produced in a product-focused facility [see Figure 7.2(c)]. At Frito-Lay, corn, potatoes, water, and seasoning are the relatively few inputs, but outputs (like Cheetos, Ruffles, Tostitos, and Fritos) vary in seasoning and packaging within the product family.

A product-focused facility produces high volume and low variety. The specialized nature of the facility requires high fixed cost, but low variable costs reward high facility utilization.

Mass Customization Focus

Mass customization

Rapid, low-cost production that caters to constantly changing unique customer desires.

Our increasingly wealthy and sophisticated world demands individualized goods and services. A peek at the rich variety of goods and services that operations managers are called on to supply is shown in Table 7.1. The explosion of variety has taken place in automobiles, movies, breakfast cereals, and thousands of other areas. Despite this proliferation of products, operations managers have improved product quality while reducing costs. Consequently, the variety of products continues to grow. Operations managers use *mass customization* to produce this vast array of goods and services. Mass customization is the rapid, low-cost production of goods and services that fulfill increasingly unique customer desires. But mass customization (see the upper-right section of Figure 7.1) is not just about variety; it is about making precisely *what* the customer wants *when* the customer wants it economically.

Mass customization brings us the variety of products traditionally provided by low-volume manufacture (a process focus) at the cost of standardized high-volume (product-focused) production. However, achieving mass customization is a challenge that requires sophisticated operational capabilities. Building agile processes that rapidly and inexpensively produce custom products requires a limited product line and modular design. The link between sales, design, production, supply chain, and logistics must be tight.

Dell Computer [see Figure 7.2(d)] has demonstrated that the payoff for mass customization can be substantial. More traditional manufacturers include Toyota, which recently announced

TABLE 7.1	Mass Customization Provides More Choices Than Ever	
	NUMBER OF CHOICES[a]	
ITEM	**1970s**	**21ST CENTURY**
Vehicle styles	18	1,212
Bicycle types	8	211,000[c]
iPhone mobile game apps	0	1,200,000[g]
Web sites	0	634,000,000[d]
Movie releases per year	267	1,551[e]
New book titles	40,530	300,000+
Houston TV channels	5	185
Breakfast cereals	160	340
Items (SKUs) in supermarkets	14,000[b]	150,000[f]
High-definition TVs	0	102

Source: Various; however, many of the data are from the Federal Reserve Bank of Dallas.
[a]Variety available in America; worldwide the variety increases even more. [b]1989.
[c]Possible combinations for one manufacturer. [d]Royal Pingdom Estimate (2015).
[e]www.the-numbers.com/movies/year/2014. [f]SKUs managed by H. E. Butts grocery chain.
[g]*Business Week*, April 26, 2015.

delivery of custom-ordered cars in 5 days. Similarly, electronic controls allow designers in the textile industry to rapidly revamp their lines and respond to changes.

The service industry is also moving toward mass customization. For instance, not very many years ago, most people had the same telephone service. Now, not only is the phone service full of options, from caller ID to voice mail, but contemporary phones are hardly phones. They may also be part camera, computer, game player, GPS, and Web browser. Insurance companies are adding and tailoring new products with shortened development times to meet the unique needs of their customers. And firms like iTunes, Spotify, Rhapsody, Amazon, and eMusic maintain a music inventory on the Internet that allows customers to select a dozen songs of their choosing and have them made into a custom playlist. Similarly, the number of new books and movies increases each year. Mass customization places new demands on operations managers who must create and align the processes that provide this expanding variety of goods and services.

Making Mass Customization Work   Mass customization suggests a high-volume system in which products are built-to-order. Build-to-order (BTO) means producing to customer orders, not forecasts. But high-volume build-to-order is difficult. Some major challenges are:

- *Product design* must be imaginative. Successful build-to-order designs include a limited product line and modules. Ping Inc., a premier golf club manufacturer, uses different combinations of club heads, grips, shafts, and angles to make 20,000 variations of its golf clubs.
- *Process design* must be flexible and able to accommodate changes in both design and technology. For instance, postponement allows for customization late in the production process. Toyota installs unique interior modules very late in production for its popular Scion, a process also typical with customized vans. Postponement is further discussed in Chapter 11.
- *Inventory management* requires tight control. To be successful with build-to-order, a firm must avoid being stuck with unpopular or obsolete components. With virtually no raw material, Dell puts custom computers together in less than a day.
- *Tight schedules* that track orders and material from design through delivery are another requirement of mass customization. Align Technology, a well-known name in orthodontics, figured out how to achieve competitive advantage by delivering custom-made clear plastic aligners within 3 weeks of the first visit to the dentist's office (see the *OM in Action* box "Mass Customization for Straight Teeth").
- *Responsive partners* in the supply chain can yield effective collaboration. Forecasting, inventory management, and ordering for JCPenney shirts are all handled for the retailer by its supplier in Hong Kong.

Mass customization/build-to-order is the new imperative for operations. There are advantages to mass customization and building to order: first, by meeting the demands of the marketplace, firms win orders and stay in business; in addition, they trim costs (from personnel to inventory to facilities) that exist because of inaccurate sales forecasting.

Build-to-order (BTO)
Produce to customer order rather than to a forecast.

Postponement
The delay of any modifications or customization to a product as long as possible in the production process.

OM in Action   Mass Customization for Straight Teeth

Align Technology of Santa Clara, California, wants to straighten your teeth with a clear plastic removable aligner. The company is a mass customizer for orthodontic treatments. Each patient is *very* custom, requiring a truly unique product; no two patients are alike. Based on dental impressions, X-rays, and photos taken at the dentist's office and sent to Align headquarters, the firm builds a precise 3-D computer model and file of the patient's mouth. This digitized file is then sent to Costa Rica, where technicians develop a comprehensive treatment plan, which is then returned to the dentist for approval. After approval, data from the virtual models and treatment plan are used to program 3-D printers to form molds. The molds are then shipped to Juarez, Mexico, where a series of customized teeth aligners—usually about 19 pairs—are made. The time required for this process: about 3 weeks from start to finish.

The clear aligners take the place of the traditional "wire and brackets." Align calls the product "complex to make, easy to use." With good OM, mass customization works, even for a very complex, very individualized product, such as teeth aligners.

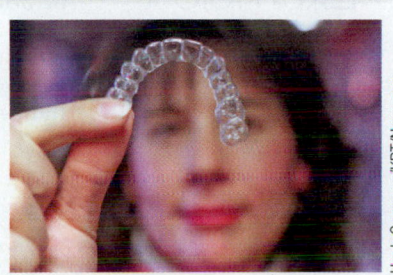

Sources: BusinessWeek (April 30, 2012); Laura Rock Kopezak and M. Eric Johnson, "Aligning the Supply Chain," Case #6-0024, Dartmouth College, 2006; and www.invisalign.com.

TABLE 7.2	Comparison of the Characteristics of Four Types of Processes		
PROCESS FOCUS (LOW VOLUME, HIGH VARIETY; e.g., ARNOLD PALMER HOSPITAL)	**REPETITIVE FOCUS (MODULAR; e.g., HARLEY-DAVIDSON)**	**PRODUCT FOCUS (HIGH VOLUME, LOW VARIETY; e.g., FRITO-LAY)**	**MASS CUSTOMIZATION (HIGH VOLUME, HIGH VARIETY; e.g., DELL COMPUTER)**
1. Small quantity and large variety of products	1. Long runs, a standardized product from modules	1. Large quantity and small variety of products	1. Large quantity and large variety of products
2. Broadly skilled operators	2. Moderately trained employees	2. Less broadly skilled operators	2. Flexible operators
3. Instructions for each job	3. Few changes in job instructions	3. Standardized job instructions	3. Custom orders requiring many job instructions
4. High inventory	4. Low inventory	4. Low inventory	4. Low inventory relative to the value of the product
5. Finished goods are made to order and not stored	5. Finished goods are made to frequent forecasts	5. Finished goods are made to a forecast and stored	5. Finished goods are build-to-order (BTO)
6. Scheduling is complex	6. Scheduling is routine	6. Scheduling is routine	6. Sophisticated scheduling accommodates custom orders
7. Fixed costs are low and variable costs high	7. Fixed costs are dependent on flexibility of the facility	7. Fixed costs are high, and variable costs low	7. Fixed costs tend to be high and variable costs low

Process Comparison

The characteristics of the four processes are shown in Table 7.2 and Figure 7.2 (on page 283), and each may provide a strategic advantage. For instance, unit costs will be less in the product (continuous) or repetitive case when high volume (and high utilization) exists. However, a low-volume differentiated product is likely to be produced more economically under process focus. And mass customization requires exceptional competence in product and process design, scheduling, supply chain, and inventory management. Proper evaluation and selection of process strategies are critical.

Crossover Charts The comparison of processes can be further enhanced by looking at the point where the total cost of the processes changes. For instance, Figure 7.3 shows three alternative processes compared on a single chart. Such a chart is sometimes called a crossover chart. Process A has the lowest cost for volumes below V_1, process B has the lowest cost between V_1 and V_2, and process C has the lowest cost at volumes above V_2.

Example 1 illustrates how to determine the exact volume where one process becomes more expensive than another.

Crossover chart

A chart of costs at the possible volumes for more than one process.

Example 1

CROSSOVER CHART

Kleber Enterprises would like to evaluate three accounting software products (A, B, and C) to support changes in its internal accounting processes. The resulting processes will have cost structures similar to those shown in Figure 7.3. The costs of the software for these processes are:

	TOTAL FIXED COST	DOLLARS REQUIRED PER ACCOUNTING REPORT
Software A	$200,000	$60
Software B	$300,000	$25
Software C	$400,000	$10

LO 7.2 *Compute* crossover points for different processes

APPROACH ▶ Solve for the crossover point for software A and B and then the crossover point for software B and C.

SOLUTION ▶ Software A yields a process that is most economical up to V_1, but to exactly what number of reports (volume)? To determine the volume at V_1, we set the cost of software A equal to the cost of software B. V_1 is the unknown volume:

$$200,000 + (60)V_1 = 300,000 + (25)V_1$$
$$35V_1 = 100,000$$
$$V_1 = 2,857$$

This means that software A is most economical from 0 reports to 2,857 reports (V_1).

Similarly, to determine the crossover point for V_2, we set the cost of software B equal to the cost of software C:

$$300,000 + (25)V_2 = 400,000 + (10)V_2$$
$$15V_2 = 100,000$$
$$V_2 = 6,666$$

This means that software B is most economical if the number of reports is between 2,857 (V_1) and 6,666 (V_2) and that software C is most economical if reports exceed 6,666 (V_2).

INSIGHT ▶ As you can see, the software and related process chosen is highly dependent on the forecasted volume.

LEARNING EXERCISE ▶ If the vendor of software A reduces the fixed cost to $150,000, what is the new crossover point between A and B? [Answer: 4,286.]

RELATED PROBLEMS ▶ 7.1, 7.2, 7.3, 7.4, 7.5, 7.6, 7.7, 7.8, 7.9, 7.10, 7.11, 7.12

ACTIVE MODEL 7.1 This example is further illustrated in Active Model 7.1 in MyOMLab.

EXCEL OM Data File **Ch07Ex1**.xls can be found in MyOMLab.

Focused Processes In an ongoing quest for efficiency, industrialized societies continue to move toward specialization. The focus that comes with specialization contributes to efficiency. Managers who focus on a limited number of activities, products, and technologies do better. As the variety of products in a facility increase, overhead costs increase even faster.

Figure **7.3**

Crossover Charts

⚠ STUDENT TIP
Different processes can be expected to have different costs. However, at any given volume, only one will have the lowest cost.

Similarly, as the variety of products, customers, and technology increases, so does complexity. The resources necessary to cope with the complexity expand disproportionately. A focus on depth of product line as opposed to breadth is typical of outstanding firms, of which Intel, L.M. Ericsson, and Bosch are world-class examples. *Focus*, defined here as specialization, simplification, and concentration, yields efficiency. Focus also contributes to building a core competence that fosters market and financial success. The focus can be:

- *Customers* (such as Winterhalter Gastronom, a German company that focuses on dishwashers for hotels and restaurants, for whom spotless glasses and dishes are critical)
- *Products* with similar attributes (such as Nucor Steel's Crawford, Ohio, plant, which processes only high-quality sheet steels, and Gallagher, a New Zealand company, which has 45% of the world market in electric fences)
- *Service* (such as Orlando's Arnold Palmer Hospital, with a focus on children and women; or Shouldice Hospital, in Canada, with a focus on hernia repair)
- *Technology* (such as Texas Instruments, with a focus on only certain specialized kinds of semiconductors; and SAP, which despite a world of opportunities, remains focused on software)

The key for the operations manager is to move continuously toward specialization, focusing on the core competence necessary to excel at that speciality.

Selection of Equipment

STUDENT TIP
A process that is going to win orders often depends on the selection of the proper equipment.

Ultimately, selection of a particular process strategy requires decisions about equipment and technology. These decisions can be complex, as alternative methods of production are present in virtually all operations functions, from hospitals, to restaurants, to manufacturing facilities. Picking the best equipment requires understanding the specific industry and available processes and technology. The choice of equipment, be it an X-ray machine for a hospital, a computer-controlled lathe for a factory, or a new computer for an office, requires considering cost, cash flow, market stability, quality, capacity, and flexibility. To make this decision, operations managers develop documentation that indicates the capacity, size, tolerances, and maintenance requirements of each option.

In this age of rapid technological change and short product life cycles, adding flexibility to the production process can be a major competitive advantage. Flexibility is the ability to respond with little penalty in time, cost, or customer value. This may mean modular, movable, or digitally controlled equipment. Honda's process flexibility, for example, has allowed it to become the industry leader at responding to market dynamics by modifying production volume and product mix.

Flexibility
The ability to respond with little penalty in time, cost, or customer value.

Building flexibility into a production process can be difficult and expensive, but if it is not present, change may mean starting over. Consider what would be required for a rather simple change—such as McDonald's adding the flexibility necessary to serve you a charbroiled hamburger. What appears to be rather straightforward would require changes in many of the 10 OM decisions. For instance, changes may be necessary in (1) purchasing (a different quality of meat, perhaps with more fat content, and supplies such as charcoal), (2) quality standards (how long and at what temperature the patty will cook), (3) equipment (the charbroiler), (4) layout (space for the new process and for new exhaust vents), (5) training, and (6) maintenance. You may want to consider the implications of another simple change, such as a change from paper menus to iPad menus as discussed in the *OM in Action* box "The iPad Menu . . . A New Process."

Changing processes or equipment can be difficult and expensive. It is best to get this critical decision right the first time.

Process Analysis and Design

STUDENT TIP
Here we look at five tools that help understand processes.

When analyzing and designing processes, we ask questions such as the following:

- Is the process designed to achieve competitive advantage in terms of differentiation, response, or low cost?
- Does the process eliminate steps that do not add value?

OM in Action | The iPad Menu ... A New Process

Mass customization begins with the order. And at restaurants from California to Boston, the order now starts with an iPad. *Stacked Restaurants* lets customers choose ingredients for their sandwiches using an iPad on the table. Diners also get a great photo of the menu item (which stimulates sales), a list of ingredients and nutritional information (a plus for those with allergies or watching their diet), and an opportunity to build their own meal (mass customization).

Some restaurants, in addition to having the enticing photo of the meal, find that they can add a description and photo of just what a medium-rare steak looks like. They can further enrich the dining experience by adding a "recipe" tab or "history" tab with descriptions of the item's origins and tradition. *Steakhouses*, a chain in San Francisco, Atlanta, and Chicago, finds the tabs great for its lengthy wine lists. Others program the system to remember the guest's meal preferences. And some customers love the

ability to order immediately, scan coupons, and swipe credit cards at the table. The instantaneous placement of the order to the kitchen is a significant advantage for those restaurants pursuing a *response strategy*.

Using iPads means developing a new process. iPads are not cheap, but they are accurate and fast, with lots of options. Restaurants using the new process find customer retention, frequency of visits, and average check size all increasing.

Sources: New York Times (June 21, 2014) and *USA Today* (February 16, 2011) and (July 25, 2012).

- ◆ Does the process maximize customer value as perceived by the customer?
- ◆ Will the process win orders?

Process analysis and design not only addresses these issues, but also related OM issues such as throughput, cost, and quality. Process is key. Examine the process; then continuously improve the process.

The following tools help us understand the complexities of process design and redesign. They are simply ways of making sense of what happens or must happen in a process. We now look at: flowcharts, time-function mapping, process charts, value-stream mapping, and service blueprinting.

Flowchart

The first tool is the flowchart, which is a schematic or drawing of the movement of material, product, or people. For instance, the flowchart in the *Global Company Profile* for this chapter shows the assembly processes for Harley-Davidson. Such charts can help understanding, analysis, and communication of a process.

Time-Function Mapping

A second tool for process analysis and design is a modified flowchart with time added on the horizontal axis. Such charts are sometimes called time-function mapping, or process mapping. With time-function mapping, nodes indicate the activities, and the arrows indicate the flow direction, with time on the horizontal axis. This type of analysis allows users to identify and eliminate waste such as extra steps, duplication, and delay. Figure 7.4 shows the use of process mapping before and after process improvement at American National Can Company. In this example, substantial reduction in waiting time and process improvement in order processing contributed to a savings of 46 days.

Process Charts

The third tool is the *process chart*. Process charts use symbols, time, and distance to provide an objective and structured way to analyze and record the activities that make up a process.[1] They allow us to focus on value-added activities. For instance, the process chart shown in Figure 7.5, which includes the present method of hamburger assembly at a fast-food restaurant, includes a value-added line to help us distinguish between value-added activities and waste. Identifying all value-added operations (as opposed to inspection, storage, delay, and transportation, which add no value) allows us to determine the percent of value added to total activities.[2] We can see from the computation at the bottom of Figure 7.5 that the percentage of value added in this case is 85.7%.

LO 7.3 *Use* the tools of process analysis

VIDEO 7.2
Alaska Airlines: 20-minute Baggage Process—Guaranteed!

Flowchart
A drawing used to analyze movement of people or material.

Time-function mapping (or process mapping)
A flowchart with time added on the horizontal axis.

Process charts
Charts that use symbols to analyze the movement of people or material.

VIDEO 7.3
Process Analysis at Arnold Palmer Hospital

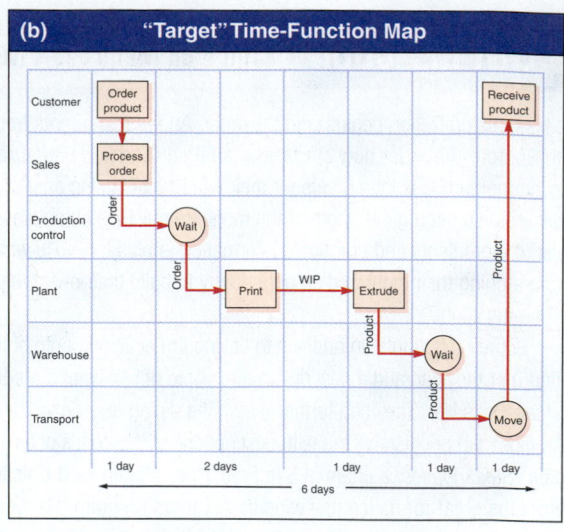

Figure **7.4**

Time-Function Mapping (Process Mapping) for a Product Requiring Printing and Extruding Operations at American National Can Company

This technique clearly shows that waiting and order processing contributed substantially to the 46 days that can be eliminated in this operation.

Source: Excerpted from Elaine J. Labach, "Faster, Better, and Cheaper," *Target* no. 5:43 with permission of the Association for Manufacturing Excellence, 380 West Palatine Road, Wheeling, IL 60090-5863, 847/520-3282. **www.ame.org**. Reprinted with permission of Target Magazine.

The operations manager's job is to reduce waste and increase the percent of value added. The non-value-added items are a waste; they are resources lost to the firm and to society forever.

Value-Stream Mapping

Value-stream mapping (VSM)

A process that helps managers understand how to add value in the flow of material and information through the entire production process.

A variation of time-function mapping is **value-stream mapping (VSM)**; however, value-stream mapping takes an expanded look at where value is added (and not added) in the entire production process, including the supply chain. As with time-function mapping, the idea is to start with the customer and understand the production process, but value-stream mapping extends the analysis back to suppliers.

Figure **7.5**

Process Chart Showing a Hamburger Assembly Process at a Fast-Food Restaurant

		PROCESS CHART		
Present Method ☒			Proposed Method ☐	

SUBJECT CHARTED *Hamburger Assembly Process*   DATE *12 / 1 / 15*
DEPARTMENT _____   CHART BY *KH*   SHEET NO. *1* OF *1*

DIST. IN FEET	TIME IN MINS.	CHART SYMBOLS	PROCESS DESCRIPTION
—	—	◯ ⇨ ▢ D ▽	*Meat Patty in Storage*
1.5	.05	◯ ⇨ ▢ D ▽	*Transfer to Broiler*
	2.50	◯ ⇨ ▢ D ▽	*Broiler*
	.05	◯ ⇨ ▢ D ▽	*Visual Inspection*
1.0	.05	◯ ⇨ ▢ D ▽	*Transfer to Rack*
	.15	◯ ⇨ ▢ D ▽	*Temporary Storage*
.5	.10	◯ ⇨ ▢ D ▽	*Obtain Buns, Lettuce, etc.*
	.20	◯ ⇨ ▢ D ▽	*Assemble Order*
.5	.05	◯ ⇨ ▢ D ▽	*Place in Finish Rack*
		◯ ⇨ ▢ D ▽	
3.5	3.15	2 4 1 — 2	TOTALS

Value-added time = Operation time/Total time = (2.50+.20)/3.15 = 85.7%

◯ = operation; ⇨ = transport; ▢ = inspect; D = delay; ▽ = storage.

Value-stream mapping takes into account not only the process but, as shown in Example 2, also the management decisions and information systems that support the process.

Example 2

VALUE-STREAM MAPPING

Motorola has received an order for 11,000 cell phones per month and wants to understand how the order will be processed through manufacturing.

APPROACH ▶ To fully understand the process from customer to supplier, Motorola prepares a value-stream map.

SOLUTION ▶ Although value-stream maps appear complex, their construction is easy. Here are the steps needed to complete the value-stream map shown in Figure 7.6.

1. Begin with symbols for customer, supplier, and production to ensure the big picture.
2. Enter customer order requirements.
3. Calculate the daily production requirements.
4. Enter the outbound shipping requirements and delivery frequency.
5. Determine inbound shipping method and delivery frequency.
6. Add the process steps (i.e., machine, assemble) in sequence, left to right.
7. Add communication methods, add their frequency, and show the direction with arrows.
8. Add inventory quantities (shown with ⚠) between every step of the entire flow.
9. Determine total working time (value-added time) and delay (non-value-added time).

Figure **7.6**

Value-Stream Mapping (VSM)

INSIGHT ▶ From Figure 7.6 we note that large inventories exist in incoming raw material and between processing steps, and that the value-added time is low as a proportion of the entire process.

LEARNING EXERCISE ▶ How might raw material inventory be reduced? [Answer: Have deliveries twice per week rather than once per week.]

RELATED PROBLEM ▶ 7.17

Service blueprinting

A process analysis technique that lends itself to a focus on the customer and the provider's interaction with the customer.

Service Blueprinting

Products with a high service content may warrant use of yet a fifth process technique. **Service blueprinting** is a process analysis technique that focuses on the customer and the provider's interaction with the customer. For instance, the activities at level one of Figure 7.7 are under the control of the customer. In the second level are activities of the service provider interacting with the customer. The third level includes those activities that are performed away from, and not immediately visible to, the customer. Each level suggests different management issues. For instance, the top level may suggest educating the customer or modifying expectations, whereas the second level may require a focus on personnel selection and training. Finally, the third level lends itself to more typical process innovations. The service blueprint shown in Figure 7.7 also notes potential failure points and shows how poka-yoke techniques can be added to improve quality. The consequences of these failure points can be greatly reduced if identified at the design stage when modifications or appropriate poka-yokes can be included. A time dimension is included in Figure 7.7 to aid understanding, extend insight, and provide a focus on customer service.

STUDENT TIP ◆

Service blueprinting helps evaluate the impact of customer interaction with the process.

Figure **7.7**

Service Blueprint for Service at Speedy Lube, Inc.

F Poka-yokes to address potential failure points

Poka-yoke: Bell in driveway in case customer arrival was unnoticed.
Poka-yoke: If customer remains in the work area, offer coffee and reading material in waiting room.

Poka-yoke: Conduct dialog with customer to identify customer expectation and assure customer acceptance.

Poka-yoke: Review checklist for compliance.
Poka-yoke: Service personnel review invoice for accuracy.

Poka-yoke: Customer approves invoice.

Poka-yoke: Customer inspects car.

Personal Greeting	Service Diagnosis	Perform Service	Friendly Close

Physical Attributes to Support Service	Parking adequate Signage clear Waiting room amenities	Employee appearance Forms	Shop cleanliness Technology	Car delivered clean Employee appearance

Level #1
Customer is in control.

Customer arrives for service. (3 min)

Customer departs.

Customer pays bill. (4 min)

Level #2
Customer interacts with service provider.

Warm greeting and obtain service request. (10 sec)

Standard request. (3 min)

Determine specifics. (5 min)

Can service be done and does customer approve? (5 min)

Notify customer and recommend an alternative provider. (7 min)

Notify customer that car is ready. (3 min)

Direct customer to waiting room.

No / Yes / No / Yes

Level #3
Service is removed from customer's control and interaction.

Perform required work. (varies)

Prepare invoice. (3 min)

Each of these five process analysis tools has strengths and variations. Flowcharts provide a quick way to view the big picture and try to make sense of the entire system. Time-function mapping adds some rigor and a time element to the macro analysis. Value-stream mapping extends beyond the immediate organization to customers and suppliers. Process charts are designed to provide a much more detailed view of the process, adding items such as value-added time, delay, distance, storage, and so forth. Service blueprinting, on the other hand, is designed to help us focus on the customer interaction part of the process. Because customer interaction is often an important variable in process design, we now examine some additional aspects of service process design.

Special Considerations for Service Process Design

Interaction with the customer often affects process performance adversely. But a service, by its very nature, implies that some interaction and customization is needed. Recognizing that the customer's unique desires tend to play havoc with a process, the more the manager designs the process to accommodate these special requirements, the more effective and efficient the process will be. The trick is to find the right combination.

The four quadrants of Figure 7.8 provide additional insight on how operations managers modify service processes to find the best level of specialization and focus while maintaining the necessary customer interaction and customization. The 10 OM decisions we introduced in Chapters 1 and 2 are used with a different emphasis in each quadrant. For instance:

- In the upper sections (quadrants) of *mass service* and *professional service*, where *labor content is high*, we expect the manager to focus extensively on human resources. This is often done with personalized services, requiring high labor involvement and therefore significant personnel selection and training issues. This is particularly true in the professional service quadrant.

LO 7.4 *Describe customer interaction in service processes*

- The quadrants with *low customization* tend to (1) standardize or restrict some offerings, as do fast-food restaurants, (2) automate, as have airlines with ticket-vending machines, or (3) remove some services, such as seat assignments, as has Southwest Airlines. Offloading some aspect of the service through automation may require innovations in process design. Such is the case with airline ticket vending, self-checkout at Home Depot, and bank ATMs. This move to standardization and automation may also require changes in other areas, such as added capital expenditure and new OM skills for the purchase and maintenance of equipment. A reduction in a customization capability will require added strength in other areas.

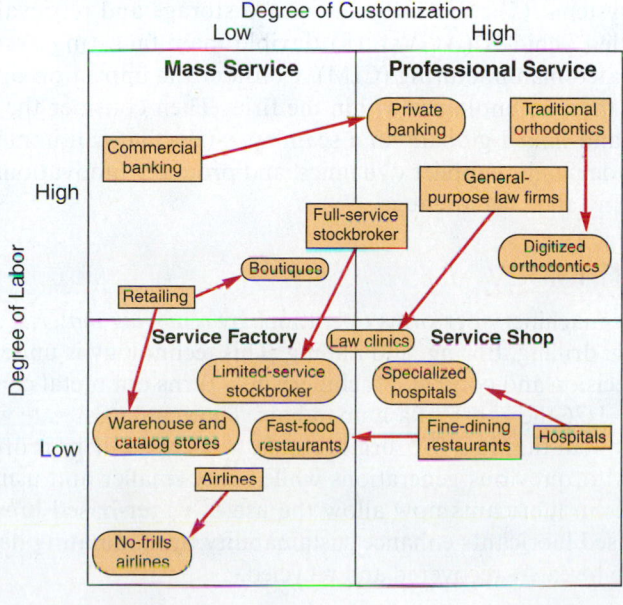

Degree of Customization

TABLE 7.3	Techniques for Improving Service Productivity	
STRATEGY	**TECHNIQUE**	**EXAMPLE**
Separation	Structuring service so customers must go where the service is offered	Bank customers go to a manager to open a new account, to loan officers for loans, and to tellers for deposits
Self-service	Self-service so customers examine, compare, and check out at their own pace	Supermarkets and department stores Internet ordering
Postponement	Customizing at delivery	Customizing vans at delivery rather than at production
Focus	Restricting the offerings	Limited-menu restaurant
Modules	Modular selection of service Modular production	Investment and insurance selection Prepackaged food modules in restaurants
Automation	Separating services that may lend themselves to some type of automation	Automatic teller machines
Scheduling	Precise personnel scheduling	Scheduling airline ticket counter personnel at 15-minute intervals
Training	Clarifying the service options Explaining how to avoid problems	Investment counselor, funeral directors After-sale maintenance personnel

◆ Because customer feedback is lower in the quadrants with *low customization*, tight control may be required to maintain quality standards.

◆ Operations with *low labor intensity* may lend themselves particularly well to innovations in process technology and scheduling.

Table 7.3 shows some additional techniques for innovative process design in services. Managers focus on designing innovative processes that enhance the service. For instance, supermarket *self-service* reduces cost while it allows customers to check for the specific features they want, such as freshness or color. Dell Computer provides another version of self-service by allowing customers to design their own product on the Web. Customers seem to like this, and it is cheaper and faster for Dell.

Production Technology

Advances in technology that enhance production and productivity are changing how things are designed, made, and serviced around the world. In this section, we introduce nine areas of technology: (1) machine technology, (2) automatic identification systems (AIS), (3) process control, (4) vision systems, (5) robots, (6) automated storage and retrieval systems (ASRSs), (7) automated guided vehicles (AGVs), (8) flexible manufacturing systems (FMSs), and (9) computer-integrated manufacturing (CIM). Consider the impact on operations managers as we digitally link these technologies within the firm. Then consider the implications when they are combined and linked globally in a seamless chain that can immediately respond to changing consumer demands, supplier dynamics, and producer innovations. The implications for the world economy and OM are huge.

LO 7.5 *Identify* recent advances in production technology

Machine Technology

Much of the world's machinery performs operations by *removing material,* performing operations such as cutting, drilling, boring, and milling. This technology is undergoing tremendous progress in both precision and control. Machinery now turns out metal components that vary less than a micron—1/76 the width of a human hair. They can accelerate water to three times the speed of sound to cut titanium for surgical tools. Such machinery is often five times more productive than that of previous generations while being smaller and using less power. And continuing advances in lubricants now allow the use of water-based lubricants rather than oil-based. Water-based lubricants enhance sustainability by eliminating hazardous waste and allowing shavings to be easily recovered and recycled.

Computer intelligence often controls this new machinery, allowing more complex and precise items to be made faster. Such machinery, with its own computer and memory, is referred to as having **computer numerical controls (CNC)**. Electronic controls increase speed by cutting change-over time, reducing waste (because of fewer mistakes), and enhancing flexibility.

Advanced versions of such technology are used on Pratt & Whitney's turbine blade plant in Connecticut. The machinery has improved the loading and alignment task so much that Pratt has cut the total time for the grinding process of a turbine blade from 10 days to 2 hours. The new machinery has also contributed to process improvements that mean the blades now travel just 1,800 feet in the plant, down from 8,100 feet, cutting throughput time from 22 days to 7 days.

New advances in machinery suggest that rather than *removing* material as has traditionally been done, *adding* material may in many cases be more efficient. **Additive manufacturing** or, as it is commonly called, 3D printing, is frequently used for design testing, prototypes, and custom products. The technology continues to advance and now supports innovative product design (variety and complexity), minimal custom tooling (little tooling is needed), minimal assembly (integrated assemblies can be "printed"), low inventory (make-to-order systems), and reduced time to market. As a result, additive manufacturing is being increasingly used to enhance production efficiency for high-volume products. In addition, production processes using numerous materials including plastics, ceramics, and even a paste of living cells are being developed. The convergence of software advances, computer technology, worldwide communication, and 3D printing seems to be putting us on the cusp of true mass customization. We can expect personalized mass markets via additive manufacturing to bring enormous changes to operations.

Automatic Identification Systems (AISs) and RFID

New equipment, from numerically controlled manufacturing machinery to ATMs, is controlled by digital electronic signals. Electrons are a great vehicle for transmitting information, but they have a major limitation—most OM data does not start out in bits and bytes. Therefore, operations managers must get the data into an electronic form. Making data digital is done via computer keyboards, bar codes, radio frequencies, optical characters, and so forth. These **automatic identification systems (AISs)** help us move data into electronic form, where it is easily manipulated.

Because of its decreasing cost and increasing pervasiveness, **radio frequency identification (RFID)** warrants special note. RFID is integrated circuitry with its own tiny antennas that use radio waves to send signals a limited range—usually a matter of yards. These RFID tags provide unique identification that enables the tracking and monitoring of parts, pallets, people, and pets—virtually everything that moves. RFID requires no line of sight between tag and reader.

Process Control

Process control is the use of information technology to monitor and control a physical process. For instance, process control is used to measure the moisture content and thickness of paper as it travels over a paper machine at thousands of feet per minute. Process control is also used to determine and control temperatures, pressures, and quantities in petroleum refineries, petrochemical processes, cement plants, steel mills, nuclear reactors, and other product-focused facilities.

Computer numerical control (CNC)
Machinery with its own computer and memory.

Additive manufacturing
The production of physical items by adding layer upon layer, much in the same way an inkjet printer lays down ink.

With RFID, a cashier could scan the entire contents of a shopping cart in seconds.

Automatic identification system (AIS)
A system for transforming data into electronic form, for example, bar codes.

Radio frequency identification (RFID)
A wireless system in which integrated circuits with antennas send radio waves.

Process control
The use of information technology to control a physical process.

Pharmaceutical companies are counting on RFID to aid the tracking and tracing of drugs in the distribution system to reduce losses that total over $30 billion a year.

Kruell/laif/Redux Pictures

The Safe Place® Infant Security Solution from RF Technologies® monitors infants with small, lightweight transmitters and soft, comfortable banding. When a protected infant approaches a monitored exit, the transmitter triggers the exit's lock and notifies staff to ensure a fast response.

Sophisticated process control is required to monitor complex processes that vary—from beer at Anheuser-Busch, to steel at Nucor, to nuclear reactors at Dominion Resources (shown here).

Process control systems operate in a number of ways, but the following are typical:

- Sensors collect data, which is read on some periodic basis, perhaps once a minute or second.
- Measurements are translated into digital signals, which are transmitted to a computer.
- Computer programs read the file and analyze the data.
- The resulting output may take numerous forms. These include messages on computer consoles or printers, signals to motors to change valve settings, warning lights or horns, or statistical process control charts.

Vision Systems

Vision systems
Systems that use video cameras and computer technology in inspection roles.

Vision systems combine video cameras and computer technology and are often used in inspection roles. Visual inspection is an important task in most food-processing and manufacturing organizations. Moreover, in many applications, visual inspection performed by humans is tedious, mind-numbing, and error prone. Thus vision systems are widely used when the items being inspected are very similar. For instance, vision systems are used to inspect Frito-Lay's potato chips so that imperfections can be identified as the chips proceed down the production line. The systems are also used to ensure that sealant is present and in the proper amount on Whirlpool's washing-machine transmissions. Vision systems are consistently accurate, do not become bored, and are of modest cost. These systems are vastly superior to individuals trying to perform these tasks.

Robots

Robot
A flexible machine with the ability to hold, move, or grab items. It functions through electronic impulses that activate motors and switches.

When a machine is flexible and has the ability to hold, move, and perhaps "grab" items, we tend to use the word *robot*. **Robots** are mechanical devices that use electronic impulses to activate motors and switches. Robots may be used effectively to perform tasks that are especially monotonous or dangerous or those that can be improved by the substitution of mechanical for human effort. Such is the case when consistency, accuracy, speed, strength, or power can be enhanced by the substitution of machines for people. The automobile industry, for example, uses robots to do virtually all the welding and painting on automobiles. And a new, more sophisticated, generation of robots are fitted with sensors and cameras that provide enough dexterity to assemble, test, and pack small parts.

Automated Storage and Retrieval Systems (ASRSs)

Automated storage and retrieval system (ASRS)
Computer-controlled warehouses that provide for the automatic placement of parts into and from designated places in a warehouse.

Because of the tremendous labor involved in error-prone warehousing, computer-controlled warehouses have been developed. These systems, known as **automated storage and retrieval systems (ASRSs)**, provide for the automatic placement and withdrawal of parts and products into and from designated places in a warehouse. Such systems are commonly used in distribution facilities of retailers such as Walmart, Tupperware, and Benetton. These systems are also found in inventory and test areas of manufacturing firms.

Automated Guided Vehicles (AGVs)

Automated guided vehicle (AGV)
Electronically guided and controlled cart used to move materials.

Automated material handling can take the form of monorails, conveyors, robots, or automated guided vehicles. **Automated guided vehicles (AGVs)** are electronically guided and controlled carts used in manufacturing and warehousing to move parts and equipment. They are also used in agriculture to distribute feed, in offices to move mail, and in hospitals and jails to deliver supplies and meals.

Flexible Manufacturing Systems (FMSs)

When a central computer provides instructions to each workstation *and* to the material-handling equipment such as robots, ASRSs, and AGVs (as just noted), the system is known as an automated work cell or, more commonly, a flexible manufacturing system (FMS). An FMS is flexible because both the material-handling devices and the machines themselves are controlled by easily changed electronic signals (computer programs). Operators simply load new programs, as necessary, to produce different products. The result is a system that can economically produce low volume but high variety. For example, the Lockheed Martin facility, near Dallas, efficiently builds one-of-a-kind spare parts for military aircraft. The costs associated with changeover and low utilization have been reduced substantially. FMSs bridge the gap between product-focused and process-focused facilities.

Flexible manufacturing system (FMS)

A system that uses electronic signals from a centralized computer to automate production and material flow.

Computer-Integrated Manufacturing (CIM)

Flexible manufacturing systems can be extended backward electronically into the engineering and inventory control departments and forward to the warehousing and shipping departments. In this way, computer-aided design (CAD) generates the necessary electronic instructions to run a numerically controlled machine. In a computer-integrated manufacturing environment, a design change initiated at a CAD terminal can result in that change being made in the part produced on the shop floor in a matter of minutes. When this capability is integrated with inventory control, warehousing, and shipping as a part of a flexible manufacturing system, the entire system is called computer-integrated manufacturing (CIM); (Figure 7.9).

Computer-integrated manufacturing (CIM)

A manufacturing system in which CAD, FMS, inventory control, warehousing, and shipping are integrated.

Management decides to make a product

Computer-aided design (CAD) designs the product and programs the automated production equipment.

OM runs production process, purchasing components, coordinating suppliers, planning and scheduling operations, overseeing quality and the workforce, and shipping to customers.

Computer-aided manufacturing (CAM) converts raw materials into components or products

ASRS (above) **and AGVs** move incoming materials and parts, work-in-process, and complete product.

Robots and specialized equipment weld, insert, and assemble components.

Robots test, package, and ship the finished product.

Material flows →
Information flows ╌►

Computer-integrated manufacturing (CIM)

Flexible manufacturing system (FMS)

Figure **7.9**

Computer-Integrated Manufacturing (CIM)

CIM includes computer-aided design (CAD), computer-aided manufacturing (CAM), flexible manufacturing systems (FMSs), automated storage and retrieval systems (ASRSs), automated guided vehicles (AGVs), and robots to provide an integrated and flexible manufacturing process.

Technology is introducing "intelligent rooms" to the hotel industry. Hotel management can now precisely track a maid's time through the use of a security system. When a maid enters a room, a card is inserted that notifies the front-desk computer of the maid's location. "We can show her a printout of how long she takes to do a room," says one manager.

Security systems also enable guests to use their own credit cards as keys to unlock their doors. There are also other uses for the system. The computer can bar a guest's access to the room after checkout time and automatically control the air conditioning or heat, turning it on at check-in and off at checkout.

Minibars are now equipped with sensors that alert the central computer system at the hotel when an item is removed. Such items are immediately billed to the room. And now, with a handheld infrared unit, housekeeping staff can check, from the hallway, to see if a room is physically occupied. This both eliminates the embarrassment of having a hotel staffer walk in on a guest and improves security for housekeepers.

At Loew's Portofino Bay Hotel at Universal Studios, Orlando, guest smart cards act as credit cards in both the theme park and the hotel, and staff smart cards (programmed for different levels of security access) create an audit trail of employee movement. At the Mandarin Oriental Hotel in Las Vegas, guests arriving in their rooms after check-in are greeted by the drapes opening, lights turning on, and the TV displaying a customized message with the guest's name. Not to be outdone, Aloft hotel in Cupertino, California, has a robot that will hustle razors, toothbrushes, snacks, or the morning paper to any of the hotel's 150 rooms in 2 to 3 minutes. And when finished it returns to the lobby for the next chore or recharging. As a result, the staff spends more time with guests.

Sources: New York Times (August 12, 2014) and (November 10, 2008); *The Wall Street Journal* (October 28, 2014); and **Hotel Marketing.com** (March 28, 2011).

Flexible manufacturing systems and computer-integrated manufacturing are reducing the distinction between low-volume/high-variety and high-volume/low-variety production. Information technology is allowing FMS and CIM to handle increasing variety while expanding to include a growing range of volumes.

Technology in Services

Just as we have seen rapid advances in technology in the manufacturing sector, so we also find dramatic changes in the service sector. These range from electronic diagnostic equipment at auto repair shops, to blood- and urine-testing equipment in hospitals, to retinal security scanners at airports. The hospitality industry provides other examples, as discussed in the *OM in Action* box "Technology Changes the Hotel Industry." The McDonald's approach is to use self-serve kiosks. The labor savings when ordering and speedier checkout service provide valuable productivity increases for both the restaurant and the customer.

In retail stores, POS terminals download prices quickly to reflect changing costs or market conditions, and sales are tracked in 15-minute segments to aid scheduling. Drug companies, such as Purdue Pharma LP, track critical medications with radio frequency identification (RFID) tags to reduce counterfeiting and theft.

Table 7.4 provides a glimpse of the impact of technology on services. Operations managers in services, as in manufacturing, must be able to evaluate the impact of technology on their firm. This ability requires particular skill when evaluating reliability, investment analysis, human resource requirements, and maintenance/service.

Process Redesign

Often a firm finds that the initial assumptions of its process are no longer valid. The world is a dynamic place, and customer desires, product technology, and product mix change. Consequently, processes are redesigned. Process redesign (sometimes called process reengineering) is the fundamental rethinking of business processes to bring about dramatic improvements in performance. Effective process redesign relies on reevaluating the purpose of the process and questioning both purpose and underlying assumptions. It works only if the basic process and its objectives are reexamined.

Process redesign also focuses on those activities that cross functional lines. Because managers are often in charge of specific "functions" or specialized areas of responsibility, those

Process redesign

The fundamental rethinking of business processes to bring about dramatic improvements in performance.

TABLE 7.4	Examples of Technology's Impact on Services
SERVICE INDUSTRY	**EXAMPLE**
Financial Services	Debit cards, electronic funds transfer, automatic teller machines, Internet stock trading, online banking via cell phone
Education	Online newspapers and journals, interactive assignments via WebCT, Blackboard, and smartphones
Utilities and government	Automated one-person garbage trucks, optical mail scanners, flood-warning systems, meters that allow homeowners to control energy usage and costs
Restaurants and foods	Wireless orders from waiters to the kitchen, robot butchering, transponders on cars that track sales at drive-throughs
Communications	Interactive TV, e-books via Kindle
Hotels	Electronic check-in/check-out, electronic key/lock systems, mobile Web bookings
Wholesale/retail trade	Point-of-sale (POS) terminals, e-commerce, electronic communication between store and supplier, bar-coded data, RFID
Transportation	Automatic toll booths, satellite-directed navigation systems, Wi-Fi in automobiles
Health care	Online patient-monitoring systems, online medical information systems, robotic surgery
Airlines	Ticketless travel, scheduling, Internet purchases, boarding passes downloaded as two-dimensional bar codes on smartphones

activities (processes) that cross from one function or specialty to another may be neglected. Redesign casts aside all notions of how the process is currently being done and focuses on dramatic improvements in cost, time, and customer value. Any process is a candidate for radical redesign. The process can be a factory layout, a purchasing procedure, a new way of processing credit applications, or a new order-fulfillment process.

Shell Lubricants, for example, reinvented its order-fulfillment process by replacing a group of people who handled different parts of an order with one individual who does it all. As a result, Shell has cut the cycle time of turning an order into cash by 75%, reduced operating expenses by 45%, and boosted customer satisfaction 105%—all by introducing a new way of handling orders. Time, cost, and customer satisfaction—the dimension of performance shaped by operations—get major boosts from operational innovation.

Summary

Effective operations managers understand how to use process strategy as a competitive weapon. They select a production process with the necessary quality, flexibility, and cost structure to meet product and volume requirements. They also seek creative ways to combine the low unit cost of high-volume, low-variety manufacturing with the customization available through low-volume, high-variety facilities. Managers use the techniques of lean production and employee participation to encourage the development of efficient equipment and processes. They design their equipment and processes to have capabilities beyond the tolerance required by their customers, while ensuring the flexibility needed for adjustments in technology, features, and volumes.

Key Terms

Process strategy (p. 282)
Process focus (p. 282)
Modules (p. 283)
Repetitive process (p. 283)
Product focus (p. 284)
Mass customization (p. 284)
Build-to-order (BTO) (p. 285)
Postponement (p. 285)
Crossover chart (p. 286)
Flexibility (p. 288)
Flowchart (p. 289)

Time-function mapping (or process mapping) (p. 289)
Process charts (p. 289)
Value-stream mapping (VSM) (p. 290)
Service blueprinting (p. 292)
Computer numerical control (CNC) (p. 295)
Additive manufacturing (3D Printing) (p. 295)
Automatic identification system (AIS) (p. 295)
Radio frequency identification (RFID) (p. 295)

Process control (p. 295)
Vision systems (p. 296)
Robot (p. 296)
Automated storage and retrieval system (ASRS) (p. 296)
Automated guided vehicle (AGV) (p. 296)
Flexible manufacturing system (FMS) (p. 297)
Computer-integrated manufacturing (CIM) (p. 297)
Process redesign (p. 298)

Ethical Dilemma

For the sake of efficiency and lower costs, Premium Standard Farms of Princeton, Missouri, has turned pig production into a standardized product-focused process. Slaughterhouses have done this for a hundred years—but after the animal was dead. Doing it while the animal is alive is a relatively recent innovation. Here is how it works.

Impregnated female sows wait for 40 days in metal stalls so small that they cannot turn around. After an ultrasound test, they wait 67 days in a similar stall until they give birth. Two weeks after delivering 10 or 11 piglets, the sows are moved back to breeding rooms for another cycle. After 3 years, the sow is slaughtered. Animal-welfare advocates say such confinement drives pigs crazy. Premium Standard replies that its hogs are in fact comfortable, arguing that only 1% die before Premium Standard wants them to and that their system helps reduce the cost of pork products.

Discuss the productivity and ethical implications of this industry and these two divergent opinions.

Glenda/Shutterstock

Discussion Questions

1. What is process strategy?
2. What type of process is used for making each of the following products?
   (a) beer
   (b) wedding invitations
   (c) automobiles
   (d) paper
   (e) Big Macs
   (f) custom homes
   (g) motorcycles
3. What is service blueprinting?
4. What is process redesign?
5. What are the techniques for improving service productivity?
6. Name the four quadrants of the service process matrix. Discuss how the matrix is used to classify services into categories.
7. What is CIM?
8. What do we mean by a process-control system, and what are the typical elements in such systems?
9. Identify *manufacturing* firms that compete on each of the four processes shown in Figure 7.1.
10. Identify the competitive advantage of each of the four firms identified in Discussion Question 9.
11. Identify *service* firms that compete on each of the four processes shown in Figure 7.1.
12. Identify the competitive advantage of each of the four firms identified in Discussion Question 11.
13. What are numerically controlled machines?
14. Describe briefly what an automatic identification system (AIS) is and how service organizations could use AIS to increase productivity and at the same time increase the variety of services offered.
15. Name some of the advances being made in technology that enhance production and productivity.
16. Explain what a flexible manufacturing system (FMS) is.
17. In what ways do CAD and FMS connect?
18. What is additive manufacturing?
19. Discuss the advantages and disadvantages of 3D printing.

Solved Problem   Virtual Office Hours help is available in MyOMLab.

SOLVED PROBLEM 7.1

Bagot Copy Shop has a volume of 125,000 black-and-white copies per month. Two salespeople have made presentations to Gordon Bagot for machines of equal quality and reliability. The *Print Shop 5* has a cost of $2,000 per month and a variable cost of $.03. The other machine (a *Speed Copy 100*) will cost only $1,500 per month, but the toner is more expensive, driving the cost per copy up to $.035. If cost and volume are the only considerations, which machine should Bagot purchase?

SOLUTION

$$2,000 + .03X = 1,500 + .035X$$
$$2,000 - 1,500 = .035X - .03X$$
$$500 = .005X$$
$$100,000 = X$$

Because Bagot expects his volume to exceed 100,000 units, he should choose the *Print Shop 5*.

Problems

Note: **P** means the problem may be solved with POM for Windows and/or Excel OM.

Problems 7.1–7.12 relate to Four Process Strategies

• **7.1** Borges Machine Shop, Inc., has a 1-year contract for the production of 200,000 gear housings for a new off-road vehicle. Owner Luis Borges hopes the contract will be extended and the volume increased next year. Borges has developed costs for three alternatives. They are general-purpose equipment (GPE), flexible manufacturing system (FMS), and expensive, but efficient, dedicated machine (DM). The cost data follow:

	GENERAL-PURPOSE EQUIPMENT (GPE)	FLEXIBLE MANUFACTURING SYSTEM (FMS)	DEDICATED MACHINE (DM)
Annual contracted units	200,000	200,000	200,000
Annual fixed cost	$100,000	$200,000	$500,000
Per unit variable cost	$ 15.00	$ 14.00	$ 13.00

Which process is best for this contract? **P**

• **7.2** Using the data in Problem 7.1, determine the most economical volume for each process. **P**

• **7.3** Using the data in Problem 7.1, determine the best process for each of the following volumes: (1) 75,000, (2) 275,000, and (3) 375,000.

• **7.4** Refer to Problem 7.1. If a contract for the second and third years is pending, what are the implications for process selection?

•• **7.5** Stan Fawcett's company is considering producing a gear assembly that it now purchases from Salt Lake Supply, Inc. Salt Lake Supply charges $4 per unit, with a minimum order of 3,000 units. Stan estimates that it will cost $15,000 to set up the process and then $1.82 per unit for labor and materials.
a) Draw a graph illustrating the crossover (or indifference) point.
b) Determine the number of units where either choice has the same cost. **P**

•• **7.6** Ski Boards, Inc., wants to enter the market quickly with a new finish on its ski boards. It has three choices: (a) Refurbish the old equipment at a cost of $800, (b) make major modifications at a cost of $1,100, or (c) purchase new equipment

Eric Limon/ Shutterstock

at a net cost of $1,800. If the firm chooses to refurbish the equipment, materials and labor will be $1.10 per board. If it chooses to make modifications, materials and labor will be $0.70 per board. If it buys new equipment, variable costs are estimated to be $0.40 per board.
a) Graph the three total cost lines on the same chart.
b) Which alternative should Ski Boards, Inc., choose if it thinks it can sell more than 3,000 boards?
c) Which alternative should the firm use if it thinks the market for boards will be between 1,000 and 2,000? **P**

•• **7.7** Tim Urban, owner/manager of Urban's Motor Court in Key West, is considering outsourcing the daily room cleanup for his motel to Duffy's Maid Service. Tim rents an average of 50 rooms for each of 365 nights (365 × 50 equals the total rooms rented for the year). Tim's cost to clean a room is $12.50. The Duffy's Maid Service quote is $18.50 per room plus a fixed cost of $25,000 for sundry items such as uniforms with the motel's name. Tim's annual fixed cost for space, equipment, and supplies is $61,000. Which is the preferred process for Tim, and why? **P**

•• **7.8** Matthew Bailey, as manager of Designs by Bailey, is upgrading his CAD software. The high-performance (HP) software rents for $3,000 per month per workstation. The standard-performance (SP) software rents for $2,000 per month per workstation. The productivity figures that he has available suggest that the HP software is faster for his kind of design. Therefore, with the HP software he will need five engineers and with the SP software he will need six. This translates into a variable cost of $200 per drawing for the HP system and $240 per drawing for the SP system. At his projected volume of 80 drawings per month, which system should he rent? **P**

••• **7.9** Metters Cabinets, Inc., needs to choose a production method for its new office shelf, the Maxistand. To help accomplish this, the firm has gathered the following production cost data:

PROCESS TYPE	ANNUALIZED FIXED COST OF PLANT & EQUIP.	VARIABLE COSTS (PER UNIT) ($)		
		LABOR	MATERIAL	ENERGY
Mass Customization	$1,260,000	30	18	12
Intermittent	$1,000,000	24	26	20
Repetitive	$1,625,000	28	15	12
Continuous	$1,960,000	25	15	10

Metters Cabinets projects an annual demand of 24,000 units for the Maxistand. The Maxistand will sell for $120 per unit.
a) Which process type will maximize the annual profit from producing the Maxistand?
b) What is the value of this annual profit? **P**

•• **7.10** California Gardens, Inc., prewashes, shreds, and distributes a variety of salad mixes in 2-pound bags. Doug Voss, Operations VP, is considering a new Hi-Speed shredder to replace the old machine, referred to in the shop as "Clunker." Hi-Speed will have a fixed cost of $85,000 per month and a variable cost of $1.25 per bag. Clunker has a fixed cost of only $44,000 per month, but a variable cost of $1.75. Selling price is $2.50 per bag.
a) What is the crossover point in units (point of indifference) for the processes?

b) What is the monthly profit or loss if the company changes to the Hi-Speed shredder and sells 60,000 bags per month?

c) What is the monthly profit or loss if the company stays with Clunker and sells 60,000 bags per month?

•• **7.11** Nagle Electric, Inc., of Lincoln, Nebraska, must replace a robotic Mig welder and is evaluating two alternatives. Machine A has a fixed cost for the first year of $75,000 and a variable cost of $16, with a capacity of 18,000 units per year. Machine B is slower, with a speed of one-half of A's, but the fixed cost is only $60,000. The variable cost will be higher, at $20 per unit. Each unit is expected to sell for $28.

a) What is the crossover point (point of indifference) in units for the two machines?

b) What is the range of units for which machine A is preferable?

c) What is the range of units for which machine B is preferable?

•• **7.12** Stapleton Manufacturing intends to increase capacity through the addition of new equipment. Two vendors have presented proposals. The fixed cost for proposal A is $65,000, and for proposal B, $34,000. The variable cost for A is $10, and for B, $14. The revenue generated by each unit is $18.

a) What is the crossover point in units for the two options?

b) At an expected volume of 8,300 units, which alternative should be chosen?

Problems 7.13–7.17 relate to Process Analysis and Design

• **7.13** Prepare a flowchart for one of the following:

a) the registration process at a school

b) the process at the local car wash

c) a shoe shine

d) some other process with the approval of the instructor

• **7.14** Prepare a process chart for one of the activities in Problem 7.13.

•• **7.15** Prepare a time-function map for one of the activities in Problem 7.13.

•• **7.16** Prepare a service blueprint for one of the activities in Problem 7.13.

•• **7.17** Using Figure 7.6 in the discussion of value-stream mapping as a starting point, analyze an opportunity for improvement in a process with which you are familiar and develop an improved process.

CASE STUDIES

Rochester Manufacturing's Process Decision

Rochester Manufacturing Corporation (RMC) is considering moving some of its production from traditional numerically controlled machines to a flexible manufacturing system (FMS). Its computer numerical control machines have been operating in a high-variety, low-volume manner. Machine utilization, as near as it can determine, is hovering around 10%. The machine tool salespeople and a consulting firm want to put the machines together in an FMS. They believe that a $3 million expenditure on machinery and the transfer machines will handle about 30% of RMC's work. There will, of course, be transition and startup costs in addition to this.

The firm has not yet entered all its parts into a comprehensive group technology system, but believes that the 30% is a good estimate of products suitable for the FMS. This 30% should fit very nicely into a "family." A reduction, because of higher utilization, should take place in the number of pieces of machinery. The firm should be able to go from 15 to about 4 machines, and personnel should go from 15 to perhaps as low as 3. Similarly, floor space reduction will go from 20,000 square feet to about 6,000.

Throughput of orders should also improve with processing of this family of parts in 1 to 2 days rather than 7 to 10. Inventory reduction is estimated to yield a one-time $750,000 savings, and annual labor savings should be in the neighborhood of $300,000.

Although the projections all look very positive, an analysis of the project's return on investment showed it to be between 10% and 15% per year. The company has traditionally had an expectation that projects should yield well over 15% and have payback periods of substantially less than 5 years.

Discussion Questions

1. As a production manager for RMC, what do you recommend? Why?

2. Prepare a case by a conservative plant manager for maintaining the status quo until the returns are more obvious.

3. Prepare the case for an optimistic sales manager that you should move ahead with the FMS now.

Process Strategy at Wheeled Coach

Video Case

Wheeled Coach, based in Winter Park, Florida, is the world's largest manufacturer of ambulances. Working four 10-hour days each week, 350 employees make only custom-made ambulances; virtually every vehicle is unique. Wheeled Coach accommodates the marketplace by providing a wide variety of options and an engineering staff accustomed to innovation and custom design. Continuing growth, which now requires that more than 20 ambulances roll off the assembly line each week, makes process design a continuing challenge. Wheeled Coach's response has been to build a focused factory: Wheeled Coach builds nothing but

ambulances. Within the focused factory, Wheeled Coach established work cells for every major module feeding an assembly line, including aluminum bodies, electrical wiring harnesses, interior cabinets, windows, painting, and upholstery.

Labor standards drive the schedule so that every work cell feeds the assembly line on schedule, just-in-time for installations. The chassis, usually that of a Ford truck, moves to a station at which the aluminum body is mounted. Then the vehicle is moved to painting. Following a custom paint job, it moves to the assembly line, where it will spend 7 days. During each of these 7 workdays, each work cell delivers its respective module to the appropriate position on the assembly line. During the first day, electrical wiring is installed; on the second day, the unit moves forward to the station at which cabinetry is delivered and installed, then to a window and lighting station, on to upholstery, to fit and finish, to further customizing, and finally to inspection and road testing. The *Global Company Profile* featuring Wheeled Coach, which opens Chapter 14, provides further details about this process.

Discussion Questions*

1. Why do you think major auto manufacturers do not build ambulances?

2. What is an alternative process strategy to the assembly line that Wheeled Coach currently uses?
3. Why is it more efficient for the work cells to prepare "modules" and deliver them to the assembly line than it would be to produce the component (e.g., interior upholstery) on the line?
4. How does Wheeled Coach manage the tasks to be performed at each work station?

*You may wish to view the video that accompanies this case before addressing these questions.

Alaska Airlines: 20-Minute Baggage Process—Guaranteed!

Video Case

Alaska Airlines is unique among the nine major U.S. carriers not only for its extensive flight coverage of remote towns throughout Alaska (it also covers the U.S., Hawaii, and Mexico from its primary hub in Seattle). It is also one of the smallest independent airlines, with 10,300 employees, including 3,000 flight attendants and 1,500 pilots. What makes it really unique, though, is its ability to build state-of-the-art processes, using the latest technology, that yield high customer satisfaction. Indeed, J. D. Power and Associates has ranked Alaska Airlines highest in North America for seven years in a row for customer satisfaction.

Alaska Airlines was the first to sell tickets via the Internet, first to offer Web check-in and print boarding passes online, and first with kiosk check-in. As Wayne Newton, Director of System Operation Control, states, "We are passionate about our processes. If it's not measured, it's not managed."

One of the processes Alaska is most proud of is its baggage handling system. Passengers can check in at kiosks, tag their own bags with bar code stickers, and deliver them to a customer service agent at the carousel, which carries the bags through the vast underground system that eventually delivers the bags to a baggage handler. En route, each bag passes through TSA automated screening and is manually opened or inspected if it appears suspicious. With the help of bar code readers, conveyer belts automatically sort and transfer bags to their location (called a "pier") at the tarmac level. A baggage handler then loads the bags onto a cart and takes it to the plane for loading by the ramp team waiting inside the cargo hold. There are different procedures for "hot bags" (bags that have less than 30 minutes between transfer) and for "cold bags" (bags with over 60 minutes between plane transfers). Hot bags are delivered directly from one plane to another (called "tail-to-tail"). Cold bags are sent back into the normal conveyer system.

The process continues on the destination side with Alaska's unique guarantee that customer luggage will be delivered to the terminal's carousel within 20 minutes of the plane's arrival at the gate. If not, Alaska grants each passenger a 2,000 frequent-flier mile bonus!

The airline's use of technology includes bar code scanners to check in the bag when a passenger arrives, and again before it is placed on the cart to the plane. Similarly, on arrival, the time the passenger door opens is electronically noted and bags are again scanned as they are placed on the baggage carousel at the destination—tracking this metric means that the "time to carousel" (TTC) deadline is seldom missed. And the process almost guarantees that the lost bag rate approaches zero. On a recent day, only one out of 100 flights missed the TTC mark. The baggage

Alaska Airlines

process relies not just on technology, though. There are detailed, documented procedures to ensure that bags hit the 20-minute timeframe. Within one minute of the plane door opening at the gate, baggage handlers must begin the unloading. The first bag must be out of the plane within three minutes of parking the plane. This means the ground crew must be in the proper location—with their trucks and ramps in place and ready to go.

Largely because of technology, flying on Alaska Airlines is remarkably reliable—even in the dead of an Alaska winter with only two hours of daylight, 50 mph winds, slippery runways, and low visibility. Alaska Airlines has had the industry's best on-time performance, with 87% if its flights landing on time.

Discussion Questions*

1. Prepare a flowchart of the process a passenger's bag follows from kiosk to destination carousel. (See Example 2 in Chapter 6 for a sample flowchart.) Include the exception process for the TSA opening of selected bags.

2. What other processes can an airline examine? Why is each important?

3. How does the kiosk alter the check-in process?

4. What metrics (quantifiable measures) are needed to track baggage?

5. What is the role of scanners in the baggage process?

*You may wish to view the video that accompanies this case before addressing these questions.

Process Analysis at Arnold Palmer Hospital

Video Case

The Arnold Palmer Hospital (APH) in Orlando, Florida, is one of the busiest and most respected hospitals for the medical treatment of children and women in the U.S. Since its opening on golfing legend Arnold Palmer's birthday September 10, 1989, more than 1.6 million children and women have passed through its doors. It is the fourth busiest labor and delivery hospital in the U.S. and one of the largest neonatal intensive care units in the Southeast. APH ranks in the top 10% of hospitals nationwide in patient satisfaction.

"Part of the reason for APH's success," says Executive Director Kathy Swanson, "is our continuous improvement process. Our goal is 100% patient satisfaction. But getting there means constantly examining and reexamining everything we do, from patient flow, to cleanliness, to layout space, to a work-friendly environment, to speed of medication delivery from the pharmacy to a patient. Continuous improvement is a huge and never-ending task."

One of the tools the hospital uses consistently is process charts [like those in Figures 7.4 to 7.7 in this chapter and Figure 6.6(e) in Chapter 6]. Staffer Diane Bowles, who carries the title "clinical practice improvement consultant," charts scores of processes. Bowles's flowcharts help study ways to improve the turnaround of a vacated room (especially important in a hospital that has pushed capacity for years), speed up the admission process, and deliver warm meals warm.

Lately, APH has been examining the flow of maternity patients (and their paperwork) from the moment they enter the hospital until they are discharged, hopefully with their healthy baby, a day or two later. The flow of maternity patients follows these steps:

1. Enter APH's Labor & Delivery (L&D) check-in desk entrance.

2. If the baby is born en route or if birth is imminent, the mother and baby are taken directly to Labor & Delivery on the second floor and registered and admitted directly at the bedside. If there are no complications, the mother and baby go to Step 6.

3. If the baby is *not* yet born, the front desk asks if the mother is pre-registered. (Most do preregister at the 28- to 30-week pregnancy mark.) If she is not, she goes to the registration office on the first floor.

4. The pregnant woman is then taken to L&D Triage on the 8th floor for assessment. If she is in active labor, she is taken to an L&D room on the 2nd floor until the baby is born. If she is not ready, she goes to Step 5.

5. Pregnant women not ready to deliver (i.e., no contractions or false alarms) are either sent home to return on a later date and reenter the system at that time, or if contractions are not yet close enough, they are sent to walk around the hospital grounds (to encourage progress) and then return to L&D Triage at a prescribed time.

6. When the baby is born, if there are no complications, after 2 hours the mother and baby are transferred to a "mother–baby care unit" room on floors 3, 4, or 5 for an average of 40–44 hours.

7. If there *are* complications with the mother, she goes to an operating room and/or intensive care unit. From there, she goes back to a mother–baby care room upon stabilization—or is discharged at another time if not stabilized. Complications for the baby may result in a stay in the neonatal intensive care unit (NICU) before transfer to the baby nursery near the mother's room. If the baby is not stable enough for discharge with the mother, the baby is discharged later.

8. Mother and/or baby, when ready, are discharged and taken by wheelchair to the discharge exit for pickup to travel home.

Discussion Questions*

1. As Diane's new assistant, you need to flowchart this process. Explain how the process might be improved once you have completed the chart.

2. If a mother is scheduled for a Caesarean-section birth (i.e., the baby is removed from the womb surgically), how would this flowchart change?

3. If *all* mothers were electronically (or manually) preregistered, how would the flowchart change? Redraw the chart to show your changes.

4. Describe in detail a process that the hospital could analyze, besides the ones mentioned in this case.

*You may wish to view the video that accompanies this case before addressing these questions.

- **Additional Case Study:** Visit MyOMLab for this free case study:
  Matthew Yachts, Inc.: Examines a possible process change as the market for yachts changes.

Endnotes

1. An additional example of a process chart is shown in Chapter 10.

2. Waste includes *inspection* (if the task is done properly, then inspection is unnecessary); *transportation* (movement of material within a process may be a necessary evil, but it adds no value); *delay* (an asset sitting idle and taking up space is waste); *storage* (unless part of a "curing" process, storage is waste).

Main Heading	Review Material	MyOMLab
FOUR PROCESS STRATEGIES (pp. 282–288)	■ **Process strategy**—An organization's approach to transforming resources into goods and services. *The objective of a process strategy is to build a production process that meets customer requirements and product specifications within cost and other managerial constraints.* Virtually every good or service is made by using some variation of one of four process strategies. ■ **Process focus**—A facility organized around processes to facilitate low-volume, high-variety production. The vast majority of global production is devoted to making low-volume, high-variety products in process-focused facilities, also known as job shops or *intermittent process* facilities. Process-focused facilities have high variable costs with extremely low utilization (5% to 25%) of facilities. ■ **Modules**—Parts or components of a product previously prepared, often in a continuous process. ■ **Repetitive process**—A product-oriented production process that uses modules. The repetitive process is the classic assembly line. It allows the firm to use modules and combine the economic advantages of the product-focused model with the customization advantages of the process-focus model. ■ **Product focus**—A facility organized around products; a product-oriented, high-volume, low-variety process. Product-focused facilities are also called *continuous processes* because they have very long, continuous production runs. The specialized nature of a product-focused facility requires high fixed cost; however, low variable costs reward high facility utilization. ■ **Mass customization**—Rapid, low-cost production that caters to constantly changing unique customer desires. ■ **Build-to-order (BTO)**—Produce to customer order rather than to a forecast. Major challenges of a build-to-order system include: *Product design, Process design, Inventory management, Tight schedules*, and *Responsive partners*. ■ **Postponement**—The delay of any modifications or customization to a product as long as possible in the production process. ■ **Crossover chart**—A chart of costs at the possible volumes for more than one process.	Concept Questions: 1.1–1.4 Problems: 7.1–7.12 **ACTIVE MODEL 7.1** **VIDEO 7.1** Process Strategy at Wheeled Coach Ambulance Virtual Office Hours for Solved Problem: 7.1
SELECTION OF EQUIPMENT (p. 288)	Picking the best equipment involves understanding the specific industry and available processes and technology. The choice requires considering cost, quality, capacity, and flexibility. ■ **Flexibility**—The ability to respond with little penalty in time, cost, or customer value.	Concept Questions: 2.1–2.3
PROCESS ANALYSIS AND DESIGN (pp. 288–293)	Five tools of process analysis are (1) flowcharts, (2) time-function mapping, (3) process charts, (4) value-stream mapping, and (5) service blueprinting. ■ **Flowchart**—A drawing used to analyze movement of people or materials. ■ **Time-function mapping** (or **process mapping**)—A flowchart with time added on the horizontal axis. ■ **Process charts**—Charts that use symbols to analyze the movement of people or material. Process charts allow managers to focus on value-added activities and to compute the percentage of value-added time (= operation time/total time). ■ **Value-stream mapping (VSM)**—A tool that helps managers understand how to add value in the flow of material and information through the entire production process. ■ **Service blueprinting**—A process analysis technique that lends itself to a focus on the customer and the provider's interaction with the customer.	Concept Questions: 3.1–3.4 Problems: 7.14–7.15 **VIDEO 7.2** Alaska Airlines 20-Minute Baggage Process–Guaranteed! **VIDEO 7.3** Process Analysis at Arnold Palmer Hospital

Main Heading	Review Material	MyOMLab
SPECIAL CONSIDERA-TIONS FOR SERVICE PROCESS DESIGN (pp. 293–294)	Services can be classified into one of four quadrants, based on relative degrees of labor and customization: 1. *Service factory* 2. *Service shop* 3. *Mass service* 4. *Professional service* Techniques for improving service productivity include: ■ *Separation*—Structuring service so customers must go where the service is offered ■ *Self-service*—Customers examining, comparing, and evaluating at their own pace ■ *Postponement*—Customizing at delivery ■ *Focus*—Restricting the offerings ■ *Modules*—Modular selection of service; modular production ■ *Automation*—Separating services that may lend themselves to a type of automation ■ *Scheduling*—Precise personnel scheduling ■ *Training*—Clarifying the service options; explaining how to avoid problems	Concept Questions: 4.1–4.4
PRODUCTION TECHNOLOGY (pp. 294–298)	■ **Computer numerical control (CNC)**—Machinery with its own computer and memory. ■ **Additive manufacturing**—The production of physical items by adding layer upon layer, much in the same way an ink jet printer lays down ink; often referred to as 3D printing. ■ **Automatic identification system (AIS)**—A system for transforming data into electronic form (e.g., bar codes). ■ **Radio frequency identification (RFID)**—A wireless system in which integrated circuits with antennas send radio waves. ■ **Process control**—The use of information technology to control a physical process. ■ **Vision systems**—Systems that use video cameras and computer technology in inspection roles. ■ **Robot**—A flexible machine with the ability to hold, move, or grab items. ■ **Automated storage and retrieval systems (ASRS)**—Computer-controlled warehouses that provide for the automatic placement of parts into and from designated places within a warehouse. ■ **Automated guided vehicle (AGV)**—Electronically guided and controlled cart used to move materials. ■ **Flexible manufacturing system (FMS)**—Automated work cell controlled by electronic signals from a common centralized computer facility. ■ **Computer-integrated manufacturing (CIM)**—A manufacturing system in which CAD, FMS, inventory control, warehousing, and shipping are integrated.	Concept Questions: 5.1–5. 4
TECHNOLOGY IN SERVICES (p. 298)	Many rapid technological developments have occurred in the service sector. These range from POS terminals and RFID to online newspapers and e-books.	Concept Questions: 6.1–6.2
PROCESS REDESIGN (pp. 298–299)	■ **Process redesign**—The fundamental rethinking of business processes to bring about dramatic improvements in performance. Process redesign often focuses on activities that cross functional lines.	Concept Questions: 7.1–7.2

Self Test

■ **Before taking the self-test,** refer to the learning objectives listed at the beginning of the chapter and the key terms listed at the end of the chapter.

LO 7.1 Low-volume, high-variety processes are also known as:
   a) continuous processes.   b) process focused.
   c) repetitive processes.   d) product focused.

LO 7.2 A crossover chart for process selection focuses on:
   a) labor costs.
   b) material cost.
   c) both labor and material costs.
   d) fixed and variable costs.
   e) fixed costs.

LO 7.3 Tools for process analysis include all of the following except:
   a) flowchart.
   b) vision systems.
   c) service blueprinting.
   d) time-function mapping.
   e) value-stream mapping.

LO 7.4 Customer feedback in process design is lower as:
   a) the degree of customization is increased.
   b) the degree of labor is increased.
   c) the degree of customization is lowered.
   d) both a and b.
   e) both b and c.

LO 7.5 Computer-integrated manufacturing (CIM) includes manufacturing systems that have:
   a) computer-aided design, direct numerical control machines, and material-handling equipment controlled by automation.
   b) transaction processing, a management information system, and decision support systems.
   c) automated guided vehicles, robots, and process control.
   d) robots, automated guided vehicles, and transfer equipment.

Answers: LO 7.1. b; LO 7.2. d; LO 7.3. b; LO 7.4. c; LO 7.5. a.

Capacity and Constraint Management

SUPPLEMENT OUTLINE

- Capacity *308*
- Bottleneck Analysis and the Theory of Constraints *314*
- Break-Even Analysis *318*
- Reducing Risk with Incremental Changes *322*
- Applying Expected Monetary Value (EMV) to Capacity Decisions *323*
- Applying Investment Analysis to Strategy-Driven Investments *324*

Alaska Airlines

Alaska Airlines

LEARNING OBJECTIVES

LO S7.1 *Define* capacity 308

LO S7.2 *Determine* design capacity, effective capacity, and utilization 310

LO S7.3 *Perform* bottleneck analysis 315

LO S7.4 *Compute* break-even 319

LO S7.5 *Determine* expected monetary value of a capacity decision 323

LO S7.6 *Compute* net present value 324

When designing a concert hall, management hopes that the forecasted capacity (the product mix—opera, symphony, and special events—and the technology needed for these events) is accurate and adequate for operation above the break-even point. However, in many concert halls, even when operating at full capacity, break-even is not achieved, and supplemental funding must be obtained.

Klaus Lang/All Canada Photos/Alamy

Capacity

LO S7.1 *Define* capacity

Capacity

The "throughput," or number of units a facility can hold, receive, store, or produce in a period of time.

What should be the seating capacity of a concert hall? How many customers per day should an Olive Garden or a Hard Rock Cafe be able to serve? How large should a Frito-Lay plant be to produce 75,000 bags of Ruffles in an 8-hour shift? In this supplement we look at tools that help a manager make these decisions.

After selection of a production process (Chapter 7), managers need to determine capacity. **Capacity** is the "throughput," or the number of units a facility can hold, receive, store, or produce in a given time. Capacity decisions often determine capital requirements and therefore a large portion of fixed cost. Capacity also determines whether demand will be satisfied or whether facilities will be idle. If a facility is too large, portions of it will sit unused and add cost to existing production. If a facility is too small, customers—and perhaps entire markets—will be lost. Determining facility size, with an objective of achieving high levels of utilization and a high return on investment, is critical.

Capacity planning can be viewed in three time horizons. In Figure S7.1 we note that long-range capacity (generally greater than 3 years) is a function of adding facilities and equipment that have a long lead time. In the intermediate range (usually 3 to 36 months), we can add equipment, personnel, and shifts; we can subcontract; and we can build or use inventory. This is the "aggregate planning" task. In the short run (usually up to 3 months), we are primarily concerned with scheduling jobs and people, as well as allocating machinery. Modifying capacity in the short run is difficult, as we are usually constrained by existing capacity.

STUDENT TIP ❗

Too little capacity loses customers and too much capacity is expensive. Like Goldilocks's porridge, capacity needs to be *just* right.

Options for Adjusting Capacity

Time Horizon	Modify capacity	Use capacity
Long-range planning	Design new production processes. Add (or sell existing) long-lead-time equipment. Acquire or sell facilities. Acquire competitors.	*
Intermediate-range planning (aggregate planning)	Subcontract. Add or sell equipment. Add or reduce shifts.	Build or use inventory. More or improved training. Add or reduce personnel.
Short-range planning (scheduling)	*	Schedule jobs. Schedule personnel. Allocate machinery.

* Difficult to adjust capacity, as limited options exist

Design and Effective Capacity

Design capacity is the maximum theoretical output of a system in a given period under ideal conditions. It is normally expressed as a rate, such as the number of tons of steel that can be produced per week, per month, or per year. For many companies, measuring capacity can be straightforward: it is the maximum number of units the company is capable of producing in a specific time. However, for some organizations, determining capacity can be more difficult. Capacity can be measured in terms of beds (a hospital), active members (a church), or billable hours (a CPA firm). Other organizations use total work time available as a measure of overall capacity.

Most organizations operate their facilities at a rate less than the design capacity. They do so because they have found that they can operate more efficiently when their resources are not stretched to the limit. For example, Ian's Bistro has tables set with 2 or 4 chairs seating a total of 270 guests. But the tables are never filled that way. Some tables will have 1 or 3 guests; tables can be pulled together for parties of 6 or 8. There are always unused chairs. *Design capacity* is 270, but *effective capacity* is often closer to 220, which is 81% of design capacity.

Effective capacity is the capacity a firm *expects* to achieve given the current operating constraints. Effective capacity is often lower than design capacity because the facility may have been designed for an earlier version of the product or a different product mix than is currently being produced. Table S7.1 further illustrates the relationship between design capacity, effective capacity, and *actual output*.

Design capacity

The theoretical maximum output of a system in a given period under ideal conditions.

Effective capacity

The capacity a firm can expect to achieve, given its product mix, methods of scheduling, maintenance, and standards of quality.

TABLE S7.1	Capacity Measurements	
MEASURE	**DEFINITION**	**EXAMPLE**
Design capacity	Ideal conditions exist during the time that the system is available.	If machines at Frito-Lay are designed to produce 1,000 bags of chips/hr., and the plant operates 16 hrs./day. **Design Capacity = 1,000 bags/hr. × 16 hrs. = 16,000 bags/day**
Effective capacity	Design capacity minus lost output because of *planned* resource unavailability (e.g., preventive maintenance, machine setups/changeovers, changes in product mix, scheduled breaks)	If Frito-Lay loses 3 hours of output per day (namely 0.5 hrs./day on preventive maintenance + 1 hr./day on employee breaks + 1.5 hrs./day setting up machines for different products). **Effective Capacity = 16,000 bags/day − (1,000 bags/hr.)(3 hrs./day) = 16,000 bags/day − 3,000 bags/day = 13,000 bags/day**
Actual output	Effective capacity minus lost output during *unplanned* resource idleness (e.g., absenteeism, machine breakdowns, unavailable parts, quality problems)	On average, if machines at Frito-Lay are not running 1 hr./day due to late parts and machine breakdowns. **Actual Output = 13,000 bags/day − (1,000 bags/hr.)(1 hr./day) = 13,000 bags/day − 1,000 bags/day = 12,000 bags/day**

Andrey Eremin/123rf

Hongqi Zhang/123rf

Hongqi Zhang/123rf

Utilization

Actual output as a percent of design capacity.

Efficiency

Actual output as a percent of effective capacity.

LO S7.2 *Determine* design capacity, effective capacity, and utilization

Two measures of system performance are particularly useful: utilization and efficiency. **Utilization** is simply the percent of *design capacity* actually achieved. **Efficiency** is the percent of *effective capacity* actually achieved. Depending on how facilities are used and managed, it may be difficult or impossible to reach 100% efficiency. Operations managers tend to be evaluated on efficiency. The key to improving efficiency is often found in correcting quality problems and in effective scheduling, training, and maintenance. Utilization and efficiency are computed below:

$$\text{Utilization} = \text{Actual output}/\text{Design capacity} \qquad \text{(S7-1)}$$

$$\text{Efficiency} = \text{Actual output}/\text{Effective capacity} \qquad \text{(S7-2)}$$

In Example S1 we determine these values.

Example S1

DETERMINING CAPACITY UTILIZATION AND EFFICIENCY

Sara James Bakery has a plant for processing *Deluxe* breakfast rolls and wants to better understand its capability. Last week the facility produced 148,000 rolls. The effective capacity is 175,000 rolls. The production line operates 7 days per week, with three 8-hour shifts per day. The line was designed to process the nut-filled, cinnamon-flavored *Deluxe* roll at a rate of 1,200 per hour. Determine the design capacity, utilization, and efficiency for this plant when producing this *Deluxe* roll.

APPROACH ▶ First compute the design capacity and then use Equation (S7-1) to determine utilization and Equation (S7-2) to determine efficiency.

SOLUTION ▶

$$\text{Design capacity} = (7 \text{ days} \times 3 \text{ shifts} \times 8 \text{ hours}) \times (1{,}200 \text{ rolls per hour}) = 201{,}600 \text{ rolls}$$

$$\text{Utilization} = \text{Actual output}/\text{Design capacity} = 148{,}000/201{,}600 = 73.4\%$$

$$\text{Efficiency} = \text{Actual output}/\text{Effective capacity} = 148{,}000/175{,}000 = 84.6\%$$

INSIGHT ▶ The bakery now has the information necessary to evaluate efficiency.

LEARNING EXERCISE ▶ If the actual output is 150,000, what is the efficiency? [Answer: 85.7%.]

RELATED PROBLEMS ▶ S7.1, S7.2, S7.3, S7.4, S7.5, S7.6, S7.7, S7.8

ACTIVE MODEL S7.1 This example is further illustrated in Active Model S7.1 in MyOMLab.

In Example S2 we see how the effectiveness of new capacity additions depends on how well management can perform on the utilization and efficiency of those additions.

Example S2

EXPANDING CAPACITY

The manager of Sara James Bakery (see Example S1) now needs to increase production of the increasingly popular *Deluxe* roll. To meet this demand, she will be adding a second production line. The second line has the same design capacity (201,600) and effective capacity (175,000) as the first line; however, new workers will be operating the second line. Quality problems and other inefficiencies stemming from the inexperienced workers are expected to reduce output on the second line to 130,000 (compared to 148,000 on the first). The utilization and efficiency were 73.4% and 84.6%, respectively, on the first line. Determine the new utilization and efficiency for the *Deluxe* roll operation after adding the second line.

APPROACH ▶ First, determine the new design capacity, effective capacity, and actual output after adding the second line. Then, use Equation (S7-1) to determine utilization and Equation (S7-2) to determine efficiency.

SOLUTION ▶ Design capacity $= 201,600 \times 2 = 403,200$ rolls

Effective capacity $= 175,000 \times 2 = 350,000$ rolls

Actual output $= 148,000 + 130,000 = 278,000$ rolls

Utilization $=$ Actual output/Design capacity $= 278,000 / 403,200 = 68.95\%$

Efficiency $=$ Actual output/Effective capacity $= 278,000 / 350,000 = 79.43\%$

INSIGHT ▶ Although adding equipment increases capacity, that equipment may not be operated as efficiently with new employees as might be the case with experienced employees. For Sara James Bakery, a doubling of equipment investment did not result in a doubling of output; other variables drove both utilization and efficiency lower.

LEARNING EXERCISE ▶ Suppose that Sara James reduces changeover time (setup time) by three fewer hours per week. What will be the new values of utilization and efficiency? [Answer: utilization is still 68.95%, efficiency now increases to 81.10%]

RELATED PROBLEMS ▶ S7.1, S7.2, S7.3, S7.4, S7.5, S7.6, S7.7, S7.8

Actual output, as used in Equation (S7-2), represents current conditions. Alternatively, with a knowledge of effective capacity and a current or target value for efficiency, the future *expected output* can be computed by reversing Equation (S7-2):

$$\text{Expected output} = \text{Effective capacity} \times \text{Efficiency}$$

If the expected output is inadequate, additional capacity may be needed. Much of the remainder of this supplement addresses how to effectively and efficiently add that capacity.

Capacity and Strategy

Sustained profits come from building competitive advantage, not just from a good financial return on a specific process. Capacity decisions must be integrated into the organization's mission and strategy. Investments are not to be made as isolated expenditures, but as part of a coordinated plan that will place the firm in an advantageous position. The questions to be asked are, "Will these investments eventually win profitable customers?" and "What competitive advantage (such as process flexibility, speed of delivery, improved quality, and so on) do we obtain?"

All 10 OM decisions we discuss in this text, as well as other organizational elements such as marketing and finance, are affected by changes in capacity. Change in capacity will have sales and cash flow implications, just as capacity changes have quality, supply chain, human resource, and maintenance implications. All must be considered.

Capacity Considerations

In addition to tight integration of strategy and investments, there are four special considerations for a good capacity decision:

1. *Forecast demand accurately:* Product additions and deletions, competition actions, product life cycle, and unknown sales volumes all add challenge to accurate forecasting.
2. *Match technology increments and sales volume:* Capacity options are often constrained by technology. Some capacity increments may be large (e.g., steel mills or power plants), while others may be small (hand-crafted Louis Vuitton handbags). Large capacity increments complicate the difficult but necessary job of matching capacity to sales.
3. *Find the optimum operating size (volume):* Economies and diseconomies of scale often dictate an optimal size for a facility. *Economies of scale* exist when average cost declines as size increases, whereas *diseconomies of scale* occur when a larger size raises the average cost. As Figure S7.2 suggests, most businesses have an optimal size—at least until someone comes along with a new business model. For decades, very large integrated steel mills were considered optimal. Then along came Nucor, CMC, and other minimills, with a new process and a new business model that radically reduced the optimum size of a steel mill.
4. *Build for change:* Managers build flexibility into facilities and equipment; changes will occur in processes, as well as products, product volume, and product mix.

STUDENT TIP
Each industry and technology has an optimum size.

Next, we note that rather than strategically manage capacity, managers may tactically manage demand.

Chitose Suzuki/AP Images

Figure **S7.2**

Economies and Diseconomies of Scale

Krispy Kreme originally had 8,000-square-foot stores but found them too large and too expensive for many markets. Then they tried tiny 1,300-square-foot stores, which required less investment, but such stores were too small to provide the mystique of seeing and smelling Krispy Kreme doughnuts being made. Krispy Kreme finally got it right with a 2,600-foot-store.

Capacity Considerations for Krispy Kreme Stores

Managing Demand

Even with good forecasting and facilities built to accomodate that forecast, there may be a poor match between the actual demand that occurs and available capacity. A poor match may mean demand exceeds capacity or capacity exceeds demand. However, in both cases, firms have options.

Demand Exceeds Capacity   When *demand exceeds capacity*, the firm may be able to curtail demand simply by raising prices, scheduling long lead times (which may be inevitable), and discouraging marginally profitable business. However, because inadequate facilities reduce revenue below what is possible, the long-term solution is usually to increase capacity.

Capacity Exceeds Demand   When *capacity exceeds demand*, the firm may want to stimulate demand through price reductions or aggressive marketing, or it may accommodate the market through product changes. When decreasing customer demand is combined with old and inflexible processes, layoffs and plant closings may be necessary to bring capacity in line with demand.

Adjusting to Seasonal Demands   A seasonal or cyclical pattern of demand is another capacity challenge. In such cases, management may find it helpful to offer products with complementary demand patterns—that is, products for which the demand is high for one when low for the other. For example, in Figure S7.3 the firm is adding a line of snowmobile motors to its line of jet skis to smooth demand. With appropriate complementing of products, perhaps the utilization of facility, equipment, and personnel can be smoothed (as we see in the *OM in Action* box "Matching Airline Capacity to Demand").

Figure **S7.3**

By Combining Products That Have Complementary Seasonal Patterns, Capacity Can Be Better Utilized

OM in Action | Matching Airline Capacity to Demand

Airlines constantly struggle to control their capital expenditures and to adapt to unstable demand patterns.

Southwest and Lufthansa have each taken their own approach to increasing capacity while holding down capital investment. To manage capacity constraints on the cheap, Southwest squeezes seven flight segments out of its typical plane schedule per day—one more than most competitors. Its operations personnel find that quick ground turnaround, long a Southwest strength, is a key to this capital-saving technique.

Lufthansa has cut hundreds of millions of dollars in new jet purchases by squashing rows of seats 2 inches closer together. On the A320, for example, Lufthansa added two rows of seats, giving the plane 174 seats instead of 162. For its European fleet, this is the equivalent of having 12 more Airbus A320 jets. But Lufthansa will tell you that squeezing in more seats is not quite as bad as it sounds, as the new generation of ultra-thin seats provides passengers with more leg room. Using a strong mesh, similar to that in fancy office chairs

(instead of inches of foam padding), and moving magazine pockets to the top of seat backs, there is actually more knee room than with the old chairs.

Unstable demands in the airline industry provide another capacity challenge. Seasonal patterns (e.g., fewer people fly in the winter), compounded by spikes in demand during major holidays and summer vacations, play havoc with efficient use of capacity. Airlines attack costly seasonality in several ways. First, they schedule more planes for maintenance and renovations during slow winter months, curtailing winter capacity; second, they seek out contra-seasonal routes. And when capacity is substantially above demand, placing planes in storage (as shown in the photo) may be the most economical answer.

Airlines also use revenue management (see Chapter 13) to maximize per-seat pricing of available capacity, regardless of current demand patterns.

Sources: The Wall Street Journal (February 29, 2012) and (October 6, 2011).

Tactics for Matching Capacity to Demand Various tactics for adjusting capacity to demand include:

1. Making staffing changes (increasing or decreasing the number of employees or shifts)
2. Adjusting equipment (purchasing additional machinery or selling or leasing out existing equipment)
3. Improving processes to increase throughput (e.g., reducing setup times at M2 Global Technology added the equivalent of 17 shifts of capacity)
4. Redesigning products to facilitate more throughput
5. Adding process flexibility to better meet changing product preferences
6. Closing facilities

The foregoing tactics can be used to adjust demand to existing facilities. The strategic issue is, of course, how to have a facility of the correct size.

Service-Sector Demand and Capacity Management

In the service sector, scheduling customers is *demand management*, and scheduling the workforce is *capacity management*.

Joe McNally/Getty Images

Recessions (e.g., 2008–2010) and terrorist attacks (e.g., September 11, 2001) can make even the best capacity decision for an airline look bad. And excess capacity for an airline can be very expensive, with storage costs running as high as $60,000 per month per aircraft. Here, as a testimonial to excess capacity, aircraft sit idle in the Mojave Desert.

Many U.S. hospitals use services abroad to manage capacity for radiologists during night shifts. Night Hawk, an Idaho-based service with 50 radiologists in Zurich and Sydney, contracts with 900 facilities (20% of all U.S. hospitals). These trained experts, wide awake and alert in their daylight hours, usually return a diagnosis in 10 to 20 minutes, with a guarantee of 30 minutes.

Demand Management   When demand and capacity are fairly well matched, demand management can often be handled with appointments, reservations, or a first-come, first-served rule. In some businesses, such as doctors' and lawyers' offices, an *appointment system* is the schedule and is adequate. *Reservations systems* work well in rental car agencies, hotels, and some restaurants as a means of minimizing customer waiting time and avoiding disappointment over unfilled service. In retail shops, a post office, or a fast-food restaurant, a *first-come, first-served* rule for serving customers may suffice. Each industry develops its own approaches to matching demand and capacity. Other more aggressive approaches to demand management include many variations of discounts: "early bird" specials in restaurants, discounts for matinee performances or for seats at odd hours on an airline, and cheap weekend hotel rooms.

Capacity Management   When managing demand is not feasible, then managing capacity through changes in full-time, temporary, or part-time staff may be an option. This is the approach in many services. For instance, hospitals may find capacity limited by a shortage of board-certified radiologists willing to cover the graveyard shifts. Getting fast and reliable radiology readings can be the difference between life and death for an emergency room patient. As the photo above illustrates, when an overnight reading is required (and 40% of CT scans are done between 8 P.M. and 8 A.M.), the image can be sent by e-mail to a doctor in Europe or Australia for immediate analysis.

Bottleneck Analysis and the Theory of Constraints

As managers seek to match capacity to demand, decisions must be made about the size of specific operations or work areas in the larger system. Each of the interdependent work areas can be expected to have its own unique capacity. Capacity analysis involves determining the throughput capacity of workstations in a system and ultimately the capacity of the entire system.

A key concept in capacity analysis is the role of a constraint or bottleneck. A bottleneck is an operation that is the limiting factor or constraint. The term *bottleneck* refers to the literal neck of a bottle that constrains flow or, in the case of a production system, constrains throughput. A bottleneck has the lowest effective capacity of any operation in the system and thus limits the system's output. Bottlenecks occur in all facets of life—from job shops where a machine is constraining the work flow to highway traffic where two lanes converge into one inadequate lane, resulting in traffic congestion.

We define the process time of a station as the time to produce a unit (or a specified batch size of units) at that workstation. For example, if 16 customers can be checked out in a supermarket line every 60 minutes, then the process time at that station is 3.75 minutes per customer (= 60/16). (Process time is simply the inverse of capacity, which in this case is 60 minutes per hour/3.75 minutes per customer = 16 customers per hour.)

Capacity analysis

A means of determining throughput capacity of workstations or an entire production system.

Bottleneck

The limiting factor or constraint in a system.

Process time

The time to produce a unit (or specified batch of units) at a workstation.

To determine the bottleneck in a production system, simply identify the station with the slowest process time. The bottleneck time is the process time of the slowest workstation (the one that takes the longest) in a production system. For example, the flowchart in Figure S7.4 shows a simple assembly line. Individual station process times are 2, 4, and 3 minutes, respectively. The bottleneck time is 4 minutes. This is because station B is the slowest station. Even if we were to speed up station A, the entire production process would not be faster. Inventory would simply pile up in front of station B even more than now. Likewise, if station C could work faster, we could not tap its excess capacity because station B will not be able to feed products to it any faster than 1 every 4 minutes.

Station A	Station B	Station C
2 min/unit	4 min/unit	3 min/unit

The throughput time, on the other hand, is the time it takes a unit to go through production from start to end, *with no waiting*. (Throughput time describes the behavior in an empty system. In contrast, flow time describes the time to go through a production process from beginning to end, including idle time waiting for stations to finish working on other units.) The throughput time to produce a new completed unit in Figure S7.4 is 9 minutes (= 2 minutes + 4 minutes + 3 minutes).

Bottleneck time and *throughput time* may be quite different. For example, a Ford assembly line may roll out a new car every minute (bottleneck time), but it may take 25 hours to actually make a car from start to finish (throughput time). This is because the assembly line has many workstations, with each station contributing to the completed car. Thus, bottleneck time determines the system's capacity (one car per minute), while its throughput time determines potential ability to produce a newly ordered product from scratch in 25 hours.

The following two examples illustrate capacity analysis for slightly more complex systems. Example S3 introduces the concept of parallel processes, and Example S4 introduces the concept of simultaneous processing.

Bottleneck time

The process time of the longest (slowest) process, i.e., the bottleneck.

Figure S7.4

Three-Station Assembly Line

A box represents an operation, a triangle represents inventory, and arrows represent precedence relationships

Throughput time

The time it takes for a product to go through the production process *with no waiting*. It is the time of the longest path through the system.

Example S3

LO S7.3 *Perform bottleneck analysis*

CAPACITY ANALYSIS WITH PARALLEL PROCESSES

Howard Kraye's sandwich shop provides healthy sandwiches for customers. Howard has two identical sandwich assembly lines. A customer first places an order, which takes 30 seconds. The order is then sent to one of the two assembly lines. Each assembly line has two workers and three operations: (1) assembly worker 1 retrieves and cuts the bread (15 seconds/sandwich), (2) assembly worker 2 adds ingredients and places the sandwich onto the toaster conveyor belt (20 seconds/sandwich), and (3) the toaster heats the sandwich (40 seconds/sandwich). Finally, another employee wraps the heated sandwich coming out of the toaster and delivers it to the customer (37.5 seconds/sandwich). A flowchart of the process is shown below. Howard wants to determine the bottleneck time and throughput time of this process.

APPROACH ▶ Clearly the toaster is the single-slowest resource in the five-step process, but is it the bottleneck? Howard should first determine the bottleneck time of each of the two assembly lines separately, then the bottleneck time of the combined assembly lines, and finally the bottleneck time of the entire operation. For throughput time, each assembly line is identical, so Howard should just sum the process times for all five operations.

SOLUTION ▶ Because each of the three assembly-line operations uses a separate resource (worker or machine), different partially completed sandwiches can be worked on simultaneously at each station. Thus, the bottleneck time of each assembly line is the longest process time of each of the three operations. In this case, the 40-second toasting time represents the bottleneck time of each assembly line. Next, the bottleneck time of the *combined* assembly line operations is 40 seconds per *two* sandwiches, or 20 seconds per sandwich. Therefore, the wrapping and delivering operation, with a process time of 37.5 seconds, appears to be the bottleneck for the entire operation. The capacity per hour equals 3,600 seconds per hour/37.5 seconds per sandwich = 96 sandwiches per hour. The throughput time equals 30 + 15 + 20 + 40 + 37.5 = 142.5 seconds (or 2 minutes and 22.5 seconds), assuming no wait time in line to begin with.

INSIGHT ▶ Doubling the resources at a workstation effectively cuts the time at that station in half. (If *n* parallel [redundant] operations are added, the process time of the combined workstation operation will equal $1/n$ times the original process time.)

LEARNING EXERCISE ▶ If Howard hires an additional wrapper, what will be the new hourly capacity? [Answer: The new bottleneck is now the order-taking station: Capacity = 3,600 seconds per hour/30 seconds per sandwich = 120 sandwiches per hour]

RELATED PROBLEMS ▶ S7.9, S7.10, S7.11, S7.12, S7.13

In Example S3, how could we claim that the process time of the toaster was 20 seconds per sandwich when it takes 40 seconds to toast a sandwich? The reason is that we had two toasters; thus, two sandwiches could be toasted every 40 seconds, for an average of one sandwich every 20 seconds. And that time for a toaster can actually be achieved if the start times for the two are *staggered* (i.e., a new sandwich is placed in a toaster every 20 seconds). In that case, even though each sandwich will sit in the toaster for 40 seconds, a sandwich could emerge from one of the two toasters every 20 seconds. As we see, doubling the number of resources effectively cuts the process time at that station in half, resulting in a doubling of the capacity of those resources.

Example S4 | CAPACITY ANALYSIS WITH SIMULTANEOUS PROCESSES

Dr. Cynthia Knott's dentistry practice has been cleaning customers' teeth for decades. The process for a basic dental cleaning is relatively straightforward: (1) the customer checks in (2 minutes); (2) a lab technician takes and develops X-rays (2 and 4 minutes, respectively); (3) the dentist processes and examines the X-rays (5 minutes) *while* the hygienist cleans the teeth (24 minutes); (4) the dentist meets with the patient to poke at a few teeth, explain the X-ray results, and tell the patient to floss more often (8 minutes); and (5) the customer pays and books her next appointment (6 minutes). A flowchart of the customer visit is shown below. Dr. Knott wants to determine the bottleneck time and throughput time of this process.

APPROACH ▶ With simultaneous processes, an order or a product is essentially *split* into different paths to be rejoined later on. To find the bottleneck time, each operation is treated separately, just as though all operations were on a sequential path. To find the throughput time, the time over *all* paths must be computed, and the throughput time is the time of the *longest* path.

SOLUTION ▶ The bottleneck in this system is the hygienist cleaning operation at 24 minutes per patient, resulting in an hourly system capacity of 60 minutes/24 minutes per patient = 2.5 patients. The throughput time is the maximum of the two paths through the system. The path through the X-ray exam is 2 + 2 + 4 + 5 + 8 + 6 = 27 minutes, while the path through the hygienist cleaning operation is 2 + 2 + 4 + 24 + 8 + 6 = 46 minutes. Thus a patient should be out the door after 46 minutes (i.e., the maximum of 27 and 46).

INSIGHT ▶ With simultaneous processing, all operation times in the entire system are not simply added together to compute throughput time because some operations are occurring simultaneously. Instead, the time of the longest path through the system is deemed the throughput time.

LEARNING EXERCISE ▶ Suppose that the same technician now has the hygienist start immediately after the X-rays are taken (allowing the hygienist to start 4 minutes sooner). The technician then develops the X-rays while the hygienist is cleaning teeth. The dentist still examines the X-rays while the teeth cleaning is occurring. What would be the new system capacity and throughput time? [Answer: The X-ray development operation is now on the parallel path with cleaning and X-ray exam, reducing the total patient visit duration by 4 minutes, for a throughput time of 42 minutes (the maximum of 27 and 42). However, the hygienist cleaning operation is still the bottleneck, so the capacity remains 2.5 patients per hour.]

RELATED PROBLEMS ▶ S7.14, S7.15

To summarize: (1) the *bottleneck* is the operation with the longest (slowest) process time, after dividing by the number of parallel (redundant) operations, (2) the *system capacity* is the inverse of the *bottleneck time*, and (3) the *throughput time* is the total time through the longest path in the system, assuming no waiting.

Theory of Constraints

The theory of constraints (TOC) has been popularized by the book *The Goal: A Process of Ongoing Improvement,* by Goldratt and Cox.[1] TOC is a body of knowledge that deals with anything that limits or constrains an organization's ability to achieve its goals. Constraints can be physical (e.g., process or personnel availability, raw materials, or supplies) or nonphysical (e.g., procedures, morale, and training). Recognizing and managing these limitations through a five-step process is the basis of TOC.

Theory of constraints (TOC)
A body of knowledge that deals with anything that limits an organization's ability to achieve its goals.

STEP 1: Identify the constraints.

STEP 2: Develop a plan for overcoming the identified constraints.

STEP 3: Focus resources on accomplishing Step 2.

STEP 4: Reduce the effects of the constraints by offloading work or by expanding capability. Make sure that the constraints are recognized by all those who can have an impact on them.

STEP 5: When one set of constraints is overcome, go back to Step 1 and identify new constraints.

Bottleneck Management

A crucial constraint in any system is the bottleneck, and managers must focus significant attention on it. We present four principles of bottleneck management:

STUDENT TIP
There are always bottlenecks; a manager must identify and manage them.

1. *Release work orders to the system at the pace set by the bottleneck's capacity:* The theory of constraints utilizes the concept of *drum, buffer, rope* to aid in the implementation of bottleneck and nonbottleneck scheduling. In brief, the *drum* is the beat of the system. It provides the schedule—the pace of production. The *buffer* is the resource, usually inventory, which may be helpful to keep the bottleneck operating at the pace of the drum. Finally, the *rope* provides the synchronization or communication necessary to pull units through the system. The rope can be thought of as signals between workstations.

2. *Lost time at the bottleneck represents lost capacity for the whole system:* This principle implies that the bottleneck should always be kept busy with work. Well-trained and cross-trained employees and inspections prior to the bottleneck can reduce lost capacity at a bottleneck.

3. *Increasing the capacity of a nonbottleneck station is a mirage:* Increasing the capacity of *nonbottleneck* stations has no impact on the system's overall capacity. Working faster on

a nonbottleneck station may just create extra inventory, with all of its adverse effects. This implies that nonbottlenecks should have planned idle time. Extra work or setups at nonbottleneck stations will not cause delay, which allows for smaller batch sizes and more frequent product changeovers at nonbottleneck stations.

4. *Increasing the capacity of the bottleneck increases capacity for the whole system:* Managers should focus improvement efforts on the bottleneck. Bottleneck capacity may be improved by various means, including offloading some of the bottleneck operations to another workstation (e.g., let the beer foam settle next to the tap at the bar, not under it, so the next beer can be poured), increasing capacity of the bottleneck (adding resources, working longer or working faster), subcontracting, developing alternative routings, and reducing setup times.

Even when managers have process and quality variability under control, changing technology, personnel, products, product mixes, and volumes can create multiple and shifting bottlenecks. Identifying and managing bottlenecks is a required operations task, but by definition, bottlenecks cannot be "eliminated." A system will always have at least one.

Break-Even Analysis

Break-even analysis

A means of finding the point, in dollars and units, at which costs equal revenues.

Break-even analysis is the critical tool for determining the capacity a facility must have to achieve profitability. The objective of break-even analysis is to find the point, in dollars and units, at which costs equal revenue. This point is the break-even point. Firms must operate above this level to achieve profitability. As shown in Figure S7.5, break-even analysis requires an estimation of fixed costs, variable costs, and revenue.

Fixed costs are costs that continue even if no units are produced. Examples include depreciation, taxes, debt, and mortgage payments. *Variable costs* are those that vary with the volume of units produced. The major components of variable costs are labor and materials. However, other costs, such as the portion of the utilities that varies with volume, are also variable costs. The difference between selling price and variable cost is *contribution*. Only when total contribution exceeds total fixed cost will there be profit.

Another element in break-even analysis is the *revenue function*. In Figure S7.5, revenue begins at the origin and proceeds upward to the right, increasing by the selling price of each unit. Where the revenue function crosses the total cost line (the sum of fixed and variable costs) is the break-even point, with a profit corridor to the right and a loss corridor to the left.

Assumptions A number of assumptions underlie the basic break-even model. Notably, costs and revenue are shown as straight lines. They are shown to increase linearly—that is,

Figure **S7.5**

Basic Break-Even Point

in direct proportion to the volume of units being produced. However, neither fixed costs nor variable costs (nor, for that matter, the revenue function) need be a straight line. For example, fixed costs change as more capital equipment or warehouse space is used; labor costs change with overtime or as marginally skilled workers are employed; the revenue function may change with such factors as volume discounts.

Single-Product Case

The formulas for the break-even point in units and dollars for a single product are shown below. Let:

LO S7.4 *Compute break-even*

$$BEP_x = \text{break-even point in units} \qquad TR = \text{total revenue} = Px$$
$$BEP_\$ = \text{break-even point in dollars} \qquad F = \text{fixed costs}$$
$$P = \text{price per unit (after all discounts)} \qquad V = \text{variable costs per unit}$$
$$x = \text{number of units produced} \qquad TC = \text{total costs} = F + Vx$$

The break-even point occurs where total revenue equals total costs. Therefore:

$$TR = TC \quad \text{or} \quad Px = F + Vx$$

Solving for x, we get:

$$\text{Break-even point in units } (BEP_x) = \frac{F}{P - V}$$

and:

$$\text{Break-even point in dollars } (BEP_\$) = BEP_x P = \frac{F}{P - V}P = \frac{F}{(P - V)/P} = \frac{F}{1 - V/P}$$

$$\text{Profit} = TR - TC = Px - (F + Vx) = Px - F - Vx = (P - V)x - F$$

Using these equations, we can solve directly for break-even point and profitability. The two break-even formulas of particular interest are:

$$\text{Break-even in units } (BEP_x) = \frac{\text{Total fixed cost}}{\text{Price} - \text{Variable cost}} = \frac{F}{P - V} \qquad \text{(S7-3)}$$

$$\text{Break-even in dollars } (BEP_\$) = \frac{\text{Total fixed cost}}{1 - \dfrac{\text{Variable cost}}{\text{Price}}} = \frac{F}{1 - \dfrac{V}{P}} \qquad \text{(S7-4)}$$

In Example S5, we determine the break-even point in dollars and units for one product.

Example S5 | SINGLE-PRODUCT BREAK-EVEN ANALYSIS

Stephens, Inc., wants to determine the minimum dollar volume and unit volume needed at its new facility to break even.

APPROACH ▶ The firm first determines that it has fixed costs of $10,000 this period. Direct labor is $1.50 per unit, and material is $.75 per unit. The selling price is $4.00 per unit.

SOLUTION ▶ The break-even point in dollars is computed as follows:

$$BEP_\$ = \frac{F}{1 - (V/P)} = \frac{\$10,000}{1 - [(1.50 + .75)/(4.00)]} = \frac{\$10,000}{.4375} = \$22,857.14$$

The break-even point in units is:

$$BEP_x = \frac{F}{P - V} = \frac{\$10,000}{4.00 - (1.50 + .75)} = 5,714$$

Note that we use total variable costs (that is, both labor and material).

Multiproduct Case

Most firms, from manufacturers to restaurants, have a variety of offerings. Each offering may have a different selling price and variable cost. Utilizing break-even analysis, we modify Equation (S7-4) to reflect the proportion of sales for each product. We do this by "weighting" each product's contribution by its proportion of sales. The formula is then:

$$\text{Break-even point in dollars } (BEP_\$) = \frac{F}{\sum \left[1 - \left(\dfrac{V_i}{P_i} \right) \times (W_i) \right]} \qquad \text{(S7-5)}$$

where V = variable cost per unit
P = price per unit
F = fixed cost

W = percent each product is of total dollar sales
i = each product

Paper machines such as the one shown here require a high capital investment. This investment results in a high fixed cost but allows production of paper at a very low variable cost. The production manager's job is to maintain utilization above the break-even point to achieve profitability.

Image Ideas/Stockbyte/Getty Images

Example S6 shows how to determine the break-even point for the multiproduct case at the Le Bistro restaurant.

Example S6

MULTIPRODUCT BREAK-EVEN ANALYSIS

Le Bistro, like most other resturants, makes more than one product and would like to know its break-even point in dollars. Information for Le Bistro follows. Fixed costs are $3,000 per month.

ITEM	ANNUAL FORECASTED SALES UNITS	PRICE	COST
Sandwich	9,000	$5.00	$3.00
Drinks	9,000	1.50	0.50
Baked potato	7,000	2.00	1.00

APPROACH ▶ With a variety of offerings, we proceed with break-even analysis just as in a single-product case, except that we weight each of the products by its proportion of total sales using Equation (S7-5).

SOLUTION ▶ Multiproduct Break-Even: Determining Contribution

1	2	3	4	5	6	7	8	9
ITEM (*i*)	ANNUAL FORECASTED SALES UNITS	SELLING PRICE (P_i)	VARIABLE COST (V_i)	(V_i/P_i)	CONTRIBUTION $1-(V_i/P_i)$	ANNUAL FORECASTED SALES $	% OF SALES (W)	WEIGHTED CONTRIBUTION (COL. 6 × COL. 8)
Sandwich	9,000	$5.00	$3.00	.60	.40	$45,000	.621	.248
Drinks	9,000	1.50	0.50	.33	.67	13,500	.186	.125
Baked potato	7,000	2.00	1.00	.50	.50	14,000	.193	.097
						$72,500	1.000	.470

Note: Revenue for sandwiches is $45,000 (= 5.00 × 9,000), which is 62.1% of the total revenue of $72,500. Therefore, the contribution for sandwiches is "weighted" by .621. The weighted contribution is .621 × .40 = .248. In this manner, its *relative* contribution is properly reflected.

Using this approach for each product, we find that the total weighted contribution is .47 for each dollar of sales, and the break-even point in dollars is $76,596:

$$BEP_\$ = \frac{F}{\sum\left[1-\left(\frac{V_i}{P_i}\right) \times (W_i)\right]} = \frac{\$3,000 \times 12}{.47} = \frac{\$36,000}{.47} = \$76,596$$

The information given in this example implies total daily sales (52 weeks at 6 days each) of:

$$\frac{\$76,596}{312 \text{ days}} = \$245.50$$

INSIGHT ▶ The management of Le Bistro now knows that it must generate average sales of $245.50 each day to break even. Management also knows that if the forecasted sales of $72,500 are correct, Le Bistro will lose money, as break-even is $76,596.

LEARNING EXERCISE ▶ If the manager of Le Bistro wants to make an additional $1,000 per month in salary, and considers this a fixed cost, what is the new break-even point in average sales per day? [Answer: $327.33.]

RELATED PROBLEMS ▶ S7.26, S7.27

Break-even figures by product provide the manager with added insight as to the realism of his or her sales forecast. They indicate exactly what must be sold each day, as we illustrate in Example S7.

Example S7

UNIT SALES AT BREAK-EVEN

Le Bistro also wants to know the break-even for the number of sandwiches that must be sold every day.

APPROACH ▶ Using the data in Example S6, we take the forecast sandwich sales of 62.1% times the daily break-even of $245.50 divided by the selling price of each sandwich ($5.00).

SOLUTION ▶ At break-even, sandwich sales must then be:

$$\frac{.621 \times \$245.50}{5.00} = \text{Number of sandwiches} = 30.5 \approx 31 \text{ sandwiches each day}$$

INSIGHT ▶   With knowledge of individual product sales, the manager has a basis for determining material and labor requirements.

LEARNING EXERCISE ▶   At a dollar break-even of $327.33 per day, how many sandwiches must Le Bistro sell each day? [Answer: ≈ 41.]

RELATED PROBLEMS ▶   S7.26b, S7.27b

Once break-even analysis has been prepared, analyzed, and judged to be reasonable, decisions can be made about the type and capacity of equipment needed. Indeed, a better judgment of the likelihood of success of the enterprise can now be made.

Reducing Risk with Incremental Changes

STUDENT TIP ◆

Capacity decisions require matching capacity to forecasts, which is always difficult.

When demand for goods and services can be forecast with a reasonable degree of precision, determining a break-even point and capacity requirements can be rather straightforward. But, more likely, determining the capacity and how to achieve it will be complicated, as many factors are difficult to measure and quantify. Factors such as technology, competitors, building restrictions, cost of capital, human resource options, and regulations make the decision interesting. To complicate matters further, demand growth is usually in small units, while capacity additions are likely to be both instantaneous and in large units. This contradiction adds to the capacity decision risk. To reduce risk, incremental changes that hedge demand forecasts may be a good option. Figure S7.6 illustrates four approaches to new capacity.

Alternative Figure S7.6(a) *leads* capacity—that is, acquires capacity to stay ahead of demand, with new capacity being acquired at the beginning of period 1. This capacity handles increased demand until the beginning of period 2. At the beginning of period 2, new capacity is again acquired, allowing the organization to stay ahead of demand until the beginning of period 3. This process can be continued indefinitely into the future. Here capacity is acquired *incrementally*—at the beginning of period 1 *and* at the beginning of period 2.

But managers can also elect to make a larger increase at the beginning of period 1 [Figure S7.6(b)]—an increase that may satisfy expected demand until the beginning of period 3. Excess capacity gives operations managers flexibility. For instance, in the hotel industry, added (extra) capacity in the form of rooms can allow a wider variety of room options and perhaps flexibility in room cleanup schedules. In manufacturing, excess capacity can be used to do more setups, shorten production runs, and drive down inventory costs.

VIDEO S7.1

Capacity Planning at Arnold Palmer Hospital

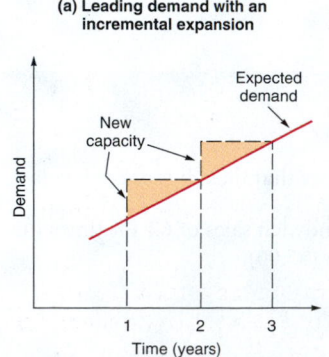

(a) Leading demand with an incremental expansion

(b) Leading demand with a one-step expansion

(c) Lagging demand with incremental expansion

(d) Attempts to have an average capacity that straddles demand with incremenal expansion

Figure **S7.6**

Four Approaches to Capacity Expansion

Figure S7.6(c) shows an option that *lags* capacity, perhaps using overtime or subcontracting to accommodate excess demand. Finally, Figure S7.6(d) *straddles* demand by building capacity that is "average," sometimes lagging demand and sometimes leading it. Both the lag and straddle option have the advantage of delaying capital expenditure.

In cases where the business climate is stable, deciding between alternatives can be relatively easy. The total cost of each alternative can be computed, and the alternative with the least total cost can be selected. However, when capacity requirements are subject to significant unknowns, "probabilistic" models may be appropriate. One technique for making successful capacity planning decisions with an uncertain demand is decision theory, including the use of expected monetary value.

⬥ STUDENT TIP
Uncertainty in capacity decisions makes EMV a helpful tool.

Applying Expected Monetary Value (EMV) to Capacity Decisions

Determining expected monetary value (EMV) requires specifying alternatives and various states of nature. For capacity-planning situations, the state of nature usually is future demand or market favorability. By assigning probability values to the various states of nature, we can make decisions that maximize the expected value of the alternatives. Example S8 shows how to apply EMV to a capacity decision.

LO S7.5 *Determine expected monetary value of a capacity decision*

Example S8 | EMV APPLIED TO CAPACITY DECISION

Southern Hospital Supplies, a company that makes hospital gowns, is considering capacity expansion.

APPROACH: ▶ Southern's major alternatives are to do nothing, build a small plant, build a medium plant, or build a large plant. The new facility would produce a new type of gown, and currently the potential or marketability for this product is unknown. If a large plant is built and a favorable market exists, a profit of $100,000 could be realized. An unfavorable market would yield a $90,000 loss. However, a medium plant would earn a $60,000 profit with a favorable market. A $10,000 loss would result from an unfavorable market. A small plant, on the other hand, would return $40,000 with favorable market conditions and lose only $5,000 in an unfavorable market. Of course, there is always the option of doing nothing.

Recent market research indicates that there is a .4 probability of a favorable market, which means that there is also a .6 probability of an unfavorable market. With this information, the alternative that will result in the highest expected monetary value (EMV) can be selected.

SOLUTION ▶ Compute the EMV for each alternative:

$$\text{EMV (large plant)} = (.4)(\$100,000) + (.6)(-\$90,000) = -\$14,000$$
$$\text{EMV (medium plant)} = (.4)(\$60,000) + (.6)(-\$10,000) = +\$18,000$$
$$\text{EMV (small plant)} = (.4)(\$40,000) + (.6)(-\$5,000) = +\$13,000$$
$$\text{EMV (do nothing)} = \$0$$

Based on EMV criteria, Southern should build a medium plant.

INSIGHT ▶ If Southern makes many decisions like this, then determining the EMV for each alternative and selecting the highest EMV is a good decision criterion.

LEARNING EXERCISE ▶ If a new estimate of the loss from a medium plant in an unfavorable market increases to –$20,000, what is the new EMV for this alternative? [Answer: $12,000, which changes the decision because the small plant EMV is now higher.]

RELATED PROBLEMS ▶ S7.32, S7.33

Applying Investment Analysis to Strategy-Driven Investments

Once the strategy implications of potential investments have been considered, traditional investment analysis is appropriate. We introduce the investment aspects of capacity next.

Investment, Variable Cost, and Cash Flow

Because capacity and process alternatives exist, so do options regarding capital investment and variable cost. Managers must choose from among different financial options as well as capacity and process alternatives. Analysis should show the capital investment, variable cost, and cash flows as well as net present value for each alternative.

Net Present Value

Net present value

A means of determining the discounted value of a series of future cash receipts.

Determining the discount value of a series of future cash receipts is known as the **net present value** technique. By way of introduction, let us consider the time value of money. Say you invest $100.00 in a bank at 5% for 1 year. Your investment will be worth $100.00 + ($100.00)(.05) = $105.00. If you invest the $105.00 for a second year, it will be worth $105.00 + ($105.00)(.05) = $110.25 at the end of the second year. Of course, we could calculate the future value of $100.00 at 5% for as many years as we wanted by simply extending this analysis. However, there is an easier way to express this relationship mathematically. For the first year:

$$\$105 = \$100(1 + .05)$$

For the second year:

$$\$110.25 = \$105(1 + .05) = \$100(1 + .05)^2$$

In general:

$$F = P(1 + i)^N \tag{S7-6}$$

where F = future value (such as $110.25 or $105)
  P = present value (such as $100.00)
  i = interest rate (such as .05)
  N = number of years (such as 1 year or 2 years)

LO S7.6 *Compute* net present value

In most investment decisions, however, we are interested in calculating the present value of a series of future cash receipts. Solving for P, we get:

$$P = \frac{F}{(1 + i)^N} \tag{S7-7}$$

When the number of years is not too large, the preceding equation is effective. However, when the number of years, N, is large, the formula is cumbersome. For 20 years, you would have to compute $(1 + i)^{20}$. Interest-rate tables, such as Table S7.2, can help. We restate the present value equation:

$$P = \frac{F}{(1 + i)^N} = FX \tag{S7-8}$$

where X = a factor from Table S7.2 defined as = $1/(1 + i)^N$ and F = future value

Thus, all we have to do is find the factor X and multiply it by F to calculate the present value, P. The factors, of course, are a function of the interest rate, i, and the number of years, N. Table S7.2 lists some of these factors.

  Equations (S7-7) and (S7-8) are used to determine the present value of one future cash amount, but there are situations in which an investment generates a series of uniform and equal

TABLE S7.2 Present Value of $1

YEAR	5%	6%	7%	8%	9%	10%	12%	14%
1	.952	.943	.935	.926	.917	.909	.893	.877
2	.907	.890	.873	.857	.842	.826	.797	.769
3	.864	.840	.816	.794	.772	.751	.712	.675
4	.823	.792	.763	.735	.708	.683	.636	.592
5	.784	.747	.713	.681	.650	.621	.567	.519
6	.746	.705	.666	.630	.596	.564	.507	.456
7	.711	.665	.623	.583	.547	.513	.452	.400
8	.677	.627	.582	.540	.502	.467	.404	.351
9	.645	.592	.544	.500	.460	.424	.361	.308
10	.614	.558	.508	.463	.422	.386	.322	.270
15	.481	.417	.362	.315	.275	.239	.183	.140
20	.377	.312	.258	.215	.178	.149	.104	.073

cash amounts. This type of investment is called an *annuity*. For example, an investment might yield $300 per year for 3 years. Easy-to-use factors have been developed for the present value of annuities. These factors are shown in Table S7.3. The basic relationship is:

$$S = RX$$

where X = factor from Table S7.3
  S = present value of a series of uniform annual receipts
  R = receipts that are received every year for the life of the investment (the annuity)

The present value of a uniform annual series of amounts is an extension of the present value of a single amount, and thus Table S7.3 can be directly developed from Table S7.2. The factors for any given interest rate in Table S7.3 are the cumulative sum of the values in Table S7.2. In Table S7.2, for example, .943, .890, and .840 are the factors for years 1, 2, and 3 when the interest rate is 6%. The cumulative sum of these factors is 2.673. Now look at the point in Table S7.3 where the interest rate is 6% and the number of years is 3. The factor for the present value of an annuity is 2.673, as you would expect. Alternatively, the PV formula in Microsoft Excel can be used: $=-PV(\text{interest rate,year,1})$, e.g., $=-PV(.06,3,1) = 2.673$.

TABLE S7.3 Present Value of an Annuity of $1

YEAR	5%	6%	7%	8%	9%	10%	12%	14%
1	.952	.943	.935	.926	.917	.909	.893	.877
2	1.859	1.833	1.808	1.783	1.759	1.736	1.690	1.647
3	2.723	2.673	2.624	2.577	2.531	2.487	2.402	2.322
4	3.546	3.465	3.387	3.312	3.240	3.170	3.037	2.914
5	4.329	4.212	4.100	3.993	3.890	3.791	3.605	3.433
6	5.076	4.917	4.766	4.623	4.486	4.355	4.111	3.889
7	5.786	5.582	5.389	5.206	5.033	4.868	4.564	4.288
8	6.463	6.210	5.971	5.747	5.535	5.335	4.968	4.639
9	7.108	6.802	6.515	6.247	5.985	5.759	5.328	4.946
10	7.722	7.360	7.024	6.710	6.418	6.145	5.650	5.216
15	10.380	9.712	9.108	8.559	8.060	7.606	6.811	6.142
20	12.462	11.470	10.594	9.818	9.128	8.514	7.469	6.623

Example S9 shows how to determine the present value of an annuity.

Example S9

DETERMINING NET PRESENT VALUE OF FUTURE RECEIPTS OF EQUAL VALUE

River Road Medical Clinic is thinking of investing in a sophisticated new piece of medical equipment. It will generate $7,000 per year in receipts for 5 years.

APPROACH ▶   Determine the present value of this cash flow; assume an interest rate of 6%.

SOLUTION ▶   The factor from Table S7.3 (4.212) is obtained by finding that value when the interest rate is 6% and the number of years is 5 (alternatively using the Excel formula $= -PV\,(.06,5,1)$):

$$S = RX = \$7,000(4.212) = \$29,484$$

INSIGHT ▶   There is another way of looking at this example. If you went to a bank and took a loan for $29,484 today, your payments would be $7,000 per year for 5 years if the bank used an interest rate of 6% compounded yearly. Thus, $29,484 is the present value.

LEARNING EXERCISE ▶   If the interest rate is 8%, what is the present value? [Answer: $27,951.]

RELATED PROBLEMS ▶   S7.34–S7.39 (S7.40–S7.45 are available in MyOMLab)

EXCEL OM Data File Ch07SExS9.xls can be found in MyOMLab.

The net present value method is straightforward: You simply compute the present value of all cash flows for each investment alternative. When deciding among investment alternatives, you pick the investment with the highest net present value. Similarly, when making several investments, those with higher net present values are preferable to investments with lower net present values.

Solved Problem S7.4 shows how to use the net present value to choose between investment alternatives.

Although net present value is one of the best approaches to evaluating investment alternatives, it does have its faults. Limitations of the net present value approach include the following:

1. Investments with the same net present value may have significantly different projected lives and different salvage values.
2. Investments with the same net present value may have different cash flows. Different cash flows may make substantial differences in the company's ability to pay its bills.
3. The assumption is that we know future interest rates, which we do not.
4. Payments are always made at the end of the period (week, month, or year), which is not always the case.

Summary

Managers tie equipment selection and capacity decisions to the organization's missions and strategy. Four additional considerations are critical: (1) accurately forecasting demand; (2) understanding the equipment, processes, and capacity increments; (3) finding the optimum operating size; and (4) ensuring the flexibility needed for adjustments in technology, product features and mix, and volumes.

Techniques that are particularly useful to operations managers when making capacity decisions include good forecasting, bottleneck analysis, break-even analysis, expected monetary value, cash flow, and net present value.

The single most important criterion for investment decisions is the contribution to the overall strategic plan and the winning of profitable orders. Successful firms select the correct process and capacity.

Key Terms

Capacity (p. 308)
Design capacity (p. 309)
Effective capacity (p. 309)
Utilization (p. 310)
Efficiency (p. 310)

Capacity analysis (p. 314)
Bottleneck (p. 314)
Process time (p. 314)
Bottleneck time (p. 315)
Throughput time (p. 315)

Theory of constraints (TOC) (p. 317)
Break-even analysis (p. 318)
Net present value (p. 324)

Discussion Questions

1. Distinguish between design capacity and effective capacity.
2. What is effective capacity?
3. What is efficiency?
4. Distinguish between effective capacity and actual output.
5. Explain why doubling the capacity of a bottleneck may not double the system capacity.
6. Distinguish between bottleneck time and throughput time.
7. What is the theory of constraints?
8. What are the assumptions of break-even analysis?
9. What keeps plotted revenue data from falling on a straight line in a break-even analysis?
10. Under what conditions would a firm want its capacity to lag demand? to lead demand?
11. Explain how net present value is an appropriate tool for comparing investments.
12. Describe the five-step process that serves as the basis of the theory of constraints.
13. What are the techniques available to operations managers to deal with a bottleneck operation? Which of these does not decrease throughput time?

Using Software for Break-Even Analysis

Excel, Excel OM, and POM for Windows all handle break-even and cost–volume analysis problems.

CREATING YOUR OWN EXCEL SPREADSHEETS

It is a straightforward task to develop the formulas to conduct a single-product break-even analysis in Excel. Although we do not demonstrate the basics here, Active Model S7.2 provides a working example. Program S7.1 illustrates how you can make an Excel model to solve Example S6, which is a multiproduct break-even analysis.

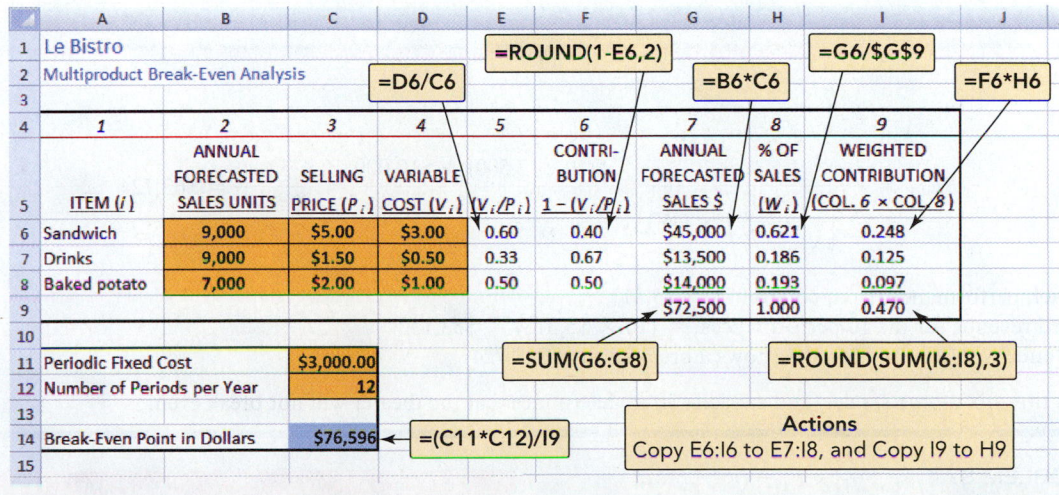

Program **S7.1**

An Excel Spreadsheet for Performing Break-Even Analysis for Example S6

✕ USING EXCEL OM

Excel OM's Break-Even Analysis module provides the Excel formulas needed to compute the break-even points, and the solution and graphical output.

P USING POM FOR WINDOWS

Similar to Excel OM, POM for Windows also contains a break-even/cost–volume analysis module.

Solved Problems   Virtual Office Hours help is available in MyOMLab.

SOLVED PROBLEM S7.1

Sara James Bakery, described in Examples S1 and S2, has decided to increase its facilities by adding one additional process line. The firm will have two process lines, each working 7 days a week, 3 shifts per day, 8 hours per shift, with effective capacity of 300,000 rolls. This addition, however, will reduce overall system efficiency to 85%. Compute the expected production with this new effective capacity.

SOLUTION

Expected production = (Effective capacity) (Efficiency)
$$= 300,000(.85)$$
$$= 255,000 \text{ rolls per week}$$

SOLVED PROBLEM S7.2

Marty McDonald has a business packaging software in Wisconsin. His annual fixed cost is $10,000, direct labor is $3.50 per package, and material is $4.50 per package. The selling price will be $12.50 per package. What is the break-even point in dollars? What is break-even in units?

SOLUTION

$$BEP_\$ = \frac{F}{1 - (V/P)} = \frac{\$10,000}{1 - (\$8.00/\$12.50)} = \frac{\$10,000}{.36} = \$27,777$$

$$BEP_x = \frac{F}{P - V} = \frac{\$10,000}{\$12.50 - \$8.00} = \frac{\$10,000}{\$4.50} = 2,222 \text{ units}$$

SOLVED PROBLEM S7.3

John has been asked to determine whether the $22.50 cost of tickets for the community dinner theater will allow the group to achieve break-even and whether the 175 seating capacity is adequate. The cost for each performance of a 10-performance run is $2,500. The facility rental cost for the entire 10 performances is $10,000. Drinks and parking are extra charges and have their own price and variable costs, as shown below:

1	2 SELLING PRICE (P)	3 VARIABLE COST (V)	4 PERCENT VARIABLE COST (V/P)	5 CONTRIBUTION 1 − (V/P)	6 ESTIMATED QUANTITY OF SALES UNITS (SALES)	7 DOLLAR SALES (SALES × P)	8 PERCENT OF SALES	9 CONTRIBUTION WEIGHTED BY PERCENT SALES (COL.5 × COL. 8)
Tickets with dinner	$22.50	$10.50	0.467	0.533	175	$3,938	0.741	0.395
Drinks	$ 5.00	$ 1.75	0.350	0.650	175	$ 875	0.165	0.107
Parking	$ 5.00	$ 2.00	0.400	0.600	100	$ 500	0.094	0.056
					450	$5,313	1.000	0.558

SOLUTION

$$BEP_\$ = \frac{F}{\sum\left[\left(1 - \frac{V_i}{P_i}\right) \times (W_i)\right]} = \frac{\$(10 \times 2,500) + \$10,000}{0.558} = \frac{\$35,000}{0.558} = \$62,724$$

Revenue for each performance (from column 7) = $5,313
Total forecasted revenue for the 10 performances = (10 × $5,313) = $53,130
Forecasted revenue with this mix of sales shows a break-even of $62,724

Thus, given this mix of costs, sales, and capacity John determines that the theater will not break even.

SOLVED PROBLEM S7.4

Your boss has told you to evaluate the cost of two machines. After some questioning, you are assured that they have the costs shown at the right. Assume:

a) The life of each machine is 3 years.
b) The company thinks it knows how to make 14% on investments no riskier than this one.

Determine via the present value method which machine to purchase.

	MACHINE A	MACHINE B
Original cost	$13,000	$20,000
Labor cost per year	2,000	3,000
Floor space per year	500	600
Energy (electricity) per year	1,000	900
Maintenance per year	2,500	500
Total annual cost	$ 6,000	$ 5,000
Salvage value	$ 2,000	$ 7,000

SOLUTION

		MACHINE A			MACHINE B		
		COLUMN 1	COLUMN 2	COLUMN 3	COLUMN 4	COLUMN 5	COLUMN 6
Now	Expense	1.000	$13,000	$13,000	1.000	$20,000	$20,000
1 yr.	Expense	.877	6,000	5,262	.877	5,000	4,385
2 yr.	Expense	.769	6,000	4,614	.769	5,000	3,845
3 yr.	Expense	.675	6,000	4,050	.675	5,000	3,375
				$26,926			$31,605
3 yr.	Salvage revenue	.675	$ 2,000	−1,350	.675	$ 7,000	−4,725
				$25,576			$26,880

We use 1.0 for payments with no discount applied against them (that is, when payments are made now, there is no need for a discount). The other values in columns 1 and 4 are from the 14% column and the respective year in Table S7.2 (for example, the intersection of 14% and 1 year is .877, etc.). Columns 3 and 6 are the products of the present value figures times the combined costs. This computation is made for each year and for the salvage value.

The calculation for machine A for the first year is:

$$.877 \times (\$2,000 + \$500 + \$1,000 + \$2,500) = \$5,262$$

The salvage value of the product is subtracted from the summed costs, because it is a receipt of cash. Because the sum of the net costs for machine B is larger than the sum of the net costs for machine A, machine A is the low-cost purchase, and your boss should be so informed.

SOLVED PROBLEM S7.5

T. Smunt Manufacturing Corp. has the process displayed below. The drilling operation occurs separately from and simultaneously with the sawing and sanding operations. The product only needs to go through one of the three assembly operations (the assembly operations are "parallel").

a) Which operation is the bottleneck?
b) What is the throughput time for the overall system?

c) If the firm operates 8 hours per day, 22 days per month, what is the monthly capacity of the manufacturing process?
d) Suppose that a second drilling machine is added, and it takes the same time as the original drilling machine. What is the new bottleneck time of the system?
e) Suppose that a second drilling machine is added, and it takes the same time as the original drilling machine. What is the new throughput time?

SOLUTION

a) The time for *assembly* is 78 minutes/3 operators = 26 minutes per unit, so the station that takes the longest time, hence the bottleneck, is *drilling*, at 27 minutes.
b) System throughput time is the maximum of (15 + 15 + 25 + 78), (27 + 25 + 78) = maximum of (133, 130) = 133 minutes
c) Monthly capacity = (60 minutes)(8 hours)(22 days)/27 minutes per unit = 10,560 minutes per month/27 minutes per unit = 391.11 units/month.
d) The bottleneck shifts to *Assembly*, with a time of 26 minutes per unit.
e) Redundancy does not affect throughput time. It is still 133 minutes.

Problems   *Note:* **Px** means the problem may be solved with POM for Windows and/or Excel OM.

Problems S7.1–S7.8 relate to Capacity

• **S7.1**   Amy Xia's plant was designed to produce 7,000 hammers per day but is limited to making 6,000 hammers per day because of the time needed to change equipment between styles of hammers. What is the utilization?

• **S7.2**   For the past month, the plant in Problem S7.1, which has an effective capacity of 6,500, has made only 4,500 hammers per day because of material delay, employee absences, and other problems. What is its efficiency?

•• **S7.3**   If a plant has an effective capacity of 6,500 and an efficiency of 88%, what is the actual (planned) output?

• **S7.4**   A plant has an effective capacity of 900 units per day and produces 800 units per day with its product mix; what is its efficiency?

• **S7.5**   Material delays have routinely limited production of household sinks to 400 units per day. If the plant efficiency is 80%, what is the effective capacity?

•• **S7.6**   The effective capacity and efficiency for the next quarter at MMU Mfg. in Waco, Texas, for each of three departments are shown:

DEPARTMENT	EFFECTIVE CAPACITY	RECENT EFFICIENCY
Design	93,600	.95
Fabrication	156,000	1.03
Finishing	62,400	1.05

Compute the expected production for next quarter for each department.

•• **S7.7**   Southeastern Oklahoma State University's business program has the facilities and faculty to handle an enrollment of 2,000 new students per semester. However, in an effort to limit class sizes to a "reasonable" level (under 200, generally), Southeastern's dean, Holly Lutze, placed a ceiling on enrollment of 1,500 new students. Although there was ample demand for business courses last semester, conflicting schedules allowed only 1,450 new students to take business courses. What are the utilization and efficiency of this system?

•• **S7.8**   Under ideal conditions, a service bay at a Fast Lube can serve 6 cars per hour. The effective capacity and efficiency of a Fast Lube service bay are known to be 5.5 and 0.880, respectively. What is the minimum number of service bays Fast Lube needs to achieve an anticipated servicing of 200 cars per 8-hour day?

Problems S7.9–S7.15 relate to Bottleneck Analysis and the Theory of Constraints

• **S7.9**   A production line at V. J. Sugumaran's machine shop has three stations. The first station can process a unit in 10 minutes. The second station has two identical machines, each of which can process a unit in 12 minutes. (Each unit only needs to be processed on one of the two machines.) The third station can process a unit in 8 minutes. Which station is the bottleneck station?

•• **S7.10**   A work cell at Chris Ellis Commercial Laundry has a workstation with two machines, and each unit produced at the station needs to be processed by both of the machines. (The same unit cannot be worked on by both machines simultaneously.) Each machine has a production capacity of 4 units per hour. What is the throughput time of the work cell?

•• **S7.11**   The three-station work cell illustrated in Figure S7.7 has a product that must go through one of the two machines at station 1 (they are parallel) before proceeding to station 2.

Figure **S7.7**

a) What is the bottleneck time of the system?
b) What is the bottleneck station of this work cell?
c) What is the throughput time?
d) If the firm operates 10 hours per day, 5 days per week, what is the weekly capacity of this work cell?

•• **S7.12**   The three-station work cell at Pullman Mfg., Inc. is illustrated in Figure S7.8. It has two machines at station 1 in parallel (i.e., the product needs to go through only one of the two machines before proceeding to station 2).

Figure **S7.8**

a) What is the throughput time of this work cell?
b) What is the bottleneck time of this work cell?
c) What is the bottleneck station?
d) If the firm operates 8 hours per day, 6 days per week, what is the weekly capacity of this work cell?

•• **S7.13**   The Pullman Mfg., Inc., three-station work cell illustrated in Figure S7.8 has two machines at station 1 in parallel. (The product needs to go through only one of the two machines before proceeding to station 2.) The manager, Ms. Hartley, has asked you to evaluate the system if she adds a parallel machine at station 2.
a) What is the throughput time of the new work cell?
b) What is the bottleneck time of the new work cell?
c) If the firm operates 8 hours per day, 6 days per week, what is the weekly capacity of this work cell?
d) How did the addition of the second machine at workstation 2 affect the performance of the work cell from Problem S7.12?

• **S7.14**   Klassen Toy Company, Inc., assembles two parts (parts 1 and 2): Part 1 is first processed at workstation A for 15 minutes per unit and then processed at workstation B for

10 minutes per unit. Part 2 is simultaneously processed at workstation C for 20 minutes per unit. Work stations B and C feed the parts to an assembler at workstation D, where the two parts are assembled. The time at workstation D is 15 minutes.

a) What is the bottleneck of this process?

b) What is the hourly capacity of the process?

•• **S7.15** A production process at Kenneth Day Manufacturing is shown in Figure S7.9. The drilling operation occurs separately from, and simultaneously with, sawing and sanding, which are independent and sequential operations. A product needs to go through only one of the three assembly operations (the operations are in parallel).

a) Which operation is the bottleneck?

b) What is the bottleneck time?

c) What is the throughput time of the overall system?

d) If the firm operates 8 hours per day, 20 days per month, what is the monthly capacity of the manufacturing process?

Figure **S7.9**

Problems S7.16–S7.31 relate to **Break-Even Analysis**

• **S7.16** Smithson Cutting is opening a new line of scissors for supermarket distribution. It estimates its fixed cost to be $500.00 and its variable cost to be $0.50 per unit. Selling price is expected to average $0.75 per unit.

a) What is Smithson's break-even point in units?

b) What is the break-even point in dollars? **Px**

• **S7.17** Markland Manufacturing intends to increase capacity by overcoming a bottleneck operation by adding new equipment. Two vendors have presented proposals. The fixed costs for proposal A are $50,000, and for proposal B, $70,000. The variable cost for A is $12.00, and for B, $10.00. The revenue generated by each unit is $20.00.

a) What is the break-even point in units for proposal A?

b) What is the break-even point in units for proposal B? **Px**

• **S7.18** Using the data in Problem S7.17:

a) What is the break-even point in dollars for proposal A if you add $10,000 installation to the fixed cost?

b) What is the break-even point in dollars for proposal B if you add $10,000 installation to the fixed cost? **Px**

• **S7.19** Given the data in Problem S7.17, at what volume (units) of output would the two alternatives yield the same profit? **Px**

•• **S7.20** Janelle Heinke, the owner of Ha'Peppas!, is considering a new oven in which to bake the firm's signature dish, vegetarian pizza. Oven type A can handle 20 pizzas an hour. The fixed costs associated with oven A are $20,000 and the variable costs are $2.00 per pizza. Oven B is larger and can handle 40 pizzas an hour. The fixed costs associated with oven B are $30,000 and the variable costs are $1.25 per pizza. The pizzas sell for $14 each.

a) What is the break-even point for each oven?

b) If the owner expects to sell 9,000 pizzas, which oven should she purchase?

c) If the owner expects to sell 12,000 pizzas, which oven should she purchase?

d) At what volume should Janelle switch ovens? **Px**

•• **S7.21** Given the following data, calculate a) BEP_x; b) $BEP_\$$; and c) the profit at 100,000 units:

$$P = \$8/\text{unit} \quad V = \$4/\text{unit} \quad F = \$50,000 \ \textbf{Px}$$

•• **S7.22** You are considering opening a copy service in the student union. You estimate your fixed cost at $15,000 and the variable cost of each copy sold at $.01. You expect the selling price to average $.05.

a) What is the break-even point in dollars?

b) What is the break-even point in units? **Px**

•• **S7.23** An electronics firm is currently manufacturing an item that has a variable cost of $.50 per unit and a selling price of $1.00 per unit. Fixed costs are $14,000. Current volume is

30,000 units. The firm can substantially improve the product quality by adding a new piece of equipment at an additional fixed cost of $6,000. Variable cost would increase to $.60, but volume should jump to 50,000 units due to a higher-quality product. Should the company buy the new equipment? **Px**

•• **S7.24** The electronics firm in Problem S7.23 is now considering the new equipment and increasing the selling price to $1.10 per unit. With the higher-quality product, the new volume is expected to be 45,000 units. Under these circumstances, should the company purchase the new equipment and increase the selling price? **Px**

•••• **S7.25** Zan Azlett and Angela Zesiger have joined forces to start A&Z Lettuce Products, a processor of packaged shredded lettuce for institutional use. Zan has years of food processing experience, and Angela has extensive commercial food preparation experience. The process will consist of opening crates of lettuce and then sorting, washing, slicing, preserving, and finally packaging the prepared lettuce. Together, with help from vendors, they think they can adequately estimate demand, fixed costs, revenues, and variable cost per 5-pound bag of lettuce. They think a largely manual process will have monthly fixed costs of $37,500 and variable costs of $1.75 per bag. A more mechanized process will have fixed costs of $75,000 per month with variable costs of $1.25 per 5-pound bag. They expect to sell the shredded lettuce for $2.50 per 5-pound bag.
a) What is the break-even quantity for the manual process?
b) What is the revenue at the break-even quantity for the manual process?
c) What is the break-even quantity for the mechanized process?
d) What is the revenue at the break-even quantity for the mechanized process?
e) What is the monthly profit or loss of the *manual* process if they expect to sell 60,000 bags of lettuce per month?
f) What is the monthly profit or loss of the *mechanized* process if they expect to sell 60,000 bags of lettuce per month?
g) At what quantity would Zan and Angela be indifferent to the process selected?
h) Over what range of demand would the *manual* process be preferred over the mechanized process? Over what range of demand would the *mechanized* process be preferred over the manual process? **Px**

•••• **S7.26** As a prospective owner of a club known as the Red Rose, you are interested in determining the volume of sales dollars necessary for the coming year to reach the break-even point. You have decided to break down the sales for the club into four categories, the first category being beer. Your estimate of the beer sales is that 30,000 drinks will be served. The selling price for each unit will average $1.50; the cost is $.75. The second major category is meals, which you expect to be 10,000 units with an average price of $10.00 and a cost of $5.00. The third major category is desserts and wine, of which you also expect to sell 10,000 units, but with an average price of $2.50 per unit sold and a cost of $1.00 per unit. The final category is lunches and inexpensive sandwiches, which you expect to total 20,000 units at an average price of $6.25 with a food cost of $3.25. Your fixed cost (i.e., rent, utilities, and so on) is $1,800 per month plus $2,000 per month for entertainment.
a) What is your break-even point in dollars per month?
b) What is the expected number of meals each day if you are open 30 days a month?

•••• **S7.27** As manager of the St. Cloud Theatre Company, you have decided that concession sales will support themselves. The following table provides the information you have been able to put together thus far:

ITEM	SELLING PRICE	VARIABLE COST	% OF REVENUE
Soft drink	$1.00	$.65	25
Wine	1.75	.95	25
Coffee	1.00	.30	30
Candy	1.00	.30	20

Last year's manager, Jim Freeland, has advised you to be sure to add 10% of variable cost as a waste allowance for all categories.

You estimate labor cost to be $250.00 (5 booths with 2 people each). Even if nothing is sold, your labor cost will be $250.00, so you decide to consider this a fixed cost. Booth rental, which is a contractual cost at $50.00 for *each* booth per night, is also a fixed cost.
a) What is the break-even volume per evening performance?
b) How much wine would you expect to sell each evening at the break-even point?

Additional problems **S7.28–S7.31** *are available in* MyOMLab.

Problems S7.32–S7.33 relate to Applying Expected Monetary Value (EMV) to Capacity Decisions

•• **S7.32** James Lawson's Bed and Breakfast, in a small historic Mississippi town, must decide how to subdivide (remodel) the large old home that will become its inn. There are three alternatives: Option A would modernize all baths and combine rooms, leaving the inn with four suites, each suitable for two to four adults. Option B would modernize only the second floor; the results would be six suites, four for two to four adults, two for two adults only. Option C (the status quo option) leaves all walls intact. In this case, there are eight rooms available, but only two are suitable for four adults, and four rooms will not have private baths. Below are the details of profit and demand patterns that will accompany each option:

ALTERNATIVES	ANNUAL PROFIT UNDER VARIOUS DEMAND PATTERNS			
	HIGH	P	AVERAGE	P
A (modernize all)	$90,000	.5	$25,000	.5
B (modernize 2nd)	$80,000	.4	$70,000	.6
C (status quo)	$60,000	.3	$55,000	.7

Which option has the highest expected monetary value? **Px**

•••• **S7.33** As operations manager of Holz Furniture, you must make a decision about adding a line of rustic furniture. In discussing the possibilities with your sales manager, Steve Gilbert, you decide that there will definitely be a market and that your firm should enter that market. However, because rustic furniture has a different finish than your standard offering, you decide you need another process line. There is no doubt in your mind about the decision, and you are sure that you should have a second process. But you do question how large to make it. A large process line is going to cost $400,000; a small process line will cost $300,000. The question, therefore, is the demand for rustic furniture. After extensive discussion with Mr. Gilbert and Tim Ireland of Ireland Market Research, Inc., you determine that the best estimate you can make is that there is a two-out-of-three chance of profit from sales as large as $600,000 and a one-out-of-three chance as low as $300,000.

With a large process line, you could handle the high figure of $600,000. However, with a small process line you could not and would be forced to expand (at a cost of $150,000), after which time your profit from sales would be $500,000 rather than the $600,000 because of the lost time in expanding the process. If you do not expand the small process, your profit from sales would be held to $400,000. If you build a small process and the demand is low, you can handle all of the demand.

Should you open a large or small process line?

Problems S7.34–S7.45 relate to Applying Investment Analysis to Strategy-Driven Investments

•• **S7.34**   What is the net present value of an investment that costs $75,000 and has a salvage value of $45,000? The annual profit from the investment is $15,000 each year for 5 years. The cost of capital at this risk level is 12%. **Px**

• **S7.35**   The initial cost of an investment is $65,000 and the cost of capital is 10%. The return is $16,000 per year for 8 years. What is the net present value? **Px**

• **S7.36**   What is the present value of $5,600 when the interest rate is 8% and the return of $5,600 will not be received for 15 years? **Px**

•• **S7.37**   Tim Smunt has been asked to evaluate two machines. After some investigation, he determines that they have the costs shown in the following table. He is told to assume that:
1. The life of each machine is 3 years.
2. The company thinks it knows how to make 12% on investments no more risky than this one.
3. Labor and maintenance are paid at the end of the year.

	MACHINE A	MACHINE B
Original cost	$10,000	$20,000
Labor per year	2,000	4,000
Maintenance per year	4,000	1,000
Salvage value	2,000	7,000

Determine, via the present value method, which machine Tim should recommend.

•••• **S7.38**   Your boss has told you to evaluate two ovens for Tink-the-Tinkers, a gourmet sandwich shop. After some questioning of vendors and receipt of specifications, you are assured that the ovens have the attributes and costs shown in the following table. The following two assumptions are appropriate:
1. The life of each machine is 5 years.
2. The company thinks it knows how to make 14% on investments no more risky than this one.
a) Determine via the present value method which machine to tell your boss to purchase.
b) What assumption are you making about the ovens?
c) What assumptions are you making in your methodology?

	THREE SMALL OVENS AT $1,250 EACH	TWO LARGE OVENS AT $2,500 EACH
Original cost	$3,750	$5,000
Labor per year in excess of larger models	$ 750 (total)	
Cleaning/ maintenance	$ 750 ($250 each)	$ 400 ($200 each)
Salvage value	$ 750 ($250 each)	$1,000 ($500 each)

•••• **S7.39**   Bold's Gym, a health club chain, is considering expanding into a new location: the initial investment would be $1 million in equipment, renovation, and a 6-year lease, and its annual upkeep and expenses would be $75,000 (paid at the beginning of the year). Its planning horizon is 6 years out, and at the end, it can sell the equipment for $50,000. Club capacity is 500 members who would pay an annual fee of $600. Bold's expects to have no problems filling membership slots. Assume that the interest rate is 10%. (See Table S7.2.)
a) What is the present value profit/loss of the deal?
b) The club is considering offering a special deal to the members in the first year. For $3,000 upfront they get a full 6-year membership (i.e., 1 year free). Would it make financial sense to offer this deal?

Additional problems **S7.40–S7.45** *are available in* MyOMLab.

CASE STUDY

Capacity Planning at Arnold Palmer Hospital

Video Case

Since opening day, Arnold Palmer Hospital has experienced an explosive growth in demand for its services. One of only six hospitals in the U.S. to specialize in health care for women and children, Arnold Palmer Hospital has cared for over 1,500,000 patients who came to the Orlando facility from all 50 states and more than 100 other countries. With patient satisfaction scores in the top 10% of U.S. hospitals surveyed (over 95% of patients would recommend the hospital to others), one of Arnold Palmer Hospital's main focuses is delivery of babies. Originally built with

281 beds and a capacity for 6,500 births per year, the hospital steadily approached and then passed 10,000 births. Looking at Table S7.4, Executive Director Kathy Swanson knew an expansion was necessary.

With continuing population growth in its market area serving 18 central Florida counties, Arnold Palmer Hospital was delivering the equivalent of a kindergarten class of babies every day and still not meeting demand. Supported with substantial additional demographic analysis, the hospital was ready to move ahead with a capacity expansion plan and a new 11-story hospital building across the street from the existing facility.

Thirty-five planning teams were established to study such issues as (1) specific forecasts, (2) services that would transfer to the new facility, (3) services that would remain in the existing facility, (4) staffing needs, (5) capital equipment, (6) pro forma accounting data, and (7) regulatory requirements. Ultimately, Arnold Palmer Hospital was ready to move ahead with a budget of $100 million and a commitment to an additional 150 beds. But given the growth of the central Florida region, Swanson decided to expand the hospital in stages: the top two floors would be empty interiors ("shell") to be completed at a later date, and the fourth-floor operating room could be doubled in size when needed. "With the new facility in place, we are now able to handle up to 16,000 births per year," says Swanson.

Discussion Questions*

1. Given the capacity planning discussion in the text (see Figure S7.6), what approach is being taken by Arnold Palmer Hospital toward matching capacity to demand?
2. What kind of major changes could take place in Arnold Palmer Hospital's demand forecast that would leave the hospital with an underutilized facility (namely, what are the risks connected with this capacity decision)?
3. Use regression analysis to forecast the point at which Swanson needs to "build out" the top two floors of the new building, namely, when demand will exceed 16,000 births.

*You may wish to view the video that accompanies the case before addressing these questions.

TABLE S7.4	Births at Arnold Palmer Hospital
YEAR	**BIRTHS**
1995	6,144
1996	6,230
1997	6,432
1998	6,950
1999	7,377
2000	8,655
2001	9,536
2002	9,825
2003	10,253
2004	10,555
2005	12,316
2006	13,070
2007	14,028
2008	14,241
2009	13,050
2010	12,571
2011	12,978
2012	13,529
2013	13,576
2014	13,994

- **Additional Case Study:** Visit MyOMLab for this free case study:
  Southwestern University (D): Requires the development of a multiproduct break-even solution.

Endnote

1. See E. M. Goldratt and J. Cox, *The Goal: A Process of Ongoing Improvement*, 3rd rev. ed., Great Barrington, MA: North River Press, 2004.

Supplement 7 *Rapid Review*

Main Heading	Review Material	MyOMLab
CAPACITY (pp. 308–314)	■ **Capacity**—The "throughput," or number of units a facility can hold, receive, store, or produce in a period of time.	Concept Questions: 1.1–1.4 Problems: S7.1–S7.8

CAPACITY (pp. 308–314)

■ **Capacity**—The "throughput," or number of units a facility can hold, receive, store, or produce in a period of time.

Capacity decisions often determine capital requirements and therefore a large portion of fixed cost. Capacity also determines whether demand will be satisfied or whether facilities will be idle.

Determining facility size, with an objective of achieving high levels of utilization and a high return on investment, is critical.

Capacity planning can be viewed in three time horizons:

1. *Long-range* (> 1 year)—Adding facilities and long lead-time equipment
2. *Intermediate-range* (3–18 months)—"Aggregate planning" tasks, including adding equipment, personnel, and shifts; subcontracting; and building or using inventory
3. *Short-range* (< 3 months)—Scheduling jobs and people, and allocating machinery

■ **Design capacity**—The theoretical maximum output of a system in a given period, under ideal conditions.

Most organizations operate their facilities at a rate less than the design capacity.

■ **Effective capacity**—The capacity a firm can expect to achieve, given its product mix, methods of scheduling, maintenance, and standards of quality.
■ **Utilization**—Actual output as a percent of design capacity.
■ **Efficiency**—Actual output as a percent of effective capacity.

$$\text{Utilization} = \text{Actual output}/\text{Design capacity} \qquad (S7\text{-}1)$$

$$\text{Efficiency} = \text{Actual output}/\text{Effective capacity} \qquad (S7\text{-}2)$$

When demand exceeds capacity, a firm may be able to curtail demand simply by raising prices, increasing lead times (which may be inevitable), and discouraging marginally profitable business.

When capacity exceeds demand, a firm may want to stimulate demand through price reductions or aggressive marketing, or it may accommodate the market via product changes.

In the service sector, scheduling customers is *demand management,* and scheduling the workforce is *capacity management.*

When demand and capacity are fairly well matched, demand management in services can often be handled with appointments, reservations, or a first-come, first-served rule. Otherwise, discounts based on time of day may be used (e.g., "early bird" specials, matinee pricing).

When managing demand in services is not feasible, managing capacity through changes in full-time, temporary, or part-time staff may be an option.

Virtual Office Hours for Solved Problem: S7.1

ACTIVE MODEL S7.1

BOTTLENECK ANALYSIS AND THE THEORY OF CONSTRAINTS (pp. 314–318)

■ **Capacity analysis**—Determining throughput capacity of workstations or an entire production system.
■ **Bottleneck**—The limiting factor or constraint in a system.
■ **Process time**—The time to produce a unit (or batch) at a workstation.
■ **Bottleneck time**—The process time of the longest (slowest) process.
■ **Throughput time**—The time it takes for a product to go through the production process *with no waiting,* i.e., the time of the longest path through the system.

If *n* parallel (redundant) operations are added, the process time of the combined operations will equal $1/n$ times the process time of the original.

With simultaneous processing, an order or product is essentially *split* into different paths to be rejoined later on. The longest path through the system is deemed the throughput time.

■ **Theory of constraints (TOC)**—A body of knowledge that deals with anything limiting an organization's ability to achieve its goals.

Concept Questions: 2.1–2.4 Problems: S7.9–S7.15

Virtual Office Hours for Solved Problem: S7.5

Main Heading	Review Material	MyOMLab
BREAK-EVEN ANALYSIS (pp. 318–322)	■ **Break-even analysis**—A means of finding the point, in dollars and units, at which costs equal revenues. *Fixed costs* are costs that exist even if no units are produced. Variable costs are those that vary with the volume of units produced. In the break-even model, costs and revenue are assumed to increase linearly. $$\text{Break-even in units} = \frac{\text{Total Fixed cost}}{\text{Price} - \text{Variable cost}} = \frac{F}{P - V} \quad (S7\text{-}3)$$ $$\text{Break-even in dollars} = \frac{\text{Total Fixed cost}}{1 - \dfrac{\text{Variable cost}}{\text{Price}}} = \frac{F}{1 - \left(\dfrac{V}{P}\right)} \quad (S7\text{-}4)$$ $$\text{Multiproduct break-even point in dollars} = BEP_{\$} = \frac{F}{\sum\left[\left(1 - \dfrac{V_i}{P_i}\right) \times (W_i)\right]} \quad (S7\text{-}5)$$	Concept Questions: 3.1–3.4 Problems: S7.16–S7.31 Virtual Office Hours for Solved Problem: S7.3 **ACTIVE** MODEL **S7.2**
REDUCING RISK WITH INCREMENTAL CHANGES (pp. 322–323)	Demand growth is usually in small units, while capacity additions are likely to be both instantaneous and in large units. To reduce risk, incremental changes that hedge demand forecasts may be a good option. Four approaches to capacity expansion are (1) *leading* strategy, with incremental expansion, (2) *leading* strategy with one step expansion, (3) *lag* strategy, and (4) *straddle* strategy. Both lag strategy and straddle strategy delay capital expenditure.	Concept Questions: 4.1–4.4 **VIDEO S7.1** Capacity Planning at Arnold Palmer Hospital
APPLYING EXPECTED MONETARY VALUE (p. 323)	Determining expected monetary value requires specifying alternatives and various states of nature (e.g., demand or market favorability). By assigning probability values to the various states of nature, we can make decisions that maximize the expected value of the alternatives.	Concept Questions: 5.1–5.4 Problems: S7.32–S7.33
APPLYING INVESTMENT ANALYSIS TO STRATEGY-DRIVEN INVESTMENTS (pp. 324–326)	■ **Net present value**—A means of determining the discounted value of a series of future cash receipts. $$F = P(1 + i)^N \quad (S7\text{-}6)$$ $$P = \frac{F}{(1 + i)^N} \quad (S7\text{-}7)$$ $$P = \frac{F}{(1 + i)^N} = FX \quad (S7\text{-}8)$$ When making several investments, those with higher net present values are preferable to investments with lower net present values.	Concept Questions: 6.1–6.4 Problems: S7.34–S7.45 Virtual Office Hours for Solved Problem: S7.4

Self Test

■ **Before taking the self-test,** refer to the learning objectives listed at the beginning of the supplement and the key terms listed at the end of the supplement.

LO S7.1 Capacity decisions should be made on the basis of:
- a) building sustained competitive advantage.
- b) good financial returns.
- c) a coordinated plan.
- d) integration into the company's strategy.
- e) all of the above.

LO S7.2 Effective capacity is:
- a) the capacity a firm expects to achieve, given the current operating constraints.
- b) the percentage of design capacity actually achieved.
- c) the percentage of capacity actually achieved.
- d) actual output.
- e) efficiency.

LO S7.3 System capacity is based on:
- a) the bottleneck.
- b) throughput time.
- c) time of the fastest station.
- d) throughput time plus waiting time.
- e) none of the above.

LO S7.4 The break-even point is:
- a) adding processes to meet the point of changing product demands.
- b) improving processes to increase throughput.
- c) the point in dollars or units at which cost equals revenue.
- d) adding or removing capacity to meet demand.
- e) the total cost of a process alternative.

LO S7.5 Expected monetary value is most appropriate:
- a) when the payoffs are equal.
- b) when the probability of each decision alternative is known.
- c) when probabilities are the same.
- d) when both revenue and cost are known.
- e) when probabilities of each state of nature are known.

LO S7.6 Net present value:
- a) is greater if cash receipts occur later rather than earlier.
- b) is greater if cash receipts occur earlier rather than later.
- c) is revenue minus fixed cost.
- d) is preferred over break-even analysis.
- e) is greater if $100 monthly payments are received in a lump sum ($1,200) at the end of the year.

Answers: LO S7.1. e; LO S7.2. a; LO S7.3. a; LO S7.4. c; LO S7.5. b; LO S7.6. b.

Location Strategies

CHAPTER OUTLINE

GLOBAL COMPANY PROFILE: *FedEx*

◆ The Strategic Importance of Location *340*

◆ Factors That Affect Location Decisions *341*

◆ Methods of Evaluating Location Alternatives *344*

◆ Service Location Strategy *350*

◆ Geographic Information Systems *351*

Alaska Airlines

Alaska Airlines

10 OM STRATEGY DECISIONS

- Design of Goods and Services
- Managing Quality
- Process Strategy
- *Location Strategies*
- Layout Strategies
- Human Resources
- Supply-Chain Management
- Inventory Management
- Scheduling
- Maintenance

CHAPTER 8

Location Provides Competitive Advantage for FedEx

Overnight-delivery powerhouse FedEx has believed in the hub concept for its 46-year existence. Even though Fred Smith, founder and CEO, got a C on his college paper proposing a hub for small-package delivery, the idea has proven extremely successful. Starting with one central location in Memphis, Tennessee (now called its *superhub*), the $45 billion firm has added a European hub in Paris, an Asian hub in Guangzhou, China, a Latin American hub in Miami, and a Canadian hub in Toronto. FedEx's fleet of 667 planes flies into 375 airports worldwide, then delivers to the door with more than 80,000 vans and trucks.

At the FedEx hub in Memphis, Tennessee, approximately 100 FedEx aircraft converge each night around midnight with more than 5 million documents and packages.

Oliver Berg/EPA/Newscom

At the preliminary sorting area, packages and documents are sorted and sent to a secondary sorting area. The Memphis facility covers 1.5 million square feet; it is big enough to hold 33 football fields. Packages are sorted and exchanged until 4 A.M.

Troy Glasgow/AP Images

Packages and documents that have already gone through the primary and secondary sorts are checked by city, state, and zip code. They are then placed in containers that are loaded onto aircraft for delivery to their final destinations in 236 countries.

FedEx's fleet of 667 planes makes it the largest airline in the world. More than 80,000 trucks complete the delivery process.

The $150 million hub opened in Guangzhou in 2009 lies in the heart of one of China's fastest-growing manufacturing districts. FedEx controls 39% of the China-to-U.S. air express market.

Why was Memphis picked as FedEx's central location? (1) It is located in the middle of the U.S. (2) It has very few hours of bad weather closures, perhaps contributing to the firm's excellent flight-safety record. (3) It provided FedEx with generous tax incentives.

Each night, except Sunday, FedEx brings to Memphis packages from throughout the world that are going to cities for which FedEx does not have direct flights. The central hub permits service to a far greater number of points with fewer aircraft than the traditional City-A-to-City-B system. It also allows FedEx to match aircraft flights with package loads each night and to reroute flights when load volume requires it, a major cost savings. Moreover, FedEx also believes that the central hub system helps reduce mishandling and delay in transit because there is total control over the packages from pickup point through delivery.

LEARNING OBJECTIVES

LO 8.1 *Identify* and explain seven major factors that affect location decisions 342

LO 8.2 *Compute* labor productivity 342

LO 8.3 *Apply* the factor-rating method 345

LO 8.4 *Complete* a locational cost–volume analysis graphically and mathematically 347

LO 8.5 *Use* the center-of-gravity method 348

LO 8.6 *Understand* the differences between service- and industrial-sector location analysis 351

VIDEO 8.1
Hard Rock's Location Selection

The Strategic Importance of Location

World markets continue to expand, and the global nature of business is accelerating. Indeed, one of the most important strategic decisions made by many companies, including FedEx, Mercedes-Benz, and Hard Rock, is where to locate their operations. When FedEx opened its Asian hub in Guangzhou, China, it set the stage for "round-the-world" flights linking its Paris and Memphis package hubs to Asia. When Mercedes-Benz announced its plans to build its first major overseas plant in Vance, Alabama, it completed a year of competition among 170 sites in 30 states and two countries. When Hard Rock Cafe opened in Moscow, it ended 3 years of advance preparation of a Russian food-supply chain. The strategic impact, cost, and international aspect of these decisions indicate how significant location decisions are.

Firms throughout the world are using the concepts and techniques of this chapter to address the location decision because location greatly affects both fixed and variable costs. Location has a major impact on the overall risk and profit of the company. For instance, depending on the product and type of production or service taking place, transportation costs alone can total as much as 25% of the product's selling price. That is, one-fourth of a firm's total revenue may be needed just to cover freight expenses of the raw materials coming in and finished products going out. Other costs that may be influenced by location include taxes, wages, raw material costs, and rents. When all costs are considered, location may alter total operating expenses as much as 50%.

The economics of transportation are so significant that companies—and even cities—have coalesced around a transportation advantage. For centuries, rivers and ports, and more recently rail hubs and then interstate highways, were a major ingredient in the location decision. Today airports are often the deciding factor, providing fast, low-cost transportation of goods and people.

Companies make location decisions relatively infrequently, usually because demand has outgrown the current plant's capacity or because of changes in labor productivity, exchange rates, costs, or local attitudes. Companies may also relocate their manufacturing or service facilities because of shifts in demographics and customer demand.

Location options include (1) expanding an existing facility instead of moving, (2) maintaining current sites while adding another facility elsewhere, or (3) closing the existing facility and moving to another location.

The location decision often depends on the type of business. For industrial location decisions, the strategy is usually minimizing costs, although locations that foster innovation and creativity may also be critical. For retail and professional service organizations, the strategy focuses on maximizing revenue. Warehouse location strategy, however, may be driven by a combination of cost and speed of delivery. *The objective of location strategy is to maximize the benefit of location to the firm.*

Location and Costs   Because location is such a significant cost and revenue driver, location often has the power to make (or break) a company's business strategy. Key multinationals in every major industry, from automobiles to cellular phones, now have or are planning a presence in each of their major markets. Location decisions to support a low-cost strategy require particularly careful consideration.

Once management is committed to a specific location, many costs are firmly in place and difficult to reduce. For instance, if a new factory location is in a region with high energy costs, even good management with an outstanding energy strategy is starting at a disadvantage. Management is in a similar bind with its human resource strategy if labor in the selected location is expensive, ill-trained, or has a poor work ethic. Consequently, hard work to determine an optimal facility location is a good investment.

Factors That Affect Location Decisions

Selecting a facility location is becoming much more complex with globalization. As we saw in Chapter 2, globalization has taken place because of the development of (1) market economics; (2) better international communications; (3) more rapid, reliable travel and shipping; (4) ease of capital flow between countries; and (5) high differences in labor costs. Many firms now consider opening new offices, factories, retail stores, or banks outside their home country. Location decisions transcend national borders. In fact, as Figure 8.1 shows, the sequence of location decisions often begins with choosing a country in which to operate.

One approach to selecting a country is to identify what the parent organization believes are key success factors (KSFs) needed to achieve competitive advantage. Six possible country KSFs are listed at the top of Figure 8.1. Using such factors (including some negative ones, such as crime) the World Economic Forum biannually ranks the global competitiveness of 144 countries (see Table 8.1). Switzerland placed first because of its high rates of saving and investment, openness to trade, quality education, and efficient government.

Once a firm decides which country is best for its location, it focuses on a region of the chosen country and a community. The final step in the location decision process is choosing a specific site within a community. The company must pick the one location that is best suited for shipping and receiving, zoning, utilities, size, and cost. Again, Figure 8.1 summarizes this series of decisions and the factors that affect them.

TABLE 8.1

Competitiveness of 144 Selected Countries, Based on Annual Surveys of 13,000 Business Executives

COUNTRY	2015 RANKING
Switzerland	1
Singapore	2
U.S.	3
Finland	4
Germany	5
Japan	6
⋮	
Canada	15
⋮	
Israel	27
China	28
⋮	
Russia	53
⋮	
Mexico	61
⋮	
Vietnam	68
⋮	
Haiti	137
⋮	
Chad	143
Guinea	144

Source: www.weforum.org, 2015. Used with permission of World Economic Forum.

Country Decision

Key Success Factors

1. Political risks, government rules, attitudes, incentives
2. Cultural and economic issues
3. Location of markets
4. Labor talent, attitudes, productivity, costs
5. Availability of supplies, communications, energy
6. Exchange rates and currency risk

Region/Community Decision

1. Corporate desires
2. Attractiveness of region (culture, taxes, climate, etc.)
3. Labor availability, costs, attitudes toward unions
4. Cost and availability of utilities
5. Environmental regulations of state and town
6. Government incentives and fiscal policies
7. Proximity to raw materials and customers
8. Land/construction costs

Site Decision

Indianapolis

1. Site size and cost
2. Air, rail, highway, and waterway systems
3. Zoning restrictions
4. Proximity of services/supplies needed
5. Environmental impact issues
6. Customer density and demographics

Figure **8.1**

Some Considerations and Factors That Affect Location Decisions

LO 8.1 *Identify* and explain seven major factors that affect location decisions

Besides globalization, a number of other factors affect the location decision. Among these are labor productivity, foreign exchange, culture, changing attitudes toward the industry, and proximity to markets, suppliers, and competitors.

Labor Productivity

LO 8.2 *Compute* labor productivity

When deciding on a location, management may be tempted by an area's low wage rates. However, wage rates cannot be considered by themselves, as Otis Elevator discovered when it opened its plant in Mexico in 1998. But by 2011, Otis found a move to an automated plant in South Carolina more advantageous. Management must also consider productivity.

As discussed in Chapter 1, differences exist in productivity in various countries. What management is really interested in is the combination of production and the wage rate. For example, if Otis Elevator pays $70 per day with 60 units produced per day in South Carolina, it will spend less on labor than at a Mexican plant that pays $25 per day with production of 20 units per day:

$$\frac{\text{Labor cost per day}}{\text{Production (units per day)}} = \text{Labor cost per unit}$$

1. Case 1: South Carolina plant:

$$\frac{\$70 \text{ Wages per day}}{60 \text{ Units produced per day}} = \frac{\$70}{60} = \$1.17 \text{ per unit}$$

2. Case 2: Juarez, Mexico, plant:

$$\frac{\$25 \text{ Wages per day}}{20 \text{ Units produced per day}} = \frac{\$25}{20} = \$1.25 \text{ per unit}$$

STUDENT TIP

Final cost is the critical factor, and low productivity can negate low wages.

Employees with poor training, poor education, or poor work habits may not be a good buy even at low wages. By the same token, employees who cannot or will not always reach their places of work are not much good to the organization, even at low wages. (Labor cost per unit is sometimes called the *labor content* of the product.)

Exchange Rates and Currency Risk

Although wage rates and productivity may make a country seem economical, unfavorable exchange rates may negate any savings. Sometimes, though, firms can take advantage of a particularly favorable exchange rate by relocating or exporting to a foreign country. However, the values of foreign currencies continually rise and fall in most countries. Such changes could well make what was a good location in 2015 a disastrous one in 2019. *Operational hedging* describes the situation where firms have excess capacity in multiple countries and then shift production levels from location to location as exchange rates change.

Costs

Tangible costs

Readily identifiable costs that can be measured with some precision.

We can divide location costs into two categories, tangible and intangible. **Tangible costs** are those costs that are readily identifiable and precisely measured. They include utilities, labor, material, taxes, depreciation, and other costs that the accounting department and management can identify. In addition, such costs as transportation of raw materials, transportation of finished goods, and site construction are all factored into the overall cost of a location. Government incentives, as we see in the *OM in Action* box "Iowa—Home of Corn and Facebook," also affect a location's cost.

Intangible costs

A category of location costs that cannot be easily quantified, such as quality of life and government.

Intangible costs are less easily quantified. They include quality of education, public transportation facilities, community attitudes toward the industry and the company, and quality and attitude of prospective employees. They also include quality-of-life variables, such as climate and sports teams, that may influence personnel recruiting.

OM in Action   Iowa—Home of Corn and Facebook

Among the big draws in Altoona, Iowa, population 15,000, are Adventureland, a Bass Pro Shop, and the Prairie Meadows casino. And now, it has Facebook's new data center. The social network recently opened the $300 million facility, a move that highlights the intense competition and lavish tax breaks available from small communities looking for technology bragging rights. The Altoona facility was built on millions of dollars of tax breaks and about 18 months of negotiation.

Facebook isn't Iowa's first high-tech catch. Microsoft is spending $2 billion on a data center nearby in Des Moines. Google is expanding a facility in Council Bluffs.

States and cities long have vied against each other to lure factories, sports teams and corporate headquarters. Iowa, the country's largest producer of corn, is among many states rolling out a green carpet for those farming bits and bytes. Officials say data centers broaden their tax base, create well-paying technical and construction jobs, and confer bragging rights that will lure companies with bigger hiring plans. They also contribute to the local economy without stressing infrastructure such as roads and sewage plants.

But it remains an open question whether the cost of these facilities, in tax breaks and services, works out in their favor. Altoona provided Facebook a 20-year exemption on paying property taxes, and Iowa agreed to $18 million in sales-tax refunds or investment-tax credits through 2023. "For the tax breaks they often receive, the centers produce few jobs or spinoff benefits," said an Iowa State University professor. Tech companies aren't looking for incentives alone. Availability and pricing of electricity, which can exceed two-thirds of the cost to run a data center, are among the most important factors.

Proponents argue that businesses expect to trade tax cuts for jobs. But a report by the John Locke foundation summarized the results of 55 studies on the impact of targeted tax incentives. More than 70% of the studies found that incentives either did not substantially contribute to economic performance or produced mixed results. Often the giveaways add up to cronyism, a misallocation of resources, and a huge bill for taxpayers.

gdbrekke/Fotolia

Sources: Wall Street Journal (Nov. 15–16, 2014) and (March 13, 2015); and *New York Times* (Dec. 1, 2012).

Political Risk, Values, and Culture

The political risk associated with national, state, and local governments' attitudes toward private and intellectual property, zoning, pollution, and employment stability may be in flux. Governmental positions at the time a location decision is made may not be lasting ones. However, management may find that these attitudes can be influenced by their own leadership.

Worker values may also differ from country to country, region to region, and small town to city. Worker views regarding turnover, unions, and absenteeism are all relevant factors. In turn, these values can affect a company's decision whether to make offers to current workers if the firm relocates to a new location. The case study at the end of this chapter, "Southern Recreational Vehicle Company," describes a St. Louis firm that actively chose *not to relocate* any of its workers when it moved to Mississippi.

One of the greatest challenges in a global operations decision is dealing with another country's culture. Cultural variations in punctuality by employees and suppliers make a marked difference in production and delivery schedules. Bribery and other forms of corruption also create substantial economic inefficiency, as well as ethical and legal problems in the global arena. As a result, operations managers face significant challenges when building effective supply chains across cultures. Table 8.2 provides one ranking of corruption in countries around the world.

Proximity to Markets

For many firms, locating near customers is extremely important. Particularly, service organizations, like drugstores, restaurants, post offices, or barbers, find that demographics and proximity to market are *the* primary location factors. Manufacturing firms find it useful to be close to customers when transporting finished goods is expensive or difficult (perhaps because they are bulky, heavy, or fragile). To be near U.S. markets, foreign-owned auto giants such as Mercedes, Honda, Toyota, and Hyundai are building millions of cars each year in the U.S.

TABLE 8.2

Ranking Corruption in Selected Countries (Score of 100 Represents a Corruption-Free Country

RANK	SCORE
1 Denmark	92
2 New Zealand	91
3 Finland	89
⋮	
10 Canada	81
⋮	
17 U.S., Hong Kong	74 (tie)
37 Israel	60
⋮	
69 Brazil, Greece	43 (tie)
⋮	
136 Russia	27
⋮	
161 Haiti	19
⋮	
174 Somalia, North Korea	8 (tie)

Source: Transparency International's 2014 survey, at **www.transparency.org**. Used with permission of Transparency International.

In addition, with just-in-time production, suppliers want to locate near users. For a firm like Coca-Cola, whose product's primary ingredient is water, it makes sense to have bottling plants in many cities rather than shipping heavy (and sometimes fragile glass) containers cross country.

Proximity to Suppliers

Firms locate near their raw materials and suppliers because of (1) perishability, (2) transportation costs, or (3) bulk. Bakeries, dairy plants, and frozen seafood processors deal with *perishable* raw materials, so they often locate close to suppliers. Companies dependent on inputs of heavy or bulky raw materials (such as steel producers using coal and iron ore) face expensive inbound *transportation costs*, so transportation costs become a major factor. And goods for which there is a *reduction in bulk* during production (e.g., trees to lumber) typically need facilities near the raw material.

Proximity to Competitors (Clustering)

Clustering

The location of competing companies near each other, often because of a critical mass of information, talent, venture capital, or natural resources.

Both manufacturing and service organizations also like to locate, somewhat surprisingly, near competitors. This tendency, called clustering, often occurs when a major resource is found in that region. Such resources include natural resources, information resources, venture capital resources, and talent resources. Table 8.3 presents nine examples of industries that exhibit clustering, and the reasons why.

Italy may be the true leader when it comes to clustering, however, with northern zones of that country holding world leadership in such specialties as ceramic tile (Modena), gold jewelry (Vicenza), machine tools (Busto Arsizio), cashmere and wool (Biella), designer eyeglasses (Belluma), and pasta machines (Parma). When it comes to clusters for innovations in slaughtering, however (see the *OM in Action* box), Denmark is the leader.

Methods of Evaluating Location Alternatives

Four major methods are used for solving location problems: the factor-rating method, locational cost–volume analysis, the center-of-gravity method, and the transportation model. This section describes these approaches.

TABLE 8.3	Clustering of Companies

INDUSTRY	LOCATIONS	REASON FOR CLUSTERING
Wine making	Napa Valley (U.S.), Bordeaux region (France)	Natural resources of land and climate
Software firms	Silicon Valley, Boston, Bangalore, Israel	Talent resources of bright graduates in scientific/technical areas, venture capitalists nearby
Clean energy	Colorado	Critical mass of talent and information, with 1,000 companies
Theme parks (e.g., Disney World, Universal Studios, and Sea World)	Orlando, Florida	A hot spot for entertainment, warm weather, tourists, and inexpensive labor
Electronics firms (e.g., Sony, IBM, HP, Motorola, and Panasonic)	Northern Mexico	NAFTA, duty-free export to U.S. (24% of all TVs are built here)
Computer hardware manufacturing	Singapore, Taiwan	High technological penetration rates and per capita GDP, skilled/educated workforce with large pool of engineers
Fast-food chains (e.g., Wendy's, McDonald's, Burger King, Pizza Hut)	Sites within 1 mile of one another	Stimulate food sales, high traffic flows
General aviation aircraft (e.g., Cessna, Learjet, Boeing, Raytheon)	Wichita, Kansas	Mass of aviation skills (60–70% of world's small planes/jets are built here)
Athletic footwear, outdoor wear	Portland, Oregon	300 companies, many spawned by Nike, deep talent pool and outdoor culture

OM in Action | Denmark's Meat Cluster

Every day, 20,000 pigs are delivered to the Danish Crown company's slaughterhouse in central Denmark. The pigs trot into the stunning room, guided by workers armed with giant fly swats. The animals are hung upside down, divided in two, shaved, and scalded clean. A machine cuts them into pieces, which are then cooled, boned, and packed.

The slaughterhouse is enormous: 10 football fields long with 7 miles of conveyor belts. Its managers attend to the tiniest detail. The workers wear green rather than white because this puts the pigs in a better mood. The cutting machine photographs a carcass before adjusting its blades to the exact carcass contours. The company calibrates not only how to carve the flesh, but also where the various parts will fetch the highest prices.

Denmark is a tiny country, with 5.6 million people and wallet-draining labor costs. But it is an agricultural giant, home to 30 million pigs and numerous global brands. Farm products make up over 20% of its goods exports—and the value of these exports is expected to grow from $5.5 billion in 2001 to $31 billion by 2020.

How is this meat-processing cluster still thriving? It is because clustering can be applied to ancient industries like slaughtering as well as to new ones. The cluster includes several big companies: Danish Crown, Arla, Rose Poultry,

and DuPont Danisco, as well as plenty of smaller firms, which act as indicators of nascent trends and incubators of new ideas. Other firms are contributing information technology tools for the cluster. Among these are LetFarm for fields, Bovisoft for stables, Agrosoft for pigs, Webstech for grain, and InOMEGA for food.

The cluster also has a collection of productivity-spurring institutions (the Cattle Research Center, for example, creates ways to boost pork productivity through robotics) and Danish Tech University, where 1,500 people work on food-related subjects.

Racorn/123rf

Sources: The Economist (Jan. 4, 2014); and *GlobalMeatNews.com* (Nov. 1, 2013).

The Factor-Rating Method

There are many factors, both qualitative and quantitative, to consider in choosing a location. Some of these factors are more important than others, so managers can use weightings to make the decision process more objective. The factor-rating method is popular because a wide variety of factors, from education to recreation to labor skills, can be objectively included. Figure 8.1 listed a few of the many factors that affect location decisions.

Factor-rating method
A location method that instills objectivity into the process of identifying hard-to-evaluate costs.

The factor-rating method (which we introduced in Chapter 2) has six steps:

1. Develop a list of relevant factors called *key success factors* (such as those in Figure 8.1).
2. Assign a weight to each factor to reflect its relative importance in the company's objectives.
3. Develop a scale for each factor (for example, 1 to 10 or 1 to 100 points).
4. Have management score each location for each factor, using the scale in Step 3.
5. Multiply the score by the weights for each factor and total the score for each location.
6. Make a recommendation based on the maximum point score, considering the results of other quantitative approaches as well.

Example 1 | **FACTOR-RATING METHOD FOR AN EXPANDING THEME PARK**

LO 8.3 *Apply* the factor-rating method

Five Flags over Florida, a U.S. chain of 10 family-oriented theme parks, has decided to expand overseas by opening its first park in Europe. It wishes to select between France and Denmark.

APPROACH ▶ The ratings sheet in Table 8.4 lists key success factors that management has decided are important; their weightings and their rating for two possible sites—Dijon, France, and Copenhagen, Denmark—are shown.

TABLE 8.4	Weights, Scores, and Solution					
KEY SUCCESS FACTOR	**WEIGHT**	**SCORES (OUT OF 100)**		**WEIGHTED SCORES**	
		FRANCE	**DENMARK**	**FRANCE**	**DENMARK**
Labor availability and attitude	.25	70	60	(.25)(70) = 17.50	(.25)(60) = 15.00
People-to-car ratio	.05	50	60	(.05)(50) = 2.50	(.05)(60) = 3.00
Per capita income	.10	85	80	(.10)(85) = 8.50	(.10)(80) = 8.00
Tax structure	.39	75	70	(.39)(75) = 29.25	(.39)(70) = 27.30
Education and health	.21	60	70	(.21)(60) = 12.60	(.21)(70) = 14.70
Totals	1.00			70.35	68.00

STUDENT TIP ◆

These weights do not need to be on a 0–1 scale or total to 1. We can use a 1–10 scale, 1–100 scale, or any other scale we prefer.

SOLUTION ▶ Table 8.4 uses weights and scores to evaluate alternative site locations. Given the option of 100 points assigned to each factor, the French location is preferable.

INSIGHT ▶ By changing the points or weights slightly for those factors about which there is some doubt, we can analyze the sensitivity of the decision. For instance, we can see that changing the scores for "labor availability and attitude" by 10 points can change the decision. The numbers used in factor weighting can be subjective, and the model's results are not "exact" even though this is a quantitative approach.

LEARNING EXERCISE ▶ If the weight for "tax structure" drops to .20 and the weight for "education and health" increases to .40, what is the new result? [Answer: Denmark is now chosen, with a 68.0 vs. a 67.5 score for France.]

RELATED PROBLEMS ▶ 8.5–8.15, 8.24, 8.25 (8.26, 8.27, 8.28, 8.33, 8.34 are available in MyOMLab)

EXCEL OM Data File **Ch08Ex1.xls** can be found in MyOMLab.

When a decision is sensitive to minor changes, further analysis of the weighting and the points assigned may be appropriate. Alternatively, management may conclude that these intangible factors are not the proper criteria on which to base a location decision. Managers therefore place primary weight on the more quantitative aspects of the decision.

Locational Cost–Volume Analysis

Locational cost–volume analysis

A method of making an economic comparison of location alternatives.

Locational cost–volume analysis is a technique for making an economic comparison of location alternatives. By identifying fixed and variable costs and graphing them for each location, we can determine which one provides the lowest cost. Locational cost–volume analysis can be done mathematically or graphically. The graphic approach has the advantage of providing the range of volume over which each location is preferable.

The three steps to locational cost–volume analysis are as follows:

1. Determine the fixed and variable cost for each location.
2. Plot the costs for each location, with costs on the vertical axis of the graph and annual volume on the horizontal axis.
3. Select the location that has the lowest total cost for the expected production volume.

Example 2

LOCATIONAL COST–VOLUME ANALYSIS FOR A PARTS MANUFACTURER

Esmail Mohebbi, owner of European Ignitions Manufacturing, needs to expand his capacity. He is considering three locations—Athens, Brussels, and Lisbon—for a new plant. The company wishes to find the most economical location for an expected volume of 2,000 units per year.

APPROACH ▶ Mohebbi conducts locational cost–volume analysis. To do so, he determines that fixed costs per year at the sites are $30,000, $60,000, and $110,000, respectively; and variable costs are $75 per unit, $45 per unit, and $25 per unit, respectively. The expected selling price of each ignition system produced is $120.

SOLUTION ▶ For each of the three locations, Mohebbi can plot the fixed costs (those at a volume of zero units) and the total cost (fixed costs + variable costs) at the expected volume of output. These lines have been plotted in Figure 8.2.

Figure **8.2**

Crossover Chart for Locational Cost–Volume Analysis

For Athens:

$$\text{Total cost} = \$30,000 + \$75(2,000) = \$180,000$$

For Brussels:

$$\text{Total cost} = \$60,000 + \$45(2,000) = \$150,000$$

For Lisbon:

$$\text{Total cost} = \$110,000 + \$25(2,000) = \$160,000$$

LO 8.4 *Complete* a locational cost–volume analysis graphically and mathematically

With an expected volume of 2,000 units per year, Brussels provides the lowest cost location. The expected profit is:

$$\text{Total revenue} - \text{Total cost} = \$120(2,000) - \$150,000 = \$90,000 \text{ per year}$$

The crossover point for Athens and Brussels is:

$$30,000 + 75(x) = 60,000 + 45(x)$$
$$30(x) = 30,000$$
$$x = 1,000$$

and the crossover point for Brussels and Lisbon is:

$$60,000 + 45(x) = 110,000 + 25(x)$$
$$20(x) = 50,000$$
$$x = 2,500$$

INSIGHT ▶ As with every other OM model, locational cost–volume analysis can be sensitive to input data. For example, for a volume of less than 1,000, Athens would be preferred. For a volume greater than 2,500, Lisbon would yield the greatest profit.

LEARNING EXERCISE ▶ The variable cost for Lisbon is now expected to be $22 per unit. What is the new crossover point between Brussels and Lisbon? [Answer: 2,174 units.]

RELATED PROBLEMS ▶ 8.16–8.19 (8.29, 8.30 are available in MyOMLab)

EXCEL **OM** Data File **Ch08Ex2.xls** can be found in MyOMLab.

Center-of-Gravity Method

Center-of-gravity method

A mathematical technique used for finding the best location for a single distribution point that services several stores or areas.

The **center-of-gravity method** is a mathematical technique used for finding the location of a distribution center that will minimize distribution costs. The method takes into account the location of markets, the volume of goods shipped to those markets, and shipping costs in finding the best location for a distribution center.

The first step in the center-of-gravity method is to place the locations on a coordinate system. This will be illustrated in Example 3. The origin of the coordinate system and the scale used are arbitrary, just as long as the relative distances are correctly represented. This can be done easily by placing a grid over an ordinary map. The center of gravity is determined using Equations (8-1) and (8-2):

$$x\text{-coordinate of the center of gravity} = \frac{\sum_i x_i Q_i}{\sum_i Q_i} \tag{8-1}$$

$$y\text{-coordinate of the center of gravity} = \frac{\sum_i y_i Q_i}{\sum_i Q_i} \tag{8-2}$$

where x_i = x-coordinate of location i
y_i = y-coordinate of location i
Q_i = Quantity of goods moved to or from location i

LO 8.5 *Use* the center-of-gravity method

Note that Equations (8-1) and (8-2) include the term Q_i, the quantity of supplies transferred to or from location i.

Because the number of containers shipped each month affects cost, distance alone should not be the principal criterion. The center-of-gravity method assumes that cost is directly proportional to both distance and volume shipped. The ideal location is that which minimizes the weighted distance between sources and destinations, where the distance is weighted by the number of containers shipped.[1]

Example 3

CENTER OF GRAVITY

Quain's Discount Department Stores, a chain of four large Target-type outlets, has store locations in Chicago, Pittsburgh, New York, and Atlanta; they are currently being supplied out of an old and inadequate warehouse in Pittsburgh, the site of the chain's first store. The firm wants to find some "central" location in which to build a new warehouse.

APPROACH ▶ Quain's will apply the center-of-gravity method. It gathers data on demand rates at each outlet (see Table 8.5).

TABLE 8.5	Demand for Quain's Discount Department Stores
STORE LOCATION	**NUMBER OF CONTAINERS SHIPPED PER MONTH**
Chicago	2,000
Pittsburgh	1,000
New York	1,000
Atlanta	2,000

Its current store locations are shown in Figure 8.3. For example, location 1 is Chicago, and from Table 8.5 and Figure 8.3, we have:

$$x_1 = 30$$
$$y_1 = 120$$
$$Q_1 = 2,000$$

Figure **8.3**

Coordinate Locations of Four Quain's Department Stores and Center of Gravity

SOLUTION ▶ Using the data in Table 8.5 and Figure 8.3 for each of the other cities, and Equations (8-1) and (8-2), we find:

x-coordinate of the center of gravity:

$$= \frac{(30)(2000) + (90)(1000) + (130)(1000) + (60)(2000)}{2000 + 1000 + 1000 + 2000} = \frac{400,000}{6,000}$$

$$= 66.7$$

y-coordinate of the center of gravity:

$$= \frac{(120)(2000) + (110)(1000) + (130)(1000) + (40)(2000)}{2000 + 1000 + 1000 + 2000} = \frac{560,000}{6,000}$$

$$= 93.3$$

This location (66.7, 93.3) is shown by the crosshairs in Figure 8.3.

INSIGHT ▶ By overlaying a U.S. map on Figure 8.3, we find this location (66.7, 93.3) is near central Ohio. The firm may well wish to consider Columbus, Ohio, or a nearby city as an appropriate location. But it is important to have both north–south and east–west interstate highways near the city selected to make delivery times quicker.

LEARNING EXERCISE ▶ The number of containers shipped per month to Atlanta is expected to grow quickly to 3,000. How does this change the center of gravity, and where should the new warehouse be located? [Answer: (65.7, 85.7), which is closer to Cincinnati, Ohio.]

RELATED PROBLEMS ▶ 8.20–8.23 (8.31, 8.32 are available in MyOMLab)

EXCEL OM Data File **Ch08Ex3.xls** can be found in MyOMLab.

ACTIVE MODEL 8.1 This example is further illustrated in Active Model 8.1 in MyOMLab.

Transportation Model

The objective of the **transportation model** is to determine the best pattern of shipments from several points of supply (sources) to several points of demand (destinations) so as to minimize total production and transportation costs. Every firm with a network of supply-and-demand points faces such a problem. The complex Volkswagen supply network (shown in Figure 8.4) provides one such illustration. We note in Figure 8.4, for example, that VW of Mexico ships vehicles for assembly and parts to VW of Nigeria, sends assemblies to VW of Brasil, and receives parts and assemblies from headquarters in Germany.

Transportation model

A technique for solving a class of linear programming problems.

→ Engines, other assemblies   → Parts
→ Finished vehicles   → Vehicles for assembly

Figure 8.4

Volkswagen, the Third Largest Automaker in the World, Finds It Advantageous to Locate Its Plants Throughout the World

This graphic shows a portion of VW's supply network. There are 61 plants in Europe, along with nine countries in the Americas, Asia, and Africa.

Although the linear programming (LP) technique can be used to solve this type of problem, more efficient, special-purpose algorithms have been developed for the transportation application. The transportation model finds an initial feasible solution and then makes step-by-step improvement until an optimal solution is reached.

Service Location Strategy

While the focus in industrial-sector location analysis is on *minimizing cost,* the focus in the service sector is on *maximizing revenue.* This is because manufacturing firms find that costs tend to vary substantially among locations, while service firms find that location often has more impact on revenue than cost. Therefore, the location focus for service firms should be on determining the volume of customers and revenue.

There are eight major determinants of volume and revenue for the service firm:

1. Purchasing power of the customer-drawing area
2. Service and image compatibility with demographics of the customer-drawing area
3. Competition in the area
4. Quality of the competition
5. Uniqueness of the firm's and competitors' locations
6. Physical qualities of facilities and neighboring businesses
7. Operating policies of the firm
8. Quality of management

Realistic analysis of these factors can provide a reasonable picture of the revenue expected. The techniques used in the service sector include regression analysis (see the *OM in Action* box, "How La Quinta Selects Profitable Hotel Sites"), traffic counts, demographic analysis, purchasing power analysis, the factor-rating method, the center-of-gravity method, and geographic information systems. Table 8.6 provides a summary of location strategies for both service and goods-producing organizations.

OM in Action | How La Quinta Selects Profitable Hotel Sites

One of the most important decisions a lodging chain makes is location. Those that pick good sites more accurately and quickly than competitors have a distinct advantage. La Quinta Inns, headquartered in San Antonio, Texas, is a moderately priced chain of 800 inns. To model motel selection behavior and predict success of a site, La Quinta turned to regression analysis.

The hotel started by testing 35 independent variables, trying to find which of them would have the highest correlation with predicted profitability, the dependent variable. Variables included: the number of hotel rooms in the vicinity and their average room rates; local attractions such as office buildings and hospitals that drew potential customers to a 4-mile-radius trade area; local population and unemployment rate; the number of inns in a region; and physical characteristics of the site, such as ease of access or sign visibility.

In the end, the regression model chosen, with an R^2 of 51%, included four predictive variables: (1) the price of the inn, (2) median income levels, (3) the state population per inn, and (4) the location of nearby colleges

(which serves as a proxy for other demand generators). La Quinta then used the regression model to predict profitability and developed a cutoff that gave the best results for predicting success or failure of a site. A spreadsheet is now used to implement the model, which applies the decision rule and suggests "build" or "don't build." The CEO likes the model so much that he no longer feels obliged to personally select new sites.

Mike Booth/Alamy

Sources: S. Kimes and J. Fitzsimmons, *Interfaces* 20, no. 2: 12–20; and G. Keller, *Statistics for Management and Economics*, 8th ed. Cincinnati-Cengage, 2008: 679.

TABLE 8.6 | Location Strategies—Service vs. Goods-Producing Organizations

SERVICE/RETAIL/PROFESSIONAL	GOODS-PRODUCING
REVENUE FOCUS	**COST FOCUS**

Volume/revenue
   Drawing area; purchasing power
   Competition; advertising/pricing
Physical quality
   Parking/access; security/lighting; appearance/image
Cost determinants
   Rent
   Management caliber
   Operation policies (hours, wage rates)
	Tangible costs
	   Transportation cost of raw material
	   Shipment cost of finished goods
	   Energy and utility cost; labor; raw material; taxes, and so on
	Intangible and future costs
	   Attitude toward union
	   Quality of life
	   Education expenditures by state
	   Quality of state and local government

TECHNIQUES	**TECHNIQUES**
Regression models to determine importance of various factors Factor-rating method Traffic counts Demographic analysis of drawing area Purchasing power analysis of area Center-of-gravity method Geographic information systems	Transportation method Factor-rating method Locational cost–volume analysis Crossover charts
ASSUMPTIONS	**ASSUMPTIONS**
Location is a major determinant of revenue High customer-interaction issues are critical Costs are relatively constant for a given area; therefore, the revenue function is critical	Location is a major determinant of cost Most major costs can be identified explicitly for each site Low customer contact allows focus on the identifiable costs Intangible costs can be evaluated

> ◆ **STUDENT TIP**
> This table helps differentiate between service- and manufacturing-sector decisions.

> **LO 8.6** *Understand* the differences between service- and industrial-sector location analysis

---

Geographic Information Systems

Geographic information systems are an important tool to help firms make successful, analytical decisions with regard to location. A geographic information system (GIS) stores, accesses, displays, and links demographic information to a geographical location. For instance, retailers,

> **Geographic information system (GIS)**
> A system that stores and displays information that can be linked to a geographic location.

banks, food chains, gas stations, and print shop franchises can all use geographically coded files from a GIS to conduct demographic analyses. By combining population, age, income, traffic flow, and density figures with geography, a retailer can pinpoint the best location for a new store or restaurant.

Here are some of the geographic databases available in many GISs:

◆ Census data by block, tract, city, county, congressional district, metropolitan area, state, and zip code

◆ Maps of every street, highway, bridge, and tunnel in the U.S.

◆ Utilities such as electrical, water, and gas lines

◆ All rivers, mountains, lakes, and forests

◆ All major airports, colleges, and hospitals

For example, airlines use GISs to identify airports where ground services are the most effective. This information is then used to help schedule and to decide where to purchase fuel, meals, and other services.

Commercial office building developers use GISs in the selection of cities for future construction. Building new office space takes several years; therefore, developers value the database approach that a GIS can offer. GIS is used to analyze factors that influence the location decisions by addressing five elements for each city: (1) residential areas, (2) retail shops, (3) cultural and entertainment centers, (4) crime incidence, and (5) transportation options.

Here are five examples of how location-scouting GIS software is turning commercial real estate into a science.

◆ *Carvel Ice Cream:* This 80-year-old chain of ice cream shops uses GIS to create a demographic profile of what a typically successful neighborhood for a Carvel looks like—mostly in terms of income and ages.

◆ *Saber Roofing:* Rather than send workers out to estimate the costs for reroofing jobs, this Redwood City, California, firm pulls up aerial shots of the building via Google Earth. The

Geographic information systems (GISs) are used by a variety of firms, including Darden Restaurants, to identify target markets by income, ethnicity, product use, age, etc. Here, data from MapInfo helps with competitive analysis for a retailer. Three concentric blue rings, each representing various mile radii, were drawn around the competitor's store. The heavy red line indicates the "drive" time to the firm's own central store (the red dot).

owner can measure roofs, evaluate their condition, and e-mail the client an estimate, saving hundreds of miles of driving daily. In one case, while on the phone, a potential client was told her roof was too steep for the company to tackle after the Saber employee quickly looked up the home on Google Earth.

- *Arby's:* As this fast-food chain learned, specific products can affect behavior. Using MapInfo, Arby's discovered that diners drove up to 20% farther for their roast beef sandwich (which they consider a "destination" product) than for its chicken sandwich.

- *Home Depot:* Wanting a store in New York City, even though Home Depot demographics are usually for customers who own big homes, the company opened in Queens when GIS software predicted it would do well. Although most people there live in apartments and very small homes, the store has become one of the chain's highest-volume outlets. Similarly, Home Depot thought it had saturated Atlanta two decades ago, but GIS analysis suggested expansion. There are now over 40 Home Depots in that area.

- *Jo-Ann Stores:* This fabric and craft retailer's 70 superstores were doing well a few years ago, but managers were afraid more big-box stores could not justify building expenses. So Jo-Ann used its GIS to create an ideal customer profile—female homeowners with families—and mapped it against demographics. The firm found it could build 700 superstores, which in turn increased the sales from $105 to $150 per square foot.

Other packages similar to MapInfo are Atlas GIS (from Strategic Mapping), ArcGIS (by Esri), SAS/GIS (by SAS Institute), Maptitude (by Caliper), and GeoMedia (by Intergraph).

These GISs can be extensive, including comprehensive sets of map and demographic data. The maps have millions of miles of streets and points of interest to allow users to locate restaurants, airports, hotels, gas stations, ATMs, museums, campgrounds, and freeway exits. Demographic data include statistics for population, age, income, education, and housing. These data can be mapped by state, county, city, zip code, or census tract.

The *Video Case Study* "Locating the Next Red Lobster Restaurant" that appears at the end of this chapter describes how that chain uses its GIS to define trade areas based on market size and population density.

VIDEO 8.2
Locating the Next Red Lobster Restaurant

Summary

Location may determine up to 50% of operating expense. Location is also a critical element in determining revenue for the service, retail, or professional firm. Industrial firms need to consider both tangible and intangible costs. Industrial location problems are typically addressed via a factor-rating method, locational cost–volume analysis, the center-of-gravity method, and the transportation method of linear programming.

For service, retail, and professional organizations, analysis is typically made of a variety of variables including purchasing power of a drawing area, competition, advertising and promotion, physical qualities of the location, and operating policies of the organization.

Key Terms

Tangible costs (p. 342)
Intangible costs (p. 342)
Clustering (p. 344)

Factor-rating method (p. 345)
Locational cost–volume analysis (p. 346)
Center-of-gravity method (p. 348)

Transportation model (p. 349)
Geographic information system (GIS) (p. 351)

Ethical Dilemma

In this chapter, we have discussed a number of location decisions. Consider another: United Airlines announced its competition to select a town for a new billion-dollar aircraft-repair base. The bidding for the prize of 7,500 jobs paying at least $25 per hour was fast and furious, with Orlando offering $154 million in incentives and Denver more than twice that amount. Kentucky's governor angrily rescinded Louisville's offer of $300 million, likening the bidding to "squeezing every drop of blood out of a turnip."

When United finally selected from among the 93 cities bidding on the base, the winner was Indianapolis and its $320 million offer of taxpayers' money.

But a few years later, with United near bankruptcy, and having fulfilled its legal obligation, the company walked away from the massive center. This left the city and state governments out all that money, with no new tenant in sight. The city now even owns the tools, neatly arranged in each of the 12 elaborately equipped hangar bays. United outsourced its maintenance to mechanics at a southern firm (which pays one-third of what United paid in salary and benefits in Indianapolis).

What are the ethical, legal, and economic implications of such location bidding wars? Who pays for such giveaways? Are local citizens allowed to vote on offers made by their cities, counties, or states? Should there be limits on these incentives?

Discussion Questions

1. How is FedEx's location a competitive advantage? Discuss.
2. Why do so many U.S. firms build facilities in other countries?
3. Why do so many foreign companies build facilities in the U.S.?
4. What is clustering?
5. How does factor weighting incorporate personal preference in location choices?
6. What are the advantages and disadvantages of a qualitative (as opposed to a quantitative) approach to location decision making?
7. Provide two examples of clustering in the service sector.
8. What are the major factors that firms consider when choosing a country in which to locate?
9. What factors affect region/community location decisions?
10. Although most organizations may make the location decision infrequently, there are some organizations that make the decision quite regularly and often. Provide one or two examples. How might their approach to the location decision differ from the norm?
11. List factors, other than globalization, that affect the location decision.
12. Explain the assumptions behind the center-of-gravity method. How can the model be used in a service facility location?
13. What are the three steps to locational cost–volume analysis?
14. "Manufacturers locate near their resources, retailers locate near their customers." Discuss this statement, with reference to the proximity-to-markets arguments covered in the text. Can you think of a counter-example in each case? Support your choices.
15. Why shouldn't low wage rates alone be sufficient to select a location?
16. List the techniques used by service organizations to select locations.
17. Contrast the location of a food distributor and a supermarket. (The distributor sends truckloads of food, meat, produce, etc., to the supermarket.) Show the relevant considerations (factors) they share; show those where they differ.
18. Elmer's Fudge Factory is planning to open 10 retail outlets in Oregon over the next 2 years. Identify (and weight) those factors relevant to the decision. Provide this list of factors and weights.

Using Software to Solve Location Problems

This section presents three ways to solve location problems with computer software. First, you can create your own spreadsheets to compute factor ratings, the center of gravity, and locational cost–volume analysis. Second, Excel OM (free with your text and found in MyOMLab) is programmed to solve all three models. Third, POM for Windows is also found in MyOMLab and can solve all problems labeled with a **P**.

CREATING YOUR OWN EXCEL SPREADSHEETS

Excel spreadsheets are easily developed to solve most of the problems in this chapter. Consider the Quain's Department Store center-of-gravity analysis in Example 3. You can see from Program 8.1 how the formulas are created.

✕ USING EXCEL OM

Excel OM may be used to solve Example 1 (with the Factor Rating module), Example 2 (with the Cost–Volume Analysis module), and Example 3 (with the Center-of-Gravity module), as well as other location problems. The factor-rating method was illustrated in Chapter 2.

P USING POM FOR WINDOWS

POM for Windows also includes three different facility location models: the factor-rating method, the center-of-gravity model, and locational cost–volume analysis. For details, refer to Appendix IV.

	A	B	C	D
1	Quain's Discount Department Stores			
2	Center-of-Gravity Method			
3				
4	STORE LOCATION	NUMBER OF CONTAINERS SHIPPED PER MONTH	x-coordinate x_i	y-coordinate y_i
5	Chicago	2,000	30	120
6	Pittsburgh	1,000	90	110
7	New York	1,000	130	130
8	Atlanta	2,000	60	40
9	Sum	6,000		
10				
11	Center of Gravity	=SUM(B5:B8)	66.7	93.3
12				
13		**Action**		
14		Copy D11 to C11		
15				
16		=SUMPRODUCT(D5:D8,$B5:$B8)/$B9		

Program **8.1**

An Excel Spreadsheet for Creating a Center-of-Gravity Analysis for Example 3, Quain's Discount Department Stores

Solved Problems   Virtual Office Hours help is available in MyOMLab.

SOLVED PROBLEM 8.1

Just as cities and communities can be compared for location selection by the weighted approach model, as we saw earlier in this chapter, so can actual site decisions within those cities. Table 8.7 illustrates four factors of importance to Washington, DC, and the health officials charged with opening that city's first public drug treatment clinic. Of primary concern (and given a weight of 5) was location of the clinic so it would be as accessible as possible to the largest number of patients. Due to a tight budget, the annual lease cost was also of some concern. A suite in the city hall, at 14th and U Streets, was highly rated because its rent would be free. An old office building near the downtown bus station received a much lower rating because of its cost. Equally important as lease cost was the need for confidentiality of patients and, therefore, for a relatively inconspicuous clinic. Finally, because so many of the staff at the clinic would be donating their time, the safety, parking, and accessibility of each site were of concern as well.

Using the factor-rating method, which site is preferred?

SOLUTION

From the three rightmost columns in Table 8.7, the weighted scores are summed. The bus terminal area has a low score and can be excluded from further consideration. The other two sites are virtually identical in total score. The city may now want to consider other factors, including political ones, in selecting between the two remaining sites.

TABLE 8.7	Potential Clinic Sites in Washington, DC						
		POTENTIAL LOCATIONS*			**WEIGHTED SCORES**		
FACTOR	IMPORTANCE WEIGHT	HOMELESS SHELTER (2ND AND D, SE)	CITY HALL (14TH AND U, NW)	BUS TERMINAL AREA (7TH AND H, NW)	HOMELESS SHELTER	CITY HALL	BUS TERMINAL AREA
Accessibility for addicts	5	9	7	7	45	35	35
Annual lease cost	3	6	10	3	18	30	9
Inconspicuous	3	5	2	7	15	6	21
Accessibility for health staff	2	3	6	2	6	12	4
					Total scores: 84	83	69

*All sites are rated on a 1 to 10 basis, with 10 as the highest score and 1 as the lowest.

SOLVED PROBLEM 8.2

Ching-Chang Kuo is considering opening a new foundry in Denton, Texas; Edwardsville, Illinois; or Fayetteville, Arkansas, to produce high-quality rifle sights. He has assembled the following fixed-cost and variable-cost data:

		PER-UNIT COSTS		
LOCATION	FIXED COST PER YEAR	MATERIAL	VARIABLE LABOR	OVERHEAD
Denton	$200,000	$ .20	$ .40	$ .40
Edwardsville	$180,000	$ .25	$ .75	$ .75
Fayetteville	$170,000	$1.00	$1.00	$1.00

a) Graph the total cost lines.
b) Over what range of annual volume is each facility going to have a competitive advantage?
c) What is the volume at the intersection of the Edwardsville and Fayetteville cost lines?

SOLUTION

a) A graph of the total cost lines is shown in Figure 8.5.
b) Below 8,000 units, the Fayetteville facility will have a competitive advantage (lowest cost); between 8,000 units and 26,666 units, Edwardsville has an advantage; and above 26,666, Denton has the advantage. (We have made the assumption in this problem that other costs—that is, delivery and intangible factors—are constant regardless of the decision.)
c) From Figure 8.5, we see that the cost line for Fayetteville and the cost line for Edwardsville cross at about 8,000. We can also determine this point with a little algebra:

$$\$180,000 + 1.75Q = \$170,000 + 3.00Q$$
$$\$10,000 = 1.25Q$$
$$8,000 = Q$$

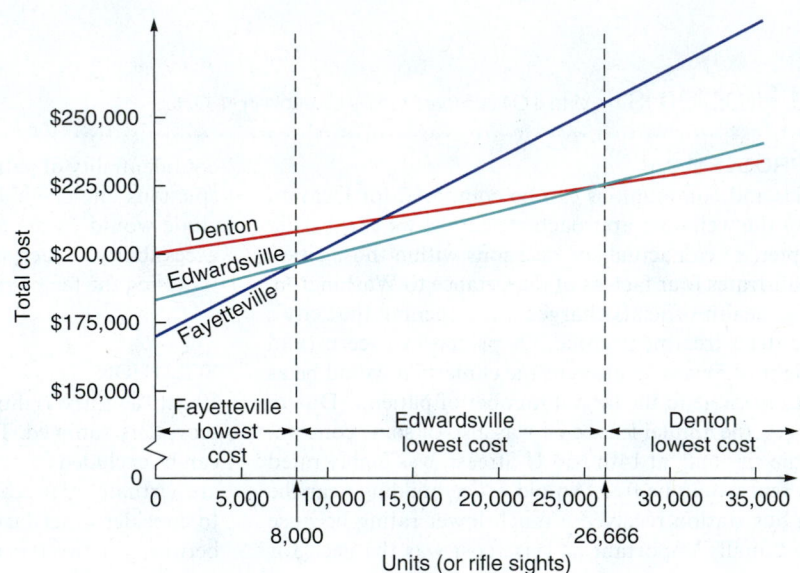

Figure 8.5

Graph of Total Cost Lines for Ching-Chang Kuo

SOLVED PROBLEM 8.3

The Metropolis Public Library plans to expand with its first major branch library in the city's growing north side. The branch will serve six census tracts. Here are the coordinates of each tract and the population within it:

CENSUS TRACT	CENTER OF TRACT	POPULATION IN TRACT
503—Logan Square	(3, 4)	45,000
519—Albany Park	(4, 5)	25,000
522—Rogers Park	(3, 6)	62,000
538—Kentwood	(4, 7)	51,000
540—Roosevelt	(2, 3)	32,000
561—Western	(5, 2)	29,000

Using the center-of-gravity method, what should be the coordinate location of the branch library?

SOLUTION

$$x\text{-coordinate} = \frac{\sum_i x_i Q_i}{\sum_i Q_i} = \frac{3(45{,}000) + 4(25{,}000) + 3(62{,}000) + 4(51{,}000) + 2(32{,}000) + 5(29{,}000)}{244{,}000} = 3.42$$

$$y\text{-coordinate} = \frac{\sum_i y_i Q_i}{\sum_i Q_i} = \frac{4(45{,}000) + 5(25{,}000) + 6(62{,}000) + 7(51{,}000) + 3(32{,}000) + 2(29{,}000)}{244{,}000} = 4.87$$

The new branch library will sit just west of Logan Square and Rogers Park, at the (3.42, 4.87) tract location.

Problems   Note: **PX** means the problem may be solved with POM for Windows and/or Excel OM.

Problems 8.1–8.4 relate to Factors That Affect Location Decisions

· **8.1** In Myanmar (formerly Burma), 6 laborers, each making the equivalent of $3 per day, can produce 40 units per day. In rural China, 10 laborers, each making the equivalent of $2 per day, can produce 45 units. In Billings, Montana, 2 laborers, each making $60 per day, can make 100 units. Based on labor costs only, which location would be most economical to produce the item?

· **8.2** Refer to Problem 8.1. Shipping cost from Myanmar to Denver, Colorado, the final destination, is $1.50 per unit. Shipping cost from China to Denver is $1 per unit, while the shipping cost from Billings to Denver is $.25 per unit. Considering both labor and transportation costs, which is the most favorable production location?

·· **8.3** You have been asked to analyze the bids for 200 polished disks used in solar panels. These bids have been submitted by three suppliers: Thailand Polishing, India Shine, and Sacramento Glow. Thailand Polishing has submitted a bid of 2,000 baht. India Shine has submitted a bid of 2,000 rupees. Sacramento Glow has submitted a bid of $200. You check with your local bank and find that $1 = 10 baht and $1 = 8 rupees. Which company should you choose?

· **8.4** Refer to Problem 8.3. If the final destination is New Delhi, India, and there is a 30% import tax, which firm should you choose?

Problems 8.5–8.34 relate to Methods of Evaluating Location Alternatives

·· **8.5** Subway, with more than 25,000 outlets in the U.S., is planning for a new restaurant in Buffalo, New York. Three locations are being considered. The following table gives the factors for each site.

FACTOR	WEIGHT	MAITLAND	BAPTIST CHURCH	NORTHSIDE MALL
Space	.30	60	70	80
Costs	.25	40	80	30
Traffic density	.20	50	80	60
Neighborhood income	.15	50	70	40
Zoning laws	.10	80	20	90

a) At which site should Subway open the new restaurant?
b) If the weights for Space and Traffic density are reversed, how would this affect the decision? **PX**

· **8.6** Ken Gilbert owns the Knoxville Warriors, a minor league baseball team in Tennessee. He wishes to move the Warriors south, to either Mobile (Alabama) or Jackson (Mississippi). The table below gives the factors that Gilbert thinks are important, their weights, and the scores for Mobile and Jackson.

FACTOR	WEIGHT	MOBILE	JACKSON
Incentive	.4	80	60
Player satisfaction	.3	20	50
Sports interest	.2	40	90
Size of city	.1	70	30

a) Which site should he select?
b) Jackson just raised its incentive package, and the new score is 75. Why doesn't this impact your decision in part (a)? **PX**

Andrea Catenaro/Shutterstock

·· **8.7** Northeastern Insurance Company is considering opening an office in the U.S. The two cities under consideration are Philadelphia and New York. The factor ratings (higher scores are better) for the two cities are given in the following table. In which city should Northeastern locate?

FACTOR	WEIGHT	PHILADELPHIA	NEW YORK
Customer convenience	.25	70	80
Bank accessibility	.20	40	90
Computer support	.20	85	75
Rental costs	.15	90	55
Labor costs	.10	80	50
Taxes	.10	90	50

•• 8.8 Marilyn Helm Retailers is attempting to decide on a location for a new retail outlet. At the moment, the firm has three alternatives—stay where it is but enlarge the facility; locate along the main street in nearby Newbury; or locate in a new shopping mall in Hyde Park. The company has selected the four factors listed in the following table as the basis for evaluation and has assigned weights as shown:

FACTOR	FACTOR DESCRIPTION	WEIGHT
1	Average community income	.30
2	Community growth potential	.15
3	Availability of public transportation	.20
4	Labor availability, attitude, and cost	.35

Helm has rated each location for each factor, on a 100-point basis. These ratings are given below:

	LOCATION		
FACTOR	PRESENT LOCATION	NEWBURY	HYDE PARK
1	40	60	50
2	20	20	80
3	30	60	50
4	80	50	50

a) What should Helm do?

b) A new subway station is scheduled to open across the street from the present location in about a month, so its third factor score should be raised to 40. How does this change your answer? **Px**

•• 8.9 A location analysis for Cook Controls, a small manufacturer of parts for high-technology cable systems, has been narrowed down to four locations. Cook will need to train assemblers, testers, and robotics maintainers in local training centers. Lori Cook, the president, has asked each potential site to offer training programs, tax breaks, and other industrial incentives. The critical factors, their weights, and the ratings for each location are shown in the following table. High scores represent favorable values.

		LOCATION			
FACTOR	WEIGHT	AKRON, OH	BILOXI, MS	CARTHAGE, TX	DENVER, CO
Labor availability	.15	90	80	90	80
Technical school quality	.10	95	75	65	85
Operating cost	.30	80	85	95	85
Land and construction cost	.15	60	80	90	70
Industrial incentives	.20	90	75	85	60
Labor cost	.10	75	80	85	75

a) Compute the composite (weighted average) rating for each location.

b) Which site would you choose?

c) Would you reach the same conclusion if the weights for operating cost and labor cost were reversed? Recompute as necessary and explain. **Px**

••• 8.10 Pan American Refineries, headquartered in Houston, must decide among three sites for the construction of a new oil-processing center. The firm has selected the six factors listed

below as a basis for evaluation and has assigned rating weights from 1 to 5 on each factor:

FACTOR	FACTOR NAME	RATING WEIGHT
1	Proximity to port facilities	5
2	Power-source availability and cost	3
3	Workforce attitude and cost	4
4	Distance from Houston	2
5	Community desirability	2
6	Equipment suppliers in area	3

Subhajit Chakraborty, the CEO, has rated each location for each factor on a 1- to 100-point basis.

FACTOR	LOCATION A	LOCATION B	LOCATION C
1	100	80	80
2	80	70	100
3	30	60	70
4	10	80	60
5	90	60	80
6	50	60	90

a) Which site will be recommended based on *total* weighted scores?

b) If location B's score for Proximity to port facilities was reset at 90, how would the result change?

c) What score would location B need on Proximity to port facilities to change its ranking? **Px**

•• 8.11 A company is planning on expanding and building a new plant in one of three Southeast Asian countries. Chris Ellis, the manager charged with making the decision, has determined that five key success factors can be used to evaluate the prospective countries. Ellis used a rating system of 1 (least desirable country) to 5 (most desirable) to evaluate each factor.

KEY SUCCESS FACTOR	WEIGHT	CANDIDATE COUNTRY RATINGS		
		TAIWAN	THAILAND	SINGAPORE
Technology	0.2	4	5	1
Level of education	0.1	4	1	5
Political and legal aspects	0.4	1	3	3
Social and cultural aspects	0.1	4	2	3
Economic factors	0.2	3	3	2

a) Which country should be selected for the new plant?

b) Political unrest in Thailand results in a lower score, 2, for Political and legal aspects. Does your conclusion change?

c) What if Thailand's score drops even further, to a 1, for Political and legal aspects? **Px**

• 8.12 Harden College is contemplating opening a European campus where students from the main campus could go to take courses for 1 of the 4 college years. At the moment, it is considering five countries: The Netherlands, Great Britain, Italy, Belgium, and Greece. The college wishes to consider eight factors in its decision. The first two factors are given weights of 0.2, while the rest are assigned weights of 0.1. The following table illustrates its assessment of each factor for each country (5 is best).

FACTOR	FACTOR DESCRIPTION	THE NETHERLANDS	GREAT BRITAIN	ITALY	BELGIUM	GREECE
1	Stability of government	5	5	3	5	4
2	Degree to which the population can converse in English	4	5	3	4	3
3	Stability of the monetary system	5	4	3	4	3
4	Communications infrastructure	4	5	3	4	3
5	Transportation infrastructure	5	5	3	5	3
6	Availability of historic/cultural sites	3	4	5	3	5
7	Import restrictions	4	4	3	4	4
8	Availability of suitable quarters	4	4	3	4	3

a) In which country should Harden College choose to set up its European campus?

b) How would the decision change if the "degree to which the population can converse in English" was not an issue? **Px**

•• **8.13** Daniel Tracy, owner of Martin Manufacturing, must expand by building a new factory. The search for a location for this factory has been narrowed to four sites: A, B, C, or D. The following table shows the results thus far obtained by Tracy by using the factor-rating method to analyze the problem. The scale used for each factor scoring is 1 through 5.

FACTOR	WEIGHT	SITE SCORES A	B	C	D
Quality of labor	10	5	4	4	5
Construction cost	8	2	3	4	1
Transportation costs	8	3	4	3	2
Proximity to markets	7	5	3	4	4
Taxes	6	2	3	3	4
Weather	6	2	5	5	4
Energy costs	5	5	4	3	3

a) Which site should Tracy choose?

b) If site D's score for Energy costs increases from a 3 to a 5, do results change?

c) If site A's Weather score is adjusted to a 4, what is the impact? What should Tracy do at this point? **Px**

••• **8.14** An American consulting firm is planning to expand globally by opening a new office in one of four countries: Germany, Italy, Spain, or Greece. The chief partner entrusted with the decision, L. Wayne Shell, has identified eight key success factors that he views as essential for the success of any consultancy. He used a rating system of 1 (least desirable country) to 5 (most desirable) to evaluate each factor.

KEY SUCCESS FACTOR	WEIGHT	CANDIDATE COUNTRY RATINGS GERMANY	ITALY	SPAIN	GREECE
Level of education					
Number of consultants	.05	5	5	5	2
National literacy rate	.05	4	2	1	1
Political aspects					
Stability of government	0.2	5	5	5	2
Product liability laws	0.2	5	2	3	5
Environmental regulations	0.2	1	4	1	3
Social and cultural aspects					
Similarity in language	0.1	4	2	1	1
Acceptability of consultants	0.1	1	4	4	3
Economic factors					
Incentives	0.1	2	3	1	5

a) Which country should be selected for the new office?

b) If Spain's score were lowered in the Stability of government factor, to a 4, how would its overall score change? On this factor, at what score for Spain *would* the rankings change? **Px**

•• **8.15** A British hospital chain wishes to make its first entry into the U.S. market by building a medical facility in the Midwest, a region with which its director, Doug Moodie, is comfortable because he got his medical degree at Northwestern University. After a preliminary analysis, four cities are chosen for further consideration. They are rated and weighted according to the factors shown below:

FACTOR	WEIGHT	CITY CHICAGO	MILWAUKEE	MADISON	DETROIT
Costs	2.0	8	5	6	7
Need for a facility	1.5	4	9	8	4
Staff availability	1.0	7	6	4	7
Local incentives	0.5	8	6	5	9

a) Which city should Moodie select?

b) Assume a minimum score of 5 is now required for all factors. Which city should be chosen? **Px**

•• **8.16** The fixed and variable costs for three potential manufacturing plant sites for a rattan chair weaver are shown:

SITE	FIXED COST PER YEAR	VARIABLE COST PER UNIT
1	$ 500	$11
2	1,000	7
3	1,700	4

a) Over what range of production is each location optimal?

b) For a production of 200 units, which site is best? **Px**

• **8.17** Peter Billington Stereo, Inc., supplies car radios to auto manufacturers and is going to open a new plant. The company is undecided between Detroit and Dallas as the site. The fixed costs in Dallas are lower due to cheaper land costs, but the variable costs in Dallas are higher because shipping distances would increase. Given the following costs:

COST	DALLAS	DETROIT
Fixed costs	$600,000	$800,000
Variable costs	$28/radio	$22/radio

a) Perform an analysis of the volume over which each location is preferable.
b) How does your answer change if Dallas's fixed costs increase by 10%? **Px**

• • • 8.18 Hyundai Motors is considering three sites—A, B, and C—at which to locate a factory to build its new-model automobile, the Hyundai Sport C150. The goal is to locate at a minimum-cost site, where cost is measured by the annual fixed plus variable costs of production. Hyundai Motors has gathered the following data:

SITE	ANNUALIZED FIXED COST	VARIABLE COST PER AUTO PRODUCED
A	$10,000,000	$2,500
B	$20,000,000	$2,000
C	$25,000,000	$1,000

The firm knows it will produce between 0 and 60,000 Sport C150s at the new plant each year, but, thus far, that is the extent of its knowledge about production plans.
a) For what values of volume, V, of production, if any, is site C a recommended site?
b) What volume indicates site A is optimal?
c) Over what range of volume is site B optimal? Why? **Px**

• • 8.19 Peggy Lane Corp., a producer of machine tools, wants to move to a larger site. Two alternative locations have been identified: Bonham and McKinney. Bonham would have fixed costs of $800,000 per year and variable costs of $14,000 per standard unit produced. McKinney would have annual fixed costs of $920,000 and variable costs of $13,000 per standard unit. The finished items sell for $29,000 each.
a) At what volume of output would the two locations have the same profit?
b) For what range of output would Bonham be superior (have higher profits)?
c) For what range would McKinney be superior?
d) What is the relevance of break-even points for these cities? **Px**

• • 8.20 The following table gives the map coordinates and the shipping loads for a set of cities that we wish to connect through a central hub.

CITY	MAP COORDINATE (X, Y)	SHIPPING LOAD
A	(5, 10)	5
B	(6, 8)	10
C	(4, 9)	15
D	(9, 5)	5
E	(7, 9)	15
F	(3, 2)	10
G	(2, 6)	5

a) Near which map coordinates should the hub be located?
b) If the shipments from city A triple, how does this change the coordinates? **Px**

• • 8.21 A chain of home health care firms in Louisiana needs to locate a central office from which to conduct internal audits and other periodic reviews of its facilities. These facilities are scattered throughout the state, as detailed in the following table. Each site, except for Houma, will be visited three times each year by a team of workers, who will drive from the central office to the site. Houma will be visited five times a year. Which coordinates represent a good central location for this office? What other factors might influence the office location decision? Where would you place this office? Explain. **Px**

CITY	MAP COORDINATES	
	x	y
Covington	9.2	3.5
Donaldsonville	7.3	2.5
Houma	7.8	1.4
Monroe	5.0	8.4
Natchitoches	2.8	6.5
New Iberia	5.5	2.4
Opelousas	5.0	3.6
Ruston	3.8	8.5

• • 8.22 A small rural county has experienced unprecedented growth over the past 6 years, and as a result, the local school district built the new 500-student North Park Elementary School. The district has three older and smaller elementary schools: Washington, Jefferson, and Lincoln. Now the growth pressure is being felt at the secondary level. The school district would like to build a centrally located middle school to accommodate students and reduce busing costs. The older middle school is adjacent to the high school and will become part of the high school campus.
a) What are the coordinates of the central location?
b) What other factors should be considered before building a school? **Px**

• • 8.23 Todd's Direct, a major TV sales chain headquartered in New Orleans, is about to open its first outlet in Mobile, Alabama, and wants to select a site that will place the new outlet in the center of Mobile's population base. Todd examines the seven census tracts in Mobile, plots the coordinates of the center of each from a map, and looks up the population base in each to use as a weighting. The information gathered appears in the following table.

CENSUS TRACT	POPULATION IN CENSUS TRACT	X, Y MAP COORDINATES
101	2,000	(25, 45)
102	5,000	(25, 25)
103	10,000	(55, 45)
104	7,000	(50, 20)
105	10,000	(80, 50)
106	20,000	(70, 20)
107	14,000	(90, 25)

a) At what center-of-gravity coordinates should the new store be located?

b) Census tracts 103 and 105 are each projected to grow by 20% in the next year. How will this influence the new store's coordinates? **Px**

•••• **8.24** Eagle Electronics must expand by building a second facility. The search has been narrowed down to locating the new facility in one of four cities: Atlanta (A), Baltimore (B), Chicago (C), or Dallas (D). The factors, scores, and weights follow:

I	FACTOR	WEIGHT (W_i)	SCORES BY SITE			
			A	B	C	D
1	Labor quality	20	5	4	4	5
2	Quality of life	16	2	3	4	1
3	Transportation	16	3	4	3	2
4	Proximity to markets	14	5	3	4	4
5	Proximity to suppliers	12	2	3	3	4
6	Taxes	12	2	5	5	4
7	Energy supplies	10	5	4	3	3

a) Using the factor-rating method, what is the recommended site for Eagle Electronics's new facility?

b) For what range of values for the weight (currently $w_7 = 10$) does the site given as the answer to part (a) remain a recommended site?

•••• **8.25** The EU has made changes in airline regulation that dramatically affect major European carriers such as British International Air (BIA), KLM, Air France, Alitalia, and Swiss International Air. With ambitious expansion plans, BIA has decided it needs a second service hub on the continent, to complement its large Heathrow (London) repair facility. The location selection is critical, and with the potential for 4,000 new skilled blue-collar jobs on the line, virtually every city in western Europe is actively bidding for BIA's business.

After initial investigations by Holmes Miller, head of the Operations Department, BIA has narrowed the list to 9 cities. Each is then rated on 12 factors, as shown in the table below.

a) Help Miller rank the top three cities that BIA should consider as its new site for servicing aircraft.

b) After further investigation, Miller decides that an existing set of hangar facilities for repairs is not nearly as important as earlier thought. If he lowers the weight of that factor to 30, does the ranking change?

c) After Miller makes the change in part (b), Germany announces it has reconsidered its offer of financial incentives, with an additional 200-million-euro package to entice BIA. Accordingly, BIA has raised Germany's rating to 10 on that factor. Is there any change in top rankings in part (b)? **Px**

> *Additional problems* **8.26–8.34** *are available in* MyOMLab.

DATA FOR PROBLEM 8.25		LOCATION								
		ITALY			FRANCE			GERMANY		
FACTOR	IMPORTANCE WEIGHT	MILAN	ROME	GENOA	PARIS	LYON	NICE	MUNICH	BONN	BERLIN
Financial incentives	85	8	8	8	7	7	7	7	7	7
Skilled labor pool	80	4	6	5	9	9	7	10	8	9
Existing facility	70	5	3	2	9	6	5	9	9	2
Wage rates	70	9	8	9	4	6	6	4	5	5
Competition for jobs	70	7	3	8	2	8	7	4	8	9
Ease of air traffic access	65	5	4	6	2	8	8	4	8	9
Real estate cost	40	6	4	7	4	6	6	3	4	5
Communication links	25	6	7	6	9	9	9	10	9	8
Attractiveness to relocating executives	15	4	8	3	9	6	6	2	3	3
Political considerations	10	6	6	6	8	8	8	8	8	8
Expansion possibilities	10	10	2	8	1	5	4	4	5	6
Union strength	10	1	1	1	5	5	5	6	6	6

CASE STUDIES

Southern Recreational Vehicle Company

In October 2015, the top management of Southern Recreational Vehicle Company of St. Louis, Missouri, announced its plans to relocate its manufacturing and assembly operations to a new plant in Ridgecrest, Mississippi. The firm, a major producer of pickup campers and camper trailers, had experienced 5 consecutive years of declining profits as a result of spiraling production costs. The costs of labor and raw materials had increased alarmingly, utility costs had gone up sharply, and taxes and transportation expenses had steadily climbed upward. Despite increased sales, the company suffered its first net loss since operations were begun in 1982.

When management initially considered relocation, it closely scrutinized several geographic areas. Of primary importance to the relocation decision were the availability of adequate transportation facilities, state and municipal tax structures, an adequate labor supply, positive community attitudes, reasonable site costs, and financial inducements. Although several communities offered essentially the same incentives, the management of Southern Recreational Vehicle Company was favorably impressed by the efforts of the Mississippi Power and Light Company to attract "clean, labor-intensive" industry and the enthusiasm exhibited by state and local officials, who actively sought to bolster the state's economy by enticing manufacturing firms to locate within its boundaries.

Two weeks prior to the announcement, management of Southern Recreational Vehicle Company finalized its relocation plans. An existing building in Ridgecrest's industrial park was selected (the physical facility had previously housed a mobile home manufacturer that had gone bankrupt due to inadequate financing and poor management); initial recruiting was begun through the state employment office; and efforts to lease or sell the St. Louis property were initiated. Among the inducements offered Southern Recreational Vehicle Company to locate in Ridgecrest were:

1. Exemption from county and municipal taxes for 5 years
2. Free water and sewage services
3. Construction of a second loading dock—free of cost—at the industrial site

4. An agreement to issue $500,000 in industrial bonds for future expansion
5. Public-financed training of workers in a local industrial trade school

In addition to these inducements, other factors weighed heavily in the decision to locate in the small Mississippi town. Labor costs would be significantly less than those incurred in St. Louis; organized labor was not expected to be as powerful (Mississippi is a right-to-work state); and utility costs and taxes would be moderate. All in all, the management of Southern Recreational Vehicle Company felt that its decision was sound.

On October 15, the following announcement was attached to each employee's paycheck:

To: Employees of Southern Recreational Vehicle Company

From: Gerald O'Brian, President

The Management of Southern Recreational Vehicle Company regretfully announces its plans to cease all manufacturing operations in St. Louis on December 31. Because of increased operating costs and the unreasonable demands forced upon the company by the union, it has become impossible to operate profitably. I sincerely appreciate the fine service that each of you has rendered to the company during the past years. If I can be of assistance in helping you find suitable employment with another firm, please let me know. Thank you again for your cooperation and past service.

Discussion Questions

1. Evaluate the inducements offered Southern Recreational Vehicle Company by community leaders in Ridgecrest, Mississippi.
2. What problems would a company experience in relocating its executives from a heavily populated industrialized area to a small rural town?
3. Evaluate the reasons cited by O'Brian for relocation. Are they justifiable?
4. What legal and ethical responsibilities does a firm have to its employees when a decision to cease operations is made?

Source: Reprinted by permission of Professor Jerry Kinard, Western Carolina University.

Locating the Next Red Lobster Restaurant

Video Case

From its first Red Lobster in 1968, the chain has grown to 705 locations, with over $2.6 billion in U.S. sales annually. The casual dining market may be crowded, with competitors such as Chili's, Ruby Tuesday, Applebee's, TGI Friday's, and Outback, but Red Lobster's continuing success means the chain thinks there is still plenty of room to grow. Robert Reiner, director of market development, is charged with identifying the sites that will maximize new store sales without cannibalizing sales at the existing Red Lobster locations.

Characteristics for identifying a good site have not changed in 40 years; they still include real estate prices, customer age, competition, ethnicity, income, family size, population density, nearby hotels, and buying behavior, to name just a few. What *has* changed is the powerful software that allows Reiner to analyze a

new site in 5 minutes, as opposed to the 8 hours he spent just a few years ago.

Red Lobster has partnered with MapInfo Corp., whose geographic information system (GIS) contains a powerful module for analyzing a trade area (see the discussion of GIS in the chapter). With the U.S. geo-coded down to the individual block, MapInfo allows Reiner to create a psychographic profile of existing and potential Red Lobster trade areas. "We can now target areas with greatest sales potential," says Reiner.

The U.S. is segmented into 72 "clusters" of customer profiles by MapInfo. If, for example, cluster #7, Equestrian Heights (see MapInfo description below), represents 1.7% of a household base within a Red Lobster trade area, but this segment also accounts for 2.4% of sales, Reiner computes that this segment is effectively spending 1.39 times more than average (Index = 2.4/1.7) and adjusts his analysis of a new site to reflect this added weight.

CLUSTER	PSYTE 2003	SNAP SHOT DESCRIPTION
7	Equestrian Heights	They may not have a stallion in the barn, but they likely pass a corral on the way home. These families with teens live in older, larger homes adjacent to, or between, suburbs but not usually tract housing. Most are married with teenagers, but 40% are empty nesters. They use their graduate and professional school education—56% are dual earners. Over 90% are white, non-Hispanic. Their mean family income is $99,000, and they live within commuting distance of central cities. They have white-collar jobs during the week but require a riding lawn mower to keep the place up on weekends.

When Reiner maps the U.S., a state, or a region for a new site, he wants one that is at least 3 miles from the nearest Red Lobster and won't negatively impact its sales by more than 8%; MapInfo pinpoints the best spot. The software also recognizes the nearness of non-Red Lobster competition and assigns a probability of success (as measured by reaching sales potential).

The specific spot selected depends on Red Lobster's seven real estate brokers, whose list of considerations include proximity to a vibrant retail area, proximity to a freeway, road visibility, nearby hotels, and a corner location at a primary intersection.

"Picking a new Red Lobster location is one of the most critical functions we can do," says Reiner. "And the software we use serves as an independent voice in assessing the quality of an existing or proposed location."

Discussion Questions*

1. Visit the Web site for PSTYE 2003 (**www.gemapping.com /downloads/targetpro_brochure.pdf**). Describe the psychological profiling (PSYTE) clustering system. Select an industry, other than restaurants, and explain how the software can be used for that industry.

2. What are the major differences in site location for a restaurant versus a retail store versus a manufacturing plant?

3. Red Lobster also defines its trade areas based on market size and population density. Here are its seven density classes:

DENSITY CLASS	DESCRIPTION	HOUSEHOLDS PER SQ. MILE
1	Super Urban	8,000+
2	Urban	4,000–7,999
3	Light Urban	2,000–3,999
4	First Tier Suburban	1,000–1,999
5	Second Tier Suburban	600–999
6	Exurban/Small	100–599
7	Rural	0–99

Note: Density classes are based on the households and land area within 3 miles of the geography (e.g., census tract) using population-weighted centroids.

The majority (92%) of the Red Lobster restaurants fall into three of these classes. Which three classes do you think the chain has the most restaurants in? Why?

*You may wish to view the video that accompanies this case before answering the questions.

Where to Place the Hard Rock Cafe

Video Case

Some people would say that Oliver Munday, Hard Rock's vice president for cafe development, has the best job in the world. Travel the world to pick a country for Hard Rock's next cafe, select a city, and find the ideal site. It's true that selecting a site involves lots of incognito walking around, visiting nice restaurants, and drinking in bars. But that is not where Mr. Munday's work begins, nor where it ends. At the front end, selecting the country and city first involves a great deal of research. At the back end, Munday not only picks the final site and negotiates the deal but then works with architects and planners and stays with the project through the opening and first year's sales.

Munday is currently looking heavily into global expansion in Europe, Latin America, and Asia. "We've got to look at political risk, currency, and social norms—how does our brand fit into the country," he says. Once the country is selected, Munday focuses on the region and city. His research checklist is extensive, as seen in the accompanying table.

Site location now tends to focus on the tremendous resurgence of "city centers," where nightlife tends to concentrate. That's what Munday selected in Moscow and Bogota, although in both locations he chose to find a local partner and franchise the operation. In these two political environments, "Hard Rock wouldn't dream of operating by ourselves," says Munday. The location decision also is at least a 10- to 15-year commitment by Hard Rock, which employs tools such as locational cost–volume

Hard Rock's Standard Market Report (for offshore sites)

A. Demographics (local, city, region, SMSA), with trend analysis
  1. Population of area
  2. Economic indicators
B. Visitor market, with trend analysis
  1. Tourists/business visitors
  2. Hotels
  3. Convention center
  4. Entertainment
  5. Sports
  6. Retail
C. Transportation
  1. Airport
  2. Rail
  3. Road
  4. Sea/river
D. Restaurants and nightclubs (a selection in key target market areas)
E. Political risk
F. Real estate market
G. Hard Rock Cafe comparable market analysis

subcategories include:
(a) age of airport
(b) no. of passengers
(c) airlines
(d) direct flights
(e) hubs

analysis to help decide whether to purchase land and build, or to remodel an existing facility.

Currently, Munday is considering four European cities for Hard Rock's next expansion. Although he could not provide the names, for competitive reasons, the following is known:

FACTOR	EUROPEAN CITY UNDER CONSIDERATION				IMPORTANCE OF THIS FACTOR AT THIS TIME
	A	B	C	D	
A. Demographics	70	70	60	90	20
B. Visitor market	80	60	90	75	20
C. Transportation	100	50	75	90	20
D. Restaurants/ nightclubs	80	90	65	65	10
E. Low political risk	90	60	50	70	10
F. Real estate market	65	75	85	70	10
G. Comparable market analysis	70	60	65	80	10

Discussion Questions*

1. From Munday's Standard Market Report checklist, select any other four categories, such as population (A1), hotels (B2), or restaurants/nightclubs (D), and provide three subcategories that should be evaluated. (See item C1 [airport] for a guide.)
2. Which is the highest rated of the four European cities under consideration, using the table?
3. Why does Hard Rock put such serious effort into its location analysis?
4. Under what conditions do you think Hard Rock prefers to franchise a cafe?

*You may wish to view the video case before answering the questions.

- **Additional Case Study:** Visit MyOMLab for this free case study:
Southwestern University (E): The university faces three choices as to where to locate its football stadium.

Endnote

1. Equations (8-1) and (8-2) compute a center of gravity (COG) under "squared Euclidean" distances and may actually result in transportation costs slightly (less than 2%) higher than an *optimal* COG computed using "Euclidean" (straight-line) distances. The latter, however, is a more complex and involved procedure mathematically, so the formulas we present are generally used as an attractive substitute. See C. Kuo and R. E. White, "A Note on the Treatment of the Center-of-Gravity Method in Operations Management Textbooks," *Decision Sciences Journal of Innovative Education* 2: 219–227.

Main Heading	Review Material	MyOMLab
THE STRATEGIC IMPORTANCE OF LOCATION (pp. 340–341)	Location has a major impact on the overall risk and profit of the company. Transportation costs alone can total as much as 25% of the product's selling price. When all costs are considered, location may alter total operating expenses as much as 50%. Companies make location decisions relatively infrequently, usually because demand has outgrown the current plant's capacity or because of changes in labor productivity, exchange rates, costs, or local attitudes. Companies may also relocate their manufacturing or service facilities because of shifts in demographics and customer demand. Location options include (1) expanding an existing facility instead of moving, (2) maintaining current sites while adding another facility elsewhere, and (3) closing the existing facility and moving to another location. For industrial location decisions, the location strategy is usually minimizing costs. For retail and professional service organizations, the strategy focuses on maximizing revenue. Warehouse location strategy may be driven by a combination of cost and speed of delivery. *The objective of location strategy is to maximize the benefit of location to the firm.* When innovation is the focus, overall competitiveness and innovation are affected by (1) the presence of high-quality and specialized inputs such as scientific and technical talent, (2) an environment that encourages investment and intense local rivalry, (3) pressure and insight gained from a sophisticated local market, and (4) local presence of related and supporting industries.	Concept Questions: 1.1–1.4 **VIDEO 8.1** Hard Rock's Location Selection
FACTORS THAT AFFECT LOCATION DECISIONS (pp. 341–344)	Globalization has taken place because of the development of (1) market economics; (2) better international communications; (3) more rapid, reliable travel and shipping; (4) ease of capital flow between countries; and (5) large differences in labor costs. Labor cost per unit is sometimes called the *labor content* of the product: Labor cost per unit = Labor cost per day ÷ Production (that is, units per day) Sometimes firms can take advantage of a particularly favorable exchange rate by relocating or exporting to (or importing from) a foreign country. ■ **Tangible costs**—Readily identifiable costs that can be measured with some precision. ■ **Intangible costs**—A category of location costs that cannot be easily quantified, such as quality of life and government. Many service organizations find that proximity to market is *the* primary location factor. Firms locate near their raw materials and suppliers because of (1) perishability, (2) transportation costs, or (3) bulk. ■ **Clustering**—Location of competing companies near each other, often because of a critical mass of information, talent, venture capital, or natural resources.	Concept Questions: 2.1–2.4 Problems: 8.1–8.4
METHODS OF EVALUATING LOCATION ALTERNATIVES (pp. 344–350)	■ **Factor-rating method**—A location method that instills objectivity into the process of identifying hard-to-evaluate costs. The six steps of the factor-rating method are: 1. Develop a list of relevant factors called *key success factors*. 2. Assign a weight to each factor to reflect its relative importance in the company's objectives. 3. Develop a scale for each factor (for example, 1 to 10 or 1 to 100 points). 4. Have management score each location for each factor, using the scale in step 3. 5. Multiply the score by the weight for each factor and total the score for each location. 6. Make a recommendation based on the maximum point score, considering the results of other quantitative approaches as well. ■ **Locational cost–volume analysis**—A method used to make an economic comparison of location alternatives. The three steps to locational cost–volume analysis are: 1. Determine the fixed and variable cost for each location. 2. Plot the costs for each location, with costs on the vertical axis of the graph and annual volume on the horizontal axis. 3. Select the location that has the lowest total cost for the expected production volume.	Concept Questions: 3.1–3.4 Problems: 8.5–8.34 Virtual Office Hours for Solved Problems: 8.1, 8.2 **ACTIVE** MODEL 8.1

Main Heading	Review Material	MyOMLab
	■ **Center-of-gravity method**—A mathematical technique used for finding the best location for a single distribution point that services several stores or areas. The center-of-gravity method chooses the ideal location that minimizes the *weighted* distance between itself and the locations it serves, where the distance is weighted by the number of containers shipped, Q_i: $$x\text{-coordinate of the center of gravity} = \sum_i x_i Q_i \div \sum_i Q_i \qquad (8\text{-}1)$$ $$y\text{-coordinate of the center of gravity} = \sum_i y_i Q_i \div \sum_i Q_i \qquad (8\text{-}2)$$ ■ **Transportation model**—A technique for solving a class of linear programming problems. The transportation model determines the best pattern of shipments from several points of supply to several points of demand to minimize total production and transportation costs.	Virtual Office Hours for Solved Problem: 8.3
SERVICE LOCATION STRATEGY (pp. 350–351)	The eight major determinants of volume and revenue for the service firm are: 1. Purchasing power of the customer-drawing area 2. Service and image compatibility with demographics of the customer-drawing area 3. Competition in the area 4. Quality of the competition 5. Uniqueness of the firm's and competitors' locations 6. Physical qualities of facilities and neighboring businesses 7. Operating policies of the firm 8. Quality of management	Concept Questions: 4.1–4.4
GEOGRAPHIC INFORMATION SYSTEMS (pp. 351–353)	■ **Geographic information system (GIS)**—A system that stores and displays information that can be linked to a geographic location. Some of the geographic databases available in many GISs include (1) census data by block, tract, city, county, congressional district, metropolitan area, state, and zip code; (2) maps of every street, highway, bridge, and tunnel in the U.S.; (3) utilities such as electrical, water, and gas lines; (4) all rivers, mountains, lakes, and forests; and (5) all major airports, colleges, and hospitals.	Concept Questions: 5.1–5.4 **VIDEO 8.2** Locating the Next Red Lobster Restaurant

Self Test

■ **Before taking the self-test,** refer to the learning objectives listed at the beginning of the chapter and the key terms listed at the end of the chapter.

LO 8.1 The factors involved in location decisions include
  a) foreign exchange.
  b) attitudes.
  c) labor productivity.
  d) all of the above.

LO 8.2 If Fender Guitar pays $30 per day to a worker in its Ensenada, Mexico, plant, and the employee completes four instruments per 8-hour day, the labor cost/unit is
  a) $30.00.
  b) $3.75.
  c) $7.50.
  d) $4.00.
  e) $8.00.

LO 8.3 Evaluating location alternatives by comparing their composite (weighted-average) scores involves
  a) factor-rating analysis.
  b) cost–volume analysis.
  c) transportation model analysis.
  d) linear regression analysis.
  e) crossover analysis.

LO 8.4 On the cost–volume analysis chart where the costs of two or more location alternatives have been plotted, the quantity at which two cost curves cross is the quantity at which:

  a) fixed costs are equal for two alternative locations.
  b) variable costs are equal for two alternative locations.
  c) total costs are equal for all alternative locations.
  d) fixed costs equal variable costs for one location.
  e) total costs are equal for two alternative locations.

LO 8.5 A regional bookstore chain is about to build a distribution center that is centrally located for its eight retail outlets. It will most likely employ which of the following tools of analysis?
  a) Assembly-line balancing
  b) Load–distance analysis
  c) Center-of-gravity model
  d) Linear programming
  e) All of the above

LO 8.6 What is the major difference in focus between location decisions in the service sector and in the manufacturing sector?
  a) There is no difference in focus.
  b) The focus in manufacturing is revenue maximization, while the focus in service is cost minimization.
  c) The focus in service is revenue maximization, while the focus in manufacturing is cost minimization.
  d) The focus in manufacturing is on raw materials, while the focus in service is on labor.

Answers: LO 8.1. d; LO 8.2. c; LO 8.3. a; LO 8.4. e; LO 8.5. c; LO 8.6. c.

Layout Strategies

CHAPTER OUTLINE

GLOBAL COMPANY PROFILE: *McDonald's*

◆ The Strategic Importance of Layout Decisions *370*

◆ Types of Layout *370*

◆ Office Layout *371*

◆ Retail Layout *372*

◆ Warehouse and Storage Layouts *375*

◆ Fixed-Position Layout *377*

◆ Process-Oriented Layout *378*

◆ Work Cells *383*

◆ Repetitive and Product-Oriented Layout *386*

Alaska Airlines

Alaska Airlines

10 OM STRATEGY DECISIONS

- Design of Goods and Services
- Managing Quality
- Process Strategy
- Location Strategies
- *Layout Strategies*
- Human Resources
- Supply-Chain Management
- Inventory Management
- Scheduling
- Maintenance

McDonald's Looks for Competitive Advantage Through Layout

In its over half-century of existence, McDonald's has revolutionized the restaurant industry by inventing the limited-menu fast-food restaurant. It has also made seven major innovations. The first, the introduction of *indoor seating* (1950s), was a layout issue, as was the second, *drive-through windows* (1970s). The third, adding *breakfasts* to the menu (1980s), was a product strategy. The fourth, *adding play areas* (late 1980s), was again a layout decision.

In the 1990s, McDonald's completed its fifth innovation, a radically new *redesign of the kitchens* in its 14,000 North American outlets to facilitate a mass customization process. Dubbed the "Made by You" kitchen system, sandwiches were assembled to order with the revamped layout.

In 2004, the chain began the rollout of its sixth innovation, a new food ordering layout: the *self-service kiosk*. Self-service kiosks have been infiltrating the service sector since the introduction of ATMs in 1985 (there are over 1.5 million ATMs in banking). Alaska Airlines was the first airline to provide self-service airport check-in, in 1996. Most passengers of the major airlines now check themselves in for flights. Kiosks take up less space than an employee and reduce waiting line time.

Now, McDonald's is working on its seventh innovation, and not surprisingly, it also deals with restaurant layout. The company, on an unprecedented scale, is redesigning all 30,000 eateries around the globe to take on a *21st-century look*. The dining area will be separated into three sections with distinct personalities: (1) the "linger" zone focuses on young adults and offers

Rick Wilking/Corbis

McDonald's finds that kiosks reduce both space requirements and waiting; order taking is faster. An added benefit is that customers like them. Also, kiosks are reliable—they don't call in sick. And, most important, sales are up 10%–15% (an average of $1) when a customer orders from a kiosk, which consistently recommends the larger size and other extras.

The redesigned kitchen of a McDonald's in Manhattan. The more efficient layout requires less labor, reduces waste, and provides faster service. A graphic of this "assembly line" is shown in Figure 9.11.

comfortable furniture and Wi-Fi connections; (2) the "grab and go" zone features tall counters, bar stools, and flat-screen TVs; and (3) the "flexible" zone has colorful family booths, flexible seating, and kid-oriented music. The cost per outlet: a whopping $300,000–$400,000 renovation fee.

As McDonald's has discovered, facility layout is indeed a source of competitive advantage. ◀

Flexible Zone ▲

This area is geared for family and larger groups, with movable tables and chairs.

Grab & Go Zone ▲

This section has tall counters with bar stools for customers who eat alone. Flat-screen TVs keep them company.

Linger Zone ▲

Cozy booths, plus Wi-Fi connections, make these areas attractive to those who want to hang out and socialize.

LEARNING OBJECTIVES

LO 9.1 *Discuss* important issues in office layout 372

LO 9.2 *Define* the objectives of retail layout 374

LO 9.3 *Discuss* modern warehouse management and terms such as ASRS, cross-docking, and random stocking 3͞ ͞

LO 9.4 *Identify* when fixed-position layouts are appropriate 378

LO 9.5 *Explain* how to achieve a good process-oriented facility layout 379

LO 9.6 *Define* work cell and the requirements of a work cell 383

LO 9.7 *Define* product-oriented layout 386

LO 9.8 *Explain* how to balance production flow in a repetitive or product-oriented facility 387

The Strategic Importance of Layout Decisions

Layout is one of the key decisions that determines the long-run efficiency of operations. Layout has strategic implications because it establishes an organization's competitive priorities in regard to capacity, processes, flexibility, and cost, as well as quality of work life, customer contact, and image. An effective layout can help an organization achieve a strategy that supports differentiation, low cost, or response. Benetton, for example, supports a *differentiation* strategy by heavy investment in warehouse layouts that contribute to fast, accurate sorting and shipping to its 5,000 outlets. Walmart store layouts support a strategy of *low cost*, as do its warehouse layouts. Hallmark's office layouts, where many professionals operate with open communication in work cells, support *rapid development* of greeting cards. *The objective of layout strategy is to develop an effective and efficient layout that will meet the firm's competitive requirements.* These firms have done so.

In all cases, layout design must consider how to achieve the following:

♦ Higher utilization of space, equipment, and people
♦ Improved flow of information, materials, and people
♦ Improved employee morale and safer working conditions
♦ Improved customer/client interaction
♦ Flexibility (whatever the layout is now, it will need to change)

In our increasingly short-life-cycle, mass-customized world, layout designs need to be viewed as dynamic. This means considering small, movable, and flexible equipment. Store displays need to be movable, office desks and partitions modular, and warehouse racks prefabricated. To make quick and easy changes in product models and in production rates, operations managers must design flexibility into layouts. To obtain flexibility in layout, managers cross-train their workers, maintain equipment, keep investments low, place workstations close together, and use small, movable equipment. In some cases, equipment on wheels is appropriate, in anticipation of the next change in product, process, or volume.

Types of Layout

Layout decisions include the best placement of machines (in production settings), offices and desks (in office settings), or service centers (in settings such as hospitals or department stores). An effective layout facilitates the flow of materials, people, and information within and between areas. To achieve these objectives, a variety of approaches has been developed. We will discuss seven of them in this chapter:

1. *Office layout:* Positions workers, their equipment, and spaces/offices to provide for movement of information.
2. *Retail layout:* Allocates display space and responds to customer behavior.
3. *Warehouse layout:* Addresses trade-offs between space and material handling.
4. *Fixed-position layout:* Addresses the layout requirements of large, bulky projects such as ships and buildings.

TABLE 9.1	Layout Strategies		
	OBJECTIVES	**EXAMPLES**	
Office	Locate workers requiring frequent contact close to one another	Allstate Insurance Microsoft Corp.	
Retail	Expose customer to high-margin items	Kroger's Supermarket Walgreens Bloomingdale's	
Warehouse (storage)	Balance low-cost storage with low cost material handling	Federal-Mogul's warehouse The Gap's distribution center	
Project (fixed position)	Move material to the limited storage areas around the site	Ingall Ship Building Corp. Trump Plaza Pittsburgh Airport	
Job shop (process oriented)	Manage varied material flow for each product	Arnold Palmer Hospital Hard Rock Cafe Olive Garden	
Work cell (product families)	Identify a product family, build teams, cross-train team members	Hallmark Cards Wheeled Coach Ambulances	
Repetitive/continuous (product oriented)	Equalize the task time at each workstation	Sony's TV assembly line Toyota Scion	

5. *Process-oriented layout:* Deals with low-volume, high-variety production (also called "job shop," or intermittent production).
6. *Work-cell layout:* Arranges machinery and equipment to focus on production of a single product or group of related products.
7. *Product-oriented layout:* Seeks the best personnel and machine utilization in repetitive or continuous production.

Examples for each of these classes of layouts are noted in Table 9.1.

Because only a few of these seven classes can be modeled mathematically, layout and design of physical facilities are still something of an art. However, we do know that a good layout requires determining the following:

◆ *Material handling equipment:* Managers must decide about equipment to be used, including conveyors, cranes, automated storage and retrieval systems, and automatic carts to deliver and store material.

◆ *Capacity and space requirements:* Only when personnel, machines, and equipment requirements are known can managers proceed with layout and provide space for each component. In the case of office work, operations managers must make judgments about the space requirements for each employee. They must also consider allowances for requirements that address safety, noise, dust, fumes, temperature, and space around equipment and machines.

◆ *Environment and aesthetics:* Layout concerns often require decisions about windows, planters, and height of partitions to facilitate air flow, reduce noise, and provide privacy.

◆ *Flows of information:* Communication is important to any organization and must be facilitated by the layout. This issue may require decisions about proximity, as well as decisions about open spaces versus half-height dividers versus private offices.

◆ *Cost of moving between various work areas:* There may be unique considerations related to moving materials or to the importance of having certain areas next to each other. For example, moving molten steel is more difficult than moving cold steel.

Office Layout

Office layouts require the grouping of workers, their equipment, and spaces to provide for comfort, safety, and movement of information. The main distinction of office layouts is the importance placed on the flow of information. Office layouts are in constant flux as the technological changes sweeping society alter the way offices function.

Office layout

The grouping of workers, their equipment, and spaces/offices to provide for comfort, safety, and movement of information.

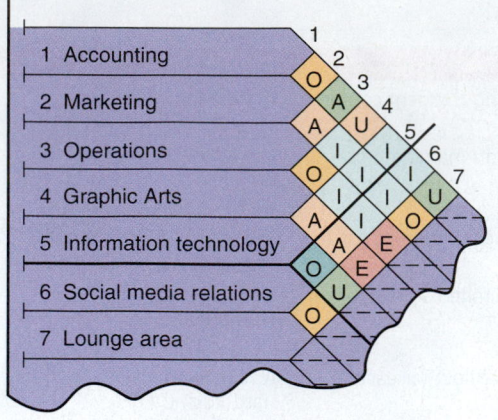

Code	CLOSENESS
A	Absolutely necessary
E	Especially important
I	Important
O	Ordinary OK
U	Unimportant
X	Not desirable

LO 9.1 *Discuss* important issues in office layout

Even though the movement of information is increasingly electronic, analysis of office layouts still requires a task-based approach. Managers therefore examine both electronic and conventional communication patterns, separation needs, and other conditions affecting employee effectiveness. A useful tool for such an analysis is the *relationship chart* (also called a Muther Grid) shown in Figure 9.1. This chart, prepared for a software firm, indicates that operations must be near accounting and marketing, but it does not need to be near the graphic arts staff.

On the other hand, some layout considerations are universal (many of which apply to factories as well as to offices). They have to do with working conditions, teamwork, authority, and status. Should offices be private or open cubicles, have low file cabinets to foster informal communication or high cabinets to reduce noise and contribute to privacy?

Workspace can inspire informal and productive encounters if it balances three physical and social aspects[1]:

- *Proximity:* Spaces should naturally bring people together.
- *Privacy:* People must be able to control access to their conversations.
- *Permission:* The culture should signal that nonwork interactions are encouraged.

As a final comment on office layout, we note two major trends. First, technology, such as smart phones, scanners, the Internet, laptop computers, and tablets, allows increasing layout flexibility by moving information electronically and allowing employees to work offsite. Second, modern firms create dynamic needs for space and services.

Here are two examples:

- When Deloitte & Touche found that 30% to 40% of desks were empty at any given time, the firm developed its "hoteling programs." Consultants lost their permanent offices; anyone who plans to be in the building (rather than out with clients) books an office through a "concierge," who hangs that consultant's name on the door for the day and stocks the space with requested supplies.
- Cisco Systems cut rent and workplace service costs by 37% and saw productivity benefits of $2.4 billion per year by reducing square footage, reconfiguring space, creating movable, everything-on-wheels offices, and designing "get away from it all" innovation areas.

Retail Layout

Retail layout

An approach that addresses flow, allocates space, and responds to customer behavior.

Retail layouts are based on the idea that sales and profitability vary directly with customer exposure to products. Thus, most retail operations managers try to expose customers to as many products as possible. Studies do show that the greater the rate of exposure, the greater the sales and the higher the return on investment. The operations manager can change

Here are five versions of the office layout.

Everett Collection

Managers and architects have pondered how to design an office to encourage productivity for more than 100 years. In the early 20th century, large offices resembled factories (see the photo of the Jack Lemmon film *The Apartment*, where clerical workers sat in long rows, often performing repetitive tasks).

Starting in the 1960s, layouts changed to foster teamwork where managers and support staff sat together, and groupings were geared toward specific tasks.

Courtesy of Herman Miller, Inc.

Chad McDermott/Fotolia

With computers, more individual work was possible and the "Cube Farm" era became ubiquitous through the '80s and '90s. An office full of high-walled cubicles offered both an open environment and personal office space.

By the turn of the century, looking for innovation and creativity to recruit and inspire college grads, technology firms created the "fun" office. Bright, casual, open office spaces, with amenities such as beanbag chairs, foosball tables, and coffee bars became the fad.

Monkey Business/Fotolia

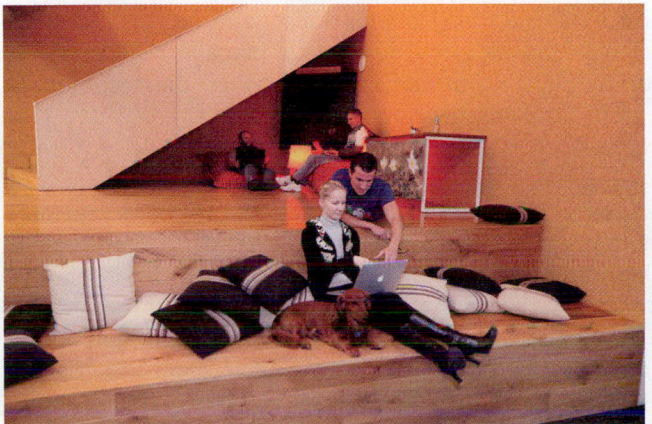

Anruth/Agencja Fotograficzna Caro/Alamy

The buzzwords today are serendipity and collaboration, as companies design office space to engineer encounters between employees. Steve Jobs designed his Pixar headquarters with the cafeteria and bathrooms in a central atrium away from work areas to encourage intermingling and collaboration. Skype achieves similar goals with open lounges.

Sources: Wall Street Journal (April 28, 2014); *USA Today* (Feb. 28, 2013); and *Harvard Business Review* (Oct. 2014).

Figure **9.2**

Store Layout with Dairy and Bakery, High-Draw Items, in Different Areas of the Store

exposure with store arrangement and the allocation of space to various products within that arrangement.

Five ideas are helpful for determining the overall arrangement of many stores:

1. Locate the high-draw items around the periphery of the store. Thus, we tend to find dairy products on one side of a supermarket and bread and bakery products on another. An example of this tactic is shown in Figure 9.2.
2. Use prominent locations for high-impulse and high-margin items. Best Buy puts fast-growing, high-margin digital goods—such as cameras and printers—in the front and center of its stores.

3. Distribute what are known in the trade as "power items"—items that may dominate a purchasing trip—to both sides of an aisle, and disperse them to increase the viewing of other items.
4. Use end-aisle locations because they have a very high exposure rate.
5. Convey the mission of the store by carefully selecting the position of the lead-off department. For instance, if prepared foods are part of a supermarket's mission, position the bakery and deli up front to appeal to convenience-oriented customers. Walmart's push to increase sales of clothes means those departments are in broad view upon entering a store.

LO 9.2 *Define* the objectives of retail layout

Once the overall layout of a retail store has been decided, products need to be arranged for sale. Many considerations go into this arrangement. However, the main *objective of retail layout is to maximize profitability per square foot of floor space* (or, in some stores, on linear foot of shelf space). Big-ticket, or expensive, items may yield greater dollar sales, but the profit per square foot may be lower. Computer programs are available to assist managers in evaluating the profitability of various merchandising plans for hundreds of categories: this technique is known as category management.

An additional, and somewhat controversial, issue in retail layout is called slotting.

Slotting fees

Fees manufacturers pay to get shelf space for their products.

Slotting fees are fees manufacturers pay to get their goods on the shelf in a retail store or supermarket chain. The result of massive new-product introductions, retailers can now demand up to $25,000 to place an item in their chain. During the last decade, marketplace economics, consolidations, and technology have provided retailers with this leverage. The competition for shelf space is advanced by POS systems and scanner technology, which improve supply-chain management and inventory control. Many small firms question the legality and ethics of slotting fees, claiming the fees stifle new products, limit their ability to expand, and cost consumers money. Walmart is one of the few major retailers that does not demand slotting fees, removing a barrier to entry. (See the *Ethical Dilemma* at the end of this chapter.)

Servicescapes

Although a major goal of retail layout is to maximize profit through product exposure, there are other aspects of the service that managers consider. The term servicescape describes the physical surroundings in which the service is delivered and how the surroundings have a humanistic effect on customers and employees. To provide a good service layout, a firm considers three elements:

1. *Ambient conditions*, which are background characteristics such as lighting, sound, smell, and temperature. All these affect workers *and* customers and can affect how much is spent and how long a person stays in the building.
2. *Spatial layout and functionality*, which involve customer circulation path planning, aisle characteristics (such as width, direction, angle, and shelf spacing), and product grouping.
3. *Signs, symbols, and artifacts*, which are characteristics of building design that carry social significance (such as carpeted areas of a department store that encourage shoppers to slow down and browse).

Examples of each of these three elements of servicescape are:

♦ *Ambient conditions:* Fine-dining restaurants with linen tablecloths and candlelit atmosphere; Mrs. Field's Cookie bakery smells permeating the shopping mall; leather chairs at Starbucks.

♦ *Layout/functionality:* Kroger's long aisles and high shelves; Best Buy's wide center aisle.

♦ *Signs, symbols, and artifacts:* Walmart's greeter at the door; Hard Rock Cafe's wall of guitars; Disneyland's entrance looking like hometown heaven.

Warehouse and Storage Layouts

The objective of warehouse layout is to find the optimum trade-off between handling cost and costs associated with warehouse space. Consequently, management's task is to maximize the utilization of the total "cube" of the warehouse—that is, utilize its full volume while maintaining low material handling costs. We define *material handling costs* as all the costs related to the transaction. This consists of incoming transport, storage, and outgoing transport of the materials to be warehoused. These costs include equipment, people, material, supervision, insurance, and depreciation. Effective warehouse layouts do, of course, also minimize the damage and spoilage of material within the warehouse.

imageBROKER/Alamy

A critical element contributing to the bottom line at Hard Rock Cafe is the layout of each cafe's retail shop space. The retail space, from 600 to 1,300 square feet in size, is laid out in conjunction with the restaurant area to create the maximum traffic flow before and after eating. The payoffs for cafes like this one in London are huge. Almost half of a cafe's annual sales are generated from these small shops, which have very high retail sales per square foot.

OM in Action | Amazon Lets Loose the Robots

Amazon's robot army is falling into place. The Seattle online retailer has outfitted several U.S. warehouses with over 10,000 short, orange, wheeled Kiva robots that move stocked shelves to workers, instead of having employees seek items amid long aisles of merchandise. This is similar to the introduction of the moving assembly line with cars moving down the line, rather than the employee moving from workstation to workstation.

At a 1.2-million-square-foot warehouse in Tracy, California, Amazon has replaced 4 floors of fixed shelving with the robots. Now, "pickers" at the facility stand in one place, and robots bring 4-foot-by-6-foot shelving units to them, sparing them what amounted to as much as 20 miles a day of walking through the warehouse. Employees at robot-equipped warehouses are now expected to pick and scan at least 300 items an hour, compared with 100 under the old system.

At the heart of the robot rollout is Amazon's relentless drive to compete with the immediacy of shopping at brick-and-mortar retailers by improving the efficiency of its logistics. If Amazon can shrink the time it takes to sort and pack goods at its 80 U.S. warehouses, it can guarantee same-day or overnight delivery for more products to more customers.

Noah Berger/Reuters

The robots save Amazon $400–$900 million a year in fulfillment costs by reducing the number of times a product is "touched." The Kiva robots pare 20% to 40% from the average $3.50-to-$3.75 cost of sorting, picking, and boxing an order.

Sources: The Wall Street Journal (Nov. 20, 2014) and (Dec. 9, 2013).

Management minimizes the sum of the resources spent on finding and moving material plus the deterioration and damage to the material itself. The variety of items stored and the number of items "picked" has direct bearing on the optimum layout. A warehouse storing a few unique items lends itself to higher density than a warehouse storing a variety of items. Modern warehouse management is, in many instances, an automated procedure using *automated storage and retrieval systems* (ASRSs).

The Stop & Shop grocery chain, with 350 supermarkets in New England, has recently completed the largest ASRS in the world. The 1.3-million-square-foot distribution center in Freetown, Massachusetts, employs 77 rotating-fork automated storage and retrieval machines. These 77 ASRS machines each access 11,500 pick slots on 90 aisles—a total of 64,000 pallets of food. The *OM in Action* box, "Amazon Lets Loose the Robots," shows another way that technology can help minimize warehouse costs.

An important component of warehouse layout is the relationship between the receiving/unloading area and the shipping/loading area. Facility design depends on the type of supplies unloaded, what they are unloaded from (trucks, rail cars, barges, and so on), and where they are unloaded. In some companies, the receiving and shipping facilities, or *docks*, as they are called, are even in the same area; sometimes they are receiving docks in the morning and shipping docks in the afternoon.

Cross-Docking

Cross-docking means to avoid placing materials or supplies in storage by processing them as they are received. In a manufacturing facility, product is received directly by the assembly line. In a distribution center, labeled and presorted loads arrive at the shipping dock for immediate rerouting, thereby avoiding formal receiving, stocking/storing, and order-selection activities. Because these activities add no value to the product, their elimination is 100% cost savings. Walmart, an early advocate of cross-docking, uses the technique as a major component of its continuing low-cost strategy. With cross-docking, Walmart reduces distribution costs and speeds restocking of stores, thereby improving customer service. Although cross-docking reduces product handling, inventory, and facility costs, it requires both (1) tight scheduling and (2) accurate inbound product identification.

INBOUND

No delay
No storage
System in place for information exchange and product movement

OUTBOUND

Cross-docking

Avoiding the placement of materials or supplies in storage by processing them as they are received for shipment.

Random Stocking

Automatic identification systems (AISs), usually in the form of bar codes, allow accurate and rapid item identification. When automatic identification systems are combined with effective management information systems, operations managers know the quantity and location of every unit. This information can be used with human operators or with automatic storage and retrieval systems to load units anywhere in the warehouse—randomly. Accurate inventory quantities and locations mean the potential utilization of the whole facility because space does not need to be reserved for certain stock-keeping units (SKUs) or part families. Computerized random stocking systems often include the following tasks:

1. Maintaining a list of "open" locations
2. Maintaining accurate records of existing inventory and its locations
3. Sequencing items to minimize the travel time required to "pick" orders
4. Combining orders to reduce picking time
5. Assigning certain items or classes of items, such as high-usage items, to particular warehouse areas so that the total distance traveled within the warehouse is minimized

Random stocking systems can increase facility utilization and decrease labor cost, but they require accurate records.

Customizing

Although we expect warehouses to store as little product as possible and hold it for as short a time as possible, we are now asking warehouses to customize products. Warehouses can be places where value is added through customizing. Warehouse customization is a particularly useful way to generate competitive advantage in markets where products have multiple configurations. For instance, a warehouse can be a place where computer components are put together, software loaded, and repairs made. Warehouses may also provide customized labeling and packaging for retailers so items arrive ready for display.

Increasingly, this type of work goes on adjacent to major airports, in facilities such as the FedEx terminal in Memphis. Adding value at warehouses adjacent to major airports also facilitates overnight delivery. For example, if your computer has failed, the replacement may be sent to you from such a warehouse for delivery the next morning. When your old machine arrives back at the warehouse, it is repaired and sent to someone else. These value-added activities at "quasi-warehouses" contribute to strategies of differentiation, low cost, and rapid response.

At Ikea's distribution center in Almhult, Sweden, pallets are stacked and retrieved through a fully automated process.

Random stocking
Used in warehousing to locate stock wherever there is an open location.

Customizing
Using warehousing to add value to a product through component modification, repair, labeling, and packaging.

Fixed-Position Layout

In a fixed-position layout, the project remains in one place, and workers and equipment come to that one work area. Examples of this type of project are a ship, a highway, a bridge, a house, and an operating table in a hospital operating room.

The techniques for addressing the fixed-position layout are complicated by three factors. First, there is limited space at virtually all sites. Second, at different stages of a project, different materials are needed; therefore, different items become critical as the project develops. Third, the volume of materials needed is dynamic. For example, the rate of use of steel panels for the hull of a ship changes as the project progresses.

Fixed-position layout
A system that addresses the layout requirements of stationary projects.

Here are three versions of the fixed-position layout.

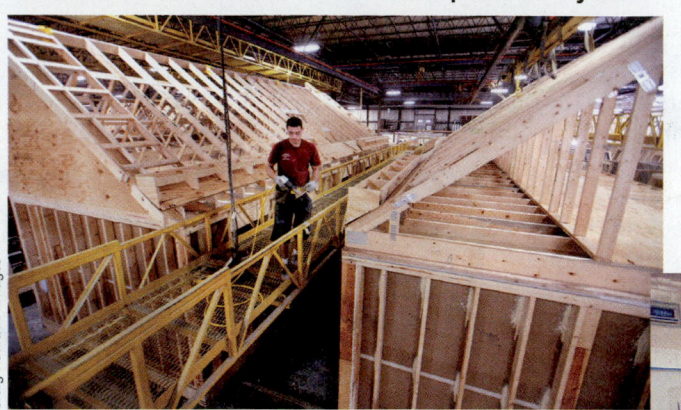

Craig Ruttle/AP Images

A house built via traditional fixed-position layout would be constructed onsite, with equipment, materials, and workers brought to the site. Then a "meeting of the trades" would assign space for various time periods. However, the home pictured here can be built at a much lower cost. The house is built in two movable modules in a factory. Scaffolding and hoists make the job easier, quicker, and cheaper, and the indoor work environment aids labor productivity.

A service example of a fixed-position layout is an operating room; the patient remains stationary on the table, and medical personnel and equipment are brought to the site.

Dick Blume/The Image Works

Tim Altevogt/Reuters/Corbis

In shipbuilding, there is limited space next to the fixed-position layout. Shipyards call these loading areas platens, and they are assigned for various time periods to each contractor.

LO 9.4 *Identify* when fixed-position layouts are appropriate

Because problems with fixed-position layouts are so difficult to solve well onsite, an alternative strategy is to complete as much of the project as possible offsite. This approach is used in the shipbuilding industry when standard units—say, pipe-holding brackets—are assembled on a nearby assembly line (a product-oriented facility). In an attempt to add efficiency to shipbuilding, Ingall Ship Building Corporation has moved toward product-oriented production when sections of a ship (modules) are similar or when it has a contract to build the same section of several similar ships. Also, as the first photo on this page shows, many home builders are moving from a fixed-position layout strategy to one that is more product oriented. About one-third of all new homes in the U.S. are built this way. In addition, many houses that are built onsite (fixed position) have the majority of components such as doors, windows, fixtures, trusses, stairs, and wallboard built as modules in more efficient offsite processes.

Process-Oriented Layout

Process-oriented layout

A layout that deals with low-volume, high-variety production in which like machines and equipment are grouped together.

A process-oriented layout can simultaneously handle a wide variety of products or services. This is the traditional way to support a product differentiation strategy. It is most efficient when making products with different requirements or when handling customers, patients, or clients with different needs. A process-oriented layout is typically the low-volume, high-variety strategy discussed in Chapter 7. In this job-shop environment, each product or each small group of products undergoes a different sequence of operations. A product or small order is produced

Figure **9.3**

An Emergency Room Process Layout Showing the Routing of Two Patients

◆**STUDENT TIP**

Patient A (broken leg) proceeds (blue arrow) to ER triage, to radiology, to surgery, to a bed, to pharmacy, to billing. Patient B (pacemaker problem) moves (red arrow) to ER triage, to surgery, to pharmacy, to lab, to a bed, to billing.

VIDEO 9.1
Laying Out Arnold Palmer Hospital's New Facility

by moving it from one department to another in the sequence required for that product. A good example of the process-oriented layout is a hospital or clinic. Figure 9.3 illustrates the process for two patients, A and B, at an emergency clinic in Chicago. An inflow of patients, each with his or her own needs, requires routing through admissions, laboratories, operating rooms, radiology, pharmacies, nursing beds, and so on. Equipment, skills, and supervision are organized around these processes.

A big advantage of process-oriented layout is its flexibility in equipment and labor assignments. The breakdown of one machine, for example, need not halt an entire process; work can be transferred to other machines in the department. Process-oriented layout is also especially good for handling the manufacture of parts in small batches, or job lots, and for the production of a wide variety of parts in different sizes or forms.

Job lots
Groups or batches of parts processed together.

The disadvantages of process-oriented layout come from the general-purpose use of the equipment. Orders take more time to move through the system because of difficult scheduling, changing setups, and unique material handling. In addition, general-purpose equipment requires high labor skills, and work-in-process inventories are higher because of imbalances in the production process. High labor-skill needs also increase the required level of training and experience, and high work-in-process levels increase capital investment.

When designing a process layout, the most common tactic is to arrange departments or work centers so as to minimize the costs of material handling. In other words, departments with large flows of parts or people between them should be placed next to one another. Material handling costs in this approach depend on (1) the number of loads (or people) to be moved between two departments during some period of time and (2) the distance-related costs of moving loads (or people) between departments. Cost is assumed to be a function of distance between departments. The objective can be expressed as follows:

LO 9.5 *Explain* how to achieve a good process-oriented facility layout

$$\text{Minimize cost} = \sum_{i=1}^{n} \sum_{j=1}^{n} X_{ij} C_{ij} \qquad (9\text{-}1)$$

where n = total number of work centers or departments
  i, j = individual departments
  X_{ij} = number of loads moved from department i to department j
  C_{ij} = cost to move a load between department i and department j

Process-oriented facilities (and fixed-position layouts as well) try to minimize loads, or trips, multiplied by distance-related costs. The term C_{ij} combines distance and other costs into one factor. We thereby assume not only that the difficulty of movement is equal but also that the pickup and setdown costs are constant. Although they are not always constant, for simplicity's sake we summarize these data (that is, distance, difficulty, and pickup and setdown costs) in this one variable, cost. The best way to understand the steps involved in designing a process layout is to look at an example.

Example 1

DESIGNING A PROCESS LAYOUT

Walters Company management wants to arrange the six departments of its factory in a way that will minimize interdepartmental material-handling costs. They make an initial assumption (to simplify the problem) that each department is 20 × 20 feet and that the building is 60 feet long and 40 feet wide.

APPROACH AND SOLUTION ▶ The process layout procedure that they follow involves six steps:

Step 1: *Construct a "from–to matrix"* showing the flow of parts or materials from department to department (see Figure 9.4).

Figure 9.4

Interdepartmental Flow of Parts

STUDENT TIP ◆

The high flows between 1 and 3 and between 3 and 6 are immediately apparent. Departments 1, 3, and 6, therefore, should be close together.

Number of loads per week

Department	Assembly (1)	Painting (2)	Machine Shop (3)	Receiving (4)	Shipping (5)	Testing (6)
Assembly (1)		50	100	0	0	20
Painting (2)			30	50	10	0
Machine Shop (3)				20	0	100
Receiving (4)					50	0
Shipping (5)						0
Testing (6)						

Step 2: *Determine the space requirements* for each department. (Figure 9.5 shows available plant space.)

Figure 9.5

Building Dimensions and One Possible Department Layout

STUDENT TIP ◆

Think of this as a starting, initial, layout. Our goal is to improve it, if possible.

Step 3: *Develop an initial schematic diagram* showing the sequence of departments through which parts must move. Try to place departments with a heavy flow of materials or parts next to one another. (See Figure 9.6.)

Figure 9.6

Interdepartmental Flow Graph Showing Number of Weekly Loads

STUDENT TIP ◆

This shows that 100 loads also move weekly between Assembly and the Machine Shop. We will probably want to move these two departments closer to one another to minimize the flow of parts through the factory.

Step 4: *Determine the cost of this layout* by using the material-handling cost equation:

$$\text{Cost} = \sum_{i=1}^{n} \sum_{j=1}^{n} X_{ij} C_{ij}$$

For this problem, Walters Company assumes that a forklift carries all interdepartmental loads. The cost of moving one load between adjacent departments is estimated to be $1. Moving a load between nonadjacent departments costs $2. Looking at Figures 9.4 and 9.5, we thus see that the handling cost between departments 1 and 2 is $50 ($1 × 50 loads), $200 between departments 1 and 3 ($2 × 100 loads), $40 between departments 1 and 6 ($2 × 20 loads), and so on. Work areas that are diagonal to one another, such as 2 and 4, are treated as adjacent. The total cost for the layout shown in Figure 9.6 is:

$$\text{Cost} = \$50 + \$200 + \$40 + \$30 + \$50$$

(1 and 2) (1 and 3) (1 and 6) (2 and 3) (2 and 4)

$$+ \$10 + \$40 + \$100 + \$50$$

(2 and 5) (3 and 4) (3 and 6) (4 and 5)

$$= \$570$$

Step 5: By trial and error (or by a more sophisticated computer program approach that we discuss shortly), *try to improve the layout* pictured in Figure 9.5 to establish a better arrangement of departments.

By looking at both the flow graph (Figure 9.6) and the cost calculations, we see that placing departments 1 and 3 closer together appears desirable. They currently are nonadjacent, and the high volume of flow between them causes a large handling expense. Looking the situation over, we need to check the effect of shifting departments and possibly raising, instead of lowering, overall costs.

One possibility is to switch departments 1 and 2. This exchange produces a second departmental flow graph (Figure 9.7), which shows a reduction in cost to $480, a savings in material handling of $90:

$$\text{Cost} = \$50 + \$100 + \$20 + \$60 + \$50$$

(1 and 2) (1 and 3) (1 and 6) (2 and 3) (2 and 4)

$$+ \$10 + \$40 + \$100 + \$50$$

(2 and 5) (3 and 4) (3 and 6) (4 and 5)

$$= \$480$$

Suppose Walters Company is satisfied with the cost figure of $480 and the flow graph of Figure 9.7. The problem may not be solved yet. Often, a sixth step is necessary:

Step 6: *Prepare a detailed plan* arranging the departments to fit the shape of the building and its nonmovable areas (such as the loading dock, washrooms, and stairways). Often this step involves ensuring that the final plan can be accommodated by the electrical system, floor loads, aesthetics, and other factors.

In the case of Walters Company, space requirements are a simple matter (see Figure 9.8).

Figure **9.8**

A Feasible Layout for Walters Company

STUDENT TIP ⬦

Here we see the departments moved to areas A–F to try to improve the flow.

Area A	Area B	Area C
Painting Department (2)	Assembly Department (1)	Machine Shop Department (3)
Receiving Department (4)	Shipping Department (5)	Testing Department (6)
Area D	Area E	Area F

INSIGHT ▶ This switch of departments is only one of a large number of possible changes. For a six-department problem, there are actually 720 (or $6! = 6 \times 5 \times 4 \times 3 \times 2 \times 1$) potential arrangements! In layout problems, we may not find the optimal solution and may have to be satisfied with a "reasonable" one.

LEARNING EXERCISE ▶ Can you improve on the layout in Figures 9.7 and 9.8? [Answer: Yes, it can be lowered to $430 by placing Shipping in area A, Painting in area B, Assembly in area C, Receiving in area D (no change), Machine Shop in area E, and Testing in area F (no change).]

RELATED PROBLEMS ▶ 9.1–9.9 (9.10 is available in MyOMLab)

EXCEL OM Data File **Ch09Ex1.xls** can be found in MyOMLab.

ACTIVE MODEL 9.1 Example 1 is further illustrated in Active Model 9.1 in MyOMLab.

Computer Software for Process-Oriented Layouts

The graphic approach in Example 1 is fine for small problems. It does not, however, suffice for larger problems. When 20 departments are involved in a layout problem, more than 600 *trillion* different department configurations are possible. Fortunately, computer programs have been written to handle large layouts. These programs (see the Flow Path Calculator graphic on the next page) often add sophistication with flowcharts, multiple-story capability, storage and container placement, material volumes, time analysis, and cost comparisons. These programs tend to be interactive—that is, require participation by the user. And most only claim to provide "good," not "optimal," solutions.

Siemens Corp. software such as this allows operations managers to quickly place factory equipment for a full three-dimensional view of the layout. Such presentations provide added insight into the issues of facility layout in terms of process, material handling, efficiency, and safety. (Images created with Tecnomatix Plant Simulation software, courtesy of Siemens PLM Software)

Julian Stratenschulte/picture-alliance/dpa/AP Images

Proplanner Software for Process-Oriented Layouts

Working with computer-aided design software, analysts with the click of a mouse can use Proplanner's Flow Path Calculator to generate material flow diagrams and calculate material handling distances, time, and cost. Variable-width flow lines, color-coded by product, part, or material handling method, allow users to identify how layouts should be arranged and where to eliminate excessive material handling.

Work Cells

A work cell reorganizes people and machines that would ordinarily be dispersed in various departments into a group so that they can focus on making a single product or a group of related products (Figure 9.9). Cellular work arrangements are used when volume warrants a special arrangement of machinery and equipment. These work cells are reconfigured as product designs change or volume fluctuates. The advantages of work cells are:

1. *Reduced work-in-process inventory* because the work cell is set up to provide one-piece flow from machine to machine.
2. *Less floor space* required because less space is needed between machines to accommodate work-in-process inventory.
3. *Reduced raw material and finished goods inventories* because less work-in-process allows more rapid movement of materials through the work cell.
4. *Reduced direct labor cost* because of improved communication among employees, better material flow, and improved scheduling.
5. *Heightened sense of employee participation* in the organization and the product: employees accept the added responsibility of product quality because it is directly associated with them and their work cell.
6. *Increased equipment and machinery utilization* because of better scheduling and faster material flow.
7. *Reduced investment in machinery and equipment* because good utilization reduces the number of machines and the amount of equipment and tooling.

Requirements of Work Cells

The requirements of cellular production include:

- Identification of families of products, often through the use of group technology codes or equivalents
- A high level of training, flexibility, and empowerment of employees
- Being self-contained, with its own equipment and resources
- Testing (poka-yoke) at each station in the cell

Work cell

An arrangement of machines and personnel that focuses on making a single product or family of related products.

LO 9.6 *Define* work cell and the requirements of a work cell

Figure **9.9**

Improving Layouts by Moving to the Work Cell Concept

Note in both (a) and (b) that U-shaped work cells can reduce material and employee movement. The U shape may also reduce space requirements, enhance communication, cut the number of workers, and make inspection easier.

(a)

Current layout—workers
are in small closed areas.

Improved layout—cross-trained
workers can assist each other.
May be able to add a third worker
as added output is needed.

(b)

Current layout—straight lines make
it hard to balance tasks because
work may not be divided evenly.

Improved layout—in U shape,
workers have better access.
Four cross-trained workers were
reduced to three.

Work cells have at least five advantages over assembly lines and focused process facilities: (1) because tasks are grouped, inspection is often immediate; (2) fewer workers are needed; (3) workers can reach more of the work area; (4) the work area can be more efficiently balanced; and (5) communication is enhanced. Work cells are sometimes organized in a U shape, as shown on the right side of Figure 9.9. The shape of the cell is secondary to the process flow. The focus should be on a flow that optimizes people, material, and communication.

Why did Canon's copier factories in Japan switch from assembly lines to work cells? First, the move freed up 12 miles of conveyor-belt space, at 54 plants, saving $280 million in real estate costs. Second, the cells enabled Canon to change its product mix more quickly, to accommodate short life cycles. And third, morale increased because workers can now assemble a whole copier, not just one part. Some of Canon's fastest workers are so admired that they have become TV celebrities!

Staffing and Balancing Work Cells

Once the work cell has the appropriate equipment located in the proper sequence, the next task is to staff and balance the cell. Efficient production in a work cell requires appropriate staffing.

Takt time

Pace of production to meet customer demands.

This involves two steps. First, determine the takt time,[2] which is the pace (frequency) of production units necessary (time per unit) to meet customer orders:

$$\text{Takt time} = \text{Total work time available/Units required to satisfy customer demand} \quad (9\text{-}2)$$

Second, determine the number of operators required. This requires dividing the total operation time in the work cell by the takt time:

$$\text{Workers required} = \text{Total operation time required/Takt time} \quad (9\text{-}3)$$

Example 2 considers these two steps when staffing work cells.

Example 2

STAFFING WORK CELLS

Stephen Hall's company in Dayton makes auto mirrors. The major customer is the Honda plant nearby. Honda expects 600 mirrors delivered daily, and the work cell producing the mirrors is scheduled for 8 hours. Hall wants to determine the takt time and the number of workers required.

APPROACH ▶ Hall uses Equations (9-2) and (9-3) and develops a work balance chart to help determine the time for each operation in the work cell, as well as total time.

SOLUTION ▶

$$\text{Takt time} = (8 \text{ hours} \times 60 \text{ minutes})/600 \text{ units} = 480/600 = .8 \text{ minute} = 48 \text{ seconds}$$

Therefore, the customer requirement is one mirror every 48 seconds.

The *work balance chart* in Figure 9.10 shows that 5 operations are necessary, for a total operation time of 140 seconds:

$$\text{Workers required} = \text{Total operation time required}/\text{Takt time}$$
$$= (50 + 45 + 10 + 20 + 15)/48$$
$$= 140/48 = 2.92$$

Figure **9.10**

Work Balance Chart for Mirror Production

INSIGHT ▶ To produce one unit every 48 seconds will require 2.92 people. With three operators this work cell will be producing one unit each 46.67 seconds (140 seconds/3 employees = 46.67) and 617 units per day (480 minutes available × 60 seconds/46.67 seconds for each unit = 617).

LEARNING EXERCISE ▶ If testing time is expanded to 20 seconds, what is the staffing requirement? [Answer: 3.125 employees.]

RELATED PROBLEM ▶ 9.11

A *work balance chart* (like the one in Example 2) is also valuable for evaluating the operation times in work cells. Some consideration must be given to determining the bottleneck operation. Bottleneck operations can constrain the flow through the cell. Imbalance in a work cell is seldom an issue if the operation is manual, as cell members by definition are part of a cross-trained team. Consequently, the inherent flexibility of work cells typically overcomes modest imbalance issues within a cell. However, if the imbalance is a machine constraint, then an adjustment in machinery, process, or operations may be necessary. In such situations the use of traditional assembly-line-balancing analysis, the topic of our next section, may be helpful.

The success of work cells is not limited to manufacturing. Kansas City's Hallmark, which has over half the U.S. greeting card market and produces some 40,000 different cards, has modified the offices into a cellular design. In the past, its 700 creative professionals would take up to 2 years to develop a new card. Hallmark's decision to create work cells consisting of artists, writers, lithographers, merchandisers, and accountants, all located in the same area, has resulted in card preparation in a fraction of the time that the old layout required. Work cells have also yielded higher performance and better service for the American Red Cross blood donation process.

The Focused Work Center and the Focused Factory

Focused work center

A permanent or semipermanent product-oriented arrangement of machines and personnel.

When a firm has *identified a family of similar products that have a large and stable demand*, it may organize a focused work center. A focused work center (also called a "plant within a plant") moves production to a large work cell that remains part of the present facility. For example, bumpers and dashboards in Toyota's Texas plant are produced in a focused work center, and the Levi's departments in JCPenney are managed and run in a stand-alone boutique setting.

Focused factory

A facility designed to produce similar products or components.

If the focused work center is in a separate facility, it is often called a focused factory. For example, separate plants that produce seat belts, fuel tanks, and exhaust systems for Toyota are focused factories. A fast-food restaurant is also a focused factory—most are easily reconfigured for adjustments to product mix and volume. Burger King changes the number of personnel and task assignments rather than moving machines and equipment. In this manner, Burger King balances the assembly line to meet changing production demands. In effect, the "layout" changes numerous times each day.

The term *focused factories* may also refer to facilities that are focused in ways other than by product line or layout. For instance, facilities may focus on their core competence, such as low cost, quality, new product introduction, or flexibility.

Focused facilities in both manufacturing and services appear to be better able to stay in tune with their customers, to produce quality products, and to operate at higher margins. This is true whether they are auto manufacturers like Toyota; restaurants like McDonald's and Burger King; or a hospital like Arnold Palmer.

Repetitive and Product-Oriented Layout

Product-oriented layouts are organized around products or families of similar high-volume, low-variety products. Repetitive production and continuous production, which are discussed in Chapter 7, use product layouts. The assumptions are that:

LO 9.7 *Define* product-oriented layout

1. Volume is adequate for high equipment utilization
2. Product demand is stable enough to justify high investment in specialized equipment
3. Product is standardized or approaching a phase of its life cycle that justifies investment in specialized equipment
4. Supplies of raw materials and components are adequate and of uniform quality (adequately standardized) to ensure that they will work with the specialized equipment

Fabrication line

A machine-paced, product-oriented facility for building components.

Assembly line

An approach that puts fabricated parts together at a series of workstations; used in repetitive processes.

Two types of a product-oriented layout are fabrication and assembly lines. The fabrication line builds components, such as automobile tires or metal parts for a refrigerator, on a series of machines, while an assembly line puts the fabricated parts together at a series of workstations. However, both are repetitive processes, and in both cases, the line must be "balanced"; that is, the time spent to perform work on one machine must equal or "balance" the time spent to perform work on the next machine in the fabrication line, just as the time spent at one workstation by one assembly-line employee must "balance" the time spent at the next workstation by the next employee. The same issues arise when designing the "disassembly lines" of slaughterhouses and automobile recyclers.

Assembly-line balancing

Obtaining output at each workstation on a production line so delay is minimized.

A well-balanced assembly line has the advantage of high personnel and facility utilization and equity among employees' workloads. Some union contracts require that workloads be nearly equal among those on the same assembly line. The term most often used to describe this process is assembly-line balancing. Indeed, the *objective of the product-oriented layout is to minimize imbalance in the fabrication or assembly line.*

The main advantages of product-oriented layout are:

1. The low variable cost per unit usually associated with high-volume, standardized products
2. Low material-handling costs
3. Reduced work-in-process inventories
4. Easier training and supervision
5. Rapid throughput

The disadvantages of product layout are:

1. The high volume required because of the large investment needed to establish the process
2. Work stoppage at any one point can tie up the whole operation
3. The process flexibility necessary for a variety of products and production rates can be a challenge

Because the problems of fabrication lines and assembly lines are similar, we focus our discussion on assembly lines. On an assembly line, the product typically moves via automated means, such as a conveyor, through a series of workstations until completed. This is the way fast-food hamburgers are made (see Figure 9.11), automobiles and some planes (see the photo of the Boeing 737 on the next page) are assembled, and television sets and ovens are produced. Product-oriented layouts use more automated and specially designed equipment than do process layouts.

VIDEO 9.2
Facility Layout at Wheeled Coach
Ambulances

Assembly-Line Balancing

Line balancing is usually undertaken to minimize imbalance between machines or personnel while meeting a required output from the line. To produce at a specified rate, management must know the tools, equipment, and work methods used. Then the time requirements for each assembly task (e.g., drilling a hole, tightening a nut, or spray-painting a part) must be determined. Management also needs to know the *precedence relationship* among the activities—that is, the sequence in which various tasks must be performed. Example 3 shows how to turn these task data into a precedence diagram.

LO 9.8 *Explain* how to balance production flow in a repetitive or product-oriented facility

Elapsed time	0:00	0:11	0:31	0:45		1:30
Task time (seconds)		11	20	14	0	45
Task	1. Order	2. Bun toasting	3. Assembly with condiments	4. Wrapping of patty with bun	5. Order picked up immediately to keep it fresh	6. Customer service (order and payment)

Buns

Order read on a video screen

More personnel added during busy periods

Toaster   Condiments

Heated cabinet for the grilled patties

Heated landing pad

Point-of-sale (POS) terminal that tracks each order (payment, time, cashier, etc.)

Figure **9.11**

McDonald's Hamburger Assembly Line

The Boeing 737, the world's most popular commercial airplane, is produced on a moving production line, traveling at 2 inches a minute through the final assembly process. The moving line, one of several lean manufacturing innovations at the Renton, Washington, facility, has enhanced quality, reduced flow time, slashed inventory levels, and cut space requirements. Final assembly is only 11 days—a time savings of 50%—and inventory is down more than 55%.

Copyright Boeing

Example 3

DEVELOPING A PRECEDENCE DIAGRAM FOR AN ASSEMBLY LINE

Boeing wants to develop a precedence diagram for an electrostatic wing component that requires a total assembly time of 65 minutes.

APPROACH ▶ Staff gather tasks, assembly times, and sequence requirements for the component in Table 9.2.

| TABLE 9.2 | Precedence Data for Wing Component |

TASK	ASSEMBLY TIME (MINUTES)	TASK MUST FOLLOW TASK LISTED BELOW	
A	10	—	This means that tasks B and E cannot be done until task A has been completed.
B	11	A	
C	5	B	
D	4	B	
E	11	A	
F	3	C, D	
G	7	F	
H	11	E	
I	3	G, H	
	Total time 65		

SOLUTION ▶ Figure 9.12 shows the precedence diagram.

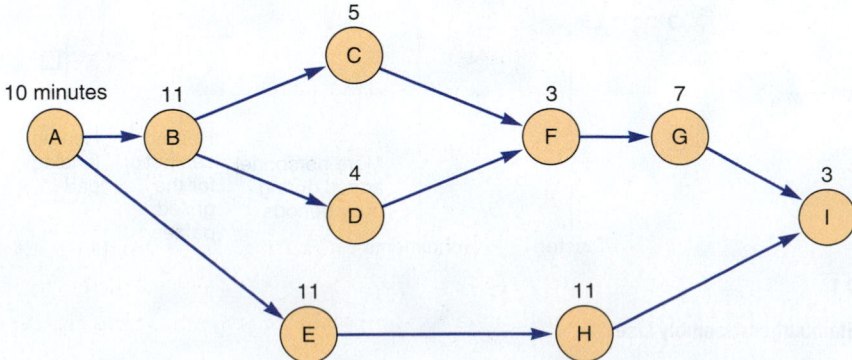

Figure **9.12**

Precedence Diagram

> **INSIGHT ▶** The diagram helps structure an assembly line and workstations, and it makes it easier to visualize the sequence of tasks.
>
> **LEARNING EXERCISE ▶** If task D had a second preceding task (C), how would Figure 9.12 change? [Answer: There would also be an arrow pointing from C to D.]
>
> **RELATED PROBLEMS ▶** 9.13a, 9.15a, 9.16a, 9.17a, 9.20a (9.25a,d, 9.26a, 9.27 are available in MyOMLab)

Once we have constructed a precedence chart summarizing the sequences and performance times, we turn to the job of grouping tasks into job stations so that we can meet the specified production rate. This process involves three steps:

1. Take the units required (demand or production rate) per day and divide them into the productive time available per day (in minutes or seconds). This operation gives us what is called the cycle time[3]—namely, the maximum time allowed at each workstation if the production rate is to be achieved:

$$\text{Cycle time} = \frac{\text{Production time available per day}}{\text{Units required per day}} \tag{9-4}$$

Cycle time
The maximum time that a product is allowed at each workstation.

2. Calculate the theoretical minimum number of workstations. This is the total task-duration time (the time it takes to make the product) divided by the cycle time. Fractions are rounded to the next higher whole number:

$$\text{Minimum number of workstations} = \frac{\sum_{i=1}^{n} \text{Time for task } i}{\text{Cycle time}} \tag{9-5}$$

where n is the number of assembly tasks.

3. Balance the line by assigning specific assembly tasks to each workstation. An efficient balance is one that will complete the required assembly, follow the specified sequence, and keep the idle time at each workstation to a minimum. A formal procedure for doing this is the following:

   a. Identify a master list of tasks.
   b. Eliminate those tasks that have been assigned.
   c. Eliminate those tasks whose precedence relationship has not been satisfied.
   d. Eliminate those tasks for which inadequate time is available at the workstation.
   e. Use one of the line-balancing "heuristics" described in Table 9.3. The five choices are (1) longest task time, (2) most following tasks, (3) ranked positional weight, (4) shortest task time, and (5) least number of following tasks. You may wish to test several of these heuristics to see which generates the "best" solution—that is, the smallest number of workstations and highest efficiency. Remember, however, that although heuristics provide solutions, they do not guarantee an optimal solution.

Heuristic
Problem solving using procedures and rules rather than mathematical optimization.

TABLE 9.3	Layout Heuristics That May Be Used to Assign Tasks to Workstations in Assembly-Line Balancing
1. *Longest task (operation) time*	From the available tasks, choose the task with the largest (longest) time.
2. *Most following tasks*	From the available tasks, choose the task with the largest number of following tasks.
3. *Ranked positional weight*	From the available tasks, choose the task for which the sum of the times for each following task is longest. (In Example 4 we see that the ranked positional weight of task C = 5(C) + 3(F) + 7(G) + 3(I) = 18, whereas the ranked positional weight of task D = 4(D) + 3(F) + 7(G) + 3(I) = 17; therefore, C would be chosen first, using this heuristic.)
4. *Shortest task (operations) time*	From the available tasks, choose the task with the shortest task time.
5. *Least number of following tasks*	From the available tasks, choose the task with the least number of subsequent tasks.

Example 4 illustrates a simple line-balancing procedure.

Example 4

BALANCING THE ASSEMBLY LINE

On the basis of the precedence diagram and activity times given in Example 3, Boeing determines that there are 480 productive minutes of work available per day. Furthermore, the production schedule requires that 40 units of the wing component be completed as output from the assembly line each day. It now wants to group the tasks into workstations.

APPROACH ▶ Following the three steps above, we compute the cycle time using Equation (9-4) and minimum number of workstations using Equation (9-5), and we assign tasks to workstations—in this case using the *most following tasks* heuristic.

SOLUTION ▶

$$\text{Cycle time (in minutes)} = \frac{480 \text{ minutes}}{40 \text{ units}}$$

$$= 12 \text{ minutes/unit}$$

$$\text{Minimum number of workstations} = \frac{\text{Total task time}}{\text{Cycle time}} = \frac{65}{12}$$

$$= 5.42, \text{ or } 6 \text{ stations}$$

Figure 9.13 shows one solution that does not violate the sequence requirements and that groups tasks into six one-person stations. To obtain this solution, activities with the most following tasks were moved into workstations to use as much of the available cycle time of 12 minutes as possible. The first workstation consumes 10 minutes and has an idle time of 2 minutes.

Figure **9.13**

A Six-Station Solution to the Line-Balancing Problem

STUDENT TIP ❗

Tasks C, D, and F can be grouped together in one workstation, provided that the physical facilities and skill levels meet the work requirements.

INSIGHT ▶ This is a reasonably well-balanced assembly line. The second and third workstations use 11 minutes. The fourth workstation groups three small tasks and balances perfectly at 12 minutes. The fifth has 1 minute of idle time, and the sixth (consisting of tasks G and I) has 2 minutes of idle time per cycle. Total idle time for this solution is 7 minutes per cycle.

LEARNING EXERCISE ▶ If task I required 6 minutes (instead of 3 minutes), how would this change the solution? [Answer: The cycle time would not change, and the *theoretical* minimum number of workstations would still be 6 (rounded up from 5.67), but it would take 7 stations to balance the line.]

RELATED PROBLEMS ▶ 9.12–9.24 (9.25–9.27 are available in MyOMLab)

EXCEL OM Data File **Ch09Ex4.xls** can be found in MyOMLab.

There are two measures of effectiveness of a balance assignment. The first measure computes the *efficiency* of a line balance by dividing the total task times by the product of the number of workstations required times the assigned (actual) cycle time of the *longest* workstation:

$$\text{Efficiency} = \frac{\Sigma \text{ Task times}}{(\textit{Actual} \text{ number of workstations}) \times (\text{Largest assigned cycle time})} \quad (9\text{-}6)$$

Operations managers compare different levels of efficiency for various numbers of workstations. In this way, a firm can determine the sensitivity of the line to changes in the production rate and workstation assignments.

The second measure computes the *idle time* for the line.

$$\text{Idle time} = (\text{Actual number of workstations} \times \text{Largest assigned cycle time}) - \Sigma \text{ Task times} \quad (9\text{-}7)$$

Example 5

DETERMINING LINE EFFICIENCY

Boeing needs to calculate the efficiency for Example 4.

APPROACH ▶ Equation (9-6) is applied.

SOLUTION ▶

$$\text{Efficiency} = \frac{65 \text{ minutes}}{(6 \text{ stations}) \times (12 \text{ minutes})} = \frac{65}{72} = 90.3\%$$

Note that opening a seventh workstation, for whatever reason, would decrease the efficiency of the balance to 77.4% (assuming that at least one of the workstations still required 12 minutes):

$$\text{Efficiency} = \frac{65 \text{ minutes}}{(7 \text{ stations}) \times (12 \text{ minutes})} = 77.4\%$$

INSIGHT ▶ Increasing efficiency may require that some tasks be divided into smaller elements and reassigned to other tasks. This facilitates a better balance between workstations and means higher efficiency. Note that we can also compute efficiency as 1 − (% Idle time), that is, [1 − (Idle time)/(Total time in workstations)].

LEARNING EXERCISE ▶ What is the efficiency if an eighth workstation is opened? [Answer: Efficiency = 67.7%.]

RELATED PROBLEMS ▶ 9.13f, 9.14c, 9.15f, 9.17c, 9.18b, 9.19b, 9.20e,g (9.25e, 9.26c, 9.27 are available in MyOMLab)

Large-scale line-balancing problems, like large process-layout problems, are often solved by computers. Computer programs such as Assembly Line Pro, Proplanner, Timer Pro, Flexible Line Balancing, and Promodel are available to handle the assignment of workstations on assembly lines with numerous work activities. Such software evaluates the thousands, or even millions, of possible workstation combinations much more efficiently than could ever be done by hand.

Summary

Layouts make a substantial difference in operating efficiency. The seven layout situations discussed in this chapter are (1) office, (2) retail, (3) warehouse, (4) fixed position, (5) process oriented, (6) work cells, and (7) product oriented. A variety of techniques have been developed to solve these layout problems. Office layouts often seek to maximize information flows, retail firms focus on product exposure, and warehouses attempt to optimize the trade-off between storage space and material handling cost.

The fixed-position layout problem attempts to minimize material handling costs within the constraint of limited space at the site. Process layouts minimize travel distances times the number of trips. Product layouts focus on reducing waste and the imbalance in an assembly line. Work cells are the result of identifying a family of products that justify a special configuration of machinery and equipment that reduces material travel and adjusts imbalances with cross-trained personnel.

Often, the issues in a layout problem are so wide-ranging that finding an optimal solution is not possible. For this reason, layout decisions, although the subject of substantial research effort, remain something of an art.

Key Terms

Office layout (p. 371)
Retail layout (p. 372)
Slotting fees (p. 374)
Servicescape (p. 375)
Warehouse layout (p. 375)
Cross-docking (p. 376)
Random stocking (p. 377)

Customizing (p. 377)
Fixed-position layout (p. 377)
Process-oriented layout (p. 378)
Job lots (p. 379)
Work cell (p. 383)
Takt time (p. 384)
Focused work center (p. 386)

Focused factory (p. 386)
Fabrication line (p. 386)
Assembly line (p. 386)
Assembly-line balancing (p. 386)
Cycle time (p. 389)
Heuristic (p. 389)

Ethical Dilemma

Although buried by mass customization and a proliferation of new products of numerous sizes and variations, grocery chains continue to seek to maximize payoff from their layout. Their layout includes a marketable commodity—shelf space—and they charge for it. This charge is known as a *slotting fee*. Recent estimates are that food manufacturers now spend some 13% of sales on trade promotions, which is paid to grocers to get them to promote and discount the manufacturer's products. A portion of these fees is for slotting, but slotting fees drive up the manufacturer's cost. They also put the small company with a new product at a disadvantage because small companies with limited resources may be squeezed out of the marketplace. Slotting fees may also mean that customers may no longer be able to find the special local brand. How ethical are slotting fees?

Image Source/Alamy

Discussion Questions

1. What are the seven layout strategies presented in this chapter?
2. What are the three factors that complicate a fixed-position layout?
3. What are the advantages and disadvantages of process layout?
4. How would an analyst obtain data and determine the number of trips in:
   (a) a hospital?
   (b) a machine shop?
   (c) an auto-repair shop?
5. What are the advantages and disadvantages of product layout?
6. What are the four assumptions (or preconditions) of establishing layout for high-volume, low-variety products?
7. What are the alternative forms of work cells discussed in this textbook?
8. What are the advantages and disadvantages of work cells?
9. What are the requirements for a focused work center or focused factory to be appropriate?
10. What are the two major trends influencing office layout?
11. What layout variables would you consider particularly important in an office layout where computer programs are written?

12. What layout innovations have you noticed recently in retail establishments?

13. What are the variables that a manager can manipulate in a retail layout?

14. Visit a local supermarket and sketch its layout. What are your observations regarding departments and their locations?

15. What is random stocking?

16. What information is necessary for random stocking to work?

17. Explain the concept of cross-docking.

18. What is a heuristic? Name several that can be used in assembly-line balancing.

Using Software to Solve Layout Problems

In addition to the many commercial software packages available for addressing layout problems, Excel OM and POM for Windows, both of which accompany this text, contain modules for the process problem and the assembly-line-balancing problem.

✗ USING EXCEL OM

Excel OM can assist in evaluating a series of department work assignments like the one we saw for the Walters Company in Example 1. The layout module can generate an optimal solution by enumeration or by computing the "total movement" cost for each layout you wish to examine. As such, it provides a speedy calculator for each flow–distance pairing.

Program 9.1 illustrates our inputs in the top two tables. We first enter department flows, then provide distances between work areas. Entering area assignments on a trial-and-error basis in the upper left of the top table generates movement computations at the bottom of the screen. Total movement is recalculated each time we try a new area assignment. It turns out that the assignment shown is optimal at 430 feet of movement.

Program **9.1**

Using Excel OM's Process Layout Module to Solve the Walters Company Problem in Example 1

P USING POM FOR WINDOWS

The POM for Windows facility layout module can be used to place up to 10 departments in 10 rooms to minimize the total distance traveled as a function of the distances between the rooms and the flow between departments. The program exchanges departments until no exchange will reduce the total amount of movement, meaning an optimal solution has been reached.

The POM for Windows and Excel OM modules for line balancing can handle a line with up to 99 tasks, each with up to six immediate predecessors. In this program, cycle time can be entered as either (1) *given*, if known, or (2) the *demand* rate can be entered with time available as shown. All five "heuristic rules" are used: (1) longest operation (task) time, (2) most following tasks, (3) ranked positional weight, (4) shortest operation (task) time, and (5) least number of following tasks. No one rule can guarantee an optimal solution, but POM for Windows displays the number of stations needed for each rule.

Appendix IV discusses further details regarding POM for Windows.

Solved Problems   Virtual Office Hours help is available in MyOMLab.

SOLVED PROBLEM 9.1

Aero Maintenance is a small aircraft engine maintenance facility located in Wichita, Kansas. Its new administrator, Ann Daniel, decides to improve material flow in the facility, using the process layout method she studied at Wichita State University. The current layout of Aero Maintenance's eight departments is shown in Figure 9.14.

The only physical restriction perceived by Daniel is the need to keep the entrance in its current location. All other departments can be moved to a different work area (each 10 feet square) if layout analysis indicates a move would be beneficial.

First, Daniel analyzes records to determine the number of material movements among departments in an average month. These data are shown in Figure 9.15. Her objective, Daniel decides, is to lay out the departments so as to minimize the total movement (distance traveled) of material in the facility. She writes her objective as:

$$\text{Minimize material movement} = \sum_{i=1}^{8}\sum_{j=1}^{8} X_{ij}C_{ij}$$

where X_{ij} = number of material movements per month (loads or trips) moving from department i to department j

C_{ij} = distance in feet between departments i and j (which, in this case, is the equivalent of cost per load to move between departments)

Note that this is only a slight modification of the cost-objective equation shown earlier in the chapter.

Daniel assumes that adjacent departments, such as entrance (now in work area A) and receiving (now in work area B), have a walking distance of 10 feet. Diagonal departments are also considered adjacent and assigned a distance of 10 feet. Nonadjacent departments, such as the entrance and parts (now in area C) or the entrance and inspection (area G) are 20 feet apart, and nonadjacent rooms, such as entrance and metallurgy (area D), are 30 feet apart. (Hence, 10 feet is considered 10 units of cost, 20 feet is 20 units of cost, and 30 feet is 30 units of cost.)

Given the above information, redesign Aero Maintenance's layout to improve its material flow efficiency.

Current Aero Maintenance Layout

Area A	Area B	Area C	Area D	
Entrance (1)	Receiving (2)	Parts (3)	Metallurgy (4)	10'
Breakdown (5)	Assembly (6)	Inspection (7)	Test (8)	10'
Area E	Area F	Area G	Area H	

← 40' →

Figure 9.14

Aero Maintenance Layout

Figure 9.15

Number of Material Movements (Loads) Between Departments in 1 Month

	Entrance (1)	Receiving (2)	Parts (3)	Metallurgy (4)	Breakdown (5)	Assembly (6)	Inspection (7)	Test (8)	Department
		100	100	0	0	0	0	0	Entrance (1)
			0	50	20	0	0	0	Receiving (2)
				30	30	0	0	0	Parts (3)
					20	0	0	20	Metallurgy (4)
						20	0	10	Breakdown (5)
							30	0	Assembly (6)
								0	Inspection (7)
									Test (8)

SOLUTION

First, establish Aero Maintenance's current layout, as shown in Figure 9.16. Then, by analyzing the current layout, compute material movement:

$$
\begin{aligned}
\text{Total movement} = &\ \underset{\text{1 to 2}}{(100 \times 10')} + \underset{\text{1 to 3}}{(100 \times 20')} + \underset{\text{2 to 4}}{(50 \times 20')} + \underset{\text{2 to 5}}{(20 \times 10')} \\
&+ \underset{\text{3 to 4}}{(30 \times 10')} + \underset{\text{3 to 5}}{(30 \times 20')} + \underset{\text{4 to 5}}{(20 \times 30')} + \underset{\text{4 to 8}}{(20 \times 10')} \\
&+ \underset{\text{5 to 6}}{(20 \times 10')} + \underset{\text{5 to 8}}{(10 \times 30')} + \underset{\text{5 to 7}}{(30 \times 10')} \\
= &\ 1{,}000 + 2{,}000 + 1{,}000 + 200 + 300 + 600 + 600 \\
&+ 200 + 200 + 300 + 300 \\
= &\ 6{,}700 \text{ feet}
\end{aligned}
$$

Figure **9.16**

Current Material Flow

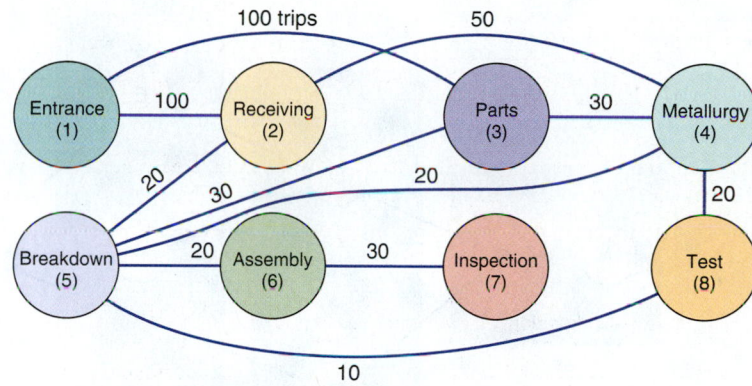

Propose a new layout that will reduce the current figure of 6,700 feet. Two useful changes, for example, are to switch departments 3 and 5 and to interchange departments 4 and 6. This change would result in the schematic shown in Figure 9.17:

$$
\begin{aligned}
\text{Total movement} = &\ \underset{\text{1 to 2}}{(100 \times 10')} + \underset{\text{1 to 3}}{(100 \times 10')} + \underset{\text{2 to 4}}{(50 \times 10')} + \underset{\text{2 to 5}}{(20 \times 10')} \\
&+ \underset{\text{3 to 4}}{(30 \times 10')} + \underset{\text{3 to 5}}{(30 \times 20')} + \underset{\text{4 to 5}}{(20 \times 10')} + \underset{\text{4 to 8}}{(20 \times 20')} \\
&+ \underset{\text{5 to 6}}{(20 \times 10')} + \underset{\text{5 to 8}}{(10 \times 10')} + \underset{\text{6 to 7}}{(30 \times 10')} \\
= &\ 1{,}000 + 1{,}000 + 500 + 200 + 300 + 600 + 200 \\
&+ 400 + 200 + 100 + 300 \\
= &\ 4{,}800 \text{ feet}
\end{aligned}
$$

Do you see any room for further improvement?

Figure **9.17**

Improved Layout

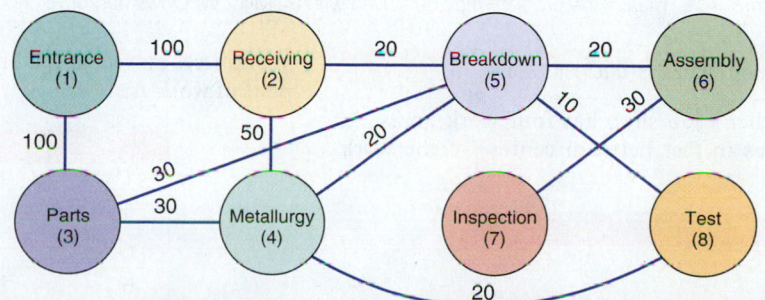

SOLVED PROBLEM 9.2

The assembly line whose activities are shown in Figure 9.18 has an 8-minute cycle time. Draw the precedence graph, and find the minimum possible number of one-person workstations. Then arrange the work activities into workstations so as to balance the line. What is the efficiency of your line balance?

TASK	PERFORMANCE TIME (MINUTES)	TASK MUST FOLLOW THIS TASK
A	5	—
B	3	A
C	4	B
D	3	B
E	6	C
F	1	C
G	4	D, E, F
H	2	G
	28	

Figure **9.18**

Four-Station Solution to the Line-Balancing Problem

SOLUTION

The theoretical minimum number of workstations is:

$$\frac{\Sigma t_i}{\text{Cycle time}} = \frac{28 \text{ minutes}}{8 \text{ minutes}} = 3.5, \text{ or 4 stations}$$

The precedence graph and one good layout are shown in Figure 9.18:

$$\text{Efficiency} = \frac{\text{Total task time}}{(\text{Actual number of workstations}) \times (\text{Largest assigned cycle time})} = \frac{28}{(4)(8)} = 87.5\%$$

Problems   *Note:* **Px** means the problem may be solved with POM for Windows and/or Excel OM.

Problems 9.1–9.10 relate to Process-Oriented Layout

•• **9.1**   Gordon Miller's job shop has four work areas, A, B, C, and D. Distances in feet between centers of the work areas are:

	A	B	C	D
A	—	4	9	7
B	—	—	6	8
C	—	—	—	10
D	—	—	—	—

Workpieces moved, in hundreds of workpieces per week, between pairs of work areas, are:

	A	B	C	D
A	—	8	7	4
B	—	—	3	2
C	—	—	—	6
D	—	—	—	—

It costs Gordon $1 to move 1 work piece 1 foot. What is the weekly total material handling cost of the layout? **Px**

•• **9.2** A Missouri job shop has four departments—machining (M), dipping in a chemical bath (D), finishing (F), and plating (P)—assigned to four work areas. The operations manager, Mary Marrs, has gathered the following data for this job shop as it is currently laid out (Plan A).

100s of Workpieces Moved Between Work Areas Each Year Plan A

	M	D	F	P
M	—	6	18	2
D	—	—	4	2
F	—	—	—	18
P	—	—	—	—

Distances Between Work Areas (Departments) in Feet

	M	D	F	P
M	—	20	12	8
D	—	—	6	10
F	—	—	—	4
P	—	—	—	—

It costs $0.50 to move 1 workpiece 1 foot in the job shop. Marrs's goal is to find a layout that has the lowest material handling cost.
a) Determine cost of the current layout, Plan A, from the data above.
b) One alternative is to switch those departments with the high loads, namely, finishing (F) and plating (P), which alters the distance between them and machining (M) and dipping (D), as follows:

Distances Between Work Areas (Departments) in Feet Plan B

	M	D	F	P
M	—	20	8	12
D	—	—	10	6
F	—	—	—	4
P	—	—	—	—

What is the cost of *this* layout?
c) Marrs now wants you to evaluate Plan C, which also switches milling (M) and drilling (D), below.

Distance Between Work Areas (Departments) in Feet Plan C

	M	D	F	P
M	—	20	10	6
D	—	—	8	12
F	—	—	—	4
P	—	—	—	—

What is the cost of *this* layout?
d) Which layout is best from a cost perspective? **Px**

• **9.3** Three departments—milling (M), drilling (D), and sawing (S)—are assigned to three work areas in Victor Berardis's machine shop in Vent, Ohio. The number of workpieces moved per day and the distances between the centers of the work areas, in feet, follow.

Pieces Moved Between Work Areas Each Day

	M	D	S
M	—	23	32
D	—	—	20
S	—	—	—

Distances Between Centers of Work Areas (Departments) in Feet

	M	D	S
M	—	10	5
D	—	—	8
S	—	—	—

It costs $2 to move 1 workpiece 1 foot.
What is the cost?

•• **9.4** Roy Creasey Enterprises, a machine shop, is planning to move to a new, larger location. The new building will be 60 feet long by 40 feet wide. Creasey envisions the building as having six distinct production areas, roughly equal in size. He feels strongly about safety and intends to have marked pathways throughout the building to facilitate the movement of people and materials. See the following building schematic.

Building Schematic (with work areas 1–6)

His foreman has completed a month-long study of the number of loads of material that have moved from one process to another in the current building. This information is contained in the following flow matrix.

Flow Matrix Between Production Processes

FROM \ TO	MATERIALS	WELDING	DRILLS	LATHES	GRINDERS	BENDERS
Materials	0	100	50	0	0	50
Welding	25	0	0	50	0	0
Drills	25	0	0	0	50	0
Lathes	0	25	0	0	20	0
Grinders	50	0	100	0	0	0
Benders	10	0	20	0	0	0

Finally, Creasey has developed the following matrix to indicate distances between the work areas shown in the building schematic.

Distance Between Work Areas

	1	2	3	4	5	6
1		20	40	20	40	60
2			20	40	20	40
3				60	40	20
4					20	40
5						20
6						

What is the appropriate layout of the new building? **Px**

•• **9.5** Adam Munson Manufacturing, in Gainesville, Florida, wants to arrange its four work centers so as to minimize interdepartmental parts handling costs. The flows and existing facility layout are shown in Figure 9.19. For example, to move a part from Work Center A to Work Center C is a 60-foot movement distance. It is 90 feet from A to D.

Parts Moved Between Work Centers

	A	B	C	D
A	—	450	550	50
B	350	—	200	0
C	0	0	—	750
D	0	0	0	—

Existing Layout

| A | B | C | D |

|—— 30' ——|—— 30' ——|—— 30' ——|

Figure 9.19

Munson Manufacturing

a) What is the "load × distance," or "movement cost," of the layout shown?

b) Provide an improved layout and compute its movement cost. **Px**

••• **9.6** You have just been hired as the director of operations for Reid Chocolates, a purveyor of exceptionally fine candies. Reid Chocolates has two kitchen layouts under consideration for its recipe making and testing department. The strategy is to provide the best kitchen layout possible so that food scientists can devote their time and energy to product improvement, not wasted effort in the kitchen. You have been asked to evaluate these two kitchen layouts and to prepare a recommendation for your boss, Mr. Reid, so that he can proceed to place the contract for building the kitchens. [See Figure 9.20(a), and Figure 9.20(b).] **Px**

Number of trips between work centers:

From: \ To:	Refrigerator 1	Counter 2	Sink 3	Storage 4	Stove 5
Refrig. 1	0	8	13	0	0
Counter 2	5	0	3	3	8
Sink 3	3	12	0	4	0
Storage 4	3	0	0	0	5
Stove 5	0	8	4	10	0

Figure 9.20(a)

Layout Options

Kitchen layout #1
Walking distance in feet

| Refrig. 1 | Counter 2 | Sink 3 | Storage 4 | Stove 5 |

4   4   4   4

Kitchen layout #2
Walking distance in feet

Figure 9.20(b)

••• **9.7** Reid Chocolates (see Problem 9.6) is considering a third layout, as shown below. Evaluate its effectiveness in trip-distance feet. **Px**

Kitchen layout #3
Walking distance in feet

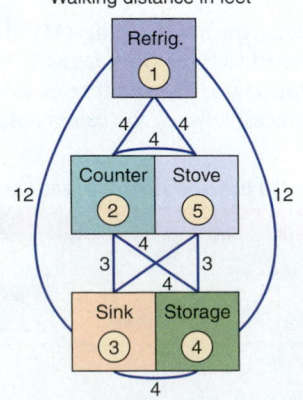

••• **9.8** Reid Chocolates (see Problems 9.6 and 9.7) has yet two more layouts to consider.
a) Layout 4 is shown below. What is the total trip distance?
b) Layout 5, which also follows, has what total trip distance?

Kitchen layout #4
Walking distance in feet

Kitchen layout #5
Walking distance in feet

•• **9.9** Six processes are to be laid out in six areas along a long corridor at Rita Gibson Accounting Services in Daytona Beach. The distance between adjacent work centers is 40 feet. The number of trips between work centers is given in the following table:

	TRIPS BETWEEN PROCESSES					
			TO			
FROM	A	B	C	D	E	F
A		18	25	73	12	54
B			96	23	31	45
C				41	22	20
D					19	57
E						48
F						

a) Assign the processes to the work areas in a way that minimizes the total flow, using a method that places processes with highest flow adjacent to each other.
b) What assignment minimizes the total traffic flow? **Px**

Additional problem 9.10 is available in MyOMLab.

Problem 9.11 relates to Work Cells

•• **9.11** After an extensive product analysis using group technology, Leon Bazil has identified a product he believes should be pulled out of his process facility and handled in a work cell. Leon has identified the following operations as necessary for the work cell. The customer expects delivery of 250 units per day, and the workday is 420 minutes.
a) What is the takt time?
b) How many employees should be cross-trained for the cell?
c) Which operations may warrant special consideration?

OPERATION	STANDARD TIME (min)
Shear	1.1
Bend	1.1
Weld	1.7
Clean	3.1
Paint	1.0

Problems 9.12–9.27 relate to Repetitive and Product-Oriented Layout

•• **9.12** Stanford Rosenberg Computing wants to establish an assembly line for producing a new product, the Personal Digital Assistant (PDA). The tasks, task times, and immediate predecessors for the tasks are as follows:

TASK	TIME (sec)	IMMEDIATE PREDECESSORS
A	12	—
B	15	A
C	8	A
D	5	B, C
E	20	D

Rosenberg's goal is to produce 180 PDAs per hour.
a) What is the cycle time?
b) What is the theoretical minimum for the number of workstations that Rosenberg can achieve in this assembly line?
c) Can the theoretical minimum actually be reached when workstations are assigned? **Px**

••• **9.13** Illinois Furniture, Inc., produces all types of office furniture. The "Executive Secretary" is a chair that has been designed using ergonomics to provide comfort during long work hours. The chair sells for $130. There are 480 minutes available during the day, and the average daily demand has been 50 chairs. There are eight tasks:

TASK	PERFORMANCE TIME (min)	TASK MUST FOLLOW TASK LISTED BELOW
A	4	—
B	7	—
C	6	A, B
D	5	C
E	6	D
F	7	E
G	8	E
H	6	F, G

a) Draw a precedence diagram of this operation.
b) What is the cycle time for this operation?
c) What is the theoretical minimum number of workstations?
d) Assign tasks to workstations.
e) What is the idle time per cycle?
f) How much total idle time is present in an 8-hour shift?
g) What is the efficiency of the assembly line, given your answer in (d)? **Px**

•• **9.14** Sue Helms Appliances wants to establish an assembly line to manufacture its new product, the Micro Popcorn Popper. The goal is to produce five poppers per hour. The tasks, task times, and immediate predecessors for producing one Micro Popcorn Popper are as follows:

TASK	TIME (min)	IMMEDIATE PREDECESSORS
A	10	—
B	12	A
C	8	A, B
D	6	B, C
E	6	C
F	6	D, E

a) What is the theoretical minimum for the smallest number of workstations that Helms can achieve in this assembly line?
b) Graph the assembly line, and assign workers to workstations. Can you assign them with the theoretical minimum?
c) What is the efficiency of your assignment? **Px**

•• **9.15** The Action Toy Company has decided to manufacture a new train set, the production of which is broken into six steps. The demand for the train is 4,800 units per 40-hour workweek:

TASK	PERFORMANCE TIME (sec)	PREDECESSORS
A	20	None
B	30	A
C	15	A
D	15	A
E	10	B, C
F	30	D, E

a) Draw a precedence diagram of this operation.
b) Given the demand, what is the cycle time for this operation?
c) What is the theoretical minimum number of workstations?
d) Assign tasks to workstations.

e) How much total idle time is present each cycle?

f) What is the efficiency of the assembly line with five stations? With six stations? **Px**

•• 9.16 The following table details the tasks required for Indiana-based Frank Pianki Industries to manufacture a fully portable industrial vacuum cleaner. The times in the table are in minutes. Demand forecasts indicate a need to operate with a cycle time of 10 minutes.

ACTIVITY	ACTIVITY DESCRIPTION	IMMEDIATE PREDECESSORS	TIME
A	Attach wheels to tub	—	5
B	Attach motor to lid	—	1.5
C	Attach battery pack	B	3
D	Attach safety cutoff	C	4
E	Attach filters	B	3
F	Attach lid to tub	A, E	2
G	Assemble attachments	—	3
H	Function test	D, F, G	3.5
I	Final inspection	H	2
J	Packing	I	2

a) Draw the appropriate precedence diagram for this production line.

b) Assign tasks to workstations and determine how much idle time is present each cycle.

c) Discuss how this balance could be improved to 100%.

d) What is the *theoretical* minimum number of workstations? **Px**

•• 9.17 Tailwind, Inc., produces high-quality but expensive training shoes for runners. The Tailwind shoe, which sells for $210, contains both gas- and liquid-filled compartments to provide more stability and better protection against knee, foot, and back injuries. Manufacturing the shoes requires 10 separate tasks. There are 400 minutes available for manufacturing the shoes in the plant each day. Daily demand is 60. The information for the tasks is as follows:

TASK	PERFORMANCE TIME (min)	TASK MUST FOLLOW TASK LISTED BELOW
A	1	—
B	3	A
C	2	B
D	4	B
E	1	C, D
F	3	A
G	2	F
H	5	G
I	1	E, H
J	3	I

a) Draw the precedence diagram.

b) Assign tasks to the minimum feasible number of workstations according to the "ranked positioned weight" decision rule.

c) What is the efficiency of the process you completed in (b)?

d) What is the idle time per cycle? **Px**

•• 9.18 The Mach 10 is a one-person sailboat manufactured by Creative Leisure. The final assembly plant is in Cupertino, California. The assembly area is available for production of the

Mach 10 for 200 minutes per day. (The rest of the time it is busy making other products.) The daily demand is 60 boats. Given the information in the table,

a) Draw the precedence diagram and assign tasks using five workstations.

b) What is the efficiency of the assembly line, using your answer to (a)?

c) What is the *theoretical* minimum number of workstations?

d) What is the idle time per boat produced? **Px**

TASK	PERFORMANCE TIME (min)	TASK MUST FOLLOW TASK LISTED BELOW
A	1	—
B	1	A
C	2	A
D	1	C
E	3	C
F	1	C
G	1	D, E, F
H	2	B
I	1	G, H

Ivan Smuk/Shutterstock

•• 9.19 Because of the expected high demand for Mach 10, Creative Leisure has decided to increase manufacturing time available to produce the Mach 10 (see Problem 9.18).

a) If demand remained the same but 300 minutes were available each day on the assembly line, how many workstations would be needed?

b) What would be the efficiency of the new system, using the actual number of workstations from (a)?

c) What would be the impact on the system if 400 minutes were available? **Px**

••• 9.20 Dr. Lori Baker, operations manager at Nesa Electronics, prides herself on excellent assembly-line balancing. She has been told that the firm needs to complete 96 instruments per 24-hour day. The assembly-line activities are:

TASK	TIME (min)	PREDECESSORS
A	3	—
B	6	—
C	7	A
D	5	A, B
E	2	B
F	4	C
G	5	F
H	7	D, E
I	1	H
J	6	E
K	4	G, I, J
	50	

a) Draw the precedence diagram.
b) If the daily (24-hour) production rate is 96 units, what is the highest allowable cycle time?
c) If the cycle time after allowances is given as 10 minutes, what is the daily (24-hour) production rate?
d) With a 10-minute cycle time, what is the theoretical minimum number of stations with which the line can be balanced?
e) With a 10-minute cycle time and six workstations, what is the efficiency?
f) What is the total idle time per cycle with a 10-minute cycle time and six workstations?
g) What is the best workstation assignment you can make without exceeding a 10-minute cycle time, and what is its efficiency? **Px**

• • 9.21 Suppose production requirements in Solved Problem 9.2 (see page 396) increase and require a reduction in cycle time from 8 minutes to 7 minutes. Balance the line once again, using the new cycle time. Note that it is not possible to combine task times so as to group tasks into the minimum number of workstations. This condition occurs in actual balancing problems fairly often. **Px**

• • 9.22 The preinduction physical examination given by the U.S. Army involves the following seven activities:

ACTIVITY	AVERAGE TIME (min)
Medical history	10
Blood tests	8
Eye examination	5
Measurements (e.g., weight, height, blood pressure)	7
Medical examination	16
Psychological interview	12
Exit medical evaluation	10

These activities can be performed in any order, with two exceptions: Medical history must be taken first, and Exit medical evaluation is last. At present, there are three paramedics and two physicians on duty during each shift. Only physicians can perform exit evaluations and conduct psychological interviews. Other activities can be carried out by either physicians or paramedics.

a) Develop a layout and balance the line.
b) How many people can be processed per hour?
c) Which activity accounts for the current bottleneck?
d) What is the total idle time per cycle?
e) If one more physician and one more paramedic can be placed on duty, how would you redraw the layout? What is the new throughput?

• • • 9.23 Samuel Smith's company wants to establish an assembly line to manufacture its new product, the iStar phone. Samuel's goal is to produce 60 iStars per hour. Tasks, task times, and immediate predecessors are as follows:

TASK	TIME (sec)	IMMEDIATE PREDECESSORS	TASK	TIME (sec)	IMMEDIATE PREDECESSORS
A	40	—	F	25	C
B	30	A	G	15	C
C	50	A	H	20	D, E
D	40	B	I	18	F, G
E	6	B	J	30	H, I

a) What is the theoretical minimum for the number of workstations that Samuel can achieve in this assembly line?
b) Use the *most following tasks* heuristic to balance an assembly line for the iStar phone.
c) How many workstations are in your answer to (b)?
d) What is the efficiency of your answer to (b)? **Px**

• • • • 9.24 As the Cottrell Bicycle Co. of St. Louis completes plans for its new assembly line, it identifies 25 different tasks in the production process. VP of Operations Jonathan Cottrell now faces the job of balancing the line. He lists precedences and provides time estimates for each step based on work-sampling techniques. His goal is to produce 1,000 bicycles per standard 40-hour workweek.

TASK	TIME (sec)	PRECEDENCE TASKS	TASK	TIME (sec)	PRECEDENCE TASKS
K3	60	—	E3	109	F3
K4	24	K3	D6	53	F4
K9	27	K3	D7	72	F9, E2, E3
J1	66	K3	D8	78	E3, D6
J2	22	K3	D9	37	D6
J3	3	—	C1	78	F7
G4	79	K4, K9	B3	72	D7, D8, D9, C1
G5	29	K9, J1	B5	108	C1
F3	32	J2	B7	18	B3
F4	92	J2	A1	52	B5
F7	21	J3	A2	72	B5
F9	126	G4	A3	114	B7, A1, A2
E2	18	G5, F3			

a) Balance this operation, using various heuristics. Which is best and why?
b) What happens if the firm can change to a 41-hour workweek? **Px**

Additional problems 9.25–9.27 are available in MyOMLab.

CASE STUDIES

State Automobile License Renewals

Henry Coupe, the manager of a metropolitan branch office of the state department of motor vehicles, attempted to analyze the driver's license-renewal operations. He had to perform several steps. After examining the license-renewal process, he identified those steps and associated times required to perform each step, as shown in the following table:

State Automobile License Renewal Process Times

STEP	AVERAGE TIME TO PERFORM (sec)
1. Review renewal application for correctness	15
2. Process and record payment	30
3. Check file for violations and restrictions	60
4. Conduct eye test	40
5. Photograph applicant	20
6. Issue temporary license	30

Coupe found that each step was assigned to a different person. Each application was a separate process in the sequence shown. He determined that his office should be prepared to accommodate a maximum demand of processing 120 renewal applicants per hour.

He observed that work was unevenly divided among clerks and that the clerk responsible for checking violations tended to shortcut her task to keep up with the others. Long lines built up during the maximum-demand periods.

Coupe also found that Steps 1 to 4 were handled by general clerks who were each paid $12 per hour. Step 5 was performed by a photographer paid $16 per hour. (Branch offices were charged $10 per hour for each camera to perform photography.)

Step 6, issuing temporary licenses, was required by state policy to be handled by uniformed motor vehicle officers. Officers were paid $18 per hour but could be assigned to any job except photography.

A review of the jobs indicated that Step 1, reviewing applications for correctness, had to be performed before any other step could be taken. Similarly, Step 6, issuing temporary licenses, could not be performed until all the other steps were completed.

Henry Coupe was under severe pressure to increase productivity and reduce costs, but he was also told by the regional director that he must accommodate the demand for renewals. Otherwise, "heads would roll."

Discussion Questions

1. What is the maximum number of applications per hour that can be handled by the present configuration of the process?

2. How many applications can be processed per hour if a second clerk is added to check for violations?

3. If the second clerk could be added *anywhere* you choose (and not necessarily to check for violations, as in Question 2), what is the maximum number of applications the process can handle? What is the new configuration?

4. How would you suggest modifying the process to accommodate 120 applications per hour? What is the cost per application of this new configuration?

Source: Modified from a case by W. Earl Sasser, Paul R. Olson, and D. Daryl Wyckoff, *Management of Services Operations: Text, Cases, and Readings* (Boston: Allyn & Bacon).

Laying Out Arnold Palmer Hospital's New Facility

Video Case

When Orlando's Arnold Palmer Hospital began plans to create a new 273-bed, 11-story hospital across the street from its existing facility, which was bursting at the seams in terms of capacity, a massive planning process began. The $100 million building, opened in 2006, was long overdue, according to Executive Director Kathy Swanson: "We started Arnold Palmer Hospital in 1989, with a mission to provide quality services for children and women in a comforting, family-friendly environment. Since then we have served well over 1.5 million women and children and now deliver more than 12,000 babies a year. By 2001, we simply ran out of room, and it was time for us to grow."

The new hospital's unique, circular pod design provides a maximally efficient layout in all areas of the hospital, creating a patient-centered environment. *Servicescape* design features include a serene environment created through the use of warm colors, private rooms with pull-down Murphy beds for family members, 14-foot ceilings, and natural lighting with oversized windows in patient rooms. But these radical new features did not come easily. "This pod concept with a central nursing area and pie-shaped rooms resulted from over 1,000 planning meetings of 35 user groups, extensive motion and time studies, and computer simulations of the daily movements of nurses," says Swanson.

In a traditional linear hospital layout, called the *racetrack* design, patient rooms line long hallways, and a nurse might walk 2.7 miles per day serving patient needs at Arnold Palmer. "Some nurses spent 30% of their time simply walking. With the nursing shortage and the high cost of health care professionals, efficiency is a major concern," added Swanson. With the nursing station in the center of 10- or 12-bed circular pods, no patient room is more than 14 feet from a station. The time savings are in the 20% range. Swanson pointed to Figures 9.21 and 9.22 as examples of the old and new walking and trip distances.*

"We have also totally redesigned our neonatal rooms," says Swanson. "In the old system, there were 16 neonatal beds in a large and often noisy rectangular room. The new building features semiprivate rooms for these tiny babies. The rooms are much improved, with added privacy and a quiet, simulated night atmosphere, in addition to pull-down beds for parents to use. Our research shows that babies improve and develop much more quickly with this layout design. Layout and environment indeed impact patient care!"

*Layout and walking distances, including some of the numbers in Figures 9.21 and 9.22, have been simplified for purposes of this case.

Figure **9.21**

Traditional Hospital Layout

Patient rooms are on two linear hallways with exterior windows. Supply rooms are on interior corridors. This layout is called a "racetrack" design.

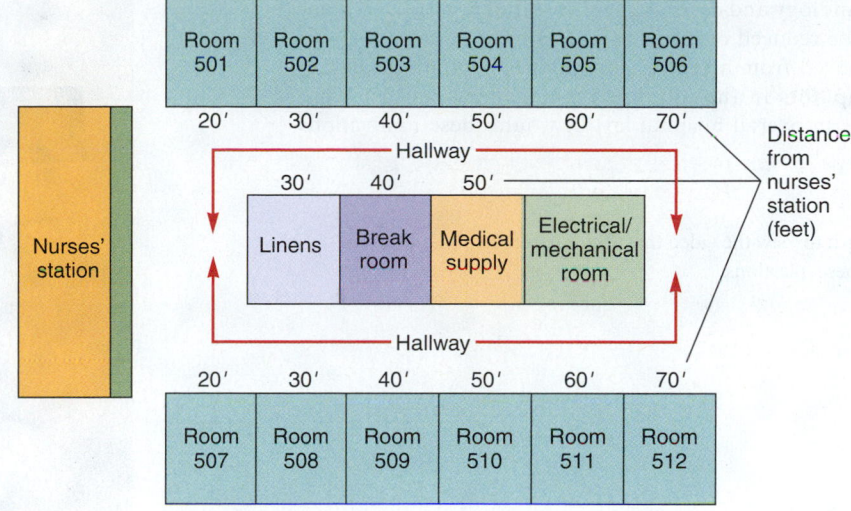

Figure **9.22**

New Pod Design for Hospital Layout

Note that each room is 14 feet from the pod's *local* nursing station. The *break rooms* and the *central medical station* are each about 60 feet from the local nursing pod. Pod *linen supply* rooms are also 14 feet from the local nursing station.

Courtesy Arnold Palmer Medical Center

Discussion Questions*

1. Identify the many variables that a hospital needs to consider in layout design.

2. What are the advantages of the circular pod design over the traditional linear hallway layout found in most hospitals?

3. Figure 9.21 illustrates a sample linear hallway layout. During a period of random observation, nurse Thomas Smith's day includes 6 trips from the nursing station to each of the 12 patient rooms (back and forth), 20 trips to the medical supply room, 5 trips to the break room, and 12 trips to the linen supply room. What is his total distance traveled in miles?

4. Figure 9.22 illustrates an architect's drawing of Arnold Palmer Hospital's new circular pod system. If nurse Susan Jones's day includes 7 trips from the nursing pod to each of the 12 rooms (back and forth), 20 trips to central medical supply, 6 trips to the break room, and 12 trips to the pod linen supply, how many miles does she walk during her shift? What are the differences in the travel times between the two nurses for this random day?

5. The concept of *servicescapes* is discussed in this chapter. Describe why this is so important at Arnold Palmer Hospital, and give examples of its use in layout design.

6. As technology and costs change, hospitals continue to innovate. The reduced cost of computers means some hospitals have moved from a central computer at the nurse's station to computers in the room or on carts (see photo). What changes in overall hospital layout would these innovations suggest?

*You may wish to view the video that accompanies this case before addressing these questions.

Rubbermaid Healthcare.

Facility Layout at Wheeled Coach

Video Case

When President Bob Collins began his career at Wheeled Coach, the world's largest manufacturer of ambulances, there were only a handful of employees. Now the firm's Florida plant has a workforce of 350. The physical plant has also expanded, with offices, R&D, final assembly, and wiring, cabinetry, and upholstery work cells in one large building. Growth has forced the painting work cell into a separate building, aluminum fabrication and body installation into another, inspection and shipping into a fourth, and warehousing into yet another.

Like many other growing companies, Wheeled Coach was not able to design its facility from scratch. And although management realizes that material handling costs are a little higher than an ideal layout would provide, Collins is pleased with the way the facility has evolved and employees have adapted. The aluminum cutting work cell lies adjacent to body fabrication, which, in turn, is located next to the body-installation work cell. And while the vehicle must be driven across a street to one building for painting and then to another for final assembly, at least the ambulance is on wheels. Collins is also satisfied with the flexibility shown in the design of the work cells. Cell construction is flexible and can accommodate changes in product mix and volume. In addition, work cells are typically small and movable, with many work benches and staging racks borne on wheels so that they can be easily rearranged and products transported to the assembly line.

Assembly-line balancing is one key problem facing Wheeled Coach and every other repetitive manufacturer. Produced on a schedule calling for four 10-hour work days per week, once an ambulance is on one of the six final assembly lines, it *must* move forward each day to the next workstation. Balancing just enough workers and tasks at each of the seven workstations is a never-ending challenge. Too many workers end up running into each other; too few can't finish an ambulance in seven days. Constant shifting of design and mix and improved analysis has led to frequent changes.

Discussion Questions*

1. What analytical techniques are available to help a company like Wheeled Coach deal with layout problems?
2. What suggestions would you make to Bob Collins about his layout?
3. How would you measure the "efficiency" of this layout?

*You may wish to view the video that accompanies this case before addressing these questions.

- **Additional Case Study:** Visit MyOMLab for this free case study:

  Microfix, Inc.: This company needs to balance its PC manufacturing assembly line and deal with sensitivity analysis of time estimates.

Endnotes

1. Fayurd, A. L., and J. Weeks. "Who Moved My Cube?" *Harvard Business Review* (July–August, 2011): 102.
2. *Takt* is German for "time," "measure," or "beat" and is used in this context as the rate at which completed units must be produced to satisfy customer demand.
3. *Cycle time* is the maximum time allowed to accomplish a task or process step. Several process steps may be necessary to complete the product. *Takt time*, discussed earlier, is determined by the customer and is the speed at which completed units must be produced to satisfy customer demand.

Chapter 9 *Rapid Review*

Main Heading	Review Material	MyOMLab
THE STRATEGIC IMPORTANCE OF LAYOUT DECISIONS (p. 370)	Layout has numerous strategic implications because it establishes an organization's competitive priorities in regard to capacity, processes, flexibility, and cost, as well as quality of work life, customer contact, and image. *The objective of layout strategy is to develop an effective and efficient layout that will meet the firm's competitive requirements.*	Concept Questions: 1.1–1.4
TYPES OF LAYOUT (pp. 370–371)	Types of layout and examples of their typical objectives include: 1. *Office layout*: Locate workers requiring frequent contact close to one another. 2. *Retail layout*: Expose customers to high-margin items. 3. *Warehouse layout*: Balance low-cost storage with low-cost material handling. 4. *Fixed-position layout*: Move material to the limited storage areas around the site. 5. *Process-oriented layout*: Manage varied material flow for each product. 6. *Work-cell layout*: Identify a product family, build teams, and cross-train team members. 7. *Product-oriented layout*: Equalize the task time at each workstation.	Concept Questions: 2.1–2.4
OFFICE LAYOUT (pp. 371–372)	■ **Office layout**—The grouping of workers, their equipment, and spaces/offices to provide for comfort, safety, and movement of information. A *relationship chart* displays a "closeness value" between each pair of people and/or departments that need to be placed in the office layout.	Concept Questions: 3.1–3.4
RETAIL LAYOUT (pp. 372–375)	■ **Retail layout**—An approach that addresses flow, allocates space, and responds to customer behavior. Retail layouts are based on the idea that sales and profitability vary directly with customer exposure to products. The main *objective of retail layout is to maximize profitability per square foot of floor space* (or, in some stores, per linear foot of shelf space). ■ **Slotting fees**—Fees manufacturers pay to get shelf space for their products. ■ **Servicescape**—The physical surroundings in which a service takes place and how they affect customers and employees.	Concept Questions: 4.1–4.4
WAREHOUSE AND STORAGE LAYOUTS (pp. 375–377)	■ **Warehouse layout**—A design that attempts to minimize total cost by addressing trade-offs between space and material handling. The variety of items stored and the number of items "picked" has direct bearing on the optimal layout. Modern warehouse management is often an automated procedure using *automated storage and retrieval systems* (ASRSs). ■ **Cross-docking**—Avoiding the placement of materials or supplies in storage by processing them as they are received for shipment. Cross-docking requires both tight scheduling and accurate inbound product identification. ■ **Random stocking**—Used in warehousing to locate stock wherever there is an open location. ■ **Customizing**—Using warehousing to add value to a product through component modification, repair, labeling, and packaging.	Concept Questions: 5.1–5.4
FIXED-POSITION LAYOUT (pp. 377–378)	■ **Fixed-position layout**—A system that addresses the layout requirements of stationary projects. Fixed-position layouts involve three complications: (1) there is limited space at virtually all sites, (2) different materials are needed at different stages of a project, and (3) the volume of materials needed is dynamic.	Concept Questions: 6.1–6.4
PROCESS-ORIENTED LAYOUT (pp. 378–383)	■ **Process-oriented layout**—A layout that deals with low-volume, high-variety production in which like machines and equipment are grouped together. ■ **Job lots**—Groups or batches of parts processed together. $$\text{Minimize cost} = \sum_{i=1}^{n}\sum_{j=1}^{n} X_{ij}C_{ij} \qquad (9\text{-}1)$$	Concept Questions: 7.1–7.4 Problems: 9.1–9.10 Virtual Office Hours for Solved Problem: 9.1 **VIDEO 9.1** Laying Out Arnold Palmer Hospital's New Facility **ACTIVE** MODEL 9.1

Main Heading	Review Material	MyOMLab
WORK CELLS (pp. 383–386)	■ **Work cell**—An arrangement of machines and personnel that focuses on making a single product or family of related products. ■ **Takt time**—Pace of production to meet customer demands. Takt time = Total work time available/ Units required to satisfy customer demand (9-2) Workers required = Total operation time required/Takt time (9-3) ■ **Focused work center**—A permanent or semipermanent product-oriented arrangement of machines and personnel. ■ **Focused factory**—A facility designed to produce similar products or components.	Concept Questions: 8.1–8.4 Problem: 9.11
REPETITIVE AND PRODUCT-ORIENTED LAYOUT (pp. 386–391)	■ **Fabrication line**—A machine-paced, product-oriented facility for building components. ■ **Assembly line**—An approach that puts fabricated parts together at a series of workstations; a repetitive process. ■ **Assembly-line balancing**—Obtaining output at each workstation on a production line in order to minimize delay. ■ **Cycle time**—The maximum time that a product is allowed at each workstation. Cycle time = Production time available per day ÷ Units required per day (9-4) Minimum number of workstations = $\sum_{i=1}^{n}$ Time for task i/(Cycle time) (9-5) ■ **Heuristic**—Problem solving using procedures and rules rather than mathematical optimization. Line-balancing heuristics include *longest task (operation) time, most following tasks, ranked positional weight, shortest task (operation) time,* and *least number of following tasks.* Efficiency = $\dfrac{\sum \text{Task times}}{(Actual \text{ number of workstations}) \times (\text{Largest assigned cycle time})}$ (9-6) Idle time = (Actual number of workstations × Largest assigned cycle time) − $\sum$ Task times (9-7)	Concept Questions: 9.1–9.4 Problems: 9.12–9.27 **VIDEO 9.2** Facility Layout at Wheeled Coach Ambulances Virtual Office Hours for Solved Problem: 9.2

Self Test

Before taking the self-test, refer to the learning objectives listed at the beginning of the chapter and the key terms listed at the end of the chapter.

LO 9.1 Which of the statements below best describes *office layout*?
a) Groups workers, their equipment, and spaces/offices to provide for movement of information.
b) Addresses the layout requirements of large, bulky projects such as ships and buildings.
c) Seeks the best personnel and machine utilization in repetitive or continuous production.
d) Allocates shelf space and responds to customer behavior.
e) Deals with low-volume, high-variety production.

LO 9.2 Which of the following does *not* support the retail layout objective of maximizing customer exposure to products?
a) Locate high-draw items around the periphery of the store.
b) Use prominent locations for high-impulse and high-margin items.
c) Maximize exposure to expensive items.
d) Use end-aisle locations.
e) Convey the store's mission with the careful positioning of the lead-off department.

LO 9.3 The major problem addressed by the warehouse layout strategy is:
a) minimizing difficulties caused by material flow varying with each product.
b) requiring frequent contact close to one another.
c) addressing trade-offs between space and material handling.
d) balancing product flow from one workstation to the next.
d) none of the above.

LO 9.4 A fixed-position layout:
a) groups workers to provide for movement of information.
b) addresses the layout requirements of large, bulky projects such as ships and buildings.

c) seeks the best machine utilization in continuous production.
d) allocates shelf space based on customer behavior.
e) deals with low-volume, high-variety production.

LO 9.5 A process-oriented layout:
a) groups workers to provide for movement of information.
b) addresses the layout requirements of large, bulky projects such as ships and buildings.
c) seeks the best machine utilization in continuous production.
d) allocates shelf space based on customer behavior.
e) deals with low-volume, high-variety production.

LO 9.6 For a focused work center or focused factory to be appropriate, the following three factors are required:
a) _____
b) _____
c) _____

LO 9.7 Before considering a product-oriented layout, it is important to be certain of:
a) _____
b) _____
c) _____
d) _____

LO 9.8 An assembly line is to be designed for a product whose completion requires 21 minutes of work. The factory works 400 minutes per day. Can a production line with five workstations make 100 units per day?
a) Yes, with exactly 100 minutes to spare.
b) No, but four workstations would be sufficient.
c) No, it will fall short even with a perfectly balanced line.
d) Yes, but the line's efficiency is very low.
e) Cannot be determined from the information given.

Answers: LO 9.1. a; LO 9.2. c; LO 9.3. c; LO 9.4. b; LO 9.5. e; LO 9.6. family of products, stable forecast (demand), volume; LO 9.7. adequate volume, stable demand, standardized product, adequate/quality supplies; LO 9.8. c.

Human Resources, Job Design, and Work Measurement

CHAPTER OUTLINE

GLOBAL COMPANY PROFILE: *Rusty Wallace's NASCAR Racing Team*

◆ Human Resource Strategy for Competitive Advantage *410*

◆ Labor Planning *411*

◆ Job Design *412*

◆ Ergonomics and the Work Environment *415*

◆ Methods Analysis *417*

◆ The Visual Workplace *420*

◆ Labor Standards *420*

◆ Ethics *430*

Alaska Airlines

Alaska Airlines

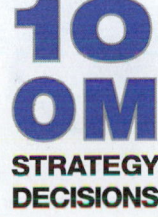

10 OM STRATEGY DECISIONS

- Design of Goods and Services
- Managing Quality
- Process Strategy
- Location Strategies
- Layout Strategies
- *Human Resources*
- Supply-Chain Management
- Inventory Management
- Scheduling
- Maintenance

High-Performance Teamwork Makes the Difference Between Winning and Losing

A new century brought new popularity to NASCAR (National Association for Stock Car Auto Racing). Hundreds of millions of TV and sponsorship dollars poured into the sport. With more money, competition increased, as did the rewards for winning on Sunday. The teams, headed by such names as Rusty Wallace, Jeff Gordon, Dale Earnhardt, Jr., and Tony Stewart, are as famous as the New York Yankees, Atlanta Hawks, or Chicago Bears.

The race car drivers may be famous, but it's the pit crews who often determine the outcome of a race. Years ago, crews were auto mechanics during the week who simply did double duty on Sundays in the pits. They did pretty well to change four tires in less than 30 seconds. Today, because NASCAR teams find competitive advantage wherever they can, taking more than 16 seconds can be disastrous. A botched pit stop is the equivalent of ramming your car against the wall—crushing all hopes for the day.

On Rusty Wallace's team, as on all the top NASCAR squads, the crewmen who go "over the wall" are now athletes, usually ex-college football or basketball players with proven agility and strength. The Evernham team, for example, includes a former defensive back from Fairleigh Dickinson (who is now a professional tire carrier) and a 300-pound lineman from East Carolina University (who handles the jack). The Chip Ganassi racing team includes baseball players from Wake Forest, football players from University of Kentucky and North Carolina, and a hockey player from Dartmouth.

Tire changers—the guys who wrench lug nuts off and on—are a scarce human resource and average $100,000 a year in salary. Jeff Gordon was reminded of the importance of coordinated

This Goodyear tire comes off Rusty Wallace's car and is no longer needed after going around the track for more than 40 laps in a June 19 Michigan International Speedway race.

Courtesy of the Orlando Sentinel, 2005

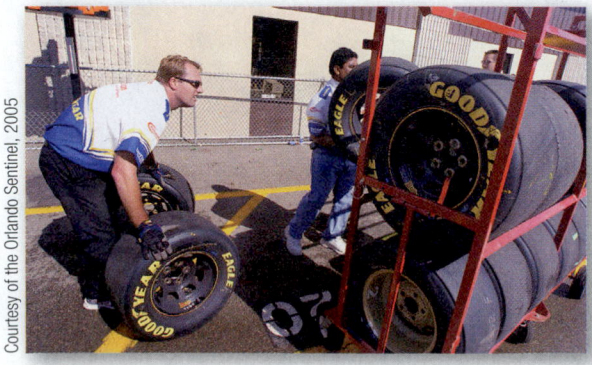

Jamie Rolewicz takes tires from a pile of used tires and puts them onto a cart.

Courtesy of the Orlando Sentinel, 2005

Lap 91—Gas is added and a tire is removed from Rusty Wallace's car.

Courtesy of the Orlando Sentinel, 2005

1 Wallace's car pulls into the pit; the crew rushes to the right side of the car to begin service.

0.0 sec.

2 Right side is jacked up, tire starts to come off; gas man is emptying his first can.

3.1 sec.

3 Action shifts to driver's side of the car; gas man carries second can of gas in.

8.9 sec.

4 The second can of gas is being emptied; driver's side tires are being changed.

13.7 sec.

5 Service is complete. The jackman drops the car, which is the signal to the Wallace driver to exit the pit.

15.4 sec.

A good pit stop will take about 16 seconds.

Movement of the pit crew members who go over the wall...

JM = Jackman

FTC = Front tire carrier

CFT = Changer front tire

RTC = Rear tire carrier

CRT = Changer rear tire

GM#1 = Gas man #1

GM#2 = Gas man #2

JM (Jackman) The jackman carries the hydraulic jack from the pit wall to raise the car's right side. After new tires are bolted on, he drops the car to the ground and repeats the process on the left side. His timing is crucial during this left side change, because when he drops the car again, it's the signal for the driver to go. The jackman has the most dangerous job of all the crew members; during the right-side change, he is exposed to oncoming traffic down pit row. **FTC (Front tire carrier)** Each tire carrier hauls a new 75-pound tire to the car's right side, places it on the wheel studs, and removes the old tire after the tire change. They repeat this process on the left side of the car with a new tire rolled to them by crew members behind the pit wall. **CFT (Changer front tire)** Tire changers run to the car's right side and, using an air impact wrench, they remove five lug nuts off the old tire and bolt on a new tire. They repeat the process on the left side. **RTC (Rear tire carrier)** Same as front tire carrier, except RTC may also adjust the rear jack bolt to alter the car's handling. **CRT (Changer rear tire)** Same as FT but on two rear tires. **Gas man #1** This gas man is usually the biggest and strongest person on the team. He goes over the wall carrying a 75-pound, 11-gallon "dump can" whose nozzle he jams into the car's fuel cell receptacle. He is then handed (or tossed) another can, and the process is repeated. **Gas man #2** Gets second gas can to Gas man #1 and catches excess fuel that spills out.

teamwork when five of his "over-the-wall" guys jumped to Dale Jarrett's organization a few years ago; it was believed to be a $500,000 per year deal.

A pit crew consists of seven men: a front-tire changer; a rear-tire changer; front- and rear-tire carriers; a man who jacks the car up; and two gas men with an 11-gallon can.

Every sport has its core competencies and key metrics—for example, the speed of a pitcher's fastball and a running back's time on the 40-yard dash. In NASCAR, a tire changer should get 5 lug nuts off in 1.2 seconds. The jackman should haul his 25-pound aluminum jack from the car's right side to left in 3.8 seconds. For tire carriers, it should take .7 seconds to get a tire from the ground to mounted on the car.

The seven men who go over the wall are coached and orchestrated. Coaches use the tools of OM and watch "game tape" of pit stops and make intricate adjustments to the choreography.

"There's a lot of pressure," says D. J. Richardson, a Rusty Wallace team tire changer—and one of the best in the business. Richardson trains daily with the rest of the crew in the

shop of the team owner. They focus on cardiovascular work and two muscle groups daily. Twice a week, they simulate pit stops—there can be from 12 to 14 variations—to work on their timing.

In a recent race in Michigan, Richardson and the rest of the Rusty Wallace team, with ergonomically designed gas cans, tools, and special safety gear, were ready. On lap 43, the split-second frenzy began, with Richardson—air gun in hand—jumping over a 2-foot white wall and sprinting to the right side of the team's Dodge. A teammate grabbed the tire and set it in place while Richardson secured it to the car. The process was repeated on the left side while the front crew followed the same procedure. Coupled with refueling, the pit stop took 12.734 seconds.

After catching their breath for a minute, Richardson and the other pit crew guys reviewed a videotape, looking for split-second flaws.

The same process was repeated on lap 91. The Wallace driver made a late charge on Jeff Burton and Kurt Busch on the last lap and went from 14th place to a 10th place finish.

LEARNING OBJECTIVES

LO 10.1 *Describe* labor-planning policies 411

LO 10.2 *Identify* the major issues in job design 412

LO 10.3 *Identify* major ergonomic and work environment issues 416

LO 10.4 *Use* the tools of methods analysis 418

LO 10.5 *Identify* four ways of establishing labor standards 421

LO 10.6 *Compute* the normal and standard times in a time study 423

LO 10.7 *Find* the proper sample size for a time study 424

Human Resource Strategy for Competitive Advantage

Good human resource strategies are expensive, difficult to achieve, and hard to sustain. But, like a NASCAR team, many organizations, from Hard Rock Cafe to Alaska Airlines, have demonstrated that sustainable competitive advantage can be built through a human resource strategy. The payoff can be significant and difficult for others to duplicate. Indeed, as the manager at London Four Seasons Hotel has noted, "We've identified that our key *competitive difference is our people*."[1] In this chapter, we will examine some of the tools available to operations managers for achieving competitive advantage via human resource management.

The objective of a human resource strategy is to manage labor and design jobs so people are effectively and efficiently utilized. As we focus on a human resource strategy, we want to ensure that people:

1. Are efficiently utilized within the constraints of other operations management decisions.
2. Have a reasonable quality of work life in an atmosphere of mutual commitment and trust.

By reasonable *quality of work life* we mean a job that is not only reasonably safe and for which the pay is equitable but that also achieves an appropriate level of both physical and psychological requirements. *Mutual commitment* means that both management and employee strive to meet common objectives. *Mutual trust* is reflected in reasonable, documented employment policies that are honestly and equitably implemented to the satisfaction of both management and employee. When management has a genuine respect for its employees and their contributions to the firm, establishing a reasonable quality of work life and mutual trust is not particularly difficult.

Constraints on Human Resource Strategy

As Figure 10.1 suggests, many decisions made about people are constrained by other decisions. First, the product mix may determine seasonality and stability of employment. Second, technology, equipment, and processes may have implications for safety and job content. Third, the location decision may have an impact on the ambient environment in which the employees work. Finally, layout decisions, such as assembly line versus work cell, influence job content.

Technology decisions impose substantial constraints. For instance, some of the jobs in foundries are dirty, noisy, and dangerous; slaughterhouse jobs may be stressful and subject workers to stomach-crunching stench; assembly-line jobs are often boring and mind numbing; and high capital investments such as those required for manufacturing semiconductor chips may require 24-hour, 7-day-a-week operation in restrictive clothing.

We are not going to change these jobs without making changes in our other strategic decisions, so the trade-offs necessary to reach a tolerable quality of work life are difficult. Effective managers consider such decisions simultaneously. The result: a system in which both individual and team performance are enhanced through optimum job design.

We now look at three distinct decision areas of human resource strategy: *labor planning, job design*, and *labor standards*.

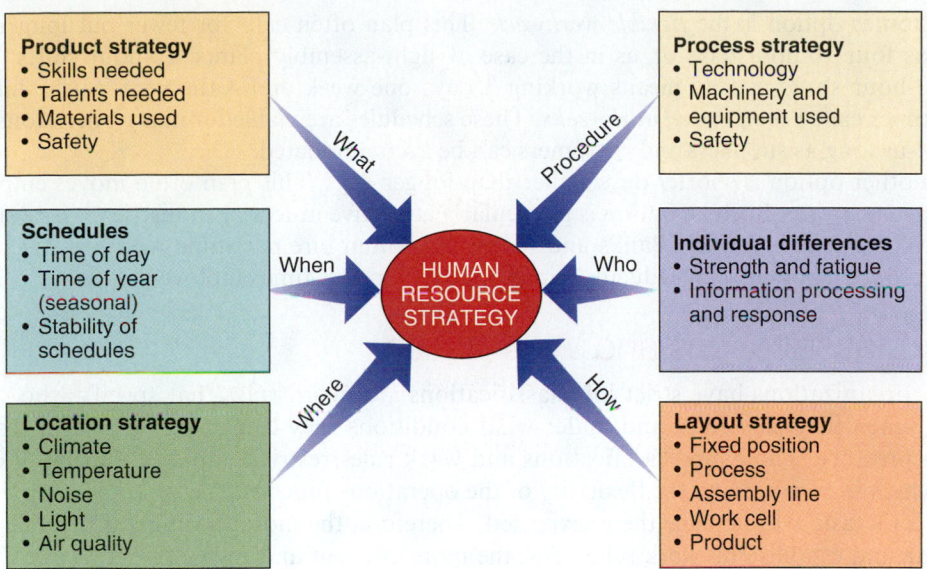

Figure **10.1**

Constraints on Human Resource Strategy

Labor Planning

Labor planning is determining staffing policies that deal with (1) employment stability, (2) work schedules, and (3) work rules.

Labor planning

A means of determining staffing policies dealing with employment stability, work schedules, and work rules.

Employment-Stability Policies

Employment stability deals with the number of employees maintained by an organization at any given time. There are two very basic policies for dealing with stability:

1. *Follow demand exactly:* Following demand exactly keeps direct labor costs tied to production but incurs other costs. These other costs include (a) hiring and layoff costs, (b) unemployment insurance, and (c) premium wages to entice personnel to accept unstable employment. This policy tends to treat labor as a variable cost.
2. *Hold employment constant:* Holding employment levels constant maintains a trained workforce and keeps hiring, layoff, and unemployment costs to a minimum. However, with employment held constant, employees may not be utilized fully when demand is low, and the firm may not have the human resources it needs when demand is high. This policy tends to treat labor as a fixed cost.

These policies are only two of many that can be efficient *and* provide a reasonable quality of work life. Firms must determine policies about employment stability.

LO 10.1 *Describe* labor-planning policies

Work Schedules

Although the standard work schedule in the U.S. is still five 8-hour days, many variations exist. A popular variation is a work schedule called flextime. *Flextime* allows employees, within limits, to determine their own schedules. A flextime policy might allow an employee (with proper notification) to be at work at 8 A.M. plus or minus 2 hours. This policy allows more autonomy and independence on the part of the employee. Some firms have found flextime a low-cost fringe benefit that enhances job satisfaction. The problem from the OM perspective is that much production work requires full staffing for efficient operations. A machine that requires three people cannot run at all if only two show up. Having a waiter show up to serve lunch at 1:30 P.M. rather than 11:30 A.M. is not much help either.

Similarly, some industries find that their process strategies severely constrain their human resource scheduling options. For instance, paper manufacturing, petroleum refining, and power stations require around-the-clock staffing except for maintenance and repair shutdown.

Another option is the *flexible workweek*. This plan often calls for fewer but longer days, such as four 10-hour days or, as in the case of light-assembly plants, 12-hour shifts. Working 12-hour shifts usually means working 3 days one week and 4 the next. Such shifts are sometimes called *compressed workweeks*. These schedules are viable for many operations functions—as long as suppliers and customers can be accommodated.

Another option is shorter days rather than longer days. This plan often moves employees to *part-time status*. Such an option is particularly attractive in service industries, where staffing for peak loads is necessary. Banks and restaurants often hire part-time workers. Also, many firms reduce labor costs by reducing fringe benefits for part-time employees.

Job Classifications and Work Rules

Many organizations have strict job classifications and work rules that specify who can do what, when they can do it, and under what conditions they can do it, often as a result of union pressure. These job classifications and work rules restrict employee flexibility on the job, which in turn reduces the flexibility of the operations function. Yet part of an operations manager's task is to manage the unexpected. Therefore, the more flexibility a firm has when staffing and establishing work schedules, the more efficient and responsive it *can* be. This is particularly true in service organizations, where extra capacity often resides in extra or flexible staff. Building morale and meeting staffing requirements that result in an efficient, responsive operation are easier if managers have fewer job classifications and work-rule constraints. If the strategy is to achieve a competitive advantage by responding rapidly to the customer, a flexible workforce may be a prerequisite.

Job Design

Job design

An approach that specifies the tasks that constitute a job for an individual or a group.

Job design specifies the tasks that constitute a job for an individual or a group. We examine five components of job design: (1) job specialization, (2) job expansion, (3) psychological components, (4) self-directed teams, and (5) motivation and incentive systems.

Labor Specialization

Labor specialization (or job specialization)

The division of labor into unique ("special") tasks.

The importance of job design as a management variable is credited to the 18th-century economist Adam Smith. Smith suggested that a division of labor, also known as **labor specialization** (or job specialization), would assist in reducing labor costs of multiskilled artisans. This is accomplished in several ways:

1. *Development of dexterity* and faster learning by the employee because of repetition
2. *Less loss of time* because the employee would not be changing jobs or tools
3. *Development of specialized tools* and the reduction of investment because each employee has only a few tools needed for a particular task

LO 10.2 *Identify* the major issues in job design

The 19th-century British mathematician Charles Babbage determined that a fourth consideration was also important for labor efficiency. Because pay tends to follow skill with a rather high correlation, Babbage suggested *paying exactly the wage needed for the particular skill required*. If the entire job consists of only one skill, then we would pay for only that skill. Otherwise, we would tend to pay for the highest skill contributed by the employee. These four advantages of labor specialization are still valid today.

A classic example of labor specialization is the assembly line. Such a system is often very efficient, although it may require employees to do short, repetitive, mind-numbing jobs. The wage rate for many of these jobs, however, is good. Given the relatively high wage rate for the modest skills required in many of these jobs, there is often a large pool of employees from which to choose.

From the manager's point of view, a major limitation of specialized jobs is their failure to bring the whole person to the job. Job specialization tends to bring only the employee's manual skills to work. In an increasingly sophisticated knowledge-based society, managers want employees to bring their mind to work as well.

Figure **10.2**

An Example of Job Enlargement (*horizontal*** job expansion) and Job Enrichment (***vertical*** job expansion)**

Job Expansion

Moving from labor specialization toward more varied job design may improve the quality of work life. The theory is that variety makes the job "better" and that the employee therefore enjoys a higher quality of work life. This flexibility thus benefits the employee and the organization.

We modify jobs in a variety of ways. The first approach is job enlargement, which occurs when we add tasks requiring similar skill to an existing job. Job rotation is a version of job enlargement that occurs when the employee is allowed to move from one specialized job to another. Variety has been added to the employee's perspective of the job. Another approach is job enrichment, which adds planning and control to the job. An example is to have department store salespeople responsible for ordering, as well as selling, their goods. Job enrichment can be thought of as *vertical expansion*, as opposed to job enlargement, which is *horizontal*. These ideas are shown in Figure 10.2.

A popular extension of job enrichment, employee empowerment is the practice of enriching jobs so employees accept responsibility for a variety of decisions normally associated with staff specialists. Empowering employees helps them take "ownership" of their jobs so they have a personal interest in improving performance.

Psychological Components of Job Design

An effective human resources strategy also requires consideration of the psychological components of job design. These components focus on how to design jobs that meet some minimum psychological requirements.

Hawthorne Studies   The Hawthorne studies introduced psychology to the workplace. They were conducted in the 1920s at Western Electric's Hawthorne plant near Chicago. These studies were initiated to determine the impact of lighting on productivity. Instead, they found the dynamic social system and distinct roles played by employees to be more important than the intensity of the lighting. They also found that individual differences may be dominant in what an employee expects from the job and what the employee thinks her or his contribution to the job should be.

Core Job Characteristics   Substantial research regarding the psychological components of job design has taken place since the Hawthorne studies. Hackman and Oldham have incorporated much of that work into five desirable characteristics of job design.[2] They suggest that jobs should include the following characteristics:

1. **Skill variety**, requiring the worker to use a variety of skills and talents
2. **Job identity**, allowing the worker to perceive the job as a whole and recognize a start and a finish
3. **Job significance**, providing a sense that the job has an impact on the organization and society
4. **Autonomy**, offering freedom, independence, and discretion
5. **Feedback**, providing clear, timely information about performance

Job enlargement
The grouping of a variety of tasks about the same skill level; horizontal enlargement.

Job rotation
A system in which an employee is moved from one specialized job to another.

Job enrichment
A method of giving an employee more responsibility that includes some of the planning and control necessary for job accomplishment; vertical expansion.

Employee empowerment
Enlarging employee jobs so that the added responsibility and authority are moved to the lowest level possible.

Figure **10.3**

Job Design Continuum

An increasing reliance on the employee's contribution can increase the responsibility accepted by the employee.

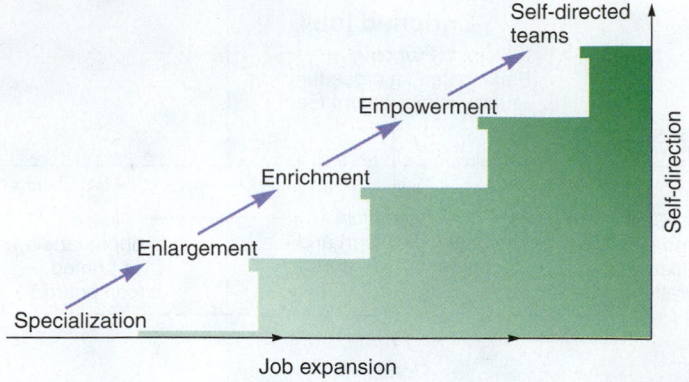

Including these five ingredients in job design is consistent with job enlargement, job enrichment, and employee empowerment. We now want to look at some of the ways in which teams can be used to expand jobs and achieve these five job characteristics.

Self-Directed Teams

Self-directed team

A group of empowered individuals working together to reach a common goal.

Many world-class organizations have adopted teams to foster mutual trust and commitment, and provide the core job characteristics. One team concept of particular note is the self-directed team: a group of empowered individuals working together to reach a common goal. These teams may be organized for long- or short-term objectives. Teams are effective primarily because they can easily provide employee empowerment, ensure core job characteristics, and satisfy many of the psychological needs of individual team members. A job design continuum is shown in Figure 10.3.

Limitations of Job Expansion   If job designs that enlarge, enrich, empower, and use teams are so good, why are they not universally used? Mostly it is because of costs. Here are a few limitations of expanded job designs:

- *Higher capital cost:* Job expansion may require additional equipment and facilities.
- *Individual differences:* Some employees opt for the less-complex jobs.
- *Higher wage rates:* Expanded jobs may well require a higher average wage.
- *Smaller labor pool:* Because expanded jobs require more skill and acceptance of more responsibility, job requirements have increased.
- *Higher training costs:* Job expansion requires training and cross-training. Therefore, training budgets need to increase.

Despite these limitations, firms are finding a substantial payoff in job expansion.

Southwest Airlines—consistently near the top of the airline pack in travel surveys, fewest lost bags and complaints, and highest profits—hires people with enthusiasm and empowers them to excel. A barefoot co-founder and chairman emeritus, Herb Kelleher, clings to the tail of a jet (left photo). Says Kelleher, "I've tried to create a culture of caring for people in the totality of their lives, not just at work. Someone can go out and buy airplanes and ticket counters, but they can't buy our culture, our *esprit de corps.*"

OM in Action | Using Incentives to Unsnarl Traffic Jams in the OR

Hospitals have long offered surgeons a precious perk: scheduling the bulk of their elective surgeries in the middle of the week so they can attend conferences, teach, or relax during long weekends. But at Boston Medical Center, St. John's Health Center (in Missouri), and Elliot Health System (in New Hampshire), this practice, one of the biggest impediments to a smooth-running hospital, is changing. "Block scheduling" jams up operating rooms, overloads nurses at peak times, and bumps scheduled patients for hours and even days.

Boston Medical Center's delays and cancellations of elective surgeries were nearly eliminated after surgeons agreed to stop block scheduling and to dedicate one OR for emergency cases. Cancellations dropped to 3, from 334, in just one 6-month period. In general, hospitals changing to the new system of spreading out elective surgeries during the week increase their surgery capacity by 10%, move patients through the operating room faster, and reduce nursing overtime.

To get doctors on board at St. John's, the hospital offered a carrot and two sticks: Doctors who were more than 10 minutes late 10% of the time lost their coveted 7:30 A.M. start times *and* were fined a portion of their fee—with proceeds going to a kitty that rewarded the best on-time performers. Surgeons' late start times quickly dropped from 16% to 5% and then to less than 1% within a year.

Sources: Executive Insight (October 4, 2011); *The Wall Street Journal* (August 10, 2005); and *Hospitals & Health Networks* (September 2005).

Motivation and Incentive Systems

Our discussion of the psychological components of job design provides insight into the factors that contribute to job satisfaction and motivation. In addition to these psychological factors, there are monetary factors. Money often serves as a psychological as well as financial motivator. Monetary rewards take the form of bonuses, profit and gain sharing, and incentive systems.

Bonuses, in cash, stock ownership, or stock options, are often used to reward employees. Almost half of U.S. employees have one or more forms of profit sharing that distributes part of the profit to employees. A variation of profit sharing is gain sharing, which rewards employees for improvements made in an organization's performance. The most popular of these is the Scanlon plan, in which any reduction in the cost of labor is shared between management and labor.

Incentive systems based on individual or group productivity are used throughout the world in a wide variety of applications, including nearly half of the manufacturing firms in America. Production incentives often require employees or crews to produce at or above a predetermined standard. The standard can be based on a "standard time" per task or number of pieces made. Both systems typically guarantee the employee at least a base rate. Incentives, of course, need not be monetary. Awards, recognition, and other kinds of preferences such as a preferred work schedule can be effective. (See the *OM in Action* box "Using Incentives to Unsnarl Traffic Jams in the OR.") Hard Rock Cafe has successfully reduced its turnover by giving every employee—from the CEO to the busboys—a $10,000 gold Rolex watch on their 10th anniversary with the firm.

With the increasing use of teams, various forms of team-based pay are also being developed. Many are based on traditional pay systems supplemented with some form of bonus or incentive system. However, because many team environments require cross training, *knowledge-based* pay systems have also been developed. Under knowledge-based (or skill-based) pay systems, a portion of the employee's pay depends on demonstrated knowledge or skills. At Wisconsin's Johnsonville Sausage Co., employees receive pay raises *only* by mastering new skills such as scheduling, budgeting, and quality control.

Ergonomics and the Work Environment

With the foundation provided by Frederick W. Taylor, the father of the era of scientific management, we have developed a body of knowledge about people's capabilities and limitations. This knowledge is necessary because humans are hand/eye animals possessing exceptional capabilities and some limitations. Because managers must design jobs that can be done, we now introduce a few of the issues related to people's capabilities and limitations.

Ergonomics   The operations manager is interested in building a good interface between humans, the environment, and machines. Studies of this interface are known as ergonomics. Ergonomics means "the study of work." (*Ergon* is the Greek word for "work.") The term

Ergonomics

The study of the human interface with the environment and machines.

With a commitment to efficiency and an understanding of ergonomics, UPS trains drivers in the company's "340 methods" that save seconds and improve safety. Here a UPS driver learns to walk on "ice" with the help of a "slip and fall" simulator.

Stephen Voss

human factors is often substituted for the word *ergonomics*. Understanding ergonomic issues helps to improve human performance.

Male and female adults come in limited configurations and abilities. Therefore, design of tools and the workplace depends on the study of people to determine what they can and cannot do. Substantial data have been collected that provide basic strength and measurement data needed to design tools and the workplace. The design of the workplace can make the job easier or impossible. In addition, we now have the ability, through the use of computer modeling, to analyze human motions and efforts. The *OM in Action* box, "The Missing Perfect Chair," discusses how the size of furniture can affect employees.

LO 10.3 *Identify* major ergonomic and work environment issues

Operator Input to Machines Operator response to machines, be they hand tools, pedals, levers, or buttons, needs to be evaluated. Operations managers need to be sure that operators have the strength, reflexes, perception, and mental capacity to provide necessary control. Such problems as *carpal tunnel syndrome* may result when a tool as simple as a

---

OM in Action | **The Missing Perfect Chair**

As you sit at your desk, are your feet dangling, or are they scrunched under the chair? In a perfectly fitting chair, your back is supported, your feet are planted on the floor, your thighs are parallel to the floor, and your knees are at a 90-degree angle. If your chair, as are many chairs, is 17.3 inches high then you should be a 68.3-inch-tall male (the 50th percentile for men). For women, the 50th percentile chair should be 15.7 inches high, and you should be 62.9 inches tall. However, if you have an adjustable chair, you are in luck as they are often designed for the 5th to the 95th percentiles.* But that still leaves millions of unlucky people at both ends of the bell curve—too small or too big for their chair.

Former Labor Secretary Robert Reich, who is 4 feet 10 inches tall, once sawed off the legs of his office chair and desk to make them fit. While he was working in the Justice Department in the 1970s, the General Services Administration (GSA) refused his request to shorten his standard-sized wooden desk and chair. "I snuck in one weekend with my saw and did it myself, and sent the stubs to the GSA administrator," Dr. Reich says. Later as Labor Secretary, his chair left his legs sticking out, so he held meetings standing up.

Managers may find that solving the "chair" problem is complicated because special chairs for only some employees can foster resentment. In addition, changing the height of a chair often means the desk must also be higher or lower, complicating desk assignments. But, manufacturers are now

offering both adjustable chairs and worktables. Some desks now include timers and a touch screen that allow you to change desk height. Other offerings include multiple work surfaces and keyboard supports, as well as repositionable computer-monitor supports.

Joe Marquette/AP Images

However, most operations managers are under heavy pressure to hold down costs, so providing special items for a few workers presents a conflict. Special chairs can list for $1,000 and adjustable desks for much more. Nevertheless, the need for adjustable chairs and desks is growing. Steelcase Inc. recently studied the body shapes and postures of 2,000 workers in 11 countries and found that "extreme size" is on the rise.

Sources: The Wall Street Journal (April 29, 2015), (May 20, 2014), and (September 21, 2011).

*For men the 5th percentile is 63.6 in., and the 95th is 72.8 in. tall; for women it is 62.9 in. and 76.1 in., respectively.

Drivers of race cars have no time to grasp for controls or to look for small hidden gauges. Controls and instrumentation for modern race cars have migrated to the steering wheel itself—the critical interface between man and machine.

keyboard is poorly designed. The photo of the race car steering wheel above shows one innovative approach to critical operator input.

Feedback to Operators   Feedback to operators is provided by sight, sound, and feel; it should not be left to chance. The mishap at the Three Mile Island nuclear facility, America's worst nuclear experience, was in large part the result of poor feedback to the operators about reactor performance. Nonfunctional groups of large, unclear instruments and inaccessible controls, combined with hundreds of confusing warning lights, contributed to that failure. Such relatively simple issues make a difference in operator response and, therefore, performance.

An important human factor/ergonomic issue in the aircraft industry is cockpit design. Newer "glass cockpits" display information in more concise form than the traditional rows of round analog dials and gauges. These displays reduce the chance of human error, which is a factor in about two-thirds of commercial air accidents.

The Work Environment   The physical environment in which employees work affects their performance, safety, and quality of work life. Illumination, noise and vibration, temperature, humidity, and air quality are work-environment factors under the control of the organization and the operations manager. The manager must approach them as controllable.

Illumination is necessary, but the proper level depends on the work being performed. Figure 10.4(a) provides some guidelines. However, other lighting factors are important. These include reflective ability, contrast of the work surface with surroundings, glare, and shadows.

Noise of some form is usually present in the work area, and most employees seem to adjust well. However, high levels of sound will damage hearing. Figure 10.4(b) provides indications of the sound generated by various activities. Extended periods of exposure to decibel levels above 85 dB are permanently damaging. The Occupational Safety and Health Administration (OSHA) requires ear protection above this level if exposure equals or exceeds eight hours. Even at low levels, noise and vibration can be distracting and can raise a person's blood pressure, so managers make substantial effort to reduce noise and vibration through good machine design, enclosures, or insulation.

Temperature and humidity parameters have also been well established. Managers with activities operating outside the established comfort zone should expect adverse effect on performance.

Methods Analysis

Methods analysis focuses on *how* a task is accomplished. Whether controlling a machine or making or assembling components, how a task is done makes a difference in performance, safety, and quality. Using knowledge from ergonomics and methods analysis, methods engineers are charged with ensuring that quality and quantity standards are achieved efficiently and safely. Methods analysis and related techniques are useful in office environments as well as in the factory. Methods techniques are used to analyze:

Methods analysis

A system that involves developing work procedures that are safe and produce quality products efficiently.

1. **Movement of individuals or material.** The analysis is performed using *flow diagrams* and *process charts* with varying amounts of detail.

Figure **10.4(a)**

Recommended Levels of Illumination (using foot-candles (ft-c) as the measure of illumination)

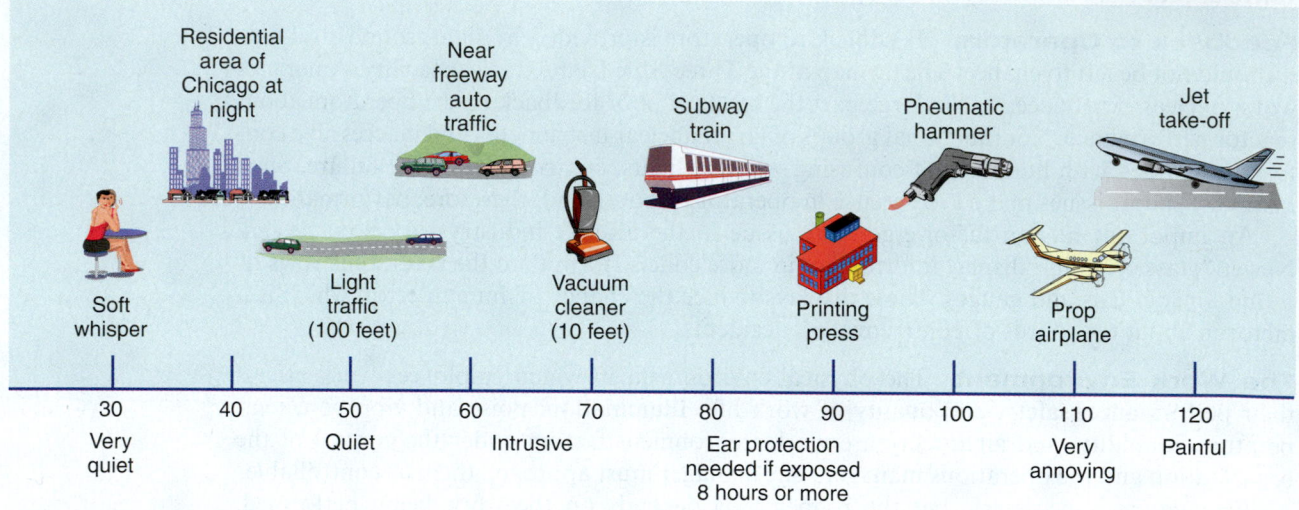

Figure **10.4(b)**

Decibel (dB) Levels for Various Sounds

Adapted from A. P. G. Peterson and E. E. Gross, Jr., *Handbook of Noise Measurement*, 7th ed. Copyright © by GenRad, LLC. Reprinted with permission.

LO 10.4 *Use* the tools of methods analysis

Flow diagram

A drawing used to analyze movement of people or material.

Process chart

Graphic representations that depict a sequence of steps for a process.

Activity chart

A way of improving utilization of an operator and a machine or some combination of operators (a crew) and machines.

Operations chart

A chart depicting right- and left-hand motions.

2. **Activity of human and machine and crew activity.** This analysis is performed using *activity charts* (also known as man–machine charts and crew charts).

3. **Body movement** (primarily arms and hands). This analysis is performed using *operations charts*.

Flow diagrams are schematics (drawings) used to investigate movement of people or material. Britain's Paddy Hopkirk Factory, which manufactures auto parts, demonstrates one version of a flow diagram in Figure 10.5. Hopkirk's old work flow is shown in Figure 10.5(a), and a new method, with improved work flow and requiring less storage and space, is shown in Figure 10.5(b). **Process charts** use symbols, as in Figure 10.5(c), to help us understand the movement of people or material. In this way non-value-added activities can be recognized and operations made more efficient. Figure 10.5(c) is a process chart used to supplement the flow diagrams shown in Figure 10.5(b).

Activity charts are used to study and improve the utilization of an operator and a machine or some combination of operators (a "crew") and machines. The typical approach is for the analyst to record the present method through direct observation and then propose the improvement on a second chart. Figure 10.6 is an activity chart to show a proposed improvement for a two-person crew at Quick Car Lube.

Body movement is analyzed by an **operations chart**. It is designed to show economy of motion by pointing out wasted motion and idle time (delay). The operations chart (also known as a *right-hand/left-hand chart*) is shown in Figure 10.7.

(a)

(c)

			PROCESS CHART
Present Method ☐			
Proposed Method ☒			

SUBJECT CHARTED _Axle-stand Production_ DATE _5 / 1 / 15_

CHART BY _JH_

CHART NO. _1_

DEPARTMENT _Work cell for axle stand_ SHEET NO. _1_ OF _1_

DIST. IN FEET	TIME IN MINS.	CHART SYMBOLS	PROCESS DESCRIPTION
50		◯⇨☐D▽	From press machine to storage bins at work cell
	3	◯⇨☐D▼	Storage bins
5		◯⇨☐D▽	Move to machine 1
	4	●⇨☐D▽	Operation at machine 1
4		◯⇨☐D▽	Move to machine 2
	2.5	●⇨☐D▽	Operation at machine 2
4		◯⇨☐D▽	Move to machine 3
	3.5	●⇨☐D▽	Operation at machine 3
4		◯⇨☐D▽	Move to machine 4
	4	●⇨☐D▽	Operation at machine 4
20		◯⇨☐D▽	Move to welding
	Poka-yoke	◯⇨☐D▽	Poka-yoke inspection at welding
	4	●⇨☐D▽	Weld
10		◯⇨☐D▽	Move to painting
	4	●⇨☐D▽	Paint
		◯⇨☐D▽	
97	25		TOTAL

◯ = operation; ⇨ = transport; ☐ = inspect; D = delay; ▽ = storage

(b)

Figure **10.5**

Flow Diagrams and Process Chart of Axle-Stand Production at Paddy Hopkirk Factory

(a) Old method; (b) new method; (c) process chart of axle-stand production using Paddy Hopkirk's new method (shown in (b)).

ACTIVITY CHART

	OPERATOR #1		OPERATOR #2	
	TIME	%	TIME	%
WORK	12	100	12	100
IDLE	0	0	0	0

OPERATION: Oil change & fluid check
EQUIPMENT: One bay/pit
OPERATOR: Two-person crew
STUDY NO.: _____ ANALYST: BR

SUBJECT _Quick Car Lube_ DATE _5-1-15_

PRESENT (PROPOSED) DEPT. SHEET 1 OF 1 CHART BY _LSA_

TIME	Operator #1	TIME	Operator #2	TIME
2	Take order		Move car to pit	
4	Vacuum car		Drain oil	
6	Clean windows		Check transmission	
8	Check under hood		Change oil filter	
	Fill with oil		Replace oil plug	
10	Complete bill		Move car to front for customer	
12	Greet next customer		Move next car to pit	
14	Vacuum car		Drain oil	
16	Clean windows		Check transmission	
18				

Repeat cycle

Figure **10.6**

Activity Chart for Two-Person Crew Doing an Oil Change in 12 Minutes at Quick Car Lube

---

OPERATIONS CHART

SYMBOLS	PRESENT		PROPOSED	
	LH	RH	LH	RH
◯ OPERATION	2	3		
⇨ TRANSPORT.	1	1		
☐ INSPECTION				
D DELAY	4	3		
▽ STORAGE				

PROCESS: Scooping Ice for Coffee
EQUIPMENT: Scoop
OPERATOR: Starbucks
STUDY NO: _____ ANALYST: CM
DATE: 5 /1 /15 SHEET NO. 1 of 2
METHOD (PRESENT / PROPOSED)
REMARKS: Partial Study

LEFT-HAND ACTIVITY Present METHOD	DIST.	SYMBOLS	SYMBOLS	DIST.	RIGHT-HAND ACTIVITY Present METHOD
1 Reach for cup		●⇨☐D▽	◯⇨☐D▽		Idle
2 Grasp cup		●⇨☐D▽	◯⇨☐D▽		Idle
3 Move cup	6"	◯⇨☐D▽	◯⇨☐D▽		Idle
4 Hold cup		◯⇨☐D▽	●⇨☐D▽		Reach for scoop
5 Hold cup		◯⇨☐D▽	●⇨☐D▽		Grasp scoop
6 Hold cup		◯⇨☐D▽	◯⇨☐D▽	8"	Move scoop to ice
7 Hold cup		◯⇨☐D▽	●⇨☐D▽		Scoop ice

Figure **10.7**

Operations Chart (right-hand/left-hand chart) for Scooping Ice to Coffee Cup

Visual utensil holder encourages housekeeping.

A "3-minute service" clock reminds employees of the goal.

Visual signals at the machine notify support personnel.

Andon — Line/machine stoppage — Parts/maintenance needed — All systems go

Reorder point →

Part A Part B Part C

Visual kanbans reduce inventory and foster JIT.

Quantities in bins indicate ongoing daily requirements, and clipboards provide information on schedule changes.

Company data, process specifications, and operating procedures are posted in each work area.

Figure **10.8**

The Visual Workplace

The Visual Workplace

Visual workplace

Uses a variety of visual communication techniques to rapidly communicate information to stakeholders.

A visual workplace uses low-cost visual devices to share information quickly and accurately. Well-designed displays and graphs root out confusion and replace difficult-to-understand printouts and paperwork. Because workplace data change quickly and often, operations managers need to share accurate and up-to-date information. Changing customer requirements, specifications, schedules, and other details must be rapidly communicated to those who can make things happen.

The visual workplace can eliminate non-value-added activities by making standards, problems, and abnormalities visual (see Figure 10.8). The visual workplace needs less supervision because employees understand the standard, see the results, and know what to do.

Labor Standards

Labor standards

The amount of time required to perform a job or part of a job.

So far in this chapter, we have discussed labor planning and job design. The third requirement of an effective human resource strategy is the establishment of labor standards. Labor standards are the amount of time required to perform a job or part of a job, and they exist, formally or informally, for all jobs. Effective manpower planning is dependent on a knowledge of the labor required.

Modern labor standards originated with the works of Frederick W. Taylor and Frank and Lillian Gilbreth at the beginning of the 20th century. At that time, a large proportion of work was manual, and the resulting labor content of products was high. Little was known about what constituted a fair day's work, so managers initiated studies to improve work methods and understand human effort. These efforts continue to this day. Although labor costs are often less than 10% of sales, labor standards remain important and continue to play a major role in both service and manufacturing organizations. They are often a beginning point for determining staffing requirements. With over half of the manufacturing plants in America using some form of labor incentive system, good labor standards are a requirement.

Effective operations management requires meaningful standards that help a firm determine:

1. Labor content of items produced (the labor cost)
2. Staffing needs (how many people it will take to meet required production)
3. Cost and time estimates prior to production (to assist in a variety of decisions, from cost estimates to make-or-buy decisions)
4. Crew size and work balance (who does what in a group activity or on an assembly line)
5. Expected production (so that both manager and worker know what constitutes a fair day's work)
6. Basis of wage-incentive plans (what provides a reasonable incentive)
7. Efficiency of employees and supervision (a standard is necessary against which to determine efficiency)

Properly set labor standards represent the amount of time that it should take an average employee to perform specific job activities under normal working conditions. Labor standards are set in four ways:

LO 10.5 *Identify* four ways of establishing labor standards

1. **Historical experience**
2. **Time studies**
3. **Predetermined time standards**
4. **Work sampling**

Historical Experience

Labor standards can be estimated based on *historical experience*—that is, how many labor-hours were required to do a task the last time it was performed. Historical standards have the advantage of being relatively easy and inexpensive to obtain. They are usually available from employee time cards or production records. However, they are not objective, and we do not know their accuracy, whether they represent a reasonable or a poor work pace, and whether unusual occurrences are included. Because these variables are unknown, their use is not recommended. Instead, time studies, predetermined time standards, and work sampling are preferred.

Time Studies

The classical stopwatch study, or **time study**, originally proposed by Frederick W. Taylor in 1881, involves timing a sample of a worker's performance and using it to set a standard. (See the *OM in Action* box, "Saving Seconds at Retail Boosts Productivity.") Stopwatch studies are

Time study

Timing a sample of a worker's performance and using it as a basis for setting a standard time.

the most widely used labor standard method. A trained and experienced person can establish a standard by following these eight steps:

1. Define the task to be studied (after methods analysis has been conducted).
2. Divide the task into precise elements (parts of a task that often take no more than a few seconds).
3. Decide how many times to measure the task (the number of job cycles or samples needed).
4. Time and record elemental times and ratings of performance.

Average observed time

The arithmetic mean of the times for each element measured, adjusted for unusual influence for each element.

5. Compute the average observed (actual) time. The average observed time is the arithmetic mean of the times for *each* element measured, adjusted for unusual influence for each element:

$$\text{Average observed time} = \frac{\text{Sum of the times recorded to perform each element}}{\text{Number of observations}} \quad (10\text{-}1)$$

Normal time

The average observed time, adjusted for pace.

6. Determine performance rating (work pace) and then compute the normal time for each element.

$$\text{Normal time} = \text{Average observed time} \times \text{Performance rating factor} \quad (10\text{-}2)$$

The performance rating adjusts the average observed time to what a trained worker could expect to accomplish working at a normal pace. For example, a worker should be able to walk 3 miles per hour. He or she should also be able to deal a deck of 52 cards into 4 equal piles in 30 seconds. A performance rating of 1.05 would indicate that the observed worker performs the task slightly *faster* than average. Numerous videos specify work pace on which professionals agree, and benchmarks have been established by the Society for the Advancement of Management. Performance rating, however, is still something of an art.

7. Add the normal times for each element to develop a total normal time for the task.

Standard time

An adjustment to the total normal time; the adjustment provides allowances for personal needs, unavoidable work delays, and fatigue.

8. Compute the standard time. This adjustment to the total normal time provides for allowances such as *personal* needs, unavoidable work *delays*, and worker *fatigue*:

$$\text{Standard time} = \frac{\text{Total normal time}}{1 - \text{Allowance factor}} \quad (10\text{-}3)$$

Personal time allowances are often established in the range of 4% to 7% of total time, depending on nearness to restrooms, water fountains, and other facilities. *Delay allowances* are often set as a result of the actual studies of the delay that occurs. *Fatigue allowances* are based on our growing knowledge of human energy expenditure under various physical and environmental conditions. A sample set of personal and fatigue allowances is shown in Table 10.1.

TABLE 10.1	Allowance Factors (in percentage) for Various Classes of Work

1. Constant allowances:
    (A) Personal allowance 5
    (B) Basic fatigue allowance 4
2. Variable allowances:
    (A) Standing allowance 2
    (B) Abnormal position allowance:
        (i) Awkward (bending) 2
        (ii) Very awkward (lying, stretching) 7
    (C) Use of force or muscular energy in
        lifting, pulling, pushing
	Weight lifted (pounds):
	    20 3
	    40 9
	    60 17
	(D) Bad light:
	    (i) Well below recommended 2
	    (ii) Quite inadequate 5
	(E) Noise level:
	    (i) Intermittent—loud 2
	    (ii) Intermittent—very loud or high pitched 5

Sources: George Kanawaty (ed.), *Introduction to Work Study*, International Labour Office, Geneva, 1992; B. W. Niebel, *Motion and Time Study*, 8th ed. (Homewood, IL: Richard D. Irwin), 1988; and Stephan Konz, *Work Design* (Columbus, Ohio: Grid Publishing, Inc.), 1979.

Example 1 illustrates the computation of standard time.

Example 1

DETERMINING NORMAL AND STANDARD TIME

The time study of a work operation at a Red Lobster restaurant yielded an average observed time of 4.0 minutes. The analyst rated the observed worker at 85%. This means the worker performed at 85% of normal when the study was made. The firm uses a 13% allowance factor. Red Lobster wants to compute the normal time and the standard time for this operation.

APPROACH ▶ The firm needs to apply Equations (10-2) and (10-3).

SOLUTION ▶

$$\text{Average observed time} = 4.0 \text{ min}$$

$$\text{Normal time} = (\text{Average observed time}) \times (\text{Performance rating factor})$$

$$= (4.0)(0.85)$$

$$= 3.4 \text{ min}$$

LO 10.6 *Compute* the normal and standard times in a time study

$$\text{Standard time} = \frac{\text{Normal time}}{1 - \text{Allowance factor}} = \frac{3.4}{1 - 0.13} = \frac{3.4}{0.87} = 3.9 \text{ min}$$

INSIGHT ▶ Because the observed worker was rated at 85% (slower than average), the normal time is less than the worker's 4.0-minute average time.

LEARNING EXERCISE ▶ If the observed worker is rated at 115% (faster than average), what are the new normal and standard times? [Answer: 4.6 min, 5.287 min.]

RELATED PROBLEMS ▶ 10.13–10.21, 10.33, 10.38 (10.39–10.40 are available in MyOMLab)

EXCEL **OM** Data File **Ch10Ex1.xls** can be found in MyOMLab.

Example 2 uses a series of actual stopwatch times for each element.

Example 2

USING TIME STUDIES TO COMPUTE STANDARD TIME

Management Science Associates promotes its management development seminars by mailing thousands of individually composed and typed letters to various firms. A time study has been conducted on the task of preparing letters for mailing. On the basis of the following observations, Management Science Associates wants to develop a time standard for this task. The firm's personal, delay, and fatigue allowance factor is 15%.

JOB ELEMENT	OBSERVATIONS (MINUTES)					PERFORMANCE RATING
	1	2	3	4	5	
(A) Compose and type letter	8	10	9	21*	11	120%
(B) Type envelope address	2	3	2	1	3	105%
(C) Stuff, stamp, seal, and sort envelopes	2	1	5*	2	1	110%

APPROACH ▶ Once the data have been collected, the procedure is to:

1. Delete unusual or nonrecurring observations.
2. Compute the *average time* for each element, using Equation (10-1).
3. Compute the *normal time* for each element, using Equation (10-2).
4. Find the total normal time.
5. Compute the *standard time*, using Equation (10-3).

SOLUTION ▶

1. Delete observations such as those marked with an asterisk (*). (These may be due to business interruptions, conferences with the boss, or mistakes of an unusual nature; they are not part of the job element, but may be personal or delay time.)

2. Average time for each job element:

$$\text{Average time for A} = \frac{8 + 10 + 9 + 11}{4} = 9.5 \text{ min}$$

$$\text{Average time for B} = \frac{2 + 3 + 2 + 1 + 3}{5} = 2.2 \text{ min}$$

$$\text{Average time for C} = \frac{2 + 1 + 2 + 1}{4} = 1.5 \text{ min}$$

3. Normal time for each job element:

$$\text{Normal time for A} = (\text{Average observed time}) \times (\text{Performance rating})$$

$$= (9.5)(1.2) \quad = 11.4 \text{ min}$$

$$\text{Normal time for B} = (2.2)(1.05) = 2.31 \text{ min}$$

$$\text{Normal time for C} = (1.5)(1.10) = 1.65 \text{ min}$$

Note: Normal times are computed for each element because the performance rating factor (work pace) may vary for each element, as it did in this case.

4. Add the normal times for each element to find the total normal time (the normal time for the whole job):

$$\text{Total normal time} = 11.40 + 2.31 + 1.65 = 15.36 \text{ min}$$

5. Standard time for the job:

$$\text{Standard time} = \frac{\text{Total normal time}}{1 - \text{Allowance factor}} = \frac{15.36}{1 - 0.15} = 18.07 \text{ min}$$

Thus, 18.07 minutes is the time standard for this job.

INSIGHT ▶ When observed times are not consistent they need to be reviewed. Abnormally short times may be the result of an observational error and are usually discarded. Abnormally long times need to be analyzed to determine if they, too, are an error. However, they may *include* a seldom occurring but legitimate activity for the element (such as a machine adjustment) or may be personal, delay, or fatigue time.

LEARNING EXERCISE ▶ If the two observations marked with an asterisk were *not* deleted, what would be the total normal time and the standard time? [Answer: 18.89 min, 22.22 min.]

RELATED PROBLEMS ▶ 10.22–10.25, 10.28a,b, 10.29a, 10.30a (10.41–10.43 are available in MyOMLab)

Time study requires a sampling process; so the question of sampling error in the average observed time naturally arises. In statistics, error varies inversely with sample size. Thus, to determine just how many "cycles" we should time, we must consider the variability of each element in the study.

LO 10.7 *Find the proper sample size for a time study*

To determine an adequate sample size, three items must be considered:

1. How accurate we want to be (e.g., is ±5% of observed time close enough?).
2. The desired level of confidence (e.g., the *z*-value; is 95% adequate or is 99% required?).
3. How much variation exists within the job elements (e.g., if the variation is large, a larger sample will be required).

The formula for finding the appropriate sample size, given these three variables, is:

$$\text{Required sample size} = n = \left(\frac{zs}{h\bar{x}}\right)^2 \tag{10-4}$$

where

h = accuracy level (acceptable error) desired in percent of the job element, expressed as a decimal (5% = .05)

z = number of standard deviations required for desired level of confidence (90% confidence = 1.65; see Table 10.2 or Appendix I for more *z*-values)

s = standard deviation of the initial sample

$\bar{x}$ = mean of the initial sample

n = required sample size

TABLE 10.2

Common z-Values

DESIRED CONFIDENCE (%)	Z-VALUE (STANDARD DEVIATION REQUIRED FOR DESIRED LEVEL OF CONFIDENCE)
90.0	1.65
95.0	1.96
95.45	2.00
99.0	2.58
99.73	3.00

We demonstrate with Example 3.

Example 3

COMPUTING SAMPLE SIZE

Thomas W. Jones Manufacturing Co. has asked you to check a labor standard prepared by a recently terminated analyst. Your first task is to determine the correct sample size. Your accuracy is to be within $\pm5\%$ and your confidence level at 95%. The standard deviation of the sample is 1.0 and the mean 3.00.

APPROACH ▶ You apply Equation (10-4).

SOLUTION ▶
$$h = 0.05 \quad \bar{x} = 3.00 \quad s = 1.0$$
$$z = 1.96 \text{ (from Table 10.2 or Appendix I)}$$
$$n = \left(\frac{zs}{h\bar{x}}\right)^2$$
$$n = \left(\frac{1.96 \times 1.0}{0.05 \times 3}\right)^2 = 170.74 \approx 171$$

Therefore, you recommend a sample size of 171.

INSIGHT ▶ Notice that as the confidence level required increases, the sample size also increases. Similarly, as the desired accuracy level increases (say, from 5% to 1%), the sample size increases.

LEARNING EXERCISE ▶ The confidence level for Jones Manufacturing Co. can be set lower, at 90%, while retaining the same $\pm5\%$ accuracy levels. What sample size is needed now? [Answer: $n = 121$.]

RELATED PROBLEMS ▶ 10.26, 10.27, 10.28c, 10.29b, 10.30b (10.44–10.46 are available in MyOMLab)

EXCEL OM Data File **Ch10Ex3.xls** can be found in MyOMLab.

Now let's look at two variations of Example 3.

First, if h, the desired accuracy, is expressed as an absolute amount of error (say, ±1 minute of error is acceptable), then substitute e for $h\bar{x}$, and the appropriate formula is:

$$n = \left(\frac{zs}{e}\right)^2 \tag{10-5}$$

where e is the absolute time amount of acceptable error.

Second, for those cases when s, the standard deviation of the sample, is not provided (which is typically the case outside the classroom), it must be computed. The formula for doing so is given in Equation (10-6):

$$s = \sqrt{\frac{\Sigma(x_i - \bar{x})^2}{n - 1}} = \sqrt{\frac{\Sigma(\text{Each sample observation} - \bar{x})^2}{\text{Number in sample} - 1}} \tag{10-6}$$

where x_i = value of each observation
$\bar{x}$ = mean of the observations
n = number of observations in the sample

An example of this computation is provided in Solved Problem 10.4 on page 433.

With the development of handheld computers, job elements, time, performance rates, and statistical confidence intervals can be easily created, logged, edited, and managed. Although time studies provide accuracy in setting labor standards (see the *OM in Action* box "UPS: The Tightest Ship in the Shipping Business"), they have two disadvantages. First, they require a trained staff of analysts. Second, these standards cannot be set before tasks are actually performed. This leads us to two alternative work-measurement techniques that we discuss next.

Predetermined Time Standards

In addition to historical experience and time studies, we can set production standards by using predetermined time standards. **Predetermined time standards** divide manual work into small basic elements that already have established times (based on very large samples of workers). To estimate the time for a particular task, the time factors for each basic element of that task are

Predetermined time standards
A division of manual work into small basic elements that have established and widely accepted times.

OM in Action   UPS: The Tightest Ship in the Shipping Business

United Parcel Service (UPS) employs 425,000 people and delivers an average of 16 million packages a day to locations throughout the U.S. and 220 other countries. To achieve its claim of "running the tightest ship in the shipping business," UPS methodically trains its delivery drivers in how to do their jobs as efficiently as possible.

Industrial engineers at UPS have time-studied each driver's route and set standards for each delivery, stop, and pickup. These engineers have recorded every second taken up by stoplights, traffic volume, detours, doorbells, walkways, stairways, and coffee breaks. Even bathroom stops are factored into the standards. All this information is then fed into company computers to provide detailed time standards for every driver, every day.

To meet their objective of 200 deliveries and pickups each day (versus only 80 at FedEx), UPS drivers must follow procedures exactly. As they approach a delivery stop, drivers unbuckle their seat belts, honk their horns, and cut their engines. Ignition keys have been dispensed with and replaced by a digital remote fob that turns off the engine and unlocks the bulkhead door that leads to the packages. In one seamless motion, drivers are required to yank up their emergency brakes and push their gearshifts into first. Then they slide to the ground with their electronic clipboards under their right arm and their packages in their left hand. They walk to the customer's door at the prescribed 3 feet per second and knock first to avoid lost seconds searching for the doorbell. After making the delivery, they do the paperwork on the way back to the truck.

Productivity experts describe UPS as one of the most efficient companies anywhere in applying effective labor standards.

Sources: Wall Street Journal (February 19, 2015), (December 26, 2011), and (September 19, 2011); and G. Niemann, *Big Brown: The Untold Story of UPS*, New York: Wiley, 2007.

---

added together. Developing a comprehensive system of predetermined time standards would be prohibitively expensive for any given firm. Consequently, a number of systems are commercially available. The most common predetermined time standard is *methods time measurement* (MTM), which is a product of the MTM Association.[3]

Therbligs

Basic physical elements of motion.

Time measurement units (TMUs)

Units for very basic micromotions in which 1 TMU = .0006 min, or 100,000 TMUs = 1 hr.

Predetermined time standards are an outgrowth of basic motions called therbligs. The term *therblig* was coined by Frank Gilbreth (*Gilbreth* spelled backwards, with the *t* and *h* reversed). Therbligs include such activities as select, grasp, position, assemble, reach, hold, rest, and inspect. These activities are stated in terms of time measurement units (TMUs), which are equal to only .00001 hour, or .0006 minute each. MTM values for various therbligs are specified in very detailed tables. Figure 10.9, for example, provides the set of time standards for the motion GET and PLACE. To use GET and PLACE, one must know what is "gotten," its approximate weight, and where and how far it is supposed to be placed.

GET and PLACE			DISTANCE RANGE IN IN.	<8	>8 <20	>20 <32
WEIGHT	CONDITIONS OF GET	PLACE ACCURACY	MTM CODE	1	2	3
<2 LB	EASY	APPROXIMATE	AA	20	35	50
		LOOSE	AB	30	45	60
		TIGHT	AC	40	55	70
	DIFFICULT	APPROXIMATE	AD	20	45	60
		LOOSE	AE	30	55	70
		TIGHT	AF	40	65	80
	HANDFUL	APPROXIMATE	AG	40	65	80
>2 LB <18 LB		APPROXIMATE	AH	25	45	55
		LOOSE	AJ	40	65	75
		TIGHT	AK	50	75	85
>18 LB <45 LB		APPROXIMATE	AL	90	106	115
		LOOSE	AM	95	120	130
		TIGHT	AN	120	145	160

Figure **10.9**

Sample MTM Table for GET and PLACE Motion

Time values are in TMUs.

Source: Copyrighted by the MTM Association for Standards and Research. No reprint permission without consent from the MTM Association, 16–01 Broadway, Fair Lawn, NJ 07410. Used with permission of MTM Association for Standards & Research.

Example 4 shows a use of predetermined time standards in setting service labor standards.

Example 4

USING PREDETERMINED TIME (MTM ANALYSIS) TO DETERMINE STANDARD TIME

General Hospital wants to set the standard time for lab technicians to pour a tube specimen using MTM.[4]

APPROACH ▶ This is a repetitive task for which the MTM data in Table 10.3 may be used to develop standard times. The sample tube is in a rack and the centrifuge tubes in a nearby box. A technician removes the sample tube from the rack, uncaps it, gets the centrifuge tube, pours, and places both tubes in the rack.

TABLE 10.3	MTM-HC Analysis: Pouring Tube Specimen	
ELEMENT DESCRIPTION	**ELEMENT**	**TIME**
Get tube from rack	AA2	35
Uncap, place on counter	AA2	35
Get centrifuge tube, place at sample tube	AD2	45
Pour (3 sec)	PT	83
Place tubes in rack (simo)	PC2	40
		Total TMU 238

.0006 × 238 = Total standard minutes = .143 or about 8.6 seconds

SOLUTION ▶ The first work element involves getting the tube from the rack. The conditions for GETTING the tube and PLACING it in front of the technician are:

- *Weight:* (less than 2 pounds)
- *Conditions of GET:* (easy)
- *Place accuracy:* (approximate)
- *Distance range:* (8 to 20 inches)

Then the MTM element for this activity is AA2 (as seen in Figure 10.9). The rest of Table 10.3 is developed from similar MTM tables.

INSIGHT ▶ Most MTM calculations are computerized, so the user need only key in the appropriate MTM codes, such as AA2 in this example.

LEARNING EXERCISE ▶ General Hospital decides that the first step in this process really involves a distance range of 4 inches (getting the tube from the rack). The other work elements are unchanged. What is the new standard time? [Answer: .134 minutes, or just over 8 seconds]

RELATED PROBLEM ▶ 10.36

Predetermined time standards have several advantages over direct time studies. First, they may be established in a laboratory environment, where the procedure will not upset actual production activities (which time studies tend to do). Second, because the standard can be set *before* a task is actually performed, it can be used for planning. Third, no performance ratings are necessary. Fourth, unions tend to accept this method as a fair means of setting standards. Finally, predetermined time standards are particularly effective in firms that do substantial numbers of studies of similar tasks. To ensure accurate labor standards, some firms use both time studies and predetermined time standards.

> **⚠ STUDENT TIP**
> Families of predetermined time standards have been developed for many occupations.

Work Sampling

The fourth method of developing labor or production standards, work sampling, was developed in England by L. Tippet in the 1930s. Work sampling estimates the percent of the time that a worker spends on various tasks. Random observations are used to record the activity that a worker is performing. The results are primarily used to determine how employees allocate their time among various activities. Knowledge of this allocation may lead to staffing changes, reassignment of duties, estimates of activity cost, and the setting of delay allowances for labor standards. When work sampling is performed to establish delay allowances, it is sometimes called a *ratio delay study*.

> **Work sampling**
> An estimate, via sampling, of the percentage of the time that a worker spends on various tasks.

Using the techniques of this chapter to develop labor standards, operations managers at Orlando's Arnold Palmer Hospital determined that nurses walked an average of 2.7 miles per day. This constitutes up to 30% of the nurse's time, a terrible waste of critical talent. Analysis resulted in a new layout design that has reduced walking distances by 20%.

The work-sampling procedure can be summarized in five steps:

1. Take a preliminary sample to obtain an estimate of the parameter value (e.g., percent of time a worker is busy).
2. Compute the sample size required.
3. Prepare a schedule for observing the worker at appropriate times. The concept of random numbers is used to provide for random observation. For example, let's say we draw the following five random numbers from a table: 07, 12, 22, 25, and 49. These can then be used to create an observation schedule of 9:07 A.M., 9:12, 9:22, 9:25, 9:49.
4. Observe and record worker activities.
5. Determine how workers spend their time (usually as a percentage).

To determine the number of observations required, management must decide on the desired confidence level and accuracy. First, however, the analyst must select a preliminary value for the parameter under study (Step 1 above). The choice is usually based on a small sample of perhaps 50 observations. The following formula then gives the sample size for a desired confidence and accuracy:

$$n = \frac{z^2 p(1-p)}{h^2} \tag{10-7}$$

where n = required sample size
z = number of standard deviations for the desired confidence level ($z = 1$ for 68.27% confidence, $z = 2$ for 95.45% confidence, and $z = 3$ for 99.73% confidence—these values are obtained from Table 10.2 or the normal table in Appendix I)
p = estimated value of sample proportion (of time worker is observed busy or idle)
h = acceptable error level, in percent (as a decimal)

Example 5 shows how to apply this formula.

Example 5

DETERMINING THE NUMBER OF WORK SAMPLE OBSERVATIONS NEEDED

The manager of Michigan County's welfare office, Dana Johnson, estimates that her employees are idle 25% of the time. She would like to take a work sample that is accurate within ±3% and wants to have 95.45% confidence in the results.

APPROACH ▶ Dana applies Equation (10-7) to determine how many observations should be taken.

SOLUTION ▶ Dana computes n:

$$n = \frac{z^2 p(1-p)}{h^2}$$

where n = required sample size
z = confidence level (2 for 95.45% confidence)
p = estimate of idle proportion = 25% = .25
h = acceptable error of 3% = .03

She finds that

$$n = \frac{(2)^2(.25)(.75)}{(.03)^2} = 833 \text{ observations}$$

INSIGHT ▶ Thus, 833 observations should be taken. If the percent of idle time observed is not close to 25% as the study progresses, then the number of observations may have to be recalculated and increased or decreased as appropriate.

LEARNING EXERCISE ▶ If the confidence level increases to 99.73%, how does the sample size change? [Answer: $n = 1,875$.]

RELATED PROBLEMS ▶ 10.31, 10.32, 10.35, 10.37

ACTIVE MODEL 10.1 This example is further illustrated in Active Model 10.1 in MyOMLab.

The focus of work sampling is to determine how workers allocate their time among various activities. This is accomplished by establishing the percent of time individuals spend on these activities rather than the exact amount of time spent on specific tasks. The analyst simply records in a random, nonbiased way the occurrence of each activity. Example 6 shows the procedure for evaluating employees at the state welfare office introduced in Example 5.

Example 6

DETERMINING EMPLOYEE TIME ALLOCATION WITH WORK SAMPLING

Dana Johnson, the manager of Michigan County's welfare office, wants to be sure her employees have adequate time to provide prompt, helpful service. She believes that service to welfare clients who phone or walk in without an appointment deteriorates rapidly when employees are busy more than 75% of the time. Consequently, she does not want her employees to be occupied with client service activities more than 75% of the time.

APPROACH ▶ The study requires several things: First, based on the calculations in Example 5, 833 observations are needed. Second, observations are to be made in a random, nonbiased way over a period of 2 weeks to ensure a true sample. Third, the analyst must define the activities that are "work." In this case, work is defined as all the activities necessary to take care of the client (filing, meetings, data entry, discussions with the supervisor, etc.). Fourth, personal time is to be included in the 25% of nonwork time. Fifth, the observations are made in a nonintrusive way so as not to distort the normal work patterns. At the end of the 2 weeks, the 833 observations yield the following results:

NO. OF OBSERVATIONS	ACTIVITY
485	On the phone or meeting with a welfare client
126	Idle
62	Personal time
23	Discussions with supervisor
137	Filing, meeting, and computer data entry
833	

SOLUTION ▶ The analyst concludes that all but 188 observations (126 idle and 62 personal) are work related. Because 22.6% (= 188/833) is less idle time than Dana believes necessary to ensure a high client service level, she needs to find a way to reduce current workloads. This could be done through a reassignment of duties or the hiring of additional personnel.

INSIGHT ▶ Work sampling is particularly helpful when determining staffing needs or the reallocation of duties (see Figure 10.10).

LEARNING EXERCISE ▶ The analyst working for Dana recategorizes several observations. There are now 450 "on the phone/meeting with client" observations, 156 "idle," and 67 "personal time" observations. The last two categories saw no changes. Do the conclusions change? [Answer: Yes; now about 27% of employee time is not work related—over the 25% Dana desires.]

RELATED PROBLEM ▶ 10.34

The results of similar studies of salespeople and assembly-line employees are shown in Figure 10.10.

Work sampling offers several advantages over time-study methods. First, because a single observer can observe several workers simultaneously, it is less expensive. Second, observers usually do not require much training, and no timing devices are needed. Third, the study can be temporarily delayed at any time with little impact on the results. Fourth, because work sampling uses instantaneous observations over a long period, the worker has little chance of affecting the study's outcome. Fifth, the procedure is less intrusive and therefore less likely to generate objections.

The disadvantages of work sampling are (1) it does not divide work elements as completely as time studies, (2) it can yield biased or incorrect results if the observer does not follow random routes of travel and observation, and (3) because it is less intrusive, it tends to be less accurate; this is particularly true when job content times are short.

Figure **10.10**

Work-Sampling Time Studies

These two work-sampling time studies were done to determine what salespeople do at a wholesale electronics distributor (left) and a composite of several auto assembly-line employees (right).

Salespeople

Sales in person **20%**

Travel **20%**

Telephone sales **12%**

Paperwork **17%**

Telephone within firm **13%**

Lunch and personal **10%**

Meetings and other **8%**

Assembly-Line Employees

Productive work **67%**

Startup/pep talk **3%**

Breaks and lunch **10%**

Dead time between tasks **13%**

Unscheduled tasks and downtime **4%**

Cleanup **3%**

Ethics

Ethics in the workplace presents some interesting challenges. As we have suggested in this chapter, many constraints influence job design. The issues of fairness, equity, and ethics are pervasive. Whether the issue is equal opportunity or safe working conditions, an operations manager is often the one responsible. Managers do have some guidelines. By knowing the law, working with OSHA,[5] MSDS,[6] state agencies, unions, trade associations, insurers, and employees, managers can often determine the parameters of their decisions. Human resource and legal departments are also available for help and guidance through the labyrinth of laws and regulations.

Management's role is to educate employees; specify the necessary equipment, work rules, and work environment; and then enforce those requirements, even when employees think it is not necessary to wear safety equipment. We began this chapter with a discussion of mutual trust and commitment, and that is the environment that managers should foster. Ethical management requires no less.

Summary

Outstanding firms know that their human resource strategy can yield a competitive advantage. Often a large percentage of employees and a large part of labor costs are under the direction of OM. Consequently, an operations manager usually has a major role to play in achieving human resource objectives. A requirement is to build an environment with mutual respect and commitment and a reasonable quality of work life. Successful organizations have designed jobs that use both the mental and physical capabilities of their employees. Regardless of the strategy chosen, the skill with which a firm manages its human resources ultimately determines its success.

Labor standards are required for an efficient operations system. They are needed for production planning, labor planning, costing, and evaluating performance. They are used throughout industry—from the factory to finance, sales, and office. They can also be used as a basis for incentive systems. Standards may be established via historical data, time studies, predetermined time standards, and work sampling.

Key Terms

Labor planning (p. 411)
Job design (p. 412)
Labor specialization (or job specialization) (p. 412)
Job enlargement (p. 413)
Job rotation (p. 413)
Job enrichment (p. 413)
Employee empowerment (p. 413)
Self-directed team (p. 414)

Ergonomics (p. 415)
Methods analysis (p. 417)
Flow diagram (p. 418)
Process chart (p. 418)
Activity chart (p. 418)
Operations chart (p. 418)
Visual workplace (p. 420)
Labor standards (p. 420)
Time study (p. 421)

Average observed time (p. 422)
Normal time (p. 422)
Standard time (p. 422)
Predetermined time standards (p. 425)
Therbligs (p. 426)
Time measurement units (TMUs) (p. 426)
Work sampling (p. 427)

Ethical Dilemma

Johnstown Foundry, Inc., with several major plants, is one of the largest makers of cast-iron water and sewer pipes in the U.S. In one of the nation's most dangerous industries, Johnstown is perhaps one of the most unsafe, with four times the injury rate of its six competitors combined. Its worker death rate is six times the industry average. In a recent 7-year period, Johnstown's plants were also found to be in violation of pollution and emission limits 450 times.

Workers who protest dangerous work conditions claim they are "bull's-eyed"—marked for termination. Supervisors have bullied injured workers and intimidated union leaders. Line workers who fail to make daily quotas get disciplinary actions. Managers have put up safety signs *after* a worker was injured to make it appear that the worker ignored posted policies. They doctor safety records and alter machines to cover up hazards. When the government investigated one worker's death recently, inspectors found the Johnstown policy "was not to correct anything until OSHA found it."

Johnstown plants have also been repeatedly fined for failing to stop production to repair broken pollution controls. Three plants have been designated "high-priority" violators by the EPA. Inside the plants, workers have repeatedly complained of blurred vision, severe headaches, and respiratory problems after being exposed, without training or protection, to chemicals used in the production process. Near one Pennsylvania plant, school crossing guards have had to wear gas masks; that location alone has averaged over a violation every month for 7 years. Johnstown's "standard procedure," according to a former plant manager, is to illegally dump industrial contaminants into local rivers and creeks. Workers wait for night or heavy rainstorms before flushing thousands of gallons from their sump pumps.

Given the following scenarios, what is your position, and what action should you take?

a) On your spouse's recent move to the area, you accepted a job, perhaps somewhat naively, as a company nurse in one of the Johnstown plants. After 2 weeks on the job, you became aware of the work environment noted above.

b) You are a contractor who has traditionally used Johnstown's products, which meet specifications. Johnstown is consistently the low bidder. Your customers are happy with the product.

c) You are Johnstown's banker.

d) You are a supplier to Johnstown.

Mark Winfrey/Shutterstock

Discussion Questions

1. How would you define a good quality of work life?

2. What are some of the worst jobs you know about? Why are they bad jobs? Why do people want these jobs?

3. If you were redesigning the jobs described in Question 2, what changes would you make? Are your changes realistic? Would they improve productivity (not just *production* but *productivity*)?

4. Can you think of any jobs that push the man–machine interface to the limits of human capabilities?

5. What are the five core characteristics of a good job design?

6. What are the differences among job enrichment, job enlargement, job rotation, job specialization, and employee empowerment?

7. Define ergonomics. Discuss the role of ergonomics in job design.

8. List the techniques available for carrying out methods analysis.

9. Identify four ways in which labor standards are set.

10. What are some of the uses to which labor standards are put?

11. How would you classify the following job elements? Are they personal, fatigue, or delay?

    a) The operator stops to talk to you.

    b) The operator lights up a cigarette.

    c) The operator opens his lunch pail (it is not lunch time), removes an apple, and takes an occasional bite.

12. How do you classify the time for a drill press operator who is idle for a few minutes at the beginning of every job waiting for the setup person to complete the setup? Some of the setup time is used in going for stock, but the operator typically returns with stock before the setup person is finished with the setup.

13. How do you classify the time for a machine operator who, between every job and sometimes in the middle of jobs, turns off the machine and goes for stock?

14. The operator drops a part, which you pick up and hand to him. Does this make any difference in a time study? If so, how?

Solved Problems   Virtual Office Hours help is available in MyOMLab.

SOLVED PROBLEM 10.1

As pit crew manager for Rusty Wallace's NASCAR team (see the *Global Company Profile* that opens this chapter), you would like to evaluate how your "Jackman" (JM) and "Gas Man #1" (GM #1) are utilized. Recent stopwatch studies have verified the following times:

PIT CREW	ACTIVITY	TIME (SECONDS)
JM	Move to right side of car and raise car	4.0
GM #1	Move to rear gas filler	2.5
JM	Wait for tire	1.0
JM	Move to left side of car and raise car	3.8
GM #1	Load fuel (per gallon)	0.5
JM	Wait for tire	1.2
JM	Move back over wall from left side	2.5
GM #1	Move back over the wall from gas filler	2.5

Use an activity chart similar to the one in Figure 10.6 as an aid.

SOLUTION

SOLVED PROBLEM 10.2

A work operation consisting of three elements has been subjected to a stopwatch time study. The recorded observations are shown in the following table. By union contract, the allowance time for the operation is personal time 5%, delay 5%, and fatigue 10%. Determine the standard time for the work operation.

JOB ELEMENT	OBSERVATIONS (MINUTES)						PERFORMANCE RATING (%)
	1	2	3	4	5	6	
A	.1	.3	.2	.9	.2	.1	90
B	.8	.6	.8	.5	3.2	.7	110
C	.5	.5	.4	.5	.6	.5	80

SOLUTION

First, delete the two observations that appear to be very unusual (.9 minute for job element A and 3.2 minutes for job element B). Then:

$$\text{A's average observed time} = \frac{.1 + .3 + .2 + .2 + .1}{5} = 0.18 \text{ min}$$

$$\text{B's average observed time} = \frac{.8 + .6 + .8 + .5 + .7}{5} = 0.68 \text{ min}$$

$$\text{C's average observed time} = \frac{.5 + .5 + .4 + .5 + .6 + .5}{6} = 0.50 \text{ min}$$

A's normal time = (0.18)(0.90) = 0.16 min

B's normal time = (0.68)(1.10) = 0.75 min

C's normal time = (0.50)(0.80) = 0.40 min

Normal time for job = 0.16 + 0.75 + 0.40 = 1.31 min

Note, the total allowance factor = 0.05 + 0.05 + 0.10 = 0.20

$$\text{Then: Standard time} = \frac{1.31}{1 - 0.20} = 1.64 \text{ min}$$

SOLVED PROBLEM 10.3

The preliminary work sample of an operation indicates the following:

Number of times operator working	60
Number of times operator idle	40
Total number of preliminary observations	100

What is the required sample size for a 99.73% confidence level with ±4% precision?

SOLUTION

$z = 3$ for 99.73 confidence; $p = \dfrac{60}{100} = 0.6$; $h = 0.04$

So:

$$n = \frac{z^2 p(1-p)}{h^2} = \frac{(3)^2(0.6)(0.4)}{(0.04)^2} = 1{,}350 \text{ sample size}$$

SOLVED PROBLEM 10.4

Amor Manufacturing Co. of Geneva, Switzerland, has just observed a job in its laboratory in anticipation of releasing the job to the factory for production. The firm wants rather good accuracy for costing and labor forecasting. Specifically, it wants to provide a 99% confidence level and a cycle time that is within 3% of the true value. How many observations should it make? The data collected so far are as follows:

OBSERVATION	TIME
1	1.7
2	1.6
3	1.4
4	1.4
5	1.4

SOLUTION

First, solve for the mean, $\bar{x}$, and the sample standard deviation, s:

$$s = \sqrt{\frac{\sum(\text{Each sample observation} - \bar{x})^2}{\text{Number in sample} - 1}}$$

OBSERVATION	x_i	$\bar{x}$	$x_i - \bar{x}$	$(x_i - \bar{x})^2$
1	1.7	1.5	.2	0.04
2	1.6	1.5	.1	0.01
3	1.4	1.5	−.1	0.01
4	1.4	1.5	−.1	0.01
5	1.4	1.5	−.1	0.01
	$\bar{x} = 1.5$			$0.08 = \sum(x_i - \bar{x})^2$

$$s = \sqrt{\frac{0.08}{n-1}} = \sqrt{\frac{0.08}{4}} = 0.141$$

Then, solve for $n = \left(\dfrac{zs}{h\bar{x}}\right)^2 = \left[\dfrac{(2.58)(0.141)}{(0.03)(1.5)}\right]^2 = 65.3$

where $\bar{x} = 1.5$
$s = 0.141$
$z = 2.58$ (from Table 10.2)
$h = 0.03$

Therefore, you round up to 66 observations.

SOLVED PROBLEM 10.5

At Maggard Micro Manufacturing, Inc., workers press semiconductors into predrilled slots on printed circuit boards. The elemental motions for normal time used by the company are as follows:

Reach 6 inches for semiconductors	40 TMU
Grasp the semiconductor	10 TMU
Move semiconductor to printed circuit board	30 TMU
Position semiconductor	35 TMU
Press semiconductor into slots	65 TMU
Move board aside	20 TMU

(Each time measurement unit is equal to .0006 min.) Determine the normal time for this operation in minutes and in seconds.

SOLUTION

Add the time measurement units:

$$40 + 10 + 30 + 35 + 65 + 20 = 200$$
$$\text{Time in minutes} = (200)(.0006 \text{ min.}) = 0.12 \text{ min}$$
$$\text{Time in seconds} = (0.12)(60 \text{ sec}) = 7.2 \text{ sec}$$

SOLVED PROBLEM 10.6

To obtain the estimate of time a worker is busy for a work sampling study, a manager divides a typical workday into 480 minutes. Using a random-number table to decide what time to go to an area to sample work occurrences, the manager records observations on a tally sheet like the following:

STATUS	TALLY
Productively working	$\cancel{||||}$ $\cancel{||||}$ $\cancel{||||}$ $|$
Idle	$||||$

SOLUTION

In this case, the supervisor made 20 observations and found that employees were working 80% of the time. So, out of 480 minutes in an office workday, 20%, or 96 minutes, was idle time, and 384 minutes were productive. Note that this procedure describes that a worker is busy, not necessarily doing what he or she *should* be doing.

Problems
Note: **P𝗫** means the problem may be solved with POM for Windows and/or Excel.

Problem 10.1 relates to Job Design

• **10.1** Rate a job you have had using Hackman and Oldham's core job characteristics (see page 413) on a scale from 1 to 10. What is your total score? What about the job could have been changed to make you give it a higher score?

Problems 10.2–10.12 relate to Methods Analysis

• **10.2** Make a process chart for changing the right rear tire on an automobile.

• **10.3** Draw an activity chart for a machine operator with the following operation. The relevant times are as follows:

Prepare mill for loading (cleaning, oiling, and so on)	.50 min
Load mill	1.75 min
Mill operating (cutting material)	2.25 min
Unload mill	.75 min

••• **10.4** Draw an activity chart (a crew chart similar to Figure 10.6) for a concert (for example, Tim McGraw, Linkin Park, Lil' Wayne, or Bruce Springsteen) and determine how to put together the concert so the star has reasonable breaks. For instance, at what point is there an instrumental number, a visual effect, a duet, a dance moment, that allows the star to pause and rest physically or at least rest his or her voice? Do other members of the show have moments of pause or rest?

Fernando Medina

•• **10.5** Make an operations chart of one of the following:
a) Putting a new eraser in (or on) a pencil
b) Putting a paper clip on two pieces of paper
c) Putting paper in a printer

• **10.6** Develop a process chart for installing a new memory board in your personal computer.

•• **10.7** Using the data in Solved Problem 10.1, prepare an activity chart like the one in the Solved Problem, but a second Gas Man also delivers 11 gallons.

•• **10.8** Prepare a process chart for the Jackman in Solved Problem 10.1.

•• **10.9** Draw an activity chart for changing the right rear tire on an automobile with:
a) Only one person working
b) Two people working

••• **10.10** Draw an activity chart for washing the dishes in a double-sided sink. Two people participate, one washing, the other rinsing and drying. The rinser dries a batch of dishes from the drip rack as the washer fills the right sink with clean but unrinsed dishes. Then the rinser rinses the clean batch and places them on the drip rack. All dishes are stacked before being placed in the cabinets.

••• **10.11** Your campus club is hosting a car wash. Due to demand, three people are going to be scheduled per wash line. (Three people have to wash each vehicle.) Design an activity chart for washing and drying a typical sedan. You must wash the wheels but ignore the cleaning of the interior, because this part of the operation will be done at a separate vacuum station.

•••• **10.12** Design a process chart for printing a short document on a laser printer at an office. Unknown to you, the printer in the hallway is out of paper. The paper is located in a supply room at the other end of the hall. You wish to make five stapled copies of the document once it is printed. The copier, located next to the printer, has a sorter but no stapler. How could you make the task more efficient with the existing equipment?

Problems 10.13–10.46 relate to Labor Standards

• **10.13** If Charlene Brewster has times of 8.4, 8.6, 8.3, 8.5, 8.7, and 8.5 and a performance rating of 110%, what is the normal time for this operation? Is she faster or slower than normal? **P𝗫**

• **10.14** If Charlene, the worker in Problem 10.13, has a performance rating of 90%, what is the normal time for the operation? Is she faster or slower than normal? **P𝗫**

•• **10.15** Refer to Problem 10.13.
a) If the allowance factor is 15%, what is the standard time for this operation?
b) If the allowance factor is 18% and the performance rating is now 90%, what is the standard time for this operation? **P𝗫**

•• **10.16** Claudine Soosay recorded the following times assembling a watch. Determine (a) the average time, (b) the normal time, and (c) the standard time taken by her, using a performance rating of 95% and a personal allowance of 8%.

Assembly Times Recorded

OBSERVATION NO.	TIME (MINUTES)	OBSERVATION NO.	TIME (MINUTES)
1	0.11	9	0.12
2	0.10	10	0.09
3	0.11	11	0.12
4	0.10	12	0.11
5	0.14	13	0.10
6	0.10	14	0.12
7	0.10	15	0.14
8	0.09	16	0.09

• **10.17** A Northeast Airlines gate agent, Chip Gilliken, gives out seat assignments to ticketed passengers. He takes an average of 50 seconds per passenger and is rated 110% in performance. How long should a *typical* agent be expected to take to make seat assignments? **P𝗫**

• **10.18** After being observed many times, Beverly Demarr, a hospital lab analyst, had an average observed time for blood tests of 12 minutes. Beverly's performance rating is 105%. The hospital has a personal, fatigue, and delay allowance of 16%.
a) Find the normal time for this process.
b) Find the standard time for this blood test. **P𝗫**

• **10.19** Jell Lee Beans is famous for its boxed candies, which are sold primarily to businesses. One operator had the following observed times for gift wrapping in minutes: 2.2, 2.6, 2.3, 2.5, 2.4. The operator has a performance rating of 105% and an allowance factor of 10%. What is the standard time for gift wrapping? **P𝗫**

• **10.20** After training, Mary Fernandez, a computer technician, had an average observed time for memory-chip tests of 12 seconds. Mary's performance rating is 100%. The firm has a personal fatigue and delay allowance of 15%.
a) Find the normal time for this process.
b) Find the standard time for this process. **PX**

•• **10.21** Susan Cottenden clocked the observed time for welding a part onto truck doors at 5.3 minutes. The performance rating of the worker timed was estimated at 105%. Find the normal time for this operation.

Note: According to the local union contract, each welder is allowed 3 minutes of personal time per hour and 2 minutes of fatigue time per hour. Further, there should be an average delay allowance of 1 minute per hour. Compute the allowance factor and then find the standard time for the welding activity. **PX**

•• **10.22** A hotel housekeeper, Alison Harvey, was observed five times on each of four task elements, as shown in the following table. On the basis of these observations, find the standard time for the process. Assume a 10% allowance factor.

ELEMENT	PERFORMANCE RATING (%)	OBSERVATIONS (MINUTES PER CYCLE)				
		1	2	3	4	5
Check minibar	100	1.5	1.6	1.4	1.5	1.5
Make one bed	90	2.3	2.5	2.1	2.2	2.4
Vacuum floor	120	1.7	1.9	1.9	1.4	1.6
Clean bath	100	3.5	3.6	3.6	3.6	3.2

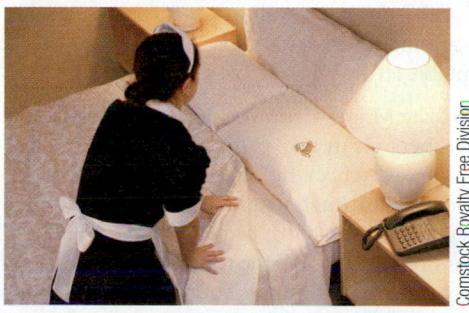

Comstock Royalty Free Division

•• **10.23** Virginia College promotes a wide variety of executive-training courses for firms in the Arlington, Virginia, region. Director Wendy Tate believes that individually written letters add a personal touch to marketing. To prepare letters for mailing, she conducts a time study of her secretaries. On the basis of the observations shown in the following table, she wishes to develop a time standard for the whole job.

The college uses a total allowance factor of 12%. Tate decides to delete all unusual observations from the time study. What is the standard time?

ELEMENT	OBSERVATIONS (MINUTES)						PERFORMANCE RATING (%)
	1	2	3	4	5	6	
Typing letter	2.5	3.5	2.8	2.1	2.6	3.3	85
Typing envelope	.8	.8	.6	.8	3.1[a]	.7	100
Stuffing envelope	.4	.5	1.9[a]	.3	.6	.5	95
Sealing, sorting	1.0	2.9[b]	.9	1.0	4.4[b]	.9	125

[a]Disregard—secretary stopped to answer the phone.
[b]Disregard—interruption by supervisor. **PX**

• **10.24** The results of a time study to perform a quality control test are shown in the following table. On the basis of these observations, determine the normal and standard time for the test, assuming a 23% allowance factor. **PX**

TASK ELEMENT	PERFORMANCE RATING (%)	OBSERVATIONS (MINUTES)				
		1	2	3	4	5
1	97	1.5	1.8	2.0	1.7	1.5
2	105	.6	.4	.7	3.7[a]	.5
3	86	.5	.4	.6	.4	.4
4	90	.6	.8	.7	.6	.7

[a]Disregard—employee is smoking a cigarette (included in personal time).

•• **10.25** Peter Rourke, a loan processor at Wentworth Bank, has been timed performing four work elements, with the results shown in the following table. The allowances for tasks such as this are personal, 7%; fatigue, 10%; and delay, 3%.

TASK ELEMENT	PERFORMANCE RATING (%)	OBSERVATIONS (MINUTES)				
		1	2	3	4	5
1	110	.5	.4	.6	.4	.4
2	95	.6	.8	.7	.6	.7
3	90	.6	.4	.7	.5	.5
4	85	1.5	1.8	2.0	1.7	1.5

a) What is the normal time?
b) What is the standard time? **PX**

•• **10.26** Each year, Lord & Taylor, Ltd., sets up a gift-wrapping station to assist its customers with holiday shopping. Preliminary observations of one worker at the station produced the following sample time (in minutes per package): 3.5, 3.2, 4.1, 3.6, 3.9. Based on this small sample, what number of observations would be necessary to determine the true cycle time with a 95% confidence level and an accuracy of ±5%? **PX**

•• **10.27** A time study of a factory worker has revealed an average observed time of 3.20 minutes, with a standard deviation of 1.28 minutes. These figures were based on a sample of 45 observations. Is this sample adequate in size for the firm to be 99% confident that the standard time is within ±5% of the true value? If not, what should be the proper number of observations? **PX**

•• **10.28** Based on a careful work study in the Hofstetter Corp., the results shown in the following table have been observed:

ELEMENT	OBSERVATIONS (MINUTES)					PERFORMANCE RATING (%)
	1	2	3	4	5	
Prepare daily reports	35	40	33	42	39	120
Photocopy results	12	10	36[a]	15	13	110
Label and package reports	3	3	5	5	4	90
Distribute reports	15	18	21	17	45[b]	85

[a]Photocopying machine broken; included as delay in the allowance factor.
[b]Power outage; included as delay in the allowance factor.

a) Compute the normal time for each work element.
b) If the allowance for this type of work is 15%, what is the standard time?
c) How many observations are needed for a 95% confidence level within ±5% accuracy? (*Hint:* Calculate the sample size of each element.)

•• **10.29** The Dubuque Cement Company packs 80-pound bags of concrete mix. Time-study data for the filling activity are shown in the following table. Because of the high physical demands of the job, the company's policy is a 23% allowance for workers.
a) Compute the standard time for the bag-packing task.
b) How many observations are necessary for 99% confidence, within ±5% accuracy?

ELEMENT	OBSERVATIONS (SECONDS)					PERFORMANCE RATING (%)
	1	2	3	4	5	
Grasp and place bag	8	9	8	11	7	110
Fill bag	36	41	39	35	112[a]	85
Seal bag	15	17	13	20	18	105
Place bag on conveyor	8	6	9	30[b]	35[b]	90

[a]Bag breaks open; included as delay in the allowance factor.
[b]Conveyor jams; included as delay in the allowance factor.

•• 10.30 Installing mufflers at the O'Sullivan Garage in Golden, Colorado, involves five work elements. Jill O'Sullivan has timed workers performing these tasks seven times, with the results shown in the following table:

JOB ELEMENT	OBSERVATIONS (MINUTES)							PERFORMANCE RATING (%)
	1	2	3	4	5	6	7	
1. Select correct mufflers	4	5	4	6	4	15[a]	4	110
2. Remove old muffler	6	8	7	6	7	6	7	90
3. Weld/install new muffler	15	14	14	12	15	16	13	105
4. Check/inspect work	3	4	24[a]	5	4	3	18[a]	100
5. Complete paperwork	5	6	8	—	7	6	7	130

[a]Employee has lengthy conversations with boss (not job related).

By agreement with her workers, Jill allows a 10% fatigue factor and a 10% personal-time factor, but no time for delay. To compute standard time for the work operation, Jill excludes all observations that appear to be unusual or nonrecurring. She does not want an error of more than ±5%.

a) What is the standard time for the task?
b) How many observations are needed to assure a 95% confidence level? **Px**

••10.31 Bank manager Art Hill wants to determine the percent of time that tellers are working and idle. He decides to use work sampling, and his initial estimate is that the tellers are idle 15% of the time. How many observations should Hill take to be 95.45% confident that the results will not be more than ±4% from the true result? **Px**

••10.32 Supervisor Kenneth Peterson wants to determine the percent of time a machine in his area is idle. He decides to use work sampling, and his initial estimate is that the machine is idle 20% of the time. How many observations should Peterson take to be 98% confident that the results will be less than 5% from the true results?

•••10.33 Tim Nelson's job as an inspector for La-Z-Boy is to inspect 130 chairs per day.

a) If he works an 8-hour day, how many minutes is he allowed for each inspection (i.e., what is his "standard time")?
b) If he is allowed a 6% fatigue allowance, a 6% delay allowance, and 6% for personal time, what is the normal time that he is assumed to take to perform each inspection?

•••10.34 A random work sample of operators taken over a 160-hour work month at Tele-Marketing, Inc., has produced the following results. What is the percentage of time spent working?

On phone with customer	858
Idle time	220
Personal time	85

••10.35 A total of 300 observations of Bob Ramos, an assembly-line worker, were made over a 40-hour workweek. The sample also showed that Bob was busy working (assembling the parts) during 250 observations.

a) Find the percentage of time Bob was working.
b) If you want a confidence level of 95%, and if ±3% is an acceptable error, what size should the sample be?
c) Was the sample size adequate? **Px**

• 10.36 Sharpening your pencil is an operation that may be divided into eight small elemental motions. In MTM terms, each element may be assigned a certain number of TMUs:

Reach 4 inches for the pencil	6 TMU
Grasp the pencil	2 TMU
Move the pencil 6 inches	10 TMU
Position the pencil	20 TMU
Insert the pencil into the sharpener	4 TMU
Sharpen the pencil	120 TMU
Disengage the pencil	10 TMU
Move the pencil 6 inches	10 TMU

What is the total normal time for sharpening one pencil? Convert your answer into minutes and seconds.

••10.37 Supervisor Tom Choi at Tempe Equipment Company is concerned that material is not arriving as promptly as needed at work cells. A new kanban system has been installed, but there seems to be some delay in getting the material moved to the work cells so that the job can begin promptly. Choi is interested in determining how much delay there is on the part of his highly paid machinists. Ideally, the delay would be close to zero. He has asked his assistant to determine the delay factor among his 10 work cells. The assistant collects the data on a random basis over the next 2 weeks and determines that of the 1,200 observations, 105 were made while the operators were waiting for materials. Use a 95% confidence level and a ±3% acceptable error. What report does he give to Choi? **Px**

••••10.38 The Miami Central Hotel has 400 rooms. Every day, the housekeepers clean any room that was occupied the night before. If a guest is checking out of the hotel, the housekeepers give the room a thorough cleaning to get it ready for the next guest. This takes 30 minutes. If a guest is staying another night, the housekeeper only "refreshes" the room, which takes 15 minutes.

Each day, each housekeeper reports for her 6-hour shift, then prepares her cart. She pushes the cart to her floor and begins work. She usually has to restock the cart once per day; then she pushes it back to the storeroom at the end of the day and delivers dirty laundry, etc. Here is a timetable:

1) Arrive at work and stock cart (0.10 hrs).
2) Push cart to floor (0.10 hrs).
3) Take morning break (0.33 hrs).
4) Stop for lunch (0.50 hrs).
5) Restock cart (0.30 hrs).
6) Take afternoon break (0.33 hrs).
7) Push cart back to laundry and store items (0.33 hrs).

Last night, the hotel was full (all 400 rooms were occupied). People are checking out of 200 rooms. Their rooms will need to be thoroughly cleaned. The other 200 rooms will need to be refreshed.

a) How many minutes per day of actual room cleaning can each housekeeper do?
b) How many minutes of room cleaning will the Miami Central Hotel need today?
c) How many housekeepers will be needed to clean the hotel today?
d) If *all* the guests checked out this morning, how many housekeepers would be needed to clean the 400 rooms?

Additional problems **10.39–10.46** *are available in* MyOMLab.

CASE STUDIES

Jackson Manufacturing Company

Kathleen McFadden, vice president of operations at Jackson Manufacturing Company, has just received a request for quote (RFQ) from DeKalb Electric Supply for 400 units per week of a motor armature. The components are standard and either easy to work into the existing production schedule or readily available from established suppliers on a JIT basis. But there is some difference in assembly. Ms. McFadden has identified eight tasks that Jackson must perform to assemble the armature. Seven of these tasks are very similar to ones performed by Jackson in the past; therefore, the average time and resulting labor standard of those tasks is known.

The eighth task, an *overload* test, requires performing a task that is very different from any performed previously, however. Kathleen has asked you to conduct a time study on the task to determine the standard time. Then an estimate can be made of the cost to assemble the armature. This information, combined with other cost data, will allow the firm to put together the information needed for the RFQ.

To determine a standard time for the task, an employee from an existing assembly station was trained in the new assembly process. Once proficient, the employee was then asked to perform the task 17 times so a standard could be determined. The actual times observed (in minutes) were as follows:

1	2	3	4	5	6	7	8	9	10	11	12	13	14	15	16	17
2.05	1.92	2.01	1.89	1.77	1.80	1.86	1.83	1.93	1.96	1.95	2.05	1.79	1.82	1.85	1.85	1.99

The worker had a 115% performance rating. The task can be performed in a sitting position at a well-designed ergonomic work-station in an air-conditioned facility. Although the armature itself weighs 10.5 pounds, there is a carrier that holds it so that the operator need only rotate the armature. But the detail work remains high; therefore, the fatigue allowance should be 8%. The company has an established personal allowance of 6%. Delay should be very low. Previous studies of delay in this department average 2%. This standard is to use the same figure.

The workday is 7.5 hours, but operators are paid for 8 hours at an average of $12.50 per hour.

Discussion Questions

In your report to Ms. McFadden, you realize you will want to address several factors:

1. How big should the sample be for a statistically accurate standard (at, say, the 99.73% confidence level and accuracy of $\pm 5\%$)?
2. Is the sample size adequate?
3. How many units should be produced at this workstation per day?
4. What is the cost per unit for this task in direct labor cost?

Source: Professor Hank Maddux, Sam Houston State University

The "People" Focus: Human Resources at Alaska Airlines

Video Case

With thousands of employees spread across nearly 100 locations in the United States, Mexico, and Canada, building a committed and cohesive workforce is a challenge. Yet Alaska Airlines is making it work. The company's "people" focus states:

> While airplanes and technology enable us to do what we do, we recognize this is fundamentally a people business, and our future depends on how we work together to win in this extremely competitive environment. As we grow, we want to strengthen our small company feel ... We will succeed where others fail because of our pride and passion, and because of the way we treat our customers, our suppliers and partners, and each other.

Managerial excellence requires a committed workforce. Alaska Airlines' pledge of respect for people is one of the key elements of a world-class operation.

Effective organizations require talented, committed, and trained personnel. Alaska Airlines conducts comprehensive training at all levels. Its "Flight Path" leadership training for all 10,000 employees is now being followed by "Gear Up" training for 800 front-line managers. In addition, training programs have been developed for Lean and Six Sigma as well as for the unique requirements for pilots, flight attendants, baggage, and ramp personnel. Because the company only hires pilots into first officer positions—the right seat in the cockpit, it offers a program called

the "Fourth Stripe" to train for promotion into the captain's seat on the left side, along with all the additional responsibility that entails (see exterior and interior photos of one of Alaska Airlines' flight simulators on the opening page of this chapter).

Customer service agents receive specific training on the company's "Empowerment Toolkit." Like the Ritz-Carlton's famous customer service philosophy, agents have the option of awarding customers hotel and meal vouchers or frequent flier miles when the customer has experienced a service problem.

Because many managers are cross-trained in operational duties outside the scope of their daily positions, they have the ability to pitch in to ensure that customer-oriented processes go smoothly. Even John Ladner, Director of Seattle Airport Operations, who is a fully licensed pilot, has left his desk to cover a flight at the last minute for a sick colleague.

Along with providing development and training at all levels, managers recognize that inherent personal traits can make a huge difference. For example, when flight attendants are hired, the ones who are still engaged, smiling, and fresh at the end of a very long interview day are the ones Alaska wants on the team. Why? The job requires these behaviors and attitudes to fit with the Alaska Airlines team—and smiling and friendly flight attendants are particularly important at the end of a long flight.

Visual workplace tools also complement and close the loop that matches training to performance. Alaska Airlines makes full use of color-coded graphs and charts to report performance against key metrics to employees. Twenty top managers gather weekly in an operations leadership meeting, run by Executive VP of Operations, Ben Minicucci, to review activity consolidated into visual summaries. Key metrics are color-coded and posted prominently in every work area.

Alaska's training approach results in empowered employees who are willing to assume added responsibility and accept the unknowns that come with that added responsibility.

Discussion Questions*

1. Summarize Alaska Airlines' human resources focus in your own words.
2. Why is employee empowerment useful to companies such as Alaska Airlines?
3. What tools discussed in the chapter might be employed to enhance the company's training and performance efforts? Why?

*Before answering these questions, you may wish to view the video that accompanies this case.

Hard Rock's Human Resource Strategy

 Video Case

Everyone—managers and hourly employees alike—who goes to work for Hard Rock Cafe takes Rock 101, an initial 2-day training class. The Hard Rock value system is to bring a fun, healthy, nurturing environment into the Hard Rock Cafe culture. This initial course and many other courses help employees develop both personally and professionally. The human resource department plays a critical role in any service organization, but at Hard Rock, with its "experience strategy," the human resource department takes on added importance.

Long before Jim Knight, manager of corporate training, begins the class, the human resource strategy of Hard Rock has had an impact. Hard Rock's strategic plan includes building a culture that allows for acceptance of substantial diversity and individuality. From a human resource perspective, this has the benefit of enlarging the pool of applicants as well as contributing to the Hard Rock culture.

Creating a work environment above and beyond a paycheck is a unique challenge. Outstanding pay and benefits are a start, but the key is to provide an environment that works for the employees. This includes benefits that start for part-timers who work at least 19 hours per week (while others in the industry start at 35 hours per week); a unique respect for individuality; continuing training; and a high level of internal promotions—some 60% of the managers are promoted from hourly employee ranks. The company's training is very specific, with job-oriented interactive DVDs covering kitchen, retail, and front-of-the-house service. Outside volunteer work is especially encouraged to foster a bond between the workers, their community, and issues of importance to them.

Applicants also are screened on their interest in music and their ability to tell a story. Hard Rock builds on a hiring criterion of bright, positive-attitude, self-motivated individuals with an employee bill of rights and substantial employee empowerment. The result is a unique culture and work environment, which no doubt contributes to the low turnover of hourly people—one-half the industry average.

The layout, memorabilia, music, and videos are important elements in the Hard Rock "experience," but it falls on the waiters and waitresses to make the experience come alive. They are particularly focused on providing an authentic and memorable dining experience. Like Alaska Airlines, Hard Rock is looking for people with a cause—people who like to serve. By succeeding with its human resource strategy, Hard Rock obtains a competitive advantage.

Discussion Questions*

1. What has Hard Rock done to lower employee turnover to half the industry average?
2. How does Hard Rock's human resource department support the company's overall strategy?
3. How would Hard Rock's value system work for automobile assembly line workers? (*Hint:* Consider Hackman and Oldham's core job characteristics.)
4. How might you adjust a traditional assembly line to address more "core job characteristics"?

*Before answering these questions, you may wish to view the video that accompanies this case.

- **Additional Case Studies:** Visit MyOMLab for these free case studies:
  Chicago Southern Hospital: Examines the requirements for a work-sampling plan for nurses.
  The Fleet That Wanders: Requires a look at ergonomic issues for truck drivers.

Endnotes

1. *Four Seasons Magazine*, Annabell Shaw, Jan. 3, 2011.
2. See "Motivation Through the Design of Work," in Jay Richard Hackman and Greg R. Oldham, eds., *Work Redesign* (Reading, MA: Addison-Wesley, 1980); and A. Thomas, W. C. Buboltz, and C. Winkelspecht, "Job Characteristics and Personality as Predictors of Job Satisfaction," *Organizational Analysis*, 12, no. 2 (2004): 205–219.
3. MTM is really a family of products available from the Methods Time Measurement Association. For example, MTM-HC deals with the health care industry, MTM-C handles clerical activities, MTM-M involves microscope activities, MTM-V deals with machine shop tasks, and so on.
4. A. S. Helms, B. W. Shaw, and C. A. Lindner, "The Development of Laboratory Workload Standards through Computer-Based Work Measurement Technique, Part I," *Journal of Methods-Time Measurement* 12: 43. Used with permission of MTM Association for Standards and Research.
5. The Occupational Safety and Health Administration (OSHA) is a federal government agency whose task is to ensure the safety and health of U.S. workers.
6. Material safety data sheets (MSDSs) contain details of hazards associated with chemicals and give information on their safe use.

Chapter 10 *Rapid* Review

Main Heading	Review Material	MyOMLab
HUMAN RESOURCE STRATEGY FOR COMPETITIVE ADVANTAGE (pp. 410–411)	*The objective of a human resource strategy is to manage labor and design jobs so people are effectively and efficiently utilized.* *Quality of work life* refers to a job that is not only reasonably safe with equitable pay but that also achieves an appropriate level of both physical and psychological requirements. *Mutual commitment* means that both management and employees strive to meet common objectives. *Mutual trust* is reflected in reasonable, documented employment policies that are honestly and equitably implemented to the satisfaction of both management and employees.	Concept Questions: 1.1–1.4 **VIDEO 10.1** The "People" Focus: Human Resources at Alaska Airlines **VIDEO 10.2** Human Resources at Hard Rock Cafe
LABOR PLANNING (pp. 411–412)	■ **Labor planning**—A means of determining staffing policies dealing with employment stability, work schedules, and work rules. *Flextime* allows employees, within limits, to determine their own schedules. *Flexible* (or *compressed*) *workweeks* often call for fewer but longer workdays. *Part-time status* is particularly attractive in service industries with fluctuating demand loads.	Concept Questions: 2.1–2.4
JOB DESIGN (pp. 412–415)	■ **Job design**—Specifies the tasks that constitute a job for an individual or group. ■ **Labor specialization** (or **job specialization**)—The division of labor into unique ("special") tasks. ■ **Job enlargement**—The grouping of a variety of tasks about the same skill level; horizontal enlargement. ■ **Job rotation**—A system in which an employee is moved from one specialized job to another. ■ **Job enrichment**—A method of giving an employee more responsibility that includes some of the planning and control necessary for job accomplishment; vertical expansion. ■ **Employee empowerment**—Enlarging employee jobs so that the added responsibility and authority are moved to the lowest level possible. ■ **Self-directed team**—A group of empowered individuals working together to reach a common goal.	Concept Questions: 3.1–3.4
ERGONOMICS AND THE WORK ENVIRONMENT (pp. 415–417)	■ **Ergonomics**—The study of the human interface with the environment and machines. The physical environment affects performance, safety, and quality of work life. Illumination, noise and vibration, temperature, humidity, and air quality are controllable by management.	Concept Questions: 4.1–4.4
METHODS ANALYSIS (pp. 417–419)	■ **Methods analysis**—A system that involves developing work procedures that are safe and produce quality products efficiently. ■ **Flow diagram**—A drawing used to analyze movement of people or material. ■ **Process chart**—A graphic representation that depicts a sequence of steps for a process. ■ **Activity chart**—A way of improving utilization of an operator and a machine or some combination of operators (a crew) and machines. ■ **Operations chart**—A chart depicting right- and left-hand motions.	Concept Questions: 5.1–5.4 Problems: 10.2, 10.6, 10.8 Virtual Office Hours for Solved Problem: 10.1
THE VISUAL WORKPLACE (p. 420)	■ **Visual workplace**—Uses a variety of visual communication techniques to rapidly communicate information to stakeholders.	Concept Questions: 6.1–6.4
LABOR STANDARDS (pp. 420–430)	■ **Labor standards**—The amount of time required to perform a job or part of a job. Labor standards are set in four ways: (1) historical experience, (2) time studies, (3) predetermined time standards, and (4) work sampling. ■ **Time study**—Timing a sample of a worker's performance and using it as a basis for setting a standard time. ■ **Average observed time**—The arithmetic mean of the times for each element measured, adjusted for unusual influence for each element. $$\text{Average observed time} = \frac{\text{Sum of the times recorded to perform each elemen}}{\text{Number of observations}} \quad (10\text{-}1)$$ ■ **Normal time**—The average observed time, adjusted for pace: $$\text{Normal time} = (\text{Average observed time}) \times (\text{Performance rating factor}) \quad (10\text{-}2)$$	Concept Questions: 7.1–7.4 Problems: 10.13–10.46 Virtual Office Hours for Solved Problems: 10.2–10.6

Main Heading	Review Material	MyOMLab

■ **Standard time**—An adjustment to the total normal time; the adjustment provides allowances for personal needs, unavoidable work delays, and fatigue:

$$\text{Standard time} = \frac{\text{Total normal time}}{1 - \text{Allowance factor}} \qquad (10\text{-}3)$$

Personal time allowances are often established in the range of 4% to 7% of total time.

$$\text{Required sample size} = n = \left(\frac{zs}{h\bar{x}}\right)^2 \qquad (10\text{-}4)$$

$$n = \left(\frac{zs}{e}\right)^2 \qquad (10\text{-}5)$$

$$s = \sqrt{\frac{\sum(x_i - \bar{x})^2}{n-1}} = \sqrt{\frac{\sum(\text{Each sample observation} - \bar{x})^2}{\text{Number in sample} - 1}} \qquad (10\text{-}6)$$

■ **Predetermined time standards**—A division of manual work into small basic elements that have established and widely accepted times.

The most common predetermined time standard is *methods time measurement* (MTM).

■ **Therbligs**—Basic physical elements of motion.
■ **Time measurement units (TMUs)**—Units for very basic micromotions in which 1 TMU = 0.0006 min or 100,000 TMUs = 1 hr.
■ **Work sampling**—An estimate, via sampling, of the percent of the time that a worker spends on various tasks.

Work sampling sample size for a desired confidence and accuracy:

$$n = \frac{z^2 p(1-p)}{h^2} \qquad (10\text{-}7)$$

ACTIVE MODEL **10.1**

ETHICS (p. 430)	Management's role is to educate the employee; specify the necessary equipment, work rules, and work environment; and then enforce those requirements.	Concept Questions: 8.1–8.2

Self Test

■ **Before taking the self-test,** refer to the learning objectives listed at the beginning of the chapter and the key terms listed at the end of the chapter.

LO 10.1 When product demand fluctuates and yet you maintain a constant level of employment, some of your cost savings might include:
 a) reduction in hiring costs.
 b) reduction in layoff costs and unemployment insurance costs.
 c) lack of need to pay a premium wage to get workers to accept unstable employment.
 d) having a trained workforce rather than having to retrain new employees each time you hire for an upswing in demand.
 e) all of the above.

LO 10.2 The difference between *job enrichment* and *job enlargement* is that:
 a) enlarged jobs contain a larger number of similar tasks, while enriched jobs include some of the planning and control necessary for job accomplishment.
 b) enriched jobs contain a larger number of similar tasks, while enlarged jobs include some of the planning and control necessary for job accomplishment.
 c) enriched jobs enable an employee to do a number of boring jobs instead of just one.
 d) all of the above.

LO 10.3 The work environment includes these factors:
 a) Lighting, noise, temperature, and air quality
 b) Illumination, carpeting, and high ceilings
 c) Enough space for meetings and videoconferencing
 d) Noise, humidity, and number of coworkers
 e) Job enlargement and space analysis

LO 10.4 *Methods analysis* focuses on:
 a) the design of the machines used to perform a task.
 b) how a task is accomplished.
 c) the raw materials that are consumed in performing a task.
 d) reducing the number of steps required to perform a task.

LO 10.5 The least preferred method of establishing labor standards is:
 a) time studies.
 b) work sampling.
 c) historical experience.
 d) predetermined time standards.

LO 10.6 The allowance factor in a time study:
 a) adjusts normal time for errors and rework.
 b) adjusts standard time for lunch breaks.
 c) adjusts normal time for personal needs, unavoidable delays, and fatigue.
 d) allows workers to rest every 20 minutes.

LO 10.7 To set the required sample size in a time study, you must know:
 a) the number of employees.
 b) the number of parts produced per day.
 c) the desired accuracy and confidence levels.
 d) management's philosophy toward sampling.

Answers: LO 10.1. e; LO 10.2. a; LO 10.3. a; LO 10.4. b; LO 10.5. c; LO 10.6. c; LO 10.7. c.

Supply Chain Management

CHAPTER OUTLINE

GLOBAL COMPANY PROFILE: *Darden Restaurants*

◆ The Supply Chain's Strategic Importance *444*

◆ Sourcing Issues: Make-or-Buy and Outsourcing *446*

◆ Six Sourcing Strategies *447*

◆ Supply Chain Risk *449*

◆ Managing the Integrated Supply Chain *451*

◆ Building the Supply Base *454*

◆ Logistics Management *456*

◆ Distribution Management *459*

◆ Ethics and Sustainable Supply Chain Management *460*

◆ Measuring Supply Chain Performance *461*

Alaska Airlines

10 OM STRATEGY DECISIONS

- Design of Goods and Services
- Managing Quality
- Process Strategy
- Location Strategies
- Layout Strategies
- Human Resources
- *Supply Chain Management*
- Inventory Management
- Scheduling
- Maintenance

Darden's Supply Chain Yields a Competitive Edge

Darden Restaurants, Inc., is one of the largest publicly traded casual dining restaurant companies in the world with $6.3 billion in annual sales. It serves over 320 million meals annually from more than 1,500 restaurants in North America. Its well-known flagship brand—Olive Garden—generates sales of $3.6 billion annually. Darden's other brands include Bahama Breeze, Seasons 52, The Capital Grille, Eddie V's, Yard House, and LongHorn Steakhouse. The firm employs more than 150,000 people and is the 33rd largest employer in the U.S.

"Operations is typically thought of as an execution of strategy. For us it is the strategy," Darden's former chairman, Joe R. Lee, stated.

In the restaurant business, a winning strategy requires a winning supply chain. Nothing is more important than sourcing and delivering healthy, high-quality food; and there are very few

Darden Restaurants

Qualifying Worldwide Sources: Part of Darden's supply chain begins with a crab harvest in the frigid waters off the coast of Alaska. But long before a supplier is qualified to sell to Darden, a total quality team is appointed. The team provides guidance, assistance, support, and training to the suppliers to ensure that overall objectives are understood and desired results accomplished.

Aquaculture Certification: Shrimp in this Asian plant are certified to ensure traceability. The focus is on quality control certified by the Aquaculture Certification Council, of which Darden is a member. Farming and inspection practices yield safe and wholesome shrimp.

Darden Restaurants

Darden Restaurants

Product tracking: Darden's seafood inspection team developed an integral system that uses a *Lot ID* to track seafood from its origin through shipping and receipt. Darden uses a modified atmosphere packaging (MAP) process to extend the shelf life and preserve the quality of its fresh fish. The tracking includes time temperature monitoring.

other industries where supplier performance is so closely tied to the customer.

Darden sources its food from five continents and thousands of suppliers. To meet Darden's needs for fresh ingredients, the company has developed four distinct supply chains: one for seafood; one for dairy/produce/other refrigerated foods; a third for other food items, like baked goods; and a fourth for restaurant supplies (everything from dishes to ovens to uniforms). Over $2 billion is spent in these supply chains annually.

(See the *Video Case Study* at the end of this chapter for details.)

Darden's four supply channels have some common characteristics. They all require *supplier qualification*, have *product tracking*, are subject to *independent audits*, and employ *just-in-time delivery*. With best-in-class techniques and processes, Darden creates worldwide supply chain partnerships and alliances that are rapid, transparent, and efficient. Darden achieves competitive advantage through its superior supply chain.

JIT Delivery: For many products, temperature monitoring begins immediately and is tracked through the entire supply chain, to the kitchen at each of Darden's 1,500 restaurants, and ultimately to the guest.

LEARNING OBJECTIVES

LO 11.1 *Explain* the strategic importance of the supply chain 445

LO 11.2 *Identify* six sourcing strategies 447

LO 11.3 *Explain* issues and opportunities in the supply chain 451

LO 11.4 *Describe* the steps in supplier selection 454

LO 11.5 *Explain* major issues in logistics management 456

LO 11.6 *Compute* the percentage of assets committed to inventory and inventory turnover 461

The Supply Chain's Strategic Importance

Like Darden, most firms spend a huge portion of their sales dollars on purchases. Because an increasing percentage of an organization's costs are determined by purchasing, relationships with suppliers are increasingly integrated and long term. Combined efforts that improve innovation, speed design, and reduce costs are common. Such efforts, when part of a corporate-wide strategy, can dramatically improve all partners' competitiveness. This integrated focus places added emphasis on managing supplier relationships.

Supply chain management

The coordination of all supply chain activities involved in enhancing customer value.

Supply chain management describes the coordination of all supply chain activities, starting with raw materials and ending with a satisfied customer. Thus, a supply chain includes suppliers; manufacturers and/or service providers; and distributors, wholesalers, and/or retailers who deliver the product and/or service to the final customer. Figure 11.1 provides an example of the breadth of links and activities that a supply chain may cover.

The objective of supply chain management is to structure the supply chain to maximize its competitive advantage and benefits to the ultimate consumer. Just as with championship teams, a central feature of successful supply chains is members acting in ways that benefit the team (the supply chain).

Figure **11.1**

A Supply Chain for Beer

The supply chain includes all the interactions among suppliers, manufacturers, distributors, and customers. A well-functioning supply chain has information flowing between all partners. The chain includes transportation, scheduling information, cash and credit transfers, as well as ideas, designs, and material transfers. Even can and bottle manufacturers have their own tiers of suppliers providing components such as lids, labels, packing containers, etc. (Costs are approximate and include substantial taxes.)

With collaboration, costs for both buyers and suppliers can drop. For example, when both parties are willing to share sales and cost information, profit can increase for both. Examples of supply chain coordination include:

- Walmart cooperates with its top 200 supplier factories in China to reach the goal of 20% energy efficiency improvement.
- Mercury Marine, the large boat-engine producer, uses the Internet to enhance design with boat builders and engine dealers as it fights off competition from Honda, Yamaha, and Volvo.
- Unifi, the leading U.S. maker of synthetic yarn, shares daily production-scheduling and quality-control information with raw materials supplier DuPont.
- Amazon, to reduce logistics costs, has moved its fulfillment activities for Procter and Gamble products directly into Procter and Gamble's warehouse.

As Table 11.1 indicates, a huge part of a firm's revenue is typically spent on purchases, so supply chains are a good place to look for savings. Example 1 further illustrates the amount of leverage available to the operations manager through the supply chain. These percentages indicate the strong role that supply chains play in potential profitability. Effective cost cutting may help a firm reach its profit goals more easily than would an increased sales effort.

TABLE 11.1

Supply Chain Costs as a Percentage of Sales

INDUSTRY	% PURCHASED
Automobile	67
Beverages	52
Chemical	62
Food	60
Lumber	61
Metals	65
Paper	55
Petroleum	79
Restaurants	35
Transportation	62

Example 1

SUPPLY CHAIN STRATEGY VS. SALES STRATEGY TO ACHIEVE A TARGET PROFIT

Hau Lee Furniture, Inc., spends 60% of its sales dollars in the supply chain and has a current gross profit of $10,000. Hau wishes to increase gross profit by $5,000 (50%). He would like to compare two strategies: reducing material costs vs. increasing sales.

APPROACH ▶ Use the table below to make the analysis.

SOLUTION ▶ The current material costs and production costs are 60% and 20%, respectively, of sales dollars, with fixed cost at a constant $10,000. Analysis indicates that an improvement in the supply chain that would *reduce material costs by 8.3%* ($5,000/$60,000) would produce a 50% net profit gain for Hau, whereas a *much larger 25% increase in sales* ($25,000/$100,000) would be required to produce the same result.

	CURRENT SITUATION	SUPPLY CHAIN STRATEGY	SALES STRATEGY
Sales	$100,000	$100,000	$125,000
Cost of materials	$60,000 (60%)	$55,000 (55%)	$75,000 (60%)
Production costs	$20,000 (20%)	$20,000 (20%)	$25,000 (20%)
Fixed costs	$10,000 (10%)	$10,000 (10%)	$10,000 (8%)
Profit	$10,000 (10%)	$15,000 (15%)	$15,000 (12%)

INSIGHT ▶ Supply chain savings flow directly to the bottom line. In general, supply chain costs need to shrink by a much lower percentage than sales revenue needs to increase to attain a profit goal. Effective management of the supply chain can generate substantial benefits.

LEARNING EXERCISE ▶ If Hau wants to double the original gross profits (from $10,000 to $20,000), what would be required of the supply chain and sales strategies? [Answer: Supply chain strategy = 16.7% *reduction* in material costs; sales strategy = 50% *increase* in sales.]

RELATED PROBLEMS ▶ 11.2, 11.3

As firms strive to increase their competitiveness via product customization, high quality, cost reductions, and speed to market, added emphasis is placed on the supply chain. Through long-term strategic relationships, suppliers become "partners" as they contribute to competitive advantage.

To ensure that the supply chain supports a firm's strategy, managers need to consider the supply chain issues shown in Table 11.2. Activities of supply chain managers cut across the accounting, finance, marketing, and operations disciplines. Just as the OM function supports the firm's overall strategy, the supply chain must support the OM strategy. Strategies of low

LO 11.1 *Explain* the strategic importance of the supply chain

A Rose Is a Rose, but Only If It Is Fresh

Supply chains for food and flowers must be fast, and they must be good. When the food supply chain has a problem, the best that can happen is the customer does not get fed on time; the worst that happens is the customer gets food poisoning and dies. In the floral industry, the timing and temperature are also critical. Indeed, flowers are the most perishable agricultural item—even more so than fish. Flowers not only need to move fast, but they must also be kept cool, at a constant temperature of 33 to 37 degrees. And they must be provided preservative-treated water while in transit. Roses are especially delicate, fragile, and perishable.

Eighty percent of the roses sold in the U.S. market arrive by air from rural Colombia and Ecuador. Roses move through this supply chain via an intricate but fast transportation network. This network stretches from growers who cut, grade, bundle, pack, and ship; to importers who make the deal; to the U.S. Department of Agriculture personnel who quarantine and inspect for insects, diseases, and parasites; to U.S. Customs agents who inspect

Africa Studio/Fotolia

and approve; to facilitators who provide clearance and labeling; to wholesalers who distribute; to retailers who arrange and sell; and finally to the customer. Each and every minute the product is deteriorating. The time and temperature sensitivity of perishables like roses requires sophistication and refined standards in the supply chain. Success yields quality and low losses. After all, when it's Valentine's Day, what good is a shipment of roses that arrives wilted or late? This is a difficult supply chain; only an excellent one will get the job done.

Sources: NPR (Feb. 13, 2015); *Supply Chain 24/7* (Feb. 13, 2014); and *The Star-Ledger* (Feb. 6, 2011).

---

cost or rapid response demand different things from a supply chain than a strategy of differentiation. For instance, a low-cost strategy, as Table 11.2 indicates, requires suppliers be selected based primarily on cost. Such suppliers should have the ability to design low-cost products that meet the functional requirements, minimize inventory, and drive down lead times. However, if you want roses that are fresh, build a supply chain that focuses on response (see the *OM in Action* box "A Rose Is a Rose, but Only If It Is Fresh").

Firms must achieve integration of strategy up and down the supply chain. And they must expect that strategy to be different for different products and to change as products move through their life cycle. Darden Restaurants, as noted in the opening *Global Company Profile*, has mastered worldwide product and service complexity by segmenting its supply chain and at the same time integrating four unique supply chains into its overall strategy.

VIDEO 11.1
Darden's Global Supply Chain

Sourcing Issues: Make-or-Buy and Outsourcing

As suggested in Table 11.2, a firm needs to determine strategically how to design the supply chain. However, prior to embarking on supply chain design, operations managers must first consider the "make-or-buy" and outsourcing decisions.

TABLE 11.2	How Corporate Strategy Impacts Supply Chain Decisions*		
	LOW-COST STRATEGY	**RESPONSE STRATEGY**	**DIFFERENTIATION STRATEGY**
Primary supplier selection criteria	• Cost	• Capacity • Speed • Flexibility	• Product development skills • Willing to share information • Jointly and rapidly develop products
Supply chain inventory	• Minimize inventory to hold down costs	• Use buffer stocks to ensure speedy supply	• Minimize inventory to avoid product obsolescence
Distribution network	• Inexpensive transportation • Sell through discount distributors/retailers	• Fast transportation • Provide premium customer service	• Gather and communicate market research data • Knowledgeable sales staff
Product design characteristics	• Maximize performance • Minimize cost	• Low setup time • Rapid production ramp-up	• Modular design to aid product differentiation

*See related table and discussion in Marshall L. Fisher, "What Is the Right Supply Chain for Your Product?" *Harvard Business Review* (March–April 1997): 105.

Make-or-Buy Decisions

A wholesaler or retailer buys everything that it sells; a manufacturing operation hardly ever does. Manufacturers, restaurants, and assemblers of products buy components and subassemblies that go into final products. As we saw in Chapter 5, choosing products and services that can be advantageously obtained *externally* as opposed to produced *internally* is known as the make-or-buy decision. Supply chain personnel evaluate alternative suppliers and provide current, accurate, and complete data relevant to the buy alternative.

Outsourcing

Outsourcing transfers some of what are traditional internal activities and resources of a firm to outside vendors, making it slightly different from the traditional make-or-buy decision. Outsourcing, discussed in Chapter 2, is part of the continuing trend toward using the efficiency that comes with specialization. The vendor performing the outsourced service is an expert in that particular specialty. This leaves the outsourcing firm to focus on its key success factors and its core competencies.

Make-or-buy decision
A choice between producing a component or service in-house or purchasing it from an outside source.

Outsourcing
Transferring a firm's activities that have traditionally been internal to external suppliers.

Six Sourcing Strategies

Having decided *what* to outsource, managers have six strategies to consider.

LO 11.2 *Identify* six sourcing strategies

Many Suppliers

With the many-suppliers strategy, a supplier responds to the demands and specifications of a "request for quotation," with the order usually going to the low bidder. This is a common strategy when products are commodities. This strategy plays one supplier against another and places the burden of meeting the buyer's demands on the supplier. Suppliers aggressively compete with one another. This approach holds the supplier responsible for maintaining the necessary technology, expertise, and forecasting abilities, as well as cost, quality, and delivery competencies. Long-term "partnering" relationships are not the goal.

⬥ **STUDENT TIP**

Supply chain strategies come in many varieties; choosing the correct one is the trick.

Few Suppliers

A strategy of few suppliers implies that rather than looking for short-term attributes, such as low cost, a buyer is better off forming a long-term relationship with a few dedicated suppliers. Long-term suppliers are more likely to understand the broad objectives of the procuring firm and the end customer. Using few suppliers can create value by allowing suppliers to have economies of scale and a learning curve that yields both lower transaction costs and lower production costs. This strategy also encourages those suppliers to provide design innovations and technological expertise.

Ford chooses suppliers even before parts are designed. Motorola evaluates suppliers on rigorous criteria, but in many instances has eliminated traditional supplier bidding, placing added emphasis on quality and reliability. On occasion these relationships yield contracts that extend through the product's life cycle. The British retailer Marks & Spencer finds that cooperation with its suppliers yields new products that win customers for the supplier and themselves. The move toward tight integration of the suppliers and purchasers is occurring in both manufacturing and services.

As with all other strategies, a downside exists. With few suppliers, the cost of changing partners is huge, so both buyer and supplier run the risk of becoming captives of the other. Poor supplier performance is only one risk the purchaser faces. The purchaser must also be concerned about trade secrets and suppliers that make other alliances or venture out on their own. This happened when the U.S. Schwinn Bicycle Co., needing additional capacity, taught Taiwan's Giant Manufacturing Company to make and sell bicycles. Giant Manufacturing is now the largest bicycle manufacturer in the world, and Schwinn was acquired out of bankruptcy by Pacific Cycle LLC.

VIDEO 11.2
Supply Chain Management at Regal Marine

Figure **11.2**

Vertical Integration Can Be Forward or Backward

Vertical Integration

Vertical integration

Developing the ability to produce goods or services previously purchased or actually buying a supplier or a distributor.

Purchasing can be extended to take the form of vertical integration. By **vertical integration**, we mean developing the ability to produce goods or services previously purchased or to actually buy a supplier or a distributor. As shown in Figure 11.2, vertical integration can take the form of *forward* or *backward integration*.

Backward integration suggests a firm purchase its suppliers, as in the case of Apple deciding to manufacture its own semiconductors. Apple also uses forward integration by establishing its own revolutionary retail stores.

Vertical integration can offer a strategic opportunity for the operations manager. For firms with the capital, managerial talent, and required demand, vertical integration may provide substantial opportunities for cost reduction, higher quality, timely delivery, and inventory reduction. Vertical integration appears to work best when the organization has a large market share and the management talent to operate an acquired vendor successfully.

The relentless march of specialization continues, meaning that a model of "doing everything" or "vertical integration" is increasingly difficult. Backward integration may be particularly dangerous for firms in industries undergoing technological change if management cannot keep abreast of those changes or invest the financial resources necessary for the next wave of technology. Research and development costs are too high and technology changes too rapid for one company to sustain leadership in every component. Most organizations are better served concentrating on their own specialty and leveraging suppliers' contributions.

Joint Ventures

Because vertical integration is so dangerous, firms may opt for some form of formal collaboration. As we noted in Chapter 5, firms may engage in collaboration to enhance their new product prowess or technological skills. But firms also engage in collaboration to secure supply or reduce costs. One version of a joint venture is the current Daimler–BMW effort to develop and produce standard automobile components. Given the global consolidation of the auto industry, these two rivals in the luxury segment of the automobile market are at a disadvantage in volume. Their relatively low volume means fewer units over which to spread fixed costs, hence the interest in consolidating to cut development and production costs. As in all other such collaborations, the trick is to cooperate without diluting the brand or conceding a competitive advantage.

Keiretsu Networks

Keiretsu

A Japanese term that describes suppliers who become part of a company coalition.

Many large Japanese manufacturers have found another strategy: it is part collaboration, part purchasing from few suppliers, and part vertical integration. These manufacturers are often financial supporters of suppliers through ownership or loans. The supplier becomes part of a company coalition known as a *keiretsu*. Members of the *keiretsu* are assured long-term relationships and are therefore expected to collaborate as partners, providing technical expertise and stable quality production to the manufacturer. Members of the *keiretsu* can also have second- and even third-tier suppliers as part of the coalition.

Virtual Companies

Virtual companies rely on a variety of good, stable supplier relationships to provide services on demand. Suppliers may provide a variety of services that include doing the payroll, hiring personnel, designing products, providing consulting services, manufacturing components, conducting tests, or distributing products. The relationships may be short- or long-term and may include true partners, collaborators, or simply able suppliers and subcontractors. Whatever the formal relationship, the result can be exceptionally lean performance. The advantages of virtual companies include specialized management expertise, low capital investment, flexibility, and speed. The result is efficiency.

The apparel business provides a *traditional* example of virtual organizations. The designers of clothes seldom manufacture their designs; rather, they license the manufacture. The manufacturer may then rent space, lease sewing machines, and contract for labor. The result is an organization that has low overhead, remains flexible, and can respond rapidly to the market.

A *contemporary* example is exemplified by Vizio, Inc., a California-based producer of flat-screen TVs that has fewer than 100 employees but huge sales. Vizio uses modules to assemble its own brand of TVs. Because the key components of TVs are now readily available and sold almost as commodities, innovative firms such as Vizio can specify the components, hire a contract manufacturer, and market the TVs with very little startup cost. In a virtual company, the supply chain is the company. Managing it is dynamic and demanding.

> **Virtual companies**
> Companies that rely on a variety of supplier relationships to provide services on demand. Also known as hollow corporations or network companies.

Supply Chain Risk

In this age of increasing specialization, low communication cost, and fast transportation, companies are making less and buying more. This means more reliance on supply chains and more risk. Managing integrated supply chains is a strategic challenge. Having fewer suppliers makes the supplier and customer more dependent on each other, increasing risk for both.

Supply chain risks arise in many ways. As this mishap illustrates, expected shipments can literally sink into the ocean.

This risk is compounded by globalization and logistical complexity. In any supply chain, vendor reliability and quality may be challenging. But the new model of a tight, fast, low-inventory supply chain, operating across political and cultural boundaries, adds a new dimension to risk. As organizations go global, shipping time (lead time) may increase, logistics may be less reliable, and tariffs and quotas may block companies from doing business. In addition, international supply chains complicate information flows and increase political/currency risks.

Risks and Mitigation Tactics

Supply chain risks arise in numerous ways, and you cannot outsource risk! Table 11.3 identifies major categories of risks and tactics to help manage them. The development of a successful strategic plan for supply chain management requires careful research, a thorough assessment of the risks involved, and innovative planning. Companies need to focus not only on reducing potential disruptions but also on how to prepare for responses to inevitable negative events. Flexible, secure supply chains and sufficient insurance against a variety of disruptions are a start. They may also choose to diversify their supplier base by using multiple sources for critical components. Cross-sourcing represents a hybrid technique where two suppliers each provide a different component, but they have the capability of producing each other's component—that is, each acting as a backup source. Another option is to create excess capacity that can be used in response to problems in the supply chain. Such contingency plans can reduce risk.

Cross-sourcing

Using one supplier for a component and a second supplier for another component, where each supplier acts as a backup for the other.

TABLE 11.3	Supply Chain Risks and Tactics	
RISK	**RISK REDUCTION TACTICS**	**EXAMPLE**
Supplier failure to deliver	Use multiple suppliers; effective contracts with penalties; subcontractors on retainer; preplanning	**McDonald's** planned its supply chain 6 years before its opening in Russia. Every plant—bakery, meat, chicken, fish, and lettuce—is closely monitored to ensure strong links.
Supplier quality failures	Careful supplier selection, training, certification, and monitoring	**Darden Restaurants** has placed extensive controls, including third-party audits, on supplier processes and logistics to ensure constant monitoring and reduction of risk.
Outsourcing	Take over production; provide or perform the service yourself	**Tyson** took over chicken farm production in China to mitigate product quality and safety concerns related to using independent farmers.
Logistics delays or damage	Multiple/redundant transportation modes and warehouses; secure packaging; effective contracts with penalties	**Walmart,** with its own trucking fleet and numerous distribution centers located throughout the U.S., finds alternative origins and delivery routes bypassing problem areas.
Distribution	Careful selection, monitoring, and effective contracts with penalties	**Toyota** trains its dealers around the world, invoking principles of the Toyota Production System to help dealers improve customer service, used-car logistics, and body and paint operations.
Information loss or distortion	Redundant databases; secure IT systems; training of supply chain partners on the proper interpretations and uses of information	**Boeing** utilizes a state-of-the-art international communication system that transmits engineering, scheduling, and logistics data to Boeing facilities and suppliers worldwide.
Political	Political risk insurance; cross-country diversification; franchising and licensing	**Hard Rock Café** reduces political risk by franchising and licensing, rather than owning, when the political and cultural barriers seem significant.
Economic	Hedging to combat exchange rate risk; purchasing contracts that address price fluctuations	**Honda and Nissan** are moving more manufacturing out of Japan as the exchange rate for the yen makes Japanese-made autos more expensive.
Natural catastrophes	Insurance; alternate sourcing; cross-country diversification	**Toyota,** after its experience with fires, earthquakes, and tsunamis, now attempts to have at least two suppliers, each in a different geographical region, for each component.
Theft, vandalism, and terrorism	Insurance; patent protection; security measures including RFID and GPS; diversification	**Domestic Port Radiation Initiative:** The U.S. government has set up radiation portal monitors that scan nearly all imported containers for radiation.

As this photo of the port of Charleston suggests, with over 16 million containers entering the U.S. annually, tracking location, content, and condition of trucks and containers is a challenge. But new technology may improve both security and JIT shipments.

Security and JIT

There is probably no society more open than the U.S. This includes its borders and ports—but they are swamped. Millions of containers enter U.S. ports each year, along with thousands of planes, cars, and trucks each day. Even under the best of conditions, some 5% of the container movements are misrouted, stolen, damaged, or excessively delayed.

Since the September 11, 2001, terrorist attacks, supply chains have become more complex. However, technological innovations in the supply chain are improving both security and inventory management, making logistics more reliable. Technology is now capable of knowing truck and container location, content, and condition. New devices can even detect broken container seals. Motion detectors can also be installed inside containers. Other sensors record interior data including temperature, shock, radioactivity, and whether a container is moving. Tracking lost containers, identifying delays, or just reminding individuals in the supply chain that a shipment is on its way will help expedite shipments.

Managing the Integrated Supply Chain

As managers move toward integration of the supply chain, substantial efficiencies are possible. The cycle of materials—as they flow from suppliers, to production, to warehousing, to distribution, to the customer—takes place among separate and often very independent organizations. It can lead to actions that may not optimize the entire chain. On the other hand, the supply chain is full of opportunities to reduce waste and enhance value. We now look at some of the significant *issues* and *opportunities*.

VIDEO 11.3
Arnold Palmer Hospital's Supply Chain

Issues in Managing the Integrated Supply Chain

Three issues complicate development of an efficient, integrated supply chain: local optimization, incentives, and large lots.

LO 11.3 *Explain* issues and opportunities in the supply chain

Local Optimization   Members of the chain are inclined to focus on maximizing local profit or minimizing immediate cost based on their limited knowledge. Slight upturns in demand are overcompensated for because no one wants to be caught short. Similarly, slight downturns are overcompensated for because no one wants to be caught holding excess inventory. So fluctuations are magnified. For instance, a pasta distributor does not want to run out of pasta for its retail customers; the natural response to an extra large order from the retailer is to compensate with an even larger order to the manufacturer on the assumption that retail sales are picking up. Neither the distributor nor the manufacturer knows that the retailer had a major one-time promotion that moved a lot of pasta. This is exactly the issue that complicated the implementation of efficient distribution at the Italian pasta maker Barilla.

Incentives (Sales Incentives, Quantity Discounts, Quotas, and Promotions) Incentives push merchandise into the chain for sales that have not occurred. This generates fluctuations that are ultimately expensive to all members of the chain.

Large Lots There is often a bias toward large lots because large lots tend to reduce unit costs. A logistics manager wants to ship large lots, preferably in full trucks, and a production manager wants long production runs. Both actions drive down unit shipping and production costs, but they increase holding costs and fail to reflect actual sales.

These three common occurrences—local optimization, incentives, and large lots—contribute to distortions of information about what is really occurring in the supply chain. A well-running supply system needs to be based on accurate information about how many products are truly being pulled through the chain. The inaccurate information is unintentional, but it results in distortions and fluctuations, causing what is known as the bullwhip effect.

> **Bullwhip effect**
> The increasing fluctuation in orders that often occurs as orders move through the supply chain.

The bullwhip effect occurs as orders are relayed from retailers, to distributors, to wholesalers, to manufacturers, with fluctuations increasing at each step in the sequence. The "bullwhip" fluctuations in the supply chain increase the costs associated with inventory, transportation, shipping, and receiving, while decreasing customer service and profitability. A number of specific opportunities exist for reducing the bullwhip effect and improving supply chain performance. The bullwhip effect is discussed more thoroughly in the supplement to this chapter.

Opportunities in Managing the Integrated Supply Chain

Opportunities for effective management in the supply chain include the following 10 items.

> **Pull data**
> Accurate sales data that initiate transactions to "pull" product through the supply chain.

Accurate "Pull" Data Accurate pull data are generated by sharing (1) point-of-sales (POS) information so that each member of the chain can schedule effectively and (2) computer-assisted ordering (CAO). This implies using POS systems that collect sales data and then adjusting that data for market factors, inventory on hand, and outstanding orders. Then a net order is sent directly to the supplier, who is responsible for maintaining the finished-goods inventory.

Lot Size Reduction Lot sizes are reduced through aggressive management. This may include (1) developing economical shipments of less than truckload lots; (2) providing discounts based on total annual volume rather than size of individual shipments; and (3) reducing the cost of ordering through techniques such as standing orders and various forms of electronic purchasing.

> **Single-stage control of replenishment**
> Fixing responsibility for monitoring and managing inventory for the retailer.

Single-Stage Control of Replenishment Single-stage control of replenishment means designating a member in the chain as responsible for monitoring and managing inventory in the supply chain based on the "pull" from the end user. This approach removes distorted information and multiple forecasts that create the bullwhip effect. Control may be in the hands of:

◆ A sophisticated **retailer** who understands demand patterns. Walmart does this for some of its inventory with radio frequency ID (RFID) tags.

◆ A distributor who manages the inventory for a particular distribution area. Distributors who handle grocery items, beer, and soft drinks may do this. Anheuser-Busch manages beer inventory and delivery for many of its customers.

◆ A manufacturer who has a well-managed forecasting, manufacturing, and distribution system. TAL Apparel Ltd., discussed in the *OM in Action* box, "The JCPenney Supply Chain for Dress Shirts," does this for JCPenney.

> **Vendor-managed inventory (VMI)**
> A system in which a supplier maintains material for the buyer, often delivering directly to the buyer's using department.

Vendor-Managed Inventory Vendor-managed inventory (VMI) means the use of a local supplier (usually a distributor) to maintain inventory for the manufacturer or retailer. The supplier delivers directly to the purchaser's using department rather than to a receiving dock or stockroom. If the supplier can maintain the stock of inventory for a variety of customers who use

OM in Action | The JCPenney Supply Chain for Dress Shirts

Purchase a white Stafford wrinkle-free dress shirt, size 17 neck, 34/35 sleeve at JCPenney at Atlanta's Northlake Mall on a Tuesday, and the supply chain responds. Within a day, TAL Apparel Ltd. in Hong Kong downloads a record of the sale. After a run through its forecasting model, TAL decides how many shirts to make and in what styles, colors, and sizes. By Wednesday afternoon, the replacement shirt is packed to be shipped directly to the JCPenney Northlake Mall store. The system bypasses the JCPenney warehouse—indeed all warehouses—as well as the JCPenney corporate decision makers.

In a second instance, two shirts are sold, leaving none in stock. TAL, after downloading the data, runs its forecasting model but comes to the decision that this store needs to have two in stock. Without consulting JCPenney, a TAL factory in Taiwan makes two new shirts. It sends one by ship, but because of the outage, the other goes by air.

As retailers deal with mass customization, fads, and seasonal swings, they also strive to cut costs—making a responsive supply chain critical. Before globalization of the supply chain, JCPenney would have had thousands of shirts warehoused across the country. Now JCPenney stores, like those of

many retailers, hold a very limited inventory of shirts.

JCPenney's supplier, TAL, is providing both sales forecasting and inventory management, a situation not acceptable to many retailers. But what is most startling is that TAL also places its own orders! A supply chain like this

Pavel L Photo and Video/Shutterstock

works only when there is trust between partners. The rapid changes in supply chain management not only place increasing technical demands on suppliers but also increase demands for trust between the parties.

Sources: Fortune (June 10, 2013); Apparel (April 2006); and The Wall Street Journal (September 11, 2003).

---

the same product or whose differences are very minor (say, at the packaging stage), then there should be a net savings. These systems work without the immediate direction of the purchaser.

Collaborative Planning, Forecasting, and Replenishment (CPFR) As with single-stage control and vendor-managed inventory, collaborative planning, forecasting, and replenishment (CPFR) is another effort to manage inventory in the supply chain. With CPFR, members of the supply chain share planning, demand, forecasting, and inventory information. Partners in a CPFR effort begin with collaboration on product definition and a joint marketing plan. Promotion, advertising, forecasts, joint order commitments, and timing of shipments are all included in the plan in a concerted effort to drive down inventory and related costs. CPFR can help to significantly reduce the bullwhip effect.

Blanket Orders Blanket orders are unfilled orders with a vendor and are also called "open orders" or "incomplete orders." A blanket order is a contract to purchase certain items from a vendor. It is not an authorization to ship anything. Shipment is made only on receipt of an agreed-on document, perhaps a shipping requisition or shipment release.

Standardization The purchasing department should make special efforts to increase levels of standardization. That is, rather than obtaining a variety of similar components with labeling, coloring, packaging, or perhaps even slightly different engineering specifications, the purchasing agent should try to have those components standardized.

Postponement Postponement withholds any modification or customization to the product (keeping it generic) as long as possible. The concept is to minimize internal variety while maximizing external variety. For instance, after analyzing the supply chain for its printers, Hewlett-Packard (HP) determined that if the printer's power supply was moved out of the printer itself and into a power cord, HP could ship the basic printer anywhere in the world. HP modified the printer, its power cord, its packaging, and its documentation so that only the power cord and documentation needed to be added at the final distribution point. This modification allowed the firm to manufacture and hold centralized inventories of the generic printer for shipment as demand changed. Only the unique power system and documentation had to be held in each country. This understanding of the entire supply chain reduced both risk and inventory investment. Similarly, Benetton leaves a portion of each style of its sweaters white so that they can be dyed the color the market is demanding at the last possible moment.

Electronic Ordering and Funds Transfer Electronic ordering and bank transfers are traditional approaches to speeding transactions and reducing paperwork. Transactions

Collaborative planning, forecasting, and replenishment (CPFR)
A system in which members of a supply chain share information in a joint effort to reduce supply chain costs.

Blanket order
A long-term purchase commitment to a supplier for items that are to be delivered against short-term releases to ship.

Postponement
Delaying any modifications or customization to a product as long as possible in the production process.

between firms often use electronic data interchange (EDI), which is a standardized data-transmittal format for computerized communications between organizations. EDI also provides for the use of advanced shipping notice (ASN), which notifies the purchaser that the vendor is ready to ship. Although some firms are still moving to EDI and ASN, the Internet's ease of use and lower cost is proving more popular.

Drop Shipping and Special Packaging **Drop shipping** means the supplier will ship directly to the end consumer, rather than to the seller, saving both time and reshipping costs. Other cost-saving measures include the use of special packaging, labels, and optimal placement of labels and bar codes on containers. The final location down to the department and number of units in each shipping container can also be indicated. Substantial savings can be obtained through management techniques such as these. Some of these techniques can be of particular benefit to wholesalers and retailers by reducing shrinkage (lost, damaged, or stolen merchandise) and handling cost.

For instance, Walmart Marketplace (Walmart.com) provides customers access to hundreds of thousands of additional products through approved retailers. Although orders from these retailers are combined in a common payment to Walmart.com, all shipping and returns are handled by the affiliate retailers.

> **Drop shipping**
>
> Shipping directly from the supplier to the end consumer rather than from the seller, saving both time and reshipping costs.

Building the Supply Base

> **LO 11.4** *Describe* the steps in supplier selection

For those goods and services a firm buys, suppliers, also known as *vendors,* must be selected and actively managed. Supplier selection considers numerous factors, such as strategic fit, supplier competence, delivery, and quality performance. Because a firm may have some competence in all areas and may have exceptional competence in only a few, selection can be challenging. Procurement policies also need to be established. Those might address issues such as percent of business done with any one supplier or with minority businesses. We now examine supplier selection as a four-stage process: (1) supplier evaluation, (2) supplier development, (3) negotiations, and (4) contracting.

Supplier Evaluation

The first stage of supplier selection, *supplier evaluation,* involves finding potential suppliers and determining the likelihood of their becoming *good* suppliers. If good suppliers are not selected, then all other supply chain efforts are wasted. As firms move toward long-term suppliers, the issues of financial strength, quality, management, research, technical ability, and potential for a close, long-term relationship play an increasingly important role. Evaluation criteria critical to the firm might include these categories as well as production process capability, location, and information systems. The supplement to this chapter provides an example of the commonly used *factor weighting* approach to supplier evaluation.

Supplier Certification International quality certifications such as ISO 9000 and ISO 14000 are designed to provide an external verification that a firm follows sound quality management and environmental management standards. Buying firms can use such certifications to pre-qualify potential suppliers. Despite the existence of the ISO standards, firms often create their own supplier certification programs. Buyers audit potential suppliers and award a certified status to those that meet the specified qualification. A certification process often involves three steps: (1) qualification, (2) education, and (3) the certification performance process. Once certified, the supplier may be awarded special treatment and priority, allowing the buying firm to reduce or eliminate incoming inspection of materials. Such an arrangement may facilitate JIT production for the buying firm. Most large companies use some sort of supplier certification program.

Supplier Development

The second stage of supplier selection is *supplier development*. Assuming that a firm wants to proceed with a particular supplier, how does it integrate this supplier into its system?

The buyer makes sure the supplier has an appreciation of quality requirements, product specifications, schedules and delivery, and procurement policies. Supplier development may include everything from training, to engineering and production help, to procedures for information transfer.

Negotiations

Although the prices that consumers pay are often inflexible (printed on the price tag, listed in the catalog, etc.), a significant number of final prices paid in business-to-business transactions are negotiated. In addition to the price itself, several other aspects of the full product "package" must be determined. These may include credit and delivery terms, quality standards, and cooperative advertising agreements. In fact, negotiation represents a significant element in a purchasing manager's job, and well-honed negotiation skills are highly valued.

Here are three classic types of negotiation strategies: the cost-based model, the market-based price model, and competitive bidding.

Cost-Based Price Model The cost-based price model requires that the supplier open its books to the purchaser. The contract price is then based on time and materials or on a fixed cost with an escalation clause to accommodate changes in the vendor's labor and materials cost.

Market-Based Price Model In the market-based price model, price is based on a published, auction, or index price. Many commodities (agricultural products, paper, metal, etc.) are priced this way. Paperboard prices, for instance, are available via the *Official Board Markets* weekly publication (**www.advanstar.com**).

Competitive Bidding When suppliers are not willing to discuss costs or where near-perfect markets do not exist, competitive bidding is often appropriate. Competitive bidding is the typical policy in many firms for the majority of their purchases. Bidding policies usually require that the purchasing agent have several potential suppliers and quotations from each. The major disadvantage of this method, as mentioned earlier, is that the development of long-term relations between buyer and seller is hindered. It may also make difficult the communication and performance that are vital for engineering changes, quality, and delivery.

Yet a fourth approach is *to combine one or more* of the preceding negotiation techniques. The supplier and purchaser may agree to review cost data, accept some form of market-based cost, or agree that the supplier will "remain competitive."

Contracting

Supply chain partners often develop contracts to spell out terms of the relationship. Contracts are designed to share risks, share benefits, and create incentive structures to encourage supply chain members to adopt policies that are optimal for the entire chain. The idea is to make the total pie (of supply chain profits) bigger and then divide the bigger pie among all participants. The goal is collaboration. Some common features of contracts include *quantity discounts* (lower prices for larger orders), *buybacks* (common in the magazine and book business where there is a buyback of unsold units), and *revenue sharing* (where both partners share the risk of uncertainty by sharing revenue).

Centralized Purchasing

Companies with multiple facilities (e.g., multiple manufacturing plants or multiple retail outlets) must determine which items to purchase centrally and which to allow local sites to purchase for themselves. Unmonitored decentralized purchasing can create havoc. For example, different plants for Nestle USA's brands used to pay 29 different prices for its vanilla ingredient *to the same supplier*! Important cost, efficiency, and "single-voice" benefits often accrue from a centralized purchasing function. Typical benefits include:

- Leverage purchase volume for better pricing
- Develop specialized staff expertise
- Develop stronger supplier relationships
- Maintain professional control over the purchasing process

◆ Devote more resources to the supplier selection and negotiation process
◆ Reduce the duplication of tasks
◆ Promote standardization

However, local managers enjoy having their own purchasing control, and decentralized purchasing can offer certain inventory control, transportation cost, or lead-time benefits. Often firms use a hybrid approach—using centralized purchasing for some items and/or sites while allowing local purchasing for others.

E-Procurement

E-procurement

Purchasing facilitated through the Internet.

E-procurement speeds purchasing, reduces costs, and integrates the supply chain. It reduces the traditional barrage of paperwork and, at the same time, provides purchasing personnel with an extensive database of supplier, delivery, and quality data.

Online Catalogs and Exchanges   Purchase of standard items is often accomplished via online catalogs. Such catalogs support cost comparisons and incorporate voice and video clips, making the process efficient for both buyers and sellers.

Online exchanges are typically industry-specific Internet sites that bring buyers and sellers together. Marriott and Hyatt created one of the first, Avendra (**www.avendra.com**), which facilitates economic purchasing of the huge range of goods needed by the 5,000 hospitality industry customers now in the exchange. Online catalogs and exchanges can help move companies from a multitude of individual phone calls, faxes, and emails to a centralized system and drive billions of dollars of waste out of the supply chain.

Online Auctions   In addition to catalogs, some suppliers and buyers have established online auction sites. Operations managers find online auctions a fertile area for disposing of excess raw material and discontinued or excess inventory. Online auctions lower entry barriers, encourage sellers to join, and simultaneously increase the potential number of buyers. The key for intermediaries is to find and build a huge base of potential bidders, improve client buying procedures, and qualify new suppliers.

In a traditional auction, a seller offers a product or service and generates competition between bidders—bidding the price up. In contrast, buyers often utilize online *reverse auctions* (or *Dutch auctions*). In reverse auctions, a buyer initiates the process by submitting a description of the desired product or service. Potential suppliers then submit bids, which may include price and other delivery information. Thus, price competition occurs on the selling side of the transaction—bidding the price down. Note that, as with traditional supplier selection decisions, price is important but may not be the only factor in winning the bid.

Logistics Management

Logistics management

An approach that seeks efficiency of operations through the integration of all material acquisition, movement, and storage activities.

Procurement activities may be combined with various shipping, warehousing, and inventory activities to form a logistics system. The purpose of logistics management is to obtain efficiency of operations through the integration of all material acquisition, movement, and storage activities. When transportation and inventory costs are substantial on both the input and output sides of the production process, an emphasis on logistics may be appropriate. Many firms opt for outsourcing the logistics function, as logistics specialists can often bring expertise not available in-house. For instance, logistics companies often have tracking technology that reduces transportation losses and supports delivery schedules that adhere to precise delivery windows. The potential for competitive advantage is found via both reduced costs and improved customer service.

Shipping Systems

LO 11.5 *Explain* major issues in logistics management

Firms recognize that the transportation of goods to and from their facilities can represent as much as 25% of the cost of products. Because of this high cost, firms constantly evaluate their means of shipping. Six major means of shipping are trucking, railroads, airfreight, waterways, pipelines, and multimodal.

Trucking   The vast majority of manufactured goods moves by truck. The flexibility of shipping by truck is only one of its many advantages. Companies that have adopted JIT programs in recent years have put increased pressure on truckers to pick up and deliver on time, with no damage, with paperwork in order, and at low cost. Trucking firms are using computers to monitor weather, find the most effective route, reduce fuel cost, and analyze the most efficient way to unload. To improve logistics efficiency, the industry is establishing Web sites such as Schneider National's connection (**www.schneider.com**), which lets shippers and truckers find each other to use some of this idle capacity.

Railroads   Railroads in the U.S. employ 235,000 people and ship 40% of the ton-miles of all commodities, including 93% of coal, 57% of cereal grains, and 52% of basic chemicals. Containerization has made shipping of truck trailers on railroad flat cars a popular means of distribution. The equivalent of 47 million trailer loads are moved in the U.S. each year by rail.

Airfreight   Airfreight represents less than 1% of tonnage shipped in the U.S. However, the proliferation of airfreight carriers such as FedEx, UPS, and DHL makes it a fast-growing mode of shipping. Clearly, for national and international movement of lightweight items, such as medical and emergency supplies, flowers, fruits, and electronic components, airfreight offers speed and reliability.

Waterways   Waterways are one of the nation's oldest means of freight transportation, dating back to construction of the Erie Canal in 1817. Included in U.S. waterways are the nation's rivers, canals, the Great Lakes, coastlines, and oceans connecting to other countries. The usual cargo on internal waterways is bulky, low-value cargo such as iron ore, grains, cement, coal, chemicals, limestone, and petroleum products. Internationally, millions of containers holding all sorts of industrial and consumer goods are shipped at very low cost via huge oceangoing ships each year. Water transportation is often preferred when cost is more important than speed.

Pipelines   Pipelines are an important form of transporting crude oil, natural gas, and other petroleum and chemical products.

Multimodal   Multimodal shipping combines shipping methods, and is a common means of getting a product to its final destination, particularly for international shipments. The use of standardized containers facilitates easy transport from truck to rail to ship and back again, without having to unload products from the containers until the very end.

   While freight rates are often based on very complicated pricing systems, in general, clients pay for speed. Faster methods such as airfreight tend to be much more expensive, while slower methods, such as waterways, provide a much cheaper shipping rate per unit. The size of shipments follows a similar pattern. The faster methods tend to involve smaller shipment sizes, while the slower methods involve very large shipment sizes.

STUDENT TIP
Logistics represents a substantial part of the economy, as logistics cost comprises 11.3% of the U.S. gross domestic product.

Warehousing

Warehousing often adds 8–10% to the cost of a product, making warehousing a significant expense for many firms. Warehouses come in all shapes and sizes, from tiny rooms in the back of a store to enormous facilities that could fit multiple football fields. Warehouses may be extremely expensive to operate, but the alternatives (e.g., either no storage at all or storage at local operating facilities, along with the related logistics issues) may be much more costly.

   The fundamental purpose of a warehouse is to store goods. However, some warehouses also provide other crucial functions. For example, a warehouse can serve as a *consolidation point,* gathering shipments from multiple sources to send outbound in one cheaper, fully loaded truck. Alternatively, a warehouse can provide a *break-bulk* function by accepting a cheaper full truckload inbound shipment and then dividing it for distribution to individual sites. Further, similar to a major airport hub, a warehouse can serve simply as a *cross-docking* facility—accepting shipments from a variety of sources and recombining them for distribution to a variety of destinations, often without actually storing any goods during the transition. Finally, a warehouse can serve as a point of *postponement* in the process, providing final customer-specific value-added processing to the product before final shipment.

   Channel assembly represents one way to implement postponement. Channel assembly sends individual components and modules, rather than finished products, to the distributor.

Channel assembly
Postpones final assembly of a product so the distribution channel can assemble it.

OM in Action   DHL's Role in the Supply Chain

It's the dead of night at DHL International's air express hub in Brussels, yet the massive building is alive with busy forklifts and sorting workers. The boxes going on and off the DHL plane range from Dell computers and Cisco routers to Caterpillar mufflers and Komatsu hydraulic pumps. Sun Microsystems computers from California are earmarked for Finland; DVDs from Teac's plant in Malaysia are destined for Bulgaria.

The door-to-door movement of time-sensitive packages is key to the global supply chain. JIT, short product life cycles, mass customization, and reduced inventories depend on logistics firms such as DHL, FedEx, and UPS. These powerhouses are in continuous motion.

With a decentralized network covering 220 countries and territories (more than are in the UN), DHL is a true multinational. The Brussels headquarters has under 2,000 of the company's 325,000 employees but includes 26 nationalities.

DHL has assembled an extensive global network of express logistics centers for strategic goods. In its Brussels logistics center, for instance, DHL upgrades, repairs, and configures Fijitsu computers, InFocus projectors, and Johnson & Johnson medical equipment. It stores and provides parts for EMC and Hewlett-Packard and replaces Nokia and Philips phones. "If something breaks down on a Thursday at 4 o'clock, the relevant warehouse knows at 4:05, and the part is on a DHL plane at 7 or 8 that evening," says Robert Kuijpers, DHL International's CEO.

Sources: www.dhl.com (2015); *The Wall Street Journal* (July 19, 2012); *Materials Handling World* (December 14, 2011); and www.dhlsupplychainmatters.com.

The distributor then assembles, tests, and ships. Channel assembly treats distributors more as manufacturing partners than as distributors. This technique has proven successful in industries where products are undergoing rapid change, such as PCs. With this strategy, finished-goods inventory is reduced because units are built to a shorter, more accurate forecast. Consequently, market response is better, with lower investment—a nice combination.

Third-Party Logistics (3PL)

Third-party logistics, as is the case with most specialization, tends to bring added innovation and expertise to the logistics system. Consequently, supply chain managers outsource logistics to meet three goals: (1) drive down inventory investment, (2) lower delivery costs, and (3) improve delivery reliability and speed. Specialized logistics firms support these goals by creatively coordinating the supplier's inventory system with the service capabilities of the delivery firm. FedEx, for example, has a successful history of using the Internet for online tracking. At **fedex.com**, a customer can compute shipping costs, print labels, adjust invoices, and track package status. FedEx, UPS, and DHL play a core role in other firms' logistics processes. For instance, UPS works with Nike at a shipping hub in Louisville, Kentucky, to store and immediately expedite shipments. The *OM in Action* box "DHL's Role in the Supply Chain"

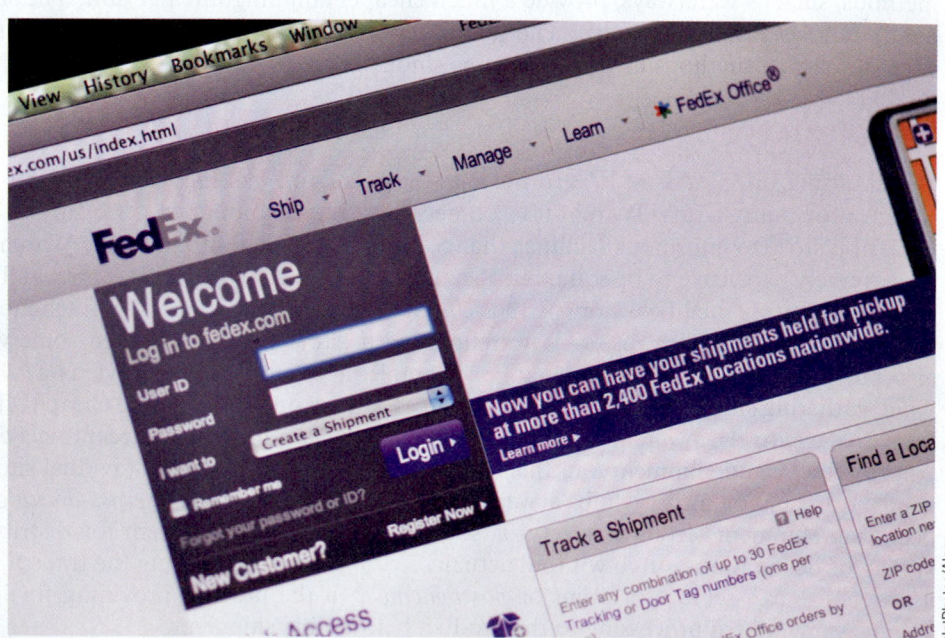

Speed and accuracy in the supply chain are supported by bar-code tracking of shipments. At each step of a journey, from initial pickup (left) to final destination, bar codes are read and stored. Within seconds, this tracking information is available online to customers worldwide (right).

provides another example of how outsourcing logistics can reduce costs while shrinking inventory and delivery times.

Distribution Management

Management of the supply chain focuses on incoming materials, but just as important, *distribution management* focuses on the outbound flow of products. Designing distribution networks to meet customer expectations suggests three criteria: (1) *rapid response,* (2) *product choice,* and (3) *service.*

Office Depot, for example, addresses these customer concerns by having several stores in a town for convenience and quick response time. But it also offers an online shopping presence to accommodate customers requiring a much larger selection of products (**www.officedepot.com**). It may even offer delivery directly to large customers. These varying customer expectations suggest both different distribution channels and multiple outlets.

So how many stores should Office Depot open in a town? As Figure 11.3(a) indicates, an increase in the number of facilities generally implies a quicker response and increased customer satisfaction. On the cost side, three logistics-related costs [see Figure 11.3(b)] are shown: *inventory costs*, *transportation costs*, and *facility costs*. Taken together, *total logistics costs* tend to follow the top curve, first declining, and then rising. For this particular example, it appears that total logistics costs are minimized with three facilities. However, when revenue is considered [see Figure 11.3(c)], we note that profit is maximized with four facilities.

Whether creating a network of warehouses or retail outlets, finding the optimal number of facilities represents a critical and often dynamic decision. For instance, barely a year after adding 3 million square feet of warehouse capacity, market dynamics caused Amazon.com to close three of its U.S. distribution centers.

Just as firms need an effective *supplier management* program, an effective *distribution management* program may make the difference between supply chain success and failure. For example, in addition to facilities, packaging and logistics are necessary for the network to perform well. Packaging and logistics are also important distribution decisions because the manufacturer is usually held responsible for breakages and serviceability. Further, selection and development of dealers or retailers are necessary to ensure ethical and enthusiastic representation of the firm's products. Top-notch supply chain performance requires good *downstream* (distributors and retailers) management, just as it does good *upstream* (suppliers) management.

Figure **11.3**

Number of Facilities in a Distribution Network

The focus should be on profit maximization (c) rather than cost minimization (b).

Ethics and Sustainable Supply Chain Management

Let's look at two issues that OM managers must address every day when dealing with supply chains: ethics and sustainability.

Supply Chain Management Ethics

We consider three aspects of ethics: personal ethics, ethics within the supply chain, and ethical behavior regarding the environment. As the supply chain becomes increasingly international, each of these becomes even more significant.

Personal Ethics Ethical decisions are critical to the long-term success of any organization. However, the supply chain is particularly susceptible to ethical lapses. With sales personnel anxious to sell and purchasing agents spending huge sums, temptations abound. Salespeople become friends with customers, do favors for them, take them to lunch, or present small (or large) gifts. Determining when tokens of friendship become bribes can be challenging. Many companies have strict rules and codes of conduct that limit what is acceptable.

Recognizing these issues, the Institute for Supply Management has developed the following principles and standards to be used as guidelines for ethical behavior:

◆ *Promote and uphold* responsibilities to one's employer; positive supplier and customer relationships; sustainability and social responsibility; protection of confidential and proprietary information; applicable laws, regulations, and trade agreements; and development of professional competence.

◆ *Avoid* perceived impropriety; conflicts of interest; behaviors that negatively influence supply chain decisions; and improper reciprocal agreements.

Ethics Within the Supply Chain In this age of hyper-specialization, much of any organization's resources are purchased, putting great stress on ethics in the supply chain. Managers may be tempted to ignore ethical lapses by suppliers or offload pollution to suppliers. But firms must establish standards for their suppliers, just as they have established standards for themselves. Society expects ethical performance throughout the supply chain. For instance, Gap, Inc., reported that of its 3,000-plus factories worldwide, about 90% failed their initial evaluation. Gap found that 10% to 25% of its Chinese factories engaged in psychological or verbal abuse, and more than 50% of the factories in sub-Saharan Africa operated without proper safety devices. The challenge of enforcing ethical standards is significant, but responsible firms such as Gap are finding ways to deal with this difficult issue.

Ethical Behavior Regarding the Environment While ethics on both a personal basis and in the supply chain are important, so is ethical behavior in regard to the environment. Good ethics extends to doing business in a way that supports conservation and renewal of resources. This requires evaluation of the entire environmental impact, from raw material, to manufacture, through use and final disposal. For instance, Darden Restaurants and Walmart both require their shrimp and fish suppliers in Southeast Asia to abide by the standards of the Global Aquaculture Alliance. These standards must be met if suppliers want to maintain the business relationship. Operations managers also ensure that sustainability is reflected in the performance of second- and third-tier suppliers. Enforcement can be done by in-house inspectors, third-party auditors, governmental agencies, or nongovernmental watchdog organizations. All four approaches are used.

Establishing Sustainability in Supply Chains

The incoming supply chain garners most of the attention, but it is only part of the challenge of sustainability. The "return" supply chain is also significant. Reverse logistics involves the processes for sending returned products back up the supply chain for resale, repair, reuse, remanufacture, recycling, or disposal. The operations manager's goal should be to limit burning or

TABLE 11.4	Management Challenges of Reverse Logistics	
ISSUE	**FORWARD LOGISTICS**	**REVERSE LOGISTICS**
Forecasting	Relatively straightforward	More uncertain
Product quality	Uniform	Not uniform
Product packaging	Uniform	Often damaged
Pricing	Relatively uniform	Dependent on many factors
Speed	Often very important	Often not a priority
Distribution costs	Easily visible	Less directly visible
Inventory management	Consistent	Not consistent

Adapted from the Reverse Logistics Executive Council (**www.rlec.org**).

burying of returned products and instead strive for reuse. Reverse logistics initiates a new set of challenges, as shown in Table 11.4.

Although sometimes used as a synonym for reverse logistics, a **closed-loop supply chain** refers more to the proactive design of a supply chain that tries to optimize all forward and reverse flows. A closed-loop supply chain prepares for returns prior to product introduction. For instance, IBM has recognized that components often have much longer life cycles than the original products that they go into. So the company has established a systematic method for dismantling returns and used equipment to extract components that still have value, such as boards, cards, and hard-disk assemblies. IBM has realized millions of dollars of savings in procurement costs by exploiting its "dismantling channel" of used parts.

Closed-loop supply chain
A supply chain designed to optimize both forward and reverse flows.

Measuring Supply Chain Performance

❗ STUDENT TIP
If you can't measure it, you can't control it.

Like all other managers, supply chain managers require standards (or *metrics*, as they are often called) to evaluate performance. For example, the large grocery chain HEB tracks metrics such as total freight cost per $1 million of sales, errors and returns in distribution, and lead-time compliance. Lancers, a beverage dispenser manufacturer, tracks metrics such as on-time delivery percentage, defects per million, and lead time. We now introduce several financial-based inventory metrics.

Assets Committed to Inventory

Supply chain managers make scheduling and quantity decisions that determine the assets committed to inventory. Three specific measures can be helpful here. The first is the amount of money invested in inventory, usually expressed as a percentage of assets, as shown in Equation (11-1) and Example 2:

LO 11.6 *Compute* the percentage of assets committed to inventory and inventory turnover

$$\text{Percentage invested in inventory} = (\text{Average inventory investment}/\text{Total assets}) \times 100 \quad (11\text{-}1)$$

Example 2 — TRACKING HOME DEPOT'S INVENTORY INVESTMENT

Home Depot's management wishes to track its investment in inventory as one of its performance measures. Recently, Home Depot had $11.4 billion invested in inventory and total assets of $44.4 billion.

APPROACH ▶ Determine the investment in inventory and total assets and then use Equation (11-1).

SOLUTION ▶ Percent invested in inventory = (11.4/44.4) × 100 = 25.7%

INSIGHT ▶ Over one-fourth of Home Depot assets are committed to inventory.

LEARNING EXERCISE ▶ If Home Depot can drive its investment down to 20% of assets, how much money will it free up for other uses? [Answer: 11.4 − (44.4 × 0.2) = $2.52 billion.]

RELATED PROBLEMS ▶ 11.5b, 11.6b

Inventory turnover

Cost of goods sold divided by average inventory.

TABLE 11.5

Inventory as Percentage of Total Assets (with examples of exceptional performance)

Manufacturer (Toyota 5%)	15%
Wholesale (Coca-Cola 2.9%)	34%
Restaurants (McDonald's .05%)	2.9%
Retail (Home Depot 25.7%)	27%

Specific comparisons with competitors may assist evaluation. Total assets committed to inventory in manufacturing approach 15%, in wholesale 34%, and retail 27%—with wide variations, depending on the specific business model, the business cycle, and management (see Table 11.5).

The second common measure of supply chain performance is *inventory turnover* (see Table 11.6). Its reciprocal, *weeks of supply*, is the third. **Inventory turnover** is computed on an annual basis, using Equation (11-2):

$$\text{Inventory turnover} = \text{Cost of goods sold/Average inventory investment} \qquad (11\text{-}2)$$

Cost of goods sold is the cost to produce the goods or services sold for a given period. Inventory investment is the average inventory value for the same period. This may be the average of several periods of inventory or beginning and ending inventory added together and divided by 2. Often, average inventory investment is based on nothing more than the inventory investment at the end of the period—typically at year-end.[1]

In Example 3, we look at inventory turnover applied to PepsiCo.

Example 3

INVENTORY TURNOVER AT PEPSICO, INC.

PepsiCo, Inc., manufacturer and distributor of drinks, Frito-Lay, and Quaker Foods, provides the following in a recent annual report (shown here in $ billions). Determine PepsiCo's turnover.

Net revenue		$32.5
Cost of goods sold		$14.2
Inventory:		
Raw material inventory	$.74	
Work-in-process inventory	$.11	
Finished goods inventory	$.84	
Total average inventory investment		$1.69

APPROACH ▶ Use the inventory turnover computation in Equation (11-2) to measure inventory performance. Cost of goods sold is $14.2 billion. Total inventory is the sum of raw material at $.74 billion, work-in-process at $.11 billion, and finished goods at $.84 billion, for total average inventory investment of $1.69 billion.

SOLUTION ▶
$$\text{Inventory turnover} = \text{Cost of goods sold/Average inventory investment}$$
$$= 14.2/1.69$$
$$= 8.4$$

INSIGHT ▶ We now have a standard, popular measure by which to evaluate performance.

LEARNING EXERCISE ▶ If Coca-Cola's cost of goods sold is $10.8 billion and inventory investment is $.76 billion, what is its inventory turnover? [Answer: 14.2.]

RELATED PROBLEMS ▶ 11.5a, 11.6c, 11.7

Weeks of supply, as shown in Example 4, may have more meaning in the wholesale and retail portions of the service sector than in manufacturing. It is computed below as the reciprocal of inventory turnover:

$$\text{Weeks of supply} = \text{Average inventory investment/(Annual cost of goods sold/52 weeks)} \quad (11\text{-}3)$$

Example 4

DETERMINING WEEKS OF SUPPLY AT PEPSICO

Using the PepsiCo data in Example 3, management wants to know the weeks of supply.

APPROACH ▶ We know that inventory investment is $1.69 billion and that weekly sales equal annual cost of goods sold ($14.2 billion) divided by 52 = $14.2/52 = $.273 billion.

SOLUTION ▶ Using Equation (11-3), we compute weeks of supply as:

$$\text{Weeks of supply} = (\text{Average inventory investment}/\text{Average weekly cost of goods sold})$$
$$= 1.69/.273 = 6.19 \text{ weeks}$$

INSIGHT ▶ We now have a standard measurement by which to evaluate a company's continuing performance or by which to compare companies.

LEARNING EXERCISE ▶ If Coca-Cola's average inventory investment is $.76 billion and its average weekly cost of goods sold is $.207 billion, what is the firm's weeks of supply? [Answer: 3.67 weeks.]

RELATED PROBLEMS ▶ 11.6a, 11.8

Supply chain management is critical in driving down inventory investment. The rapid movement of goods is key. Walmart, for example, has set the pace in the retailing sector with its world-renowned supply chain management. By doing so, it has established a competitive advantage. With its own truck fleet, distribution centers, and a state-of-the-art communication system, Walmart (with the help of its suppliers) replenishes store shelves an average of twice per week. Competitors resupply every other week. Economical and speedy resupply means both rapid response to product changes and customer preferences, as well as lower inventory investment. Similarly, while many manufacturers struggle to move inventory turnover up to 10 times per year, Dell Computer has inventory turns exceeding 90 and supply measured in *days*—not weeks. Supply chain management provides a competitive advantage when firms effectively respond to the demands of global markets and global sources.

Benchmarking the Supply Chain

While metric values convey their own meaning and are useful when compared to past data, another important use compares these values to those of benchmark firms. Several organizations and websites allow companies to submit their own data and receive reports on how they stack up against other firms in their own industry or against world-class firms from any industry. Table 11.7 provides a few examples of metric values for typical firms and for benchmark firms in the consumer packaged goods industry. World-class benchmarks are the result of well-managed supply chains that drive down costs, lead times, late deliveries, and shortages while improving service levels.

TABLE 11.6

Examples of Annual Inventory Turnover

FOOD, BEVERAGE, RETAIL	
Anheuser Busch	15
Coca-Cola	14
Home Depot	5
McDonald's	112
MANUFACTURING	
Dell Computer	90
Johnson Controls	22
Toyota (overall)	13
Nissan (assembly)	150

TABLE 11.7	Supply Chain Metrics in the Consumer Packaged Goods Industry	
	TYPICAL FIRMS	**BENCHMARK FIRMS**
Order fill rate	71%	98%
Order fulfillment lead time (days)	7	3
Cash-to-cash cycle time (days)	100	30
Inventory days of supply	50	20

Source: Institute for Industrial Engineers

The SCOR Model

Perhaps the best-known benchmarking system is the five-part **Supply Chain Operations Reference (SCOR) model**. As shown in Figure 11.4, the five parts are Plan (planning activities for supply and demand), Source (purchasing activities), Make (production activities), Deliver

Supply Chain Operations Reference (SCOR) model

A set of processes, metrics, and best practices developed by the APICS Supply Chain Council.

Figure **11.4**

The Supply Chain Operations Reference (SCOR) Model

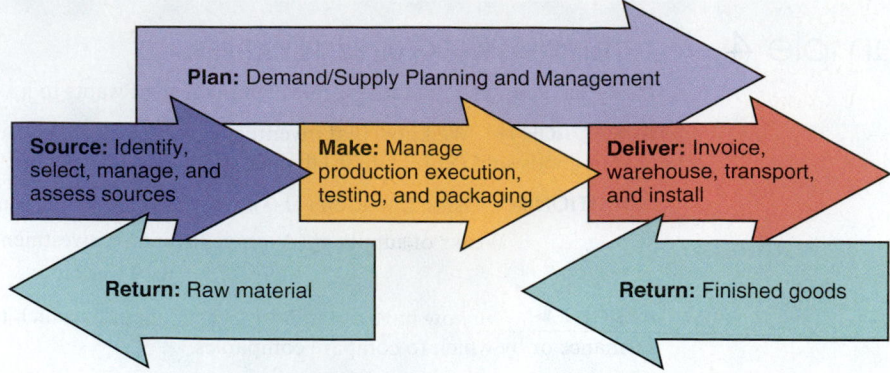

(distribution activities), and Return (closed-loop supply chain activities). The system is maintained by the APICS Supply Chain Council (**www.apics.org/sites/apics-supply-chain-council**). Firms use SCOR to identify, measure, reorganize, and improve supply chain processes.

The SCOR model defines over 200 process elements, 550 measurable metrics, and 500 best practices. The best practices describe the techniques used by benchmark firms that have scored very well on the metrics. SCOR combines these metrics with "Performance Attributes" (see Table 11.8) to facilitate comparisons of companies that compete by using different strategies (for example, low cost vs. responsiveness).

TABLE 11.8   SCOR Model Metrics to Help Firms Benchmark Performance Against the Industry

PERFORMANCE ATTRIBUTE	SAMPLE METRIC	CALCULATION
Supply chain reliability	Perfect order fulfillment	(Total perfect orders)/(Total number of orders)
Supply chain responsiveness	Average order fulfillment cycle time	(Sum of actual cycle times for all orders delivered)/ (Total number of orders delivered)
Supply chain agility	Upside supply chain flexibility	Time required to achieve an unplanned 20% increase in delivered quantities
Supply chain costs	Supply chain management cost	Cost to plan + Cost to source + Cost to deliver + Cost to return
Supply chain asset management	Cash-to-cash cycle time	Inventory days of supply + Days of receivables outstanding − Days of payables outstanding

Benchmarking can be very useful, but it is not always adequate for excellence in the supply chain. Audits based on continuing communication, understanding, trust, performance, and corporate strategy are necessary. The relationships should manifest themselves in the mutual belief that "we are in this together" and go well beyond written agreements.

Summary

Competition is no longer between companies but between supply chains. The key to success is to collaborate with members on both the supply side and the distribution side of the supply chain to make decisions that will benefit the whole channel. For many firms, the supply chain determines a substantial portion of product cost and quality, as well as opportunities for responsiveness and differentiation. The challenge of building a great supply chain is significant, but with good sourcing tactics, a thoughtful logistics plan, and active management of the distribution network, each link in the chain can be firmly forged. A number of metrics are available to help managers evaluate their supply chain performance and benchmark against the industry. Skillful supply chain management provides a great strategic opportunity for competitive advantage.

Key Terms

Supply chain management (p. 444)
Make-or-buy decision (p. 447)
Outsourcing (p. 447)
Vertical integration (p. 448)
Keiretsu (p. 448)
Virtual companies (p. 449)
Cross-sourcing (p. 450)
Bullwhip effect (p. 452)
Pull data (p. 452)

Single-stage control of
  replenishment (p. 452)
Vendor-managed inventory (VMI)
  (p. 452)
Collaborative planning, forecasting,
  and replenishment (CPFR) (p. 453)
Blanket order (p. 453)
Postponement (p. 453)
Drop shipping (p. 454)

E-procurement (p. 456)
Logistics management (p. 456)
Channel assembly (p. 457)
Reverse logistics (p. 460)
Closed-loop supply chain (p. 461)
Inventory turnover (p. 462)
Supply Chain Operations Reference
  (SCOR) model (p. 463)

Ethical Dilemma

As a buyer for a discount retail chain, you find yourself caught in a maelstrom. Just last month, your chain began selling an economy-priced line of clothing endorsed by a famous movie star. To be price competitive, you have followed the rest of the industry and sourced the clothing from a low-wage region of Asia. Initial sales have been brisk; however, the movie star has recently called you screaming and crying because an investigative news outlet has reported that the clothes with her name on them are being made by children.

Outraged, you fly to the outsourcing manufacturing facility only to find that conditions are not quite as clear-cut as the news had reported. You feel uncomfortable riding through the streets. Poverty is everywhere. Children are chasing foreigners and begging for money. When you enter the plant, you observe a very clean facility. The completely female workforce appears to be very industrious, but many of them do appear to be young. You confront the plant manager and explain your firm's strict international sourcing policies. You demand to know why these girls aren't in school. The manager provides the following response: "The truth is that some of these workers may be underage. We check IDs, but the use of falsified records is commonplace in this country. Plus, you don't understand the alternatives. If you shut this plant down, you will literally take food off the table for these families. There are no other opportunities in this town at this time, and there's no comprehensive welfare system in our country. As for the young women, school is not an option. In this town, only boys receive an education past the sixth grade. If you shut us down, these girls will be out on the street, begging, stealing, or prostituting themselves. Your business offers them a better existence. Please don't take that away!"

What do you say to your company, the movie star, the media, and the protestors picketing your stores? Is the best option to shut down and try someplace else?

Discussion Questions

1. Define *supply chain management*.
2. What are the objectives of supply chain management?
3. What is the objective of logistics management?
4. How do we distinguish between the types of risk in the supply chain?
5. What is vertical integration? Give examples of backward and forward integration.
6. What are three basic approaches to negotiations?
7. How does a traditional adversarial relationship with suppliers change when a firm makes a decision to move to a few suppliers?
8. What is the difference between postponement and channel assembly?
9. What is CPFR?
10. What is the value of online auctions in e-commerce?
11. Explain how FedEx uses the Internet to meet requirements for quick and accurate delivery.
12. How does Walmart use drop shipping?
13. What are blanket orders? How do they differ from invoiceless purchasing?
14. What can purchasing do to implement just-in-time deliveries?
15. What is e-procurement?
16. How does Darden Restaurants, described in the *Global Company Profile*, find competitive advantage in its supply chain?
17. What is SCOR, and what purpose does it serve?

Solved Problems   Virtual Office Hours help is available in MyOMLab.

SOLVED PROBLEM 11.1

Jack's Pottery Outlet has total end-of-year assets of $5 million. The first-of-the-year inventory was $375,000, with a year-end inventory of $325,000. The annual cost of goods sold was $7 million. The owner, Eric Jack, wants to evaluate his supply chain performance by measuring his percent of assets in inventory, his inventory turnover, and his weeks of supply. We use Equations (11-1), (11-2), and (11-3) to provide these measures.

SOLUTION

First, determine *average inventory*:

$$(\$375,000 + \$325,000)/2 = \$350,000$$

Then, use Equation (11-1) to determine percent invested in inventory:

$$\text{Percent invested in inventory} = (\text{Average inventory investment}/\text{Total assets}) \times 100$$
$$= (350,000/5,000,000) \times 100$$
$$= 7\%$$

Third, determine inventory turnover, using Equation (11-2):

$$\text{Inventory turnover} = \text{Cost of goods sold}/\text{Average inventory investment}$$
$$= 7,000,000/350,000$$
$$= 20$$

Finally, to determine weeks of inventory, use Equation (11-3), adjusted to weeks:

$$\text{Weeks of inventory} = \text{Average inventory investment}/\text{Weekly cost of goods sold}$$
$$= 350,000/(7,000,000/52)$$
$$= 350,000/134,615$$
$$= 2.6$$

We conclude that Jack's Pottery Outlet has 7% of its assets invested in inventory, that the inventory turnover is 20, and that weeks of supply is 2.6.

Problems

Problems 11.1–11.3 relate to The Supply Chain's Strategic Importance

•• **11.1** Choose a local establishment that is a member of a relatively large chain. From interviews with workers and information from the Internet, identify the elements of the supply chain. Determine whether the supply chain supports a low-cost, rapid response, or differentiation strategy (refer to Chapter 2). Are the supply chain characteristics significantly different from one product to another?

••• **11.2** Hau Lee Furniture, Inc., described in Example 1 of this chapter, finds its current profit of $10,000 inadequate. The bank is insisting on an improved profit picture prior to approval of a loan for some new equipment. Hau would like to improve the profit line to $25,000 so he can obtain the bank's approval for the loan.
a) What percentage improvement is needed in the *supply chain strategy* for profit to improve to $25,000? What is the cost of material with a $25,000 profit?
b) What percentage improvement is needed in the *sales strategy* for profit to improve to $25,000? What must sales be for profit to improve to $25,000?

•••• **11.3** Kamal Fatehl, production manager of Kennesaw Manufacturing, finds his profit at $15,000 (as shown in the statement below)—inadequate for expanding his business. The bank is insisting on an improved profit picture prior to approval of a loan for some new equipment. Kamal would like to improve the profit line to $25,000 so he can obtain the bank's approval for the loan.

		% OF SALES
Sales	$250,000	100%
Cost of supply chain purchases	175,000	70%
Other production costs	30,000	12%
Fixed costs	30,000	12%
Profit	15,000	6%

a) What percentage improvement is needed in a *supply chain strategy* for profit to improve to $25,000? What is the cost of material with a $25,000 profit?
b) What percentage improvement is needed in a *sales strategy* for profit to improve to $25,000? What must sales be for profit to improve to $25,000? (*Hint:* See Example 1.)

Problem 11.4 relates to Six Sourcing Strategies

•• **11.4** Using sources from the Internet, identify some of the problems faced by a company of your choosing as it moves toward, or operates as, a virtual organization. Does its operating as a virtual organization simply exacerbate old problems, or does it create new ones?

Problems 11.5–11.8 relate to Measuring Supply Chain Performance

•• **11.5** Baker Mfg. Inc. (see Table 11.9) wishes to compare its inventory turnover to those of industry leaders, who have turnover of about 13 times per year and 8% of their assets invested in inventory.
a) What is Baker's inventory turnover?
b) What is Baker's percent of assets committed to inventory?
c) How does Baker's performance compare to the industry leaders?

TABLE 11.9	For Problems 11.5 and 11.6
ARROW DISTRIBUTING CORP.	
Net revenue	$16,500
Cost of sales	$13,500
Inventory	$ 1,000
Total assets	$ 8,600
BAKER MFG. INC.	
Net revenue	$27,500
Cost of sales	$21,500
Inventory	$ 1,250
Total assets	$16,600

•• **11.6** Arrow Distributing Corp. (see Table 11.9) likes to track inventory by using weeks of supply as well as by inventory turnover.
a) What is its weeks of supply?
b) What percent of Arrow's assets are committed to inventory?
c) What is Arrow's inventory turnover?
d) Is Arrow's supply chain performance, as measured by these inventory metrics, better than that of Baker in Problem 11.5?

• **11.7** The grocery industry has an annual inventory turnover of about 14 times. Organic Grocers, Inc. had a cost of goods sold last year of $10.5 million; its average inventory was $1.0 million. What was Organic Grocers' inventory turnover, and how does that performance compare with that of the industry?

•• **11.8** Mattress Wholesalers, Inc., is constantly trying to reduce inventory in its supply chain. Last year, cost of goods sold was $7.5 million and inventory was $1.5 million. This year, cost of goods sold is $8.6 million and inventory investment is $1.6 million.

a) What were the weeks of supply last year?

b) What are the weeks of supply this year?

c) Is Mattress Wholesalers making progress in its inventory-reduction effort?

Tyler Olson/Fotolia

CASE STUDIES

Darden's Global Supply Chains

Video Case

Darden Restaurants (subject of the *Global Company Profile* at the beginning of this chapter), owner of popular brands such as Olive Garden and LongHorn Steakhouse, requires unique supply chains to serve more than 300 million meals annually. Darden's strategy is operations excellence, and Senior VP Jim Lawrence's task is to ensure competitive advantage via Darden's supply chains. For a firm with purchases exceeding $1.8 billion, managing the supply chains is a complex and challenging task.

Darden, like other casual dining restaurants, has unique supply chains that reflect its menu options. Darden's supply chains are rather shallow, often having just one tier of suppliers. But it has four distinct supply chains.

First, "smallware" is a restaurant industry term for items such as linens, dishes, tableware and kitchenware, and silverware. These are purchased, with Darden taking title as they are received at the Darden Direct Distribution (DDD) warehouse in Orlando, Florida. From this single warehouse, smallware items are shipped via common carrier (trucking companies) to Olive Garden, Bahama Breeze, and Seasons 52 restaurants.

Second, frozen, dry, and canned food products are handled economically by Darden's 11 distribution centers in North America, which are managed by major U.S. food distributors, such as MBM, Maines, and Sygma. This is Darden's second supply line.

Third, the fresh food supply chain (not frozen and not canned), where product life is measured in days, includes dairy products, produce, and meat. This supply chain is B2B, where restaurant managers directly place orders with a preselected group of independent suppliers.

Fourth, Darden's worldwide seafood supply chain is the final link. Here Darden has developed independent suppliers of salmon, shrimp, tilapia, scallops, and other fresh fish that are source inspected by Darden's overseas representatives to ensure quality. These fresh products are flown to the U.S. and shipped to 16 distributors, with 22 locations, for quick delivery to the restaurants. With suppliers in 35 countries, Darden must be on the cutting edge when it comes to collaboration, partnering, communication, and food safety. It does this with heavy travel schedules for purchasing and quality control personnel, native-speaking employees onsite, and aggressive communication. Communication is a critical element; Darden tries to develop as much forecasting transparency as possible. "Point of sale (POS) terminals," says Lawrence, "feed actual sales every night to suppliers."

Discussion Questions*

1. What are the advantages of each of Darden's four supply chains?

2. What are the complications of having four supply chains?

3. Where would you expect ownership/title to change in each of Darden's four supply chains?

4. How do Darden's four supply chains compare with those of other firms, such as Dell or an automobile manufacturer? Why do the differences exist, and how are they addressed?

*You may wish to view the video that accompanies this case before answering the questions.

Supply Chain Management at Regal Marine

Video Case

Like most other manufacturers, Regal Marine finds that it must spend a huge portion of its revenue on purchases. Regal has also found that the better its suppliers understand its end users, the better are both the supplier's product and Regal's final product. As one of the 10 largest U.S. power boat manufacturers, Regal is trying to differentiate its products from the vast number of boats supplied by 300 other companies. Thus, the firm works closely with suppliers to ensure innovation, quality, and timely delivery.

Regal has done a number of things to drive down costs while driving up quality, responsiveness, and innovation. First, working on partnering relationships with suppliers ranging from providers of windshields to providers of instrument panel controls, Regal has brought timely innovation at reasonable cost to its product. Key vendors are so tightly linked with the company that they meet with designers to discuss material changes to be incorporated into new product designs.

Second, the company has joined about 15 other boat manufacturers in a purchasing group, known as American Boat Builders Association, to work with suppliers on reducing the costs of large purchases. Third, Regal is working with a number of local vendors to supply hardware and fasteners directly to the assembly line on a just-in-time basis. In some of these cases, Regal has worked out an arrangement with the vendor so that title does not transfer until parts are used by Regal. In other cases, title transfers when items are delivered to the property. This practice drives down total inventory and the costs associated with large-lot delivery.

Finally, Regal works with a personnel agency to outsource part of the recruiting and screening process for employees. In all these cases, Regal is demonstrating innovative approaches to supply chain management that help the firm and, ultimately, the end user. The *Global Company Profile* featuring Regal Marine (which opens Chapter 5) provides further background on Regal's operations.

Discussion Questions*

1. What other techniques might Regal use to improve supply chain management?
2. What kind of response might members of the supply chain expect from Regal because of their "partnering" in the supply chain?
3. Why is supply chain management important to Regal?

*You may wish to view the video that accompanies this case before answering the questions.

Arnold Palmer Hospital's Supply Chain

Video Case

Arnold Palmer Hospital, one of the nation's top hospitals dedicated to serving women and children, is a large business with over 2,000 employees working in a 431-bed facility totaling 676,000 square feet in Orlando, Florida. Like many other hospitals, and other companies, Arnold Palmer Hospital had been a long-time member of a large buying group, one servicing 900 members. But the group did have a few limitations. For example, it might change suppliers for a particular product every year (based on a new lower-cost bidder) or stock only a product that was not familiar to the physicians at Arnold Palmer Hospital. The buying group was also not able to negotiate contracts with local manufacturers to secure the best pricing.

So in 2003, Arnold Palmer Hospital, together with seven other partner hospitals in central Florida, formed its own much smaller, but still powerful (with $200 million in annual purchases) Healthcare Purchasing Alliance (HPA) corporation. The new alliance saved the HPA members $7 million in its first year with two main changes. First, it was structured and staffed to ensure that the bulk of the savings associated with its contracting efforts went to its eight members. Second, it struck even better deals with vendors by guaranteeing a *committed* volume and signing not 1-year deals but 3- to 5-year contracts. "Even with a new internal cost of $400,000 to run HPA, the savings and ability to contract for what our member hospitals really want makes the deal a winner," says George DeLong, head of HPA.

Effective supply chain management in manufacturing often focuses on development of new product innovations and efficiency through buyer–vendor collaboration. However, the approach in a service industry has a slightly different emphasis. At Arnold Palmer Hospital, supply chain opportunities often manifest themselves through the Medical Economic Outcomes Committee. This committee (and its subcommittees) consists of users (including the medical and nursing staff) who evaluate purchase options with a goal of better medicine while achieving economic targets. For instance, the heart pacemaker negotiation by the cardiology subcommittee allowed for the standardization to two manufacturers, with annual savings of $2 million for just this one product.

Arnold Palmer Hospital is also able to develop custom products that require collaboration down to the third tier of the supply chain. This is the case with custom packs that are used in the operating room. The custom packs are delivered by a distributor, McKesson General Medical, but assembled by a pack company that uses materials the hospital wanted purchased from specific manufacturers. The HPA allows Arnold Palmer Hospital to be creative in this way. With major cost savings, standardization, blanket purchase orders, long-term contracts, and more control of product development, the benefits to the hospital are substantial.

Discussion Questions*

1. How does this supply chain differ from that in a manufacturing firm?
2. What are the constraints on making decisions based on economics alone at Arnold Palmer Hospital?
3. What role do doctors and nurses play in supply chain decisions in a hospital? How is this participation handled at Arnold Palmer Hospital?
4. Doctor Smith just returned from the Annual Physician's Orthopedic Conference, where she saw a new hip joint replacement demonstrated. She decides she wants to start using the replacement joint at Arnold Palmer Hospital. What process will Dr. Smith have to go through at the hospital to introduce this new product into the supply chain for future surgical use?

*You may wish to view the video that accompanies this case before answering these questions.

Endnote

1. Inventory quantities often fluctuate wildly, and various types of inventory exist (e.g., raw material; work-in-process; finished goods; and maintenance, repair, and operating supplies [MRO]). Therefore, care must be taken when using inventory values; they may reflect more than just supply chain performance.

Main Heading	Review Material	MyOMLab
THE SUPPLY CHAIN'S STRATEGIC IMPORTANCE (pp. 444–446)	Most firms spend a huge portion of their sales dollars on purchases. ■ **Supply chain management**—Management of activities related to procuring materials and services, transforming them into intermediate goods and final products, and delivering them through a distribution system. *The objective is to build a chain of suppliers that focuses on maximizing value to the ultimate customer.* Competition is no longer between companies; it is between supply chains.	Concept Questions: 1.1–1.4 Problems: 11.2–11.3 **VIDEO 11.1** Darden's Global Supply Chain
SOURCING ISSUES: MAKE-OR-BUY AND OUTSOURCING (pp. 446–447)	■ **Make-or-buy decision**—A choice between producing a component or service within the firm or purchasing it from an outside source. ■ **Outsourcing**—Transferring to external suppliers a firm's activities that have traditionally been internal.	Concept Questions: 2.1–2.4
SIX SOURCING STRATEGIES (pp. 447–449)	Six supply chain strategies for goods and services to be obtained from outside sources are: 1. Negotiating with many suppliers and playing one supplier against another 2. Developing long-term partnering relationships with a few suppliers 3. Vertical integration 4. Joint ventures 5. Developing *keiretsu* networks 6. Developing virtual companies that use suppliers on an as-needed basis. ■ **Vertical integration**—Developing the ability to produce goods or services previously purchased or actually buying a supplier or a distributor. ■ *Keiretsu*—A Japanese term that describes suppliers who become part of a company coalition. ■ **Virtual companies**—Companies that rely on a variety of supplier relationships to provide services on demand. Also known as hollow corporations or network companies.	Concept Questions: 3.1–3.4 **VIDEO 11.2** Supply Chain Management at Regal Marine
SUPPLY CHAIN RISK (pp. 449–451)	The development of a supply chain plan requires a thorough assessment of the risks involved. ■ **Cross-sourcing**—Using one supplier for a component and a second supplier for another component, where each supplier acts as a backup for the other.	Concept Questions: 4.1–4.4
MANAGING THE INTEGRATED SUPPLY CHAIN (pp. 451–454)	Supply chain integration success begins with mutual agreement on goals, followed by mutual trust, and continues with compatible organizational cultures. Three issues complicate the development of an efficient, integrated supply chain: local optimization, incentives, and large lots. ■ **Bullwhip effect**—Increasing fluctuation in orders or cancellations that often occurs as orders move through the supply chain. ■ **Pull data**—Accurate sales data that initiate transactions to "pull" product through the supply chain. ■ **Single-stage control of replenishment**—Fixing responsibility for monitoring and managing inventory for the retailer. ■ **Vendor-managed inventory (VMI)**—A system in which a supplier maintains material for the buyer, often delivering directly to the buyer's using department. ■ **Collaborative planning, forecasting, and replenishment (CPFR)**—A system in which members of a supply chain share information in a joint effort to reduce supply chain costs. ■ **Blanket order**—A long-term purchase commitment to a supplier for items that are to be delivered against short-term releases to ship. The purchasing department should make special efforts to increase levels of standardization. ■ **Postponement**—Delaying any modifications or customization to a product as long as possible in the production process. Postponement strives to minimize internal variety while maximizing external variety. ■ **Drop shipping**—Shipping directly from the supplier to the end consumer rather than from the seller, saving both time and reshipping costs. Online catalogs move companies from a multitude of individual phone calls, faxes, and e-mails to a centralized online system and drive billions of dollars of waste out of the supply chain.	Concept Questions: 5.1–5.4 **VIDEO 11.3** Arnold Palmer Hospital's Supply Chain
BUILDING THE SUPPLY BASE (pp. 454–456)	Supplier selection is a four-stage process: (1) supplier evaluation, (2) supplier development, (3) negotiations, and (4) contracting. *Supplier evaluation* involves finding potential vendors and determining the likelihood of their becoming good suppliers. *Supplier development* may include everything from training, to engineering and production help, to procedures for information transfer.	Concept Questions: 6.1–6.4

Main Heading	Review Material	MyOMLab
	Negotiations involve approaches taken by supply chain personnel to set prices. Three classic types of negotiation strategies are (1) the cost-based price model, (2) the market-based price model, and (3) competitive bidding. *Contracting* involves a design to share risks, share benefits, and create incentives so as to optimize the whole supply chain. ■ **E-procurement**—Purchasing facilitated through the Internet.	
LOGISTICS MANAGEMENT (pp. 456–459)	■ **Logistics management**—An approach that seeks efficiency of operations through the integration of all material acquisition, movement, and storage activities. Six major means of distribution are trucking, railroads, airfreight, waterways, pipelines, and multimodal. The vast majority of manufactured goods move by truck. Third-party logistics involves the outsourcing of the logistics function. ■ **Channel assembly**—A system that postpones final assembly of a product so the distribution channel can assemble it.	Concept Questions: 7.1–7.4
DISTRIBUTION MANAGEMENT (p. 459)	Distribution management focused on the outbound flow of final products. Total logistics costs are the sum of facility costs, inventory costs, and transportation costs (Figure 11.3). The optimal number of distribution facilities focuses on maximizing profit.	Concept Questions: 8.1–8.4
ETHICS AND SUS-TAINABLE SUPPLY CHAIN MANAGEMENT (pp. 460–461)	Ethics includes personal ethics, ethics within the supply chain, and ethical behavior regarding the environment. The Institute for Supply Management has developed a set of Principles and Standards for ethical conduct. ■ **Reverse logistics**—The process of sending returned products back up the supply chain for value recovery or disposal. ■ **Closed-loop supply chain**—A supply chain designed to optimize all forward and reverse flows.	Concept Questions: 9.1–9.4
MEASURING SUPPLY CHAIN PERFORMANCE (pp. 461–464)	Typical supply chain benchmark metrics include lead time, time spent placing an order, percent of late deliveries, percent of rejected material, and number of shortages per year: Percent invested in inventory = (Average inventory investment/Total assets) × 100 (11-1) ■ **Inventory turnover**—Cost of goods sold divided by average inventory: Inventory turnover = Cost of goods sold ÷ Average inventory investment (11-2) Weeks of supply = Average inventory investment ÷ (Annual cost of goods sold/52 weeks) (11-3) ■ **Supply Chain Operations Reference (SCOR) model**—A set of processes, metrics, and best practices developed by the APICS Supply Chain Council. The five parts of the SCOR model are Plan, Source, Make, Deliver, and Return.	Concept Questions: 10.1–10.4 Problems: 11.5–11.8 Virtual Office Hours for Solved Problem: 11.1

Self Test

■ **Before taking the self-test,** refer to the learning objectives listed at the beginning of the chapter and the key terms listed at the end of the chapter.

LO 11.1 The objective of supply chain management is to _____.

LO 11.2 The term *vertical integration* means to:
   a) develop the ability to produce products that complement or supplement the original product.
   b) produce goods or services previously purchased.
   c) develop the ability to produce the specified good more efficiently.
   d) all of the above.

LO 11.3 The bullwhip effect can be aggravated by:
   a) local optimization.
   b) sales incentives.
   c) quantity discounts.
   d) promotions.
   e) all of the above.

LO 11.4 Supplier selection requires:
   a) supplier evaluation and effective third-party logistics.
   b) supplier development and logistics.

   c) negotiations, supplier evaluation, supplier development, and contracts.
   d) an integrated supply chain.
   e) inventory and supply chain management.

LO 11.5 A major issue in logistics is:
   a) cost of purchases.
   b) supplier evaluation.
   c) product customization.
   d) cost of shipping alternatives.
   e) excellent e-procurement.

LO 11.6 Inventory turnover =
   a) Cost of goods sold ÷ Weeks of supply
   b) Weeks of supply ÷ Annual cost of goods sold
   c) Annual cost of goods sold ÷ 52 weeks
   d) Average inventory investment ÷ Cost of goods sold
   e) Cost of goods sold ÷ Average inventory investment

Answers: LO 11.1. build a chain of suppliers that focuses on maximizing value to the ultimate customer; LO 11.2. b; LO 11.3. e; LO 11.4. c; LO 11.5. d; LO 11.6. e.

Supply Chain Management Analytics

SUPPLEMENT OUTLINE

◆ Techniques for Evaluating Supply Chains *472*

◆ Evaluating Disaster Risk in the Supply Chain *472*

◆ Managing the Bullwhip Effect *474*

◆ Supplier Selection Analysis *476*

◆ Transportation Mode Analysis *477*

◆ Warehouse Storage *478*

Alaska Airlines

LEARNING OBJECTIVES

LO S11.1 *Use* a decision tree to determine the best number of suppliers to manage disaster risk 472

LO S11.2 *Explain* and measure the bullwhip effect 475

LO S11.3 *Describe* the factor-weighting approach to supplier evaluation 477

LO S11.4 *Evaluate* cost-of-shipping alternatives 478

LO S11.5 *Allocate* items to storage locations in a warehouse 479

The 2011 Tōhoku earthquake and tsunami devastated eastern sections of Japan. The economic impact was felt around the globe, as manufacturers had been relying heavily—in some cases exclusively—on suppliers located in the affected zones. In the month immediately following the earthquake, the Japanese-built vehicle outputs for both Toyota and Honda were down 63%. Plants in other countries ceased or reduced operations due to part shortages. Manufacturers in several industries worldwide took 6 months or longer before they saw their supply chains working normally again. Although disasters such as this one occur relatively infrequently, supply chain managers should consider their probabilities and repercussions when determining the makeup of the supply base.

mTaira/Shutterstock

Techniques for Evaluating Supply Chains

Many supply chain metrics exist that can be used to evaluate performance within a company as well as for its supply chain partners. This supplement introduces five techniques that are aimed at ways to build and evaluate performance of the supply chain.

Evaluating Disaster Risk in the Supply Chain

Disasters that disrupt supply chains can take many forms, including tornadoes, fires, hurricanes, typhoons, tsunamis, earthquakes, and terrorism. When you are deciding whether to purchase collision insurance for your car, the amount of insurance must be weighed against the probability of a minor accident occurring and the potential financial worst-case scenario if an accident happens (e.g., "totaling" of the car). Similarly, firms often use multiple suppliers for important components to mitigate the risks of total supply disruption.

LO S11.1 *Use* a decision tree to determine the best number of suppliers to manage disaster risk

As shown in Example S1, a decision tree can be used to help operations managers make this important decision regarding the number of suppliers. We will use the following notation for a given supply cycle:

S = the probability of a "super-event" that would disrupt *all* suppliers simultaneously

U = the probability of a "unique-event" that would disrupt only one supplier

L = the financial loss incurred in a supply cycle if *all* suppliers were disrupted

C = the marginal cost of managing a supplier

All suppliers will be disrupted simultaneously if either the super-event occurs or the super-event does not occur but a unique-event occurs for all of the suppliers. Assuming that the probabilities are all independent of each other, the probability of all n suppliers being disrupted simultaneously equals:

$$P(n) = S + (1 - S)U^n \tag{S11-1}$$

Example S1

HOW MANY SUPPLIERS ARE BEST FOR MANAGING RISK?

Xiaotian Geng, president of Shanghai Manufacturing Corp., wants to create a portfolio of suppliers for the motors used in her company's products that will represent a reasonable balance between costs and risks. While she knows that the single-supplier approach has many potential benefits with respect to quality management and just-in-time production, she also worries about the risk of fires, natural disasters, or other catastrophes at supplier plants disrupting her firm's performance. Based on historical data and climate and geological forecasts, Xiaotian estimates the probability of a "super-event" that would negatively impact all suppliers simultaneously to be 0.5% (i.e., probability = 0.005) during the supply cycle. She further estimates the "unique-event" risk for any of the potential suppliers to be 4% (probability = .04). Assuming that the marginal cost of managing an additional supplier is $10,000, and the financial loss incurred if a disaster caused all suppliers to be down simultaneously is $10,000,000, how many suppliers should Xiaotian use? Assume that up to three nearly identical suppliers are available.

APPROACH ▶ Use of a decision tree seems appropriate, as Shanghai Manufacturing Corp. has the basic data: a choice of decisions, probabilities, and payoffs (costs).

SOLUTION ▶ We draw a decision tree (Figure S11.1) with a branch for each of the three decisions (one, two, or three suppliers), assign the respective probabilities [using Equation (S11-1)] and payoffs for each branch, and then compute the respective expected monetary values (EMVs). The EMVs have been identified at each step of the decision tree.

Using Equation (S11-1), the probability of a total disruption equals:

One supplier: $0.005 + (1 - 0.005)0.04 = 0.005 + 0.0398 = 0.044800$, or 4.4800%

Two suppliers: $0.005 + (1 - 0.005)0.04^2 = 0.005 + 0.001592 = 0.006592$, or 0.6592%

Three suppliers: $0.005 + (1 - 0.005)0.04^3 = 0.005 + 0.000064 = 0.005064$, or 0.5064%

INSIGHT ▶ Even with significant supplier management costs and unlikely probabilities of disaster, a large enough financial loss incurred during a total supplier shutdown will suggest that multiple suppliers may be needed.

Figure **S11.1**

Decision Tree for Selection of Suppliers Under Risk

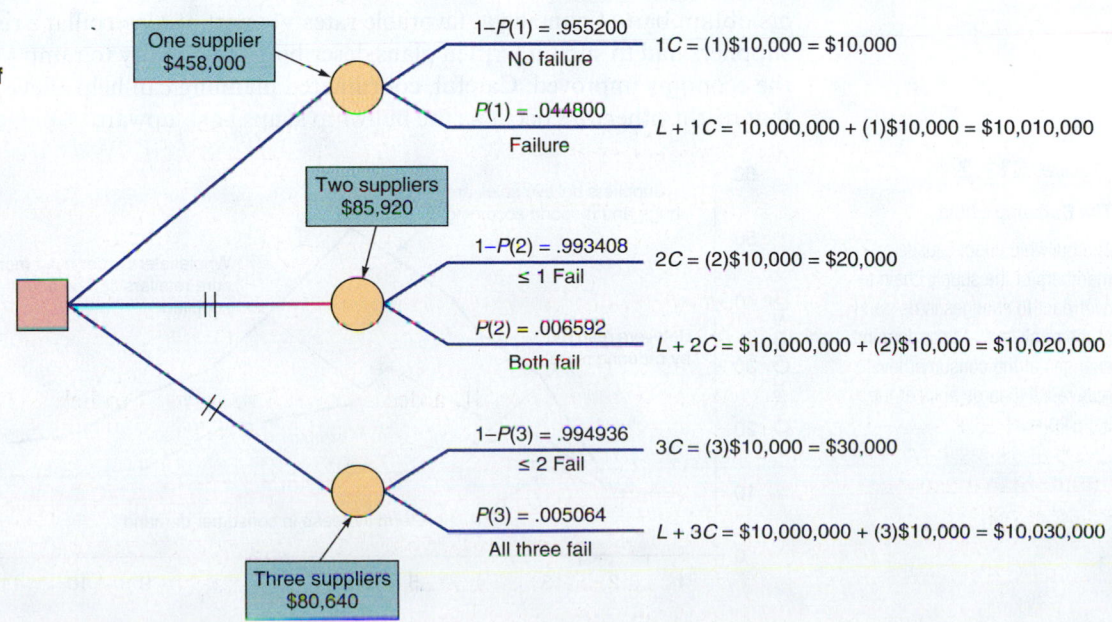

LEARNING EXERCISE ▶ Suppose that the probability of a super-event increases to 50%. How many suppliers are needed now? [Answer: 2.] Using the 50% probability of a super-event, suppose that the financial loss of a complete supplier shutdown drops to $500,000. Now how many suppliers are needed? [Answer: 1.]

RELATED PROBLEMS ▶ S11.1, S11.2, S11.3, S11.4, S11.5

An interesting implication of Equation (S11-1) is that as the probability of a super-event (S) increases, the advantage of utilizing multiple suppliers diminishes (all would be knocked out anyway). On the other hand, large values of the unique event (U) increase the likelihood of needing more suppliers. These two phenomena taken together suggest that when multiple suppliers are used, managers may consider using ones that are geographically dispersed to lessen the probability of all failing simultaneously.

Managing the Bullwhip Effect

Figure S11.2 provides an example of the *bullwhip effect*, which describes the tendency for larger order size fluctuations as orders are relayed to the supply chain from retailers. "Bullwhip" fluctuations create unstable production schedules, resulting in expensive capacity change adjustments such as overtime, subcontracting, extra inventory, backorders, hiring and laying off of workers, equipment additions, underutilization, longer lead times, or obsolescence of overproduced items.

Procter & Gamble found that although the use of Pampers diapers was steady and the retail-store orders had little fluctuation, as orders moved through the supply chain, fluctuations increased. By the time orders were initiated for raw material, the variability was substantial. Similar behavior has been observed and documented at many companies, including Campbell Soup, Hewlett-Packard, Barilla SpA, and Applied Materials.

The bullwhip effect can occur when orders decrease as well as when they increase. Table S11.1 identifies some of the major causes and remedies of the bullwhip effect. Often the human tendency to overreact to stimuli causes managers to make decisions that exacerbate the phenomenon. The overarching solution to the bullwhip effect is simply for supply-chain members to share information and work together, as in the *OM in Action* box "RFID Helps Control the Bullwhip."

Supplier coordination can help with demand shifts. During the recent worldwide recession, but prior to experiencing the economic recovery and increasing sales, Caterpillar started ordering more supplies. It also worked proactively with its suppliers to prepare them for a sharp increase in output. Caterpillar visited key suppliers individually. In some cases it helped suppliers obtain bank financing at favorable rates. As part of Caterpillar's risk assessment activities, suppliers had to submit written plans describing their ability to ramp production back up once the economy improved. Careful, coordinated planning can help alleviate shortages and delays that might otherwise occur as the bullwhip snaps back upward.

Figure **S11.2**

The Bullwhip Effect

The bullwhip effect causes members of the supply chain to overreact to changes in demand at the retail level. Minor demand changes at the consumer level may result in large ones at the supplier level.

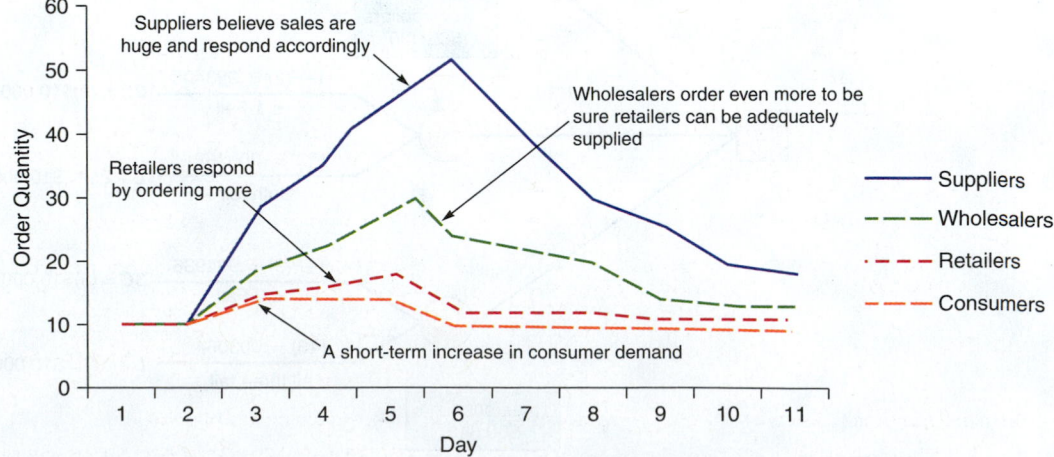

TABLE S11.1 | **The Bullwhip Effect**

CAUSE	REMEDY
Demand forecast errors (cumulative uncertainty in the supply chain)	Share demand information throughout the supply chain.
Order batching (large, infrequent orders leading suppliers to order even larger amounts)	Channel coordination: Determine lot sizes as though the full supply chain was one company.
Price fluctuations (buying in advance of demand to take advantage of low prices, discounts, or sales)	Price stabilization (everyday low prices).
Shortage gaming (hoarding supplies for fear of a supply shortage)	Allocate orders based on past demand.

A Bullwhip Effect Measure

A straightforward way to analyze the extent of the bullwhip effect at any link in the supply chain is to calculate the *bullwhip measure*:

$$\text{Bullwhip} = \frac{\text{Variance of orders}}{\text{Variance of demand}} = \frac{\sigma^2_{\text{orders}}}{\sigma^2_{\text{demand}}} \tag{S11-2}$$

LO S11.2 *Explain and measure the bullwhip effect*

Variance *amplification* (i.e., the bullwhip effect) is present if the bullwhip measure is greater than 1. This means the size of a company's orders fluctuate more than the size of its incoming demand. If the measure equals 1, then no amplification is present. A value less than 1 would imply a *smoothing* or *dampening* scenario as orders move up the supply chain toward suppliers. Example S2 illustrates how to use Equation (S11-2) to analyze the extent of the bullwhip effect at each stage in the supply chain.

OM in Action   RFID Helps Control the Bullwhip

Supply chains work smoothly when sales are steady, but often break down when confronted by a sudden surge or rapid drop in demand. Radio frequency ID (RFID) tags can change that by providing real-time information about what's happening on store shelves. Here's how the system works for Procter & Gamble's (P&G's) Pampers.

1. A special promotion causes Walmart shoppers to snap up boxes of Pampers Baby-Dry.

2. Each box of Pampers has an RFID tag. Shelf-mounted scanners alert the stockroom of urgent need for restock.

3. Walmart's inventory management system tracks and links its in-store stock and its warehouse stock, prompting quicker replenishment and providing accurate real-time data.

4. Walmart's systems are linked to the P&G supply-chain management system. Demand spikes reported by RFID tags are immediately visible throughout the supply chain.

5. P&G's logistics software tracks its trucks with GPS locators, and tracks their contents with RFID tag readers. Regional managers can reroute trucks to fill urgent needs.

6. P&G suppliers also use RFID tags and readers on their raw materials, giving P&G visibility several tiers down the supply chain, and giving suppliers the ability to accurately forecast demand and production.

Sources: Supply Chain Digest (July 21, 2012); Arkansas Business (July 2, 2012); and Business 2.0 (May 2002).

The U.S. *Cash for Clunkers* program produced an unintended bullwhip effect in the automobile industry. In an effort to stimulate the economy and improve fuel efficiency, the U.S. offered attractive rebates for trading old cars in exchange for new, more fuel-efficient vehicles. The $3 billion, 8-week program proved to be very popular with consumers. Fearing a shortage and assuming that they would not receive 100% of their orders, some dealers inflated orders for new cars to try to receive a larger pool of allocated vehicles. In one month, *Cash for Clunkers* increased demand by 50% for automakers, many of whom had already cut capacity significantly. Almost overnight, manufacturers and parts suppliers had to transform from a shift reduction mode to an overtime mode.

Paul Brennan/Shutterstock

Example S2

CALCULATING THE BULLWHIP EFFECT

Chieh Lee Metals, Inc. orders sheet metal and transforms it into 50 formed tabletops that are sold to furniture manufacturers. The table below shows the weekly variance of demand and orders for each major company in this supply chain for tables. Each firm has one supplier and one customer, so the order variance for one firm will equal the demand variance for its supplier. Analyze the relative contributions to the bullwhip effect in this supply chain.

FIRM	VARIANCE OF DEMAND	VARIANCE OF ORDERS	BULLWHIP MEASURE
Furniture Mart, Inc.	100	110	110/100 = 1.10
Furniture Distributors, Inc.	110	180	180/110 = 1.64
Furniture Makers of America	180	300	300/180 = 1.67
Chieh Lee Metals, Inc.	300	750	750/300 = 2.50
Metal Suppliers Ltd.	750	2000	2000/750 = 2.67

APPROACH ▶ Use Equation (S11-2) to calculate the bullwhip measure for each firm in the chain.

SOLUTION ▶ The last column of the table displays the bullwhip measure for each firm.

INSIGHT ▶ This supply chain exhibits a classic bullwhip effect. Despite what might be a very stable demand pattern at the retail level, order sizes to suppliers vary significantly. Chieh Lee should attempt to identifiy the causes for her own firm's order amplification, and she should attempt to work with her supply chain partners to try to reduce amplification at every level of the chain.

LEARNING EXERCISE ▶ Suppose that Chieh Lee is able to reduce her bullwhip measure from 2.50 to 1.20. If the measure for all other firms remained the same, what would be the new reduced variance of orders from Metal Suppliers? [Answer: 961.]

RELATED PROBLEMS ▶ S11.6, S11.7, S11.8, S11.9

Supplier Selection Analysis

Selecting suppliers from among a multitude of candidates can be a daunting task. Choosing suppliers simply based on the lowest bid has become a somewhat rare approach. Various, sometimes competing, factors often play a role in the decision. Buyers may consider such supplier characteristics as product quality, delivery speed, delivery reliability, customer service, and financial performance.

The *factor-weighting* technique, presented here, simultaneously considers multiple supplier criteria. Each factor must be assigned an importance *weight,* and then each potential supplier is *scored* on each factor. The weights typically sum to 100%. Factors are scored using the same scale (e.g., 1–10). Sometimes a key is provided for supplier raters that converts qualitative ratings into numerical scores (e.g., "Very good" = 8). Example S3 illustrates the weighted criteria in comparing two competing suppliers.

LO S11.3 *Describe the factor-weighting approach to supplier evaluation*

Example S3

FACTOR-WEIGHTING APPROACH TO SUPPLIER EVALUATION

Erick Davis, president of Creative Toys in Palo Alto, California, is interested in evaluating suppliers who will work with him to make nontoxic, environmentally friendly paints and dyes for his line of children's toys. This is a critical strategic element of his supply chain, and he desires a firm that will contribute to his product.

APPROACH ▶ Erick has narrowed his choices to two suppliers: Faber Paint and Smith Dye. He will use the factor-weighting approach to supplier evaluation to compare the two.

SOLUTION ▶ Erick develops the following list of selection criteria. He then assigns the weights shown to help him perform an objective review of potential suppliers. His staff assigns the scores and computes the total weighted score.

CRITERION	WEIGHT	FABER PAINT SCORE (1–5) (5 HIGHEST)	FABER PAINT WEIGHT × SCORE	SMITH DYE SCORE (1–5) (5 HIGHEST)	SMITH DYE WEIGHT × SCORE
Engineering/innovation skills	.20	5	1.0	5	1.0
Production process capability	.15	4	0.6	5	0.75
Distribution capability	.05	4	0.2	3	0.15
Quality performance	.10	2	0.2	3	0.3
Facilities/location	.05	2	0.1	3	0.15
Financial strength	.15	4	0.6	5	0.75
Information systems	.10	2	0.2	5	0.5
Integrity	.20	5	1.0	3	0.6
Total	1.00		3.9		4.2

Smith Dye received the higher score of 4.2 and, based on this analysis, would be the preferred vendor.

INSIGHT ▶ The use of a factor-weighting approach can help firms systematically identify the features that are important to them and evaluate potential suppliers in an objective manner. A certain degree of subjectivity remains in the process, however, with regard to the criteria chosen, the weights applied to those criteria, and the supplier scores that are applied to each criterion.

LEARNING EXERCISE ▶ If Erick believes that integrity should be twice as important while production process capability and financial strength should both only be 1/3 as important, how does the analysis change? [Answer: Faber Paint's score becomes 4.1, while Smith Dye's score becomes 3.8, so Faber Paint is now the preferred vendor.]

RELATED PROBLEMS ▶ S11.10, S11.11, S11.12 (S11.13 is available in MyOMLab)

Transportation Mode Analysis

The longer a product is in transit, the longer the firm has its money invested. But faster shipping is usually more expensive than slow shipping. A simple way to obtain some insight into this trade-off is to evaluate holding cost against shipping options. We do this in Example S4.

Example S4

DETERMINING DAILY COST OF HOLDING

A shipment of new connectors for semiconductors needs to go from San Jose to Singapore for assembly. The value of the connectors is $1,750, and holding cost is 40% per year. One airfreight carrier can ship the connectors 1 day faster than its competitor, at an extra cost of $20.00. Which carrier should be selected?

APPROACH ▶ First we determine the daily holding cost and then compare the daily holding cost with the cost of faster shipment.

SOLUTION ▶ Daily cost of holding the product = (Annual holding cost × Product value)/365

$$= (.40 × \$1,750)/365$$

$$= \$1.92$$

LO S11.4 *Evaluate* cost-of-shipping alternatives

Because the cost of saving one day is $20.00, which is much more than the daily holding cost of $1.92, we decide on the less costly of the carriers and take the extra day to make the shipment. This saves $18.08 ($20.00 − $1.92).

INSIGHT ▶ The solution becomes radically different if the 1-day delay in getting the connectors to Singapore delays delivery (making a customer angry) or delays payment of a $150,000 final product. (Even 1 day's interest on $150,000 or an angry customer makes a savings of $18.08 insignificant.)

LEARNING EXERCISE ▶ If the holding cost is 100% per year, what is the decision? [Answer: Even with a holding cost of $4.79 per day, the less costly carrier is selected.]

RELATED PROBLEMS ▶ S11.14, S11.15, S11.16, S11.17

Example S4 looks only at holding cost versus shipping cost. For the operations or logistics manager there are many other considerations, including ensuring *on-time delivery*, coordinating shipments to maintain a schedule, getting a new product to market, and keeping a customer happy. Estimates of these other costs can be added to the estimate of the daily holding cost. Determining the impact and cost of these considerations makes the evaluation of shipping alternatives a challenging OM task.

Warehouse Storage

Storage represents a significant step for many items as they travel through their respective supply chains. The U.S. alone has more than 13,000 buildings dedicated to warehouse and storage. Some exceed the size of several connected football fields. In fact, more than 35% have over 100,000 square feet of floor space.

Care should be taken when determining which items to store in various locations in a warehouse. In large warehouses in particular, hundreds or thousands of trips are made each day along very long aisles. Proper placement of items can improve efficiency by shaving significant travel time for workers. In Example S5, we observe a simple way to determine storage locations in a warehouse.

Example S5

DETERMINING STORAGE LOCATIONS IN A WAREHOUSE

Erika Marsillac manages a warehouse for a local chain of specialty hardware stores. As seen in Figure S11.3, the single-aisle rectangular warehouse has a dock for pickup and delivery, along with 16 equal-sized storage blocks for inventory items.

Figure S11.3

Storage Locations in the Warehouse

The following table shows: (1) the category of each item stored in the warehouse, (2) the estimated number of times per month (trips) that workers need to either store or retrieve those items, and (3) the area (number of specialized blocks) required to store the items. Erika wishes to assign items to the storage blocks to minimize average distance traveled.

ITEM	MONTHLY TRIPS TO STORAGE	BLOCKS OF STORAGE SPACE NEEDED
Lumber	600	5
Paint	260	2
Tools	150	3
Small hardware	400	2
Chemical bags	90	3
Lightbulbs	220	1

LO S11.5 *Allocate items to storage locations in a warehouse*

APPROACH ▶ For each item, calculate the ratio of the number of trips to blocks of storage area needed. Rank the items according to this ratio, and place the *highest*-ranked items closest to the dock.

SOLUTION ▶ The following table calculates the ratio for each item and ranks the items from highest to lowest. Based on the ranking, items are assigned to the remaining blocks that are as close to the dock as possible. (Where applicable, given a choice between two equidistant blocks, items should be placed next to items of the same type rather than across the aisle from them.)

ITEM	TRIPS/BLOCKS	RANKING	ASSIGNED BLOCKS
Lumber	600/5 = 120	4	6, 7, 8, 9, 10
Paint	260/2 = 130	3	3, 5
Tools	150/3 = 50	5	11, 12, 13
Small hardware	400/2 = 200	2	2, 4
Chemical bags	90/3 = 30	6	14, 15, 16
Lightbulbs	220/1 = 220	1	1

INSIGHT ▶ This procedure allocates items with the highest "bang-for-the-buck" first. The "bang" (value) here is the number of trips. Because we want to minimize travel, we would like to place items with high-frequency visits near the front. The storage space represents the "buck" (cost). We want items that take up a lot of space moved toward the back because if they were placed near the front, we would have to travel past their multiple blocks every time we needed to store or retrieve an item from a different category. This bang versus buck trade-off is neatly accommodated by using the trips/blocks ratio (column 2 of the solution table). In this example, even though lumber has the highest number of trips, the lumber takes up so much storage space that it is placed further back, toward the middle of the warehouse.

LEARNING EXERCISE ▶ Order frequency for paint is expected to increase to 410 trips per month. How will that change the storage plan? [Answer: Paint and small hardware will switch storage locations.]

RELATED PROBLEMS ▶ S11.18, S11.19, S11.20

Summary

Myriad tools have been developed to help supply-chain managers make well-informed decisions. We have provided a small sampling in this supplement. A decision tree can help determine the best number of suppliers to protect against supply disruption from potential disasters. The bullwhip measure can identify each supply chain member's contribution to exacerbating ordering fluctuations.

The factor-weighting approach can be used to help select suppliers based on multiple criteria. Inventory holding costs can be computed for various shipping alternatives to better compare their overall cost impact. Finally, items can be ranked according to the ratio of (trips/blocks of storage) to determine their best placement in a warehouse.

Discussion Questions

1. What is the difference between "unique-event" risk and "super-event" risk?
2. If the probability of a "super-event" increases, does the "unique-event" risk increase or decrease in importance? Why?
3. If the probability of a "super-event" decreases, what happens to the likelihood of needing multiple suppliers?
4. Describe some ramifications of the bullwhip effect.
5. Describe causes of the bullwhip effect and their associated remedies.
6. Describe how the bullwhip measure can be used to analyze supply chains.
7. Describe some potentially useful categories to include in a factor-weighting analysis for supplier selection.
8. Describe some potential pitfalls in relying solely on the results of a factor-weighting analysis for supplier selection.
9. Describe some disadvantages of using a slow shipping method.
10. Besides warehouse layout decisions, what are some other applications where ranking items according to "bang/buck" might make sense?

Solved Problems   Virtual Office Hours help is available in MyOMLab.

SOLVED PROBLEM S11.1

Jon Jackson Manufacturing is searching for suppliers for its new line of equipment. Jon has narrowed his choices to two sets of suppliers. Believing in diversification of risk, Jon would select two suppliers under each choice. However, he is still concerned about the risk of both suppliers failing at the same time. The "San Francisco option" uses both suppliers in San Francisco. Both are stable, reliable, and profitable firms, so Jon calculates the "unique-event" risk for either of them to be 0.5%. However, because San Francisco is in an earthquake zone, he estimates the probability of an event that would knock out both suppliers to be 2%. The "North American option" uses one supplier in Canada and another in Mexico. These are upstart firms; John calculates the "unique-event" risk for either of them to be 10%. But he estimates the "super-event" probability that would knock out both of these suppliers to be only 0.1%. Purchasing costs would be $500,000 per year using the San Francisco option and $510,000 per year using the North American option. A total disruption would create an annualized loss of $800,000. Which option seems best?

SOLUTION

Using Equation (S11-1), the probability of a total disruption (i.e., the probability of incurring the $800,000 loss) equals:

$$\text{San Francisco option: } 0.02 + (1 - 0.02)0.005^2 = 0.02 + 0.0000245 = 0.0200245, \text{ or } 2.00245\%$$

$$\text{North American option: } 0.001 + (1 - 0.001)0.1^2 = 0.001 + 0.0099 = 0.01099, \text{ or } 1.099\%$$

$$\text{Total annual expected costs} = \text{Annual purchasing costs} + \text{Expected annualized disruption costs}$$

$$\text{San Francisco option: } \$500,000 + \$800,000(0.0200245) = \$500,000 + \$16,020 = \$516,020$$

$$\text{North American option: } \$510,000 + \$800,000(0.01099) = \$510,000 + \$8,792 = \$518,792$$

In this case, the San Francisco option appears to be slightly cheaper.

SOLVED PROBLEM S11.2

Over the past 10 weeks, demand for gears at Michael's Metals has been 140, 230, 100, 175, 165, 220, 200, and 178. Michael has placed weekly orders of 140, 250, 90, 190, 140, 240, 190, and 168 units.

The sample variance of a data set can be found by using the VAR.S function in Excel or by plugging each value (x) of the data set into the formula: $\text{Variance} = \dfrac{\Sigma(x - \bar{x})^2}{(n - 1)}$, where $\bar{x}$ is the mean of the data set and n is the number of values in the set. Using Equation (S11-2), calculate the bullwhip measure for Michael's Metals over the 10-week period.

SOLUTION

Mean demand $= (140 + 230 + 100 + 175 + 165 + 220 + 200 + 178)/8 = 1,408/8 = 176$

Variance of demand

$$= \frac{(140 - 176)^2 + (230 - 176)^2 + (100 - 176)^2 + (175 - 176)^2 + (165 - 176)^2 + (220 - 176)^2 + (200 - 176)^2 + (178 - 176)^2}{(8 - 1)}$$

$$= \frac{36^2 + 54^2 + 76^2 + 1^2 + 11^2 + 44^2 + 24^2 + 2^2}{7} = \frac{1,296 + 2,916 + 5,776 + 1 + 121 + 1,936 + 576 + 4}{7}$$

$$= \frac{12,626}{7} = 1,804$$

Mean orders $= (140 + 250 + 90 + 190 + 140 + 240 + 190 + 168)/8 = 1,408/8 = 176$

Variance of orders

$$= \frac{(140 - 176)^2 + (250 - 176)^2 + (90 - 176)^2 + (190 - 176)^2 + (140 - 176)^2 + (240 - 176)^2 + (190 - 176)^2 + (168 - 176)^2}{(8 - 1)}$$

$$= \frac{36^2 + 74^2 + 86^2 + 14^2 + 36^2 + 64^2 + 14^2 + 8^2}{7} = \frac{1,296 + 5,476 + 7,396 + 196 + 1,296 + 4,096 + 196 + 64}{7}$$

$$= \frac{20,016}{7} = 2,859$$

From Equation (S11-2), the bullwhip measure = 2,859/1,804 = 1.58.
Since 1.58 > 1, Michael's Metals is contributing to the bullwhip effect in its supply chain.

SOLVED PROBLEM S11.3

Victor Pimentel, purchasing manager of Office Supply Center of Mexico, is searching for a new supplier for its paper. The most important supplier criteria for Victor include paper quality, delivery reliability, customer service, and financial condition, and he believes that paper quality is twice as important as each of the other three criteria. Victor has narrowed the choice to two suppliers, and his staff has rated each supplier on each criterion (using a scale of 1 to 100, with 100 being highest), as shown in the following table:

	PAPER QUALITY	DELIVERY RELIABILITY	CUSTOMER SERVICE	FINANCIAL CONDITION
Monterrey Paper	85	70	65	80
Papel Grande	80	90	95	75

Use the factor-weighting approach to determine the best supplier choice.

SOLUTION

To determine the appropriate weights for each category, create a simple algebraic relationship:

Let x = weight for criteria 2, 3, and 4.
Then $2x + x + x + x = 100\%$, i.e., $5x = 100\%$, or $x = 0.2 = 20\%$

Thus, paper quality has a weight of 2(20%) = 40%, and the other three criteria each have a weight of 20%.

The following table presents the factor-weighting analysis:

CRITERION	WEIGHT	MONTERREY PAPER SCORE (1–100) (100 HIGHEST)	MONTERREY PAPER WEIGHT × SCORE	PAPEL GRANDE SCORE (1–100) (100 HIGHEST)	PAPEL GRANDE WEIGHT × SCORE
Paper quality	.40	85	34	80	32
Delivery reliability	.20	70	14	90	18
Customer service	.20	65	13	95	19
Financial condition	.20	80	16	75	15
Total	1.00		77		84

Since 84 > 77, Papel Grande should be the chosen supplier according to the factor-weighting method.

SOLVED PROBLEM S11.4

A French car company ships 120,000 cars annually to the United Kingdom. The current method of shipment uses ferries to cross the English Channel and averages 10 days. The firm is considering shipping by rail through the Chunnel (the tunnel that goes through the English Channel) instead. That transport method would average approximately 2 days. Shipping through the Chunnel costs $80 more per vehicle. The firm has a holding cost of 25% per year. The average value of each car shipped is $20,000. Which transportation method should be selected?

SOLUTION

Daily cost of holding the product = (.25 × $20,000)/365 = $13.70

Total holding cost savings by using the Chunnel = (10 − 2) × $13.70 = $110 (rounded)

Since the $110 savings exceeds the $80 higher shipping cost, the Chunnel option appears best.
This switch would save the firm (120,000)($110 − $80) = $3,600,000 per year.

Problems

Problems S11.1–S11.5 relate to Evaluating Disaster Risk in the Supply Chain

• **S11.1** How would you go about attempting to come up with the probability of a "super-event" or the probability of a "unique-event?" What factors would you consider?

•• **S11.2** Phillip Witt, president of Witt Input Devices, wishes to create a portfolio of local suppliers for his new line of keyboards. As the suppliers all reside in a location prone to hurricanes, tornadoes, flooding, and earthquakes, Phillip believes that the probability in any year of a "super-event" that might shut down all suppliers at the same time for at least 2 weeks is 3%. Such a total shutdown would cost the company approximately $400,000. He estimates the "unique-event" risk for any of the suppliers to be 5%. Assuming that the marginal cost of managing an additional supplier is $15,000 per year, how many suppliers should Witt Input Devices use? Assume that up to three nearly identical local suppliers are available.

•• **S11.3** Still concerned about the risk in Problem S11.2, suppose that Phillip is willing to use one local supplier and up to two more located in other territories within the country. This would reduce the probability of a "super-event" to 0.5%, but due to increased distance the annual costs for managing each of the distant suppliers would be $25,000 (still $15,000 for the local supplier). Assuming that the local supplier would be the first one chosen, how many suppliers should Witt Input Devices use now?

•• **S11.4** Johnson Chemicals is considering two options for its supplier portfolio. Option 1 uses two local suppliers. Each has a "unique-event" risk of 5%, and the probability of a "super-event" that would disable both at the same time is estimated to be 1.5%. Option 2 uses two suppliers located in different countries. Each has a "unique-event" risk of 13%, and the probability of a "super-event" that would disable both at the same time is estimated to be 0.2%.
a) What is the probability that both suppliers will be disrupted using option 1?
b) What is the probability that both suppliers will be disrupted using option 2?
c) Which option would provide the lowest risk of a total shutdown?

•• **S11.5** Bloom's Jeans is searching for new suppliers, and Debbie Bloom, the owner, has narrowed her choices to two sets. Debbie is very concerned about supply disruptions, so she has chosen to use three suppliers no matter what. For option 1, the suppliers are well established and located in the same country. Debbie calculates the "unique-event" risk for each of them to be 4%. She estimates the probability of a nationwide event that would knock out all three suppliers to be 2.5%. For option 2, the suppliers are newer but located in three different countries. Debbie calculates the "unique-event" risk for each of them to be 20%. She estimates the "super-event" probability that would knock out all three of these suppliers to be 0.4%. Purchasing and transportation costs would be $1,000,000 per year using option 1 and $1,010,000 per year using option 2. A total disruption would create an annualized loss of $500,000.
a) What is the probability that all three suppliers will be disrupted using option 1?
b) What is the probability that all three suppliers will be disrupted using option 2?

c) What is the total annual purchasing and transportation cost plus expected annualized disruption cost for option 1?
d) What is the total annual purchasing and transportation cost plus expected annualized disruption cost for option 2?
e) Which option seems best?

Problems S11.6–S11.9 relate to Managing the Bullwhip Effect

•• **S11.6** Consider the supply chain illustrated below:

Last year, the retailer's weekly variance of demand was 200 units. The variance of orders was 500, 600, 750, and 1,350 units for the retailer, wholesaler, distributor, and manufacturer, respectively. (Note that the variance of orders equals the variance of demand for that firm's supplier.)
a) Calculate the bullwhip measure for the retailer.
b) Calculate the bullwhip measure for the wholesaler.
c) Calculate the bullwhip measure for the distributor.
d) Calculate the bullwhip measure for the manufacturer.
e) Which firm appears to be contributing the most to the bullwhip effect in this supply chain?

•• **S11.7** Over the past 5 weeks, demand for wine at Winston's Winery has been 1,000, 2,300, 3,200, 1,750, and 1,200 bottles. Winston has placed weekly orders for glass bottles of 1,100, 2,500, 4,000, 1,000, and 900 units. (Recall that the sample variance of a data set can be found by using the VAR.S function in Excel or by plugging each x value of the data set into the formula: Variance $= \dfrac{\Sigma(x - \bar{x})^2}{(n-1)}$, where $\bar{x}$ is the mean of the data set and n is the number of values in the set.)

a) What is the variance of demand for Winston's Winery?
b) What is the variance of orders from Winston's Winery for glass bottles?
c) What is the bullwhip measure for glass bottles for Winston's Winery?
d) Is Winston's Winery providing an amplifying or smoothing effect?

•• **S11.8** Over the past 12 months, Super Toy Mart has experienced a demand variance of 10,000 units and has produced an order variance of 12,000 units.
a) What is the bullwhip measure for Super Toy Mart?
b) If Super Toy Mart had made a perfect forecast of demand over the past 12 months and had decided to order 1/12 of that annual demand each month, what would its bullwhip measure have been?

••• **S11.9** Consider a three-firm supply chain consisting of a retailer, manufacturer, and supplier. The retailer's demand over an 8-week period was 100 units each of the first 2 weeks, 200 units each of the second 2 weeks, 300 units each of the third 2 weeks, and 400 units each of the fourth 2 weeks. The following table presents the orders placed by each firm in the supply chain. Notice, as is often the case in supply chains due to economies of scale, that total units are the same in each case, but firms further up the supply chain (away from the retailer) place larger, less frequent, orders.

WEEK	RETAILER	MANUFACTURER	SUPPLIER
1	100	200	600
2	100		
3	200	400	
4	200		
5	300	600	1400
6	300		
7	400	800	
8	400		

Recall that the sample variance of a data set can be found by using the VAR.S function in Excel or by plugging each x value of the data set into the formula: Variance $= \dfrac{\Sigma(x - \bar{x})^2}{(n - 1)}$, where $\bar{x}$ is the mean of the data set and n is the number of values in the set.

a) What is the bullwhip measure for the retailer?

b) What is the bullwhip measure for the manufacturer?

c) What is the bullwhip measure for the supplier?

d) What conclusions can you draw regarding the impact that economies of scale may have on the bullwhip effect?

Problems S11.10–S11.13 relate to Supplier Selection Analysis

•• **S11.10** As purchasing agent for Eynan Enterprises in Richmond, Virginia, you ask your buyer to provide you with a ranking of "excellent," "good," "fair," or "poor" for a variety of characteristics for two potential vendors. You suggest that the "Products" total be weighted 40% and the other three categories totals be weighted 20% each. The buyer has returned the rankings shown in Table S11.2.

Which of the two vendors would you select? **Px**

•• **S11.11** Using the data in Problem S11.10, assume that both Donna, Inc. and Kay Corp. are able to move all their "poor" ratings to "fair." How would you then rank the two firms? **Px**

•• **S11.12** Develop a vendor-rating form that represents your comparison of the education offered by universities in which you considered (or are considering) enrolling. Fill in the necessary data, and identify the "best" choice. Are you attending that "best" choice? If not, why not?

> *Additional problem **S11.13** is available in* MyOMLab.

Problems S11.14–S11.17 relate to Transportation Mode Analysis

•• **S11.14** Your options for shipping $100,000 of machine parts from Baltimore to Kuala Lumpur, Malaysia, are (1) use a ship that will take 30 days at a cost of $3,800 or (2) truck the parts to Los Angeles and then ship at a total cost of $4,800. The second option will take only 20 days. You are paid via a letter of credit the day the parts arrive. Your holding cost is estimated at 30% of the value per year.

a) Which option is more economical?

b) What customer issues are not included in the data presented?

•• **S11.15** If you have a third option for the data in Problem S11.14 and it costs only $4,000 and also takes 20 days, what is your most economical plan?

•• **S11.16** Monczka-Trent Shipping is the logistics vendor for Handfield Manufacturing Co. in Ohio. Handfield has daily shipments of a power-steering pump from its Ohio plant to an auto assembly line in Alabama. The value of the standard shipment is $250,000. Monczka-Trent has two options: (1) its standard 2-day shipment or (2) a subcontractor who will team drive overnight with an effective delivery of one day. The extra driver costs $175. Handfield's holding cost is 35% annually for this kind of inventory.

a) Which option is more economical?

b) What production issues are not included in the data presented?

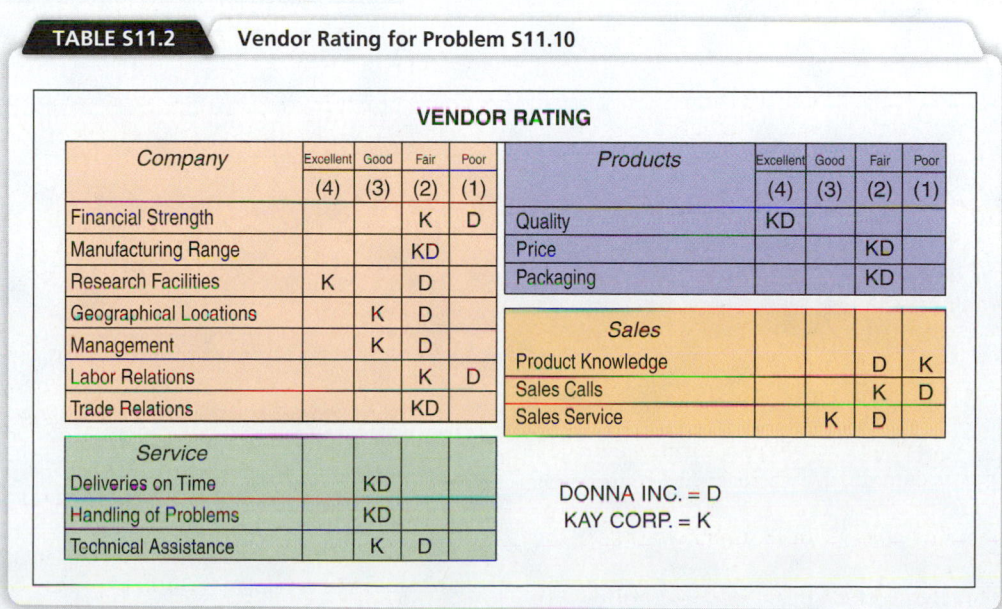

| TABLE S11.2 | Vendor Rating for Problem S11.10 |

VENDOR RATING

Company	Excellent (4)	Good (3)	Fair (2)	Poor (1)
Financial Strength			K	D
Manufacturing Range			KD	
Research Facilities	K		D	
Geographical Locations		K	D	
Management		K	D	
Labor Relations			K	D
Trade Relations			KD	

Service	Excellent (4)	Good (3)	Fair (2)	Poor (1)
Deliveries on Time		KD		
Handling of Problems		KD		
Technical Assistance		K	D	

Products	Excellent (4)	Good (3)	Fair (2)	Poor (1)
Quality	KD			
Price			KD	
Packaging			KD	

Sales	Excellent (4)	Good (3)	Fair (2)	Poor (1)
Product Knowledge			D	K
Sales Calls			K	D
Sales Service		K	D	

DONNA INC. = D
KAY CORP. = K

•••**S11.17** Recently, Abercrombie & Fitch (A&F) began shifting a large portion of its Asian deliveries to the U.S. from air freight to slower but cheaper ocean freight. Shipping costs have been cut dramatically, but shipment times have gone from days to weeks. In addition to having less control over inventory and being less responsive to fashion changes, the holding costs have risen for the goods in transport. Meanwhile, Central America might offer an inexpensive manufacturing alternative that could reduce shipping time through the Panama Canal to, say, 6 days, compared to, say, 27 days from Asia. Suppose that A&F uses an annual holding rate of 30%. Suppose further that the product costs $20 to produce in Asia. Assuming that the transportation cost via ocean liner would be approximately the same whether coming from Asia or Central America, what would the maximum production cost in Central America need to be in order for that to be a competitive source compared to the Asian producer?

ITEM CATEGORY	MONTHLY TRIPS	AREA NEEDED (BLOCKS)
Paper Products	50	2
Dishes, Glasses, and Silverware	16	4
Cleaning Agents	6	2
Cooking Oils and Seasonings	30	2
Pots and Pans	12	6

The following picture of the warehouse provides an identification number for each of the 16 storage blocks. For each item category, indicate into which blocks it should be stored.

Problems S11.18–S11.20 relate to Warehouse Storage

• **S11.18** The items listed in the following table are stored in a warehouse.

ITEM	WEEKLY TRIPS	AREA NEEDED (BLOCKS)
A	300	60
B	219	3
C	72	1
D	90	10
E	24	3

a) Which item should be stored at the very front (closest to the dock)?
b) Which item should be stored at the very back (furthest from the dock)?

••**S11.19** Amy Zeng, owner of Zeng's Restaurant Distributions, supplies nonperishable goods to restaurants around the metro area. She stores all the goods in a warehouse. The goods are divided into five categories according to the following table. The table indicates the number of trips per month to store or retrieve items in each category, as well as the number of storage blocks taken up by each.

••**S11.20** The items listed in the following table are stored in a warehouse.

ITEM	WEEKLY TRIPS	AREA NEEDED (BLOCKS)
A	2	1
B	160	8
C	16	1
D	40	4
E	24	2
F	15	1
G	4	1

Using the following figure, indicate the best storage location for each item to minimize average distance traveled.

Supplement 11 *Rapid Review*

Main Heading	Review Material	MyOMLab
TECHNIQUES FOR EVALUATING SUPPLY CHAINS (p. 472)	Many supply chain metrics exist that can be used to evaluate performance within a company and for its supply chain partners. The 2011 Tōhoku earthquake and tsunami devastated eastern sections of Japan. The economic impact was felt around the globe, as manufacturers had been relying heavily, in some cases exclusively, on suppliers located in the affected zones. Manufacturers in several industries worldwide took 6 months or longer before they saw their supply chains working normally again.	Concept Question: 1.1
EVALUATING DISASTER RISK IN THE SUPPLY CHAIN (pp. 472–474)	Disasters that disrupt supply chains can take on many forms, including tornadoes, fires, hurricanes, typhoons, tsunamis, earthquakes, and terrorism. Firms often use multiple suppliers for important components to mitigate the risks of total supply disruption. *The probability of all n suppliers being disrupted simultaneously*: $$P(n) = S + (1 - S)U^n \qquad \text{(S11-1)}$$ where: S = probability of a "super-event" disrupting all suppliers simultaneously U = probability of a "unique-event" disrupting only one supplier L = financial loss incurred in a supply chain if all suppliers were disrupted C = marginal cost of managing a supplier All suppliers will be disrupted simultaneously if either the super-event occurs or the super-event does not occur but a unique-event occurs for all of the suppliers. As the probability of a super-event (S) increases, the advantage of utilizing multiple suppliers diminishes (all would be knocked out anyway). On the other hand, large values of the unique event (U) increase the likelihood of needing more suppliers. These two phenomena taken together suggest that when multiple suppliers are used, managers may consider using ones that are geographically dispersed to lessen the probability of all failing simultaneously. A decision tree can be used to help operations managers make this important decision regarding number of suppliers. 	Concept Questions: 2.1–2.4 Problems: S11.1–S11.5 Virtual Office Hours for Solved Problem: S11.1
MANAGING THE BULLWHIP EFFECT (pp. 474–476)	*Demand forecast updating, order batching, price fluctuations,* and *shortage gaming* can all produce inaccurate information, resulting in distortions and fluctuations in the supply chain and causing the *bullwhip effect*. ■ **Bullwhip effect**—The increasing fluctuation in orders that often occurs as orders move through the supply chain. "Bullwhip" fluctuations create unstable production schedules, resulting in expensive capacity change adjustments such as overtime, subcontracting, extra inventory, backorders, hiring and laying off of workers, equipment additions, equipment underutilization, longer lead times, or obsolescence of overproduced items. The bullwhip effect can occur when orders decrease as well as when they increase. Often the human tendency to overreact to stimuli causes managers to make decisions that exacerbate the phenomenon.	Concept Questions: 3.1–3.4 Problems: S11.6–S11.9 Virtual Office Hours for Solved Problem: S11.2

Main Heading	Review Material	MyOMLab
	The overarching solution to the bullwhip effect is simply for supply chain members to share information and work together. *Specific remedies for the four primary causes include:* Demand forecast errors → *Share demand information throughout the chain* Order batching → *Think of the supply chain as one firm when choosing order sizes* Price fluctuations → *Institute everyday low prices* Shortage gaming → *Allocate orders based on past demand* A straightforward way to measure the extent of the bullwhip effect at any link in the supply chain is to calculate the *bullwhip measure*: $$\text{Bullwhip} = \frac{\text{Variance of orders}}{\text{Variance of demand}} = \frac{\sigma^2_{\text{orders}}}{\sigma^2_{\text{demand}}} \qquad (S11\text{-}2)$$ Variance *amplification* (i.e., the bullwhip effect) is present if the bullwhip measure is greater than 1. That means the size of a company's orders fluctuate more than the size of its incoming demand. If the measure equals 1, then no amplification is present. A value less than 1 would imply a *smoothing* or *dampening* scenario as orders move up the supply chain from the retailer toward suppliers.	
SUPPLIER SELECTION ANALYSIS (pp. 476–477)	Choosing suppliers simply based on the lowest bid has become a somewhat rare approach. Various, sometimes competing, factors often play a role in the decision. Buyers may consider such supplier characteristics as product quality, delivery speed, delivery reliability, customer service, and financial performance. The *factor-weighting* technique simultaneously considers multiple supplier criteria. Each factor must be assigned an importance *weight*, and then each potential supplier is *scored* on each factor. The weights typically sum to 100%. Factors are scored using the same scale (e.g., 1–10). Sometimes a key is provided for supplier raters that converts qualitative ratings into numerical scores (e.g., "Very good" = 8).	Concept Questions: 4.1–4.2 Problems: S11.10–S11.11, S11.13 Virtual Office Hours for Solved Problem: S11.3
TRANSPORTATION MODE ANALYSIS (pp. 477–478)	The longer a product is in transit, the longer the firm has its money invested. But faster shipping is usually more expensive than slow shipping. A simple way to obtain some insight into this trade-off is to evaluate holding cost against shipping options. *Daily cost of holding the product*: (Annual holding cost × Product value)/365 There are many other considerations beyond holding vs. shipping costs when choosing the appropriate transportation mode and carrier, including ensuring *on-time delivery* (whether fast or slow), coordinating shipments to maintain a schedule, getting a new product to market, and keeping a customer happy. Estimates of these other costs can be added to the estimate of the daily holding cost.	Concept Questions: 5.1–5.2 Problems: S11.14–S11.17 Virtual Office Hours for Solved Problem: S11.4
WAREHOUSE STORAGE (pp. 478–479)	When determining storage locations for items in a warehouse, rank the items according to the ratio: (Number of trips/Blocks of storage needed) Place the items with the *highest* ratios closest to the dock.	Concept Questions: 6.1–6.2 Problems: S11.18–S11.20

Self Test

■ **Before taking the self-test,** refer to the learning objectives listed at the beginning of the supplement.

LO S11.1 Which of the following combinations would result in needing to utilize the largest number of suppliers?
  a) a high value of S and high value of U
  b) a high value of S and low value of U
  c) a low value of S and high value of U
  d) a low value of S and low value of U

LO S11.2 Typically, the bullwhip effect is most pronounced at which level of the supply chain?
  a) consumers   b) suppliers
  c) wholesalers   d) retailers

LO S11.3 Which of the following is not a characteristic of the factor-weighting approach to supplier evalution?
  a) it applies quantitative scores to qualitative criteria
  b) the weights typically sum to 100%
  c) multiple criteria can be considered simultaneously
  d) subjective judgment is often involved
  e) it applies qualitative assessments to quantitative criteria

LO S11.4 A more expensive shipper tends to provide:
  a) faster shipments and lower holding costs
  b) faster shipments and higher holding costs
  c) slower shipments and lower holding costs
  d) slower shipments and higher holding costs

LO S11.5 Which of the following items is most likely to be stored at the back of a warehouse, furthest away from the shipping dock?
  a) low number of trips and low number of storage blocks
  b) low number of trips and high number of storage blocks
  c) high number of trips and low number of storage blocks
  d) high number of trips and high number of storage blocks

Answers: LO S11.1. c; LO S11.2. b; LO S11.3. e; LO S11.4. a; LO S11.5. b.

Inventory Management

CHAPTER OUTLINE

GLOBAL COMPANY PROFILE: *Amazon.com*

◆ The Importance of Inventory *490*

◆ Managing Inventory *491*

◆ Inventory Models *495*

◆ Inventory Models for Independent Demand *496*

◆ Probabilistic Models and Safety Stock *508*

◆ Single-Period Model *513*

◆ Fixed-Period (*P*) Systems *514*

Alaska Airlines

10 OM STRATEGY DECISIONS

- Design of Goods and Services
- Managing Quality
- Process Strategy
- Location Strategies
- Layout Strategies
- Human Resources
- Supply-Chain Management

- **Inventory Management**
  - ■ *Independent Demand (Ch. 12)*
  - ■ Dependent Demand (Ch. 14)
  - ■ Lean Operations (Ch. 16)

- Scheduling
- Maintenance

CHAPTER 12

Inventory Management Provides Competitive Advantage at Amazon.com

When Jeff Bezos opened his revolutionary business in 1995, Amazon.com was intended to be a "virtual" retailer—no inventory, no warehouses, no overhead—just a bunch of computers taking orders for books and authorizing others to fill them. Things clearly didn't work out that way. Now, Amazon stocks millions of items of inventory, amid hundreds of thousands of bins on shelves in over 150 warehouses around the world. Additionally, Amazon's

Marilyn Newton/Reno Gazette-Journal

1. You order three items, and a computer in Seattle takes charge. A computer assigns your order—a book, a game, and a digital camera—to one of Amazon's massive U.S. distribution centers.

2. The "flow meister" at the distribution center receives your order. She determines which workers go where to fill your order.

Bernhard Classen/Alamy

3. Amazon's current system doubles the picking speed of manual operators and drops the error rate to nearly zero.

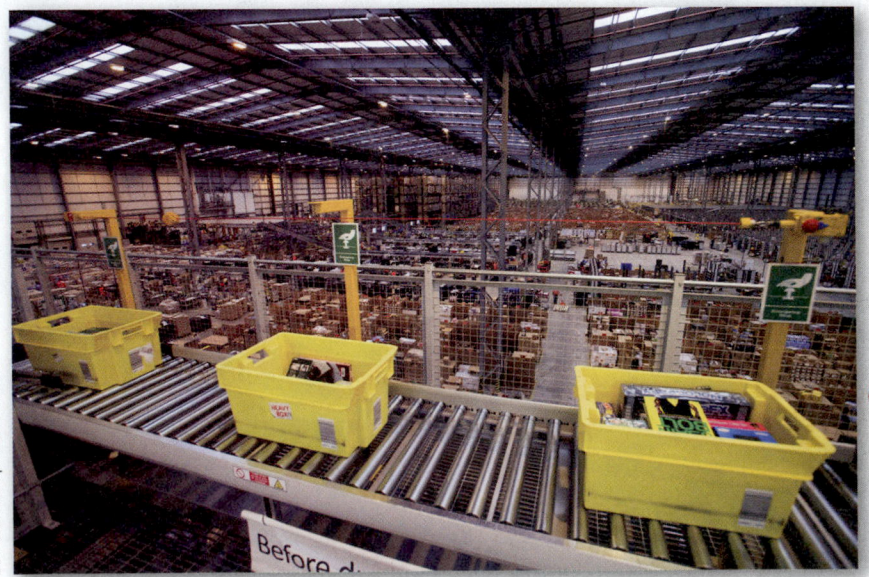

Ben Cawthra/Sipa USA/Newscom

4. Your items are put into crates on moving belts. Each item goes into a large yellow crate that contains many customers' orders. When full, the crates ride a series of conveyor belts that wind more than 10 miles through the plant at a constant speed of 2.9 feet per second. The bar code on each item is scanned 15 times, by machines and by many of the 600 workers. The goal is to reduce errors to zero—returns are very expensive.

5. All three items converge in a chute and then inside a box. All the crates arrive at a central point where bar codes are matched with order numbers to determine who gets what. Your three items end up in a 3-foot-wide chute—one of several thousand—and are placed into a corrugated box with a new bar code that identifies your order. Picking is sequenced to reduce operator travel.

6. Any gifts you've chosen are wrapped by hand. Amazon trains an elite group of gift wrappers, each of whom processes 30 packages an hour.

software is so good that Amazon sells its order taking, processing, and billing expertise to others. It is estimated that 200 million items are now available via the Amazon Web site.

Bezos expects the customer experience at Amazon to be one that yields the lowest price, the fastest delivery, and an error-free order fulfillment process so no other contact with Amazon is necessary. Exchanges and returns are very expensive.

Managing this massive inventory precisely is the key for Amazon to be the world-class leader in warehouse automation and management. The time to receive, process, and position the stock in storage and to then accurately "pull" and package an order requires a labor investment of less than 3 minutes. And 70% of these orders are multiproduct orders. This underlines the high benchmark that Amazon has achieved. This is world-class performance.

When you place an order with Amazon.com, you are doing business with a company that obtains competitive advantage through inventory management. This *Global Company Profile* shows how Amazon does it. ◀

7. The box is packed, taped, weighed, and labeled before leaving the warehouse in a truck. A typical plant is designed to ship as many as 200,000 pieces a day. About 60% of orders are shipped via the U.S. Postal Service; nearly everything else goes through United Parcel Service.

8. Your order arrives at your doorstep. In 1 or 2 days, your order is delivered.

LEARNING OBJECTIVES

LO 12.1 *Conduct* an ABC analysis 492

LO 12.2 *Explain* and use cycle counting 493

LO 12.3 *Explain* and use the EOQ model for independent inventory demand 496

LO 12.4 *Compute* a reorder point and explain safety stock 502

LO 12.5 *Apply* the production order quantity model 503

LO 12.6 *Explain* and use the quantity discount model 505

LO 12.7 *Understand* service levels and probabilistic inventory models 511

The Importance of Inventory

As Amazon.com well knows, inventory is one of the most expensive assets of many companies, representing as much as 50% of total invested capital. Operations managers around the globe have long recognized that good inventory management is crucial. On the one hand, a firm can reduce costs by reducing inventory. On the other hand, production may stop and customers become dissatisfied when an item is out of stock. *The objective of inventory management is to strike a balance between inventory investment and customer service.* You can never achieve a low-cost strategy without good inventory management.

All organizations have some type of inventory planning and control system. A bank has methods to control its inventory of cash. A hospital has methods to control blood supplies and pharmaceuticals. Government agencies, schools, and, of course, virtually every manufacturing and production organization are concerned with inventory planning and control.

In cases involving physical products, the organization must determine whether to produce goods or to purchase them. Once this decision has been made, the next step is to forecast demand, as discussed in Chapter 4. Then operations managers determine the inventory necessary to service that demand. In this chapter, we discuss the functions, types, and management of inventory. We then address two basic inventory issues: how much to order and when to order.

Functions of Inventory

VIDEO 12.1
Managing Inventory at Frito-Lay

Inventory can serve several functions that add flexibility to a firm's operations. The four functions of inventory are:

1. *To provide a selection of goods for anticipated customer demand and to separate the firm from fluctuations in that demand.* Such inventories are typical in retail establishments.
2. To *decouple various parts of the production process.* For example, if a firm's supplies fluctuate, extra inventory may be necessary to decouple the production process from suppliers.
3. To *take advantage of quantity discounts,* because purchases in larger quantities may reduce the cost of goods or their delivery.
4. To *hedge against inflation* and upward price changes.

Types of Inventory

Raw material inventory
Materials that are usually purchased but have yet to enter the manufacturing process.

Work-in-process (WIP) inventory
Products or components that are no longer raw materials but have yet to become finished products.

Maintenance/repair/operating (MRO) inventory
Maintenance, repair, and operating materials.

To accommodate the functions of inventory, firms maintain four types of inventories: (1) raw material inventory, (2) work-in-process inventory, (3) maintenance/repair/operating supply (MRO) inventory, and (4) finished-goods inventory.

Raw material inventory has been purchased but not processed. This inventory can be used to decouple (i.e., separate) suppliers from the production process. However, the preferred approach is to eliminate supplier variability in quality, quantity, or delivery time so that separation is not needed. Work-in-process (WIP) inventory is components or raw material that have undergone some change but are not completed. WIP exists because of the time it takes for a product to be made (called *cycle time*). Reducing cycle time reduces inventory. Often this task is not difficult: during most of the time a product is "being made," it is in fact sitting idle. As Figure 12.1 shows, actual work time, or "run" time, is a small portion of the material flow time, perhaps as low as 5%.

MROs are inventories devoted to maintenance/repair/operating supplies necessary to keep machinery and processes productive. They exist because the need and timing for maintenance and

Cycle time

95%   5%

Input → | Wait for inspection | Wait to be moved | Move time | Wait in queue for operator | Setup time | Run time | → Output

Figure 12.1

The Material Flow Cycle

Most of the time that work is in-process (95% of the cycle time) is not productive time.

repair of some equipment are unknown. Although the demand for MRO inventory is often a function of maintenance schedules, other unscheduled MRO demands must be anticipated. Finished-goods inventory is completed product awaiting shipment. Finished goods may be inventoried because future customer demands are unknown.

Managing Inventory

Operations managers establish systems for managing inventory. In this section, we briefly examine two ingredients of such systems: (1) how inventory items can be classified (called *ABC analysis*) and (2) how accurate inventory records can be maintained. We will then look at inventory control in the service sector.

ABC Analysis

ABC analysis divides on-hand inventory into three classifications on the basis of annual dollar volume. ABC analysis is an inventory application of what is known as the *Pareto principle* (named after Vilfredo Pareto, a 19th-century Italian economist). The Pareto principle states that there are a "critical few and trivial many." The idea is to establish inventory policies that focus resources on the *few critical* inventory parts and not the many trivial ones. It is not realistic to monitor inexpensive items with the same intensity as very expensive items.

To determine annual dollar volume for ABC analysis, we measure the *annual demand* of each inventory item times the *cost per unit*. Class A items are those on which the annual dollar volume is high. Although such items may represent only about 15% of the total inventory items, they represent 70% to 80% of the total dollar usage. *Class B* items are those inventory items of medium annual dollar volume. These items may represent about 30% of inventory items and 15% to 25% of the total value. Those with low annual dollar volume are *Class C*, which may represent only 5% of the annual dollar volume but about 55% of the total inventory items.

Graphically, the inventory of many organizations would appear as presented in Figure 12.2.

A items

B items

C items

Percentage of annual dollar usage

80 70 60 50 40 30 20 10 0

10 20 30 40 50 60 70 80 90 100

Percentage of inventory items

An example of the use of ABC analysis is shown in Example 1.

Example 1

LO 12.1 *Conduct* an ABC analysis

ABC ANALYSIS FOR A CHIP MANUFACTURER

Silicon Chips, Inc., maker of superfast DRAM chips, wants to categorize its 10 major inventory items using ABC analysis.

APPROACH ▶ ABC analysis organizes the items on an annual dollar-volume basis. Shown below (in columns 1–4) are the 10 items (identified by stock numbers), their annual demands, and unit costs.

SOLUTION ▶ Annual dollar volume is computed in column 5, along with the percentage of the total represented by each item in column 6. Column 7 groups the 10 items into A, B, and C categories.

ABC Calculation

(1) ITEM STOCK NUMBER	(2) PERCENTAGE OF NUMBER OF ITEMS STOCKED	(3) ANNUAL VOLUME (UNITS)	×	(4) UNIT COST	=	(5) ANNUAL DOLLAR VOLUME	(6) PERCENTAGE OF ANNUAL DOLLAR VOLUME		(7) CLASS
#10286	20%	1,000		$ 90.00		$ 90,000	38.8%	72%	A
#11526		500		154.00		77,000	33.2%		A
#12760	30%	1,550		17.00		26,350	11.3%	23%	B
#10867		350		42.86		15,001	6.4%		B
#10500		1,000		12.50		12,500	5.4%		B
#12572	50%	600		14.17		8,502	3.7%	5%	C
#14075		2,000		.60		1,200	.5%		C
#01036		100		8.50		850	.4%		C
#01307		1,200		.42		504	.2%		C
#10572		250		.60		150	.1%		C
		8,550				$232,057	100.0%		

INSIGHT ▶ The breakdown into A, B, and C categories is not hard and fast. The objective is to try to separate the "important" from the "unimportant."

LEARNING EXERCISE ▶ The unit cost for Item #10286 has increased from $90.00 to $120.00. How does this impact the ABC analysis? [Answer: The total annual dollar volume increases by $30,000, to $262,057, and the two A items now comprise 75% of that amount.]

RELATED PROBLEMS ▶ 12.1, 12.2, 12.3 (12.5–12.6 are available in MyOMLab)

EXCEL OM Data File **Ch12Ex1.xls** can be found in MyOMLab.

Criteria other than annual dollar volume can determine item classification. For instance, high shortage or holding cost, anticipated engineering changes, delivery problems, or quality problems may dictate upgrading items to a higher classification. The advantage of dividing inventory items into classes allows policies and controls to be established for each class.

Policies that may be based on ABC analysis include the following:

1. Purchasing resources expended on supplier development should be much higher for individual A items than for C items.
2. A items, as opposed to B and C items, should have tighter physical inventory control; perhaps they belong in a more secure area, and perhaps the accuracy of inventory records for A items should be verified more frequently.
3. Forecasting A items may warrant more care than forecasting other items.

Better forecasting, physical control, supplier reliability, and an ultimate reduction in inventory can all result from classification systems such as ABC analysis.

OM in Action | Inventory Accuracy at Milton Bradley

Milton Bradley, a division of Hasbro, Inc., has been manufacturing toys for 150 years. Founded by Milton Bradley in 1860, the company started by making a lithograph of Abraham Lincoln. Using his printing skills, Bradley developed games, including The Game of Life, Chutes and Ladders, Candy Land, Scrabble, and Lite Brite. Today, the company produces hundreds of games, requiring billions of plastic parts.

Once Milton Bradley has determined the optimal quantities for each production run, it must make them and assemble them as a part of the proper game. Some games require literally hundreds of plastic parts, including spinners, hotels, people, animals, cars, and so on. According to Gary Brennan, director of manufacturing, getting the right number of pieces to the right toys and production lines is the most important issue for the credibility of the company. Some orders can require 20,000 or more perfectly assembled games delivered to their warehouses in a matter of days.

Games with the incorrect number of parts and pieces can result in some very unhappy customers. It is also time-consuming and expensive for Milton Bradley to

Anthony Labbe/Photofulcrum.com

supply the extra parts or to have toys or games returned. When shortages are found during the assembly stage, the entire production run is stopped until the problem is corrected.

Counting parts by hand or machine is not always accurate. As a result, Milton Bradley now weighs pieces and completed games to determine if the correct number of parts have been included. If the weight is not exact, there is a problem that is resolved before shipment. Using highly accurate digital scales, Milton Bradley is now able to get the right parts in the right game at the right time. Without this simple innovation, the company's most sophisticated production schedule would be meaningless.

Sources: Forbes (February 7, 2011); and *The Wall Street Journal* (April 15, 1999).

Record Accuracy

Record accuracy is a prerequisite to inventory management, production scheduling, and, ultimately, sales. Accuracy can be maintained by either periodic or perpetual systems. *Periodic systems* require regular (periodic) checks of inventory to determine quantity on hand. Some small retailers and facilities with vendor-managed inventory (the vendor checks quantity on hand and resupplies as necessary) use these systems. However, the downside is lack of control between reviews and the necessity of carrying extra inventory to protect against shortages.

A variation of the periodic system is a *two-bin system*. In practice, a store manager sets up two containers (each with adequate inventory to cover demand during the time required to receive another order) and places an order when the first container is empty.

Alternatively, *perpetual inventory* tracks both receipts and subtractions from inventory on a continuing basis. Receipts are usually noted in the receiving department in some semiautomated way, such as via a bar-code reader, and disbursements are noted as items leave the stockroom or, in retailing establishments, at the point-of-sale (POS) cash register.

Regardless of the inventory system, record accuracy requires good incoming and outgoing record keeping as well as good security. Stockrooms will have limited access, good housekeeping, and storage areas that hold fixed amounts of inventory. In both manufacturing and retail facilities, bins, shelf space, and individual items must be stored and labeled accurately. Meaningful decisions about ordering, scheduling, and shipping, are made only when the firm knows what it has on hand. (See the *OM in Action* box, "Inventory Accuracy at Milton Bradley.")

Omnicell

In this hospital, these vertically rotating storage carousels provide rapid access to hundreds of critical items and at the same time save floor space. This Omnicell inventory management carousel is also secure and has the added advantage of printing bar code labels.

Cycle Counting

Even though an organization may have made substantial efforts to record inventory accurately, these records must be verified through a continuing audit. Such audits are known as cycle counting. Historically, many firms performed annual physical inventories. This practice often meant shutting down the facility and having inexperienced people count parts and material. Inventory records should instead be verified via cycle counting. Cycle counting uses inventory classifications developed through ABC analysis. With cycle counting procedures, items are counted, records are verified, and inaccuracies are periodically documented. The cause of inaccuracies is then traced and appropriate remedial action taken to ensure integrity of the inventory system. **A** items will be counted frequently, perhaps once a month; **B** items will be counted less frequently, perhaps once a quarter; and **C** items will be counted perhaps once every 6 months. Example 2 illustrates how to compute the number of items of each classification to be counted each day.

Cycle counting
A continuing reconciliation of inventory with inventory records.

LO 12.2 *Explain* and *use cycle counting*

Example 2

CYCLE COUNTING AT COLE'S TRUCKS, INC.

Cole's Trucks, Inc., a builder of high-quality refuse trucks, has about 5,000 items in its inventory. It wants to determine how many items to cycle count each day.

APPROACH ▶   After hiring Matt Clark, a bright young OM student, for the summer, the firm determined that it has 500 A items, 1,750 B items, and 2,750 C items. Company policy is to count all A items every month (every 20 working days), all B items every quarter (every 60 working days), and all C items every 6 months (every 120 working days). The firm then allocates some items to be counted each day.

SOLUTION ▶

ITEM CLASS	QUANTITY	CYCLE-COUNTING POLICY	NUMBER OF ITEMS COUNTED PER DAY
A	500	Each month (20 working days)	500/20 = 25/day
B	1,750	Each quarter (60 working days)	1,750/60 = 29/day
C	2,750	Every 6 months (120 working days)	2,750/120 = 23/day
			77/day

Each day, 77 items are counted.

INSIGHT ▶   This daily audit of 77 items is much more efficient and accurate than conducting a massive inventory count once a year.

LEARNING EXERCISE ▶   Cole's reclassifies some B and C items so there are now 1,500 B items and 3,000 C items. How does this change the cycle count? [Answer: B and C both change to 25 items each per day, for a total of 75 items per day.]

RELATED PROBLEM ▶   12.4

In Example 2, the particular items to be cycle counted can be sequentially or randomly selected each day. Another option is to cycle count items when they are reordered.

Cycle counting also has the following advantages:

Shrinkage

Retail inventory that is unaccounted for between receipt and sale.

Pilferage

A small amount of theft.

1. Eliminates the shutdown and interruption of production necessary for annual physical inventories.
2. Eliminates annual inventory adjustments.
3. Trained personnel audit the accuracy of inventory.
4. Allows the cause of the errors to be identified and remedial action to be taken.
5. Maintains accurate inventory records.

Robin Nelson/ZUMA Press, Inc./Alamy

Pharmaceutical distributor McKesson Corp., which is one of Arnold Palmer Hospital's main suppliers of surgical materials, makes heavy use of bar-code readers to automate inventory control. The device on the warehouse worker's arm combines a scanner, a computer, and a two-way radio to check orders. With rapid and accurate data, items are easily verified, improving inventory and shipment accuracy.

Control of Service Inventories

Although we may think of the service sector of our economy as not having inventory, that is seldom the case. Extensive inventory is held in wholesale and retail businesses, making inventory management crucial. In the food-service business, control of inventory is often the difference between success and failure. Moreover, inventory that is in transit or idle in a warehouse is lost value. Similarly, inventory damaged or stolen prior to sale is a loss. In retailing, inventory that is unaccounted for between receipt and time of sale is known as shrinkage. Shrinkage occurs from damage and theft as well as from sloppy paperwork. Inventory theft is also known as pilferage. Retail inventory loss of 1% of sales is considered good, with losses in many stores exceeding 3%. Because the impact on profitability is substantial, inventory accuracy and control are critical. Applicable techniques include the following:

1. *Good personnel selection, training, and discipline:* These are never easy but very necessary in food-service, wholesale, and retail operations, where employees have access to directly consumable merchandise.

2. *Tight control of incoming shipments:* This task is being addressed by many firms through the use of Universal Product Code (or bar code) and radio frequency ID (RFID) systems that read every incoming shipment and automatically check tallies against purchase orders. When properly designed, these systems—where each stock keeping unit (SKU; pronounced "skew") has its own identifier—can be very hard to defeat.

3. *Effective control of all goods leaving the facility:* This job is accomplished with bar codes, RFID tags, or magnetic strips on merchandise, and via direct observation. Direct observation can be personnel stationed at exits (as at Costco and Sam's Club wholesale stores) and in potentially high-loss areas or can take the form of one-way mirrors and video surveillance.

A handheld reader can scan RFID tags, aiding control of both incoming and outgoing shipments.

Successful retail operations require very good store-level control with accurate inventory in its proper location. Major retailers lose 10% to 25% of overall profits due to poor or inaccurate inventory records.[1] (See the *OM in Action* box, "Retail's Last 10 Yards.")

Inventory Models

We now examine a variety of inventory models and the costs associated with them.

VIDEO 12.2
Inventory Control at Wheeled Coach Ambulance

Independent vs. Dependent Demand

Inventory control models assume that demand for an item is either independent of or dependent on the demand for other items. For example, the demand for refrigerators is *independent* of the demand for toaster ovens. However, the demand for toaster oven components is *dependent* on the requirements of toaster ovens.

This chapter focuses on managing inventory where demand is *independent*. Chapter 14 presents *dependent* demand management.

Holding, Ordering, and Setup Costs

Holding costs are the costs associated with holding or "carrying" inventory over time. Therefore, holding costs also include obsolescence and costs related to storage, such as insurance, extra staffing, and interest payments. Table 12.1 shows the kinds of costs that need to be evaluated to determine holding costs. Many firms fail to include all the inventory holding costs. Consequently, inventory holding costs are often understated.

Ordering cost includes costs of supplies, forms, order processing, purchasing, clerical support, and so forth. When orders are being manufactured, ordering costs also exist, but they are a part

Holding cost
The cost to keep or carry inventory in stock.

Ordering cost
The cost of the ordering process.

TABLE 12.1	Determining Inventory Holding Costs	
CATEGORY		COST (AND RANGE) AS A PERCENTAGE OF INVENTORY VALUE
Housing costs (building rent or depreciation, operating cost, taxes, insurance)		6% (3–10%)
Material-handling costs (equipment lease or depreciation, power, operating cost)		3% (1–3.5%)
Labor cost (receiving, warehousing, security)		3% (3–5%)
Investment costs (borrowing costs, taxes, and insurance on inventory)		11% (6–24%)
Pilferage, scrap, and obsolescence (much higher in industries undergoing rapid change like tablets and smart phones)		3% (2–5%)
Overall carrying cost		26%

Note: All numbers are approximate, as they vary substantially depending on the nature of the business, location, and current interest rates.

of what is called setup costs. Setup cost is the cost to prepare a machine or process for manufacturing an order. This includes time and labor to clean and change tools or holders. Operations managers can lower ordering costs by reducing setup costs and by using such efficient procedures as electronic ordering and payment.

In manufacturing environments, setup cost is highly correlated with setup time. Setups usually require a substantial amount of work even before a setup is actually performed at the work center. With proper planning, much of the preparation required by a setup can be done prior to shutting down the machine or process. Setup times can thus be reduced substantially. Machines and processes that traditionally have taken hours to set up are now being set up in less than a minute by the more imaginative world-class manufacturers. Reducing setup times is an excellent way to reduce inventory investment and to improve productivity.

Setup cost

The cost to prepare a machine or process for production.

Setup time

The time required to prepare a machine or process for production.

Inventory Models for Independent Demand

In this section, we introduce three inventory models that address two important questions: *when to order* and *how much to order*. These *independent* demand models are:

1. Basic economic order quantity (EOQ) model
2. Production order quantity model
3. Quantity discount model

The Basic Economic Order Quantity (EOQ) Model

The economic order quantity (EOQ) model is one of the most commonly used inventory-control techniques. This technique is relatively easy to use but is based on several assumptions:

Economic order quantity (EOQ) model

An inventory-control technique that minimizes the total of ordering and holding costs.

1. Demand for an item is known, reasonably constant, and independent of decisions for other items.
2. Lead time—that is, the time between placement and receipt of the order—is known and consistent.
3. Receipt of inventory is instantaneous and complete. In other words, the inventory from an order arrives in one batch at one time.
4. Quantity discounts are not possible.
5. The only variable costs are the cost of setting up or placing an order (setup or ordering cost) and the cost of holding or storing inventory over time (holding or carrying cost). These costs were discussed in the previous section.
6. Stockouts (shortages) can be completely avoided if orders are placed at the right time.

LO 12.3 *Explain* and use the EOQ model for independent inventory demand

With these assumptions, the graph of inventory usage over time has a sawtooth shape, as in Figure 12.3. In Figure 12.3, *Q* represents the amount that is ordered. If this amount is 500 dresses, all 500 dresses arrive at one time (when an order is received). Thus, the inventory

Figure **12.3**

Inventory Usage over Time

STUDENT TIP

If the maximum we can ever have is Q (say, 500 units) and the minimum is zero, then if inventory is used (or sold) at a fairly steady rate, the average $= (Q + 0)/2 = Q/2$.

level jumps from 0 to 500 dresses. In general, an inventory level increases from 0 to Q units when an order arrives.

Because demand is constant over time, inventory drops at a uniform rate over time. (Refer to the sloped lines in Figure 12.3.) Each time the inventory is received, the inventory level again jumps to Q units (represented by the vertical lines). This process continues indefinitely over time.

Minimizing Costs

The objective of most inventory models is to minimize total costs. With the assumptions just given, significant costs are setup (or ordering) cost and holding (or carrying) cost. All other costs, such as the cost of the inventory itself, are constant. Thus, if we minimize the sum of setup and holding costs, we will also be minimizing total costs. To help you visualize this, in Figure 12.4 we graph total costs as a function of the order quantity, Q. The optimal order size, Q^*, will be the quantity that minimizes the total costs. As the quantity ordered increases, the total number of orders placed per year will decrease. Thus, as the quantity ordered increases, the annual setup or ordering cost will decrease [Figure 12.4(a)]. But as the order quantity increases, the holding cost will increase due to the larger average inventories that are maintained [Figure 12.4(b)].

STUDENT TIP

Figure 12.4 is the heart of EOQ inventory modeling. We want to find the smallest total cost (top curve), which is the sum of the two curves below it.

As we can see in Figure 12.4(c), a reduction in either holding or setup cost will reduce the total cost curve. A reduction in the setup cost curve also reduces the optimal order quantity (lot size). In addition, smaller lot sizes have a positive impact on quality and production flexibility. At Toshiba, the $77 billion Japanese conglomerate, workers can make as few as 10 laptop computers before changing models. This lot-size flexibility has allowed Toshiba to move toward a "build-to-order" mass customization system, an important ability in an industry that has product life cycles measured in months, not years.

You should note that in Figure 12.4(c), the optimal order quantity occurs at the point where the ordering-cost curve and the carrying-cost curve intersect. This was not by chance. With the EOQ model, the optimal order quantity will occur at a point where the total setup cost is equal

(a) Annual setup (order) cost   (b) Annual holding cost   (c) Total costs

Figure **12.4**

Costs as a Function of Order Quantity

to the total holding cost.[2] We use this fact to develop equations that solve directly for Q^*. The necessary steps are:

1. Develop an expression for setup or ordering cost.
2. Develop an expression for holding cost.
3. Set setup (order) cost equal to holding cost.
4. Solve the equation for the optimal order quantity.

Using the following variables, we can determine setup and holding costs and solve for Q^*:

$$Q = \text{Number of units per order}$$
$$Q^* = \text{Optimum number of units per order (EOQ)}$$
$$D = \text{Annual demand in units for the inventory item}$$
$$S = \text{Setup or ordering cost for each order}$$
$$H = \text{Holding or carrying cost per unit per year}$$

1. Annual setup cost = (Number of orders placed per year) × (Setup or order cost per order)

$$= \left(\frac{\text{Annual demand}}{\text{Number of units in each order}} \right)(\text{Setup or order cost per order})$$

$$= \left(\frac{D}{Q} \right)(S) = \frac{D}{Q}S$$

2. Annual holding cost = (Average inventory level) × (Holding cost per unit per year)

$$= \left(\frac{\text{Order quantity}}{2} \right)(\text{Holding cost per unit per year})$$

$$= \left(\frac{Q}{2} \right)(H) = \frac{Q}{2}H$$

3. Optimal order quantity is found when annual setup (order) cost equals annual holding cost, namely:

$$\frac{D}{Q}S = \frac{Q}{2}H$$

4. To solve for Q^*, simply cross-multiply terms and isolate Q on the left of the equal sign:

$$2DS = Q^2H$$

$$Q^2 = \frac{2DS}{H}$$

$$Q^* = \sqrt{\frac{2DS}{H}} \tag{12-1}$$

Now that we have derived the equation for the optimal order quantity, Q^*, it is possible to solve inventory problems directly, as in Example 3.

Example 3

FINDING THE OPTIMAL ORDER SIZE AT SHARP, INC.

Sharp, Inc., a company that markets painless hypodermic needles to hospitals, would like to reduce its inventory cost by determining the optimal number of hypodermic needles to obtain per order.

APPROACH ▶ The annual demand is 1,000 units; the setup or ordering cost is $10 per order; and the holding cost per unit per year is $.50.

SOLUTION ▶ Using these figures, we can calculate the optimal number of units per order:

$$Q^* = \sqrt{\frac{2DS}{H}}$$

$$Q^* = \sqrt{\frac{2(1,000)(10)}{0.50}} = \sqrt{40,000} = 200 \text{ units}$$

INSIGHT ▶ Sharp, Inc., now knows how many needles to order per order. The firm also has a basis for determining ordering and holding costs for this item, as well as the number of orders to be processed by the receiving and inventory departments.

LEARNING EXERCISE ▶ If D increases to 1,200 units, what is the new Q^*? [Answer: $Q^* = 219$ units.]

RELATED PROBLEMS ▶ 12.7, 12.8, 12.9, 12.10, 12.11, 12.14, 12.15, 12.17, 12.29 (12.31, 12.32, 12.33a, 12.35a are available in MyOMLab)

EXCEL OM Data File **Ch12Ex3.xls** can be found in MyOMLab.

ACTIVE MODEL 12.1 This example is further illustrated in Active Model 12.1 in MyOMLab.

We can also determine the expected number of orders placed during the year (N) and the expected time between orders (T), as follows:

$$\text{Expected number of orders} = N = \frac{\text{Demand}}{\text{Order quantity}} = \frac{D}{Q^*} \qquad (12\text{-}2)$$

$$\text{Expected time between orders} = T = \frac{\text{Number of working days per year}}{N} \qquad (12\text{-}3)$$

Example 4 illustrates this concept.

Example 4

COMPUTING NUMBER OF ORDERS AND TIME BETWEEN ORDERS AT SHARP, INC.

Sharp, Inc. (in Example 3) has a 250-day working year and wants to find the number of orders (N) and the expected time between orders (T).

APPROACH ▶ Using Equations (12-2) and (12-3), Sharp enters the data given in Example 3.

SOLUTION ▶

$$N = \frac{\text{Demand}}{\text{Order quantity}}$$

$$= \frac{1,000}{200} = 5 \text{ orders per year}$$

$$T = \frac{\text{Number of working days per year}}{\text{Expected number of orders}}$$

$$= \frac{250 \text{ working days per year}}{5 \text{ orders}} = 50 \text{ days between orders}$$

INSIGHT ▶ The company now knows not only how many needles to order per order but that the time between orders is 50 days and that there are five orders per year.

LEARNING EXERCISE ▶ If $D = 1,200$ units instead of 1,000, find N and T. [Answer: $N \cong 5.48$, $T = 45.62$.]

RELATED PROBLEMS ▶ 12.14, 12.15, 12.17 (12.35c,d are available in MyOMLab)

As mentioned earlier in this section, the total annual variable inventory cost is the sum of setup and holding costs:

$$\text{Total annual cost} = \text{Setup (order) cost} + \text{Holding cost} \qquad (12\text{-}4)$$

In terms of the variables in the model, we can express the total cost TC as:

$$TC = \frac{D}{Q}S + \frac{Q}{2}H \qquad (12\text{-}5)$$

Example 5 shows how to use this formula.

Example 5

COMPUTING COMBINED COST OF ORDERING AND HOLDING

Sharp, Inc. (from Examples 3 and 4) wants to determine the combined annual ordering and holding costs.

APPROACH ▶ Apply Equation (12-5), using the data in Example 3.

SOLUTION ▶

$$TC = \frac{D}{Q}S + \frac{Q}{2}H$$

$$= \frac{1,000}{200}(\$10) + \frac{200}{2}(\$.50)$$

$$= (5)(\$10) + (100)(\$.50)$$

$$= \$50 + \$50 = \$100$$

INSIGHT ▶ These are the annual setup and holding costs. The $100 total does not include the actual cost of goods. Notice that in the EOQ model, holding costs always equal setup (order) costs.

LEARNING EXERCISE ▶ Find the total annual cost if $D = 1,200$ units in Example 3. [Answer: $109.54.]

RELATED PROBLEMS ▶ 12.11, 12.14, 12.15, 12.16 (12.33b,c; 12.35e; 12.36a,b are available in MyOMLab)

Inventory costs may also be expressed to include the actual cost of the material purchased. If we assume that the annual demand and the price per hypodermic needle are known values (e.g., 1,000 hypodermics per year at $P = \$10$) and total annual cost should include purchase cost, then Equation (12-5) becomes:

$$TC = \frac{D}{Q}S + \frac{Q}{2}H + PD$$

Because material cost does not depend on the particular order policy, we still incur an annual material cost of $D \times P = (1,000)(\$10) = \$10,000$. (Later in this chapter we will discuss the case in which this may not be true—namely, when a quantity discount is available.)[3]

Robust

Giving satisfactory answers even with substantial variation in the parameters.

Robust Model A benefit of the EOQ model is that it is robust. By robust we mean that it gives satisfactory answers even with substantial variation in its parameters. As we have observed, determining accurate ordering costs and holding costs for inventory is often difficult. Consequently, a robust model is advantageous. The total cost of the EOQ changes little in the neighborhood of the minimum. The curve is very shallow. This means that variations in setup costs, holding costs, demand, or even EOQ make relatively modest differences in total cost. Example 6 shows the robustness of EOQ.

Example 6

EOQ IS A ROBUST MODEL

Management in the Sharp, Inc., examples underestimates total annual demand by 50% (say demand is actually 1,500 needles rather than 1,000 needles) while using the same Q. How will the annual inventory cost be impacted?

APPROACH ▶ We will solve for annual costs twice. First, we will apply the wrong EOQ; then we will recompute costs with the correct EOQ.

SOLUTION ▶ If demand in Example 5 is actually 1,500 needles rather than 1,000, but management uses an order quantity of $Q = 200$ (when it should be $Q = 244.9$ based on $D = 1,500$), the sum of holding and ordering cost increases to $125:

$$\text{Annual cost} = \frac{D}{Q}S + \frac{Q}{2}H$$

$$= \frac{1,500}{200}(\$10) + \frac{200}{2}(\$.50)$$

$$= \$75 + \$50 = \$125$$

However, had we known that the demand was for 1,500 with an EOQ of 244.9 units, we would have spent $122.47, as shown:

$$\text{Annual cost} = \frac{1,500}{244.9}(\$10) + \frac{244.9}{2}(\$.50)$$

$$= 6.125(\$10) + 122.45(\$.50)$$

$$= \$61.25 + \$61.22 = \$122.47$$

INSIGHT ▶ Note that the expenditure of $125.00, made with an estimate of demand that was substantially wrong, is only 2% ($2.52/$122.47) higher than we would have paid had we known the actual demand and ordered accordingly. Note also that were it not due to rounding, the annual holding costs and ordering costs would be exactly equal.

LEARNING EXERCISE ▶ Demand at Sharp remains at 1,000, H is still $.50, and we order 200 needles at a time (as in Example 5). But if the true order cost = S = $15 (rather than $10), what is the annual cost? [Answer: Annual order cost increases to $75, and annual holding cost stays at $50. So the total cost = $125.]

RELATED PROBLEMS ▶ 12.10b, 12.16 (12.36a,b are available in MyOMLab)

We may conclude that the EOQ is indeed robust and that significant errors do not cost us very much. This attribute of the EOQ model is most convenient because our ability to accurately determine demand, holding cost, and ordering cost is limited.

Reorder Points

Now that we have decided *how much* to order, we will look at the second inventory question, *when* to order. Simple inventory models assume that receipt of an order is instantaneous. In other words, they assume (1) that a firm will place an order when the inventory level for that particular item reaches zero and (2) that it will receive the ordered items immediately. However, the time between placement and receipt of an order, called **lead time**, or delivery time, can be as short as a few hours or as long as months. Thus, the when-to-order decision is usually expressed in terms of a **reorder point (ROP)**—the inventory level at which an order should be placed (see Figure 12.5).

The reorder point (ROP) is given as:

ROP = Demand per day ×

Lead time for a new order in days

$$\text{ROP} = d \times L \tag{12-6}$$

This equation for ROP *assumes that demand during lead time and lead time itself are constant.* When this is not the case, extra stock, often called **safety stock (ss)**, should be added. The reorder point with safety stock then becomes:

ROP = Expected demand during lead time +

Safety stock

The demand per day, d, is found by dividing the annual demand, D, by the number of working days in a year:

$$d = \frac{D}{\text{Number of working days in a year}}$$

Lead time

In purchasing systems, the time between placing an order and receiving it; in production systems, the wait, move, queue, setup, and run times for each component produced.

Reorder point (ROP)

The inventory level (point) at which action is taken to replenish the stocked item.

Safety stock (ss)

Extra stock to allow for uneven demand; a buffer.

Figure 12.5

The Reorder Point (ROP)

Q^* is the optimum order quantity, and lead time represents the time between placing and receiving an order.

Computing the reorder point is demonstrated in Example 7.

Example 7

COMPUTING REORDER POINTS (ROP) FOR IPHONES WITH AND WITHOUT SAFETY STOCK

LO 12.4 *Compute* a reorder point and explain safety stock

An Apple store has a demand (D) for 8,000 iPhones per year. The firm operates a 250-day working year. On average, delivery of an order takes 3 working days, but has been known to take as long as 4 days. The store wants to calculate the reorder point without a safety stock and then with a one-day safety stock.

APPROACH ▶ First compute the daily demand and then apply Equation (12-6) for the ROP. Then compute the ROP with safety stock.

SOLUTION ▶

$$d = \frac{D}{\text{Number of working days in a year}} = \frac{8,000}{250} = 32 \text{ units}$$

$$ROP = \text{Reorder point} = d \times L = 32 \text{ units per day} \times 3 \text{ days} = 96 \text{ units}$$

ROP with safety stock adds 1 day's demand (32 units) to the ROP (for 128 units).

INSIGHT ▶ When iPhone inventory stock drops to 96 units, an order should be placed. If the safety stock for a possible one-day delay in delivery is added, the ROP is 128 (= 96 + 32).

LEARNING EXERCISE ▶ If there are only 200 working days per year, what is the correct ROP, without safety stock and with safety stock? [Answer: 120 iPhones without safety stock and 160 with safety stock.]

RELATED PROBLEMS ▶ 12.11d, 12.12, 12.13, 12.15f (12.33d, 12.34, 12.35f, 12.36c are available in MyOMLab)

When demand is not constant or variability exists in the supply chain, safety stock can be critical. We discuss safety stock in more detail later in this chapter.

Production Order Quantity Model

In the previous inventory model, we assumed that the entire inventory order was received at one time. There are times, however, when the firm may receive its inventory over a period of time. Such cases require a different model, one that does not require the instantaneous-receipt assumption. This model is applicable under two situations: (1) when inventory continuously flows or builds up over a period of time after an order has been placed or (2) when units are produced and sold simultaneously. Under these circumstances, we take into account daily production (or inventory-flow) rate and daily demand rate. Figure 12.6 shows inventory levels as a function of time (and inventory dropping to zero between orders).

Production order quantity model

An economic order quantity technique applied to production orders.

Because this model is especially suitable for the production environment, it is commonly called the production order quantity model. It is useful when inventory continuously builds up over time, and traditional economic order quantity assumptions are valid. We derive this model by setting ordering or setup costs equal to holding costs and solving for optimal order size, Q^*. Using the following symbols, we can determine the expression for annual inventory holding cost for the production order quantity model:

Figure 12.6

Change in Inventory Levels over Time for the Production Model

Q = Number of units per order

H = Holding cost per unit per year

p = Daily production rate

d = Daily demand rate, or usage rate

t = Length of the production run in days

1. $\left(\begin{array}{c}\text{Annual inventory}\\\text{holding cost}\end{array}\right)$ = (Average inventory level) $\times \left(\begin{array}{c}\text{Holding cost}\\\text{per unit per year}\end{array}\right)$

LO 12.5 *Apply* the production order quantity model

2. (Average inventory level) = (Maximum inventory level)/2

3. $\left(\begin{array}{c}\text{Maximum}\\\text{inventory level}\end{array}\right) = \left(\begin{array}{c}\text{Total production during}\\\text{the production run}\end{array}\right) - \left(\begin{array}{c}\text{Total used during}\\\text{the production run}\end{array}\right)$

$$= pt - dt$$

However, Q = total produced = pt, and thus $t = Q/p$. Therefore:

$$\text{Maximum inventory level} = p\left(\frac{Q}{p}\right) - d\left(\frac{Q}{p}\right) = Q - \frac{d}{p}Q$$

$$= Q\left(1 - \frac{d}{p}\right)$$

4. Annual inventory holding cost (or simply holding cost) =

$$\frac{\text{Maximum inventory level}}{2}(H) = \frac{Q}{2}\left[1 - \left(\frac{d}{p}\right)\right]H$$

⚠ STUDENT TIP

Note in Figure 12.6 that inventory buildup is not instantaneous but gradual. So the formula reduces the average inventory and thus the holding cost by the ratio of that buildup.

Using this expression for holding cost and the expression for setup cost developed in the basic EOQ model, we solve for the optimal number of pieces per order by equating setup cost and holding cost:

$$\text{Setup cost} = (D/Q)S \qquad\qquad \text{Holding cost} = \tfrac{1}{2}HQ[1 - (d/p)]$$

Set ordering cost equal to holding cost to obtain Q_p^*:

$$\frac{D}{Q}S = \tfrac{1}{2}HQ[1 - (d/p)]$$

$$Q^2 = \frac{2DS}{H[1 - (d/p)]}$$

$$Q_p^* = \sqrt{\frac{2DS}{H[1 - (d/p)]}} \qquad\qquad (12\text{-}7)$$

Dmitry Kalinovsky/Shutterstock

Each order may require a change in the way a machine or process is set up. Reducing setup time usually means a reduction in setup cost, and reductions in setup costs make smaller batches (lots) economical to produce. Increasingly, setup (and operation) is performed by computer-controlled machines, such as this one, operating from previously written programs.

In Example 8, we use the above equation, Q_p^*, to solve for the optimum order or production quantity when inventory is consumed as it is produced.

Example 8

A PRODUCTION ORDER QUANTITY MODEL

Nathan Manufacturing, Inc., makes and sells specialty hubcaps for the retail automobile aftermarket. Nathan's forecast for its wire-wheel hubcap is 1,000 units next year, with an average daily demand of 4 units. However, the production process is most efficient at 8 units per day. So the company produces 8 per day but uses only 4 per day. The company wants to solve for the optimum number of units per order. (*Note:* This plant schedules production of this hubcap only as needed, during the 250 days per year the shop operates.)

APPROACH ▶ Gather the cost data and apply Equation (12-7):

$$\text{Annual demand} = D = 1,000 \text{ units}$$
$$\text{Setup costs} = S = \$10$$
$$\text{Holding cost} = H = \$0.50 \text{ per unit per year}$$
$$\text{Daily production rate} = p = 8 \text{ units daily}$$
$$\text{Daily demand rate} = d = 4 \text{ units daily}$$

SOLUTION ▶

$$Q_p^* = \sqrt{\frac{2DS}{H[1 - (d/p)]}}$$

$$Q_p^* = \sqrt{\frac{2(1,000)(10)}{0.50[1 - (4/8)]}}$$

$$= \sqrt{\frac{20,000}{0.50(1/2)}} = \sqrt{80,000} = 282.8 \text{ hubcaps, or } 283 \text{ hubcaps}$$

INSIGHT ▶ The difference between the production order quantity model and the basic EOQ model is that the effective annual holding cost per unit is reduced in the production order quantity model because the entire order does not arrive at once.

LEARNING EXERCISE ▶ If Nathan can increase its daily production rate from 8 to 10, how does Q_p^* change? [Answer: $Q_p^* = 258$.]

RELATED PROBLEMS ▶ 12.18, 12.19, 12.20, 12.30 (12.37 is available in MyOMLab)

EXCEL OM Data File **Ch12Ex8.xls** can be found in MyOMLab.

ACTIVE MODEL 12.2 This example is further illustrated in Active Model 12.2 in MyOMLab.

You may want to compare this solution with the answer in Example 3, which had identical D, S, and H values. Eliminating the instantaneous-receipt assumption, where $p = 8$ and $d = 4$, resulted in an increase in Q^* from 200 in Example 3 to 283 in Example 8. This increase in Q^* occurred because holding cost dropped from $\$.50$ to $[\$.50 \times (1 - d/p)]$, making a larger order quantity optimal. Also note that:

$$d = 4 = \frac{D}{\text{Number of days the plant is in operation}} = \frac{1,000}{250}$$

We can also calculate Q_p^* when *annual* data are available. When annual data are used, we can express Q_p^* as:

$$Q_p^* = \sqrt{\frac{2DS}{H\left(1 - \dfrac{\text{Annual demand rate}}{\text{Annual production rate}}\right)}} \tag{12-8}$$

Quantity Discount Models

Quantity discounts appear everywhere—you cannot go into a grocery store without seeing them on nearly every shelf. In fact, researchers have found that *most* companies either offer or receive quantity discounts for at least some of the products that they sell or purchase. A **quantity discount** is simply a reduced price (*P*) for an item when it is purchased in larger quantities. A typical quantity discount schedule appears in Table 12.2. As can be seen in the table, the normal price of the item is $100. When 120 to 1,499 units are ordered at one time, the price per unit drops to $98; when the quantity ordered at one time is 1,500 units or more, the price is $96 per unit. The 120 quantity and the 1,500 quantity are called *price-break quantities* because they represent the first order amount that would lead to a new lower price. As always, management must decide when and how much to order. However, given these quantity discounts, how does the operations manager make these decisions?

Quantity discount
A reduced price for items purchased in large quantities.

As with other inventory models, the objective is to minimize total cost. Because the unit cost for the second discount in Table 12.2 is the lowest, you may be tempted to order 1,500 units. Placing an order for that quantity, however, even with the greatest discount price, may not minimize total inventory cost. This is because holding cost increases. Thus, the major trade-off when considering quantity discounts is between *reduced product cost* and *increased holding cost*. When we include the cost of the product, the equation for the total annual inventory cost can be calculated as follows:

Total annual cost = Annual setup (ordering) cost + Annual holding cost
+ Annual product cost,

or

LO 12.6 *Explain* and use the quantity discount model

$$TC = \frac{D}{Q}S + \frac{Q}{2}IP + PD \tag{12-9}$$

where   *Q* = Quantity ordered
   D = Annual demand in units
   S = Setup or ordering cost per order
   P = Price per unit
   I = Holding cost per unit per year expressed as a percent of price *P*

Note that holding cost is *IP* instead of *H* as seen in the regular EOQ model. Because the price of the item is a factor in annual holding cost, we do not assume that the holding cost is a constant when the price per unit changes for each quantity discount. Thus, it is common to express the holding cost as a percent (*I*) of unit price (*P*) when evaluating costs of quantity discount schedules.

The EOQ formula (12-1) is modified for the quantity discount problem as follows:

$$Q^* = \sqrt{\frac{2DS}{IP}} \tag{12-10}$$

The solution procedure uses the concept of a *feasible EOQ*. An EOQ is feasible if it lies in the quantity range that leads to the same price *P* used to compute it in Equation (12-10). For example, suppose that *D* = 5,200, *S* = $200, and *I* = 28%. Using Table 12.2 and Equation (12-10), the EOQ for the $96 price equals $\sqrt{2(5,200)(200)/[(.28)(96)]}$ = 278 units. Because 278 < 1,500 (the price-break quantity needed to receive the $96 price), the EOQ for the $96 price is *not feasible*. On the other hand, the EOQ for the $98 price equals 275 units. This amount is *feasible* because if 275 units were actually ordered, the firm would indeed receive the $98 purchase price.

TABLE 12.2	A Quantity Discount Schedule	
PRICE RANGE	**QUANTITY ORDERED**	**PRICE PER UNIT P**
Initial price	1–119	$100
Discount price 1	120–1,499	$ 98
Discount price 2	1,500 and over	$ 96

Figure **12.7**

EOQs and Possible Best Order Quantities for the Quantity Discount Problem with Three Prices in Table 12.2

The solid black curves represent the realized total annual setup plus holding plus purchasing cost at the applicable order quantities. The black curve drops to the total cost curve for the next discount level when each price-break quantity is reached.

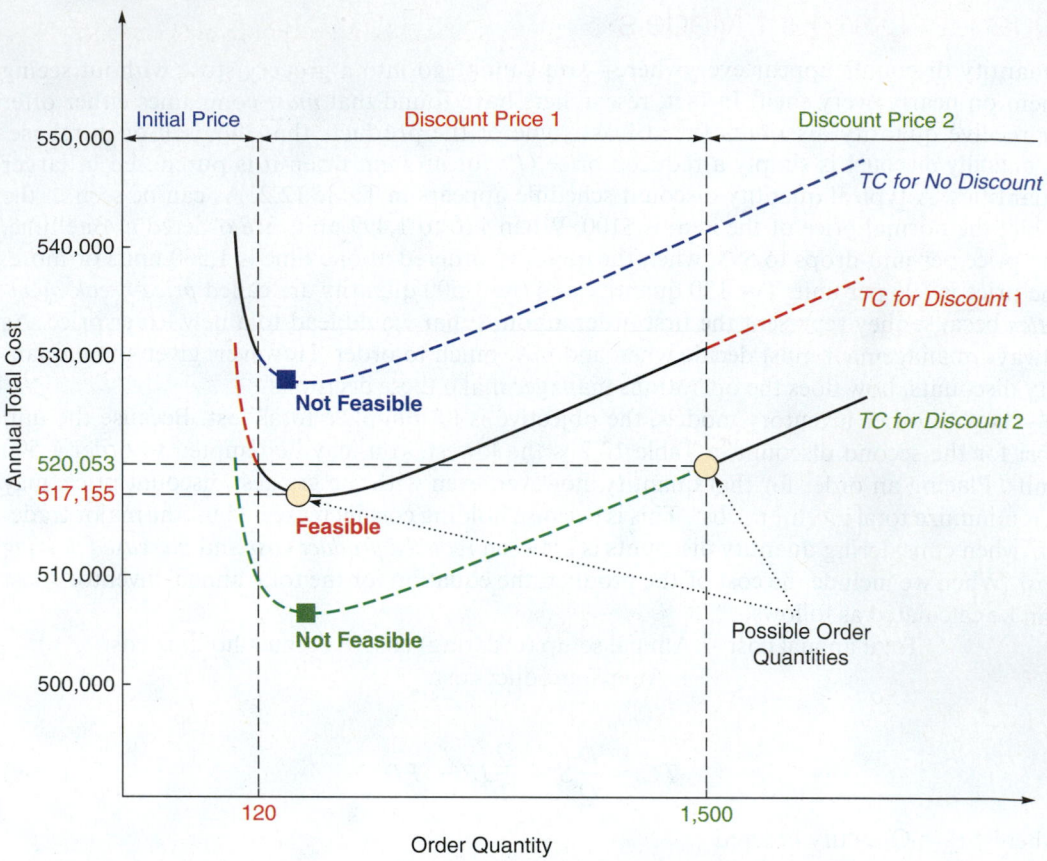

Now we have to determine the quantity that will minimize the total annual inventory cost. Because there are a few discounts, this process involves two steps. In Step 1, we identify all possible order quantities that could be the best solution. In Step 2, we calculate the total cost of all possible best order quantities, and the least expensive order quantity is selected.

Solution Procedure

STEP 1: Starting with the *lowest* possible purchase price in a quantity discount schedule and working toward the highest price, keep calculating Q^* from Equation (12-10) until the first feasible EOQ is found. The first feasible EOQ is a possible best order quantity, along with all price-break quantities for all *lower* prices.

STEP 2: Calculate the total annual cost TC using Equation (12-9) for each of the possible best order quantities determined in Step 1. Select the quantity that has the lowest total cost.

Note that no quantities need to be considered for any prices greater than the first feasible EOQ found in Step 1. This occurs because if an EOQ for a given price is feasible, then the EOQ for any *higher* price *cannot* lead to a lower cost (*TC* is guaranteed to be higher).

Figure 12.7 provides a graphical illustration of Step 1 using the three price ranges from Table 12.2. In that example, the EOQ for the lowest price is infeasible, but the EOQ for the second-lowest price is feasible. So the EOQ for the second-lowest price, along with the price-break quantity for the lowest price, are the possible best order quantities. Finally, the highest price (no discount) can be ignored because a feasible EOQ has already been found for a lower price.

Example 9 illustrates how the full solution procedure can be applied.

Example 9 | QUANTITY DISCOUNT MODEL

Chris Beehner Electronics stocks toy remote control flying drones. Recently, the store has been offered a quantity discount schedule for these drones. This quantity schedule was shown in Table 12.2. Furthermore, setup cost is $200 per order, annual demand is 5,200 units, and annual inventory carrying charge as a percent of cost, I, is 28%. What order quantity will minimize the total inventory cost?

APPROACH ▶ We will follow the two steps just outlined for the quantity discount model.

SOLUTION ▶ First we calculate the Q^* for the lowest possible price of $96, as we did earlier:

$$Q^*_{\$96} = \sqrt{\frac{2(5,200)(\$200)}{(.28)(\$96)}} = 278 \text{ flying drones per order}$$

Because $278 < 1,500$, this EOQ is *infeasible* for the $96 price. So now we calculate Q^* for the next-higher price of $98:

$$Q^*_{\$98} = \sqrt{\frac{2(5,200)(\$200)}{(.28)(\$98)}} = 275 \text{ flying drones per order}$$

Because 275 is between 120 and 1,499 units, this EOQ is *feasible* for the $98 price. Thus, the possible best order quantities are 275 (the first feasible EOQ) and 1,500 (the price-break quantity for the lower price of $96). We need not bother to compute Q^* for the initial price of $100 because we found a feasible EOQ for a lower price.

Step 2 uses Equation (12-9) to compute the total cost for each of the possible best order quantities. This step is taken with the aid of Table 12.3.

TABLE 12.3	Total Cost Computations for Chris Beehner Electronics				
ORDER QUANTITY	UNIT PRICE	ANNUAL ORDERING COST	ANNUAL HOLDING COST	ANNUAL PRODUCT COST	TOTAL ANNUAL COST
275	$98	$3,782	$ 3,773	$509,600	$517,155
1,500	$96	$ 693	$20,160	$499,200	$520,053

Because the total annual cost for 275 units is lower, 275 units should be ordered. The costs for this example are shown in Figure 12.7.

INSIGHT ▶ Even though Beehner Electronics could save more than $10,000 in annual product costs, ordering 1,500 units (28.8% of annual demand) at a time would generate even more than that in increased holding costs. So in this example it is not in the store's best interest to order enough to attain the lowest possible purchase price per unit. On the other hand, if the price-break quantity for the $96 had been 1,000 units rather than 1,500 units, then total annual costs would have been $513,680, which would have been cheaper than ordering 275 units at $98.

LEARNING EXERCISE ▶ Resolve the problem with $D = 2,000$, $S = \$5$, $I = 50\%$, discount price 1 = $99, and discount price 2 = $98. [Answer: only 20 units should be ordered each time, which is the EOQ at the $100 price.]

RELATED PROBLEMS ▶ 12.21–12.28 (12.38–12.40 are available in MyOMLab)

EXCEL OM Data file **Ch12Ex9.xls** can be found in MyOMLab.

In this section we have studied the most popular form of single-purchase quantity discount called the *all-units discount*. In practice, quantity discounts appear in a variety of forms. For example, *incremental quantity discounts* apply only to those units purchased beyond the price-break quantities rather than to all units. *Fixed fees*, such as a fixed shipping and processing cost for a catalog order or a $5,000 tooling setup cost for any order placed with a manufacturer, encourage buyers to purchase more units at a time. Some discounts are *aggregated* over items or time. *Item aggregation* bases price breaks on total units or dollars purchased. *Time aggregation* applies to total items or dollars spent over a specific time period such as one year. *Truckload discounts*, *buy-one-get-one-free offers*, and *one-time-only sales* also represent types of quantity discounts in that they provide price incentives for buyers to purchase more units at one time. Most purchasing managers deal with some form of quantity discounts on a regular basis.

Probabilistic Models and Safety Stock

Probabilistic model

A statistical model applicable when product demand or any other variable is not known but can be specified by means of a probability distribution.

Service level

The probability that demand will not be greater than supply during lead time. It is the complement of the probability of a stockout.

All the inventory models we have discussed so far make the assumption that demand for a product is constant and certain. We now relax this assumption. The following inventory models apply when product demand is not known but can be specified by means of a probability distribution. These types of models are called probabilistic models. Probabilistic models are a real-world adjustment because demand and lead time won't always be known and constant.

An important concern of management is maintaining an adequate service level in the face of uncertain demand. The service level is the *complement* of the probability of a stockout. For instance, if the probability of a stockout is 0.05, then the service level is .95. Uncertain demand raises the possibility of a stockout. One method of reducing stockouts is to hold extra units in inventory. As we noted earlier such inventory is referred to as safety stock. Safety stock involves adding a number of units as a buffer to the reorder point. As you recall:

$$\text{Reorder point} = \text{ROP} = d \times L$$

where d = Daily demand

L = Order lead time, or number of working days it takes to deliver an order

The inclusion of safety stock (ss) changed the expression to:

$$\text{ROP} = d \times L + ss \tag{12-11}$$

The amount of safety stock maintained depends on the cost of incurring a stockout and the cost of holding the extra inventory. Annual stockout cost is computed as follows:

$$\text{Annual stockout costs} = \text{The sum of the units short for each demand level}$$
$$\times \text{The probability of that demand level} \times \text{The stockout cost/unit}$$
$$\times \text{The number of orders per year} \tag{12-12}$$

Example 10 illustrates this concept.

Example 10

DETERMINING SAFETY STOCK WITH PROBABILISTIC DEMAND AND CONSTANT LEAD TIME

David Rivera Optical has determined that its reorder point for eyeglass frames is 50 ($d \times L$) units. Its carrying cost per frame per year is $5, and stockout (or lost sale) cost is $40 per frame. The store has experienced the following probability distribution for inventory demand during the lead time (reorder period). The optimum number of orders per year is six.

NUMBER OF UNITS	PROBABILITY
30	.2
40	.2
ROP → 50	.3
60	.2
70	.1
	1.0

How much safety stock should David Rivera keep on hand?

APPROACH ▶   The objective is to find the amount of safety stock that minimizes the sum of the additional inventory holding costs and stockout costs. The annual holding cost is simply the holding cost per unit multiplied by the units added to the ROP. For example, a safety stock of 20 frames, which implies that the new ROP, with safety stock, is 70 (= 50 + 20), raises the annual carrying cost by $5(20) = $100.

However, computing annual stockout cost is more interesting. For any level of safety stock, stockout cost is the expected cost of stocking out. We can compute it, as in Equation (12-12), by multiplying the number of frames short (Demand – ROP) by the probability of demand at that level, by the stockout cost, by the number of times per year the stockout can occur (which in our case is the number of orders per year). Then we add stockout costs for each possible stockout level for a given ROP.[4]

SOLUTION ▶ We begin by looking at zero safety stock. For this safety stock, a shortage of 10 frames will occur if demand is 60, and a shortage of 20 frames will occur if the demand is 70. Thus the stockout costs for zero safety stock are:

$$(10 \text{ frames short})(.2)(\$40 \text{ per stockout})(6 \text{ possible stockouts per year})$$
$$+ (20 \text{ frames short})(.1)(\$40)(6) = \$960$$

The following table summarizes the total costs for each of the three alternatives:

SAFETY STOCK	ADDITIONAL HOLDING COST	STOCKOUT COST		TOTAL COST
20	(20)($5) = $100		$ 0	$100
10	(10)($5) = $ 50	(10) (.1) ($40) (6)	= $240	$290
0	$ 0	(10) (.2) ($40) (6) + (20) (.1) ($40) (6) = $960		$960

The safety stock with the lowest total cost is 20 frames. Therefore, this safety stock changes the reorder point to 50 + 20 = 70 frames.

INSIGHT ▶ The optical company now knows that a safety stock of 20 frames will be the most economical decision.

LEARNING EXERCISE ▶ David Rivera's holding cost per frame is now estimated to be $20, while the stockout cost is $30 per frame. Does the reorder point change? [Answer: Safety stock = 10 now, with a total cost of $380, which is the lowest of the three. ROP = 60 frames.]

RELATED PROBLEMS ▶ 12.43, 12.44, 12.45

When it is difficult or impossible to determine the cost of being out of stock, a manager may decide to follow a policy of keeping enough safety stock on hand to meet a prescribed customer service level. For instance, Figure 12.8 shows the use of safety stock when demand (for hospital resuscitation kits) is probabilistic. We see that the safety stock in Figure 12.8 is 16.5 units, and the reorder point is also increased by 16.5.

The manager may want to define the service level as meeting 95% of the demand (or, conversely, having stockouts only 5% of the time). Assuming that demand during lead time (the reorder period) follows a normal curve, only the mean and standard deviation are needed to define the inventory requirements for any given service level. Sales data are usually adequate for computing the mean and standard deviation. Example 11 uses a normal curve with a known mean (μ) and standard deviation (σ) to determine the reorder point and safety stock necessary

Figure **12.8**

Probabilistic Demand for a Hospital Item

Expected number of kits needed during lead time is 350, but for a 95% service level, the reorder point should be raised to 366.5.

for a 95% service level. We use the following formula:

$$\text{ROP} = \text{Expected demand during lead time} + Z\sigma_{dLT} \qquad (12\text{-}13)$$

where
$$Z = \text{Number of standard deviations}$$
$$\sigma_{dLT} = \text{Standard deviation of demand during lead time}$$

Example 11

SAFETY STOCK WITH PROBABILISTIC DEMAND

Memphis Regional Hospital stocks a "code blue" resuscitation kit that has a normally distributed demand during the reorder period. The mean (average) demand during the reorder period is 350 kits, and the standard deviation is 10 kits. The hospital administrator wants to follow a policy that results in stockouts only 5% of the time.

(a) What is the appropriate value of Z? (b) How much safety stock should the hospital maintain? (c) What reorder point should be used?

APPROACH ▶ The hospital determines how much inventory is needed to meet the demand 95% of the time. The figure in this example may help you visualize the approach. The data are as follows:

$$\mu = \text{Mean demand} = 350 \text{ kits}$$
$$\sigma_{dLT} = \text{Standard deviation of demand during lead time} = 10 \text{ kits}$$
$$Z = \text{Number of standard normal deviations}$$

STUDENT TIP ⬤
Recall that the service level is 1 minus the risk of a stockout.

SOLUTION ▶

a) We use the properties of a standardized normal curve to get a Z-value for an area under the normal curve of .95 (or $1 - .05$). Using a normal table (see Appendix I) or the Excel formula =NORMSINV(.95), we find a Z-value of 1.645 standard deviations from the mean.

b) Because: Safety stock $= x - \mu$

and:
$$Z = \frac{x - \mu}{\sigma_{dLT}}$$

then: Safety stock $= Z\sigma_{dLT}$ $\qquad (12\text{-}14)$

Solving for safety stock, as in Equation (12-14), gives:

$$\text{Safety stock} = 1.645(10) = 16.5 \text{ kits}$$

This is the situation illustrated in Figure 12.8.

c) The reorder point is:

$$\text{ROP} = \text{Expected demand during lead time} + \text{Safety stock}$$
$$= 350 \text{ kits} + 16.5 \text{ kits of safety stock} = 366.5, \text{ or } 367 \text{ kits}$$

INSIGHT ▶ The cost of the inventory policy increases dramatically (exponentially) with an increase in service levels.

LEARNING EXERCISE ▶ What policy results in stockouts 10% of the time? [Answer: $Z = 1.28$; safety stock $= 12.8$; ROP $= 363$ kits.]

RELATED PROBLEMS ▶ 12.41, 12.42, 12.49 (12.50 is available in MyOMLab)

Other Probabilistic Models

Equations (12-13) and (12-14) assume that both an estimate of expected demand during lead times and its standard deviation are available. When data on lead time demand are *not* available, the preceding formulas cannot be applied. However, three other models are available. We need to determine which model to use for three situations:

1. Demand is variable and lead time is constant
2. Lead time is variable and demand is constant
3. Both demand and lead time are variable

All three models assume that demand and lead time are independent variables. Note that our examples use days, but weeks can also be used. Let us examine these three situations separately, because a different formula for the ROP is needed for each.

LO 12.7 *Understand service levels and probabilistic inventory models*

Demand Is Variable and Lead Time Is Constant   (See Example 12.) When *only the demand is variable*, then:[5]

$$\text{ROP} = (\textit{Average daily demand} \times \text{Lead time in days}) + Z\sigma_{dLT} \quad (12\text{-}15)$$

where σ_{dLT} = Standard deviation of demand during lead time = $\sigma_d\sqrt{\text{Lead time}}$

and σ_d = Standard deviation of demand per day

Example 12

ROP FOR VARIABLE DEMAND AND CONSTANT LEAD TIME

The *average* daily demand for Lenovo laptop computers at a Circuit Town store is 15, with a standard deviation of 5 units. The lead time is constant at 2 days. Find the reorder point if management wants a 90% service level (i.e., risk stockouts only 10% of the time). How much of this is safety stock?

APPROACH ▶   Apply Equation (12-15) to the following data:

Average daily demand (normally distributed) = 15

Lead time in days (constant) = 2

Standard deviation of daily demand = σ_d = 5

Service level = 90%

SOLUTION ▶   From the normal table (Appendix I) or the Excel formula =NORMSINV(.90), we derive a Z-value for 90% of 1.28. Then:

$$\text{ROP} = (15 \text{ units} \times 2 \text{ days}) + Z\sigma_d\sqrt{\text{Lead time}}$$
$$= 30 + 1.28(5)(\sqrt{2})$$
$$= 30 + 1.28(5)(1.41) = 30 + 9.02 = 39.02 \cong 39$$

Thus, safety stock is about 9 Lenovo computers.

INSIGHT ▶   The value of Z depends on the manager's stockout risk level. The smaller the risk, the higher the Z.

LEARNING EXERCISE ▶   If the Circuit Town manager wants a 95% service level, what is the new ROP? [Answer: ROP = 41.63, or 42.]

RELATED PROBLEM ▶   12.46

Lead Time Is Variable and Demand Is Constant   When the demand is constant and *only the lead time is variable*, then:

$$\text{ROP} = (\text{Daily demand} \times \textit{Average} \text{ lead time in days}) + Z \times \text{Daily demand} \times \sigma_{LT} \quad (12\text{-}16)$$

where σ_{LT} = Standard deviation of lead time in days

Example 13

ROP FOR CONSTANT DEMAND AND VARIABLE LEAD TIME

The Circuit Town store in Example 12 sells about 10 digital cameras a day (almost a constant quantity). Lead time for camera delivery is normally distributed with a mean time of 6 days and a standard deviation of 1 day. A 98% service level is set. Find the ROP.

APPROACH ▶ Apply Equation (12-16) to the following data:

Daily demand = 10

Average lead time = 6 days

Standard deviation of lead time = σ_{LT} = 1 day

Service level = 98%, so Z (from Appendix I or the Excel formula =NORMSINV(.98)) = 2.055

SOLUTION ▶ From the equation we get:

$$\text{ROP} = (10 \text{ units} \times 6 \text{ days}) + 2.055(10 \text{ units})(1)$$
$$= 60 + 20.55 = 80.55$$

The reorder point is about 81 cameras.

INSIGHT ▶ Note how the very high service level of 98% drives the ROP up.

LEARNING EXERCISE ▶ If a 90% service level is applied, what does the ROP drop to? [Answer: ROP = 60 + (1.28)(10)(1) = 60 + 12.8 = 72.8 because the Z-value is only 1.28.]

RELATED PROBLEM ▶ 12.47

Both Demand and Lead Time Are Variable When both the demand and lead time are variable, the formula for reorder point becomes more complex:[6]

$$\text{ROP} = (\text{Average daily demand} \times \text{Average lead time in days}) + Z\sigma_{dLT} \qquad (12\text{-}17)$$

where

$$\sigma_d = \text{Standard deviation of demand per day}$$
$$\sigma_{LT} = \text{Standard deviation of lead time in days}$$

and $\sigma_{dLT} = \sqrt{(\text{Average lead time} \times \sigma_d^2) + (\text{Average daily demand})^2 \sigma_{LT}^2}$

Example 14

ROP FOR VARIABLE DEMAND AND VARIABLE LEAD TIME

The Circuit Town store's most popular item is six-packs of 9-volt batteries. About 150 packs are sold per day, following a normal distribution with a standard deviation of 16 packs. Batteries are ordered from an out-of-state distributor; lead time is normally distributed with an average of 5 days and a standard deviation of 1 day. To maintain a 95% service level, what ROP is appropriate?

APPROACH ▶ Determine a quantity at which to reorder by applying Equation (12-17) to the following data:

Average daily demand = 150 packs

Standard deviation of demand = σ_d = 16 packs

Average lead time = 5 days

Standard deviation of lead time = σ_{LT} = 1 day

Service level = 95%, so Z =1.645 (from Appendix I or the Excel formula =NORMSINV(.95))

SOLUTION ▶ From the equation we compute:

$$\text{ROP} = (150 \text{ packs} \times 5 \text{ days}) + 1.645\,\sigma_{dLT}$$

where
$$\sigma_{dLT} = \sqrt{(5 \text{ days} \times 16^2) + (150^2 \times 1^2)}$$
$$= \sqrt{(5 \times 256) + (22{,}500 \times 1)}$$
$$= \sqrt{1{,}280 + 22{,}500} = \sqrt{23{,}780} \cong 154$$

So ROP $= (150 \times 5) + 1.645(154) \cong 750 + 253 = 1{,}003$ packs

INSIGHT ▶ When both demand and lead time are variable, the formula looks quite complex. But it is just the result of squaring the standard deviations in Equations (12-15) and (12-16) to get their variances, then summing them, and finally taking the square root.

LEARNING EXERCISE ▶ For an 80% service level, what is the ROP? [Answer: $Z = .84$ and ROP $= 879$ packs.]

RELATED PROBLEM ▶ 12.48

Single-Period Model

Single-period inventory model

A system for ordering items that have little or no value at the end of a sales period (perishables).

A **single-period inventory model** describes a situation in which *one* order is placed for a product. At the end of the sales period, any remaining product has little or no value. This is a typical problem for Christmas trees, seasonal goods, bakery goods, newspapers, and magazines. (Indeed, this inventory issue is often called the "newsstand problem.") In other words, even though items at a newsstand are ordered weekly or daily, they cannot be held over and used as inventory in the next sales period. So our decision is how much to order at the beginning of the period.

Because the exact demand for such seasonal products is never known, we consider a probability distribution related to demand. If the normal distribution is assumed, and we stocked and sold an average (mean) of 100 Christmas trees each season, then there is a 50% chance we would stock out and a 50% chance we would have trees left over. To determine the optimal stocking policy for trees before the season begins, we also need to know the standard deviation and consider these two marginal costs:

C_s = Cost of shortage (we underestimated) = Sales price per unit − Cost per unit

C_o = Cost of overage (we overestimated) = Cost per unit − Salvage value per unit (if there is any)

The service level, that is, the probability of *not* stocking out, is set at:

$$\text{Service level} = \frac{C_s}{C_s + C_o} \tag{12-18}$$

Therefore, we should consider increasing our order quantity until the service level is equal to or more than the ratio of $[C_s/(C_s + C_o)]$.

This model, illustrated in Example 15, is used in many service industries, from hotels to airlines to bakeries to clothing retailers.

Example 15 | SINGLE-PERIOD INVENTORY DECISION

Chris Ellis's newsstand, just outside the Smithsonian subway station in Washington, DC, usually sells 120 copies of the *Washington Post* each day. Chris believes the sale of the *Post* is normally distributed, with a standard deviation of 15 papers. He pays 70 cents for each paper, which sells for $1.25. The *Post* gives him a 30-cent credit for each unsold paper. He wants to determine how many papers he should order each day and the stockout risk for that quantity.

APPROACH ▶ Chris's data are as follows:

C_s = cost of shortage = $1.25 − $.70 = $.55

C_o = cost of overage = $.70 − $.30 (salvage value) = $.40

Chris will apply Equation (12-18) and the normal table, using $\mu = 120$ and $\sigma = 15$.

SOLUTION ▶

a) Service level $= \dfrac{C_s}{C_s + C_o} = \dfrac{.55}{.55 + .40} = \dfrac{.55}{.95} = .579$

b) Chris needs to find the Z score for his normal distribution that yields a probability of .579.

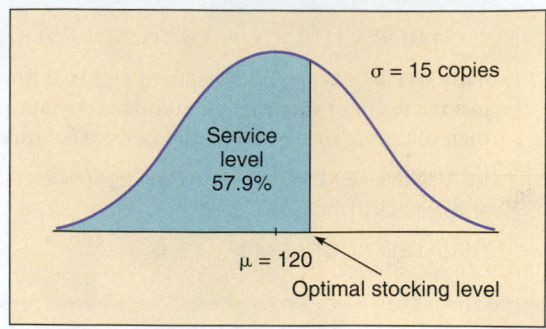

σ = 15 copies

Service level 57.9%

μ = 120

Optimal stocking level

So 57.9% of the area under the normal curve must be to the left of the optimal stocking level.

c) Using Appendix I or the Excel formula =NORMSINV(.578), for an area of .578, the Z value ≅ .195.

Then, the optimal stocking level $= 120$ copies $+ (.195)(\sigma)$

$= 120 + (.195)(15) = 120 + 3 = 123$ papers

The stockout risk if Chris orders 123 copies of the *Post* each day is $1 -$ Service level $= 1 - .578 = .422 = 42.2\%$.

INSIGHT ▶   If the service level is ever under .50, Chris should order fewer than 120 copies per day.

LEARNING EXERCISE ▶   How does Chris's decision change if the *Post* changes its policy and offers *no credit* for unsold papers, a policy many publishers are adopting?

[Answer: Service level $= .44$, $Z = -.15$. Therefore, stock $120 + (-.15)(15) = 117.75$, or 118 papers.]

RELATED PROBLEMS ▶   12.51, 12.52, 12.53

Fixed-quantity (*Q*) system

An ordering system with the same order amount each time.

Perpetual inventory system

A system that keeps track of each withdrawal or addition to inventory continuously, so records are always current.

Fixed-period (*P*) system

A system in which inventory orders are made at regular time intervals.

Fixed-Period (*P*) Systems

The inventory models that we have considered so far are fixed-quantity, or *Q*, systems. That is, the same fixed amount is added to inventory every time an order for an item is placed. We saw that orders are event triggered. When inventory decreases to the reorder point (ROP), a new order for *Q* units is placed.

To use the fixed-quantity model, inventory must be continuously monitored.[7] This requires a perpetual inventory system. Every time an item is added to or withdrawn from inventory, records must be updated to determine whether the ROP has been reached. In a fixed-period system (also called a periodic review, or *P* system), on the other hand, inventory is ordered at the end of a given period. Then, and only then, is on-hand inventory counted. Only the amount necessary to bring total inventory up to a prespecified target level (*T*) is ordered. Figure 12.9 illustrates this concept.

Fixed-period systems have several of the same assumptions as the basic EOQ fixed-quantity system:

- The only relevant costs are the ordering and holding costs.
- Lead times are known and constant.
- Items are independent of one another.

The downward-sloped lines in Figure 12.9 again represent on-hand inventory levels. But now, when the time between orders (*P*) passes, we place an order to raise inventory up to the target quantity (*T*).

Figure 12.9

Inventory Level in a Fixed-Period (*P*) System

Various amounts (Q_1, Q_2, Q_3, etc.) are ordered at regular time intervals (*P*) based on the quantity necessary to bring inventory up to the target quantity (*T*).

The amount ordered during the first period may be Q_1, the second period Q_2, and so on. The Q_i value is the difference between current on-hand inventory and the target inventory level.

The advantage of the fixed-period system is that there is no physical count of inventory items after an item is withdrawn—this occurs only when the time for the next review comes up. This procedure is also convenient administratively.

A fixed-period (P) system is appropriate when vendors make routine (i.e., at fixed-time interval) visits to customers to take fresh orders or when purchasers want to combine orders to save ordering and transportation costs (therefore, they will have the same review period for similar inventory items). For example, a vending machine company may come to refill its machines every Tuesday. This is also the case at Anheuser-Busch, whose sales reps may visit a store every 5 days.

The disadvantage of the P system is that because there is no tally of inventory during the review period, there is the possibility of a stockout during this time. This scenario is possible if a large order draws the inventory level down to zero right after an order is placed. Therefore, a higher level of safety stock (as compared to a fixed-quantity system) needs to be maintained to provide protection against stockout during both the time between reviews and the lead time.

Summary

Inventory represents a major investment for many firms. This investment is often larger than it should be because firms find it easier to have "just-in-case" inventory rather than "just-in-time" inventory. Inventories are of four types:

1. Raw material and purchased components
2. Work-in-process
3. Maintenance, repair, and operating (MRO)
4. Finished goods

In this chapter, we discussed independent inventory, ABC analysis, record accuracy, cycle counting, and inventory models used to control independent demands. The EOQ model, production order quantity model, and quantity discount model can all be solved using Excel, Excel OM, or POM for Windows software.

Key Terms

Raw material inventory (p. 490)
Work-in-process (WIP) inventory (p. 490)
Maintenance/repair/operating (MRO) inventory (p. 490)
Finished-goods inventory (p. 491)
ABC analysis (p. 491)
Cycle counting (p. 493)
Shrinkage (p. 494)
Pilferage (p. 494)

Holding cost (p. 495)
Ordering cost (p. 495)
Setup cost (p. 496)
Setup time (p. 496)
Economic order quantity (EOQ) model (p. 496)
Robust (p. 500)
Lead time (p. 501)
Reorder point (ROP) (p. 501)

Safety stock (ss) (p. 501)
Production order quantity model (p. 502)
Quantity discount (p. 505)
Probabilistic model (p. 508)
Service level (p. 508)
Single-period inventory model (p. 513)
Fixed-quantity (Q) system (p. 514)
Perpetual inventory system (p. 514)
Fixed-period (P) system (p. 514)

Ethical Dilemma

Wayne Hills Hospital in tiny Wayne, Nebraska, faces a problem common to large, urban hospitals as well as to small, remote ones like itself. That problem is deciding how much of each type of whole blood to keep in stock. Because blood is expensive and has a limited shelf life (up to 5 weeks under 1–6°C refrigeration), Wayne Hills naturally wants to keep its stock as low as possible. Unfortunately, past disasters such as a major tornado and a train wreck demonstrated that lives would be lost when not enough blood was available to handle massive needs. The hospital administrator wants to set an 85% service level based on demand over the past decade. Discuss the implications of this decision. What is the hospital's responsibility with regard to stocking lifesaving medicines with short shelf lives? How would you set the inventory level for a commodity such as blood?

Discussion Questions

1. Describe the four types of inventory.
2. With the advent of low-cost computing, do you see alternatives to the popular ABC classifications?
3. What is the purpose of the ABC classification system?
4. Identify and explain the types of costs that are involved in an inventory system.
5. Explain the major assumptions of the basic EOQ model.
6. What is the relationship of the economic order quantity to demand? To the holding cost? To the setup cost?
7. Explain why it is not necessary to include product cost (price or price times quantity) in the EOQ model, but the quantity discount model requires this information.

8. What are the advantages of cycle counting?

9. What impact does a decrease in setup time have on EOQ?

10. When quantity discounts are offered, why is it not necessary to check discount points that are below the EOQ or points above the EOQ that are not discount points?

11. What is meant by "service level"?

12. Explain the following: All things being equal, the production order quantity will be larger than the economic order quantity.

13. Describe the difference between a fixed-quantity (Q) and a fixed-period (P) inventory system.

14. Explain what is meant by the expression "robust model." Specifically, what would you tell a manager who exclaimed, "Uh-oh, we're in trouble! The calculated EOQ is wrong; actual demand is 10% greater than estimated."

15. What is "safety stock"? What does safety stock provide safety against?

16. When demand is not constant, the reorder point is a function of what four parameters?

17. How are inventory levels monitored in retail stores?

18. State a major advantage, and a major disadvantage, of a fixed-period (P) system.

Using Software to Solve Inventory Problems

This section presents three ways to solve inventory problems with computer software. First, you can create your own Excel spreadsheets. Second, you can use the Excel OM software that comes free with this text. Third, POM for Windows, also free with this text, can solve all problems marked with a **P** .

CREATING YOUR OWN EXCEL SPREADSHEETS

Program 12.1 illustrates how you can make an Excel model to solve Example 8, which is a production order quantity model.

Program **12.1**

Using Excel for a Production Model, with Data from Example 8

Program 12.2 illustrates how you can make an Excel model to solve Example 15, which is a single-period inventory model.

Program **12.2**

Using Excel for a Single-Period Inventory Model, with Data from Example 15

✗ USING EXCEL OM

Excel OM allows us to easily model inventory problems ranging from ABC analysis, to the basic EOQ model, to the production model, to quantity discount situations.

Program 12.3 shows the input data, selected formulas, and results for an ABC analysis, using data from Example 1. After the data are entered, we use the *Data* and *Sort* Excel commands to rank the items from largest to smallest dollar volumes.

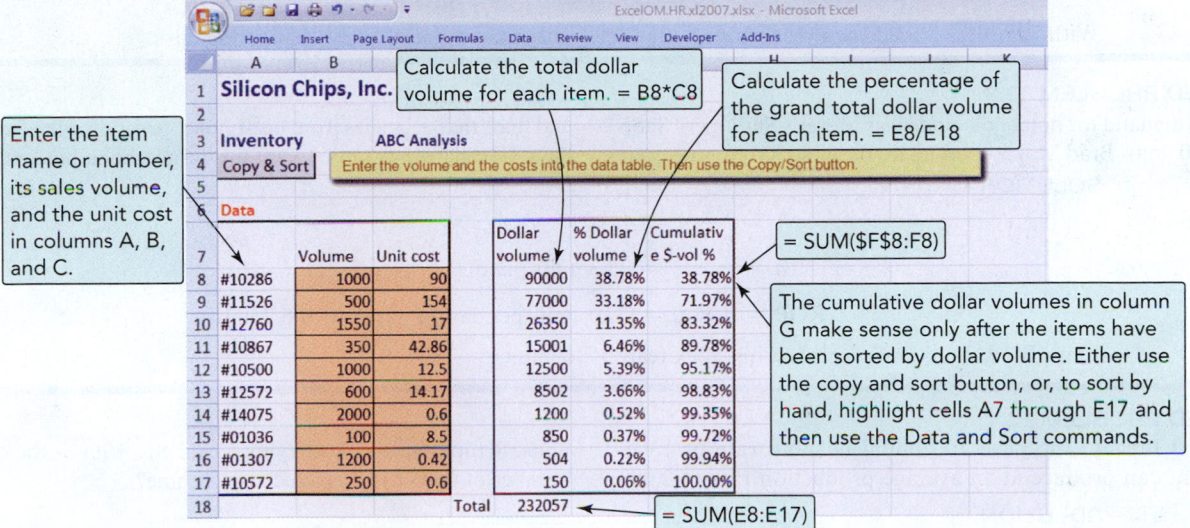

Program 12.3

Using Excel OM for an ABC Analysis, with Data from Example 1

P USING POM FOR WINDOWS

The POM for Windows Inventory module can also solve the entire EOQ family of problems. Please refer to Appendix IV for further details.

Solved Problems   Virtual Office Hours help is available in MyOMLab.

SOLVED PROBLEM 12.1

David Alexander has compiled the following table of six items in inventory at Angelo Products, along with the unit cost and the annual demand in units:

IDENTIFICATION CODE	UNIT COST ($)	ANNUAL DEMAND (UNITS)
XX1	5.84	1,200
B66	5.40	1,110
3CPO	1.12	896
33CP	74.54	1,104
R2D2	2.00	1,110
RMS	2.08	961

Use ABC analysis to determine which item(s) should be carefully controlled using a quantitative inventory technique and which item(s) should not be closely controlled.

SOLUTION

The item that needs strict control is 33CP, so it is an A item. Items that do not need to be strictly controlled are 3CPO, R2D2, and RMS; these are C items. The B items will be XX1 and B66.

CODE	ANNUAL DOLLAR VOLUME = UNIT COST × DEMAND
XX1	$ 7,008.00
B66	$ 5,994.00
3CPO	$ 1,003.52
33CP	$82,292.16
R2D2	$ 2,220.00
RMS	$ 1,998.88

Total cost = $100,516.56
70% of total cost = $70,347.92

SOLVED PROBLEM 12.2

The Warren W. Fisher Computer Corporation purchases 8,000 transistors each year as components in minicomputers. The unit cost of each transistor is $10, and the cost of carrying one transistor in inventory for a year is $3. Ordering cost is $30 per order.

What are (a) the optimal order quantity, (b) the expected number of orders placed each year, and (c) the expected time between orders? Assume that Fisher operates on a 200-day working year.

SOLUTION

a) $Q^* = \sqrt{\dfrac{2DS}{H}} = \sqrt{\dfrac{2(8,000)(30)}{3}} = 400$ units

b) $N = \dfrac{D}{Q^*} = \dfrac{8,000}{400} = 20$ orders

c) Time between orders $= T = \dfrac{\text{Number of working days}}{N} = \dfrac{200}{20} = 10$ working days

With 20 orders placed each year, an order for 400 transistors is placed every 10 working days.

SOLVED PROBLEM 12.3

Annual demand for notebook binders at Meyer's Stationery Shop is 10,000 units. Brad Meyer operates his business 300 days per year and finds that deliveries from his supplier generally take 5 working days. Calculate the reorder point for the notebook binders.

SOLUTION

$$L = 5 \text{ days}$$

$$d = \dfrac{10,000}{300} = 33.3 \text{ units per day}$$

$$\text{ROP} = d \times L = (33.3 \text{ units per day})(5 \text{ days}) = 166.7 \text{ units}$$

Thus, Brad should reorder when his stock reaches 167 units.

SOLVED PROBLEM 12.4

Leonard Presby, Inc., has an annual demand rate of 1,000 units but can produce at an average production rate of 2,000 units. Setup cost is $10; carrying cost is $1. What is the optimal number of units to be produced each time?

SOLUTION

$$Q_p^* = \sqrt{\dfrac{2DS}{H\left(1 - \dfrac{\text{Annual demand rate}}{\text{Annual production rate}}\right)}} = \sqrt{\dfrac{2(1,000)(10)}{1[1 - (1,000/2,000)]}}$$

$$= \sqrt{\dfrac{20,000}{1/2}} = \sqrt{40,000} = 200 \text{ units}$$

SOLVED PROBLEM 12.5

Whole Nature Foods sells a gluten-free product for which the annual demand is 5,000 boxes. At the moment, it is paying $6.40 for each box; carrying cost is 25% of the unit cost; ordering costs are $25. A new supplier has offered to sell the same item for $6.00 if Whole Nature Foods buys at least 3,000 boxes per order. Should the firm stick with the old supplier, or take advantage of the new quantity discount?

SOLUTION

Step 1, under the lowest possible price of $6.00 per box:
Economic order quantity, using Equation (12-10):

$$Q^*_{\$6.00} = \sqrt{\dfrac{2(5,000)(25)}{(0.25)(6.00)}}$$

$$= 408.25, \text{ or } 408 \text{ boxes}$$

Because $408 < 3,000$, this EOQ is *infeasible* for the $6.00 price. So now we calculate Q^* for the next-higher price of $6.40, which equals 395 boxes (and is feasible). Thus, the best possible order quantities are 395 (the first feasible EOQ) and 3,000 (the price-break quantity for the lower price of $6.00).

Step 2 uses Equation (12-9) to compute the total cost for both of the possible best order quantities:

$$TC_{395} = \dfrac{5,000}{395}(\$25) + \dfrac{395}{2}(0.25)(\$6.40) + \$6.40(5,000)$$

$$= \$316 + \$316 + \$32,000$$

$$= \$32,632$$

And under the quantity discount price of $6.00 per box:

$$TC_{3,000} = \dfrac{5,000}{3,000}(\$25) + \dfrac{3,000}{2}(0.25)(\$6.00) + \$6.00(5,000)$$

$$= \$42 + \$2,250 + \$30,000$$

$$= \$32,292$$

Therefore, the new supplier with which Whole Nature Foods would incur a total cost of $32,292 is preferable, but not by a large amount. If buying 3,000 boxes at a time raises problems of storage or freshness, the company may very well wish to stay with the current supplier.

SOLVED PROBLEM 12.6

Children's art sets are ordered once each year by Ashok Kumar, Inc., and the reorder point, without safety stock (dL), is 100 art sets. Inventory carrying cost is $10 per set per year, and the cost of a stockout is $50 per set per year. Given the following demand probabilities during the lead time, how much safety stock should be carried?

DEMAND DURING LEAD TIME	PROBABILITY
0	.1
50	.2
ROP → 100	.4
150	.2
200	.1
	1.0

SOLUTION

SAFETY STOCK	INCREMENTAL COSTS		
	CARRYING COST	STOCKOUT COST	TOTAL COST
0	0	50 × (50 × 0.2 + 100 × 0.1) = 1,000	$1,000
50	50 × 10 = 500	50 × (0.1 × 50) = 250	750
100	100 × 10 = 1,000	0	1,000

The safety stock that minimizes total incremental cost is 50 sets. The reorder point then becomes 100 sets + 50 sets, or 150 sets.

SOLVED PROBLEM 12.7

What safety stock should Ron Satterfield Corporation maintain if mean sales are 80 during the reorder period, the standard deviation is 7, and Ron can tolerate stockouts 10% of the time?

SOLUTION

10% area under the normal curve

Safety stock

$\mu = 80$
$\sigma_{dLT} = 7$

From Appendix I, Z at an area of .9 (or $1 - .10$) = 1.28, and Equation (12-14):

Safety stock $= Z\sigma_{dLT}$
$= 1.28(7) = 8.96$ units, or 9 units

SOLVED PROBLEM 12.8

The daily demand for 52" flat-screen TVs at Sarah's Discount Emporium is normally distributed, with an average of 5 and a standard deviation of 2 units. The lead time for receiving a shipment of new TVs is 10 days and is fairly constant. Determine the reorder point and safety stock for a 95% service level.

SOLUTION

The ROP for this variable demand and constant lead time model uses Equation (12-15):

$$\text{ROP} = (\text{Average daily demand} \times \text{Lead time in days}) + Z\sigma_{dLT}$$

where $\sigma_{dLT} = \sigma_d \sqrt{\text{Lead time}}$

So, with $Z = 1.645$,

$$\text{ROP} = (5 \times 10) + 1.645(2)\sqrt{10}$$
$$= 50 + 10.4 = 60.4 \cong 60 \text{ TVs, or rounded up to 61 TVs}$$

The safety stock is 10.4, which can be rounded up to 11 TVs.

SOLVED PROBLEM 12.9

The demand at Arnold Palmer Hospital for a specialized surgery pack is 60 per week, virtually every week. The lead time from McKesson, its main supplier, is normally distributed, with a mean of 6 weeks for this product and a standard deviation of 2 weeks. A 90% weekly service level is desired. Find the ROP.

SOLUTION

Here the demand is constant and lead time is variable, with data given in weeks, not days. We apply Equation (12-16):

$$\text{ROP} = (\text{Weekly demand} \times \text{Average lead time in weeks}) + Z(\text{Weekly demand})\sigma_{LT}$$

where $\sigma_{LT} = $ standard deviation of lead time in weeks = 2

So, with $Z = 1.28$, for a 90% service level:

$$\text{ROP} = (60 \times 6) + 1.28(60)(2)$$
$$= 360 + 153.6 = 513.6 \cong 514 \text{ surgery packs}$$

Problems

Note: **Px** means the problem may be solved with POM for Windows and/or Excel OM.

Problems 12.1–12.6 relate to Managing Inventory

•• **12.1** L. Houts Plastics is a large manufacturer of injection-molded plastics in North Carolina. An investigation of the company's manufacturing facility in Charlotte yields the information presented in the table below. How would the plant classify these items according to an ABC classification system? **Px**

L. Houts Plastics' Charlotte Inventory Levels

ITEM CODE #	AVERAGE INVENTORY (UNITS)	VALUE ($/UNIT)
1289	400	3.75
2347	300	4.00
2349	120	2.50
2363	75	1.50
2394	60	1.75
2395	30	2.00
6782	20	1.15
7844	12	2.05
8210	8	1.80
8310	7	2.00
9111	6	3.00

•• **12.2** Boreki Enterprises has the following 10 items in inventory. Theodore Boreki asks you, a recent OM graduate, to divide these items into ABC classifications.

ITEM	ANNUAL DEMAND	COST/UNIT
A2	3,000	$ 50
B8	4,000	12
C7	1,500	45
D1	6,000	10
E9	1,000	20
F3	500	500
G2	300	1,500
H2	600	20
I5	1,750	10
J8	2,500	5

a) Develop an ABC classification system for the 10 items.
b) How can Boreki use this information?
c) Boreki reviews the classification and then places item A2 into the A category. Why might he do so? **Px**

•• **12.3** Jean-Marie Bourjolly's restaurant has the following inventory items that it orders on a weekly basis:

INVENTORY ITEM	$ VALUE/CASE	# ORDERED/WEEK
Ribeye steak	135	3
Lobster tail	245	3
Pasta	23	12
Salt	3	2
Napkins	12	2
Tomato sauce	23	11
French fries	43	32

cont'd

(cont'd)

INVENTORY ITEM	$ VALUE/CASE	# ORDERED/WEEK
Pepper	3	3
Garlic powder	11	3
Trash can liners	12	3
Table cloths	32	5
Fish filets	143	10
Prime rib roasts	166	6
Oil	28	2
Lettuce (case)	35	24
Chickens	75	14
Order pads	12	2
Eggs (case)	22	7
Bacon	56	5
Sugar	4	2

a) Which is the most expensive item, using annual dollar volume?
b) Which are C items?
c) What is the annual dollar volume for all 20 items? **Px**

• **12.4** Lindsay Electronics, a small manufacturer of electronic research equipment, has approximately 7,000 items in its inventory and has hired Joan Blasco-Paul to manage its inventory. Joan has determined that 10% of the items in inventory are A items, 35% are B items, and 55% are C items. She would like to set up a system in which all A items are counted monthly (every 20 working days), all B items are counted quarterly (every 60 working days), and all C items are counted semiannually (every 120 working days). How many items need to be counted each day?

> Additional problems **12.5–12.6** are available in MyOMLab.

Problems 12.7–12.40 relate to Inventory Models for Independent Demand

• **12.7** William Beville's computer training school, in Richmond, stocks workbooks with the following characteristics:

$$\text{Demand } D = 19{,}500 \text{ units/year}$$
$$\text{Ordering cost } S = \$25/\text{order}$$
$$\text{Holding cost } H = \$4/\text{unit/year}$$

a) Calculate the EOQ for the workbooks.
b) What are the annual holding costs for the workbooks?
c) What are the annual ordering costs? **Px**

• **12.8** If $D = 8{,}000$ per month, $S = \$45$ per order, and $H = \$2$ per unit per month,
a) What is the economic order quantity?
b) How does your answer change if the holding cost doubles?
c) What if the holding cost drops in half? **Px**

•• **12.9** Henry Crouch's law office has traditionally ordered ink refills 60 units at a time. The firm estimates that carrying cost is 40% of the $10 unit cost and that annual demand is about 240 units per year. The assumptions of the basic EOQ model are thought to apply.
a) For what value of ordering cost would its action be optimal?
b) If the true ordering cost turns out to be much greater than your answer to (a), what is the impact on the firm's ordering policy?

• **12.10** Matthew Liotine's Dream Store sells beds and assorted supplies. His best-selling bed has an annual demand of 400 units. Ordering cost is $40; holding cost is $5 per unit per year.

a) To minimize the total cost, how many units should be ordered each time an order is placed?

b) If the holding cost per unit was $6 instead of $5, what would be the optimal order quantity? **Px**

• **12.11** Southeastern Bell stocks a certain switch connector at its central warehouse for supplying field service offices. The yearly demand for these connectors is 15,000 units. Southeastern estimates its annual holding cost for this item to be $25 per unit. The cost to place and process an order from the supplier is $75. The company operates 300 days per year, and the lead time to receive an order from the supplier is 2 working days.

a) Find the economic order quantity.

b) Find the annual holding costs.

c) Find the annual ordering costs.

d) What is the reorder point? **Px**

• **12.12** Lead time for one of your fastest-moving products is 21 days. Demand during this period averages 100 units per day.

a) What would be an appropriate reorder point?

b) How does your answer change if demand during lead time doubles?

c) How does your answer change if demand during lead time drops in half?

• **12.13** Annual demand for the notebook binders at Duncan's Stationery Shop is 10,000 units. Dana Duncan operates her business 300 days per year and finds that deliveries from her supplier generally take 5 working days.

a) Calculate the reorder point for the notebook binders that she stocks.

b) Why is this number important to Duncan?

•• **12.14** Thomas Kratzer is the purchasing manager for the headquarters of a large insurance company chain with a central inventory operation. Thomas's fastest-moving inventory item has a demand of 6,000 units per year. The cost of each unit is $100, and the inventory carrying cost is $10 per unit per year. The average ordering cost is $30 per order. It takes about 5 days for an order to arrive, and the demand for 1 week is 120 units. (This is a corporate operation, and there are 250 working days per year.)

a) What is the EOQ?

b) What is the average inventory if the EOQ is used?

c) What is the optimal number of orders per year?

d) What is the optimal number of days in between any two orders?

e) What is the annual cost of ordering and holding inventory?

f) What is the total annual inventory cost, including the cost of the 6,000 units? **Px**

•• **12.15** Joe Henry's machine shop uses 2,500 brackets during the course of a year. These brackets are purchased from a supplier 90 miles away. The following information is known about the brackets:

Annual demand:	2,500
Holding cost per bracket per year:	$1.50
Order cost per order:	$18.75
Lead time:	2 days
Working days per year:	250

a) Given the above information, what would be the economic order quantity (EOQ)?

b) Given the EOQ, what would be the average inventory? What would be the annual inventory holding cost?

c) Given the EOQ, how many orders would be made each year? What would be the annual order cost?

d) Given the EOQ, what is the total annual cost of managing the inventory?

e) What is the time between orders?

f) What is the reorder point (ROP)? **Px**

•• **12.16** Abey Kuruvilla, of Parkside Plumbing, uses 1,200 of a certain spare part that costs $25 for each order, with an annual holding cost of $24.

a) Calculate the total cost for order sizes of 25, 40, 50, 60, and 100.

b) Identify the economic order quantity and consider the implications for making an error in calculating economic order quantity. **Px**

••• **12.17** M. Cotteleer Electronics supplies microcomputer circuitry to a company that incorporates microprocessors into refrigerators and other home appliances. One of the components has an annual demand of 250 units, and this is constant throughout the year. Carrying cost is estimated to be $1 per unit per year, and the ordering (setup) cost is $20 per order.

a) To minimize cost, how many units should be ordered each time an order is placed?

b) How many orders per year are needed with the optimal policy?

c) What is the average inventory if costs are minimized?

d) Suppose that the ordering (setup) cost is not $20, and Cotteleer has been ordering 150 units each time an order is placed. For this order policy (of $Q = 150$) to be optimal, determine what the ordering (setup) cost would have to be. **Px**

•• **12.18** Race One Motors is an Indonesian car manufacturer. At its largest manufacturing facility, in Jakarta, the company produces subcomponents at a rate of 300 per day, and it uses these subcomponents at a rate of 12,500 per year (of 250 working days). Holding costs are $2 per item per year, and ordering (setup) costs are $30 per order.

a) What is the economic production quantity?

b) How many production runs per year will be made?

c) What will be the maximum inventory level?

d) What percentage of time will the facility be producing components?

e) What is the annual cost of ordering and holding inventory? **Px**

•• **12.19** Radovilsky Manufacturing Company, in Hayward, California, makes flashing lights for toys. The company operates its production facility 300 days per year. It has orders for about 12,000 flashing lights per year and has the capability of producing 100 per day. Setting up the light production costs $50. The cost of each light is $1. The holding cost is $0.10 per light per year.

a) What is the optimal size of the production run?

b) What is the average holding cost per year?

c) What is the average setup cost per year?

d) What is the total cost per year, including the cost of the lights? **Px**

•• **12.20** Arthur Meiners is the production manager of Wheel-Rite, a small producer of metal parts. Wheel-Rite supplies Cal-Tex, a larger assembly company, with 10,000 wheel bearings each year. This order has been stable for some time. Setup cost for Wheel-Rite is $40, and holding cost is $.60 per wheel bearing per year. Wheel-Rite can produce 500 wheel bearings per day. Cal-Tex is a just-in-time manufacturer and requires that 50 bearings be shipped to it each business day.

a) What is the optimum production quantity?

b) What is the maximum number of wheel bearings that will be in inventory at Wheel-Rite?

c) How many production runs of wheel bearings will Wheel-Rite have in a year?

d) What is the total setup + holding cost for Wheel-Rite? **Px**

•• 12.21 Cesar Rego Computers, a Mississippi chain of computer hardware and software retail outlets, supplies both educational and commercial customers with memory and storage devices. It currently faces the following ordering decision relating to purchases of very high-density disks:

$$D = 36,000 \text{ disks}$$
$$S = \$25$$
$$H = \$0.45$$
$$\text{Purchase price} = \$.85$$
$$\text{Discount price} = \$0.82$$

Quantity needed to qualify for the discount = 6,000 disks

Should the discount be taken? **Px**

•• 12.22 Bell Computers purchases integrated chips at $350 per chip. The holding cost is $35 per unit per year, the ordering cost is $120 per order, and sales are steady, at 400 per month. The company's supplier, Rich Blue Chip Manufacturing, Inc., decides to offer price concessions in order to attract larger orders. The price structure is shown below.

Rich Blue Chip's Price Structure

QUANTITY PURCHASED	PRICE/UNIT
1–99 units	$350
100–199 units	$325
200 or more units	$300

a) What is the optimal order quantity and the minimum annual cost for Bell Computers to order, purchase, and hold these integrated chips?

b) Bell Computers wishes to use a 10% holding cost rather than the fixed $35 holding cost in (a). What is the optimal order quantity, and what is the optimal annual cost? **Px**

•• 12.23 Wang Distributors has an annual demand for an airport metal detector of 1,400 units. The cost of a typical detector to Wang is $400. Carrying cost is estimated to be 20% of the unit cost, and the ordering cost is $25 per order. If Ping Wang, the owner, orders in quantities of 300 or more, he can get a 5% discount on the cost of the detectors. Should Wang take the quantity discount? **Px**

•• 12.24 The catering manager of La Vista Hotel, Lisa Ferguson, is disturbed by the amount of silverware she is losing every week. Last Friday night, when her crew tried to set up for a banquet for 500 people, they did not have enough knives. She decides she needs to order some more silverware, but wants to take advantage of any quantity discounts her vendor will offer.

For a small order (2,000 or fewer pieces), her vendor quotes a price of $1.80/piece.

If she orders 2,001–5,000 pieces, the price drops to $1.60/piece. 5,001–10,000 pieces brings the price to $1.40/piece, and 10,001 and above reduces the price to $1.25.

Lisa's order costs are $200 per order, her annual holding costs are 5%, and the annual demand is 45,000 pieces. For the best option:

a) What is the optimal order quantity?

b) What is the annual holding cost?

c) What is the annual ordering (setup) cost?

d) What are the annual costs of the silverware itself with an optimal order quantity?

e) What is the total annual cost, including ordering, holding, and purchasing the silverware? **Px**

•• 12.25 Rocky Mountain Tire Center sells 20,000 go-cart tires per year. The ordering cost for each order is $40, and the holding cost is 20% of the purchase price of the tires per year. The purchase price is $20 per tire if fewer than 500 tires are ordered, $18 per tire if 500 or more—but fewer than 1,000—tires are ordered, and $17 per tire if 1,000 or more tires are ordered.

a) How many tires should Rocky Mountain order each time it places an order?

b) What is the total cost of this policy? **Px**

•• 12.26 M. P. VanOyen Manufacturing has gone out on bid for a regulator component. Expected demand is 700 units per month. The item can be purchased from either Allen Manufacturing or Baker Manufacturing. Their price lists are shown in the table. Ordering cost is $50, and annual holding cost per unit is $5.

ALLEN MFG.		BAKER MFG.	
QUANTITY	UNIT PRICE	QUANTITY	UNIT PRICE
1–499	$16.00	1–399	$16.10
500–999	15.50	400–799	15.60
1,000+	15.00	800+	15.10

a) What is the economic order quantity?

b) Which supplier should be used? Why?

c) What is the optimal order quantity and total annual cost of ordering, purchasing, and holding the component? **Px**

••• 12.27 Chris Sandvig Irrigation, Inc., has summarized the price list from four potential suppliers of an underground control valve. See the accompanying table. Annual usage is 2,400 valves; order cost is $10 per order; and annual inventory holding costs are $3.33 per unit.

Which vendor should be selected and what order quantity is best if Sandvig Irrigation wants to minimize total cost? **Px**

VENDOR A		VENDOR B	
QUANTITY	PRICE	QUANTITY	PRICE
1–49	$35.00	1–74	$34.75
50–74	34.75	75–149	34.00
75–149	33.55	150–299	32.80
150–299	32.35	300–499	31.60
300–499	31.15	500+	30.50
500+	30.75		

VENDOR C		VENDOR D	
QUANTITY	PRICE	QUANTITY	PRICE
1–99	$34.50	1–199	$34.25
100–199	33.75	200–399	33.00
200–399	32.50	400+	31.00
400+	31.10		

••• 12.28 Emery Pharmaceutical uses an unstable chemical compound that must be kept in an environment where both temperature and humidity can be controlled. Emery uses 800 pounds per month of the chemical, estimates the holding cost to be 50% of the purchase price (because of spoilage), and estimates order costs to be $50 per order. The cost schedules of two suppliers are as follows:

VENDOR 1		VENDOR 2	
QUANTITY	PRICE/LB	QUANTITY	PRICE/LB
1–499	$17.00	1–399	$17.10
500–999	16.75	400–799	16.85
1,000+	16.50	800–1,199	16.60
		1,200+	16.25

a) What is the economic order quantity for each supplier?

b) What quantity should be ordered, and which supplier should be used?

c) What is the total cost for the most economic order size?

d) What factor(s) should be considered besides total cost? **P✗**

• • • 12.29 Kim Clark has asked you to help him determine the best ordering policy for a new product. The demand for the new product has been forecasted to be about 1,000 units annually. To help you get a handle on the carrying and ordering costs, Kim has given you the list of last year's costs. He thought that these costs might be appropriate for the new product.

COST FACTOR	COST ($)	COST FACTOR	COST ($)
Taxes for the warehouse	2,000	Warehouse supplies	280
Receiving and incoming inspection	1,500	Research and development	2,750
New product development	2,500	Purchasing salaries & wages	30,000
Acct. Dept. costs to pay invoices	500	Warehouse salaries & wages	12,800
Inventory insurance	600	Pilferage of inventory	800
Product advertising	800	Purchase order supplies	500
Spoilage	750	Inventory obsolescence	300
Sending purchasing orders	800	Purchasing Dept. overhead	1,000

He also told you that these data were compiled for 10,000 inventory items that were carried or held during the year. You have also determined that 200 orders were placed last year. Your job as a new operations management graduate is to help Kim determine the economic order quantity for the new product.

• • • • 12.30 Emarpy Appliance is a company that produces all kinds of major appliances. Bud Banis, the president of Emarpy, is concerned about the production policy for the company's best-selling refrigerator. The annual demand has been about 8,000 units each year, and this demand has been constant throughout the year. The production capacity is 200 units per day. Each time production starts, it costs the company $120 to move materials into place, reset the assembly line, and clean the equipment. The holding cost of a refrigerator is $50 per year. The current production plan calls for 400 refrigerators to be produced in each production run. Assume there are 250 working days per year.

a) What is the daily demand of this product?

b) If the company were to continue to produce 400 units each time production starts, how many days would production continue?

c) Under the current policy, how many production runs per year would be required? What would the annual setup cost be?

d) If the current policy continues, how many refrigerators would be in inventory when production stops? What would the average inventory level be?

e) If the company produces 400 refrigerators at a time, what would the total annual setup cost and holding cost be?

f) If Bud Banis wants to minimize the total annual inventory cost, how many refrigerators should be produced in each production run? How much would this save the company in inventory costs compared to the current policy of producing 400 in each production run? **P✗**

Additional problems **12.31–12.40** *are available in* MyOMLab.

Problems 12.41–12.50 relate to Probabilistic Models and Safety Stock

• • 12.41 Barbara Flynn is in charge of maintaining hospital supplies at General Hospital. During the past year, the mean lead time demand for bandage BX-5 was 60 (and was normally distributed). Furthermore, the standard deviation for BX-5 was 7. Ms. Flynn would like to maintain a 90% service level.

a) What safety stock level do you recommend for BX-5?

b) What is the appropriate reorder point? **P✗**

• • 12.42 Based on available information, lead time demand for PC jump drives averages 50 units (normally distributed), with a standard deviation of 5 drives. Management wants a 97% service level.

a) What value of Z should be applied?

b) How many drives should be carried as safety stock?

c) What is the appropriate reorder point? **P✗**

• • • 12.43 Authentic Thai rattan chairs (shown in the photo) are delivered to Gary Schwartz's chain of retail stores, called The Kathmandu Shop, once a year. The reorder point, without safety stock, is 200 chairs. Carrying cost is $30 per unit per year, and the cost of a stockout is $70 per chair per year. Given the following demand probabilities during the lead time, how much safety stock should be carried?

Barry Render

DEMAND DURING LEAD TIME	PROBABILITY
0	0.2
100	0.2
200	0.2
300	0.2
400	0.2

• • 12.44 Tobacco is shipped from North Carolina to a cigarette manufacturer in Cambodia once a year. The reorder point, without safety stock, is 200 kilos. The carrying cost is $15 per kilo per year, and the cost of a stockout is $70 per kilo per year. Given the following demand probabilities during the lead time, how much safety stock should be carried?

DEMAND DURING LEAD TIME (KILOS)	PROBABILITY
0	0.1
100	0.1
200	0.2
300	0.4
400	0.2

••• **12.45** Mr. Beautiful, an organization that sells weight training sets, has an ordering cost of $40 for the BB-1 set. (BB-1 stands for Body Beautiful Number 1.) The carrying cost for BB-1 is $5 per set per year. To meet demand, Mr. Beautiful orders large quantities of BB-1 seven times a year. The stockout cost for BB-1 is estimated to be $50 per set. Over the past several years, Mr. Beautiful has observed the following demand during the lead time for BB-1:

DEMAND DURING LEAD TIME	PROBABILITY
40	.1
50	.2
60	.2
70	.2
80	.2
90	.1
	1.0

The reorder point for BB-1 is 60 sets. What level of safety stock should be maintained for BB-1?

•• **12.46** Chicago's Hard Rock Hotel distributes a mean of 1,000 bath towels per day to guests at the pool and in their rooms. This demand is normally distributed with a standard deviation of 100 towels per day, based on occupancy. The laundry firm that has the linens contract requires a 2-day lead time. The hotel expects a 98% service level to satisfy high guest expectations.
a) What is the safety stock?
b) What is the ROP?

•• **12.47** First Printing has contracts with legal firms in San Francisco to copy their court documents. Daily demand is almost constant at 12,500 pages of documents. The lead time for paper delivery is normally distributed with a mean of 4 days and a standard deviation of 1 day. A 97% service level is expected. Compute First's ROP.

••• **12.48** Gainesville Cigar stocks Cuban cigars that have variable lead times because of the difficulty in importing the product: lead time is normally distributed with an average of 6 weeks and a standard deviation of 2 weeks. Demand is also a variable and normally distributed with a mean of 200 cigars per week and a standard deviation of 25 cigars.
a) For a 90% service level, what is the ROP?
b) What is the ROP for a 95% service level?

c) Explain what these two service levels mean. Which is preferable?

•••• **12.49** A gourmet coffee shop in downtown San Francisco is open 200 days a year and sells an average of 75 pounds of Kona coffee beans a day. (Demand can be assumed to be distributed normally, with a standard deviation of 15 pounds per day.) After ordering (fixed cost = $16 per order), beans are always shipped from Hawaii within exactly 4 days. Per-pound annual holding costs for the beans are $3.
a) What is the economic order quantity (EOQ) for Kona coffee beans?
b) What are the total annual holding costs of stock for Kona coffee beans?
c) What are the total annual ordering costs for Kona coffee beans?
d) Assume that management has specified that no more than a 1% risk during stockout is acceptable. What should the reorder point (ROP) be?
e) What is the safety stock needed to attain a 1% risk of stockout during lead time?
f) What is the annual holding cost of maintaining the level of safety stock needed to support a 1% risk?
g) If management specified that a 2% risk of stockout during lead time would be acceptable, would the safety stock holding costs decrease or increase?

Additional problem **12.50** is available in MyOMLab.

Problems 12.51–12.53 relate to Single-Period Model

•• **12.51** Cynthia Knott's oyster bar buys fresh Louisiana oysters for $5 per pound and sells them for $9 per pound. Any oysters not sold that day are sold to her cousin, who has a nearby grocery store, for $2 per pound. Cynthia believes that demand follows the normal distribution, with a mean of 100 pounds and a standard deviation of 15 pounds. How many pounds should she order each day?

•• **12.52** Henrique Correa's bakery prepares all its cakes between 4 A.M. and 6 A.M. so they will be fresh when customers arrive. Day-old cakes are virtually always sold, but at a 50% discount off the regular $10 price. The cost of baking a cake is $6, and demand is estimated to be normally distributed, with a mean of 25 and a standard deviation of 4. What is the optimal stocking level?

••• **12.53** University of Florida football programs are printed 1 week prior to each home game. Attendance averages 90,000 screaming and loyal Gators fans, of whom two-thirds usually buy the program, following a normal distribution, for $4 each. Unsold programs are sent to a recycling center that pays only 10 cents per program. The standard deviation is 5,000 programs, and the cost to print each program is $1.
a) What is the cost of underestimating demand for each program?
b) What is the overage cost per program?
c) How many programs should be ordered per game?
d) What is the stockout risk for this order size?

CASE STUDIES

Zhou Bicycle Company

Zhou Bicycle Company (ZBC), located in Seattle, is a wholesale distributor of bicycles and bicycle parts. Formed in 1981 by University of Washington Professor Yong-Pin Zhou, the firm's primary retail outlets are located within a 400-mile radius of the distribution center. These retail outlets receive the order from ZBC within 2 days after notifying the distribution center, provided that the stock is available. However, if an order is not fulfilled by the company, no backorder is placed; the retailers arrange to get their shipment from other distributors, and ZBC loses that amount of business.

The company distributes a wide variety of bicycles. The most popular model, and the major source of revenue to the company, is the AirWing. ZBC receives all the models from a single manufacturer in China, and shipment takes as long as 4 weeks from the time an order is placed. With the cost of communication, paperwork, and customs clearance included, ZBC estimates that each time an order is placed, it incurs a cost of $65. The purchase price paid by ZBC, per bicycle, is roughly 60% of the suggested retail price for all the styles available, and the inventory carrying cost is 1% per month (12% per year) of the purchase price paid by ZBC. The retail price (paid by the customers) for the AirWing is $170 per bicycle.

ZBC is interested in making an inventory plan for 2016. The firm wants to maintain a 95% service level with its customers to minimize the losses on the lost orders. The data collected for the past 2 years are summarized in the following table. A forecast for AirWing model sales in 2016 has been developed and will be used to make an inventory plan for ZBC.

Demands For Airwing Model

MONTH	2014	2015	FORECAST FOR 2016
January	6	7	8
February	12	14	15

MONTH	2014	2015	FORECAST FOR 2016
March	24	27	31
April	46	53	59
May	75	86	97
June	47	54	60
July	30	34	39
August	18	21	24
September	13	15	16
October	12	13	15
November	22	25	28
December	38	42	47
Total	343	391	439

Discussion Questions

1. Develop an inventory plan to help ZBC.
2. Discuss ROPs and total costs.
3. How can you address demand that is not at the level of the planning horizon?

Source: Professor Kala Chand Seal, Loyola Marymount University.

Parker Hi-Fi Systems

Parker Hi-Fi Systems, located in Wellesley, Massachusetts, a Boston suburb, assembles and sells the very finest home theater systems. The systems are assembled with components from the best manufacturers worldwide. Although most of the components are procured from wholesalers on the East Coast, some critical items, such as LCD screens, come directly from their manufacturer. For instance, the LCD screens are shipped via air from Foxy, Ltd., in Taiwan, to Boston's Logan airport, and the top-of-the-line speakers are purchased from the world-renowned U.S. manufacturer Boss.

Parker's purchasing agent, Raktim Pal, submits an order release for LCD screens once every 4 weeks. The company's annual requirements total 500 units (2 per working day), and Parker's per unit cost is $1,500. (Because of Parker's relatively low volume and the quality focus—rather than volume focus—of many of Parker's suppliers, Parker is seldom able to obtain quantity discounts.) Because Foxy promises delivery within 1 week following receipt of an order release, Parker has never had a shortage of LCDs. (Total time between date of the release and date of receipt is 1 week or 5 working days.)

Parker's activity-based costing system has generated the following inventory-related costs. Procurement costs, which amount to $500 per order, include the actual labor costs involved in ordering, customs inspection, arranging for airport pickup, delivery to the plant, maintaining inventory records, and arranging for the bank to issue a check. Parker's holding costs take into account storage, damage, insurance, taxes, and so forth on a square-foot basis. These costs equal $150 per LCD per year.

With added emphasis being placed on efficiencies in the supply chain, Parker's president has asked Raktim to seriously evaluate the purchase of the LCDs. One area to be closely scrutinized for possible cost savings is inventory procurement.

Discussion Questions

1. What is the optimal order number of LCDs that should be placed in each order?
2. What is the optimal reorder point (ROP) for LCDs?
3. What cost savings will Parker realize if it implements an order plan based on EOQ?

Managing Inventory at Frito-Lay

Video Case

Frito-Lay has flourished since its origin—the 1931 purchase of a small San Antonio firm for $100 that included a recipe, 19 retail accounts, and a hand-operated potato ricer. The multibillion-dollar company, headquartered in Dallas, now has 41 products—15 with sales of over $100 million per year and 7 at over $1 billion in sales. Production takes place in 36 product-focused plants in the U.S. and Canada, with 48,000 employees.

Inventory is a major investment and an expensive asset in most firms. Holding costs often exceed 25% of product value, but in Frito-Lay's prepared food industry, holding cost can be much higher because the raw materials are perishable. In the food industry, inventory spoils. So poor inventory management is not only expensive but can also yield an unsatisfactory product that in the extreme can also ruin market acceptance.

Major ingredients at Frito-Lay are corn meal, corn, potatoes, oil, and seasoning. Using potato chips to illustrate rapid inventory flow: potatoes are moved via truck from farm, to regional plants for processing, to warehouse, to the retail store. This happens in a matter of hours—not days or weeks. This keeps freshness high and holding costs low.

Frequent deliveries of the main ingredients at the Florida plant, for example, take several forms:

- Potatoes are delivered in 10 truckloads per day, with 150,000 lbs consumed in one shift: the entire potato storage area will only hold 7½ hours' worth of potatoes.
- Oil inventory arrives by rail car, which lasts only 4½ days.
- Corn meal arrives from various farms in the Midwest, and inventory typically averages 4 days' production.
- Seasoning inventory averages 7 days.
- Packaging inventory averages 8 to 10 days.

Frito-Lay's product-focused facility represents a major capital investment. That investment must achieve high utilization to be efficient. The capital cost must be spread over a substantial volume to drive down total cost of the snack foods produced. This demand for high utilization requires reliable equipment and tight schedules. Reliable machinery requires an inventory of critical components: this is known as MRO, or maintenance, repair, and operating supplies. MRO inventory of motors, switches, gears, bearings, and other critical specialized components can be costly but is necessary.

Frito-Lay's non-MRO inventory moves rapidly. Raw material quickly becomes work-in-process, moving through the system and out the door as a bag of chips in about $1\frac{1}{2}$ shifts. Packaged finished products move from production to the distribution chain in less than 1.4 days.

Discussion Questions*

1. How does the mix of Frito-Lay's inventory differ from those at a machine or cabinet shop (a process-focused facility)?
2. What are the major inventory items at Frito-Lay, and how rapidly do they move through the process?
3. What are the four types of inventory? Give an example of each at Frito-Lay.
4. How would you rank the dollar investment in each of the four types (from the most investment to the least investment)?
5. Why does inventory flow so quickly through a Frito-Lay plant?
6. Why does the company keep so many plants open?
7. Why doesn't Frito-Lay make all its 41 products at each of its plants?

*You may wish to view the video that accompanies this case before addressing these questions.

Inventory Control at Wheeled Coach

Video Case

Controlling inventory is one of Wheeled Coach's toughest problems. Operating according to a strategy of mass customization and responsiveness, management knows that success is dependent on tight inventory control. Anything else results in an inability to deliver promptly, chaos on the assembly line, and a huge inventory investment. Wheeled Coach finds that almost 50% of the cost of every ambulance it manufactures is purchased materials. A large proportion of that 50% is in chassis (purchased from Ford), aluminum (from Reynolds Metal), and plywood used for flooring and cabinetry construction (from local suppliers). Wheeled Coach tracks these A inventory items quite carefully, maintaining tight security/control and ordering carefully so as to maximize quantity discounts while minimizing on-hand stock. Because of long lead times and scheduling needs at Reynolds, aluminum must actually be ordered as much as 8 months in advance.

In a crowded ambulance industry in which it is the only giant, its 45 competitors don't have the purchasing power to draw the same discounts as Wheeled Coach. But this competitive cost advantage cannot be taken lightly, according to President Bob Collins. "Cycle counting in our stockrooms is critical. No part can leave the locked stockrooms without appearing on a bill of materials."

Accurate bills of material (BOM) are a requirement if products are going to be built on time. Additionally, because of the custom nature of each vehicle, most orders are won only after a bidding process. Accurate BOMs are critical to cost estimation and the resulting bid. For these reasons, Collins was emphatic that Wheeled Coach maintain outstanding inventory control. The *Global Company Profile* featuring Wheeled Coach (which opens Chapter 14) provides further details about the ambulance inventory control and production process.

Discussion Questions*

1. Explain how Wheeled Coach implements ABC analysis.
2. If you were to take over as inventory control manager at Wheeled Coach, what additional policies and techniques would you initiate to ensure accurate inventory records?
3. How would you go about implementing these suggestions?

*You may wish to view the video that accompanies this case before addressing these questions.

- **Additional Case Studies:** Visit MyOMLab for these free case studies:
  Southwestern University (F): The university must decide how many football day programs to order, and from whom.
  LaPlace Power and Light: This utility company is evaluating its current inventory policies.

Endnotes

1. See E. Malykhina, "Retailers Take Stock," *Information Week* (February 7, 2005): 20–22, and A. Raman, N. DeHoratius, and Z. Ton, "Execution: The Missing Link in Retail Operations," *California Management Review* 43, no. 3 (Spring 2001): 136–141.
2. This is the case when holding costs are linear and begin at the origin—that is, when inventory costs do not decline (or they increase) as inventory volume increases and all holding costs are in small increments. In addition, there is probably some learning each time a setup (or order) is executed—a fact that lowers subsequent setup costs. Consequently, the EOQ model is probably a special case. However, we abide by the conventional wisdom that this model is a reasonable approximation.
3. The formula for the economic order quantity (Q^*) can also be determined by finding where the total cost curve is at a minimum (i.e., where the slope of the total cost curve is zero). Using calculus, we set the derivative of the total cost with respect to Q^* equal to 0. The calculations for finding the minimum of

$$TC = \frac{D}{Q}S + \frac{Q}{2}H + PD$$

are $$\frac{d(TC)}{dQ} = \left(\frac{-DS}{Q^2}\right) + \frac{H}{2} + 0 = 0$$

Thus, $$Q^* = \sqrt{\frac{2DS}{H}}$$

4. The number of units short, Demand–ROP, is true only when Demand–ROP is non-negative.
5. Equations (12-15), (12-16), and (12-17) are expressed in days; however, they could equivalently be expressed in weeks, months, or even years. Just be consistent, and use the same time units for all terms in the equations.
6. Note that Equation (12-17) can also be expressed as:

    ROP = Average daily demand × Average lead time +

    $$Z\sqrt{(\text{Average lead time} \times \sigma_d^2) + \overline{d}^2\sigma_{LT}^2}.$$

7. OM managers also call these *continuous review systems*.

Main Heading	Review Material	MyOMLab
THE IMPORTANCE OF INVENTORY (pp. 490–491)	Inventory is one of the most expensive assets of many companies. *The objective of inventory management is to strike a balance between inventory investment and customer service.* The two basic inventory issues are how much to order and when to order. ■ **Raw material inventory**—Materials that are usually purchased but have yet to enter the manufacturing process. ■ **Work-in-process (WIP) inventory**—Products or components that are no longer raw materials but have yet to become finished products. ■ **MRO inventory**—Maintenance, repair, and operating materials. ■ **Finished-goods inventory**—An end item ready to be sold but still an asset on the company's books.	Concept Questions: 1.1–1.4 **VIDEO 12.1** Managing Inventory at Frito-Lay
MANAGING INVENTORY (pp. 491–495)	■ **ABC analysis**—A method for dividing on-hand inventory into three classifications based on annual dollar volume. ■ **Cycle counting**—A continuing reconciliation of inventory with inventory records. ■ **Shrinkage**—Retail inventory that is unaccounted for between receipt and sale. ■ **Pilferage**—A small amount of theft.	Concept Questions: 2.1–2.4 Problems: 12.1–12.6 Virtual Office Hours for Solved Problem: 12.1
INVENTORY MODELS (pp. 495–496)	■ **Holding cost**—The cost to keep or carry inventory in stock. ■ **Ordering cost**—The cost of the ordering process. ■ **Setup cost**—The cost to prepare a machine or process for production. ■ **Setup time**—The time required to prepare a machine or process for production.	Concept Questions: 3.1–3.4 **VIDEO 12.2** Inventory Control at Wheeled Coach Ambulance
INVENTORY MODELS FOR INDEPENDENT DEMAND (pp. 496–507)	■ **Economic order quantity (EOQ) model**—An inventory-control technique that minimizes the total of ordering and holding costs: $$Q^* = \sqrt{\frac{2DS}{H}} \qquad (12\text{-}1)$$ $$\text{Expected number of orders} = N = \frac{\text{Demand}}{\text{Order quantity}} = \frac{D}{Q^*} \qquad (12\text{-}2)$$ $$\text{Expected time between orders} = T = \frac{\text{Number of working days per year}}{N} \qquad (12\text{-}3)$$ $$\text{Total annual cost} = \text{Setup (order) cost} + \text{Holding cost} \qquad (12\text{-}4)$$ $$TC = \frac{D}{Q}S + \frac{Q}{2}H \qquad (12\text{-}5)$$ ■ **Robust**—Giving satisfactory answers even with substantial variation in the parameters. ■ **Lead time**—In purchasing systems, the time between placing an order and receiving it; in production systems, the wait, move, queue, setup, and run times for each component produced. ■ **Reorder point (ROP)**—The inventory level (point) at which action is taken to replenish the stocked item. *ROP for known demand:* $$\text{ROP} = \text{Demand per day} \times \text{Lead time for a new order in days} = d \times L \qquad (12\text{-}6)$$ ■ **Safety stock (ss)**—Extra stock to allow for uneven demand; a buffer. ■ **Production order quantity model**—An economic order quantity technique applied to production orders: $$Q_p^* = \sqrt{\frac{2DS}{H[1 - (d/p)]}} \qquad (12\text{-}7)$$ $$Q_p^* = \sqrt{\frac{2DS}{H\left(1 - \dfrac{\text{Annual demand rate}}{\text{Annual production rate}}\right)}} \qquad (12\text{-}8)$$ ■ **Quantity discount**—A reduced price for items purchased in large quantities: $$TC = \frac{D}{Q}S + \frac{Q}{2}H + PD \qquad (12\text{-}9)$$ $$Q^* = \sqrt{\frac{2DS}{IP}} \qquad (12\text{-}10)$$	Concept Questions: 4.1–4.4 Problems: 12.7–12.40 Virtual Office Hours for Solved Problems: 12.2–12.5 **ACTIVE MODELS 12.1, 12.2**

Main Heading	Review Material	MyOMLab
PROBABILISTIC MODELS AND SAFETY STOCK (pp. 508–513)	■ **Probabilistic model**—A statistical model applicable when product demand or any other variable is not known but can be specified by means of a probability distribution. ■ **Service level**—The complement of the probability of a stockout. *ROP for unknown demand:* $$\text{ROP} = d \times L + ss \quad (12\text{-}11)$$ Annual stockout costs = The sum of the units short for each demand level $\times$ The probability of that demand level $\times$ The stockout cost/unit $\quad$ (12-12) $\times$ The number of orders per year *ROP for unknown demand and given service level:* $$\text{ROP} = \text{Expected demand during lead time} + Z\sigma_{dLT} \quad (12\text{-}13)$$ $$\text{Safety stock} = Z\sigma_{dLT} \quad (12\text{-}14)$$ *ROP for variable demand and constant lead time:* $$\text{ROP} = (\text{Average daily demand} \times \text{Lead time in days}) + Z\sigma_{dLT} \quad (12\text{-}15)$$ *ROP for constant demand and variable lead time:* $$\text{ROP} = (\text{Daily demand} \times \text{Average lead time in days}) + Z \times \text{Daily demand} \times \sigma_{LT} \quad (12\text{-}16)$$ *ROP for variable demand and variable lead time:* $$\text{ROP} = (\text{Average daily demand} \times \text{Average lead time in days}) + Z\sigma_{dLT} \quad (12\text{-}17)$$ In each case, $\sigma_{dLT} = \sqrt{(\text{Average lead time} \times \sigma_d^2) + \overline{d}^2\sigma_{LT}^2}$ but under constant demand: $\sigma_d^2 = 0$, and under constant lead time: $\sigma_{LT}^2 = 0$.	Concept Questions: 5.1–5.4 Problems: 12.41–12.50 Virtual Office Hours for Solved Problems: 12.6–12.9
SINGLE-PERIOD MODEL (pp. 513–514)	■ **Single-period inventory model**—A system for ordering items that have little or no value at the end of the sales period: $$\text{Service level} = \frac{C_s}{C_s + C_o} \quad (12\text{-}18)$$	Concept Questions: 6.1–6.4 Problems: 12.51–12.53
FIXED-PERIOD (P) SYSTEMS (pp. 514–515)	■ **Fixed-quantity (Q) system**—An ordering system with the same order amount each time. ■ **Perpetual inventory system**—A system that keeps track of each withdrawal or addition to inventory continuously, so records are always current. ■ **Fixed-period (P) system**—A system in which inventory orders are made at regular time intervals.	Concept Questions: 7.1–7.4

Self Test

■ **Before taking the self-test,** refer to the learning objectives listed at the beginning of the chapter and the key terms listed at the end of the chapter.

LO 12.1 ABC analysis divides on-hand inventory into three classes, based on:
  a) unit price.
  b) the number of units on hand.
  c) annual demand.
  d) annual dollar values.

LO 12.2 Cycle counting:
  a) provides a measure of inventory turnover.
  b) assumes that all inventory records must be verified with the same frequency.
  c) is a process by which inventory records are periodically verified.
  d) all of the above.

LO 12.3 The two most important inventory-based questions answered by the typical inventory model are:
  a) when to place an order and the cost of the order.
  b) when to place an order and how much of an item to order.
  c) how much of an item to order and the cost of the order.
  d) how much of an item to order and with whom the order should be placed.

LO 12.4 Extra units in inventory to help reduce stockouts are called:
  a) reorder point.
  b) safety stock.
  c) just-in-time inventory.
  d) all of the above.

LO 12.5 The difference(s) between the basic EOQ model and the production order quantity model is(are) that:
  a) the production order quantity model does not require the assumption of known, constant demand.
  b) the EOQ model does not require the assumption of negligible lead time.
  c) the production order quantity model does not require the assumption of instantaneous delivery.
  d) all of the above.

LO 12.6 The EOQ model with quantity discounts attempts to determine:
  a) the lowest amount of inventory necessary to satisfy a certain service level.
  b) the lowest purchase price.
  c) whether to use a fixed-quantity or fixed-period order policy.
  d) how many units should be ordered.
  e) the shortest lead time.

LO 12.7 The appropriate level of safety stock is typically determined by:
  a) minimizing an expected stockout cost.
  b) choosing the level of safety stock that assures a given service level.
  c) carrying sufficient safety stock so as to eliminate all stockouts.
  d) annual demand.

Answers: LO 12.1. d; LO 12.2. c; LO 12.3. b; LO 12.4. b; LO 12.5. c; LO 12.6. d; LO 12.7. b.

Aggregate Planning and S&OP

CHAPTER OUTLINE

GLOBAL COMPANY PROFILE: *Frito-Lay*

- The Planning Process *532*
- Sales and Operations Planning *533*
- The Nature of Aggregate Planning *534*
- Aggregate Planning Strategies *535*

- Methods for Aggregate Planning *538*
- Aggregate Planning in Services *545*
- Revenue Management *547*

Alaska Airlines

10 OM STRATEGY DECISIONS

- Design of Goods and Services
- Managing Quality
- Process Strategy
- Location Strategies
- Layout Strategies
- Human Resources
- Supply-Chain Management
- Inventory Management
- Scheduling
  - *Aggregate/S&OP (Ch. 13)*
  - Short-Term (Ch. 15)
- Maintenance

CHAPTER 13

Aggregate Planning Provides a Competitive Advantage at Frito-Lay

Like other organizations throughout the world, Frito-Lay relies on effective aggregate planning to match fluctuating multi-billion-dollar demand to capacity in its 36 North American plants. Planning for the intermediate term (3 to 18 months) is the heart of aggregate planning. Effective aggregate planning combined with tight scheduling, effective maintenance, and efficient employee and facility scheduling are the keys to high plant utilization. High utilization is a critical factor in facilities such as Frito-Lay, where capital investment is substantial.

Frito-Lay has more than three dozen brands of snacks and chips, 15 of which sell more than $100 million annually and 7 of which sell over $1 billion. Its brands include such well-known names as Fritos, Lay's, Doritos, Sun Chips, Cheetos, Tostitos, Flat Earth, and Ruffles. Unique processes using specially designed equipment are required to produce each of these products. Because these specialized processes generate high fixed cost, they must operate at very high volume. But such product-focused facilities benefit by having low variable costs. High utilization and performance above the break-even point require a good match between demand and capacity. Idle equipment is disastrous.

At Frito-Lay's headquarters near Dallas, planners create a total demand profile. They use historical product sales, forecasts of new products, product innovations, product promotions,

The aggregate plan adjusts for farm location, yield, and quantities for timely delivery of Frito-Lay's unique varieties of potatoes. During harvest times, potatoes go directly to the plant. During non-harvest months, potatoes are stored in climate-controlled environments to maintain quality, texture, and taste.

Frito-Lay North America

Frito-Lay North America

Frito-Lay North America

As potatoes arrive at the plant, they are promptly washed and peeled to ensure freshness and taste.

After peeling, potatoes are cut into thin slices, rinsed of excess starch, and cooked in sunflower and/or corn oil.

Frito-Lay North America

and dynamic local demand data from account managers to forecast demand. Planners then match the total demand profile to existing capacity, capacity expansion plans, and cost. This becomes the aggregate plan. The aggregate plan is communicated to each of the firm's 17 regions and to the 36 plants. Every quarter, headquarters and each plant modify the respective plans to incorporate changing market conditions and plant performance.

Each plant uses its quarterly plan to develop a 4-week plan, which in turn assigns specific products to specific product lines for production runs. Finally, each week raw materials and labor are assigned to each process. Effective aggregate planning is a major factor in high utilization and low cost. As the company's 60% market share indicates, excellent aggregate planning yields a competitive advantage at Frito-Lay.

After cooking is complete, inspection, bagging, weighing, and packing operations prepare Lay's potato chips for shipment to customers—all in a matter of hours.

Frito-Lay North America

531

LEARNING OBJECTIVES

LO 13.1 *Define* sales and operations planning 533

LO 13.2 *Define* aggregate planning 534

LO 13.3 *Identify* optional strategies for developing an aggregate plan 535

LO 13.4 *Prepare* a graphical aggregate plan 538

LO 13.5 *Solve* an aggregate plan via the transportation method 544

LO 13.6 *Understand* and solve a revenue management problem 548

The Planning Process

In Chapter 4, we saw that demand forecasting can address long-, medium-, and short-range decisions. Figure 13.1 illustrates how managers translate these forecasts into long-, intermediate-, and short-range plans. Long-range forecasts, the responsibility of top management, provide data for a firm's multi-year plans. These long-range plans require policies and strategies related to issues such as capacity and capital investment (Supplement 7), facility location (Chapter 8), new products (Chapter 5) and processes (Chapter 7), and supply-chain development (Chapter 11).

Intermediate plans are designed to be consistent with top management's long-range plans and strategy, and work within the resource constraints determined by earlier strategic decisions. The challenge is to have these plans match production to the ever-changing demands of the market. Intermediate plans are the job of the operations manager, working with other functional areas of the firm. In this chapter we deal with intermediate plans, typically measured in months.

Short-range plans are usually for less than 3 months. These plans are also the responsibility of operations personnel. Operations managers work with supervisors and foremen to translate

Figure 13.1

Planning Tasks and Responsibilities

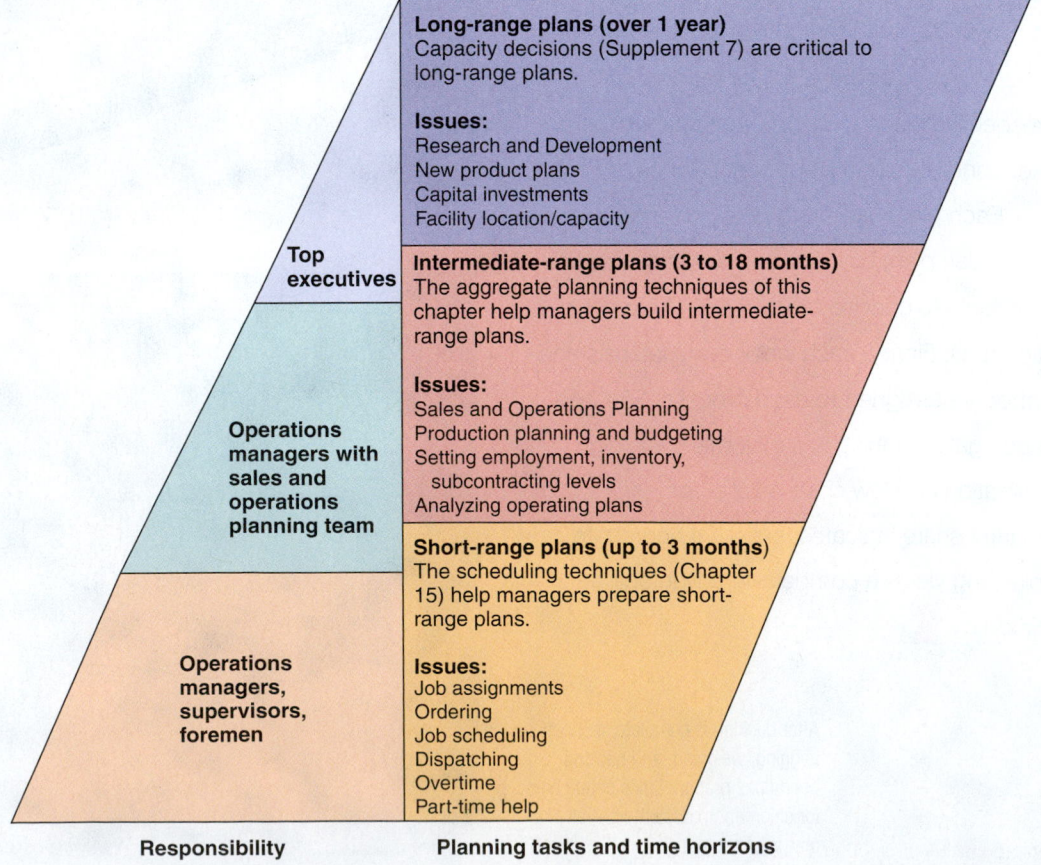

Responsibility | **Planning tasks and time horizons**

Top executives — **Long-range plans (over 1 year)** Capacity decisions (Supplement 7) are critical to long-range plans.

Issues: Research and Development, New product plans, Capital investments, Facility location/capacity

Operations managers with sales and operations planning team — **Intermediate-range plans (3 to 18 months)** The aggregate planning techniques of this chapter help managers build intermediate-range plans.

Issues: Sales and Operations Planning, Production planning and budgeting, Setting employment, inventory, subcontracting levels, Analyzing operating plans

Operations managers, supervisors, foremen — **Short-range plans (up to 3 months)** The scheduling techniques (Chapter 15) help managers prepare short-range plans.

Issues: Job assignments, Ordering, Job scheduling, Dispatching, Overtime, Part-time help the intermediate plan into short-term plans consisting of weekly, daily, and hourly schedules. Short-term planning techniques are discussed in Chapter 15.

Intermediate planning is initiated by a process known as *sales and operations planning (S&OP)*.

Sales and Operations Planning

Good intermediate planning requires the coordination of demand forecasts with functional areas of a firm and its supply chain. And because each functional part of a firm and the supply chain has its own limitations and constraints, the coordination can be difficult. This coordinated planning effort has evolved into a process known as sales and operations planning (S&OP). As Figure 13.2 shows, S&OP receives input from a variety of sources both internal and external to the firm. Because of the diverse inputs, S&OP is typically done by cross-functional teams that align the competing constraints.

One of the tasks of S&OP is to determine which plans are feasible in the coming months and which are not. Any limitations, both within the firm and in the supply chain, must be reflected in an intermediate plan that brings day-to-day sales and operational realities together. When the resources appear to be substantially at odds with market expectations, S&OP provides advanced warning to top management. If the plan cannot be implemented in the short run, the planning exercise is useless. And if the plan cannot be supported in the long run, strategic changes need to be made. To keep aggregate plans current and to support its intermediate planning role, S&OP uses rolling forecasts that are frequently updated—often weekly or monthly.

The output of S&OP is called an *aggregate plan*. The aggregate plan is concerned with determining the quantity and timing of production for the intermediate future, often from 3 to

Sales and operations planning (S&OP)
A process of balancing resources and forecasted demand, aligning an organization's competing demands from supply chain to final customer, while linking strategic planning with operations over all planning horizons.

LO 13.1 *Define* sales and operations planning

Aggregate plan
A plan that includes forecast levels for families of products of finished goods, inventory, shortages, and changes in the workforce.

Figure **13.2**

Relationships of S&OP and the Aggregate Plan

18 months ahead. Aggregate plans use information regarding product families or product lines rather than individual products. These plans are concerned with the total, or *aggregate,* of the individual product lines.

Rubbermaid, Office Max, and Rackspace have developed formal systems for S&OP, each with its own planning focus. Rubbermaid may use S&OP with a focus on production decisions; Office Max may focus S&OP on supply chain and inventory decisions; while Rackspace, a data storage firm, tends to have its S&OP focus on its critical and expensive investments in capacity. In *all* cases, though, the decisions must be tied to strategic planning and integrated with *all* areas of the firm over *all* planning horizons. Specifically, S&OP is aimed at (1) the coordination and integration of the internal and external resources necessary for a successful aggregate plan and (2) communication of the plan to those charged with its execution. The added advantage of S&OP and an aggregate plan is that they can be effective tools to engage members of the supply chain in achieving the firm's goals.

Besides being representative, timely, and comprehensive, an effective S&OP process needs these four additional features to generate a useful aggregate plan:

◆ A logical unit for measuring sales and output, such as pounds of Doritos at Frito-Lay, air-conditioning units at GE, or terabytes of storage at Rackspace
◆ A forecast of demand for a reasonable intermediate planning period in aggregate terms
◆ A method to determine the relevant costs
◆ A model that combines forecasts and costs so scheduling decisions can be made for the planning period

In this chapter we describe several techniques that managers use when developing an aggregate plan for both manufacturing and service-sector firms. For manufacturers, an aggregate schedule ties a firm's strategic goals to production plans. For service organizations, an aggregate schedule ties strategic goals to workforce schedules.

LO 13.2 *Define* aggregate planning

The Nature of Aggregate Planning

An S&OP team builds an aggregate plan that satisfies forecasted demand by adjusting production rates, labor levels, inventory levels, overtime work, subcontracting rates, and other controllable variables. The plan can be for Frito-Lay, Whirlpool, hospitals, colleges, or Pearson Education, the company that publishes this textbook. Regardless of the firm, *the objective of aggregate planning is usually to meet forecast demand while minimizing cost over the planning period.* However, other strategic issues may be more important than low cost. These strategies may be to smooth employment, to drive down inventory levels, or to meet a high level of service, regardless of cost.

Let's look at Snapper, which produces many different models of lawn mowers. Snapper makes walk-behind mowers, rear-engine riding mowers, garden tractors, and many more, for a total of 145 models. For each month in the upcoming 3 quarters, the aggregate plan for Snapper might have the following output (in units of production) for Snapper's "family" of mowers:

QUARTER 1			QUARTER 2			QUARTER 3		
Jan.	Feb.	March	April	May	June	July	Aug.	Sept.
150,000	120,000	110,000	100,000	130,000	150,000	180,000	150,000	140,000

Briggs & Stratton Power Products Marketing

S&OP builds an aggregate plan using the total expected demand for all of the family products, such as 145 models at Snapper (a few of which are shown above). Only when the forecasts are assembled in the aggregate plan does the company decide how to meet the total requirement with the available resources. These resource constraints include facility capacity, workforce size, supply-chain limitations, inventory issues, and financial resources.

OM in Action | Building the Plan at Snapper

Every bright-red Snapper lawn mower sold anywhere in the world comes from a factory in McDonough, Georgia. Ten years ago, the Snapper line had about 40 models of mowers, leaf blowers, and snow blowers. Today, reflecting the demands of mass customization, the product line is much more complex. Snapper designs, manufactures, and sells 145 models. This means that aggregate planning and the related short-term scheduling have become more complex, too.

In the past, Snapper met demand by carrying a huge inventory for 52 regional distributors and thousands of independent dealerships. It manufactured and shipped tens of thousands of lawn mowers, worth tens of millions of dollars, without quite knowing when they would be sold—a very expensive approach to meeting demand. Some changes were necessary. The new plan's goal is for each distribution center to receive only the minimum inventory necessary to meet demand. Today, operations managers at Snapper evaluate production

capacity and use frequent data from the field as inputs to sophisticated software to forecast sales. The new system tracks customer demand and aggregates forecasts for every model in every region of the country. It even adjusts for holidays and weather. And the number of distribution centers has been cut from 52 to 4.

Once evaluation of the aggregate plan against capacity determines the plan to be feasible, Snapper's planners break down the plan into production needs for each model. Production by model is accomplished by building rolling monthly and weekly plans. These plans track the pace at which various units are selling. Then, the final step requires juggling work assignments to various work centers for each shift, such as 265 lawn mowers in an 8-hour shift. That's a new Snapper every 109 seconds.

Sources: Fair Disclosure Wire (January 17, 2008); *The Wall Street Journal* (July 14, 2006); *Fast Company* (January/February 2006); and **www.snapper.com**.

Note that the plan looks at production *in the aggregate* (the family of mowers), not as a product-by-product breakdown. Likewise, an aggregate plan for BMW tells the auto manufacturer how many cars to make but not how many should be two-door vs. four-door or red vs. green. It tells Nucor Steel how many tons of steel to produce but does not differentiate grades of steel. (We extend the discussion of planning at Snapper in the *OM in Action* box "Building the Plan at Snapper.")

In a manufacturing environment, the process of breaking the aggregate plan down into greater detail is called **disaggregation**. Disaggregation results in a **master production schedule**, which provides input to material requirements planning (MRP) systems. The master production schedule addresses the purchasing or production of major parts or components (see Chapter 14). It is *not* a sales forecast. Detailed work schedules for people and priority scheduling for products result as the final step of the production planning system (and are discussed in Chapter 15).

Disaggregation
The process of breaking an aggregate plan into greater detail.

Master production schedule
A timetable that specifies what is to be made and when.

Aggregate Planning Strategies

When generating an aggregate plan, the operations manager must answer several questions:

1. Should inventories be used to absorb changes in demand during the planning period?
2. Should changes be accommodated by varying the size of the workforce?
3. Should part-timers be used, or should overtime and idle time absorb fluctuations?
4. Should subcontractors be used on fluctuating orders so a stable workforce can be maintained?
5. Should prices or other factors be changed to influence demand?

All of these are legitimate planning strategies. They involve the manipulation of inventory, production rates, labor levels, capacity, and other controllable variables. We will now examine eight options in more detail. The first five are called *capacity options* because they do not try to change demand but attempt to absorb demand fluctuations. The last three are *demand options* through which firms try to smooth out changes in the demand pattern over the planning period.

STUDENT TIP
Managers can meet aggregate plans by adjusting either capacity or demand.

LO 13.3 *Identify* optional strategies for developing an aggregate plan

Capacity Options

A firm can choose from the following basic capacity (production) options:

1. *Changing inventory levels:* Managers can increase inventory during periods of low demand to meet high demand in future periods. If this strategy is selected, costs associated with storage, insurance, handling, obsolescence, pilferage, and capital invested will increase.

John Deere and Company, the "granddaddy" of farm equipment manufacturers, uses sales incentives to smooth demand. During the fall and winter off-seasons, sales are boosted with price cuts and other incentives. About 70% of Deere's big machines are ordered in advance of seasonal use—about double the industry rate. Incentives hurt margins, but Deere keeps its market share and controls costs by producing more steadily all year long. Similarly, service businesses like L.L. Bean offer customers free shipping on orders placed before the Christmas rush.

Stefan Kiefer/imageBROKER/Alamy

On the other hand, with low inventory on hand and increasing demand, shortages can occur, resulting in longer lead times and poor customer service.

2. *Varying workforce size by hiring or layoffs:* One way to meet demand is to hire or lay off production workers to match production rates. However, new employees need to be trained, and productivity drops temporarily as they are absorbed into the workforce. Layoffs or terminations, of course, lower the morale of all workers and also lead to lower productivity.

3. *Varying production rates through overtime or idle time:* Keeping a constant workforce while varying working hours may be possible. Yet when demand is on a large upswing, there is a limit on how much overtime is realistic. Overtime pay increases costs, and too much overtime can result in worker fatigue and a drop in productivity. Overtime also implies added overhead costs to keep a facility open. On the other hand, when there is a period of decreased demand, the company must somehow absorb workers' idle time—often a difficult and expensive process.

4. *Subcontracting:* A firm can acquire temporary capacity by subcontracting work during peak demand periods. Subcontracting, however, has several pitfalls. First, it may be costly; second, it risks opening the door to a competitor. Third, developing the perfect subcontract supplier can be a challenge.

5. *Using part-time workers:* Especially in the service sector, part-time workers can fill labor needs. This practice is common in restaurants, retail stores, and supermarkets.

Demand Options

The basic demand options are:

1. *Influencing demand:* When demand is low, a company can try to increase demand through advertising, promotion, personal selling, and price cuts. Airlines and hotels have long offered weekend discounts and off-season rates; theaters cut prices for matinees; some colleges give discounts to senior citizens; and air conditioners are least expensive in winter. However, even special advertising, promotions, selling, and pricing are not always able to balance demand with production capacity.

2. *Back ordering during high-demand periods:* Back orders are orders for goods or services that a firm accepts but is unable (either on purpose or by chance) to fill at the moment.

| TABLE 13.1 | Aggregate Planning Options: Advantages and Disadvantages |

OPTION	ADVANTAGES	DISADVANTAGES	COMMENTS
Changing inventory levels	Changes in human resources are gradual or none; no abrupt production changes.	Inventory holding costs may increase. Shortages may result in lost sales.	Applies mainly to production, not service, operations.
Varying workforce size by hiring or layoffs	Avoids the costs of other alternatives.	Hiring, layoff, and training costs may be significant.	Used where size of labor pool is large.
Varying production rates through overtime or idle time	Matches seasonal fluctuations without hiring/training costs.	Overtime premiums; tired workers; may not meet demand.	Allows flexibility within the aggregate plan.
Subcontracting	Permits flexibility and smoothing of the firm's output.	Loss of quality control; reduced profits; potential loss of future business.	Applies mainly in production settings.
Using part-time workers	Is less costly and more flexible than full-time workers.	High turnover/training costs; quality suffers; scheduling difficult.	Good for unskilled jobs in areas with large temporary labor pools.
Influencing demand	Tries to use excess capacity. Discounts draw new customers.	Uncertainty in demand. Hard to match demand to supply exactly.	Creates marketing ideas. Overbooking used in some businesses.
Back ordering during high-demand periods	May avoid overtime. Keeps capacity constant.	Customer must be willing to wait, but goodwill is lost.	Many companies back order.
Counterseasonal product and service mixing	Fully utilizes resources; allows stable workforce.	May require skills or equipment outside firm's areas of expertise.	Risky finding products or services with opposite demand patterns.

If customers are willing to wait without loss of their goodwill or order, back ordering is a possible strategy. Many firms back order, but the approach often results in lost sales.

3. *Counterseasonal product and service mixing:* A widely used active smoothing technique among manufacturers is to develop a product mix of counterseasonal items. Examples include companies that make both furnaces and air conditioners or lawn mowers and snowblowers. However, companies that follow this approach may find themselves involved in products or services beyond their area of expertise or beyond their target market.

These eight options, along with their advantages and disadvantages, are summarized in Table 13.1.

Mixing Options to Develop a Plan

Although each of the five capacity options and three demand options discussed above may produce an effective aggregate schedule, some combination of capacity options and demand options may be better.

Many manufacturers assume that the use of the demand options has been fully explored by the marketing department and those reasonable options incorporated into the demand forecast. The operations manager then builds the aggregate plan based on that forecast. However, using the five capacity options at his command, the operations manager still has a multitude of possible plans. These plans can embody, at one extreme, a *chase strategy* and, at the other, a *level-scheduling strategy*. They may, of course, fall somewhere in between.

Chase Strategy A chase strategy typically attempts to achieve output rates for each period that match the demand forecast for that period. This strategy can be accomplished in a variety of ways. For example, the operations manager can vary workforce levels by hiring or laying off or can vary output by means of overtime, idle time, part-time employees, or subcontracting. Many service organizations favor the chase strategy because the changing inventory levels option is difficult or impossible to adopt. Industries that have moved toward a chase strategy include education, hospitality, and construction.

Chase strategy
A planning strategy that sets production equal to forecast demand.

Level scheduling
Maintaining a constant output rate, production rate, or workforce level over the planning horizon.

Level Strategy A level strategy (or level scheduling) is an aggregate plan in which production is uniform from period to period. Firms like Toyota and Nissan attempt to keep production at uniform levels and may (1) let the finished-goods inventory vary to buffer the difference between demand and production or (2) find alternative work for employees. Their philosophy is that a stable workforce leads to a better-quality product, less turnover and absenteeism, and more employee commitment to corporate goals. Other hidden savings include more experienced employees, easier scheduling and supervision, and fewer dramatic startups and shutdowns. Level scheduling works well when demand is reasonably stable.

Mixed strategy
A planning strategy that uses two or more controllable variables to set a feasible production plan.

For most firms, neither a chase strategy nor a level strategy is likely to prove ideal, so a combination of the eight options (called a mixed strategy) must be investigated to achieve minimum cost. However, because there are a huge number of possible mixed strategies, managers find that aggregate planning can be a challenging task. Finding the one "optimal" plan is not always possible, but as we will see in the next section, a number of techniques have been developed to aid the aggregate planning process.

Methods for Aggregate Planning

In this section, we introduce techniques that operations managers use to develop aggregate plans. They range from the widely used graphical method to the transportation method of linear programming.

Graphical Methods

Graphical techniques
Aggregate planning techniques that work with a few variables at a time to allow planners to compare projected demand with existing capacity.

Graphical techniques are popular because they are easy to understand and use. These plans work with a few variables at a time to allow planners to compare projected demand with existing capacity. They are trial-and-error approaches that do not guarantee an optimal production plan, but they require only limited computations and can be performed by clerical staff. Following are the five steps in the graphical method:

LO 13.4 *Prepare a graphical aggregate plan*

1. Determine the demand in each period.
2. Determine capacity for regular time, overtime, and subcontracting each period.
3. Find labor costs, hiring and layoff costs, and inventory holding costs.
4. Consider company policy that may apply to the workers or to stock levels.
5. Develop alternative plans and examine their total costs.

These steps are illustrated in Examples 1 through 4.

Example 1

GRAPHICAL APPROACH TO AGGREGATE PLANNING FOR A ROOFING SUPPLIER

A Juarez, Mexico, manufacturer of roofing supplies has developed monthly forecasts for a family of products. Data for the 6-month period January to June are presented in Table 13.2. The firm would like to begin development of an aggregate plan.

TABLE 13.2 Monthly Forecasts

MONTH	EXPECTED DEMAND	PRODUCTION DAYS	DEMAND PER DAY (COMPUTED)
Jan.	900	22	41
Feb.	700	18	39
Mar.	800	21	38
Apr.	1,200	21	57
May	1,500	22	68
June	1,100	20	55
	6,200	124	

APPROACH ▶ Plot daily and average demand to illustrate the nature of the aggregate planning problem.

SOLUTION ▶ First, compute demand per day by dividing the expected monthly demand by the number of production days (working days) each month and drawing a graph of those forecast demands (Figure 13.3). Second, draw a dotted line across the chart that represents the production rate required to meet average demand over the 6-month period. The chart is computed as follows:

$$\text{Average requirement} = \frac{\text{Total expected demand}}{\text{Number of production days}} = \frac{6{,}200}{124} = 50 \text{ units per day}$$

Figure **13.3**

Graph of Forecast and Average Forecast Demand

INSIGHT ▶ Changes in the production rate become obvious when the data are graphed. Note that in the first 3 months, expected demand is lower than average, while expected demand in April, May, and June is above average.

LEARNING EXERCISE ▶ If demand for June increases to 1,200 (from 1,100), what is the impact on Figure 13.3? [Answer: The daily rate for June will go up to 60, and average production will increase to 50.8 (6,300/124).]

RELATED PROBLEM ▶ 13.1

The graph in Figure 13.3 illustrates how the forecast differs from the average demand. Some strategies for meeting the forecast were listed earlier. The firm, for example, might staff in order to yield a production rate that meets *average* demand (as indicated by the dashed line). Or it might produce a steady rate of, say, 30 units and then subcontract excess demand to other roofing suppliers. Other plans might combine overtime work with subcontracting to absorb demand or vary the workforce by hiring and laying off. Examples 2 to 4 illustrate three possible strategies.

Example 2

PLAN 1 FOR THE ROOFING SUPPLIER—A CONSTANT WORKFORCE

One possible strategy (call it plan 1) for the manufacturer described in Example 1 is to maintain a constant workforce throughout the 6-month period. A second (plan 2) is to maintain a constant workforce at a level necessary to meet the lowest demand month (March) and to meet all demand above this level by subcontracting. Both plan 1 and plan 2 have level production and are, therefore, called *level strategies*. Plan 3 is to hire and lay off workers as needed to produce exact monthly requirements—*a chase strategy*. Table 13.3 provides cost information necessary for analyzing these three alternatives.

TABLE 13.3   **Cost Information**

Inventory carrying cost	$ 5 per unit per month
Subcontracting cost per unit	$ 20 per unit
Average pay rate	$ 10 per hour ($80 per day)
Overtime pay rate	$ 17 per hour (above 8 hours per day)
Labor-hours to produce a unit	1.6 hours per unit
Cost of increasing daily production rate (hiring and training)	$300 per unit
Cost of decreasing daily production rate (layoffs)	$600 per unit

ANALYSIS OF PLAN 1 APPROACH ▶   Here we assume that 50 units are produced per day and that we have a constant workforce, no overtime or idle time, no safety stock, and no subcontractors. The firm accumulates inventory during the slack period of demand, January through March, and depletes it during the higher-demand warm season, April through June. We assume beginning inventory = 0 and planned ending inventory = 0.

SOLUTION ▶   We construct the table below and accumulate the costs:

MONTH	PRODUCTION DAYS	PRODUCTION AT 50 UNITS PER DAY	DEMAND FORECAST	MONTHLY INVENTORY CHANGE	ENDING INVENTORY
Jan.	22	1,100	900	+200	200
Feb.	18	900	700	+200	400
Mar.	21	1,050	800	+250	650
Apr.	21	1,050	1,200	−150	500
May	22	1,100	1,500	−400	100
June	20	1,000	1,100	−100	0
					1,850

Total units of inventory carried over from one month to the next month = 1,850 units

Workforce required to produce 50 units per day = 10 workers

Because each unit requires 1.6 labor-hours to produce, each worker can make 5 units in an 8-hour day. Therefore, to produce 50 units, 10 workers are needed.

    Finally, the costs of plan 1 are computed as follows:

COST		CALCULATIONS
Inventory carrying	$ 9,250	(= 1,850 units carried × $5 per unit)
Regular-time labor	99,200	(= 10 workers × $80 per day × 124 days)
Other costs (overtime, hiring, layoffs, subcontracting)	0	
Total cost	$108,450	

INSIGHT ▶   Note the significant cost of carrying the inventory.

LEARNING EXERCISE ▶   If demand for June decreases to 1,000 (from 1,100), what is the change in cost? [Answer: Total inventory carried will increase to 1,950 at $5, for an inventory cost of $9,750 and total cost of $108,950.]

RELATED PROBLEMS ▶   13.2–13.12, 13.19 (13.23 is available in MyOMLab)

EXCEL OM Data File **Ch13Ex2.xls** can be found in MyOMLab.

ACTIVE MODEL 13.1 This example is further illustrated in Active Model 13.1 in MyOMLab.

Figure **13.4**

Cumulative Graph for Plan 1

The graph for Example 2 was shown in Figure 13.3. Some planners prefer a *cumulative* graph to display visually how the forecast deviates from the average requirements. Such a graph is provided in Figure 13.4. Note that both the level production line and the forecast line produce the same total production.

Example 3

PLAN 2 FOR THE ROOFING SUPPLIER—USE OF SUBCONTRACTORS WITHIN A CONSTANT WORKFORCE

ANALYSIS OF PLAN 2 APPROACH ▶ Although a constant workforce is also maintained in plan 2, it is set low enough to meet demand only in March, the lowest demand-per-day month. To produce 38 units per day (800/21) in-house, 7.6 workers are needed. (You can think of this as 7 full-time workers and 1 part-timer.) *All* other demand is met by subcontracting. Subcontracting is thus required in every other month. No inventory holding costs are incurred in plan 2.

SOLUTION ▶ Because 6,200 units are required during the aggregate plan period, we must compute how many can be made by the firm and how many must be subcontracted:

$$\text{In-house production} = 38 \text{ units per day} \times 124 \text{ production days}$$
$$= 4,712 \text{ units}$$
$$\text{Subcontract units} = 6,200 - 4,712 = 1,488 \text{ units}$$

The costs of plan 2 are computed as follows:

COST		CALCULATIONS
Regular-time labor	$ 75,392	(= 7.6 workers × $80 per day × 124 days)
Subcontracting	29,760	(= 1,488 units × $20 per unit)
Total cost	$105,152	

INSIGHT ▶ Note the lower cost of regular labor but the added subcontracting cost.

LEARNING EXERCISE ▶ If demand for June increases to 1,200 (from 1,100), what is the change in cost? [Answer: Subcontracting requirements increase to 1,588 at $20 per unit, for a subcontracting cost of $31,760 and a total cost of $107,152.]

RELATED PROBLEMS ▶ 13.2–13.12, 13.19 (13.23 is available in MyOMLab)

Example 4

PLAN 3 FOR THE ROOFING SUPPLIER—HIRING AND LAYOFFS

ANALYSIS OF PLAN 3 APPROACH ▶   The final strategy, plan 3, involves varying the workforce size by hiring and layoffs as necessary. The production rate will equal the demand, and there is no change in production from the previous month, December.

SOLUTION ▶   Table 13.4 shows the calculations and the total cost of plan 3. Recall that it costs $600 per unit produced to reduce production from the previous month's daily level and $300 per unit change to increase the daily rate of production through hirings.

TABLE 13.4			Cost Computations for Plan 3			
MONTH	FORECAST (UNITS)	DAILY PRODUCTION RATE	BASIC PRODUCTION COST (DEMAND ×1.6 HR PER UNIT × $10 PER HR)	EXTRA COST OF INCREASING PRODUCTION (HIRING COST)	EXTRA COST OF DECREASING PRODUCTION (LAYOFF COST)	TOTAL COST
Jan.	900	41	$14,400	—	—	$ 14,400
Feb.	700	39	11,200	—	$1,200 (= 2 × $600)	12,400
Mar.	800	38	12,800	—	$ 600 (= 1 × $600)	13,400
Apr.	1,200	57	19,200	$5,700 (= 19 × $300)	—	24,900
May	1,500	68	24,000	$3,300 (= 11 × $300)	—	27,300
June	1,100	55	17,600	—	$7,800 (= 13 × $600)	$ 25,400
			$99,200	$9,000	$9,600	$117,800

Thus, the total cost, including production, hiring, and layoff, for plan 3 is $117,800.

INSIGHT ▶   Note the substantial cost associated with changing (both increasing and decreasing) the production levels.

LEARNING EXERCISE ▶   If demand for June increases to 1,200 (from 1,100), what is the change in cost? [Answer: Daily production for June is 60 units, which is a decrease of 8 units in the daily production rate from May's 68 units, so the new June layoff cost is $4,800 (= 8 × $600), but an additional production cost for 100 units is $1,600 (100 × 1.6 × $10) with a total plan 3 cost of $116,400.]

RELATED PROBLEMS ▶   13.2–13.12, 13.19 (13.23 is available in MyOMLab)

The final step in the graphical method is to compare the costs of each proposed plan and to select the approach with the least total cost. A summary analysis is provided in Table 13.5. We see that because plan 2 has the lowest cost, it is the best of the three options.

TABLE 13.5	Comparison of the Three Plans		
COST	PLAN 1 (CONSTANT WORKFORCE OF 10 WORKERS)	PLAN 2 (WORKFORCE OF 7.6 WORKERS PLUS SUBCONTRACTORS)	PLAN 3 (HIRING AND LAYOFFS TO MEET DEMAND)
Inventory carrying	$ 9,250	$ 0	$ 0
Regular labor	99,200	75,392	99,200
Overtime labor	0	0	0
Hiring	0	0	9,000
Layoffs	0	0	9,600
Subcontracting	0	29,760	0
Total cost	$108,450	$105,152	$117,800

Of course, many other feasible strategies can be considered in a problem like this, including combinations that use some overtime. Although graphing is a popular management tool, its help is in evaluating strategies, not generating them. To generate strategies, a systematic approach that considers all costs and produces an effective solution is needed.

Mathematical Approaches

This section briefly describes mathematical approaches to aggregate planning.

The Transportation Method of Linear Programming   When an aggregate planning problem is viewed as one of allocating operating capacity to meet forecast demand, it can be formulated in a linear programming format. The transportation method of linear programming is not a trial-and-error approach like graphing but rather produces an optimal plan for minimizing costs. It is also flexible in that it can specify regular and overtime production in each time period, the number of units to be subcontracted, extra shifts, and the inventory carryover from period to period.

In Example 5, the supply consists of on-hand inventory and units produced by regular time, overtime, and subcontracting. Costs per unit, in the upper-right corner of each cell of the matrix in Table 13.7, relate to units produced in a given period or units carried in inventory from an earlier period.

> **Transportation method of linear programming**
> A way of solving for the optimal solution to an aggregate planning problem.

Example 5

AGGREGATE PLANNING WITH THE TRANSPORTATION METHOD

Farnsworth Tire Company would like to develop an aggregate plan via the transportation method. Data that relate to production, demand, capacity, and cost at its West Virginia plant are shown in Table 13.6.

TABLE 13.6 Farnsworth's Production, Demand, Capacity, and Cost Data

	SALES PERIOD		
	MAR.	**APR.**	**MAY**
Demand	800	1,000	750
Capacity:			
Regular	700	700	700
Overtime	50	50	50
Subcontracting	150	150	130
Beginning inventory	100 tires		

COSTS	
Regular time	$40 per tire
Overtime	$50 per tire
Subcontract	$70 per tire
Carrying cost	$ 2 per tire per month

APPROACH ▶   Solve the aggregate planning problem by minimizing the costs of matching production in various periods to future demands.

SOLUTION ▶   Table 13.7 illustrates the structure of the transportation table and an initial feasible solution.

| TABLE 13.7 | Farnsworth's Transportation Table[a] |

		DEMAND FOR				TOTAL CAPACITY AVAILABLE (supply)
SUPPLY FROM		Period 1 (Mar.)	Period 2 (Apr.)	Period 3 (May)	Unused Capacity (dummy)	
Beginning inventory		0 / 100	2	4	0	100
Period 1	Regular time	40 / 700	42	44	0	700
	Overtime	50	52 / 50	54	0	50
	Subcontract	70	72 / 150	74	0	150
Period 2	Regular time	×	40 / 700	42	0	700
	Overtime	×	50 / 50	52	0	50
	Subcontract	×	70 / 50	72	0 / 100	150
Period 3	Regular time	×	×	40 / 700	0	700
	Overtime	×	×	50 / 50	0	50
	Subcontract	×	×	70	0 / 130	130
TOTAL DEMAND		800	1,000	750	230	2,780

[a]Cells with an *x* indicate that back orders are not used at Farnsworth. When using Excel OM or POM for Windows to solve, you must insert a *very* high cost (e.g., 9999) in each cell that is not used for production.

When setting up and analyzing this table, you should note the following:

1. Carrying costs are $2/tire per month. Tires produced in 1 period and held for 1 month will have a $2 higher cost. Because holding cost is linear, 2 months' holdover costs $4. So when you move across a row from left to right, regular time, overtime, and subcontracting costs are lowest when output is used in the same period it is produced. If goods are made in one period and carried over to the next, holding costs are incurred. Beginning inventory, however, is generally given a unit cost of 0 if it is used to satisfy demand in period 1.

2. Transportation problems require that supply equals demand, so a dummy column called "unused capacity" has been added. Costs of not using capacity are zero.

3. Because back ordering is not a viable alternative for this particular company, no production is possible in those cells that represent production in a period to satisfy demand in a past period (i.e., those periods with an "×"). If back ordering is allowed, costs of expediting, loss of goodwill, and loss of sales revenues are summed to estimate backorder cost.

4. Quantities in red in each column of Table 13.7 designate the levels of inventory needed to meet demand requirements (shown in the bottom row of the table). Demand of 800 tires in March is met by using 100 tires from beginning inventory and 700 tires from regular time.

5. In general, to complete the table, allocate as much production as you can to a cell with the smallest cost without exceeding the unused capacity in that row or demand in that column. If there is still some demand left in that row, allocate as much as you can to the next-lowest-cost cell. You then repeat this process for periods 2 and 3 (and beyond, if necessary). When you are finished, the sum of all your entries in a row must equal the total row capacity, and the sum of all entries in a column must equal the demand for that period. (This step can be accomplished by the transportation method or by using POM for Windows or Excel OM software.)

LO 13.5 *Solve* an aggregate plan via the transportation method

Try to confirm that the cost of this initial solution is $105,900. The initial solution is not optimal, however. See if you can find the production schedule that yields the least cost (which turns out to be $105,700) using software or by hand.

INSIGHT ▶ The transportation method is flexible when costs are linear but does not work when costs are nonlinear.

LEARNING EXAMPLE ▶ What is the impact on this problem if there is no beginning inventory? [Answer: Total capacity (units) available is reduced by 100 units and the need to subcontract increases by 100 units.]

RELATED PROBLEMS ▶ 13.13–13.18 (13.20–13.22 are available in MyOMLab)

EXCEL OM Data File **Ch13Ex5.xls** can be found in MyOMLab.

The transportation method of linear programming described in the preceding example works well when analyzing the effects of holding inventories, using overtime, and subcontracting. However, it does not work when nonlinear or negative factors are introduced. Thus, when other factors such as hiring and layoffs are introduced, the more general method of linear programming must be used. Similarly, computer simulation models look for a minimum-cost combination of values.

A number of commercial S&OP software packages that incorporate the techniques of this chapter are available to ease the mechanics of aggregate planning. These include Arkieva's S&OP *Workbench* for process industries, Demand Solutions's *S&OP Software,* and Steelwedge's *S&OP Suite.*

Aggregate Planning in Services

Some service organizations conduct aggregate planning in exactly the same way as we did in Examples 1 through 5 in this chapter, but with demand management taking a more active role. Because most services pursue *combinations* of the eight capacity and demand options discussed earlier, they usually formulate mixed aggregate planning strategies. In industries such as banking, trucking, and fast foods, aggregate planning may be easier than in manufacturing.

Controlling the cost of labor in service firms is critical. Successful techniques include:

1. Accurate scheduling of labor-hours to ensure quick response to customer demand
2. An on-call labor resource that can be added or deleted to meet unexpected demand
3. Flexibility of individual worker skills that permits reallocation of available labor
4. Flexibility in rate of output or hours of work to meet changing demand

These options may seem demanding, but they are not unusual in service industries, in which labor is the primary aggregate planning vehicle. For instance:

⚠ STUDENT TIP
The major variable in capacity management for services is labor.

- Excess capacity is used to provide study and planning time by real estate and auto salespersons.
- Police and fire departments have provisions for calling in off-duty personnel for major emergencies. Where the emergency is extended, police or fire personnel may work longer hours and extra shifts.
- When business is unexpectedly light, restaurants and retail stores send personnel home early.
- Supermarket stock clerks work cash registers when checkout lines become too lengthy.
- Experienced waitresses increase their pace and efficiency of service as crowds of customers arrive.

Approaches to aggregate planning differ by the type of service provided. Here we discuss five service scenarios.

Restaurants

In a business with a highly variable demand, such as a restaurant, aggregate scheduling is directed toward (1) smoothing the production rate and (2) finding the optimal size of the workforce. The general approach usually requires building very modest levels of inventory during slack periods and depleting inventory during peak periods, but using labor to accommodate most of the changes in demand. Because this situation is very similar to those found in manufacturing, traditional aggregate planning methods may be applied to restaurants as well. One difference is that even modest amounts of inventory may be perishable. In addition, the relevant units of time may be much smaller than in manufacturing. For example, in fast-food restaurants, peak and slack periods may be measured in fractions of an hour, and the "product" may be inventoried for as little as 10 minutes.

Hospitals

Hospitals face aggregate planning problems in allocating money, staff, and supplies to meet the demands of patients. Michigan's Henry Ford Hospital, for example, plans for bed capacity and personnel needs in light of a patient-load forecast developed by moving averages. The necessary labor focus of its aggregate plan has led to the creation of a new floating staff pool serving each nursing pod.

National Chains of Small Service Firms

With the advent of national chains of small service businesses such as funeral homes, oil change outlets, and photocopy/printing centers, the question of aggregate planning versus independent planning at each business establishment becomes an issue. Both purchases and production capacity may be centrally planned when demand can be influenced through special promotions. This approach to aggregate scheduling is often advantageous because it reduces costs and helps manage cash flow at independent sites.

Miscellaneous Services

Most "miscellaneous" services—financial, transportation, and many communication and recreation services—provide intangible output. Aggregate planning for these services deals mainly with planning for human resource requirements and managing demand. The twofold goal is to level demand peaks and to design methods for fully utilizing labor resources during low-demand periods. Example 6 illustrates such a plan for a legal firm.

Example 6

AGGREGATE PLANNING IN A LAW FIRM

Klasson and Avalon, a medium-size Tampa law firm of 32 legal professionals, wants to develop an aggregate plan for the next quarter. The firm has developed 3 forecasts of billable hours for the next quarter for each of 5 categories of legal business it performs (column 1, Table 13.8). The 3 forecasts (best, likely, and worst) are shown in columns 2, 3, and 4 of Table 13.8.

TABLE 13.8 — Labor Allocation at Klasson and Avalon, Forecasts for Coming Quarter (1 lawyer = 500 hours of labor)

	FORECASTED LABOR-HOURS REQUIRED			CAPACITY CONSTRAINTS	
(1) CATEGORY OF LEGAL BUSINESS	(2) BEST (HOURS)	(3) LIKELY (HOURS)	(4) WORST (HOURS)	(5) MAXIMUM DEMAND FOR PERSONNEL	(6) NUMBER OF QUALIFIED PERSONNEL
Trial work	1,800	1,500	1,200	3.6	4
Legal research	4,500	4,000	3,500	9.0	32
Corporate law	8,000	7,000	6,500	16.0	15
Real estate law	1,700	1,500	1,300	3.4	6
Criminal law	3,500	3,000	2,500	7.0	12
Total hours	19,500	17,000	15,000		
Lawyers needed	39	34	30		

APPROACH ▶ If we make some assumptions about the workweek and skills, we can provide an aggregate plan for the firm. Assuming a 40-hour workweek and that 100% of each lawyer's hours are billed, about 500 billable hours are available from each lawyer this fiscal quarter.

SOLUTION ▶ We divide hours of billable time (which is the demand) by 500 to provide a count of lawyers needed (lawyers represent the capacity) to cover the estimated demand. Capacity then is shown to be 39, 34, and 30 for the three forecasts, best, likely, and worst, respectively. For example, the best-case scenario of 19,500 total hours, divided by 500 hours per lawyer, equals 39 lawyers needed. Because all 32 lawyers at Klasson and Avalon are qualified to perform basic legal research, this skill has maximum scheduling flexibility (column 6). The most highly skilled (and capacity-constrained) categories are trial work and corporate law. The firm's best-case forecast just barely covers trial work, with 3.6 lawyers needed (see column 5) and 4 qualified (column 6). And corporate law is short 1 full person.

Overtime may be used to cover the excess this quarter, but as business expands, it may be necessary to hire or develop talent in both of these areas. Available staff adequately covers real estate and criminal practice, as long as other needs do not use their excess capacity. With its current legal staff of 32, Klasson and Avalon's best-case forecast will increase the workload by [(39 − 32)/32 =] 21.8% (assuming no new hires). This represents 1 extra day of work per lawyer per week. The worst-case scenario will result in about a 6% underutilization of talent. For both of these scenarios, the firm has determined that available staff will provide adequate service.

INSIGHT ▶ While our definitions of demand and capacity are different than for a manufacturing firm, aggregate planning is as appropriate, useful, and necessary in a service environment as in manufacturing.

LEARNING EXERCISE ▶ If the criminal law best-case forecast increases to 4,500 hours, what happens to the number of lawyers needed? [Answer: The demand for lawyers increases to 41.]

RELATED PROBLEMS ▶ 13.24, 13.25

Source: Based on Glenn Bassett, *Operations Management for Service Industries* (Westport, CT: Quorum Books): 110.

Airline Industry

Airlines and auto-rental firms also have unique aggregate scheduling problems. Consider an airline that has its headquarters in New York, two hub sites in cities such as Atlanta and Dallas, and 150 offices in airports throughout the country. This planning is considerably more complex than aggregate planning for a single site or even for a number of independent sites.

Aggregate planning consists of schedules for (1) number of flights into and out of each hub; (2) number of flights on all routes; (3) number of passengers to be serviced on all flights; (4) number of air personnel and ground personnel required at each hub and airport; and (5) determining the seats to be allocated to various fare classes. Techniques for determining seat allocation are called revenue (or yield) management, our next topic.

Revenue Management

Most operations models, like most business models, assume that firms charge all customers the same price for a product. In fact, many firms work hard at charging different prices. The idea is to match capacity and demand by charging different prices based on the customer's willingness to pay. The management challenge is to identify those differences and price accordingly. The technique for multiple price points is called revenue management.

Revenue (or yield) management is the aggregate planning process of allocating the company's scarce resources to customers at prices that will maximize revenue. Popular use of the technique dates to the 1980s, when American Airlines's reservation system (called SABRE) allowed the airline to alter ticket prices, in real time and on any route, based on demand information. If it looked like demand for expensive seats was low, more discounted seats were offered. If demand for full-fare seats was high, the number of discounted seats was reduced.

◆ **STUDENT TIP**
Revenue management changes the focus of aggregate planning from capacity management to demand management.

Revenue (or yield) management
Capacity decisions that determine the allocation of resources to maximize revenue or yield.

OM in Action | Revenue Management Makes Disney the "King" of the Broadway Jungle

Disney accomplished the unthinkable for long-running Broadway musicals: *The Lion King* transformed from a declining money-maker into the top-grossing Broadway show. How? Hint: It's not because the show added performances after 16 years.

The show's producers are using a previously undisclosed computer algorithm to recommend the highest ticket prices that audiences would be likely to pay for each of the 1,700 seats. Other shows also employ this dynamic pricing model to raise seat prices during tourist-heavy holiday weeks, but only Disney has reached the level of sophistication achieved in the airline and hotel industries. By continually using its algorithm to calibrate prices based on ticket demand and purchasing patterns, Disney was able to achieve the 2013 sales record.

By charging $10 more here, $20 more there, *The Lion King* stunned Broadway at year's end as the No. 1 earner for the first time since 2003, bumping off the champ, *Wicked*. And Disney even managed to do it by charging half as much for top tickets as some rivals. "Credit the management science experts at Disney's corporate offices—a data army that no Broadway producer could ever match—for helping develop the winning formula," writes *The New York Times*. Disney's algorithm, a software tool that draws on *Lion King* data for 11.5 million past customers, recommends prices for multiple categories of performances—

© JTB MEDIA CREATION, Inc. / Alamy Stock Photo

peak dates such as Christmas, off-peak dates such as a weeknight in February, and various periods in between. "The Lion King" is widely believed to have sold far more seats for $227 than most Broadway shows sell at their top rates, a situation that bolsters its grosses.

Sources: NY Daily News (September 22, 2014); and *The New York Times* (March 17, 2014).

American Airlines' success in revenue management spurred many other companies and industries to adopt the concept. Revenue management in the hotel industry began in the late 1980s at Marriott International, which now claims an additional $400 million a year in profit from its management of revenue. The competing Omni hotel chain uses software that performs more than 100,000 calculations every night at each facility. The Dallas Omni, for example, charges its highest rates on weekdays but heavily discounts on weekends. Its sister hotel in San Antonio, which is in a more tourist-oriented destination, reverses this rating scheme, with better deals for its consumers on weekdays. Similarly, Walt Disney World has multiple prices: an annual admission "premium" pass for an adult was recently quoted at $779, but for a Florida resident, $691, with different discounts for AAA members and active-duty military. The *OM in Action* box, "Revenue Management Makes Disney the 'King' of the Broadway Jungle," describes this practice in the live theatre industry. The video case at the end of this chapter addresses revenue management for the Orlando Magic.

Organizations that have *perishable inventory*, such as airlines, hotels, car rental agencies, cruise lines, and even electrical utilities, have the following shared characteristics that make yield management of interest:[1]

1. Service or product can be sold in advance of consumption
2. Fluctuating demand
3. Relatively fixed resource (capacity)
4. Segmentable demand
5. Low variable costs and high fixed costs

VIDEO 13.1
Using Revenue Management to Set Orlando Magic Ticket Prices

LO 13.6 *Understand and solve a revenue management problem*

Example 7 illustrates how revenue management works in a hotel.

Example 7 | REVENUE MANAGEMENT

The Cleveland Downtown Inn is a 100-room hotel that has historically charged one set price for its rooms, $150 per night. The variable cost of a room being occupied is low. Management believes the cleaning, air-conditioning, and incidental costs of soap, shampoo, and so forth, are $15 per room per night. Sales average 50 rooms per night. Figure 13.5 illustrates the current pricing scheme. Net sales are $6,750 per night with a single price point.

APPROACH ▶ Analyze pricing from the perspective of revenue management. We note in Figure 13.5 that some guests would have been willing to spend more than $150 per room—"money left on the table." Others would be willing to pay more than the variable cost of $15 but less than $150—"passed-up contribution."

Figure **13.5**

Hotel Sets Only One Price Level

Room Sales

Demand curve

Potential customers exist who are willing to pay more than the $15 variable cost of the room, but not $150.

Passed-up contribution

Some customers who paid $150 were actually willing to pay more for the room.

Total $ contribution = (Price) × (50 rooms) = ($150 − $15)(50) = $6,750

Money left on the table

$15 Variable cost of room (e.g., cleaning, A/C)

$150 Price charged for room

Price

SOLUTION ▶ In Figure 13.6, the inn decides to set *two* price levels. It estimates that 30 rooms per night can be sold at $100 and another 30 rooms at $200, using revenue management software that is widely available.

Figure **13.6**

Hotel with Two Price Levels

Room Sales

Demand curve

Total $ contribution = (1st price) × 30 rooms + (2nd price) × 30 rooms = ($100 − $15) × 30 + ($200 − $15) × 30 = $2,550 + $5,550 = $8,100

$15 Variable cost of room

$100 Price 1 for room

$200 Price 2 for room

Price

INSIGHT ▶ Revenue management has increased total contribution to $8,100 ($2,550 from $100 rooms and $5,550 from $200 rooms). It may be that even more price levels are called for at Cleveland Downtown Inn.

LEARNING EXERCISE ▶ If the hotel develops a third price of $150 and can sell half of the $100 rooms at the increased rate, what is the contribution? [Answer: $8,850 = (15 × $85) + (15 × $135) + (30 × $185).]

RELATED PROBLEM ▶ 13.26

Industries traditionally associated with revenue management include hotels, airlines, and rental cars. They are able to apply variable pricing for their product and control product use or availability (number of airline seats or hotel rooms sold at economy rates). Others, such as movie theaters, arenas, or performing arts centers have less pricing flexibility but still use time (evening or matinee) and location (orchestra, side, or balcony) to manage revenue. In both cases, management has control over the amount of the resource used—both the quantity and the duration of the resource.

The manager's job is more difficult in facilities such as restaurants and on golf courses because the duration and the use of the resource is less controllable. However, with imagination, managers are using excess capacity even for these industries. For instance, the golf course may sell less desirable tee times at a reduced rate, and the restaurant may have an "early bird" special to generate business before the usual dinner hour.

To make revenue management work, the company needs to manage three issues:

1. *Multiple pricing structures:* These structures must be feasible and appear logical (and preferably fair) to the customer. Such justification may take various forms, for example, first-class seats on an airline or the preferred starting time at a golf course. (See the Ethical Dilemma at the end of this chapter.)
2. *Forecasts of the use and duration of the use:* How many economy seats should be available? How much will customers pay for a room with an ocean view?
3. *Changes in demand:* This means managing the increased use as more capacity is sold. It also means dealing with issues that occur because the pricing structure may not seem logical and fair to all customers. Finally, it means managing new issues, such as overbooking because the forecast was not perfect.

Precise pricing through revenue management has substantial potential, and several firms sell software available to address the issue. These include NCR's *Teradata,* SPS, *DemandTec,* and Oracle with *Profit Logic.*

Summary

Sales and operations planning (S&OP) can be a strong vehicle for coordinating the functional areas of a firm as well as for communication with supply-chain partners. The output of S&OP is an *aggregate plan.* An aggregate plan provides both manufacturing and service firms the ability to respond to changing customer demands and produce with a winning strategy.

Aggregate schedules set levels of inventory, production, subcontracting, and employment over an intermediate time range, usually 3 to 18 months. This chapter describes two aggregate planning techniques: the popular graphical approach and the transportation method of linear programming.

The aggregate plan is an important responsibility of an operations manager and a key to efficient use of existing resources. It leads to the more detailed master production schedule, which becomes the basis for disaggregation, detail scheduling, and MRP systems.

Restaurants, airlines, and hotels are all service systems that employ aggregate plans. They also have an opportunity to implement revenue management.

Regardless of the industry or planning method, the S&OP process builds an aggregate plan that a firm can implement and suppliers endorse.

Key Terms

Sales and operations planning (S&OP) (p. 533)
Aggregate plan (p. 533)
Disaggregation (p. 535)
Master production schedule (p. 535)

Chase strategy (p. 537)
Level scheduling (p. 538)
Mixed strategy (p. 538)
Graphical techniques (p. 538)

Transportation method of linear programming (p. 543)
Revenue (or yield) management (p. 547)

Ethical Dilemma

Airline passengers today stand in numerous lines, are crowded into small seats on mostly full airplanes, and often spend time on taxiways because of air-traffic problems or lack of open gates. But what gripes travelers almost as much as these annoyances is finding out that the person sitting next to them paid a much lower fare than they did for their seat. This concept of *revenue management* results in ticket pricing that can range from free to thousands of dollars on the same plane. Figure 13.7

illustrates what passengers recently paid for various seats on an 11:35 A.M. flight from Minneapolis to Anaheim, California, on an Airbus A320.

Make the case for, and then against, this pricing system. Does the general public seem to accept revenue management? What would happen if you overheard the person in front of you in line getting a better room rate at a Hilton Hotel? How do customers manipulate the airline systems to get better fares?

Sales	Fare	Seats
First class	$817	1
Full fare	792	4
Corporate discount	491	5
21-day advance	273	20
Deep discounts	190	33
Frequent flyer program	0	7
Connections	—	53
Empty	—	27

Figure 13.7

Revenue Management Seat Costs on a Typical Flight

Discussion Questions

1. Define *sales* and *operations planning*.
2. Why are S&OP teams typically cross-functional?
3. Define *aggregate planning*.
4. Explain what the term *aggregate* in "aggregate planning" means.
5. List the strategic objectives of aggregate planning. Which one of these is most often addressed by the quantitative techniques of aggregate planning? Which one of these is generally the most important?
6. Define *chase strategy*.
7. What is level scheduling? What is the basic philosophy underlying it?
8. Define *mixed strategy*. Why would a firm use a mixed strategy instead of a simple pure strategy?
9. What are the advantages and disadvantages of varying the size of the workforce to meet demand requirements each period?
10. How does aggregate planning in service differ from aggregate planning in manufacturing?
11. What is the relationship between the aggregate plan and the master production schedule?
12. Why are graphical aggregate planning methods useful?
13. What are major limitations of using the transportation method for aggregate planning?
14. How does revenue management impact an aggregate plan?

Using Software for Aggregate Planning

This section illustrates the use of Excel, Excel OM, and POM for Windows in aggregate planning.

CREATING YOUR OWN EXCEL SPREADSHEETS

Program 13.1 illustrates how you can make an Excel model to solve Example 5, which uses the transportation method for aggregate planning.

Program 13.1

Using Excel for Aggregate Planning Via the Transportation Method, with Data from Example 5

Excel comes with an Add-In called Solver that offers the ability to analyze linear programs such as the transportation problem. To ensure that Solver always loads when Excel is loaded, go to: **File→Options→Add-Ins**. Next to **Manage:** at the bottom, make sure that **Excel Add-ins** is selected, and click on the **<Go...>** button. Check **Solver Add-in**, and click **<OK>**. Once in Excel, the Solver dialog box will appear by clicking on: **Data→Analysis: Solver**. The following screen shot shows how to use Solver to find the optimal (very best) solution to Example 4. Click on **<Solve>**, and the solution will automatically appear in the Transportation Table, yielding a cost of $105,700.

X USING EXCEL OM

Excel OM's Aggregate Planning module is demonstrated in Program 13.2. Using data from Example 2, Program 13.2 provides input and some of the formulas used to compute the costs of regular time, overtime, subcontracting, holding, shortage, and increase or decrease in production. The user must provide the production plan for Excel OM to analyze.

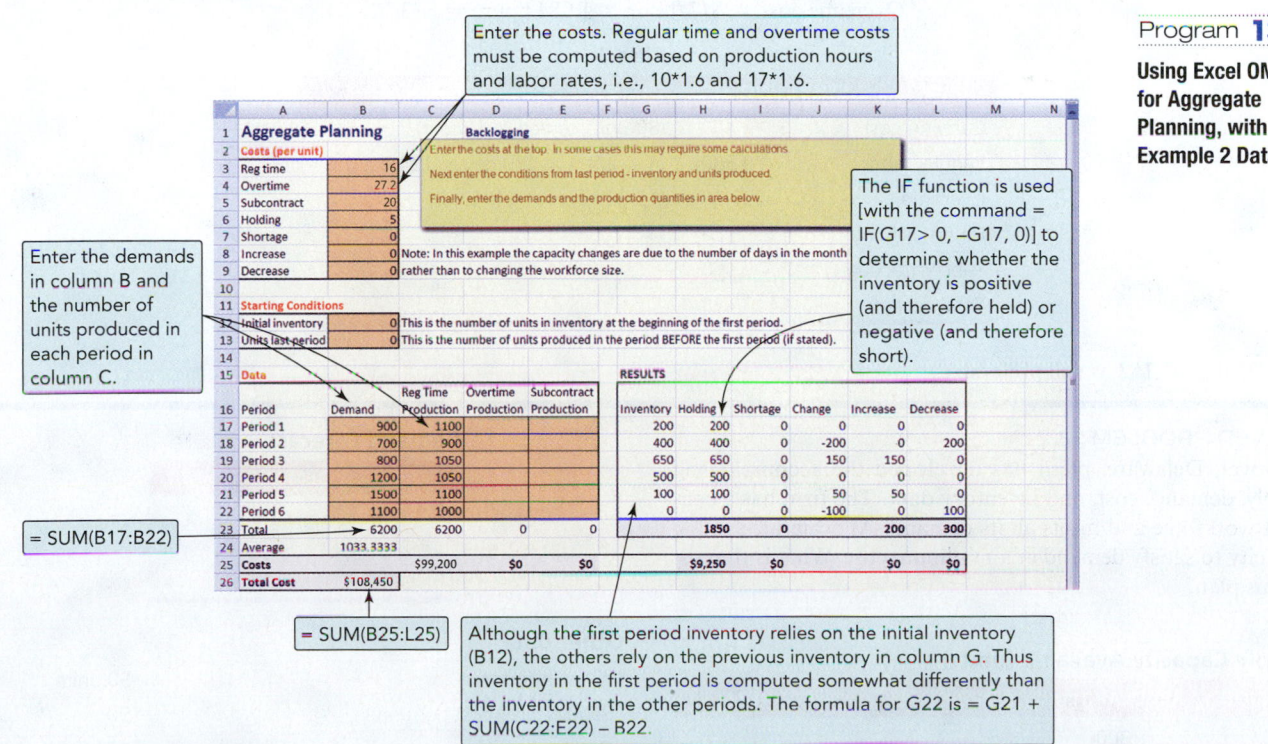

Program 13.2

Using Excel OM for Aggregate Planning, with Example 2 Data

P USING POM FOR WINDOWS

The POM for Windows Aggregate Planning module performs aggregate or production planning for up to 90 time periods. Given a set of demands for future periods, you can try various plans to determine the lowest-cost plan based on holding, shortage, production, and changeover costs. Four methods are available for planning. More help is available on each after you choose the method. See Appendix IV for further details.

Solved Problems Virtual Office Hours help is available in MyOMLab.

SOLVED PROBLEM 13.1

The roofing manufacturer described in Examples 1 to 4 of this chapter wishes to consider yet a fourth planning strategy (plan 4). This one maintains a constant workforce of eight people and uses overtime whenever necessary to meet demand. Use the information found in Table 13.3 on page 540. Again, assume beginning and ending inventories are equal to zero.

SOLUTION

Employ eight workers and use overtime when necessary. Note that carrying costs will be encountered in this plan.

MONTH	PRODUCTION DAYS	PRODUCTION AT 40 UNITS PER DAY	BEGINNING-OF-MONTH INVENTORY	FORECAST DEMAND THIS MONTH	OVERTIME PRODUCTION NEEDED	ENDING INVENTORY
Jan.	22	880	—	900	20 units	0 units
Feb.	18	720	0	700	0 units	20 units
Mar.	21	840	20	800	0 units	60 units
Apr.	21	840	60	1,200	300 units	0 units
May	22	880	0	1,500	620 units	0 units
June	20	800	0	1,100	300 units	0 units
					1,240 units	80 units

Carrying cost totals = 80 units × $5/unit/month = $400

Regular pay:

8 workers × $80/day × 124 days = $79,360

Overtime pay:

To produce 1,240 units at overtime rate requires 1,240 × 1.6 hours/unit = 1,984 hours.

Overtime cost = $17/hour × 1,984 hours = $33,728

Plan 4

COSTS (WORKFORCE OF 8 PLUS OVERTIME)		
Carrying cost	$ 400	(80 units carried × $5/unit)
Regular labor	79,360	(8 workers × $80/day × 124 days)
Overtime	33,728	(1,984 hours × $17/hour)
Hiring or firing	0	
Subcontracting	0	
Total costs	$113,488	

Plan 2, at $105,152, is still preferable.

SOLVED PROBLEM 13.2

A Dover, Delaware, plant has developed the accompanying supply, demand, cost, and inventory data. The firm has a constant workforce and meets all its demand. Allocate production capacity to satisfy demand at a minimum cost. What is the cost of this plan?

Demand Forecast

PERIOD	DEMAND (UNITS)
1	450
2	550
3	750

Supply Capacity Available (units)

PERIOD	REGULAR TIME	OVERTIME	SUBCONTRACT
1	300	50	200
2	400	50	200
3	450	50	200

Other data

Initial inventory	50 units
Regular-time cost per unit	$50
Overtime cost per unit	$65
Subcontract cost per unit	$80
Carrying cost per unit per period	$ 1
Back order cost per unit per period	$ 4

SOLUTION

SUPPLY FROM		DEMAND FOR				
		Period 1	Period 2	Period 3	*Unused Capacity (dummy)*	TOTAL CAPACITY AVAILABLE (supply)
Beginning inventory		0	1	2	0	
		50				50
Period 1	Regular time	50	51	52	0	
		300				300
	Overtime	65	66	67	0	
		50				50
	Subcontract	80	81	82	0	
		50			150	200
Period 2	Regular time	54	50	51	0	
			400			400
	Overtime	69	65	66	0	
			50			50
	Subcontract	84	80	81	0	
			100	50	50	200
Period 3	Regular time	58	54	50	0	
				450		450
	Overtime	73	69	65	0	
				50		50
	Subcontract	88	84	80	0	
				200		200
TOTAL DEMAND		450	550	750	200	1,950

Cost of plan:

Period 1:   50($0) + 300($50) + 50($65) +   50($80) = $22,250
Period 2:   400($50) + 50($65) + 100($80) = $31,250
Period 3: 50($81) + 450($50) + 50($65) + 200($80) = $45,800*
                                                  Total cost $99,300

*Includes 50 units of subcontract and carrying cost.

Problems   *Note:* **PX** means the problem may be solved with POM for Windows and/or Excel OM.

Problems 13.1–13.23 relate to Methods for Aggregate Planning

• **13.1** Prepare a graph of the monthly forecasts and average forecast demand for Chicago Paint Corp., a manufacturer of specialized paint for artists.

MONTH	PRODUCTION DAYS	DEMAND FORECAST
January	22	1,000
February	18	1,100
March	22	1,200
April	21	1,300
May	22	1,350
June	21	1,350
July	21	1,300
August	22	1,200
September	21	1,100
October	22	1,100
November	20	1,050
December	20	900

•• **13.2** Develop another plan for the Mexican roofing manufacturer described in Examples 1 to 4 (pages 538–542) and Solved Problem 13.1 (page 554).

a) For this plan, plan 5, the firm wants to maintain a constant workforce of six, using subcontracting to meet remaining demand. Is this plan preferable?

b) The same roofing manufacturer in Examples 1 to 4 and Solved Problem 13.1 has yet a sixth plan. A constant workforce of seven is selected, with the remainder of demand filled by subcontracting.

c) Is this better than plans 1–5? **PX**

••• **13.3** The president of Hill Enterprises, Terri Hill, projects the firm's aggregate demand requirements over the next 8 months as follows:

Jan.	1,400		May	2,200
Feb.	1,600		June	2,200
Mar.	1,800		July	1,800
Apr.	1,800		Aug.	1,800

Her operations manager is considering a new plan, which begins in January with 200 units on hand. Stockout cost of lost sales is $100 per unit. Inventory holding cost is $20 per unit per month. Ignore any idle-time costs. The plan is called plan A.

Plan A: Vary the workforce level to execute a strategy that produces the quantity demanded in the *prior* month. The December demand and rate of production are both 1,600 units per month. The cost of hiring additional workers is $5,000 per 100 units. The cost of laying off workers is $7,500 per 100 units. Evaluate this plan. **PX**

Note: Both hiring and layoff costs are incurred in the month of the change. For example, going from 1,600 in January to 1,400 in February incurs a cost of layoff for 200 units in February.

•• **13.4** Using the information in Problem 13.3, develop plan B. Produce at a constant rate of 1,400 units per month, which will meet minimum demands. Then use subcontracting, with additional units at a premium price of $75 per unit. Evaluate this plan by computing the costs for January through August. **PX**

•• **13.5** Hill is now considering plan C: Keep a stable workforce by maintaining a constant production rate equal to the average requirements and allow varying inventory levels. Beginning inventory, stockout costs, and holding costs are provided in Problem 13.3.

Plot the demand with a graph that also shows average requirements. Conduct your analysis for January through August. **PX**

••• **13.6** Hill's operations manager (see Problems 13.3 through 13.5) is also considering two mixed strategies for January–August: Produce in overtime or subcontracting only when there is no inventory.

◆ *Plan D:* Keep the current workforce stable at producing 1,600 units per month. Permit a maximum of 20% overtime at an additional cost of $50 per unit. A warehouse now constrains the maximum allowable inventory on hand to 400 units or less.

◆ *Plan E:* Keep the current workforce, which is producing 1,600 units per month, and subcontract to meet the rest of the demand.

Evaluate plans D and E and make a recommendation. **PX**

Note: Do not produce in overtime if production or inventory are adequate to cover demand.

••• **13.7** Consuelo Chua, Inc., is a disk drive manufacturer in need of an aggregate plan for July through December. The company has gathered the following data:

COSTS	
Holding cost	$8/disk/month
Subcontracting	$80/disk
Regular-time labor	$12/hour
Overtime labor	$18/hour for hours above 8 hours/worker/day
Hiring cost	$40/worker
Layoff cost	$80/worker

DEMAND*	
July	400
Aug.	500
Sept.	550
Oct.	700
Nov.	800
Dec.	700

*No costs are incurred for unmet demand, but unmet demand (backorders) must be handled in the following period. If half or more of a worker is needed, round up.

OTHER DATA	
Current workforce (June)	8 people
Labor-hours/disk	4 hours
Workdays/month	20 days
Beginning inventory	150 disks**
No requirement for ending inventory	0 disks

**Note that there is no holding cost for June.

What will each of the two following strategies cost?
a) Vary the workforce so that production meets demand. Chua had eight workers on board in June.
b) Vary overtime only and use a constant workforce of eight. **PX**

•• **13.8** You manage a consulting firm down the street from Consuelo Chua, Inc., and to get your foot in the door, you have told Ms. Chua (see Problem 13.7) that you can do a better job at aggregate planning than her current staff. She said, "Fine. You do that, and you have a one year contract." You now have to make good on your boast using the data in Problem 13.7. You decide to hire 5 workers in August and 5 more in October. Your results?

••• **13.9** The S&OP team at Kansas Furniture, has received the following estimates of demand requirements:

July	Aug.	Sept.	Oct.	Nov.	Dec.
1,000	1,200	1,400	1,800	1,800	1,800

Stephanie Klein-Davis/The Roanoke Times/AP Images

a) Assuming one-time stockout costs for lost sales of $100 per unit, inventory carrying costs of $25 per unit per month, and zero beginning and ending inventory, evaluate these two plans on an *incremental* cost basis:

◆ *Plan A:* Produce at a steady rate (equal to minimum requirements) of 1,000 units per month and subcontract additional units at a $60 per unit premium cost.

◆ *Plan B:* Vary the workforce, to produce the prior month's demand. The firm produced 1,300 units in June. The cost of hiring additional workers is $3,000 per 100 units produced. The cost of layoffs is $6,000 per 100 units cut back.

Note: Both hiring and layoff costs are incurred in the month of the change, (i.e. going from production of 1,300 in July to 1,000 in August requires a layoff (and related costs) of 300 units in August, just as going from production of 1,000 in August to 1,200 in September requires hiring (and related costs) of 200 units in September). **PX**

b) Which plan is best and why?

••• **13.10** The S&OP team (see Problem 13.9) is considering two more mixed strategies. Using the data in Problem 13.9, compare plans C and D with plans A and B and make a recommendation.

◆ *Plan C:* Keep the current workforce steady at a level producing 1,300 units per month. Subcontract the remainder to meet demand. Assume that 300 units remaining from June are available in July.

◆ *Plan D:* Keep the current workforce at a level capable of producing 1,300 units per month. Permit a maximum of 20% overtime at a premium of $40 per unit. Assume that warehouse limitations permit no more than a 180-unit carryover from month to month. This plan means that any time inventories reach 180, the plant is kept idle. Idle time per unit is $60. Any additional needs are subcontracted at a cost of $60 per incremental unit.

••• **13.11** Deb Bishop Health and Beauty Products has developed a new shampoo, and you need to develop its aggregate schedule. The cost accounting department has supplied you the costs relevant to the aggregate plan, and the marketing department has provided a four-quarter forecast. All are shown as follows:

QUARTER	FORECAST
1	1,400
2	1,200
3	1,500
4	1,300

COSTS	
Previous quarter's output	1,500 units
Beginning inventory	0 units
Stockout cost for backorders	$50 per unit
Inventory holding cost	$10 per unit for every unit held at the end of the quarter
Hiring workers	$40 per unit
Layoff workers	$80 per unit
Unit cost	$30 per unit
Overtime	$15 extra per unit
Subcontracting	Not available

Your job is to develop an aggregate plan for the next four quarters.
a) First, try hiring and layoffs (to meet the forecast) as necessary.
b) Then try a plan that holds employment steady.
c) Which is the more economical plan for Deb Bishop Health and Beauty Products? **Px**

••• **13.12** Southeast Soda Pop, Inc., has a new fruit drink for which it has high hopes. John Mittenthal, the production planner, has assembled the following cost data and demand forecast:

QUARTER	FORECAST
1	1,800
2	1,100
3	1,600
4	900

COSTS/OTHER DATA	
Previous quarter's output = 1,300 cases	
Beginning inventory = 0 cases	
Stockout cost = $150 per case	
Inventory holding cost = $40 per case at end of quarter	
Hiring employees = $40 per case	
Terminating employees = $80 per case	
Subcontracting cost = $60 per case	
Unit cost on regular time = $30 per case	
Overtime cost = $15 extra per case	
Capacity on regular time = 1,800 cases per quarter	

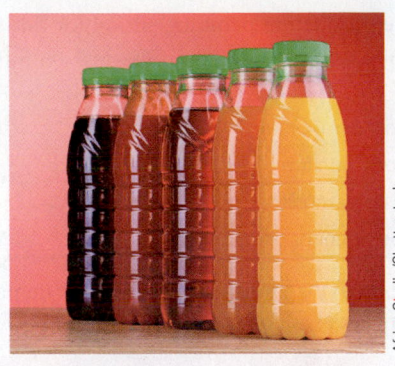
Africa Studio/Shutterstock

John's job is to develop an aggregate plan. The three initial options he wants to evaluate are:

◆ *Plan A:* a strategy that hires and fires personnel as necessary to meet the forecast.
◆ *Plan B:* a level strategy.
◆ *Plan C:* a level strategy that produces 1,200 cases per quarter and meets the forecast demand with inventory and subcontracting.

a) Which strategy is the lowest-cost plan?
b) If you are John's boss, the VP for operations, which plan do you implement and why? **Px**

•• **13.13** Ram Roy's firm has developed the following supply, demand, cost, and inventory data. Allocate production capacity to meet demand at a minimum cost using the transportation method. What is the cost? Assume that the initial inventory has no holding cost in the first period and backorders are not permitted.

Supply Available

PERIOD	REGULAR TIME	OVERTIME	SUBCONTRACT	DEMAND FORECAST
1	30	10	5	40
2	35	12	5	50
3	30	10	5	40

Initial inventory	20 units
Regular-time cost per unit	$100
Overtime cost per unit	$150
Subcontract cost per unit	$200
Carrying cost per unit per month	$ 4

Px

••**13.14** Jerusalem Medical Ltd., an Israeli producer of portable kidney dialysis units and other medical products, develops a 4-month aggregate plan. Demand and capacity (in units) are forecast as follows:

CAPACITY SOURCE	MONTH 1	MONTH 2	MONTH 3	MONTH 4
Labor				
Regular time	235	255	290	300
Overtime	20	24	26	24
Subcontract	12	15	15	17
Demand	255	294	321	301

The cost of producing each dialysis unit is $985 on regular time, $1,310 on overtime, and $1,500 on a subcontract. Inventory carrying cost is $100 per unit per month. There is to be no beginning or ending inventory in stock and backorders are not permitted. Set up a production plan that minimizes cost using the transportation method. **Px**

•• **13.15** The production planning period for flat-screen monitors at Louisiana's Roa Electronics, Inc., is 4 months. Cost data are as follows:

Regular-time cost per monitor	$ 70
Overtime cost per monitor	$110
Subcontract cost per monitor	$120
Carrying cost per monitor per month	$ 4

For each of the next 4 months, capacity and demand for flat-screen monitors are as follows:

	PERIOD			
	MONTH 1	MONTH 2	MONTH 3[a]	MONTH 4
Demand	2,000	2,500	1,500	2,100
Capacity				
Regular time	1,500	1,600	750	1,600
Overtime	400	400	200	400
Subcontract	600	600	600	600

[a]Factory closes for 2 weeks of vacation.

CEO Mohan Roa expects to enter the planning period with 500 monitors in stock. Back ordering is not permitted (meaning, for example, that monitors produced in the second month cannot be used to cover first month's demand). Develop a production plan that minimizes costs using the transportation method. **Px**

••**13.16** A large St. Louis feed mill, Robert Orwig Processing, prepares its 6-month aggregate plan by forecasting demand for 50-pound bags of cattle feed as follows: January, 1,000 bags; February, 1,200; March, 1,250; April, 1,450; May, 1,400; and June, 1,400. The feed mill plans to begin the new year with no inventory left over from the previous year, and backorders are not permitted. It projects that capacity (during regular hours) for producing bags of feed will remain constant at 800 until the end of April, and then increase to 1,100 bags per month when a planned expansion is completed on May 1. Overtime capacity is set at 300 bags per month until the expansion, at which time it will increase to 400 bags per month. A friendly competitor in Sioux City, Iowa, is also available as a backup source to meet demand—but can provide only 500 bags total during the 6-month period. Develop a 6-month production plan for the feed mill using the transportation method.

Cost data are as follows:

Regular-time cost per bag (until April 30)	$12.00
Regular-time cost per bag (after May 1)	$11.00
Overtime cost per bag (during entire period)	$16.00
Cost of outside purchase per bag	$18.50
Carrying cost per bag per month	$ 1.00

Px

•• **13.17** Yu Amy Xia has developed a specialized airtight vacuum bag to extend the freshness of seafood shipped to restaurants. She has put together the following demand cost data:

QUARTER	FORECAST (UNITS)	REGULAR TIME	OVERTIME	SUB-CONTRACT
1	500	400	80	100
2	750	400	80	100
3	900	800	160	100
4	450	400	80	100

Initial inventory = 250 units
Regular time cost = $1.00/unit
Overtime cost = $1.50/unit
Subcontracting cost = $2.00/unit
Carrying cost = $0.20/unit/quarter
Back order cost = $0.50/unit/quarter

Yu decides that the initial inventory of 250 units will incur the 20¢/unit cost from each prior quarter (unlike the situation in most other companies, where a 0 unit cost is assigned).
a) Find the optimal plan using the transportation method.
b) What is the cost of the plan?
c) Does any regular time capacity go unused? If so, how much in which periods?
b) What is the extent of backordering in units and dollars? **Px**

••• **13.18** José Martinez of El Paso has developed a polished stainless steel tortilla machine that makes it a "showpiece" for display in Mexican restaurants. He needs to develop a 5-month aggregate plan. His forecast of capacity and demand follows:

	MONTH				
	1	2	3	4	5
Demand	150	160	130	200	210
Capacity					
Regular	150	150	150	150	150
Overtime	20	20	10	10	10

Subcontracting: 100 units available over the 5-month period
Beginning inventory: 0 units
Ending inventory required: 20 units

COSTS	
Regular-time cost per unit	$100
Overtime cost per unit	$125
Subcontract cost per unit	$135
Inventory holding cost per unit per month	$ 3

Assume that backorders are not permitted. Using the transportation method, what is the total cost of the optimal plan? **Px**

•••• **13.19** Dwayne Cole, owner of a Florida firm that manufactures display cabinets, develops an 8-month aggregate plan. Demand and capacity (in units) are forecast as follows:

CAPACITY SOURCE (UNITS)	JAN.	FEB.	MAR.	APR.	MAY	JUNE	JULY	AUG.
Regular time	235	255	290	300	300	290	300	290
Overtime	20	24	26	24	30	28	30	30
Subcontract	12	16	15	17	17	19	19	20
Demand	255	294	321	301	330	320	345	340

The cost of producing each unit is $1,000 on regular time, $1,300 on overtime, and $1,800 on a subcontract. Inventory carrying cost is $200 per unit per month. There is no beginning or ending inventory in stock, and no backorders are permitted from period to period.

Let the production (workforce) vary by using regular time first, then overtime, and then subcontracting.
a) Set up a production plan that minimizes cost by producing exactly what the demand is each month. This plan allows no backorders or inventory. What is this plan's cost?
b) Through better planning, regular-time production can be set at exactly the same amount, 275 units, per month. If demand cannot be met there is no cost assigned to shortages and they will not be filled. Does this alter the solution?

c) If overtime costs per unit rise from $1,300 to $1,400, will your answer to (a) change? What if overtime costs then fall to $1,200?

Additional problems **13.20–13.23** are available in MyOMLab.

Problems 13.24–13.25 relate to Aggregate Planning in Services

• • • **13.24** Forrester and Cohen is a small accounting firm, managed by Joseph Cohen since the retirement in December of his partner Brad Forrester. Cohen and his 3 CPAs can together bill 640 hours per month. When Cohen or another accountant bills more than 160 hours per month, he or she gets an additional "overtime" pay of $62.50 for each of the extra hours: this is above and beyond the $5,000 salary each draws during the month. (Cohen draws the same base pay as his employees.) Cohen strongly discourages any CPA from working (billing) more than 240 hours in any given month. The demand for billable hours for the firm over the next 6 months is estimated below:

MONTH	ESTIMATE OF BILLABLE HOURS
Jan.	600
Feb.	500
Mar.	1,000
Apr.	1,200
May	650
June	590

Cohen has an agreement with Forrester, his former partner, to help out during the busy tax season, if needed, for an hourly fee of $125. Cohen will not even consider laying off one of his colleagues in the case of a slow economy. He could, however, hire another CPA at the same salary, as business dictates.
a) Develop an aggregate plan for the 6-month period.
b) Compute the cost of Cohen's plan of using overtime and Forrester.
c) Should the firm remain as is, with a total of 4 CPAs?

• • **13.25** Refer to the CPA firm in Problem 13.24. In planning for next year, Cohen estimates that billable hours will increase by 10% in each of the 6 months. He therefore proceeds to hire a fifth CPA. The same regular time, overtime, and outside consultant (i.e., Forrester) costs still apply.
a) Develop the new aggregate plan and compute its costs.
b) Comment on the staffing level with five accountants. Was it a good decision to hire the additional accountant?

Problem 13.26 relates to Revenue Management

• • **13.26** Southeastern Airlines's daily flight from Atlanta to Charlotte uses a Boeing 737, with all-coach seating for 120 people. In the past, the airline has priced every seat at $140 for the one-way flight. An average of 80 passengers are on each flight. The variable cost of a filled seat is $25. Aysajan Eziz, the new operations manager, has decided to try a yield revenue approach, with seats priced at $80 for early bookings and at $190 for bookings within 1 week of the flight. He estimates that the airline will sell 65 seats at the lower price and 35 at the higher price. Variable cost will not change. Which approach is preferable to Mr. Eziz?

CASE STUDIES

Andrew-Carter, Inc.

Andrew-Carter, Inc. (A-C), is a major Canadian producer and distributor of outdoor lighting fixtures. Its products are distributed throughout South and North America and have been in high demand for several years. The company operates three plants to manufacture fixtures and distribute them to five distribution centers (warehouses).

During the present global slowdown, A-C has seen a major drop in demand for its products, largely because the housing market has declined. Based on the forecast of interest rates, the head of operations feels that demand for housing and thus for A-C's products will remain depressed for the foreseeable future. A-C is considering closing one of its plants, as it is now operating with a forecast excess capacity of 34,000 units per week. The forecast weekly demands for the coming year are as follows:

Warehouse 1	9,000 units
Warehouse 2	13,000
Warehouse 3	11,000
Warehouse 4	15,000
Warehouse 5	8,000

Plant capacities, in units per week, are as follows:

Plant 1, regular time	27,000 units
Plant 1, on overtime	7,000
Plant 2, regular time	20,000
Plant 2, on overtime	5,000
Plant 3, regular time	25,000
Plant 3, on overtime	6,000

If A-C shuts down any plants, its weekly costs will change, because fixed costs will be lower for a nonoperating plant. Table 13.9 shows production costs at each plant, both variable at regular time and overtime, and fixed when operating and shut down. Table 13.10 shows distribution costs from each plant to each distribution center.

Discussion Questions

1. Evaluate the various configurations of operating and closed plants that will meet weekly demand. Determine which configuration minimizes total costs.
2. Discuss the implications of closing a plant.

| TABLE 13.9 | Andrew-Carter, Inc., Variable Costs and Fixed Production Costs per Week |

| PLANT | VARIABLE COST (PER UNIT) | FIXED COST PER WEEK | |
		OPERATING	NOT OPERATING
1, regular time	$2.80	$14,000	$6,000
1, overtime	3.52	——	——
2, regular time	2.78	12,000	5,000
2, overtime	3.48	——	——
3, regular time	2.72	15,000	7,500
3, overtime	3.42	——	——

| TABLE 13.10 | Andrew-Carter, Inc., Distribution Costs per Unit |

| FROM PLANTS | TO DISTRIBUTION CENTERS | | | | |
	W1	W2	W3	W4	W5
1	$.50	$.44	$.49	$.46	$.56
2	.40	.52	.50	.56	.57
3	.56	.53	.51	.54	.35

Source: Reprinted by permission of Professor Michael Ballot, University of the Pacific, Stockton, CA. Copyright © by Michael Ballot.

Using Revenue Management to Set Orlando Magic Ticket Prices

Video Case 📷

Revenue management was once the exclusive domain of the airline industry. But it has since spread its wings into the hotel business, auto rentals, and now even professional sports, with the San Francisco Giants, Boston Celtics, and Orlando Magic as leaders in introducing dynamic pricing into their ticketing systems. Dynamic pricing means looking at unsold tickets for every single game, every day, to see if the current ticket price for a particular seat needs to be lowered (because of slow demand) or raised (because of higher-than-expected demand).

Pricing can be impacted by something as simple as bad weather or by whether the team coming to play in the arena is on a winning streak or has just traded for a new superstar player. For example, a few years ago, a basketball star was traded in midseason to the Denver Nuggets; this resulted in an immediate runup in unsold ticket prices for the teams the Nuggets were facing on the road. Had the Nuggets been visiting the Orlando Magic 2 weeks after the trade and the Magic not raised prices, they would have been "leaving money on the table" (as shown in Figure 13.5).

As the Magic became more proficient in revenue management, they evolved from (l) setting the price for each seat at the start of the season and never changing it; to (2) setting the prices for each seat at season onset, based on the popularity of the opponent, the day of the week, and the time of season (see the Video Case in Chapter 4)—but keeping the prices frozen once the season began (see Table 13.11); to (3) pricing tickets based on projected demand, but adjusting them frequently to match market demand as the season progressed.

To track market demand, the Magic use listed prices on Stub Hub and other online ticket exchange services. The key is to sell out all 18,500 seats every home game, keeping the pressure on Anthony Perez, the director of business strategy, and Chris Dorso, the Magic's vice president of sales.

Perez and Dorso use every tool available to collect information on demand, including counting unique page views at the Ticketmaster Web site. If, for example, there are 5,000 page views for the Miami Heat game near Thanksgiving, it indicates enough demand that prices of unsold seats can be notched up. If there are only 150 Ticketmaster views for the Utah Jazz game 3 days later, there may not be sufficient information to make any changes yet.

| TABLE 13.11 | An Example of Variable Pricing for a $68 Terrace V seat in Zone 103 |

OPPONENT POPULARITY RATING	NUMBER OF GAMES IN THIS CATEGORY	PRICE
Tier I	3	$187
Tier II	3	$170
Tier III	4	$ 85
Tier IV	6	$ 75
Tier V	14	$ 60
Tier VI	9	$ 44
Tier VII	6	$ 40
Average		$ 68

With a database of 650,000, the Magic can use e-mail blasts to react quickly right up to game day. The team may discount seat prices, offer other perks, or just point out that prime seats are still available for a game against an exciting opponent.

Discussion Questions*

1. After researching revenue (yield) management in airlines, describe how the Magic system differs from that of American or other air carriers.
2. The Magic used its original pricing systems of several years ago and set the price for a Terrace V, Zone 103 seat at $68 per game. There were 230 such seats *not* purchased as part of season ticket packages and thus available to the public. If the team switched to the 7-price dynamic system (illustrated in Table 13.11), how would the profit-contribution for the 45-game season change? (Note that the 45-game season includes 4 preseason games.)
3. What are some concerns the team needs to consider when using dynamic pricing with frequent changes in price?

*You may wish to view the video that accompanies this case before addressing these questions.

- **Additional Case Studies:** Visit MyOMLab for these free case studies:
  Cornwell Glass: Involves setting a production schedule for an auto glass producer.
  Southwestern University: (G) Requires developing an aggregate plan for a university police department.

Endnote

1. R. Oberwetter, "Revenue Management," *OR/MS Today* (June 2001): 41–44.

Main Heading	Review Material	MyOMLab
THE PLANNING PROCESS (pp. 532–533)	■ *Long-range plans* develop policies and strategies related to location, capacity, products and process, supply chain, research, and capital investment. ■ *Intermediate planning* develops plans that match production to demand. ■ *Short-run planning* translates intermediate plans into weekly, daily, and hourly schedules.	Concept Questions: 1.1–1.4
SALES AND OPERATIONS PLANNING (pp. 533–534)	■ **Sales and operation planning (S&OP)**—Balances resources and forecasted demand, and aligns the organization's competing demands, from supply chain to final customer, while linking strategic planning with operations over all planning horizons. ■ **Aggregate planning**—An approach to determine the quantity and timing of production for the intermediate future (usually 3 to 18 months ahead). Four things are needed for aggregate planning: 1. A logical unit for measuring sales and output 2. A forecast of demand for a reasonable intermediate planning period in these aggregate terms 3. A method for determining the relevant costs 4. A model that combines forecasts and costs so that scheduling decisions can be made for the planning period	Concept Questions: 2.1–2.4
THE NATURE OF AGGREGATE PLANNING (pp. 534–535)	Usually, *the objective of aggregate planning is to meet forecasted demand while minimizing cost over the planning period.* An aggregate plan looks at production *in the aggregate* (a family of products), not as a product-by-product breakdown. ■ **Disaggregation**—The process of breaking an aggregate plan into greater detail. ■ **Master production schedule**—A timetable that specifies what is to be made and when.	Concept Questions: 3.1–3.4
AGGREGATE PLANNING STRATEGIES (pp. 535–538)	The basic aggregate planning capacity (production) options are: ■ *Changing inventory levels* ■ *Varying workforce size by hiring or layoffs* ■ *Varying production rates through overtime or idle time* ■ *Subcontracting* ■ *Using part-time workers* The basic aggregate planning demand options are: ■ *Influencing demand* ■ *Back ordering during high-demand periods* ■ *Counterseasonal product and service mixing* ■ **Chase strategy**—A planning strategy that sets production equal to forecast demand. Many service organizations favor the chase strategy because the inventory option is difficult or impossible to adopt. ■ **Level scheduling**—Maintaining a constant output rate, production rate, or workforce level over the planning horizon. Level scheduling works well when demand is reasonably stable. ■ **Mixed strategy**—A planning strategy that uses two or more controllable variables to set a feasible production plan.	Concept Questions: 4.1–4.4
METHODS FOR AGGREGATE PLANNING (pp. 538–545)	■ **Graphical techniques**—Aggregate planning techniques that work with a few variables at a time to allow planners to compare projected demand with existing capacity. Graphical techniques are trial-and-error approaches that do not guarantee an optimal production plan, but they require only limited computations. A *cumulative* graph displays visually how the forecast deviates from the average requirements. ■ **Transportation method of linear programming**—A way of solving for the optimal solution to an aggregate planning problem. The transportation method of linear programming is flexible in that it can specify regular and overtime production in each time period, the number of units to be subcontracted, extra shifts, and the inventory carryover from period to period. Transportation problems require that supply equals demand, so when it does not, a dummy column called "unused capacity" may be added. Costs of not using capacity are zero.	Concept Questions: 5.1–5.4 Problems: 13.2–13.23 Virtual Office Hours for Solved Problems: 13.1, 13.2 **ACTIVE MODEL 13.1**

Main Heading	Review Material	MyOMLab
	Demand requirements are shown in the bottom row of a transportation table. Total capacity available (supply) is shown in the far right column. In general, to complete a transportation table, allocate as much production as you can to a cell with the smallest cost, without exceeding the unused capacity in that row or demand in that column. If there is still some demand left in that row, allocate as much as you can to the next-lowest-cost cell. You then repeat this process for periods 2 and 3 (and beyond, if necessary). When you are finished, the sum of all your entries in a row must equal total row capacity, and the sum of all entries in a column must equal the demand for that period. The transportation method does not work when nonlinear or negative factors are introduced.	
AGGREGATE PLANNING IN SERVICES (pp. 545–547)	Successful techniques for controlling the cost of labor in service firms include: 1. Accurate scheduling of labor-hours to ensure quick response to customer demand. 2. An on-call labor resource that can be added or deleted to meet unexpected demand. 3. Flexibility of individual worker skills that permits reallocation of available labor. 4. Flexibility in rate of output or hours of work to meet changing demand.	Concept Questions: 6.1–6.4 Problems: 13.24–13.25
REVENUE MANAGEMENT (pp. 547–550)	■ **Revenue** (or **yield**) **management**—Capacity decisions that determine the allocation of resources to maximize revenue. Organizations that have *perishable inventory*, such as airlines, hotels, car rental agencies, and cruise lines, have the following shared characteristics that make revenue management of interest: 1. Service or product can be sold in advance of consumption 2. Fluctuating demand 3. Relatively fixed resource (capacity) 4. Segmentable demand 5. Low variable costs and high fixed costs To make revenue management work, the company needs to manage three issues: 1. *Multiple pricing structures.* 2. *Forecasts of the use and duration of the use.* 3. *Changes in demand.*	Concept Questions: 7.1–7.4 Problem: 13.26 **VIDEO 13.1** Using Revenue Management to Set Orlando Magic Ticket Prices

Self Test

■ **Before taking the self-test,** refer to the learning objectives listed at the beginning of the chapter and the key terms listed at the end of the chapter.

LO 13.1 The outputs from an S&OP process are:
 a) long-run plans.
 b) detail schedules.
 c) aggregate plans.
 d) revenue management plans.
 e) short-run plans.

LO 13.2 Aggregate planning is concerned with determining the quantity and timing of production in the:
 a) short term.
 b) intermediate term.
 c) long term.
 d) all of the above.

LO 13.3 Aggregate planning deals with a number of constraints. These typically are:
 a) job assignments, job ordering, dispatching, and overtime help.
 b) part-time help, weekly scheduling, and SKU production scheduling.
 c) subcontracting, employment levels, inventory levels, and capacity.
 d) capital investment, expansion or contracting capacity, and R&D.
 e) facility location, production budgeting, overtime, and R&D.

LO 13.4 Which of the following is not one of the graphical method steps?
 a) Determine the demand in each period.
 b) Determine capacity for regular time, overtime, and subcontracting each period.
 c) Find labor costs, hiring and layoff costs, and inventory holding costs.
 d) Construct the transportation table.
 e) Consider company policy that may apply to the workers or stock levels.
 f) Develop alternative plans and examine their total costs.

LO 13.5 When might a dummy column be added to a transportation table?
 a) When supply does not equal demand
 b) When overtime is greater than regular time
 c) When subcontracting is greater than regular time
 d) When subcontracting is greater than regular time plus overtime
 e) When production needs to spill over into a new period

LO 13.6 Revenue management requires management to deal with:
 a) multiple pricing structures.
 b) changes in demand.
 c) forecasts of use.
 d) forecasts of duration of use.
 e) all of the above.

Answers: LO 13.1. c; LO 13.2. b; LO 13.3. c; LO 13.4. d; LO 13.5. a; LO 13.6. e.

Material Requirements Planning (MRP) and ERP

CHAPTER OUTLINE

GLOBAL COMPANY PROFILE: *Wheeled Coach*

- Dependent Demand **566**
- Dependent Inventory Model Requirements **566**
- MRP Structure **571**
- MRP Management **575**

- Lot-Sizing Techniques **576**
- Extensions of MRP **580**
- MRP in Services **583**
- Enterprise Resource Planning (ERP) **584**

Alaska Airlines

10 OM STRATEGY DECISIONS

- Design of Goods and Services
- Managing Quality
- Process Strategy
- Location Strategies
- Layout Strategies
- Human Resources
- Supply-Chain Management

- *Inventory Management*
  - Independent Demand (Ch. 12)
  - ***Dependent Demand (Ch. 14)***
  - Lean Operations (Ch. 16)
- Scheduling
- Maintenance

CHAPTER 14

MRP Provides a Competitive Advantage for Wheeled Coach

Wheeled Coach, headquartered in Winter Park, Florida, is the largest manufacturer of ambulances in the world. The $200 million firm is an international competitor that sells more than 25% of its vehicles to markets outside the U.S. Twelve major ambulance designs are produced on assembly lines (i.e., a repetitive process) at the Florida plant, using 18,000 different

This cutaway of one ambulance interior indicates the complexity of the product, which for some rural locations may be the equivalent of a hospital emergency room in miniature. To complicate production, virtually every ambulance is custom ordered. This customization necessitates precise orders, excellent bills of materials, exceptional inventory control from supplier to assembly, and an MRP system that works.

Wheeled Coach Industries Incorporated

Wheeled Coach uses work cells to feed the assembly line. It maintains a complete carpentry shop (to provide interior cabinetry), a paint shop (to prepare, paint, and detail each vehicle), an electrical shop (to provide for the complex electronics in a modern ambulance), an upholstery shop (to make interior seats and benches), and as shown here, a metal fabrication shop (to construct the shell of the ambulance).

Wheeled Coach Industries Incorporated

inventory items, of which 6,000 are manufactured and 12,000 purchased. Most of the product line is custom designed and assembled to meet the specific and often unique requirements demanded by the ambulance's application and customer preferences.

This variety of products and the nature of the process demand good material requirements planning (MRP). Effective use of an MRP system requires accurate bills of material and inventory records. The Wheeled Coach system provides daily updates and has reduced inventory by more than 30% in just two years.

Wheeled Coach insists that four key tasks be performed properly. First, the material plan must meet both the requirements of the master schedule and the capabilities of the production facility. Second, the plan must be executed as designed. Third, inventory investment must be minimized through effective "time-phased" material deliveries, consignment inventories, and a constant review of purchase methods. Finally, excellent record integrity must be maintained. Record accuracy is recognized as a fundamental ingredient of Wheeled Coach's successful MRP program. Its cycle counters are charged with material audits that not only correct errors but also investigate and correct problems.

Wheeled Coach Industries uses MRP as the catalyst for low inventory, high quality, tight schedules, and accurate records. Wheeled Coach has found competitive advantage via MRP. ◀

On five parallel lines, ambulances move forward each day to the next workstation. The MRP system makes certain that just the materials needed at each station arrive overnight for assembly the next day.

Here an employee is installing the wiring for an ambulance. There are an average of 15 miles of wire in a Wheeled Coach vehicle. This compares to 17 miles of wire in a sophisticated F-16 fighter jet.

Wheeled Coach Industries Incorporated

Wheeled Coach Industries Incorporated

LEARNING OBJECTIVES

LO 14.1 *Develop* a product structure 569

LO 14.2 *Build* a gross requirements plan 572

LO 14.3 *Build* a net requirements plan 573

LO 14.4 *Determine* lot sizes for lot-for-lot, EOQ, and POQ 577

LO 14.5 *Describe* MRP II 580

LO 14.6 *Describe* closed-loop MRP 582

LO 14.7 *Describe* ERP 584

Dependent Demand

STUDENT TIP ◆

"Dependent demand" means the demand for one item is related to the demand for another item.

Wheeled Coach, the subject of the *Global Company Profile*, and many other firms have found important benefits in material requirements planning (MRP). These benefits include (1) better response to customer orders as the result of improved adherence to schedules, (2) faster response to market changes, (3) improved utilization of facilities and labor, and (4) reduced inventory levels. Better response to customer orders and to the market wins orders and market share. Better utilization of facilities and labor yields higher productivity and return on investment. Less inventory frees up capital and floor space for other uses. These benefits are the result of a strategic decision to use a *dependent* inventory scheduling system. Demand for every component of an ambulance is dependent.

Demand for items is dependent when the relationship between the items can be determined. Therefore, once management receives an order or makes a forecast for the final product, quantities for all components can be computed. All components are dependent items. The Boeing Aircraft operations manager who schedules production of one plane per week, for example, knows the requirements down to the last rivet. For any product, all components of that product are dependent demand items. *More generally, for any product for which a schedule can be established, dependent techniques should be used.*

When the requirements of MRP are met, dependent models are preferable to the models for independent demand (EOQ) described in Chapter 12.[1] Dependent models are better not only for manufacturers and distributors but also for a wide variety of firms from restaurants to hospitals. The dependent technique used in a production environment is called material requirements planning (MRP).

Material requirements planning (MRP)

A dependent demand technique that uses a bill-of-material, inventory, expected receipts, and a master production schedule to determine material requirements.

Because MRP provides such a clean structure for dependent demand, it has evolved as the basis for Enterprise Resource Planning (ERP). ERP is an information system for identifying and planning the enterprise-wide resources needed to take, make, ship, and account for customer orders. We will discuss ERP in the latter part of this chapter.

Dependent Inventory Model Requirements

Effective use of dependent inventory models requires that the operations manager know the following:

1. Master production schedule (what is to be made and when)
2. Specifications or bill of material (materials and parts required to make the product)
3. Inventory availability (what is in stock)
4. Purchase orders outstanding (what is on order, also called expected receipts)
5. Lead times (how long it takes to get various components)

We now discuss each of these requirements in the context of material requirements planning.

Figure **14.1**

The Planning Process

Master Production Schedule

A master production schedule (MPS) specifies what is to be made (e.g., the number of finished products or items) and when. The schedule must be in accordance with an aggregate plan. The aggregate plan sets the overall level of output in broad terms (e.g., product families, standard hours, or dollar volume). The plan, usually developed by the sales and operations planning team, includes a variety of inputs, including financial data, customer demand, engineering capabilities, labor availability, inventory fluctuations, supplier performance, and other considerations. Each of these inputs contributes in its own way to the aggregate plan, as shown in Figure 14.1.

As the planning process moves from the aggregate plan to execution, each of the lower-level plans must be feasible. When one is not, feedback to the next higher level is required to make the necessary adjustment. One of the major strengths of MRP is its ability to determine precisely the feasibility of a schedule within aggregate capacity constraints. This planning process can yield excellent results. The aggregate plan sets the upper and lower bounds on the master production schedule.

The master production schedule tells us how to satisfy demand by specifying what items to make and when. It *disaggregates* the aggregate plan. While the *aggregate plan* (as discussed in Chapter 13) is established in gross terms such as families of products or tons of steel, the *master production schedule* is established in terms of specific products. Figure 14.2 shows the master production schedules for three stereo models that flow from the aggregate plan for a family of stereo amplifiers.

Master production schedule (MPS)

A timetable that specifies what is to be made (usually finished goods) and when.

Aggregate Plan (Shows the total quantity of amplifiers)	Months				January				February			
						1,500				1,200		

Master Production **Schedule** (Shows the specific type and quantity of amplifier to be produced)	Weeks	1	2	3	4	5	6	7	8
	240-watt amplifier	100		100		100		100	
	150-watt amplifier		500		500		450		450
	75-watt amplifier			300				100	

Figure **14.2**

The Aggregate Plan Is the Basis for Development of the Master Production Schedule

TABLE 14.1	Master Production Schedule for Chef John's Buffalo Chicken Mac & Cheese								
GROSS REQUIREMENTS FOR CHEF JOHN'S BUFFALO CHICKEN MAC & CHEESE									
Day	6	7	8	9	10	11	12	13	14	and so on
Quantity	450		200	350	525		235	375		

Managers must adhere to the schedule for a reasonable length of time (usually a major portion of the production cycle—the time it takes to produce a product). Many organizations establish a master production schedule and establish a policy of not changing ("fixing") the near-term portion of the plan. This near-term portion of the plan is then referred to as the "fixed," "firm," or "frozen" schedule. Wheeled Coach, the subject of the *Global Company Profile* for this chapter, fixes the last 14 days of its schedule. Only changes farther out, beyond the fixed schedule, are permitted. The master production schedule is a "rolling" production schedule. For example, a fixed 7-week plan has an additional week added to it as each week is completed, so a 7-week fixed schedule is maintained. Note that the master production schedule is a statement of *what is to be produced;* it is *not* a forecast. The master schedule can be expressed in the following terms:

♦ A *customer order* in a job shop (make-to-order) company (examples: print shops, machine shops, fine-dining restaurants)
♦ *Modules* in a repetitive (assemble-to-order or forecast) company (examples: Harley-Davidson motorcycles, TVs, fast-food restaurant)
♦ An *end item* in a continuous (stock-to-forecast) company (examples: steel, beer, bread, light bulbs, paper)

A master production schedule for Chef John's "Buffalo Chicken Mac & Cheese" at the Orlando Magic's Amway Center is shown in Table 14.1.

Bills of Material

Defining what goes into a product may seem simple, but it can be difficult in practice. As we noted in Chapter 5, to aid this process, manufactured items are defined via a bill of material. A bill of material (BOM) is a list of quantities of components, ingredients, and materials required to make a product. Individual drawings describe not only physical dimensions but also any special processing as well as the raw material from which each part is made. Chef John's recipe for Buffalo Chicken Mac & Cheese specifies ingredients and quantities, just as Wheeled Coach has a full set of drawings for an ambulance. Both are bills of material (although we call one a recipe, and they do vary somewhat in scope).

One way a bill of material defines a product is by providing a product structure. Example 1 shows how to develop the product structure and "explode" it to reveal the requirements for each component. A bill of material for item A in Example 1 consists of items B and C. Items above any level are called *parents*; items below any level are called *components* or *children*. By convention, the top level in a BOM is the 0 level.

VIDEO 14.1
When 18,500 Orlando Magic Fans Come to Dinner

Bill of material (BOM)

A listing of the components, their description, and the quantity of each required to make one unit of a product.

VIDEO 14.2
MRP at Wheeled Coach Ambulances

Example 1

DEVELOPING A PRODUCT STRUCTURE AND GROSS REQUIREMENTS

Speaker Kits, Inc., packages high-fidelity components for mail order. Components for the top-of-the-line speaker kit, "Awesome" (A), include 2 Bs and 3 Cs.

Each B consists of 2 Ds and 2 Es. Each of the Cs has 2 Fs and 2 Es. Each F includes 2 Ds and 1 G. It is an *awesome* sound system. (Most purchasers require hearing aids within 3 years, and at least one court case is pending because of structural damage to a men's dormitory.) As we can see, the demand for B, C, D, E, F, and G is completely dependent on the master production schedule for A—the Awesome speaker kits.

LO 14.1 *Develop* a
product structure

APPROACH ▶ Given the preceding information, we construct a product structure and "explode" the requirements.

SOLUTION ▶ This structure has four levels: 0, 1, 2, and 3. There are four parents: A, B, C, and F. Each parent item has at least one level below it. Items B, C, D, E, F, and G are components because each item has at least one level above it. In this structure, B, C, and F are both parents and components. The number in parentheses indicates how many units of that particular item are needed to make the item immediately above it. Thus, $B_{(2)}$ means that it takes two units of B for every unit of A, and $F_{(2)}$ means that it takes two units of F for every unit of C.

Level   Product structure for "Awesome" (A)

Dragon_Fang/Shutterstock

Once we have developed the product structure, we can determine the number of units of each item required to satisfy demand for a new order of 50 Awesome speaker kits. We "explode" the requirements as shown:

Part B:	2 × number of As =	(2)(50) =	100
Part C:	3 × number of As =	(3)(50) =	150
Part D:	2 × number of Bs + 2 × number of Fs =	(2)(100) + (2)(300) =	800
Part E:	2 × number of Bs + 2 × number of Cs =	(2)(100) + (2)(150) =	500
Part F:	2 × number of Cs =	(2)(150) =	300
Part G:	1 × number of Fs =	(1)(300) =	300

INSIGHT ▶ We now have a visual picture of the Awesome speaker kit requirements and knowledge of the quantities required. Thus, for 50 units of A, we will need 100 units of B, 150 units of C, 800 units of D, 500 units of E, 300 units of F, and 300 units of G.

LEARNING EXERCISE ▶ If there are 100 Fs in stock, how many Ds do you need? [Answer: 600.]

RELATED PROBLEMS ▶ 14.1–14.4, 14.5a,b, 14.13a,b, 14.17a,b (14.20a,b are available in MyOMLab)

Bills of material not only specify requirements but also are useful for costing, and they can serve as a list of items to be issued to production or assembly personnel. When bills of material are used in this way, they are usually called *pick lists*.

Modular Bills   Bills of material may be organized around product modules (see Chapter 5). *Modules* are not final products to be sold, but are components that can be produced and assembled into units. They are often major components of the final product or product options. Bills of material for modules are called modular bills. Modular bills are convenient because production scheduling and production are often facilitated by organizing around relatively few modules rather than a multitude of final assemblies. For instance, a firm may make 138,000 different final products but may have only 40 modules that are mixed and matched to produce those 138,000 final products. The firm builds an aggregate production plan and prepares its master production schedule for the 40 modules, not the 138,000

Modular bills

Bills of material organized by major subassemblies or by product options.

configurations of the final product. This approach allows the MPS to be prepared for a reasonable number of items. The 40 modules can then be configured for specific orders at final assembly.

Planning Bills and Phantom Bills Two other special kinds of bills of material are planning bills and phantom bills. Planning bills (sometimes called "pseudo" bills, or super bills) are created in order to assign an artificial parent to the bill of material. Such bills are used (1) when we want to group subassemblies so the number of items to be scheduled is reduced and (2) when we want to issue "kits" to the production department. For instance, it may not be efficient to issue inexpensive items such as washers and cotter pins with each of numerous subassemblies, so we call this a *kit* and generate a planning bill. The planning bill specifies the *kit* to be issued. Consequently, a planning bill may also be known as kitted material, or kit. Phantom bills of material are bills of material for components, usually subassemblies, that exist only temporarily. These components go directly into another assembly and are never inventoried. Therefore, components of phantom bills of material are coded to receive special treatment; lead times are zero, and they are handled as an integral part of their parent item. An example is a transmission shaft with gears and bearings assembly that is placed directly into a transmission.

Low-Level Coding Low-level coding of an item in a BOM is necessary when identical items exist at various levels in the BOM. Low-level coding means that the item is coded at the lowest level at which it occurs. For example, item D in Example 1 is coded at the lowest level at which it is used. Item D could be coded as part of B and occur at level 2. However, because D is also part of F, and F is level 2, item D becomes a level-3 item. Low-level coding is a convention to allow easy computing of the requirements of an item.

Accurate Inventory Records

As we saw in Chapter 12, knowledge of what is in stock is the result of good inventory management. Good inventory management is an absolute necessity for an MRP system to work. If the firm does not exceed 99% record accuracy, then material requirements planning will not work.[2]

Purchase Orders Outstanding

Knowledge of outstanding orders exists as a by-product of well-managed purchasing and inventory-control departments. When purchase orders are executed, records of those orders and their scheduled delivery dates must be available to production personnel. Only with good purchasing data can managers prepare meaningful production plans and effectively execute an MRP system.

Lead Times for Components

Once managers determine when products are needed, they determine when to acquire them. The time required to acquire (that is, purchase, produce, or assemble) an item is known as lead time. Lead time for a manufactured item consists of *move*, *setup*, and *assembly* or *run times* for each component. For a purchased item, the lead time includes the time between recognition of need for an order and when it is available for production.

When the bill of material for Awesome speaker kits (As), in Example 1, is turned on its side and modified by adding lead times for each component (see Table 14.2), we then have a *time-phased product structure*. Time in this structure is shown on the horizontal axis of Figure 14.3 with item A due for completion in week 8. Each component is then offset to accommodate lead times.

Planning bills (or kits)

Material groupings created in order to assign an artificial parent to a bill of material; also called "pseudo" bills.

Phantom bills of material

Bills of material for components, usually assemblies, that exist only temporarily; they are never inventoried.

Low-level coding

A number that identifies items at the lowest level at which they occur.

Lead time

In purchasing systems, the time between recognition of the need for an order and receiving it; in production systems, it is the order, wait, move, queue, setup, and run times for each component.

TABLE 14.2

Lead Times for Awesome Speaker Kits (As)

COMPONENT	LEAD TIME
A	1 week
B	2 weeks
C	1 week
D	1 week
E	2 weeks
F	3 weeks
G	2 weeks

Figure **14.3**

Time-Phased Product Structure

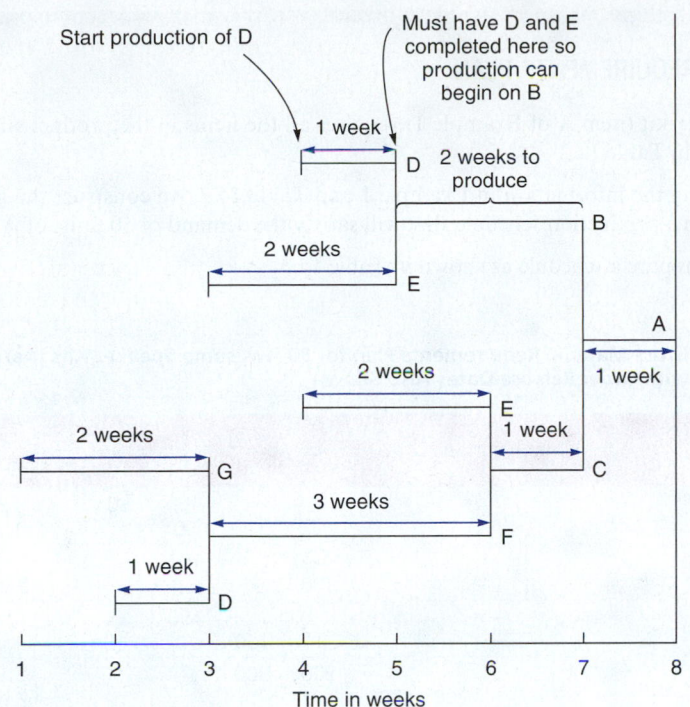

STUDENT TIP

This is a product structure on its side, with lead times.

MRP Structure

Although most MRP systems are computerized, the MRP procedure is straightforward, and we can illustrate a small one by hand. A master production schedule, a bill of material, inventory and purchase records, and lead times for each item are the ingredients of a material requirements planning system (see Figure 14.4).

Once these ingredients are available and accurate, the next step is to construct a gross material requirements plan. The gross material requirements plan is a schedule, as shown in Example 2. It combines a master production schedule (that requires one unit of A in week 8) and the time-phased schedule (Figure 14.3). It shows when an item must be ordered from suppliers if there is no inventory on hand or when the production of an item must be started to satisfy demand for the finished product by a particular date.

Gross material requirements plan

A schedule that shows the total demand for an item (prior to subtraction of on-hand inventory and scheduled receipts) and (1) when it must be ordered from suppliers, or (2) when production must be started to meet its demand by a particular date.

Figure **14.4**

Structure of the MRP System

Data Files   **Output Reports**

STUDENT TIP

MRP software programs are popular because manual approaches are slow and error prone.

Example 2

BUILDING A GROSS REQUIREMENTS PLAN

Each Awesome speaker kit (item A of Example 1) requires all the items in the product structure for A. Lead times are shown in Table 14.2.

APPROACH ▶ Using the information in Example 1 and Table 14.2, we construct the gross material requirements plan with a production schedule that will satisfy the demand of 50 units of A by week 8.

SOLUTION ▶ We prepare a schedule as shown in Table 14.3.

TABLE 14.3 Gross Material Requirements Plan for 50 Awesome Speaker Kits (As) with Order Release Dates Also Shown

	WEEK								LEAD TIME
	1	2	3	4	5	6	7	8	
A. Required date								50	
Order release date							50		1 week
B. Required date							100		
Order release date					100				2 weeks
C. Required date							150		
Order release date						150			1 week
E. Required date					200	300			
Order release date			200	300					2 weeks
F. Required date						300			
Order release date			300						3 weeks
D. Required date			600		200				
Order release date		600		200					1 week
G. Required date			300						
Order release date	300								2 weeks

You can interpret the gross material requirements shown in Table 14.3 as follows: If you want 50 units of A at week 8, you must start assembling A in week 7. Thus, in week 7, you will need 100 units of B and 150 units of C. These two items take 2 weeks and 1 week, respectively, to produce. Production of B, therefore, should start in week 5, and production of C should start in week 6 (lead time subtracted from the required date for these items). Working backward, we can perform the same computations for all of the other items. Because D and E are used in two different places in Awesome speaker kits, there are two entries in each data record.

INSIGHT ▶ The gross material requirements plan shows when production of each item should begin and end in order to have 50 units of A at week 8. Management now has an initial plan.

LEARNING EXERCISE ▶ If the lead time for G decreases from 2 weeks to 1 week, what is the new order release date for G? [Answer: 300 in week 2.]

RELATED PROBLEMS ▶ 14.6, 14.8, 14.10a, 14.11a

EXCEL OM Data File **Ch14Ex2.xls** can be found in **MyOMLab**.

LO 14.2 *Build* a gross requirements plan

Net requirements plan

The result of adjusting gross requirements for inventory on hand and scheduled receipts.

So far, we have considered *gross material requirements*, which assumes that there is no inventory on hand. A net requirements plan adjusts for on-hand inventory. When considering on-hand inventory, we must realize that many items in inventory contain subassemblies or parts. If the gross requirement for Awesome speaker kits (As) is 100 and there are 20 of those speakers on hand, the net requirement for As is 80 (that is, 100 − 20). However, each Awesome speaker kit on hand contains 2 Bs. As a result, the requirement for Bs drops by 40 Bs (20 A kits on hand × 2 Bs per A). Therefore, if inventory is on hand for a parent item, the requirements for the parent item and all its components decrease because each Awesome kit contains the components for lower-level items. Example 3 shows how to create a net requirements plan.

Example 3 — DETERMINING NET REQUIREMENTS

Speaker Kits, Inc., developed a product structure from a bill of material in Example 1. Example 2 developed a gross requirements plan. Given the following on-hand inventory, Speaker Kits, Inc., now wants to construct a net requirements plan. The gross requirement remains 50 units in week 8, and component requirements are as shown in the product structure in Example 1.

LO 14.3 *Build* a net requirements plan

ITEM	ON HAND	ITEM	ON HAND
A	10	E	10
B	15	F	5
C	20	G	0
D	10		

Net Material Requirements Plan for 50 Units of Product A in Week 8. *(The superscript is the source of the demand)*

Lot Size	Lead Time (weeks)	On Hand	Safety Stock	Allocated	Low-Level Code	Item Identification		Week 1	2	3	4	5	6	7	8
Lot-for-Lot	1	10	—	—	0	A	Gross Requirements								50
							Scheduled Receipts								
							Projected On Hand 10	10	10	10	10	10	10	10	10
							Net Requirements								40
							Planned Order Receipts								40
							Planned Order Releases							40	
Lot-for-Lot	2	15	—	—	1	B	Gross Requirements								80^A
							Scheduled Receipts								
			2 × number of As = 80				Projected On Hand 15	15	15	15	15	15	15	15	15
							Net Requirements								65
							Planned Order Receipts								65
							Planned Order Releases							65	
Lot-for-Lot	1	20	—	—	1	C	Gross Requirements								120^A
							Scheduled Receipts								
			3 × number of As = 120				Projected On Hand 20	20	20	20	20	20	20	20	20
							Net Requirements								100
							Planned Order Receipts								100
							Planned Order Releases							100	
Lot-for-Lot	2	10	—	—	2	E	Gross Requirements							130^B	200^C
							Scheduled Receipts								
			2 × number of Bs = 130				Projected On Hand 10	10	10	10	10	10			
			2 × number of Cs = 200				Net Requirements							120	200
							Planned Order Receipts							120	200
							Planned Order Releases					120	200		
Lot-for-Lot	3	5	—	—	2	F	Gross Requirements								200^C
							Scheduled Receipts								
			2 × number of Cs = 200				Projected On Hand 5	5	5	5	5	5	5		
							Net Requirements							195	
							Planned Order Receipts							195	
							Planned Order Releases					195			
Lot-for-Lot	1	10	—	—	3	D	Gross Requirements						390^F	130^B	
							Scheduled Receipts								
			2 × number of Bs = 130				Projected On Hand 10	10	10	10					
			2 × number of Fs = 390				Net Requirements						380	130	
							Planned Order Receipts						380	130	
							Planned Order Releases				380		130		
Lot-for-Lot	2	0	—	—	3	G	Gross Requirements						195^F		
							Scheduled Receipts								
			1 × number of Fs = 195				Projected On Hand 0						0		
							Net Requirements						195		
							Planned Order Receipts						195		
							Planned Order Releases				195				

APPROACH ▶ A net material requirements plan includes gross requirements, on-hand inventory, net requirements, planned order receipt, and planned order release for each item. We begin with A and work backward through the components.

SOLUTION ▶ Shown in the MRP format on the previous page is the net material requirements plan for product A.

Constructing a net requirements plan is similar to constructing a gross requirements plan. Starting with item A, we work backward to determine net requirements for all items. To do these computations, we refer to the product structure, on-hand inventory, and lead times. The gross requirement for A is 50 units in week 8. Ten items are on hand; therefore, the net requirements and the scheduled **planned order receipt** are both 40 items in week 8. Because of the one-week lead time, the **planned order release** is 40 items in week 7 (see the arrow connecting the order receipt and order release). Referring to week 7 and the product structure in Example 1, we can see that 80 (2 × 40) items of B and 120 (3 × 40) items of C are required in week 7 to have a total for 50 items of A in week 8. The letter superscripted A to the right of the gross figure for items B and C was generated as a result of the demand for the parent, A. Performing the same type of analysis for B and C yields the net requirements for D, E, F, and G. Note the on-hand inventory in row E in week 6 is zero. It is zero because the on-hand inventory (10 units) was used to make B in week 5. By the same token, the inventory for D was used to make F in week 3.

INSIGHT ▶ Once a net requirement plan is completed, management knows the quantities needed, an ordering schedule, and a production schedule for each component.

LEARNING EXERCISE ▶ If the on-hand inventory quantity of component F is 95 rather than 5, how many units of G will need to be ordered in week 1? [Answer: 105 units.]

RELATED PROBLEMS ▶ 14.9, 14.10b, 14.11b, 14.12, 14.13c, 14.14b, 14.15a,b,c, 14.16a,b, 14.17c (14.18–14.21 are available in MyOMLab)

ACTIVE MODEL 14.1 This example is further illustrated in Active Model 14.1 in MyOMLab.

EXCEL OM Data File **Ch14Ex3.xls** can be found in MyOMLab.

Planned order receipt
The quantity planned to be received at a future date.

Planned order release
The scheduled date for an order to be released.

STUDENT TIP ❗
MRP gross requirements can combine multiple products, spare parts, and items sold directly.

Examples 2 and 3 considered only product A, the Awesome speaker kit, and its completion only in week 8. Fifty units of A were required in week 8. Normally, however, there is a demand for many products over time. For each product, management must prepare a master production schedule (as we saw earlier, in Table 14.1). Scheduled production of each product is added to the master schedule and ultimately to the net material requirements plan. Figure 14.5 shows how several product schedules, including requirements for components sold directly, can contribute to one gross material requirements plan.

Most inventory systems also note the number of units in inventory that have been assigned to specific future production but not yet used or issued from the stockroom. Such items are often

Figure **14.5**

Several Schedules Contributing to a Gross Requirements Schedule for B

One B is in each A, and one B is in each S; in addition, 10 Bs sold directly are scheduled in week 1, and 10 more that are sold directly are scheduled in week 2.

Lot Size	Lead Time	On Hand	Safety Stock	Allocated	Low-Level Code	Item ID		Period							
								1	2	3	4	5	6	7	8
Lot For Lot	1	0	0	10	0	Z	Gross Requirements								80 90
							Scheduled Receipts								0
							Projected On Hand 0	0	0	0	0	0	0	0	0
							Net Requirements								90
							Planned Order Receipts								90
							Planned Order Releases							90	

Figure **14.6**

Sample MRP Planning Sheet for Item Z

referred to as *allocated* items. Allocated items increase requirements as shown in Figure 14.6, where gross requirements have been increased from 80 to 90 to reflect the 10 allocated items.

Safety Stock   The continuing task of operations managers is to remove variability. This is the case in MRP systems as in other operations systems. Realistically, however, managers need to realize that bills of material and inventory records, like purchase and production quantities, as well as lead times, may not be perfect. This means that some consideration of safety stock may be prudent. Because of the significant domino effect of any change in requirements, safety stock should be minimized, with a goal of ultimate elimination. When safety stock is deemed absolutely necessary, the usual policy is to build it into (increase) the inventory requirement of the MRP logic. Distortion can be minimized when safety stock is held at the finished goods or module level and at the purchased component or raw material level.

MRP Management

Now let's look at the dynamics and limitations of MRP.

MRP Dynamics

The inputs to MRP (the master schedule, BOM, lead times, purchasing, and inventory) frequently change. Conveniently, a central strength of MRP systems is timely and accurate replanning. However, many firms find they do not want to respond to minor scheduling or quantity changes even if they are aware of them. These frequent changes generate what is called system nervousness and can create havoc in purchasing and production departments if implemented. Consequently, OM personnel reduce such nervousness by evaluating the need and impact of changes prior to disseminating requests to other departments. Two tools are particularly helpful when trying to reduce MRP system nervousness.

The first is time fences. Time fences allow a segment of the master schedule to be designated as "not to be rescheduled." This segment of the master schedule is therefore not changed during the periodic regeneration of schedules. The second tool is pegging. Pegging means tracing upward in the BOM from the component to the parent item. By pegging upward, the production planner can determine the cause for the requirement and make a judgment about the necessity for a change in the schedule.

With MRP, the operations manager *can* react to the dynamics of the real world. If the nervousness is caused by legitimate changes, then the proper response may be to investigate the production environment—not adjust via MRP.

MRP Limitations

MRP does not do detailed scheduling—it plans. MRP is an excellent tool for product-focused and repetitive facilities, but it has limitations in process (make-to-order) environments. MRP will tell you that a job needs to be completed on a certain week or day but does not tell you

System nervousness

Frequent changes in an MRP system.

Time fences

A means for allowing a segment of the master schedule to be designated as "not to be rescheduled."

Pegging

In material requirements planning systems, tracing upward the bill of material from the component to the parent item.

that Job X needs to run on Machine A at 10:30 A.M. and be completed by 11:30 A.M. so that Job X can then run on Machine B. MRP is also a planning technique with *fixed* lead times that loads work into *infinite* size "buckets." The buckets are time units, usually one week. MRP puts work into these buckets without regard to capacity. Consequently, MRP is considered an *infinite* scheduling technique. Techniques for the alternative, *finite* scheduling, are discussed in Chapter 15.

Buckets

Time units in a material requirements planning system.

Lot-Sizing Techniques

An MRP system is an excellent way to do production planning and determine net requirements. But net requirements still demand a decision about *how much and when* to order. This decision is called a lot-sizing decision. There are a variety of ways to determine lot sizes in an MRP system; commercial MRP software usually includes the choice of several lot-sizing techniques. We now review a few of them.

Lot-sizing decision

The process of, or techniques used in, determining lot size.

Lot-for-Lot   In Example 3, we used a lot-sizing technique known as lot-for-lot, which produced exactly what was required. This decision is consistent with the objective of an MRP system, which is to meet the requirements of *dependent* demand. Thus, an MRP system should produce units only as needed, with no safety stock and no anticipation of further orders. When frequent orders are economical (i.e., when setup costs are low) and just-in-time inventory techniques implemented, lot-for-lot can be very efficient. However, when setup costs are significant, lot-for-lot can be expensive. Example 4 uses the lot-for-lot criteria and determines cost for 10 weeks of demand.

Lot-for-lot

A lot-sizing technique that generates exactly what is required to meet the plan.

Example 4

LOT SIZING WITH LOT-FOR-LOT

Speaker Kits, Inc., wants to compute its ordering and carrying cost of inventory on lot-for-lot criteria.

APPROACH ▶   With lot-for-lot, we order material only as it is needed. Once we have the cost of ordering (setting up), the cost of holding each unit for a given time period, and the production schedule, we can assign orders to our net requirements plan.

SOLUTION ▶   Speaker Kits has determined that, for **component B,** setup cost is $100 and holding cost is $1 per period. The production schedule, as reflected in net requirements for assemblies, is as follows:

MRP Lot Sizing: Lot-for-Lot Technique*

WEEK		1	2	3	4	5	6	7	8	9	10
Gross requirements		35	30	40	0	10	40	30	0	30	55
Scheduled receipts											
Projected on hand	35	35	0	0	0	0	0	0	0	0	0
Net requirements		0	30	40	0	10	40	30	0	30	55
Planned order receipts			30	40		10	40	30		30	55
Planned order releases		30	40		10	40	30		30	55	

*Holding costs = $1/unit/week; setup cost = $100; gross requirements average per week = 27; lead time = 1 week.

The lot-sizing solution using the lot-for-lot technique is shown in the table. The holding cost is zero as there is never any end-of-period inventory. (Inventory in the first period is used immediately and therefore has no holding cost.) But seven separate setups (one associated with each order) yield a total cost of $700. (Holding cost = 0 × 1 = 0; ordering cost = 7 × 100 = 700.)

INSIGHT ▶   When supply is reliable and frequent orders are inexpensive, but holding cost or obsolescence is high, lot-for-lot ordering can be very efficient.

LEARNING EXERCISE ▶   What is the impact on total cost if holding cost is $2 per period rather than $1? [Answer: Total holding cost remains zero, as no units are held from one period to the next with lot-for-lot.]

RELATED PROBLEMS ▶   14.22, 14.25, 14.26a, 14.27a (14.28b is available in MyOMLab)

This Nissan line in Smyrna, Tennessee, has little inventory because Nissan schedules to a razor's edge. At Nissan, MRP helps reduce inventory to world-class standards. World-class automobile assembly requires that purchased parts have a turnover of slightly more than once a day and that overall turnover approaches 150 times per year.

John Russell/AP Images

Economic Order Quantity (EOQ) We now extend our discussion of EOQ in Chapter 12 to use it as a lot-sizing technique for MRP systems. As we indicated there, EOQ is useful when we have relatively constant demand. However, demand may change every period in MRP systems. Therefore, EOQ lot sizing often does not perform well in MRP. Operations managers should take advantage of demand information when it is known, rather than assuming a constant demand. EOQ is used to do lot sizing in Example 5 for comparison purposes.

LO 14.4 *Determine* lot sizes for lot-for-lot, EOQ, and POQ

Example 5

LOT SIZING WITH EOQ

With a setup cost of $100 and a holding cost per week of $1, Speaker Kits, Inc., wants to examine its cost for **component B,** with lot sizes based on an EOQ criteria.

APPROACH ▶ Using the same cost and production schedule as in Example 4, we determine net requirements and EOQ lot sizes.

SOLUTION ▶ Ten-week usage equals a gross requirement of 270 units; therefore, weekly usage equals 27, and 52 weeks (annual usage) equals 1,404 units. From Chapter 12, the EOQ model is:

$$Q^* = \sqrt{\frac{2DS}{H}}$$

where D = annual usage = 1,404

   S = setup cost = $100

   H = holding (carrying) cost, on an annual basis per unit

   = 1×52 weeks = $52

   $Q^* = 73$ units

Therefore, place an order of 73 units, as necessary, to avoid a stockout.

MRP Lot Sizing: EOQ Technique*

WEEK		1	2	3	4	5	6	7	8	9	10
Gross requirements		35	30	40	0	10	40	30	0	30	55
Scheduled receipts											
Projected on hand	35	35	0	43	3	3	66	26	69	69	39
Net requirements		0	30	0	0	7	0	4	0	0	16
Planned order receipts			73			73		73			73
Planned order releases		73			73		73		73		

*Holding costs = $1/unit/week; setup cost = $100; gross requirements average per week = 27; lead time = 1 week.

For the 10-week planning period:

Holding cost = 375 units × $1 = $375 (includes 57 remaining at the end of week 10)

Ordering cost = 4 × $100 = $400

Total = $375 + $400 = $775

INSIGHT ▶   EOQ can be a reasonable lot-sizing technique when demand is relatively constant. However, notice that actual holding cost will vary substantially depending on the rate of actual usage. If any stockouts had occurred, these costs too would need to be added to our actual EOQ cost of $775.

LEARNING EXERCISE ▶   What is the impact on total cost if holding cost is $2 per period rather than $1? [Answer: The EOQ quantity becomes 52, the theoretical annual total cost becomes $5,404, and the 10-week cost is $1,039 ($5,404 × (10/52).]

RELATED PROBLEMS ▶   14.23, 14.25, 14.26b, 14.27c (14.28a is available in MyOMLab)

Periodic order quantity (POQ)

An inventory ordering technique that issues orders on a predetermined time interval, with the order quantity covering the total of the interval's requirements.

Periodic Order Quantity   Periodic order quantity (POQ) is a lot-sizing technique that orders the quantity needed during a predetermined time between orders, such as every 3 weeks. We define the *POQ interval* as the EOQ divided by the average demand per period (e.g., one week).[3] The POQ is the order quantity that covers the specific demand for that interval. *Each order quantity is recalculated at the time of the order release*, never leaving extra inventory. An application of POQ is shown in Example 6.

Example 6

LOT SIZING WITH POQ

With a setup cost of $100 and a holding cost per week of $1, Speaker Kits, Inc., wants to examine its cost for **component B,** with lot sizes based on POQ.

APPROACH ▶   Using the same cost and production schedule as in Example 5, we determine net requirements and POQ lot sizes.

SOLUTION ▶   Ten-week usage equals a gross requirement of 270 units; therefore, average weekly usage equals 27, and from Example 5, we know the EOQ is 73 units.

We set the *POQ interval* equal to the EOQ divided by the average weekly usage.

Therefore:

POQ interval = EOQ/Average weekly usage = 73/27 = 2.7, or 3 weeks.

The *POQ order size* will vary by the quantities required in the respective weeks, as shown in the following table, with first planned order release in week 1.

Note: Orders are postponed if no demand exists, which is why week 7's order is postponed until week 8.

MRP Lot Sizing: POQ Technique*

WEEK		1	2	3	4	5	6	7	8	9	10
Gross requirements		35	30	40	0	10	40	30	0	30	55
Scheduled receipts											
Projected on hand	35	35	0	40	0	0	70	30	0	0	55
Net requirements		0	30	0	0	10	0	0	0	55	0
Planned order receipts			70				80		0		85	0
Planned order releases		70				80			85		

*Holding costs = $1/unit/week; setup cost = $100; gross requirements average per week = 27; lead time = 1 week.

$$\text{Setups} = 3 \times \$100 = \$300$$

$$\text{Holding cost} = (40 + 70 + 30 + 55) \text{ units} \times \$1 \text{ each} = \$195$$

$$\text{The POQ solution yields a computed 10-week cost of } \$300 + \$195 = \$495$$

INSIGHT ▶ Because POQ tends to produce a balance between holding and ordering costs with no excess inventory, POQ typically performs much better than EOQ. Notice that even with frequent recalculations, actual holding cost can vary substantially, depending on the demand fluctuations. We are assuming no stockouts. In this and similar examples, we are also assuming no safety stock; such costs would need to be added to our actual cost.

LEARNING EXERCISE ▶ What is the impact on total cost if holding cost is $2 per period rather than $1? [Answer: EOQ = 52; POQ interval = 52/27 = 1.93 ≈ 2 weeks; holding cost = $270; setups = $400. The POQ total cost becomes $670.]

RELATED PROBLEMS ▶ 14.24, 14.25, 14.26c, 14.27b (14.28c is available in MyOMLab)

Other lot-sizing techniques, known as *dynamic lot-sizing*, are similar to periodic order quantity as they attempt to balance the lot size against the setup cost. These are *part period balancing* (also called *least total cost*), *least unit cost,* and *least period cost* (also called *Silver-Meal*). Another technique, *Wagner-Whitin*, takes a different approach by using dynamic programming to optimize ordering over a finite time horizon.[4]

Lot-Sizing Summary In the three speaker kits lot-sizing examples, we found the following costs:

	COSTS		
	SETUP	**HOLDING**	**TOTAL**
Lot-for-lot	$700	$0	$700
Economic order quantity (EOQ)	$400	$375	$775
Periodic order quantity (POQ)	$300	$195	$495

These examples should not, however, lead operations personnel to hasty conclusions about the preferred lot-sizing technique. In theory, new lot sizes should be computed whenever there is a schedule or lot-size change anywhere in the MRP hierarchy. In practice, such changes cause the instability and system nervousness referred to earlier in this chapter. Consequently, such frequent changes are not made. This means that all lot sizes are wrong because the production system cannot and should not respond to frequent changes. Note that there are no "shortage" (out of stock) charges in any of these lot-sizing techniques. This limitation places added demands on accurate forecasts and "time fences."

In general, the lot-for-lot approach should be used whenever low-cost setup can be achieved. Lot-for-lot is the goal. Lots can be modified as necessary for scrap allowances, process constraints (for example, a heat-treating process may require a lot of a given size), or raw material purchase lots (for example, a truckload of chemicals may be available in only one lot size). However, caution should be exercised prior to any modification of lot size because the modification can cause substantial distortion of actual requirements at lower levels in the MRP hierarchy. When setup costs are significant and demand is reasonably smooth, POQ or even EOQ should provide satisfactory results. Too much concern with lot sizing yields false accuracy because of MRP dynamics. A correct lot size can be determined only after the fact, based on what actually happened in terms of requirements.

Extensions of MRP

In this section, we review three extensions of MRP.

Material Requirements Planning II (MRP II)

Material requirements planning II is an extremely powerful technique. Once a firm has MRP in place, requirements data can be enriched by resources other than just components. When MRP is used this way, *resource* is usually substituted for *requirements*, and MRP becomes **MRP II**. It then stands for material resource planning.

So far in our discussion of MRP, we have scheduled products and their components. However, products require many resources, such as energy and money, beyond the product's tangible components. In addition to these resource inputs, *outputs* can be generated as well. Outputs can include such things as scrap, packaging waste, effluent, and carbon emissions. As OM becomes increasingly sensitive to environmental and sustainability issues, identifying and managing by-products takes on more significance. MRP II provides a vehicle for doing so. Table 14.4 provides an example of labor-hours, machine-hours, grams of greenhouse gas emissions, pounds of scrap, and cash, in the format of a gross requirements plan. With MRP II, management can identify both the inputs and outputs as well as the relevant schedule. MRP II provides another tool in OM's battle for sustainable operations.

Material requirements planning II (MRP II)
A system that allows, with MRP in place, inventory data to be augmented by other resource variables; in this case, MRP becomes *material resource planning*.

LO 14.5 *Describe* MRP II

Many MRP programs, such as *Resource Manager for Excel*, are commercially available. *Resource Manager's* initial menu screen is shown here.

A demo program is available for student use at **www.usersolutions.com**.

Jim Convis, User Solutions, Inc.

TABLE 14.4	Material Resource Planning (MRP II)					
				Weeks		
	LEAD TIME	5	6	7	8	
Computer *Labor-hours:* .2 each *Machine-hours:* .2 each *GHG Emissions:* .25 each *Scrap:* 1 ounce fiberglass each *Payables:* $0	1				100 20 20 25 grams 6.25 lb $0	
PC board (1 each) *Labor-hours:* .15 each *Machine-hours:* .1 each *GHG Emissions:* 2.5 each *Scrap:* .5 ounces copper each *Payables:* raw material at $5 each	2			100 15 10 250 grams 3.125 lb $500		
Processors (5 each) *Labor-hours:* .2 each *Machine-hours:* .2 each *GHG Emissions:* .50 each *Scrap:* .01 ounces of acid waste each *Payables:* processor components at $10 each	4	500 100 100 25,000 grams 0.3125 lb $5,000				

By utilizing the logic of MRP, resources such as labor, machine-hours, greenhouse gas emissions, scrap, and cost can be accurately determined and scheduled. Weekly demand for labor, machine-hours, greenhouse gas emissions, scrap, and payables for 100 computers are shown.

MRP II systems are seldom stand-alone programs. Most are tied into other computer software. Purchasing, production scheduling, capacity planning, inventory, and warehouse management systems are a few examples of this data integration.

Closed-Loop MRP

Closed-loop material requirements planning implies an MRP system that provides feedback to scheduling from the inventory control system. Specifically, a closed-loop MRP system provides information to the capacity plan, master production schedule, and ultimately to the production plan (as shown in Figure 14.7). Virtually all commercial MRP systems are closed-loop.

Closed-loop MRP system

A system that provides feedback to the capacity plan, master production schedule, and production plan so planning can be kept valid at all times.

Capacity Planning

In keeping with the definition of closed-loop MRP, feedback about workload is obtained from each work center. Load reports show the resource requirements in a work center for all work currently assigned to the work center, all work planned, and expected orders.

Load report

A report showing the resource requirements in a work center for all work currently assigned there as well as all planned and expected orders.

Figure **14.7**

Closed-Loop Material Requirements Planning

Figure **14.8**

(a) Initial Resource
Requirements Profile for a
Work Center
(b) Smoothed Resource
Requirements Profile for
a Work Center

(a)   (b)

LO 14.6 *Describe
closed-loop MRP*

Figure 14.8(a) shows that the initial load in the milling center exceeds capacity on days 2, 3, and 5. Closed-loop MRP systems allow production planners to move the work between time periods to smooth the load or at least bring it within capacity. (This is the "capacity planning" part of Figure 14.7.) The closed-loop MRP system can then reschedule all items in the net requirements plan (see Figure 14.8[b]).

Tactics for smoothing the load and minimizing the impact of changed lead time include the following:

1. *Overlapping,* which reduces the lead time, sends pieces to the second operation before the entire lot is completed on the first operation.
2. *Operations splitting* sends the lot to two different machines for the same operation. This involves an additional setup, but results in shorter throughput times because only part of the lot is processed on each machine.
3. *Order splitting,* or *lot splitting,* involves breaking up the order and running part of it earlier (or later) in the schedule.

Example 7 shows a brief detailed capacity scheduling example using order splitting to improve utilization.

Example 7

ORDER SPLITTING

Kevin Watson, the production planner at Wiz Products, needs to develop a capacity plan for a work center. He has the production orders shown below for the next 5 days. There are 12 hours available in the work cell each day. The parts being produced require 1 hour each.

Day	1	2	3	4	5
Orders	10	14	13	10	14

APPROACH ▶ Compute the time available in the work center and the time necessary to complete the production requirements.

SOLUTION ▶

DAY	UNITS ORDERED	CAPACITY REQUIRED (HOURS)	CAPACITY AVAILABLE (HOURS)	UTILIZATION: OVER/ (UNDER) (HOURS)	PRODUCTION PLANNER'S ACTION	NEW PRODUCTION SCHEDULE
1	10	10	12	(2)		12
2	14	14	12	2	Split order: move 2 units to day 1	12
3	13	13	12	1	Split order: move 1 unit to day 6 or request overtime	13
4	10	10	12	(2)		12
5	14	14	12	2	Split order: move 2 units to day 4	12
	61					

INSIGHT ▶ By moving orders, the production planner is able to utilize capacity more effectively and still meet the order requirements, with only 1 order produced on overtime in day 3.

LEARNING EXERCISE ▶ If the units ordered for day 5 increase to 16, what are the production planner's options? [Answer: In addition to moving 2 units to day 4, move 2 units of production to day 6, or request overtime.]

RELATED PROBLEMS ▶ 14.29, 14.30

When the workload consistently exceeds work-center capacity, the tactics just discussed are not adequate. This may mean adding capacity via personnel, machinery, overtime, or subcontracting.

MRP in Services

The demand for many services or service items is classified as dependent demand when it is directly related to or derived from the demand for other services. Such services often require product-structure trees, bills of material and labor, and scheduling. Variations of MRP systems can make a major contribution to operational performance in such services. Examples from restaurants, hospitals, and hotels follow.

Restaurants In restaurants, ingredients and side dishes (bread, vegetables, and condiments) are typically meal components. These components are dependent on the demand for meals. The meal is an end item in the master schedule. Figure 14.9 shows (a) a product-structure tree and

(a) PRODUCT STRUCTURE TREE

Figure **14.9**

Product Structure Tree and Bill of Material for Chef John's Buffalo Chicken Mac & Cheese

(b) BILL OF MATERIALS

Production Specification	Buffalo Chicken Mac & Cheese (6 portions)				
Ingredients	Quantity	Measure	Unit Cost	Total Cost	Labor Hrs.
Elbow Macaroni (large, uncooked)	20.00	oz.	$ 0.09	$ 1.80	
Cheese—Pepper Jack (grated)	10.00	oz.	0.17	1.70	
Mac and Cheese Base (from refrigerator)	32.00	oz.	0.80	25.60	
Milk	4.00	oz.	0.03	0.12	
Smoked Pulled Chicken	2.00	lb.	2.90	5.80	
Buffalo Sauce	8.00	oz.	0.09	0.72	
Blue Cheese Crumbles	4.00	oz.	0.19	0.76	
Scallions	2.00	oz.	0.18	0.36	
Total Labor Hours					0.2 hrs

(b) bill of material (here called a *product specification*) for 6 portions of *Buffalo Chicken Mac & Cheese,* a popular dish prepared by Chef John for Orlando Magic fans at the Amway Center.

Hospitals MRP is also applied in hospitals, especially when dealing with surgeries that require known equipment, materials, and supplies. Houston's Park Plaza Hospital and many hospital suppliers, for example, use the technique to improve the scheduling and management of expensive surgical inventory.

Hotels Marriott develops a bill of material and a bill of labor when it renovates each of its hotel rooms. Marriott managers explode the BOM to compute requirements for materials, furniture, and decorations. MRP then provides net requirements and a schedule for use by purchasing and contractors.

Distribution Resource Planning (DRP)

When dependent techniques are used in the supply chain, they are called distribution resource planning (DRP). Distribution resource planning (DRP) is a time-phased stock-replenishment plan for all levels of the supply chain.

DRP procedures and logic are analogous to MRP. With DRP, expected demand becomes gross requirements. Net requirements are determined by allocating available inventory to gross requirements. The DRP procedure starts with the forecast at the retail level (or the most distant point of the distribution network being supplied). All other levels are computed. As is the case with MRP, inventory is then reviewed with an aim to satisfying demand. So that stock will arrive when it is needed, net requirements are offset by the necessary lead time. A planned order release quantity becomes the gross requirement at the next level down the distribution chain.

DRP *pulls* inventory through the system. Pulls are initiated when the retail level orders more stock. Allocations are made to the retail level from available inventory and production after being adjusted to obtain shipping economies. Effective use of DRP requires an integrated information system to rapidly convey planned order releases from one level to the next. The goal of the DRP system is small and frequent replenishment within the bounds of economical ordering and shipping.

Enterprise Resource Planning (ERP)

Advances in MRP II systems that tie customers and suppliers to MRP II have led to the development of enterprise resource planning (ERP) systems. Enterprise resource planning (ERP) is software that allows companies to (1) automate and integrate many of their business processes, (2) share a common database and business practices throughout the enterprise, and (3) produce information in real time. A schematic showing some of these relationships for a manufacturing firm appears in Figure 14.10.

The objective of an ERP system is to coordinate a firm's entire business, from supplier evaluation to customer invoicing. This objective is seldom achieved, but ERP systems are umbrella systems that tie together a variety of specialized systems. This is accomplished by using a centralized database to assist the flow of information among business functions. Exactly what is tied together, and how, varies on a case-by-case basis. In addition to the traditional components of MRP, ERP systems usually provide financial and human resource (HR) management information. ERP systems may also include:

LO 14.7 *Describe* ERP

♦ *Supply-chain management (SCM)* software to support sophisticated vendor communication, e-commerce, and those activities necessary for efficient warehousing and logistics. The idea is to tie operations (MRP) to procurement, to materials management, and to suppliers, providing the tools necessary for effective management of all four areas.

♦ *Customer relationship management (CRM)* software for the incoming side of the business. CRM is designed to aid analysis of sales, target the most profitable customers, and manage the sales force.

♦ *Sustainability* software to tie together sustainable workforce issues and provide transparency for supply-chain sustainability issues, as well as monitor health and safety activities, energy use and efficiency, emissions (carbon footprint, greenhouse gases), and environmental compliance.

Figure **14.10**

MRP and ERP Information Flows, Showing Customer Relationship Management (CRM), Supply-Chain Management (SCM), and Finance/Accounting

Other functions such as human resources and sustainability are often also included in ERP systems.

◆ **STUDENT TIP**

ERP tries to integrate all of a firm's information to ensure data integrity.

In addition to data integration, ERP software promises reduced transaction costs and fast, accurate information. A strategic emphasis on just-in-time systems and supply chain integration drives the desire for enterprise-wide software. The *OM in Action* box "Managing Benetton with ERP Software" provides an example of how ERP software helps integrate company operations.

OM in Action   Managing Benetton with ERP Software

Thanks to ERP, the Italian sportswear company Benetton can probably claim to have the world's fastest factory and the most efficient distribution in the garment industry. Located in Ponzano, Italy, Benetton makes and ships 50 million pieces of clothing each year. That is 30,000 boxes every day—boxes that must be filled with exactly the items ordered going to the correct store of the 5,000 Benetton outlets in 60 countries. This highly automated distribution center uses only 19 people. Without ERP, hundreds of people would be needed.

Here is how ERP software works:

1. *Ordering:* A salesperson in the south Boston store finds that she is running out of a best-selling blue sweater. Using a laptop PC, her local Benetton sales agent taps into the ERP sales module.

2. *Availability:* ERP's inventory software simultaneously forwards the order to the mainframe in Italy and finds that half the order can be filled immediately from the Italian warehouse. The rest will be manufactured and shipped in 4 weeks.

3. *Production:* Because the blue sweater was originally created by computer-aided design (CAD), ERP manufacturing software passes the specifications to a knitting machine. The knitting machine makes the sweaters.

4. *Warehousing:* The blue sweaters are boxed with a radio frequency ID (RFID) tag addressed to the Boston store and placed in one of the 300,000 slots in the Italian warehouse. A robot flies by, reading RFID tags, picks out any and all boxes ready for the Boston store, and loads them for shipment.

5. *Order tracking:* The Boston salesperson logs onto the ERP system through the Internet and sees that the sweater (and other items) are completed and being shipped.

6. *Planning:* Based on data from ERP's forecasting and financial modules, Benetton's chief buyer decides that blue sweaters are in high demand and quite profitable. She decides to add three new hues.

Sources: Forbes (December 2, 2011); *The Wall Street Journal* (April 10, 2007); *Information Week* (June 13, 2005); and *MIT Sloan Management Review* (Fall 2001).

In an ERP system, data are entered only once into a common, complete, and consistent database shared by all applications. For example, when a Nike salesperson enters an order into his ERP system for 20,000 pairs of sneakers for Foot Locker, the data are instantly available on the manufacturing floor. Production crews start filling the order if it is not in stock, accounting prints Foot Locker's invoice, and shipping notifies Foot Locker of the future delivery date. The salesperson, or even the customer, can check the progress of the order at any point. This is all accomplished using the same data and common applications. To reach this consistency, however, the data fields must be defined identically across the entire enterprise. In Nike's case, this means integrating operations at production sites from Vietnam to China to Mexico, at business units across the globe, in many currencies, and with reports in a variety of languages.

Each ERP vendor produces unique products. The major vendors, SAP AG (a German firm), BEA (Canada), SSAGlobal, American Software, PeopleSoft/Oracle, and CMS Software (all U.S. firms), sell software or modules designed for specific industries (a set of SAP's modules is shown in Figure 14.11). However, companies must determine if their way of doing business will fit the standard ERP module. If they determine that the product will not fit the standard ERP product, they can change the way they do business to accommodate the software. But such a change can have an adverse impact on their business process, reducing a competitive advantage.

Alternatively, ERP software can be customized to meet their specific process requirements. Although the vendors build the software to keep the customization process simple, many companies spend up to five times the cost of the software to customize it. In addition to the expense, the major downside of customization is that when ERP vendors provide an upgrade or enhancement to the software, the customized part of the code must be rewritten to fit into the new version. ERP programs cost from a minimum of $300,000 for a small company to

CASH TO CASH

Covers all financial related activity:

| Accounts receivable | General ledger | Cash management |
| Accounts payable | Treasury | Asset management |

PROMOTE TO DELIVER
Covers front-end customer-oriented activities:

Marketing

Quote and order processing

Transportation

Documentation and labeling

After sales service

Warranty and guarantees

DESIGN TO MANUFACTURE
Covers internal production activities:

Design engineering	Shop floor reporting
Production engineering	Contract/project management
Plant maintenance	Subcontractor management

RECRUIT TO RETIRE
Covers all HR- and payroll-oriented activity:

| Time and attendance | Payroll |
| Travel and expenses | |

PROCURE TO PAY
Covers sourcing activities:

Vendor sourcing

Purchase requisitioning

Purchase ordering

Purchase contracts

Inbound logistics

Supplier invoicing/matching

Supplier payment/settlement

Supplier performance

DOCK TO DISPATCH

Covers internal inventory management:

| Warehousing | Forecasting | Physical inventory |
| Distribution planning | Replenishment planning | Material handling |

Figure **14.11**

SAP's Modules for ERP

Source: www.sap.com.

hundreds of millions of dollars for global giants like Ford and Coca-Cola. It is easy to see, then, that ERP systems are expensive, full of hidden issues, and time-consuming to install.

ERP in the Service Sector

ERP vendors have developed a series of service modules for such markets as health care, government, retail stores, and financial services. Springer-Miller Systems, for example, has created an ERP package for the hotel market with software that handles all front- and back-office functions. This system integrates tasks such as maintaining guest histories, booking room and dinner reservations, scheduling golf tee times, and managing multiple properties in a chain. PeopleSoft/Oracle combines ERP with supply chain management to coordinate airline meal preparation. In the grocery industry, these supply chain systems are known as *efficient consumer response* (ECR) systems. Efficient consumer response systems tie sales to buying, to inventory, to logistics, and to production.

Efficient consumer response (ECR)

Supply chain management systems in the grocery industry that tie sales to buying, to inventory, to logistics, and to production.

Summary

Material requirements planning (MRP) schedules production and inventory when demand is dependent. For MRP to work, management must have a master schedule, precise requirements for all components, accurate inventory and purchasing records, and accurate lead times.

When properly implemented, MRP can contribute in a major way to reduction in inventory while improving customer service levels. MRP techniques allow the operations manager to schedule and replenish stock on a "need-to-order" basis rather than simply a "time-to-order" basis.

Many firms using MRP systems find that lot-for-lot can be the low-cost lot-sizing option.

The continuing development of MRP systems has led to its use with lean manufacturing techniques. In addition, MRP can integrate production data with a variety of other activities, including the supply chain and sales. As a result, we now have integrated database-oriented enterprise resource planning (ERP) systems. These expensive and difficult-to-install ERP systems, when successful, support strategies of differentiation, response, and cost leadership.

Key Terms

Material requirements planning (MRP) (p. 566)
Master production schedule (MPS) (p. 567)
Bill of material (BOM) (p. 568)
Modular bills (p. 569)
Planning bills (or kits) (p. 570)
Phantom bills of material (p. 570)
Low-level coding (p. 570)
Lead time (p. 570)

Gross material requirements plan (p. 571)
Net requirements plan (p. 572)
Planned order receipt (p. 574)
Planned order release (p. 574)
System nervousness (p. 575)
Time fences (p. 575)
Pegging (p. 575)
Buckets (p. 576)
Lot-sizing decision (p. 576)
Lot-for-lot (p. 576)

Periodic order quantity (POQ) (p. 578)
Material requirements planning II (MRP II) (p. 580)
Closed-loop MRP system (p. 581)
Load report (p. 581)
Distribution resource planning (DRP) (p. 584)
Enterprise resource planning (ERP) (p. 584)
Efficient consumer response (ECR) (p. 587)

Ethical Dilemma

For many months your prospective ERP customer has been analyzing the hundreds of assumptions built into the $900,000 ERP software you are selling. So far, you have knocked yourself out to try to make this sale. If the sale goes through, you will reach your yearly quota and get a nice bonus. On the other hand, loss of this sale may mean you start looking for other employment.

The accounting, human resource, supply chain, and marketing teams put together by the client have reviewed the specifications and finally recommended purchase of the software. However, as you looked over their shoulders and helped them through the evaluation process, you began to realize that their purchasing procedures—with much of the purchasing being done at hundreds of regional stores—were not a good fit for the software. At the very least, the customizing will add $250,000 to the implementation and training cost. The team is not aware of the issue, and you know that the necessary $250,000 is not in the budget.

What do you do?

Discussion Questions

1. What is the difference between a *gross* requirements plan and a *net* requirements plan?

2. Once a material requirements plan (MRP) has been established, what other managerial applications might be found for the technique?

3. What are the similarities between MRP and DRP?

4. How does MRP II differ from MRP?

5. Which is the best lot-sizing policy for manufacturing organizations?

6. What impact does ignoring carrying cost in the allocation of stock in a DRP system have on lot sizes?

7. MRP is more than an inventory system; what additional capabilities does MRP possess?

8. What are the options for the production planner who has:
   a) scheduled more than capacity in a work center next week?
   b) a consistent lack of capacity in that work center?

9. Master schedules are expressed in three different ways depending on whether the process is continuous, a job shop, or repetitive. What are these three ways?

10. What functions of the firm affect an MRP system? How?

11. What is the rationale for (a) a phantom bill of material, (b) a planning bill of material, and (c) a pseudo bill of material?

12. Identify five specific requirements of an effective MRP system.

13. What are the typical benefits of ERP?

14. What are the distinctions between MRP, DRP, and ERP?

15. As an approach to inventory management, how does MRP differ from the approach taken in Chapter 12, dealing with economic order quantities (EOQ)?

16. What are the disadvantages of ERP?

17. Use the Web or other sources to:
   a) Find stories that highlight the advantages of an ERP system.
   b) Find stories that highlight the difficulties of purchasing, installing, or failure of an ERP system.

18. Use the Web or other sources to identify what an ERP vendor (SAP, PeopleSoft/Oracle, American Software, etc.) includes in these software modules:
   a) Customer relationship management.
   b) Supply-chain management.
   c) Product life cycle management.

19. The structure of MRP systems suggests "buckets" and infinite loading. What is meant by these two terms?

Using Software to Solve MRP Problems

There are many commercial MRP software packages, for companies of all sizes. MRP software for small and medium-size companies includes User Solutions, Inc., a demo of which is available at **www.usersolutions.com,** and MAX, from Exact Software North America, Inc. Software for larger systems is available from SAP, CMS, BEA, Oracle, i2 Technologies, and many others. The Excel OM software that accompanies this text includes an MRP module, as does POM for Windows. The use of both is explained in the following sections.

✖ USING EXCEL OM

Using Excel OM's MRP module requires the careful entry of several pieces of data. The initial MRP screen is where we enter (1) the total number of occurrences of items in the BOM (including the top item), (2) what we want the BOM items to be called (e.g., Item no., Part), (3) total number of periods to be scheduled, and (4) what we want the periods called (e.g., days, weeks).

Excel OM's second MRP screen provides the data entry for an indented bill of material. Here we enter (1) the name of each item in the BOM, (2) the quantity of that item in the assembly, and (3) the correct indent (e.g., parent/child relationship) for each item. The indentations are critical, as they provide the logic for the BOM explosion. The indentations should follow the logic of the product structure tree with indents for each assembly item in that assembly.

Excel OM's third MRP screen repeats the indented BOM and provides the standard MRP tableau for entries. This is shown in Program 14.1 using the data from Examples 1, 2, and 3.

▶ USING POM FOR WINDOWS

The POM for Windows MRP module can also solve Examples 1 to 3. Up to 18 periods can be analyzed. Here are the inputs required:

1. *Item names:* The item names are entered in the left column. The same item name will appear in more than one row if the item is used by two parent items. Each item must follow its parents.

2. *Item level:* The level in the indented BOM must be given here. The item *cannot* be placed at a level more than one below the item immediately above.

3. *Lead time:* The lead time for an item is entered here. The default is 1 week.

4. *Number per parent:* The number of units of this subassembly needed for its parent is entered here. The default is 1.

5. *On hand:* List current inventory on hand once, even if the subassembly is listed twice.

6. *Lot size:* The lot size can be specified here. A 0 or 1 will perform lot-for-lot ordering. If another number is placed here, then all orders for that item will be in integer multiples of that number.

7. *Demands:* The demands are entered in the end item row in the period in which the items are demanded.

8. *Scheduled receipts:* If units are scheduled to be received in the future, they should be listed in the appropriate time period (column) and item (row). (An entry here in level 1 is a demand; all other levels are receipts.)

Further details regarding POM for Windows are seen in Appendix IV.

Program 14.1

Using Excel OM's MRP Module to Solve Examples 1, 2, and 3

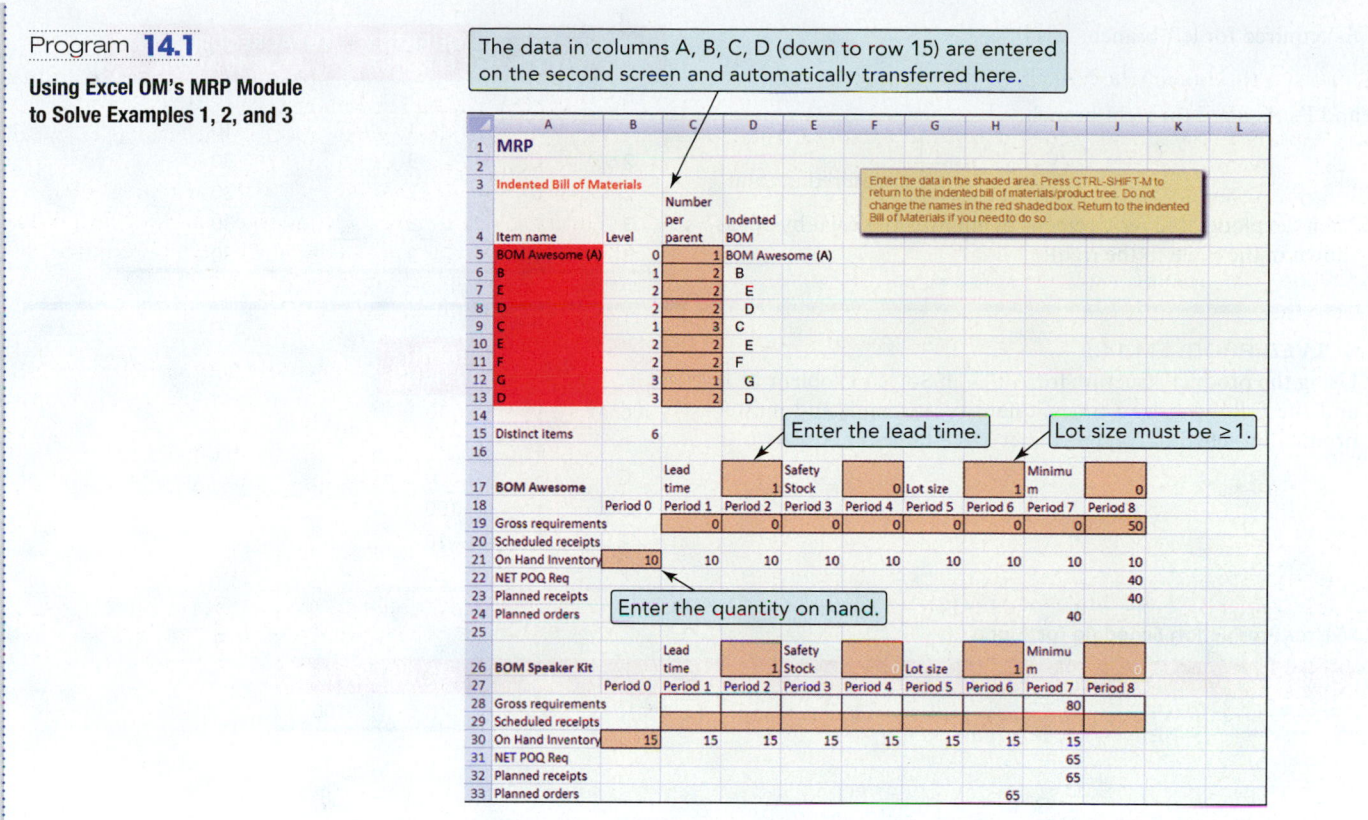

> The data in columns A, B, C, D (down to row 15) are entered on the second screen and automatically transferred here.

Solved Problems

Virtual Office Hours help is available in MyOMLab.

SOLVED PROBLEM 14.1

Determine the low-level coding and the quantity of each component necessary to produce 10 units of an assembly we will call Alpha. The product structure and quantities of each component needed for each assembly are noted in parentheses.

SOLUTION

Redraw the product structure with low-level coding. Then multiply down the structure until the requirements of each branch are determined. Then add across the structure until the total for each is determined.

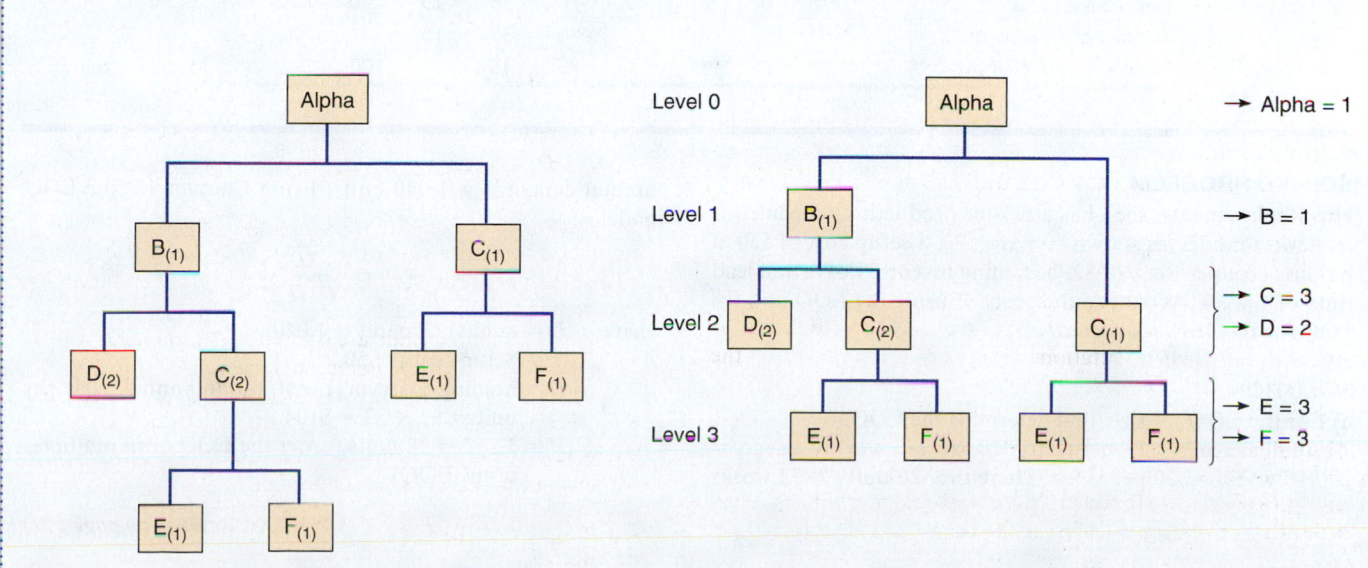

Es required for left branch:

$$(1_{alpha} \times 1_B \times 2_C \times 1_E) = 2 \text{ Es}$$

and Es required for right branch:

$$(1_{alpha} \times 1_C \times 1_E) = \underline{1 \text{ E}}$$
$$3 \text{ Es required in total}$$

Then "explode" the requirement by multiplying each by 10, as shown in the table to the right:

LEVEL	ITEM	QUANTITY PER UNIT	TOTAL REQUIREMENTS FOR 10 ALPHA
0	Alpha	1	10
1	B	1	10
2	C	3	30
2	D	2	20
3	E	3	30
3	F	3	30

SOLVED PROBLEM 14.2

Using the product structure for Alpha in Solved Problem 14.1, and the following lead times, quantity on hand, and master production schedule, prepare a net MRP table for Alphas.

ITEM	LEAD TIME	QUANTITY ON HAND
Alpha	1	10
B	2	20
C	3	0
D	1	100
E	1	10
F	1	50

Master Production Schedule for Alpha

PERIOD	6	7	8	9	10	11	12	13
Gross requirements			50			50		100

SOLUTION

See the chart on following page.

SOLVED PROBLEM 14.3

Hip Replacements, Inc., has a master production schedule for its newest model, as shown below, a setup cost of $50, a holding cost per week of $2, beginning inventory of 0, and lead time of 1 week. What are the costs of using lot-for-lot for this 10-week period?

SOLUTION

Holding cost = $0 (as there is never any end-of-period inventory)

Ordering costs = 4 orders × $50 = $200

Total cost for lot-for-lot = $0 + $200 = $200

WEEK	1	2	3	4	5	6	7	8	9	10
Gross requirements	0	0	50	0	0	35	15	0	100	0
Scheduled receipts										
Projected on hand	0	0	0	0	0	0	0	0	0	0	0
Net requirements		0	0	50	0	0	35	15	0	100	
Planned order receipts			50			35	15		100	
Planned order releases		50			35	15		100		

SOLVED PROBLEM 14.4

Hip Replacements, Inc., has a master production schedule for its newest model, as shown on page 592, a setup cost of $50, a holding cost per week of $2, beginning inventory of 0, and lead time of 1 week. What are the costs of using (a) EOQ and (b) POQ for this 10-week period?

SOLUTION

a) For the **EOQ** lot size, first determine the EOQ.

Annual usage = 200 units for 10 weeks; weekly usage = 200/10 weeks = 20 per week. Therefore, 20 units × 52 weeks

(annual demand) = 1,040 units. From Chapter 12, the EOQ model is:

$$Q^* = \sqrt{\frac{2DS}{H}}$$

where D = annual demand = 1,040
  S = Setup cost = $50
  H = holding (carrying) cost, on an annual basis per unit = $2 × 52 = $104
  Q^* = 31.62 ≈ 32 units (order the EOQ or in multiples of the EOQ)

(*Continued on page 592*)

Net Material Requirements Planning Sheet for Alpha for Solved Problem 14.2

The letter in parentheses (A) is the source of the demand.

Lot Size	Lead Time (# of Periods)	On Hand	Safety Stock	Allocated	Low-Level Code	Item ID		Period (week, day)												
								1	2	3	4	5	6	7	8	9	10	11	12	13
Lot-for-Lot	1	10	—	—	0	Alpha (A)	Gross Requirements								50			50		100
							Scheduled Receipts													
							Projected On Hand 10	10	10	10	10	10	10	10	0	0	0	0	0	0
							Net Requirements								40			50		100
							Planned Order Receipts								40			50		100
							Planned Order Releases							40			50		100	
Lot-for-Lot	2	20	—	—	1	B	Gross Requirements							40(A)			50(A)		100(A)	
							Scheduled Receipts													
							Projected On Hand 20	20	20	20	20	20	20	0	0	0	0	0	0	0
							Net Requirements							20			50		100	
							Planned Order Receipts							20			50		100	
							Planned Order Releases					20			50		100			
Lot-for-Lot	3	0	—	—	2	C	Gross Requirements					40(B)		40(A)	100(B)		200(B) + 50(A)		100(A)	
							Scheduled Receipts													
							Projected On Hand 0	0	0	0	0	0	0	0	0	0	0	0	0	0
							Net Requirements					40		40	100		250		100	
							Planned Order Receipts					40		40	100		250		100	
							Planned Order Releases		40		40	100		250		100				
Lot-for-Lot	1	100	—	—	2	D	Gross Requirements					40(B)			100(B)		200(B)			
							Scheduled Receipts													
							Projected On Hand 100	100	100	100	100	60	60	60	0	0	0	0	0	0
							Net Requirements								40		200			
							Planned Order Receipts								40		200			
							Planned Order Releases							40		200				
Lot-for-Lot	1	10	—	—	3	E	Gross Requirements		40(C)		40(C)	100(C)		250(C)		100(C)				
							Scheduled Receipts													
							Projected On Hand 10	10	0	0	0	0	0	0	0	0	0	0	0	0
							Net Requirements		30		40	100		250		100				
							Planned Order Receipts		30		40	100		250		100				
							Planned Order Releases	30		40	100		250		100					
Lot-for-Lot	1	50	—	—	3	F	Gross Requirements		40(C)		40(C)	100(C)		250(C)		100(C)				
							Scheduled Receipts													
							Projected On Hand 50	50	10	10	0	0	0	0	0	0	0	0	0	0
							Net Requirements				30	100		250		100				
							Planned Order Receipts				30	100		250		100				
							Planned Order Releases			30	100		250		100					

WEEK		1	2	3	4	5	6	7	8	9	10	
Gross requirements		0	0	50	0	0	35	15	0	100	0	
Scheduled receipts												
Projected on hand	0	0	0	0	14	14	14	11	28	28	24	24
Net requirements		0	0	50	0	0	21	0	0	72	0	
Planned order receipts				64			32	32		96		
Planned order releases			64			32	32		96			

Holding cost = 157 units × $2 = $314 (note the 24 units available in period 11, for which there is an inventory charge as they are in on-hand inventory at the end of period 10)

Ordering costs = 4 orders × $50 = $200

Total cost for EOQ lot sizing = $314 + $200 = $514

b) For the **POQ** lot size we use the EOQ computed above to find the time period between orders:

Period interval = EOQ/average weekly usage = 32/20 = 1.6 ≈ 2 periods

POQ order size = Demand required in the 2 periods, postponing orders in periods with no demand.

WEEK		1	2	3	4	5	6	7	8	9	10
Gross requirements		0	0	50	0	0	35	15	0	100	0
Scheduled receipts											
Projected on hand	0	0	0	0	0	0	0	15	0	0	
Net requirements		0	0	50	0	0	50	0	0	100	0
Planned order receipts				50			50			100	
Planned order releases			50			50			100		

Holding cost = 15 units × $2 = $30

Ordering costs = 3 orders × $50 = $150

Total cost for POQ lot sizing = $30 + $150 = $180

Problems*

Note: **Px** means the problem may be solved with POM for Windows and/or Excel OM. Many of the exercises in this chapter (14.1 through 14.16 and 14.29 through 14.32) can be done on *Resource Manager for Excel,* a commercial system made available by User Solutions, Inc. Access to a trial version of the software and a set of notes for the user are available at **www.usersolutions.com.**

Problems 14.1–14.4 relate to Dependent Inventory Model Requirements

• **14.1** You have developed the following simple product structure of items needed for your gift bag for a rush party for prospective pledges in your organization. You forecast 200 attendees. Assume that there is no inventory on hand of any of the items. Explode the bill of material. (Subscripts indicate the number of units required.)

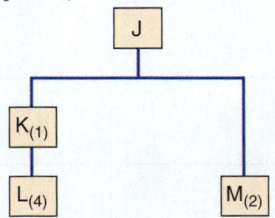

•• **14.2** You are expected to have the gift bags in Problem 14.1 ready at 5 P.M. However, you need to personalize the items (monogrammed pens, note pads, literature from the printer, etc.). The lead time is 1 hour to assemble 200 Js once the other items are prepared. The other items will take a while as well. Given the volunteers you have, the other time estimates are item K (2 hours), item L (1 hour), and item M (4 hours). Develop a time-phased assembly plan to prepare the gift bags.

•• **14.3** As the production planner for Xiangling Hu Products, Inc., you have been given a bill of material for a bracket that is

made up of a base, two springs, and four clamps. The base is assembled from one clamp and two housings. Each clamp has one handle and one casting. Each housing has two bearings and one shaft. There is no inventory on hand.
a) Design a product structure noting the quantities for each item and show the low-level coding.
b) Determine the gross quantities needed of each item if you are to assemble 50 brackets.
c) Compute the net quantities needed if there are 25 of the base and 100 of the clamp in stock. **Px**

•• **14.4** Your boss at Xiangling Hu Products, Inc., has just provided you with the schedule and lead times for the bracket in Problem 14.3. The unit is to be prepared in week 10. The lead times for the components are bracket (1 week), base (1 week), spring (1 week), clamp (1 week), housing (2 weeks), handle (1 week), casting (3 weeks), bearing (1 week), and shaft (1 week).
a) Prepare the time-phased product structure for the bracket.
b) In what week do you need to start the castings? **Px**

Problems 14.5–14.21 relate to MRP Structure

•• **14.5** The demand for subassembly S is 100 units in week 7. Each unit of S requires 1 unit of T and 2 units of U. Each unit of T requires 1 unit of V, 2 units of W, and 1 unit of X. Finally, each unit of U requires 2 units of Y and 3 units of Z. One firm manufactures all items. It takes 2 weeks to make S, 1 week to make T,

2 weeks to make U, 2 weeks to make V, 3 weeks to make W, 1 week to make X, 2 weeks to make Y, and 1 week to make Z.
a) Construct a product structure. Identify all levels, parents, and components.
b) Prepare a time-phased product structure.

•• **14.6**   Using the information in Problem 14.5, construct a gross material requirements plan. **Px**

•• **14.7**   Using the information in Problem 14.5, construct a net material requirements plan using the following on-hand inventory.

ITEM	ON-HAND INVENTORY	ITEM	ON-HAND INVENTORY
S	20	W	30
T	20	X	25
U	40	Y	240
V	30	Z	40 **Px**

•• **14.8**   Refer again to Problems 14.5 and 14.6. In addition to 100 units of S, there is also a demand for 20 units of U, which is a component of S. The 20 units of U are needed for maintenance purposes. These units are needed in week 6. Modify the *gross material requirements plan* to reflect this change. **Px**

•• **14.9**   Refer again to Problems 14.5 and 14.7. In addition to 100 units of S, there is also a demand for 20 units of U, which is a component of S. The 20 units of U are needed for maintenance purposes. These units are needed in week 6. Modify the *net material requirements plan* to reflect this change. **Px**

•• **14.10**
a) Given the product structure and master production schedule (Figure 14.12 below), develop a gross requirements plan for all items.
b) Given the preceding product structure, master production schedule, and inventory status (Figure 14.12), develop a net materials requirements (planned order release) for all items. **Px**

••• **14.11** Given the product structure, master production schedule, and inventory status in Figure 14.13 on the next page and assuming the requirements for each BOM item is 1:
a) develop a gross requirements plan for Item C;
b) develop a net requirements plan for Item C. **Px**

•••• **14.12** Based on the data in Figure 14.13, complete a net material requirements schedule for:
a) All items (10 schedules in all), assuming the requirement for each BOM item is 1.
b) All 10 items, assuming the requirement for all items is 1, except B, C, and F, which require *2 each*. **Px**

••• **14.13** Electro Fans has just received an order for one thousand 20-inch fans due week 7. Each fan consists of a housing assembly, two grills, a fan assembly, and an electrical unit. The housing assembly consists of a frame, two supports, and a handle. The fan assembly consists of a hub and five blades. The electrical unit consists of a motor, a switch, and a knob. The following table gives lead times, on-hand inventory, and scheduled receipts.
a) Construct a product structure.
b) Construct a time-phased product structure.
c) Prepare a net material requirements plan. **Px**

Data Table for Problem 14.13

COMPONENT	LEAD TIME	ON-HAND INVENTORY	LOT SIZE*	SCHEDULED RECEIPT
20" Fan	1	100	—	
Housing	1	100	—	
Frame	2	—	—	
Supports (2)	1	50	100	
Handle	1	400	500	
Grills (2)	2	200	500	
Fan Assembly	3	150	—	
Hub	1	—	—	
Blades (5)	2	—	100	
Electrical Unit	1	—	—	
Motor	1	—	—	
Switch	1	20	12	
Knob	1	—	25	200 knobs in week 2

* Lot-for-lot unless otherwise noted.

••• **14.14** A part structure, lead time (weeks), and on-hand quantities for product A are shown in Figure 14.14. From the information shown, generate:
a) An indented bill of material for product A (see Figure 5.9 in Chapter 5 as an example of a BOM).
b) Net requirements for each part to produce 10 As in week 8 using lot-for-lot. **Px**

••• **14.15** You are product planner for product A (in Problem 14.14 and Figure 14.14). The field service manager, Al Trostel, has just called and told you that the requirements for B and F should each be increased by 10 units for his repair requirements in the field.
a) Prepare a list showing the quantity of each part required to produce the requirements for the service manager *and* the production request of 10 Bs and Fs.
b) Prepare a net requirement plan by date for the new requirements (for both production and field service), assuming that the field service manager wants his 10 units of B and F in week 6 and the 10 production units of A in week 8. **Px**

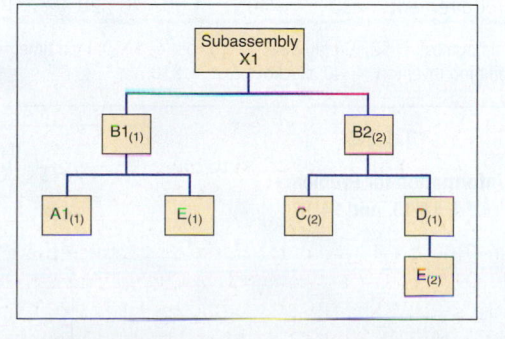

Master Production Schedule for X1

PERIOD	7	8	9	10	11	12
Gross requirements		50		20		100

ITEM	LEAD TIME	ON HAND		ITEM	LEAD TIME	ON HAND
X1	1	50		C	1	0
B1	2	20		D	1	0
B2	2	20		E	3	10
A1	1	5				

Figure 14.12

Information for Problem 14.10

PERIOD	8	9	10	11	12
Gross requirements: A	100		50		150
Gross requirements: H		100		50	

ITEM	ON HAND	LEAD TIME	ITEM	ON HAND	LEAD TIME
A	0	1	F	75	2
B	100	2	G	75	1
C	50	2	H	0	1
D	50	1	J	100	2
E	75	2	K	100	2

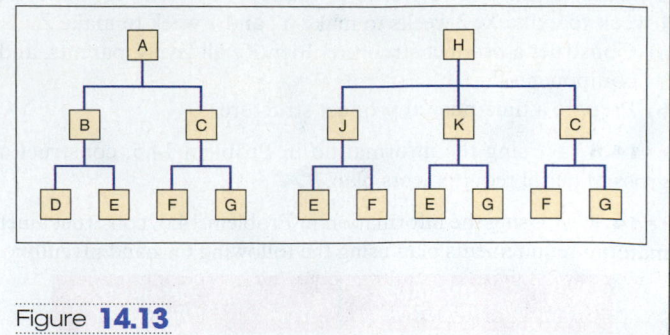

Figure **14.13**

Information for Problems 14.11 and 14.12

••• **14.16** You have just been notified via fax that the lead time for component G of product A (Problem 14.15 and Figure 14.14) has been increased to 4 weeks.
a) Which items have changed, and why?
b) What are the implications for the production plan?
c) As production planner, what can you do? **Px**

•• **14.17** Heather Adams, production manager for a Colorado exercise equipment manufacturer, needs to schedule an order for 50 UltimaSteppers, which are to be shipped in week 8. Subscripts indicate quantity required for each parent. Assume lot-for-lot ordering. Below is information about the steppers:

ITEM	LEAD TIME	ON-HAND INVENTORY	COMPONENTS
Stepper	2	20	$A_{(1)}, B_{(3)}, C_{(2)}$
A	1	10	$D_{(1)}, F_{(2)}$
B	2	30	$E_{(1)}, F_{(3)}$
C	3	10	$D_{(2)}, E_{(3)}$
D	1	15	
E	2	5	
F	2	20	

a) Develop a product structure for Heather.
b) Develop a time-phased structure.
c) Develop a net material requirements plan for F. **Px**

> *Additional problems* **14.18–14.21** *are available in* MyOMLab.

Problems 14.22–14.28 relate to Lot-Sizing Techniques

Data Table for Problems 14.22 through 14.25*

PERIOD	1	2	3	4	5	6	7	8	9	10	11	12
Gross requirements	30		40			30	70	20		10	80		50

*Holding cost = $2.50/unit/week; setup cost = $150; lead time = 1 week; beginning inventory = 40; stockout cost = $10.

••• **14.22** Develop a lot-for-lot solution and calculate total relevant costs for the data in the preceding table. **Px**

••• **14.23** Develop an EOQ solution and calculate total relevant costs for the data in the preceding table. **Px**

••• **14.24** Develop a POQ solution and calculate total relevant costs for the data in the preceding table. **Px**

••• **14.25** Using your answers for the lot sizes computed in Problems 14.22, 14.23, and 14.24, which is the best technique and why?

•• **14.26** M. de Koster, of Rene Enterprises, has the master production plan shown below:

Period (weeks)	1	2	3	4	5	6	7	8	9
Gross requirements		15		20		10			25

Lead time = 1 period; setup cost = $200; holding cost = $10 per week; stockout cost = $10 per week. Your job is to develop an ordering plan and costs for:

a) Lot-for-lot.   b) EOQ.
c) POQ.   d) Which plan has the lowest cost? **Px**

14.27 Grace Greenberg, production planner for Science and Technology Labs, in New Jersey, has the master production plan shown below:

Period (weeks)	1	2	3	4	5	6	7	8	9	10	11	12
Gross requirements		35		40		10			25	10		45

Lead time = 1 week; setup costs = $200; holding cost = $10 per week; stockout cost = $10 per week. Develop an ordering plan and costs for Grace, using these techniques:

a) Lot-for-lot.   b) EOQ.
c) POQ.   d) Which plan has the lowest cost? **Px**

Figure **14.14**

Information for Problems 14.14, 14.15, and 14.16

PART	INVENTORY ON HAND
A	0
B	2
C	10
D	5
E	4
F	5
G	1
H	10

PART STRUCTURE TREE

LT = lead time in weeks
(1) = All quantities = 1

Additional problem **14.28** *is available in* MyOMLab.

Problems 14.29–14.32 relate to **Extensions of MRP**

•••**14.29** Karl Knapps, Inc., has received the following orders:

Period	1	2	3	4	5	6	7	8	9	10
Order size	0	40	30	40	10	70	40	10	30	60

The entire fabrication for these units is scheduled on one machine. There are 2,250 usable minutes in a week, and each unit will take 65 minutes to complete. Develop a capacity plan, using lot splitting, for the 10-week time period.

•••**14.30** Coleman Rich, Ltd., has received the following orders:

Period	1	2	3	4	5	6	7	8	9	10
Order size	60	30	10	40	70	10	40	30	40	0

The entire fabrication for these units is scheduled on one machine. There are 2,250 usable minutes in a week, and each unit will take 65 minutes to complete. Develop a capacity plan, using lot splitting, for the 10-week time period.

•••**14.31** Courtney Kamauf schedules production of a popular Rustic Coffee Table at Kamauf Enterprises, Inc. The table requires a top, four legs, $\frac{1}{8}$ gallon of stain, $\frac{1}{16}$ gallon of glue, 2 short braces between the legs and 2 long braces between the legs, and a brass cap that goes on the bottom of each leg. She has 100 gallons of glue in inventory, but none of the other components. All items except the brass caps, stain, and glue are ordered on a lot-for-lot basis. The caps are purchased in quantities of 1,000, stain and glue by the gallon. Lead time is 1 day for each item. Schedule the order releases necessary to produce 640 coffee tables on days 5 and 6, and 128 on days 7 and 8. **Px**

••••**14.32** Using the data for the coffee table in Problem 14.31, build a labor schedule when the labor standard for each top is 2 labor-hours; each leg including brass cap installation requires $\frac{1}{4}$ hour, as does each pair of braces. Base assembly requires 1 labor-hour, and final assembly requires 2 labor-hours. What is the total number of labor-hours required each day, and how many employees are needed each day at 8 hours per day?

CASE STUDIES

When 18,500 Orlando Magic Fans Come to Dinner

Video Case

With vast experience at venues such as the American Airlines Arena (in Miami), the Kentucky Derby, and Super Bowls, Chef John Nicely now also plans huge culinary events at Orlando's Amway Center, home of the Orlando Magic basketball team. With his unique talent and exceptional operations skills, Nicely serves tens of thousands of cheering fans at some of the world's largest events. And when more than 18,500 basketball fans show up for a game, expecting great food and great basketball, he puts his creative as well as operations talent to work.

Chef John must be prepared. This means determining not only a total demand for all 18,500 fans, but also translating that demand into specific menu items and beverages. He prepares a forecast from current ticket sales, history of similar events at other venues, and his own records, which reflect the demand with this particular opponent, night of week, time of year, and even time of day. He then breaks the demand for specific menu items and quantities into items to be available at each of the 22 concession stands, 7 restaurants, and 68 suites. He must also be prepared to accommodate individual requests from players on both teams.

Chef John frequently changes the menu to keep it interesting for the fans who attend many of the 41 regular season home games each season. Even the culinary preference of the opponent's fans who may be attending influences the menu. Additionally, when entertainment other than the Magic is using the Amway Center, the demographic mix is likely to be different, requiring additional tweaking of the menu. The size of the wait staff and the kitchen staff change to reflect the size of the crowd; Chef John may be supervising as many as 90 people working in the kitchen. Similarly, the concessions stands, 40% of which have their own grills and fryers, present another challenge, as they are managed by volunteers from nonprofit organizations. The use of these volunteers adds the need for special training and extra enforcement of strict quality standards.

Once deciding on the overall demand and the menu, Chef John must prepare the production specifications (a bill of material) for each item. For the evening game with the Celtics, Chef John is preparing his unique *Cheeto Crusted Mac & Cheese* dish. The ingredients, quantity, costs, and labor requirements are shown below:

Production Specifications

CHEETO CRUSTED MAC & CHEESE (6 PORTIONS)					
INGREDIENTS	QUANTITY	MEASURE	UNIT COST	TOTAL COST	LABOR-HOURS
Elbow macaroni (large, uncooked)	20.00	oz.	$0.09	$1.80	
Cheese—cheddar shredded	10.00	oz.	0.16	1.60	
Mac and cheese base (see recipe)	44.00	oz.	0.80	35.20	
Milk	4.00	oz.	0.03	0.12	
Cheetos, crushed	6.00	oz.	0.27	1.62	
Sliced green onion—garnish	0.50	oz.	0.18	0.09	
Whole Cheetos—garnish	2.00	oz.	0.27	0.54	
Total labor hours					0.2 hours

The yield on this dish is 6 portions, and labor cost is $15 per hour, with fringes. The entire quantity required for the evening is prepared prior to the game and kept in warming ovens until needed. Demand for each basketball game is divided into 5 periods: prior to the game, first quarter, second quarter, half-time, and second half. At the Magic vs. Celtics game next week, the demand (number of portions) in each period is 60, 36, 48, 60, and 12 for the Cheeto Crusted Mac & Cheese dish, respectively.

Discussion Questions*

1. Prepare a bill of material explosion and total cost for the 216 portions of Cheeto Crusted Mac & Cheese.

2. What is the cost per portion? How much less expensive is the Cheeto Crusted Mac & Cheese than Chef John's alternative creation, the Buffalo Chicken Mac & Cheese, shown in Figure 14.9 of this chapter?

3. Assuming that there is no beginning inventory of the Cheeto Crusted Mac & Cheese and cooking time for the entire 216 portions is 0.6 hours, when must preparation begin?

*You may wish to view the video that accompanies this case before answering the questions.

MRP at Wheeled Coach

Video Case

Wheeled Coach, the world's largest manufacturer of ambulances, builds thousands of different and constantly changing configurations of its products. The custom nature of its business means lots of options and special designs—and a potential scheduling and inventory nightmare. Wheeled Coach addressed such problems, and succeeded in solving a lot of them, with an MRP system (described in the *Global Company Profile* that opens this chapter). As with most MRP installations, however, solving one set of problems uncovers a new set.

One of the new issues that had to be addressed by plant manager Lynn Whalen was newly discovered excess inventory. Managers discovered a substantial amount of inventory that was not called for in any finished products. Excess inventory was evident because of the new level of inventory accuracy required by the MRP system. The other reason was a new series of inventory reports generated by the IBM MAPICS MRP system purchased by Wheeled Coach. One of those reports indicates where items are used and is known as the "Where Used" report. Interestingly, many inventory items were not called out on bills of material (BOMs) for any current products. In some cases, the reason some parts were in the stockroom remained a mystery.

The discovery of this excess inventory led to renewed efforts to ensure that the BOMs were accurate. With substantial work,

BOM accuracy increased and the number of engineering change notices (ECNs) decreased. Similarly, purchase-order accuracy, with regard to both part numbers and quantities ordered, was improved. Additionally, receiving department and stockroom accuracy went up, all helping to maintain schedule, costs, and ultimately, shipping dates and quality.

Eventually, Lynn Whalen concluded that the residual amounts of excess inventory were the result, at least in part, of rapid changes in ambulance design and technology. Another source was customer changes made after specifications had been determined and materials ordered. This latter excess occurs because, even though Wheeled Coach's own throughput time is only 17 days, many of the items that it purchases require much longer lead times.

Discussion Questions*

1. Why is accurate inventory such an important issue at Wheeled Coach?

2. Why does Wheeled Coach have excess inventory, and what kind of a plan would you suggest for dealing with it?

3. Be specific in your suggestions for reducing inventory and how to implement them.

*You may wish to view the video that accompanies this case before answering the questions.

- **Additional Case Studies:** Visit MyOMLab for these free case studies:
  Ikon's attempt at ERP: The giant office technology firm faces hurdles with ERP implementation.
  Hill's Automotive, Inc.: An after-market producer and distributor of auto replacement parts has trouble making MRP work.

Endnotes

1. The inventory models (EOQ) discussed in Chapter 12 assumed that the demand for one item was independent of the demand for another item. For example, EOQ assumes the demand for refrigerator parts is *independent* of the demand for refrigerators and that demand for parts is constant. MRP makes neither of these assumptions.

2. Record accuracy of 99% may sound good, but note that even when each component has an availability of 99% and a product

has only seven components, the likelihood of a product being completed is only .932 (because $.99^7 = .932$).

3. Using EOQ is a convenient approach for determining the time between orders, but other rules can be used.

4. *Part period balancing, Silver-Meal,* and *Wagner-Whitin* are included in the software POM for Windows and ExcelOM, available with this text.

Main Heading	Review Material	MyOMLab
DEPENDENT DEMAND (p. 566)	Demand for items is *dependent* when the relationship between the items can be determined. For any product, all components of that product are dependent demand items. ■ **Material requirements planning (MRP)**—A dependent demand technique that uses a bill-of-material, inventory, expected receipts, and a master production schedule to determine material requirements.	Concept Questions: 1.1–1.4
DEPENDENT INVENTORY MODEL REQUIREMENTS (pp. 566–571)	Dependent inventory models require that the operations manager know the: (1) Master production schedule; (2) Specifications or bill of material; (3) Inventory availability; (4) Purchase orders outstanding; and (5) Lead times. ■ **Master production schedule (MPS)**—A timetable that specifies what is to be made and when. The MPS is a statement of *what is to be produced*, not a forecast of demand. ■ **Bill of material (BOM)**—A listing of the components, their description, and the quantity of each required to make one unit of a product. Items above any level in a BOM are called *parents*; items below any level are called *components*, or *children*. The top level in a BOM is the 0 level. ■ **Modular bills**—Bills of material organized by major subassemblies or by product options. ■ **Planning bills (or kits)**—Material groupings created in order to assign an artificial parent to a bill of material; also called "pseudo" bills. ■ **Phantom bills of material**—Bills of material for components, usually subassemblies, that exist only temporarily; they are never inventoried. ■ **Low-level coding**—A number that identifies items at the lowest level at which they occur. ■ **Lead time**—In purchasing systems, the time between recognition of the need for an order and receiving it; in production systems, it is the order, wait, move, queue, setup, and run times for each component. When a bill of material is turned on its side and modified by adding lead times for each component, it is called a *time-phased product structure*.	Concept Questions: 2.1–2.4 Problems: 14.1–14.4 Virtual Office Hours for Solved Problem: 14.1 **VIDEO 14.1** When 18,500 Orlando Magic Fans Come to Dinner **VIDEO 14.2** MRP at Wheeled Coach Ambulances
MRP STRUCTURE (pp. 571–575)	■ **Gross material requirements plan**—A schedule that shows the total demand for an item (prior to subtraction of on-hand inventory and scheduled receipts) and (1) when it must be ordered from suppliers, or (2) when production must be started to meet its demand by a particular date. ■ **Net material requirements**—The result of adjusting gross requirements for inventory on hand and scheduled receipts. ■ **Planned order receipt**—The quantity planned to be received at a future date. ■ **Planned order release**—The scheduled date for an order to be released. Net requirements = Gross requirements + Allocations − (On hand + Scheduled receipts)	Concept Questions: 3.1–3.4 Problems: 14.5–14.9, 14.11, 14.16–14.21 Virtual Office Hours for Solved Problem: 14.2 **ACTIVE MODEL 14.1**
MRP MANAGEMENT (pp. 575–576)	■ **System nervousness**—Frequent changes in an MRP system. ■ **Time fences**—A means for allowing a segment of the master schedule to be designated as "not to be rescheduled." ■ **Pegging**—In material requirements planning systems, tracing upward the bill of material from the component to the parent item. Four approaches for integrating MRP and JIT are (1) finite capacity scheduling, (2) small buckets, (3) balanced flow, and (4) supermarkets. ■ **Buckets**—Time units in a material requirements planning system. Finite capacity scheduling (FCS) considers department and machine capacity. FCS provides the precise scheduling needed for rapid material movement.	Concept Questions: 4.1–4.4
LOT-SIZING TECHNIQUES (pp. 576–580)	■ **Lot-sizing decision**—The process of, or techniques used in, determining lot size. ■ **Lot-for-lot**—A lot-sizing technique that generates exactly what is required to meet the plan. ■ **Periodic order quantity (POQ)**—A lot-sizing technique that issues orders on a predetermined time interval with an order quantity equal to all of the interval's requirements. In general, the lot-for-lot approach should be used whenever low-cost deliveries setup can be achieved.	Concept Questions: 5.1–5.4 Problems: 14.22, 14.26, 14.28

Main Heading	Review Material	MyOMLab
EXTENSIONS OF MRP (pp. 580–583)	■ **Material requirements planning II (MRP II)**—A system that allows, with MRP in place, inventory data to be augmented by other resource variables; in this case, MRP becomes *material resource planning*. ■ **Closed-loop MRP system**—A system that provides feedback to the capacity plan, master production schedule, and production plan so planning can be kept valid at all times. ■ **Load report**—A report for showing the resource requirements in a work center for all work currently assigned there as well as all planned and expected orders. Tactics for smoothing the load and minimizing the impact of changed lead time include: *overlapping, operations splitting,* and *order splitting,* or *lot splitting.*	Concept Questions: 6.1–6.4 Problem: 14.32
MRP IN SERVICES (pp. 583–584)	■ **Distribution resource planning (DRP)**—A time-phased stock-replenishment plan for all levels of a distribution network.	Concept Questions: 7.1–7.4
ENTERPRISE RESOURCE PLANNING (ERP) (pp. 584–587)	■ **Enterprise resource planning (ERP)**—An information system for identifying and planning the enterprise-wide resources needed to take, make, ship, and account for customer orders. In an ERP system, data are entered only once into a common, complete, and consistent database shared by all applications. ■ **Efficient consumer response (ECR)**—Supply-chain management systems in the grocery industry that tie sales to buying, to inventory, to logistics, and to production.	Concept Questions: 8.1–8.4

Self Test

■ **Before taking the self-test,** refer to the learning objectives listed at the beginning of the chapter and the key terms listed at the end of the chapter.

LO 14.1 In a product structure diagram:
a) parents are found only at the top level of the diagram.
b) parents are found at every level in the diagram.
c) children are found at every level of the diagram except the top level.
d) all items in the diagrams are both parents and children.
e) all of the above.

LO 14.2 The difference between a gross material requirements plan (gross MRP) and a net material requirements plan (net MRP) is:
a) the gross MRP may not be computerized, but the net MRP must be computerized.
b) the gross MRP includes consideration of the inventory on hand, whereas the net MRP doesn't include the inventory consideration.
c) the net MRP includes consideration of the inventory on hand, whereas the gross MRP doesn't include the inventory consideration.
d) the gross MRP doesn't take taxes into account, whereas the net MRP includes the tax considerations.
e) the net MRP is only an estimate, whereas the gross MRP is used for actual production scheduling.

LO 14.3 Net requirements =
a) Gross requirements + Allocations − On-hand inventory + Scheduled receipts.
b) Gross requirements − Allocations − On-hand inventory − Scheduled receipts.
c) Gross requirements − Allocations − On-hand inventory + Scheduled receipts.
d) Gross requirements + Allocations − On-hand inventory − Scheduled receipts.

LO 14.4 A lot-sizing procedure that orders on a predetermined time interval with the order quantity equal to the total of the interval's requirement is:
a) periodic order quantity.
b) part period balancing.
c) economic order quantity.
d) all of the above.

LO 14.5 MRP II stands for:
a) material resource planning.
b) management requirements planning.
c) management resource planning.
d) material revenue planning.
e) material risk planning.

LO 14.6 A(n) _____ MRP system provides information to the capacity plan, to the master production schedule, and ultimately to the production plan.
a) dynamic
b) closed-loop
c) continuous
d) retrospective
e) introspective

LO 14.7 Which system extends MRP II to tie in customers and suppliers?
a) MRP III
b) JIT
c) IRP
d) ERP
e) Enhanced MRP II

Answers: LO 14.1. c; LO 14.2. c; LO 14.3. d; LO 14.4. a; LO 14.5. a; LO 14.6. b; LO 14.7. d.

Short-Term Scheduling

CHAPTER OUTLINE

GLOBAL COMPANY PROFILE: *Alaska Airlines*

◆ The Importance of Short-Term Scheduling *602*

◆ Scheduling Issues *602*

◆ Scheduling Process-Focused Facilities *605*

◆ Loading Jobs *605*

◆ Sequencing Jobs *611*

◆ Finite Capacity Scheduling (FCS) *617*

◆ Scheduling Services *618*

Alaska Airlines

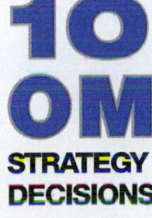

10 OM STRATEGY DECISIONS

- Design of Goods and Services
- Managing Quality
- Process Strategy
- Location Strategies
- Layout Strategies
- Human Resources
- Supply-Chain Management
- Inventory Management
- *Scheduling*
  - Aggregate/S&OP (Ch. 13)
  - *Short-Term (Ch. 15)*
- Maintenance

Scheduling Flights When Weather Is the Enemy

Seattle–Tacoma International Airport (SEA) is the 15th busiest in the U.S. in passenger traffic. Served by 24 airlines that fly non-stop to 76 domestic and 19 international destinations, it is a weather forecaster's nightmare, raining 5 inches a month in the winter season. But it is also the top-ranked U.S. airport in on-time departures, at 85.8%. Much of the credit goes to Alaska Airlines, which dominates traffic at SEA with over 50% of all domestic flights. Alaska's scheduling is critical to efficiency and passenger service.

4 A.M.
FORECAST:
Rain with a chance of light snow for Seattle.

ACTION:
Discuss status of planes and possible need for cancellations.

10 A.M.
FORECAST:
Freezing rain after 5 P.M.

ACTION:
Ready deicing trucks; develop plans to cancel 50% to 80% of flights after 6 P.M.

1:30 P.M.
FORECAST:
Rain changing to snow.

ACTION:
Cancel half the flights from 6 P.M. to 10 A.M.; notify passengers and reroute planes.

5 P.M.
FORECAST:
Less snow than expected.

ACTION:
Continue calling passengers and arrange alternate flights.

10 P.M.
FORECAST:
Snow tapering off.

ACTION:
Find hotels for 600 passengers stranded by the storm.

This is typical of what Alaska Air officials had to do one December day when a storm bore down on Seattle.

Managers at airlines, such as Alaska, learn to expect the unexpected. Events that require rapid rescheduling are a regular part of life. Throughout the ordeals of hurricanes, tornadoes, ice storms, snow storms, and more, airlines around the globe struggle to cope with delays, cancellations, and furious passengers. The inevitable schedule changes often create a ripple effect that impacts passengers at dozens of airports.

Alaska Airlines

To improve flight rescheduling efforts, Alaska Air employees monitor numerous screens that display flights in progress, meteorological charts, and weather patterns at its Flight Operations Department in Seattle. Note the many *andon* signal lights used to indicate "status OK" (green), "needs attention" (yellow), or "major issue—emergency" (red).

Weather-related disruptions can create major scheduling and expensive snow removal issues for airlines (left), just as they create major inconveniences for passengers (right).

To maintain schedules, Alaska Airlines uses elaborate equipment and motivated personnel for snow and ice removal.

Alaska Air's quest to provide passenger and freight service to the state of Alaska complicates its scheduling even more than that of other airlines. Here are just three examples: (1) Juneau's airport is surrounded by mountains, so the approach is often buffeted by treacherous wind shears; (2) Sitka's one small runway is on a narrow strip of land surrounded by water; and (3) in Kodiak, the landing strip ends abruptly at a mountainside. The airport approach is so tricky that first officers are not allowed to land there—only captains are trusted to do so.

Alaska Air takes the sting out of the scheduling nightmares that come from weather-related problems by using the latest technology on its planes and in its Flight Operations Department, located near the Seattle airport. From computers to telecommunications systems to deicers, the department reroutes flights, gets its jets in the air, and quickly notifies customers of schedule changes. The department's job is to keep flights flowing despite the disruptions. Alaska estimates that it saves $18 million a year by using its technology to reduce cancellations and delays.

With mathematical scheduling models such as the ones described in this text, Alaska quickly develops alternate schedules and route changes. This may mean coordinating incoming and outgoing aircraft, ensuring crews are on hand, and making sure information gets to passengers as soon as possible. Weather may be the enemy, but Alaska Airlines has learned how to manage it.

LEARNING OBJECTIVES

LO 15.1 *Explain* the relationship between short-term scheduling, capacity planning, aggregate planning, and a master schedule 603

LO 15.2 *Draw* Gantt loading and scheduling charts 607

LO 15.3 *Apply* the assignment method for loading jobs 608

LO 15.4 *Name* and describe each of the priority sequencing rules 613

LO 15.5 *Use* Johnson's rule 616

LO 15.6 *Define* finite capacity scheduling 617

LO 15.7 *Use* the cyclical scheduling technique 620

The Importance of Short-Term Scheduling

Alaska Airlines doesn't just schedule its 150 aircraft every day; it also schedules over 4,500 pilots and flight attendants to accommodate passengers seeking timely arrival at their destinations. This schedule, developed with huge computer programs, plays a major role in meeting customer expectations. Alaska finds competitive advantage with its ability to make last-minute adjustments to demand fluctuations and weather disruptions.

Scheduling decisions for five organizations—an airline, a hospital, a college, a sports arena, and a manufacturer—are shown in Table 15.1. These decisions all deal with the timing of operations.

When manufacturing firms make schedules that match resources to customer demands, scheduling competence focuses on making parts on a just-in-time basis, with low setup times, little work-in-process, and high facility utilization. Efficient scheduling is how manufacturing companies drive down costs and meet promised due dates.

The strategic importance of scheduling is clear:

- Internally effective scheduling means faster movement of goods and services through a facility and greater use of assets. The result is greater capacity per dollar invested, which translates into lower costs.

- Externally good scheduling provides faster throughput, added flexibility, and more dependable delivery, improving customer service.

Scheduling Issues

Figure 15.1 shows that a series of decisions affects scheduling. Schedule decisions begin with planning capacity, which defines the facility and equipment resources available (discussed in Supplement 7). **Capacity plans** are usually made over a period of years as new equipment

VIDEO 15.1
From the Eagles to the Magic: Converting the Amway Center

TABLE 15.1	Scheduling Decisions
ORGANIZATION	**MANAGERS SCHEDULE THE FOLLOWING**
Alaska Airlines	Maintenance of aircraft Departure timetables Flight crews, catering, gate, and ticketing personnel
Arnold Palmer Hospital	Operating room use Patient admissions Nursing, security, maintenance staffs Outpatient treatments
University of Alabama	Classrooms and audiovisual equipment Student and instructor schedules Graduate and undergraduate courses
Amway Center	Ushers, ticket takers, food servers, security personnel Delivery of fresh foods and meal preparation Orlando Magic games, concerts, arena football
Lockheed Martin factory	Production of goods Purchases of materials Workers

Capacity Planning
(Long term; years)
Changes in facilities
Changes in equipment
See Chapter 7 and Supplement 7

Capacity Plan for New Facilities
Adjust capacity to the demand suggested by strategic plan

Myrleen Pearson/Alamy

Figure **15.1**

The Relationship Between Capacity Planning, Aggregate Planning, Master Schedule, and Short-Term Scheduling for a Bike Company

Aggregate Planning
(Intermediate term; quarterly or monthly)
Facility utilization
Personnel changes
Subcontracting
See Chapter 13

Aggregate Production Plan for All Bikes
(Determine personnel or subcontracting necessary to match aggregate demand to existing facilities/capacity)

Month	1	2
Bike Production	800	850

Master Schedule
(Intermediate term; weekly)
Material requirements planning
Disaggregate the aggregate plan
See Chapters 13 and 14

Master Production Schedule for Bike Models
(Determine weekly capacity schedule)

		Month 1				Month 2		
Week	1	2	3	4	5	6	7	8
Model 22		200		200		200		200
Model 24	100		100		150		100	
Model 26	100		100		100		100	

Short-Term Scheduling
(Short term; days, hours, minutes)
Work center loading
Job sequencing/dispatching
See this chapter

Work Assigned to Specific Personnel and Work Centers
Make finite capacity schedule by matching specific tasks to specific people and machines

Assemble Model 22 in work center 6

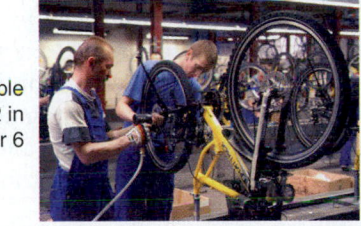

Peter Endig/dpa/Landov

and facilities are designed, built, purchased, or shut down. **Aggregate plans** (Chapter 13) are the result of a Sales and Operating Planning team that makes decisions regarding the use of facilities, inventory, people, and outside contractors. Aggregate plans are typically for 3 to 18 months, and resources are allocated in terms of an aggregate measure such as total units, tons, or shop hours. The **master schedule** breaks down the aggregate plan and develops weekly schedules for specific products or product lines. **Short-term schedules** then translate capacity decisions, aggregate (intermediate) plans, and master schedules into job sequences and specific assignments of personnel, materials, and machinery. In this chapter, we focus on this last step, scheduling goods and services in the *short run* (that is, matching daily or hourly demands to specific personnel and equipment capacity). See the *OM in Action* box "Prepping for the Orlando Magic Basketball Game."

The objective of scheduling is to allocate and prioritize demand (generated by either forecasts or customer orders) to available facilities. Three factors are pervasive in scheduling: (1) generating the schedule forward or backward, (2) finite and infinite loading, and (3) the criteria (priorities) for sequencing jobs. We discuss these topics next.

LO 15.1 *Explain* the relationship between short-term scheduling, capacity planning, aggregate planning, and a master schedule

Forward and Backward Scheduling

Scheduling can be initiated forward or backward. Forward scheduling starts the schedule *as soon as the job requirements are known.* Forward scheduling is used in organizations such as hospitals, clinics, restaurants, and machine tool manufacturers. In these facilities, jobs are performed to customer order, and delivery is typically scheduled at the earliest possible date.

Forward Scheduling

Now   Due date

Backward Scheduling

Now — Due date

Backward scheduling *begins with the due date,* scheduling the *final* operation first. Steps within the job are then scheduled, one at a time, in reverse order. By subtracting the time needed for each item, the start time is obtained. Backward scheduling is used in manufacturing environments, as well as service environments such as catering a banquet or scheduling surgery. In practice, a combination of forward and backward scheduling is often used to find a reasonable trade-off between capacity constraints and customer expectations.

Finite and Infinite Loading

Loading

The assigning of jobs to work or processing centers.

Loading is the process of assigning jobs to work stations or processes. Scheduling techniques that load (or assign) work only up to the capacity of the process are called *finite loading*. The advantage of finite loading is that, in theory, all of the work assigned can be accomplished. However, because only work that can be accomplished is loaded into workstations—when in fact there may be more work than capacity—the due dates may be pushed out to an unacceptable future time.

Techniques that load work without regard for the capacity of the process are *infinite loading*. All the work that needs to be accomplished in a given time period is assigned. The capacity of the process is not considered. Most material requirements planning (MRP) systems (discussed in Chapter 14) are infinite loading systems. The advantage of infinite loading is an initial schedule that meets due dates. Of course, when the workload exceeds capacity, either the capacity or the schedule must be adjusted.

Scheduling Criteria

The correct scheduling technique depends on the volume of orders, the nature of operations, and the overall complexity of jobs, as well as the importance placed on each of four criteria:

1. *Minimize completion time:* Evaluated by determining the average completion time.
2. *Maximize utilization:* Evaluated by determining the percent of the time the facility is utilized.
3. *Minimize work-in-process (WIP) inventory:* Evaluated by determining the average number of jobs in the system. The relationship between the number of jobs in the system and

TABLE 15.2	Different Processes Suggest Different Approaches to Scheduling

Process-focused facilities (job shops)
- Scheduling to customer orders where changes in both volume and variety of jobs/clients/patients are frequent.
- Schedules are often due-date focused, with loading refined by finite loading techniques.
- *Examples:* foundries, machine shops, cabinet shops, print shops, many restaurants, and the fashion industry.

Repetitive facilities (assembly lines)
- Schedule module production and product assembly based on frequent forecasts.
- Finite loading with a focus on generating a forward-looking schedule.
- JIT techniques are used to schedule components that feed the assembly line.
- *Examples:* assembly lines for washing machines at Whirlpool and automobiles at Ford.

Product-focused facilities (continuous)
- Schedule high-volume finished products of limited variety to meet a reasonably stable demand within existing fixed capacity.
- Finite loading with a focus on generating a forward-looking schedule that can meet known setup and run times for the limited range of products.
- *Examples:* huge paper machines at International Paper, beer in a brewery at Anheuser-Busch, and potato chips at Frito-Lay.

WIP inventory will be high. Therefore, the fewer the number of jobs that are in the system, the lower the inventory.

4. *Minimize customer waiting time:* Evaluated by determining the average number of late periods (e.g., days or hours).

These four criteria are used in this chapter, as they are in industry, to evaluate scheduling performance. In addition, good scheduling techniques should be simple, clear, easily understood, easy to carry out, flexible, and realistic.

Scheduling is further complicated by machine breakdowns, absenteeism, quality problems, shortages, and other factors. Consequently, assignment of a date does not ensure that the work will be performed according to the schedule. Many specialized techniques have been developed to aid in preparing reliable schedules. Table 15.2 provides an overview of approaches to scheduling for three different processes.

In this chapter, we first examine the scheduling of process-focused facilities and then the challenge of scheduling employees in the service sector.

Scheduling Process-Focused Facilities

Process-focused facilities (also known as *intermittent*, or *job-shop, facilities*) are common in high-variety, low-volume manufacturing and service organizations. These facilities produce make-to-order products or services and include everything from auto repair garages and hospitals to beauty salons. The production items themselves differ considerably, as do the talents, material, and equipment required to make them. Scheduling requires that the sequence of work (its routing), time required for each item, and the capacity and availability of each work center be known. The variety of products and unique requirements means that scheduling is often complex. In this section we look at some of the tools available to managers for loading and sequencing work for these facilities.

Loading Jobs

Operations managers assign jobs to work centers so that costs, idle time, or completion times are kept to a minimum. "Loading" work centers takes two forms. One is oriented to capacity; the second is related to assigning specific jobs to work centers.

First, we examine loading from the perspective of capacity via a technique known as *input–output* control. Then, we present two approaches used for loading: *Gantt charts* and the *assignment method* of linear programming.

Input–Output Control

Input–output control

A system that allows operations personnel to manage facility work flows.

Many firms have difficulty scheduling (that is, achieving effective throughput) because they overload the production processes. This often occurs because they do not know actual performance in the work centers. Effective scheduling depends on matching the schedule to performance. Lack of knowledge about capacity and performance causes reduced throughput.

Input–output control is a technique that allows operations personnel to manage facility work flows. If the work is arriving faster than it is being processed, the facility is overloaded, and a backlog develops. Overloading causes crowding in the facility, leading to inefficiencies and quality problems. If the work is arriving at a slower rate than jobs are being performed, the facility is underloaded, and the work center may run out of work. Underloading the facility results in idle capacity and wasted resources. Example 1 shows the use of input–output controls.

Example 1

Figure **15.2**

Input–Output Control

INPUT–OUTPUT CONTROL

Bronson Machining, Inc., manufactures driveway security fences and gates. It wants to develop an input–output control report for its welding work center for 5 weeks (weeks 6/6 through 7/4). The planned input is 280 standard hours per week. The actual input is close to this figure, varying between 250 and 285. Output is scheduled at 320 standard hours, which is the assumed capacity. A backlog exists in the work center.

APPROACH ▶ Bronson uses schedule information to create Figure 15.2, which monitors the workload–capacity relationship at the work center.

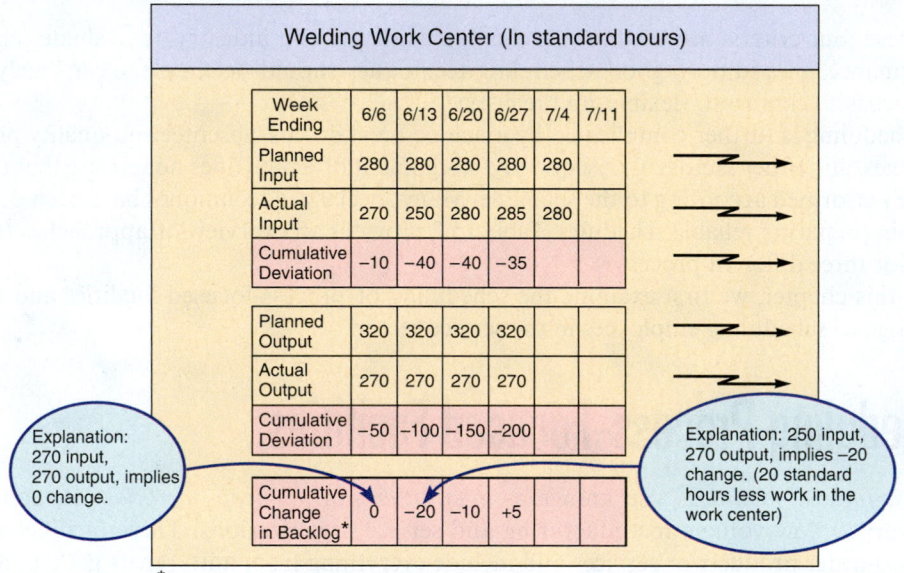

Welding Work Center (In standard hours)

Week Ending	6/6	6/13	6/20	6/27	7/4	7/11
Planned Input	280	280	280	280	280	
Actual Input	270	250	280	285	280	
Cumulative Deviation	−10	−40	−40	−35		
Planned Output	320	320	320	320		
Actual Output	270	270	270	270		
Cumulative Deviation	−50	−100	−150	−200		
Cumulative Change in Backlog*	0	−20	−10	+5		

Explanation: 270 input, 270 output, implies 0 change.

Explanation: 250 input, 270 output, implies −20 change. (20 standard hours less work in the work center)

*Sum of actual inputs minus sum of actual outputs = cumulative change in backlog

SOLUTION ▶ The deviations between scheduled input and actual output are shown in Figure 15.2. Actual output (270 hours) is substantially less than planned. Therefore, neither the input plan nor the output plan is being achieved.

INSIGHT ▶ The backlog of work in this work center has actually increased by 5 hours by week 6/27. This increases work-in-process inventory, complicating the scheduling task and indicating the need for manager action.

LEARNING EXERCISE ▶ If actual output for the week of 6/27 was 275 (instead of 270), what changes? [Answer: Output cumulative deviation now is −195, and cumulative change in backlog is 0.]

RELATED PROBLEM ▶ 15.10

ConWIP cards

Cards that control the amount of work in a work center, aiding input–output control.

Input–output control can be maintained by a system of **ConWIP cards**, which control the amount of work in a work center. ConWIP is an acronym for *constant work-in-process*. The ConWIP card travels with a job (or batch) through the work center. When the job is finished, the card is released and returned to the initial workstation, authorizing the entry of a new batch into the work center. The ConWIP card effectively limits the amount of work in the work center, controls lead time, and monitors the backlog.

Gantt Charts

Gantt charts are visual aids that are useful in loading and scheduling. The name is derived from Henry Gantt, who developed them in the late 1800s. The charts show the use of resources, such as work centers and labor.

When used in *loading*, Gantt charts show the loading and idle times of several departments, machines, or facilities. They display the relative workloads in the system so that the manager knows what adjustments are appropriate. For example, when one work center becomes overloaded, employees from a low-load center can be transferred temporarily to increase the workforce. Or if waiting jobs can be processed at different work centers, some jobs at high-load centers can be transferred to low-load centers. Versatile equipment may also be transferred among centers. Example 2 illustrates a simple Gantt load chart.

Gantt charts

Planning charts used to schedule resources and allocate time.

Example 2

GANTT LOAD CHART

A New Orleans washing machine manufacturer accepts special orders for machines to be used in such unique facilities as submarines, hospitals, and large industrial laundries. The production of each machine requires varying tasks and durations. The company wants to build a load chart for the week of March 8.

APPROACH ▶ The Gantt chart is selected as the appropriate graphical tool.

SOLUTION ▶ Figure 15.3 shows the completed Gantt chart.

Figure **15.3**

Gantt Load Chart for the Week of March 8

Work Center \ Day	Monday	Tuesday	Wednesday	Thursday	Friday
Metalworks	Job 349	✕	◄— Job 350 —►		
Mechanical		◄— Job 349 —►		Job 408	
Electronics	Job 408			Job 349	
Painting	◄— Job 295 —►		Job 408	✕	Job 349

Processing Unscheduled Center not available (e.g., maintenance time, repairs, shortages)

INSIGHT ▶ The four work centers process several jobs during the week. This particular chart indicates that the metalworks and painting centers are completely loaded for the entire week. The mechanical and electronic centers have some idle time scattered during the week. We also note that the metalworks center is unavailable on Tuesday, and the painting center is unavailable on Thursday, perhaps for preventive maintenance.

LEARNING EXERCISE ▶ What impact results from the electronics work center closing on Tuesday for preventive maintenance? [Answer: None.]

RELATED PROBLEM ▶ 15.1b

The Gantt *load chart* has a major limitation: it does not account for production variability such as unexpected breakdowns or human errors that require reworking a job. Consequently, the chart must also be updated regularly to account for new jobs and revised time estimates.

A Gantt *schedule chart* is used to monitor jobs in progress (and is also used for project scheduling). It indicates which jobs are on schedule and which are ahead of or behind schedule. In practice, many versions of the chart are found. The schedule chart in Example 3 places jobs in progress on the vertical axis and time on the horizontal axis.

LO 15.2 *Draw* Gantt loading and scheduling charts

Example 3

Figure **15.4**

Gantt Scheduling Chart for Jobs A, B, and C at First Printing

GANTT SCHEDULING CHART

First Printing in Winter Park, Florida, wants to use a Gantt chart to show the scheduling of three orders, jobs A, B, and C.

APPROACH ▶ In Figure 15.4, each pair of brackets on the time axis denotes the estimated starting and finishing of a job enclosed within it. The solid bars reflect the actual status or progress of the job. We are just finishing day 5.

SOLUTION ▶

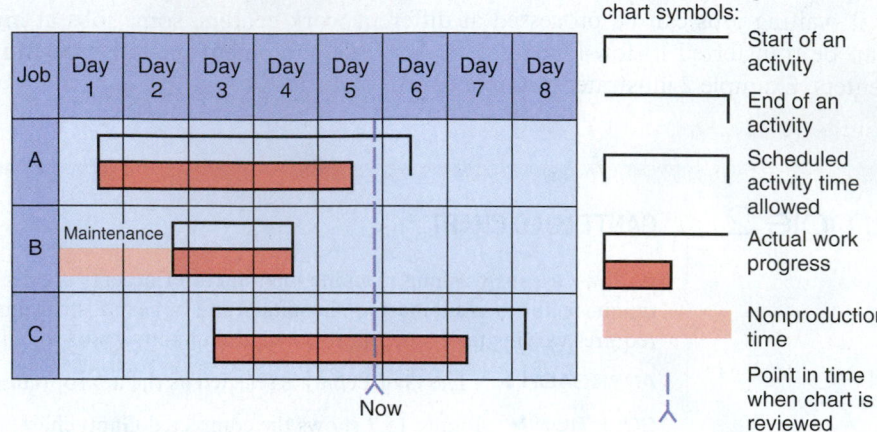

INSIGHT ▶ Figure 15.4 illustrates that job A is about a half-day behind schedule at the end of day 5. Job B was completed after equipment maintenance. We also see that job C is ahead of schedule.

LEARNING EXERCISE ▶ Redraw the Gantt chart to show that job A is a half-day *ahead* of schedule. [Answer: The orangish bar now extends all the way to the end of the activity.]

RELATED PROBLEMS ▶ 15.1a, 15.2

Assignment Method

Assignment method

A special class of linear programming models that involves assigning tasks or jobs to resources.

The **assignment method** involves assigning tasks or jobs to resources. Examples include assigning jobs to machines, contracts to bidders, people to projects, and salespeople to territories. The objective is most often to minimize total costs or time required to perform the tasks at hand. One important characteristic of assignment problems is that only one job (or worker) is assigned to one machine (or project).

Each assignment problem uses a table. The numbers in the table will be the costs or times associated with each particular assignment. For example, if First Printing has three available typesetters (A, B, and C) and three new jobs to be completed, its table might appear as follows. The dollar entries represent the firm's estimate of what it will cost for each job to be completed by each typesetter.

LO 15.3 *Apply* the assignment method for loading jobs

JOB	TYPESETTER		
	A	B	C
R-34	$11	$14	$ 6
S-66	$ 8	$10	$11
T-50	$ 9	$12	$ 7

The assignment method involves adding and subtracting appropriate numbers in the table to find the lowest *opportunity cost*[1] for each assignment. There are four steps to follow:

1. Subtract the smallest number in each row from every number in that row and then, from the resulting matrix, subtract the smallest number in each column from every number in that column. This step has the effect of reducing the numbers in the table until a series

of zeros, meaning *zero opportunity costs*, appear. Even though the numbers change, this reduced problem is equivalent to the original one, and the same solution will be optimal.

2. Draw the minimum number of vertical and horizontal straight lines necessary to cover all zeros in the table. If the number of lines equals either the number of rows or the number of columns in the table, then we can make an optimal assignment (see Step 4). If the number of lines is less than the number of rows or columns, we proceed to Step 3.

3. Subtract the smallest number not covered by a line from every other uncovered number. Add the same number to any number(s) lying at the intersection of any two lines. Do not change the value of the numbers that are covered by only one line. Return to Step 2 and continue until an optimal assignment is possible.

4. Optimal assignments will always be at zero locations in the table. One systematic way of making a valid assignment is first to select a row or column that contains only one zero square. We can make an assignment to that square and then draw lines through its row and column. From the uncovered rows and columns, we choose another row or column in which there is only one zero square. We make that assignment and continue the procedure until we have assigned each person or machine to one task.

Example 4 shows how to use the assignment method.

Example 4

ASSIGNMENT METHOD

First Printing wants to find the minimum total cost assignment of 3 jobs to 3 typesetters.

APPROACH ▶ The cost table shown earlier in this section is repeated here, and steps 1 through 4 are applied.

JOB \ TYPESETTER	A	B	C
R-34	$11	$14	$ 6
S-66	$ 8	$10	$11
T-50	$ 9	$12	$ 7

SOLUTION ▶

Step 1A: Using the previous table, subtract the smallest number in each row from every number in the row. The result is shown in the table on the left.

JOB \ TYPESETTER	A	B	C
R-34	5	8	0
S-66	0	2	3
T-50	2	5	0

JOB \ TYPESETTER	A	B	C
R-34	5	6	0
S-66	0	0	3
T-50	2	3	0

Step 1B: Using the above left table, subtract the smallest number in each column from every number in the column. The result is shown in the table on the right.

Step 2: Draw the minimum number of vertical and horizontal straight lines needed to cover all zeros. Because two lines suffice, the solution is not optimal.

JOB \ TYPESETTER	A	B	C
R-34	5	6	0
S-66	0	0	3
T-50	②	3	0

Smallest uncovered number

Step 3: Subtract the smallest uncovered number (2 in this table) from every other uncovered number and add it to numbers at the intersection of two lines.

JOB \ TYPESETTER	A	B	C
R-34	3	4	0
S-66	0	0	5
T-50	0	1	0

Return to step 2. Cover the zeros with straight lines again.

JOB \ TYPESETTER	A	B	C
R-34	3	4	0
S-66	0	0	
T-50	0	1	0

Because three lines are necessary, an optimal assignment can be made (see Step 4). Assign R-34 to person C, S-66 to person B, and T-50 to person A. Referring to the original cost table, we see that:

$$\text{Minimum cost} = \$6 + \$10 + \$9 = \$25$$

INSIGHT ▶ If we had assigned S-66 to typesetter A, we could not assign T-50 to a zero location.

LEARNING EXERCISE ▶ If it costs \$10 for Typesetter C to complete Job R-34 (instead of \$6), how does the solution change? [Answer: R-34 to A, S-66 to B, T-50 to C; cost = \$28.]

RELATED PROBLEMS ▶ 15.3–15.9 (15.11–15.14 are available in MyOMLab)

EXCEL OM Data File **Ch15Ex4.xls** can be found in MyOMLab.

Some assignment problems entail *maximizing* profit, effectiveness, or payoff of an assignment of people to tasks or of jobs to machines. An equivalent minimization problem can be obtained by converting every number in the table to an *opportunity loss*. To convert a maximizing problem to an equivalent minimization problem, we create a minimizing table by subtracting every number in the original payoff table from the largest single number in that table. We then proceed to step 1 of the four-step assignment method. Minimizing the opportunity loss produces the same assignment solution as the original maximization problem.

The problem of scheduling major league baseball umpiring crews from one series of games to the next is complicated by many restrictions on travel. The league strives to achieve two conflicting objectives: (1) balance crew assignments relatively evenly among all teams over the course of a season and (2) minimize travel costs. Using the assignment method, the time it takes the league to generate a schedule has been significantly decreased, and the quality of the schedule has improved.

Nicholas D. Cacchione/Shutterstock

Sequencing Jobs

Once jobs are *loaded* in a work center, as we just discussed, managers decide the *sequence* in which they are to be completed. Sequencing (often called *dispatching*) is accomplished by specifying the priority rules to use to release (dispatch) jobs to each work center.

Priority Rules for Sequencing Jobs

Priority rules are especially applicable for process-focused facilities such as clinics, print shops, and manufacturing job shops. The most popular priority rules are:

- **FCFS:** first come, first served. Jobs are completed in the order they arrived.
- **SPT:** shortest processing time. Jobs with the shortest processing times are assigned first.
- **EDD:** earliest due date. Earliest due date jobs are assigned first.
- **LPT:** longest processing time. Jobs with the longest processing time are assigned first.

Performance Criteria The choice of which priority rule to choose depends in part on how each rule performs on four criteria: the priority rules try to minimize *completion time*, maximize *facility utilization*, minimize *number of jobs in the system*, and minimize *job lateness*. These performance criteria incorporate the concept of flow time, which measures the time each job spends waiting plus time being processed. For example, if Job B waits 6 days for Job A to be processed and then takes 2 more days of operation time itself, its flow time would be $6 + 2 = 8$ days. The performance criteria are measured as:

$$\text{Average completion time} = \frac{\text{Sum of total flow time}}{\text{Number of jobs}} \quad (15\text{-}1)$$

$$\text{Utilization metric} = \frac{\text{Total job work (processing) time}}{\text{Sum of total flow time}} \quad (15\text{-}2)$$

$$\text{Average number of jobs in the system} = \frac{\text{Sum of total flow time}}{\text{Total job work (processing) time}} \quad (15\text{-}3)$$

$$\text{Average job lateness} = \frac{\text{Total late days}}{\text{Number of jobs}} \quad (15\text{-}4)$$

Computing the lateness of a particular job involves assumptions about the start time during the day and the timing of delivering a completed job. Equation (15-5) assumes that today is a work day, work has not yet begun today, and a job finished by the end of a day can be delivered to the customer that same day.

$$\text{Job lateness} = \text{Max}\{0, \text{yesterday} + \text{flow time} - \text{due date}\} \quad (15\text{-}5)$$

For example, suppose that today is day 20 (thus yesterday was day 19). Job A is due tomorrow (day 21) and has a flow time of 1 day. That job would be considered to be completed on time, i.e., not late:

$$\text{Max}\{0, 19 + 1 - 21\} = \text{Max}\{0, -1\} = 0 \text{ days late.}$$

Meanwhile, Job B is due on day 32 and has a flow time of 15 days. The lateness of Job B would be:

$$\text{Max}\{0, 19 + 15 - 32\} = \text{Max}\{0, 2\} = 2 \text{ days late.}$$

We will examine four of the most popular priority rules in Example 5.

Sequencing
Determining the order in which jobs should be done at each work center.

Priority rules
Rules used to determine the sequence of jobs in process-oriented facilities.

Flow time
The time between the release of a job to a work center until the job is finished.

Example 5 | PRIORITY RULES FOR DISPATCHING

Five architectural rendering jobs are waiting to be assigned at Avanti Sethi Architects. Their work (processing) times and due dates are given in the following table. The firm wants to determine the sequence of processing according to (1) FCFS, (2) SPT, (3) EDD, and (4) LPT rules. Jobs were assigned a letter in the order they arrived. Today is day 1, and work begins today.

JOB	JOB WORK (PROCESSING) TIME (DAYS)	JOB DUE DATE (DAYS)
A	6	8
B	2	6
C	8	18
D	3	15
E	9	23

APPROACH ▶   Each of the four priority rules is examined in turn. Four measures of effectiveness can be computed for each rule and then compared to see which rule is best for the company.

SOLUTION ▶

1. The *FCFS* sequence shown in the next table is simply A–B–C–D–E.

JOB SEQUENCE	JOB WORK (PROCESSING) TIME	FLOW TIME	JOB DUE DATE	JOB LATENESS
A	6	6	8	0
B	2	8	6	2
C	8	16	18	0
D	3	19	15	4
E	9	28	23	5
	28	77		11

The FCFS rule results in the following measures of effectiveness:

a. Average completion time $= \dfrac{\text{Sum of total flow time}}{\text{Number of jobs}}$

$= \dfrac{77 \text{ days}}{5} = 15.4 \text{ days}$

b. Utilization metric $= \dfrac{\text{Total job work (processing) time}}{\text{Sum of total flow time}}$

$= \dfrac{28}{77} = 36.4\%$

c. Average number of jobs in the system $= \dfrac{\text{Sum of total flow time}}{\text{Total job work (processing) time}}$

$= \dfrac{77 \text{ days}}{28 \text{ days}} = 2.75 \text{ jobs}$

d. Average job lateness $= \dfrac{\text{Total late days}}{\text{Number of jobs}} = \dfrac{11}{5} = 2.2 \text{ days}$

2. The *SPT* rule shown in the next table results in the sequence B–D–A–C–E. Orders are sequenced according to processing time, with the highest priority given to the shortest job.

JOB SEQUENCE	JOB WORK (PROCESSING) TIME	FLOW TIME	JOB DUE DATE	JOB LATENESS
B	2	2	6	0
D	3	5	15	0
A	6	11	8	3
C	8	19	18	1
E	9	28	23	5
	28	65		9

Measurements of effectiveness for SPT are:

a. Average completion time $= \dfrac{65}{5} = 13 \text{ days}$

b. Utilization metric $= \dfrac{28}{65} = 43.1\%$

c. Average number of jobs in the system $= \dfrac{65}{28} = 2.32 \text{ jobs}$

d. Average job lateness $= \dfrac{9}{5} = 1.8 \text{ days}$

LO 15.4 *Name* and describe each of the priority sequencing rules

3. The *EDD* rule shown in the next table gives the sequence B–A–D–C–E. Note that jobs are ordered by earliest due date first.

JOB SEQUENCE	JOB WORK (PROCESSING) TIME	FLOW TIME	JOB DUE DATE	JOB LATENESS
B	2	2	6	0
A	6	8	8	0
D	3	11	15	0
C	8	19	18	1
E	9	28	23	5
	28	68		6

Measurements of effectiveness for EDD are:

a. Average completion time $= \dfrac{68}{5} = 13.6$ days

b. Utilization metric $= \dfrac{28}{68} = 41.2\%$

c. Average number of jobs in the system $= \dfrac{68}{28} = 2.43$ jobs

d. Average job lateness $= \dfrac{6}{5} = 1.2$ days

4. The *LPT* rule shown in the next table results in the order E–C–A–D–B.

JOB SEQUENCE	JOB WORK (PROCESSING) TIME	FLOW TIME	JOB DUE DATE	JOB LATENESS
E	9	9	23	0
C	8	17	18	0
A	6	23	8	15
D	3	26	15	11
B	2	28	6	22
	28	103		48

Measures of effectiveness for LPT are:

a. Average completion time $= \dfrac{103}{5} = 20.6$ days

b. Utilization metric $= \dfrac{28}{103} = 27.2\%$

c. Average number of jobs in the system $= \dfrac{103}{28} = 3.68$ jobs

d. Average job lateness $= \dfrac{48}{5} = 9.6$ days

The results of these four rules are summarized in the following table:

RULE	AVERAGE COMPLETION TIME (DAYS)	UTILIZATION METRIC (%)	AVERAGE NUMBER OF JOBS IN SYSTEM	AVERAGE LATENESS (DAYS)
FCFS	15.4	36.4	2.75	2.2
SPT	13.0	43.1	2.32	1.8
EDD	13.6	41.2	2.43	1.2
LPT	20.6	27.2	3.68	9.6

INSIGHT ▶ LPT is the least effective measurement for sequencing for the Avanti Sethi firm. SPT is superior in 3 measures, and EDD is superior in the fourth (average lateness).

LEARNING EXERCISE ▶ If job A takes 7 days (instead of 6), how do the 4 measures of effectiveness change under the FCFS rule? [Answer: 16.4 days, 35.4%, 2.83 jobs, 2.8 days late.]

RELATED PROBLEMS ▶ 15.15, 15.17a–d, 15.18, 15.19 (15.15 alternate, 15.24 are available in MyOMLab)

EXCEL OM Data File Ch15Ex5.xls can be found in MyOMLab.

ACTIVE MODEL 15.1 This example is further illustrated in Active Model 15.1 in MyOMLab.

Your doctor may use a first-come, first-served priority rule satisfactorily. However, such a rule may be less than optimal for this emergency room. What priority rule might be best, and why? What priority rule is often used on TV hospital dramas?

Tyler Olson/Fotolia

The results in Example 5 are typically true in the real world also. No one sequencing rule always excels on all criteria. Experience indicates the following:

1. **Shortest processing time** is generally the best technique for minimizing job flow and minimizing the average number of jobs in the system. Its chief disadvantage is that long-duration jobs may be continuously pushed back in priority in favor of short-duration jobs. Customers may view this dimly, and a periodic adjustment for longer jobs must be made.
2. **First come, first served** does not score well on most criteria (but neither does it score particularly poorly). It has the advantage, however, of appearing fair to customers, which is important in service systems.
3. **Earliest due date** minimizes maximum tardiness, which may be necessary for jobs that have a very heavy penalty after a certain date. In general, EDD works well when lateness is an issue.

Critical Ratio

Critical ratio (CR)

A sequencing rule that is an index number computed by dividing the time remaining until due date by the work time remaining.

For organizations that have due dates (such as manufacturers and many firms like your local printer and furniture re-upholsterer), the critical ratio for sequencing jobs is beneficial. The **critical ratio (CR)** is an index number computed by dividing the time remaining until due date by the work time remaining. As opposed to the priority rules, critical ratio is dynamic and easily updated. It tends to perform better than FCFS, SPT, EDD, or LPT on the average job-lateness criterion.

The critical ratio gives priority to jobs that must be done to keep shipping on schedule. A job with a low critical ratio (less than 1.0) is one that is falling behind schedule. If CR is exactly 1.0, the job is on schedule. A CR greater than 1.0 means the job is ahead of schedule and has some slack.

The formula for critical ratio is:

$$CR = \frac{\text{Time remaining}}{\text{Workdays remaining}} = \frac{\text{Due date} - \text{Today's date}}{\text{Work (lead) time remaining}} \tag{15-6}$$

Example 6 shows how to use the critical ratio.

Example 6

CRITICAL RATIO

Today is day 25 on Zyco Medical Testing Laboratories' production schedule. Three jobs are on order, as indicated here:

JOB	DUE DATE	WORKDAYS REMAINING
A	30	4
B	28	5
C	27	2

APPROACH ▶ Zyco wants to compute the critical ratios, using the formula for CR.

SOLUTION ▶

JOB	CRITICAL RATIO	PRIORITY ORDER
A	(30 − 25)/4 = 1.25	3
B	(28 − 25)/5 = .60	1
C	(27 − 25)/2 = 1.00	2

INSIGHT ▶ Job B has a critical ratio of less than 1, meaning it will be late unless expedited. Thus, it has the highest priority. Job C is on time, and job A has some slack. Once job B has been completed, we would recompute the critical ratios for jobs A and C to determine whether their priorities have changed.

LEARNING EXERCISE ▶ Today is day 24 (a day earlier) on Zyco's schedule. Recompute the CRs and determine the priorities. [Answer: 1.5, 0.8, 1.5; B is still number 1, but now jobs A and C are tied for second.]

RELATED PROBLEMS ▶ 15.16, 15.17e, 15.21

In most production scheduling systems, the critical-ratio rule can help do the following:

1. Determine the status of a specific job.
2. Establish relative priority among jobs on a common basis.
3. Adjust priorities (and revise schedules) automatically for changes in both demand and job progress.
4. Dynamically track job progress.

Sequencing *N* Jobs on Two Machines: Johnson's Rule

The next step in complexity is the case in which *N* jobs (where *N* is 2 or more) must go through two different machines or work centers in the same order. (Each work center only works on one job at a time.) This is called the *N*/2 problem.

Johnson's rule can be used to minimize the time for sequencing a group of jobs through two work centers. It also minimizes total idle time on the machines. *Johnson's rule* involves four steps:

Johnson's rule
An approach that minimizes the total time for sequencing a group of jobs through two work centers while minimizing total idle time in the work centers.

1. All jobs are to be listed, and the time that each requires on a machine is to be shown.
2. Select the job with the shortest activity time. If the shortest time lies with the first machine, the job is scheduled first. If the shortest time lies with the second machine, schedule the job last. Ties in activity times can be broken arbitrarily.
3. Once a job is scheduled, eliminate it.
4. Apply steps 2 and 3 to the remaining jobs, working toward the center of the sequence.

Example 7 shows how to apply Johnson's rule.

Example 7 | JOHNSON'S RULE

Five specialty jobs at a La Crosse, Wisconsin, tool and die shop must be processed through two work centers (drill press and lathe). The time for processing each job follows:

Work (processing) Time for Jobs (hours)

JOB	WORK CENTER 1 (DRILL PRESS)	WORK CENTER 2 (LATHE)
A	5	2
B	3	6
C	8	4
D	10	7
E	7	12

The owner, Niranjan Pati, wants to set the sequence to minimize his total time for the five jobs.

APPROACH ▶ Pati applies the four steps of Johnson's rule.

SOLUTION ▶

1. The job with the shortest processing time is A, in work center 2 (with a time of 2 hours). Because it is at the second center, schedule A last. Eliminate it from consideration.

				A

2. Job B has the next shortest time (3 hours). Because that time is at the first work center, we schedule it first and eliminate it from consideration.

B				A

LO 15.5 *Use Johnson's rule*

3. The next shortest time is job C (4 hours) on the second machine. Therefore, it is placed as late as possible.

B			C	A

4. There is a tie (at 7 hours) for the shortest remaining job. We can place E, which was on the first work center, first. Then D is placed in the last sequencing position:

B	E	D	C	A

The sequential times are:

Work center 1	3	7	10	8	5
Work center 2	6	12	7	4	2

The time-phased flow of this job sequence is best illustrated graphically:

Thus, the five jobs are completed in 35 hours.

INSIGHT ▶ The second work center will wait 3 hours for its first job, and it will also wait 1 hour after completing job B.

LEARNING EXERCISE ▶ If job C takes 8 hours in work center 2 (instead of 4 hours), what sequence is best? [Answer: B–E–C–D–A.]

RELATED PROBLEMS ▶ 15.20, 15.22, 15.23 (15.25 is available in MyOMLab)

EXCEL OM Data File **Ch15Ex7.xls** can be found in MyOMLab.

Limitations of Rule-Based Sequencing Systems

The scheduling techniques just discussed are rule-based techniques, but rule-based systems have a number of limitations. Among these are the following:

1. Scheduling is dynamic; therefore, rules need to be revised to adjust to changes in orders, process, equipment, product mix, and so forth.

2. Rules do not look upstream or downstream; idle resources and bottleneck resources in other departments may not be recognized.
3. Rules do not look beyond due dates. For instance, two orders may have the same due date. One order involves restocking a distributor and the other is a custom order that will shut down the customer's factory if not completed. Both may have the same due date, but clearly the custom order is more important.

Despite these limitations, schedulers often use sequencing rules such as SPT, EDD, or critical ratio. They apply these methods at each work center and then modify the sequence to deal with a multitude of real-world variables. They may do this manually or with finite capacity scheduling software.

Finite Capacity Scheduling (FCS)

Short-term scheduling systems are also called finite capacity scheduling.[2] Finite capacity scheduling (FCS) overcomes the disadvantages of systems based exclusively on rules by providing the scheduler with interactive computing and graphic output. In dynamic scheduling environments such as job shops (with high variety, low volume, and shared resources) we expect changes. But changes disrupt schedules. Operations managers are moving toward FCS systems that allow virtually instantaneous change by the operator. Improvements in communication on the shop floor are also enhancing the accuracy and speed of information necessary for effective control in job shops. Computer-controlled machines can monitor events and collect information in near real-time. This means the scheduler can make schedule changes based on up-to-the-minute information. These schedules are often displayed in Gantt chart form. In addition to including priority rule options, many of the current FCS systems also combine an "expert system" or simulation techniques and allow the scheduler to assign costs to various options. The scheduler has the flexibility to handle any situation, including order, labor, or machine changes.

The combining of planning and FCS data, priority rules, models to assist analysis, and Gantt chart output is shown in Figure 15.5.

Finite capacity scheduling allows delivery requirements to be based on today's conditions and today's orders, not according to some predefined rule. The scheduler determines what constitutes a "good" schedule. FCS software packages such as Lekin (shown in Figure 15.6), ProPlanner, Preactor, Asprova, Schedlyzer, and Jobplan are currently used at over 60% of U.S. plants.

Finite capacity scheduling (FCS)

Computerized short-term scheduling that overcomes the disadvantage of rule-based systems by providing the user with graphical interactive computing.

LO 15.6 *Define* finite capacity scheduling

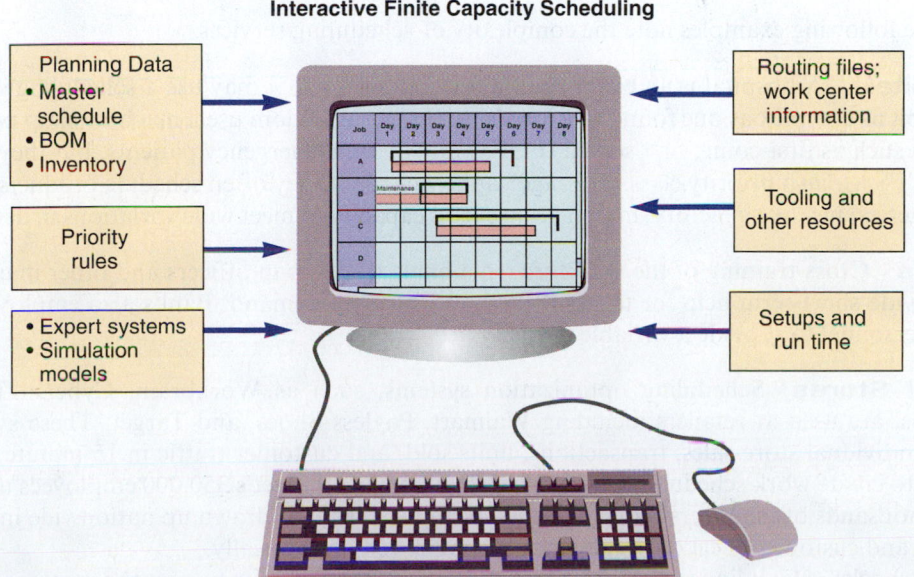

Interactive Finite Capacity Scheduling

Figure **15.5**

Finite Capacity Scheduling Systems Use Production Data to Generate Gantt Load Charts, and Work-in-Process Data That Can Be Manipulated by the User to Evaluate Schedule Alternatives

Screenshot from Lekin® Finite Capacity Scheduling Software. Reprinted with permission.

Figure **15.6**

Finite Capacity Scheduling (FCS) System

This Lekin® finite capacity scheduling software presents a schedule of the five jobs and the two work centers shown in Example 7 (pages 615–616) in Gantt chart form. The software is capable of using a variety of priority rules and many jobs. The Lekin software is available for free at **http://community.stern.nyu.edu/om/software/lekin/download.html** and can solve many of the problems at the end of this chapter.

Scheduling Services

STUDENT TIP ◆

Scheduling people to perform services can be even more complex than scheduling machines.

Scheduling service systems differs from scheduling manufacturing systems in several ways:

◆ In manufacturing, the scheduling emphasis is on machines and materials; in services, it is on staffing levels.

◆ Inventories can help smooth demand for manufacturers, but many service systems do not maintain inventories.

◆ Services are labor intensive, and the demand for this labor can be highly variable.

◆ Legal considerations, such as wage and hour laws and union contracts that limit hours worked per shift, week, or month, constrain scheduling decisions.

◆ Because services usually schedule people (rather than material), social, fatigue, seniority, and status issues complicate scheduling.

The following examples note the complexity of scheduling services.

VIDEO 15.2
Scheduling at Hard Rock Cafe

Hospitals A hospital is an example of a service facility that may use a scheduling system every bit as complex as one found in a job shop. Hospitals seldom use a machine shop priority system such as first come, first served (FCFS) for treating emergency patients, but they often use FCFS *within* a priority class, a "triage" approach. And they often schedule products (such as surgeries) just like a factory, maintaining excess capacity to meet wide variations in demand.

Banks Cross-training of the workforce in a bank allows loan officers and other managers to provide short-term help for tellers if there is a surge in demand. Banks also employ part-time personnel to provide a variable capacity.

Retail Stores Scheduling optimization systems, such as Workbrain, Cybershift, and Kronos, are used at retailers including Walmart, Payless Shoes, and Target. These systems track individual store sales, transactions, units sold, and customer traffic in 15-minute increments to create work schedules. Walmart's 2.2 million and Target's 350,000 employees used to take thousands of managers' hours to schedule; now staffing is drawn up nationwide in a few hours, and customer checkout experience has improved dramatically.

Starbucks' scheduling software is discussed in the *OM in Action* box on the next page.

OM in Action | Starbucks' Controversial Scheduling Software

Starbucks recently announced revisions to the way the company schedules its 130,000 baristas, saying it wanted to improve "stability and consistency" in work hours from week to week. The company intends to curb the much-loathed practice of "clopening," or workers closing the store late at night and returning just a few hours later to reopen. All work hours must be posted at least one week in advance, a policy that has been only loosely followed in the past. Baristas with more than an hour's commute will be given the option to transfer to more convenient locations, and scheduling software will be revised to allow more input from managers.

The revisions came in response to a newspaper article about a single mother struggling to keep up with erratic hours set by automated software. A growing push to curb scheduling practices, enabled by sophisticated software, has caused havoc in employees' lives: giving only a few days' notice of working hours; sending workers home early when sales are slow; and shifting hours significantly from week to week. Those practices have been common at Starbucks. And many other chains use even more severe methods, such as requiring workers to have "open availability," or be able to work anytime they are needed, or to stay "on call," meaning they only find out that morning if they are needed.

Starbucks prides itself on progressive labor practices, such as offering health benefits, free online degrees at Arizona State University, and stock. But baristas across the country say that their actual working conditions vary

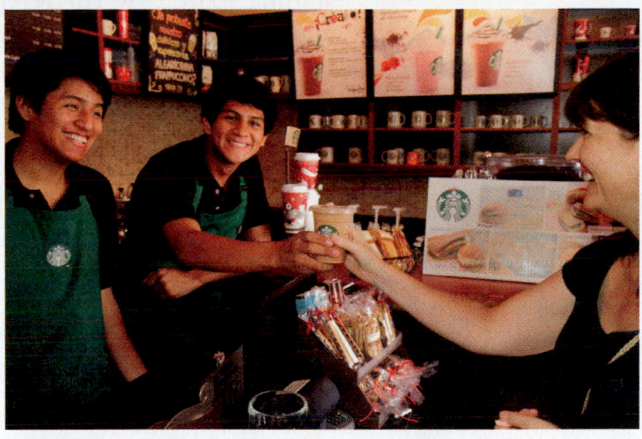

RosalreneBetancourt 7/Alamy

wildly, and that the company often fails to live up to its professed ideals, by refusing to offer any guaranteed hours to part-time workers and keeping many workers' pay at minimum wage. Scheduling has been an issue for years. Said a former company executive: "Labor is the biggest controllable cost for front-line operators, who are under incredible pressure to hit financial targets."

Sources: New York Times (September 24, 2015 and August 15, 2014) and *BloombergBusinessweek* (August 15, 2014).

Airlines   Two of the constraints airlines face when scheduling flight crews are: (1) a complex set of FAA work-time limitations and (2) union contracts that guarantee crew pay for some number of hours each day or each trip. Planners must also make efficient use of their other expensive resource: aircraft. These schedules are typically built using linear programming models.

24/7 Operations   Emergency hotlines, police/fire departments, telephone operations, and mail-order businesses (such as L.L.Bean) schedule employees 24 hours a day, 7 days a week. To allow management flexibility in staffing, sometimes part-time workers can be employed. This provides both benefits (in using odd shift lengths or matching anticipated workloads) and difficulties (from the large number of possible alternatives in terms of days off, lunch hour times, rest periods, starting times). Most companies use computerized scheduling systems to cope with these complexities.

Patricia McDonnell/AP Images

Good scheduling in the health care industry can help keep nurses happy and costs contained. Here, nurses in Boston protest nurse-staffing levels in Massachusetts hospitals. Shortages of qualified nurses is a chronic problem.

Scheduling Service Employees with Cyclical Scheduling

A number of techniques and algorithms exist for scheduling service-sector employees when staffing needs vary. This is typically the case for police officers, nurses, restaurant staff, tellers, and retail sales clerks. Managers, trying to set a timely and efficient schedule that keeps personnel happy, can spend substantial time each month developing employee schedules. Such schedules often consider a fairly long planning period (say, 6 weeks). One approach that is workable yet simple is *cyclical scheduling*.

LO 15.7 *Use the cyclical scheduling technique*

Cyclical Scheduling Cyclical scheduling focuses on developing varying (inconsistent) schedules with the minimum number of workers. In these cases, each employee is assigned to a shift and has prescribed time off. Let's look at Example 8.

Example 8

CYCLICAL SCHEDULING

Hospital administrator Doris Laughlin wants to staff the oncology ward using a standard 5-day work-week with two consecutive days off, but also wants to minimize the staff. However, as in most hospitals, she faces an inconsistent demand. Weekends have low usage. Doctors tend to work early in the week, and patients peak on Wednesday then taper off.

APPROACH ▶ Doris must first establish staffing requirements. Then the following five-step process is applied.

SOLUTION ▶

1. Doris has determined that the necessary daily staffing requirements are:

DAY	MONDAY	TUESDAY	WEDNESDAY	THURSDAY	FRIDAY	SATURDAY	SUNDAY
Staff required	5	5	6	5	4	3	3

2. Identify the two consecutive days that have the *lowest total requirement* and circle these. Assign these two days off to the first employee. In this case, the first employee has Saturday and Sunday off because 3 plus 3 is the *lowest sum* of any 2 days. In the case of a tie, choose the days with the lowest adjacent requirement, or by first assigning Saturday and Sunday as an "off" day. If there are more than one, make an arbitrary decision.

3. We now have an employee working each of the uncircled days; therefore, make a new row for the next employee by subtracting 1 from the first row (because one day has been worked)—except for the circled days (which represent the days not worked) and any day that has a zero. That is, do not subtract from a circled day or a day that has a value of zero.

4. In the new row, identify the two consecutive days that have the lowest total requirement and circle them. Assign the next employee to the remaining days.

5. Repeat the process (Steps 3 and 4) until all staffing requirements are met.

	MONDAY	TUESDAY	WEDNESDAY	THURSDAY	FRIDAY	SATURDAY	SUNDAY
Employee 1	5	5	6	5	4	③	③
Employee 2	4	4	5	4	3	③	③
Employee 3	3	3	4	3	②	③	3
Employee 4	2	2	3	②	②	3	2
Employee 5	①	①	2	2	2	2	1
Employee 6	1	1	1	1	1	①	⓪
Employee 7						1	
Capacity (measured in number of employees)	5	5	6	5	4	3	3
Excess capacity	0	0	0	0	0	1	0

Doris needs six full-time employees to meet the staffing needs and one employee to work Saturday.

Notice that capacity (number of employees) equals requirements, provided an employee works overtime on Saturday, or a part-time employee is hired for Saturday.

INSIGHT ▶ Doris has implemented an efficient scheduling system that accommodates 2 consecutive days off for every employee.

LEARNING EXERCISE ▶ If Doris meets the staffing requirement for Saturday with a full-time employee, how does she schedule that employee? [Answer: That employee can have any 2 days off, except Saturday, and capacity will exceed requirements by 1 person each day the employee works (except Saturday).]

RELATED PROBLEMS ▶ 15.26, 15.27

Using the approach in Example 8, Colorado General Hospital saved an average of 10 to 15 hours a month and found these added advantages: (1) no computer was needed, (2) the nurses were happy with the schedule, (3) the cycles could be changed seasonally to accommodate avid skiers, and (4) recruiting was easier because of predictability and flexibility. This approach yields an optimum, although there may be multiple optimal solutions.

Other cyclical scheduling techniques have been developed to aid service scheduling. Some approaches use linear programming: This is how Hard Rock Cafe schedules its services (see the Video Case Study at the end of this chapter). There is a natural bias in scheduling to use tools that are understood and yield solutions that are accepted.

Summary

Scheduling involves the timing of operations to achieve the efficient movement of units through a system. This chapter addressed the issues of short-term scheduling in process-focused and service environments. We saw that process-focused facilities are production systems in which products are made to order and that scheduling tasks in them can become complex. Several aspects and approaches to scheduling, loading, and sequencing of jobs were introduced. These ranged from Gantt charts and the assignment method of scheduling to a series of priority rules, the critical-ratio rule, Johnson's rule for sequencing, and finite capacity scheduling.

Service systems generally differ from manufacturing systems. This leads to the use of first-come, first-served rules and appointment and reservation systems, as well as linear programming for matching capacity to demand in service environments.

Key Terms

Loading (p. 604)
Input–output control (p. 606)
ConWIP cards (p. 606)
Gantt charts (p. 607)
Assignment method (p. 608)
Sequencing (p. 611)
Priority rules (p. 611)
Flow time (p. 611)
Critical ratio (CR) (p. 614)
Johnson's rule (p. 615)
Finite capacity scheduling
(FCS) (p. 617)

Ethical Dilemma

Scheduling people to work second and third shifts (evening and "graveyard") is a problem in almost every 24-hour company. Medical and ergonomic data indicate the body does not respond well to significant shifts in its natural circadian rhythm of sleep.

There are also significant long-run health issues with frequent changes in work and sleep cycles.

Consider yourself the manager of a nonunion steel mill that must operate 24-hour days, and where the physical demands are such that 8-hour days are preferable to 10- or 12-hour days.

Your empowered employees have decided that they want to work weekly rotating shifts. That is, they want a repeating work cycle of 1 week, 7 A.M. to 3 P.M., followed by a second week from 3 P.M. to 11 P.M., and the third week from 11 P.M. to 7 P.M. You are sure this is not a good idea in terms of both productivity and the long-term health of the employees. If you do not accept their decision, you undermine the work empowerment program, generate a morale issue, and perhaps, more significantly, generate few more votes for a union. What is the ethical position and what do you do?

Marcel Mooij/Shutterstock

Discussion Questions

1. What is the overall objective of scheduling?
2. List the four criteria for determining the effectiveness of a *scheduling* decision. How do these criteria relate to the four criteria for *sequencing* decisions?
3. Describe what is meant by "loading" work centers. What are the two ways work centers can be loaded? What are two techniques used in loading?
4. Name five priority sequencing rules. Explain how each works to assign jobs.
5. What are the advantages and disadvantages of the shortest processing time (SPT) rule?
6. What is a due date?
7. Explain the terms *flow time* and *lateness*.
8. Which shop-floor scheduling rule would you prefer to apply if you were the leader of the only team of experts charged with defusing several time bombs scattered throughout your building? You can see the bombs; they are of different types. You can tell how long each one will take to defuse. Discuss.
9. When is Johnson's rule best applied in job-shop scheduling?
10. State the four effectiveness measures for dispatching rules.
11. What are the steps of the assignment method of linear programming?
12. What are the advantages to finite capacity scheduling?
13. What is input–output control?

Using Software for Short-Term Scheduling

In addition to the commercial software we noted in this chapter, short-term scheduling problems can be solved with the Excel OM software that comes free with this text. POM for Windows also includes a scheduling module. The use of each of these programs is explained next.

✘ USING EXCEL OM

Excel OM has two modules that help solve short-term scheduling problems: Assignment and Job Shop Scheduling. The Assignment module is illustrated in Programs 15.1 and 15.2. The input screen, using the Example 4 data, appears first, as Program 15.1. Once the data are all entered, we choose the **Data tab** command, followed by the **Solver** command. Excel's Solver uses linear programming to optimize assignment problems. (So select Simplex LP.)

The constraints are also shown in Program 15.1. We then select the **Solve** command; the solution appears in Program 15.2.

Excel OM's Job Shop Scheduling module is illustrated in Program 15.3. Program 15.3 uses Example 5's data. Because jobs are listed in the sequence in which they arrived (see column A), the results are for the FCFS rule. Program 15.3 also shows some of the formulas (columns F, G, H, I, J) used in the calculations.

To solve with the SPT rule, we need four intermediate steps: (1) Select (that is, highlight) the data in columns A, B, C for all jobs; (2) invoke the **Data** command; (3) invoke the **Sort** command; and (4) sort by **Time** (column C) in *ascending* order. To solve for EDD, Step 4 changes to sort by **Due Date** (column D) in *ascending* order. Finally, for an LPT solution, Step 4 becomes sort by **Due Date** (column D) in *descending* order.

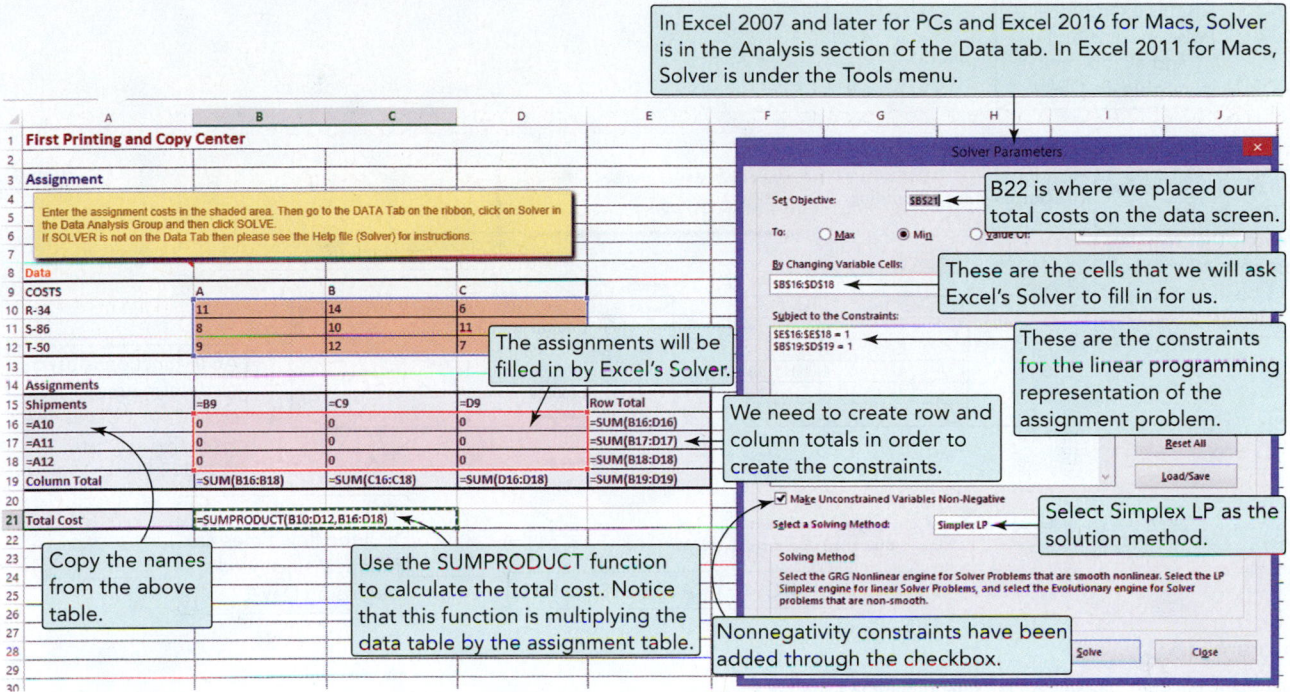

Program **15.1**

Excel OM's Assignment Module Using Example 4's Data

After entering the problem data in the yellow area, select Data, then Solver.

Program **15.2**

Excel OM Output Screen for Assignment Problem Described in Program 15.1

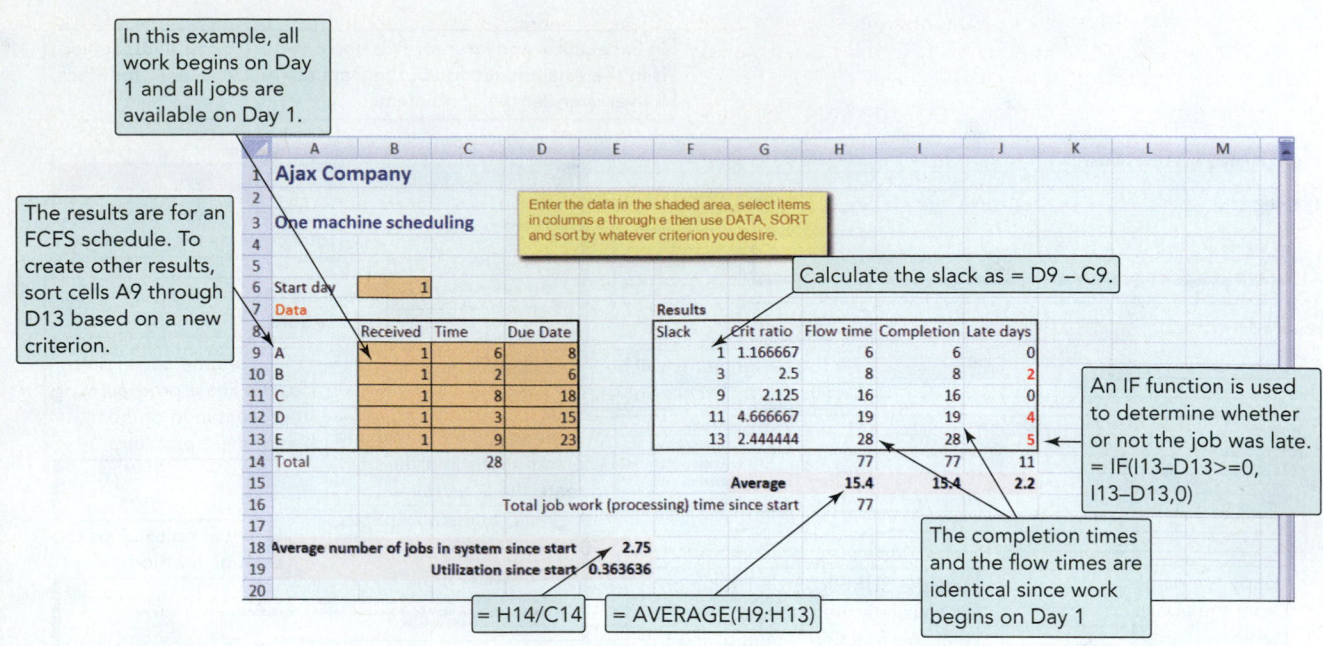

Program 15.3

Excel OM's Job Shop Scheduling Module Applied to Example 5's Data

P USING POM FOR WINDOWS

POM for Windows can handle both categories of scheduling problems we see in this chapter. Its Assignment module is used to solve the traditional one-to-one assignment problem of people to tasks, machines to jobs, and so on. Its Job Shop Scheduling module can solve a one- or two-machine job-shop problem. Available priority rules include SPT, FCFS, EDD, and LPT. Each can be examined in turn once the data are all entered. Refer to Appendix IV for specifics regarding POM for Windows.

Solved Problems   Virtual Office Hours help is available in MyOMLab.

SOLVED PROBLEM 15.1

King Finance Corporation, headquartered in New York, wants to assign three recently hired college graduates, Julie Jones, Al Smith, and Pat Wilson, to regional offices. However, the firm also has an opening in New York and would send one of the three there if it were more economical than a move to Omaha, Dallas, or Miami. It will cost $1,000 to relocate Jones to New York, $800 to relocate Smith there, and $1,500 to move Wilson. What is the optimal assignment of personnel to offices?

HIREE \ OFFICE	OMAHA	MIAMI	DALLAS
Jones	$800	$1,100	$1,200
Smith	$500	$1,600	$1,300
Wilson	$500	$1,000	$2,300

SOLUTION

a) The cost table has a fourth column to represent New York. To "balance" the problem, we add a "dummy" row (person) with a zero relocation cost to each city.

HIREE \ OFFICE	OMAHA	MIAMI	DALLAS	NEW YORK
Jones	$800	$1,100	$1,200	$1,000
Smith	$500	$1,600	$1,300	$ 800
Wilson	$500	$1,000	$2,300	$1,500
Dummy	0	0	0	0

b) Subtract the smallest number in each row and cover all zeros (column subtraction of each column's zero will give the same numbers and therefore is not necessary):

HIREE \ OFFICE	OMAHA	MIAMI	DALLAS	NEW YORK
Jones	0	300	400	200
Smith	0	1,100	800	300
Wilson	0	500	1,800	1,000
Dummy	0	0	0	0

c) Only 2 lines cover, so subtract the smallest uncovered number (200) from all uncovered numbers, and add it to each square where two lines intersect. Then cover all zeros:

OFFICE / HIRE	OMAHA	MIAMI	DALLAS	NEW YORK
Jones	0	100	200	0
Smith	0	900	600	100
Wilson	0	300	1,600	800
Dummy	200	0	0	0

d) Only 3 lines cover, so subtract the smallest uncovered number (100) from all uncovered numbers, and add it to each square where two lines intersect. Then cover all zeros:

OFFICE / HIRE	OMAHA	MIAMI	DALLAS	NEW YORK
Jones	0	0	100	0
Smith	0	800	500	100
Wilson	0	200	1,500	800
Dummy	300	0	0	100

e) Still only 3 lines cover, so subtract the smallest uncovered number (100) from all uncovered numbers, add it to squares where two lines intersect, and cover all zeros:

OFFICE / HIRE	OMAHA	MIAMI	DALLAS	NEW YORK
Jones	100	0	100	0
Smith	0	700	400	0
Wilson	0	100	1,400	700
Dummy	400	0	0	100

f) Because it takes four lines to cover all zeros, an optimal assignment can be made at zero squares. We assign:

Wilson to Omaha
Jones to Miami
Dummy (no one) to Dallas
Smith to New York

$$\text{Cost} = \$500 + \$1,100 + \$0 + \$800$$
$$= \$2,400$$

SOLVED PROBLEM 15.2

A defense contractor in Dallas has six jobs awaiting processing. Processing time and due dates are given in the table. Assume that jobs arrive in the order shown. Set the processing sequence according to FCFS and evaluate. Start date is day 1.

JOB	JOB PROCESSING TIME (DAYS)	JOB DUE DATE (DAYS)
A	6	22
B	12	14
C	14	30
D	2	18
E	10	25
F	4	34

SOLUTION

FCFS has the sequence A–B–C–D–E–F.

JOB SEQUENCE	JOB PROCESSING TIME	FLOW TIME	DUE DATE	JOB LATENESS
A	6	6	22	0
B	12	18	14	4
C	14	32	30	2
D	2	34	18	16
E	10	44	25	19
F	4	48	34	14
	48	182		55

1. Average completion time = 182/6 = 30.33 days
2. Average number of jobs in system = 182/48 = 3.79 jobs
3. Average job lateness = 55/6 = 9.16 days
4. Utilization = 48/182 = 26.4%

SOLVED PROBLEM 15.3

The Dallas firm in Solved Problem 15.2 also wants to consider job sequencing by the SPT priority rule. Apply SPT to the same data, and provide a recommendation.

SOLUTION

SPT has the sequence D–F–A–E–B–C.

JOB SEQUENCE	JOB PROCESSING TIME	FLOW TIME	DUE DATE	JOB LATENESS
D	2	2	18	0
F	4	6	34	0
A	6	12	22	0
E	10	22	25	0
B	12	34	14	20
C	14	48	30	18
	48	124		38

1. Average completion time = 124/6 = 20.67 days
2. Average number of jobs in system = 124/48 = 2.58 jobs
3. Average job lateness = 38/6 = 6.33 days
4. Utilization = 48/124 = 38.7%

SPT is superior to FCFS in this case on all four measures. If we were to also analyze EDD, we would, however, find its average job lateness to be lowest at 5.5 days. SPT is a good recommendation. SPT's major disadvantage is that it makes long jobs wait, sometimes for a long time.

SOLVED PROBLEM 15.4

Use Johnson's rule to find the optimum sequence for processing the jobs shown through two work centers. Times at each center are in hours.

JOB	WORK CENTER 1	WORK CENTER 2
A	6	12
B	3	7
C	18	9
D	15	14
E	16	8
F	10	15

SOLUTION

B	A	F	D	C	E

The sequential times are:

Work center 1	3	6	10	15	18	16
Work center 2	7	12	15	14	9	8

SOLVED PROBLEM 15.5

Illustrate the throughput time and idle time at the two work centers in Solved Problem 15.4 by constructing a time-phased chart.

SOLUTION

Problems   *Note:* **Px** means the problem may be solved with POM for Windows and/or Excel OM.

Problems 15.1–15.14 relate to Loading Jobs

··15.1   Ron Satterfield's excavation company uses both Gantt scheduling charts and Gantt load charts.

a) Today, which is the end of day 7, Ron is reviewing the Gantt chart depicting these schedules:
- Job #151 was scheduled to begin on day 3 and to take 6 days. As of now, it is 1 day ahead of schedule.
- Job #177 was scheduled to begin on day 1 and take 4 days. It is currently on time.
- Job #179 was scheduled to start on day 7 and take 2 days. It actually got started on day 6 and is progressing according to plan.
- Job #211 was scheduled to begin on day 5, but missing equipment delayed it until day 6. It is progressing as expected and should take 3 days.
- Job #215 was scheduled to begin on day 4 and take 5 days. It got started on time but has since fallen behind 2 days.

Draw the Gantt scheduling chart for the activities above.

b) Ron now wants to use a Gantt load chart to see how much work is scheduled in each of his three work teams: Able, Baker, and Charlie. Five jobs constitute the current workload for these three work teams: Job #250, requiring 48 hours and #275 requiring 32 hours for Work Team Able; Jobs #210 and #280, requiring 16 and 24 hours, respectively, for Team Baker; and Job #225, requiring 40 hours, for Team Charlie.

Prepare the Gantt load chart for these activities.

··15.2   First Printing and Copy Center has 4 more jobs to be scheduled, in addition to those shown in Example 3 in the chapter. Production scheduling personnel are reviewing the Gantt chart at the end of day 4.
- Job D was scheduled to begin early on day 2 and to end on the middle of day 9. As of now (the review point after day 4), it is 2 days ahead of schedule.
- Job E should begin on day 1 and end on day 3. It is on time.
- Job F was to begin on day 3, but maintenance forced a delay of 1½ days. The job should now take 5 full days. It is now on schedule.
- Job G is a day behind schedule. It started at the beginning of day 2 and should require 6 days to complete.

Develop a Gantt schedule chart for First Printing and Copy Center.

·15.3   The Green Cab Company has a taxi waiting at each of four cabstands in Evanston, Illinois. Four customers have called and requested service. The distances, in miles, from the waiting taxis to the customers are given in the following table. Find the optimal assignment of taxis to customers so as to minimize total driving distances to the customers.

	CUSTOMER			
CAB SITE	**A**	**B**	**C**	**D**
Stand 1	7	3	4	8
Stand 2	5	4	6	5
Stand 3	6	7	9	6
Stand 4	8	6	7	4	**Px**

·15.4   J.C. Howard's medical testing company in Kansas wishes to assign a set of jobs to a set of machines. The following table provides the production data of each machine when performing the specific job:

	MACHINE			
JOB	**A**	**B**	**C**	**D**
1	7	9	8	10
2	10	9	7	6
3	11	5	9	6
4	9	11	5	8

a) Determine the assignment of jobs to machines that will *maximize* total production.

b) What is the total production of your assignments? **Px**

·15.5   The Johnny Ho Manufacturing Company in Columbus, Ohio, is putting out four new electronic components. Each of Ho's four plants has the capacity to add one more product to its current line of electronic parts. The unit-manufacturing costs for producing the different parts at the four plants are shown in the accompanying table. How should Ho assign the new products to the plants to minimize manufacturing costs?

ELECTRONIC COMPONENT	PLANT			
	1	**2**	**3**	**4**
C53	$0.10	$0.12	$0.13	$0.11
C81	0.05	0.06	0.04	0.08
D5	0.32	0.40	0.31	0.30
D44	0.17	0.14	0.19	0.15	**Px**

·15.6   Jamison Day Consultants has been entrusted with the task of evaluating a business plan that has been divided into four sections—marketing, finance, operations, and human resources. Chris, Steve, Juana, and Rebecca form the evaluation team. Each of them has expertise in a certain field and tends to finish that section faster. The estimated times taken by each team member for each section have been outlined in the table below. Further information states that each of these individuals is paid $60/hour.

a) Assign each member to a different section such that Jamison Consultants's overall cost is minimized.

b) What is the total cost of these assignments?

Times Taken by Team Members for Different Sections (minutes)

	MARKETING	FINANCE	OPERATIONS	HR
Chris	80	120	125	140
Steve	20	115	145	160
Juana	40	100	85	45
Rebecca	65	35	25	75	**Px**

··15.7   The Baton Rouge Police Department has five detective squads available for assignment to five open crime cases. The chief of detectives, Jose Noguera, wishes to assign the squads so that the total time to conclude the cases is minimized. The average number of days, based on past performance, for each squad to complete each case is as follows:

	CASE				
SQUAD	**A**	**B**	**C**	**D**	**E**
1	14	7	3	7	27
2	20	7	12	6	30
3	10	3	4	5	21
4	8	12	7	12	21
5	13	25	24	26	8

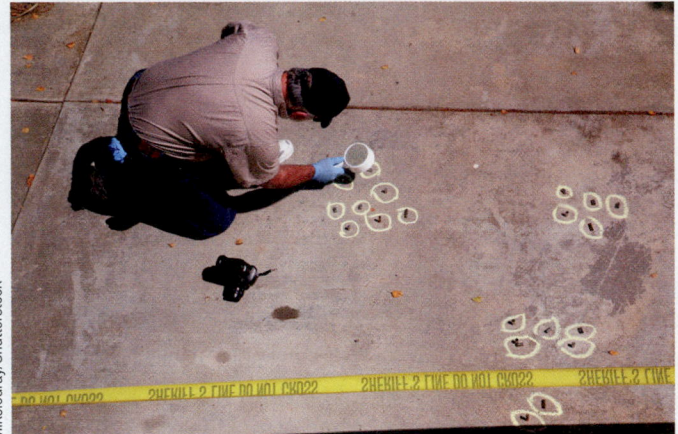

Mikeledray/Shutterstock

Each squad is composed of different types of specialists, and whereas one squad may be very effective in certain types of cases, it may be almost useless in others.

a) Solve the problem by using the assignment method.

b) Assign the squads to the above cases, but with the constraint that squad 5 cannot work on case E because of a conflict. **Px**

• **15.8** Tigers Sports Club has to select four separate co-ed doubles teams to participate in an inter-club table tennis tournament. The pre-selection results in the selection of a group of four men—Raul, Jack, Gray, and Ajay—and four women—Barbara, Dona, Stella, and Jackie. Now, the task ahead lies in pairing these men and women in the best fashion. The table below shows a matrix that has been designed for this purpose, indicating how each of the men complements the game of each of the women. A higher score indicates a higher degree of compatibility in the games of the two individuals concerned. Find the best pairs.

Game Compatibility Matrix

	BARBARA	DONA	STELLA	JACKIE
Raul	30	20	10	40
Jack	70	10	60	70
Gray	40	20	50	40
Ajay	60	70	30	90

Px

••• **15.9** Daniel Glaser, chairman of the College of San Antonio's business department, needs to assign professors to courses next semester. As a criterion for judging who should teach each course, Professor Glaser reviews the past 2 years' teaching evaluations (which were filled out by students). Since each of the four professors taught each of the four courses at one time or another during the 2-year period, Glaser is able to record a course rating for each instructor. These ratings are shown in the following table.

a) Find the assignment of professors to courses to maximize the overall teaching rating.

b) Assign the professors to the courses with the exception that Professor Fisher cannot teach statistics. **Px**

	COURSE			
PROFESSOR	STATISTICS	MANAGEMENT	FINANCE	ECONOMICS
W. W. Fisher	90	65	95	40
D. Golhar	70	60	80	75
Z. Hug	85	40	80	60
N. K. Rustagi	55	80	65	55

•• **15.10** Lifang Wu owns an automated machine shop that makes precision auto parts. He has just compiled an input–output

report for the grinding work center. Complete this report and analyze the results.

Input–Output Report

PERIOD	1	2	3	4	TOTAL
Planned input	80	80	100	100	
Actual input	85	85	85	85	
Deviation					
Planned output	90	90	90	90	
Actual output	85	85	80	80	
Deviation					
Initial backlog: 30					

Additional problems **15.11–15.14** *are available in* MyOMLab.

Problems 15.15–15.25 relate to Sequencing Jobs

•• **15.15** The following jobs are waiting to be processed at the same machine center. Jobs are logged as they arrive:

JOB	DUE DATE	DURATION (DAYS)
A	313	8
B	312	16
C	325	40
D	314	5
E	314	3

In what sequence would the jobs be ranked according to the following decision rules: (a) FCFS, (b) EDD, (c) SPT, and (d) LPT? All dates are specified as manufacturing planning calendar days. Assume that all jobs arrive on day 275. Which decision is best and why? **Px**

• **15.16** The following 5 overhaul jobs are waiting to be processed at Avianic's Engine Repair Inc. These jobs were logged as they arrived. All dates are specified as planning calendar days. Assume that all jobs arrived on day 180; today's date is 200.

JOB	DUE DATE	REMAINING TIME (DAYS)
103	214	10
205	223	7
309	217	11
412	219	5
517	217	15

Using the critical ratio scheduling rule, in what sequence would the jobs be processed? **Px**

•• **15.17** An Alabama lumberyard has four jobs on order, as shown in the following table. Today is day 205 on the yard's schedule.

JOB	DUE DATE	REMAINING TIME (DAYS)
A	212	6
B	209	3
C	208	3
D	210	8

Px

In what sequence would the jobs be ranked according to the following decision rules:

a) FCFS   b) SPT   c) LPT
d) EDD   e) Critical ratio

Which is best and why? Which has the minimum lateness?

•• **15.18** The following jobs are waiting to be processed at Rick Solano's machine center. Solano's machine center has a relatively long backlog and sets a fresh schedule every 2 weeks, which does not disturb earlier schedules. Below are the jobs received during the previous 2 weeks. They are ready to be scheduled today, which is day 241 (day 241 is a work day). Job names refer to names of clients and contract numbers.

JOB	DATE JOB RECEIVED	PRODUCTION DAYS NEEDED	DATE JOB DUE
BR-02	228	15	300
CX-01	225	25	270
DE-06	230	35	320
RG-05	235	40	360
SY-11	231	30	310

a) Complete the following table. (Show your supporting calculations.)
b) Which dispatching rule has the best score for flow time?
c) Which dispatching rule has the best score for utilization metric?
d) Which dispatching rule has the best score for lateness?
e) Which dispatching rule would you select? Support your decision.

DISPATCHING RULE	JOB SEQUENCE	FLOW TIME	UTILIZATION METRIC	AVERAGE NUMBER OF JOBS	AVERAGE LATENESS
EDD					
SPT					
LPT					
FCFS					

•• **15.19** The following jobs are waiting to be processed at Julie Morel's machine center:

JOB	DATE ORDER RECEIVED	PRODUCTION DAYS NEEDED	DATE ORDER DUE
A	110	20	180
B	120	30	200
C	122	10	175
D	125	16	230
E	130	18	210

In what sequence would the jobs be ranked according to the following rules: (a) FCFS, (b) EDD, (c) SPT, and (d) LPT? All dates are according to shop calendar days. Today on the planning calendar is day 130, and none of the jobs have been started or scheduled. Which rule is best? **Px**

•• **15.20** Sunny Park Tailors has been asked to make three different types of wedding suits for separate customers. The table below highlights the time taken in hours for (1) cutting and sewing and (2) delivery of each of the suits. Which schedule finishes sooner: first come, first served (123) or a schedule using Johnson's rule?

Times Taken for Different Activities (hours)

SUIT	CUT AND SEW	DELIVER
1	4	2
2	7	7
3	6	5

•• **15.21** The following jobs are waiting to be processed at Jeremy LaMontagne's machine center. Today is day 250.

JOB	DATE JOB RECEIVED	PRODUCTION DAYS NEEDED	DATE JOB DUE
1	215	30	260
2	220	20	290
3	225	40	300
4	240	50	320
5	250	20	340

Using the critical ratio scheduling rule, in what sequence would the jobs be processed? **Px**

•••• **15.22** The following set of seven jobs is to be processed through two work centers at George Heinrich's printing company. The sequence is first printing, then binding. Processing time at each of the work centers is shown in the following table:

JOB	PRINTING (HOURS)	BINDING (HOURS)
T	15	3
U	7	9
V	4	10
W	7	6
X	10	9
Y	4	5
Z	7	8

a) What is the optimal sequence for these jobs to be scheduled?
b) Chart these jobs through the two work centers.
c) What is the total length of time of this optimal solution?
d) What is the idle time in the binding shop, given the optimal solution?
e) How much would the binding machine's idle time be cut by splitting Job Z in half? **Px**

••• **15.23** Six jobs are to be processed through a two-step operation. The first operation involves sanding, and the second involves painting. Processing times are as follows:

JOB	OPERATION 1 (HOURS)	OPERATION 2 (HOURS)
A	10	5
B	7	4
C	5	7
D	3	8
E	2	6
F	4	3

Determine a sequence that will minimize the total completion time for these jobs. Illustrate graphically. **Px**

Additional problems **15.24–15.25** are available in MyOMLab.

Problems 15.26–15.27 relate to Scheduling Services

•• **15.26** Daniel's Barber Shop at Newark Airport is open 7 days a week but has fluctuating demand. Daniel Ball is interested in treating his barbers as well as he can with steady work and preferably 5 days of work with two consecutive days off. His analysis of his staffing needs resulted in the following plan. Schedule Daniel's staff with the minimum number of barbers.

	DAY						
	MON.	TUE.	WED.	THU.	FRI.	SAT.	SUN.
Barbers needed	6	5	5	5	6	4	3

•• **15.27** Given the following demand for waiters and waitresses at S. Ghosh Bar and Grill, determine the minimum wait staff needed with a policy of 2 consecutive days off.

	DAY						
	MON.	TUE.	WED.	THU.	FRI.	SAT.	SUN.
Wait staff needed	3	4	4	5	6	7	4

CASE STUDIES

Old Oregon Wood Store

In 2015, George Wright started the Old Oregon Wood Store to manufacture Old Oregon tables. Each table is carefully constructed by hand using the highest-quality oak. Old Oregon tables can support more than 500 pounds, and since the start of the Old Oregon Wood Store, not one table has been returned because of faulty workmanship or structural problems. In addition to being rugged, each table is beautifully finished using a urethane varnish that George developed over 20 years of working with wood-finishing materials.

The manufacturing process consists of four steps: preparation, assembly, finishing, and packaging. Each step is performed by one person. In addition to overseeing the entire operation, George does all of the finishing. Tom Surowski performs the preparation step, which involves cutting and forming the basic components of the tables. Leon Davis is in charge of the assembly, and Cathy Stark performs the packaging.

Although each person is responsible for only one step in the manufacturing process, everyone can perform any one of the steps. It is George's policy that occasionally everyone should complete several tables on his or her own without any help or assistance. A small competition is used to see who can complete an entire table in the least amount of time. George maintains average total and intermediate completion times. The data are shown in Figure 15.7.

It takes Cathy longer than the other employees to construct an Old Oregon table. In addition to being slower than the other employees, Cathy is also unhappy about her current responsibility of packaging, which leaves her idle most of the day. Her first preference is finishing, and her second preference is preparation.

In addition to quality, George is concerned with costs and efficiency. When one of the employees misses a day, it causes major scheduling problems. In some cases, George assigns another employee overtime to complete the necessary work. At other times, George simply waits until the employee returns to work to complete his or her step in the manufacturing process. Both solutions cause problems. Overtime is expensive, and waiting causes delays and sometimes stops the entire manufacturing process.

To overcome some of these problems, Randy Lane was hired. Randy's major duties are to perform miscellaneous jobs and to help out if one of the employees is absent. George has given Randy training in all phases of the manufacturing process, and he is pleased with the speed at which Randy has been able to learn how to completely assemble Old Oregon tables. Randy's average total and intermediate completion times are given in Figure 15.8.

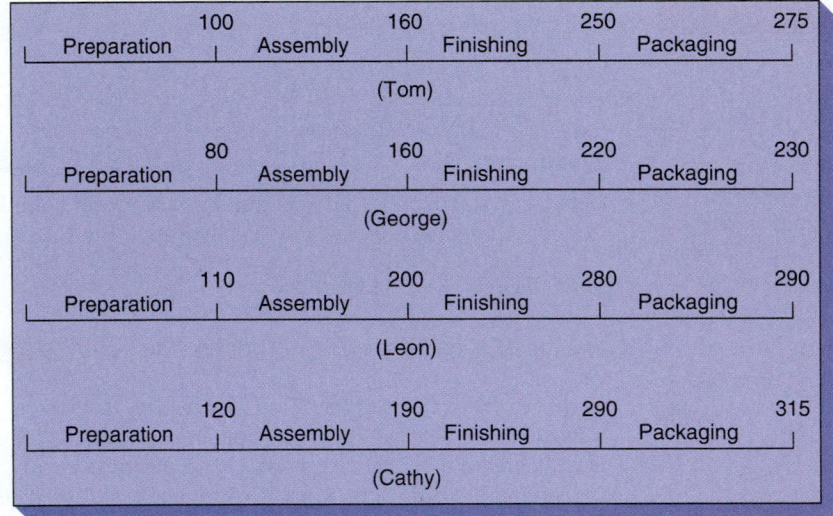

Figure **15.7**

Manufacturing Time in Minutes

Figure **15.8**

Randy's Completion Times in Minutes

Discussion Questions

1. What is the fastest way to manufacture Old Oregon tables using the original crew? How many could be made per day?
2. Would production rates and quantities change significantly if George would allow Randy to perform one of the four functions and make one of the original crew the backup person?
3. What is the fastest time to manufacture a table with the original crew if Cathy is moved to either preparation or finishing?
4. Whoever performs the packaging function is severely underutilized. Can you find a better way of utilizing the four- or five-person crew than either giving each a single job or allowing each to manufacture an entire table? How many tables could be manufactured per day with this scheme?

From the Eagles to the Magic: Converting the Amway Center

The massive 875,000-square-foot Amway Center in Orlando, Florida, is a state-of-the-art sports entertainment center. While it is the home of the Orlando Magic basketball team, it is a flexible venue designed to accommodate a vast array of entertainment. The facility is used for everything from a concert by the Eagles or Britney Spears, to ice hockey, to arena football, to conventions, as well as 41 regular season home games played by its major tenant, the National Basketball Association's Orlando Magic.

The building is a LEED-certified (Leadership in Energy and Environmental Design), sustainable, environmentally friendly design, with unmatched technology. Dispersed throughout the building are over 1,000 digital monitors, the latest in broadcasting technology, and the tallest high-definition video board in an NBA venue. To fully utilize this nearly $500 million complex, conversions from one event to the next must be done rapidly—often in a matter of hours. Letting the facility sit idle because of delays in conversion is not an option.

Well-executed conversions help maximize facility revenue and at the same time minimize expenses. Fast and efficient conversions are critical. Like any other process, a conversion can be analyzed and separated into its component activities, each requiring its own human and capital resources. The operations manager must determine when to do the conversion, how to train and schedule the crew, which tools and capital equipment are necessary, and the specific steps necessary to break down the current event and set up for the next. In addition to trying to maintain a stable crew (typically provided by local staffing companies) and to maintain

Fernando Medina

control during the frenzied pace of a conversion, managers divide the workforce into cross-trained crews, with each crew operating in its own uniquely colored shirt.

At the Amway Center, Charlie Leone makes it happen. Charlie is the operations manager, and as such, he knows that any conversion is loaded with complications and risks. Concerts add a special risk because each concert has its own idiosyncrasies—and the breakdown for the Eagles concert will be unique. Charlie and his crews must anticipate and eliminate any potential problems. Charlie's immediate issue is making a schedule for converting the Eagles' concert venue to an NBA basketball venue. The activities and the time for various tasks have been determined and are shown in Table 15.3.

TABLE 15.3	CONCERT-TO-BASKETBALL CONVERSION TASKS

Available crew size = 16, including two fork truck drivers

TIME ALLOWED	TASKS	CREW AND TIME REQUIRED
3 to 4 hr	**11:20 PM** Performance crew begins teardown of concert stage & equipment	Concert's Responsibility
45 min	**11:20 PM Clear Floor Crew**	
	Get chair carts from storage	10 for 15 min
	Clear all chairs on floor, loading carts starting at south end, working north	16 for 30 min
	Move chair carts to north storage and stack as they become full	(includes 1 fork truck operator)
15 min	**11:50 PM** *(Or as soon as area under rigging is cleared)*	6 for 15 min
	Set up retractable basketball seating on north end	
	Take down railing above concert stage	
	Place railings on cart and move to storage	
2.5 hr	**12:05 AM Basketball Floor Crew**	8
	Position 15 basketball floor carts on floor	
	Mark out arena floor for proper placement of basketball floor	
	Position basketball floor by section	
	Assemble/join flooring/lay carpets over concrete	
	Position basketball nets in place	
	Set up scorer tables	
	Install risers for all courtside seating	
	Install 8-ft tables on east side of court	
2.5 hr	**Seating Unit Crew** *Starts same time as Basketball Floor Crew*	8
	Set up retractable basketball seating on north end	(includes 2 fork truck operators)
	Set up retractable basketball seating on south end	
	(Can only be done after concert stage and equipment is out of way)	
	Install stairs to Superstar Seating	
2 hr	**Board Crew** *Starts after Seating Unit Crew finishes*	4
	Install dasher board on south end	
	Move stairs to storage	

(Continued)

TABLE 15.3   **Continued**

TIME ALLOWED	TASKS	CREW AND TIME REQUIRED
2 hr	**Chair Crew** *Starts after Seating Unit Crew finishes*	12
	Get chair carts from storage	
	Position chair carts on floor	
	Position chairs behind goals, courtside, and scorer tables	
	Clean, sweep, and place carts in order	
45 min	**End-of-Shift Activities** *Starts after Chair Crew finishes*	12
	Perform checklist items	
	Ensure that steps and stairways and railings are in place and tight	
	Check all seats are in upright position and locked in place	
	Report any damaged seats or armrests in need of repair	
	Verify exact number of chairs behind goals, courtside, and scorer tables	
15 min	**Check Out** *Starts after End-of-Shift Activities*	16
	Check for next conversion date and time and inform crew	
	Report any injuries Punch out all employees before leaving **8:00 AM** Floor ready for Magic practice	

Discussion Questions*

1. Make a Gantt chart to help Charlie organize his crew to perform the concert-to-basketball conversion. *Note*: Do not include the teardown of the concert stage and equipment, as that is the responsibility of the concert crew.

2. What time will the floor be ready?

3. Does Charlie have any extra personnel or a shortage of personnel? If so how many?

*You may wish to view the video that accompanies this case before answering the questions.

Scheduling at Hard Rock Cafe

Video Case

Whether it's scheduling nurses at Mayo Clinic, pilots at Southwest Airlines, classrooms at UCLA, or servers at a Hard Rock Cafe, it's clear that good scheduling is important. Proper schedules use an organization's assets (1) more effectively, by serving customers promptly, and (2) more efficiently, by lowering costs.

Hard Rock Cafe at Universal Studios, Orlando, is the world's largest restaurant, with 1,100 seats on two main levels. With typical turnover of employees in the restaurant industry at 80% to 100% per year, Hard Rock General Manager Ken Hoffman takes scheduling very seriously. Hoffman wants his 160 servers to be effective, but he also wants to treat them fairly. He has done so with scheduling software and flexibility that has increased productivity while contributing to turnover that is half the industry average. His goal is to find the fine balance that gives employees financially productive daily work shifts while setting the schedule tight enough so as to not overstaff between lunch and dinner.

The weekly schedule begins with a sales forecast. "First, we examine last year's sales at the cafe for the same day of the week," says Hoffman. "Then we adjust our forecast for this year based on a variety of closely watched factors. For example, we call the Orlando Convention Bureau every week to see what major groups will be in town. Then we send two researchers out to check on the occupancy of nearby hotels. We watch closely to see what

concerts are scheduled at Hard Rock Live—the 3,000-seat concert stage next door. From the forecast, we calculate how many people we need to have on duty each day for the kitchen, the bar, as hosts, and for table service."

Once Hard Rock determines the number of staff needed, servers submit request forms, which are fed into the software's linear programming mathematical model. Individuals are given priority rankings from 1 to 9, based on their seniority and how important they are to fill each day's schedule. Schedules are then posted by day and by workstation. Trades are handled between employees, who understand the value of each specific shift and station.

Hard Rock employees like the system, as does the general manager, since sales per labor-hour are rising and turnover is dropping.

Discussion Questions*

1. Name and justify several factors that Hoffman could use in forecasting weekly sales.
2. What can be done to lower turnover in large restaurants?
3. Why is seniority important in scheduling servers?
4. How does the schedule impact productivity?

*You may wish to view the video that accompanies this case before answering the questions.

- **Additional Case Study:** Visit MyOMLab for this free case study:
  Payroll Planning, Inc.: Describes setting a schedule for handling the accounting for dozens of client firms.

Endnotes

1. Opportunity costs are those profits forgone or not obtained.
2. Finite capacity scheduling (FCS) systems go by a number of names, including finite scheduling and advance planning systems

(APS). The name manufacturing execution systems (MES) may also be used, but MES tends to suggest an emphasis on the reporting system from shop operations back to the scheduling activity.

Chapter 15 *Rapid Review*

Main Heading	Review Material	MyOMLab
THE IMPORTANCE OF SHORT-TERM SCHEDULING (p. 602)	The strategic importance of scheduling is clear: ■ Effective scheduling means *faster movement* of goods and services through a facility. This means greater use of assets and hence greater capacity per dollar invested, which, in turn, *lowers cost.* ■ Added capacity, faster throughput, and the related flexibility mean better customer service through *faster delivery.* ■ Good scheduling contributes to realistic commitments, hence *dependable delivery.*	Concept Questions: 1.1–1.2
SCHEDULING ISSUES (pp. 602–605)	*The objective of scheduling is to allocate and prioritize demand (generated by either forecasts or customer orders) to available facilities.* ■ Forward scheduling—Begins the schedule as soon as the requirements are known. ■ Backward scheduling—Begins with the due date by scheduling the final operation first and the other job steps in reverse order. ■ Loading—The assigning of jobs to work or processing centers. The four scheduling criteria are (1) *minimize completion time,* (2) *maximize utilization,* (3) *minimize work-in-process (WIP) inventory,* and (4) *minimize customer waiting time.*	Concept Questions: 2.1–2.4 **VIDEO 15.1** From the Eagles to the Magic: Converting the Amway Center
SCHEDULING PROCESS-FOCUSED FACILITIES (p. 605)	A process-focused facility is a high-variety, low-volume system commonly found in manufacturing and services. It is also called an intermittent, or job shop, facility.	Concept Questions: 3.1–3.4
LOADING JOBS (pp. 605–610)	■ **Input–output control**—A system that allows operations personnel to manage facility work flows by tracking work added to a work center and its work completed. ■ **ConWIP cards**—Cards that control the amount of work in a work center, aiding input/output control. ConWIP is an acronym for *constant work-in-process.* A ConWIP card travels with a job (or batch) through the work center. When the job is finished, the card is released and returned to the initial workstation, authorizing the entry of a new batch into the work center. ■ **Gantt charts**—Planning charts used to schedule resources and allocate time. The Gantt *load chart* shows the loading and idle times of several departments, machines, or facilities. It displays the relative workloads in the system so that the manager knows what adjustments are appropriate. The Gantt *schedule chart* is used to monitor jobs in progress (and is also used for project scheduling). It indicates which jobs are on schedule and which are ahead of or behind schedule. ■ **Assignment method**—A special class of linear programming models that involves assigning tasks or jobs to resources. In assignment problems, only one job (or worker) is assigned to one machine (or project). The assignment method involves adding and subtracting appropriate numbers in the table to find the lowest *opportunity cost* for each assignment.	Concept Questions: 4.1–4.4 Problems: 15.1–15.14 Virtual Office Hours for Solved Problem: 15.1
SEQUENCING JOBS (pp. 611–617)	■ **Sequencing**—Determining the order in which jobs should be done at each work center. ■ **Priority rules**—Rules used to determine the sequence of jobs in process-oriented facilities. ■ **First come, first served (FCFS)**—Jobs are completed in the order in which they arrived. ■ **Shortest processing time (SPT)**—Jobs with the shortest processing times are assigned first. ■ **Earliest due date**—Earliest due date jobs are performed first. ■ **Longest processing time (LPT)**—Jobs with the longest processing time are completed first. $$\text{Average completion time} = \frac{\text{Sum of total flow time}}{\text{Number of jobs}} \quad (15\text{-}1)$$ $$\text{Utilization metric} = \frac{\text{Total job work (processing) time}}{\text{Sum of total flow time}} \quad (15\text{-}2)$$	Concept Questions: 5.1–5.4 Problems: 15.15–15.25 Virtual Office Hours for Solved Problems: 15.2–15.5 **ACTIVE MODEL 15.1**

Main Heading	Review Material	MyOMLab

$$\text{Average number of jobs in the system} = \frac{\text{Sum of total flow time}}{\text{Total job work (processing) time}} \quad (15\text{-}3)$$

$$\text{Average job lateness} = \frac{\text{Total late days}}{\text{Number of jobs}} \quad (15\text{-}4)$$

$$\text{Job lateness} = \text{Max}\{0, \text{yesterday} + \text{flow time} - \text{due date}\} \quad (15\text{-}5)$$

SPT is the best technique for minimizing job flow and average number of jobs in the system.

FCFS performs about average on most criteria, and it appears fair to customers.

EDD minimizes maximum tardiness.

- **Flow time**—The time each job spends waiting plus the time being processed.
- **Critical ratio (CR)**—A sequencing rule that is an index number computed by dividing the time remaining until due date by the work time remaining:

$$CR = \frac{\text{Time remaining}}{\text{Workdays remaining}} = \frac{\text{Due date} - \text{Today's date}}{\text{Work (lead) time remaining}} \quad (15\text{-}6)$$

As opposed to the priority rules, the critical ratio is dynamic and easily updated. It tends to perform better than FCFS, SPT, EDD, or LPT on the average job-lateness criterion.

- **Johnson's rule**—An approach that minimizes processing time for sequencing a group of jobs through two work centers while minimizing total idle time in the work centers.

Rule-based scheduling systems have the following limitations: (1) Scheduling is dynamic, (2) rules do not look upstream or downstream, and (3) rules do not look beyond due dates.

Main Heading	Review Material	MyOMLab
FINITE CAPACITY SCHEDULING (FCS) (pp. 617–618)	■ **Finite capacity scheduling (FCS)**—Computerized short-term scheduling that overcomes the disadvantage of rule-based systems by providing the user with graphical interactive computing.	Concept Questions: 6.1–6.2
SCHEDULING SERVICES (pp. 618–621)	Cyclical scheduling with inconsistent staffing needs is often the case in services. The objective focuses on developing a schedule with the minimum number of workers. In these cases, each employee is assigned to a shift and has time off.	Concept Questions: 7.1–7.4 **VIDEO 15.2** Scheduling at Hard Rock Cafe Problems: 15.26–15.27

Self Test

- **Before taking the self-test,** refer to the learning objectives listed at the beginning of the chapter and the key terms listed at the end of the chapter.

LO 15.1 Which of the following decisions covers the longest time period?
 a) Short-term scheduling
 b) Capacity planning
 c) Aggregate planning
 d) A master schedule

LO 15.2 A visual aid used in loading and scheduling jobs is a:
 a) Gantt chart.
 b) planning file.
 c) bottleneck.
 d) load-schedule matrix.
 e) level material chart.

LO 15.3 The assignment method involves adding and subtracting appropriate numbers in the table to find the lowest _____ for each assignment.
 a) profit
 b) number of steps
 c) number of allocations
 d) range per row
 e) opportunity cost

LO 15.4 The most popular priority rules include:
 a) FCFS.   b) EDD.
 c) SPT.   d) all of the above.

LO 15.5 The job that should be scheduled last when using Johnson's rule is the job with the:
 a) largest total processing time on both machines.
 b) smallest total processing time on both machines.
 c) longest activity time if it lies with the first machine.
 d) longest activity time if it lies with the second machine.
 e) shortest activity time if it lies with the second machine.

LO 15.6 What is computerized short-term scheduling that overcomes the disadvantage of rule-based systems by providing the user with graphical interactive computing?
 a) LPT   b) FCS
 c) CSS   d) FCFS
 e) GIC

LO 15.7 Cyclical scheduling is used to schedule:
 a) jobs.   b) machines.
 c) shipments.   d) employees.

Answers: LO 15.1. b; LO 15.2. a; LO 15.3. e; LO 15.4. d; LO 15.5. e; LO 15.6. b; LO 15.7. d.

Lean Operations

CHAPTER OUTLINE

GLOBAL COMPANY PROFILE: *Toyota Motor Corporation*

◆ Lean Operations *638*
◆ Lean and Just-in-Time *640*
◆ Lean and the Toyota Production System *649*

◆ Lean Organizations *650*
◆ Lean in Services *652*

Alaska Airlines

10 OM STRATEGY DECISIONS

- Design of Goods and Services
- Managing Quality
- Process Strategy
- Location Strategies
- Layout Strategies
- Human Resources
- Supply-Chain Management
- *Inventory Management*
  - Independent Demand (Ch. 12)
  - Dependent Demand (Ch. 14)
  - **Lean Operations (Ch. 16)**
- Scheduling
- Maintenance

Achieving Competitive Advantage with Lean Operations at Toyota Motor Corporation

Toyota Motor Corporation, with $250 billion in annual sales of over 9 million cars and trucks, is one of the largest vehicle manufacturers in the world. Two Lean techniques, just-in-time (JIT) and the Toyota Production System (TPS), have been instrumental in its growth. Toyota, with a wide range of vehicles, competes head-to-head with successful, long-established companies in Europe and the U.S. Taiichi Ohno, a former vice president of Toyota, created the basic framework for two of the world's most discussed systems for improving productivity, JIT and TPS. These two concepts provide much of the foundation for Lean operations:

◆ Central to JIT is a philosophy of continuous problem solving. In practice, JIT means making only what is needed, when it is needed. JIT provides an excellent vehicle for finding and eliminating problems because problems are easy to find in a system that eliminates the slack that inventory generates. When excess inventory is eliminated, shortcomings related to quality, layout, scheduling, and supplier performance become immediately evident—as does excess production.

◆ Central to TPS is employee learning and a continuing effort to create and produce products under ideal conditions. Ideal conditions exist only when management

Railway lines bring in engines from a Toyota plant in Alabama, axles from a supplier in Arkansas, and ship out finished trucks.

Tundras go from main assembly complex to test track or to staging area where they are shipped by truck or rail.

Toyota Logistics Services coordinates the shipment of finished Tundras by truck or rail.

Completed trucks exit here

Main assembly complex
Tundras are built here.

Land available for Toyota expansion

Supplier buildings surround main assembly complex.

Reception entrance

Large supplier sites for future expansion.

1 **Metalsa**
Truck frames

2 **Kautex**
Fuel tanks

3 **Tenneco Automotive**
Exhaust systems

4 **Curtis-Maruyasu America Inc.**
Tubing

5 **Millenium Steel Service Texas LLC**
Steel processing

6 **Green Metals Inc.**
Scrap steel recycling

7 **Avanzar Interior Technologies**
Seats and interior parts

8 **Toyotetsu Texas**
Stamped parts

9 **Futaba Industrial Texas Corp.**
Stamped parts

10 **Toyoda-Gosei Texas LLC**
Interior/exterior parts

11 **Reyes-Amtex**
Interior parts

12 **Vutex Inc.**
Assembly services

13 **Takumi Stamping Texas Inc.**
Stamped parts

14 **MetoKote**
E-coater

14 Suppliers outside the main plant

Outside: Toyota has a 2,000-acre site with 14 of the 21 onsite suppliers, adjacent rail lines, and nearby interstate highway. The site provides expansion space for both Toyota and for its suppliers — and provides an environment for just-in-time.

Assembly Components
Placed in cab for easy access rather than on shelves adjacent to the assembly line.

Andon
Problem display board that communicates abnormalities.

Pull System
Units produced only when more production is needed.

Kanban
Signal that indicates production of small batches of components.

Respect for People
Employees treated as knowledge workers.

Empowered Employees
Can stop production, ideas solicited, quality circles, etc.

Standard Work Practices
Rigorous, agreed upon, documented procedures for production.

JIT
Parts and supplies delivered just as needed in the quantity needed.

Minimal Machines
Proprietary machines designed for specific Toyota applications.

Level Schedules
Models mixed on production lines to meet customer orders.

Jidoka
Monitoring performance, making judgements, and even stopping the line as necessary.

Kaizen Area
An area where suggestions are tested and evaluated.

KAIZEN AREA

1 AGC Automotive Americas
Glass assemblies

3 HERO Assemblers LLP
Assembly of tire onto wheel

5 PPG Industries Inc.
Glass assemblies

7 Tokai Rika
Functional parts

2 ARK Inc.
Industrial waste management, recycling

4 HERO Logistics LLP
Logistics

6 Reyes Automotive Group
Interior/exterior parts

Seven suppliers inside the main plant

Toyota's San Antonio plant has about 2 million interior sq. ft., providing facilities within the final assembly building for 7 of the 21 onsite suppliers, and capacity to build 200,000 pick-up trucks annually. But most importantly, Toyota practices the world-class Toyota Production System and expects its suppliers to do the same thing, wherever they are.

brings facilities, machines, and people together to add value without waste. Waste undermines productivity by diverting resources to excess inventory, unnecessary processing, and poor quality. Respect for people, extensive training, cross-training, and standard work practices of empowered employees focusing on driving out waste are fundamental to TPS.

Toyota's implementation of TPS and JIT is present at its 2,000-acre San Antonio, Texas, facility, the largest Toyota land site for an automobile assembly plant in the U.S. Interestingly, despite its large site and annual production capability of 200,000, a throughput time of 20½ hours, and the output of a truck every 63 seconds, the building itself is one of the smallest in the industry. Modern automobiles have 30,000 parts, but at Toyota, independent suppliers combine many of these parts into subassemblies. Twenty-one of these suppliers are on site at the San Antonio facility and transfer components to the assembly line on a JIT basis.

Operations such as these taking place in the San Antonio plant are why Toyota continues to perform near the top in quality and maintain the lowest labor-hour assembly time in the industry. Lean operations *do* work—and they provide a competitive advantage for Toyota Motor Corporation. ◤

LEARNING OBJECTIVES

LO 16.1 *Define* Lean operations 638

LO 16.2 *Define* the seven wastes and the 5Ss 638

LO 16.3 *Identify* the concerns of suppliers when moving to supplier partnerships 642

LO 16.4 *Determine* optimal setup time 645

LO 16.5 *Define* kanban 647

LO 16.6 *Compute* the required number of kanbans 648

LO 16.7 *Identify* six attributes of Lean organizations 651

LO 16.8 *Explain* how Lean applies to services 652

Lean Operations

LO 16.1 *Define* Lean operations

Lean operations

Eliminates waste through continuous improvement and focus on exactly what the customer wants.

Just-in-time (JIT)

Continuous and forced problem solving via a focus on throughput and reduced inventory.

Toyota Production System (TPS)

Focus on continuous improvement, respect for people, and standard work practices.

As shown in the *Global Company Profile*, the Toyota Production System (TPS) contributes to a world-class operation at Toyota Motor Corporation. In this chapter, we discuss Lean operations, including JIT and TPS, as approaches to continuous improvement that lead to world-class operations.

Lean operations supply the customer with exactly what the customer wants when the customer wants it, without waste, through continuous improvement. Lean operations are driven by workflow initiated by the "pull" of the customer's order. **Just-in-time (JIT)** is an approach of continuous and forced problem solving via a focus on throughput and reduced inventory. The **Toyota Production System (TPS)**, with its emphasis on continuous improvement, respect for people, and standard work practices, is particularly suited for assembly lines.

In this chapter we use the term *Lean operations* to encompass all the related approaches and techniques of both JIT and TPS. When implemented as a comprehensive operations strategy, Lean sustains competitive advantage and results in increased overall returns to stakeholders.

Regardless of the approach and label, operations managers address three issues that are fundamental to operations improvement: *eliminate waste, remove variability,* and *improve throughput.* We now introduce these three issues and then discuss the major attributes of Lean operations. Finally, we look at Lean applied to services.

Eliminate Waste

Lean producers set their sights on perfection: *no* bad parts, *no* inventory, *only* value-added activities, and *no* waste. Any activity that does not add value in the eyes of the customer is a waste. The customer defines product value. If the customer does not want to pay for it, it is a waste. Taiichi Ohno, noted for his work on the Toyota Production System, identified seven categories of waste. These categories have become popular in Lean organizations and cover many of the ways organizations waste or lose money. Ohno's **seven wastes** are:

Seven wastes

Overproduction
Queues
Transportation
Inventory
Motion
Overprocessing
Defective product

- *Overproduction:* Producing more than the customer orders or producing early (before it is demanded) is waste.
- *Queues:* Idle time, storage, and waiting are wastes (they add no value).
- *Transportation:* Moving material between plants or between work centers and handling it more than once is waste.
- *Inventory:* Unnecessary raw material, work-in-process (WIP), finished goods, and excess operating supplies add no value and are wastes.
- *Motion:* Movement of equipment or people that adds no value is waste.

LO 16.2 *Define* the seven wastes and the 5Ss

- *Overprocessing:* Work performed on the product that adds no value is waste.
- *Defective product:* Returns, warranty claims, rework, and scrap are wastes.

A broader perspective—one that goes beyond immediate production—suggests that other resources, such as energy, water, and air, are often wasted but should not be. Efficient, sustainable production minimizes inputs and maximizes outputs, wasting nothing.

For over a century, managers have pursued "housekeeping" for a neat, orderly, and efficient workplace and as a means of reducing waste. Operations managers have embellished "housekeeping" to include a checklist—now known as the 5Ss.[1] The Japanese developed the initial 5Ss. Not only are the 5Ss a good checklist for Lean operations, but they also provide an easy vehicle with which to assist the culture change that is often necessary to bring about Lean operations. The 5Ss follow:

Alaska Airlines

In keeping with 5S, airports, like many other facilities, specify with painted guidelines exactly where tools and equipment such as this fuel pump are to be positioned.

- ◆ *Sort/segregate:* Keep what is needed and remove everything else from the work area; when in doubt, throw it out. Identify nonvalue items and remove them. Getting rid of these items makes space available and usually improves workflow.

- ◆ *Simplify/straighten:* Arrange and use methods analysis tools (see Chapter 7 and Chapter 10) to improve workflow and reduce wasted motion. Consider long-run and short-run ergonomic issues. Label and display for easy use only what is needed in the immediate work area. (For examples of visual displays, see Chapter 10, Figure 10.8 and the adjacent photo of equipment located within prescribed lines on the tarmac at Seattle's airport.)

- ◆ *Shine/sweep:* Clean daily; eliminate all forms of dirt, contamination, and clutter from the work area.

- ◆ *Standardize:* Remove variations from the process by developing standard operating procedures and checklists; good standards make the abnormal obvious. Standardize equipment and tooling so that cross-training time and cost are reduced. Train and retrain the work team so that when deviations occur, they are readily apparent to all.

- ◆ *Sustain/self-discipline:* Review periodically to recognize efforts and to motivate to sustain progress. Use visuals wherever possible to communicate and sustain progress.

U.S. managers often add two additional Ss that contribute to establishing and maintaining a Lean workplace:

- ◆ *Safety:* Build good safety practices into the preceding five activities.
- ◆ *Support/maintenance:* Reduce variability, unplanned downtime, and costs. Integrate daily *shine* tasks with preventive maintenance.

The Ss support continuous improvement and provide a vehicle with which employees can identify. Operations managers need think only of the examples set by a well-run hospital emergency room or the spit-and-polish of a fire department for a benchmark. Offices and retail stores, as well as manufacturers, have successfully used the 5Ss in their respective efforts to eliminate waste and move to Lean operations. A place for everything and everything in its place does make a difference in a well-run office. And retail stores successfully use the Ss to reduce misplaced merchandise and improve customer service. An orderly workplace reduces waste, releasing assets for other, more productive, purposes.

Remove Variability

Managers seek to remove variability caused by both internal and external factors. Variability is any deviation from the optimum process that delivers a perfect product on time, every time. Variability is a polite word for problems. The less variability in a system, the less waste in the system. Most variability is caused by tolerating waste or by poor management. Among the many sources of variability are:

- Poor processes that allow employees and suppliers to produce improper quantities or non-conforming units
- Inadequate maintenance of facilities and processes
- ◆ Unknown and changing customer demands
- ◆ Incomplete or inaccurate drawings, specifications, and bills of material

5Ss

A Lean production checklist:
Sort
Simplify
Shine
Standardize
Sustain

Variability

Any deviation from the optimum process that delivers a perfect product on time, every time.

Inventory reduction via JIT is an effective tool for identifying causes of variability. The precise timing of JIT makes variability evident, just as reducing inventory exposes variability. Defeating variability allows managers to move good materials on schedule, add value at each step of the process, drive down costs, and ultimately win orders.

Improve Throughput

Throughput

The rate at which units move through a process.

Throughput is the rate at which units move through a process. Each minute that products remain on the books, costs accumulate, and competitive advantage is lost. Time is money. The time that an order is in the shop is called **manufacturing cycle time**. This is the time between the arrival of raw materials and the shipping of finished product. For example, phone-system manufacturer Nortel had materials pulled directly from qualified suppliers to the assembly line. This effort reduced a segment of the manufacturing cycle time from 3 weeks to just 4 hours, the incoming inspection staff from 47 to 24, and problems on the shop floor caused by defective materials by 97%. Driving down manufacturing cycle time can make a major improvement in throughput.

Manufacturing cycle time

The time between the arrival of raw materials and the shipping of finished products.

A technique for increasing throughput is a pull system. A **pull system** *pulls* a unit to where it is needed just as it is needed. Pull systems are a standard tool of Lean. Pull systems use signals to request production and delivery from supplying stations to stations that have production capacity available. The pull concept is used both within the immediate production process and with suppliers. By *pulling* material through the system in very small lots—just as it is needed— waste and inventory are removed. As inventory is removed, clutter is reduced, problems become evident, and continuous improvement is emphasized. Removing the cushion of inventory also reduces both investment in inventory and manufacturing cycle time. A *push* system dumps orders on the next downstream workstation, regardless of timeliness and resource availability. Push systems are the antithesis of Lean. Pulling material through a production process as it is needed rather than in a "push" mode typically lowers cost and improves schedule performance, enhancing customer satisfaction.

Pull system

A concept that results in material being produced only when requested and moved to where it is needed just as it is needed.

Lean and Just-in-Time

STUDENT TIP ◗

JIT places added demands on performance, but that is why it pays off.

Just-in-time (JIT), with its focus on rapid throughput and reduced inventory, is a powerful component of Lean. With the inclusion of JIT in Lean, materials arrive *where* they are needed only *when* they are needed. When good units do not arrive just as needed, a "problem" has been identified. This is the reason this aspect of Lean is so powerful—it focuses attention on *problems*. By driving out waste and delay, JIT reduces inventory, cuts variability and waste, and improves throughput. Every moment material is held, an activity that adds value should be occurring. Consequently, as Figure 16.1 suggests, JIT often yields a competitive advantage.

A well-executed Lean program requires a meaningful buyer–supplier partnership.

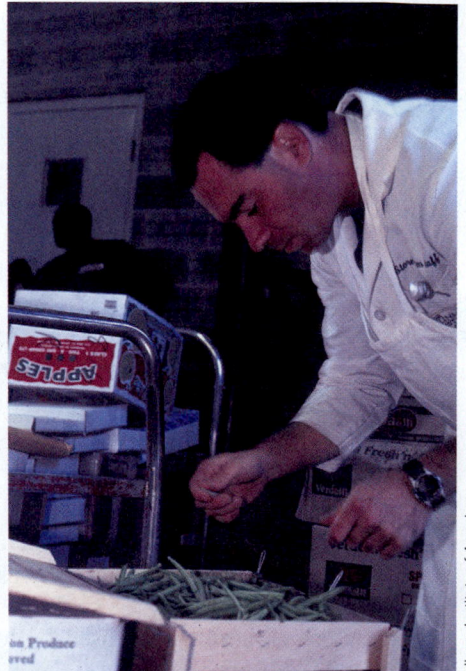

Culinary Institute of America

Many services have adopted Lean techniques as a normal part of their business. Restaurants like Olive Garden expect and receive JIT deliveries. Both buyer and supplier expect fresh, high-quality produce delivered without fail just when it is needed. The system doesn't work any other way.

Supplier Partnerships

Supplier partnerships

Partnerships of suppliers and purchasers that remove waste and drive down costs for mutual benefits.

Supplier partnerships exist when a supplier and a purchaser work together with open communication and a goal of removing waste and driving down costs. Trust and close collaboration are critical to

Figure **16.1**

Lean Contributes to Competitive Advantage

the success of Lean. Figure 16.2 shows the characteristics of supplier partnerships. Some specific goals are:

- *Removal of unnecessary activities*, such as receiving, incoming inspection, and paperwork related to bidding, invoicing, and payment.
- *Removal of in-plant inventory* by delivery in small lots directly to the using department as needed.

Figure **16.2**

Characteristics of Supplier Partnerships

OM in Action | Lean Production at Cessna Aircraft Company

When Cessna Aircraft opened its new plant in Independence, Kansas, it saw the opportunity to switch from craftwork to a Lean manufacturing system. The initial idea was to focus on three Lean concepts: (1) vendor-managed inventory, (2) cross-training of employees, and (3) using technology and manufacturing cells to move away from batch processing.

After several years, with these goals accomplished, Cessna began working on the next phase of Lean. This phase focuses on *Team Build* and *Area Team Development*.

Team Build at Cessna empowers employees to expand their skills, sequence their own work, and then sign off on it. This reduces wait time, inventory, part shortages, rework, and scrap, all contributing to improved productivity.

Area Team Development (ATD) provides experts when a factory employee cannot complete his or her standard work in the time planned. Team

members trained in the ATD process are called Skill Coaches. Skill Coaches provide support throughout each area to improve response time to problems. Andon boards and performance metrics are used for evaluating daily performance.

Cessna Aircraft Company

These commitments to Lean manufacturing are a major contributor to Cessna being the world's largest manufacturer of single-engine aircraft.

Sources: Interviews with Cessna executives, 2013.

◆ *Removal of in-transit inventory* by encouraging suppliers to locate nearby and provide frequent small shipments. The shorter the flow of material in the resource pipeline, the less inventory. Inventory can also be reduced through a technique known as *consignment*. **Consignment inventory** (see the *OM in Action* box, "Lean Production at Cessna Aircraft Company"), a variation of vendor-managed inventory (Chapter 11), means the supplier maintains the title to the inventory until it is used.

◆ *Obtain improved quality and reliability* through long-term commitments, communication, and cooperation.

Consignment inventory
An arrangement in which the supplier maintains title to the inventory until it is used.

Leading organizations view suppliers as extensions of their own organizations and expect suppliers to be fully committed to constant improvement. However, supplier concerns can be significant and must be addressed. These concerns include:

1. *Diversification:* Suppliers may not want to tie themselves to long-term contracts with one customer. The suppliers' perception is that they reduce their risk if they have a variety of customers.

2. *Scheduling:* Many suppliers have little faith in the purchaser's ability to produce orders to a smooth, coordinated schedule.

3. *Lead time:* Engineering or specification changes can play havoc with JIT because of inadequate lead time for suppliers to implement the necessary changes.

4. *Quality:* Suppliers' capital budgets, processes, or technology may limit ability to respond to changes in product and quality.

5. *Lot sizes:* Suppliers may see frequent delivery in small lots as a way to transfer buyers' holding costs to suppliers.

LO 16.3 *Identify* the concerns of suppliers when moving to supplier partnerships

As the foregoing concerns suggest, good supplier partnerships require a high degree of trust and respect by both supplier and purchaser—in a word, collaboration. Many firms establish this trust and collaborate very successfully. Two such firms are McKesson-General and Baxter International, who provide surgical supplies for hospitals on a JIT basis. They deliver prepackaged surgical supplies based on hospital operating schedules. Moreover, the surgical packages themselves are prepared so supplies are available in the sequence in which they will be used during surgery.

Lean Layout

Lean layouts reduce another kind of waste—movement. The movement of material on a factory floor (or paper in an office) does not add value. Consequently, managers want flexible layouts that reduce the movement of both people and material. Lean layouts place material directly in the location where needed. For instance, an assembly line should be designed with delivery points next to the line so material need not be delivered first to a receiving department and then moved again. Toyota has gone one step further and places components in the chassis of each vehicle moving down the assembly line. This is not only convenient, but it also allows Toyota to save space and opens areas adjacent to the assembly line previously occupied by shelves. When a layout reduces distance, firms often save labor and space and may have the added bonus of eliminating potential areas for accumulation of unwanted inventory. Table 16.1 provides a list of Lean layout tactics.

Distance Reduction   Reducing distance is a major contribution of work cells, work centers, and focused factories (see Chapter 9). The days of long production lines and huge economic lots, with goods passing through monumental, single-operation machines, are gone. Now firms use work cells, often arranged in a U shape, containing several machines performing different operations. These work cells are often based on group technology codes (as discussed in Chapter 5). Group technology codes help identify components with similar characteristics so they can be grouped into families. Once families are identified, work cells are built for them. The result can be thought of as a small product-oriented facility where the "product" is actually a group of similar products—a family of products. The cells produce one good unit at a time, and ideally, they produce the units *only* after a customer orders them.

Increased Flexibility   Modern work areas are designed so they can be easily rearranged to adapt to changes in volume and product changes. Almost nothing is bolted down. This concept of layout flexibility applies to both factory and office environments. Not only is furniture and equipment movable, but so are walls, computer connections, and telecommunications. Equipment is modular. Layout flexibility aids the changes that result from product *and* process improvements that are inevitable at a firm with a philosophy of continuous improvement.

Impact on Employees   When layouts provide for sequential operations, feedback, including quality issues, can be immediate, allowing employees working together to tell each other about problems and opportunities for improvement. When workers produce units one at a time, they test each product or component at each subsequent production stage. Work processes with self-testing *poka-yoke* functions detect defects automatically. Before Lean, defective products were replaced from inventory. Because surplus inventory is not kept in Lean facilities, there are no such buffers. Employees learn that getting it right the first time is critical. Indeed, Lean layouts allow cross-trained employees to bring flexibility and efficiency to the work area, reducing defects. Defects are waste.

Reduced Space and Inventory   Because Lean layouts reduce travel distance, they also reduce inventory. When there is little space, inventory travels less and must be moved in very small lots or even single units. Units are always moving because there is no storage. For instance, each month a Bank of America focused facility sorts 7 million checks, processes 5 million statements, and mails 190,000 customer statements. With a Lean layout, mail-processing time has been reduced by 33%, annual salary costs by tens of thousands of dollars, floor space by 50%, and in-process waiting lines by 75% to 90%. Storage, including shelves and drawers, has been removed.

Lean Inventory

Inventories in production and distribution systems often exist "just in case" something goes wrong. That is, they are used just in case some variation from the production plan occurs. The "extra" inventory is then used to cover variations or problems. Lean inventory tactics require "just in time," not "just in case." Lean inventory is the minimum inventory necessary to keep a perfect system running. With Lean inventory, the exact amount of goods arrives at the moment it is needed, not a minute before or a minute after. Some useful Lean inventory tactics are shown in Table 16.2 and discussed in more detail in the following sections.

Reduce Inventory and Variability   Operations managers move toward Lean by first reducing inventory. The idea is to eliminate variability in the production system hidden by inventory. Reducing inventory uncovers the "rocks" in Figure 16.3(a) that represent the variability and problems currently being tolerated. With reduced inventory, management chips away at the exposed problems. After the lake is lowered, managers make additional cuts

TABLE 16.1
LEAN LAYOUT TACTICS
Build work cells for families of products
Include a large number of operations in a small area
Minimize distance
Design little space for inventory
Improve employee communication
Use *poka-yoke* devices
Build flexible or movable equipment
Cross-train workers to add flexibility

TABLE 16.2
LEAN INVENTORY TACTICS
Use a pull system to move inventory
Reduce lot size
Develop just-in-time delivery systems with suppliers
Deliver directly to the point of use
Perform to schedule
Reduce setup time
Use group technology

Lean inventory
The minimum inventory necessary to keep a perfect system running.

◆ STUDENT TIP

Accountants book inventory as an asset, but operations managers know it is a cost.

Figure **16.3**

High levels of inventory hide problems (a), but as we reduce inventory, problems are exposed (b), and finally after reducing inventory and removing problems, we have lower inventory, lower costs, and smooth sailing (c).

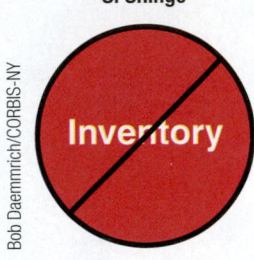

"Inventory is evil."
S. Shingo

in inventory and continue to chip away at the next level of exposed problems [see Figure 16.3(b, c)]. Ultimately, there will be little inventory and few problems (variability).

Firms with technology-sensitive products estimate that the rapid product innovations can cost as much as $\frac{1}{2}$% to 2% of the values of inventory *each week*. Shigeo Shingo, codeveloper of the Toyota JIT system, says, "Inventory is evil." He is not far from the truth. If inventory itself is not evil, it hides evil at great cost.

Reduce Lot Sizes   Lean also reduces waste by cutting the investment in inventory. A key to slashing inventory is to produce good product in small lot sizes. Reducing the size of batches can be a major help in reducing inventory and inventory costs. As we saw in Chapter 12, when inventory usage is constant, the average inventory level is the sum of the maximum inventory plus the minimum inventory divided by 2. Figure 16.4 shows that lowering the order size increases the number of orders, but drops inventory levels.

Ideally, in a Lean environment, order size is one and single units are being pulled from one adjacent process to another. More realistically, analysis of the process, transportation time, and physical attributes such as size of containers used for transport are considered when determining lot size. Such analysis typically results in a small lot size, but a lot size larger than one. Once a lot size has been determined, the EOQ production order quantity model can be modified to determine the desired setup time. We saw in Chapter 12 that the production order quantity model takes the form:

$$Q_p^* = \sqrt{\frac{2DS}{H[1 - (d/p)]}} \qquad (16\text{-}1)$$

where
D = Annual demand d = Daily demand
S = Setup cost p = Daily production
H = Holding cost

Figure **16.4**

Frequent Orders Reduce Average Inventory

A lower order size increases the number of orders and total ordering cost but reduces average inventory and total holding cost.

Q_1 When average order size = 200 average inventory is 100

Q_2 When average order size = 100 average inventory is 50

Example 1 shows how to determine the desired setup time.

Example 1

LO 16.4 *Determine optimal setup time*

DETERMINING OPTIMAL SETUP TIME

Crate Furniture, Inc., a firm that produces rustic furniture, desires to move toward a reduced lot size. Crate Furniture's production analyst, Aleda Roth, determined that a 2-hour production cycle would be acceptable between two departments. Further, she concluded that a setup time that would accommodate the 2-hour cycle time should be achieved.

APPROACH ▶ Roth developed the following data and procedure to determine optimum setup time analytically:

D = Annual demand = 400,000 units
d = Daily demand = 400,000 per 250 days = 1,600 units per day
p = Daily production rate = 4,000 units per day
Q_p = EOQ desired = 400 (which is the 2-hour demand; that is, 1,600 per day per four 2-hour periods)
H = Holding cost = \$20 per unit per year
S = Setup cost (to be determined)

Hourly labor rate = \$30.00

SOLUTION ▶ Roth determines that the cost and related time per setup should be:

$$Q_p = \sqrt{\frac{2DS}{H(1 - d/p)}}$$

$$Q_p^2 = \frac{2DS}{H(1 - d/p)}$$

$$S = \frac{(Q_p^2)(H)(1 - d/p)}{2D} \tag{16-2}$$

$$= \frac{(400)^2(20)(1 - 1,600/4,000)}{2(400,000)} = \frac{(3,200,000)(0.6)}{800,000} = \$2.40$$

Setup time = \$2.40/(hourly labor rate)
= \$2.40/(\$30 per hour)
= 0.08 hour, or 4.8 minutes

INSIGHT ▶ Now, rather than produce components in large lots, Crate Furniture can produce in a 2-hour cycle with the advantage of an inventory turnover of four *per day*.

LEARNING EXERCISE ▶ If labor cost goes to \$40 per hour, what should be the setup time? [Answer: 0.06 hours, or 3.6 minutes.]

RELATED PROBLEMS ▶ 16.1, 16.2, 16.3

Only two changes need to be made for small-lot material flow to work. First, material handling and work flow need to be improved. With short production cycles, there can be very little wait time. Improving material handling is usually easy and straightforward. The second change is more challenging, and that is a radical reduction in setup times. We discuss setup reduction next.

Reduce Setup Costs   Both the quantity of inventory and the cost of holding it go down as the inventory-reorder quantity and the maximum inventory level drop. However, because inventory requires incurring an ordering or setup cost that is applied to the units produced, managers tend to purchase (or produce) large orders; the larger the order the less the cost to be absorbed by each unit. Consequently, the way to drive down lot sizes *and* reduce inventory cost is to reduce setup cost, which in turn lowers the optimum order size.

The effect of reduced setup costs on total cost and lot size is shown in Figure 16.5. Moreover, smaller lot sizes hide fewer problems. In many environments, setup cost is highly correlated with setup time. In a manufacturing facility, setups usually require a substantial amount of preparation. Much of the preparation required by a setup can be done prior to shutting down

⬥ STUDENT TIP
Reduced lot sizes must be accompanied by reduced setup times.

Figure **16.5**

Lower Setup Costs Will Lower Total Cost

More frequent orders require reducing setup costs; otherwise, inventory costs will rise. As the setup costs are lowered (from S_1 to S_2), total inventory costs also fall (from T_1 to T_2).

the machine or process. Setup times can be reduced substantially, as shown in Figure 16.6. For example in one Kodak plant in Mexico, the setup time to change a bearing was reduced from 12 hours to 6 minutes! This is the kind of progress that is typical of world-class manufacturers.

Just as setup costs can be reduced at a machine in a factory, setup time can also be reduced during the process of getting the order ready in the office. Driving down factory setup time from hours to minutes does little good if orders are going to take weeks to process or "set up" in the office. This is exactly what happens in organizations that forget that Lean concepts have applications in offices as well as in the factory. Reducing setup time (and cost) is an excellent way to reduce inventory investment, improve productivity, and speed throughput.

STUDENT TIP ◆ Effective scheduling is required for effective use of capital and personnel.

Lean Scheduling

Effective schedules, communicated to those within the organization as well as to outside suppliers, support Lean. Better scheduling also improves the ability to meet customer orders, drives down inventory by allowing smaller lot sizes, and reduces work-in-process. For instance, many companies, such as Ford, now tie suppliers to their final assembly schedule. Ford communicates its schedules to bumper manufacturer Polycon Industries from the Ford production control system. The scheduling system describes the style and color of the bumper needed for each vehicle moving down the final assembly line. The scheduling system transmits the information to portable terminals carried by Polycon warehouse personnel, who load the bumpers onto conveyors leading to the loading dock. The bumpers are then trucked 50 miles to the Ford plant. Total time is 4 hours. However, as we saw in our opening *Global Company Profile*, Toyota has moved its bumper supplier *inside* the new Tundra plant; techniques such as this drive down delivery time even further.

Table 16.3 suggests several items that can contribute to achieving these goals, but two techniques (in addition to communicating schedules) are paramount. They are *level schedules* and *kanban*.

Figure **16.6**

Steps for Reducing Setup Times

Reduced setup times are a major component of Lean.

JIT Level Material-Use Approach

AA BBB C AA BBB C AA BBB C AA BBB C AA BBB C AA BBB C AA BBB C AA BBB C

Large-Lot Approach

AAAAAA BBBBBBBBB CCC AAAAAA BBBBBBBBB CCC AAAAAA BBBBBBBBB CCC

Time

Figure **16.7**

Scheduling Small Lots of Parts A, B, and C Increases Flexibility to Meet Customer Demand and Reduces Inventory

The Lean approach to scheduling, described as heijunka by the Japanese, produces just as many of each model per time period as the large-lot approach, provided setup times are lowered.

Level Schedules Level schedules process frequent small batches rather than a few large batches. Figure 16.7 contrasts a traditional large-lot approach using large batches with a level schedule using many small batches. The operations manager's task is to make and move small lots so the level schedule is economical. This requires success with the issues discussed in this chapter that allow small lots. As lots get smaller, the constraints may change and become increasingly challenging. At some point, processing a unit or two may not be feasible. The constraint may be the way units are sold and shipped (four to a carton), or an expensive paint changeover (on an automobile assembly line), or the proper number of units in a sterilizer (for a food-canning line).

The scheduler may find that *freezing*, that is holding a portion of the schedule near due dates constant, allows the production system to function and the schedule to be met. Operations managers expect the schedule to be achieved with no deviations.

Kanban One way to achieve small lot sizes is to move inventory through the shop only as needed rather than *pushing* it on to the next workstation whether or not the personnel there are ready for it. As noted earlier, when inventory is moved only as needed, it is referred to as a *pull* system, and the ideal lot size is one. The Japanese call this system *kanban*. Kanbans allow arrivals at a work center to match (or nearly match) the processing time.

Kanban is a Japanese word for *card*. In their effort to reduce inventory, the Japanese use systems that "pull" inventory through work centers. They often use a "card" to signal the need for another container of material—hence the name *kanban*. The card is the authorization for the next container of material to be produced. Typically, a kanban signal exists for each container of items to be obtained. An order for the container is then initiated by each kanban and "pulled" from the producing department or supplier. A sequence of kanbans "pulls" the material through the plant.

The system has been modified in many facilities so that even though it is called a *kanban*, the card itself does not exist. In some cases, an empty position on the floor is sufficient indication that the next container is needed. In other cases, some sort of signal, such as a flag or rag (Figure 16.8), alerts that it is time for the next container.

When there is visual contact between producer and user, the process works like this:

1. The user removes a standard-size container of parts from a small storage area, as shown in Figure 16.8.
2. The signal at the storage area is seen by the producing department as authorization to replenish the using department or storage area. Because there is an optimum lot size, the producing department may make several containers at a time.

A kanban system is similar to the resupply that occurs in your neighborhood supermarket: the customer buys; the stock clerk observes the shelf or receives notice from the end-of-day sales list and restocks. When the store's limited supply is depleted, a "pull" signal is sent to the warehouse, distributor, or manufacturer for resupply, usually that night. The complicating factor in a manufacturing firm is the time needed for actual manufacturing (production) to take place.

Level schedules

Scheduling products so that each day's production meets the demand for that day.

TABLE 16.3
LEAN SCHEDULING TACTICS
Make level schedules
Use kanbans
Communicate schedules to suppliers
Freeze part of the schedule
Perform to schedule
Seek one-piece-make and one-piece-move
Eliminate waste
Produce in small lots
Each operation produces a perfect part

Kanban

The Japanese word for *card*, which has come to mean "signal"; a kanban system moves parts through production via a "pull" from a signal.

LO 16.5 *Define* kanban

Signal marker hanging on post for part Z405 shows that production should start for that part. The post is located so that workers in normal locations can easily see it.

Signal marker on stack of boxes.

Part numbers mark location of specific part.

Figure **16.8**

Diagram of Storage Area with Warning-Signal Marker

Donna Shader

A kanban need not be as formal as signal lights or empty carts. The cook in a fast-food restaurant knows that when six cars are in line, eight meat patties and six orders of french fries should be cooking.

LO 16.6 *Compute the required number of kanbans*

Several additional points regarding kanbans may be helpful:

◆ When the producer and user are not in visual contact, a card can be used; otherwise, a light, flag, or empty spot on the floor may be adequate.

◆ Usually each card controls a specific quantity of parts, although multiple card systems are used if the work cell produces several components or if the lot size is different from the move size.

◆ The kanban cards provide a direct control (limit) on the amount of work-in-process between cells.

Determining the Number of Kanban Cards or Containers The number of kanban cards, or containers, sets the amount of authorized inventory. To determine the number of containers moving back and forth between the using area and the producing areas, management first sets the size of each container. This is done by computing the lot size, using a model such as the production order quantity model [discussed in Chapter 12 and shown again on page 644 in Equation (16-1)]. Setting the number of containers involves knowing: (1) lead time needed to produce a container of parts and (2) the amount of safety stock needed to account for variability or uncertainty in the system. The number of kanban cards is computed as follows:

$$\text{Number of kanbans (containers)} = \frac{\text{Demand during lead time} + \text{Safety stock}}{\text{Size of container}} \tag{16-3}$$

Example 2 illustrates how to calculate the number of kanbans needed.

Example 2

DETERMINING THE NUMBER OF KANBAN CONTAINERS

Hobbs Bakery produces short runs of cakes that are shipped to grocery stores. The owner, Ken Hobbs, wants to try to reduce inventory by changing to a kanban system. He has developed the following data and asked you to finish the project.

$$\text{Production lead time} = \text{Wait time} + \text{Material handling time} + \text{Processing time} = 2 \text{ days}$$

$$\text{Daily demand} = 500 \text{ cakes}$$

$$\text{Safety stock} = \tfrac{1}{2} \text{ day}$$

$$\text{Container size (determined on a production order size EOQ basis)} = 250 \text{ cakes}$$

APPROACH ▶ Having determined that the EOQ size is 250, we then determine the number of kanbans (containers) needed.

SOLUTION ▶ Demand during lead time =

$$\text{Lead time} \times \text{Daily demand} = 2 \text{ days} \times 500 \text{ cakes} = 1,000$$

$$\text{Safety stock} = \tfrac{1}{2} \times \text{Daily demand} = 250$$

Number of kanbans (containers) needed =

$$\frac{\text{Demand during lead time} + \text{Safety stock}}{\text{Container size}} = \frac{1,000 + 250}{250} = 5$$

INSIGHT ▶ Once the reorder point is hit, five containers should be released.

LEARNING EXERCISE ▶ If lead time drops to 1 day, how many containers are needed? [Answer: 3.]

RELATED PROBLEMS ▶ 16.4, 16.5, 16.6, 16.7, 16.8, 16.9, 16.10 (16.11, 16.12 are available in MyOMLab)

Advantages of Kanban Containers are typically very small, usually a matter of a few hours' worth of production. Such a system requires tight schedules, with small quantities being produced several times a day. The process must run smoothly with little variability in quality or lead time because any shortage has an almost immediate impact on the entire system. Kanban places added emphasis on meeting schedules, reducing the time and cost required by setups, and economical material handling.

In-plant kanban systems often use standardized, reusable containers that protect the specific quantities to be moved. Such containers are also desirable in the supply chain. Standardized containers reduce weight and disposal costs, generate less wasted space, and require less labor to pack, unpack, and prepare items.

Lean Quality

There is no Lean without quality. And Lean's "pull" production, smaller batch sizes, and low inventory all enhance quality by exposing bad quality. Savings occur because scrap, rework, inventory investment, and poor product are no longer buried in inventory. This means fewer bad units are produced. In short, whereas inventory *hides* bad quality, Lean *exposes* it.

As Lean shrinks queues and lead time, it keeps evidence of errors fresh and limits the number of potential sources of error. In effect, Lean creates an early warning system for quality problems so that fewer bad units are produced and feedback is immediate. This advantage accrues both within the firm and with goods received from outside vendors.

In addition, better quality means fewer buffers are needed, and therefore, a better, easier-to-maintain inventory system can exist. Often the purpose of keeping inventory is to protect against unreliable quality. But, when consistent quality exists, Lean firms can reduce all costs associated with inventory. Table 16.4 suggests some tactics for quality in a Lean environment.

⬥ STUDENT TIP
Good quality costs less.

TABLE 16.4

LEAN QUALITY TACTICS

Use statistical process control

Empower employees

Build fail-safe methods (poka-yoke, checklists, etc.)

Expose poor quality with small lots

Provide immediate feedback

Lean and the Toyota Production System

Toyota Motor's Eiji Toyoda and Taiichi Ohno are given credit for the Toyota Production System (TPS; see the *Global Company Profile* that opens this chapter). Three components of TPS are *continuous improvement*, *respect for people*, and *standard work practice*, which are now considered an integral part of Lean.

Continuous Improvement

Continuous improvement under TPS means building an organizational culture and instilling in its people a value system stressing that processes can be improved—indeed, that improvement is an integral part of every employee's job. This process is formalized in TPS by kaizen, the Japanese word for change for the good, or what is more generally known as *continuous improvement*. Kaizen is often implemented by a kaizen event. A kaizen event occurs when members of a work cell group or team meet to develop innovative ways to immediately implement improvements in the work area or process. In application, kaizen means making a multitude of small or incremental changes as one seeks elusive perfection. (See the *OM in Action* box, "Toyota's New Challenge.") Instilling the mantra of continuous improvement begins at personnel recruiting and continues through extensive and continuing training. One of the reasons continuous improvement works at Toyota, we should note, is because of another core value at Toyota, Toyota's respect for people.

Kaizen
A focus on continuous improvement.

Kaizen event
Members of a work cell or team meet to develop improvements in the process.

Respect for People

Toyota, like other Lean organizations, recruits, trains, and treats people as knowledge workers. Aided by aggressive cross-training and few job classifications, Lean firms engage the mental as well as physical capacities of employees in the challenging task of improving operations. Employees are empowered. They are empowered not only to make improvements, but also to stop machines and processes when quality problems exist. Indeed, empowered employees are an integral part of Lean. This means that those tasks that have traditionally been assigned to staff are moved to employees. Toyota recognizes that employees know more about their jobs than anyone else. Lean firms respect employees by giving them the opportunity to enrich both their jobs and their lives.

⬥ STUDENT TIP
Respect for people brings the entire person to work.

With the generally high value of the yen, making a profit on cars built in Japan but sold in foreign markets is a challenge. As a result, Honda and Nissan are moving plants overseas, closer to customers. But Toyota, despite marginal profit on cars produced for export, is maintaining its current Japanese capacity. Toyota, which led the way with JIT and the TPS, is doubling down on its manufacturing prowess and continuous improvement. For an organization that traditionally does things slowly and step-by-step, the changes are radical. With its first new plant in Japan in 18 years, Toyota believes it can once again set new production benchmarks. It is drastically reforming its production processes in a number of ways:

- The assembly line has cars sitting side-by-side, rather than bumper-to-bumper, shrinking the length of the line by 35% and requiring fewer steps by workers.
- Instead of having car chassis dangling from overhead conveyors, they are perched on raised platforms, reducing heating and cooling costs by 40%.

Conventional

Toyota: Side-by-side

- Retooling permits faster changeovers, allowing for shorter product runs of components, supporting level scheduling.
- The assembly line uses quiet friction rollers with fewer moving parts, requiring less maintenance than conventional lines and reducing worker fatigue.

These TPS innovations, efficient production with small lot sizes, rapid changeover, level scheduling, half the workers, and half the square footage, are being duplicated in Toyota's new plant in Blue Springs, Mississippi.

Sources: Forbes (July 29, 2012); *Automotive News* (February, 2011); and *The Wall Street Journal* (November 29, 2011).

This Porsche assembly line, like most other Lean facilities, empowers employees so they can stop the entire production line, what the Japanese call *jidoka*, if any quality problems are spotted.

Processes and Standard Work Practice

Building effective and efficient processes requires establishing what Toyota calls standard work practices. The underlying principles are:

- Work is completely specified as to content, sequence, timing, and outcome; this is fundamental to a good process.
- Supplier connections for both internal and external customers are direct, specifying personnel, methods, timing, and quantity.
- Material and service flows are simple and directed to a specific person or machine.
- Process improvements are made only after rigorous analysis at the lowest possible level in the organization.

Lean requires that activities, connections, and flows include built-in tests (or poka-yokes) to signal problems. When a problem or defect occurs, production is stopped. Japanese call the practice of stopping production because of a defect, *jidoka*. The dual focus on (1) education and training of employees and (2) the responsiveness of the system to problems make the seemingly rigid system flexible and adaptable. The result is continuous improvement.

Lean Organizations

Lean organizations understand the customer and the customer's expectations. Moreover, Lean organizations have functional areas that communicate and collaborate to verify that customer expectations are not only understood, but also met efficiently. This means identifying and delivering the customer's value expectation by implementing the tools of Lean throughout the organization.

STUDENT TIP

Lean drives out non-value-added activities.

Building a Lean Organization

Building Lean organizations is difficult, requiring exceptional leadership. Such leaders imbue the organization not just with the tools of Lean, but with a *culture* of continuous improvement. Building such a culture requires open communication and destroying isolated functional disciplines that act as independent "silos." There is no substitute for open two-way communication that fosters effective and efficient processes. Such an organizational culture will have a demonstrated respect for people and a management willing to fully understand how and where the work is performed. Lean firms sometimes use the Japanese term Gemba or Gemba walk to refer to going to where the work is actually performed.

Gemba or Gemba walk
Going to where the work is actually performed.

Building organizational cultures that foster ongoing improvement and that accept the constant change and improvement that makes improvement habitual is a challenge. However, such organizations exist. They understand the customer and drive out activities that do not add value in the eyes of the customer. They include industry leaders such as United Parcel Service, Alaska Airlines, and, of course, Toyota. Even traditionally idiosyncratic organizations such as hospitals (see the *OM in Action* box, "Lean Delivers the Medicine") find improved productivity with Lean operations. Lean operations adopt a philosophy of minimizing waste by striving for perfection through continuous learning, creativity, and teamwork. They tend to share the following attributes:

VIDEO 16.1
Lean Operations at Alaska Airlines

◆ *Respect and develop employees* by improving job design, providing constant training, instilling commitment, and building teamwork.

◆ *Empower employees* with jobs that are made challenging by pushing responsibility to the lowest level possible.

◆ *Develop worker flexibility* through cross-training and reducing job classifications.

◆ *Build processes* that destroy variability by helping employees produce a perfect product every time.

◆ *Develop collaborative partnerships with suppliers*, helping them not only to understand the needs of the ultimate customer, but also to accept responsibility for satisfying those needs.

LO 16.7 *Identify* six attributes of Lean organizations

◆ *Eliminate waste by performing only value-added activities.* Material handling, inspection, inventory, travel time, wasted space, and rework are targets, as they do not add value.

Success requires leadership as well as the full commitment and involvement of managers, employees, and suppliers. The rewards that Lean producers reap are spectacular. Lean producers often become benchmark performers.

OM in Action | Lean Delivers the Medicine

Using kaizen techniques straight out of Lean, a team of employees at San Francisco General Hospital target and then analyze a particular area within the hospital for improvement. Hospitals today are focusing on throughput and quality in the belief that excelling on these measures will drive down costs and push up patient satisfaction. Doctors and nurses now work together in teams that immerse themselves in a weeklong kaizen event. These events generate plans that make specific improvements in flow, quality, costs, or the patients' experience.

One recent kaizen event focused on the number of minutes it takes from the moment a patient is wheeled into the operating room to when the first incision is made. A team spent a week coming up with ways to whittle 10 minutes off this "prep" time. Every minute saved reduces labor cost and opens up critical facilities. Another kaizen event targeted the Urgent Care Center, dropping the average wait from 5 hours down to 2.5, primarily by adding an on-site X-ray machine instead of requiring patients to walk 15 minutes to the main radiology department. Similarly, wait times in the Surgical Clinic dropped from 2.5 hours to 70 minutes. The operating room now uses a *5S* protocol and has implemented *Standard Work* for the preoperation process.

As hospitals focus on improving medical quality and patient satisfaction, they are exposed to some Japanese terms associated with Lean, many of which do not have a direct English translation: **Gemba,** the place where work is actually performed; **Hansei,** a period of critical self-reflection; **Heijunka,** a level production schedule that provides balance and smooths day-to-day

Franck Boston/Fotolia

variation; **Jidoka,** using both human intelligence and technology to stop a process at the first sign of a potential problem; **Kaizen,** continuous improvement; and **Muda,** anything that consumes resources, but provides no value.

Lean systems are increasingly being adopted by hospitals as they try to reduce costs while improving quality and increasing patient satisfaction—and as San Francisco General has demonstrated, Lean techniques are working.

Sources: San Francisco Chronicle (Oct. 14, 2013) and *San Francisco General Hospital & Trauma Center Annual Report*, 2012–2013.

Lean Sustainability

Lean and sustainability are two sides of the same coin. Both seek to maximize resource and economic efficiency. However, if Lean focuses on only the immediate process and system, then managers may miss the sustainability issues beyond the firm. As we discussed in Supplement 5, sustainability requires examining the systems in which the firm and its stakeholders operate. When this is done, both Lean and sustainability achieve higher levels of performance.

Lean drives out waste because waste adds nothing for the customer. Sustainability drives out waste because waste is both expensive and has an adverse effect on the environment. Driving out waste is the common ground of Lean sustainability.

STUDENT TIP ◆
Lean began in factories, but is now also used in services throughout the world.

Lean in Services

LO 16.8 *Explain* how Lean applies to services

The features of Lean apply to services—from hospitals to amusement parks and airlines—directly influencing the customers' received value. The Lean attributes of respect for people, efficient processes with rigorous standard practices that drive out waste, and a focus on continuous improvement are pervasive vehicles for consistently generating value for all stakeholders. If there is any change in focus of Lean between manufacturing and services, it may be that the high level of customer interaction places added emphasis on enabling people through training, motivation, and empowerment to contribute to their fullest. However, in addition to the customer interaction aspect of services, here are some specific applications of Lean applied to suppliers, layout, inventory, and scheduling in the service sector.

Suppliers   Virtually every restaurant deals with its suppliers on a JIT basis. Those that do not are usually unsuccessful. The waste is too evident—food spoils, and customers complain, get sick, and may die. Similarly, JIT is basic to the financial sector that processes your deposits, withdrawals, and brokerage activities on a JIT basis. That is the industry standard.

Layouts   Lean layouts are required in restaurant kitchens, where cold food must be served cold and hot food hot. McDonald's, for example, has reconfigured its kitchen layout, at great expense, to drive seconds out of the production process, thereby speeding delivery to customers. With the new process, McDonald's can produce made-to-order hamburgers in 45 seconds. Layouts also make a difference at Alaska Airline's baggage claim, where customers expect their bags in 20 minutes or less.

Inventory   Stockbrokers drive inventory down to nearly zero every day. Most sell and buy orders occur on an immediate basis because an unexecuted sell or buy order is not acceptable to the client. A broker may be in serious trouble if left holding an unexecuted trade. Similarly, McDonald's reduces inventory waste by maintaining a time-stamped finished-goods inventory of only a few minutes; after that, it is thrown away. Hospitals, such as Arnold Palmer (described in this chapter's *Video Case Study*), manage JIT inventory and low safety stocks for many items. For instance, critical supplies such as pharmaceuticals may be held to low levels by developing community networks as backup. In this manner, if one pharmacy runs out of a needed drug, another member of the network can supply it until the next day's shipment arrives.

VIDEO 16.2
JIT at Arnold Palmer Hospital

Scheduling   Airlines must adjust to fluctuations in customer demand. But rather than adjusting by changes in inventory, demand is satisfied by personnel availability. Through elaborate scheduling, personnel show up just in time to cover peaks in customer demand. In other words, rather than "things" being inventoried, personnel are scheduled. At a salon, the focus is only slightly different: prompt service is assured by scheduling both the *customer* and the staff. At McDonald's and Walmart, scheduling of personnel is down to 15-minute increments, based on precise forecasting of demand. Notice that in these organizations scheduling is a key ingredient of Lean. Excellent forecasts drive those schedules. Such forecasts may be very elaborate, with seasonal, daily, and even hourly components in the case of the airline ticket counter (holiday sales, flight time, etc.), seasonal and weekly components at the salon (holidays and Fridays create special problems), and down to a few minutes (to respond to the daily meal cycle) at McDonald's.

To deliver goods and services to customers under continuously changing demand, suppliers need to be reliable, inventories low, cycle times short, and schedules nimble. Lean engages and empowers employees to create and deliver the customer's perception of value, eliminating whatever does not contribute to this goal. Lean techniques are widely used in both goods-producing and service-producing firms; they just look different.

Summary

Lean operations, including JIT and TPS, focuses on continuous improvement to eliminate waste. Because waste is found in anything that does not add value, organizations that implement these techniques are adding value more efficiently than other firms. The expectation of lean firms is that empowered employees work with committed management to build systems that respond to customers with ever-increasing efficiency and higher quality.

Key Terms

Lean operations (p. 638)
Just-in-time (JIT) (p. 638)
Toyota Production System (TPS) (p. 638)
Seven wastes (p. 638)
5Ss (p. 639)
Variability (p. 639)

Throughput (p. 640)
Manufacturing cycle time (p. 640)
Pull system (p. 640)
Supplier partnerships (p. 640)
Consignment inventory (p. 642)
Lean inventory (p. 643)

Level schedules (p. 647)
Kanban (p. 647)
Kaizen (p. 649)
Kaizen event (p. 649)
Gemba or Gemba walk (p. 651)

Ethical Dilemma

In this Lean operations world, in an effort to lower handling costs, speed delivery, and reduce inventory, retailers are forcing their suppliers to do more and more in the way of preparing their merchandise for their cross-docking warehouses, shipment to specific stores, and shelf presentation. Your company, a small manufacturer of aquarium decorations, is in a tough position. First, Mega-Mart wanted you to develop bar-code technology, then special packaging, then small individual shipments bar coded for each store. (This way when the merchandise hits the warehouse, it is cross-docked immediately to the truck destined for that store, and upon arrival the merchandise is ready for shelf placement.) And now Mega-Mart wants you to develop RFID—immediately.

Mega-Mart has made it clear that suppliers that cannot keep up with the technology will be dropped.

Earlier, when you didn't have the expertise for bar codes, you had to borrow money and hire an outside firm to do the development, purchase the technology, and train your shipping clerk. Then, meeting the special packaging requirement drove you into a loss for several months, resulting in a loss for last year. Now it appears that the RFID request is impossible. Your business, under the best of conditions, is marginally profitable, and the bank may not be willing to bail you out again. Over the years, Mega-Mart has slowly become your major customer and without it, you are probably out of business. What are the ethical issues, and what do you do?

Discussion Questions

1. What is a Lean producer?
2. What is JIT?
3. What is TPS?
4. What is level scheduling?
5. JIT attempts to remove delays, which do not add value. How, then, does JIT cope with weather and its impact on crop harvest and transportation times?
6. What are three ways in which Lean and quality are related?
7. What is kaizen, and what is a kaizen event?
8. What are the characteristics of supplier partnerships with respect to suppliers?
9. Discuss how the Japanese word for *card* has application in the study of JIT.
10. Standardized, reusable containers have obvious benefits for shipping. What is the purpose of these devices within the plant?
11. Does Lean production work in the service sector? Provide an example.
12. Which Lean techniques work in both the manufacturing *and* service sectors?

Solved Problem   Virtual Office Hours help is available in MyOMLab.

SOLVED PROBLEM 16.1

Krupp Refrigeration, Inc., is trying to reduce inventory and wants you to install a kanban system for compressors on one of its assembly lines. Determine the size of the kanban and the number of kanbans (containers) needed.

Setup cost = $10
Annual holding cost per compressor = $100
Daily production = 200 compressors
Annual usage = 25,000 (50 weeks × 5 days each × daily usage of 100 compressors)
Lead time = 3 days
Safety stock = $\frac{1}{2}$ day's production of compressors

SOLUTION

First, we must determine kanban container size. To do this, we determine the production order quantity [see discussion in Chapter 12 or Equation (16-1)], which determines the kanban size:

$$Q_p^* = \sqrt{\frac{2DS}{H\left(1 - \dfrac{d}{p}\right)}} = \sqrt{\frac{2(25,000)(10)}{H\left(1 - \dfrac{d}{p}\right)}} = \sqrt{\frac{500,000}{100\left(1 - \dfrac{100}{200}\right)}} = \sqrt{\frac{500,000}{50}}$$

$$= \sqrt{10,000} = 100 \text{ compressors. So the production order size and the size of the kanban container} = 100.$$

Then we determine the number of kanbans:

$$\text{Demand during lead time} = 300 \, (= 3 \text{ days} \times \text{daily usage of } 100)$$

$$\text{Safety stock} = 100 \, (= \tfrac{1}{2} \times \text{daily production of } 200)$$

$$\text{Number of kanbans} = \frac{\text{Demand during lead time} + \text{Safety stock}}{\text{Size of container}}$$

$$= \frac{300 + 100}{100} = \frac{400}{100} = 4 \text{ containers}$$

Problems

Note: **PX** means the problem may be solved with POM for Windows and/or Excel OM.

Problems 16.1–16.12 relate to Lean and Just-in-Time

• • • **16.1** Carol Cagle has a repetitive manufacturing plant producing trailer hitches in Arlington, Texas. The plant has an average inventory turnover of only 12 times per year. She has therefore determined that she will reduce her component lot sizes. She has developed the following data for one component, the safety chain clip:

$$\text{Annual demand} = 31,200 \text{ units}$$
$$\text{Daily demand} = 120 \text{ units}$$
$$\text{Daily production (in 8 hours)} = 960 \text{ units}$$
$$\text{Desired lot size (1 hour of production)} = 120 \text{ units}$$
$$\text{Holding cost per unit per year} = \$12$$
$$\text{Setup labor cost per hour} = \$20$$

How many minutes of setup time should she have her plant manager aim for regarding this component?

• • • **16.2** Given the following information about a product at Michael Gibson's firm, what is the appropriate setup time?

$$\text{Annual demand} = 39,000 \text{ units}$$
$$\text{Daily demand} = 150 \text{ units}$$
$$\text{Daily production} = 1,000 \text{ units}$$
$$\text{Desired lot size} = 150 \text{ units}$$
$$\text{Holding cost per unit per year} = \$10$$
$$\text{Setup labor cost per hour} = \$40$$

• • • **16.3** Rick Wing has a repetitive manufacturing plant producing automobile steering wheels. Use the following data to prepare for a reduced lot size. The firm uses a work year of 305 days.

Annual demand for steering wheels	30,500
Daily demand	100
Daily production (8 hours)	800
Desired lot size (2 hours of production)	200
Holding cost per unit per year	$10

a) What is the setup cost, based on the desired lot size?
b) What is the setup time, based on $40 per hour setup labor?

• **16.4** Hartley Electronics, Inc., in Nashville, produces short runs of custom airwave scanners for the defense industry. The owner, Janet Hartley, has asked you to reduce inventory by introducing a kanban system. After several hours of analysis, you develop the following data for scanner connectors used in one work cell. How many kanbans do you need for this connector?

Daily demand	1,000 connectors
Lead time	2 days
Safety stock	$\frac{1}{2}$ day
Kanban size	500 connectors

• **16.5** Tej Dhakar's company wants to establish kanbans to feed a newly established work cell. The following data have been provided. How many kanbans are needed?

Daily demand	250 units
Lead time	$\frac{1}{2}$ day
Safety stock	$\frac{1}{4}$ day
Kanban size	50 units

• • **16.6** Pauline Found Manufacturing, Inc., is moving to kanbans to support its telephone switching-board assembly lines. Determine the size of the kanban for subassemblies and the number of kanbans needed.

$$\text{Setup cost} = \$30$$
$$\text{Annual holding cost} = \$120 \text{ per subassembly}$$
$$\text{Daily production} = 20 \text{ subassemblies}$$
$$\text{Annual usage} = 2,500 \, (50 \text{ weeks} \times 5 \text{ days each}$$
$$\times \text{ daily usage of 10 subassemblies)}$$
$$\text{Lead time} = 16 \text{ days}$$
$$\text{Safety stock} = 4 \text{ days' production of subassemblies} \, \textbf{PX}$$

•• **16.7** Maggie Moylan Motorcycle Corp. uses kanbans to support its transmission assembly line. Determine the size of the kanban for the mainshaft assembly and the number of kanbans needed.

$$\text{Setup cost} = \$20$$

$$\begin{array}{r} \text{Annual holding cost} \\ \text{of mainshaft assembly} = \$250 \text{ per unit} \end{array}$$

$$\text{Daily production} = 300 \text{ mainshafts}$$

$$\begin{array}{r} \text{Annual usage} = 20,000 \ (= 50 \text{ weeks} \times 5 \text{ days each} \\ \times \text{ daily usage of } 80 \text{ mainshafts}) \end{array}$$

$$\text{Lead time} = 3 \text{ days}$$

$$\text{Safety stock} = \tfrac{1}{2} \text{ day's production of mainshafts} \ \mathbf{Px}$$

• **16.8** Discount-Mart, a major East Coast retailer, wants to determine the economic order quantity (see Chapter 12 for EOQ formulas) for its halogen lamps. It currently buys all halogen lamps from Specialty Lighting Manufacturers in Atlanta. Annual demand is 2,000 lamps, ordering cost per order is $30, and annual carrying cost per lamp is $12.

a) What is the EOQ?
b) What are the total annual costs of holding and ordering (managing) this inventory?
c) How many orders should Discount-Mart place with Specialty Lighting per year? **Px**

••• **16.9** Discount-Mart (see Problem 16.8), as part of its new Lean program, has signed a long-term contract with Specialty Lighting and will place orders electronically for its halogen lamps. Ordering costs will drop to $.50 per order, but Discount-Mart also reassessed its carrying costs and raised them to $20 per lamp.

a) What is the new economic order quantity?
b) How many orders will now be placed?
c) What is the total annual cost of managing the inventory with this policy? **Px**

•• **16.10** How do your answers to Problems 16.8 and 16.9 provide insight into a collaborative purchasing strategy?

Additional problems **16.11–16.12** *are available in* MyOMLab.

CASE STUDIES

Lean Operations at Alaska Airlines

Video Case

Alaska Airlines operates in a land of rugged beauty, crystal clear lakes, spectacular glaciers, majestic mountains, and bright blue skies. But equally awesome is its operating performance. Alaska Airlines consistently provides the industry's number one overall ranking and best on-time performance. A key ingredient of this excellent performance is Alaska Airlines' Lean initiative.

With an aggressive implementation of Lean, Ben Minicucci, Executive VP for Operations, is finding ever-increasing levels of performance. He pushes this initiative throughout the company with: (1) a focus on continuous improvement, (2) metrics that measure performance against targets, and (3) making performance relevant to Alaska Airlines' empowered employees.

With leadership training that includes a strong focus on participative management, Minicucci has created a seven-person Lean Department. The department provides extensive training in Lean via one-week courses, participative workshops, and two-week classes that train employees to become a Six Sigma Green Belt. Some employees even pursue the next step, Black Belt certification.

A huge part of any airline's operations is fuel cost, but capital utilization and much of the remaining cost is dependent upon ground equipment and crews that handle aircraft turnaround and maintenance, in-flight services, and customer service.

As John Ladner, Director of Seattle Airport Operations, has observed, "Lean eliminates waste, exposes non-standard work, and is forcing a focus on variations in documented best practices and work time."

Lean is now part of the Alaska Airlines corporate culture, with some 60 ongoing projects. Kaizen events (called "Accelerated Improvement Workshops" at Alaska Airlines), Gemba Walks (called "waste walks" by Alaska Airlines), and 5S are now a part of everyday conversation at Alaska Airlines. Lean projects have included:

♦ Applying 5S to identify aircraft ground equipment and its location on the tarmac.
♦ Improving preparation for and synchronization of the arrival and departure sequences; time to open the front door after arrival has been reduced from 4.5 to 1 min.
♦ Redefining the disconnect procedure for tow bars used to "push back" aircraft at departure time; planes now depart 2–3 minutes faster.
♦ Revising the deicing process, meaning less time for the plane to be on the tarmac.
♦ Improving pilot staffing, making Alaska's pilot productivity the highest in the industry. Every 1% improvement in productivity leads to a $5 million savings on a recurring basis. Alaska Airlines has achieved a 7% productivity improvement over the last five years.

Alaska Airlines

Another current Lean project is passenger unloading and loading. Lean instructor Allison Fletcher calls this "the most unique project I have worked on." One exciting aspect of deplaning is Alaska's solar-powered "switchback" staircase for unloading passengers through the rear door (see photo). Alaska is saving two minutes, or nearly 17%, off previous unloading time with this new process. Alaska Airlines' Lean culture has made it a leader in the industry.

Discussion Questions*

1. What are the key ingredients of Lean, as identified at Alaska Airlines?
2. As an initial phase of a kaizen event, discuss the many ways passengers can be loaded and unloaded from airplanes.
3. Document the research that is being done on the aircraft passenger-loading problem.

* You may wish to view the video that accompanies this case before addressing these questions.

JIT at Arnold Palmer Hospital

Video Case

Orlando's Arnold Palmer Hospital, founded in 1989, specializes in treatment of women and children and is renowned for its high-quality rankings (top 10% of 2000 benchmarked hospitals), its labor and delivery volume (more than 14,000 births per year), and its neonatal intensive care unit (one of the highest survival rates in the nation). But quality medical practices and high patient satisfaction require costly inventory—some $30 million per year and thousands of SKUs.* With pressure on medical care to manage and reduce costs, Arnold Palmer Hospital has turned toward controlling its inventory with just-in-time (JIT) techniques.

Within the hospital, for example, drugs are now distributed at the nursing stations via dispensing machines (almost like vending machines) that electronically track patient usage and post the related charge to each patient. Each night, based on patient demand and prescriptions written by doctors, the dispensing stations are refilled.

To address JIT issues externally, Arnold Palmer Hospital turned to a major distribution partner, McKesson General Medical, which as a first-tier supplier provides the hospital with about one-quarter of all its medical/surgical inventory. McKesson supplies sponges, basins, towels, Mayo stand covers, syringes, and hundreds of other medical/surgical items. To ensure coordinated daily delivery of inventory purchased from McKesson, an account executive has been assigned to the hospital on a full-time basis, as well as two other individuals who address customer service and product issues. The result has been a drop in Central Supply average daily inventory from $400,000 to $114,000 since JIT.

JIT success has also been achieved in the area of *custom surgical packs*. Custom surgical packs are the sterile coverings, disposable plastic trays, gauze, and the like, specialized to each type of surgical procedure. Arnold Palmer Hospital uses 10 different custom packs for various surgical procedures. "Over 50,000 packs are used each year, for a total cost of about $1.5 million," says George DeLong, head of Supply-Chain Management.

The packs are not only delivered in a JIT manner, but packed that way as well. That is, they are packed in the reverse order they are used so each item comes out of the pack in the sequence it is

needed. The packs are bulky, are expensive, and must remain sterile. Reducing the inventory and handling while maintaining an ensured sterile supply for scheduled surgeries presents a challenge to hospitals.

Here is how the supply chain works: Custom packs are *assembled* by a packing company with *components supplied* primarily from manufacturers selected by the hospital, and *delivered* by McKesson from its local warehouse. Arnold Palmer Hospital works with its own surgical staff (through the Medical Economics Outcome Committee) to identify and standardize the custom packs to reduce the number of custom pack SKUs. With this integrated system, pack safety stock inventory has been cut to one day.

The procedure to drive the custom surgical pack JIT system begins with a "pull" from the doctors' daily surgical schedule. Then, Arnold Palmer Hospital initiates an electronic order to McKesson between 1:00 and 2:00 P.M. daily. At 4:00 A.M. the next day, McKesson delivers the packs. Hospital personnel arrive at 7:00 A.M. and stock the shelves for scheduled surgeries. McKesson then reorders from the packing company, which in turn "pulls" necessary inventory for the quantity of packs needed from the manufacturers.

Arnold Palmer Hospital's JIT system reduces inventory investment, expensive traditional ordering, and bulky storage and supports quality with a sterile delivery.

Discussion Questions**

1. What do you recommend be done when an error is found in a pack as it is opened for an operation?
2. How might the procedure for custom surgical packs described here be improved?
3. When discussing JIT in services, the text notes that suppliers, layout, inventory, and scheduling are all used. Provide an example of each of these at Arnold Palmer Hospital.
4. When a doctor proposes a new surgical procedure, how do you recommend the SKU for a new custom pack be entered into the hospital's supply-chain system?

**You may wish to view the video that accompanies this case before answering these questions.

*SKU = stock keeping unit

- **Additional Case Studies:** Visit MyOMLab for these case studies:
  JIT after a Catastrophe: How Caterpillar responded after a tornado tore apart its Oxford plant.
  Mutual Insurance Company of Iowa: Applying JIT in an insurance office.

Endnote

1. The term 5S comes from the Japanese words seiri (*sort* and clear out), seiton (*straighten* and configure), seiso (*scrub* and clean up), seiketsu (maintain *sanitation* and cleanliness of self and workplace), and shitsuke (*self-discipline and standardization* of these practices).

Main Heading	Review Material	MyOMLab
LEAN OPERATIONS (pp. 638–640)	■ **Lean operations**—Eliminates waste through continuous improvement and focus on exactly what the customer wants. ■ **Just-in-time (JIT)**—Continuous and forced problem solving via a focus on throughput and reduced inventory. ■ **Toyota Production System (TPS)**—Focus on continuous improvement, respect for people, and standard work practices. *When implemented as a comprehensive manufacturing strategy, Lean, JIT, and TPS systems sustain competitive advantage and result in increased overall returns.* ■ **Seven wastes**—Overproduction, queues, transportation, inventory, motion, overprocessing, and defective product. ■ **5Ss**—A Lean production checklist: sort, simplify, shine, standardize, and sustain. U.S. managers often add two additional *S*s to the 5 original ones: *safety* and *support/maintenance*. ■ **Variability**—Any deviation from the optimum process that delivers perfect product on time, every time. Both JIT and inventory reduction are effective tools for identifying causes of variability. ■ **Throughput**—The rate at which units move through a process. ■ **Manufacturing cycle time**—The time between the arrival of raw materials and the shipping of finished products. ■ **Pull system**—A concept that results in material being produced only when requested and moved to where it is needed just as it is needed. Pull systems use signals to request production and delivery from supplying stations to stations that have production capacity available.	Concept Questions: 1.1–1.4
LEAN AND JUST-IN-TIME (pp. 640–649)	■ **Supplier partnerships**—Suppliers and purchasers work together to remove waste and drive down costs for mutual benefit. Some specific goals of supplier partnerships are *removal of unnecessary activities, removal of in-plant inventory, removal of in-transit inventory,* and *obtain improved quality and reliability*. ■ **Consignment inventory**—An arrangement in which the supplier maintains title to the inventory until it is used. Concerns of suppliers in suppler partnerships include (1) *diversification*, (2) *scheduling*, (3) *lead time*, (4) *quality*, and (5) *lot sizes*. *Lean layout tactics* include building work cells for families of products, including a large number of operations in a small area, minimizing distance, designing little space for inventory, improving employee communication, using poka-yoke devices, building flexible or movable equipment, and cross-training workers to add flexibility. ■ **Lean inventory**—The minimum inventory necessary to keep a perfect system running. The idea behind JIT is to eliminate inventory that hides variability in the production system. *Lean inventory tactics* include using a pull system to move inventory, reducing lot size, developing just-in-time delivery systems with suppliers, delivering directly to the point of use, performing to schedule, reducing setup time, and using group technology. $$Q_p^* = \sqrt{\frac{2DS}{H[1-(d/p)]}} \qquad (16\text{-}1)$$ Using Equation (16-1), for a given desired lot size, *Q*, we can solve for the optimal setup cost, *S*: $$S = \frac{(Q^2)(H)(1-d/p)}{2D} \qquad (16\text{-}2)$$ *Lean scheduling tactics* include communicate schedules to suppliers, make level schedules, freeze part of the schedule, perform to schedule, seek one-piece-make and one-piece-move, eliminate waste, produce in small lots, use kanbans, and make each operation produce a perfect part. ■ **Level schedules**—Scheduling products so that each day's production meets the demand for that day. ■ **Kanban**—The Japanese word for *card*, which has come to mean "signal"; a kanban system moves parts through production via a "pull" from a signal. $$\text{Number of kanbans (containers)} = \frac{\text{Demand during lead time + Safety stock}}{\text{Size of container}} \qquad (16\text{-}3)$$ *Lean quality*—whereas inventory *hides* bad quality, Lean immediately *exposes* it. Lean quality tactics include using statistical process control, empowering employees, building fail-safe methods (poka-yoke, checklists, etc.), exposing poor quality with small lots, and providing immediate feedback.	Concept Questions: 2.1–2.4 Problems: 16.1–16.3 Problems: 16.4–16.9, 16.11, 16.12 Virtual Office Hours for Solved Problem: 16.1

Main Heading	Review Material	MyOMLab
LEAN AND THE TOYOTA PRODUCTION SYSTEM (pp. 649–650)	▪ **Kaizen**—A focus on continuous improvement. ▪ **Kaizen event**—Members of a work cell or team meet to develop improvements in the process. Toyota recruits, trains, and treats people as knowledge workers. They are empowered. TPS employs aggressive cross-training and few job classifications.	Concept Questions: 3.1–3.4
LEAN ORGANIZATIONS (pp. 650–652)	Lean operations tend to share the following attributes: *respect and develop employees* by improving job design, providing constant training, instilling commitment, and building teamwork; *empower employees* by pushing responsibility to the lowest level possible; *develop worker flexibility* through cross-training and reducing job classifications; *build processes* that destroy variability; *develop collaborative partnerships with suppliers* to help them accept responsibility for satisfying end customer needs; and *eliminate waste by performing only value-added activities.* ▪ **Gemba** or **Gemba walk**—Going to where the work is actually performed.	Concept Questions: 4.1–4.4 **VIDEO 16.1** Lean Operations at Alaska Airlines
LEAN IN SERVICES (p. 652)	The features of Lean operations apply to services just as they do in other sectors. Forecasts in services may be very elaborate, with seasonal, daily, hourly, or even shorter components.	Concept Questions: 5.1–5.4 **VIDEO 16.2** JIT at Arnold Palmer Hospital

Self Test

▪ **Before taking the self-test,** refer to the learning objectives listed at the beginning of the chapter and the key terms listed at the end of the chapter.

LO 16.1 Match Lean Operations, JIT, and TPS with the concepts shown below:
  a) Continuous improvement and a focus on exactly what the customer wants, and when.
  b) Supply the customer with exactly what the customer wants when the customer wants it, without waste, through continuous improvement.
  c) Emphasis on continuous improvement, respect for people, and standard work practices.

LO 16.2 Define the seven wastes and the 5Ss. The seven wastes are _____, _____, _____, _____, _____, _____, and _____, and the 5Ss are _____, _____, _____, _____, and _____.

LO 16.3 Concerns of suppliers when moving to Supplier Partnerships include:
  a) small lots sometimes seeming economically prohibitive.
  b) realistic quality demands.
  c) changes without adequate lead time.
  d) erratic schedules.
  e) all of the above.

LO 16.4 What is the formula for optimal setup time?
  a) $\sqrt{2DQ/[H(1 - d/p)]}$
  b) $\sqrt{Q^2H(1 - d/p)/(2D)}$
  c) $QH(1 - d/p)/(2D)$
  d) $Q^2H(1 - d/p)/(2D)$
  e) $H(1 - d/p)$

LO 16.5 Kanban is the Japanese word for:
  a) car.
  b) pull.
  c) card.
  d) continuous improvement.
  e) level schedule.

LO 16.6 The required number of kanbans equals:
  a) 1.
  b) Demand during lead time / Q
  c) Size of container.
  d) Demand during lead time.
  e) Demand during lead time + Safety stock / Size of container

LO 16.7 The six attributes of Lean organizations are: _____, _____, _____, _____, _____, and _____.

LO 16.8 Lean applies to services:
  a) only in rare instances.
  b) except in terms of the supply chain.
  c) except in terms of employee issues.
  d) except in terms of both supply chain issues and employee issues.
  e) just as it applies to manufacturing.

Answers: LO 16.1. Lean = a, JIT = b, TPS = c; LO 16.2. overproduction, queues, transportation, inventory, motion, overprocessing, defective product; sort, simplify, shine, standardize, sustain; LO 16.3. e; LO 16.4. d; LO 16.5. c; LO 16.6. e; LO 16.7. respect and develop people, empower employees, develop worker flexibility, build excellent processes, develop collaborative partnerships with suppliers, eliminate waste; LO 16.8. e.

Maintenance and Reliability

CHAPTER OUTLINE

GLOBAL COMPANY PROFILE: *Orlando Utilities Commission*

◆ The Strategic Importance of Maintenance and Reliability *662*

◆ Reliability *663*

◆ Maintenance *667*

◆ Total Productive Maintenance *671*

Alaska Airlines

10 OM STRATEGY DECISIONS

- Design of Goods and Services
- Managing Quality
- Process Strategy
- Location Strategies
- Layout Strategies
- Human Resources
- Supply-Chain Management
- Inventory Management
- Scheduling
- *Maintenance*

Maintenance Provides a Competitive Advantage for the Orlando Utilities Commission

The Orlando Utilities Commission (OUC) owns and operates power plants that supply power to two central Florida counties. Every year, OUC takes each one of its power-generating units off-line for 1 to 3 weeks to perform maintenance work.

In addition, each unit is also taken off-line every 3 years for a complete overhaul and turbine generator inspection. Overhauls are scheduled for spring and fall, when the weather is mildest and demand for power is low. These overhauls last from 6 to 8 weeks.

Units at OUC's Stanton Energy Center require that maintenance personnel perform approximately 12,000 repair and preventive maintenance tasks a year. To accomplish these tasks efficiently, many of these jobs are scheduled daily via a computerized maintenance management program. The computer generates preventive maintenance work orders and lists of required materials.

Every day that a plant is down for maintenance costs OUC about $110,000 extra for the replacement cost of power that must be generated elsewhere. However, these costs pale beside the costs associated with a forced outage. An unexpected outage could cost OUC an additional $350,000 to $600,000 each day!

Scheduled overhauls are not easy; each one has 1,800 distinct tasks and requires 72,000 labor-hours. But the value of preventive maintenance was illustrated by the first overhaul of a new turbine generator. Workers discovered a cracked rotor blade, which could have destroyed a $27 million piece of equipment. To find such cracks, which are invisible to the naked eye, metals are examined using dye tests, X-rays, and ultrasound.

At OUC, preventive maintenance is worth its weight in gold. As a result, OUC's electric distribution system has been ranked number one in the Southeast U.S. by PA Consulting Group—a leading consulting firm. Effective maintenance provides a competitive advantage for the Orlando Utilities Commission.

Orlando Utilities Commission

The Stanton Energy Center in Orlando.

Orlando Utilities Commission

Two employees are on scaffolding near the top of Stanton Energy Center's 23-story high boiler, checking and repairing super heaters.

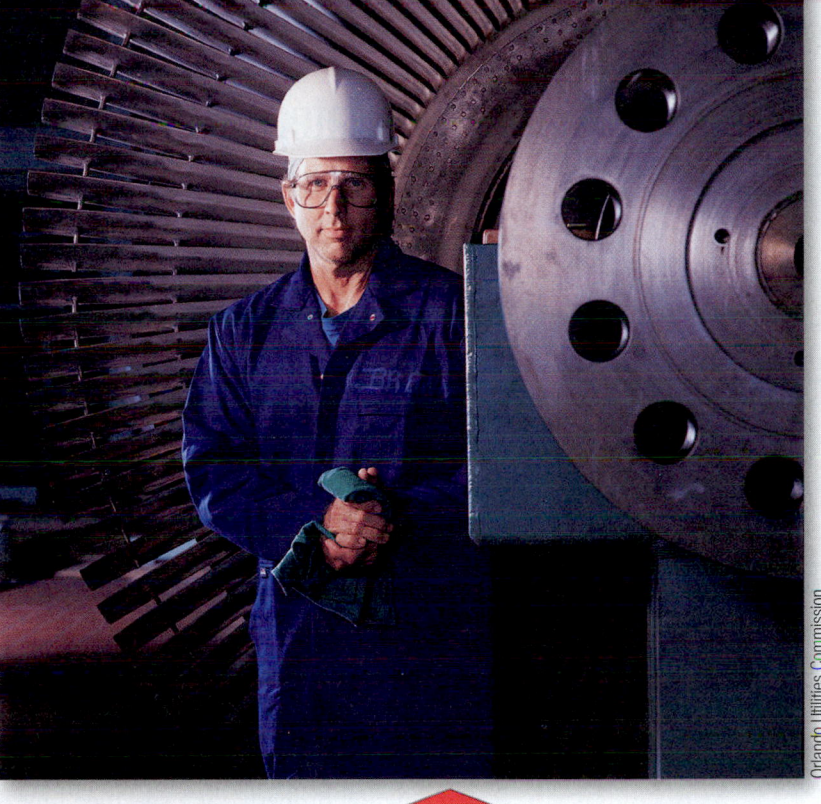

Orlando Utilities Commission

This inspector is examining a low-pressure section of turbine. The tips of these turbine blades will travel at supersonic speeds of 1,300 miles per hour when the plant is in operation. A crack in one of the blades can cause catastrophic failure.

Monty Rakusen Cultura/Newscom

Maintenance of capital-intensive facilities requires good planning to minimize downtime. Here, turbine overhaul is under way. Organizing the thousands of parts and pieces necessary for a shutdown is a major effort.

LEARNING OBJECTIVES

LO 17.1 *Describe* how to improve system reliability 663

LO 17.2 *Determine* system reliability 664

LO 17.3 *Determine* mean time between failures (MTBF) 665

LO 17.4 *Distinguish* between preventive and breakdown maintenance 667

LO 17.5 *Describe* how to improve maintenance 668

LO 17.6 *Compare* preventive and breakdown maintenance costs 669

LO 17.7 *Define* autonomous maintenance 670

The Strategic Importance of Maintenance and Reliability

VIDEO 17.1
Maintenance Drives Profits at Frito-Lay

Managers at Orlando Utilities Commission (OUC), the subject of the chapter-opening *Global Company Profile*, fight for reliability to avoid the undesirable results of equipment failure. At OUC, a generator failure is very expensive for both the company and its customers. Power outages are instantaneous, with potentially devastating consequences. Similarly, managers at Frito-Lay, Walt Disney Company, and United Parcel Service (UPS) are intolerant of failures or breakdowns. Maintenance is critical at Frito-Lay to achieve high plant utilization and excellent sanitation. At Disney, sparkling-clean facilities and safe rides are necessary to retain its standing as one of the most popular vacation destinations in the world. Likewise, UPS's famed maintenance strategy keeps its delivery vehicles operating and looking as good as new for 20 years or more.

STUDENT TIP ◆

If a system is not reliable, the other OM decisions are more difficult.

These companies, like most others, know that poor maintenance can be disruptive, inconvenient, wasteful, and expensive in dollars and even in lives. As Figure 17.1 illustrates, the interdependency of operator, machine, and mechanic is a hallmark of successful maintenance and reliability. Good maintenance and reliability management enhances a firm's performance and protects its investment.

Maintenance

The activities involved in keeping a system's equipment in working order.

The objective of maintenance and reliability is to maintain the capability of the system. Good maintenance removes variability. Systems must be designed and maintained to reach expected performance and quality standards. Maintenance includes all activities involved in keeping a system's equipment in working order. Reliability is the probability that a machine part or product will function properly for a specified time under stated conditions.

Reliability

The probability that a machine part or product will function properly for a specified time under stated conditions.

In this chapter, we examine four important tactics for improving the reliability and maintenance not only of products and equipment but also of the systems that produce them. The four tactics are organized around reliability and maintenance.

Employee Involvement

- Autonomous maintenance (partnering with maintenance personnel)
- Skill training
- Reward system
- Employee empowerment
- Continuous improvement

Maintenance and Reliability Procedures

- Clean and lubricate
- Monitor and adjust
- Make minor repairs
- Keep accurate records

Results

- Reduced variability
- Reduced inventory
- Improved quality
- Improved capacity
- Protecting investment in plant and equipment

Yields

- Enhanced productivity
- Winning products
- Improved profitability

Figure **17.1**

Good Maintenance and Reliability Management Requires Employee Involvement and Good Procedures

The reliability tactics are:

1. Improving individual components
2. Providing redundancy

The maintenance tactics are:

1. Implementing or improving preventive maintenance
2. Increasing repair capabilities or speed

We will now discuss these tactics.

Reliability

Systems are composed of a series of individual interrelated components, each performing a specific job. If any *one* component fails to perform, for whatever reason, the overall system (for example, an airplane or machine) can fail. First, we discuss system reliability and then improvement via redundancy.

System Reliability

Because failures do occur in the real world, understanding their occurrence is an important reliability concept. We now examine the impact of failure in a series. Figure 17.2 shows that as the number of components in a *series* increases, the reliability of the whole system declines very quickly. A system of $n = 50$ interacting parts, each of which has a 99.5% reliability, has an overall reliability of 78%. If the system or machine has 100 interacting parts, each with an individual reliability of 99.5%, the overall reliability will be only about 60%!

To measure reliability in a system in which each component may have its own unique reliability, we cannot use the reliability curve in Figure 17.2. However, the method of computing system reliability (R_s) is simple. It consists of finding the product of individual reliabilities as follows:

$$R_s = R_1 \times R_2 \times R_3 \times \ldots \times R_n \tag{17-1}$$

where R_1 = reliability of component 1
         R_2 = reliability of component 2

and so on.

Equation (17-1) assumes that the reliability of an individual component does not depend on the reliability of other components (that is, each component is *independent*). In addition, in this equation, as in most reliability discussions, reliabilities are presented as *probabilities*. Thus, a .90 reliability means that the unit will perform as intended 90% of the time. It also means that

LO 17.1 *Describe how to improve system reliability*

Figure **17.2**

Overall System Reliability as a Function of Number of *n* Components (Each with the Same Reliability) and Component Reliability with Components in a Series

it will fail $1 - .90 = .10 = 10\%$ of the time. We can use this method to evaluate the reliability of a service or a product, such as the one we examine in Example 1.

Example 1

RELIABILITY IN A SERIES

The National Bank of Greeley, Colorado, processes loan applications through three clerks (each checking different sections of the application in series), with reliabilities of .90, .80, and .99. It wants to find the system reliability.

APPROACH ▶ Apply Equation (17-1) to solve for R_s.

SOLUTION ▶ The reliability of the loan process is:

$$R_s = R_1 \times R_2 \times R_3 = (.90)(.80)(.99) = .713, \text{ or } 71.3\%$$

LO 17.2 *Determine system reliability*

INSIGHT ▶ Because each clerk in the series is less than perfect, the error probabilities are cumulative and the resulting reliability for this series is .713, which is less than any one clerk.

LEARNING EXERCISE ▶ If the lowest-performing clerk (.80) is replaced by a clerk performing at .95 reliability, what is the new expected reliability? [Answer: .846.]

RELATED PROBLEMS ▶ 17.1, 17.2, 17.3, 17.9 (17.16 and 17.17 are available in MyOMLab)

ACTIVE MODEL 17.1 This example is further illustrated in Active Model 17.1 in MyOMLab.

EXCEL OM Data File **Ch17Ex1.xls** can be found in MyOMLab.

The basic unit of measure for reliability is the *product failure rate* (FR). Firms producing high-technology equipment often provide failure-rate data on their products. As shown in Equations (17-2) and (17-3), the failure rate measures the percent of failures among the total number of products tested, FR(%), or a number of failures during a period of operating time, FR(N):

$$\text{FR(\%)} = \frac{\text{Number of failures}}{\text{Number of units tested}} \times 100\% \tag{17-2}$$

$$\text{FR}(N) = \frac{\text{Number of failures}}{\text{Number of unit-hours of operating time}} \tag{17-3}$$

Mean time between failures (MTBF)

The expected time between a repair and the next failure of a component, machine, process, or product.

Perhaps the most common term in reliability analysis is the **mean time between failures (MTBF)**, which is the reciprocal of FR(N):

$$\text{MTBF} = \frac{1}{\text{FR}(N)} \tag{17-4}$$

In Example 2, we compute the percentage of failure FR(%), number of failures FR(N), and mean time between failures (MTBF).

Example 2

DETERMINING MEAN TIME BETWEEN FAILURES

Twenty air-conditioning systems designed for use by astronauts in Russia's Soyuz spacecraft were operated for 1,000 hours at a Russian test facility. Two of the systems failed during the test—one after 200 hours and the other after 600 hours.

APPROACH ▶ To determine the percent of failures [FR(%)], the number of failures per unit of time [FR(N)], and the mean time between failures (MTBF), we use Equations (17-2), (17-3), and (17-4), respectively.

SOLUTION ▶ Percentage of failures:

$$FR(\%) = \frac{\text{Number of failures}}{\text{Number of units tested}} = \frac{2}{20}(100\%) = 10\%$$

Number of failures per operating hour:

$$FR(N) = \frac{\text{Number of failures}}{\text{Number of unit-hours of operating time}}$$

where

$$\text{Total time} = (1,000 \text{ hr})(20 \text{ units})$$
$$= 20,000 \text{ unit-hour}$$

$$\text{Nonoperating time} = 800 \text{ hr for 1st failure} + 400 \text{ hr for 2nd failure}$$
$$= 1,200 \text{ unit-hour}$$

$$\text{Number of unit-hours of operating time} = \text{Total time} - \text{Nonoperating time}$$

$$FR(N) = \frac{2}{20,000 - 1,200} = \frac{2}{18,800}$$

$$= .000106 \text{ failure/unit-hour}$$

Because $MTBF = \dfrac{1}{FR(N)}$:

$$MTBF = \frac{1}{.000106} = 9,434 \text{ hr}$$

LO 17.3 *Determine* mean time between failures (MTBF)

If the typical Soyuz shuttle trip to the International Space Station lasts 6 days, Russia may note that the failure rate per trip is:

$$\text{Failure rate} = (\text{Failures/unit-hr})(24 \text{ hr/day})(6 \text{ days/trip})$$
$$= (.000106)(24)(6)$$
$$= .0153 \text{ failure/trip}$$

INSIGHT ▶ Mean time between failures (MTBF) is the standard means of stating reliability.

LEARNING EXERCISE ▶ If nonoperating time drops to 800, what is the new MTBF? [Answer: 9,606 hr.]

RELATED PROBLEMS ▶ 17.4, 17.5

If the failure rate recorded in Example 2 is too high, Russia will have to increase systems reliability by either increasing the reliability of individual components or by redundancy.

Providing Redundancy

To increase the reliability of systems, redundancy is added in the form of *backup* components or *parallel paths*. Redundancy is provided to ensure that if one component or path fails, the system has recourse to another.

Redundancy
The use of backup components or parallel paths to raise reliability.

Backup Redundancy Assume that reliability of a component is .80 and we back it up with another component with reliability of .75. The resulting reliability is the probability of the first component working plus the probability of the backup component working multiplied by the probability of needing the backup component $(1 - .8 = .2)$. Therefore:

$$R_s = \begin{pmatrix} \text{Probability} \\ \text{of first} \\ \text{component} \\ \text{working} \end{pmatrix} + \left[\begin{pmatrix} \text{Probability} \\ \text{of second} \\ \text{component} \\ \text{working} \end{pmatrix} \times \begin{pmatrix} \text{Probability} \\ \text{of needing} \\ \text{second} \\ \text{component} \end{pmatrix} \right] = \qquad (17\text{-}5)$$

$$(.8) \qquad + \qquad [\ (.75) \qquad \times \qquad (1 - .8)\ ] \qquad = .8 + .15 = .95$$

Example 3 shows how redundancy, in the form of backup components, can improve the reliability of the loan process presented in Example 1.

Example 3

RELIABILITY WITH BACKUP

The National Bank is disturbed that its loan-application process has a reliability of only .713 (see Example 1) and would like to improve this situation.

APPROACH ▶ The bank decides to provide redundancy for the two least reliable clerks, with clerks of equal competence.

SOLUTION ▶ This procedure results in the following system:

$$
\begin{array}{ccc}
R_1 & R_2 & R_3 \\
\boxed{0.90} & \boxed{0.80} & \\
\downarrow & \downarrow & \\
0.90 \rightarrow & 0.80 \rightarrow & 0.99
\end{array}
$$

$$
\begin{aligned}
R_s &= [.9 + .9(1 - .9)] \times [.8 + .8(1 - .8)] \times .99 \\
&= [.9 + (.9)(.1)] \times [.8 + (.8)(.2)] \times .99 \\
&= .99 \times .96 \times .99 = .94
\end{aligned}
$$

INSIGHT ▶ By providing redundancy for two clerks, National Bank has increased reliability of the loan process from .713 to .94.

LEARNING EXERCISE ▶ What happens when the bank replaces both R_2 clerks with one new clerk who has a reliability of .90? [Answer: $R_s = .88$.]

RELATED PROBLEMS ▶ 17.7, 17.10, 17.12, 17.13, 17.14, 17.15

ACTIVE MODEL 17.2 This example is further illustrated in Active Model 17.2 in MyOMLab.

EXCEL OM Data File **Ch17Ex3.xls** can be found in MyOMLab.

Parallel Redundancy Another way to enhance reliability is to provide parallel paths. In a parallel system, the paths are assumed to be independent; therefore, success on any one path allows the system to perform. In Example 4, we determine the reliability of a process with three parallel paths.

Example 4

RELIABILITY WITH PARALLEL REDUNDANCY

A new iPad design that is more reliable because of its parallel circuits is shown below. What is its reliability?

APPROACH ▶ Identify the reliability of each path, then compute the likelihood of needing additional paths (likelihood of failure), and finally subtract the product of those failures from 1.

SOLUTION ▶

Reliability for the middle path $= R_2 \times R_3 = .975 \times .975 = .9506$

Then determine the probability of *failure* for all 3 paths $= (1 - 0.95) \times (1 - .9506) \times (1 - 0.95)$

$$= (.05) \times (.0494) \times (.05) = .00012$$

Therefore the reliability of the new design is 1 minus the probability of failures, or

$$= 1 - .00012 = .99988$$

INSIGHT ▶ Even in a system where no component has reliability over .975, the parallel design increases reliability to over .999. Parallel paths can add substantially to reliability.

LEARNING EXERCISE ▶ If reliability of *all* components is only .90, what is the new reliability? [Answer: .9981]

RELATED PROBLEMS ▶ 17.6, 17.8, 17.11

ACTIVE MODEL 17.3 This example is further illustrated in Active Model 17.3 in MyOMLab.

Managers often use a combination of backup components or parallel paths to improve reliability.

Maintenance

There are two types of maintenance: preventive maintenance and breakdown maintenance. Preventive maintenance involves monitoring equipment and facilities, performing routine inspections, servicing, and keeping facilities in good repair. These activities are intended to build a system that will reduce variability, find potential failures, and make changes or repairs that will maintain efficient processes. The current generation of sophisticated sensors allows managers to build systems that can detect the slightest unusual vibration, minute changes in temperature or pressure, and slight changes in oil viscosity or chemical components. Preventive maintenance involves designing technical and human systems that will keep the productive process working within tolerance; it allows the system to perform as designed. Breakdown maintenance occurs when preventive maintenance fails and equipment/facilities must be repaired on an emergency or priority basis.

> **Preventive maintenance**
> A plan that involves monitoring, routine inspections, servicing, and keeping facilities in good repair.

Implementing Preventive Maintenance

Preventive maintenance implies that we can determine when a system needs service or will need repair. Therefore, to perform preventive maintenance, we must know when a system requires service or when it is likely to fail. Failures occur at different rates during the life of a product. A high initial failure rate, known as infant mortality, may exist for many products. This is why many electronic firms "burn in" their products prior to shipment: that is to say, they execute a variety of tests (such as a full wash cycle at Whirlpool) to detect "startup" problems prior to shipment. Firms may also provide 90-day warranties. We should note that many infant mortality failures are not product failures per se, but rather failure due to improper use. This fact points up the importance in many industries of operations management's building an after-sales service system that includes installing and training.

> **Breakdown maintenance**
> Remedial maintenance that occurs when preventive maintenance fails and equipment/facilities must be repaired on an emergency or priority basis.

> **Infant mortality**
> The failure rate early in the life of a product or process.

Once the product, machine, or process "settles in," a study can be made of the MTBF (mean time between failures) distribution. Such distributions often follow a normal curve. When these distributions exhibit small standard deviations, then we know we have a candidate for preventive maintenance, even if the maintenance is expensive.

> **LO 17.4** *Distinguish* between preventive and breakdown maintenance

Once our firm has a candidate for preventive maintenance, we want to determine *when* preventive maintenance is economical. Typically, the more expensive the maintenance, the narrower must be the MTBF distribution (that is, have a small standard deviation). In addition, if the process is no more expensive to repair when it breaks down than the cost of preventive maintenance, perhaps we should let the process break down and then do the repair. However, the consequence of the breakdown must be fully considered. Even some relatively minor breakdowns have catastrophic consequences. At the other extreme, preventive maintenance costs may be so incidental that preventive maintenance is appropriate even if the MTBF distribution is rather flat (that is, it has a large standard deviation).

With good reporting techniques, firms can maintain records of individual processes, machines, or equipment. Such records can provide a profile of both the kinds of maintenance required and the timing of maintenance needed. Maintaining equipment history is an important part of a preventive maintenance system, as is a record of the time and cost to make the repair. Such records can also provide information about the family of equipment and suppliers.

Figure **17.3**

A Computerized Maintenance System

Data Files

Equipment file with parts list

Maintenance and work order schedule

Repair history file

Inventory of spare parts

Personnel data with skills, wages, etc.

Data entry
• Work requests
• Purchase requests
• Time reporting
• Contract work

Computer

Output Reports

Inventory and purchasing reports

Equipment parts list

Equipment history reports

Costs analysis (actual vs. standard)

Work orders

LO 17.5 *Describe* how to improve maintenance

Reliability and maintenance are of such importance that most maintenance management systems are now computerized. Figure 17.3 shows the major components of such a system with files to be maintained on the left and reports generated on the right.

Companies from Boeing to Ford are improving product reliability via their maintenance information systems. Boeing monitors the health of planes in flight by relaying relevant information in real-time to the ground. This provides a head start on reliability and maintenance issues. Similarly, with wireless satellite service, millions of car owners are alerted to thousands of diagnostic issues, from faulty airbag sensors to the need for an oil change. These real-time systems provide immediate data that are used to head off quality issues before customers even notice a problem. The technology enhances reliability and customer satisfaction. And catching problems early saves millions of dollars in warranty costs.

Figure 17.4(a) shows a traditional view of the relationship between preventive maintenance and breakdown maintenance. In this view, operations managers consider a *balance* between the two costs. Allocating more resources to preventive maintenance will reduce the number of breakdowns. At some point, however, the decrease in breakdown maintenance costs may be less than the increase in preventive maintenance costs. At this point, the total cost curve begins to rise. Beyond this optimal point, the firm will be better off waiting for breakdowns to occur and repairing them when they do.

Unfortunately, cost curves such as in Figure 17.4(a) seldom consider the *full costs of a breakdown*. Many costs are ignored because they are not *directly* related to the immediate breakdown. For instance, the cost of inventory maintained to compensate for downtime is not typically

(a) **Traditional View of Maintenance**

Total costs

Preventive maintenance costs

Breakdown maintenance costs

Costs

Maintenance commitment

Optimal point (lowest-cost maintenance policy)

(b) **Full Cost View of Maintenance**

Total costs

Full cost of breakdowns

Preventive maintenance costs

Costs

Maintenance commitment

Optimal point (lowest-cost maintenance policy)

Figure **17.4**

Maintenance Costs

considered. Moreover, downtime can have a devastating effect on safety and morale. Employees may also begin to believe that "performance to standard" and maintaining equipment are not important. Finally, downtime adversely affects delivery schedules, destroying customer relations and future sales. When the full impact of breakdowns is considered, Figure 17.4(b) may be a better representation of maintenance costs. In Figure 17.4(b), total costs are at a minimum when the system only breaks down due to unanticipated extraordinary events.

● **STUDENT TIP**

When all breakdown costs are considered, much more maintenance may be advantageous.

Assuming that all potential costs associated with downtime have been identified, the operations staff can compute the optimal level of maintenance activity on a theoretical basis. Such analysis, of course, also requires accurate historical data on maintenance costs, breakdown probabilities, and repair times. Example 5 shows how to compare preventive and breakdown maintenance costs to select the least expensive maintenance policy.

Example 5

COMPARING PREVENTIVE AND BREAKDOWN MAINTENANCE COSTS

Farlen & Halikman is a CPA firm specializing in payroll preparation. The firm has been successful in automating much of its work, using high-speed printers for check processing and report preparation. The computerized approach, however, has problems. Over the past 20 months, the printers have broken down at the rate indicated in the following table:

NUMBER OF BREAKDOWNS	NUMBER OF MONTHS THAT BREAKDOWNS OCCURRED
0	2
1	8
2	6
3	4
	Total: 20

Each time the printers break down, Farlen & Halikman estimates that it loses an average of $300 in production time and service expenses. One alternative is to purchase a service contract for preventive maintenance. Even if Farlen & Halikman contracts for preventive maintenance, there will still be breakdowns, *averaging* one breakdown per month. The price for this service is $150 per month.

LO 17.6 *Compare preventive and breakdown maintenance costs*

APPROACH ▶ To determine if the CPA firm should follow a "run until breakdown" policy or contract for preventive maintenance, we follow a 4-step process:

Step 1 Compute the *expected number* of breakdowns (based on past history) if the firm continues as is, without the service contract.

Step 2 Compute the expected breakdown cost per month with no preventive maintenance contract.

Step 3 Compute the cost of preventive maintenance.

Step 4 Compare the two options and select the one that will cost less.

SOLUTION ▶

Step 1

NUMBER OF BREAKDOWNS	FREQUENCY	NUMBER OF BREAKDOWNS	FREQUENCY
0	2/20 = .1	2	6/20 = 0.3
1	8/20 = .4	3	4/20 = 0.2

$$\begin{pmatrix} \text{Expected number} \\ \text{of breakdowns} \end{pmatrix} = \Sigma \left[\begin{pmatrix} \text{Number of} \\ \text{breakdowns} \end{pmatrix} \times \begin{pmatrix} \text{Corresponding} \\ \text{frequency} \end{pmatrix} \right]$$

$$= (0)(.1) + (1)(.4) + (2)(.3) + (3)(.2)$$

$$= 0 + .4 + .6 + .6$$

$$= 1.6 \text{ breakdowns/month}$$

Step 2

$$\text{Expected breakdown cost} = \begin{pmatrix} \text{Expected number} \\ \text{of breakdowns} \end{pmatrix} \times \begin{pmatrix} \text{Cost per} \\ \text{breakdown} \end{pmatrix}$$

$$= (1.6)(\$300)$$

$$= \$480/\text{month}$$

Step 3

$$\begin{pmatrix} \text{Preventive} \\ \text{maintenance cost} \end{pmatrix} = \begin{pmatrix} \text{Cost of expected} \\ \text{breakdowns if service} \\ \text{contract signed} \end{pmatrix} + \begin{pmatrix} \text{Cost of} \\ \text{service contract} \end{pmatrix}$$

$$= (1 \text{ breakdown/month})(\$300) + \$150/\text{month}$$

$$= \$450/\text{month}$$

Step 4   Because it is less expensive overall to hire a maintenance service firm ($450) than to not do so ($480), Farlen & Halikman should hire the service firm.

INSIGHT ▶   Determining the expected number of breakdowns for each option is crucial to making a good decision. This typically requires good maintenance records.

LEARNING EXERCISE ▶   What is the best decision if the preventive maintenance contract cost increases to $195 per month? [Answer: At $495 (= $300 + $195) per month, "run until breakdown" becomes less expensive (assuming that all costs are included in the $300 per breakdown cost).]

RELATED PROBLEMS ▶   17.18–17.21 (17.22–17.24 are available in MyOMLab)

Using variations of the technique shown in Example 5, operations managers can examine maintenance policies.

Increasing Repair Capabilities

Because reliability and preventive maintenance are seldom perfect, most firms opt for some level of repair capability. Enlarging repair facilities or improving maintenance management may be an excellent way to get the system back in operation faster.

However, not all repairs can be done in the firm's facility. Managers must, therefore, decide where repairs are to be performed. Figure 17.5 provides a continuum of options and how they rate in terms of speed, cost, and competence. Moving to the right in Figure 17.5 may improve the competence of the repair work, but at the same time it increases costs and replacement time.

LO 17.7 *Define* autonomous maintenance

Autonomous Maintenance

Autonomous maintenance

Operators partner with maintenance personnel to observe, check, adjust, clean, and notify.

Preventive maintenance policies and techniques must include an emphasis on employees accepting responsibility for the "observe, check, adjust, clean, and notify" type of equipment maintenance. Such policies are consistent with the advantages of employee empowerment. This approach is known as autonomous maintenance. Employees can predict failures, prevent breakdowns, and prolong equipment life. With autonomous maintenance, the manager is making a step toward both employee empowerment and maintaining system performance.

Figure 17.5

The Operations Manager Determines How Maintenance Will Be Performed

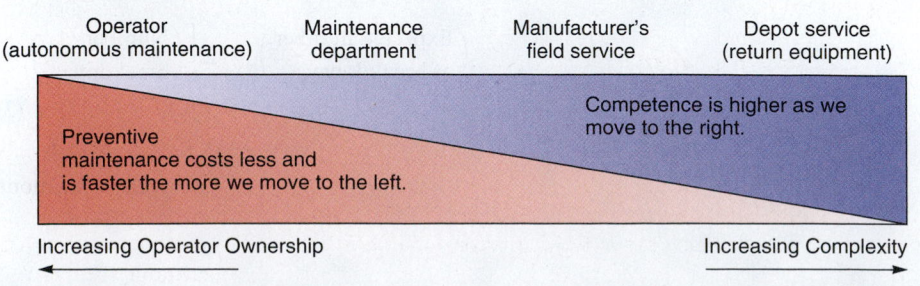

Operator (autonomous maintenance) — Maintenance department — Manufacturer's field service — Depot service (return equipment)

Competence is higher as we move to the right.

Preventive maintenance costs less and is faster the more we move to the left.

Increasing Operator Ownership   Increasing Complexity

Total Productive Maintenance

Many firms have moved to bring total quality management concepts to the practice of preventive maintenance with an approach known as total productive maintenance (TPM). It involves the concept of reducing variability through autonomous maintenance and excellent maintenance practices. Total productive maintenance includes:

◆ Designing machines that are reliable, easy to operate, and easy to maintain

◆ Emphasizing total cost of ownership when purchasing machines, so that service and maintenance are included in the cost

◆ Developing preventive maintenance plans that utilize the best practices of operators, maintenance departments, and depot service

◆ Training for autonomous maintenance so operators maintain their own machines and partner with maintenance personnel

High utilization of facilities, tight scheduling, low inventory, and consistent quality demand reliability. Total productive maintenance, which continues to improve with recent advances in the use of simulation, expert systems, and sensors, is the key to reducing variability and improving reliability.

Total productive maintenance (TPM)

Combines total quality management with a strategic view of maintenance from process and equipment design to preventive maintenance.

◆ **STUDENT TIP**

Maintenance improves productivity.

Summary

Operations managers focus on design improvements, backup components, and parallel paths to improve reliability. Reliability improvements also can be obtained through the use of preventive maintenance and excellent repair facilities.

Firms give employees "ownership" of their equipment. When workers repair or do preventive maintenance on their own machines, breakdowns are less common. Well-trained and empowered employees ensure reliable systems through preventive maintenance. In turn, reliable, well-maintained equipment not only provides higher utilization but also improves quality and performance to schedule. Top firms build and maintain systems that drive out variability so that customers can rely on products and services to be produced to specifications and on time.

Key Terms

Maintenance (p. 662)
Reliability (p. 662)
Mean time between failures
  (MTBF) (p. 664)

Redundancy (p. 665)
Preventive maintenance (p. 667)
Breakdown maintenance (p. 667)
Infant mortality (p. 667)

Autonomous maintenance (p. 670)
Total productive maintenance
  (TPM) (p. 671)

Ethical Dilemma

The space shuttle *Columbia* disintegrated over Texas on its 2003 return to Earth. The *Challenger* exploded shortly after launch in 1986. And the *Apollo 1* spacecraft imploded in fire on the launch pad in 1967. In each case, the lives of all crew members were lost. The hugely complex shuttle may have looked a bit like an airplane but was very different. In reality, its overall statistical reliability is such that about 1 out of every 50 flights had a major malfunction. As one aerospace manager stated, "Of course, you can be perfectly safe and never get off the ground."

Given the huge reliability and maintenance issues NASA faced (seals cracking in cold weather, heat shielding tiles falling off, tools left in the capsule), should astronauts have been allowed to fly? (In earlier *Atlas* rockets, men were inserted not out of necessity but because test pilots and politicians thought they should be there.) What are the pros and cons of staffed space exploration from an ethical perspective? Should the U.S. spend billions of dollars to return an astronaut to the moon or send one to Mars?

Discussion Questions

1. What is the objective of maintenance and reliability?
2. How does one identify a candidate for preventive maintenance?
3. Explain the notion of "infant mortality" in the context of product reliability.
4. How could simulation be a useful technique for maintenance problems?
5. What is the trade-off between operator-performed maintenance versus supplier-performed maintenance?
6. How can a manager evaluate the effectiveness of the maintenance function?
7. How does machine design contribute to either increasing or alleviating the maintenance problem?

8. What roles can computerized maintenance management systems play in the maintenance function?
9. During an argument as to the merits of preventive maintenance at Windsor Printers, the company owner asked, "Why fix it before it breaks?" How would you, as the director of maintenance, respond?
10. Will preventive maintenance eliminate *all* breakdowns?

Using Software to Solve Reliability Problems

PX Excel OM and POM for Windows may be used to solve reliability problems. The reliability module allows us to enter (1) number of systems (components) in the series (1 through 10); (2) number of backup, or parallel, components (1 through 12); and (3) component reliability for both series and parallel data.

Solved Problems   Virtual Office Hours help is available at MyOMLab.

SOLVED PROBLEM 17.1

The semiconductor used in the Sullivan Wrist Calculator has five circuits, each of which has its own reliability rate. Component 1 has a reliability of .90; component 2, .95; component 3, .98; component 4, .90; and component 5, .99. What is the reliability of one semiconductor?

SOLUTION

Semiconductor reliability, $R_s = R_1 \times R_2 \times R_3 \times R_4 \times R_5$
$$= (.90)(.95)(.98)(.90)(.99)$$
$$= .7466$$

SOLVED PROBLEM 17.2

A recent engineering change at Sullivan Wrist Calculator places a backup component in each of the two least reliable transistor circuits. The new circuits will look like the following:

What is the reliability of the new system?

SOLUTION

$$\text{Reliability} = [.9 + (1 - .9) \times .9] \times .95 \times .98 \times [.9 + (1 - .9) \times .9] \times .99$$
$$= [.9 + .09] \times .95 \times .98 \times [.9 + .09] \times .99$$
$$= .99 \times .95 \times .98 \times .99 \times .99$$
$$= .903$$

Problems   Note: **PX** means the problem may be solved with POM for Windows and/or Excel OM.

Problems 17.1–17.17 relate to Reliability

• **17.1**   The Beta II computer's electronic processing unit contains 50 components in series. The average reliability of each component is 99.0%. Using Figure 17.2, determine the overall reliability of the processing unit.

• **17.2.**   A testing process at Boeing Aircraft has 400 components in series. The average reliability of each component is 99.5%. Use Figure 17.2 to find the overall reliability of the whole testing process.

•• **17.3**   A new aircraft control system is being designed that must be 98% reliable. This system consists of three components in series. If all three of the components are to have the same level of reliability, what level of reliability is required? **PX**

•• **17.4**   Robert Klassan Manufacturing, a medical equipment manufacturer, subjected 100 heart pacemakers to 5,000 hours of testing. Halfway through the testing, 5 pacemakers failed. What was the failure rate in terms of the following:
a) Percentage of failures?
b) Number of failures per unit-hour?
c) Number of failures per unit-year?
d) If 1,100 people receive pacemaker implants, how many units can we expect to fail during the following year?

•• **17.5**   A manufacturer of disk drives for notebook computers wants an MTBF of at least 50,000 hours. Recent test results for 10 units were one failure at 10,000 hours, another at 25,000 hours,

and two more at 45,000 hours. The remaining units were still running at 60,000 hours. Determine the following:
a) Percent of failures
b) Number of failures per unit-hour
c) MTBF at this point in the testing

•• 17.6 What is the reliability of the following parallel production process? $R_1 = 0.95$, $R_2 = 0.90$, $R_3 = 0.98$.

•• 17.7 What is the overall reliability that bank loans will be processed accurately if each of the 5 clerks shown in the chart has the reliability shown?

Hint: The three paths are done in parallel, followed by an additional independent step.

•• 17.8 Merrill Kim Sharp has a system composed of three components in parallel. The components have the following reliabilities:

$$R_1 = 0.90, \quad R_2 = 0.95, \quad R_3 = 0.85$$

What is the reliability of the system? (*Hint:* See Example 4.) **Px**

• 17.9 A medical control system has three components in series with individual reliabilities (R_1, R_2, R_3) as shown:

What is the reliability of the system? **Px**

•• 17.10 What is the reliability of the system shown?

• 17.11 How much would reliability improve if the medical control system shown in Problem 17.9 changed to the redundant parallel system shown in Problem 17.10?

•• 17.12 Elizabeth Irwin's design team has proposed the following system with component reliabilities as indicated:

What is the reliability of the system? **Px**
Hint: The system functions if either R_2 or R_3 work.

•• 17.13 Rick Wing, salesperson for Wave Soldering Systems, Inc. (WSSI), has provided you with a proposal for improving the temperature control on your present machine. The machine uses a hot-air knife to cleanly remove excess solder from printed circuit

boards; this is a great concept, but the hot-air temperature control lacks reliability. According to Wing, engineers at WSSI have improved the reliability of the critical temperature controls. The new system still has the four sensitive integrated circuits controlling the temperature, but the new machine has a backup for each. The four integrated circuits have reliabilities of .90, .92, .94, and .96. The four backup circuits all have a reliability of .90.
a) What is the reliability of the new temperature controller?
b) If you pay a premium, Wing says he can improve all four of the backup units to .93. What is the reliability of this option? **Px**

•••• 17.14 As VP for operations at Méndez-Piñero Engineering, you must decide which product design, A or B, has the higher reliability. B is designed with backup units for components R_3 and R_4. What is the reliability of each design? **Px**

•••• 17.15 A typical retail transaction consists of several smaller steps, which can be considered components subject to failure. A list of such components might include:

COMPONENT	DESCRIPTION	DEFINITION OF FAILURE
1	Find product in proper size, color, etc.	Can't find product
2	Enter cashier line	No lines open; lines too long; line experiencing difficulty
3	Scan product UPC for name, price, etc.	Won't scan; item not on file; scans incorrect name or price
4	Calculate purchase total	Wrong weight; wrong extension; wrong data entry; wrong tax
5	Make payment	Customer lacks cash; check not acceptable; credit card refused
6	Make change	Makes change incorrectly
7	Bag merchandise	Damages merchandise while bagging; bag splits
8	Conclude transaction and exit	No receipt; unfriendly, rude, or aloof clerk

Let the eight probabilities of success be .92, .94, .99, .99, .98, .97, .95, and .96. What is the reliability of the system; that is, the probability that there will be a satisfied customer? If you were the store manager, what do you think should be an acceptable value for this probability? Which components would be good candidates for backup, which for redesign?

Additional problems **17.16–17.17** *are available in* MyOMLab.

Problems 17.18–17.24 relate to Maintenance

• 17.18 What are the *expected* number of yearly breakdowns for the power generator at Orlando Utilities that has exhibited the following data over the past 20 years? **Px**

Number of breakdowns	0	1	2	3	4	5	6
Number of years in which breakdown occurred	2	2	5	4	5	2	0

· 17.19 Each breakdown of a graphic plotter table at Airbus Industries costs $50. Find the expected daily breakdown cost, given the following data: **Px**

Number of breakdowns	0	1	2	3	4
Daily breakdown probability	.1	.2	.4	.2	.1

·· 17.20 David Hall, chief of the maintenance department at Mechanical Dynamics, has presented you with the following failure curve. What does it suggest?

··· 17.21 The fire department has a number of failures with its oxygen masks and is evaluating the possibility of outsourcing preventive maintenance to the manufacturer. Because of the risk associated with a failure, the cost of each failure is estimated at $2,000. The current maintenance policy (with station employees performing maintenance) has yielded the following history:

Number of breakdowns	0	1	2	3	4	5
Number of years in which breakdowns occurred	4	3	1	5	5	0

This manufacturer will guarantee repairs on any and all failures as part of a service contract. The cost of this service is $5,000 per year.

a) What is the expected number of breakdowns per year with station employees performing maintenance?

b) What is the cost of the current maintenance policy?

c) What is the more economical policy?

Additional problems **17.22–17.24** *are available in MyOMLab.*

CASE STUDY

Maintenance Drives Profits at Frito-Lay

Video Case

Frito-Lay, the multi-billion-dollar subsidiary of food and beverage giant PepsiCo, maintains 36 plants in the U.S. and Canada. These facilities produce dozen of snacks, including the well-known Lay's, Fritos, Cheetos, Doritos, Ruffles, and Tostitos brands, each of which sells over $1 billion per year.

Frito-Lay plants produce in the high-volume, low-variety process model common to commercial baked goods, steel, glass, and beer industries. In this environment, preventive maintenance of equipment takes a major role by avoiding costly downtime. Tom Rao, vice president for Florida operations, estimates that each 1% of downtime has a negative annual profit impact of $200,000. He is proud of the $1\frac{1}{2}$% unscheduled downtime his plant is able to reach—well below the 2% that is considered the "world-class" benchmark. This excellent performance is possible because the maintenance department takes an active role in setting the parameters for preventive maintenance. This is done with weekly input to the production schedule.

Maintenance policy impacts energy use as well. The Florida plant's technical manager, Jim Wentzel, states, "By reducing production interruptions, we create an opportunity to bring energy and utility use under control. Equipment maintenance and a solid production schedule are keys to utility efficiency. With every production interruption, there is substantial waste."

As a part of its total productive maintenance (TPM) program,* Frito-Lay empowers employees with what it calls the "Run Right" system. Run Right teaches employees to "identify and do." This

*At Frito-Lay, preventive maintenance, autonomous maintenance, and total productive maintenance are part of a Frito-Lay program known as total productive manufacturing.

means each shift is responsible for identifying problems and making the necessary corrections, when possible. This is accomplished through (1) a "power walk" at the beginning of the shift to ensure that equipment and process settings are performing to standard, (2) mid-shift and post-shift reviews of standards and performance, and (3) posting of any issues on a large whiteboard in the shift office. Items remain on the whiteboard until corrected, which is seldom more than a shift or two.

With good manpower scheduling and tight labor control to hold down variable costs, making time for training is challenging. But supervisors, including the plant manager, are available to fill in on the production line when that is necessary to free an employee for training.

The 30 maintenance personnel hired to cover 24/7 operations at the Florida plant all come with multi-craft skills (e.g., welding, electrical, plumbing). "Multi-craft maintenance personnel are harder to find and cost more," says Wentzel, "but they more than pay for themselves."

Discussion Questions**

1. What might be done to help take Frito-Lay to the next level of outstanding maintenance? Consider factors such as sophisticated software.

2. What are the advantages and disadvantages of giving more responsibility for machine maintenance to the operator?

3. Discuss the pros and cons of hiring multi-craft maintenance personnel.

**You may wish to view the video that accompanies this case before answering these questions.

· **Additional Case Studies:** Visit MyOMLab for these free case studies:

Cartak's Department Store: Requires the evaluation of the impact of an additional invoice verifier.

Worldwide Chemical Company: The maintenance department in this company is in turmoil.

Main Heading	Review Material	MyOMLab
THE STRATEGIC IMPORTANCE OF MAINTENANCE AND RELIABILITY (pp. 662–663)	Poor maintenance can be disruptive, inconvenient, wasteful, and expensive in dollars and even in lives. The interdependency of operator, machine, and mechanic is a hallmark of successful maintenance and reliability. Good maintenance and reliability management requires employee involvement and good procedures; it enhances a firm's performance and protects its investment. *The objective of maintenance and reliability is to maintain the capability of the system.* ■ **Maintenance**—All activities involved in keeping a system's equipment in working order. ■ **Reliability**—The probability that a machine part or product will function properly for a specified time under stated conditions. The two main tactics for improving reliability are: 1. Improving individual components 2. Providing redundancy The two main tactics for improving maintenance are: 1. Implementing or improving preventive maintenance 2. Increasing repair capabilities or speed	Concept Questions: 1.1–1.4 **VIDEO 17.1** Maintenance Drives Profits at Frito-Lay
RELIABILITY (pp. 663–667)	A system is composed of a series of individual interrelated components, each performing a specific job. If any *one* component fails to perform, the overall system can fail. As the number of components in a *series* increases, the reliability of the whole system declines very quickly: $$R_s = R_1 \times R_2 \times R_3 \times \ldots \times R_n \qquad (17\text{-}1)$$ where R_1 = reliability of component 1, R_2 = reliability of component 2, and so on. Equation (17-1) assumes that the reliability of an individual component does not depend on the reliability of other components. A .90 reliability means that the unit will perform as intended 90% of the time, and it will fail 10% of the time. The basic unit of measure for reliability is the *product failure rate* (FR). FR(%) is the percent of failures among the total number of products tested, and FR(N) is the number of failures during a period of time: $$FR(\%) = \frac{\text{Number of failures}}{\text{Number of units tested}} \times 100\% \qquad (17\text{-}2)$$ $$FR(N) = \frac{\text{Number of failures}}{\text{Number of unit-hours of operating time}} \qquad (17\text{-}3)$$ ■ **Mean time between failures (MTBF)**—The expected time between a repair and the next failure of a component, machine, process, or product. $$MTBF = \frac{1}{FR(N)} \qquad (17\text{-}4)$$ ■ **Redundancy**—The use of components in parallel to raise reliability. The reliability of a component along with its backup equals: (Probability that 1st component works) + [(Prob. that backup works) $\times$ (Prob. that 1st fails)] $\qquad (17\text{-}5)$	Concept Questions: 2.1–2.4 Problems: 17.1–17.17 Virtual Office Hours for Solved Problems: 17.1, 17.2 **ACTIVE MODELS 17.1, 17.2, 17.3**
MAINTENANCE (pp. 667–670)	■ **Preventive maintenance**—Involves routine inspections, monitoring, servicing, and keeping facilities in good repair. ■ **Breakdown maintenance**—Remedial maintenance that occurs when preventive maintenance fails and equipment/facilities must be repaired on an emergency or priority basis. ■ **Infant mortality**—The failure rate early in the life of a product or process. Consistent with job enrichment practices, machine operators must be held responsible for preventive maintenance of their own equipment and tools. Reliability and maintenance are of such importance that most maintenance systems are now computerized.	Concept Questions: 3.1–3.4 Problems: 17.18–17.24

Main Heading	Review Material	
	Costs of a breakdown that may get ignored include: 1. The cost of inventory maintained to compensate for downtime 2. Downtime, which can have a devastating effect on safety and morale and which adversely affects delivery schedules, destroying customer relations and future sales ■ **Autonomous maintenance**—Operators partner with maintenance personnel to observe, check, adjust, clean, and notify. Employees can predict failures, prevent breakdowns, and prolong equipment life. With autonomous maintenance, the manager is making a step toward both employee empowerment and maintaining system performance.	
TOTAL PRODUCTIVE MAINTENANCE (p. 671)	■ **Total productive maintenance (TPM)**—Combines total quality management with a strategic view of maintenance from process and equipment design to preventive maintenance. Total productive maintenance includes: 1. Designing machines that are reliable, easy to operate, and easy to maintain 2. Emphasizing total cost of ownership when purchasing machines, so that service and maintenance are included in the cost 3. Developing preventive maintenance plans that utilize the best practices of operators, maintenance departments, and depot service 4. Training for autonomous maintenance so operators maintain their own machines and partner with maintenance personnel Three techniques that have proven beneficial to effective maintenance are simulation, expert systems, and sensors.	Concept Questions: 4.1–4.4

Self Test

■ **Before taking the self-test,** refer to the learning objectives listed at the beginning of the chapter and the key terms listed at the end of the chapter.

LO 17.1 The two main tactics for improving reliability are _____ and _____.

LO 17.2 The reliability of a system with *n* independent components equals:
   a) the sum of the individual reliabilities.
   b) the minimum reliability among all components.
   c) the maximum reliability among all components.
   d) the product of the individual reliabilities.
   e) the average of the individual reliabilities.

LO 17.3 What is the formula for the mean time between failures?
   a) Number of failures ÷ Number of unit-hours of operating time
   b) Number of unit-hours of operating time ÷ Number of failures
   c) (Number of failures ÷ Number of units tested) × 100%
   d) (Number of units tested ÷ Number of failures) × 100%
   e) $1 \div FR(\%)$

LO 17.4 The process that is intended to find potential failures and make changes or repairs is known as:
   a) breakdown maintenance.
   b) failure maintenance.
   c) preventive maintenance.
   d) all of the above.

LO 17.5 The two main tactics for improving maintenance are _____ and _____.

LO 17.6 The appropriate maintenance policy is developed by balancing preventive maintenance costs with breakdown maintenance costs. The problem is that:
   a) preventive maintenance costs are very difficult to identify.
   b) full breakdown costs are seldom considered.
   c) preventive maintenance should be performed, regardless of the cost.
   d) breakdown maintenance must be performed, regardless of the cost.

LO 17.7 _____ maintenance partners operators with maintenance personnel to observe, check, adjust, clean, and notify.
   a) Partnering
   b) Operator
   c) Breakdown
   d) Six Sigma
   e) Autonomous

Answers: LO 17.1. improving individual components, providing redundancy; LO 17.2. d; LO 17.3. b; LO 17.4. c; LO 17.5. implementing or improving preventive maintenance, increasing repair capabilities or speed; LO 17.6. b; LO 17.7. e.

Decision-Making Tools

A MODULE

MODULE OUTLINE

- The Decision Process in Operations *678*
- Fundamentals of Decision Making *679*
- Decision Tables *680*
- Types of Decision-Making Environments *681*
- Decision Trees *684*

Alaska Airlines

Alaska Airlines

LEARNING OBJECTIVES

LO A.1 *Create* a simple decision tree 680

LO A.2 *Build* a decision table 680

LO A.3 *Explain* when to use each of the three types of decision-making environments 681

LO A.4 *Calculate* an expected monetary value (EMV) 682

LO A.5 *Compute* the expected value of perfect information (EVPI) 683

LO A.6 *Evaluate* the nodes in a decision tree 686

LO A.7 *Create* a decision tree with sequential decisions 687

WOULD *YOU* GO ALL IN?

At the Legends of Poker tournament in Los Angeles, veteran T.J. Cloutier opens with a $60,000 bet. (Antes and required bets of $39,000 are already on the table.) Former Go2net CTO Paul Phillips ponders going "all in"—betting virtually all his chips. Using decision theory, here's how he decided.

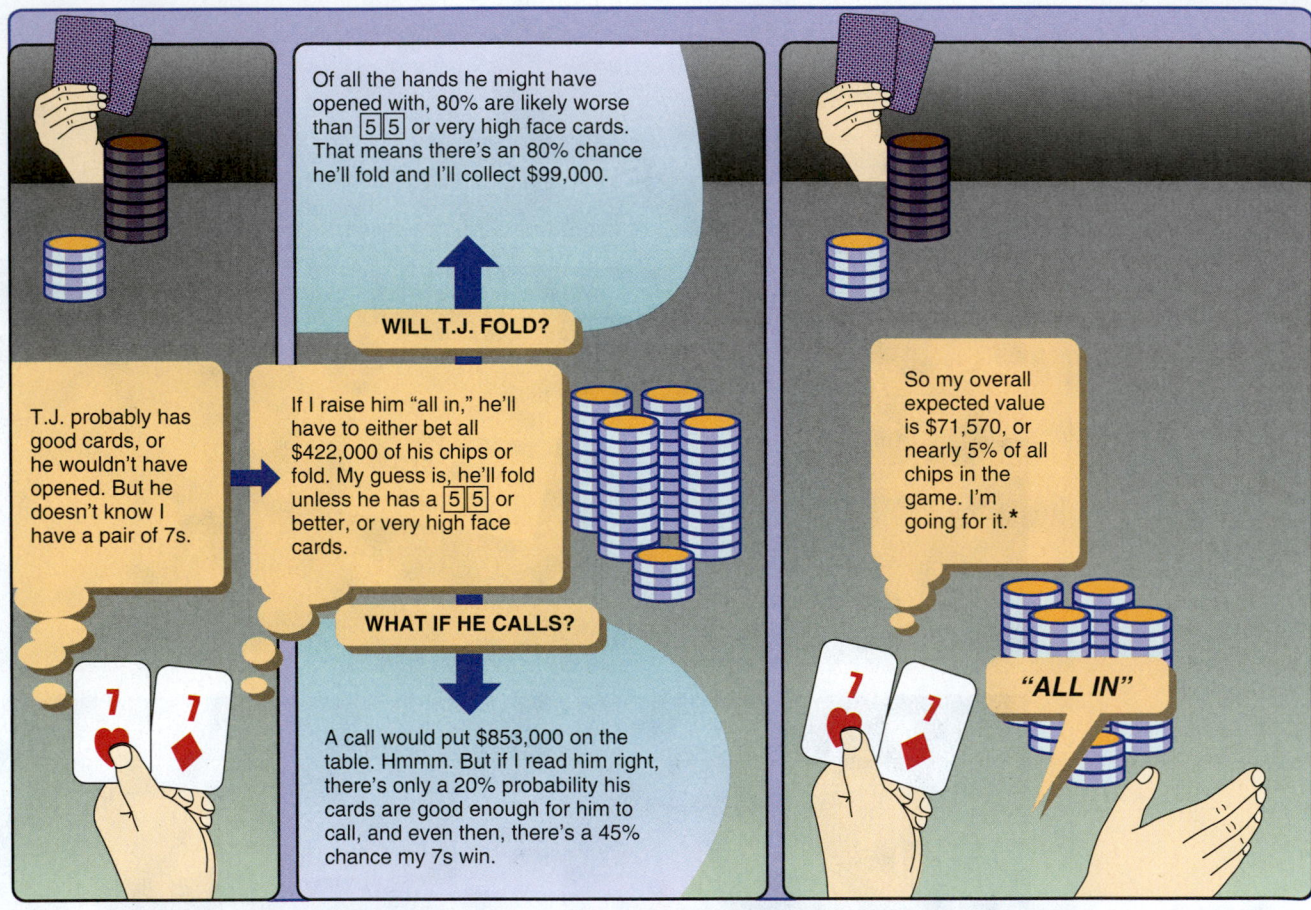

Source: Based on *Business 2.0* (November 2003): 128–134.

*To see the details of Phillips's decision, see Example A8.

The Decision Process in Operations

Operations managers are not gamblers. But they are decision makers. To achieve the goals of their organizations, managers must understand how decisions are made and know which decision-making tools to use. To a great extent, the success or failure of both people and companies depends on the quality of their decisions. Overcoming uncertainty is a manager's challenge.

What makes the difference between a good decision and a bad decision? A "good" decision—one that uses analytic decision making—is based on logic and considers all available data and possible alternatives. It also follows these six steps:

1. Clearly define the problem and the factors that influence it.
2. Develop specific and measurable objectives.
3. Develop a model—that is, a relationship between objectives and variables (which are measurable quantities).
4. Evaluate each alternative solution based on its merits and drawbacks.
5. Select the best alternative.
6. Implement and evaluate the decision and then set a timetable for completion.

So analytic decision making requires models, objectives, and quantifiable variables, often in the form of probabilities and payoffs. Such information is not always easy to obtain or derive from existing data. This challenge exists because of either a lack of data or an overabundance of data. However, because data are now easily generated and stored in digital form, we tend to have the latter—massive volumes of data. Data are collected automatically from production processes, as well as from websites, credit cards, point-of-sale records, and social media. Although this mass of data is a potential source of information, it requires sophistication in how it is stored, processed, and analyzed. Big data is the term used to describe this huge amount of data, which often cannot be efficiently processed by traditional data techniques.

Throughout this text, we have introduced a broad range of mathematical models and tools that help operations managers make better decisions. Because good decisions require data that can be analyzed and turned into information, decision makers appreciate the potential of big data. This module provides an introduction to the challenges facing managers by introducing two of the tools of decision making—decision tables and decision trees. These two tools are used in numerous OM situations, ranging from new-product analysis, to capacity planning, to location planning, to supply-chain disaster planning, to scheduling, and to maintenance planning.

Big data
The huge amount of economic, production, and consumer data now being collected in digital form.

Fundamentals of Decision Making

Regardless of the complexity of a decision or the sophistication of the technique used to analyze it, all decision makers are faced with alternatives and "states of nature." The following notation will be used in this module:

1. Terms:
   a. *Alternative*—A course of action or strategy that may be chosen by a decision maker (e.g., not carrying an umbrella tomorrow).
   b. *State of nature*—An occurrence or a situation over which the decision maker has little or no control (e.g., tomorrow's weather).
2. Symbols used in a decision tree:
   a. ▢—Decision node from which one of several alternatives may be selected.
   b. ◯—A state-of-nature node out of which one state of nature will occur.

To present a manager's decision alternatives, we can develop *decision trees* using the above symbols. When constructing a decision tree, we must be sure that all alternatives and states of nature are in their correct and logical places and that we include *all* possible alternatives and states of nature.

Example A1 | A SIMPLE DECISION TREE

Getz Products Company is investigating the possibility of producing and marketing backyard storage sheds. Undertaking this project would require the construction of either a large or a small manufacturing plant. The market for the product produced—storage sheds—could be either favorable or unfavorable. Getz, of course, has the option of not developing the new product line at all.

APPROACH ▶ Getz decides to build a decision tree.

SOLUTION ▶ Figure A.1 illustrates Getz's decision tree.

Figure **A.1**

Getz Products' Decision Tree

Figure **A.1**

Getz Products' Decision Tree

LO A.1 *Create* a simple decision tree

INSIGHT ▶ We never want to overlook the option of "doing nothing," as that is usually a possible decision.

LEARNING EXERCISE ▶ Getz now considers constructing a medium-sized plant as a fourth option. Redraw the tree in Figure A.1 to accommodate this. [Answer: Your tree will have a new node and branches between "Construct large plant" and "Construct small plant."]

RELATED PROBLEMS ▶ A.2e, A.8b, A.22–A.25

Decision Tables

Decision table

A tabular means of analyzing decision alternatives and states of nature.

We may also develop a decision or payoff table to help Getz Products define its alternatives. For any alternative and a particular state of nature, there is a *consequence* or *outcome*, which is usually expressed as a monetary value. This is called a *conditional value*. Note that all of the alternatives in Example A2 are listed down the left side of the table, that states of nature (outcomes) are listed across the top, and that conditional values (payoffs) are in the body of the decision table.

Example A2

A DECISION TABLE

Getz Products now wishes to organize the following information into a table. With a favorable market, a large facility will give Getz Products a net profit of $200,000. If the market is unfavorable, a $180,000 net loss will occur. A small plant will result in a net profit of $100,000 in a favorable market, but a net loss of $20,000 will be encountered if the market is unfavorable.

LO A.2 *Build* a decision table

APPROACH ▶ These numbers become conditional values in the decision table. We list alternatives in the left column and states of nature across the top of the table.

SOLUTION ▶ The completed table is shown in Table A.1.

TABLE A.1	Decision Table with Conditional Values for Getz Products	
	STATES OF NATURE	
ALTERNATIVES	**FAVORABLE MARKET**	**UNFAVORABLE MARKET**
Construct large plant	$200,000	−$180,000
Construct small plant	$100,000	−$ 20,000
Do nothing	$ 0	$ 0

STUDENT TIP ◆

Decision tables force logic into decision making.

INSIGHT ▶ The toughest part of decision tables is obtaining the data to analyze.

LEARNING EXERCISE ▶ In Examples A3 and A4, we see how to use decision tables to make decisions.

Types of Decision-Making Environments

The types of decisions people make depend on how much knowledge or information they have about the situation. There are three decision-making environments:

◆ Decision making under uncertainty
◆ Decision making under risk
◆ Decision making under certainty

LO A.3 *Explain* when to use each of the three types of decision-making environments

Decision Making Under Uncertainty

When there is complete *uncertainty* as to which state of nature in a decision environment may occur (i.e., when we cannot even assess probabilities for each possible outcome), we rely on three decision methods:

1. **Maximax**: This method finds an alternative that *max*imizes the *max*imum outcome for every alternative. First, we find the maximum outcome within every alternative, and then we pick the alternative with the maximum number. Because this decision criterion locates the alternative with the *highest* possible *gain*, it has been called an "optimistic" decision criterion.

2. **Maximin**: This method finds the alternative that *max*imizes the *min*imum outcome for every alternative. First, we find the minimum outcome within every alternative, and then we pick the alternative with the maximum number. Because this decision criterion locates the alternative that has the *least* possible *loss*, it has been called a "pessimistic" decision criterion.

3. **Equally likely**: This method finds the alternative with the highest average outcome. First, we calculate the average outcome for every alternative, which is the sum of all outcomes divided by the number of outcomes. We then pick the alternative with the maximum number. The equally likely approach assumes that each state of nature is equally likely to occur.

Maximax
A criterion that finds an alternative that maximizes the maximum outcome.

Maximin
A criterion that finds an alternative that maximizes the minimum outcome.

Equally likely
A criterion that assigns equal probability to each state of nature.

Example A3 | A DECISION TABLE ANALYSIS UNDER UNCERTAINTY

Getz Products Company would like to apply each of these three approaches now.

APPROACH ▶ Given Getz's decision table from Example A2, he determines the maximax, maximin, and equally likely decision criteria.

SOLUTION ▶ Table A.2 provides the solution.

TABLE A.2 Decision Table for Decision Making Under Uncertainty

ALTERNATIVES	STATES OF NATURE FAVORABLE MARKET	STATES OF NATURE UNFAVORABLE MARKET	MAXIMUM IN ROW	MINIMUM IN ROW	ROW AVERAGE
Construct large plant	$200,000	−$180,000	$200,000	−180,000	$10,000
Construct small plant	$100,000	−$ 20,000	$100,000	−$20,000	$40,000
Do nothing	$ 0	$ 0	$ 0	$ 0	$ 0
			Maximax	Maximin	Equally likely

1. The maximax choice is to construct a large plant. This is the *max*imum of the *max*imum number within each row, or alternative.

2. The maximin choice is to do nothing. This is the *maximum* of the *minimum* number within each row, or alternative.
3. The equally likely choice is to construct a small plant. This is the maximum of the average outcome of each alternative. This approach assumes that all outcomes for any alternative are *equally likely*.

INSIGHT ▶ There are optimistic decision makers ("maximax") and pessimistic ones ("maximin"). Maximax and maximin present best case–worst case planning scenarios.

LEARNING EXERCISE ▶ Getz reestimates the outcome for constructing a large plant when the market is favorable and raises it to $250,000. What numbers change in Table A.2? Do the decisions change? [Answer: The maximax is now $250,000, and the row average is $35,000 for large plant. No decision changes.]

RELATED PROBLEMS ▶ A.1, A.2b–d, A.4, A.6 (A.15 is available in MyOMLab)

Decision Making Under Risk

Decision making under risk, a more common occurrence, relies on probabilities. Several possible states of nature may occur, each with an assumed probability. The states of nature must be mutually exclusive and collectively exhaustive and their probabilities must sum to 1.[1] Given a decision table with conditional values and probability assessments for all states of nature, we can determine the **expected monetary value (EMV)** for each alternative. This figure represents the expected value or *mean* return for each alternative *if we could repeat this decision (or similar types of decisions) a large number of times*.

The EMV for an alternative is the sum of all possible payoffs from the alternative, each weighted by the probability of that payoff occurring:

$$\text{EMV (Alternative } i) = (\text{Payoff of 1st state of nature})$$
$$\times (\text{Probability of 1st state of nature})$$
$$+ (\text{Payoff of 2nd state of nature})$$
$$\times (\text{Probability of 2nd state of nature})$$
$$+ \ldots + (\text{Payoff of last state of nature})$$
$$\times (\text{Probability of last state of nature})$$

Example A4 illustrates how to compute the maximum EMV.

Expected monetary value (EMV)

The expected payout or value of a variable that has different possible states of nature, each with an associated probability.

LO A.4 *Calculate* an expected monetary value (EMV)

Example A4

EXPECTED MONETARY VALUE

Getz would like to find the EMV for each alternative.

APPROACH ▶ Getz Products' operations manager believes that the probability of a favorable market is 0.6, and that of an unfavorable market is 0.4. He can now determine the EMV for each alternative (see Table A.3).

SOLUTION ▶

1. EMV (A_1) = $(0.6)(\$200,000) + (0.4)(-\$180,000) = \$48,000$
2. EMV (A_2) = $(0.6)(\$100,000) + (0.4)(-\$20,000) = \$52,000$
3. EMV (A_3) = $(0.6)(\$0) + (0.4)(\$0) = \$0$

TABLE A.3	Decision Table for Getz Products	
	STATES OF NATURE	
ALTERNATIVES	**FAVORABLE MARKET**	**UNFAVORABLE MARKET**
Construct large plant (A_1)	$200,000	−$180,000
Construct small plant (A_2)	$100,000	−$ 20,000
Do nothing (A_3)	$ 0	$ 0
Probabilities	0.6	0.4

INSIGHT ▶ The maximum EMV is seen in alternative A_2. Thus, according to the EMV decision criterion, Getz would build the small facility.

LEARNING EXERCISE ▶ What happens to the three EMVs if Getz increases the conditional value on the "large plant/favorable market" result to $250,000? [Answer: EMV ($A_1$) = $78,000. A_1 is now the preferable decision.]

RELATED PROBLEMS ▶ A.2e, A.3a, A.5a, A.7a, A.8, A.9a, A.10, A.11, A.12, A.13a, A.14, A.22b,c (A.16, A.17, A.18, A.19, A.20 are available in MyOMLab)

EXCEL OM Data File **ModAExA4.xls** can be found in MyOMLab.

Decision Making Under Certainty

Now suppose that the Getz operations manager has been approached by a marketing research firm that proposes to help him make the decision about whether to build the plant to produce storage sheds. The marketing researchers claim that their technical analysis will tell Getz with certainty whether the market is favorable for the proposed product. In other words, it will change Getz's environment from one of decision making *under risk* to one of decision making *under certainty*. This information could prevent Getz from making a very expensive mistake. The marketing research firm would charge Getz $65,000 for the information. What would you recommend? Should the operations manager hire the firm to make the study? Even if the information from the study is perfectly accurate, is it worth $65,000? What might it be worth? Although some of these questions are difficult to answer, determining the value of such *perfect information* can be very useful. It places an upper bound on what you would be willing to spend on information, such as that being sold by a marketing consultant. This is the concept of the expected value of perfect information (EVPI), which we now introduce.

Expected Value of Perfect Information (EVPI)

LO A.5 *Compute* the expected value of perfect information (EVPI)

If a manager were able to determine which state of nature would occur, then he or she would know which decision to make. Once a manager knows which decision to make, the payoff increases because the payoff is now a certainty, not a probability. Because the payoff will increase with knowledge of which state of nature will occur, this knowledge has value. Therefore, we now look at how to determine the value of this information. We call this difference between the payoff under perfect information and the payoff under risk the expected value of perfect information (EVPI).

Expected value of perfect information (EVPI)

The difference between the payoff under perfect information and the payoff under risk.

$$\text{EVPI} = \text{Expected value with perfect information} - \text{Maximum EMV}$$

To find the EVPI, we must first compute the expected value *with* perfect information (EVwPI), which is the expected (average) return if we have perfect information before a decision has to be made.

Expected value *with* perfect information (EVwPI)

The expected (average) return if perfect information is available.

To calculate this value, we choose the best alternative for each state of nature and multiply its payoff times the probability of occurrence of that state of nature:

Expected value *with*
perfect information (EVwPI) = (Best outcome or consequence for 1st state of nature)

$\times$ (Probability of 1st state of nature)

+ (Best outcome for 2nd state of nature)

$\times$ (Probability of 2nd state of nature)

+ ... + (Best outcome for last state of nature)

$\times$ (Probability of last state of nature)

In Example A5 we use the data and decision table from Example A4 to examine the expected value of perfect information.

Example A5

EXPECTED VALUE OF PERFECT INFORMATION

The Getz operations manager would like to calculate the maximum that he would pay for information—that is, the expected value of perfect information, or EVPI.

APPROACH ▶ Referring to Table A.3 in Example 4, he follows a two-stage process. First, the expected value *with* perfect information (EVwPI) is computed. Then, using this information, the EVPI is calculated.

SOLUTION ▶

1. The best outcome for the state of nature "favorable market" is "build a large facility" with a payoff of $200,000. The best outcome for the state of nature "unfavorable market" is "do nothing" with a payoff of $0. Expected value *with* perfect information = ($200,000)(0.6) + ($0)(0.4) = $120,000. Thus, if we had perfect information, we would expect (on the average) $120,000 if the decision could be repeated many times.

2. The maximum EMV is $52,000 for A_2, which is the expected outcome without perfect information. Thus:

$$EVPI = EVwPI - \text{Maximum EMV}$$
$$= \$120,000 - \$52,000 = \$68,000$$

INSIGHT ▶ The *most* Getz should be willing to pay for perfect information is $68,000. This conclusion, of course, is again based on the assumption that the probability of the first state of nature is 0.6 and the second is 0.4.

STUDENT TIP ◉
EVPI places an upper limit on what you should pay for information.

LEARNING EXERCISE ▶ How does the EVPI change if the "large plant/favorable market" conditional value is $250,000? [Answer: EVPI = $72,000.]

RELATED PROBLEMS ▶ A.3b, A.5b, A.7, A.9, A.13, A.22c

Decision Trees

STUDENT TIP ◉
Decision trees can become complex, so we illustrate two of them in this section.

Decision tree
A graphical means of analyzing decision alternatives and states of nature.

Decisions that lend themselves to display in a decision table also lend themselves to display in a decision tree. We will therefore analyze some decisions using decision trees. Although the use of a decision table is convenient in problems having one set of decisions and one set of states of nature, many problems include *sequential* decisions and states of nature.

When there are two or more sequential decisions, and later decisions are based on the outcome of prior ones, the decision tree approach becomes appropriate. A decision tree is a graphic display of the decision process that indicates decision alternatives, states of nature and their respective probabilities, and payoffs for each combination of decision alternative and state of nature.

Expected monetary value (EMV) is the most commonly used criterion for decision tree analysis. One of the first steps in such analysis is to graph the decision tree and to specify the monetary consequences of all outcomes for a particular problem.

Screenshot from DPL Software. Reprinted with permission.

When Tomco Oil had to decide which of its new Kentucky lease areas to drill for oil, it turned to decision tree analysis. The 74 different factors, including geological, engineering, economic, and political factors, became much clearer. Decision tree software such as DPL (shown here), Tree Plan, and Supertree allow decision problems to be analyzed with less effort and greater depth than ever before.

Analyzing problems with *decision trees* involves five steps:

1. Define the problem.
2. Structure or draw the decision tree.
3. Assign probabilities to the states of nature.
4. Estimate payoffs for each possible combination of decision alternatives and states of nature.
5. Solve the problem by computing the expected monetary values (EMV) for each state-of-nature node. This is done by working *backward*—that is, by starting at the right of the tree and working back to decision nodes on the left.

Example A6

SOLVING A TREE FOR EMV

Getz wants to develop a completed and solved decision tree.

APPROACH ▶ The payoffs are placed at the right-hand side of each of the tree's branches (see Figure A.2). The probabilities (first used by Getz in Example A4) are placed in parentheses next to each

Figure **A.2**

Completed and Solved Decision Tree for Getz Products

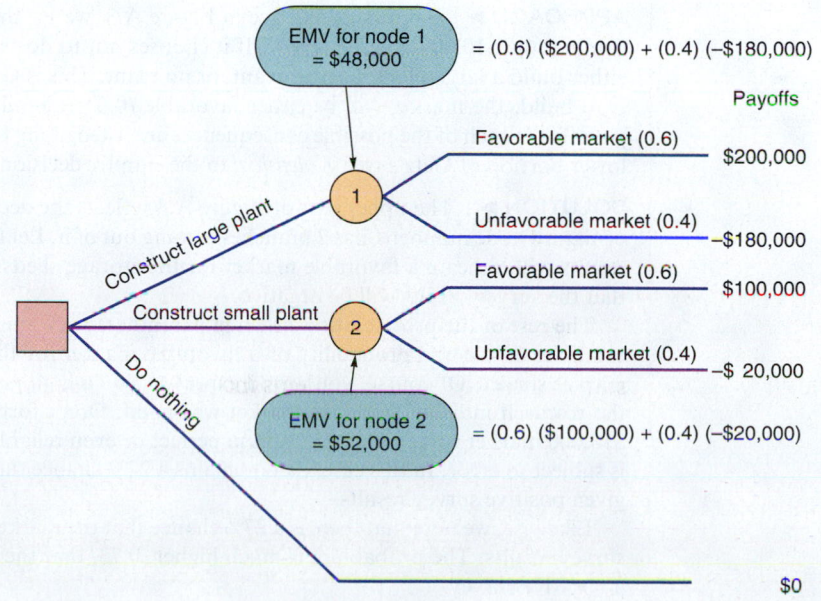

EMV for node 1 = $48,000 = (0.6) ($200,000) + (0.4) (−$180,000)

Payoffs

Favorable market (0.6) $200,000

Unfavorable market (0.4) −$180,000

Favorable market (0.6) $100,000

Unfavorable market (0.4) −$ 20,000

Construct large plant

Construct small plant

Do nothing

EMV for node 2 = $52,000 = (0.6) ($100,000) + (0.4) (−$20,000)

$0

LO A.6 *Evaluate* the nodes in a decision tree

state of nature. The expected monetary values for each state-of-nature node are then calculated and placed by their respective nodes. The EMV of the first node is $48,000. This represents the branch from the decision node to "construct a large plant." The EMV for node 2, to "construct a small plant," is $52,000. The option of "doing nothing" has, of course, a payoff of $0.

SOLUTION ▶ The branch leaving the decision node leading to the state-of-nature node with the highest EMV will be chosen. In Getz's case, a small plant should be built.

INSIGHT ▶ This graphical approach is an excellent way for managers to understand all the options in making a major decision. Visual models are often preferred over tables.

LEARNING EXERCISE ▶ Correct Figure A.2 to reflect a $250,000 payoff for "construct large plant/favorable market." [Answer: Change one payoff and recompute the EMV for node 1.]

RELATED PROBLEMS ▶ A.2e, A.8b, A.22a,b, A.24, A.25

EXCEL OM Data File **ModAExA6.xls** can be found in MyOMLab.

A More Complex Decision Tree

When a *sequence* of decisions must be made, decision trees are much more powerful tools than are decision tables. Let's say that Getz Products has two decisions to make, with the second decision dependent on the outcome of the first. Before deciding about building a new plant, Getz has the option of conducting its own marketing research survey, at a cost of $10,000. The information from this survey could help it decide whether to build a large plant, to build a small plant, or not to build at all. Getz recognizes that although such a survey will not provide it with *perfect* information, it may be extremely helpful.

Getz's new decision tree is represented in Figure A.3 of Example A7. Take a careful look at this more complex tree. Note that *all possible outcomes and alternatives* are included in their logical sequence. This procedure is one of the strengths of using decision trees. The manager is forced to examine all possible outcomes, including unfavorable ones. He or she is also forced to make decisions in a logical, sequential manner.

Example A7

A DECISION TREE WITH SEQUENTIAL DECISIONS

Getz Products wishes to develop the new tree for this sequential decision.

APPROACH ▶ Examining the tree in Figure A.3, we see that Getz's first decision point is whether to conduct the $10,000 market survey. If it chooses not to do the study (the lower part of the tree), it can either build a large plant, a small plant, or no plant. This is Getz's second decision point. If the decision is to build, the market will be either favorable (0.6 probability) or unfavorable (0.4 probability). The payoffs for each of the possible consequences are listed along the right-hand side. As a matter of fact, this lower portion of Getz's tree is *identical* to the simpler decision tree shown in Figure A.2.

SOLUTION ▶ The upper part of Figure A.3 reflects the decision to conduct the market survey. State-of-nature node number 1 has 2 branches coming out of it. Let us say there is a 45% chance that the survey results will indicate a favorable market for the storage sheds. We also note that the probability is 0.55 that the survey results will be negative.

The rest of the probabilities shown in parentheses in Figure A.3 are all *conditional* probabilities. For example, 0.78 is the probability of a favorable market for the sheds given a favorable result from the market survey. Of course, you would expect to find a high probability of a favorable market given that the research indicated that the market was good. Don't forget, though: There is a chance that Getz's $10,000 market survey did not result in perfect or even reliable information. Any market research study is subject to error. In this case, there remains a 22% chance that the market for sheds will be unfavorable given positive survey results.

Likewise, we note that there is a 27% chance that the market for sheds will be favorable given negative survey results. The probability is much higher, 0.73, that the market will actually be unfavorable given a negative survey.

Figure **A.3**

Getz Products Decision Tree with Probabilities and EMVs Shown

LO A.7 *Create* a decision tree with sequential decisions

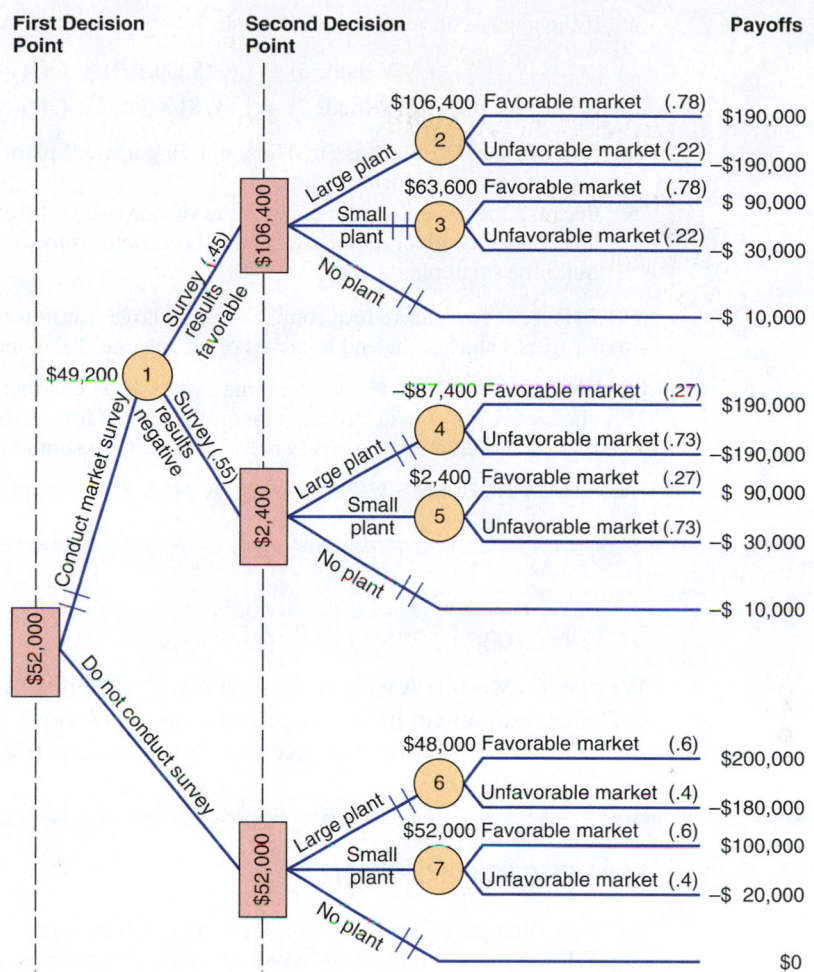

Finally, when we look to the payoff column in Figure A.3, we see that $10,000—the cost of the marketing study—has been subtracted from each of the top 10 tree branches. Thus, a large plant constructed in a favorable market would normally net a $200,000 profit. Yet because the market study was conducted, this figure is reduced by $10,000. In the unfavorable case, the loss of $180,000 would increase to $190,000. Similarly, conducting the survey and building *no plant* now results in a −$10,000 payoff.

With all probabilities and payoffs specified, we can start calculating the expected monetary value of each branch. We begin at the end or right-hand side of the decision tree and work back toward the origin. When we finish, the best decision will be known.

1. Given favorable survey results:

$$\text{EMV (node 2)} = (.78)(\$190{,}000) + (.22)(-\$190{,}000) = \$106{,}400$$

$$\text{EMV (node 3)} = (.78)(\$90{,}000) + (.22)(-\$30{,}000) = \$63{,}600$$

The EMV of no plant in this case is −$10,000. Thus, if the survey results are favorable, a large plant should be built.

2. Given negative survey results:

$$\text{EMV (node 4)} = (.27)(\$190{,}000) + (.73)(-\$190{,}000) = -\$87{,}400$$

$$\text{EMV (node 5)} = (.27)(\$90{,}000) + (.73)(-\$30{,}000) = \$2{,}400$$

The EMV of no plant is again −$10,000 for this branch. Thus, given a negative survey result, Getz should build a small plant with an expected value of $2,400.

3. Continuing on the upper part of the tree and moving backward, we compute the expected value of conducting the market survey:

$$\text{EMV (node 1)} = (.45)(\$106{,}400) + (.55)(\$2{,}400) = \$49{,}200$$

4. If the market survey is *not* conducted:

$$EMV \text{ (node 6)} = (.6)(\$200{,}000) + (.4)(-\$180{,}000) = \$48{,}000$$
$$EMV \text{ (node 7)} = (.6)(\$100{,}000) + (.4)(-\$20{,}000) = \$52{,}000$$

The EMV of no plant is \$0. Thus, building a small plant is the best choice, given the marketing research is not performed.

5. Because the expected monetary value of not conducting the survey is \$52,000—vs. an EMV of \$49,200 for conducting the study—the best choice is to *not seek marketing information*. Getz should build the small plant.

INSIGHT ▶ You can reduce complexity in a large decision tree by viewing and solving a number of smaller trees—start at the end branches of a large one. Take one decision at a time.

LEARNING EXERCISE ▶ Getz estimates that if he conducts a market survey, there is really only a 35% chance the results will indicate a favorable market for the sheds. How does the tree change? [Answer: The EMV of conducting the survey = \$38,800, so Getz should still not do it.]

RELATED PROBLEMS ▶ A.21, A.25–A.29 (A.31, A.32 are available in MyOMLab)

The Poker Decision Process

We opened Module A with ex-dot-commer Paul Phillips's decision to go "all in" at the Legends of Poker tournament in Los Angeles. Example A8 shows how he computed the expected value. Problem A.30 gives you a chance to create a decision tree for this process.

Example A8

PHILLIPS'S POKER DECISION

As on the first page in this module, Paul Phillips is deciding whether to bet all his chips against poker star T.J. Cloutier. Phillips holds a pair of 7s. Phillips reasons that T.J. will fold (with 80% probability) if he does not have a pair of 5s or better, or very high cards like a jack, queen, king, or ace. But he also figures that a call would put \$853,000 into the pot and surmises that even then, there is 45% chance his pair of 7s will win.

APPROACH ▶ Phillips does an expected monetary analysis.

SOLUTION ▶ If T.J. folds,

The amount of money already in the pot

$$EMV = (.80)(\$99{,}000)$$
$$= \$79{,}200$$

If T.J. calls,

the chance T.J. will call

$$EMV = .20[(.45)(\$853{,}000) - \text{Phillips's bet of } \$422{,}000]$$
$$= .20[\$383{,}850 - \$422{,}000]$$
$$= .20[-\$38{,}150] = -\$7{,}630$$

Overall EMV = \$79,200 − \$7,630 = \$71,570

INSIGHT ▶ The overall EMV of \$71,570 indicates that if this decision were to be made many times, the average payoff would be large. So Phillips decides to bet almost all of his chips. As it turns out, T.J. was holding a pair of jacks. Even though Phillips's decision in this instance did not work out, his analysis and procedure was the correct one.

LEARNING EXERCISE ▶ What would happen if the amount of money already in the pot were only \$39,000? [Answer: The overall EMV = \$23,570.]

RELATED PROBLEM ▶ A.30

Summary

This module examines two of the most widely used decision techniques—decision tables and decision trees. These techniques are especially useful for making decisions under risk. Many decisions in research and development, plant and equipment, and even new buildings and structures can be analyzed with these decision models. Problems in inventory control, aggregate planning, maintenance, scheduling, and production control also lend themselves to decision table and decision tree applications.

Key Terms

Big data (p. 679)
Decision table (p. 680)
Maximax (p. 681)
Maximin (p. 681)

Equally likely (p. 681)
Expected monetary value (EMV) (p. 682)
Expected value of perfect information (EVPI) (p. 683)

Expected value *with* perfect information (EVwPI) (p. 683)
Decision tree (p. 684)

Discussion Questions

1. Identify the six steps in the decision process.
2. Give an example of a good decision you made that resulted in a bad outcome. Also give an example of a bad decision you made that had a good outcome. Why was each decision good or bad?
3. What is the *equally likely* decision model?
4. Discuss the differences between decision making under certainty, under risk, and under uncertainty.
5. What is a decision tree?
6. Explain how decision trees might be used in several of the 10 OM decisions.
7. What is the expected value of perfect information (EVPI)?
8. What is the expected value *with* perfect information (EVwPI)?
9. Identify the five steps in analyzing a problem using a decision tree.
10. Why are the maximax and maximin strategies considered to be optimistic and pessimistic, respectively?
11. The expected value criterion is considered to be the rational criterion on which to base a decision. Is this true? Is it rational to consider risk?
12. When are decision trees most useful?

Using Software for Decision Models

Analyzing decision tables is straightforward with Excel, Excel OM, and POM for Windows. When decision trees are involved, Excel OM or commercial packages such as DPL, Tree Plan, and Supertree provide flexibility, power, and ease. POM for Windows will also analyze trees but does not have graphic capabilities.

CREATING AN EXCEL SPREADSHEET TO EVALUATE A DECISION TABLE

In Program A.1, we illustrate how you can build your own Excel spreadsheet to analyze decision making under uncertainty and under risk. The data from Getz Products in Examples A3 and A4 are used. Maximax, maximin, equally likely, and EMV are computed, along with EVPI.

✘ USING EXCEL OM

Excel OM allows decision makers to evaluate decisions quickly and to perform sensitivity analysis on the results. Program A.2 uses Excel OM to create the decision tree for Getz Products shown earlier in Example A6. The tool to create the tree is seen in the window on the right.

P USING POM FOR WINDOWS

POM for Windows can be used to calculate all of the information described in the decision tables and decision trees in this module. For details on how to use this software, please refer to Appendix IV.

Program A.1

An Excel Spreadsheet for Analyzing Data in Examples A3 and A4 for Getz Products

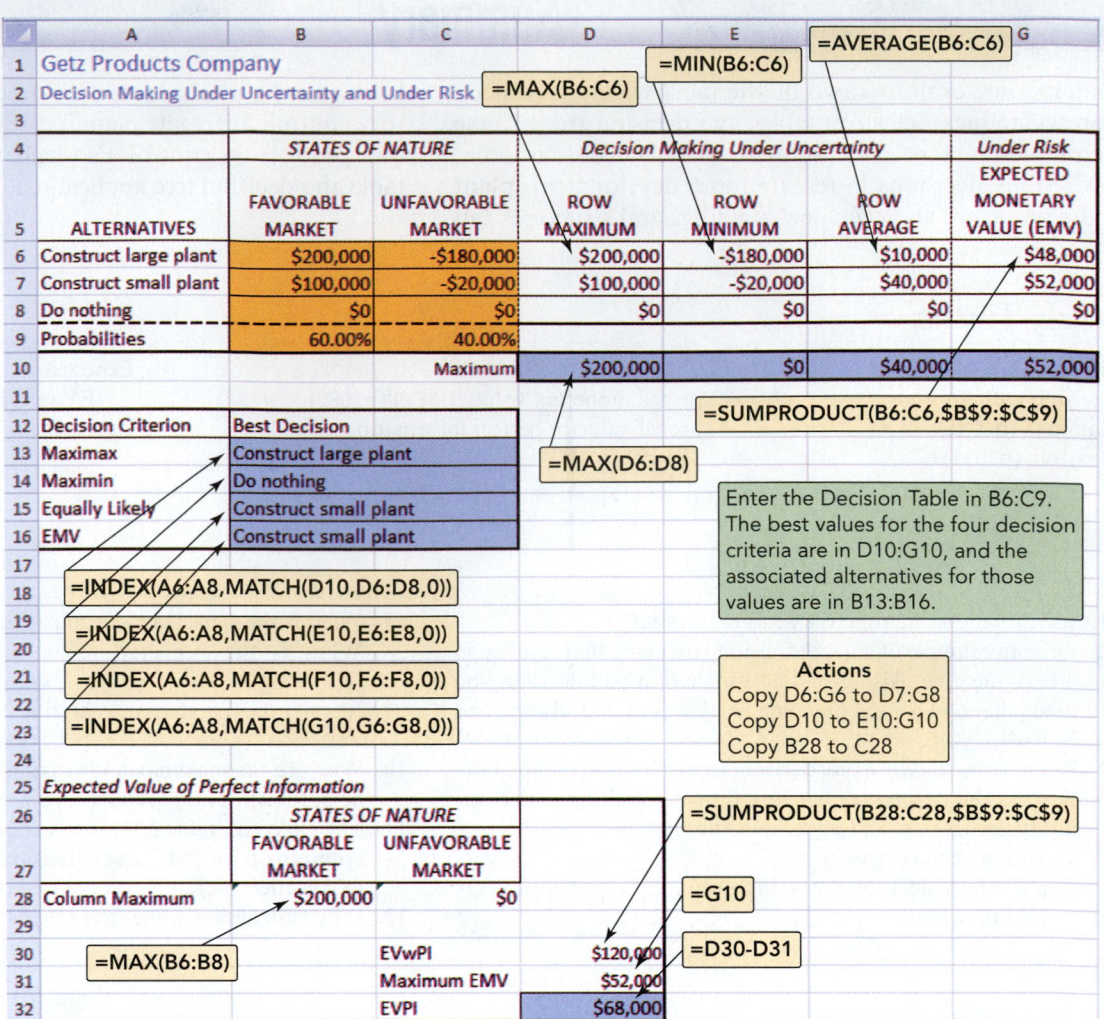

=AVERAGE(B6:C6)

=MIN(B6:C6)

=MAX(B6:C6)

=MAX(D6:D8)

=SUMPRODUCT(B6:C6,$B$9:$C$9)

=INDEX(A6:A8,MATCH(D10,D6:D8,0))

=INDEX(A6:A8,MATCH(E10,E6:E8,0))

=INDEX(A6:A8,MATCH(F10,F6:F8,0))

=INDEX(A6:A8,MATCH(G10,G6:G8,0))

=SUMPRODUCT(B28:C28,$B$9:$C$9)

=G10

=D30-D31

=MAX(B6:B8)

Enter the Decision Table in B6:C9. The best values for the four decision criteria are in D10:G10, and the associated alternatives for those values are in B13:B16.

Actions
Copy D6:G6 to D7:G8
Copy D10 to E10:G10
Copy B28 to C28

	A	B	C	D	E	F	G
1	Getz Products Company						
2	Decision Making Under Uncertainty and Under Risk						
3							
4		STATES OF NATURE		Decision Making Under Uncertainty			Under Risk
5	ALTERNATIVES	FAVORABLE MARKET	UNFAVORABLE MARKET	ROW MAXIMUM	ROW MINIMUM	ROW AVERAGE	EXPECTED MONETARY VALUE (EMV)
6	Construct large plant	$200,000	-$180,000	$200,000	-$180,000	$10,000	$48,000
7	Construct small plant	$100,000	-$20,000	$100,000	-$20,000	$40,000	$52,000
8	Do nothing	$0	$0	$0	$0	$0	$0
9	Probabilities	60.00%	40.00%				
10			Maximum	$200,000	$0	$40,000	$52,000
11							
12	Decision Criterion	Best Decision					
13	Maximax	Construct large plant					
14	Maximin	Do nothing					
15	Equally Likely	Construct small plant					
16	EMV	Construct small plant					
17							
18							
19							
20							
21							
22							
23							
24							
25	Expected Value of Perfect Information						
26		STATES OF NATURE					
27		FAVORABLE MARKET	UNFAVORABLE MARKET				
28	Column Maximum	$200,000	$0				
29							
30			EVwPI	$120,000			
31			Maximum EMV	$52,000			
32			EVPI	$68,000			

Maximum Profit = MAX(D7 + C9, D15 + C1)

Use the branch that leads to node 3 in order to achieve the maximum profit.

Expected profit for the small plant = F15*F13 + F19*F17

Use this Decision Tree Creation window to create the tree.

Program A.2

Getz Products' Decision Tree Using Excel OM

Solved Problems   Virtual Office Hours help is available in MyOMLab.

SOLVED PROBLEM A.1

Stella Yan Hua is considering the possibility of opening a small dress shop on Fairbanks Avenue, a few blocks from the university. She has located a good mall that attracts students. Her options are to open a small shop, a medium-sized shop, or no shop at all. The market for a dress shop can be good, average, or bad. The probabilities for these three possibilities are .2 for a good market, .5 for an average market, and .3 for a bad market. The net profit or loss for the medium-sized or small shops for the various market conditions are given in the adjacent table. Building no shop at all yields no loss and no gain. What do you recommend?

	STATES OF NATURE		
ALTERNATIVES	GOOD MARKET ($)	AVERAGE MARKET ($)	BAD MARKET ($)
Small shop	75,000	25,000	−40,000
Medium-sized shop	100,000	35,000	−60,000
No shop	0	0	0
Probabilities	.20	.50	.30

SOLUTION

The problem can be solved by computing the expected monetary value (EMV) for each alternative:

$$\text{EMV (Small shop)} = (.2)(\$75,000) + (.5)(\$25,000) + (.3)(-\$40,000) = \$15,500$$
$$\text{EMV (Medium-sized shop)} = (.2)(\$100,000) + (.5)(\$35,000) + (.3)(-\$60,000) = \$19,500$$
$$\text{EMV (No shop)} = (.2)(\$0) + (.5)(\$0) + (.3)(\$0) = \$0$$

As you can see, the best decision is to build the medium-sized shop. The EMV for this alternative is $19,500.

SOLVED PROBLEM A.2

T.S. Amer's Ski Shop in Nevada has a 100-day season. T.S. has established the probability of various store traffic, based on historical records of skiing conditions, as indicated in the table to the right. T.S. has four merchandising plans, each focusing on a popular name brand. Each plan yields a daily net profit as noted in the table. He also has a meteorologist friend who, for a small fee, will accurately tell tomorrow's weather so T.S. can implement one of his four merchandising plans.
a) What is the expected monetary value (EMV) under risk?
b) What is the expected value *with* perfect information (EVwPI)?
c) What is the expected value of perfect information (EVPI)?

DECISION ALTERNATIVES (MERCHANDISING PLAN FOCUSING ON:)	TRAFFIC IN STORE BECAUSE OF SKI CONDITIONS (STATES OF NATURE)			
	1	2	3	4
Patagonia	$40	92	20	48
North Face	50	84	10	52
Cloud Veil	35	80	40	64
Columbia	45	72	10	60
Probabilities	.20	.25	.30	.25

SOLUTION

a) The highest expected monetary value under risk is:

$$\text{EMV (Patagonia)} = .20(40) + .25(92) + .30(20) + .25(48) = \$49$$
$$\text{EMV (North Face)} = .20(50) + .25(84) + .30(10) + .25(52) = \$47$$
$$\text{EMV (Cloud Veil)} = .20(35) + .25(80) + .30(40) + .25(64) = \$55$$
$$\text{EMV (Columbia)} = .20(45) + .25(72) + .30(10) + .25(60) = \$45$$

So the maximum EMV = $55

b) The expected value *with* perfect information is:

$$\text{EVwPI} = .20(50) + .25(92) + .30(40) + .25(64)$$
$$= 10 + 23 + 12 + 16 = \$61$$

c) The expected value of perfect information is:

$$\text{EVPI} = \text{EVwPI} - \text{Maximum EMV} = 61 - 55 = \$6$$

SOLVED PROBLEM A.3

Daily demand for cases of Tidy Bowl cleaner at Ravinder Nath's Supermarket has always been 5, 6, or 7 cases. Develop a decision tree that illustrates her decision alternatives as to whether to stock 5, 6, or 7 cases.

SOLUTION

The decision tree is shown in Figure A.4.

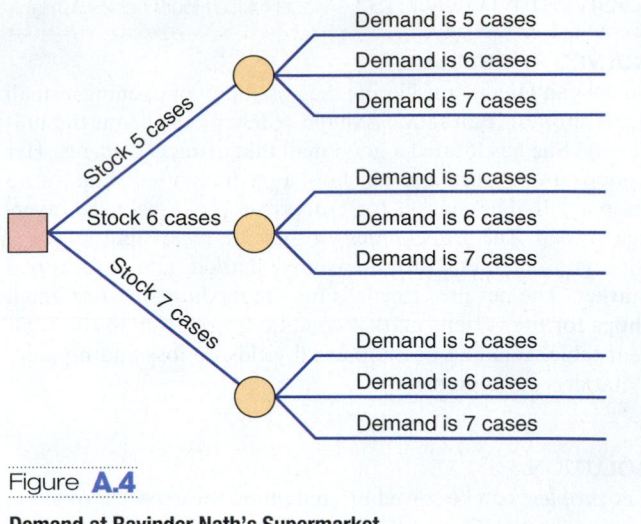

Figure **A.4**

Demand at Ravinder Nath's Supermarket

Problems   *Note:* **Px** means the problem may be solved with POM for Windows and/or Excel OM.

Problems A.1–A.20 relate to Types of Decision-Making Environments

• **A.1**   Given the following conditional value table, determine the appropriate decision under uncertainty using:
a) Maximax
b) Maximin
c) Equally likely **Px**

	STATES OF NATURE		
ALTERNATIVES	VERY FAVORABLE MARKET	AVERAGE MARKET	UNFAVORABLE MARKET
Build new plant	$350,000	$240,000	–$300,000
Subcontract	$180,000	$ 90,000	–$ 20,000
Overtime	$110,000	$ 60,000	–$ 10,000
Do nothing	$ 0	$ 0	$ 0

• • • **A.2**   Even though independent gasoline stations have been having a difficult time, Ian Langella has been thinking about starting his own independent gasoline station. Ian's problem is to decide how large his station should be. The annual returns will depend on both the size of his station and a number of marketing factors related to the oil industry and demand for gasoline. After a careful analysis, Ian developed the following table:

SIZE OF FIRST STATION	GOOD MARKET ($)	FAIR MARKET ($)	POOR MARKET ($)
Small	50,000	20,000	–10,000
Medium	80,000	30,000	–20,000
Large	100,000	30,000	–40,000
Very large	300,000	25,000	–160,000

For example, if Ian constructs a small station and the market is good, he will realize a profit of $50,000.
a) Develop a decision table for this decision, like the one illustrated in Table A.2 earlier.
b) What is the maximax decision?
c) What is the maximin decision?

d) What is the equally likely decision?
e) Develop a decision tree. Assume each outcome is equally likely, then find the highest EMV. **Px**

• **A.3**   Andrew Thomas, a sandwich vendor at Hard Rock Cafe's annual Rockfest, created a table of conditional values for the various alternatives (stocking decision) and states of nature (size of crowd):

	STATES OF NATURE (DEMAND)		
ALTERNATIVES	BIG	AVERAGE	SMALL
Large stock	$22,000	$12,000	–$2,000
Average stock	$14,000	$10,000	$6,000
Small stock	$ 9,000	$ 8,000	$4,000

The probabilities associated with the states of nature are 0.3 for a big demand, 0.5 for an average demand, and 0.2 for a small demand.
a) Determine the alternative that provides Andrew the greatest expected monetary value (EMV).
b) Compute the expected value of perfect information (EVPI).

• • **A.4**   Jeffrey Helm owns a health and fitness center called Bulk-Up in Harrisburg. He is considering adding more floor space to meet increasing demand. He will either add no floor space (N), a moderate area of floor space (M), a large area of floor space (L), or an area of floor space that doubles the size of the facility (D). Demand will either stay fixed, increase slightly, or increase greatly. The following are the changes in Bulk-Up's annual profits under each combination of expansion level and demand change level:

	EXPANSION LEVEL			
DEMAND CHANGE	N	M	L	D
Fixed	$ 0	–$4,000	–$10,000	–$50,000
Slight increase	$2,000	$8,000	$ 6,000	$ 4,000
Major increase	$3,000	$9,000	$20,000	$40,000

Jeffrey is risk averse and wishes to use the maximin criterion.
a) What are his decision alternatives and what are the states of nature?
b) What should he do? **Px**

• **A.5** Howard Weiss, Inc., is considering building a sensitive new radiation scanning device. His managers believe that there is a probability of 0.4 that the ATR Co. will come out with a competitive product. If Weiss adds an assembly line for the product and ATR Co. does not follow with a competitive product, Weiss's expected profit is $40,000; if Weiss adds an assembly line and ATR follows suit, Weiss still expects $10,000 profit. If Weiss adds a new plant addition and ATR does not produce a competitive product, Weiss expects a profit of $600,000; if ATR does compete for this market, Weiss expects a loss of $100,000.
a) Determine the EMV of each decision.
b) Compute the expected value of perfect information. **Px**

••• **A.6** Jerry Bildery's factory is considering three approaches for meeting an expected increase in demand. These three approaches are increasing capacity, using overtime, and buying more equipment. Demand will increase either slightly (S), moderately (M), or greatly (G). The profits for each approach under each possible scenario are as follows:

	DEMAND SCENARIO		
APPROACH	S	M	G
Increasing capacity	$700,000	$700,000	$ 700,000
Using overtime	$500,000	$600,000	$1,000,000
Buying equipment	$600,000	$800,000	$ 800,000

Since the goal is to maximize, and Jerry is risk-neutral, he decides to use the *equally likely* decision criterion to make the decision as to which approach to use. According to this criterion, which approach should be used?

• **A.7** The following payoff table provides profits based on various possible decision alternatives and various levels of demand at Robert Klassan's print shop:

	DEMAND	
	LOW	HIGH
Alternative 1	$10,000	$30,000
Alternative 2	$ 5,000	$40,000
Alternative 3	–$ 2,000	$50,000

The probability of low demand is 0.4, whereas the probability of high demand is 0.6.
a) What is the highest possible expected monetary value?
b) What is the expected value *with* perfect information (EVwPI)?
c) Calculate the expected value of perfect information for this situation. **Px**

• **A.8** Leah Johnson, director of Urgent Care of Brookline, wants to increase capacity to provide low-cost flu shots but must decide whether to do so by hiring another full-time nurse or by using part-time nurses. The table below shows the expected *costs* of the two options for three possible demand levels:

	STATES OF NATURE		
ALTERNATIVES	LOW DEMAND	MEDIUM DEMAND	HIGH DEMAND
Hire full-time	$300	$500	$ 700
Hire part-time	$ 0	$350	$1,000
Probabilities	.2	.5	.3

a) Using expected value, what should Ms. Johnson do?
b) Draw an appropriate decision tree showing payoffs and probabilities. **Px**

•• **A.9** Zhu Manufacturing is considering the introduction of a family of new products. Long-term demand for the product group is somewhat predictable, so the manufacturer must be concerned with the risk of choosing a process that is inappropriate. Faye Zhu is VP of operations. She can choose among batch manufacturing or custom manufacturing, or she can invest in group technology. Faye won't be able to forecast demand accurately until after she makes the process choice. Demand will be classified into four compartments: poor, fair, good, and excellent. The table below indicates the payoffs (profits) associated with each process/demand combination, as well as the probabilities of each long-term demand level:

	POOR	FAIR	GOOD	EXCELLENT
Probability	.1	.4	.3	.2
Batch	–$ 200,000	$1,000,000	$1,200,000	$1,300,000
Custom	$ 100,000	$ 300,000	$ 700,000	$ 800,000
Group technology	–$1,000,000	–$ 500,000	$ 500,000	$2,000,000

a) Based on expected value, what choice offers the greatest gain?
b) What would Faye Zhu be willing to pay for a forecast that would accurately determine the level of demand in the future? **Px**

•• **A.10** Consider the following decision table, which Joe Blackburn has developed for Vanderbilt Enterprises:

	STATES OF NATURE		
DECISION ALTERNATIVES	LOW	MEDIUM	HIGH
A	$40	$100	$60
B	$85	$ 60	$70
C	$60	$ 70	$70
D	$65	$ 75	$70
E	$70	$ 65	$80
Probability	.40	.20	.40

Which decision alternative maximizes the expected value of the payoff? **Px**

•• **A.11** The University of Miami bookstore stocks textbooks in preparation for sales each semester. It normally relies on departmental forecasts and preregistration records to determine how many copies of a text are needed. Preregistration shows 90 operations management students enrolled, but bookstore manager Vaidy Jayaraman has second thoughts, based on his intuition and some historical evidence. Vaidy believes that the distribution of sales may range from 70 to 90 units, according to the following probability model:

Demand	70	75	80	85	90
Probability	.15	.30	.30	.20	.05

This textbook costs the bookstore $82 and sells for $112. Any unsold copies can be returned to the publisher, less a restocking fee and shipping, for a net refund of $36.
a) Construct the table of conditional profits.
b) How many copies should the bookstore stock to achieve highest expected value? **Px**

•• **A.12**   Palmer Jam Company is a small manufacturer of several different jam products. One product is an organic jam that has no preservatives, sold to retail outlets. Susan Palmer must decide how many cases of jam to manufacture each month. The probability that demand will be 6 cases is .1, for 7 cases it is .3, for 8 cases it is .5, and for 9 cases it is .1. The cost of every case is $45, and the price Susan gets for each case is $95. Unfortunately, any cases not sold by the end of the month are of no value as a result of spoilage. How many cases should Susan manufacture each month? **PX**

•• **A.13**   Deborah Hollwager, a concessionaire for the Amway Center in Orlando, has developed a table of conditional values for the various alternatives (stocking decisions) and states of nature (size of crowd):

	STATES OF NATURE (SIZE OF CROWD)		
ALTERNATIVES	LARGE	AVERAGE	SMALL
Large inventory	$20,000	$10,000	–$2,000
Average inventory	$15,000	$12,000	$6,000
Small inventory	$ 9,000	$ 6,000	$5,000

If the probabilities associated with the states of nature are 0.3 for a large crowd, 0.5 for an average crowd, and 0.2 for a small crowd, determine:
a) The alternative that provides the greatest expected monetary value (EMV).
b) The expected value of perfect information (EVPI). **PX**

•••• **A.14** The city of Belgrade, Serbia, is contemplating building a second airport to relieve congestion at the main airport and is considering two potential sites, X and Y. Hard Rock Hotels would like to purchase land to build a hotel at the new airport. The value of land has been rising in anticipation and is expected to skyrocket once the city decides between sites X and Y. Consequently, Hard Rock would like to purchase land now. Hard Rock will sell the land if the city chooses not to locate the airport nearby. Hard Rock has four choices: (1) buy land at X, (2) buy land at Y, (3) buy land at both X and Y, or (4) do nothing. Hard Rock has collected the following data (which are in millions of euros):

	SITE X	SITE Y
Current purchase price	27	15
Profits if airport and hotel built at this site*	45	30
Sale price if airport not built at this site	9	6

*The second row of the table represents net operating profits from the hotel, not including the upfront cost of land.

Hard Rock determines there is a 45% chance the airport will be built at X (hence, a 55% chance it will be built at Y).
a) Set up the decision table.
b) What should Hard Rock decide to do to maximize total net profit? **PX**

Additional problems **A.15–A.20** are available in MyOMLab.

Problems A.21–A.32 relate to Decision Trees

•••**A.21**   Ronald Lau, chief engineer at South Dakota Electronics, has to decide whether to build a new state-of-the-art processing facility. If the new facility works, the company could realize a profit of $200,000. If it fails, South Dakota Electronics could lose $180,000. At this time, Lau estimates a 60% chance that the new process will fail.

The other option is to build a pilot plant and then decide whether to build a complete facility. The pilot plant would cost $10,000 to build. Lau estimates a 50–50 chance that the pilot plant will work. If the pilot plant works, there is a 90% probability that the complete plant, if it is built, will also work. If the pilot plant does not work, there is only a 20% chance that the complete project (if it is constructed) will work. Lau faces a dilemma. Should he build the plant? Should he build the pilot project and then make a decision? Help Lau by analyzing this problem. **PX**

•• **A.22**   Dwayne Whitten, president of Whitten Industries, is considering whether to build a manufacturing plant in north Texas. His decision is summarized in the following table:

ALTERNATIVES	FAVORABLE MARKET	UNFAVORABLE MARKET
Build large plant	$400,000	–$300,000
Build small plant	$ 80,000	–$ 10,000
Don't build	$ 0	$ 0
Market probabilities	0.4	0.6

a) Construct a decision tree.
b) Determine the best strategy using expected monetary value (EMV).
c) What is the expected value of perfect information (EVPI)? **PX**

•• **A.23**   Deborah Kellogg buys Breathalyzer test sets for the Winter Park Police Department. The quality of the test sets from her two suppliers is indicated in the following table:

PERCENT DEFECTIVE	PROBABILITY FOR WINTER PARK TECHNOLOGY	PROBABILITY FOR DAYTON ENTERPRISES
1	.70	.30
3	.20	.30
5	.10	.40

For example, the probability of getting a batch of tests that are 1% defective from Winter Park Technology is .70. Because Kellogg orders 10,000 tests per order, this would mean that there is a .70 probability of getting 100 defective tests out of the 10,000 tests if Winter Park Technology is used to fill the order. A defective Breathalyzer test set can be repaired for $0.50. Although the quality of the test sets of the second supplier, Dayton Enterprises, is lower, it will sell an order of 10,000 test sets for $37 less than Winter Park.

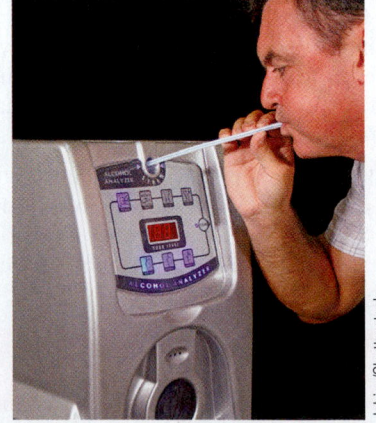

Jabiru/Shutterstock

a) Develop a decision tree.
b) Which supplier should Kellogg use? **PX**

• **A.24** Joseph Biggs owns his own ice cream truck and lives 30 miles from a Florida beach resort. The sale of his products is highly dependent on his location and on the weather. At the resort, his profit will be $120 per day in fair weather, $10 per day in bad weather. At home, his profit will be $70 in fair weather and $55 in bad weather. Assume that on any particular day, the weather service suggests a 40% chance of foul weather.

a) Construct Joseph's decision tree.

b) What decision is recommended by the expected value criterion? **Px**

•• **A.25** Jonatan Jelen is considering opening a bicycle shop in New York City. Jonatan enjoys biking, but this is to be a business endeavor from which he expects to make a living. He can open a small shop, a large shop, or no shop at all. Because there will be a 5-year lease on the building that Jonatan is thinking about using, he wants to make sure he makes the correct decision. Jonatan is also thinking about hiring his old marketing professor to conduct a marketing research study to see if there is a market for his services. The results of such a study could be either favorable or unfavorable. Develop a decision tree for Jonatan. **Px**

•• **A.26** F. J. Brewerton Retailers, Inc., must decide whether to build a small or a large facility at a new location in Omaha. Demand at the location will either be low or high, with probabilities 0.4 and 0.6, respectively. If Brewerton builds a small facility and demand proves to be high, he then has the option of expanding the facility. If a small facility is built and demand proves to be high, and then the retailer expands the facility, the payoff is $270,000. If a small facility is built and demand proves to be high, but Brewerton then decides not to expand the facility, the payoff is $223,000.

If a small facility is built and demand proves to be low, then there is no option to expand and the payoff is $200,000. If a large facility is built and demand proves to be low, Brewerton then has the option of stimulating demand through local advertising. If he does not exercise this option, then the payoff is $40,000. If he does exercise the advertising option, then the response to advertising will either be modest or sizable, with probabilities of 0.3 and 0.7, respectively. If the response is modest, the payoff is $20,000. If it is sizable, the payoff is $220,000. Finally, if a large facility is built and demand proves to be high, then no advertising is needed and the payoff is $800,000.

a) What should Brewerton do to maximize his expected payoff?

b) What is the value of this expected payoff?

••• **A.27** Philip Musa can build either a large electronics section or a small one in his Birmingham drugstore. He can also gather additional information or simply do nothing. If he gathers additional information, the results could suggest either a favorable or an unfavorable market, but it would cost him $3,000 to gather the information. Musa believes that there is a 50–50 chance that the information will be favorable. If the market is favorable, Musa will earn $15,000 with a large section or $5,000 with a small one. With an unfavorable electronics market, however, Musa could lose $20,000 with a large section or $10,000 with a small section. Without gathering additional information, Musa estimates that the probability of a favorable market is .7. A favorable report from the study would increase the probability of a favorable market to .9. Furthermore, an unfavorable report from the additional information would decrease the probability of a favorable market to .4. Of course, Musa could ignore these numbers and do nothing. What is your advice to Musa?

•••• **A.28** Jeff Kaufmann's machine shop sells a variety of machines for job shops. A customer wants to purchase a model XPO2 drilling machine from Jeff's store. The model XPO2 sells for $180,000, but Jeff is out of XPO2s. The customer says he will wait for Jeff to get a model XPO2 in stock. Jeff knows that there is a wholesale market for XPO2s from which he can purchase an XPO2. Jeff can buy an XPO2 today for $150,000, or he can wait a day and buy an XPO2 (if one is available) tomorrow for $125,000. If at least one XPO2 is still available tomorrow, Jeff can wait until the day after tomorrow and buy an XPO2 (if one is still available) for $110,000.

There is a 0.40 probability that there will be no model XPO2s available tomorrow. If there are model XPO2s available tomorrow, there is a 0.70 probability that by the day after tomorrow, there will be no model XPO2s available in the wholesale market. Three days from now, it is certain that no model XPO2s will be available on the wholesale market. What is the maximum expected profit that Jeff can achieve? What should Jeff do?

•••• **A.29** Louisiana is busy designing new lottery scratch-off games. In the latest game, Bayou Boondoggle, the player is instructed to scratch off one spot: A, B, or C. A can reveal "Loser," "Win $1," or "Win $50." B can reveal "Loser" or "Take a Second Chance." C can reveal "Loser" or "Win $500." On the second chance, the player is instructed to scratch off D or E. D can reveal "Loser" or "Win $1." E can reveal "Loser" or "Win $10." The probabilities at A are .9, .09, and .01. The probabilities at B are .8 and .2. The probabilities at C are .999 and .001. The probabilities at D are .5 and .5. Finally, the probabilities at E are .95 and .05. Draw the decision tree that represents this scenario. Use proper symbols and label all branches clearly. Calculate the expected value of this game.

•••• **A.30** On the opening page of Module A and in Example A8, we follow the poker decision made by Paul Phillips against veteran T.J. Cloutier. Create a decision tree that corresponds with the decision made by Phillips. **Px**

Additional problems **A.31–A.32** *are available in* MyOMLab.

CASE STUDY

Warehouse Tenting at the Port of Miami

The Collector's Choice Inc. (CCI), a luxury car import company, has an old warehouse at the Port of Miami, Florida, where it temporarily stores expensive sports cars and automotive parts that arrive from Europe. This summer, CCI has noticed that the termite infestation in the warehouse has escalated to a point where tenting cannot be postponed anymore. (Tenting is the process of wrapping a building inside a huge tent that is subsequently filled with a poisonous gas capable of killing most forms of life inside, including insects, plants, pets, and human beings.) CCI's pest control company's contract specifies a to-do list of pre-tenting tasks, which include:

- Turning off all air-conditioning units and opening all windows of the warehouse
- Turning off all internal and external lights, including those operating on a timer
- Pruning all outdoor vegetation at least 18″ away from the warehouse
- Soaking the soil around the warehouse on the first day of tenting

Halima Ahkdar/Shutterstock

The requirement of opening all windows is particularly worrisome to CCI because it means turning off the alarm system, leaving the warehouse vulnerable to burglary for 48 hours—the required amount of time for the poisonous gas to do its job. Therefore, Alex Ferrari, the warehouse manager, is thinking about hiring a security company to monitor the facility during that period. CCI's property insurance deductible is $25,000, and Alex is assuming that if thieves are willing to enter a building full of poisonous gas to steal something, they would certainly take more than $25,000 worth of parts—or even an entire car!

After making a few phone calls, Alex gets in touch with ProGuard, a trustworthy local security company that charges $150 per hour to have a security guard stationed outside their warehouse. The city of Miami police records indicate that about 30% of businesses that left their facilities unattended during tenting reported stolen property in the past 3 years. Although Alex thinks ProGuard's prices are reasonable, and having a guard outside the warehouse would certainly help, he is still not sure whether it is worth spending the extra money. After all, ProGuard's contract does not guarantee the protection it provides is infallible. In fact, an analysis of the company's records indicates that 3% of their clients were burglarized over the past 3 years. (Despite this figure, ProGuard is still the best security company in the area.)

Discussion Questions

1. Create a decision tree analysis to help decide whether Alex Ferrari should hire ProGuard's services.
2. Come up with a simple rule of thumb that can be applied to decisions of this nature, given any deductible amount d, extra surveillance cost c, and burglary probabilities p_1 (without surveillance) and p_2 (with surveillance).
3. Does your decision based on the tree guarantee success? Why or why not?

Source: Professor Tallys Yunes, University of Miami. Reprinted with permission.

- **Additional Case Studies:** Visit MyOMLab for these additional free case studies:
  Arctic, Inc.: A refrigeration company has several major options with regard to capacity and expansion.
  Ski Right Corp.: Which of four manufacturers should be selected to manufacture ski helmets?
  Tom Tucker's Liver Transplant: An executive must decide whether or not to opt for a dangerous surgery.

Endnote

1. To review these other statistical terms, refer to Tutorial 1, "Statistical Review for Managers," in MyOMLab.

Module A *Rapid Review*

Main Heading	Review Material	MyOMLab
THE DECISION PROCESS IN OPERATIONS (pp. 678–679)	To achieve the goals of their organizations, managers must understand how decisions are made and know which decision-making tools to use. Overcoming uncertainty is a manager's mission. Decision tables and decision trees are used in a wide number of OM situations. ■ **Big data**—The huge amount of economic, production, and consumer data now being collected in digital form.	Concept Questions: 1.1–1.4
FUNDAMENTALS OF DECISION MAKING (pp. 679–680)	*Alternative*—A course of action or strategy that may be chosen by a decision maker. *State of nature*—An occurrence or a situation over which a decision maker has little or no control. Symbols used in a decision tree: 1. ▢—A decision node from which one of several alternatives may be selected. 2. ◯—A state-of-nature node out of which one state of nature will occur. When constructing a decision tree, we must be sure that all alternatives and states of nature are in their correct and logical places and that we include *all* possible alternatives and states of nature, usually including the "do nothing" option.	Concept Questions: 2.1–2.4
DECISION TABLES (p. 680)	■ **Decision table**—A tabular means of analyzing decision alternatives and states of nature. A decision table is sometimes called a payoff table. For any alternative and a particular state of nature, there is a *consequence*, or an *outcome*, which is usually expressed as a monetary value; this is called the *conditional value*.	Concept Questions: 3.1–3.4
TYPES OF DECISION-MAKING ENVIRONMENTS (pp. 681–684)	There are three decision-making environments: (1) decision making under uncertainty, (2) decision making under risk, and (3) decision making under certainty. When there is complete *uncertainty* about which state of nature in a decision environment may occur (i.e., when we cannot even assess probabilities for each possible outcome), we rely on three decision methods: (1) maximax, (2) maximin, and (3) equally likely. ■ **Maximax**—A criterion that finds an alternative that maximizes the maximum outcome. ■ **Maximin**—A criterion that finds an alternative that maximizes the minimum outcome. ■ **Equally likely**—A criterion that assigns equal probability to each state of nature. Maximax is also called an "optimistic" decision criterion, while maximin is also called a "pessimistic" decision criterion. Maximax and maximin present best case/worst case planning scenarios. Decision making under risk relies on probabilities. The states of nature must be mutually exclusive and collectively exhaustive, and their probabilities must sum to 1. ■ **Expected monetary value (EMV)**—The expected payout or value of a variable that has different possible states of nature, each with an associated probability. The EMV represents the expected value or *mean* return for each alternative *if we could repeat this decision (or similar types of decisions) a large number of times*. The EMV for an alternative is the sum of all possible payoffs from the alternative, each weighted by the probability of that payoff occurring: $$\text{EMV (Alternative } i) = \text{(Payoff of 1st state of nature)}$$ $$\times \text{(Probability of 1st of state of nature)}$$ $$+ \text{(Payoff of 2nd state of nature)} \times \text{(Probability of 2nd state of nature)}$$ $$+ \ldots + \text{(Payoff of last state of nature)} \times \text{(Probability of last state of nature)}$$ ■ **Expected value of perfect information (EVPI)**—The difference between the payoff under perfect information and the payoff under risk. ■ **Expected value *with* perfect information (EVwPI)**—The expected (average) return if perfect information is available. EVPI represents an upper bound on what you would be willing to spend on state-of-nature information: $$\text{EVPI} = \text{EVwPI} - \text{Maximum EMV}$$ $$\text{EVwPI} = \text{(Best outcome for 1st state of nature)} \times \text{(Probability of 1st state of nature)}$$ $$+ \text{(Best outcome for 2nd state of nature)} \times \text{(Probability of 2nd state of nature)}$$ $$+ \ldots + \text{(Best outcome for last state of nature)} \times \text{(Probability of last state of nature)}$$	Concept Questions: 4.1–4.4 Problems: A.1–A.20 Virtual Office Hours for Solved Problems: A.1, A.2

Main Heading	Review Material	MyOMLab
DECISION TREES (pp. 684–688)	When there are two or more sequential decisions, and later decisions are based on the outcome of prior ones, the decision tree (as opposed to decision table) approach becomes appropriate.	Concept Questions: 5.1–5.4 Problems: A.21–A.32

- **Decision tree**—A graphical means of analyzing decision alternatives and states of nature.

Analyzing problems with *decision trees* involves five steps:

1. Define the problem.
2. Structure or draw the decision tree.
3. Assign probabilities to the states of nature.
4. Estimate payoffs for each possible combination of decision alternatives and states of nature.
5. Solve the problem by computing the expected monetary values (EMV) for each state-of-nature node. This is done by working *backward*—that is, by starting at the right of the tree and working back to decision nodes on the left:

Virtual Office Hours for Solved Problem: A.3

Decision trees force managers to examine all possible outcomes, including unfavorable ones. A manager is also forced to make decisions in a logical, sequential manner. Short parallel lines on a decision tree mean "prune" that branch, as it is less favorable than another available option and may be dropped.

Self Test

- **Before taking the self-test,** refer to the learning objectives listed at the beginning of the module and the key terms listed at the end of the module.

LO A.1 On a decision tree, at each state-of-nature node:
a) the alternative with the greatest EMV is selected.
b) an EMV is calculated.
c) all probabilities are added together.
d) the branch with the highest probability is selected.

LO A.2 In decision table terminology, a course of action or a strategy that may be chosen by a decision maker is called a(n):
a) payoff.
b) alternative.
c) state of nature.
d) all of the above.

LO A.3 If probabilities are available to the decision maker, then the decision-making environment is called:
a) certainty.   b) uncertainty.
c) risk.   d) none of the above.

LO A.4 What is the EMV for Alternative 1 in the following decision table?

	STATE OF NATURE	
Alternative	*S1*	*S2*
A1	$15,000	$20,000
A2	$10,000	$30,000
Probability	0.30	0.70

a) $15,000   b) $17,000
c) $17,500   d) $18,500
e) $20,000

LO A.5 The most that a person should pay for perfect information is:
a) the EVPI.
b) the maximum EMV minus the minimum EMV.
c) the minimum EMV.
d) the maximum EMV.

LO A.6 On a decision tree, once the tree has been drawn and the payoffs and probabilities have been placed on the tree, the analysis (computing EMVs and selecting the best alternative):
a) is done by working backward (starting on the right and moving to the left).
b) is done by working forward (starting on the left and moving to the right).
c) is done by starting at the top of the tree and moving down.
d) is done by starting at the bottom of the tree and moving up.

LO A.7 A decision tree is preferable to a decision table when:
a) a number of sequential decisions are to be made.
b) probabilities are available.
c) the maximax criterion is used.
d) the objective is to maximize regret.

Answers: LO A.1. b; LO A.2. b; LO A.3. c; LO A.4. d; LO A.5. a; LO A.6. a; LO A.7. a.

Linear Programming

B MODULE

MODULE OUTLINE

- Why Use Linear Programming? *700*
- Requirements of a Linear Programming Problem *701*
- Formulating Linear Programming Problems *701*
- Graphical Solution to a Linear Programming Problem *702*
- Sensitivity Analysis *705*
- Solving Minimization Problems *708*
- Linear Programming Applications *710*
- The Simplex Method of LP *713*
- Integer and Binary Variables *713*

Alaska Airlines

Alaska Airlines

LEARNING OBJECTIVES

LO B.1 *Formulate* linear programming models, including an objective function and constraints 702

LO B.2 *Graphically* solve an LP problem with the iso-profit line method 704

LO B.3 *Graphically* solve an LP problem with the corner-point method 705

LO B.4 *Interpret* sensitivity analysis and shadow prices 706

LO B.5 *Construct* and solve a minimization problem 709

LO B.6 *Formulate* production-mix, diet, and labor scheduling problems 710

The storm front closed in quickly on Boston's Logan Airport, shutting it down without warning. The heavy snowstorms and poor visibility sent airline passengers and ground crew scurrying. Because airlines use linear programming (LP) to schedule flights, hotels, crews, and refueling, LP has a direct impact on profitability. If an airline gets a major weather disruption at one of its hubs, a lot of flights may get canceled, which means a lot of crews and airplanes in the wrong places. LP is the tool that helps airlines unsnarl and cope with this weather mess.

Paul Italiano/Alamy

Why Use Linear Programming?

Many operations management decisions involve trying to make the most effective use of an organization's resources. Resources typically include machinery (such as planes, in the case of an airline), labor (such as pilots), money, time, and raw materials (such as jet fuel). These resources may be used to produce products (such as machines, furniture, food, or clothing) or services (such as airline schedules, advertising policies, or investment decisions). **Linear programming (LP)** is a widely used mathematical technique designed to help operations managers plan and make the decisions necessary to allocate resources.

A few examples of problems in which LP has been successfully applied in operations management are:

Linear programming (LP)

A mathematical technique designed to help operations managers plan and make decisions necessary to allocate resources.

1. Scheduling school buses to *minimize* the total distance traveled when carrying students
2. Allocating police patrol units to high crime areas to *minimize* response time to 911 calls
3. Scheduling tellers at banks so that needs are met during each hour of the day while *minimizing* the total cost of labor
4. Selecting the product mix in a factory to make best use of machine- and labor-hours available while *maximizing* the firm's profit
5. Picking blends of raw materials in feed mills to produce finished feed combinations at *minimum* cost
6. Determining the distribution system that will *minimize* total shipping cost from several warehouses to various market locations
7. Developing a production schedule that will satisfy future demands for a firm's product and at the same time *minimize* total production and inventory costs
8. Allocating space for a tenant mix in a new shopping mall to *maximize* revenues to the leasing company

VIDEO B.1

Scheduling Challenges at Alaska Airlines

Requirements of a Linear Programming Problem

All LP problems have four requirements: an objective, constraints, alternatives, and linearity:

1. LP problems seek to *maximize* or *minimize* some quantity (usually profit or cost). We refer to this property as the objective function of an LP problem. The major objective of a typical firm is to maximize dollar profits in the long run. In the case of a trucking or airline distribution system, the objective might be to minimize shipping costs.

2. The presence of restrictions, or constraints, limits the degree to which we can pursue our objective. For example, deciding how many units of each product in a firm's product line to manufacture is restricted by available labor and machinery. We want, therefore, to maximize or minimize a quantity (the objective function) subject to limited resources (the constraints).

3. There must be *alternative courses of action* to choose from. For example, if a company produces three different products, management may use LP to decide how to allocate among them its limited production resources (of labor, machinery, and so on). If there were no alternatives to select from, we would not need LP.

4. The objective and constraints in linear programming problems must be expressed in terms of *linear equations* or inequalities. Linearity implies proportionality and additivity. If x_1 and x_2 are decision variables, there can be no products (e.g., $x_1 x_2$) or powers (e.g., x_1^3) in the objective or constraints. For example, the expression $5x_1 + 8x_2 \leq 250$ is linear; however, the expression $5x_1 + 8x_2 - 2x_1 x_2 \leq 300$ is not linear.

Objective function
A mathematical expression in linear programming that maximizes or minimizes some quantity (often profit or cost, but any goal may be used).

Constraints
Restrictions that limit the degree to which a manager can pursue an objective.

Formulating Linear Programming Problems

One of the most common linear programming applications is the *product-mix problem*. Two or more products are usually produced using limited resources. The company would like to determine how many units of each product it should produce to maximize overall profit given its limited resources. Let's look at an example.

> **STUDENT TIP**
> Here we set up an LP example that we will follow for most of this module.

Glickman Electronics Example

The Glickman Electronics Company in Washington, DC, produces two products: (1) the Glickman x-pod and (2) the Glickman BlueBerry. The production process for each product is similar in that both require a certain number of hours of electronic work and a certain number of labor-hours in the assembly department. Each x-pod takes 4 hours of electronic work and 2 hours in the assembly shop. Each BlueBerry requires 3 hours in electronics and 1 hour in assembly. During the current production period, 240 hours of electronic time are available, and 100 hours of assembly department time are available. Each x-pod sold yields a profit of $7; each BlueBerry produced may be sold for a $5 profit.

Glickman's problem is to determine the best possible combination of x-pods and BlueBerrys to manufacture to reach the maximum profit. This product-mix situation can be formulated as a linear programming problem.

We begin by summarizing the information needed to formulate and solve this problem (see Table B.1). Further, let's introduce some simple notation for use in the objective function and constraints. Let:

X_1 = number of x-pods to be produced

X_2 = number of BlueBerrys to be produced

ACTIVE MODEL B.1

This example is further illustrated in Active Model B.1 in MyOMLab.

TABLE B.1	Glickman Electronics Company Problem Data		
	HOURS REQUIRED TO PRODUCE ONE UNIT		
DEPARTMENT	**X-PODS (X_1)**	**BLUEBERRYS (X_2)**	**AVAILABLE HOURS THIS WEEK**
Electronic	4	3	240
Assembly	2	1	100
Profit per unit	$7	$5	

Now we can create the LP *objective function* in terms of X_1 and X_2:

$$\text{Maximize profit} = \$7X_1 + \$5X_2$$

Our next step is to develop mathematical relationships to describe the two constraints in this problem. One general relationship is that the amount of a resource used is to be less than or equal to ($\leq$) the amount of resource *available*.

First constraint: Electronic time used is $\leq$ Electronic time available.

$$4X_1 + 3X_2 \leq 240 \text{ (hours of electronic time)}$$

Second constraint: Assembly time used is $\leq$ Assembly time available.

$$2X_1 + 1X_2 \leq 100 \text{ (hours of assembly time)}$$

Both these constraints represent production capacity restrictions and, of course, affect the total profit. For example, Glickman Electronics cannot produce 70 x-pods during the production period because if $X_1 = 70$, both constraints will be violated. It also cannot make $X_1 = 50$ x-pods and $X_2 = 10$ BlueBerrys. This constraint brings out another important aspect of linear programming; that is, certain interactions will exist between variables. The more units of one product that a firm produces, the fewer it can make of other products.

LO B.1 *Formulate* linear programming models, including an objective function and constraints

Graphical Solution to a Linear Programming Problem

The easiest way to solve a small LP problem such as that of the Glickman Electronics Company is the **graphical solution approach**. The graphical procedure can be used only when there are two **decision variables** (such as number of x-pods to produce, X_1, and number of BlueBerrys to produce, X_2). When there are more than two variables, it is *not* possible to plot the solution on a two-dimensional graph; we then must turn to more complex approaches described later in this module.

Graphical solution approach

A means of plotting a solution to a two-variable problem on a graph.

Decision variables

Choices available to a decision maker.

Graphical Representation of Constraints

To find the optimal solution to a linear programming problem, we must first identify a set, or region, of feasible solutions. The first step in doing so is to plot the problem's constraints on a graph.

The variable X_1 (x-pods, in our example) is usually plotted as the horizontal axis of the graph, and the variable X_2 (BlueBerrys) is plotted as the vertical axis. The complete problem may be restated as:

$$\text{Maximize profit} = \$7X_1 + \$5X_2$$

Subject to the constraints:

$$4X_1 + 3X_2 \leq 240 \text{ (\textit{electronics constraint})}$$
$$2X_1 + 1X_2 \leq 100 \text{ (\textit{assembly constraint})}$$
$$X_1 \geq 0 \text{ (\textit{number of x-pods produced is greater than or equal to 0})}$$
$$X_2 \geq 0 \text{ (\textit{number of BlueBerrys produced is greater than or equal to 0})}$$

(These last two constraints are also called *nonnegativity constraints*.)

The first step in graphing the constraints of the problem is to convert the constraint *inequalities* into *equalities* (or equations):

$$\text{Constraint A:} \quad 4X_1 + 3X_2 = 240$$
$$\text{Constraint B:} \quad 2X_1 + 1X_2 = 100$$

The equation for constraint A is plotted in Figure B.1 and for constraint B in Figure B.2.

To plot the line in Figure B.1, all we need to do is to find the points at which the line $4X_1 + 3X_2 = 240$ intersects the X_1 and X_2 axes. When $X_1 = 0$ (the location where the line touches the X_2 axis), it implies that $3X_2 = 240$ and that $X_2 = 80$. Likewise, when $X_2 = 0$, we see that $4X_1 = 240$ and that $X_1 = 60$. Thus, constraint A is bounded by the line running from ($X_1 = 0$, $X_2 = 80$) to ($X_1 = 60$, $X_2 = 0$). The shaded area represents all points that satisfy the original *inequality*.

Constraint B is illustrated similarly in Figure B.2. When $X_1 = 0$, then $X_2 = 100$; and when $X_2 = 0$, then $X_1 = 50$. Constraint B, then, is bounded by the line between

STUDENT TIP

We named the decision variables X_1 and X_2 here, but any notations (e.g., *x-p* and B or *X* and *Y*) would do as well.

Figure B.1

Constraint A

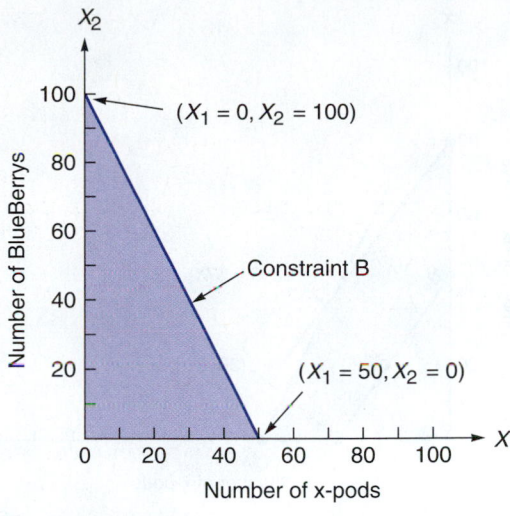

Figure B.2

Constraint B

$(X_1 = 0, X_2 = 100)$ and $(X_1 = 50, X_2 = 0)$. The shaded area represents the original inequality.

Figure B.3 shows both constraints together (along with the nonnegativity constraints). The shaded region is the part that satisfies all restrictions. The shaded region in Figure B.3 is called the *area of feasible solutions*, or simply the feasible region. This region must satisfy *all* conditions specified by the program's constraints and is thus the region where all constraints overlap. Any point in the region would be a *feasible solution* to the Glickman Electronics Company problem. Any point outside the shaded area would represent an *infeasible solution*. Hence, it would be feasible to manufacture 30 x-pods and 20 BlueBerrys ($X_1 = 30, X_2 = 20$), but it would violate the constraints to produce 70 x-pods and 40 BlueBerrys. This can be seen by plotting these points on the graph of Figure B.3.

Feasible region

The set of all feasible combinations of decision variables.

Iso-Profit Line Solution Method

Now that the feasible region has been graphed, we can proceed to find the *optimal* solution to the problem. The optimal solution is the point lying in the feasible region that produces the highest profit.

Once the feasible region has been established, several approaches can be taken in solving for the optimal solution. The speediest one to apply is called the iso-profit line method.[1]

We start by letting profits equal some arbitrary but small dollar amount. For the Glickman Electronics problem, we may choose a profit of $210. This is a profit level that can easily be obtained without violating either of the two constraints. The objective function can be written as $210 = 7X_1 + 5X_2$.

This expression is just the equation of a line; we call it an *iso-profit line*. It represents all combinations (of X_1, X_2) that will yield a total profit of $210. To plot the profit line, we proceed exactly as we did to plot a constraint line. First, let $X_1 = 0$ and solve for the point at which the line crosses the X_2 axis:

$$\$210 = \$7(0) + \$5X_2$$
$$X_2 = 42 \text{ BlueBerrys}$$

Then let $X_2 = 0$ and solve for X_1:

$$\$210 = \$7X_1 + \$5(0)$$
$$X_1 = 30 \text{ x-pods}$$

Figure B.3

Feasible Solution Region for the Glickman Electronics Company Problem

Iso-profit line method
An approach to solving a linear programming maximization problem graphically.

Figure **B.4**

A Profit Line of $210 Plotted for the Glickman Electronics Company

Figure **B.5**

Four Iso-Profit Lines Plotted for the Glickman Electronics Company

LO B.2 *Graphically solve an LP problem with the iso-profit line method*

We can now connect these two points with a straight line. This profit line is illustrated in Figure B.4. All points on the line represent feasible solutions that produce a profit of $210.

We see, however, that the iso-profit line for $210 does not produce the highest possible profit to the firm. In Figure B.5, we try graphing three more lines, each yielding a higher profit. The middle equation, $\$280 = \$7X_1 + \$5X_2$, was plotted in the same fashion as the lower line. When $X_1 = 0$:

$$\$280 = \$7(0) + \$5X_2$$
$$X_2 = 56 \text{ BlueBerrys}$$

When $X_2 = 0$:

$$\$280 = \$7X_1 + \$5(0)$$
$$X_1 = 40 \text{ x-pods}$$

Again, any combination of x-pods (X_1) and BlueBerrys (X_2) on this iso-profit line will produce a total profit of $280.

Note that the third line generates a profit of $350, even more of an improvement. The farther we move from the 0 origin, the higher our profit will be. Another important point to note is that these iso-profit lines are parallel. We now have two clues how to find the optimal solution to the original problem. We can draw a series of parallel profit lines (by carefully moving our ruler in a plane parallel to the first profit line). The highest profit line that still touches some point of the feasible region will pinpoint the optimal solution. Notice that the fourth line ($420) is too high to count because it does not touch the feasible region.

The highest possible iso-profit line is illustrated in Figure B.6. It touches the tip of the feasible region at the point where the two resource constraints intersect. To find its coordinates *accurately*, we will have to solve for the intersection of the two constraint lines. As you may recall from algebra, we can apply the method of *simultaneous equations* to the two constraint equations:

$$4X_1 + 3X_2 = 240 \quad (electronics\ time)$$
$$2X_1 + 1X_2 = 100 \quad (assembly\ time)$$

To solve these equations simultaneously, we multiply the second equation by -2:

$$-2(2X_1 + 1X_2 = 100) = -4X_1 - 2X_2 = -200$$

Figure **B.6**

Optimal Solution for the Glickman Electronics Problem

and then add it to the first equation:

$$+4X_1 + 3X_2 = 240$$
$$-4X_1 - 2X_2 = -200$$
$$+ 1X_2 = 40$$

or:

$$X_2 = 40$$

Doing this has enabled us to eliminate one variable, X_1, and to solve for X_2. We can now substitute 40 for X_2 in either of the original constraint equations and solve for X_1. Let us use the first equation. When $X_2 = 40$, then:

$$4X_1 + 3(40) = 240$$
$$4X_1 + 120 = 240$$
$$4X_1 = 120$$
$$X_1 = 30$$

Thus, the optimal solution has the coordinates ($X_1 = 30$, $X_2 = 40$). The profit at this point is $7(30) + $5(40) = $410.

Corner-Point Solution Method

A second approach to solving linear programming problems employs the corner-point method. This technique is simpler in concept than the iso-profit line approach, but it involves looking at the profit at every corner point of the feasible region.

Corner-point method
A method for solving graphical linear programming problems.

The mathematical theory behind linear programming states that an optimal solution to any problem (that is, the values of X_1, X_2 that yield the maximum profit) will lie at a *corner point*, or *extreme point*, of the feasible region. Hence, it is necessary to find only the values of the variables at each corner; the maximum profit or optimal solution will lie at one (or more) of them.

Once again we can see (in Figure B.7) that the feasible region for the Glickman Electronics Company problem is a four-sided polygon with four corner, or extreme, points. These points are labeled ①, ②, ③, and ④ on the graph. To find the (X_1, X_2) values producing the maximum profit, we find out what the coordinates of each corner point are, then determine and compare their profit levels. (We showed how to find the coordinates for point ③ in the previous section describing the iso-profit line solution method.)

Figure **B.7**

The Four Corner Points of the Feasible Region

Point ①: ($X_1 = 0$, $X_2 = 0$)   Profit $7(0) + $5(0) = $0
Point ②: ($X_1 = 0$, $X_2 = 80$)   Profit $7(0) + $5(80) = $400
Point ③: ($X_1 = 30$, $X_2 = 40$) Profit $7(30) + $5(40) = $410
Point ④: ($X_1 = 50$, $X_2 = 0$)   Profit $7(50) + $5(0) = $350

Because point ③ produces the highest profit of any corner point, the product mix of $X_1 = 30$ x-pods and $X_2 = 40$ BlueBerrys is the optimal solution to the Glickman Electronics problem. This solution will yield a profit of $410 per production period; it is the same solution we obtained using the iso-profit line method.

LO B.3 *Graphically solve an LP problem with the corner-point method*

Sensitivity Analysis

Operations managers are usually interested in more than the optimal solution to an LP problem. In addition to knowing the value of each decision variable (the X_is) and the value of the objective function, they want to know how sensitive these answers are to input parameter changes. For example, what happens if the coefficients of the objective function are not exact, or if they change by 10% or 15%? What happens if the right-hand-side values of the constraints

Parameter
Numerical value that is given in a model.

Sensitivity analysis
An analysis that projects how much a solution may change if there are changes in the variables or input data.

change? Because solutions are based on the assumption that input parameters are constant, the subject of sensitivity analysis comes into play. Sensitivity analysis, or postoptimality analysis, is the study of how sensitive solutions are to parameter changes.

There are two approaches to determining just how sensitive an optimal solution is to changes. The first is simply a trial-and-error approach. This approach usually involves resolving the entire problem, preferably by computer, each time one input data item or parameter is changed. It can take a long time to test a series of possible changes in this way.

The approach we prefer is the analytic postoptimality method. After an LP problem has been solved, we determine a range of changes in problem parameters that will not affect the optimal solution or change the variables in the solution. This is done without resolving the whole problem. LP software, such as Excel's Solver or POM for Windows, has this capability. Let us examine several scenarios relating to the Glickman Electronics example.

Program B.1 is part of the Excel Solver computer-generated output available to help a decision maker know whether a solution is relatively insensitive to reasonable changes in one or more of the parameters of the problem. (The complete computer run for these data, including input and full output, is illustrated in Programs B.3 and B.4 later in this module.)

STUDENT TIP

Here we look at the sensitivity of the final answers to changing inputs.

LO B.4 *Interpret sensitivity analysis and shadow prices*

Sensitivity Report

The Excel *Sensitivity Report* for the Glickman Electronics example in Program B.1 has two distinct components: (1) a table titled Variable Cells and (2) a table titled Constraints. These tables permit us to answer several what-if questions regarding the problem solution.

It is important to note that while using the information in the sensitivity report to answer what-if questions, we assume that we are considering a change to only a *single* input data value at a time. That is, the sensitivity information does not always apply to simultaneous changes in several input data values.

The *Variable Cells* table presents information regarding the impact of changes to the objective function coefficients (i.e., the unit profits of $7 and $5) on the optimal solution. The *Constraints* table presents information related to the impact of changes in constraint right-hand-side (RHS) values (i.e., the 240 hours and 100 hours) on the optimal solution. Although different LP software packages may format and present these tables differently, the programs all provide essentially the same information.

Changes in the Resources or Right-Hand-Side Values

The right-hand-side values of the constraints often represent resources available to the firm. The resources could be labor-hours or machine time or perhaps money or production materials available. In the Glickman Electronics example, the two resources are hours available of

Program **B.1**

Sensitivity Analysis for Glickman Electronics, Using Excel's Solver

Microsoft Excel 15.0 Sensitivity Report
Report Created: 9:22:18 AM

The solution values for the variables appear. We should make 30 x-pods and 40 BlueBerrys.

Variable Cells

Cell	Name	Final Value	Reduced Cost	Objective Coefficient	Allowable Increase	Allowable Decrease
$B$5	Variable Values x-pods	30	0	7	3	0.333333333
$C$5	Variable Values BlueBerrys	40	0	5	0.25	1.5

Constraints

Cell	Name	Final Value	Shadow Price	Constraint R.H. Side	Allowable Increase	Allowable Decrease
$D$8	Electronic Time Available	240	1.5	240	60	40
$D$9	Assembly Time Available	100	0.5	100	20	20

We will use 240 hours and 100 hours of Electronics and Assembly time, respectively.

If we use 1 more Electronics hour, our profit will increase by $1.50. This is true for up to 60 more hours. The profit will fall by $1.50 for each Electronics hour less than 240 hours, down to as low as 200 hours.

electronics time and hours of assembly time. If additional hours were available, a higher total profit could be realized. How much should the company be willing to pay for additional hours? Is it profitable to have some additional electronics hours? Should we be willing to pay for more assembly time? Sensitivity analysis about these resources will help us answer these questions.

If the right-hand side of a constraint is changed, the feasible region will change (unless the constraint is redundant), and often the optimal solution will change. In the Glickman example, there were 100 hours of assembly time available each week and the maximum possible profit was $410. If the available assembly hours are *increased* to 110 hours, the new optimal solution seen in Figure B.8(a) is (45,20) and the profit is $415. Thus, the extra 10 hours of time resulted in an increase in profit of $5 or $0.50 per hour. If the hours are *decreased* to 90 hours as shown in Figure B.8(b), the new optimal solution is (15,60) and the profit is $405. Thus, reducing the hours by 10 results in a decrease in profit of $5 or $0.50 per hour. This $0.50 per hour change in profit that resulted from a change in the hours available is called the shadow price, or **dual value**. The shadow price for a constraint is the improvement in the objective function value that results from a one-unit increase in the right-hand side of the constraint.

Shadow price (or dual value)
The value of one additional unit of a scarce resource in LP.

Validity Range for the Shadow Price   Given that Glickman Electronics' profit increases by $0.50 for each additional hour of assembly time, does it mean that Glickman can do this indefinitely, essentially earning infinite profit? Clearly, this is illogical. How far can Glickman increase its assembly time availability and still earn an extra $0.50 profit per hour? That is, for what level of increase in the RHS value of the assembly time constraint is the shadow price of $0.50 valid?

The shadow price of $0.50 is valid as long as the available assembly time stays in a range within which all current corner points continue to exist. The information to compute the upper and lower limits of this range is given by the entries labeled Allowable Increase and Allowable Decrease in the *Sensitivity Report* in Program B.1. In Glickman's case, these values show that the shadow price of $0.50 for assembly time availability is valid for an increase of up to 20 hours from the current value and a decrease of up to 20 hours. That is, the available assembly time can range from a low of 80 (= 100 − 20) to a high of 120 (= 100 + 20) for the shadow price of $0.50 to be valid. Note that the allowable decrease implies that for each hour of assembly time that Glickman loses (up to 20 hours), its profit decreases by $0.50.

Changes in the Objective Function Coefficient

Let us now focus on the information provided in Program B.1 titled Variable Cells. Each row in the Variable Cells table contains information regarding a decision variable (i.e., x-pods or BlueBerrys) in the LP model.

Figure **B.8**

Glickman Electronics Sensitivity Analysis on the Right-Hand Side (RHS) of the Assembly Resource Constraint

Allowable Ranges for Objective Function Coefficients   As the unit profit contribution of either product changes, the slope of the iso-profit lines we saw earlier in Figure B.5 changes. The size of the feasible region, however, remains the same. That is, the locations of the corner points do not change.

The limits to which the profit coefficient of x-pods or BlueBerrys can be changed without affecting the optimality of the current solution is revealed by the values in the Allowable Increase and Allowable Decrease columns of the *Sensitivity Report* in Program B.1. The allowable increase in the objective function coefficient for BlueBerrys is only $0.25. In contrast, the allowable decrease is $1.50. Hence, if the unit profit of BlueBerrys drops to $4 (i.e., a decrease of $1 from the current value of $5), it is still optimal to produce 30 x-pods and 40 BlueBerrys. The total profit will drop to $370 (from $410) because each BlueBerry now yields less profit (of $1 per unit). However, if the unit profit drops below $3.50 per BlueBerry (i.e., a decrease of more than $1.50 from the current $5 profit), the current solution is no longer optimal. The LP problem will then have to be resolved using Solver, or other software, to find the new optimal corner point.

STUDENT TIP ◑

LP problems can be structured to minimize costs as well as maximize profits.

Solving Minimization Problems

Many linear programming problems involve *minimizing* an objective such as cost instead of maximizing a profit function. A restaurant, for example, may wish to develop a work schedule to meet staffing needs while minimizing the total number of employees. Also, a manufacturer may seek to distribute its products from several factories to its many regional warehouses in a way that minimizes total shipping costs.

Iso-cost

An approach to solving a linear programming minimization problem graphically.

Minimization problems can be solved graphically by first setting up the feasible solution region and then using either the corner-point method or an iso-cost line approach (which is analogous to the iso-profit approach in maximization problems) to find the values of X_1 and X_2 that yield the minimum cost.

Example B1 shows how to solve a minimization problem.

Example B1

A MINIMIZATION PROBLEM WITH TWO VARIABLES

Cohen Chemicals, Inc., produces two types of photo-developing fluids. The first, a black-and-white picture chemical, costs Cohen $2,500 per ton to produce. The second, a color photo chemical, costs $3,000 per ton.

Based on an analysis of current inventory levels and outstanding orders, Cohen's production manager has specified that at least 30 tons of the black-and-white chemical and at least 20 tons of the color chemical must be produced during the next month. In addition, the manager notes that an existing inventory of a highly perishable raw material needed in both chemicals must be used within 30 days. To avoid wasting the expensive raw material, Cohen must produce a total of at least 60 tons of the photo chemicals in the next month.

APPROACH ▶   Formulate this information as a minimization LP problem.

Let:

$$X_1 = \text{number of tons of black-and-white photo chemical produced}$$
$$X_2 = \text{number of tons of color photo chemical produced}$$
$$\text{Objective: Minimize cost} = \$2,500X_1 + \$3,000X_2$$

Subject to:

$$X_1 \geq 30 \text{ tons of black-and-white chemical}$$
$$X_2 \geq 20 \text{ tons of color chemical}$$
$$X_1 + X_2 \geq 60 \text{ tons total}$$
$$X_1, X_2 \geq 0 \text{ nonnegativity requirements}$$

SOLUTION ▶   To solve the Cohen Chemicals problem graphically, we construct the problem's feasible region, shown in Figure B.9.

Figure **B.9**

Cohen Chemicals' Feasible Region

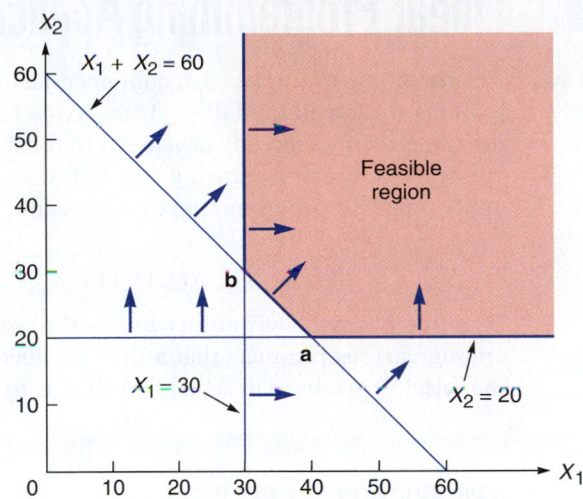

LO B.5 *Construct* and solve a minimization problem

Minimization problems are often unbounded outward (that is, on the right side and on the top), but this characteristic causes no problem in solving them. As long as they are bounded inward (on the left side and the bottom), we can establish corner points. The optimal solution will lie at one of the corners.

In this case, there are only two corner points, **a** and **b**, in Figure B.9. It is easy to determine that at point **a**, $X_1 = 40$ and $X_2 = 20$, and that at point **b**, $X_1 = 30$ and $X_2 = 30$. The optimal solution is found at the point yielding the lowest total cost.

Thus:

$$\text{Total cost at } \mathbf{a} = 2{,}500X_1 + 3{,}000X_2$$
$$= 2{,}500(40) + 3{,}000(20)$$
$$= \$160{,}000$$
$$\text{Total cost at } \mathbf{b} = 2{,}500X_1 + 3{,}000X_2$$
$$= 2{,}500(30) + 3{,}000(30)$$
$$= \$165{,}000$$

The lowest cost to Cohen Chemicals is at point **a**. Hence the operations manager should produce 40 tons of the black-and-white chemical and 20 tons of the color chemical.

INSIGHT ▶ The area is either not bounded to the right or above in a minimization problem (as it is in a maximization problem).

LEARNING EXERCISE ▶ Cohen's second constraint is recomputed and should be $X_2 \geq 15$. Does anything change in the answer? [Answer: Now $X_1 = 45$, $X_2 = 15$, and total cost = \$157,500.]

RELATED PROBLEMS ▶ B.25–B.31 (B.32, B.33 are available in MyOMLab)

EXCEL OM Data File **ModBExB1.xls** can be found in MyOMLab.

OM in Action   LP at UPS

On an *average* day, the \$58.2 billion shipping giant UPS delivers 18 million packages to 8.2 million customers in 220 countries. On a *really* busy day, say a few days before Christmas, it handles almost twice that number, or 300 packages per second. It does all this with a fleet of 600+ owned and chartered planes, making it one of the largest airline operators in the world.

When UPS decided it should use linear programming to map its entire operation—every pickup and delivery center and every sorting facility (now nearly 2,000 locations)—to find the best routes to move the millions of packages, it invested close to a decade in developing VOLCANO. This LP-based optimization system (which stands for *Volume*, *Location*, and *Aircraft Network Optimization*) is used to determine the least-cost set of routes, fleet assignments, and package flows.

Constraints include the number of planes, airport restrictions, and plane aircraft speed, capacity, and range.

The VOLCANO system is credited with saving UPS hundreds of millions of dollars. But that's just the start. UPS is investing \$600 million more to optimize the whole supply chain to include drivers—the employees closest to the customer—so they will be able to update schedules, priorities, and time conflicts on the fly.

The UPS "airline" is not alone. Southwest runs its massive LP model (called *ILOG Optimizer*) every day to schedule its thousands of flight legs. The program has 90,000 constraints and 2 million variables. United's LP program is called *OptSolver*, and Delta's is called *Coldstart*. Airlines, like many other firms, manage their millions of daily decisions with LP.

Sources: ups.com (June 2015); *Aviation Daily* (February 9, 2004); and *Interfaces* (January–February 2004).

Linear Programming Applications

The foregoing examples each contained just two variables (X_1 and X_2). Most real-world problems (as we saw in the UPS *OM in Action* box) contain many more variables, however. Let's use the principles already developed to formulate a few more-complex problems. The practice you will get by "paraphrasing" the following LP situations should help develop your skills for applying linear programming to other common operations situations.

LO B.6 *Formulate production-mix, diet, and labor scheduling problems*

Production-Mix Example

Example B2 involves another *production-mix* decision. Limited resources must be allocated among various products that a firm produces. The firm's overall objective is to manufacture the selected products in such quantities as to maximize total profits.

Example B2

A PRODUCTION-MIX PROBLEM

Failsafe Electronics Corporation primarily manufactures four highly technical products, which it supplies to aerospace firms that hold NASA contracts. Each of the products must pass through the following departments before they are shipped: wiring, drilling, assembly, and inspection. The time requirements in each department (in hours) for each unit produced and its corresponding profit value are summarized in this table:

PRODUCT	WIRING	DRILLING	ASSEMBLY	INSPECTION	UNIT PROFIT
XJ201	.5	3	2	.5	$ 9
XM897	1.5	1	4	1.0	$12
TR29	1.5	2	1	.5	$15
BR788	1.0	3	2	.5	$11

The production time available in each department each month and the minimum monthly production requirement to fulfill contracts are as follows:

DEPARTMENT	CAPACITY (HOURS)	PRODUCT	MINIMUM PRODUCTION LEVEL
Wiring	1,500	XJ201	150
Drilling	2,350	XM897	100
Assembly	2,600	TR29	200
Inspection	1,200	BR788	400

APPROACH ▶ Formulate this production-mix situation as an LP problem. The production manager first specifies production levels for each product for the coming month. He lets:

X_1 = number of units of XJ201 produced
X_2 = number of units of XM897 produced
X_3 = number of units of TR29 produced
X_4 = number of units of BR788 produced

SOLUTION ▶ The LP formulation is:

Objective: Maximize profit = $9X_1 + 12X_2 + 15X_3 + 11X_4$
subject to:
$.5X_1 + 1.5X_2 + 1.5X_3 + 1X_4 \leq 1{,}500$ hours of wiring available
$3X_1 + 1X_2 + 2X_3 + 3X_4 \leq 2{,}350$ hours of drilling available
$2X_1 + 4X_2 + 1X_3 + 2X_4 \leq 2{,}600$ hours of assembly available
$.5X_1 + 1X_2 + .5X_3 + .5X_4 \leq 1{,}200$ hours of inspection
$X_1 \geq 150$ units of XJ201
$X_2 \geq 100$ units of XM897
$X_3 \geq 200$ units of TR29
$X_4 \geq 400$ units of BR788
$X_1, X_2, X_3, X_4 \geq 0$

INSIGHT ▶ There can be numerous constraints in an LP problem. The constraint right-hand sides may be in different units, but the objective function uses one common unit—dollars of profit, in this case. Because there are more than two decision variables, this problem is not solved graphically.

LEARNING EXERCISE ▶ Solve this LP problem as formulated. What is the solution? [Answer: $X_1 = 150$, $X_2 = 300$, $X_3 = 200$, $X_4 = 400$.]

RELATED PROBLEMS ▶ B.5–B.8, B.10–B.14, B.37 (B.15, B.17, B.19, B.21, B.24 are available in MyOMLab)

Diet Problem Example

Example B3 illustrates the *diet problem*, which was originally used by hospitals to determine the most economical diet for patients. Known in agricultural applications as the *feed-mix problem*, the diet problem involves specifying a food or feed ingredient combination that will satisfy stated nutritional requirements at a minimum cost level.

Example B3

A DIET PROBLEM

The Feed 'N Ship feedlot fattens cattle for local farmers and ships them to meat markets in Kansas City and Omaha. The owners of the feedlot seek to determine the amounts of cattle feed to buy to satisfy minimum nutritional standards and, at the same time, minimize total feed costs.

Each grain stock contains different amounts of four nutritional ingredients: A, B, C, and D. Here are the ingredient contents of each grain, in *ounces per pound of grain*:

INGREDIENT	FEED		
	STOCK X	STOCK Y	STOCK Z
A	3 oz	2 oz	4 oz
B	2 oz	3 oz	1 oz
C	1 oz	0 oz	2 oz
D	6 oz	8 oz	4 oz

The cost per pound of grains X, Y, and Z is $0.02, $0.04, and $0.025, respectively. The minimum requirement per cow per month is 64 ounces of ingredient A, 80 ounces of ingredient B, 16 ounces of ingredient C, and 128 ounces of ingredient D.

The feedlot faces one additional restriction—it can obtain only 500 pounds of stock Z per month from the feed supplier, regardless of its need. Because there are usually 100 cows at the Feed 'N Ship feedlot at any given time, this constraint limits the amount of stock Z for use in the feed of each cow to no more than 5 pounds, or 80 ounces, per month.

APPROACH ▶ Formulate this as a minimization LP problem.

Let: X_1 = number of pounds of stock X purchased per cow each month
X_2 = number of pounds of stock Y purchased per cow each month
X_3 = number of pounds of stock Z purchased per cow each month

SOLUTION ▶

Objective: Minimize cost = $.02X_1 + .04X_2 + .025X_3$
subject to: Ingredient A requirement: $3X_1 + 2X_2 + 4X_3 \geq 64$
Ingredient B requirement: $2X_1 + 3X_2 + 1X_3 \geq 80$
Ingredient C requirement: $1X_1 + 0X_2 + 2X_3 \geq 16$
Ingredient D requirement: $6X_1 + 8X_2 + 4X_3 \geq 128$
Stock Z limitation: $X_3 \leq 5$
$X_1, X_2, X_3 \geq 0$

The cheapest solution is to purchase 40 pounds of grain X_1, at a cost of $0.80 per cow.

INSIGHT ▶ Because the cost per pound of stock X is so low, the optimal solution excludes grains Y and Z.

LEARNING EXERCISE ▶ The cost of a pound of stock X just increased by 50%. Does this affect the solution? [Answer: Yes, when the cost per pound of grain X is $0.03, $X_1 = 16$ pounds, $X_2 = 16$ pounds, $X_3 = 0$, and cost = $1.12 per cow.]

RELATED PROBLEMS ▶ B.27, B.28, B.40 (B.33 is available in MyOMLab)

Labor Scheduling Example

Labor scheduling problems address staffing needs over a specific time period. They are especially useful when managers have some flexibility in assigning workers to jobs that require overlapping or interchangeable talents. Large banks and hospitals frequently use LP to tackle their labor scheduling. Example B4 describes how one bank uses LP to schedule tellers.

Example B4 | SCHEDULING BANK TELLERS

Mexico City Bank of Commerce and Industry is a busy bank that has requirements for between 10 and 18 tellers depending on the time of day. Lunchtime, from noon to 2 P.M., is usually heaviest. The table below indicates the workers needed at various hours that the bank is open.

TIME PERIOD	NUMBER OF TELLERS REQUIRED	TIME PERIOD	NUMBER OF TELLERS REQUIRED
9 A.M.–10 A.M.	10	1 P.M.–2 P.M.	18
10 A.M.–11 A.M.	12	2 P.M.–3 P.M.	17
11 A.M.–Noon	14	3 P.M.–4 P.M.	15
Noon–1 P.M.	16	4 P.M.–5 P.M.	10

The bank now employs 12 full-time tellers, but many people are on its roster of available part-time employees. A part-time employee must put in exactly 4 hours per day but can start anytime between 9 A.M. and 1 P.M. Part-timers are a fairly inexpensive labor pool because no retirement or lunch benefits are provided them. Full-timers, on the other hand, work from 9 A.M. to 5 P.M. but are allowed 1 hour for lunch. (Half the full-timers eat at 11 A.M., the other half at noon.) Full-timers thus provide 35 hours per week of productive labor time.

By corporate policy, the bank limits part-time hours to a maximum of 50% of the day's total requirement.

Part-timers earn $6 per hour (or $24 per day) on average, whereas full-timers earn $75 per day in salary and benefits on average.

APPROACH ▶ The bank would like to set a schedule, using LP, that would minimize its total manpower costs. It will release 1 or more of its full-time tellers if it is profitable to do so.

We can let:

$$F = \text{full-time tellers}$$
$$P_1 = \text{part-timers starting at 9 A.M. (leaving at 1 P.M.)}$$
$$P_2 = \text{part-timers starting at 10 A.M. (leaving at 2 P.M.)}$$
$$P_3 = \text{part-timers starting at 11 A.M. (leaving at 3 P.M.)}$$
$$P_4 = \text{part-timers starting at noon (leaving at 4 P.M.)}$$
$$P_5 = \text{part-timers starting at 1 P.M. (leaving at 5 P.M.)}$$

SOLUTION ▶ Objective function:

$$\text{Minimize total daily manpower cost} = \$75F + \$24(P_1 + P_2 + P_3 + P_4 + P_5)$$

Constraints: For each hour, the available labor-hours must be at least equal to the required labor-hours:

$$
\begin{aligned}
F + P_1 &\geq 10 && (\textit{9 A.M. to 10 A.M. needs}) \\
F + P_1 + P_2 &\geq 12 && (\textit{10 A.M. to 11 A.M. needs}) \\
\tfrac{1}{2}F + P_1 + P_2 + P_3 &\geq 14 && (\textit{11 A.M. to noon needs}) \\
\tfrac{1}{2}F + P_1 + P_2 + P_3 + P_4 &\geq 16 && (\textit{noon to 1 P.M. needs}) \\
F + P_2 + P_3 + P_4 + P_5 &\geq 18 && (\textit{1 P.M. to 2 P.M. needs}) \\
F + P_3 + P_4 + P_5 &\geq 17 && (\textit{2 P.M. to 3 P.M. needs}) \\
F + P_4 + P_5 &\geq 15 && (\textit{3 P.M. to 4 P.M. needs}) \\
F + P_5 &\geq 10 && (\textit{4 P.M. to 5 P.M. needs})
\end{aligned}
$$

Only 12 full-time tellers are available, so:

$$F \leq 12$$

Part-time worker-hours cannot exceed 50% of total hours required each day, which is the sum of the tellers needed each hour:

$$4(P_1 + P_2 + P_3 + P_4 + P_5) \leq .50(10 + 12 + 14 + 16 + 18 + 17 + 15 + 10)$$

or:

$$4P_1 + 4P_2 + 4P_3 + 4P_4 + 4P_5 \leq 0.50(112)$$
$$F, P_1, P_2, P_3, P_4, P_5 \geq 0$$

There are two alternative optimal schedules that Mexico City Bank can follow. The first is to employ only 10 full-time tellers ($F = 10$) and to start 7 part-timers at 10 A.M. ($P_2 = 7$), 2 part-timers at 11 A.M. and noon ($P_3 = 2$ and $P_4 = 2$), and 3 part-timers at 1 P.M. ($P_5 = 3$). No part-timers would begin at 9 A.M.

The second solution also employs 10 full-time tellers, but starts 6 part-timers at 9 A.M. ($P_1 = 6$), 1 part-timer at 10 A.M. ($P_2 = 1$), 2 part-timers at 11 A.M. and noon ($P_3 = 2$ and $P_4 = 2$), and 3 part-timers at 1 P.M. ($P_5 = 3$). The cost of either of these two policies is $1,086 per day.

INSIGHT ▶   It is not unusual for multiple optimal solutions to exist in large LP problems. In this case, it gives management the option of selecting, at the same cost, between schedules. To find an alternate optimal solution, you may have to enter the constraints in a different sequence.

LEARNING EXERCISE ▶   The bank decides to give part-time employees a raise to $7 per hour. Does the solution change? [Answer: Yes, cost = $1,142, $F = 10$, $P_1 = 6$, $P_2 = 1$, $P_3 = 2$, $P_4 = 5$, $P_5 = 0$.]

RELATED PROBLEMS ▶   B.36

The Simplex Method of LP

Simplex method

An algorithm for solving linear programming problems of all sizes.

Most real-world linear programming problems have more than two variables and thus are too complex for graphical solution. A procedure called the simplex method may be used to find the optimal solution to such problems. The simplex method is actually an algorithm (or a set of instructions) with which we examine corner points in a methodical fashion until we arrive at the best solution—highest profit or lowest cost. Computer programs (such as Excel OM and POM for Windows) and Excel spreadsheets are available to solve linear programming problems via the simplex method.

For details regarding the algebraic steps of the simplex algorithm, see Tutorial 3 at our text student download site or in MyOMLab, or refer to a management science textbook.[2]

Integer and Binary Variables

Binary variables

Decision variables that can only take on the value of 0 or 1.

All the examples we have seen in this module so far have produced integer solutions. But it is very common to see LP solutions where the decision variables are not whole numbers. Computer software provides a simple way to guarantee only integer solutions. In addition, computers allow us to create special decision variables called binary variables that can only take on the values of 0 or 1. Binary variables allow us to introduce "yes-or-no" decisions into our linear programs and to introduce special logical conditions.

Creating Integer and Binary Variables

If we wish to ensure that decision variable values are integers rather than fractions, it is generally *not* good practice to simply round the solutions to the nearest integer values. The rounded solutions may not be optimal and, in fact, may not even be feasible. Fortunately, all LP software programs have simple ways to add constraints that enforce some or all of the decision variables to be either integer or binary. The main disadvantage of introducing such constraints is that larger programs may take longer to solve. The same LP that may take 3 seconds to solve on a computer could take several hours or more to solve if many of its variables are forced to be integer or binary. For relatively small programs, though, the difference may be unnoticeable.

Using Excel's Solver (see *Using Software to Solve LP Problems* later in this module), integer and binary constraints can be added by clicking **Add** from the main Solver dialog box. Using the Add Constraint dialog box (see Program B.2), highlight the decision variables themselves under Cell Reference:. Then select **int** or **bin** to ensure that those variables are integer or binary, respectively, in the optimal solution.

Linear Programming Applications with Binary Variables

In the written formulation of a linear program, binary variables are usually defined using the following form:

$$Y = \begin{cases} 1 & \text{if some condition holds} \\ 0 & \text{otherwise} \end{cases}$$

Sometimes we designate decision variables as binary if we are making a yes-or-no decision; for example, "Should we undertake this particular project?" "Should we buy that machine?" or "Should we locate a facility in Arkansas?" Other times, we create binary variables to introduce additional logic into our programs.

Limiting the Number of Alternatives Selected   One common use of 0-1 variables involves limiting the number of projects or items that are selected from a group. Suppose a firm is required to select no more than two of three potential projects. This could be modeled with the following constraint:

$$Y_1 + Y_2 + Y_3 \leq 2$$

If we wished to force the selection of *exactly* two of the three projects for funding, the following constraint should be used:

$$Y_1 + Y_2 + Y_3 = 2$$

This forces exactly two of the variables to have values of 1, whereas the other variable must have a value of 0.

Dependent Selections   At times the selection of one project depends in some way on the selection of another project. This situation can be modeled with the use of 0-1 variables. Suppose G.E.'s new catalytic converter could be purchased ($Y_1 = 1$) only if the software was also purchased ($Y_2 = 1$). The following constraint would force this to occur:

$$Y_1 \leq Y_2$$

or, equivalently,

$$Y_1 - Y_2 \leq 0$$

Thus, if the software is not purchased, the value of Y_2 is 0, and the value of Y_1 must also be 0 because of this constraint. However, if the software is purchased ($Y_2 = 1$), then it is possible that the catalytic converter could also be purchased ($Y_1 = 1$), although this is not required.

If we wished for the catalytic converter and the software projects to either both be selected or both not be selected, we should use the following constraint:

$$Y_1 = Y_2$$

or, equivalently,

$$Y_1 - Y_2 = 0$$

Thus, if either of these variables is equal to 0, the other must also be 0. If either of these is equal to 1, the other must also be 1.

A Fixed-Charge Integer Programming Problem

Often businesses are faced with decisions involving a fixed charge that will affect the cost of future operations. Building a new factory or entering into a long-term lease on an existing facility would involve a fixed cost that might vary depending on the size of the facility and the location. Once a factory is built, the variable production costs will be affected by the labor cost in the particular city where it is located. Example B5 provides an illustration.

Example B5

A FIXED-CHARGE PROBLEM USING BINARY VARIABLES

Sitka Manufacturing is planning to build at least one new plant, and three cities are being considered: Baytown, Texas; Lake Charles, Louisiana; and Mobile, Alabama. Once the plant or plants have been constructed, the company wishes to have sufficient capacity to produce at least 38,000 units each year. The costs associated with the possible locations are given in the following table.

SITE	ANNUAL FIXED COST	VARIABLE COST PER UNIT	ANNUAL CAPACITY
Baytown, TX	$340,000	$32	21,000
Lake Charles, LA	$270,000	$33	20,000
Mobile, AL	$290,000	$30	19,000

APPROACH ▶ In modeling this as an integer program, the objective function is to minimize the total of the fixed costs and the variable costs. The constraints are: (1) total production capacity is at least 38,000; (2) the number of units produced at the Baytown plant is 0 if the plant is not built, and it is no more than 21,000 if the plant is built; (3) the number of units produced at the Lake Charles plant is 0 if the plant is not built, and it is no more than 20,000 if the plant is built; and (4) the number of units produced at the Mobile plant is 0 if the plant is not built, and it is no more than 19,000 if the plant is built.

Then, we define the decision variables as

$$Y_1 = \begin{cases} 1 & \text{if factory is built in Baytown} \\ 0 & \text{otherwise} \end{cases}$$

$$Y_2 = \begin{cases} 1 & \text{if factory is built in Lake Charles} \\ 0 & \text{otherwise} \end{cases}$$

$$Y_3 = \begin{cases} 1 & \text{if factory is built in Mobile} \\ 0 & \text{otherwise} \end{cases}$$

X_1 = number of units produced at the Baytown plant

X_2 = number of units produced at the Lake Charles plant

X_3 = number of units produced at the Mobile plant

SOLUTION ▶ The integer programming problem formulation becomes

Objective: Minimize cost = $340,000 Y_1 + 270,000 Y_2 + 290,000 Y_3 + 32 X_1 + 33 X_2 + 30 X_3$

subject to:
$$X_1 + X_2 + X_3 \geq 38,000$$
$$X_1 \leq 21,000 Y_1$$
$$X_2 \leq 20,000 Y_2$$
$$X_3 \leq 19,000 Y_3$$
$$X_1, X_2, X_3 \geq 0 \text{ and integer}$$
$$Y_1, Y_2, Y_3 = 0 \text{ or } 1$$

INSIGHT ▶ Examining the second constraint, the objective function will try to set the binary variable Y_1 equal to 0 because it wants to minimize cost. However, if $Y_1 = 0$, then the constraint will force X_1 to equal 0, in which case no units will be produced, and the plant will not be opened. Alternatively, if the rest of the program deems it worthwhile or necessary to produce some units of X_1, then Y_1 will have to equal 1 for the constraint to hold. And when $Y_1 = 1$, the firm will be charged the fixed cost of $340,000, and production will be limited to the capacity of 21,000 units. The same logic applies for constraints 3 and 4.

LEARNING EXERCISE ▶ Solve this integer program as formulated. What is the solution? [Answer: $Y_1 = 0$, $Y_2 = 1$, $Y_3 = 1$, $X_1 = 0$, $X_2 = 19,000$, $X_3 = 19,000$; Total Cost = $1,757,000.]

RELATED PROBLEMS ▶ B.41, B.42

Summary

This module introduces a special kind of model, linear programming. LP has proven to be especially useful when trying to make the most effective use of an organization's resources.

The first step in dealing with LP models is problem formulation, which involves identifying and creating an objective function and constraints. The second step is to solve the problem. If there are only two decision variables, the problem can be solved graphically, using the corner-point method or the iso-profit/iso-cost line method. With either approach, we first identify the feasible region, then find the corner point yielding the greatest profit or least cost. LP is used in a wide variety of business applications, as the examples and homework problems in this module reveal.

Key Terms

Linear programming (LP) (p. 700)
Objective function (p. 701)
Constraints (p. 701)
Graphical solution approach (p. 702)
Decision variables (p. 702)

Feasible region (p. 703)
Iso-profit line method (p. 703)
Corner-point method (p. 705)
Parameter (p. 705)
Sensitivity analysis (p. 706)

Shadow price (or dual value) (p. 707)
Iso-cost (p. 708)
Simplex method (p. 713)
Binary variables (p. 713)

Discussion Questions

1. List at least four applications of linear programming problems.
2. What is a "corner point"? Explain why solutions to linear programming problems focus on corner points.
3. Define the feasible region of a graphical LP problem. What is a feasible solution?
4. Each linear programming problem that has a feasible region has an infinite number of solutions. Explain.
5. Under what circumstances is the objective function more important than the constraints in a linear programming model?
6. Under what circumstances are the constraints more important than the objective function in a linear programming model?
7. Why is the diet problem, in practice, applicable for animals but not particularly for people?
8. How many feasible solutions are there in a linear program? Which ones do we need to examine to find the optimal solution?

9. Define shadow price (or dual value).
10. Explain how to use the iso-cost line in a graphical minimization problem.
11. Compare how the corner-point and iso-profit line methods work for solving graphical problems.
12. Where a constraint crosses the vertical or horizontal axis, the quantity is fairly obvious. How does one go about finding the quantity coordinates where two constraints cross, not at an axis?
13. Suppose a linear programming (maximation) problem has been solved and that the optimal value of the objective function is $300. Suppose an additional constraint is added to this problem. Explain how this might affect each of the following:
    a) The feasible region.
    b) The optimal value of the objective function.

Using Software to Solve LP Problems

All LP problems can be solved with the simplex method, using software such as Excel, Excel OM, or POM for Windows.

✗ CREATING YOUR OWN EXCEL SPREADSHEETS

Excel offers the ability to analyze linear programming problems using built-in problem-solving tools. Excel's tool is named *Solver*.

We use Excel to set up the Glickman Electronics problem in Program B.3. The objective and constraints are repeated here:

Objective function: Maximize profit = $7(No. of x-pods) + $5(No. of BlueBerrys)

$$\text{Subject to: } 4(\text{x-pods}) + 3(\text{BlueBerrys}) \le 240$$

$$2(\text{x-pods}) + 1(\text{BlueBerry}) \le 100$$

Program B.3

Using Excel to Formulate the Glickman Electronics Problem

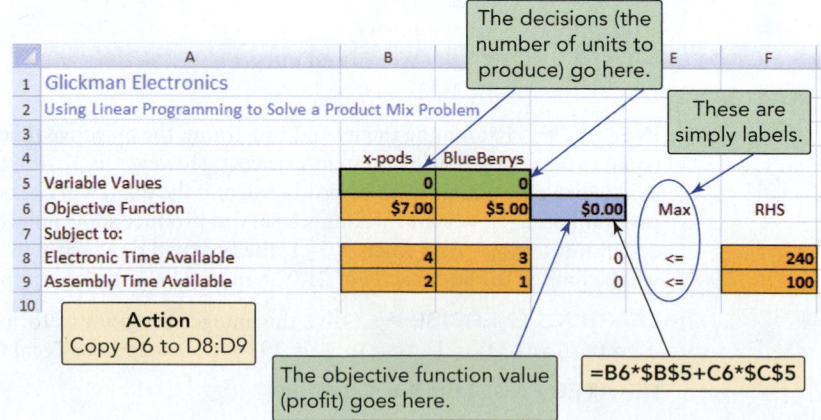

To ensure that Solver always loads when Excel is loaded, click on **FILE**, then **Options**, then **Add-Ins**. Next to **Manage:** at the bottom, make sure that **Excel Add-Ins** is selected, and click on the **Go...** button. Check **Solver Add-In**, and click **OK**. Once in Excel, the Solver dialog box will appear by clicking on: **Data**, then **Analysis: Solver**. (Or if using Excel for Mac, select **Tools**, **Solver**.) Program B.4 shows how to use Solver to find the optimal (very best) solution to the Glickman Electronics problem. Click on **Solve**, and the solution will automatically appear in the spreadsheet in the green and blue cells.

Program **B.4**

Solver Dialog Boxes for the Glickman Electronics Problem

The Excel screen in Program B.5 shows Solver's solution to the Glickman Electronics Company problem. Note that the optimal solution is now shown in cells B5 and C5, which serve as the variables. The Reports selections perform more extensive analysis of the solution and its environment. Excel's sensitivity analysis capability was illustrated earlier in Program B.1.

	A	B	C	D	E	F
1	Glickman Electronics					
2	Using Linear Programming to Solve a Product Mix Problem					
3						
4		x-pods	BlueBerrys			
5	Variable Values	30	40			
6	Objective Function	$7.00	$5.00	$410.00	Max	RHS
7	Subject to:					
8	Electronic Time Available	4	3	240	<=	240
9	Assembly Time Available	2	1	100	<=	100

Program **B.5**

Excel Solution to Glickman Electronics LP Problem

Solved Problems   Virtual Office Hours help is available in MyOMLab.

SOLVED PROBLEM B.1

Smith's, a Niagara, New York, clothing manufacturer that produces men's shirts and pajamas, has two primary resources available: sewing-machine time (in the sewing department) and cutting-machine time (in the cutting department). Over the next month, owner Barbara Smith can schedule up to 280 hours of work on sewing machines and up to 450 hours of work on cutting machines. Each shirt produced requires 1.00 hour of sewing time and 1.50 hours of cutting time. Producing each pair of pajamas requires .75 hours of sewing time and 2 hours of cutting time.

To express the LP constraints for this problem mathematically, we let:

$$X_1 = \text{number of shirts produced}$$
$$X_2 = \text{number of pajamas produced}$$

SOLUTION

First constraint: $1X_1 + .75X_2 \leq 280$ hours of sewing-machine time available—our first scarce resource

Second constraint: $1.5X_1 + 2X_2 \leq 450$ hours of cutting-machine time available—our second scarce resource

Note: This means that each pair of pajamas takes 2 hours of the cutting resource. Smith's accounting department analyzes cost and sales figures and states that each shirt produced will yield a $4 contribution to profit and that each pair of pajamas will yield a $3 contribution to profit.

This information can be used to create the LP *objective function* for this problem:

Objective function: Maximize total contribution to profit $= \$4X_1 + \$3X_2$

SOLVED PROBLEM B.2

We want to solve the following LP problem for Kevin Caskey Wholesale Inc. using the corner-point method:

Objective: Maximize profit $= \$9X_1 + \$7X_2$

Constraints: $2X_1 + 1X_2 \leq 40$

$X_1 + 3X_2 \leq 30$

$X_1, X_2 \geq 0$

SOLUTION

Figure B.10 illustrates these constraints:

Corner-point **a**: $(X_1 = 0, X_2 = 0)$ Profit $= 0$

Corner-point **b**: $(X_1 = 0, X_2 = 10)$ Profit $= 9(0) + 7(10) = \$70$

Corner-point **d**: $(X_1 = 20, X_2 = 0)$ Profit $= 9(20) + 7(0) = \$180$

Corner-point **c** is obtained by solving equations $2X_1 + 1X_2 = 40$ and $X_1 + 3X_2 = 30$ simultaneously. Multiply the second equation by -2 and add it to the first.

$$
\begin{array}{r}
2X_1 + 1X_2 = 40 \\
-2X_1 - 6X_2 = -60 \\
\hline
-5X_2 = -20
\end{array}
$$

Thus $X_2 = 4$

And $X_1 + 3(4) = 30$ or $X_1 + 12 = 30$ or $X_1 = 18$
Corner-point **c**: $(X_1 = 18, X_2 = 4)$ Profit $= 9(18) + 7(4) = \$190$
Hence the optimal solution is:

$(x_1 = 18, x_2 = 4)$ Profit $= \$190$

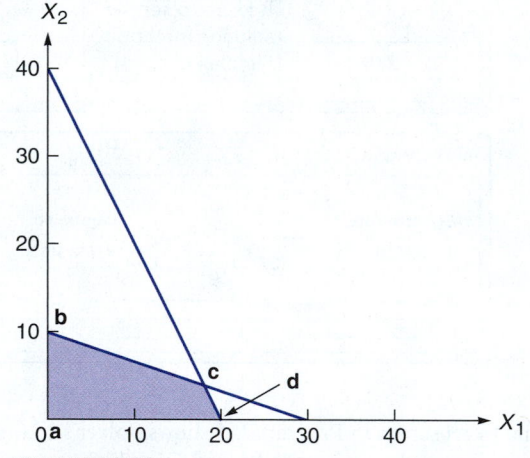

Figure B.10

K. Caskey Wholesale Inc.'s Feasible Region

SOLVED PROBLEM B.3

Holiday Meal Turkey Ranch is considering buying two different types of turkey feed. Each feed contains, in varying proportions, some or all of the three nutritional ingredients essential for fattening turkeys. Brand Y feed costs the ranch $.02 per pound. Brand Z costs $.03 per pound. The rancher would like to determine the lowest-cost diet that meets the minimum monthly intake requirement for each nutritional ingredient.

The following table contains relevant information about the composition of brand Y and brand Z feeds, as well as the minimum monthly requirement for each nutritional ingredient per turkey.

| INGREDIENT | COMPOSITION OF EACH POUND OF FEED | | |
	BRAND Y FEED	BRAND Z FEED	MINIMUM MONTHLY REQUIREMENT
A	5 oz	10 oz	90 oz
B	4 oz	3 oz	48 oz
C	.5 oz	0	1.5 oz
Cost/lb	$.02	$.03	

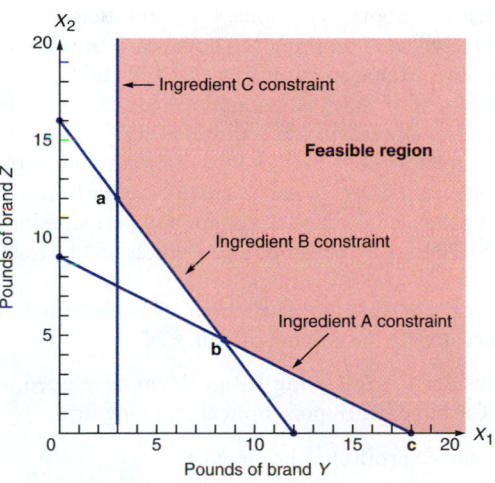

Figure **B.11**

Feasible Region for the Holiday Meal Turkey Ranch Problem

STUDENT TIP ◆

Note that the last line parallel to the 54¢ iso-cost line that touches the feasible region indicates the optimal corner point.

SOLUTION

If we let:

X_1 = number of pounds of brand Y feed purchased
X_2 = number of pounds of brand Z feed purchased

then we may proceed to formulate this linear programming problem as follows:

Objective: Minimize cost (in cents) = $2X_1 + 3X_2$

subject to these constraints:

$$5X_1 + 10X_2 \geq 90 \text{ oz} \qquad (ingredient\ A\ constraint)$$
$$4X_1 + 3X_2 \geq 48 \text{ oz} \qquad (ingredient\ B\ constraint)$$
$$\tfrac{1}{2}X_1 \geq 1\tfrac{1}{2} \text{ oz} \qquad (ingredient\ C\ constraint)$$

Figure B.11 illustrates these constraints.

The iso-cost line approach may be used to solve LP minimization problems such as that of the Holiday Meal Turkey Ranch. As with iso-profit lines, we need not compute the cost at each corner point, but instead draw a series of parallel cost lines. The last cost point to touch the feasible region provides us with the optimal solution corner.

For example, we start in Figure B.12 by drawing a 54¢ cost line, namely, $54 = 2X_1 + 3X_2$. Obviously, there are many points in the feasible region that would yield a lower total cost. We proceed to move our iso-cost line toward the lower left, in a plane parallel to the 54¢ solution line. The last point we touch while still in contact with the feasible region is the same as corner point **b** of Figure B.11. It has the coordinates ($X_1 = 8.4, X_2 = 4.8$) and an associated cost of 31.2 cents.

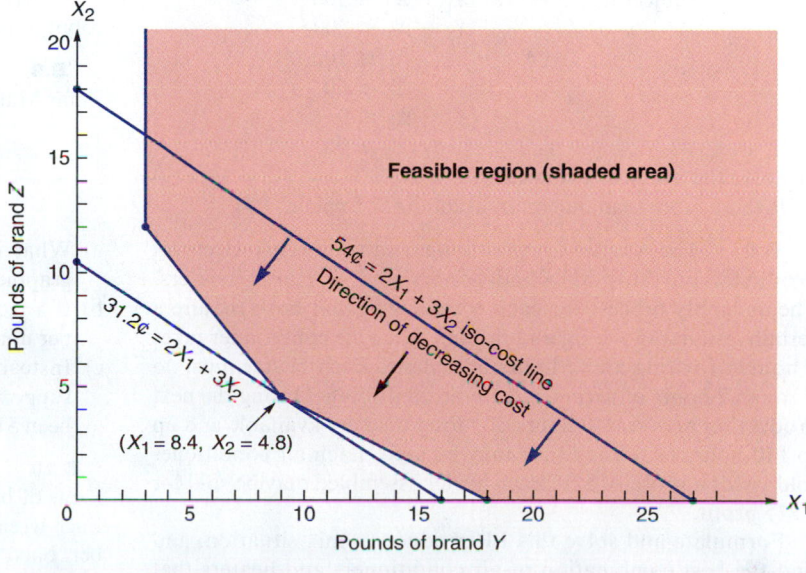

Figure **B.12**

Graphical Solution to the Holiday Meal Turkey Ranch Problem Using the Iso-Cost Line

Problems   *Note:* **PX** means the problem may be solved with POM for Windows and/or Excel OM.

• **B.1**   The LP relationships that follow were formulated by Richard Martin at the Long Beach Chemical Company. Which ones are invalid for use in a linear programming problem, and why?

$$\text{Maximize} = 6X_1 + \tfrac{1}{2}X_1X_2 + 5X_3$$
$$\text{Subject to:} \quad 4X_1X_2 + 2X_3 \leq 70$$
$$7.9X_1 - 4X_2 \geq 15.6$$
$$3X_1 + 3X_2 + 3X_3 \geq 21$$
$$19X_2 - \tfrac{1}{3}X_3 = 17$$
$$-X_1 - X_2 + 4X_3 = 5$$
$$4X_1 + 2X_2 + 3\sqrt{X_3} \leq 80$$

• **B.2**   Solve the following linear programming problem graphically:

$$\text{Maximize profit} = 4X + 6Y$$
$$\text{Subject to:} \quad X + 2Y \leq 8$$
$$5X + 4Y \leq 20$$
$$X, Y \geq 0 \quad \textbf{PX}$$

• **B.3**   Solve the following linear programming problem graphically:

$$\text{Maximize profit} = X + 10Y$$
$$\text{Subject to:} \quad 4X + 3Y \leq 36$$
$$2X + 4Y \leq 40$$
$$Y \geq 3$$
$$X, Y \geq 0 \quad \textbf{PX}$$

•• **B.4**   Consider the following linear programming problem:

$$\text{Maximize profit} = 30X_1 + 10X_2$$
$$\text{Subject to:} \quad 3X_1 + X_2 \leq 300$$
$$X_1 + X_2 \leq 200$$
$$X_1 \leq 100$$
$$X_2 \geq 50$$
$$X_1 - X_2 \leq 0$$
$$X_1, X_2 \geq 0$$

a) Solve the problem graphically.
b) Is there more than one optimal solution? Explain. **PX**

• **B.5**   The Attaran Corporation manufactures two electrical products: portable air conditioners and portable heaters. The assembly process for each is similar in that both require a certain amount of wiring and drilling. Each air conditioner takes 3 hours of wiring and 2 hours of drilling. Each heater must go through 2 hours of wiring and 1 hour of drilling. During the next production period, 240 hours of wiring time are available and up to 140 hours of drilling time may be used. Each air conditioner sold yields a profit of $25. Each heater assembled may be sold for a $15 profit.

Formulate and solve this LP production-mix situation, and find the best combination of air conditioners and heaters that yields the highest profit. **PX**

• **B.6**   The Chris Beehner Company manufactures two lines of designer yard gates, called model A and model B. Every gate requires blending a certain amount of steel and zinc; the company has available a total of 25,000 lb of steel and 6,000 lb of zinc. Each model A gate requires a mixture of 125 lb of steel and 20 lb of zinc, and each yields a profit of $90. Each model B gate requires 100 lb of steel and 30 lb of zinc and can be sold for a profit of $70.

Find by graphical linear programming the best production mix of yard gates. **PX**

•• **B.7**   Green Vehicle Inc. manufactures electric cars and small delivery trucks. It has just opened a new factory where the C1 car and the T1 truck can both be manufactured. To make either vehicle, processing in the assembly shop and in the paint shop are required. It takes 1/40 of a day and 1/60 of a day to paint a truck of type T1 and a car of type C1 in the paint shop, respectively. It takes 1/50 of a day to assemble either type of vehicle in the assembly shop.

A T1 truck and a C1 car yield profits of $300 and $220, respectively, per vehicle sold.

a) Define the objective function and constraint equations.
b) Graph the feasible region.
c) What is a maximum-profit daily production plan at the new factory?
d) How much profit will such a plan yield, assuming whatever is produced is sold? **PX**

• **B.8**   The Lifang Wu Corporation manufactures two models of industrial robots, the Alpha 1 and the Beta 2. The firm employs 5 technicians, working 160 hours each per month, on its assembly line. Management insists that full employment (that is, *all* 160 hours of time) be maintained for each worker during next month's operations. It requires 20 labor-hours to assemble each Alpha 1 robot and 25 labor-hours to assemble each Beta 2 model. Wu wants to see at least 10 Alpha 1s and at least 15 Beta 2s produced during the production period. Alpha 1s generate a $1,200 profit per unit, and Beta 2s yield $1,800 each.

Determine the most profitable number of each model of robot to produce during the coming month. **PX**

•• **B.9**   Consider the following LP problem developed at Zafar Malik's Carbondale, Illinois, optical scanning firm:

$$\text{Maximize profit} = \$1X_1 + \$1X_2$$
$$\text{Subject to:} \quad 2X_1 + 1X_2 \leq 100$$
$$1X_1 + 2X_2 \leq 100$$

a) What is the optimal solution to this problem? Solve it graphically.
b) If a technical breakthrough occurred that raised the profit per unit of X_1 to $3, would this affect the optimal solution?
c) Instead of an increase in the profit coefficient X_1 to $3, suppose that profit was overestimated and should only have been $1.25. Does this change the optimal solution? **PX**

• **B.10**   A craftsman named William Barnes builds two kinds of birdhouses, one for wrens and a second for bluebirds. Each wren birdhouse takes 4 hours of labor and 4 units of lumber. Each bluebird house requires 2 hours of labor and 12 units of lumber. The craftsman has available 60 hours of labor and 120 units of lumber. Wren houses yield a profit of $6 each, and bluebird houses yield a profit of $15 each.

a) Write out the objective and constraints.
b) Solve graphically. **PX**

•• **B.11** Each coffee table produced by Kevin Watson Designers nets the firm a profit of $9. Each bookcase yields a $12 profit. Watson's firm is small and its resources limited. During any given production period (of 1 week), 10 gallons of varnish and 12 lengths of high-quality redwood are available. Each coffee table requires approximately 1 gallon of varnish and 1 length of redwood. Each bookcase takes 1 gallon of varnish and 2 lengths of wood.

Formulate Watson's production-mix decision as a linear programming problem, and solve. How many tables and bookcases should be produced each week? What will the maximum profit be? **P✗**

• **B.12** Par, Inc., produces a standard golf bag and a deluxe golf bag on a weekly basis. Each golf bag requires time for cutting and dyeing and time for sewing and finishing, as shown in the following table:

HOURS REQUIRED PER BAG		
PRODUCT	CUTTING AND DYEING	SEWING AND FINISHING
Standard bag	1/2	1
Deluxe bag	1	2/3

The profits per bag and weekly hours available for cutting and dyeing and for sewing and finishing are as follows:

PRODUCT	PROFIT PER UNIT ($)
Standard bag	10
Deluxe bag	8

ACTIVITY	WEEKLY HOURS AVAILABLE
Cutting and dyeing	300
Sewing and finishing	360

Par, Inc., will sell whatever quantities it produces of these two products.
a) Find the mix of standard and deluxe golf bags to produce per week that maximizes weekly profit from these activities.
b) What is the value of the profit? **P✗**

•• **B.13** The Denver advertising agency promoting the new Breem dishwashing detergent wants to get the best exposure possible for the product within the $100,000 advertising budget ceiling placed on it. To do so, the agency needs to decide how much of the budget to spend on each of its two most effective media: (1) television spots during the afternoon hours and (2) large ads in the city's Sunday newspaper. Each television spot costs $3,000; each Sunday newspaper ad costs $1,250. The expected exposure, based on industry ratings, is 35,000 viewers for each TV commercial and 20,000 readers for each newspaper advertisement. The agency director, Deborah Kellogg, knows from experience that it is important to use both media in order to reach the broadest spectrum of potential Breem customers. She decides that at least 5 but no more than 25 television spots should be ordered, and that at least 10 newspaper ads should be contracted. How many times should each of the two media be used to obtain maximum exposure while staying within the budget? Use the graphical method to solve. **P✗**

•••• **B.14** Baton Rouge's Mt. Cedar Hospital is a large, private, 600-bed facility complete with laboratories, operating rooms, and X-ray equipment. In seeking to increase revenues, Mt. Cedar's administration has decided to make a 90-bed addition on a portion of adjacent land currently used for staff parking. The administrators feel that the labs, operating rooms, and X-ray department are not being fully utilized at present and do not need to be expanded to handle additional patients. The addition of 90 beds, however, involves deciding how many beds should be allocated to the medical staff (for medical patients) and how many to the surgical staff (for surgical patients).

The hospital's accounting and medical records departments have provided the following pertinent information: The average hospital stay for a medical patient is 8 days, and the average medical patient generates $2,280 in revenues. The average surgical patient is in the hospital 5 days and generates $1,515 in revenues. The laboratory is capable of handling 15,000 tests per year more than it *was* handling. The average medical patient requires 3.1 lab tests, the average surgical patient 2.6 lab tests. Furthermore, the average medical patient uses 1 X-ray, the average surgical patient 2 X-rays. If the hospital were expanded by 90 beds, the X-ray department could handle up to 7,000 X-rays without significant additional cost. Finally, the administration estimates that up to 2,800 additional operations could be performed in existing operating-room facilities. Medical patients, of course, require no surgery, whereas each surgical patient generally has one surgery performed.

Formulate this problem so as to determine how many medical beds and how many surgical beds should be added to maximize revenues. Assume that the hospital is open 365 days per year. **P✗**

Additional problems **B.15–B.21** are available in MyOMLab.

Problems B.22–B.24 relate to Sensitivity Analysis

•• **B.22** Kalyan Singhal Corp. makes three products, and it has three machines available as resources as given in the following LP problem:

Maximize contribution $= 4X_1 + 4X_2 + 7X_3$

Subject to: $1X_1 + 7X_2 + 4X_3 \leq 100$ (hours on machine 1)
$2X_1 + 1X_2 + 7X_3 \leq 110$ (hours on machine 2)
$8X_1 + 4X_2 + 1X_3 \leq 100$ (hours on machine 3)

a) Determine the optimal solution using LP software.
b) Is there unused time available on any of the machines with the optimal solution?
c) What would it be worth to the firm to make an additional hour of time available on the third machine?
d) How much would the firm's profit increase if an extra 10 hours of time were made available on the second machine at no extra cost? **P✗**

•••• **B.23** A fertilizer manufacturer has to fulfill supply contracts to its two main customers (650 tons to Customer A and 800 tons to Customer B). It can meet this demand by shipping existing inventory from any of its three warehouses. Warehouse 1 (W1) has 400 tons of inventory on hand, Warehouse 2 (W2) has 500 tons, and Warehouse 3 (W3) has 600 tons. The company would like to arrange the shipping for the lowest cost possible, where the per-ton transit costs are as follows:

	W1	W2	W3
Customer A	$7.50	$6.25	$6.50
Customer B	$6.75	$7.00	$8.00

a) Explain what each of the six decision variables (V) is: (*Hint:* Look at the Solver report below.)

V A1: _____

V A2: _____

V A3: _____

V B1: _____

V B2: _____

V B3: _____

b) Write out the objective function in terms of the variables (V A1, V A2, etc.) and the objective coefficients.

c) Aside from nonnegativity of the variables, what are the five constraints? Write a short description for each constraint, and write out the formula (and circle the type of equality/inequality).

	Description	Variables and Coefficients	What Type?	RHS
C1:	_____	Formula: _____	(= >| = | = <)	_____
C2:	_____	Formula: _____	(= >| = | = <)	_____
C3:	_____	Formula: _____	(= >| = | = <)	_____
C4:	_____	Formula: _____	(= >| = | = <)	_____
C5:	_____	Formula: _____	(= >| = | = <)	_____

After you formulate and enter the linear program for Problem B.23 in Excel, the Solver gives you the following sensitivity report:

Variable Cells

CELL	NAME	FINAL VALUE	REDUCED COST	OBJECTIVE COEFFICIENT	ALLOWABLE INCREASE	ALLOWABLE DECREASE
$B$6	V A1	0	1.5	7.5	1E+30	1.5
$C$6	V A2	100	0	6.25	0.25	0.75
$D$6	V A3	550	0	6.5	0.75	0.25
$E$6	V B1	400	0	6.75	0.5	1E+30
$F$6	V B2	400	0	7	0.75	0.5
$G$6	V B3	0	0.75	8	1E+30	0.75

Constraints

CELL	NAME	FINAL VALUE	SHADOW PRICE	CONSTRAINT R.H. SIDE	ALLOWABLE INCREASE	ALLOWABLE DECREASE
$H$7	C1	650	6.5	650	50	550
$H$8	C2	800	7.25	800	50	400
$H$9	C3	400	−0.5	400	400	50
$H$10	C4	500	−0.25	500	550	50
$H$11	C5	550	0	600	1E+30	50

d) How many of the constraints are binding?

e) What is the range of optimality on variable V A3?

f) If we could ship 10 tons less to Customer A, how much money *might* we be able to save? If we could choose to short *either* Customer A or Customer B by 10 tons, which would we prefer to short? Why? **Px**

> Additional problem **B.24** is available in MyOMLab.

Problems B.25–B.33 relate to Solving Minimization Problems

• **B.25** Solve the following linear program graphically:

$$\text{Minimize cost} = X_1 + X_2$$
$$8X_1 + 16X_2 \geq 64$$
$$X_1 \geq 0$$
$$X_2 \geq -2 \;\textbf{Px}$$

(*Note:* X_2 values can be negative in this problem.)

• **B.26** Solve the following LP problem graphically:

$$\text{Minimize cost} = 24X + 15Y$$
Subject to:
$$7X + 11Y \geq 77$$
$$16X + 4Y \geq 80$$
$$X, Y \geq 0$$

•• **B.27** Doug Turner Food Processors wishes to introduce a new brand of dog biscuits composed of chicken- and liver-flavored biscuits that meet certain nutritional requirements. The liver-flavored biscuits contain 1 unit of nutrient A and 2 units of nutrient B; the chicken-flavored biscuits contain 1 unit of nutrient A and 4 units of nutrient B. According to federal requirements, there must be at least 40 units of nutrient A and 60 units of nutrient B in a package of the new mix. In addition, the company has decided that there can be no more than 15 liver-flavored biscuits in a package. If it costs 1¢ to make 1 liver-flavored biscuit and 2¢ to make 1 chicken-flavored, what is the optimal product mix for a package of the biscuits to minimize the firm's cost?

a) Formulate this as a linear programming problem.
b) Solve this problem graphically, giving the optimal values of all variables.
c) What is the total cost of a package of dog biscuits using the optimal mix? **Px**

· **B.28**   The Sweet Smell Fertilizer Company markets bags of manure labeled "not less than 60 lb dry weight." The packaged manure is a combination of compost and sewage wastes. To provide good-quality fertilizer, each bag should contain at least 30 lb of compost but no more than 40 lb of sewage. Each pound of compost costs Sweet Smell 5¢ and each pound of sewage costs 4¢. Use a graphical LP method to determine the least-cost blend of compost and sewage in each bag. **Px**

· **B.29**   Consider Paul Jordan's following linear programming formulation:

$$\text{Minimize cost} = \$1X_1 + \$2X_2$$
$$\text{Subject to:} \quad X_1 + 3X_2 \geq 90$$
$$8X_1 + 2X_2 \geq 160$$
$$3X_1 + 2X_2 \geq 120$$
$$X_2 \leq 70$$

a) Graphically illustrate the feasible region to indicate to Jordan which corner point produces the optimal solution.
b) What is the cost of this solution? **Px**

· **B.30**   Solve the following linear programming problem graphically:

$$\text{Minimize cost} = 4X_1 + 5X_2$$
$$\text{Subject to:} \quad X_1 + 2X_2 \geq 80$$
$$3X_1 + X_2 \geq 75$$
$$X_1, X_2 \geq 0 \; \textbf{Px}$$

·· **B.31**   How many corner points are there in the feasible region of the following problem?

$$\text{Minimize cost} = X - Y$$
$$\text{Subject to:} \quad X \leq 4$$
$$-X \leq 2$$
$$X + 2Y \leq 6$$
$$-X + 2Y \leq 8$$
$$Y \geq 0$$

(*Note: X* values can be negative in this problem.)

Additional problems **B.32–B.33** are available in MyOMLab.

Problems B.34–B.40 relate to Linear Programming Applications

··· **B.34**   The Hills County, Michigan, superintendent of education is responsible for assigning students to the three high schools in his county. He recognizes the need to bus a certain number of students, because several sectors, A–E, of the county are beyond walking distance to a school. The superintendent partitions the county into five geographic sectors as he attempts to establish a plan that will minimize the total number of student miles traveled by bus. He also recognizes that if a student happens to live in a certain sector and is assigned to the high school in that sector, there is no need to bus him because he can walk to school. The three schools are located in sectors B, C, and E.

Hans Magelssen/Shutterstock

The accompanying table reflects the number of high-school-age students living in each sector and the distance in miles from each sector to each school:

	DISTANCE TO SCHOOL			
SECTOR	SCHOOL IN SECTOR B	SCHOOL IN SECTOR C	SCHOOL IN SECTOR E	NUMBER OF STUDENTS
A	5	8	6	700
B	0	4	12	500
C	4	0	7	100
D	7	2	5	800
E	12	7	0	400
				2,500

Each high school has a capacity of 900 students.

a) Set up the objective function and constraints of this problem using linear programming so that the total number of student miles traveled by bus is minimized.
b) Solve the problem. **Px**

·· **B.35**   The Rio Credit Union has $250,000 available to invest in a 12-month commitment. The money can be placed in Brazilian treasury notes yielding an 8% return or in riskier high-yield bonds at an average rate of return of 9%. Credit union regulations require diversification to the extent that at least 50% of the investment be placed in Treasury notes. It is also decided that no more than 40% of the investment be placed in bonds. How much should the Rio Credit Union invest in each security so as to maximize its return on investment? **Px**

·· **B.36**   Wichita's famous Sethi Restaurant is open 24 hours a day. Servers report for duty at 3 A.M., 7 A.M., 11 A.M., 3 P.M., 7 P.M., or 11 P.M., and each works an 8-hour shift. The following table shows the minimum number of workers needed during the 6 periods into which the day is divided:

PERIOD	TIME	NUMBER OF SERVERS REQUIRED
1	3 A.M.–7 A.M.	3
2	7 A.M.–11 A.M.	12
3	11 A.M.–3 P.M.	16
4	3 P.M.–7 P.M.	9
5	7 P.M.–11 P.M.	11
6	11 P.M.–3 A.M.	4

Owner Avanti Sethi's scheduling problem is to determine how many servers should report for work at the start of each time period in order to minimize the total staff required for one day's operation. (*Hint:* Let X_i equal the number of servers beginning work in time period *i*, where $i = 1, 2, 3, 4, 5, 6$.) **Px**

•• B.37 Leach Distributors packages and distributes industrial supplies. A standard shipment can be packaged in a class A container, a class K container, or a class T container. A single class A container yields a profit of $9; a class K container, a profit of $7; and a class T container, a profit of $15. Each shipment prepared requires a certain amount of packing material and a certain amount of time.

RESOURCES NEEDED PER STANDARD SHIPMENT		
CLASS OF CONTAINER	PACKING MATERIAL (POUNDS)	PACKING TIME (HOURS)
A	2	2
K	1	6
T	3	4

Total resource available each week: 130 pounds   240 hours

Hugh Leach, head of the firm, must decide the optimal number of each class of container to pack each week. He is bound by the previously mentioned resource restrictions but also decides that he must keep his 6 full-time packers employed all 240 hours (6 workers × 40 hours) each week.

Formulate and solve this problem using LP software. **Px**

•••B.38 Tri-State Manufacturing has three factories (1, 2, and 3) and three warehouses (A, B, and C). The following table shows the shipping costs between each factory and warehouse, the factory manufacturing capabilities (in thousands), and the warehouse capacities (in thousands). Management would like to keep the warehouses filled to capacity in order to generate demand.

TO FROM	WAREHOUSE A	WAREHOUSE B	WAREHOUSE C	PRODUCTION CAPABILITY
Factory 1	$ 6	$ 5	$ 3	6
Factory 2	$ 8	$10	$ 8	8
Factory 3	$11	$14	$18	10
Capacity	7	12	5	

a) Write the objective function and the constraint equations. Let X_{1A} = 1,000s of units shipped from factory 1 to warehouse A, and so on.
b) Solve by computer. **Px**

••••B.39 Bowman Builders manufactures steel storage sheds for commercial use. Joe Bowman, president of Bowman Builders, is contemplating producing sheds for home use. The activities necessary to build an experimental model and related data are given in Table B.2.
a) What is the project normal time completion date? (See Chapter 3 for a review of project management.)
b) Formulate an LP problem to crash this project to 10 weeks.

TABLE B.2   **Data for Problem B.39**

ACTIVITY	NORMAL TIME	CRASH TIME	NORMAL COST ($)	CRASH COST ($)	IMMEDIATE PREDECESSORS
A	3	2	1,000	1,600	—
B	2	1	2,000	2,700	—
C	1	1	300	300	—
D	7	3	1,300	1,600	A
E	6	3	850	1,000	B
F	2	1	4,000	5,000	C
G	4	2	1,500	2,000	D, E

••••B.40 You have just been hired as a planner for the municipal school system, and your first assignment is to redesign the subsidized lunch program. In particular, you are to formulate the least expensive lunch menu that will still meet all state and federal nutritional guidelines.

The guidelines are as follows: A meal must be between 500 and 800 calories. It must contain at least 200 calories of protein, at least 200 calories of carbohydrates, and no more than 400 calories of fat. It also needs to have at least 200 calories of a food classified as a fruit or vegetable.

Table B.3 provides a list of the foods you can consider as possible menu items, with contract-determined prices and nutritional information. Note that all percentages sum to 100% per food—as all calories are protein, carbohydrate, or fat calories. For example, a serving of applesauce has 100 calories, all of which are carbohydrates, and it counts as a fruit/veg food. You are allowed to use fractional servings, such as 2.25 servings of turkey breast and a 0.33 portion of salad. Costs and nutritional attributes scale likewise: e.g., a 0.33 portion of salad costs $.30 and has 33 calories.

TABLE B.3	Data for Problem B.40					
FOOD	**COST/SERVING**	**CALORIES/SERVING**	**% PROTEIN**	**% CARBS**	**% FAT**	**FRUIT/VEG**
Applesauce	$0.30	100	0%	100%	0%	Y
Canned corn	$0.40	150	20%	80%	0%	Y
Fried chicken	$0.90	250	55%	5%	40%	N
French fries	$0.20	400	5%	35%	60%	N
Mac and cheese	$0.50	430	20%	30%	50%	N
Turkey breast	$1.50	300	67%	0%	33%	N
Garden salad	$0.90	100	15%	40%	45%	Y

Formulate and solve as a linear problem. Print out your formulation in Excel showing the objective function coefficients and constraint matrix in standard form.

- ◆ Display, on a separate page, the full *Answer Report* as generated by Excel Solver.
- ◆ Highlight *and label as Z* the objective value for the optimal solution on the Answer Report.
- ◆ Highlight the nonzero decision variables for the optimal solution on the Answer Report.
- ◆ Display, on a separate page, the full *Sensitivity Report* as generated by Excel Solver. **Px**

Problems B.41–B.42 relate to Integer and Binary Variables

•• **B.41** Rollins Publishing needs to decide what textbooks from the following table to publish.

TEXT-BOOK	DEMAND	FIXED COST	VARIABLE COST	SELLING PRICE
Book 1	9,000	$12,000	$19	$40
Book 2	8,000	$21,000	$28	$60
Book 3	5,000	$15,000	$30	$52
Book 4	6,000	$10,000	$20	$34
Book 5	7,000	$18,000	$20	$45

For each book, the maximum demand, fixed cost of publishing, variable cost, and selling price are provided. Rollins has the capacity to publish a total of 20,000 books.

a) Formulate this problem to determine which books should be selected and how many of each should be published to maximize profit.
b) Solve using computer software. **Px**

•• **B.42** Porter Investments needs to develop an investment portfolio for Mrs. Singh from the following list of possible investments:

INVESTMENT	COST	EXPECTED RETURN
A	$10,000	$ 700
B	$12,000	$1,000
C	$ 3,500	$ 390
D	$ 5,000	$ 500
E	$ 8,500	$ 750
F	$ 8,000	$ 640
G	$ 4,000	$ 300

Mrs. Singh has a total of $60,000 to invest. The following conditions must be met: (1) If investment F is chosen, then investment G must also be part of the portfolio, (2) at least four investments should be chosen, and (3) of investments A and B, exactly one must be included. Formulate and solve this problem using LP software to determine which stocks should be included in Mrs. Singh's portfolio. **Px**

CASE STUDIES

Quain Lawn and Garden, Inc.

Bill and Jeanne Quain spent a career as a husband-and-wife real estate investment partnership in Atlantic City, New Jersey. When they finally retired to a 25-acre farm in nearby Cape May County, they became ardent amateur gardeners. Bill planted shrubs and fruit trees, and Jeanne spent her hours potting all sizes of plants. When the volume of shrubs and plants reached the point that the Quains began to think of their hobby in a serious vein, they built a greenhouse adjacent to their home and installed heating and watering systems.

By 2012, the Quains realized their retirement from real estate had really only led to a second career—in the plant and shrub business—and they filed for a New Jersey business license. Within

a matter of months, they asked their attorney to file incorporation documents and formed the firm Quain Lawn and Garden, Inc.

Early in the new business's existence, Bill Quain recognized the need for a high-quality commercial fertilizer that he could blend himself, both for sale and for his own nursery. His goal was to keep his costs to a minimum while producing a top-notch product that was especially suited to the New Jersey climate.

Working with chemists at Rutgers University, Quain blended "Quain-Grow." It consists of four chemical compounds, C-30, C-92, D-21, and E-11. The cost per pound for each compound is indicated in the table on the next page:

CHEMICAL COMPOUND	COST PER POUND
C-30	$.12
C-92	.09
D-21	.11
E-11	.04

The specifications for Quain-Grow are established as:

a) Chemical E-11 must constitute at least 15% of the blend.

b) C-92 and C-30 must together constitute at least 45% of the blend.

c) D-21 and C-92 can together constitute no more than 30% of the blend.

d) Quain-Grow is packaged and sold in 50-lb bags.

Discussion Questions

1. Formulate an LP problem to determine what blend of the four chemicals will allow Quain to minimize the cost of a 50-lb bag of the fertilizer.

2. Solve to find the best solution.

Scheduling Challenges at Alaska Airlines

Video Case

Good airline scheduling is essential to delivering outstanding customer service with high plane utilization rates. Airlines must schedule pilots, flight attendants, aircraft, baggage handlers, customer service agents, and ramp crews. At Alaska Airlines, it all begins with seasonal flight schedules that are developed 330 days in advance.

Revenue and marketing goals drive the potential routing decisions, but thousands of constraints impact these schedules. Using SABRE scheduling optimizer software, Alaska considers the number of planes available, seat capacity, ranges, crew availability, union contracts that dictate hours that crews can fly, and maintenance regulations that regularly take planes out of service, just to name a few. Alaska's scheduling department sends preliminary schedules to the human resources, maintenance, operations, customer service, marketing, and other departments for feedback before finalizing flight schedules.

Alaska Airlines' historic mission is to serve its extremely loyal customer base in the remote and unreachable small towns in Alaska. Serving many airports in Alaska is especially complex because the airline requires its pilots to have special skills to deal with extremely adverse weather, tight mountain passes, and short runways. Some airports lack full-time TSA agents or strong ground support and may not even be open 24 hours per day. In some cases, runways are not plowed because the village plow is busy clearing the roads for school buses. Navigational technology developed by Alaska Airlines has significantly reduced weather-related cancelled flights as Alaska can now land where many other carriers cannot.

After the SABRE optimizer schedules thousands of flights, scheduling activity turns to the next step: crew optimizing. The crew optimizer (Alaska uses Jeppersen software developed by Boeing and based on linear programming) attempts to eliminate unnecessary layovers and crew idle time while adhering to FAA and union restrictions. Alaska leads the industry in pilot "hard time" (i.e., the amount of time a pilot is being paid when passengers are actually being moved). After the crew requirements for every flight are determined, the 3,000 flight attendants and 1,500 pilots rank their preferred routings on a monthly basis. Personnel are assigned to each flight using seniority and feasibility.

Interestingly, not every pilot or flight attendant always bids on the Hawaii routes (about 20% of all flights), the long-haul East Coast routes, or the Mexico flights. Some prefer the flying challenge of the "milk run" flights to Ketchikan, Sitka, Juneau, Fairbanks, Anchorage, and back to Seattle, which are in keeping with the culture and contact with local residents.

As an airline that accentuates risk taking and empowers employees to think "out of the box," Alaska recently decided to experiment with a schedule change on its Seattle-to-Chicago route. Given crew restrictions on flying hours per day, the flight had previously included a crew layover in Chicago. When a company analyst documented the feasibility of running the same crew on the two 4-hour legs of the round trip (which implied an *extremely* tight turnaround schedule in Chicago), his data indicated that on 98.7% of the round trip flights, the crew would not "time out." His boss gave the go-ahead.

Discussion Questions*

1. Why is scheduling for Alaska more complex than for other airlines?

2. What operational considerations may prohibit Alaska from adding flights and more cities to its network?

3. What were the risks of keeping the same crew on the Seattle—Chicago—Seattle route?

4. Estimate the direct costs to the airline should the crew "time out" and not be able to fly its Boeing 737 back to Seattle from Chicago on the same day. These direct variable costs should include moving and parking the plane overnight along with hotel and meal costs for the crew and passengers. Do you think this is more advantageous than keeping a spare crew in Chicago?

*You may wish to view the video that accompanies this case before addressing these questions.

• **Additional Case Studies:** Visit MyOMLab for these free case studies:

Chase Manhattan Bank: This scheduling case involves finding the optimal number of full-time versus part-time employees at a bank.

Coastal States Chemical: The company must prepare for a shortage of natural gas.

Endnotes

1. *Iso* means "equal" or "similar." Thus, an iso-profit line represents a line with all profits the same, in this case $210.

2. See, for example, Barry Render, Ralph M. Stair, Michael Hanna, and T. Hale, *Quantitative Analysis for Management*, 12th ed. (Pearson Education, Inc., Upper Saddle River, NJ, 2013):

Chapters 7–9; or Raju Balakrishnan, Barry Render, and Ralph M. Stair, *Managerial Decision Modeling with Spreadsheets*, 3rd ed. (Pearson Education, Inc., Upper Saddle River, NJ, 2012): Chapters 2–4.

Module B *Rapid Review*

Main Heading	Review Material	MyOMLab
WHY USE LINEAR PROGRAMMING? (p. 700)	■ **Linear programming (LP)**—A mathematical technique designed to help operations managers plan and make decisions relative to allocation of resources.	Concept Questions: 1.1–1.4 **VIDEO B.1** Scheduling Challenges at Alaska Airlines
REQUIREMENTS OF A LINEAR PROGRAMMING PROBLEM (p. 701)	■ **Objective function**—A mathematical expression in linear programming that maximizes or minimizes some quantity (often profit or cost, but any goal may be used). ■ **Constraints**—Restrictions that limit the degree to which a manager can pursue an objective. All LP problems have four properties in common: 1. LP problems seek to *maximize* or *minimize* some quantity. We refer to this property as the *objective function* of an LP problem. 2. The presence of restrictions, or *constraints*, limits the degree to which we can pursue our objective. We want, therefore, to maximize or minimize a quantity (the objective function) subject to limited resources (the constraints). 3. There must be *alternative courses of action* to choose from. 4. The objective and constraints in linear programming problems must be expressed in terms of *linear equations* or inequalities.	Concept Questions: 2.1–2.4 Problem: B.1
FORMULATING LINEAR PROGRAMMING PROBLEMS (pp. 701–702)	One of the most common linear programming applications is the *product-mix problem*. Two or more products are usually produced using limited resources. For example, a company might like to determine how many units of each product it should produce to maximize overall profit, given its limited resources. An important aspect of linear programming is that certain interactions will exist between variables. The more units of one product that a firm produces, the fewer it can make of other products.	Concept Questions: 3.1–3.4 Virtual Office Hours for Solved Problem: B.1 **ACTIVE MODEL B.1**
GRAPHICAL SOLUTION TO A LINEAR PROGRAMMING PROBLEM (pp. 702–705)	■ **Graphical solution approach**—A means of plotting a solution to a two-variable problem on a graph. ■ **Decision variables**—Choices available to a decision maker. Constraints of the form $X \geq 0$ are called *nonnegativity constraints*. ■ **Feasible region**—The set of all feasible combinations of decision variables. Any point inside the feasible region represents a *feasible solution*, while any point outside the feasible region represents an *infeasible solution*. ■ **Iso-profit line method**—An approach to identifying the optimum point in a graphic linear programming problem. The line that touches a particular point of the feasible region will pinpoint the optimal solution. ■ **Corner-point method**—Another method for solving graphical linear programming problems. The mathematical theory behind linear programming states that an optimal solution to any problem will lie at a *corner point*, or an *extreme point*, of the feasible region. Hence, it is necessary to find only the values of the variables at each corner; the optimal solution will lie at one (or more) of them. This is the corner-point method.	Concept Questions: 4.1–4.4 Problems: B.2–B.21 Virtual Office Hours for Solved Problem: B.2
SENSITIVITY ANALYSIS (pp. 705–708)	■ **Parameter**—A numerical value that is given in a model. ■ **Sensitivity analysis**—An analysis that projects how much a solution may change if there are changes in the variables or input data. Sensitivity analysis is also called *postoptimality analysis*. There are two approaches to determining just how sensitive an optimal solution is to changes: (1) a trial-and-error approach and (2) the analytic postoptimality method.	Concept Questions: 5.1–5.4 Problems: B.22–B.24

Main Heading	Review Material	MyOMLab
	To use the analytic postoptimality method, after an LP problem has been solved, we determine a range of changes in problem parameters that will not affect the optimal solution or change the variables in the solution. LP software has this capability. While using the information in a sensitivity report to answer what-if questions, we assume that we are considering a change to only a *single* input data value at a time. That is, the sensitivity information does not generally apply to simultaneous changes in several input data values. ■ **Shadow price** (or **dual value**)—The value of one additional unit of a scarce resource in LP. The shadow price is valid as long as the right-hand side of the constraint stays in a range within which all current corner points continue to exist. The information to compute the upper and lower limits of this range is given by the entries labeled Allowable Increase and Allowable Decrease in the sensitivity report.	
SOLVING MINIMIZATION PROBLEMS (pp. 708–709)	■ **Iso-cost**—An approach to solving a linear programming minimization problem graphically. The iso-cost line approach to solving minimization problems is analogous to the iso-profit approach for maximization problems, but successive iso-cost lines are drawn *inward* instead of outward.	Concept Questions: 6.1–6.3 Problems: B.25–B.33 Virtual Office Hours for Solved Problem: B.3
LINEAR PROGRAM- MING APPLICATIONS (pp. 710–713)	The *diet problem*, known in agricultural applications as the *feed-mix problem*, involves specifying a food or feed ingredient combination that will satisfy stated nutritional requirements at a minimum cost level. *Labor scheduling problems* address staffing needs over a specific time period. They are especially useful when managers have some flexibility in assigning workers to jobs that require overlapping or interchangeable talents.	Concept Questions: 7.1–7.3 Problems: B.34–B.40
THE SIMPLEX METHOD OF LP (p. 713)	■ **Simplex method**—An algorithm for solving linear programming problems of all sizes. The simplex method is actually a set of instructions with which we examine corner points in a methodical fashion until we arrive at the best solution—highest profit or lowest cost. Computer programs (such as Excel OM and POM for Windows) and Excel's Solver add-in are available to solve linear programming problems via the simplex method.	Concept Questions: 8.1–8.2 Virtual Office Hours for Solved Problem: C.1 (note that this Module C video is an LP application of the transportation problem)
INTEGER AND BINARY VARIABLES (pp. 713–715)	■ **Binary variables**—Decision variables that can only take on the value of 0 or 1. Using computer software, decision variables for linear programs can be forced to be integer or even binary. Binary variables extend the flexibility of linear programs to include such options as mutually exclusive alternatives, either-or constraints, contingent decisions, fixed-charge problems, and threshold levels.	Concept Questions: 9.1–9.4 Problems: B.41–B.42

Self Test

■ **Before taking the self-test,** refer to the learning objectives listed at the beginning of the module and the key terms listed at the end of the module.

LO B.1 Which of the following is *not* a valid LP constraint formulation?
a) $3X + 4Y \leq 12$ b) $2X \times 2Y \leq 12$
c) $3Y + 2Z = 18$ d) $100 \geq X + Y$
e) $2.5X + 1.5Z = 30.6$

LO B.2 Using a *graphical solution procedure* to solve a maximization problem requires that we:
a) move the iso-profit line up until it no longer intersects with any constraint equation.
b) move the iso-profit line down until it no longer intersects with any constraint equation.
c) apply the method of simultaneous equations to solve for the intersections of constraints.
d) find the value of the objective function at the origin.

LO B.3 Consider the following linear programming problem:
Maximize $4X + 10Y$
Subject to: $3X + 4Y \leq 480$
$4X + 2Y \leq 360$
$X, Y \geq 0$
The feasible corner points are (48,84), (0,120), (0,0), and (90,0). What is the maximum possible value for the objective function?
a) 1,032   b) 1,200   c) 360   d) 1,600   e) 840

LO B.4 A zero shadow price for a resource ordinarily means that:
a) the resource is scarce.
b) the resource constraint was redundant.
c) the resource has not been used up.
d) something is wrong with the problem formulation.
e) none of the above.

LO B.5 For these two constraints, which point is in the feasible region of this minimization problem?
$$14x + 6y \geq 42 \quad \text{and} \quad x + y \geq 3$$
a) $x = -1, y = 1$ b) $x = 0, y = 4$
c) $x = 2, y = 1$ d) $x = 5, y = 1$
e) $x = 2, y = 0$

LO B.6 When applying LP to diet problems, the objective function is usually designed to:
a) maximize profits from blends of nutrients.
b) maximize ingredient blends.
c) minimize production losses.
d) maximize the number of products to be produced.
e) minimize the costs of nutrient blends.

Answers: LO B.1. b; LO B.2. a; LO B.3. b; LO B.4. c; LO B.5. d; LO B.6. e.

Transportation Models

MODULE OUTLINE

◆ Transportation Modeling *730*

◆ Developing an Initial Solution *732*

◆ The Stepping-Stone Method *734*

◆ Special Issues in Modeling *737*

Alaska Airlines

Alaska Airlines

LEARNING OBJECTIVES

LO C.1   **Develop** an initial solution to a transportation model with the northwest-corner and intuitive lowest-cost methods 732

LO C.2   **Solve** a problem with the stepping-stone method 734

LO C.3   **Balance** a transportation problem 737

LO C.4   **Deal** with a problem that has degeneracy 737

The problem facing rental companies like Avis, Hertz, and National is cross-country travel. Lots of it. Cars rented in New York end up in Chicago, cars from L.A. come to Philadelphia, and cars from Boston come to Miami. The scene is repeated in over 100 cities around the U.S. As a result, there are too many cars in some cities and too few in others. Operations managers have to decide how many of these rentals should be trucked (by costly auto carriers) from each city with excess capacity to each city that needs more rentals. The process requires quick action for the most economical routing, so rental car companies turn to transportation modeling.

Transportation Modeling

Because location of a new factory, warehouse, or distribution center is a strategic issue with substantial cost implications, most companies consider and evaluate several locations. With a wide variety of objective and subjective factors to be considered, rational decisions are aided by a number of techniques. One of those techniques is transportation modeling.

The transportation models described in this module prove useful when considering alternative facility locations *within the framework of an existing distribution system*. Each new potential plant, warehouse, or distribution center will require a different allocation of shipments, depending on its own production and shipping costs and the costs of each existing facility. The choice of a new location depends on which will yield the minimum cost *for the entire system*.

Transportation modeling finds the least-cost means of shipping supplies from several origins to several destinations. *Origin points* (or *sources*) can be factories, warehouses, car rental agencies like Avis, or any other points from which goods are shipped. *Destinations* are any points that receive goods. To use the transportation model, we need to know the following:

Transportation modeling

An iterative procedure for solving problems that involves minimizing the cost of shipping products from a series of sources to a series of destinations.

1. The origin points and the capacity or supply per period at each.
2. The destination points and the demand per period at each.
3. The cost of shipping one unit from each origin to each destination.

The transportation model is one form of the linear programming models discussed in Business Analytics Module B. Software is available to solve both transportation problems and the more general class of linear programming problems. To fully use such programs, though, you need to understand the assumptions that underlie the model. To illustrate the transportation problem, we now look at a company called Arizona Plumbing, which makes, among other products,

TABLE C.1	Transportation Costs Per Bathtub for Arizona Plumbing		
FROM \ **TO**	**ALBUQUERQUE**	**BOSTON**	**CLEVELAND**
Des Moines	$5	$4	$3
Evansville	$8	$4	$3
Fort Lauderdale	$9	$7	$5

a full line of bathtubs. In our example, the firm must decide which of its factories should supply which of its warehouses. Relevant data for Arizona Plumbing are presented in Table C.1 and Figure C.1. Table C.1 shows, for example, that it costs Arizona Plumbing $5 to ship one bathtub from its Des Moines factory to its Albuquerque warehouse, $4 to Boston, and $3 to Cleveland.

Figure **C.1**

Transportation Problem

Likewise, we see in Figure C.1 that the 300 units required by Arizona Plumbing's Albuquerque warehouse may be shipped in various combinations from its Des Moines, Evansville, and Fort Lauderdale factories.

The first step in the modeling process is to set up a *transportation matrix*. Its purpose is to summarize all relevant data and to keep track of algorithm computations. Using the information displayed in Figure C.1 and Table C.1, we can construct a transportation matrix as shown in Figure C.2.

From \ To	Albuquerque	Boston	Cleveland	Factory capacity	
Des Moines	$5	$4	$3	100	← Des Moines capacity constraint
Evansville	$8	$4	$3	300	← Cell representing a possible source-to-destination shipping assignment (Evansville to Cleveland)
Fort Lauderdale	$9	$7	$5	300	
Warehouse requirement	300	200	200	700	

Cost of shipping 1 unit from Fort Lauderdale factory to Boston warehouse

Cleveland warehouse demand

Total demand and total supply

Figure **C.2**

Transportation Matrix for Arizona Plumbing

Developing an Initial Solution

Once the data are arranged in tabular form, we must establish an initial feasible solution to the problem. A number of different methods have been developed for this step. We now discuss two of them, the northwest-corner rule and the intuitive lowest-cost method.

The Northwest-Corner Rule

Northwest-corner rule

A procedure in the transportation model where one starts at the upper-left-hand cell of a table (the northwest corner) and systematically allocates units to shipping routes.

The northwest-corner rule requires that we start in the upper-left-hand cell (or northwest corner) of the table and allocate units to shipping routes as follows:

1. Exhaust the supply (factory capacity) of each row (e.g., Des Moines: 100) before moving down to the next row.
2. Exhaust the (warehouse) requirements of each column (e.g., Albuquerque: 300) before moving to the next column on the right.
3. Check to ensure that all supplies and demands are met.

Example C1 applies the northwest-corner rule to our Arizona Plumbing problem.

Example C1

THE NORTHWEST-CORNER RULE

Arizona Plumbing wants to use the northwest-corner rule to find an initial solution to its problem.

APPROACH ▶ Follow the three steps listed above. See Figure C.3.

SOLUTION ▶ To make the initial solution, these five assignments are made:

1. Assign 100 tubs from Des Moines to Albuquerque (exhausting Des Moines's supply).
2. Assign 200 tubs from Evansville to Albuquerque (exhausting Albuquerque's demand).
3. Assign 100 tubs from Evansville to Boston (exhausting Evansville's supply).
4. Assign 100 tubs from Fort Lauderdale to Boston (exhausting Boston's demand).
5. Assign 200 tubs from Fort Lauderdale to Cleveland (exhausting Cleveland's demand and Fort Lauderdale's supply).

Figure C.3

Northwest-Corner Solution to Arizona Plumbing Problem

From \ To	(A) Albuquerque	(B) Boston	(C) Cleveland	Factory capacity
(D) Des Moines	$5 — 100	$4	$3	100
(E) Evansville	$8 — 200	$4 — 100	$3	300
(F) Fort Lauderdale	$9	$7 — (100)	$5 — 200	300
Warehouse requirement	300	200	200	700

Means that the firm is shipping 100 bathtubs from Fort Lauderdale to Boston

The total cost of this shipping assignment is $4,200 (see Table C.2).

TABLE C.2 Computed Shipping Cost

ROUTE				
FROM	TO	TUBS SHIPPED	COST PER UNIT	TOTAL COST
D	A	100	$5	$ 500
E	A	200	8	1,600
E	B	100	4	400
F	B	100	7	700
F	C	200	5	$1,000
				Total: $4,200

INSIGHTS ▶ The solution given is feasible because it satisfies all demand and supply constraints. The northwest-corner rule is easy to use, but it totally ignores costs, and therefore should only be considered as a starting position.

LEARNING EXERCISE ▶ Does the shipping assignment change if the cost from Des Moines to Albuquerque increases from $5 per unit to $10 per unit? Does the total cost change? [Answer: The initial assignment is the same, but cost = $4,700.]

RELATED PROBLEMS ▶ C.1a, C.3a, C.15

The Intuitive Lowest-Cost Method

The **intuitive method** makes initial allocations based on lowest cost. This straightforward approach uses the following steps:

Intuitive method
A cost-based approach to finding an initial solution to a transportation problem.

1. Identify the cell with the lowest cost. Break any ties for the lowest cost arbitrarily.
2. Allocate as many units as possible to that cell without exceeding the supply or demand. Then cross out that row or column (or both) that is exhausted by this assignment.
3. Find the cell with the lowest cost from the remaining (not crossed out) cells.
4. Repeat Steps 2 and 3 until all units have been allocated.

Example C2

THE INTUITIVE LOWEST-COST APPROACH

Arizona Plumbing now wants to apply the intuitive lowest-cost approach.

APPROACH ▶ Apply the 4 steps listed above to the data in Figure C.2.

SOLUTION ▶ When the firm uses the intuitive approach on the data (rather than the northwest-corner rule) for its starting position, it obtains the solution seen in Figure C.4.

The total cost of this approach = $3(100) + $3(100) + $4(200) + $9(300) = $4,100.
(D to C)　　(E to C)　　(E to B)　　(F to A)

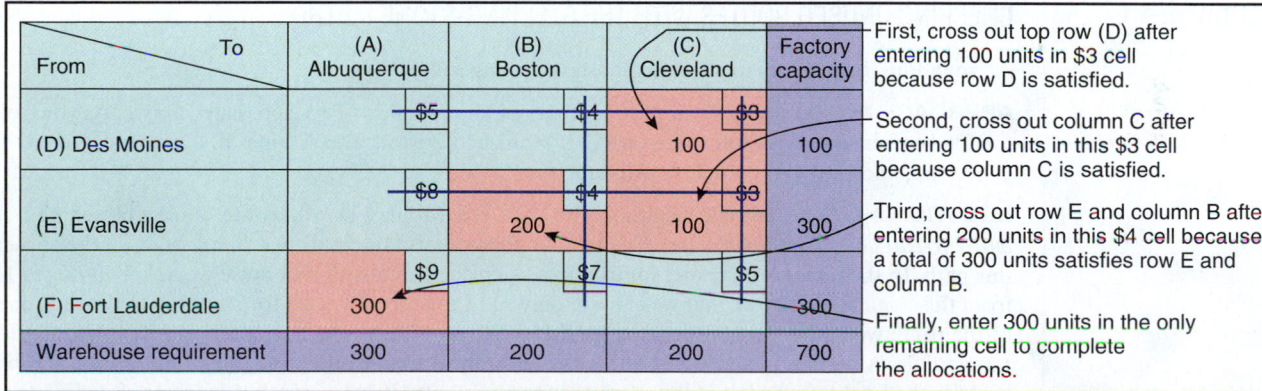

Figure **C.4**

Intuitive Lowest-Cost Solution to Arizona Plumbing Problem

INSIGHT ▶ This method's name is appropriate as most people find it intuitively correct to include costs when making an initial assignment.

LEARNING EXERCISE ▶ If the cost per unit from Des Moines to Cleveland is not $3, but rather $6, does this initial solution change? [Answer: Yes, now D − B = 100, D − C = 0, E − B = 100, E − C = 200, F − A = 300. Others unchanged at zero. Total cost stays the same.]

RELATED PROBLEMS ▶ C.1b, C.2, C.3b

Although the likelihood of a minimum-cost solution *does* improve with the intuitive method, we would have been fortunate if the intuitive solution yielded the minimum cost. In this case, as in the northwest-corner solution, it did not. Because the northwest-corner and the intuitive lowest-cost approaches are meant only to provide us with a starting point, we often will have to employ an additional procedure to reach an *optimal* solution.

The Stepping-Stone Method

Stepping-stone method

An iterative technique for moving from an initial feasible solution to an optimal solution in the transportation method.

LO C.2 *Solve* a problem with the stepping-stone method

The stepping-stone method will help us move from an initial feasible solution to an optimal solution. It is used to evaluate the cost effectiveness of shipping goods via transportation routes not currently in the solution. When applying it, we test each unused cell, or square, in the transportation table by asking: What would happen to total shipping costs if one unit of the product (for example, one bathtub) was tentatively shipped on an unused route? We conduct the test as follows:

1. Select any unused square to evaluate.
2. Beginning at this square, trace a closed path back to the original square via squares that are currently being used (only horizontal and vertical moves are permissible). You may, however, step over either an empty or an occupied square.
3. Beginning with a plus (+) sign at the unused square, place alternating minus signs and plus signs on each corner square of the closed path just traced.
4. Calculate an improvement index by first adding the unit-cost figures found in each square containing a plus sign and then by subtracting the unit costs in each square containing a minus sign.
5. Repeat Steps 1 through 4 until you have calculated an improvement index for all unused squares. If all indices computed are *greater than or equal to zero*, you have reached an optimal solution. If not, the current solution can be improved further to decrease total shipping costs.

Example C3 illustrates how to use the stepping-stone method to move toward an optimal solution. We begin with the northwest-corner initial solution developed in Example C1.

Example C3

CHECKING UNUSED ROUTES WITH THE STEPPING-STONE METHOD

Arizona Plumbing wants to evaluate unused shipping routes.

APPROACH ▶ Start with Example C1's Figure C.3 and follow the 5 steps listed above. As you can see, the four currently unassigned routes are Des Moines to Boston, Des Moines to Cleveland, Evansville to Cleveland, and Fort Lauderdale to Albuquerque.

SOLUTION ▶ **Steps 1 and 2.** Beginning with the Des Moines–Boston route, trace a closed path *using only currently occupied squares* (see Figure C.5). Place alternating plus and minus signs in the corners of this path. In the upper-left square, for example, we place a minus sign because we have *subtracted* 1 unit from the original 100. Note that we can use only squares currently used for shipping to turn the corners of the route we are tracing. Hence, the path Des Moines–Boston to Des Moines–Albuquerque to Fort Lauderdale–Albuquerque to Fort Lauderdale–Boston to Des Moines–Boston would not be acceptable because the Fort Lauderdale–Albuquerque square is empty. It turns out that *only one closed route exists for each empty square*. Once this one closed path is identified, we can begin assigning plus and minus signs to these squares in the path.

  Step 3. How do we decide which squares get plus signs and which squares get minus signs? The answer is simple. Because we are testing the cost-effectiveness of the Des Moines–Boston shipping route, we try shipping 1 bathtub from Des Moines to Boston. This is 1 *more* unit than we *were* sending between the two cities, so place a plus sign in the box. However, if we ship 1 more unit than before from Des Moines to Boston, we end up sending 101 bathtubs out of the Des Moines factory. Because the Des Moines factory's capacity is only 100 units, we must ship 1 bathtub less from Des Moines to Albuquerque. This change prevents us from violating the capacity constraint.

  To indicate that we have reduced the Des Moines–Albuquerque shipment, place a minus sign in its box. As you continue along the closed path, notice that we are no longer meeting our Albuquerque warehouse requirement for 300 units. In fact, if we reduce the Des Moines–Albuquerque shipment to 99 units, we must increase the Evansville–Albuquerque load by 1 unit, to 201 bathtubs. Therefore, place a plus sign in that box to indicate the increase. You may also observe that those squares in which we turn a corner (and only those squares) will have plus or minus signs.

Figure C.5

Stepping-Stone Evaluation of Alternative Routes for Arizona Plumbing

Evaluation of Des Moines to Boston square

Result of proposed shift in allocation = $1 \times \$4 - 1 \times \$5 + 1 \times \$8 - 1 \times \$4 = +\$3$

From \ To	(A) Albuquerque	(B) Boston	(C) Cleveland	Factory capacity
(D) Des Moines	100 $5	Start $4	$3	100
(E) Evansville	200 $8	100 $4	$3	300
(F) Fort Lauderdale	$9	100 $7	200 $5	300
Warehouse requirement	300	200	200	700

Finally, note that if we assign 201 bathtubs to the Evansville–Albuquerque route, then we must reduce the Evansville–Boston route by 1 unit, to 99 bathtubs, to maintain the Evansville factory's capacity constraint of 300 units. To account for this reduction, we thus insert a minus sign in the Evansville–Boston box. By so doing, we have balanced supply limitations among all four routes on the closed path.

Step 4. Compute an improvement index for the Des Moines–Boston route by adding unit costs in squares with plus signs and subtracting costs in squares with minus signs.

$$\text{Des Moines–Boston index} = \$4 - \$5 + \$8 - \$4 = +\$3$$

This means that for every bathtub shipped via the Des Moines–Boston route, total transportation costs will increase by $3 over their current level.

Let us now examine the unused Des Moines–Cleveland route, which is slightly more difficult to trace with a closed path (see Figure C.6). Again, notice that we turn each corner along the path only at squares on the existing route. Our path, for example, can go through the Evansville–Cleveland box but cannot turn a corner; thus we cannot place a plus or minus sign there. We may use occupied squares only as stepping-stones:

$$\text{Des Moines–Cleveland index} = \$3 - \$5 + \$8 - \$4 + \$7 - \$5 = +\$4$$

Figure C.6

Testing Des Moines to Cleveland

From \ To	(A) Albuquerque	(B) Boston	(C) Cleveland	Factory capacity
(D) Des Moines	100 $5	$4	Start $3	100
(E) Evansville	200+ $8	100 $4	$3	300
(F) Fort Lauderdale	$9	100 $7	200 $5	300
Warehouse requirement	300	200	200	700

Again, opening this route fails to lower our total shipping costs.

Two other routes can be evaluated in a similar fashion:

$$\text{Evansville–Cleveland index} = \$3 - \$4 + \$7 - \$5 = +\$1$$
$$(\text{Closed path} = EC - EB + FB - FC)$$
$$\text{Fort Lauderdale–Albuquerque index} = \$9 - \$7 + \$4 - \$8 = -\$2$$
$$(\text{Closed path} = FA - FB + EB - EA)$$

INSIGHT ▶ Because this last index is negative, we can realize cost savings by using the (currently unused) Fort Lauderdale–Albuquerque route.

LEARNING EXERCISE ▶ What would happen to total cost if Arizona used the shipping route from Des Moines to Cleveland? [Answer: Total cost of the current solution would increase by $400.]

RELATED PROBLEMS ▶ C.1c, C.3c, C.4–C.11 (C.12, C.13 are available in MyOMLab)

EXCEL OM Data File **ModCExC3.xls** can be found in MyOMLab.

In Example C3, we see that a better solution is indeed possible because we can calculate a negative improvement index on one of our unused routes. *Each negative index represents the amount by which total transportation costs could be decreased if one unit was shipped by the source–destination combination.* The next step, then, is to choose that route (unused square) with the *largest* negative improvement index. We can then ship the maximum allowable number of units on that route and reduce the total cost accordingly.

What is the maximum quantity that can be shipped on our new money-saving route? That quantity is found by referring to the closed path of plus signs and minus signs drawn for the route and then selecting the *smallest number found in the squares containing minus signs*. To obtain a new solution, we add this number to all squares on the closed path with plus signs and subtract it from all squares on the path to which we have assigned minus signs.

One iteration of the stepping-stone method is now complete. Again, of course, we must test to see if the solution is optimal or whether we can make any further improvements. We do this by evaluating each unused square, as previously described. Example C4 continues our effort to help Arizona Plumbing arrive at a final solution.

Example C4

IMPROVEMENT INDICES

Arizona Plumbing wants to continue solving the problem.

APPROACH ▶ Use the improvement indices calculated in Example C3. We found in Example C3 that the largest (and only) negative index is on the Fort Lauderdale–Albuquerque route (which is the route depicted in Figure C.7).

SOLUTION ▶ The maximum quantity that may be shipped on the newly opened route, Fort Lauderdale–Albuquerque (FA), is the smallest number found in squares containing minus signs—in this case, 100 units. Why 100 units? Because the total cost decreases by $2 per unit shipped, we know we would like to ship the maximum possible number of units. Previous stepping-stone calculations indicate that each unit shipped over the FA route results in an increase of 1 unit shipped from Evansville (E) to Boston (B) and a decrease of 1 unit in amounts shipped both from F to B (now 100 units) and from E to A (now 200 units). Hence, the maximum we can ship over the FA route is 100 units. This solution results in zero units being shipped from F to B. Now we take the following four steps:

1. Add 100 units (to the zero currently being shipped) on route FA.
2. Subtract 100 from route FB, leaving zero in that square (though still balancing the row total for F).
3. Add 100 to route EB, yielding 200.
4. Finally, subtract 100 from route EA, leaving 100 units shipped.

Note that the new numbers still produce the correct row and column totals as required. The new solution is shown in Figure C.8.

Total shipping cost has been reduced by (100 units) × ($2 saved per unit) = $200 and is now $4,000. This cost figure, of course, can also be derived by multiplying the cost of

Figure **C.7**

**Transportation Table:
Route FA**

To From	(A) Albuquerque	(B) Boston	(C) Cleveland	Factory capacity
(D) Des Moines	$5 100	$4	$3	100
(E) Evansville	$8 200	$4 100	$3	300
(F) Fort Lauderdale	$9	$7 100	$5 200	300
Warehouse demand	300	200	200	700

STUDENT TIP

FA has a negative index:
FA (+9) to FB (−7) to EB (+4)
to EA (−8) = −$2

Figure **C.8**

**Solution at Next Iteration
(Still Not Optimal)**

To From	(A) Albuquerque	(B) Boston	(C) Cleveland	Factory capacity
(D) Des Moines	$5 100	$4	$3	100
(E) Evansville	$8 100	$4 200	$3	300
(F) Fort Lauderdale	$9 100	$7	$5 200	300
Warehouse demand	300	200	200	700

shipping each unit by the number of units transported on its respective route, namely: 100($5) + 100($8) + 200($4) + 100($9) + 200($5) = $4,000.

INSIGHT ▶ Looking carefully at Figure C.8, however, you can see that it, too, is not yet optimal. Route EC (Evansville–Cleveland) has a negative cost improvement index of –$1. Closed path = EC − EA + FA − FC.

LEARNING EXERCISE ▶ Find the final solution for this route on your own. [Answer: Programs C.1 and C.2, at the end of this module, provide an Excel OM solution.]

RELATED PROBLEMS ▶ C.4–C.11 (C.12–C.13 are available in MyOMLab)

Special Issues in Modeling

Demand Not Equal to Supply

A common situation in real-world problems is the case in which total demand is not equal to total supply. We can easily handle these so-called unbalanced problems with the solution procedures that we have just discussed by introducing *dummy sources* or *dummy destinations*. If total supply is greater than total demand, we make demand exactly equal the surplus by creating a dummy destination. Conversely, if total demand is greater than total supply, we introduce a dummy source (factory) with a supply equal to the excess of demand. Because these units will not in fact be shipped, we assign cost coefficients of zero to each square on the dummy location. In each case, then, the cost is zero.

LO C.3 *Balance* a transportation problem

Degeneracy

To apply the stepping-stone method to a transportation problem, we must observe a rule about the number of shipping routes being used: *The number of occupied squares in any solution (initial or later) must be equal to the number of rows in the table plus the number of columns minus 1.* Solutions that do not satisfy this rule are called *degenerate.*

LO C.4 *Deal* with a problem that has degeneracy

Degeneracy

An occurrence in transportation models in which too few squares or shipping routes are being used, so that tracing a closed path for each unused square becomes impossible.

Degeneracy occurs when too few squares or shipping routes are being used. As a result, it becomes impossible to trace a closed path for one or more unused squares. The Arizona Plumbing problem we just examined was *not* degenerate, as it had 5 assigned routes (3 rows or factories + 3 columns or warehouses − 1).

To handle degenerate problems, we must artificially create an occupied cell: That is, we place a zero or a *very* small amount (representing a fake shipment) in one of the unused squares and *then treat that square as if it were occupied.* The chosen square must be in such a position as to allow all stepping-stone paths to be closed.

Summary

The transportation model, a form of linear programming, is used to help find the least-cost solutions to system-wide shipping problems. The northwest-corner method (which begins in the upper-left corner of the transportation table) or the intuitive lowest-cost method may be used for finding an initial feasible solution. The stepping-stone algorithm is then used for finding optimal solutions. Unbalanced problems are those in which the total demand and total supply are not equal. Degeneracy refers to the case in which the number of rows + the number of columns −1 is not equal to the number of occupied squares. The transportation model approach is one of the four location models described earlier in Chapter 8 and is one of the two aggregate planning models discussed in Chapter 13. Additional solution techniques are presented in Tutorial 4 in MyOMLab.

Key Terms

Transportation modeling (p. 730)
Northwest-corner rule (p. 732)
Intuitive method (p. 733)
Stepping-stone method (p. 734)
Degeneracy (p. 738)

Discussion Questions

1. What are the three information needs of the transportation model?
2. What are the steps in the intuitive lowest-cost method?
3. Identify the three "steps" in the northwest-corner rule.
4. How do you know when an optimal solution has been reached?
5. Which starting technique generally gives a better initial solution, and why?
6. The more sources and destinations there are for a transportation problem, the smaller the percentage of all cells that will be used in the optimal solution. Explain.
7. All of the transportation examples appear to apply to long distances. Is it possible for the transportation model to apply on a much smaller scale, for example, within the departments of a store or the offices of a building? Discuss.
8. Develop a *northeast*-corner rule and explain how it would work. Set up an initial solution for the Arizona Plumbing problem analyzed in Example C1.
9. What is meant by an unbalanced transportation problem, and how would you balance it?
10. How many occupied cells must all solutions use?
11. Explain the significance of a negative improvement index in a transportation-minimizing problem.
12. How can the transportation method address production costs in addition to transportation costs?
13. Explain what is meant by the term *degeneracy* within the context of transportation modeling.

Using Software to Solve Transportation Problems

Excel, Excel OM, and POM for Windows may all be used to solve transportation problems. Excel uses Solver, which requires that you enter your own constraints. Excel OM also uses Solver but is prestructured so that you need enter only the actual data. POM for Windows similarly requires that only demand data, supply data, and shipping costs be entered.

✗ USING EXCEL OM

Excel OM's Transportation module uses Excel's built-in Solver routine to find optimal solutions to transportation problems. Program C.1 illustrates the input data (from Arizona Plumbing) and total-cost formulas. In Excel 2007, 2010, and 2013 **Solver** is in the **Analysis** section of the **Data** tab. Be certain that the solving method is "Simplex LP." The output appears in Program C.2.

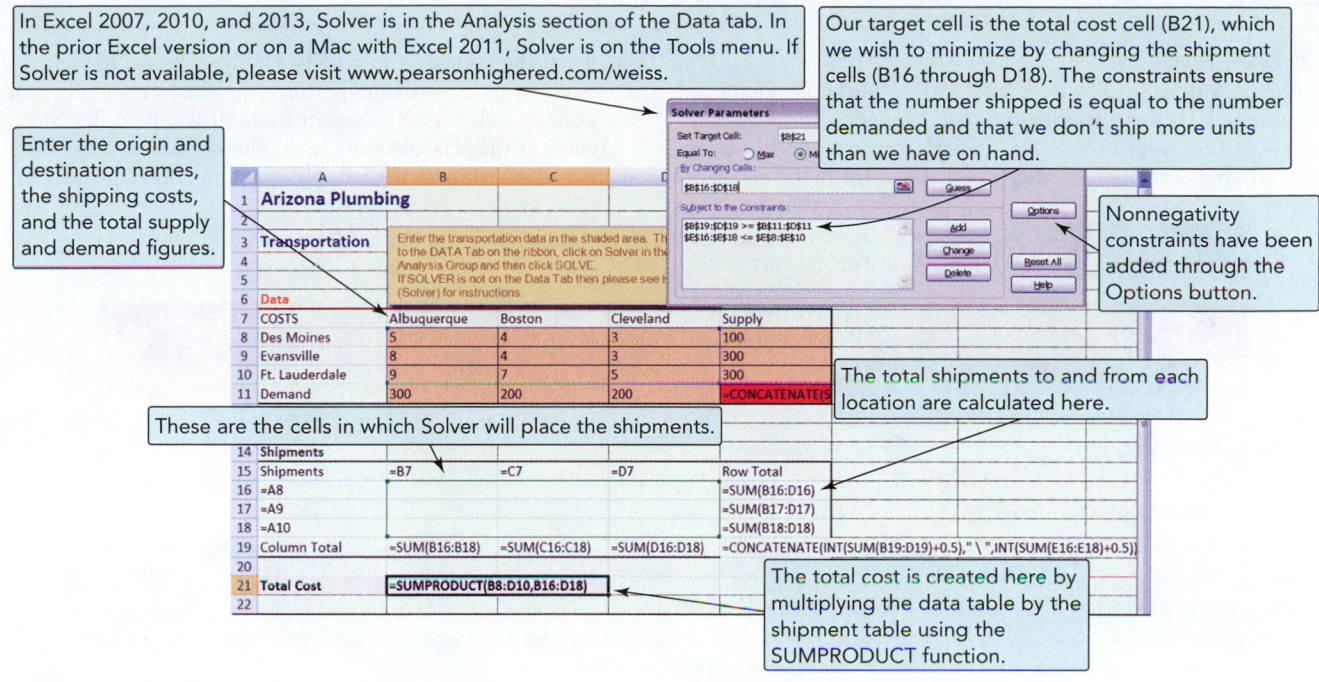

Program **C.1**

Excel OM Input Screen and Formulas, Using Arizona Plumbing Data

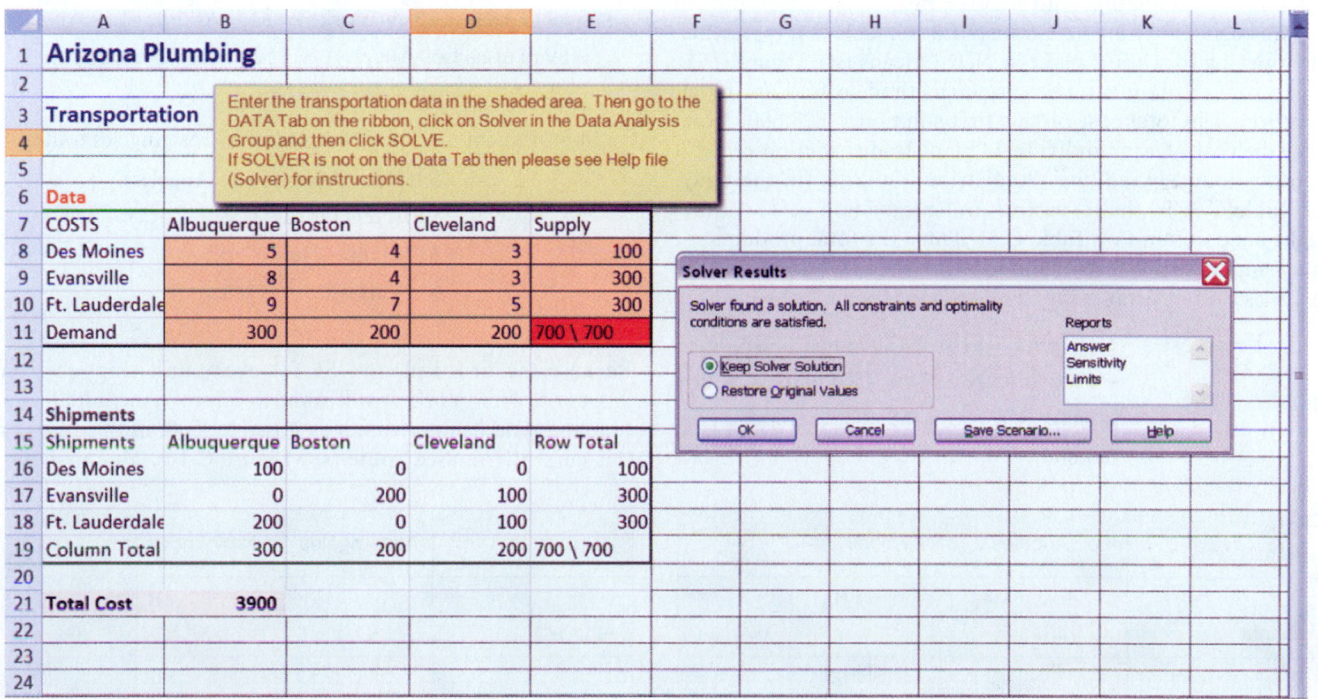

Program **C.2**

Output from Excel OM with Optimal Solution to Arizona Plumbing Problem

P USING POM FOR WINDOWS

The POM for Windows Transportation module can solve both maximization and minimization problems by a variety of methods. Input data are the demand data, supply data, and unit shipping costs. See Appendix IV for further details.

Solved Problems   Virtual Office Hours help is available in MyOMLab.

SOLVED PROBLEM C.1

Williams Auto Top Carriers currently maintains plants in Atlanta and Tulsa to supply auto top carriers to distribution centers in Los Angeles and New York. Because of expanding demand, Williams has decided to open a third plant and has narrowed the choice to one of two cities—New Orleans and Houston. Table C.3 provides pertinent production and distribution costs as well as plant capacities and distribution demands.

Which of the new locations, in combination with the existing plants and distribution centers, yields a lower cost for the firm?

TABLE C.3	Production Costs, Distribution Costs, Plant Capabilities, and Market Demands for Williams Auto Top Carriers			
	TO DISTRIBUTION CENTERS			
FROM PLANTS	**LOS ANGELES**	**NEW YORK**	**NORMAL PRODUCTION**	**UNIT PRODUCTION COST**
Existing plants				
Atlanta	$8	$5	600	$6
Tulsa	$4	$7	900	$5
Proposed locations				
New Orleans	$5	$6	500	$4 (anticipated)
Houston	$4	$6[a]	500	$3 (anticipated)
Forecast demand	800	1,200	2,000	

[a]Indicates distribution cost (shipping, handling, storage) will be $6 per carrier between Houston and New York.

SOLUTION

To answer this question, we must solve two transportation problems, one for each combination. We will recommend the location that yields a lower total cost of distribution and production in combination with the existing system.

We begin by setting up a transportation table that represents the opening of a third plant in New Orleans (see Figure C.9). Then we use the northwest-corner method to find an initial solution. The total cost of this first solution is $23,600. Note that the cost of each individual "plant-to-distribution-center" route is found by adding the distribution costs (in the body of Table C.3) to the respective unit production costs (in the right-hand column of Table C.3). Thus, the total production-plus-shipping cost of one auto top carrier from Atlanta to Los Angeles is $14 ($8 for shipping plus $6 for production).

$$\text{Total cost} = (600 \text{ units} \times \$14) + (200 \text{ units} \times \$9)$$
$$+ (700 \text{ units} \times \$12) + (500 \text{ units} \times \$10)$$
$$= \$8,400 + \$1,800 + \$8,400 + \$5,000$$
$$= \$23,600$$

Is this initial solution (in Figure C.9) optimal? We can use the stepping-stone method to test it and compute improvement indices for unused routes:

Improvement index for Atlanta–New York route:

$$= +\$11 \text{ (Atlanta–New York)} - \$14 \text{ (Atlanta–Los Angeles)}$$
$$+ \$9 \text{ (Tulsa–Los Angeles)} - \$12 \text{ (Tulsa–New York)}$$
$$= -\$6$$

Improvement index for New Orleans–Los Angeles route:

$$= +\$9 \text{ (New Orleans–Los Angeles)}$$
$$- \$10 \text{ (New Orleans–New York)}$$
$$+ \$12 \text{ (Tulsa–New York)}$$
$$- \$9 \text{ (Tulsa–Los Angeles)}$$
$$= \$2$$

Because the firm can save $6 for every unit shipped from Atlanta to New York, it will want to improve the initial solution and send as many units as possible (600, in this case) on this currently unused route (see Figure C.10). You may also

From \ To	Los Angeles	New York	Production capacity
Atlanta	$14 / 600	$11	600
Tulsa	$9 / 200	$12 / 700	900
New Orleans	$9	$10 / 500	500
Demand	800	1,200	2,000

Figure **C.9**

Initial Williams Transportation Table for New Orleans

From \ To	Los Angeles	New York	Production capacity
Atlanta	$14	$11 / 600	600
Tulsa	$9 / 800	$12 / 100	900
New Orleans	$9	$10 / 500	500
Demand	800	1,200	2,000

Figure **C.10**

Improved Transportation Table for Williams

want to confirm that the total cost is now $20,000, a savings of $3,600 over the initial solution.

Next, we must test the two unused routes to see if their improvement indices are also negative numbers:

Index for Atlanta–Los Angeles:

$$= \$14 - \$11 + \$12 - \$9 = \$6$$

Index for New Orleans–Los Angeles:

$$= \$9 - \$10 + \$12 - \$9 = \$2$$

Because both indices are greater than zero, we have already reached our optimal solution for the New Orleans location. If Williams elects to open the New Orleans plant, the firm's total production and distribution cost will be $20,000.

This analysis, however, provides only half the answer to Williams's problem. The same procedure must still be followed to determine the minimum cost if the new plant is built in Houston. Determining this cost is left as a homework problem. You can help provide complete information and recommend a solution by solving Problem C.7 (on p. 742).

SOLVED PROBLEM C.2

In Solved Problem C.1, we examined the Williams Auto Top Carriers problem by using a transportation table. An alternative approach is to structure the same decision analysis using linear programming (LP), which we explained in detail in Business Analytics Module B.

SOLUTION

Using the data in Figure C.9 (p. 740), we write the objective function and constraints as follows:

$$\text{Minimize total cost} = \$14X_{Atl,LA} + \$11X_{Atl,NY} + \$9X_{Tul,LA} + \$12X_{Tul,NY} + \$9X_{NO,LA} + \$10X_{NO,NY}$$

$$
\begin{aligned}
\text{Subject to:}\quad X_{Atl,LA} + X_{Atl,NY} &\le 600 &&\text{(production capacity at Atlanta)}\\
X_{Tul,LA} + X_{Tul,NY} &\le 900 &&\text{(production capacity at Tulsa)}\\
X_{NO,LA} + X_{NO,NY} &\le 500 &&\text{(production capacity at New Orleans)}\\
X_{Atl,LA} + X_{Tul,LA} + X_{NO,LA} &\ge 800 &&\text{(Los Angeles demand constraint)}\\
X_{Atl,NY} + X_{Tul,NY} + X_{NO,NY} &\ge 1200 &&\text{(New York demand constraint)}
\end{aligned}
$$

Problems

Note: **P✕** means the problem may be solved with POM for Windows and/or Excel OM.

Problems C.1–C.3 relate to Developing an Initial Solution

• **C.1**   Find an initial solution to the following transportation problem.

	TO			
FROM	LOS ANGELES	CALGARY	PANAMA CITY	SUPPLY
Mexico City	$ 6	$18	$ 8	100
Detroit	$17	$13	$19	60
Ottawa	$20	$10	$24	40
Demand	50	80	70	

a) Use the northwest-corner method. What is its total cost?
b) Use the intuitive lowest-cost approach. What is its total cost?
c) Using the stepping-stone method, find the optimal solution. Compute the total cost. **P✕**

• **C.2**   Consider the transportation table at right. Unit costs for each shipping route are in dollars. What is the total cost of the basic feasible solution that the intuitive lowest-cost method would find for this problem? **P✕**

	Destination					
Source	A	B	C	D	E	Supply
1	12	8	5	10	4	18
2	6	11	3	7	9	14
Demand	6	8	12	4	2	

• **C.3**   Refer to the table that follows.
a) Use the northwest-corner method to find an initial feasible solution. What must you do before beginning the solution steps?
b) Use the intuitive lowest-cost approach to find an initial feasible solution. Is this approach better than the northwest-corner method?
c) Find the optimal solution using the stepping-stone method.

FROM	TO A	B	C	SUPPLY
X	$10	$18	$12	100
Y	$17	$13	$ 9	50
Z	$20	$18	$14	75
Demand	50	80	70	

Problems C.4–C.13 relate to The Stepping-Stone Method

• **C.4** Consider the transportation table below. The solution displayed was obtained by performing some iterations of the transportation method on this problem. What is the total cost of the shipping plan that would be obtained by performing *one more iteration* of the stepping-stone method on this problem?

Destination

Source	Denver	Yuma	Miami	Supply
Houston	$2 10	$8	$1	10
St. Louis	$4 10	$5 10	$6	20
Chicago	$6	$3 10	$2 20	30
Demand	20	20	20	

•• **C.5** The following table is the result of one or more iterations.

From \ To	1	2	3	Capacity
A	30 40	30	5 10	50
B	10	10 30	10	30
C	20	10 30	25 45	75
Demand	40	60	55	155

a) Complete the next iteration using the stepping-stone method.
b) Calculate the "total cost" incurred if your results were to be accepted as the final solution. **Px**

•• **C.6** The three blood banks in Seminole County, Florida, are coordinated through a central office that facilitates blood delivery to four hospitals in the region. The cost to ship a standard container of blood from each bank to each hospital is shown in the table below. Also given are the biweekly number of containers available at each bank and the biweekly number of containers of blood needed at each hospital. How many shipments should be made biweekly from each blood bank to each hospital so that total shipment costs are minimized?

Minerva Studio/Fotolia

FROM	TO HOSP. 1	HOSP. 2	HOSP. 3	HOSP. 4	SUPPLY
Bank 1	$ 8	$ 9	$11	$16	50
Bank 2	$12	$ 7	$ 5	$ 8	80
Bank 3	$14	$10	$ 6	$ 7	120
Demand	90	70	40	50	250

Px

•• **C.7** In Solved Problem C.1 (page 740), Williams Auto Top Carriers proposed opening a new plant in either New Orleans or Houston. Management found that the total system cost (of production plus distribution) would be $20,000 for the New Orleans site. What would be the total cost if Williams opened a plant in Houston? At which of the two proposed locations (New Orleans or Houston) should Williams open the new facility? **Px**

•• **C.8** The Donna Mosier Clothing Group owns factories in three towns (W, Y, and Z), which distribute to three retail dress shops in three other cities (A, B, and C). The following table summarizes factory availabilities, projected store demands, and unit shipping costs:

From \ To	Dress Shop A	Dress Shop B	Dress Shop C	Factory availability
Factory W	$4	$3	$3	35
Factory Y	$6	$7	$6	50
Factory Z	$8	$2	$5	50
Store demand	30	65	40	135

a) Complete the analysis, determining the optimal solution for shipping at the Mosier Clothing Group.
b) How do you know whether it is optimal or not? **Px**

•••**C.9** Captain Borders Corp. manufacturers fishing equipment. Currently, the company has a plant in Los Angeles and a plant in New Orleans. William Borders, the firm's owner, is deciding where to build a new plant—Philadelphia or Seattle. Use the following table to find the total shipping costs for each potential site. Which should Borders select?

	WAREHOUSE			
PLANT	**PITTSBURGH**	**ST. LOUIS**	**DENVER**	**CAPACITY**
Los Angeles	$100	$75	$50	150
New Orleans	$ 80	$60	$90	225
Philadelphia	$ 40	$50	$90	350
Seattle	$110	$70	$30	350
Demand	200	100	400	

••C.10 Dana Johnson Corp. is considering adding a fourth plant to its three existing facilities in Decatur, Minneapolis, and Carbondale. Both St. Louis and East St. Louis are being considered. Evaluating only the transportation costs per unit as shown in the table, decide which site is best.

	FROM EXISTING PLANTS			
TO	**DECATUR**	**MINNEAPOLIS**	**CARBONDALE**	**DEMAND**
Blue Earth	$20	$17	$21	250
Ciro	$25	$27	$20	200
Des Moines	$22	$25	$22	350
Capacity	300	200	150	

	FROM PROPOSED PLANTS	
TO	**EAST ST. LOUIS**	**ST. LOUIS**
Blue Earth	$29	$27
Ciro	$30	$28
Des Moines	$30	$31
Capacity	150	150

••C.11 Using the data from Problem C.10 and the unit production costs in the following table, show which locations yield the lowest cost.

LOCATION	PRODUCTION COSTS ($)
Decatur	$50
Minneapolis	60
Carbondale	70
East St. Louis	40
St. Louis	50

Additional problems **C.12–C.13** are available in MyOMLab.

Problems C.14–C.18 relate to Special Issues in Modeling

••C.14 Allen Air Conditioning manufactures room air conditioners at plants in Houston, Phoenix, and Memphis. These are sent to regional distributors in Dallas, Atlanta, and Denver. The shipping costs vary, and the company would like to find the least-cost way to meet the demands at each of the distribution centers. Dallas needs to receive 800 air conditioners per month, Atlanta needs 600, and Denver needs 200. Houston has 850 air conditioners available each month, Phoenix has 650, and Memphis has 300. The shipping cost per unit from Houston to Dallas is $8, to Atlanta $12, and to Denver $10. The cost per unit from Phoenix to Dallas is $10, to Atlanta $14, and to Denver $9. The cost per unit from Memphis to Dallas is $11, to Atlanta $8, and to Denver $12. How many units should owner Stephen Allen ship from each plant to each regional distribution center? What is the total transportation cost? (Note that a "dummy" destination is needed to balance the problem.) Px

••C.15 For the following Gregory Bier Corp. data, find the starting solution and initial cost using the northwest-corner method. What must you do to balance this problem?

	TO				
FROM	**W**	**X**	**Y**	**Z**	**SUPPLY**
A	$132	$116	$250	$110	220
B	$220	$230	$180	$178	300
C	$152	$173	$196	$164	435
Demand	160	120	200	230	

Additional problems **C.16–C.18** are available in MyOMLab.

CASE STUDY

Custom Vans, Inc.

Custom Vans, Inc., specializes in converting standard vans into campers. Depending on the amount of work and customizing to be done, the customizing can cost from less than $1,000 to more than $5,000. In less than 4 years, Tony Rizzo was able to expand his small operation in Gary, Indiana, to other major outlets in Chicago, Milwaukee, Minneapolis, and Detroit.

Innovation was the major factor in Tony's success in converting a small van shop into one of the largest and most profitable custom van operations in the Midwest. Tony seemed to have a special ability to design and develop unique features and devices that were always in high demand by van owners. An example was Shower-Rific, which was developed by Tony only 6 months after Custom Vans, Inc., was started. These small showers were completely self-contained, and they could be placed in almost any type of van and in a number of different locations within a van. Shower-Rific was made of fiberglass, and contained towel racks,

built-in soap and shampoo holders, and a unique plastic door. Each Shower-Rific took 2 gallons of fiberglass and 3 hours of labor to manufacture.

Most of the Shower-Rifics were manufactured in Gary in the same warehouse where Custom Vans, Inc., was founded. The manufacturing plant in Gary could produce 300 Shower-Rifics in a month, but this capacity never seemed to be enough. Custom Van shops in all locations were complaining about not getting enough Shower-Rifics, and because Minneapolis was farther away from Gary than the other locations, Tony was always inclined to ship Shower-Rifics to the other locations before Minneapolis. This infuriated the manager of Custom Vans at Minneapolis, and after many heated discussions, Tony decided to start another manufacturing plant for Shower-Rifics at Fort Wayne, Indiana. The manufacturing plant at Fort Wayne could produce 150 Shower-Rifics per month.

The manufacturing plant at Fort Wayne was still not able to meet current demand for Shower-Rifics, and Tony knew that the demand for his unique camper shower would grow rapidly in the next year. After consulting with his lawyer and banker, Tony concluded that he should open two new manufacturing plants as soon as possible. Each plant would have the same capacity as the Fort Wayne manufacturing plant. An initial investigation into possible manufacturing locations was made, and Tony decided that the two new plants should be located in Detroit, Michigan; Rockford, Illinois; or Madison, Wisconsin. Tony knew that selecting the best location for the two new manufacturing plants would be difficult. Transportation costs and demands for the various locations would be important considerations.

The Chicago shop was managed by Bill Burch. This shop was one of the first established by Tony, and it continued to outperform the other locations. The manufacturing plant at Gary was supplying 200 Shower-Rifics each month, although Bill knew that the demand for the showers in Chicago was 300 units. The transportation cost per unit from Gary was $10, and although the transportation cost from Fort Wayne was double that amount, Bill was always pleading with Tony to get an additional 50 units from the Fort Wayne manufacturer. The two additional manufacturing plants would certainly be able to supply Bill with the additional 100 showers he needed. The transportation costs would, of course, vary, depending on which two locations Tony picked. The transportation cost per shower would be $30 from Detroit, $5 from Rockford, and $10 from Madison.

Wilma Jackson, manager of the Custom Van shop in Milwaukee, was the most upset about not getting an adequate supply of showers. She had a demand for 100 units, and at the present time, she was only getting half of this demand from the Fort Wayne manufacturing plant. She could not understand why Tony didn't ship her all 100 units from Gary. The transportation cost per unit from Gary was only $20, while the transportation cost from Fort Wayne was $30. Wilma was hoping that Tony would select Madison for one of the manufacturing locations. She would be able to get all the showers needed, and the transportation cost per unit would only be $5. If not in Madison, a new plant in Rockford would be able to supply her total needs, but the transportation cost per unit would be twice as much as it would be from Madison. Because the transportation cost per unit from Detroit would be $40, Wilma speculated that even if Detroit became one of the new plants, she would not be getting any units from Detroit.

Custom Vans, Inc., of Minneapolis was managed by Tom Poanski. He was getting 100 showers from the Gary plant. Demand was 150 units. Tom faced the highest transportation costs of all locations. The transportation cost from Gary was $40 per unit. It would cost $10 more if showers were sent from the Fort Wayne location. Tom was hoping that Detroit would not be one of the new plants, as the transportation cost would be $60 per unit. Rockford and Madison would have a cost of $30 and $25, respectively, to ship one shower to Minneapolis.

The Detroit shop's position was similar to Milwaukee's—only getting half of the demand each month. The 100 units that Detroit did receive came directly from the Fort Wayne plant. The transportation cost was only $15 per unit from Fort Wayne, while it cost $25 from Gary. Dick Lopez, manager of Custom Vans, Inc., of Detroit, placed the probability of having one of the new plants in Detroit fairly high. The factory would be located across town, and the transportation cost would be only $5 per unit. He could get 150 showers from the new plant in Detroit and the other 50 showers from Fort Wayne. Even if Detroit was not selected, the other two locations were not intolerable. Rockford had a transportation cost per unit of $35, and Madison had a transportation cost of $40.

Tony pondered the dilemma of locating the two new plants for several weeks before deciding to call a meeting of all the managers of the van shops. The decision was complicated, but the objective was clear—to minimize total costs. The meeting was held in Gary, and everyone was present except Wilma.

Tony: Thank you for coming. As you know, I have decided to open two new plants at Rockford, Madison, or Detroit. The two locations, of course, will change our shipping practices, and I sincerely hope that they will supply you with the Shower-Rifics that you have been wanting. I know you could have sold more units, and I want you to know that I am sorry for this situation.

Dick: Tony, I have given this situation a lot of consideration, and I feel strongly that at least one of the new plants should be located in Detroit. As you know, I am now only getting half of the showers that I need. My brother, Leon, is very interested in running the plant, and I know he would do a good job.

Tom: Dick, I am sure that Leon could do a good job, and I know how difficult it has been since the recent layoffs by the auto industry. Nevertheless, we should be considering total costs and not personalities. I believe that the new plants should be located in Madison and Rockford. I am farther away from the other plants than any other shop, and these locations would significantly reduce transportation costs.

Dick: That may be true, but there are other factors. Detroit has one of the largest suppliers of fiberglass, and I have checked prices. A new plant in Detroit would be able to purchase fiberglass for $2 per gallon less than any of the other existing or proposed plants.

Tom: At Madison, we have an excellent labor force. This is due primarily to the large number of students attending the University of Wisconsin. These students are hard workers, and they will work for $1 less per hour than the other locations that we are considering.

Bill: Calm down, you two. It is obvious that we will not be able to satisfy everyone in locating the new plants. Therefore, I would like to suggest that we vote on the two best locations.

Tony: I don't think that voting would be a good idea. Wilma was not able to attend, and we should be looking at all of these factors together in some type of logical fashion.

Discussion Question

Where would you locate the two new plants? Why?

Source: From *Quantitative Analysis for Management*, B. Render, R. M. Stair, M. Hanna, and T. Hale. 12th ed. Copyright © 2015. Reprinted by permission of Pearson Publishing, Upper Saddle River, NJ.

• **Additional Case Study:** Visit MyOMLab for this free case study:
  Consolidated Bottling (B): This case involves determining where to add bottling capacity.

Module C *Rapid Review*

Main Heading	Review Material	MyOMLab
TRANSPORTATION MODELING (pp. 730–731)	The transportation models described in this module prove useful when considering alternative facility locations *within the framework of an existing distribution system.* The choice of a new location depends on which will yield the minimum cost for the entire system.	Concept Questions: 1.1–1.4

TRANSPORTATION MODELING (pp. 730–731)

The transportation models described in this module prove useful when considering alternative facility locations *within the framework of an existing distribution system.* The choice of a new location depends on which will yield the minimum cost for the entire system.

- **Transportation modeling**—An iterative procedure for solving problems that involves minimizing the cost of shipping products from a series of sources to a series of destinations.

Origin points (or *sources*) can be factories, warehouses, car rental agencies, or any other points from which goods are shipped.

Destinations are any points that receive goods.

To use the transportation model, we need to know the following:

1. The origin points and the capacity or supply per period at each.
2. The destination points and the demand per period at each.
3. The cost of shipping one unit from each origin to each destination.

The transportation model is a type of linear programming model.

A *transportation matrix* summarizes all relevant data and keeps track of algorithm computations. Shipping costs from each origin to each destination are contained in the appropriate cross-referenced box.

TO / FROM	DESTINATION 1	DESTINATION 2	DESTINATION 3	CAPACITY
Source A				
Source B				
Source C				
Demand				

Concept Questions: 1.1–1.4

DEVELOPING AN INITIAL SOLUTION (pp. 732–734)

Two methods for establishing an initial feasible solution to the problem are the northwest-corner rule and the intuitive lowest-cost method.

- **Northwest-corner rule**—A procedure in the transportation model where one starts at the upper-left-hand cell of a table (the northwest corner) and systematically allocates units to shipping routes.

The northwest-corner rule requires that we:

1. Exhaust the supply (origin capacity) of each row before moving down to the next row.
2. Exhaust the demand requirements of each column before moving to the next column to the right.
3. Check to ensure that all supplies and demands are met.

The northwest-corner rule is easy to use and generates a feasible solution, but it totally ignores costs and therefore should be considered only as a starting position.

- **Intuitive method**—A cost-based approach to finding an initial solution to a transportation problem.

The intuitive method uses the following steps:

1. Identify the cell with the lowest cost. Break any ties for the lowest cost arbitrarily.
2. Allocate as many units as possible to that cell, without exceeding the supply or demand. Then cross out that row or column (or both) that is exhausted by this assignment.
3. Find the cell with the lowest cost from the remaining (not crossed out) cells.
4. Repeat Steps 2 and 3 until all units have been allocated.

Concept Questions: 2.1–2.4

Problems: C.1–C.3, C.15

THE STEPPING-STONE METHOD (pp. 734–737)

- **Stepping-stone method**—An iterative technique for moving from an initial feasible solution to an optimal solution in the transportation method.

The stepping-stone method is used to evaluate the cost-effectiveness of shipping goods via transportation routes not currently in the solution. When applying it, we test each unused cell, or square, in the transportation table by asking: What would happen to total shipping costs if one unit of the product were tentatively shipped on an unused route? We conduct the test as follows:

1. Select any unused square to evaluate.
2. Beginning at this square, trace a closed path back to the original square via squares that are currently being used (only horizontal and vertical moves are permissible). You may, however, step over either an empty or an occupied square.

Concept Questions: 3.1–3.4

Problems: C.4–C.13

Virtual Office Hours for Solved Problem: C.1

Main Heading	Review Material	MyOMLab

3. Beginning with a plus (+) sign at the unused square, place alternative minus signs and plus signs on each corner square of the closed path just traced.
4. Calculate an improvement index by first adding the unit-cost figures found in each square containing a plus sign and then subtracting the unit costs in each square containing a minus sign.
5. Repeat Steps 1 through 4 until you have calculated an improvement index for all unused squares. If all indices computed are *greater than or equal to zero*, you have reached an optimal solution. If not, the current solution can be improved further to decrease total shipping costs.

Each negative index represents the amount by which total transportation costs could be decreased if one unit was shipped by the source–destination combination. The next step, then, is to choose that route (unused square) with the *largest* negative improvement index. We can then ship the maximum allowable number of units on that route and reduce the total cost accordingly. That maximum quantity is found by referring to the closed path of plus signs and minus signs drawn for the route and then selecting the *smallest number found in the squares containing minus signs.* To obtain a new solution, we add this number to all squares on the closed path with plus signs and subtract it from all squares on the path to which we have assigned minus signs. From this new solution, a new test of unused squares needs to be conducted to see if the new solution is optimal or whether we can make further improvements.

SPECIAL ISSUES IN MODELING (pp. 737–738)	*Dummy sources*—Artificial shipping source points created when total demand is greater than total supply to effect a supply equal to the excess of demand over supply. *Dummy destinations*—Artificial destination points created when the total supply is greater than the total demand; they serve to equalize the total demand and supply. Because units from dummy sources or to dummy destinations will not in fact be shipped, we assign cost coefficients of zero to each square on the dummy location. If you are solving a transportation problem by hand, be careful to decide first whether a dummy source (row) or a dummy destination (column) is needed. When applying the stepping-stone method, *the number of occupied squares in any solution (initial or later) must be equal to the number of rows in the table plus the number of columns minus 1.* Solutions that do not satisfy this rule are called *degenerate.* ■ **Degeneracy**—An occurrence in transportation models in which too few squares or shipping routes are being used, so that tracing a closed path for each unused square becomes impossible. To handle degenerate problems, we must artificially create an occupied cell: That is, we place a zero (representing a fake shipment) into one of the unused squares and *then treat that square as if it were occupied.* Remember that the chosen square must be in such a position as to allow all stepping-stone paths to be closed.	Concept Questions: 4.1–4.4 Problems: C.14–C.18 Virtual Office Hours for Solved Problem: C.2

Self Test

■ **Before taking the self-test,** refer to the learning objectives listed at the beginning of the module and the key terms listed at the end of the module.

LO C.1 With the transportation technique, the initial solution can be generated in any fashion one chooses. The only restriction(s) is that:
  a) the solution be optimal.
  b) one use the northwest-corner method.
  c) the edge constraints for supply and demand be satisfied.
  d) the solution not be degenerate.
  e) all of the above.

LO C.2 The purpose of the stepping-stone method is to:
  a) develop the initial solution to a transportation problem.
  b) identify the relevant costs in a transportation problem.
  c) determine whether a given solution is feasible.
  d) assist one in moving from an initial feasible solution to the optimal solution.
  e) overcome the problem of degeneracy.

LO C.3 The purpose of a *dummy source* or a *dummy destination* in a transportation problem is to:
  a) provide a means of representing a dummy problem.
  b) obtain a balance between total supply and total demand.
  c) prevent the solution from becoming degenerate.
  d) make certain that the total cost does not exceed some specified figure.
  e) change a problem from maximization to minimization.

LO C.4 If a solution to a transportation problem is degenerate, then:
  a) it will be impossible to evaluate all empty cells without removing the degeneracy.
  b) a dummy row or column must be added.
  c) there will be more than one optimal solution.
  d) the problem has no feasible solution.
  e) increase the cost of each cell by 1.

Answers: LO C.1. c; LO C.2. d; LO C.3. b; LO C.4. a.

Waiting-Line Models

MODULE

D

MODULE OUTLINE

◆ Queuing Theory *748*

◆ Characteristics of a Waiting-Line System *749*

◆ Queuing Costs *753*

◆ The Variety of Queuing Models *754*

◆ Other Queuing Approaches *765*

Alaska Airlines

Alaska Airlines

LEARNING OBJECTIVES

LO D.1 *Describe* the characteristics of arrivals, waiting lines, and service systems 749

LO D.2 *Apply* the single-server queuing model equations 754

LO D.3 *Conduct* a cost analysis for a waiting line 757

LO D.4 *Apply* the multiple-server queuing model formulas 757

LO D.5 *Apply* the constant-service-time model equations 762

LO D.6 *Perform* a finite-population model analysis 763

Paris's EuroDisney, Tokyo's Disney Japan, and the U.S.'s Disney World and Disneyland all have one feature in common—long lines and seemingly endless waits. However, Disney is one of the world's leading companies in the scientific analysis of queuing theory. It analyzes queuing behaviors and can predict which rides will draw what length crowds. To keep visitors happy, Disney makes lines appear to be constantly moving forward, entertains people while they wait, and posts signs telling visitors how many minutes until they reach each ride.

Joshua Sudock/ZUMA Press/Corbis

Queuing Theory

Queuing theory

A body of knowledge about waiting lines.

Waiting line (queue)

Items or people in a line awaiting service.

The body of knowledge about waiting lines, often called queuing theory, is an important part of operations and a valuable tool for the operations manager. Waiting lines are a common situation—they may, for example, take the form of cars waiting for repair at a Midas Muffler Shop, copying jobs waiting to be completed at a FedEx office, or vacationers waiting to enter a ride at Disney. Table D.1 lists just a few OM uses of waiting-line models.

Waiting-line models are useful in both manufacturing and service areas. Analysis of queues in terms of waiting-line length, average waiting time, and other factors helps us to understand service systems (such as bank teller stations), maintenance activities (that might repair broken machinery), and shop-floor control activities. Indeed, patients waiting in a doctor's office and broken drill presses waiting in a repair facility have a lot in common from an OM perspective.

TABLE D.1	Common Queuing Situations	
SITUATION	**ARRIVALS IN QUEUE**	**SERVICE PROCESS**
Supermarket	Grocery shoppers	Checkout clerks at cash register
Highway toll booth	Automobiles	Collection of tolls at booth
Doctor's office	Patients	Treatment by doctors and nurses
Computer system	Programs to be run	Computer processes jobs
Telephone company	Callers	Switching equipment forwards calls
Bank	Customers	Transactions handled by teller
Machine maintenance	Broken machines	Repair people fix machines
Harbor	Ships and barges	Dock workers load and unload

Both use human and equipment resources to restore valuable production assets (people and machines) to good condition.

Characteristics of a Waiting-Line System

In this section, we take a look at the three parts of a waiting-line, or queuing, system (as shown in Figure D.1):

1. *Arrivals or inputs to the system:* These have characteristics such as population size, behavior, and a statistical distribution.
2. *Queue discipline, or the waiting line itself:* Characteristics of the queue include whether it is limited or unlimited in length and the discipline of people or items in it.
3. *The service facility:* Its characteristics include its design and the statistical distribution of service times.

We now examine each of these three parts.

LO D.1 *Describe* the characteristics of arrivals, waiting lines, and service systems

Arrival Characteristics

The input source that generates arrivals or customers for a service system has three major characteristics:

1. *Size* of the arrival population
2. *Behavior* of arrivals
3. *Pattern* of arrivals (statistical distribution)

Size of the Arrival (Source) Population   Population sizes are considered either either unlimited (essentially infinite) or limited (finite). When the number of customers or arrivals on hand at any given moment is just a small portion of all potential arrivals, the arrival population is considered unlimited, or infinite. Examples of unlimited populations include cars arriving at a big-city car wash, shoppers arriving at a supermarket, and students arriving to register for classes at a large university. Most queuing models assume such an infinite arrival population. An example of a limited, or finite, population is found in a copying shop that has, say, eight copying machines. Each of the copiers is a potential "customer" that may break down and require service.

Pattern of Arrivals at the System   Customers arrive at a service facility either according to some known schedule (for example, one patient every 15 minutes or one student every half hour) or else they arrive *randomly*. Arrivals are considered random when they are

Unlimited, or infinite, population

A queue in which a virtually unlimited number of people or items could request the services, or in which the number of customers or arrivals on hand at any given moment is a very small portion of potential arrivals.

Limited, or finite, population

A queue in which there are only a limited number of potential users of the service.

Arrival Characteristics
- Size of arrival population
- Behavior of arrivals
- Statistical distribution of arrivals

Waiting-Line Characteristics
- Limited vs. unlimited
- Queue discipline

Service Characteristics
- Service design
- Statistical distribution of service

Figure D.1

Three Parts of a Waiting Line, or Queuing System, at Dave's Car Wash

independent of one another and their occurrence cannot be predicted exactly. Frequently in queuing problems, the number of arrivals per unit of time can be estimated by a probability distribution known as the Poisson distribution.[1] For any given arrival time (such as 2 customers per hour or 4 trucks per minute), a discrete Poisson distribution can be established by using the formula:

Poisson distribution

A discrete probability distribution that often describes the arrival rate in queuing theory.

$$P(x) = \frac{e^{-\lambda}\lambda^x}{x!} \quad \text{for } x = 0, 1, 2, 3, 4, \ldots \qquad \text{(D-1)}$$

where $P(x)$ = probability of x arrivals
    x = number of arrivals per unit of time
    λ = average arrival rate
    e = 2.7183 (which is the base of the natural logarithms)

With the help of the table in Appendix II, which gives the value of $e^{-\lambda}$ for use in the Poisson distribution, these values are easy to compute. Figure D.2 illustrates the Poisson distribution for $\lambda = 2$ and $\lambda = 4$. This means that if the average arrival rate is $\lambda = 2$ customers per hour, the probability of 0 customers arriving in any random hour is about 0.13 (13%), probability of 1 customer is about 27%, 2 customers about 27%, 3 customers about 18%, 4 customers about 9%, and so on. The chances that 9 or more will arrive are virtually nil. Arrivals, of course, are not always Poisson distributed (they may follow some other distribution). Patterns, therefore, should be examined to make certain that they are well approximated by Poisson before that distribution is applied.

Behavior of Arrivals

Most queuing models assume that an arriving customer is a patient customer. Patient customers are people or machines that wait in the queue until they are served and do not switch between lines. Unfortunately, life is complicated by the fact that people have been known to balk or to renege. Customers who *balk* refuse to join the waiting line because it is too long to suit their needs or interests. *Reneging* customers are those who enter the queue but then become impatient and leave without completing their transaction. Actually, both of these situations just serve to highlight the need for queuing theory and waiting-line analysis.

Waiting-Line Characteristics

The waiting line itself is the second component of a queuing system. The length of a line can be either limited or unlimited. A queue is *limited* when it cannot, either by law or because of physical restrictions, increase to an infinite length. A small barbershop, for example, will have only a limited number of waiting chairs. Queuing models are treated in this module under an assumption of *unlimited* queue length. A queue is *unlimited* when its size is unrestricted, as in the case of the toll booth serving arriving automobiles.

A second waiting-line characteristic deals with *queue discipline*. This refers to the rule by which customers in the line are to receive service. Most systems use a queue discipline known

Figure **D.2**

Two Examples of the Poisson Distribution for Arrival Times

$$\text{Probability} = P(x) = \frac{e^{-\lambda}\lambda^x}{x!}$$

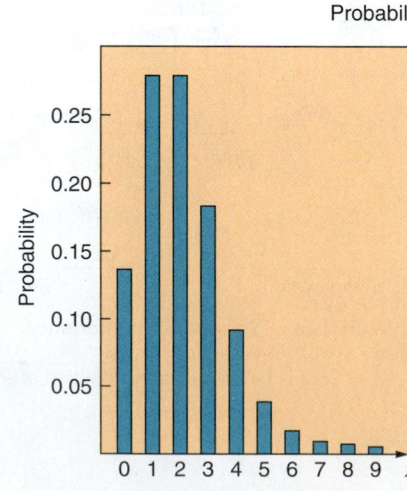

Distribution for $\lambda = 2$

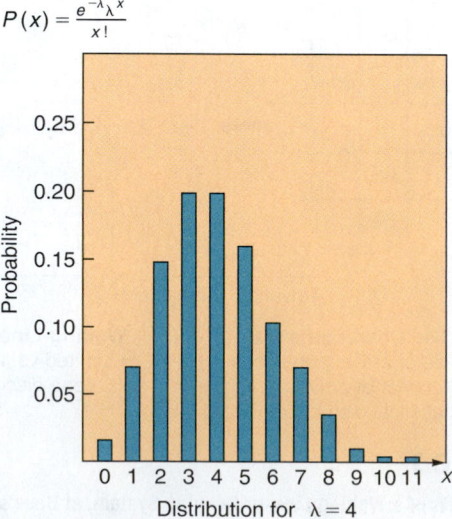

Distribution for $\lambda = 4$

as the first-in, first-out (FIFO) rule. In a hospital emergency room or an express checkout line at a supermarket, however, various assigned priorities may preempt FIFO. Patients who are critically injured will move ahead in treatment priority over patients with broken fingers or noses. Shoppers with fewer than 10 items may be allowed to enter the express checkout queue (but are *then* treated as first-come, first-served). Computer-programming runs also operate under priority scheduling. In most large companies, when computer-produced paychecks are due on a specific date, the payroll program gets highest priority.[2]

First-in, first-out (FIFO) rule

A queue discipline in which the first customers in line receive the first service.

Service Characteristics

The third part of any queuing system is the service characteristics. Two basic properties are important: (1) design of the service system and (2) the distribution of service times.

Basic Queuing System Designs   Service systems are usually classified in terms of their number of *servers* (number of channels) and number of *phases* (number of service stops that must be made). See Figure D.3. A single-server (or single-channel) queuing system, with one server, is typified by the drive-in bank with only one open teller. If, on the other hand, the

Single-server queuing system

A service system with one line and one server.

Example

A family dentist's office

Single-server, single-phase system

A McDonald's dual-window drive-through

Single-server, multiphase system

Most bank and post office service windows

Multiple-server, single-phase system

Some college cafeterias

Multiple-server, multiphase system

Figure **D.3**

Basic Queuing System Designs

bank has several tellers on duty, with each customer waiting in one common line for the first available teller, then we would have a multiple-server (or multiple channel) queuing system. Most banks today are multiple-server systems, as are most large barbershops, airline ticket counters, and post offices.

In a single-phase system, the customer receives service from only one station and then exits the system. A fast-food restaurant in which the person who takes your order also brings your food and takes your money is a single-phase system. So is a driver's license agency in which the person taking your application also grades your test and collects your license fee. However, say the restaurant requires you to place your order at one station, pay at a second, and pick up your food at a third. In this case, it is a multiphase system. Likewise, if the driver's license agency is large or busy, you will probably have to wait in one line to complete your application (the first service stop), queue again to have your test graded, and finally go to a third counter to pay your fee. To help you relate the concepts of servers and phases, Figure D.3 presents these four possible configurations.

Service Time Distribution   Service patterns are like arrival patterns in that they may be either constant or random. If service time is constant, it takes the same amount of time to take care of each customer. This is the case in a machine-performed service operation such as an automatic car wash. More often, service times are randomly distributed. In many cases, we can assume that random service times are described by the negative exponential probability distribution.

Figure D.4 shows that if *service times* follow a negative exponential distribution, the probability of any very long service time is low. For example, when an average service time is 20 minutes (or three customers per hour), seldom if ever will a customer require more than 1.5 hours in the service facility. If the mean service time is 1 hour, the probability of spending more than 3 hours in service is quite low.

Measuring a Queue's Performance

Queuing models help managers make decisions that balance service costs with waiting-line costs. Queuing analysis can obtain many measures of a waiting-line system's performance, including the following:

1. Average time that each customer or object spends in the queue
2. Average queue length
3. Average time that each customer spends in the system (waiting time plus service time)
4. Average number of customers in the system
5. Probability that the service facility will be idle
6. Utilization factor for the system
7. Probability of a specific number of customers in the system

Figure **D.4**

Two Examples of the Negative Exponential Distribution for Service Times

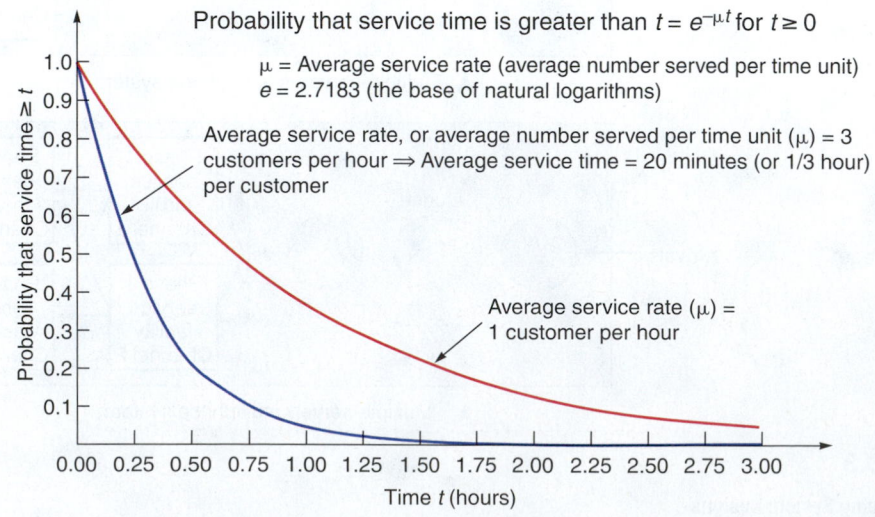

Probability that service time is greater than $t = e^{-\mu t}$ for $t \geq 0$

μ = Average service rate (average number served per time unit)
e = 2.7183 (the base of natural logarithms)

Average service rate, or average number served per time unit (μ) = 3 customers per hour $\Rightarrow$ Average service time = 20 minutes (or 1/3 hour) per customer

Average service rate (μ) = 1 customer per hour

Probability that service time $\geq t$ — y-axis: 0.1, 0.2, 0.3, 0.4, 0.5, 0.6, 0.7, 0.8, 0.9, 1.0

Time t (hours) — x-axis: 0.00 0.25 0.50 0.75 1.00 1.25 1.50 1.75 2.00 2.25 2.50 2.75 3.00

OM in Action — Zero Wait Time Guarantee at This Michigan Hospital's ER

Other hospitals smirked a few years ago when Michigan's Oakwood Healthcare chain rolled out an emergency room (ER) guarantee that promised a written apology and movie tickets to patients not seen by a doctor within 30 minutes. Even employees cringed at what sounded like a cheap marketing ploy.

But if you have visited an ER lately and watched some patients wait for hours on end—the *official* average wait is 47 minutes—you can understand why Oakwood's patient satisfaction levels have soared. The 30-minute guarantee was such a huge success that fewer than 1% of the 191,000 ER patients asked for free tickets. The following year, Oakwood upped the stakes again, offering a 15-minute guarantee. Then Oakwood started its Zero Wait Program in the ERs. Patients who enter any Oakwood emergency department are *immediately* cared for by a healthcare professional.

Oakwood's CEO even extended the ER guarantee to on-time surgery, 45-minute meal service orders, and other custom room services. "Medicine is a service business," says Larry Alexander, the head of an ER in Sanford, Florida. "And people are in the mindset of the fast-food industry."

How did Oakwood make good on its promise to eliminate the ER queue? It first studied queuing theory, then reengineered its billing, records, and lab operations to drive down service time. Then, to improve service capability, Oakwood upgraded its technical staff. Finally, it replaced its ER physicians with a crew willing to work longer hours.

Sources: Wall Street Journal (October 19, 2010); *Time* (January 26, 2011); and **unitiv.com** (February 27, 2014).

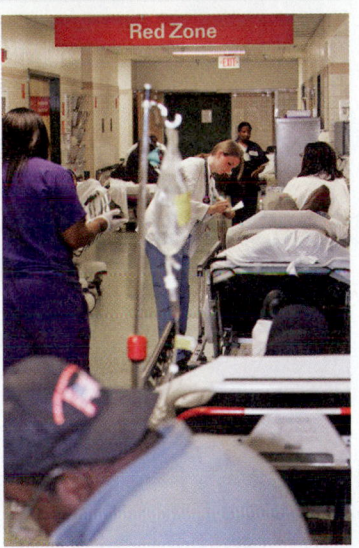

Queuing Costs

As described in the *OM in Action* box "Zero Wait Time Guarantee at This Michigan Hospital's ER," operations managers must recognize the trade-off that takes place between two costs: the cost of providing good service and the cost of customer or machine waiting time. Managers want queues that are short enough so that customers do not become unhappy and either leave without buying, or buy, but never return. However, managers may be willing to allow some waiting if it is balanced by a significant savings in service costs.

One means of evaluating a service facility is to look at total expected cost. Total cost is the sum of expected service costs plus expected waiting costs.

As you can see in Figure D.5, service costs increase as a firm attempts to raise its level of service. Managers in *some* service centers can vary capacity by having standby personnel and machines that they can assign to specific service stations to prevent or shorten excessively long lines. In grocery stores, for example, managers and stock clerks can open extra checkout counters. In banks and airport check-in points, part-time workers may be called in to help. As the level of service improves (that is, speeds up), however, the cost of time spent

Figure **D.5**

The Trade-off Between Waiting Costs and Service Costs

waiting in lines decreases. (Refer to Figure D.5.) Waiting cost may reflect lost productivity of workers while tools or machines await repairs or may simply be an estimate of the cost of customers lost because of poor service and long queues. In some service systems (for example, an emergency ambulance service), the cost of long waiting lines may be intolerably high.

The Variety of Queuing Models

A wide variety of queuing models may be applied in operations management. We will introduce you to four of the most widely used models. These are outlined in Table D.2, and examples of each follow in the next few sections. More complex models are described in queuing theory textbooks or can be developed through the use of simulation (the topic of Module F). Note that all four queuing models listed in Table D.2 have three characteristics in common. They all assume:

STUDENT TIP ◆

This is the main section of Module D. We illustrate four important queuing models.

1. Poisson distribution arrivals
2. FIFO discipline
3. A single-service phase

In addition, they all describe service systems that operate under steady, ongoing conditions. This means that arrival and service rates remain stable during the analysis.

Model A (M/M/1): Single-Server Queuing Model with Poisson Arrivals and Exponential Service Times

LO D.2 *Apply* the single-server queuing model equations

The most common case of queuing problems involves the *single-server* (also called single-channel) waiting line. In this situation, arrivals form a single line to be serviced by a single station (see Figure D.3 on p. 751). We assume that the following conditions exist in this type of system:

1. Arrivals are served on a first-in, first-out (FIFO) basis, and every arrival waits to be served, regardless of the length of the line or queue.
2. Arrivals are independent of preceding arrivals, but the average number of arrivals (*arrival rate*) does not change over time.
3. Arrivals are described by a Poisson probability distribution and come from an infinite (or very, very large) population.

TABLE D.2   Queuing Models Described in This Chapter

MODEL	NAME (TECHNICAL NAME IN PARENTHESES)	EXAMPLE	NUMBER OF SERVERS (CHANNELS)	NUMBER OF PHASES	ARRIVAL RATE PATTERN	SERVICE TIME PATTERN	POPULATION SIZE	QUEUE DISCIPLINE
A	Single-server system (M/M/1)	Information counter at department store	Single	Single	Poisson	Negative exponential	Unlimited	FIFO
B	Multiple-server (M/M/S)	Airline ticket counter	Multi-server	Single	Poisson	Negative exponential	Unlimited	FIFO
C	Constant service (M/D/1)	Automated car wash	Single	Single	Poisson	Constant	Unlimited	FIFO
D	Finite population (M/M/1 with finite source)	Shop with only a dozen machines that might break	Single	Single	Poisson	Negative exponential	Limited	FIFO

The giant Moscow McDonald's boasts 900 seats, 800 workers, and $80 million in annual sales (vs. less than $2 million in a U.S. outlet). Americans would balk at the average waiting time of 45 minutes, but Russians are used to such long lines. McDonald's represents good service in Moscow. Some people have even had their wedding receptions there.

4. Service times vary from one customer to the next and are independent of one another, but their average rate is known and follows the negative exponential distribution.
5. Service times occur according to the negative exponential probability distribution.
6. The service rate is faster than the arrival rate.

When these conditions are met, the series of equations shown in Table D.3 can be developed. Examples D1 and D2 illustrate how Model A (which in technical journals is known as the M/M/1 model) may be used.[3]

TABLE D.3	Queuing Formulas for Model A: Single-Server System, also Called M/M/1

λ = average number of arrivals per time period

μ = average number of people or items served per time period (average service rate)

L_s = average number of units (customers) in the system (waiting and being served)

$$= \frac{\lambda}{\mu - \lambda}$$

W_s = average time a unit spends in the system (waiting time plus service time)

$$= \frac{1}{\mu - \lambda}$$

L_q = average number of units waiting in the queue

$$= \frac{\lambda^2}{\mu(\mu - \lambda)}$$

W_q = average time a unit spends waiting in the queue

$$= \frac{\lambda}{\mu(\mu - \lambda)} = \frac{L_q}{\lambda}$$

ρ = utilization factor for the system

$$= \frac{\lambda}{\mu}$$

P_0 = probability of 0 units in the system (that is, the service unit is idle)

$$= 1 - \frac{\lambda}{\mu}$$

$P_{n>k}$ = probability of more than k units in the system, where n is the number of units in the system

$$= \left(\frac{\lambda}{\mu}\right)^{k+1}$$

Example D1

A SINGLE-SERVER QUEUE

Tom Jones, the mechanic at Golden Muffler Shop, is able to install new mufflers at an average rate of 3 per hour (or about 1 every 20 minutes), according to a negative exponential distribution. Customers seeking this service arrive at the shop on the average of 2 per hour, following a Poisson distribution. They are served on a first-in, first-out basis and come from a very large (almost infinite) population of possible buyers.

We would like to obtain the operating characteristics of Golden Muffler's queuing system.

APPROACH ▶ This is a single-server (M/M/1) system, and we apply the formulas in Table D.3.

SOLUTION ▶

$$\lambda = 2 \text{ cars arriving per hour}$$

$$\mu = 3 \text{ cars serviced per hour}$$

$$L_s = \frac{\lambda}{\mu - \lambda} = \frac{2}{3 - 2} = \frac{2}{1}$$

$$= 2 \text{ cars in the system, on average}$$

$$W_s = \frac{1}{\mu - \lambda} = \frac{1}{3 - 2} = 1$$

$$= 1\text{-hour average time in the system}$$

$$L_q = \frac{\lambda^2}{\mu(\mu - \lambda)} = \frac{2^2}{3(3 - 2)} = \frac{4}{3(1)} = \frac{4}{3}$$

$$= 1.33 \text{ cars waiting in line, on average}$$

$$W_q = \frac{\lambda}{\mu(\mu - \lambda)} = \frac{2}{3(3 - 2)} = \frac{2}{3} \text{ hour}$$

$$= 40\text{-minute average waiting time per car}$$

$$\rho = \frac{\lambda}{\mu} = \frac{2}{3}$$

$$= 66.6\% \text{ of time mechanic is busy}$$

$$P_0 = 1 - \frac{\lambda}{\mu} = 1 - \frac{2}{3}$$

$$= .33 \text{ probability there are 0 cars in the system}$$

Probability of More Than *K* Cars in The system

K	$P_{n > k} = (2/3)^{k+1}$
0	.667 ← Note that this is equal to $1 - P_0 = 1 - .33 = .667$.
1	.444
2	.296
3	.198 ← Implies that there is a 19.8% chance that more than 3 cars are in the system.
4	.132
5	.088
6	.058
7	.039

INSIGHT ▶ Recognize that arrival and service times are converted to the same rate. For example, a service time of 20 minutes is stated as an average *rate* of 3 mufflers *per hour*. It's also important to differentiate between time in the *queue* and time in the *system*.

LEARNING EXERCISE ▶ If $\mu = 4$ cars/hour instead of the current 3 arrivals, what are the new values of L_s, W_s, L_q, W_q, and P_0? [Answer: 1 car, 30 min., .5 cars, 15 min., 50%, .50.]

RELATED PROBLEMS ▶ D.1–D.4, D.6–D.8, D.9a–e, D.10, D.11a–c, D.12a–d (D.31–D.33, D.34a–e, D.35a–e, D.36, D.38, D.39 are available in MyOMLab)

EXCEL OM Data File **ModDExD1.xls** can be found in MyOMLab.

ACTIVE MODEL D.1 This example is further illustrated in Active Model D.1 in MyOMLab.

Once we have computed the operating characteristics of a queuing system, it is often important to do an economic analysis of their impact. Although the waiting-line model just described is valuable in predicting potential waiting times, queue lengths, idle times, and so on, it does not identify optimal decisions or consider cost factors. As we saw earlier, the solution to a queuing problem may require management to make a trade-off between the increased cost of providing better service and the decreased waiting costs derived from providing that service.

Example D2 examines the costs involved in Example D1.

Example D2

ECONOMIC ANALYSIS OF EXAMPLE D1

Golden Muffler Shop's owner is interested in cost factors as well as the queuing parameters computed in Example D1. He estimates that the cost of customer waiting time, in terms of customer dissatisfaction and lost goodwill, is $15 per hour spent *waiting* in line. Jones, the mechanic, is paid $11 per hour.

APPROACH ▶ First compute the average daily customer waiting time, then the daily salary for Jones, and finally the total expected cost.

LO D.3 *Conduct* a cost analysis for a waiting line

SOLUTION ▶ Because the average car has a $\frac{2}{3}$-hour wait (W_q) and because there are approximately 16 cars serviced per day (2 arrivals per hour times 8 working hours per day), the total number of hours that customers spend waiting each day for mufflers to be installed is:

$$\frac{2}{3}(16) = \frac{32}{3} = 10\frac{2}{3} \text{ hour}$$

Hence, in this case:

$$\text{Customer waiting-time cost} = \$15\left(10\frac{2}{3}\right) = \$160 \text{ per day}$$

The only other major cost that Golden's owner can identify in the queuing situation is the salary of Jones, the mechanic, who earns $11 per hour, or $88 per day. Thus:

$$\text{Total expected costs} = \$160 + \$88$$
$$= \$248 \text{ per day}$$

This approach will be useful in Solved Problem D.2 on page 767.

INSIGHT ▶ L_q and W_q are the two most important queuing parameters when it comes to cost analysis. Calculating customer wait times, we note, is based on average time waiting in the queue (W_q) times the number of arrivals per hour (λ) times the number of hours per day. This is because this example is set on a daily basis. This is the same as using L_q because $L_q = W_q\lambda$.

LEARNING EXERCISE ▶ If the customer waiting time is actually $20 per hour and Jones gets a salary increase to $15 per hour, what are the total daily expected costs? [Answer: $333.33.]

RELATED PROBLEMS ▶ D.12e–f, D.13, D.22, D.23, D.24 (D.37 is available in MyOMLab)

Model B (M/M/S): Multiple-Server Queuing Model

Now let's turn to a multiple-server (multiple-channel) queuing system in which two or more servers are available to handle arriving customers. We still assume that customers awaiting service form one single line and then proceed to the first available server. Multiple-server, single-phase waiting lines are found in many banks today: a common line is formed, and the customer at the head of the line proceeds to the first free teller. (Refer to Figure D.3 on p. 751 for a typical multiple-server configuration.)

LO D.4 *Apply* the multiple-server queuing model formulas

The multiple-server system presented in Example D3 again assumes that arrivals follow a Poisson probability distribution and that service times are negative exponentially distributed. Service is first-come, first-served, and all servers are assumed to perform at the same rate. Other assumptions listed earlier for the single-server model also apply.

The queuing equations for Model B (which also has the technical name M/M/S) are shown in Table D.4. These equations are obviously more complex than those used in the single-server model, yet they are used in exactly the same fashion and provide the same type of information as the simpler model. (*Note:* The POM for Windows and Excel OM software described later in this chapter can prove very useful in solving multiple-server and other queuing problems.)

To shorten lines (or wait times), each Costco register is staffed with two employees. This approach has improved efficiency by 20–30%.

Photo courtesy of Costco Wholesale, 2012

TABLE D.4	Queuing Formulas for Model B: Multiple-Server System, also Called M/M/S

M = number of servers (channels) open
λ = average number of arrivals per time period (average arrival rate)
μ = average service rate at each server (channel)
The probability that there are zero people or units in the system is:

$$P_0 = \frac{1}{\left[\displaystyle\sum_{n=0}^{M-1}\frac{1}{n!}\left(\frac{\lambda}{\mu}\right)^n\right] + \frac{1}{M!}\left(\frac{\lambda}{\mu}\right)^M \frac{M\mu}{M\mu - \lambda}} \quad \text{for } M\mu > \lambda$$

The average number of people or units in the system is:

$$L_s = \frac{\lambda\mu(\lambda/\mu)^M}{(M-1)!(M\mu - \lambda)^2}P_0 + \frac{\lambda}{\mu}$$

The average time a unit spends in the waiting line and being serviced (namely, in the system) is:

$$W_s = \frac{\mu(\lambda/\mu)^M}{(M-1)!(M\mu - \lambda)^2}P_0 + \frac{1}{\mu} = \frac{L_s}{\lambda}$$

The average number of people or units in line waiting for service is:

$$L_q = L_s - \frac{\lambda}{\mu}$$

The average time a person or unit spends in the queue waiting for service is:

$$W_q = W_s - \frac{1}{\mu} = \frac{L_q}{\lambda}$$

Example D3

A MULTIPLE-SERVER QUEUE

The Golden Muffler Shop has decided to open a second garage bay and hire a second mechanic to handle installations. Customers, who arrive at the rate of about $\lambda = 2$ per hour, will wait in a single line until 1 of the 2 mechanics is free. Each mechanic installs mufflers at the rate of about $\mu = 3$ per hour.

The company wants to find out how this system compares with the old single-server waiting-line system.

APPROACH ▶ Compute several operating characteristics for the $M = 2$ server system, using the equations in Table D.4, and compare the results with those found in Example D1.

SOLUTION ▶

$$P_0 = \cfrac{1}{\left[\displaystyle\sum_{n=0}^{1} \frac{1}{n!}\left(\frac{2}{3}\right)^n\right] + \frac{1}{2!}\left(\frac{2}{3}\right)^2 \frac{2(3)}{2(3)-2}}$$

$$= \cfrac{1}{1 + \frac{2}{3} + \frac{1}{2}\left(\frac{4}{9}\right)\left(\frac{6}{6-2}\right)} = \cfrac{1}{1 + \frac{2}{3} + \frac{1}{3}} = \frac{1}{2}$$

$$= .5 \text{ probability of zero cars in the system}$$

Then:

$$L_s = \frac{(2)(3)(2/3)^2}{1!\,[\,2(3)-2\,]^2}\left(\frac{1}{2}\right) + \frac{2}{3} = \frac{8/3}{16}\left(\frac{1}{2}\right) + \frac{2}{3} = \frac{3}{4}$$

$$= .75 \text{ average number of cars in the system}$$

$$W_s = \frac{L_s}{\lambda} = \frac{3/4}{2} = \frac{3}{8} \text{ hour}$$

$$= 22.5 \text{ minutes average time a car spends in the system}$$

$$L_q = L_s - \frac{\lambda}{\mu} = \frac{3}{4} - \frac{2}{3} = \frac{9}{12} - \frac{8}{12} = \frac{1}{12}$$

$$= .083 \text{ average number of cars in the queue (waiting)}$$

$$W_q = \frac{L_q}{\lambda} = \frac{.083}{2} = .0415 \text{ hour}$$

$$= 2.5 \text{ minutes average time a car spends in the queue (waiting)}$$

INSIGHT ▶ It is very interesting to see the big differences in service performance when an additional server is added.

LEARNING EXERCISE ▶ If $\mu = 4$ per hour, instead of $\mu = 3$, what are the new values for P_0, L_s, W_s, L_q, and W_q? [Answers: 0.6, .53 cars, 16 min, .033 cars, 1 min.]

RELATED PROBLEMS ▶ D.7h, D.9f, D.11d, D.15, D.20 (D.35f, D.36 are available in MyOMLab)

EXCEL OM Data File **ModDEx.xls** can be found in MyOMLab.

ACTIVE MODEL D.2 This example is further illustrated in Active Model D.2 in MyOMLab.

We can summarize the characteristics of the two-server model in Example D3 and compare them to those of the single-server model in Example D1 as follows:

MEASURE		SINGLE SERVER	TWO SERVERS (CHANNELS)
Probability of 0 units in the system	P_0	.33	.5
Number of units in the system	L_s	2 cars	.75 car
Average time in the system	W_s	60 minutes	22.5 minutes
Average number in the queue	L_q	1.33 cars	.083 car
Average time in the queue	W_q	40 minutes	2.5 minutes

The increased service has a dramatic effect on almost all characteristics. For instance, note that the time spent waiting in line drops from 40 minutes to only 2.5 minutes.

Use of Waiting-Line Tables   Imagine the work a manager would face in dealing with $M = 3$-, 4-, or 5- server waiting-line models if a computer was not readily available. The arithmetic becomes increasingly troublesome. Fortunately, much of the burden of manually examining multiple-server queues can be avoided by using Table D.5. This table, the result of hundreds of computations, represents the relationship between three things: (1) a ratio, λ/μ, (2) number of servers open, and (3) the average number of customers in the queue, L_q (which is what we'd like to find). For any combination of the ratio λ/μ and $M = 1, 2, 3, 4$, or 5 servers, you can quickly look in the body of the table to read off the appropriate value for L_q.

TABLE D.5	Values of L_q for M = 1–5 Servers (channels) and Selected Values of λ/μ

| | POISSON ARRIVALS, EXPONENTIAL SERVICE TIMES | | | | |
| | NUMBER OF SERVERS (CHANNELS), M | | | | |
λ/μ	1	2	3	4	5
.10	.0111				
.15	.0264	.0008			
.20	.0500	.0020			
.25	.0833	.0039			
.30	.1285	.0069			
.35	.1884	.0110			
.40	.2666	.0166			
.45	.3681	.0239	.0019		
.50	.5000	.0333	.0030		
.55	.6722	.0449	.0043		
.60	.9000	.0593	.0061		
.65	1.2071	.0767	.0084		
.70	1.6333	.0976	.0112		
.75	2.2500	.1227	.0147		
.80	3.2000	.1523	.0189		
.85	4.8166	.1873	.0239	.0031	
.90	8.1000	.2285	.0300	.0041	
.95	18.0500	.2767	.0371	.0053	
1.0		.3333	.0454	.0067	
1.2		.6748	.0904	.0158	
1.4		1.3449	.1778	.0324	.0059
1.6		2.8444	.3128	.0604	.0121
1.8		7.6734	.5320	.1051	.0227
2.0			.8888	.1739	.0398
2.2			1.4907	.2770	.0659
2.4			2.1261	.4305	.1047
2.6			4.9322	.6581	.1609
2.8			12.2724	1.0000	.2411
3.0				1.5282	.3541
3.2				2.3856	.5128
3.4				3.9060	.7365
3.6				7.0893	1.0550
3.8				16.9366	1.5184
4.0					2.2164
4.2					3.3269
4.4					5.2675
4.6					9.2885
4.8					21.6384

Example D4 illustrates the use of Table D.5.

Example D4 | USE OF WAITING-LINE TABLES

Alaska National Bank is trying to decide how many drive-in teller windows to open on a busy Saturday. CEO Ted Eschenbach estimates that customers arrive at a rate of about $\lambda = 18$ per hour, and that each teller can service about $\mu = 20$ customers per hour.

APPROACH ▶ Ted decides to use Table D.5 to compute L_q and W_q.

SOLUTION ▶ The ratio is $\lambda/\mu = \frac{18}{20} = .90$. Turning to the table, under $\lambda/\mu = .90$, Ted sees that if only $M = 1$ service window is open, the average number of customers in line will be 8.1. If two windows are open, L_q drops to .2285 customers, to .03 for $M = 3$ tellers, and to .0041 for $M = 4$ tellers. Adding more open windows at this point will result in an average queue length of 0.

It is also a simple matter to compute the average waiting time in the queue, W_q, since $W_q = L_q/\lambda$. When one service window is open, $W_q = 8.1$ customers/(18 customers per hour) = .45 hours = 27 minutes waiting time; when two tellers are open, $W_q = .2285$ customers/(18 customers per hour) = .0127 hours $\cong \frac{3}{4}$ minute; and so on.

INSIGHT ▶ If a computer is not readily available, Table D.5 makes it easy to find L_q and to then compute W_q. Table D.5 is especially handy to compare L_q for different numbers of servers (M).

LEARNING EXERCISE ▶ The number of customers arriving on a Thursday afternoon at Alaska National is 15/hour. The service rate is still 20 customers/hour. How many people are in the queue if there are 1, 2, or 3 servers? [Answer: 2.25, .1227, .0147.]

RELATED PROBLEM ▶ D.5

You might also wish to check the calculations in Example D3 against tabled values just to practice the use of Table D.5. You may need to interpolate if your exact value is not found in the first column. Other common operating characteristics besides L_q are published in tabular form in queuing theory textbooks.

Long check-in lines (left photo) such as at Los Angeles International (LAX) are a common airport sight. This is an M/M/S model—passengers wait in a single queue for one of several agents. But at Anchorage International Airport (right photo), Alaska Air has jettisoned the traditional wall of ticket counters. Instead, 1.2 million passengers per year use self-service check-in machines and staffed "bag drop" stations. Looking nothing like a typical airport, the new system doubled the airline's check-in capacity and cut staff needs in half, all while speeding travelers through in less than 15 minutes, even during peak hours.

LO D.5 *Apply* the constant-service-time model equations

Model C (M/D/1): Constant-Service-Time Model

Some service systems have constant, instead of exponentially distributed, service times. When customers or equipment are processed according to a fixed cycle, as in the case of an automatic car wash or an amusement park ride, constant service times are appropriate. Because constant rates are certain, the values for L_q, W_q, L_s, and W_s are always less than they would be in Model A, which has variable service rates. As a matter of fact, both the average queue length and the average waiting time in the queue are halved with Model C. Constant-service-model formulas are given in Table D.6. Model C also has the technical name M/D/1 in the literature of queuing theory.

TABLE D.6	Queuing Formulas for Model C: Constant Service, also Called M/D/1

Average length of queue: $L_q = \dfrac{\lambda^2}{2\mu(\mu - \lambda)}$

Average waiting time in queue: $W_q = \dfrac{\lambda}{2\mu(\mu - \lambda)}$

Average number of customers in system: $L_s = L_q + \dfrac{\lambda}{\mu}$

Average time in system: $W_s = W_q + \dfrac{1}{\mu}$

Example D5 gives a constant-service-time analysis.

Example D5

A CONSTANT-SERVICE-TIME MODEL

Inman Recycling, Inc., collects and compacts aluminum cans and glass bottles in Reston, Louisiana. Its truck drivers currently wait an average of 15 minutes before emptying their loads for recycling. The cost of driver and truck time while they are in queues is valued at $60 per hour. A new automated compactor can be purchased to process truckloads at a *constant* rate of 12 trucks per hour (that is, 5 minutes per truck). Trucks arrive according to a Poisson distribution at an average rate of 8 per hour. If the new compactor is put in use, the cost will be amortized at a rate of $3 per truck unloaded.

APPROACH ▶ CEO Tony Inman hires a summer college intern to conduct an analysis to evaluate the costs versus benefits of the purchase. The intern uses the equation for W_q in Table D.6.

SOLUTION ▶

Current waiting cost/trip = (1/4 hr waiting now)($60/hr cost) = $15/trip

New system: λ = 8 trucks/hr arriving μ = 12 trucks/hr served

$$\text{Average waiting time in queue} = W_q = \frac{\lambda}{2\mu(\mu - \lambda)} = \frac{8}{2(12)(12 - 8)} = \frac{1}{12}\,\text{hr}$$

Waiting cost/trip with new compactor = (1/12 hr wait)($60/hr cost) = $5/trip

Savings with new equipment = $15(current system) − $5(new system) = $10/trip

Cost of new equipment amortized: = $ 3/trip

Net savings = $ 7/trip

INSIGHT ▶ Constant service times, usually attained through automation, help control the variability inherent in service systems. This can lower average queue length and average waiting time. Note the 2 in the denominator of the equations for L_q and W_q in Table D.6.

LEARNING EXERCISE ▶ With the new constant-service-time system, what are the average waiting time in the queue, average number of trucks in the system, and average waiting time in the system? [Answer: 0.0833 hours, 1.33 trucks, 0.1667 hours.]

RELATED PROBLEMS ▶ D.14, D.16, D.21 (D.34f is found in MyOMLab)

EXCEL OM Data File **ModDExD5.xls** can be found in MyOMLab.

ACTIVE MODEL D.3 This example is further illustrated in Active Model D.3 in MyOMLab.

Little's Law

A practical and useful relationship in queuing for any system in a *steady state* is called Little's Law. A steady state exists when a queuing system is in its normal operating condition (e.g., after customers waiting at the door when a business opens in the morning are taken care of). Little's Law can be written as either:

$$L_s = \lambda W_s \text{ (which is the same as } W_s = L_s/\lambda) \tag{D-2}$$

or:

$$L_q = \lambda W_q \text{ (which is the same as } W_q = L_q/\lambda) \tag{D-3}$$

The advantage of these formulas is that once two of the parameters are known, the other one can easily be found. This is important because in certain waiting-line situations, one of these might be easier to determine than the other.

Example D6 | LITTLE'S LAW

Customers walk into the local U.S. Post Office at an average rate of 20 per hour. On average, there are 5 people waiting in line to be served. The probability distributions that describe arrival and service times are unknown. The manager, Vicky Luo, wishes to determine how long customers are waiting in line.

APPROACH ▶ Even though the probability distributions and even the number of servers are unknown, Vicky can use Little's Law to quickly determine the average waiting time.

SOLUTION ▶ $\lambda = 20$ customers per hour

$L_q = 5$ customers

Using Equation (D-3), $W_q = L_q/\lambda$

$$= 5/20 = 0.25 \text{ hours}$$

And $(0.25 \text{ hours})(60 \text{ minutes/hour}) = 15 \text{ minutes}$

INSIGHT ▶ It can be relatively easy to count the number of arriving customers per hour, and the average number of customers in line can be estimated by counting the line length throughout the day and taking the average of those lengths. However, it would take more effort to keep track of the time that the customers enter the facility and the time that they begin being served. Little's Law eliminates the need to track actual waiting times.

LEARNING EXERCISE ▶ Vicky believes that 15 minutes is an unreasonable waiting time. She adds a server to help during busy times, and the average number of customers in line reduces to 1.2 customers. Now how long do customers wait? [Answer: 3.6 minutes.]

RELATED PROBLEMS ▶ D.25–D.30

Little's Law is also important because it makes no assumptions about the probability distributions for arrivals and service times, the number of servers, or service priority rules. The law applies to all the queuing systems discussed in this module, except the finite-population model, which we discuss next.

Model D (M/M/1 with Finite Source): Finite-Population Model

When there is a limited (or finite) population of potential customers for a service facility, we must consider a different queuing model. This model would be used, for example, if we were considering equipment repairs in a factory that has 5 machines, if we were in charge of maintenance for a fleet of 10 commuter airplanes, or if we ran a hospital ward that has 20 beds. The finite-population model allows any number of repair people (servers) to be considered.

This model differs from the three earlier queuing models because there is now a *dependent* relationship between the length of the queue and the arrival rate. Let's illustrate the extreme situation: If your factory had five machines and all were broken and awaiting repair, the arrival rate would drop to zero. In general, then, as the *waiting line* becomes longer in the finite population model, the *arrival rate* of customers or machines drops.

LO D.6 *Perform* a finite-population model analysis

The finite calling population model has the following assumptions:

1. There is only one server.
2. The population of units seeking service is finite.[4]
3. Arrivals follow a Poisson distribution, and service times are negative exponentially distributed.
4. Customers are served on a first-come, first-served basis.

Table D.7 displays the queuing formulas for the finite-population model.

TABLE D.7	**Queuing Formulas for Model D: Finite-Population, also called M/M/1 with Finite Source**

λ = average arrival rate μ = average service rate N = size of the population	Average waiting time in the queue: $$W_q = \frac{L_q}{(N - L_s)\lambda}$$
Probability that the system is empty: $$P_0 = \frac{1}{\sum\limits_{n=0}^{N} \frac{N!}{(N - n)!}\left(\frac{\lambda}{\mu}\right)^n}$$	Average time in the system: $$W_s = W_q + \frac{1}{\mu}$$
Average length of the queue: $$L_q = N - \left(\frac{\lambda + \mu}{\lambda}\right)(1 - P_0)$$	Probability of n units in the system: $$P_n = \frac{N!}{(N - n)!}\left(\frac{\lambda}{\mu}\right)^n P_0 \text{ for } n = 0, 1, ..., N$$
Average number of customers (units) in the system: $$L_s = L_q + (1 - P_0)$$	

Example D7 illustrates Model D.

Example D7 | A FINITE-POPULATION MODEL

Past records indicate that each of the 5 massive laser computer printers at the U.S. Department of Energy (DOE), in Washington, DC, needs repair after about 20 hours of use. Breakdowns have been determined to be Poisson distributed. The one technician on duty can service a printer in an average of 2 hours, following an exponential distribution. Printer downtime costs $120 per hour. The technician is paid $25 per hour.

APPROACH ▶ To compute the system's operation characteristics we note that the mean arrival rate is $\lambda = 1/20 = 0.05$ printers/hour. The mean service rate is $\mu = 1/2 = 0.50$ printers/hour.

SOLUTION ▶

1. $P_0 = \dfrac{1}{\sum\limits_{n=0}^{5} \dfrac{5!}{(5 - n)!}\left(\dfrac{0.05}{0.5}\right)^n} = 0.564$ (we leave these calculations for you to confirm)

2. $L_q = 5 - \left(\dfrac{0.05 + 0.5}{0.05}\right)(1 - P_0) = 5 - (11)(1 - 0.564) = 5 - 4.8 = 0.2$ printers

3. $L_s = 0.2 + (1 - 0.564) = 0.64$ printers

4. $W_q = \dfrac{0.2}{(5 - 0.64)(0.05)} = \dfrac{0.2}{0.22} = 0.91$ hours

5. $W_s = 0.91 + \dfrac{1}{0.50} = 2.91$ hours

We can also compute the total cost per hour:

Total hourly cost = (Average number of printers down) (Cost per downtime hour)

$\qquad\qquad\qquad$ + Cost per technician hour

$\qquad\qquad$ = (0.64)($120) + $25 = $76.80 + $25.00 = $101.80

INSIGHT ▶ Management can now determine whether these costs and wait times are acceptable. Perhaps it is time to add a second technician.

Other Queuing Approaches

Many practical waiting-line problems that occur in service systems have characteristics like those of the four mathematical models already described. Often, however, *variations* of these specific cases are present in an analysis. Service times in an automobile repair shop, for example, tend to follow the normal probability distribution instead of the exponential. A college registration system in which seniors have first choice of courses and hours over other students is an example of a first-come, first-served model with a preemptive priority queue discipline. A physical examination for military recruits is an example of a multiphase system, one that differs from the single-phase models discussed earlier in this module. A recruit first lines up to have blood drawn at one station, then waits for an eye exam at the next station, talks to a psychiatrist at the third, and is examined by a doctor for medical problems at the fourth. At each phase, the recruit must enter another queue and wait his or her turn. Many models, some very complex, have been developed to deal with situations such as these.

STUDENT TIP
When the assumptions of the 4 models we just introduced do not hold true, there are other approaches still available to us.

Summary

Queues are an important part of the world of operations management. In this module, we describe several common queuing systems and present mathematical models for analyzing them.

The most widely used queuing models include Model A (M/M/1), the basic single-server, single-phase system with Poisson arrivals and negative exponential service times; Model B (M/M/S), the multiple-server equivalent of Model A; Model C (M/D/1), a constant-service-rate model; and Model D, a finite-population system (M/M/1 with finite source). All four models allow for Poisson arrivals; first-in, first-out service; and a single-service phase. Typical operating characteristics we examine include average time spent waiting in the queue and system, average number of customers in the queue and system, idle time, and utilization rate.

A variety of queuing models exists for which all the assumptions of the traditional models need not be met. In these cases, we use more complex mathematical models or turn to a technique called *simulation*. The application of simulation to problems of queuing systems is addressed in Module F.

Key Terms

Queuing theory (p. 748)
Waiting line (queue) (p. 748)
Unlimited, or infinite, population (p. 749)
Limited, or finite, population (p. 749)
Poisson distribution (p. 750)
First-in, first-out (FIFO) rule (p. 751)
Single-server queuing system (p. 751)
Multiple-server queuing system (p. 752)
Single-phase system (p. 752)
Multiphase system (p. 752)
Negative exponential probability distribution (p. 752)

Discussion Questions

1. Name the three parts of a typical queuing system.
2. When designing a waiting line system, what "qualitative" concerns need to be considered?
3. Name the three factors that govern the structure of "arrivals" in a queuing system.
4. State the seven common measures of queuing system performance.
5. State the assumptions of the "basic" single-server queuing model (Model A, or M/M/1).
6. Is it good or bad to operate a supermarket bakery system on a strict first-come, first-served basis? Why?
7. Describe what is meant by the waiting-line terms *balk* and *renege*. Provide an example of each.
8. Which is larger, W_s or W_q? Explain.
9. Briefly describe three situations in which the first-in, first-out (FIFO) discipline rule is not applicable in queuing analysis.
10. Describe the behavior of a waiting line where $\lambda > \mu$. Use both analysis and intuition.
11. Discuss the likely outcome of a waiting line system where $\mu > \lambda$ but only by a tiny amount (e.g., $\mu = 4.1$, $\lambda = 4$).

12. Provide examples of four situations in which there is a limited, or finite, waiting line.
13. What are the components of the following queuing systems? Draw and explain the configuration of each.
    a) Barbershop
    b) Car wash
    c) Laundromat
    d) Small grocery store
14. Do doctors' offices generally have random arrival rates for patients? Are service times random? Under what circumstances might service times be constant?

15. What happens if two single-server systems have the same mean arrival and service rates, but the service time is constant in one and exponential in the other?
16. What dollar value do you place on yourself per hour that you spend waiting in lines? What value do your classmates place on themselves? Why do the values differ?
17. Why is Little's Law a useful queuing concept?

Using Software to Solve Queuing Problems

Both Excel OM and POM for Windows may be used to analyze all but the last two homework problems in this module.

✕ USING EXCEL OM

Excel OM's Waiting-Line program handles all four of the models developed in this module. Program D.1 illustrates our first model, the M/M/1 system, using the data from Example D1.

Program **D.1**

Using Excel OM for Queuing

Example D1's (Golden Muffler Shop) data are illustrated in the M/M/1 model.

P USING POM FOR WINDOWS

There are several POM for Windows queuing models from which to select in that program's Waiting-Line module. The program can include an economic analysis of cost data, and, as an option, you may display probabilities of various numbers of people/items in the system. See Appendix IV for further details.

Solved Problems   Virtual Office Hours help is available in MyOMLab.

SOLVED PROBLEM D.1

Sid Das Brick Distributors in Jamaica currently employs 1 worker whose job is to load bricks on outgoing company trucks. An average of 24 trucks per day, or 3 per hour, arrive at the loading platform, according to a Poisson distribution. The worker loads them at a rate of 4 trucks per hour, following approximately the exponential distribution in his service times.

Das believes that adding an additional brick loader will substantially improve the firm's productivity. He estimates that a 2-person crew loading each truck will double the loading rate (μ) from 4 trucks per hour to 8 trucks per hour. Analyze the effect on the queue of such a change, and compare the results to those achieved with one worker. What is the probability that there will be more than 3 trucks either being loaded or waiting?

SOLUTION

	NUMBER OF BRICK LOADERS	
	1	**2**
Truck arrival rate (λ)	3/hr	3/hr
Loading rate (μ)	4/hr	8/hr
Average number in system (L_s)	3 trucks	.6 truck
Average time in system (W_s)	1 hr	.2 hr
Average number in queue (L_q)	2.25 trucks	.225 truck
Average time in queue (W_q)	.75 hr	.075 hr
Utilization rate (ρ)	.75	.375
Probability system empty (P_0)	.25	.625

Probability of More than *k* Trucks in System

	PROBABILITY N > K	
K	**1 LOADER**	**2 LOADERS**
0	.75	.375
1	.56	.141
2	.42	.053
3	.32	.020

These results indicate that when only one loader is employed, the average truck must wait three-quarters of an hour before it is loaded. Furthermore, there is an average of 2.25 trucks waiting in line to be loaded. This situation may be unacceptable to management. Note also the decline in queue size after the addition of a second loader.

SOLVED PROBLEM D.2

Truck drivers working for Sid Das (see Solved Problem D.1) earn an average of $10 per hour. Brick loaders receive about $6 per hour. Truck drivers waiting *in the queue or at the loading platform* are drawing a salary but are productively idle and unable to generate revenue during that time. What would be the *hourly* cost savings to the firm if it employed 2 loaders instead of 1?

Referring to the data in Solved Problem D.1, we note that the average number of trucks *in the system* is 3 when there is only 1 loader and .6 when there are 2 loaders.

SOLUTION

	NUMBER OF LOADERS	
	1	**2**
Truck driver idle time costs [(Average number of trucks) × (Hourly rate)] = (3)($10) =	$30	$ 6 = (.6)($10)
Loading costs	6	12 = (2)($6)
Total expected cost per hour	$36	$18

The firm will save $18 per hour by adding another loader.

SOLVED PROBLEM D.3

Sid Das is considering building a second platform or gate to speed the process of loading trucks. This system, he thinks, will be even more efficient than simply hiring another loader to help out on the first platform (as in Solved Problem D.1).

Assume that the worker at each platform will be able to load 4 trucks per hour each and that trucks will continue to arrive at the rate of 3 per hour. Then apply the appropriate equations to find the waiting line's new operating conditions. Is this new approach indeed speedier than hiring a second loader, as Das has considered in the Solved Problems above?

SOLUTION

$$P_0 = \cfrac{1}{\left[\sum_{n=0}^{1} \frac{1}{n!}\left(\frac{3}{4}\right)^n\right] + \frac{1}{2!}\left(\frac{3}{4}\right)^2 \frac{2(4)}{2(4)-3}}$$

$$= \cfrac{1}{1 + \frac{3}{4} + \frac{1}{2}\left(\frac{3}{4}\right)^2\left(\frac{8}{8-3}\right)} = .4545$$

$$L_s = \frac{3(4)(3/4)^2}{(1)!(8-3)^2}(.4545) + \frac{3}{4} = .873$$

$$W_s = \frac{.873}{3} = .291 \text{ hr}$$

$$L_q = .873 - 3/4 = .123$$

$$W_q = \frac{.123}{3} = .041 \text{ hr}$$

Looking back at Solved Problem D.1, we see that although length of the *queue* and average time in the queue are lowest when a second platform is open, the average number of trucks in the *system* and average time spent waiting in the system are smallest when two workers are employed at a *single* platform. Thus, we would probably recommend not building a second platform.

SOLVED PROBLEM D.4

Mount Sinai Hospital's orthopedic care unit has 5 beds, which are virtually always occupied by patients who have just undergone orthopedic surgery. One registered nurse is on duty in the unit in each of the three 8-hour shifts. About every 2 hours (following a Poisson distribution), one of the patients requires a nurse's attention. The nurse will then spend an average of 30 minutes (negative exponentially distributed) assisting the patient and updating medical records regarding the problem and care provided.

Because immediate service is critical to the 5 patients, two important questions are: What is the average number of patients either waiting for or being attended by the nurse? What is the average time that a patient spends waiting for the nurse to arrive?

SOLUTION

$$\lambda = .5 \text{ arrivals/hour}$$
$$\mu = 2 \text{ served/hour}$$
$$N = 5 \text{ patients}$$

$$P_0 = \cfrac{1}{\displaystyle\sum_{n=0}^{5} \frac{5!}{(5-n)!}\left(\frac{.5}{2}\right)^n} = 0.20$$

$$L_q = 5 - \left(\frac{.5+2}{.5}\right)(1 - 0.20) = 1 \text{ patient}$$

$$L_s = 1 + (1 - 0.20) = 1.8 \text{ patients}$$

$$W_q = \frac{1}{(5-1.8)(.5)} = .62 \text{ hours} = 37.28 \text{ min.}$$

$$W_s = .62 + \frac{1}{2} = 1.12 \text{ hours} = 67.28 \text{ min}$$

So the average number of patients in the system = 1.8
Average wait time in the queue = .62 hours = 37.28 minutes

Problems

Note: **PX** means the problem may be solved with POM for Windows and/or Excel OM.

Problems D.1–D.39 relate to The Variety of Queuing Models

- **D.1** Customers arrive at Rich Dunn's Styling Shop at a rate of 3 per hour, distributed in a Poisson fashion. Rich's service times follow a negative exponential distribution, and Rich can complete an average of 5 haircuts per hour.
  a) Find the average number of customers waiting for haircuts.
  b) Find the average number of customers in the shop.
  c) Find the average time a customer waits until it is his or her turn.
  d) Find the average time a customer spends in the shop.
  e) Find the percentage of time that Rich is busy. **PX**

- **D.2** There is only one copying machine in the student lounge of the business school. Students arrive at the rate of $\lambda = 40$ per hour (according to a Poisson distribution). Copying takes an average of 40 seconds, or $\mu = 90$ per hour (according to a negative exponential distribution). Compute the following:
  a) The percentage of time that the machine is used.
  b) The average length of the queue.
  c) The average number of students in the system.
  d) The average time spent waiting in the queue.
  e) The average time in the system. **PX**

- **D.3** Paul Fenster owns and manages a chili-dog and soft-drink stand near the Kean U. campus. While Paul can service 30 customers per hour on the average (μ), he gets only 20 customers per hour (λ). Because Paul could wait on 50% more customers than actually visit his stand, it doesn't make sense to him that he should have any waiting lines.

  Paul hires you to examine the situation and to determine some characteristics of his queue. After looking into the problem, you find it follows the six conditions for a single-server waiting line (as seen in Model A). What are your findings? **PX**

- **D.4** Dr. Tarun Gupta, a Michigan vet, is running a rabies vaccination clinic for dogs at the local grade school. Tarun can "shoot" a dog every 3 minutes. It is estimated that the dogs will arrive independently and randomly throughout the day at a rate of one dog every 6 minutes according to a Poisson distribution. Also assume that Tarun's shooting times are negative exponentially distributed. Compute the following:
  a) The probability that Tarun is idle.
  b) The proportion of the time that Tarun is busy.
  c) The average number of dogs being vaccinated and waiting to be vaccinated.
  d) The average number of dogs waiting to be vaccinated.
  e) The average time a dog waits before getting vaccinated.

  f) The average amount of time a dog spends waiting in line and being vaccinated. **PX**

- **D.5** The pharmacist at Arnold Palmer Hospital, Wende Huehn-Brown, receives 12 requests for prescriptions each hour, Poisson distributed. It takes her a mean time of 4 minutes to fill each, following a negative exponential distribution. Use the waiting-line table, Table D.5, and $W_q = L_q/\lambda$, to answer these questions.
  a) What is the average number of prescriptions in the queue?
  b) How long will the average prescription spend in the queue?
  c) Wende decides to hire a second pharmacist, Ajay Aggerwal, with whom she went to school and who operates at the same speed in filling prescriptions. How will the answers to parts (a) and (b) change? **PX**

- **D.6** Calls arrive at Lynn Ann Fish's hotel switchboard at a rate of 2 per minute. The average time to handle each is 20 seconds. There is only one switchboard operator at the current time. The Poisson and negative exponential distributions appear to be relevant in this situation.
  a) What is the probability that the operator is busy?
  b) What is the average time that a customer must wait before reaching the operator?
  c) What is the average number of calls waiting to be answered? **PX**

- **D.7** Automobiles arrive at the drive-through window at the downtown Baton Rouge, Louisiana, post office at the rate of 4 every 10 minutes. The average service time is 2 minutes. The Poisson distribution is appropriate for the arrival rate and service times are negative exponentially distributed.
  a) What is the average time a car is in the system?
  b) What is the average number of cars in the system?
  c) What is the average number of cars waiting to receive service?
  d) What is the average time a car is in the queue?
  e) What is the probability that there are no cars at the window?
  f) What percentage of the time is the postal clerk busy?
  g) What is the probability that there are exactly 2 cars in the system?
  h) By how much would your answer to part (a) be reduced if a second drive-through window, with its own server, were added? **PX**

- **D.8** Virginia's Ron McPherson Electronics Corporation retains a service crew to repair machine breakdowns that occur on average $\lambda = 3$ per 8-hour workday (approximately Poisson in nature). The crew can service an average of $\mu = 8$ machines per workday, with a repair time distribution that resembles the negative exponential distribution.
  a) What is the utilization rate of this service system?
  b) What is the average downtime for a broken machine?

c) How many machines are waiting to be serviced at any given time?

d) What is the probability that more than 1 machine is in the system? The probability that more than 2 are broken and waiting to be repaired or being serviced? More than 3? More than 4? **Px**

•• **D.9** Neve Commercial Bank is the only bank in the town of York, Pennsylvania. On a typical Friday, an average of 10 customers per hour arrive at the bank to transact business. There is currently one teller at the bank, and the average time required to transact business is 4 minutes. It is assumed that service times may be described by the negative exponential distribution. If a single teller is used, find:

a) The average time in the line.

b) The average number in the line.

c) The average time in the system.

d) The average number in the system.

e) The probability that the bank is empty.

f) CEO Benjamin Neve is considering adding a second teller (who would work at the same rate as the first) to reduce the waiting time for customers. A single line would be used, and the customer at the front of the line would go to the first available bank teller. He assumes that this will cut the waiting time in half. If a second teller is added, find the new answers to parts (a) to (e). **Px**

•• **D.10** Beate Klingenberg manages a Poughkeepsie, New York, movie theater complex called Cinema 8. Each of the eight auditoriums plays a different film; the schedule staggers starting times to avoid the large crowds that would occur if all four movies started at the same time. The theater has a single ticket booth and a cashier who can maintain an average service rate of 280 patrons per hour. Service times are assumed to follow a negative exponential distribution. Arrivals on a normally active day are Poisson distributed and average 210 per hour.

To determine the efficiency of the current ticket operation, Beate wishes to examine several queue-operating characteristics.

a) Find the average number of moviegoers waiting in line to purchase a ticket.

b) What percentage of the time is the cashier busy?

c) What is the average time that a customer spends in the system?

d) What is the average time spent waiting in line to get to the ticket window?

e) What is the probability that there are more than two people in the system? More than three people? More than four? **Px**

•• **D.11** Bill Youngdahl has been collecting data at the TU student grill. He has found that, between 5:00 P.M. and 7:00 P.M., students arrive at the grill at a rate of 25 per hour (Poisson distributed) and service time takes an average of 2 minutes (negative exponential distribution). There is only 1 server, who can work on only 1 order at a time.

a) What is the average number of students in line?

b) What is the average time a student is in the grill area?

c) Suppose that a second server can be added to team up with the first (and, in effect, act as 1 faster server). This would reduce the average service time to 90 seconds. How would this affect the average time a student is in the grill area?

d) Suppose a second server is added and the 2 servers act independently, with *each* taking an average of 2 minutes. What would be the average time a student is in the system?

••• **D.12** The wheat harvesting season in the American Midwest is short, and farmers deliver their truckloads of wheat to a giant central storage bin within a 2-week span. Because of this, wheat-filled trucks waiting to unload and return to the fields have been known to back up for a block at the receiving bin. The central bin is owned cooperatively, and it is to every farmer's benefit to make the unloading/storage process as efficient as possible. The cost of grain deterioration caused by unloading delays and the cost of truck rental and idle driver time are significant concerns to the cooperative members. Although farmers have difficulty quantifying crop damage, it is easy to assign a waiting and unloading cost for truck and driver of $18 per hour. During the 2-week harvest season, the storage bin is open and operated 16 hours per day, 7 days per week, and can unload 35 trucks per hour according to a negative exponential distribution. Full trucks arrive all day long (during the hours the bin is open) at a rate of about 30 per hour, following a Poisson pattern.

To help the cooperative get a handle on the problem of lost time while trucks are waiting in line or unloading at the bin, find the following:

a) The average number of trucks in the unloading system

b) The average time per truck in the system

c) The utilization rate for the bin area

d) The probability that there are more than three trucks in the system at any given time

e) The total daily cost to the farmers of having their trucks tied up in the unloading process

f) As mentioned, the cooperative uses the storage bin heavily only 2 weeks per year. Farmers estimate that enlarging the bin would cut unloading costs by 50% next year. It will cost $9,000 to do so during the off-season. Would it be worth the expense to enlarge the storage area? **Px**

••• **D.13** Janson's Department Store in Stark, Ohio, maintains a successful catalog sales department in which a clerk takes orders by telephone. If the clerk is occupied on one line, incoming phone calls to the catalog department are answered automatically by a recording machine and asked to wait. As soon as the clerk is free, the party who has waited the longest is transferred and serviced first. Calls come in at a rate of about 12 per hour. The clerk can take an order in an average of 4 minutes. Calls tend to follow a Poisson distribution, and service times tend to be negative exponential.

The cost of the clerk is $10 per hour, but because of lost goodwill and sales, Janson's loses about $25 per hour of customer time spent waiting for the clerk to take an order.

a) What is the average time that catalog customers must wait before their calls are transferred to the order clerk?

b) What is the average number of customers waiting to place an order?

c) Pamela Janson is considering adding a second clerk to take calls. The store's cost would be the same $10 per hour. Should she hire another clerk? Explain your decision. **Px**

• **D.14** Altug's Coffee Shop decides to install an automatic coffee vending machine outside one of its stores to reduce the number of people standing in line inside. Mehmet Altug charges $3.50 per cup. However, it takes too long for people to make change. The service time is a constant 3 minutes, and the arrival rate is 15 per hour (Poisson distributed).

a) What is the average wait in line?

b) What is the average number of people in line?

c) Mehmet raises the price to $5 per cup and takes 60 seconds off the service time. However, because the coffee is now so expensive, the arrival rate drops to 10 per hour. Now what are the average wait time and the average number of people in the queue (waiting)? **Px**

••• **D.15** The typical subway station in Washington, DC, has six turnstiles, each of which can be controlled by the station manager to be used for either entrance or exit control—but never for both. The manager must decide at different times of the day how many turnstiles to use for entering passengers and how many to use for exiting passengers.

At the George Washington University (GWU) Station, passengers enter the station at a rate of about 84 per minute between the hours of 7 A.M. and 9 A.M. Passengers exiting trains at the stop reach the exit turnstile area at a rate of about 48 per minute during the same morning rush hours. Each turnstile can allow an average of 30 passengers per minute to enter or exit. Arrival and service times have been thought to follow Poisson and negative exponential distributions, respectively. Assume riders form a common queue at both entry and exit turnstile areas and proceed to the first empty turnstile.

Kuosumo/Fotolia

The GWU station manager, Gerald Aase, does not want the average passenger at his station to have to wait in a turnstile line for more than 6 seconds, nor does he want more than 8 people in any queue at any average time.
a) How many turnstiles should be opened in each direction every morning?
b) Discuss the assumptions underlying the solution of this problem using queuing theory. **Px**

•• **D.16** Renuka Jain's Car Wash takes a constant time of 4.5 minutes in its automated car wash cycle. Autos arrive following a Poisson distribution at the rate of 10 per hour. Renuka wants to know:
a) The average waiting time in line.
b) The average length of the line.

••• **D.17** Debra Bishop's cabinet-making shop, in Des Moines, has five tools that automate the drilling of holes for the installation of hinges. Each machine needs an average of 3 "resettings" every 8-hour day, following the Poisson distribution. There is a single technician for setting these machines. Her service times are negative exponential, averaging 2 hours each.
a) What is the probability this system is empty?
b) What is the average number of machines in the system (i.e., being reset or waiting to be reset)?
c) What is the average waiting time in the queue? **Px**

••• **D.18** A technician monitors a group of 5 computers that run an automated manufacturing facility. It takes an average of 15 minutes (negative exponentially distributed) to adjust a computer that develops a problem. On average, one of the computers requires adjustment every 85 minutes. Determine the following:
a) The average number of computers waiting for adjustment (i.e., in the queue)
b) The average number in the system
c) The probability no computer needs adjustment **Px**

••• **D.19** One mechanic services 5 drilling machines for a steel plate manufacturer. Machines break down on an average of once every 6 working days, and breakdowns tend to follow a Poisson distribution. The mechanic can handle an average of one repair job per day. Repairs follow a negative exponential distribution.

a) On the average, how many machines are waiting for service?
b) On the average, what is the *waiting* time to be serviced? **Px**

••• **D.20** Ted Glickman, the administrator at D.C. General Hospital emergency room, faces the problem of providing treatment for patients who arrive at different rates during the day. There are four doctors available to treat patients when needed. If not needed, they can be assigned other responsibilities (such as doing lab tests, reports, X-ray diagnoses) or else rescheduled to work at other hours.

It is important to provide quick and responsive treatment, and Ted thinks that, on the average, patients should not have to sit in the waiting area for more than 5 minutes before being seen by a doctor. Patients are treated on a first-come, first-served basis and see the first available doctor after waiting in the queue. The arrival pattern for a typical day is as follows:

TIME	ARRIVAL RATE
9 A.M.–3 P.M.	6 patients/hour
3 P.M.–8 P.M.	4 patients/hour
8 P.M.–midnight	12 patients/hour

Arrivals follow a Poisson distribution, and treatment times, 12 minutes on the average, follow the negative exponential pattern.
a) How many doctors should be on duty during each period to maintain the level of patient care expected?
b) What condition would exist if only one doctor were on duty between 9 A.M. and 3 P.M.? **Px**

••• **D.21** The Pontchartrain Bridge is a 16-mile toll bridge that crosses Lake Pontchartrain in New Orleans. Currently, there are 7 toll booths, each staffed by an employee. Since Hurricane Katrina, the Port Authority has been considering replacing the employees with machines. Many factors must be considered because the employees are unionized. However, one of the Port Authority's concerns is the effect that replacing the employees with machines will have on the times that drivers spend in the system. Customers arrive to any one toll booth at a rate of 10 per minute. In the exact change lanes with employees, the service time is essentially constant at 5 seconds for each driver. With machines, the average service time would still be 5 seconds, but it would be negative exponential rather than constant, because it takes time for the coins to rattle around in the machine. Contrast the two systems for a single lane. **Px**

••• **D.22** The registration area has just opened at a large convention of dentists in Tallahassee, Florida. There are 200 people arriving per hour (Poisson distributed), and the cost of their waiting time in the queue is valued at $100 per person per hour. The Tallahassee Convention Center provides servers to register guests at a fee of $15 per person per hour. It takes about one minute to register an attendee (negative exponentially distributed). A single waiting line, with multiple servers, is set up.
a) What is the minimum number of servers for this system?
b) What is the optimal number of servers for this system?
c) What is the cost for the system, per hour, at the optimum number of servers?
d) What is the server utilization rate with the minimum number of servers? **Px**

•• **D.23** Refer to Problem D.22. A new registration manager, Dwayne Cole, is hired who initiates a program to entertain the people in line with a juggler whom he pays $15/hour. This reduces the waiting costs to $50 per hour.
a) What is the optimal number of servers?
b) What is the cost for the system, per hour, at the optimal service level?

•••• **D.24** The Chattanooga Furniture store gets an average of 50 customers per shift. Marilyn Helms, the manager, wants to calculate whether she should hire 1, 2, 3, or 4 salespeople. She has determined that average waiting times will be 7 minutes with one salesperson, 4 minutes with two salespeople, 3 minutes with three salespeople, and 2 minutes with four salespeople. She has estimated the cost per minute that customers wait at $1. The cost per salesperson per shift (including fringe benefits) is $70.

How many salespeople should be hired?

•• **D.25** During the afternoon peak hours the First Bank of Dubuque has an average of 40 customers arriving every hour. There is also an average of 8 customers at First Bank at any time. The probability of the arrival distribution is unknown. How long does the average customer spend in the bank?

•• **D.26** An average of 9 cars can be seen in the system (both the drive-through line and the drive-through window) at Burger Universe. Approximately every 20 seconds, a car attempts to enter the drive-through line; however, 40% of cars simply leave the restaurant because they're discouraged by the length of the line. On average, how long does a car spend going through the drive-through at Burger Universe?

•• **D.27** Lobster World stores approximately 1,000 pounds of fish on average. In a typical day, the busy restaurant cooks and sells 360 (raw) pounds of fish. How long do the fish stay in storage on average?

•• **D.28** Gamma Bank processes a typical loan application in 2.4 weeks. Customers fill out 30 loan applications per week. On average how many loan applications are being processed somewhere in the system at Gamma Bank?

•• **D.29** Fisher's Furniture Store sells $800,000 worth of furniture to customers on credit each month. The Accounts Receivable balance in the accounting books averages $2 million. On average, how long are customers taking to pay their bills?

•• **D.30** Vacation Inns, a chain of hotels operating in the southeastern region of the U.S., uses a toll-free telephone number to take reservations for all of its hotels. An average of 12 calls are received per hour. The probability distribution that describes the arrivals is unknown. Over a period of time, it is determined that the average caller spends 6 minutes on hold waiting for service. Find the average number of callers in the queue by using Little's Law.

Additional problems **D.31–D.39** *are available in* My**OM**Lab.

CASE STUDIES

New England Foundry

For more than 75 years, New England Foundry, Inc. (NEFI), has manufactured wood stoves for home use. In recent years, with increasing energy prices, president George Mathison has seen sales triple. This dramatic increase has made it difficult for George to maintain quality in all his wood stoves and related products.

Unlike other companies manufacturing wood stoves, NEFI is in the business of making *only* stoves and stove-related products. Its major products are the Warmglo I, the Warmglo II, the Warmglo III, and the Warmglo IV. The Warmglo I is the smallest wood stove, with a heat output of 30,000 BTUs, and the Warmglo IV is the largest, with a heat output of 60,000 BTUs.

The Warmglo III outsold all other models by a wide margin. Its heat output and available accessories were ideal for the typical home. The Warmglo III also had a number of other outstanding features that made it one of the most attractive and heat-efficient stoves on the market. These features, along with the accessories, resulted in expanding sales and prompted George to build a new factory to manufacture the Warmglo III model. An overview diagram of the factory is shown in Figure D.6.

The new foundry used the latest equipment, including a new Disamatic that helped in manufacturing stove parts. Regardless of new equipment or procedures, casting operations have remained basically unchanged for hundreds of years. To begin with, a wooden pattern is made for every cast-iron piece in the stove. The wooden pattern is an exact duplicate of the cast-iron piece that is to be manufactured. All NEFI patterns are made by Precision Patterns, Inc. and are stored in the pattern shop and maintenance room. Next, a specially formulated sand is molded around the wooden pattern. There can be two or more sand molds for each pattern. The sand is mixed and the molds are made in the molding room. When the wooden pattern is removed, the resulting sand molds form a negative image of the desired casting. Next, molds are transported to the casting room, where molten iron is poured into them and allowed to cool. When the iron has solidified, the molds are moved into the cleaning, grinding, and preparation room, where they are dumped into large vibrators that shake most of the sand from the casting. The rough castings are then subjected to both sandblasting to remove the rest of the sand and grinding to finish some of their surfaces. Castings are then painted with a special heat-resistant paint, assembled into workable stoves, and inspected for manufacturing defects that may have gone undetected. Finally, finished stoves are moved to storage and shipping, where they are packaged and transported to the appropriate locations.

At present, the pattern shop and the maintenance department are located in the same room. One large counter is used by both maintenance personnel, who store tools and parts (which are mainly used by the casting department), and sand molders, who need various patterns for the molding operation. Pete Nawler and Bob Dillman, who work behind the counter, can service a total of 10 people per hour (about 5 per hour each). On average, 4 people from casting and 3 from molding arrive at the counter each hour. People from molding and casting departments arrive randomly, and to be served, they form a single line.

Pete and Bob have always had a policy of first come, first served. Because of the location of the pattern shop and maintenance department, it takes an average of 3 minutes for an individual from the casting department to walk to the pattern and maintenance room, and it takes about 1 minute for an individual to walk from the molding department to the pattern and maintenance room.

After observing the operation of the pattern shop and maintenance room for several weeks, George decided to make some changes to the factory layout. An overview of these changes appears in Figure D.7.

Separating the maintenance shop from the pattern shop would have a number of advantages. It would take people from the casting department only 1 minute instead of 3 to get to the new maintenance room. The time from molding to the pattern shop would be unchanged. Using motion and time studies, George was also able to determine that improving the layout of the maintenance room would allow Bob to serve 6 people from the casting department per hour; improving the layout of the pattern department would allow Pete to serve 7 people from the molding shop per hour.

Discussion Questions

1. How much time would the new layout save?
2. If casting personnel were paid $9.50 per hour and molding personnel were paid $11.75 per hour, how much could be saved per hour with the new factory layout?
3. Should George have made the change in layout?

The Winter Park Hotel

Lori Cook, manager of the Winter Park Hotel, is considering how to restructure the front desk to reach an optimum level of staff efficiency and guest service. At present, the hotel has five clerks on duty, each with a separate waiting line, during peak check-in time of 3:00 P.M. to 5:00 P.M. Observation of arrivals during this period shows that an average of 90 guests arrive each hour (although there is no upward limit on the number that could arrive at any given time). It takes an average of 3 minutes for the front-desk clerk to register each guest.

Ms. Cook is considering three plans for improving guest service by reducing the length of time that guests spend waiting in line. The first proposal would designate one employee as a quick-service clerk for guests registering under corporate accounts, a market segment that fills about 30% of all occupied rooms. Because corporate guests are preregistered, their registration takes just 2 minutes. With these guests separated from the rest of the clientele, the average time for registering a typical guest would climb to 3.4 minutes. Under this plan, noncorporate guests would choose any of the remaining four lines.

The second plan is to implement a single-line system. All guests could form a single waiting line to be served by whichever of five clerks became available. This option would require sufficient lobby space for what could be a substantial queue.

The use of an automatic teller machine (ATM) for check-ins is the basis of the third proposal. This ATM would provide about the same service rate as would a clerk. Because initial use of this technology might be minimal, Cook estimates that 20% of customers, primarily frequent guests, would be willing to use the machines. (This might be a conservative estimate if guests perceive direct benefits from using the ATM, as bank customers do. Citibank reports that some 95% of its Manhattan customers use its ATMs.) Ms. Cook would set up a single queue for customers who prefer human check-in clerks. This line would be served by the five clerks, although Cook is hopeful that the ATM will allow a reduction to four.

Discussion Questions

1. Determine the average amount of time that a guest spends checking in. How would this change under each of the stated options?
2. Which option do you recommend?

- **Additional Case Study:** Visit MyOMLab for this additional free case study:
  Pantry Shopper: The case requires the redesign of a checkout system for a supermarket.

Endnotes

1. When the arrival rates follow a Poisson process with mean arrival rate, λ, the time between arrivals follows a negative exponential distribution with mean time between arrivals of $1/\lambda$. The negative exponential distribution, then, is also representative of a Poisson process but describes the time between arrivals and specifies that these time intervals are completely random.

2. The term *FIFS* (first-in, first-served) is often used in place of FIFO. Another discipline, LIFS (last-in, first-served), also called last-in, first-out (LIFO), is common when material is stacked or piled so that the items on top are used first.

3. In queuing notation, the first letter refers to the arrivals (where M stands for Poisson distribution); the second letter refers to service (where M is again a Poisson distribution, which is the same as an exponential rate for service—and D is a constant service rate); the third symbol refers to the number of servers. So an M/D/1 system (our Model C) has Poisson arrivals, constant service, and one server.

4. Although there is no definite number that we can use to divide finite from infinite populations, the general rule of thumb is this: If the number in the queue is a significant proportion of the calling population, use a finite queuing model.

Module D *Rapid Review*

Main Heading	Review Material	MyOMLab
QUEUING THEORY (pp. 748–749)	■ **Queuing theory**—A body of knowledge about waiting lines. ■ **Waiting line (queue)**—Items or people in a line awaiting service.	Concept Questions: 1.1–1.3
CHARACTERISTICS OF A WAITING-LINE SYSTEM (pp. 749–752)	The three parts of a waiting-line, or queuing, system are: *Arrivals or inputs to the system; queue discipline, or the waiting line itself;* and *the service facility.* ■ **Unlimited, or infinite, population**—A queue in which a virtually unlimited number of people or items could request the services, or in which the number of customers or arrivals on hand at any given moment is a very small portion of potential arrivals. ■ **Limited, or finite, population**—A queue in which there are only a limited number of potential users of the service. ■ **Poisson distribution**—A discrete probability distribution that often describes the arrival rate in queuing theory: $$P(x) = \frac{e^{-\lambda}\lambda^x}{x!} \text{ for } x = 0, 1, 2, 3, 4, \ldots \qquad \text{(D-1)}$$ A queue is *limited* when it cannot, either by law or because of physical restrictions, increase to an infinite length. A queue is *unlimited* when its size is unrestricted. *Queue discipline* refers to the rule by which customers in the line are to receive service: ■ **First-in, first-out (FIFO) rule**—A queue discipline in which the first customers in line receive the first service. ■ **Single-server (single-channel) queuing system**—A service system with one line and one server. ■ **Multiple-server (multiple-channel) queuing system**—A service system with one waiting line but with more than one server (channel). ■ **Single-phase system**—A system in which the customer receives service from only one station and then exits the system. ■ **Multiphase system**—A system in which the customer receives services from several stations before exiting the system. ■ **Negative exponential probability distribution**—A continuous probability distribution often used to describe the service time in a queuing system.	Concept Questions: 2.1–2.4
QUEUING COSTS (pp. 753–754)	Operations managers must recognize the trade-off that takes place between two costs: the cost of providing good service and the cost of customer or machine waiting time.	Concept Questions: 3.1–3.4
THE VARIETY OF QUEUING MODELS (pp. 754–765)	*Model A: Single-Server System (M/M/1):* *Queuing Formulas:* $\quad \lambda$ = mean number of arrivals per time period $\quad \mu$ = mean number of people or items served per time period $\quad L_s$ = average number of units in the system = $\lambda/(\mu - \lambda)$ $\quad W_s$ = average time a unit spends in the system = $1/(\mu - \lambda)$ $\quad L_q$ = average number of units waiting in the queue = $\lambda^2/[\mu(\mu - \lambda)]$ $\quad W_q$ = average time a unit spends waiting in the queue = $\lambda/[\mu(\mu - \lambda)] = L_q/\lambda$ $\quad \rho$ = utilization factor for the system = λ/μ $\quad P_0$ = probability of 0 units in the system (i.e., the service unit is idle) = $1 - (\lambda/\mu)$ $\quad P_{n>k}$ = probability of > k units in the system = $(\lambda/\mu)^{k+1}$ *Model B: Multiple-Server System (M/M/S):* $$P_0 = \frac{1}{\left[\sum_{n=0}^{M-1}\frac{1}{n!}\left(\frac{\lambda}{\mu}\right)^n\right] + \frac{1}{M!}\left(\frac{\lambda}{\mu}\right)^M \frac{M\mu}{M\mu - \lambda}} \text{ for } M\mu > \lambda$$ $$L_s = \frac{\lambda\mu(\lambda/\mu)^M}{(M-1)!(M\mu - \lambda)^2}P_0 + \frac{\lambda}{\mu}$$ $$W_s = L_s/\lambda \quad L_q = L_s - (\lambda/\mu) \quad W_q = L_q/\lambda$$ *Model C: Constant Service (M/D/1):* $$L_q = \lambda^2/[2\mu(\mu - \lambda)] \qquad W_q = \lambda/[2\mu(\mu - \lambda)]$$ $$L_s = L_q + (\lambda/\mu) \qquad W_s = W_q + (1/\mu)$$	Concept Questions: 4.1–4.4 Problems: D.1–D.14, D.16–D.21, D.24–D.39 Virtual Office Hours for Solved Problems: D.1–D.4 **ACTIVE** MODELS **D.1, D.2, D.3**

Main Heading   **Review Material**

Little's Law

A useful relationship in queuing for any system in a steady state is called Little's Law:

$$L_s = \lambda W_s \text{ (which is the same as } W_s = L_s/\lambda) \qquad \text{(D-2)}$$

$$L_q = \lambda W_q \text{ (which is the same as } W_q = L_q/\lambda) \qquad \text{(D-3)}$$

Model D: *Finite Population (M/M/1 with finite source)*

With a limited, or finite, population, there is a *dependent* relationship between the length of the queue and the arrival rate. As the *waiting* line becomes longer, the *arrival rate* drops.

N = size of the popuation

$$P_0 = \cfrac{1}{\sum\limits_{n=0}^{N} \cfrac{N!}{(N-n)!}\left(\cfrac{\lambda}{\mu}\right)^n}$$

$$L_q = N - \left(\frac{\lambda + \mu}{\lambda}\right)(1 - P_0)$$

$$L_s = L_q + (1 - P_0)$$

$$W_q = \frac{L_q}{(N - L_s)\lambda}$$

$$W_s = W_q + \frac{1}{\mu}$$

$$P_n = \frac{N!}{(N-n)!}\left(\frac{\lambda}{\mu}\right)^n P_0 \quad \text{for } n = 0, 1,..., N$$

OTHER QUEUING APPROACHES (p. 765)

Often, *variations* of the four basic queuing models are present in an analysis. Many models, some very complex, have been developed to deal with such variations.

Concept Question: 5.1

Self Test

- **Before taking the self-test,** refer to the learning objectives listed at the beginning of the module and the key terms listed at the end of the module.

LO D.1 Which of the following is *not* a key operating characteristic for a queuing system?
a) Utilization rate
b) Percent idle time
c) Average time spent waiting in the system and in the queue
d) Average number of customers in the system and in the queue
e) Average number of customers who renege

LO D.2 Customers enter the waiting line at a cafeteria's only cash register on a first-come, first-served basis. The arrival rate follows a Poisson distribution, while service times follow an exponential distribution. If the average number of arrivals is 6 per minute and the average service rate of a single server is 10 per minute, what is the average number of customers in the system?
a) 0.6
b) 0.9
c) 1.5
d) 0.25
e) 1.0

LO D.3 In performing a cost analysis of a queuing system, the waiting time cost is sometimes based on the time in the queue and sometimes based on the time in the system. The waiting cost should be based on time in the system for which of the following situations?
a) Waiting in line to ride an amusement park ride
b) Waiting to discuss a medical problem with a doctor
c) Waiting for a picture and an autograph from a rock star
d) Waiting for a computer to be fixed so it can be placed back in service

LO D.4 Which of the following is *not* an assumption in a multiple-server queuing model?
a) Arrivals come from an infinite, or very large, population.
b) Arrivals are Poisson distributed.
c) Arrivals are treated on a first-in, first-out basis and do not balk or renege.
d) Service times follow the exponential distribution.
e) Servers each perform at their own individual speeds.

LO D.5 If everything else remains the same, including the mean arrival rate and service rate, except that the service time becomes constant instead of exponential:
a) the average queue length will be halved.
b) the average waiting time will be doubled.
c) the average queue length will increase.
d) we cannot tell from the information provided.

LO D.6 A company has one computer technician who is responsible for repairs on the company's 20 computers. As a computer breaks, the technician is called to make the repair. If the repairperson is busy, the machine must wait to be repaired. This is an example of:
a) a multiple-server system.
b) a finite population system.
c) a constant service rate system.
d) a multiphase system.
e) all of the above.

Answers: LO D.1. e; LO D.2. c; LO D.3. d; LO D.4. e; LO D.5. a; LO D.6. b.

Learning Curves

E M O D U L E

MODULE OUTLINE

◆ What Is a Learning Curve? *776*
◆ Learning Curves in Services and Manufacturing *777*
◆ Applying the Learning Curve *778*

◆ Strategic Implications of Learning Curves *782*
◆ Limitations of Learning Curves *783*

Alaska Airlines

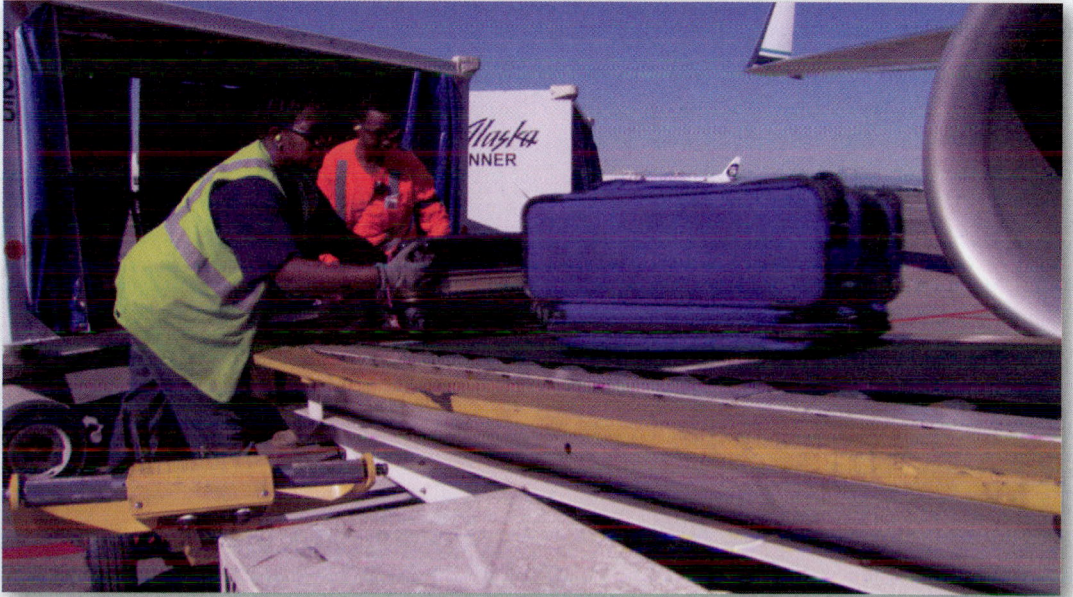

Alaska Airlines

LEARNING	LO E.1	*Define* learning curve 776
OBJECTIVES	LO E.2	*Use* the doubling concept to estimate times 778
	LO E.3	*Compute* learning-curve effects with the formula and learning-curve table approaches 779
	LO E.4	*Describe* the strategic implications of learning curves 782

Medical procedures such as heart surgery follow a learning curve. Research indicates that the death rate from heart transplants drops at a 79% learning curve, a learning rate not unlike that in many industrial settings. It appears that as doctors and medical teams improve with experience, so do your odds as a patient. If the death rate is halved every three operations, practice may indeed make perfect.

Derege/Fotolia

What Is a Learning Curve?

Most organizations learn and improve over time. As firms and employees perform a task over and over, they learn how to perform more efficiently. This means that task times and costs decrease.

Learning curves

The premise that people and organizations get better at their tasks as the tasks are repeated; sometimes called experience curves.

Learning curves are based on the premise that people and organizations become better at their tasks as the tasks are repeated. A learning curve graph (illustrated in Figure E.1) displays cost (or time) per unit versus the cumulative number of units produced. From it we see that the time needed to produce a unit decreases, usually following a negative exponential curve (part a), as the person or company produces more units. In other words, *it takes less time to complete each additional unit a firm produces*. However, we also see in Figure E.1 that the time *savings* in completing each subsequent unit *decreases*. These are the major attributes of the learning curve.

Learning curves were first applied to industry in a report by T. P. Wright of Curtis-Wright Corp. in 1936.[1] Wright described how direct labor costs of making a particular airplane decreased with learning, a theory since confirmed by other aircraft manufacturers. Regardless of the time needed to produce the first plane, learning curves are found to apply to various categories of air frames (e.g., jet fighters versus passenger planes versus bombers). Learning curves have since been applied not only to labor but also to a wide variety of other costs, including material and purchased components. The power of the learning curve is so significant that it plays a major role in many strategic decisions related to employment levels, costs, capacity, and pricing.

LO E.1 *Define* learning curve

776

(a) Exponential graph of learning

(b) Log-log graph of learning

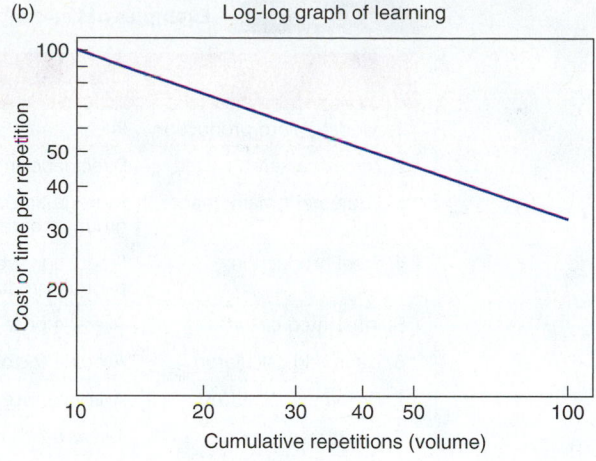

Figure **E.1**

The Learning-Curve Effect States That Time per Repetition Decreases as the Number of Repetitions Increases

Both curves show that the labor-hours to build an airplane decline by 20% each time the production volume doubles. The left graph (a) shows the exponential decline. The log-log graph (b) yields a straight line that is easier to extrapolate.

The learning curve is based on a *doubling* of production: That is, when production doubles, the decrease in time per unit affects the rate of the learning curve. So, if the learning curve is an 80% rate, the second unit takes 80% of the time of the first unit, the fourth unit takes 80% of the time of the second unit, the eighth unit takes 80% of the time of the fourth unit, and so forth. This principle is shown as:

$$T \times L^n = \text{Time required for the } n\text{th unit} \qquad \text{(E-1)}$$

where T = unit cost or unit time of the first unit
L = learning curve rate
n = number of times T is doubled

If the first unit of a particular product took 10 labor-hours, and if a 70% learning curve is present, the hours the fourth unit will take require doubling twice—from 1 to 2 to 4. Therefore, the formula is:

$$\text{Hours required for unit 4} = 10 \times (.7)^2 = 4.9 \text{ hours}$$

Learning Curves in Services and Manufacturing

Different organizations—indeed, different products—have different learning curves. The rate of learning varies depending on the quality of management and the potential of the process and product. *Any change in process, product, or personnel disrupts the learning curve.* Therefore, caution should be exercised in assuming that a learning curve is continuing and permanent.

As you can see in Table E.1, industry learning curves vary widely. The lower the number (say, 70% compared to 90%), the steeper the slope and the faster the drop in costs. By tradition, learning curves are defined in terms of the *complements* of their improvement rates. For example, a 70% learning curve implies a 30% decrease in time each time the number of repetitions is doubled. A 90% curve means there is a corresponding 10% rate of improvement.

Stable, standardized products and processes tend to have costs that decline more steeply than others. Between 1920 and 1955, for instance, the steel industry was able to reduce labor-hours per unit to 79% each time cumulative production doubled.

Learning curves have application in services as well as industry. As was noted in the caption for the opening photograph, 1-year death rates of heart transplant patients at Temple

TABLE E.1	Examples of Learning-Curve Effects		
EXAMPLE	**IMPROVING PARAMETER**	**CUMULATIVE PARAMETER**	**LEARNING-CURVE SLOPE (%)**
1. Model-T Ford production	Price	Units produced	86
2. Aircraft assembly	Direct labor-hours per unit	Units produced	80
3. Equipment maintenance at GE	Average time to replace a group of parts	Number of replacements	76
4. Steel production	Production worker labor-hours per unit produced	Units produced	79
5. Integrated circuits	Average price per unit	Units produced	72[a]
6. Handheld calculator	Average factory selling price	Units produced	74
7. Disk memory drives	Average price per bit	Number of bits	76
8. Heart transplants	1-year death rates	Transplants completed	79
9. Cesarean section baby deliveries	Average operation time	Number of surgeries	93

[a]Constant dollars.

University Hospital follow a 79% learning curve. The results of that hospital's 3-year study of 62 patients receiving transplants found that every three operations resulted in a halving of the 1-year death rate. As more hospitals face pressure from both insurance companies and the government to enter fixed-price negotiations for their services, their ability to learn from experience becomes increasingly critical. In addition to having applications in both services and industry, learning curves are useful for a variety of purposes. These include:

1. **Internal:** Labor forecasting, scheduling, establishing costs and budgets.
2. **External:** Supply-chain negotiations (see the SMT case study at the end of this module).
3. **Strategic:** Evaluation of company and industry performance, including costs and pricing.

The consequences of learning curves can be far-reaching. For instance, for Boeing's 787 (the world's fastest-selling commercial jet) to reach break-even at 1,000 planes, the unit cost must drop to $113 million, down from the $184 million it cost to make the 45th unit. This can be accomplished only with a very aggressive learning curve rate of 76%. If Boeing follows the 84% learning curve seen for its jumbo 777 model, losses will be in the billions. In addition, there may be major problems in scheduling if the learning improvement is not considered: labor and plants may sit idle a portion of the time. Firms may also refuse more work because they ignore their own efficiency improvements.

Applying the Learning Curve

STUDENT TIP
Here are the three ways of solving learning curve problems.

A mathematical relationship enables us to express the time required to produce a certain unit. This relationship is a function of how many units have been produced before the unit in question and how long it took to produce them. To gain a mastery of this relationship, we will work through learning curve scenarios using three different methods: the doubling approach, formula approach, and learning curve table approach.

Doubling Approach

LO E.2 *Use the* doubling concept to estimate times

The doubling approach is the simplest approach to learning-curve problems. As noted earlier, each time production doubles, labor per unit declines by a constant factor, known as the learning curve rate. So, if we know that the learning curve rate is 80% and that the first unit produced took 100 hours, the hours required to produce the 2nd, 4th, 8th, and 16th units are as follows:

*N*TH UNIT PRODUCED	HOURS FOR *N*TH UNIT
1	100.0
2	80.0 = (.8 × 100)
4	64.0 = (.8 × 80)
8	51.2 = (.8 × 64)
16	41.0 = (.8 × 51.2)

As long as we wish to find the hours required to produce *N* units and *N* is one of the doubled values, then this approach works. The doubling approach does not tell us how many hours will be needed to produce other units. For this flexibility, we turn to the formula approach.

Formula Approach

The formula approach allows us to determine labor for *any* unit, T_N, by the formula:

$$T_N = T_1(N^b) \tag{E-2}$$

where
T_N = time for the *N*th unit
T_1 = time to produce the first unit
b = (log of the learning rate)/(log 2) = slope of the learning curve

Some of the values for *b* are presented in Table E.2. Example E1 shows how this formula works.

TABLE E.2

Learning-Curve Values of *b*

LEARNING RATE (%)	*b*
70	−.515
75	−.415
80	−.322
85	−.234
90	−.152

Example E1

USING LOGS TO COMPUTE LEARNING CURVES

The learning-curve rate for a typical CPA to conduct a dental practice audit is 80%. Greg Lattier, a new graduate of Lee College, completed his first audit in 100 hours. If the dental offices he audits are about the same, how long should he take to finish his third job?

APPROACH ▶ We will use the formula approach in Equation (E-2).

SOLUTION ▶
$$T_N = T_1(N^b)$$
$$T_3 = (100 \text{ hours})(3^b)$$
$$= (100)(3^{\log .8/\log 2})$$
$$= (100)(3^{-.322}) = 70.2 \text{ labor-hours}$$

INSIGHT ▶ Greg improved quickly from his first to his third audit. An 80% learning-curve rate means that from just the first to second jobs, his time decreased by 20%.

LEARNING EXERCISE ▶ If Greg's learning-curve rate were only 90%, how long would the third audit take? [Answer: 84.621 hours.]

RELATED PROBLEMS ▶ E.1, E.2, E.9, E.10, E.11, E.16

EXCEL OM Data File **ModEExE1.xls** can be found in **MyOMLab**.

The formula approach allows us to determine the hours required for *any* unit produced, but there *is* a simpler method.

Learning-Curve Table Approach

The learning-curve table technique uses Table E.3 (to provide the coefficient *C*) and the following equation:

$$T_N = T_1C \tag{E-3}$$

where
T_N = number of labor-hours required to produce the *N*th unit
T_1 = number of labor-hours required to produce the first unit
C = learning-curve coefficient found in Table E.3

LO E.3 *Compute learning-curve effects with the formula and learning-curve table approaches*

The learning-curve coefficient, C, depends on both the learning curve rate (70%, 75%, 80%, and so on) and the unit number of interest.

Example E2 uses the preceding equation and Table E.3 to calculate learning-curve effects.

Example E2

USING LEARNING-CURVE COEFFICIENTS

It took a Korean shipyard 125,000 labor-hours to produce the first of several tugboats that you expect to purchase for your shipping company, Great Lakes, Inc. Boats 2 and 3 have been produced by the Koreans with a learning factor of 85%. At $40 per hour, what should you, as purchasing agent, expect to pay for the fourth unit?

APPROACH ▶ First, search Table E.3 for the fourth unit and a learning-curve rate of 85%. The learning-curve coefficient, C, is .723.

SOLUTION ▶ To produce the fourth unit, then, takes:

$$T_N = T_1 C$$
$$T_4 = (125{,}000 \text{ hours})(.723)$$
$$= 90{,}375 \text{ hours}$$

To find the cost, multiply by $40:

$$90{,}375 \text{ hours} \times \$40 \text{ per hour} = \$3{,}615{,}000$$

INSIGHT ▶ The learning-curve table approach is very easy to apply. If we had not factored learning into our cost estimates, the price would have been 125,000 hours × $40 per hour (same as the first boat) = $6,000,000.

LEARNING EXERCISE ▶ If the learning factor improved to 80%, how would the cost change? [Answer: It would drop to $3,200,000.]

RELATED PROBLEMS ▶ E.1, E.2, E.3a, E.5a,c, E.6a,b, E.9, E.10, E.11, E.14, E.16, E.22 (E.26, E.27, E.28, E.30, E.31 are available in MyOMLab)

EXCEL **OM** Data File **ModEExE2.xls** can be found in MyOMLab.

ACTIVE **MODEL E.1** This example is further illustrated in Active Model E.1 in MyOMLab.

Table E.3 also shows *cumulative values*. These allow us to compute the total number of hours needed to complete a specified number of units. Again, the computation is straightforward. Just multiply the table coefficient value by the time required for the first unit. Example E3 illustrates this concept.

Example E3

USING CUMULATIVE COEFFICIENTS

Example E2 computed the time to complete the fourth tugboat that Great Lakes plans to buy. How long will *all four* boats require?

APPROACH ▶ We look at the "Total Time Coefficient" column in Table E.3 and find that the cumulative coefficient for 4 boats with an 85% learning-curve factor is 3.345.

SOLUTION ▶ The time required is:

$$T_N = T_1 C$$
$$T_4 = (125{,}000)(3.345) = 418{,}125 \text{ hours in total for all 4 boats}$$

INSIGHT ▶ For an illustration of how Excel OM can be used to solve Examples E2 and E3, see Program E.1 at the end of this module.

LEARNING EXERCISE ▶ What is the value of T_4 if the learning-curve factor is 80% instead of 85%? [Answer: 392,750 hours.]

RELATED PROBLEMS ▶ E.3b, E.4, E.5b,c, E.6c, E.7, E.15, E.19, E.20a

| TABLE E.3 | | Learning-Curve Coefficients, Where Coefficient C = N (LOG OF LEARNING RATE/LOG 2) | | | | | | | | | |

UNIT NUMBER (N)	70%		75%		80%		85%		90%	
	UNIT TIME CO-EFFICIENT	TOTAL TIME CO-EFFICIENT	UNIT TIME CO-EFFICIENT	TOTAL TIME CO-EFFICIENT	UNIT TIME CO-EFFICIENT	TOTAL TIME CO-EFFICIENT	UNIT TIME CO-EFFICIENT	TOTAL TIME CO-EFFICIENT	UNIT TIME CO-EFFICIENT	TOTAL TIME CO-EFFICIENT
1	1.000	1.000	1.000	1.000	1.000	1.000	1.000	1.000	1.000	1.000
2	.700	1.700	.750	1.750	.800	1.800	.850	1.850	.900	1.900
3	.568	2.268	.634	2.384	.702	2.502	.773	2.623	.846	2.746
4	.490	2.758	.562	2.946	.640	3.142	.723	3.345	.810	3.556
5	.437	3.195	.513	3.459	.596	3.738	.686	4.031	.783	4.339
6	.398	3.593	.475	3.934	.562	4.299	.657	4.688	.762	5.101
7	.367	3.960	.446	4.380	.534	4.834	.634	5.322	.744	5.845
8	.343	4.303	.422	4.802	.512	5.346	.614	5.936	.729	6.574
9	.323	4.626	.402	5.204	.493	5.839	.597	6.533	.716	7.290
10	.306	4.932	.385	5.589	.477	6.315	.583	7.116	.705	7.994
11	.291	5.223	.370	5.958	.462	6.777	.570	7.686	.695	8.689
12	.278	5.501	.357	6.315	.449	7.227	.558	8.244	.685	9.374
13	.267	5.769	.345	6.660	.438	7.665	.548	8.792	.677	10.052
14	.257	6.026	.334	6.994	.428	8.092	.539	9.331	.670	10.721
15	.248	6.274	.325	7.319	.418	8.511	.530	9.861	.663	11.384
16	.240	6.514	.316	7.635	.410	8.920	.522	10.383	.656	12.040
17	.233	6.747	.309	7.944	.402	9.322	.515	10.898	.650	12.690
18	.226	6.973	.301	8.245	.394	9.716	.508	11.405	.644	13.334
19	.220	7.192	.295	8.540	.388	10.104	.501	11.907	.639	13.974
20	.214	7.407	.288	8.828	.381	10.485	.495	12.402	.634	14.608
25	.191	8.404	.263	10.191	.355	12.309	.470	14.801	.613	17.713
30	.174	9.305	.244	11.446	.335	14.020	.450	17.091	.596	20.727
35	.160	10.133	.229	12.618	.318	15.643	.434	19.294	.583	23.666
40	.150	10.902	.216	13.723	.305	17.193	.421	21.425	.571	26.543
45	.141	11.625	.206	14.773	.294	18.684	.410	23.500	.561	29.366
50	.134	12.307	.197	15.776	.284	20.122	.400	25.513	.552	32.142

Using Table E.3 requires that we know how long it takes to complete the first unit. Yet, what happens if our most recent or most reliable information available pertains to some other unit? The answer is that we must use these data to find a revised estimate for the first unit and then apply the table coefficient to that number. Example E4 illustrates this concept.

Example E4

REVISING LEARNING-CURVE ESTIMATES

Great Lakes, Inc., believes that unusual circumstances in producing the first boat (see Example E2) imply that the time estimate of 125,000 hours is not as valid a base as the time required to produce the third boat. Boat number 3 was completed in 100,000 hours. It wants to solve for the revised estimate for boat number 1.

APPROACH ▶ We return to Table E.3, with a unit value of $N = 3$ and a learning-curve coefficient of $C = .773$ in the 85% column.

SOLUTION ▶ To find the revised estimate, divide the actual time for boat number 3, 100,000 hours, by $C = .773$:

$$\frac{100,000}{.773} = 129,366 \text{ hours}$$

So 129,366 hours is the new (revised) estimate for boat 1.

INSIGHT ▶ Any change in product, process, or personnel will change the learning curve. The new estimate for boat 1 suggests that related cost and volume estimates need to be revised.

LEARNING EXERCISE ▶ Boat 4 was just completed in 90,000 hours. Great Lakes thinks the 85% learning-curve rate is valid but isn't sure about the 125,000 hours for the first boat. Find a revised estimate for boat 1. [Answer: 124,481, suggesting that boat 1's time was fairly accurate after all.]

RELATED PROBLEMS ▶ E.8, E.12, E.13, E.17, E.18, E.20b, E.21, E.23

EXCEL OM Data File **ModEExE4.xls** can be found in MyOMLab.

Examples E1 through E4 all assume that the learning curve rate is known. For a new product, this can be a major assumption. If a firm has observed the cost or time of any two products already produced, it's easy to work backward from Equation (E-3) and Table E.3 to impute the actual learning curve *rate*. Example E5 illustrates this concept.

Example E5

COMPUTING THE LEARNING-CURVE RATE FROM OBSERVED PRODUCTION

In 2012, Boeing completed production on its forty-fifth 787 airliner, at a cost of $184 million. The first plane off the assembly line, in 2010, cost $448 million. What is Boeing's learning-curve rate for this model?

APPROACH ▶   We use Equation (E-3), with costs for T_1 and T_{45} known, and then find the learning-curve coefficient (C) in Table E.3.

SOLUTION ▶   Equation (E-3) is $T_N = T_1 C$. We solve for $C = \dfrac{T_N}{T_1}$.

$$C = \frac{184}{448} = .41$$

In Table E.3, we follow the "Unit Number" row for $N = 45$, and we see that .41 falls under the 85% learning-curve rate for unit times (or costs, in this case).

INSIGHT ▶   Boeing's goal is to reach a 76% learning-curve rate, so OM must begin to lower costs dramatically. Progress should be checked with each plane from this point on.

LEARNING EXERCISE ▶   Let's say Boeing's fifth 787 cost $350 million. What was the learning-curve rate at that time relative to plane number 1? [Answer: C = $350 million/$448 million = .78. This suggests a 90% learning-curve rate, so Boeing's performance has deteriorated.]

RELATED PROBLEMS ▶   E.20, E.26 (E.29, E.32 are available in MyOMLab)

LO E.4 *Describe* the strategic implications of learning curves

Strategic Implications of Learning Curves

So far, we have shown how operations managers can forecast labor-hour requirements for a product. We have also shown how purchasing agents can determine a supplier's cost, knowledge that can help in price negotiations. Another important application of learning curves concerns strategic planning.

An example of a company cost line and industry price line are so labeled in Figure E.2. These learning curves are straight because both scales are log scales. When the *rate* of change is constant, a log-log graph yields a straight line. If an organization believes its cost line to be the "company cost" line, and the industry price is indicated by the dashed horizontal line, then the company must have costs at the points below the dashed line (for example, point *a* or *b*) or else operate at a loss (point *c*).

STUDENT TIP

Both the vertical and horizontal axes of this figure are log scales in this log-log graph.

Figure E.2

Industry Learning Curve for Price Compared with Company Learning Curve for Cost

Lower costs are not automatic; they must be managed down. When a firm's strategy is to pursue a learning curve steeper than the industry average (the company cost line in Figure E.2), it does this by:

1. Following an aggressive pricing policy
2. Focusing on continuing cost reduction and productivity improvement
3. Building on shared experience
4. Keeping capacity growing ahead of demand

Costs may drop as a firm pursues the learning curve, but volume must increase for the learning curve to exist. Moreover, managers must understand competitors before embarking on a learning-curve strategy. Weak competitors are undercapitalized, stuck with high costs, or do not understand the logic of learning curves. However, strong and dangerous competitors control their costs, have solid financial positions for the large investments needed, and have a track record of using an aggressive learning-curve strategy. Taking on such a competitor in a price war may help only the consumer.

Limitations of Learning Curves

Before using learning curves, some cautions are in order:

◆ Because learning curves differ from company to company, as well as industry to industry, estimates for each organization should be developed rather than applying someone else's.

◆ Learning curves are often based on the time necessary to complete the early units; therefore, those times must be accurate. As current information becomes available, reevaluation is appropriate.

◆ Any changes in personnel, design, or procedure can be expected to alter the learning curve, causing the curve to spike up for a short time, even if it is going to drop in the long run.

◆ While workers and processes may improve, the same learning curves do not always apply to indirect labor and material.

◆ The culture of the workplace, as well as resource availability and changes in the process, may alter the learning curve. For instance, as a project nears its end, worker interest and effort may drop, curtailing progress down the curve.

⚠ STUDENT TIP
Determining accurate rates of learning requires careful analysis.

Summary

The learning curve is a powerful tool for an operations manager. This tool can assist operations managers in determining future cost standards for items produced as well as purchased. In addition, the learning curve can provide understanding about company and industry performance. We saw three approaches to learning curves: the doubling approach, formula approach, and learning-curve table approach. Software can also help analyze learning curves.

Key Term

Learning curves (p. 776)

Discussion Questions

1. What are some of the limitations of learning curves?
2. Identify three applications of the learning curve.
3. What are the approaches to solving learning-curve problems?
4. Refer to Example E2. What are the implications for Great Lakes, Inc., if the engineering department wants to change the engine in the third and subsequent tugboats that the firm purchases?
5. Why isn't the learning-curve concept as applicable in a high-volume assembly line as it is in most other human activities?
6. What are the elements that can disrupt the learning curve?
7. Explain the concept of the doubling effect in learning curves.
8. What techniques can a firm use to move to a steeper learning curve?

Using Software for Learning Curves

Excel, Excel OM, and POM for Windows may all be used in analyzing learning curves. You can use the ideas in the following section on Excel OM to build your own Excel spreadsheet if you wish.

✖ USING EXCEL OM

Program E.1 shows how Excel OM develops a spreadsheet for learning-curve calculations. The input data come from Examples E2 and E3. In cell B7, we enter the unit number for the base unit (which does not have to be 1), and in B8 we enter the time for this unit. Learning-curve rates can also be developed from observed times or costs, as illustrated in Example E5.

These are used for computations. Do not touch these cells. In cell B11, the time for the first unit is computed, allowing us to use initial units other than unit 1. In cell B12, the power to be raised to is computed, making the formulas in the rest of column B much simpler.

=$B$11*POWER(1,$B$12)

=SUM($B$16:B16)

Program **E.1**

Excel OM's Learning Curve Module, Using Data from Examples E2 and E3

P USING POM FOR WINDOWS

The POM for Windows Learning Curve module computes the length of time that future units will take, given the time required for the base unit and the learning rate (expressed as a number between 0 and 1). As an option, if the times required for the first and Nth units are already known, the learning *rate* can be computed. See Appendix IV for further details.

Solved Problems   Virtual Office Hours help is available in MyOMLab.

SOLVED PROBLEM E.1

Digicomp produces a new telephone system with built-in TV screens. Its learning-curve rate is 80%.

a) If the first one took 56 hours, how long will it take Digicomp to make the eleventh system?

b) How long will the first 11 systems take in total?

c) As a purchasing agent, you expect to buy units 12 through 15 of the new phone system. What would be your expected cost for the units if Digicomp charges $30 for each labor-hour?

SOLUTION

from Table E.3, coefficient for 80% unit time

a) $T_N = T_1 C$
    $T_{11} = (56 \text{ hours})(.462) = 25.9 \text{ hours}$

b) Total time for the first 11 units = (56 hours)(6.777) = 379.5 hours

from Table E.3, coefficient for 80% total time

c) To find the time for units 12 through 15, we take the total cumulative time for units 1 to 15 and subtract the total time for units 1 to 11, which was computed in part (b). Total time for the first 15 units = (56 hours)(8.511) = 476.6 hours. So the time for units 12 through 15 is 476.6 − 379.5 = 97.1 hours. (This figure could also be confirmed by computing the times for units 12, 13, 14, and 15 separately using the unit-time coefficient column and then adding them.) Expected cost for units 12 through 15 = (97.1 hours)($30 per hour) = $2,913.

SOLVED PROBLEM E.2

If the first time you performed a job took 60 minutes, how long will the eighth job take if you are on an 80% learning curve?

SOLUTION

Three doublings from 1 to 2 to 4 to 8 implies $.8^3$. Therefore, we have:

$$60 \times (.8)^3 = 60 \times .512 = 30.72 \text{ minutes}$$

or, using Table E.3, we have $C = .512$. Therefore:

$$60 \times .512 = 30.72 \text{ minutes}$$

Problems

Note: **PX** *means the problem may be solved with POM for Windows and/or Excel OM.*

Problems E.1–E.32 relate to Applying the Learning Curve

• **E.1** Susan Sherer, an IRS auditor, took 45 minutes to process her first tax return. The IRS uses an 85% learning curve. How long will the:
a) 2nd return take?
b) 4th return take?
c) 8th return take? **PX**

• **E.2** Temple Trucking Co. just hired Ed Rosenthal to verify daily invoices and accounts payable. He took 9 hours and 23 minutes to complete his task on the first day. Prior employees in this job have tended to follow a 90% learning curve. How long will the task take at the end of:
a) the 2nd day?
b) the 4th day?
c) the 8th day?
d) the 16th day? **PX**

• **E.3** If Professor Laurie Macdonald takes 15 minutes to grade the first exam and follows an 80% learning curve, how long will it take her:
a) to grade the 25th exam?
b) to grade the first 10 exams? **PX**

• **E.4** If it took 563 minutes to complete a hospital's first cornea transplant, and the hospital uses a 90% learning rate, what is the cumulative time to complete:
a) the first 3 transplants?
b) the first 6 transplants?
c) the first 8 transplants?
d) the first 16 transplants? **PX**

•• **E.5** Beth Zion Hospital has received initial certification from the state of California to become a center for liver transplants. The hospital, however, must complete its first 18 transplants under great scrutiny and at no cost to the patients. The very first transplant, just completed, required 30 hours. On the basis of research at the hospital, Beth Zion estimates that it will have an 80% learning curve. Estimate the time it will take to complete:
a) the 5th liver transplant.
b) all of the first 5 transplants.
c) the 18th transplant.
d) all 18 transplants. **PX**

•• **E.6** Refer to Problem E.5. Beth Zion Hospital has just been informed that only the first 10 transplants must be performed at the hospital's expense. The cost per hour of surgery is estimated to be $5,000. Again, the learning rate is 80% and the first surgery took 30 hours.
a) How long will the 10th surgery take?
b) How much will the 10th surgery cost?
c) How much will all 10 cost the hospital? **PX**

• **E.7** Manceville Air has just produced the first unit of a large industrial compressor that incorporated new technology in the control circuits and a new internal venting system. The first unit took 112 hours of labor to manufacture. The company knows from past experience that this labor content will decrease significantly as more units are produced. In reviewing past production data, it appears that the company has experienced a 90% learning curve when producing similar designs. The company is interested in estimating the total time to complete the next 7 units. Your job as the production cost estimator is to prepare the estimate. **PX**

• **E.8** Elizabeth Perry, a student at SUNY, bought 6 bookcases for her dorm room. Each required unpacking of parts and assembly, which included some nailing and bolting.

doble.d/Fotolia

Elizabeth completed the first bookcase in 5 hours and the second in 4 hours.

a) What is her learning rate?

b) Assuming that the same rate continues, how long will the 3rd bookcase take?

c) The 4th, 5th, and 6th cases?

d) All 6 cases? **PX**

•• E.9 Professor Mary Beth Marrs took 6 hours to prepare the first lecture in a new course. Traditionally, she has experienced a 90% learning curve. How much time should it take her to prepare the 15th lecture? **PX**

• E.10 The first vending machine that William Kine, Inc., assembled took 80 labor-hours. Estimate how long the fourth machine will require for each of the following learning rates:

a) 95%

b) 87%

c) 72% **PX**

• E.11 D. Shimshak Systems is installing networks for Advantage Insurance. The first installation took 46 labor-hours to complete. Estimate how long the 4th and the 8th installations will take for each of the following learning rates:

a) 92%

b) 84%

c) 77% **PX**

••• E.12 Providence Assessment Center screens and trains employees for a computer assembly firm in Boston. The progress of all trainees is tracked, and those not showing the proper progress are moved to less demanding programs. By the tenth repetition trainees must be able to complete the assembly task in 1 hour or less. Susan Sweaney has just spent 5 hours on the fourth unit and 4 hours completing her eighth unit, while another trainee, Julie Burgmeier, took 4 hours on the third and 3 hours on the sixth unit. Should you encourage either or both of the trainees to continue? Why? **PX**

•• E.13 The better students at Providence Assessment Center (see Problem E.12) have an 80% learning curve and can do a task in 20 minutes after just six times. You would like to weed out the weak students sooner and decide to evaluate them after the third unit. How long should the third unit take? **PX**

•• E.14 Suad Alwan, the purchasing agent for Dubai Airlines, is interested in determining what he can expect to pay for airplane number 4 if the third plane took 20,000 hours to produce. What would Alwan expect to pay for plane number 5? Number 6? Use an 85% learning curve and a $40-per-hour labor charge. **PX**

•• E.15 Using the data from Problem E.14, how long will it take to complete the 12th plane? The 15th plane? How long will it take to complete planes 12 through 15 inclusive? At $40 per hour, what can Alwan, as purchasing agent, expect to pay for planes 12 through 15? **PX**

•• E.16 Central Electronics Corp. produces semiconductors and has a learning curve of .7. The price per bit is 100 millicents when the volume is $.7 \times 10^{12}$ bits. What is the expected price at 1.4×10^{12} bits? What is the expected price at 89.6×10^{12} bits? **PX**

•• E.17 Regional Power owns 25 small power generating plants. It has contracted with Genco Services to overhaul the power turbines of each of the plants. The number of hours that Genco billed Regional to complete the third turbine was 460. Regional pays Genco $60 per hour for its services. As the maintenance manager for Regional, you are trying to estimate the cost of overhauling the fourth turbine. How much would you expect to pay for the overhaul of number 5 and number 6? All the turbines are similar, and an 80% learning curve is appropriate. **PX**

•• E.18 If it took Boeing 28,718 hours to produce the eighth 787 jet and the learning-curve factor is 80%, how long did it take to produce the tenth 787? **PX**

•• E.19 Richard Dulski's firm is about to bid on a new radar system. Although the product uses new technology, Dulski believes that a learning rate of 75% is appropriate. The first unit is expected to take 700 hours, and the contract is for 40 units. **PX**

a) What is the total amount of hours to build the 40 units?

b) What is the average time to build each of the 40 units?

c) Assume that a worker works 2,080 hours per year. How many workers should be assigned to this contract to complete it in a year? **PX**

••• E.20 As the estimator for Rajendra Tibrewala Enterprises, your job is to prepare an estimate for a potential customer service contract. The contract is for the service of diesel locomotive cylinder heads. The shop has done some of these in the past on a sporadic basis. The time required to service the first cylinder head in each job has been exactly 4 hours, and similar work has been accomplished at an 85% learning curve. The customer wants you to quote the total time in batches of 12 and 20.

a) Prepare the quote.

b) After preparing the quote, you find a labor ticket for this customer for five locomotive cylinder heads. From the notations on the labor ticket, you conclude that the fifth unit took 2.5 hours. What do you conclude about the learning curve and your quote? **PX**

•• E.21 Girish Shambu and William Reisel are teammates at a discount store; their new job is assembling bicycles for customers. Assembly of a bike has a learning rate of 90%. They forgot to time their effort on the first bike, but spent 4 hours on the second set. They have 6 more bikes to do. Determine approximately how much time will be (was) required for:

a) the 1st unit

b) the 8th unit

c) all 8 units **PX**

•• E.22 Kelly-Lambing, Inc., a builder of government-contracted small ships, has a steady work force of 10 very skilled craftspeople. These workers can supply 2,500 labor-hours each per year. Kelly-Lambing is about to undertake a new contract, building a new style of boat. The first boat is expected to take 6,000 hours to complete. The firm thinks that 90% is the expected learning rate.

a) What is the firm's "capacity" to make these boats—that is, how many units can the firm make in 1 year?

b) If the operations manager can increase the learning rate to 85% instead of 90%, how many units can the firm make? **PX**

• • • **E.23**   The service times for a new data entry clerk have been measured and sequentially recorded as shown below:

REPORT	TIME (MINUTES)
1	66
2	56
3	53
4	48
5	47
6	45
7	44
8	41

a) What is the learning curve rate, based on this information?

b) Using an 85% learning curve rate and the above times, estimate the length of time the clerk will take to complete the 48th report. **Px**

• • **E.24**   If the first unit of a production run takes 1 hour and the firm is on an 80% learning curve, how long will unit 100 take? (*Hint:* Apply the coefficient in Table E.3 twice.) **Px**

• • • **E.25**   Boeing spent $270 million to make the eleventh 787 in its production line. The first 787 cost $448 million. What was the learning curve rate at this point?

Additional problems **E.26–E.32** *are available in* MyOMLab.

Problem E.33 relates to Strategic Implications of Learning Curves

• • • • **E.33** Using the accompanying log-log graph, answer the following questions:

a) What are the implications for management if it has forecast its cost on the optimum line?

b) What could be causing the fluctuations above the optimum line?

c) If management forecasted the 10th unit on the optimum line, what was that forecast in hours?

d) If management built the 10th unit as indicated by the actual line, how many hours did it take?

CASE STUDY

SMT's Negotiation with IBM

IBM asked SMT and one other, much larger company to bid on 80 more units of a particular computer product. The RFQ (request for quote) asked that the overall bid be broken down to show the hourly rate, the parts and materials component in the price, and any charges for subcontracted services. SMT quoted $1.62 million and supplied the cost breakdown as requested. The second company submitted only one total figure, $5 million, with no cost breakdown. The decision was made to negotiate with SMT.

The IBM negotiating team included two purchasing managers and two cost engineers. One cost engineer had developed manufacturing cost estimates for every component, working from engineering drawings and cost-data books that he had built up from previous experience and that contained time factors, both setup and run times, for a large variety of operations. He estimated material costs by working both from data supplied by the IBM corporate purchasing staff and from purchasing journals. He visited SMT facilities to see the tooling available so that he would know what processes were being used. He assumed that there would be perfect conditions and trained operators, and he developed cost estimates for the 158th unit (previous orders were for 25, 15, and 38 units). He added 5% for scrap-and-flow loss; 2% for the use of temporary tools, jigs, and fixtures; 5% for quality

control; and 9% for purchasing burden. Then, using an 85% learning curve, he backed up his costs to get an estimate for the first unit. He next checked the data on hours and materials for the 25, 15, and 38 units already made and found that his estimate for the first unit was within 4% of actual cost. His check, however, had indicated a 90% learning-curve effect on hours per unit.

In the negotiations, SMT was represented by one of the two owners of the business, two engineers, and one cost estimator. The sessions opened with a discussion of learning curves. The IBM cost estimator demonstrated that SMT had in fact been operating on a 90% learning curve. But, he argued, it should be possible to move to an 85% curve, given the longer runs, reduced setup time, and increased continuity of workers on the job that would be possible with an order for 80 units. The owner agreed with this analysis and was willing to reduce his price by 4%.

However, as each operation in the manufacturing process was discussed, it became clear that some IBM cost estimates were too low because certain crating and shipping expenses had been overlooked. These oversights were minor, however, and in the following discussions, the two parties arrived at a common understanding of specifications and reached agreements on the costs of each manufacturing operation.

At this point, SMT representatives expressed great concern about the possibility of inflation in material costs. The IBM negotiators volunteered to include a form of price escalation in the contract, as previously agreed among themselves. IBM representatives suggested that if overall material costs changed by more than 10%, the price could be adjusted accordingly. However, if one party took the initiative to have the price revised, the other could require an analysis of *all* parts and materials invoices in arriving at the new price.

Another concern of the SMT representatives was that a large amount of overtime and subcontracting would be required to meet IBM's specified delivery schedule. IBM negotiators thought that a relaxation in the delivery schedule might be possible if a price concession could be obtained. In response, the SMT team offered a 5% discount, and this was accepted. As a result of these negotiations, the SMT price was reduced almost 20% below its original bid price.

In a subsequent meeting called to negotiate the prices of certain pipes to be used in the system, it became apparent to an IBM cost estimator that SMT representatives had seriously underestimated their costs. He pointed out this apparent error because he could not understand why SMT had quoted such a low figure. He wanted to be sure that SMT was using the correct manufacturing process. In any case, if SMT estimators had made a mistake, it should be noted. It was IBM's policy to seek a fair price both for itself and for its suppliers. IBM procurement managers believed that if a vendor was losing money on a job, there would be a tendency to cut corners. In addition, the IBM negotiator felt that by pointing out the error, he generated some goodwill that would help in future sessions.

Discussion Questions

1. What are the advantages and disadvantages to IBM and SMT from this approach?
2. How does SMT's proposed learning rate compare with that of other industries?
3. What are the limitations of the learning curve in this case?

Source: Based on E. Raymond Corey, *Procurement Management: Strategy, Organization, and Decision Making* (New York: Van Nostrand Reinhold).

Endnote

1. T. P. Wright, "Factors Affecting the Cost of Airplanes," *Journal of the Aeronautical Sciences* (February 1936).

Module E *Rapid* Review

Main Heading	Review Material	MyOMLab
WHAT IS A LEARNING CURVE? (pp. 776–777)	■ **Learning curves**—The premise that people and organizations get better at their tasks as the tasks are repeated; sometimes called experience curves.	Concept Questions: 1.1–1.4

WHAT IS A LEARNING CURVE?
(pp. 776–777)

■ **Learning curves**—The premise that people and organizations get better at their tasks as the tasks are repeated; sometimes called experience curves.

Learning usually follows a negative exponential curve.

It takes less time to complete each additional unit a firm produces; however, the time *savings* in completing each subsequent unit *decreases.*

Learning curves were first applied to industry in a report by T. P. Wright of Curtis-Wright Corp. in 1936. Wright described how direct labor costs of making a particular airplane decreased with learning.

Learning curves have been applied not only to labor but also to a wide variety of other costs, including material and purchased components.

The power of the learning curve is so significant that it plays a major role in many strategic decisions related to employment levels, costs, capacity, and pricing.

The learning curve is based on a *doubling* of production: That is, when production doubles, the decrease in time per unit affects the rate of the learning curve.

$$T \times L^n = \text{Time required for the } n\text{th unit} \qquad \text{(E-1)}$$

where
T = unit cost or time of the first unit
L = learning curve rate
n = number of times T is doubled

Concept Questions: 1.1–1.4

LEARNING CURVES IN SERVICES AND MANUFACTURING
(pp. 777–778)

Different organizations—indeed, different products—have different learning curves. The rate of learning varies, depending on the quality of management and the potential of the process and product. *Any change in process, product, or personnel disrupts the learning curve.* Therefore, caution should be exercised in assuming that a learning curve is continuing and permanent.

The steeper the slope of the learning curve, the faster the drop in costs.

By tradition, learning curves are defined in terms of the *complements* of their improvement rates (i.e., a 75% learning rate is better than an 85% learning rate).

Stable, standardized products and processes tend to have costs that decline more steeply than others.

Learning curves are useful for a variety of purposes, including:

1. *Internal:* Labor forecasting, scheduling, establishing costs and budgets
2. *External:* Supply-chain negotiations
3. *Strategic:* Evaluation of company and industry performance, including costs and pricing

Concept Questions: 2.1–2.4

APPLYING THE LEARNING CURVE
(pp. 778–782)

If learning curve improvement is ignored, potential problems could arise, such as scheduling mismatches, leading to idle labor and productive facilities, refusal to accept new orders because capacity is assumed to be full, or missing an opportunity to negotiate with suppliers for lower purchase prices as a result of large orders.

Three ways to approach the mathematics of learning curves are (1) doubling approach, (2) formula approach, and (3) learning-curve table approach.

The doubling approach uses the production doubling Equation (E-1).

The formula approach allows us to determine labor for *any* unit, T_N, by the formula:

$$T_N = T_1(N^b) \qquad \text{(E-2)}$$

where
T_N = time for the Nth unit
T_1 = time to produce the first unit
b = (log of the learning rate)/(log 2) = slope of the learning curve

The learning-curve table approach makes use of Table E.3 and uses the formula:

$$T_N = T_1 C \qquad \text{(E-3)}$$

where
T_N = number of labor-hours required to produce the Nth unit
T_1 = number of labor-hours required to produce the first unit
C = learning-curve coefficient found in Table E.3

The learning-curve coefficient, C, depends on both the learning rate and the unit number of interest.

Concept Questions: 3.1–3.4

Problems: E.1–E.32

Virtual Office Hours for Solved Problems: E.1, E.2

ACTIVE MODEL E.1

MyOMLab

Main Heading	Review Material	
	Formula (E-3) can also use the "Total Time Coefficient" columns of Table E.3 to provide the total cumulative number of hours needed to complete the specified number of units.	
	If the most recent or most reliable information available pertains to some unit other than the first, these data should be used to find a revised estimate for the first unit, and then the applicable formulas should be applied to that revised number.	
STRATEGIC IMPLICATIONS OF LEARNING CURVES (pp. 782–783)	When a firm's strategy is to pursue a learning cost curve steeper than the industry average, it can do this by: 1. Following an aggressive pricing policy 2. Focusing on continuing cost reduction and productivity improvement 3. Building on shared experience 4. Keeping capacity growing ahead of demand Managers must understand competitors before embarking on a learning-curve strategy. For example, taking on a strong competitor in a price war may help only the consumer.	Concept Questions: 4.1–4.3 Problem: E.33
LIMITATIONS OF LEARNING CURVES (p. 783)	Before using learning curves, some cautions are in order: ■ Because learning curves differ from company to company, as well as industry to industry, estimates for each organization should be developed rather than applying someone else's. ■ Learning curves are often based on the time necessary to complete the early units; therefore, those times must be accurate. As current information becomes available, reevaluation is appropriate. ■ Any changes in personnel, design, or procedure can be expected to alter the learning curve, causing the curve to spike up for a short time, even if it is going to drop in the long run. ■ While workers and process may improve, the same learning curves do not always apply to indirect labor and material. ■ The culture of the workplace, as well as resource availability and changes in the process, may alter the learning curve. For instance, as a project nears its end, worker interest and effort may drop, curtailing progress down the curve.	Concept Questions: 5.1–5.4

Self Test

- **Before taking the self-test,** refer to the learning objectives listed at the beginning of the module and the key term listed at the end of the module.

LO E.1 A learning curve describes:
  a) the rate at which an organization acquires new data.
  b) the amount of production time per unit as the total number of units produced increases.
  c) the increase in production time per unit as the total number of units produced increases.
  d) the increase in number of units produced per unit time as the total number of units produced increases.

LO E.2 A surgical procedure with a 90% learning curve required 20 hours for the initial patient. The fourth patient should require approximately how many hours?
  a) 18
  b) 16.2
  c) 28
  d) 30
  e) 54.2

LO E.3 The first transmission took 50 hours to rebuild at Bob's Auto Repair, and the learning rate is 80%. How long will it take to rebuild the third unit? (Use at least three decimals in the exponent if you use the formula approach.)
  a) under 30 hours
  b) about 32 hours
  c) about 35 hours
  d) about 60 hours
  e) about 45 hours

LO E.4 Which one of the following courses of action would *not* be taken by a firm wanting to pursue a learning curve steeper than the industry average?
  a) Following an aggressive pricing policy
  b) Focusing on continuing cost reduction
  c) Keeping capacity equal to demand to control costs
  d) Focusing on productivity improvement
  e) Building on shared experience

Answers: LO E.1. b; LO E.2. b; LO E.3. c; LO E.4. c.

Simulation

MODULE OUTLINE

- What Is Simulation? *792*
- Advantages and Disadvantages of Simulation *793*

- Monte Carlo Simulation *794*
- Simulation with Two Decision Variables: An Inventory Example *797*

Alaska Airlines

Alaska Airlines

Kaiser/Agencja Fotograficzna Caro/Alamy

Micro Saint® Sharp image used with permission of Alion Science and Technolgy Corp.

When Bay Medical Center faced severe overcrowding at its outpatient clinic, it turned to computer simulation to try to reduce bottlenecks and improve patient flow. A simulation language called Micro Saint analyzed current data relating to patient service times between clinic rooms. By simulating different numbers of doctors and staff, simulating the use of another clinic for overflow, and simulating a redesign of the existing clinic, Bay Medical Center was able to make decisions based on an understanding of both costs and benefits. This resulted in better patient service at lower cost.

Source: Micro Analysis and Design Simulation Software, Inc., Boulder, CO.

What Is Simulation?

Simulation models abound in our world. The city of Atlanta, for example, uses them to control traffic. Europe's Airbus Industries uses them to test the aerodynamics of proposed jets. The U.S. Army simulates war games on computers. Business students use management gaming to simulate realistic business competition. And thousands of organizations like Bay Medical Center develop simulation models to help make operations decisions.

Most of the large companies in the world use simulation models. Table F.1 lists just a few areas in which simulation is now being applied.

Simulation is the attempt to duplicate the features, appearance, and characteristics of a real system. In this module, we will show how to simulate part of an operations management system by building a mathematical model that comes as close as possible to representing the reality

Simulation

The attempt to duplicate the features, appearance, and characteristics of a real system, usually via a computerized model.

TABLE F.1	Some Applications of Simulation
Ambulance location and dispatching	Bus scheduling
Assembly-line balancing	Design of library operations
Parking lot and harbor design	Taxi, truck, and railroad dispatching
Distribution system design	Production facility scheduling
Scheduling aircraft	Plant layout
Labor-hiring decisions	Capital investments
Personnel scheduling	Production scheduling
Traffic-light timing	Sales forecasting
Voting pattern prediction	Inventory planning and control

of the system. The model will then be used to estimate the effects of various actions. The idea behind simulation is threefold:

1. To imitate a real-world situation mathematically
2. Then to study its properties and operating characteristics
3. Finally, to draw conclusions and make action decisions based on the results of the simulation

In this way, a real-life system need not be touched until the advantages and disadvantages of a major policy decision are first measured on the model.

To use simulation, an OM manager should:

1. Define the problem.
2. Introduce the important variables associated with the problem.
3. Construct a numerical model.
4. Set up possible courses of action for testing by specifying values of variables.
5. Run the experiment.
6. Consider the results (possibly modifying the model or changing data inputs).
7. Decide what course of action to take.

These steps are illustrated in Figure F.1.

The problems tackled by simulation may range from very simple to extremely complex, from bank-teller lines to an analysis of the U.S. economy. Although small simulations can be conducted by hand, effective use of the technique requires a computer. Large-scale models, simulating perhaps years of business decisions, are virtually all handled by computer.

In this module, we examine the basic principles of simulation and then tackle some problems in the areas of waiting-line analysis and inventory control. Why do we use simulation in these areas when mathematical models described in other chapters can solve similar problems? The answer is that simulation provides an alternative approach for problems that are very complex mathematically. It can handle, for example, inventory problems in which demand or lead time is not constant.

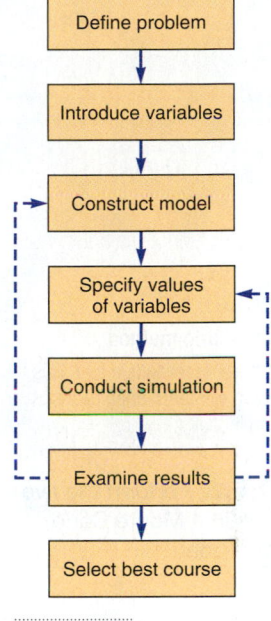

Figure **F.1**

The Process of Simulation

Advantages and Disadvantages of Simulation

Simulation is a tool that has become widely accepted by managers for several reasons. The main *advantages* of simulation are as follows:

1. It can be used to analyze large and complex real-world situations that cannot be solved by conventional operations management models.
2. Real-world complications can be included that most OM models cannot permit. For example, simulation can use *any* probability distribution the user defines; it does not require standard distributions.
3. "Time compression" is possible. The effects of OM policies over many months or years can be obtained by computer simulation in a short time.
4. Simulation allows "what-if?" types of questions. Managers like to know in advance what options will be most attractive. With a computerized model, a manager can try out several policy decisions within a matter of minutes.
5. Simulations do not interfere with real-world systems. It may be too disruptive, for example, to experiment physically with new policies or ideas in a hospital or manufacturing plant.

The main *disadvantages* of simulation are as follows:

1. Good simulation models can take a long time to develop.
2. It is a repetitive approach that may produce different solutions in repeated runs. It does not generate optimal solutions to problems (as does linear programming).
3. Managers must generate all of the conditions and constraints for solutions that they want to examine. The simulation model does not produce answers without adequate, realistic input.
4. Each simulation model is unique. Its solutions and inferences are not usually transferable to other problems.

LO F.1 *List* the advantages and disadvantages of modeling with simulation

Computer simulation models have been developed to address a variety of productivity issues at fast-food restaurants such as Burger King. In one, the ideal distance between the drive-through order station and the pickup window was simulated. For example, because a longer distance reduced waiting time, 12 to 13 additional customers could be served per hour—a benefit of about $20,000 in extra sales per restaurant per year. In another simulation, a second drive-through window was considered. This model predicted a sales increase of 15%.

Donna Shader

Monte Carlo Simulation

Monte Carlo method

A simulation technique that uses random elements when chance exists in their behavior.

When a system contains elements that exhibit *chance* in their behavior, the Monte Carlo method of simulation may be applied. The basis of Monte Carlo simulation is experimentation on chance (or *probabilistic*) elements by means of random sampling.

The technique breaks down into five simple steps:

LO F.2 *Perform* the five steps in a Monte Carlo simulation

1. Setting up a probability distribution for important variables.
2. Building a cumulative probability distribution for each variable.
3. Establishing an interval of random numbers for each variable.
4. Generating random numbers.
5. Actually simulating a series of trials.

Let's examine these steps in turn.

Step 1. Establishing Probability Distributions. The basic idea in the Monte Carlo simulation is to generate values for the variables making up the model under study. In real-world systems, a lot of variables are probabilistic in nature. To name just a few: inventory demand; lead time for orders to arrive; times between machine breakdowns; times between customer arrivals at a service facility; service times; times required to complete project activities; and number of employees absent from work each day.

One common way to establish a *probability distribution* for a given variable is to examine historical outcomes. We can find the probability, or relative frequency, for each possible outcome of a variable by dividing the frequency of observation by the total number of observations. Here's an example.

The daily demand for radial tires at Barry's Auto Tire over the past 200 days is shown in columns 1 and 2 of Table F.2. Assuming that past arrival rates will hold in the future, we can convert this demand to a probability distribution by dividing each demand frequency by the total demand, 200. The results are shown in column 3.

Cumulative probability distribution

The accumulation of individual probabilities of a distribution.

Step 2. Building a Cumulative Probability Distribution for Each Variable. The conversion from a regular probability distribution, such as in column 3 of Table F.2, to a cumulative probability distribution is an easy job. In column 4, we see that the cumulative probability for each level of demand is the sum of the number in the probability column (column 3) added to the previous cumulative probability.

TABLE F.2	Demand for Barry's Auto Tire		
(1) **DEMAND FOR TIRES**	**(2)** **FREQUENCY**	**(3)** **PROBABILITY OF OCCURRENCE**	**(4)** **CUMULATIVE PROBABILITY**
0	10	10/200 = .05	.05
1	20	20/200 = .10	.15
2	40	40/200 = .20	.35
3	60	60/200 = .30	.65
4	40	40/200 = .20	.85
5	30	30/200 = .15	1.00
	200 days	200/200 = 1.00	

STUDENT TIP ◆

To establish a probability distribution for tires, we assume that historical demand is a good indicator of future demand.

TABLE F.3	The Assignment of Random-Number Intervals for Barry's Auto Tire		
DAILY DEMAND	**PROBABILITY**	**CUMULATIVE PROBABILITY**	**INTERVAL OF RANDOM NUMBERS**
0	.05	.05	01 through 05
1	.10	.15	06 through 15
2	.20	.35	16 through 35
3	.30	.65	36 through 65
4	.20	.85	66 through 85
5	.15	1.00	86 through 00

 STUDENT TIP

You may start random-number intervals at either 01 or 00, but the text starts at 01 so that the top of each range is the cumulative probability.

Step 3. Setting Random-Number Intervals. Once we have established a cumulative probability distribution for each variable in the simulation, we must assign a set of numbers to represent each possible value or outcome. These are referred to as random-number intervals. Basically, a random number is a series of digits (say, two digits from 01, 02, . . . , 98, 99, 00) that have been selected by a totally random process—a process in which each random number has an equal chance of being selected.

If, for example, there is a 5% chance that demand for Barry's radial tires will be 0 units per day, then we will want 5% of the random numbers available to correspond to a demand of 0 units. If a total of 100 two-digit numbers is used in the simulation, we could assign a demand of 0 units to the first 5 random numbers: 01, 02, 03, 04, and 05.[1] Then a simulated demand for 0 units would be created every time one of the numbers 01 to 05 was drawn. If there is also a 10% chance that demand for the same product will be 1 unit per day, we could let the next 10 random numbers (06, 07, 08, 09, 10, 11, 12, 13, 14, and 15) represent that demand—and so on for other demand levels.

Similarly, we can see in Table F.3 that the length of each interval on the right corresponds to the probability of 1 of each of the possible daily demands. Thus, in assigning random numbers

Random-number intervals

A set of numbers to represent each possible value or outcome in a computer simulation.

Random number

A series of digits that have been selected by a totally random process.

TABLE F.4	Table of 2-Digit Random Numbers																
52	06	50	88	53	30	10	47	99	37	66	91	35	32	00	84	57	07
37	63	28	02	74	35	24	03	29	60	74	85	90	73	59	55	17	60
82	57	68	28	05	94	03	11	27	79	90	87	92	41	09	25	36	77
69	02	36	49	71	99	32	10	75	21	95	90	94	38	97	71	72	49
98	94	90	36	06	78	23	67	89	85	29	21	25	73	69	34	85	76
96	52	62	87	49	56	59	23	78	71	72	90	57	01	98	57	31	95
33	69	27	21	11	60	95	89	68	48	17	89	34	09	93	50	44	51
50	33	50	95	13	44	34	62	64	39	55	29	30	64	49	44	30	16
88	32	18	50	62	57	34	56	62	31	15	40	90	34	51	95	26	14
90	30	36	24	69	82	51	74	30	35	36	85	01	55	92	64	09	85
50	48	61	18	85	23	08	54	17	12	80	69	24	84	92	16	49	59
27	88	21	62	69	64	48	31	12	73	02	68	00	16	16	46	13	85
45	14	46	32	13	49	66	62	74	41	86	98	92	98	84	54	33	40
81	02	01	78	82	74	97	37	45	31	94	99	42	49	27	64	89	42
66	83	14	74	27	76	03	33	11	97	59	81	72	00	64	61	13	52
74	05	81	82	93	09	96	33	52	78	13	06	28	30	94	23	37	39
30	34	87	01	74	11	46	82	59	94	25	34	32	23	17	01	58	73
59	55	72	33	62	13	74	68	22	44	42	09	32	46	71	79	45	89
67	09	80	98	99	25	77	50	03	32	36	63	65	75	94	19	95	88
60	77	46	63	71	69	44	22	03	85	14	48	69	13	30	50	33	24
60	08	19	29	36	72	30	27	50	64	85	72	75	29	87	05	75	01
80	45	86	99	02	34	87	08	86	84	49	76	24	08	01	86	29	11
53	84	49	63	26	65	72	84	85	63	26	02	75	26	92	62	40	67
69	84	12	94	51	36	17	02	15	29	16	52	56	43	26	22	08	62
37	77	13	10	02	18	31	19	32	85	31	94	81	43	31	58	33	51

Source: Adapted from *A Million Random Digits with 100,000 Normal Deviates.* New York: The Free Press, 1995. Used by permission.

to the daily demand for 3 radial tires, the range of the random-number interval (36 through 65) corresponds *exactly* to the probability (or proportion) of that outcome. A daily demand for 3 radial tires occurs 30% of the time. All of the 30 random numbers greater than 35 up to and including 65 are assigned to that event.

Step 4. Generating Random Numbers. Random numbers may be generated for simulation problems in two ways. If the problem is large and the process under study involves many simulation trials, computer programs are available to generate the needed random numbers. If the simulation is being done by hand, the numbers may be selected from a table of random digits.

Step 5. Simulating the Experiment. We may simulate outcomes of an experiment by simply selecting random numbers from Table F.4. Beginning anywhere in the table, we note the interval in Table F.3 into which each number falls. For example, if the random number chosen is 81 and the interval 66 through 85 represents a daily demand for 4 tires, then we select a demand of 4 tires. Example F1 carries the simulation further.

Example F1

SIMULATING DEMAND

Barry's Auto Tire wants to simulate 10 days of demand for radial tires.

APPROACH ▶ Earlier, we went through Steps 1 and 2 in the Monte Carlo method (in Table F.2) and Step 3 (in Table F.3). Now we need to generate random numbers (Step 4) and simulate demand (Step 5).

SOLUTION ▶ We select the random numbers needed from Table F.4, starting in the upper-left-hand corner and continuing down the first column, and record the corresponding daily demand:

DAY NUMBER	RANDOM NUMBER	SIMULATED DAILY DEMAND
1	52	3
2	37	3
3	82	4
4	69	4
5	98	5
6	96	5
7	33	2
8	50	3
9	88	5
10	90	5
		39 Total 10-day demand
		39/10 = 3.9 = tires average daily demand

INSIGHT ▶ It is interesting to note that the average demand of 3.9 tires in this 10-day simulation differs substantially from the *expected* daily demand, which we may calculate from the data in Table F.3:

$$\text{Expected demand} = \sum_{i=0}^{5} (\text{probability of } i \text{ units}) \times (\text{demand of } i \text{ units})$$

$$= (.05)(0) + (.10)(1) + (.20)(2) + (.30)(3) + (.20)(4) + (.15)(5)$$

$$= 0 + .1 + .4 + .9 + .8 + .75$$

$$= 2.95 \text{ tires}$$

However, if this simulation was repeated hundreds or thousands of times, the average *simulated* demand would be nearly the same as the *expected* demand.

LEARNING EXERCISE ▶ Resimulate the 10 days, this time with random numbers from column 2 of Table F.4. What is the average daily demand? [Answer: 2.5.]

RELATED PROBLEMS ▶ F.1–F.12 (F.13–F.15 are available in MyOMLab)

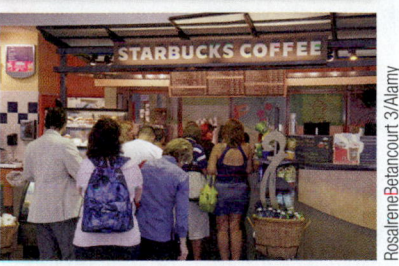
Naturally, it would be risky to draw any hard and fast conclusions about the operation of a firm from only a short simulation like Example F1. Seldom would anyone actually want to go to the effort of simulating such a simple model containing only one variable. Simulating by hand does, however, demonstrate the important principles involved and may be useful in small-scale studies.

Simulation with Two Decision Variables:
An Inventory Example

Often, there is more than one variable to be simulated. In Example F1 it was demand for tires. But many OM decisions have multiple variables. In a queuing situation, it may be arrival times and service times. In an inventory problem, as we saw in Chapter 12, both demand and lead time might be variable (not constant).

In this section, we present an inventory problem with two decision variables and two probabilistic components. The owner of the hardware store in Example F2 would like to establish *order quantity* and *reorder point* decisions for a particular product that has probabilistic (uncertain) daily demand and reorder lead time. He wants to make a series of simulation runs, trying out various order quantities and reorder points, to minimize his total inventory cost for the item. Inventory costs in this case will include ordering, holding, and stockout costs.

STUDENT TIP

Most real-world inventory systems have probabilistic events and benefit from a simulation approach.

Example F2   AN INVENTORY SIMULATION WITH TWO VARIABLES

Simkin's Hardware Store, in Reno, sells the Ace model electric drill. Daily demand for this particular product is relatively low but subject to some variability. Lead times tend to be variable as well. Mark Simkin wants to develop a simulation to test an inventory policy of ordering 10 drills, with a reorder point of 5. In other words, every time the on-hand inventory level at the end of the day is 5 or less, Simkin will call his supplier that evening and place an order for 10 more drills. Simkin notes that if the lead time is 1 day, the order will not arrive the next morning but rather at the beginning of the following workday. Stockouts become lost sales, not backorders.

APPROACH ▶   Simkin wants to follow the 5 steps in the Monte Carlo simulation process.

SOLUTION ▶   Over the past 300 days, Simkin has observed the sales shown in column 2 of Table F.5. He converts this historical frequency into a probability distribution for the variable daily demand (column 3). A cumulative probability distribution is formed in column 4 of Table F.5. Finally, Simkin establishes an interval of random numbers to represent each possible daily demand (column 5).

When Simkin places an order to replenish his inventory of drills, there is a delivery lag of from 1 to 3 days. This means that lead time may also be considered a probabilistic variable. The number of days

| TABLE F.5 | Probabilities and Random-Number Intervals for Daily Ace Drill Demand |

(1) DEMAND FOR ACE DRILL	(2) FREQUENCY	(3) PROBABILITY	(4) CUMULATIVE PROBABILITY	(5) INTERVAL OF RANDOM NUMBERS
0	15	.05	.05	01 through 05
1	30	.10	.15	06 through 15
2	60	.20	.35	16 through 35
3	120	.40	.75	36 through 75
4	45	.15	.90	76 through 90
5	30	.10	1.00	91 through 00
	300 days	1.00		

LO F.3 *Simulate* an inventory problem

that it took to receive the past 50 orders is presented in Table F.6. In a fashion similar to the creation of the demand variable, Simkin establishes a probability distribution for the lead time variable (column 3 of Table F.6), computes the cumulative distribution (column 4), and assigns random-number intervals for each possible time (column 5).

| TABLE F.6 | Probabilities and Random-Number Intervals for Reorder Lead Time |

(1) LEAD TIME (DAYS)	(2) FREQUENCY	(3) PROBABILITY	(4) CUMULATIVE PROBABILITY	(5) RANDOM-NUMBER INTERVAL
1	10	.20	.20	01 through 20
2	25	.50	.70	21 through 70
3	15	.30	1.00	71 through 00
	50 orders	1.00		

The entire process is simulated in Table F.7 for a 10-day period. We assume that beginning inventory (column 3) is 10 units on day 1. We took the random numbers (column 4) from column 2 of Table F.4.

| TABLE F.7 | Simkin Hardware's First Inventory Simulation. Order Quantity = 10 Units; Reorder Point = 5 Units |

(1) DAY	(2) UNITS RECEIVED	(3) BEGINNING INVENTORY	(4) RANDOM NUMBER	(5) DEMAND	(6) ENDING INVENTORY	(7) LOST SALES	(8) ORDER?	(9) RANDOM NUMBER	(10) LEAD TIME
1		10	06	1	9	0	No		
2	0	9	63	3	6	0	No		
3	0	6	57	3	3[a]	0	Yes	02[b]	1
4	0	3	94[c]	5	0	2	No[d]		
5	10[e]	10	52	3	7	0	No		
6	0	7	69	3	4	0	Yes	33	2
7	0	4	32	2	2	0	No		
8	0	2	30	2	0	0	No		
9	10[f]	10	48	3	7	0	No		
10	0	7	88	4	3	0	Yes	14	1
					Totals: 41	2			

[a]This is the first time inventory dropped to the reorder point of five drills. Because no prior order was outstanding, an order is placed.

[b]The random number 02 is generated to represent the first lead time. It was drawn from column 2 of Table F.4 as the next number in the list being used. A separate column could have been used from which to draw lead-time random numbers if we had wanted to do so, but in this example, we did not do so.

[c]Again, notice that the random digits 02 were used for lead time (see footnote b). So the next number in the column is 94.

[d]No order is placed on day 4 because there is an order outstanding from the previous day that has not yet arrived.

[e]The lead time for the first order placed is 1 day, but as noted in the text, an order does not arrive the next morning but rather the beginning of the following day. Thus, the first order arrives at the start of day 5.

[f]This is the arrival of the order placed at the close of business on day 6. Fortunately for Simkin, no lost sales occurred during the 2-day lead time before the order arrived.

Table F.7 was filled in by proceeding 1 day (or line) at a time, working from left to right. It is a four-step process:

1. Begin each simulated day by checking to see whether any ordered inventory has just arrived. If it has, increase current inventory by the quantity ordered (10 units, in this case).
2. Generate a daily demand from the demand probability distribution for the selected random number.
3. Compute: Ending inventory = Beginning inventory minus Demand. If on-hand inventory is insufficient to meet the day's demand, satisfy as much demand as possible and note the number of lost sales.
4. Determine whether the day's ending inventory has reached the reorder point (5 units). If it has, and if there are no outstanding orders, place an order. Lead time for a new order is simulated for the selected random number corresponding to the distribution in Table F.6.

INSIGHTS ▶ Simkin's inventory simulation yields some interesting results. The average daily ending inventory is:

$$\text{Average ending inventory} = \frac{41 \text{ total units}}{10 \text{ days}} = 4.1 \text{ units/day}$$

We also note the average lost sales and number of orders placed per day:

$$\text{Average lost sales} = \frac{2 \text{ sales lost}}{10 \text{ days}} = .2 \text{ units/day}$$

$$\text{Average number of orders placed} = \frac{3 \text{ orders}}{10 \text{ days}} = .3 \text{ orders/day}$$

LEARNING EXERCISE ▶ How would these 3 averages change if the random numbers for day 10 were 04 and 93 instead of 88 and 14? [Answer: 4.4, .2 (no change), and .2.]

RELATED PROBLEMS ▶ F.16–F.21 (F.22–F.25 are available in MyOMLab)

Now that we have worked through Example F2 we want to emphasize something very important: This simulation should be extended many more days before we draw any conclusions as to the cost of the order policy being tested. If a hand simulation is being conducted, 100 days would provide a better representation. If a computer is doing the calculations, 1,000 days would be helpful in reaching accurate cost estimates. (Moreover, remember that even with a 1,000-day simulation, the generated distribution should be compared with the desired distribution to ensure valid results.)

Summary

Simulation involves building mathematical models that attempt to act like real operating systems. In this way, a real-world situation can be studied without imposing on the actual system. Although simulation models can be developed manually, simulation by computer is generally more desirable. The Monte Carlo approach uses random numbers to represent variables, such as inventory demand or people waiting in line, which are then simulated in a series of trials. Simulation is widely used as an operations tool because its advantages usually outweigh its disadvantages.

Key Terms

Simulation (p. 792)
Monte Carlo method (p. 794)
Cumulative probability distribution (p. 794)
Random-number intervals (p. 795)
Random number (p. 795)

Discussion Questions

1. State the seven steps, beginning with "Defining the Problem," that an operations manager should perform when using simulation to analyze a problem.
2. List the advantages of simulation.
3. List the disadvantages of simulation.
4. Explain the difference between *simulated* average demand and *expected* average demand.
5. What is the role of random numbers in a Monte Carlo simulation?
6. Why might the results of a simulation differ each time you make a run?
7. What is Monte Carlo simulation? What principles underlie its use, and what steps are followed in applying it?
8. List six ways that simulation can be used in business.

9. Why is simulation such a widely used technique?

10. What are the advantages of special-purpose simulation languages (see below)?

11. In the simulation of an order policy for drills at Simkin's hardware (Example F2, pp. 797–799), would the results (of Table F.7) change significantly if a longer period were simulated? Why is the 10-day simulation valid or invalid?

12. Why is a computer necessary in conducting a real-world simulation?

13. Why might a manager be forced to use simulation instead of an analytical model in dealing with a problem of:
a) inventory order policy?
b) ships docking in a port to unload?
c) bank-teller service windows?
d) the U.S. economy?

Using Software in Simulation

Computers are critical in simulating complex tasks. They can generate random numbers, simulate thousands of time periods in a matter of seconds or minutes, and provide management with reports that improve decision making. A computer approach is almost a necessity in order to draw valid conclusions from a simulation.

Computer programming languages can help the simulation process. *General-purpose languages*, such as BASIC or C++, constitute one approach. *Special-purpose simulation languages*, such as GPSS and SIMSCRIPT, have a few advantages: (1) they require less programming time for large simulations, (2) they are usually more efficient and easier to check for errors, and (3) random-number generators are already built in as subroutines.

Commercial, easy-to-use prewritten simulation programs are also available. Some are generalized to handle a wide variety of situations ranging from queuing to inventory. These include programs such as Extend, Modsim, Witness, MAP/1, Enterprise Dynamics, Simfactory, ProModel, Micro Saint, and ARENA.

Spreadsheet software such as Excel can also be used to develop simulations quickly and easily. Such packages have built-in random-number generators and develop outputs through "data-fill" table commands.

✖ USING EXCEL SPREADSHEETS

The ability to generate random numbers and then "look up" these numbers in a table to associate them with a specific event makes spreadsheets excellent tools for conducting simulations. Program F.1 illustrates an Excel simulation for Example F1.

Notice that the cumulative probabilities are calculated in column E of Program F.1. This procedure reduces the chance of error and is useful in larger simulations involving more levels of demand.

The **VLOOKUP** function in column I looks up the random number (generated in column H) in the leftmost column of the defined lookup table. The **VLOOKUP** function moves downward through this column until it finds a cell that is bigger than the random number. It then goes to the previous row and gets the value from column B of the table.

LO F.4 *Use* Excel spreadsheets to create a simulation

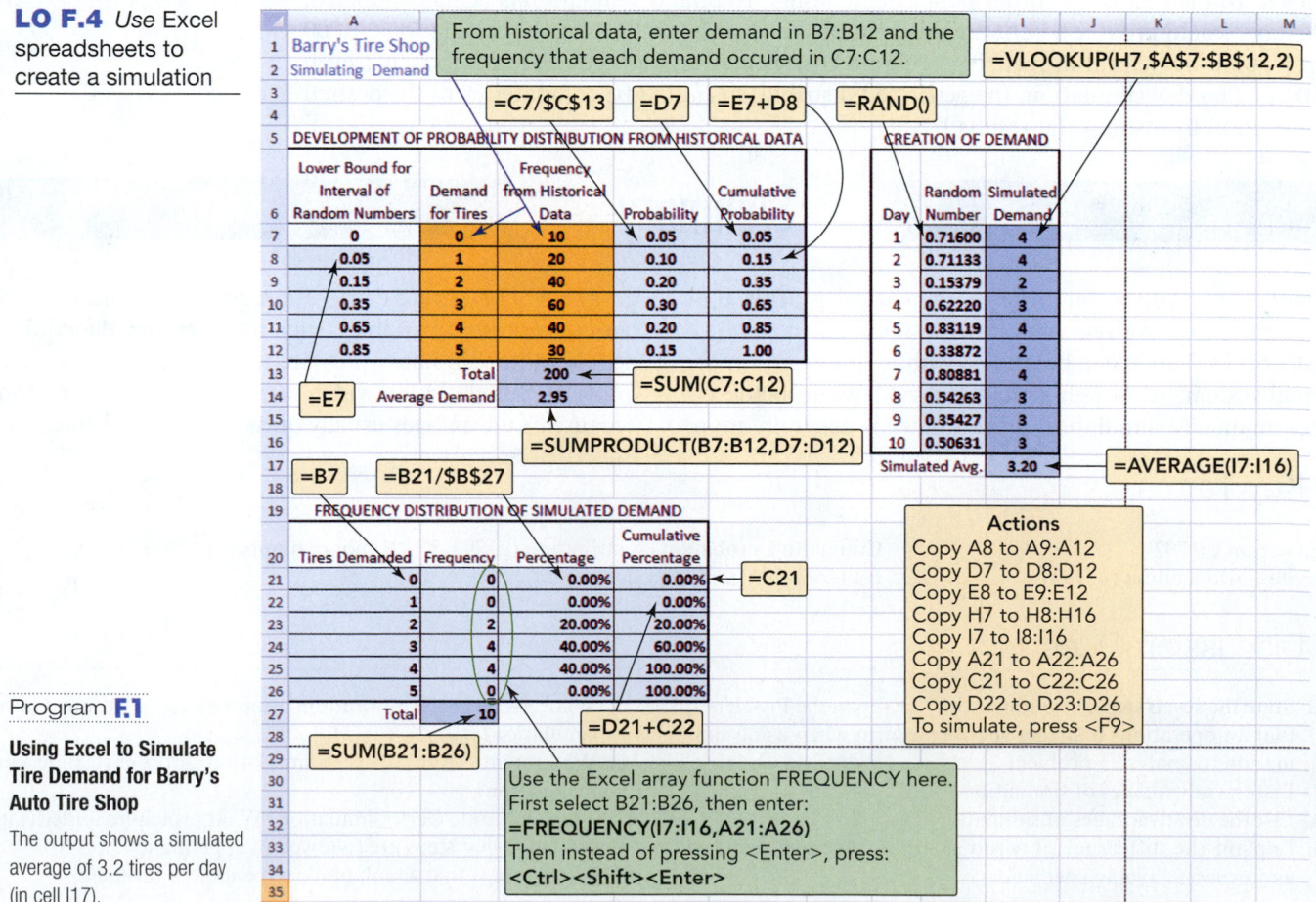

Program F.1

Using Excel to Simulate Tire Demand for Barry's Auto Tire Shop

The output shows a simulated average of 3.2 tires per day (in cell I17).

In column H, for example, the first random number shown is .716. Excel looked down the left-hand column of the lookup table ($A$7:$B$12) of Program F.1 until it found .85. From the previous row it retrieved the value in column B which is 4. Pressing the F9 function key recalculates the random numbers and the simulation.

Px USING POM FOR WINDOWS AND EXCEL OM

POM for Windows and Excel OM are capable of handling any simulation that contains only one random variable, such as Example F1. For further details, please refer to Appendix IV.

Solved Problems   Virtual Office Hours help is available in MyOMLab.

SOLVED PROBLEM F.1

Higgins Plumbing and Heating maintains a stock of 30-gallon water heaters that it sells to homeowners and installs for them. Owner Jim Higgins likes the idea of having a large supply on hand to meet any customer demand. However, he also recognizes that it is expensive to do so. He examines water heater sales over the past 50 weeks and notes the following:

WATER HEATER SALES PER WEEK	NUMBER OF WEEKS THIS NUMBER WAS SOLD
4	6
5	5
6	9
7	12
8	8
9	7
10	3
	50 weeks total data

a) If Higgins maintains a constant supply of 8 water heaters in any given week, how many times will he stockout during a 20-week simulation? We use random numbers from the 7th column of Table F.4 (on p. 795), beginning with the random digit 10.

b) What is the average number of sales per week over the 20-week period?

c) Using an analytic nonsimulation technique, determine the expected number of sales per week. How does this compare with the answer in part (b)?

SOLUTION

HEATER SALES	PROBABILITY	CUMULATIVE PROBABILITY	RANDOM-NUMBER INTERVALS
4	.12	.12	01 through 12
5	.10	.22	13 through 22
6	.18	.40	23 through 40
7	.24	.64	41 through 64
8	.16	.80	65 through 80
9	.14	.94	81 through 94
10	.06	1.00	95 through 00
	1.00		

a)

WEEK	RANDOM NUMBER	SIMULATED SALES	WEEK	RANDOM NUMBER	SIMULATED SALES
1	10	4	11	08	4
2	24	6	12	48	7
3	03	4	13	66	8
4	32	6	14	97	10
5	23	6	15	03	4
6	59	7	16	96	10
7	95	10	17	46	7
8	34	6	18	74	8
9	34	6	19	77	8
10	51	7	20	44	7

With a supply of 8 heaters, Higgins will stock out three times during the 20-week period (in weeks 7, 14, and 16).

b) Average sales by simulation = total sales/20 weeks − 135/20 = 6.75 per week

c) Using expected values, we obtain:

E (sales) = .12(4 heaters) + .10(5) + .18(6) + .24(7) + .16(8) + .14(9) + .06(10) = 6.88 heaters

With a longer simulation, these two approaches will lead to even closer values.

SOLVED PROBLEM F.2

Random numbers may be used to simulate continuous distributions. As a simple example, assume that fixed cost equals $300, profit contribution equals $10 per item sold, and you expect an equally likely chance of 0 to 99 units to be sold. That is, profit equals $-\$300 + \$10X$, where X is the number sold. The mean amount you expect to sell is 49.5 units.

a) Calculate the expected value.
b) Simulate the sale of 5 items, using the following double-digit randomly-selected numbers of items sold:
   37 77 13 10 85
c) Calculate the expected value of (b) and compare with the results of (a).

SOLUTION

a) Expected value $= -300 + 10(49.5) = \$195$

b) $-300 + \$10(37) = \$70$
   $-300 + \$10(77) = \$470$
   $-300 + \$10(13) = -\$170$
   $-300 + \$10(10) = -\$200$
   $-300 + \$10(85) = \$550$

c) The mean of these simulated sales is $144. If the sample size were larger, we would expect the two values to be closer.

Problems

Note: **PX** *means the problem may be solved with POM for Windows and/or Excel OM or Excel.*

The problems that follow involve simulations that can be done by hand. However, to obtain accurate and meaningful results, long periods must be simulated. This task is usually handled by a computer. If you are able to program some of the problems in Excel or a computer language with which you are familiar, we suggest you try to do so. If not, the hand simulations will still help you understand the simulation process.

Problems F.1–F.15 relate to Monte Carlo Simulation

• **F.1** The daily demand for tuna sandwiches at an Ohio University cafeteria vending machine is 8, 9, 10, or 11, with probabilities 0.4, 0.3, 0.2, or 0.1, respectively. Assume the following random numbers have been generated: 09, 55, 73, 67, 53, 59, 04, 23, 88, and 84. Using these numbers, generate daily sandwich sales for 10 days. **PX**

• **F.2** The number of machine breakdowns per day at Yuwen Chen's factory is 0, 1, or 2, with probabilities 0.5, 0.3, or 0.2, respectively. The following random numbers have been generated: 13, 14, 02, 18, 31, 19, 32, 85, 31, and 94. Use these numbers to generate the number of breakdowns for 10 consecutive days. What proportion of these days had at least one breakdown? **PX**

• **F.3** The table below shows the partial results of a Monte Carlo simulation. Assume that the simulation began at 8:00 A.M., and there is only one server.

CUSTOMER NUMBER	ARRIVAL TIME	SERVICE TIME
1	8:01	6
2	8:06	7
3	8:09	8
4	8:15	6
5	8:20	6

a) When does service begin for customer number 3?
b) When will customer number 5 leave?
c) What is the average waiting time in line?
d) What is the average time in the system?

• **F.4** Barbara Flynn sells papers at a newspaper stand for $.35. The papers cost her $.25, giving her a $.10 profit on each one she sells. From past experience Barbara knows that:
a) 20% of the time she sells 100 papers.
b) 20% of the time she sells 150 papers.
c) 30% of the time she sells 200 papers.
d) 30% of the time she sells 250 papers.

Assuming that Barbara believes the cost of a lost sale to be $.05 and any unsold papers cost her $.25, simulate her profit outlook over 5 days if she orders 200 papers for each of the 5 days. Use the following random numbers: 52, 06, 50, 88, and 53. **PX**

•• **F.5** Arnold Palmer Hospital is studying the number of emergency surgery kits that it uses on weekends. Over the past 40 weekends, the number of kits used was as follows:

NUMBER OF KITS	FREQUENCY
4	4
5	6
6	10
7	12
8	8

The following random numbers have been generated: 11, 52, 59, 22, 03, 03, 50, 86, 85, 15, 32, 47. Simulate 12 weekends of emergency kit usage. What is the average number of kits used during these 12 weekends? **PX**

• **F.6** Susan Sherer's grocery store has noted the following figures with regard to the number of people who arrive at the store's three checkout stands and the time it takes to check them out:

ARRIVALS/MINUTE	FREQUENCY
0	.3
1	.5
2	.2

SERVICE TIME/MINUTE	FREQUENCY
1	.1
2	.3
3	.4
4	.2

Simulate the utilization of the three checkout stands over 5 minutes, using the following random numbers: 07, 60, 77, 49, 76, 95, 51, 16, and 14. Record the results at the end of the 5-minute period. Start at time = 0. **PX**

• **F.7** A warehouse manager at Mary Beth Marrs Corp. needs to simulate the demand placed on a product that does not fit standard models. The concept being measured is "demand during lead time," where both lead time and daily demand are variable. The historical record for this product, along with the cumulative distribution, appear in the table. Random numbers have been generated to simulate the next 5 order cycles; they are 91, 45, 37, 65, and 51. What are the five demand values? What is their average?

DEMAND DURING LEAD TIME	PROBABILITY	CUMULATIVE PROBABILITY
100	.01	.01
120	.15	.16
140	.30	.46
160	.15	.61
180	.04	.65
200	.10	.75
220	.25	1.00

Px

· F.8 Phantom Controls monitors and repairs control circuit boxes on elevators installed in multistory buildings in downtown Chicago. The company has the contract for 108 buildings. When a box malfunctions, Phantom installs a new one and rebuilds the failed unit in its repair facility in Gary, Indiana. The data for failed boxes over the last 2 years is shown in the following table:

NUMBER OF FAILED BOXES PER MONTH	PROBABILITY
0	.10
1	.14
2	.26
3	.20
4	.18
5	.12

Simulate 2 years (24 months) of operation for Phantom and determine the average number of failed boxes per month from the simulation. Was it common to have fewer than 7 failures over 3 months of operation? (Start your simulation at the top of the 10th column of Table F.4 on page 795, $RN = 37$, and go down in the table.) **Px**

· F.9 The number of cars arriving at Patti Miles's Car Wash, in Orono, Maine, during the last 200 hours of operation is observed to be the following:

NUMBER OF CARS ARRIVING	FREQUENCY
3 or fewer	0
4	20
5	30
6	50
7	60
8	40
9 or more	0
	200

a) Set up a probability and cumulative-probability distribution for the variable of car arrivals.
b) Establish random-number intervals for the variable.
c) Simulate 15 hours of car arrivals and compute the average number of arrivals per hour. Select the random numbers needed from column 1, Table F.4, beginning with the digits 52. **Px**

··F.10 Leonard Presby's newsstand uses naive forecasting to order tomorrow's papers. The number of newspapers ordered corresponds to the previous day's demands. Today's demand for papers was 22. Presby buys the newspapers for $.20 and sells them for $.50. Whenever there is unsatisfied demand, Presby estimates the lost goodwill cost at $.10. Complete the accompanying table, and answer the questions that follow.

DEMAND	PROBABILITY
21	.25
22	.15
23	.10
24	.20
25	.30

DAY	PAPERS ORDERED	RANDOM NUMBER	DEMAND	REVENUE	COST	GOODWILL COST	NET PROFIT
1	22	37					
2		19					
3		52					
4		8					
5		22					
6		61					

a) What is the demand on day 3?
b) What is the total net profit at the end of the 6 days?
c) What is the lost goodwill on day 6?
d) What is the net profit on day 2?
e) How many papers has Presby ordered for day 5? **Px**

··F.11 Every home football game for the past 8 years at Southwestern University has been sold out. The revenues from ticket sales are significant, but the sale of food, beverages, and souvenirs has contributed greatly to the overall profitability of the football program. One particular souvenir is the football program for each game. The number of programs sold at each game is described by the probability distribution given in the following table.

NUMBERS OF PROGRAMS SOLD	PROBABILITY
2,300	0.15
2,400	0.22
2,500	0.24
2,600	0.21
2,700	0.18

Each program costs $.80 to produce and sells for $2.00. Any programs that are not sold are donated to a recycling center and do not produce any revenue.
a) Simulate the sales of programs at 10 football games. Use the last column in the random-number table (Table F.4 on p. 795) and begin at the top of the column.
b) If the university decided to print 2,500 programs for each game, what would the average profits be for the 10 games that were simulated?
c) If the university decided to print 2,600 programs for each game, what would the average profits be for the 10 games that were simulated? **Px**

· F.12 Refer to the data in Solved Problem F.1, on page 801, which deals with Higgins Plumbing and Heating. Higgins has now collected 100 weeks of data and finds the following distribution for sales:

WATER HEATER SALES PER WEEK	NUMBER OF WEEKS THIS NUMBER WAS SOLD	WATER HEATER SALES PER WEEK	NUMBER OF WEEKS THIS NUMBER WAS SOLD
3	2	8	12
4	9	9	12
5	10	10	10
6	15	11	5
7	25		100

a) Assuming that Higgins maintains a constant supply of 8 heaters, simulate the number of stockouts incurred over a 20-week period (using the seventh column of Table F.4).

b) Conduct this 20-week simulation two more times and compare your answers with those in (a). Did they change significantly? Why or why not?

c) What is the new expected number of sales per week? **Px**

Additional problems **F.13–F.15** are available in MyOMLab.

Problems F.16–F.25 relate to Simulation with Two Decision Variables: An Inventory Example

•• **F.16** The time between arrivals at the drive-through window of Barry Harmon's fast-food restaurant follows the distribution given in the table. The service-time distribution is also given. Use the random numbers provided to simulate the activity of the first 4 arrivals. Assume that the window opens at 11:00 A.M. and that the first arrival occurs afterward, based on the first interarrival time generated.

TIME BETWEEN ARRIVALS	PROBABILITY	SERVICE TIME	PROBABILITY
1	.2	1	.3
2	.3	2	.5
3	.3	3	.2
4	.2		

Random numbers for arrivals: 14, 74, 27, 03
Random numbers for service times: 88, 32, 36, 24
At what time does the fourth customer leave the system? **Px**

••• **F.17** Central Hospital in York, Pennsylvania, has an emergency room that is divided into six departments: (1) an initial exam station to treat minor problems or to make a diagnosis; (2) an X-ray department; (3) an operating room; (4) a cast-fitting room; (5) an observation room (for recovery and general observation before final diagnosis or release); and (6) an outprocessing department (where clerks check out patients and arrange for payment or insurance forms).

The probabilities that a patient will go from one department to another are presented in the following table:

FROM	TO	PROBABILITY
Initial exam at emergency room entrance	X-ray department	.45
	Operating room	.15
	Observation room	.10
	Outprocessing clerk	.30
X-ray department	Operating room	.10
	Cast-fitting room	.25
	Observation room	.35
	Outprocessing clerk	.30
Operating room	Cast-fitting room	.25
	Observation room	.70
	Outprocessing clerk	.05
Cast-fitting room	Observation room	.55
	X-ray department	.05
	Outprocessing clerk	.40
Observation room	Operating room	.15
	X-ray department	.15
	Outprocessing clerk	.70

a) Simulate the trail followed by 10 emergency room patients. Proceed, one patient at a time, from each one's entry at the initial exam station until he or she leaves through outprocessing. You should be aware that a patient can enter the same department more than once.

b) Using your simulation data, determine the chances that a patient enters the X-ray department twice.

••• **F.18** Connecticut Tanning has two tanning beds. One bed serves the company's regular members exclusively. The second bed serves strictly walk-in customers (those without appointments) on a first-come, first-served basis. Orv Karan, the store manager, has noticed on several occasions during the busy 5 hours of the day (2:00 P.M. until 7:00 P.M.) that potential walk-in customers will most often walk away from the store if they see one person already waiting for the second bed. He wonders if capturing this lost demand would justify adding a third bed. Leasing and maintaining a tanning bed costs Connecticut Tanning $600 per month. The price paid per customer varies according to the time in the bed, but Orv has calculated the average net income for every 10 minutes of tanning time to be $2. A study of the pattern of arrivals during the busy hours and the time spent tanning has revealed the following:

TIME BETWEEN ARRIVALS (MINUTES)	PROBABILITY	TIME IN TANNING BED (MINUTES)	PROBABILITY
5	0.30	10	0.20
10	0.25	15	0.30
15	0.20	20	0.40
20	0.15	25	0.10
25	0.10		

a) Simulate 4 hours of operation (arrivals over 4 hours). Use the 14th column of Table F.4 (p. 795) for arrival times and the 8th column for tanning times. Assume there is one person who has just entered the bed at 2:00 P.M. for a 20-minute tan. Indicate which customers balk at waiting for the bed to become available. How many customers were lost over the 4 hours (the simulation ends at 6:00 P.M.)?

b) If the store is open an average of 24 days a month, will capturing all lost sales justify adding a new tanning bed?

••• **F.19** Kathryn Marley owns and operates the largest Mercedes-Benz auto dealership in Pittsburgh. In the past 36 months, her sales have ranged from a low of 6 new cars to a high of 12 new cars, as reflected in the following table:

SALES OF NEW CARS/MONTH	FREQUENCY
6	3
7	4
8	6
9	12
10	9
11	1
12	1
	36 months

Marley believes that sales will continue during the next 24 months at about the same historical rates, and that delivery times will also continue to follow the following pace (stated in probability form):

DELIVERY TIME (MONTHS)*	PROBABILITY
1	.44
2	.33
3	.16
4	.07
	1.00

*With cars arriving at the end of the month (i.e., orders placed at the end of the 1st month, with a lead time of 2 months, will arrive at the end of the 3rd month, too late for sales in the 3rd month).

Marley's current policy is to order 14 cars at a time (two full truckloads, with 7 autos on each truck), and to place a new order whenever the stock on hand reaches 12 autos.
a) What are the results of this policy when simulated over the next 2 years?
b) Marley establishes the following relevant costs: (1) carrying cost per Mercedes per month is $600; (2) cost of a lost sale averages $4,350; and (3) cost of placing an order is $570. What is the total inventory cost of this policy?

•• F.20   Dumoor Appliance Center sells and services several brands of major appliances. Past sales for a particular model of refrigerator have resulted in the following probability distribution for demand:

Demand per week	0	1	2	3	4
Probability	0.20	0.40	0.20	0.15	0.05

The lead-time in weeks is described by the following distribution:

Lead time (weeks)	1	2	3
Probability	0.15	0.35	0.50

Based on cost considerations as well as storage space, the company has decided to order 10 of these each time an order is placed. The holding cost is $1 per week for each unit that is left in inventory at the end of the week. The stockout cost has been set at $40 per stockout. The company has decided to place an order whenever there are only two refrigerators left at the end of the week. Simulate 10 weeks of operation for Dumoor Appliance, assuming that there are currently 5 units in inventory. Determine what the weekly stockout cost and weekly holding cost would be for the problem. Use the random numbers in the first column of Table F.4 for demand and the second column for lead time.

•• F.21   Repeat the simulation in Problem F.20, assuming that the reorder point is 4 units rather than 2. Compare the costs for these two situations. Use the same random numbers as in Problem F.20.

Additional problems **F.22–F.25** *are available in* MyOMLab.

CASE STUDY

Alabama Airlines' Call Center

Alabama Airlines opened its doors in December 2015 as a commuter service with its headquarters and hub located in Birmingham. The airline was started and managed by two former pilots, David Douglas and George Devenney. It acquired a fleet of 12 used prop-jet planes and the airport gates vacated by Delta Air Lines in 2014.

TABLE F.8	Incoming Call Distribution

TIME BETWEEN CALLS (MINUTES)	PROBABILITY
1	.11
2	.21
3	.22
4	.20
5	.16
6	.10

With business growing quickly, Douglas turned his attention to Alabama Air's "800" reservations system. Between midnight and 6:00 A.M., only one telephone reservations agent had been on duty. The time between incoming calls during this period is distributed as shown in Table F.8. Carefully observing and timing the agent, Douglas estimated that the time required to process passenger inquiries is distributed as shown in Table F.9.

TABLE F.9	Service-Time Distribution

TIME TO PROCESS CUSTOMER INQUIRIES (MINUTES)	PROBABILITY
1	.20
2	.19
3	.18
4	.17
5	.13
6	.10
7	.03

All customers calling Alabama Air go "on hold" and are served in the order of the calls received unless the reservations agent is available for immediate service. Douglas is deciding whether a second agent should be on duty to cope with customer demand. To maintain customer satisfaction, Alabama Air wants a customer to be "on hold" for no more than 3 to 4 minutes; it also wants to maintain a "high" operator utilization.

Furthermore, the airline is planning a new TV advertising campaign. As a result, it expects an increase in "800" line phone inquiries. Based on similar campaigns in the past, the incoming call distribution from midnight to 6:00 A.M. is expected to be as shown in Table F.10. (The same service-time distribution will apply.)

TABLE F.10	Incoming Call Distribution

TIME BETWEEN CALLS (MINUTES)	PROBABILITY
1	.22
2	.25
3	.19
4	.15
5	.12
6	.07

Discussion Questions

1. Given the original call distribution, what would you advise Alabama Air to do for the current reservation system? Create a simulation model to investigate the scenario. Describe the model carefully, and justify the duration of the simulation, assumptions, and measures of performance.

2. What are your recommendations regarding operator utilization and customer satisfaction if the airline proceeds with the advertising campaign?

Source: Professor Zbigniew H. Przasnyski, Loyola Marymount University. Reprinted by permission.

- **Additional Case Study:** Visit MyOMLab for this free case study:
  Saigon Transport: This Vietnamese shipping company is trying to determine the ideal truck fleet size.

Endnote

1. Alternatively, we could have assigned the random numbers 00, 01, 02, 03, and 04 to represent a demand of 0 units. The 2 digits 00 can be thought of as either 0 or 100. As long as 5 numbers out of 100 are assigned to the 0 demand, it does not make any difference which 5 they are.

Module F *Rapid Review*

Main Heading	Review Material	MyOMLab
WHAT IS SIMULATION? (pp. 792–793)	Most of the large companies in the world use simulation models.	Concept Questions: 1.1–1.4

WHAT IS SIMULATION? (pp. 792–793)

Most of the large companies in the world use simulation models.

- **Simulation**—The attempt to duplicate the features, appearance, and characteristics of a real system, usually via a computerized model.

The idea behind simulation is threefold:

1. To imitate a real-world situation mathematically
2. Then to study its properties and operating characteristics
3. Finally, to draw conclusions and make action decisions based on the results of the simulation

In this way, a real-life system need not be touched until the advantages and disadvantages of a major policy decision are first measured on the model.

To use simulation, an OM manager should:

1. Define the problem.
2. Introduce the important variables associated with the problem.
3. Construct a numerical model.
4. Set up possible courses of action for testing by specifying values of variables.
5. Run the experiment.
6. Consider the results (possibly modifying the model or changing data inputs).
7. Decide what course of action to take.

Figure **F.1**

The Process of Simulation

Concept Questions: 1.1–1.4

ADVANTAGES AND DISADVANTAGES OF SIMULATION (p. 793)

The main *advantages* of simulation are:

1. It can be used to analyze large and complex real-world situations that cannot be solved using conventional operations management models.
2. Real-world complications can be included that most OM models cannot permit. For example, simulation can use any probability distribution the user defines; it does not require standard distributions.
3. "Time compression" is possible. The effects of OM policies over many months or years can be obtained by computer simulation in a short time.
4. Simulation allows "what-if?" types of questions. Managers like to know in advance what options will be most attractive. With a computerized model, a manager can try out several policy decisions within a matter of minutes.
5. Simulations do not interfere with real-world systems. It may be too disruptive, for example, to experiment physically with new policies or ideas.

The main *disadvantages* of simulation are:

1. Good simulation models can be very expensive; they may take many months to develop.
2. It is a repetitive approach that may produce different solutions in repeated runs. It does not generate optimal solutions to problems.

Concept Questions: 2.1–2.4

Main Heading	Review Material	MyOMLab
	3. Managers must generate all of the conditions and constraints for solutions that they want to examine. The simulation model does not produce answers without adequate, realistic input. 4. Each simulation model is unique. Its solutions and inferences are not usually transferable to other problems.	
MONTE CARLO SIMULATION (pp. 794–797)	■ **Monte Carlo method**—A simulation technique that selects random numbers assigned to a distribution. The Monte Carlo method breaks down into five simple steps: 1. Setting up a probability distribution for important variables 2. Building a cumulative probability distribution for each variable 3. Establishing an interval of random numbers for each variable 4. Generating random numbers 5. Actually simulating a series of trials One common way to establish a *probability distribution* for a given variable is to examine historical outcomes. We can find the probability, or relative frequency, for each possible outcome of a variable by dividing the frequency of observation by the total number of observations. ■ **Cumulative probability distribution**—The accumulation (summary) of probabilities of a distribution. ■ **Random-number intervals**—A set of numbers to represent each possible value or outcome in a computer simulation. ■ **Random number**—A series of digits that have been selected using a totally random process. Random numbers may be generated for simulation problems in two ways: (1) If the problem is large and the process under study involves many simulation trials, computer programs are available to generate the needed random numbers; or (2) if the simulation is being done by hand, the numbers may be selected from a table of random digits.	Concept Questions: 3.1–3.4 Problems: F.1–F.15 Virtual Office Hours for Solved Problems: F.1, F.2
SIMULATION WITH TWO DECISION VARIABLES: AN INVENTORY EXAMPLE (pp. 797–799)	The commonly used EOQ models are based on the assumption that both product demand and reorder lead time are known, constant values. In most real-world inventory situations, though, demand and lead time are variables, so accurate analysis becomes extremely difficult to handle by any means other than simulation.	Concept Questions: 4.1–4.4 Problems: F.16–F.25

Self Test

■ **Before taking the self-test,** refer to the learning objectives listed at the beginning of the module and the key terms listed at the end of the module.

LO F.1 Which of the following is *not* an advantage of simulation?
a) Simulation is relatively straightforward and flexible.
b) Good simulation models are usually inexpensive to develop.
c) "Time compression" is possible.
d) Simulation can study the interactive effects of individual variables.
e) Simulations do not interfere with real-world systems.

LO F.2 The five steps required to implement the Monte Carlo simulation technique are _____, _____, _____, _____, and _____.

LO F.3 Two particularly good candidates to be probabilistic components in the simulation of an inventory problem are:
a) order quantity and reorder point.
b) setup cost and holding cost.

c) daily demand and reorder lead time.
d) order quantity and reorder lead time.
e) reorder point and reorder lead time.

LO F.4 One important reason that spreadsheets are excellent tools for conducting simulations is that they can:
a) generate random numbers.
b) easily provide animation of the simulation.
c) provide more security than manual simulations.
d) prohibit "time compression" from corrupting the results.
e) be easily programmed.

Answers: LO F.1. b; LO F.2. set up a probability distribution for each of the important variables, build a cumulative probability distribution for each of the important variables, establish an interval of random numbers for each variable, generate sets of random numbers, actually simulate a set of trials; LO F.3. c; LO F.4. a.

Appendixes

APPENDIX I
Normal Curve Areas

APPENDIX II
Values of $e^{-\lambda}$ for Use in the Poisson Distribution

APPENDIX III
Table of Random Numbers

APPENDIX IV
Using Excel OM and POM for Windows

APPENDIX V
Solutions to Even-Numbered Problems

APPENDIX I

NORMAL CURVE AREAS

1.55
Standard deviations

Area is
.93943

0   1.55
Mean   Z

To find the area under the normal curve, you can apply either Table I.1 or Table I.2. In Table I.1, you must know how many standard deviations that point is to the right of the mean. Then, the area under the normal curve can be read directly from the normal table. For example, the total area under the normal curve for a point that is 1.55 standard deviations to the right of the mean is .93943.

TABLE I.1

Z	.00	.01	.02	.03	.04	.05	.06	.07	.08	.09
.0	.50000	.50399	.50798	.51197	.51595	.51994	.52392	.52790	.53188	.53586
.1	.53983	.54380	.54776	.55172	.55567	.55962	.56356	.56749	.57142	.57535
.2	.57926	.58317	.58706	.59095	.59483	.59871	.60257	.60642	.61026	.61409
.3	.61791	.62172	.62552	.62930	.63307	.63683	.64058	.64431	.64803	.65173
.4	.65542	.65910	.66276	.66640	.67003	.67364	.67724	.68082	.68439	.68793
.5	.69146	.69497	.69847	.70194	.70540	.70884	.71226	.71566	.71904	.72240
.6	.72575	.72907	.73237	.73565	.73891	.74215	.74537	.74857	.75175	.75490
.7	.75804	.76115	.76424	.76730	.77035	.77337	.77637	.77935	.78230	.78524
.8	.78814	.79103	.79389	.79673	.79955	.80234	.80511	.80785	.81057	.81327
.9	.81594	.81859	.82121	.82381	.82639	.82894	.83147	.83398	.83646	.83891
1.0	.84134	.84375	.84614	.84849	.85083	.85314	.85543	.85769	.85993	.86214
1.1	.86433	.86650	.86864	.87076	.87286	.87493	.87698	.87900	.88100	.88298
1.2	.88493	.88686	.88877	.89065	.89251	.89435	.89617	.89796	.89973	.90147
1.3	.90320	.90490	.90658	.90824	.90988	.91149	.91309	.91466	.91621	.91774
1.4	.91924	.92073	.92220	.92364	.92507	.92647	.92785	.92922	.93056	.93189
1.5	.93319	.93448	.93574	.93699	.93822	.93943	.94062	.94179	.94295	.94408
1.6	.94520	.94630	.94738	.94845	.94950	.95053	.95154	.95254	.95352	.95449
1.7	.95543	.95637	.95728	.95818	.95907	.95994	.96080	.96164	.96246	.96327
1.8	.96407	.96485	.96562	.96638	.96712	.96784	.96856	.96926	.96995	.97062
1.9	.97128	.97193	.97257	.97320	.97381	.97441	.97500	.97558	.97615	.97670
2.0	.97725	.97784	.97831	.97882	.97932	.97982	.98030	.98077	.98124	.98169
2.1	.98214	.98257	.98300	.98341	.98382	.98422	.98461	.98500	.98537	.98574
2.2	.98610	.98645	.98679	.98713	.98745	.98778	.98809	.98840	.98870	.98899
2.3	.98928	.98956	.98983	.99010	.99036	.99061	.99086	.99111	.99134	.99158
2.4	.99180	.99202	.99224	.99245	.99266	.99286	.99305	.99324	.99343	.99361
2.5	.99379	.99396	.99413	.99430	.99446	.99461	.99477	.99492	.99506	.99520
2.6	.99534	.99547	.99560	.99573	.99585	.99598	.99609	.99621	.99632	.99643
2.7	.99653	.99664	.99674	.99683	.99693	.99702	.99711	.99720	.99728	.99736
2.8	.99744	.99752	.99760	.99767	.99774	.99781	.99788	.99795	.99801	.99807
2.9	.99813	.99819	.99825	.99831	.99836	.99841	.99846	.99851	.99856	.99861
3.0	.99865	.99869	.99874	.99878	.99882	.99886	.99889	.99893	.99896	.99900
3.1	.99903	.99906	.99910	.99913	.99916	.99918	.99921	.99924	.99926	.99929
3.2	.99931	.99934	.99936	.99938	.99940	.99942	.99944	.99946	.99948	.99950
3.3	.99952	.99953	.99955	.99957	.99958	.99960	.99961	.99962	.99964	.99965
3.4	.99966	.99968	.99969	.99970	.99971	.99972	.99973	.99974	.99975	.99976
3.5	.99977	.99978	.99978	.99979	.99980	.99981	.99981	.99982	.99983	.99983
3.6	.99984	.99985	.99985	.99986	.99986	.99987	.99987	.99988	.99988	.99989
3.7	.99989	.99990	.99990	.99990	.99991	.99991	.99992	.99992	.99992	.99992
3.8	.99993	.99993	.99993	.99994	.99994	.99994	.99994	.99995	.99995	.99995
3.9	.99995	.99995	.99996	.99996	.99996	.99996	.99996	.99996	.99997	.99997

1.55 Standard deviations

Area shaded is .43943

0   1.55

Mean   Z

As an alternative to Table I.1, the numbers in Table I.2 represent the proportion of the total area away from the mean, μ, to one side. For example, the area between the mean and a point that is 1.55 standard deviations to its right is .43943.

TABLE I.2

Z	.00	.01	.02	.03	.04	.05	.06	.07	.08	.09
0.0	.00000	.00399	.00798	.01197	.01595	.01994	.02392	.02790	.03188	.03586
0.1	.03983	.04380	.04776	.05172	.05567	.05962	.06356	.06749	.07142	.07535
0.2	.07926	.08317	.08706	.09095	.09483	.09871	.10257	.10642	.11026	.11409
0.3	.11791	.12172	.12552	.12930	.13307	.13683	.14058	.14431	.14803	.15173
0.4	.15542	.15910	.16276	.16640	.17003	.17364	.17724	.18082	.18439	.18793
0.5	.19146	.19497	.19847	.20194	.20540	.20884	.21226	.21566	.21904	.22240
0.6	.22575	.22907	.23237	.23565	.23891	.24215	.24537	.24857	.25175	.25490
0.7	.25804	.26115	.26424	.26730	.27035	.27337	.27637	.27935	.28230	.28524
0.8	.28814	.29103	.29389	.29673	.29955	.30234	.30511	.30785	.31057	.31327
0.9	.31594	.31859	.32121	.32381	.32639	.32894	.33147	.33398	.33646	.33891
1.0	.34134	.34375	.34614	.34850	.35083	.35314	.35543	.35769	.35993	.36214
1.1	.36433	.36650	.36864	.37076	.37286	.37493	.37698	.37900	.38100	.38298
1.2	.38493	.38686	.38877	.39065	.39251	.39435	.39617	.39796	.39973	.40147
1.3	.40320	.40490	.40658	.40824	.40988	.41149	.41309	.41466	.41621	.41174
1.4	.41924	.42073	.42220	.42364	.42507	.42647	.42786	.42922	.43056	.43189
1.5	.43319	.43448	.43574	.43699	.43822	.43943	.44062	.44179	.44295	.44408
1.6	.44520	.44630	.44738	.44845	.44950	.45053	.45154	.45254	.45352	.45449
1.7	.45543	.45637	.45728	.45818	.45907	.45994	.46080	.46164	.46246	.46327
1.8	.46407	.46485	.46562	.46638	.46712	.46784	.46856	.46926	.46995	.47062
1.9	.47128	.47193	.47257	.47320	.47381	.47441	.47500	.47558	.47615	.47670
2.0	.47725	.47778	.47831	.47882	.47932	.47982	.48030	.48077	.48124	.48169
2.1	.48214	.48257	.48300	.48341	.48382	.48422	.48461	.48500	.48537	.48574
2.2	.48610	.48645	.48679	.48713	.48745	.48778	.48809	.48840	.48870	.48899
2.3	.48928	.48956	.48983	.49010	.49036	.49061	.49086	.49111	.49134	.49158
2.4	.49180	.49202	.49224	.49245	.49266	.49286	.49305	.49324	.49343	.49361
2.5	.49379	.49396	.49413	.49430	.49446	.49461	.49477	.49492	.49506	.49520
2.6	.49534	.49547	.49560	.49573	.49585	.49598	.49609	.49621	.49632	.49643
2.7	.49653	.49664	.49674	.49683	.49693	.49702	.49711	.49720	.49728	.49736
2.8	.49744	.49752	.49760	.49767	.49774	.49781	.49788	.49795	.49801	.49807
2.9	.49813	.49819	.49825	.49831	.49836	.49841	.49846	.49851	.49856	.49861
3.0	.49865	.49869	.49874	.49878	.49882	.49886	.49889	.49893	.49897	.49900
3.1	.49903	.49906	.49910	.49913	.49916	.49918	.49921	.49924	.49926	.49929

APPENDIX II

VALUES OF $e^{-\lambda}$ FOR USE IN THE POISSON DISTRIBUTION

Values of $e^{-\lambda}$

λ	$e^{-\lambda}$	λ	$e^{-\lambda}$	λ	$e^{-\lambda}$	λ	$e^{-\lambda}$
.0	1.0000	1.6	.2019	3.1	.0450	4.6	.0101
.1	.9048	1.7	.1827	3.2	.0408	4.7	.0091
.2	.8187	1.8	.1653	3.3	.0369	4.8	.0082
.3	.7408	1.9	.1496	3.4	.0334	4.9	.0074
.4	.6703	2.0	.1353	3.5	.0302	5.0	.0067
.5	.6065	2.1	.1225	3.6	.0273	5.1	.0061
.6	.5488	2.2	.1108	3.7	.0247	5.2	.0055
.7	.4966	2.3	.1003	3.8	.0224	5.3	.0050
.8	.4493	2.4	.0907	3.9	.0202	5.4	.0045
.9	.4066	2.5	.0821	4.0	.0183	5.5	.0041
1.0	.3679	2.6	.0743	4.1	.0166	5.6	.0037
1.1	.3329	2.7	.0672	4.2	.0150	5.7	.0033
1.2	.3012	2.8	.0608	4.3	.0136	5.8	.0030
1.3	.2725	2.9	.0550	4.4	.0123	5.9	.0027
1.4	.2466	3.0	.0498	4.5	.0111	6.0	.0025
1.5	.2231						

APPENDIX III

TABLE OF RANDOM NUMBERS

52	06	50	88	53	30	10	47	99	37	66	91	35	32	00	84	57	07
37	63	28	02	74	35	24	03	29	60	74	85	90	73	59	55	17	60
82	57	68	28	05	94	03	11	27	79	90	87	92	41	09	25	36	77
69	02	36	49	71	99	32	10	75	21	95	90	94	38	97	71	72	49
98	94	90	36	06	78	23	67	89	85	29	21	25	73	69	34	85	76
96	52	62	87	49	56	59	23	78	71	72	90	57	01	98	57	31	95
33	69	27	21	11	60	95	89	68	48	17	89	34	09	93	50	44	51
50	33	50	95	13	44	34	62	64	39	55	29	30	64	49	44	30	16
88	32	18	50	62	57	34	56	62	31	15	40	90	34	51	95	26	14
90	30	36	24	69	82	51	74	30	35	36	85	01	55	92	64	09	85
50	48	61	18	85	23	08	54	17	12	80	69	24	84	92	16	49	59
27	88	21	62	69	64	48	31	12	73	02	68	00	16	16	46	13	85
45	14	46	32	13	49	66	62	74	41	86	98	92	98	84	54	33	40
81	02	01	78	82	74	97	37	45	31	94	99	42	49	27	64	89	42
66	83	14	74	27	76	03	33	11	97	59	81	72	00	64	61	13	52
74	05	81	82	93	09	96	33	52	78	13	06	28	30	94	23	37	39
30	34	87	01	74	11	46	82	59	94	25	34	32	23	17	01	58	73
59	55	72	33	62	13	74	68	22	44	42	09	32	46	71	79	45	89
67	09	80	98	99	25	77	50	03	32	36	63	65	75	94	19	95	88
60	77	46	63	71	69	44	22	03	85	14	48	69	13	30	50	33	24
60	08	19	29	36	72	30	27	50	64	85	72	75	29	87	05	75	01
80	45	86	99	02	34	87	08	86	84	49	76	24	08	01	86	29	11
53	84	49	63	26	65	72	84	85	63	26	02	75	26	92	62	40	67
69	84	12	94	51	36	17	02	15	29	16	52	56	43	26	22	08	62
37	77	13	10	02	18	31	19	32	85	31	94	81	43	31	58	33	51

Source: Excerpted from *A Million Random Digits with 100,000 Normal Deviates*, The Free Press (1955): 7, with permission of the RAND Corporation.

APPENDIX IV

USING EXCEL OM AND POM FOR WINDOWS

Two approaches to computer-aided decision making are provided with this text: **Excel OM** and **POM** (Production and Operations Management) **for Windows**. These are the two most user-friendly software packages available to help you learn and understand operations management. Both programs can be used either to solve homework problems identified with an icon or to check answers you have developed by hand. Both software packages use the standard Windows interface and run on any IBM-compatible PC operating Windows XP or newer. Excel OM is also available for the Mac.

EXCEL OM

Excel OM has been designed to help you to better learn and understand both OM and Excel. Even though the software contains 24 modules and more than 60 submodules, the screens for every module are consistent and easy to use. The Chapter menu (Excel 2007 and later for PCs) or the Heizer menu (Excel 2011 for Macs) lists the modules in *chapter* order, as illustrated for Excel 2007 and later for PCs in Program IV.1(a). The Alphabetical menu (Excel 2007 and later for PCs) or Excel OM menu (Excel 2011 for Macs) lists the modules in alphabetical order, as illustrated for Excel OM for Macs in Program IV.1(b). The menu for Excel 2016 for Macs is slightly different and not displayed here. This software is provided at no cost to users of MyOMLab or purchasers of a new copy of this textbook. The software can also be purchased at www.pearsonhighered.com/heizer. Excel 2007 or newer must be on your PC or Excel 2011 or greater must be on your Mac.

To install Excel OM, click on the Download Center on the left side of your MyOMLab course, and follow the instructions. Default values have been assigned in the setup program, but you may change them if you like. For Windows, the default folder into which a program will be installed is

▼ **PROGRAM IV.1(a)**   **Excel OM Modules Menu in Excel OM Tab in Excel 2007 and later for PCs**

▲ **PROGRAM IV.1(b)**   **Excel OM Modules Menu in OM for Macs 2011**

named C:\Program Files(x86)\ExcelomQMv4. Generally speaking, it is simply necessary to click *Next* each time the installation asks a question. For Macs, simply unzip the zip file that is provided.

Starting the Program   To start Excel OM using Windows, double-click on the Excel OM V4 shortcut placed on the desktop during installation. The Excel OM menu will appear in an Excel OM tab that will be added to the Excel ribbon, as displayed in Program IV.1(a). To start Excel OM on the Mac, open the file excelomqmv4.xla. Be certain that you open the file from the folder that has the excelomqmv4 .lic file. On the Mac under Excel 2011, the Excel OM menu will appear in the main menu of Excel, as displayed in Program IV.1(b).

If you have Excel 2007 or later and do not see an Excel OM tab on the Ribbon, then your Excel security settings need to be revised to enable Excel OM V4. Please consult the Excel instructions at the support site, www.pearsonhighered.com/weiss, or see the document Excel.Security.pdf that has been installed in the default directory.

Excel OM serves two purposes in the learning process. First, it helps you solve problems. You enter the appropriate data, and the program provides numerical solutions. POM for Windows operates on the same principle. However, Excel OM allows for a second approach: the Excel *formulas* used to develop solutions can be modified to deal with a wider variety of problems. This "open" approach enables you to observe, understand, and even change the formulas underlying the Excel calculations—conveying Excel's power as an OM analysis tool.

POM FOR WINDOWS

POM for Windows is decision support software that is also offered free to students who use MyOMLab or who purchased this as a new text. It can also be purchased at our Web site www.pearsonhighered .com/heizer. Program IV.2 shows a list of the 25 OM modules that can be accessed from the menu tree on the left. The modules can also be accessed from the MODULE menu where they are in alphabetical order or the HEIZER menu where they are in chapter order. Once you follow the standard setup instructions, a POM for Windows program icon will be added to your desktop, and a program group will be added to your Start, All Programs menu. The program may be accessed by double-clicking on the desktop icon.

▲ **PROGRAM IV.2**   **POM for Windows Module List**

USING EXCEL OM AND POM FOR WINDOWS WITH MYOMLAB

Both Excel OM and POM for Windows have MyOMLab toolbars that make it very easy to copy from or paste to MyOMLab and very easy to set the specific number of decimals for which MyOMLab asks for any problem. To copy data from MyOMLab: after creating a model in Excel OM or POM, go to MyOMLab and click on the Copy icon. Then, in POM or in Excel OM, click on the **Paste from MyOMLab** icon on the toolbar or in the right-click menu.

Updates to POM for Windows and Excel OM are available on the Internet through the Downloads and Support links at *www.pearsonhighered.com/weiss*.

APPENDIX V
SOLUTIONS TO EVEN-NUMBERED PROBLEMS

Chapter 1

1.2 (a) 2 valves/hr.
   (b) 2.25 valves/hr.
   (c) 12.5%
1.4 (a) 20 pkg/hour
   (b) 26.6 pkg/hour
   (c) 33.0%
1.6 .078 fewer resources (7.8% improvement)
1.8 (a) 2.5 tires/hour
   (b) 0.025 tires/dollar
   (c) 2.56% increase
1.10 .000375 autos per dollar of inputs
1.12 4 workers
1.14 1.6%
1.16 $57.00 per labor hour

Chapter 2

2.2 Venezuela, China, United States, Switzerland, Denmark
2.4 Differentiation is evident when comparing most restaurants or restaurant chains.
2.6 (a) Focus more on standardization, make fewer product changes, find optimum capacity, and stabilize manufacturing process are a few possibilities
   (b) New human resource skills, added capital investment for new equipment/processes
   (c) Same as (b)
2.8 (a) Canada, 1.7
   (b) No change
2.10 (a) Worldwide, 81.5 weighted *average*, 815 weighted *total*
   (b) No change
   (c) Overnight Shipping now preferred, weighted total = 880
2.12 Company C, $1.0 \leq w \leq 25.0$

Chapter 3

3.2 Here are some detailed activities for the first two activities for Day's WBS:
   1.1.1 Set initial goals for fundraising.
   1.1.2 Set strategy, including identifying sources and solicitation.
   1.1.3 Raise the funds.
   1.2.1 Identify voters' concerns.
   1.2.2 Analyze competitor's voting record.
   1.2.3 Establish position on issues.
3.4 (a) AON network:

   (b) AOA network:

3.6

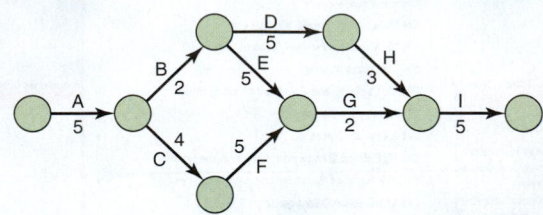

A–C–F–G–I is critical path; 21 days.
This is an AOA network.

3.8 (a)

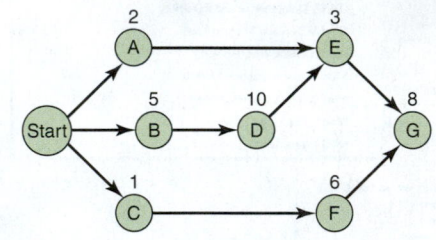

   (b) B–D–E–G
   (c) 26 days
   (d)

Activity	Slack
A	13
B	0
C	11
D	0
E	0
F	11
G	0

3.10 (a)

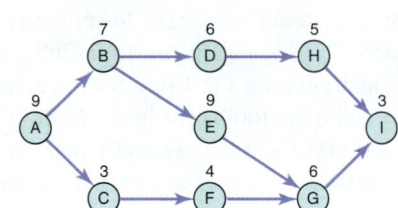

   (b) A–B–E–G–I is critical path.
   (c) 34

3.12

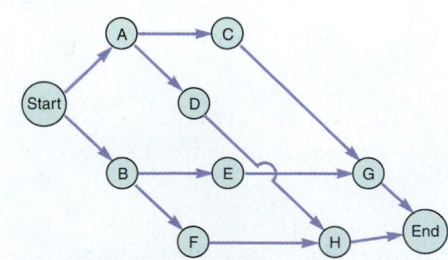

3.14 (a) List all courses you must take.
   (b) List all immediate predecessors.
   (c) Develop a network. Note the difficulty of scheduling electives.

3.16 (a)

(b) Critical path is A–B–J–K–L–M–R–S–T–U for 18 days.

(c) i. No, transmissions and drivetrains are not on the critical path.

   ii. No, halving engine-building time will reduce the critical path by only 1 day.

   iii. No, it is not on the critical path.

(d) Reallocating workers not involved with critical-path activities to activities along the critical path will reduce the critical path length.

3.18 A: 15, 1.33
B: 32, 2.33
C: 18, 0
D: 13.17, 1.83
E: 18.17, 0.5
F: 19, 1.0

3.20 (a) A: 10, 0.11
B: 10, 4
C: 10, 0.11
D: 8, 1

(b) A–C: 20 weeks
B–D: 18 weeks

(c) .22, 5

(d) 1.0

(e) 0.963

3.22 (a) 32 weeks, C-H-M-O

(b) 50%

(c) No impact

3.24 (a) A = 5, B = 6, C = 7, D = 6, E = 3, Time = 15

(b) 1, 1, 1, 4, 0; Project variance = 2

3.26 (b) Expected times are: 10.0, 7.2, 3.2, 20.0, 7.0, 10.0, 7.3, 15.0, 11.2, 7.0, 6.7, 2.2

(c) Slack times are: 0, 22.8, 19.8, 0, 19.8, 0, 17.7, 0, 10.8, 0, 0, 11.5

(d) A–D–F–H–J–K; 68.7 days

(e) 0.644

(f) 0.99934

(g) 0.99999

3.28 Crash C to 3 weeks at $200 total for one week. Now both paths are critical. Not worth it to crash further.

3.30 (a) Reduce A, cheapest path @ $600 per time period

(b) Reduce B, best choice now @ $900

(c) Total cost = $1,500

3.32 (a) Slacks are: 0, 2, 11, 0, 2, 11, 0

(b) First, crash D by 2 weeks. Then crash D and E by 2 weeks each.

(c) Minimum completion time = 7. Crash cost = $1,550.

Chapter 4

4.2 (a) None obvious.

(b) 7, 7.67, 9, 10, 11, 11, 11.33, 11, 9

(c) 6.4, 7.8, 11, 9.6, 10.9, 12.2, 10.5, 10.6, 8.4

(d) The 3-yr. moving average.

4.4 (a) 41.6

(b) 42.3

(c) Banking industry's seasonality.

4.6 (b) Naive = 23; 3-mo. moving = 21.33; 6-mo. weighted = 20.6; exponential smoothing = 20.62; trend = 20.67

(c) Trend projection

4.8 (a) 91.3

(b) 89

(c) MAD = 2.7

(d) MSE = 13.35

(e) MAPE = 2.99%

4.10 (a) 4.67, 5.00, 6.33, 7.67, 8.33, 8.00, 9.33, 11.67, 13.7

(b) 4.50, 5.00, 7.25, 7.75, 8.00, 8.25, 10.00, 12.25, 14.0

(c) Forecasts are about the same.

4.12 72

4.14 Method 1: MAD = .125; MSE = .021
Method 2: MAD = .1275; MSE = .018

4.16 (a) $y = 421 + 33.6x$. When $x = 6$, $y = 622.8$.

(b) MAD = 5.6

(c) MSE = 32.88

4.18 alpha = .25; forecast = 49

4.20 $\alpha = .1, \beta = .8$, August forecast = $71,303; MSE = 12.7 for $\beta = .8$ vs. MSE = 18.87 for $\beta = .2$ in Problem 4.19.

4.22 Confirm that you match the numbers in Table 4.1.

4.24 $y = 5 + 20x$, $y = 105$

4.26 1,680 sailboats

4.28 96.344, 132.946, 169.806, 85.204

4.30 $y = 29.76 + 3.28x$
Year 11 = 65.8, Year 12 = 69.1 (patients)
$r^2 = 0.853$

4.32 Trend adjustment does not appear to give any significant improvement based on MAD.

4.34 (a) Trend analysis: $y = -18.968 + 1.638 \times$ year
$r = .846$, MAD = 10.587

4.36 7.86

4.38 (a) 13.67, MAD = 2.20

(b) 13.17, MAD = 2.72

4.40 150,000; 126,000; 120,000; 198,000

4.42 (a) 7,000

(b) 9,000

4.44 (a) 337   (b) 380   (c) 423

4.46 (a) $y = 50 + 18x$

(b) $410

4.48 (a) 83,502

(d) 0.397

4.50 (a) $y = -.158 + .1308x$

(b) 2.719

(c) $r = .966$; $r^2 = .934$

4.52 (b) $y = 0.511 + 0.159x$

(c) 2,101,000 riders

(d) 511,000 people

(e) .404 (rounded to .407 in POM software)

(f) $r^2 = 0.840$

4.54 (a) Sales (y) = $-9.349 + .1121$ (contracts)

(b) $r = .8963$; $S_{xy} = 1.3408$

4.56 (a) $y = 1 + 1x$

(b) 0.45

(c) 3.65

4.58 Games lost = $6.41 + 0.533 \times$ rainy days

4.60 MAD = 10.875; Tracking signal = 3.586

Chapter 5

5.2 *Possible strategies:*

Tablet (growth phase):

Increase capacity and improve balance of production system.

Attempt to make production facilities more efficient.

Smart watch (introductory phase):

Increase R&D to better define required product characteristics.

Modify and improve production process.

Develop supplier and distribution systems.

Hand calculator (decline phase):

Concentrate on production and distribution cost reduction.

5.4 Shown below is a house of quality for a sports watch in the under $50 market.

5.6 Build a house of quality similar to the one shown in Example 1 in the text.

Consider customer requirements such as:

Effective Luring, Reliability, Kills Quickly, Finger Safe, etc.

Consider Manufacturing issues such as:

Luring Radius, Dead Mouse Ratio, Time to Kill, Cost, etc.

5.8 House of Quality Sequence for Ice Cream

5.10 An assembly chart for the eyeglasses is shown below:

5.12 Assembly chart for a table lamp:

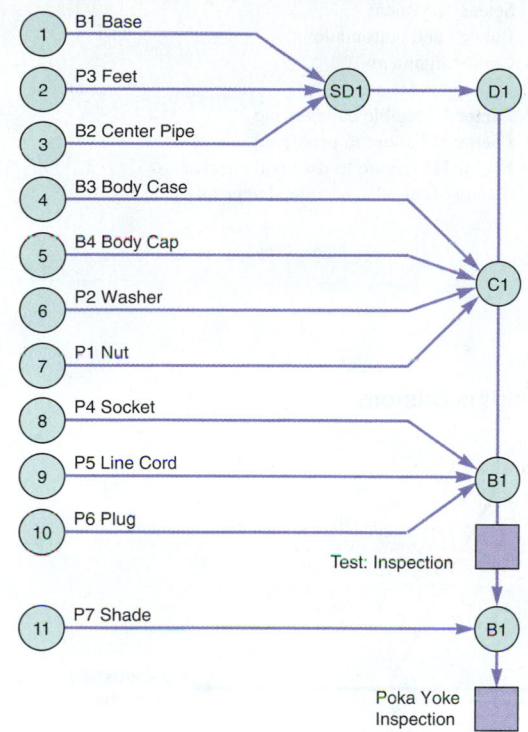

5.14 Bill of material for a wooden pencil with eraser:

Description	Quantity
Pencil	1
Wood half	2
Graphite rod	1
Band	1
Eraser	1
Yellow paint	1 gram
Glue	1 gram

5.16 The major assemblies in the bill of material for a computer mouse (GeniMouse):

Bill of Material for GeniMouse

Part Number	Description	Quantity
GM1001	GeniMouse	1
SC004	Phillips Head No. 12 0.5 inch. Screw	1
TA101	Top Mouse Assembly	1
BA101	Base Assembly	1
GML101	GeniMouse Label	1

5.18 **(a)** For computer repair service, customer interaction is a strategic choice.

Supplier				Consumer	
Supplier's Process Domain				Consumer's Process Domain	
Independent processing	Surrogate interaction	Direct interaction	Direct interaction	Surrogate interaction	Independent processing
Factory repair or remanufacturer	Local computer repair service	Repair at business or home		Computer components sold based on discussion with customer	Parts purchased online by end user

(b) Parts (b) and (c) should be prepared in a style similar to part (a).

5.20 Moving to the left is likely to be most efficient in terms of resources used (economies of scale), but there may be shipping cost and shipping time. Also, customization may be complicated.
    Moving to the right may be faster and lend itself to more customization, but it may be less efficient. It may also provide less competence (less training, specialized skills, and testing).

5.22 The company should complete the value analysis, for an expected payoff of $55,025,000.

5.24 **(a)** Best decision, buy the semiconductors. Expected Payoff (cost) = $1,500,000.

   (b) Expected monetary value, minimum cost.

   (c) Worst case: Ritz fails at mfg. and must buy. Cost of $3,500,000.

   Best case: They make the semiconductor and spend only $1,000,000.

5.26 For design A:

   EMV (Design A) = (.9)($500,000) + (.1)($1,250,000) = $450,000 + $125,000 = $575,000.

   For design B:

   EMV (Design B) = (.8)($500,000) + (.2)($500,000) = $400,000 + $100,000 = $500,000.

   The highest payoff is design option A at $575,000.

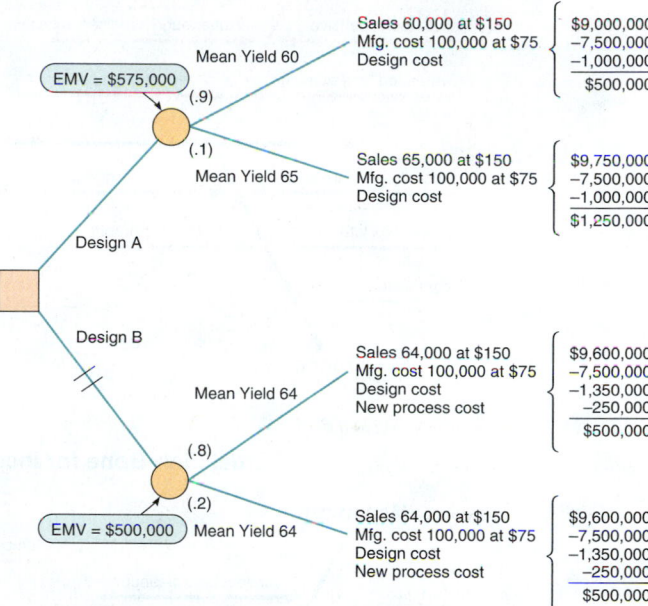

5.28 The EMV is maximized when using existing material; $8,910,000

Chapter 5 Supplement

S5.2 Brew Master revenue retrieval = $5.31 provides higher opportunity.

S5.4 $66,809

S5.6 3.57 years

S5.8 3.48 years

S5.10 66,667 miles

S5.12 **(a)** $4.53

   (b) $3.23

   (c) GF Deluxe

S5.14 **(a)** $4.53, GF Deluxe

   (b) $5.06, Premium Mate

   (c) Premium Mate model

S5.16 **(a)** 45,455 miles

   (b) gas vehicle

S5.18 42,105 miles

Chapter 6

6.2 Individual answer, in the style of Figure 6.6(b).

6.4 Individual answer, in the style of Figure 6.6(f).

6.6 Partial flowchart for planning a party:

6.8 See figure below for a partial fish-bone. Individual answer in the style of Figure 6.7 in the chapter.

6.10 Individual answer, in the style of Figure 6.7 in the chapter.

6.12 Pareto chart, in the style of Example 1 with parking/drives most frequent, pool second, etc.

6.14 See figure below.
Issues: Materials: 4, 12, 14; Methods: 3, 7, 15, 16; Manpower: 1, 5, 6, 11; Machines: 2, 8, 9, 10, 13.

6.18 Stitching
Seams alignment
Buttons and buttonholes
Collar alignment
Hem

6.20 **Factor I** Illegible handwriting
Factor II Failure to proofread
Factor III Failure to use spell checker
(Factors II and III are interchangeable.)

▼ *Figure for Problem 6.8.*

Partial Fish-Bone Chart for Dissatisfied Airline Customer

▼ *Figure for Problem 6.14.*

Partial Fish-Bone for Incorrect Formulation

6.16 (a) A scatter diagram in the style of Figure 6.6(b) that shows a strong positive relationship between shipments and defects
(b) A scatter diagram in the style of Figure 6.6(b) that shows a mild relationship between shipments and turnover
(c) A Pareto chart in the style of Figure 6.6(d) that shows frequency of each type of defect
(d) A fishbone chart in the style of Figure 6.6(c) with the 4 Ms showing possible causes of increasing defects in shipments

Chapter 6 Supplement

S6.2 (a) $UCL_{\bar{x}} = 52.31$
$LCL_{\bar{x}} = 47.69$
(b) $UCL_{\bar{x}} = 51.54$
$LCL_{\bar{x}} = 48.46$

S6.4 (a) $UCL_{\bar{x}} = 440$ calories
$LCL_{\bar{x}} = 400$ calories
(b) $UCL_{\bar{x}} = 435$ calories
$LCL_{\bar{x}} = 405$ calories

S6.6 $UCL_{\bar{x}} = 3.728$
$LCL_{\bar{x}} = 2.236$
$UCL_R = 2.336$
$LCL_R = 0.0$
The process is in control.

S6.8 (a) $UCL_{\bar{x}} = 16.08$
$LCL_{\bar{x}} = 15.92$
(b) $UCL_{\bar{x}} = 16.12$
$LCL_{\bar{x}} = 15.88$

S6.10 (a) $\sigma_{\bar{x}} = 0.61$
(b) Using $\sigma_{\bar{x}}$, $UCL_{\bar{x}} = 11.83$, and $LCL_{\bar{x}} = 8.17$.
Using A_2, $UCL_{\bar{x}} = 11.90$, and $LCL_{\bar{x}} = 8.10$.
(c) $UCL_R = 6.98$; $LCL_R = 0$
(d) Yes

S6.12 $UCL_R = 6.058$; $LCL_R = 0.442$
Averages are increasing.

S6.14

UCL	LCL
.062	0
.099	0
.132	0
.161	0
.190	.01

S6.16 $UCL_p = .0313$; $LCL_p = 0$
S6.18 (a) $UCL_p = 0.077$; $LCL_p = 0.003$
S6.20 (a) $UCL_p = .0581$
$LCL_p = 0$
(b) in control
(c) $UCL_p = .1154$
$LCL_p = 0$
S6.22 (a) c-chart
(b) $UCL_c = 13.35$
$LCL_c = 0$
(c) in control
(d) not in control
S6.24 (a) $UCL_c = 26.063$
$LCL_c = 3.137$
(b) No point out of control.
S6.26 (a) $UCL_{\bar{x}} = 61.131$, $LCL_{\bar{x}} = 38.421$, $UCL_R = 41.62$, $LCL_R = 0$
(b) Yes, the process is in control for both $\bar{x}$- and R-charts.
(c) They support West's claim. But variance from the mean needs to be reduced and controlled.
S6.28 $UCL_{\bar{x}} = 76.85$ $LCL_{\bar{x}} = 73.15$
S6.30 $UCL_{\bar{x}} = 60.924$ $LCL_{\bar{x}} = 59.076$
$UCL_R = 5.331$ $LCL_R = 0.669$
S6.32 (a) $UCL_{\bar{x}} = 20.15$ $LCL_{\bar{x}} = 19.65$
(b) $UCL_R = 0.78$ $LCL_R = 0$
S6.34 At least 29 holes that meet tolerance, but no more than 88 holes before being replaced.
S6.36 $UCL_p = 0.0209$ $LCL_p = 0.0011$
S6.38 $UCL_p = 0.154$ $LCL_p = 0.031$
Sample 16 exceeds the UCL.
S6.40 $C_p = 1.0$. The process is barely capable.
S6.42 $C_{pk} = 1.125$. Process *is* centered and will produce within tolerance.
S6.44 $C_{pk} = .1667$
S6.46 $C_{pk} = 0.33$
S6.48 Machine 1 has index of $C_{pk} = 0.83$ (not capable)
Machine 2 has index of $C_{pk} = 1.0$ (capable)
S6.50 $C_p = 1.667$ (very capable)
S6.52 AOQ = 0.02
S6.54 AOQ = 0.0117

Chapter 7

7.2 GPE is best below 100,000.
FMS is best between 100,000 and 300,000.
DM is best over 300,000.
7.4 Optimal process will change at 100,000 and 300,000.
7.6 (a)

(b) Plan c
(c) Plan b
7.8 Rent HP software since projected volume of 80 is above the crossover point of 75.
7.10 (a) 82,000 units
(b) Loss of $10,000
(c) Profit of $1,000
7.12 (a) 7,750 units
(b) Proposal A
7.14

7.16

Chapter 7 Supplement

S7.2 69.2%

S7.4 88.9%

S7.6 Design = 88,920
Fabrication = 160,680
Finishing = 65,520

S7.8 5.17 (or 6) bays

S7.10 15 min/unit

S7.12 (a) Throughput time = 40 min
(b) Bottleneck time = 12 min.
(c) Station 2
(d) Weekly capacity = 240 units

S7.14 (a) Work station C at 20 min/unit
(b) 3 units/hr

S7.16 (a) 2,000 units
(b) $1,500

S7.18 (a) $150,000
(b) $160,000

S7.20 (a) $BEP_A = 1,667$;
$BEP_B = 2,353$
(b, c) Oven A slightly more profitable
(d) 13,333 pizzas

S7.22 (a) $18,750
(b) 375,000

S7.24 Yes, purchase new equipment and raise price. Profit = $2,500

S7.26 $BEP_\$ = \$7,584.83$ per mo
Daily meals = 9

S7.28 (a) 6,250
(b) 7,000

S7.30 10,000

S7.32 Option B; $74,000

S7.34 $4,590

S7.36 NPV = $1,764

S7.38 (a) Purchase two large ovens.
(b) Equal quality, equal capacity.
(c) Payments are made at end of each time period, and future interest rates are known.

S7.40 Investment A; payoff = $24,234

S7.42 (11 percent) should not purchase; NPV = –$7,678
(4 percent) should purchase; NPV = $5,379

S7.44 Machine B; NPV = $85,983

Chapter 8

8.2 China, $1.44

8.4 India is $.05 less than elsewhere.

8.6 (a) Mobile = 53; Jackson = 60; select Jackson.
(b) Jackson now = 66.

8.8 (a) Hyde Park, with 54.5 points.
(b) Present location = 51 points.

8.10 (a) Location C, with a total *weighted* score of 1,530.
(b) Location B = 1,360
(c) B can never be in first place.

8.12 (a) Great Britain, at 4.6.
(b) Great Britain is now 3.6.

8.14 (a) Italy is highest.
(b) Spain always lowest.

8.16 (a) Site 1 up to 125, site 2 from 125 to 233, site 3 above 233
(b) Site 2

8.18 (a) Above 10,000 cars, site C is lowest cost
(b) Site A optimal from 0 to 10,000 cars.
(c) Site B is never optimal.

8.20 (a) (5.15, 7.31)
(b) (5.13, 7.67)

8.22 (a) (6.23, 6.08)
(b) safety, etc.

8.24 (a) Site C is best, with a score of 374
(b) For all positive values of w_7 such that $w_7 \le 14$

8.26 Downtown rating = 2.24
Shopping mall rating = 3.24 (best)
Coral Gables rating = 2.42
When grade A = 4, B = 3, C = 2, D = 1

8.28 Site 1 = 78.125
Site 2 = 75.0
Site 3 = 86.56 (highest)
Site 4 = 80.94

8.30 (a) Atlanta TC = $125,000 + 6x$
Burlington TC = $75,000 + 5x$
Cleveland TC = $100,000 + 4x$
Denver TC = $50,000 + 12x$
(b) Denver best from 0 to 3,571 units
(c) At 5,000 units, Burlington best

8.32 (7.97, 6.69)

8.34 England, 3.55

Chapter 9

9.2 (a) $23,400
(b) $20,600
(c) $22,000
(d) Plan B

9.4 Benders to area 1; Materials to 2; Welders to 3; Drills to 4; Grinder to 5; and Lathes to 6; Trips × Distance = 13,000 ft.

9.6 Layout #1, distance = 600 with areas fixed
Layout #2, distance = 602 with areas fixed

9.8 Layout #4, distance = 609
Layout #5, distance = 478

9.10

Entrance (1)	Exam II (3)	Lab, EKG (5)	O.R. (6)
Exam I (2)	X-ray (4)	Casts (8)	R.R. (7)

Patient movement = 4,500 feet

9.12 (a) 20 seconds
(b) 3
(c) Yes; Station 1 with A, C;
Station 2 with B, D;
Station 3 with E

9.14 (a) 4 stations
(b) Cannot be done with theoretical minimum; requires 5 stations
(c) 80% for 5 stations

9.16 (b) Station 1–A, G, B, with .5 min. left
Station 2–C, D, E with no time left
Station 3–F, H, I, J with .5 min left
(c) If stations 1 and 3 each had 0.5 min. work more to do, the line would be 100% efficient
(d) 3

9.18 (a) Station 1–A, C
Station 2–E
Station 3–B, D
Station 4–F, H
Station 5–G, I
(b) 97.6% with cycle time = 3.33 (theoretical efficiency)
87.6% is operating efficiency
(c) 4
(d) 2 min./boat

9.20 (b) 15 min.
(c) 144 units/day
(d) 5 stations
(e) 83.33%
(f) 10 min./cycle

9.22 **(b)** 3.75 patients/hour
    (c) Medical exam station, 16 min.
    (d) Paramedics are idle 2 minutes, doctors 10 minutes for each patient
    (e) 5 patients/hour

9.24 **(a)**

Algorithm	No. Workstations	Efficiency
Fewest following tasks	13	84.56%
Longest operating time	12	84.61
Most following tasks	12	84.61
Ranked positional weight	12	84.61
Shortest operating time	13	78.10

    (b)

Algorithm	No. Workstations	Efficiency
Fewest following tasks	13	77.56%
Longest operating time	12	84.02
Most following tasks	12	84.02
Ranked positional weight	11	91.66
Shortest operating time	12	84.02

9.26 **(a)**

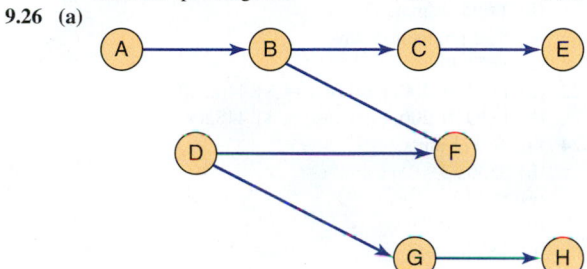

    (b) Multiple alternatives are possible
    (c) 92.5%

Chapter 10

10.2 The first 8 steps of the process chart are:

Process Chart

Charted by_____
Date:_____ Sheet_____ of_____
Problem:_____

Summary

Operation	26
Transport	4
Inspect	2
Delay	
Store	
Vert. Dist.	
Hor. Dist.	24
Time (min)	24.4

Distance (ft)	Time (mins)	Chart Symbols	Process Description
	1.0		Park auto
	0.1		Set parking brake
	0.1		Set gear shift to park
	0.1		Turn off engine
	0.2		Exit vehicle
8	0.1		Move to trunk of auto
	0.3		Open trunk
	1.0		Remove jack and spare tire

10.4 Individually prepared solution in the style of Figure 10.6
10.6 The first 8 steps of the process chart are:

Process Chart

Charted by_____
Date:___ Sheet___1___ of___1___
Problem: adding a memory board to your computer

Summary

Operation	14
Transport	4
Inspect	1
Delay	
Store	
Vert. Dist.	
Hor. Dist.	68
Time (min)	24.7

Distance (ft)	Time (mins)	Chart Symbols	Process Description
	0.2		Turn computer off
	2.0		Disconnect all cables
30	1.0		Move computer to table top
	1.5		Remove screws from cover
	1.0		Remove cover
3	0.1		Set cover on floor
	0.6		Find board to be replaced
5	0.2		Bring box with new board to table

10.8

Process Chart

Charted by _H. Molano_
Date _____ Sheet _1_ of _1_
Problem _Pit crew jack man_

Summary

Operation	2
Transport	3
Inspect	
Delay	2
Store	
Vert. Dist.	
Hor. Dist.	
Time (seconds)	12.5

Distance (feet)	Time (seconds)	Chart Symbols	Process Description
15	2.0		Move to right side of car
	2.0		Raise car
	1.0		Wait for tire exchange to finish
10	1.8		Move to left side of car
	2.0		Raise car
	1.2		Wait for tire exchange to finish
5	2.5		Move back over wall from left side

10.10 The first portion of the activity chart is shown below.

10.12 The first portion of the process chart is shown below.

PROCESS CHART

Present Method ☐
Proposed Method ☒
SUBJECT CHARTED   Printing and Copying Document
DATE _____
CHART BY _HSM_
CHART NO. _1_
DEPARTMENT _____   Clerical
SHEET NO. _1_ OF _1_

DIST. IN FEET	TIME IN MINS.	CHART SYMBOLS	PROCESS DESCRIPTION
	0.25		Click on Print Command
50	0.25		Move to Printer
	0.50		Wait for Printer
	0.10		Read Error Message
100	0.50		Move to Supply Room
	0.25		Locate Correct Paper

10.14 NT = 7.65 sec; slower than normal
10.16 **(a)** 6.525 sec
    (b) 6.2 sec
    (c) 6.739 sec
10.18 **(a)** 12.6 min
    (b) 15 min
10.20 **(a)** 12.0 sec
    (b) 14.12 sec
10.22 10.12 min
10.24 **(a)** 3.24 min
    (b) 4.208 min
10.26 n = 14.06, or 15 observations
10.28 **(a)** 45.36, 13.75, 3.6, 15.09
    (b) 91.53 min
    (c) 97 samples
10.30 **(a)** 47.6 min
    (b) 75 samples

10.32 $n = 348$
10.34 73.8%
10.36 6.55 sec
10.38 (a) 240 min
  (b) 150 hr
  (c) Clean 8 rooms; refresh 16 rooms; 38 housekeepers
  (d) 50 employees

Chapter 11

11.2 (a) 25% decrease in material costs; $45,000
  (b) 75% increase in sales; $175,000
11.4 Problems include communication, product valuation, selecting virtual partners
11.6 (a) Weeks of supply = 3.85
  (b) % of assets in inventory = 11.63%
  (c) Turnover = 13.5
  (d) No, but note they are in different industries
11.8 (a) Last year = 10.4
  (b) This year = 9.67
  (c) Yes

Chapter 11 Supplement

S11.2 Two suppliers best, $42,970
S11.4 (a) $P(2) = 0.017463$
  (b) $P(2) = 0.018866$
  (c) Option 1 (2 local suppliers) has lower risk.
S11.6 (a) 2.5
  (b) 1.2
  (c) 1.25
  (d) 1.8
  (e) Retailer
S11.8 (a) 1.20
  (b) Bullwhip = 0 if order sizes all the same.
S11.10 Donna Inc., 8.2; Kay Corp., 9.8
S11.12 Individual responses. Issues might include academics, location, financial support, size, facilities, etc.
S11.14 (a) Alternative (1) (slower shipping)
  (b) Customer satisfaction and interest earned on earlier payments
S11.16 (a) Alternative (2) (faster shipping)
  (b) Potential delay in the production process
S11.18 (a) Item B
  (b) Item A
S11.20

B	B	B	B	C	E	D	D	G
Dock		Aisle						
B	B	B	B	F	E	D	D	A

Chapter 12

12.2 (a) A items are G2 and F3; B items are A2, C7, and D1; all others are C.
12.4 108 items
12.6 (D23) A
  (D27) C
  (R02) C
  (R19) C
  (S123) C
  (U11) $5,600; B
  (U23) $1,500; C
  (V75) $6,000
12.8 (a) 600 units
  (b) 424.26 units
  (c) 848.53 units
12.10 (a) 80 units
  (b) 73 units

12.12 (a) 2,100 units
  (b) 4,200 units
  (c) 1,050 units
12.14 (a) 189.74 units
  (b) 94.87
  (c) 31.62
  (d) 7.91
  (e) $1,897.30
  (f) $601,897
12.16 (a) Order quantity variations have limited impact on total cost.
  (b) EOQ = 50
12.18 (a) 671 units
  (b) 18.63
  (c) 559 = max. inventory
  (d) 16.7%
  (e) $1,117.90
12.20 (a) 1,217 units
  (b) 1,095 = max. inventory
  (c) 8.22 production runs
  (e) $657.30
12.22 (a) EOQ = 200, total cost = $1,446,380
  (b) EOQ = 200, total cost = $1,445,880
12.24 (a) 16,971 units
  (b) $530.33
  (c) $530.33
  (d) $56,250
  (e) $57,310.66
12.26 (a) EOQ = 410
  (b) Vendor Allen has slightly lower cost.
  (c) Optimal order quantity = 1,000 @ total cost of $128,920
12.28 (a) EOQ (1) = 336; EOQ (2) = 335
  (b) Order 1,200 from Vendor 2.
  (c) At 1,200 lb., total cost = $161,275.
  (d) Storage space and perishability.
12.30 (a) 32
  (b) 2
  (c) 20; $2,400
  (d) 336; 168
  (e) $10,800
  (f) 214; $1,820
12.32 $8
12.34 7,000
12.36 (a) $1,220
  (b) $1,200
  (c) 24
12.38 (without discount) $2,200
  (with discount) $2,510
  No, do not take the discount.
12.40 Order more than 50 sheets; cost = $1,901.22
12.42 (a) $Z = 1.88$
  (b) Safety stock = $Z\sigma = 1.88(5) = 9.4$ drives
  (c) ROP = 59.4 drives
12.44 100 kilos of safety stock
12.46 (a) 291 towels
  (b) 2,291 towels
12.48 (a) ROP = 1,718 cigars
  (b) 1,868 cigars
  (c) A higher service level means a lower probability of stocking out.
12.50 55
12.52 28 cakes

Chapter 13

13.2 (a) $109,120 = total cost
  (b) $106,640 = total cost
  (c) No, plan 2 is better at $105,152.
13.4 Cost = $244,000 for plan B

13.6   (a) Plan D, $128,000
   (b) Plan E is $140,000
13.8   Extra total cost = $2,960.
13.10 (a) Plan C, $104,000; (b) plan D, $93,800, assuming initial inventory = 0
13.12 (a) Plan A: Cost is $314,000.
            Plan B: Cost is $329,000.
            Plan C: Cost is $222,000 (lowest cost).
         (b) Plan C, with lowest cost and steady employment.
13.14 $1,186,810
13.16 $100,750
13.18 $90,850
13.20 $20,400
13.22 $308,125
13.24 (b) Cost using O.T. and Forrester = $195,625.
         (c) A case could be made for either position.
13.26 Current model = $9,200 in sales; proposed model yields $9,350, which is only slightly better.

Chapter 14

14.2 The time-phased plan for the gift bags is:

Someone should start on item M by noon.

14.4 (a) Time-phased product structure for bracket with start times:

Week Activity is Scheduled to Start

(b) Castings need to start in week 4.

14.6 Gross material requirements plan:

Item		Week								Lead Time (wk)
		1	2	3	4	5	6	7	8	
S	Gross req.							100		
	Order release					100				2
T	Gross req.							100		
	Order release					100				1
U	Gross req.						200			
	Order release			200						2
V	Gross req.						100			
	Order release		100							2
W	Gross req.						200			
	Order release	200								3
X	Gross req.						100			
	Order release				100					1
Y	Gross req.					400				
	Order release	400								2
Z	Gross req.				600					
	Order release		600							1

14.8 Gross material requirements plan, modified to include the 20 units of U required for maintenance purposes:

Item		Week								Lead Time (wk)
		1	2	3	4	5	6	7	8	
S	Gross req.							100		
	Order release					100				2
T	Gross req.							100		
	Order release					100				1
U	Gross req.						200	20		
	Order release			200	20					2
V	Gross req.						100			
	Order release		100							2
W	Gross req.						200			
	Order release	200								3
X	Gross req.						100			
	Order release				100					1
Y	Gross req.					400	40			
	Order release	400	40							2
Z	Gross req.				600	60				
	Order release		600	60						1

14.10 (a) Gross material requirements plan for the first three items:

Item		Week											
		1	2	3	4	5	6	7	8	9	10	11	12
X1	Gross req.								50		20		100
	Order release							50		20		100	
B1	Gross req.								50		20		100
	Order release						50		20		100		
B2	Gross req.								100		40		200
	Order release							100		40		200	

(b) The net materials requirement plan for the first two items:

Level: 0 Item: X1	Parent: Lead Time:		Quantity: Lot Size: L4L								
Week No.	1	2	3 4 5	6	7	8 9	10	11	12		
Gross Requirement						50	20		100		
Scheduled Receipt											
On-hand Inventory						50	0		0		
Net Requirement						0	20		100		
Planned Order Receipt							20		100		
Planned Order Release						20		100			

Level: 1 Item: B1	Parent: X1 Lead Time: 2		Quantity: 1X Lot Size: L4L								
Week No.	1	2	3 4 5	6	7	8 9	10	11	12		
Gross Requirement						20		100			
Scheduled Receipt											
On-hand Inventory						20		0			
Net Requirement						0		100			
Planned Order Receipt								100			
Planned Order Release						100					

14.14 (a)

Level	Description	Qty
0	A	1
1	B	1
2	C	1
2	D	1
3	E	1
1	F	1
2	G	1
2	H	1
3	E	1
3	C	1

Note: with low-level coding "C" would be a level-3 code

(b) Solution for Items A, B, F (on next page):

14.12 (a) Net material requirements schedule (only items A and H are shown):

	Week											
	1	2 3 4	5	6	7	8	9	10	11	12		
A Gross Required						100		50		150		
On Hand						0		0		0		
Net Required						100		50		150		
Order Receipt						100		50		150		
Order Release					100		50		150			
H Gross Required						100		50				
On Hand						0		0				
Net Required						100		50				
Order Receipt						100		50				
Order Release					100		50					

(b) Net material requirements schedule (only items B and C are shown; schedule for items A and H remains the same as in part a).

	Week												
	1 2 3 4	5	6	7	8	9	10 11 12 13						
B Gross Requirements				200		100		300					
Scheduled Receipts													
Projected on Hand	100			100		0		0					
Net Requirements				100		100		300					
Planned Order Receipts				100		100		300					
Planned Order Releases			100		100		300						
C Gross Requirements				200	200	100	100	300					
Scheduled Receipts													
Projected on Hand	50			50	0	0	0	0					
Net Requirements				150	200	100	100	300					
Planned Order Receipts				150	200	100	100	300					
Planned Order Releases			150	200	100	100	300						

14.14 (b) Net material requirements schedule (only items A, B, and F are shown).

Lot Size	Lead Time	On Hand	Safety Stock	Allo-cated	Low-Level Code	Item ID		1	2	3	4	5	6	7	8
Lot	1	0	—	—	0	A	Gross Requirement								10
for							Scheduled Receipt								
Lot							Projected on Hand								0
							Net Requirement								10
							Planned Receipt								10
							Planned Release							10	
Lot	1	2	—	—	1	B	Gross Requirement								10
for							Scheduled Receipt								
Lot							Projected on Hand	2	2	2	2	2	2	2	0
							Net Requirement								8
							Planned Receipt								8
							Planned Release							8	
Lot	1	5	—	—	1	F	Gross Requirement								10
for							Scheduled Receipt								
Lot							Projected on Hand	5	5	5	5	5	5	5	0
							Net Requirement								5
							Planned Receipt								5
							Planned Release							5	

14.16 (a) Only item G changes.
(b) Component F and 4 units of A will be delayed one week.
(c) Options include: delaying 4 units of A for 1 week; asking supplier of G to expedite production.

14.18 (a)

(b)

(c)

Week	2	3	4	5	6	
Required Date				10		A
Order Release				10		
Required Date			30			D
Order Release			30			
Required Date				20		F
Order Release		20				

14.20 (a)

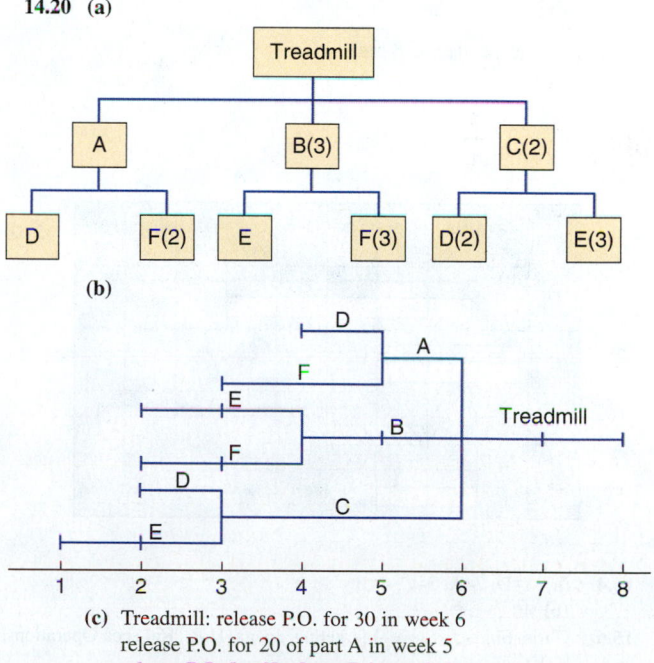

(b)

(c) Treadmill: release P.O. for 30 in week 6
release P.O. for 20 of part A in week 5
release P.O. for 60 of part B in week 4
release P.O. for 160 of part B in week 2 and 40 in week 3

14.22 Lot-for-lot: Total cost = 7 orders × $150/order + 20 units × $2.50/unit/period = $1,100.

14.24 POQ: Setup cost = 5 × $150 = $750; Holding cost = 2.50 × $170 = $425; Total $1,175

14.26 **(a)** Lot-for-lot: Setup cost = $800; Holding cost = $0.0; Total cost = $800.
(b) EOQ: EOQ = 18, Setup cost = $800; Holding cost = $370; Total cost = $1,170.
(c) POQ: EOQ = 18, POQ = 2, Setup cost = $800; Holding cost = $0.0; Total cost = $800.
(d) Lot-for-lot and POQ have the same cost.

14.28 **(a)** EOQ = 105; orders released now and in weeks 3 and 7; Actual cost = $307.50
(b) Lot-for-lot: orders released now and in weeks 1, 2, 4, 5, 6, 8, 9; Total cost = $400.

14.30 Selection for first 5 weeks:

Week	Units	Capacity Required (time)	Capacity Available (time)	Over/ (Under)	Production Scheduler's Action
1	60	3,900	2,250	1,650	Lot split. Move 300 minutes (4.3 units) to week 2 and 1,350 minutes to week 3.
2	30	1,950	2,250	(300)	
3	10	650	2,250	(1,600)	
4	40	2,600	2,250	350	Lot split. Move 250 minutes to week 3. Operations split. Move 100 minutes to another machine, overtime, or subcontract.
5	70	4,550	2,250	2,300	Lot split. Move 1,600 minutes to week 6. Overlap operations to get product out door. Operations split. Move 700 minutes to another machine, overtime, or subcontract.

14.32

Coffee Table Master Schedule	Hrs Required	Lead Time	Day 1	Day 2	Day 3	Day 4	Day 5	Day 6	Day 7	Day 8
							640	640	128	128
Table Assembly	2	1				1,280	1,280	256	256	
Top Preparation	2	1			1,280	1,280	256	256		
Assemble Base	1	1			640	640	128	128		
Long Brace (2)	0.25	1		320	320	64	64			
Short Brace (2)	0.25	1		320	320	64	64			
Leg (4)	0.25	1		640	640	128	128			
Total Hours			0	1,280	3,200	3,456	1,920	640	256	
Employees needed @ 8 hrs. each			0	160	400	432	240	80	32	

Chapter 15

15.2

15.4 **(a)** 1–D, 2–A, 3–C, 4–B
(b) 40

15.6 Chris–Finance, Steve–Marketing, Juana–H.R., Rebecca Operations, $210

15.8 Ajay–Jackie, Jack–Barbara, Gray–Stella, Raul–Dona, 230

15.10

Period	1	2	3	4
Input deviation	+5	+5	−15	−15
Output deviation	−5	−5	−10	−10
Backlog	30	30	35	40

15.12 Divorce to Attorney 3
Felony to Attorney 1
Discrimination to Attorney 2
Total cost = $2,700

15.14 G99 to 1; E2 to 2; C81 to 3;
D5 to 4; D44 to 5; C53 to 6;
E35 to 8; no component to 7.
Total cost = $1.18

15.16 Sequence 517, 103, 309, 205, 412

15.18 **(b)** SPT for best flow time
(c) SPT for best utilization
(d) EDD for best lateness
(e) LPT scores poorly on all three criteria

15.20 Johnson's Rule finishes in 21 days
First-come, First-served finishes in 23 days

15.22 **(a)** V–Y–U–Z–X–W–T
(c) 57 hours
(d) 7 hours
(e) unchanged

15.24 **(a)** 010, 020, 030, 040, 050
(b) 020, 010, 030, 040, 050 (030 could come before 010)
(c) 030, 050, 020, 040, 010
(d) 010, 040, 020, 050, 030
Average no. jobs in system: FCFS = 3.4; EDD = 3.3; SPT = 2.4; LPT = 3.6

15.26 Worker 1, M–F; Worker 2; M–F;
Worker 3, M, Th, F, S, Su; Worker 4, M-F;
Worker 5, M, T, F, S, Su; Worker 6, W, Th, F, S, Su;
Worker 7, M, T, W, S (only 4 days)

Chapter 16

16.2 Setup time = 3.675 minutes
16.4 Number of kanbans needed = 5
16.6 Production order quantity = 50; 5 Kanbans
16.8 (a) EOQ = 100 lamps
    (b) TC = $1,200
    (c) 20 orders/year
16.10 EOQ size decreases; orders increase; inventory costs can be expected to drop.
16.12 Kanban size = 158; number of kanbans needed = 10

Chapter 17

17.2 From Figure 17.2, about 13% overall reliability.
17.4 (a) 5.0%
    (b) .00001026 failures/unit-hr.
    (c) .08985
    (d) 98.83
17.6 R_s = .9941
17.8 R_p = .99925
17.10 R_p = .984
17.12 R = .7918
17.14 System B is slightly higher, at .9397.
17.16 From Figure 17.2, about 82%
17.18 2.7 breakdowns
17.20 The figure suggests that there are likely to be at least three separate modes of failure; one or more causes of infant mortality, and two modes of failure which occur at later times.
17.22 1.5 breakdowns; $15
17.24 Current cost = $1,255/week; Contract cost = $1,395; therefore, eliminate maintenance contract.

Business Analytics Module A

A.2 (a)

Size of First Station	Good Market ($)	Fair Market ($)	Poor Market ($)	EV Under Equally Likely
Small	50,000	20,000	–10,000	20,000
Medium	80,000	30,000	–20,000	30,000
Large	100,000	30,000	– 40,000	30,000
Very large	300,000	25,000	–160,000	55,000

    (b) Maximax: Build a very large station.
    (c) Maximin: Build a small station.
    (d) Equally likely: Build a very large station.
    (e)

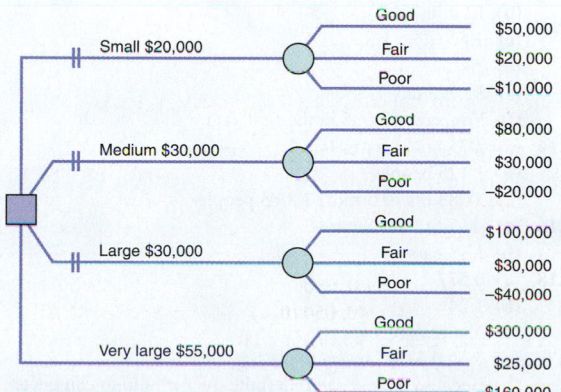

A.4 (a) Alternatives: N, M, L, D. States of nature: Fixed, Slight Increase, Major Increase
    (b) Use maximin criterion. No floor space (N).
A.6 Buying equipment at $733,333

A.8 (a) E(cost full-time) = $520
        E(cost part-timers) = $475
A.10 Alternative B; 74
A.12 8 cases; EMV = $352.50
A.14 (b) EMV(Y) = 4.2, which is best
A.16 (a) EMV(Alt. 1) = 110 = max. EMV
    (b) EVPI = 7
A.18 (a) Stock 11 cases; EMV = $385.00
    (b) Stock 13 cases; EMV = $411.25
A.20 Alternative A, with an EMV = $1,400,000
A.22 (a)

    (b) Small plant with EMV = $26,000
    (c) EVPI = $134,000
A.24 (a) Resort has higher EMV than home
    (b) EMV (Resort) = $76
A.26 (a) Build large facility
    (b) $544,000
A.28 Maximum expected profit = $33,000
    Michael should wait 1 day. Then if an XP02 is available, he should buy it. Otherwise, he should stop pursuing an XP02 on the wholesale market.
A.30

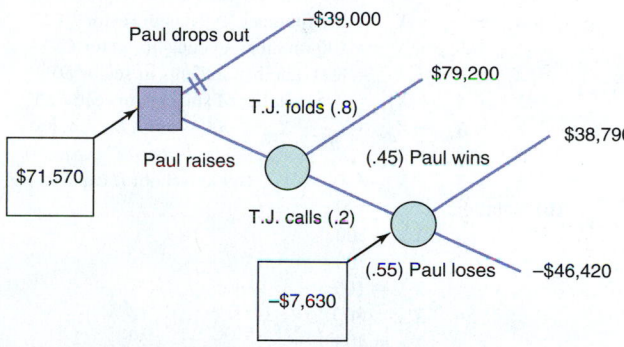

A.32 (a) Minor renovation; EMV = $10,000

Business Analytics Module B

B.2 X = 1.33, Y = 3.33; profit = $25.33
B.4 (b) Yes; P = $3,000 at (75, 75) and (50, 150)
B.6 x_1 = 200, x_2 = 0, profit = $18,000
B.8 10 Alpha 1s, 24 Beta 2s, profit = $55,200
B.10 (a) Let X = wren houses, Y = bluebird houses
        Maximize profit = $6X + 15Y$
        Subject to:
        $4X + 2Y \leq 60$
        $4X + 12Y \leq 120$
        $X, Y \geq 0$
    (b) X = 12, Y = 6; profit = $162
B.12 (a) Standard = 240, Deluxe = 180
    (b) $3,840
B.14 One approach results in 2,790 medical patients and 2,104 surgical patients, with a revenue of $9,551,659 per year (which can change slightly to $9,548,760 with rounding). This yields 61 integer medical beds and 29 integer surgical beds.
B.16 X = 4, Y = 8; profit = $52

B.18 $X_1 = 18.75$, $X_2 = 18.75$; profit = \$150

B.20 $X_1 = 2$, $X_2 = 6$; profit = \$36

B.22 (a) $x_1 = 7.95$, $x_2 = 5.95$, $x_3 = 12.59$, $P = \$143.76$

    (b) No unused time

    (c) 26¢

    (d) \$7.86

B.24 (a) A158

    (b) Nonbinding; increasing; reducing

    (c) 0

    (d) should; \$119.32

    (e) Objective function; 17.91; 49.99; 24.00; 8.88; 77.01

    (f) Constraints 7 through 11 become ≥ 0, and Constraint 12 is still ≥ 20.

B.26 $X = 3.86$, $Y = 4.54$; cost = \$160.86

B.28 Let X = number of pounds of compost in each bag

Let Y = number of pounds of sewage waste in each bag

$X = 30$, $Y = 30$; cost = \$2.70

B.30 $x_1 = 14$, $x_2 = 33$, cost = 221

B.32 Objective function: Minimize Z (in thousands) $10X_1 + 8X_2$

Constraints: $0X_1 + 1X_2 \geq 5$

             $2X_1 + 1X_2 \geq 20$

Solution: 7.5 thousand round tables, 5 thousand square tables; cost = \$115 (in thousands)

B.34 (a) Let X_{ij} = number of students bused from sector i to school j.

Objective: minimize total travel miles =

$$5X_{AB} + 8X_{AC} + 6X_{AE}$$
$$+ 0X_{BB} + 4X_{BC} + 12X_{BE}$$
$$+ 4x_{CB} + 0X_{CC} + 7X_{CE}$$
$$+ 7X_{DB} + 2X_{DC} + 5x_{DE}$$
$$+ 12X_{EB} + 7X_{EC} + 0X_{EE}$$

Subject to:

$X_{AB} + X_{AC} + X_{AE} = 700$ (number of students in sector A)

$X_{BB} + X_{BC} + X_{BE} = 500$ (number students in sector B)

$X_{CB} + X_{CC} + X_{CE} = 100$ (number of students in sector C)

$X_{DB} + X_{DC} + X_{DE} = 800$ (number of students in sector D)

$X_{EB} + X_{EC} + X_{EE} = 400$ (number of students in sector E)

$X_{AB} + X_{BB} + X_{CB} + X_{DB} + X_{EB} \leq 900$ (school B capacity)

$X_{AC} + X_{BC} + X_{CC} + X_{DC} + X_{EC} \leq 900$ (school C capacity)

$X_{AE} + X_{BE} + X_{CE} + X_{DE} + X_{EE} \leq 900$ (school E capacity)

    (b) Solution: $X_{AB} = 400$

                  $X_{AE} = 300$

                  $X_{BB} = 500$

                  $X_{CC} = 100$

                  $X_{DC} = 800$

                  $X_{EE} = 400$

Distance = 5,400 "student miles"

B.36 Hire 30 workers; three solutions are feasible; two of these are:

16 begin at 7 A.M.

9 begin at 3 P.M.

2 begin at 7 P.M.

3 begin at 11 P.M.

An alternate optimum is:

3 begin at 3 A.M.

9 begin at 7 A.M.

7 begin at 11 A.M.

2 begin at 3 P.M.

9 begin at 7 P.M.

0 begin at 11 P.M.

B.38 (a) Minimize = $6X_{1A} + 5X_{1B} + 3X_{1C} + 8X_{2A} + 10X_{2B} + 8X_{2C} + 11X_{3A} + 14X_{3B} + 18X_{3C}$

Subject to:

$X_{1A} + X_{2A} + X_{3A} = 7$

$X_{1B} + X_{2B} + X_{3B} = 12$

$X_{1C} + X_{2C} + X_{3C} = 5$

$X_{1A} + X_{1B} + X_{1C} \leq 6$

$X_{2A} + X_{2B} + X_{2C} \leq 8$

$X_{3A} + X_{3B} + X_{3C} \leq 10$

    (b) Minimum cost = \$219,000

B.40 Apple sauce = 0, Canned corn = 1.33, Fried chicken = 0.46, French fries = 0, Mac & Cheese = 1.13, Turkey = 0, Garden salad = 0, Cost = \$1.51.

B.42 Include all but investment A.; total expected return = \$3,580

Business Analytics Module C

C.2 \$208

C.4 \$170

C.6 \$2,020

C.8 Total cost = \$505

C.10 Optimal site is St. Louis, at \$17,250

C.12 D–A, 100; E–B, 200; F–A, 200; E–C, 100; F–C, 100. \$3,900 total cost.

C.14 \$14,700, Houston-Dallas, 800; Houston-Atlanta, 50; Phoenix-Atlanta, 250; Phoenix-Denver, 200; Phoenix-Dummy, 200; Memphis-Atlanta, 300.

C.16 A–1, 20; B–1, 20; B–2, 10; C–2, 50; C–3, 25; Dummy–3, 30

C.18 Dublin, \$1,535,000

Fountainbleau, \$1,530,000 (lowest cost)

Business Analytics Module D

D.2 (a) 44%

    (b) .36 people

    (c) .8 people

    (d) .53 min

    (e) 1.2 min

D.4 (a) .5

    (b) .5

    (c) 1

    (d) .5

    (e) .05 hr

    (f) .1 hr

D.6 (a) .667

    (b) .667 min

    (c) 1.33

D.8 (a) .375

    (b) 1.6 hr (or .2 days)

    (c) .225

    (d) 0.141, 0.053, 0.020, 0.007

D.10 (a) 2.25

    (b) .75

    (c) .857 min. (.014 hr)

    (d) .64 min. (.011 hr)

    (e) 42%, 32%, 24%

D.12 (a) 6 trucks

    (b) 12 min

    (c) .857

    (d) .54

    (e) \$1,728/day

    (f) Yes, save \$3,096 in the first year.

D.14 (a) .075 hrs (4.5 min)

    (b) 1.125 people

    (c) .0083 hrs (0.5 min), 0.083 people

D.16 (a) .113 hr. = 6.8 min

    (b) 1.13 cars

D.18 (a) 0.577

    (b) 1.24

    (c) 33.6%

D.20 (a) 3, 2, 4 MDs, respectively

    (b) Because $\lambda > \mu$, an indefinite queue buildup can occur.

D.22 (a) 4 servers

    (b) 6 servers

    (c) \$109

    (d) 83.33%

D.24 2 salespeople ($340)
D.26 5 min.
D.28 72 loans
D.30 1.2 callers
D.32 (a) 0.833
 (b) 1.667 hours
 (c) 4.167
 (d) 0.335
D.34 (a) 1.33 cars
 (b) 0.0667 hours
 (c) 0.10 hours
 (d) 0.667
 (e) 0.33
 (f) $L_q = 0.083$, $W_q = 0.0042$ hrs., $W_s = 0.0209$ hrs., $\rho = 0.333$, $P_0 = 0.667$
D.36 (a) 0.0377
 (b) 4.53 persons
 (c) 22.65 min.
 (d) 7.62 min. (or 0.127 hrs.)
 (e) 1.53 customers
 (f) 0.9533
D.38 (a) 4.167 cars
 (b) 0.4167 hrs.
 (c) 0.5 hrs.
 (d) 0.8333
 (e) 0.1667

Business Analytics Module E

E.2 (a) 507 min
 (b) 456 min
 (c) 410 min
 (d) 369 min
E.4 (a) 1,546 min
 (b) 2,872 min
 (c) 3,701 min
 (d) 6,779 min
E.6 (a) 14.31 hr
 (b) $71,550
 (c) $947,250
E.8 (a) 80%
 (b) 3.51
 (c) 3.2, 2.98, 2.81
 (d) 21.5
E.10 (a) 72.2 hr
 (b) 60.55 hr
 (c) 41.47 hr
E.12 Susan will take 3.67 hr and Julie 2.43 hr. Neither trainee will reach 1 hr by the 10th unit.
E.14 $748,240 for fourth, $709,960 for fifth, $679,960 for sixth
E.16 (a) 70 millicents/bit
 (b) 8.2 millicents/bit
E.18 26,755 hr
E.20 (a) 32.98 hr, 49.61 hr
 (b) Initial quote is high.
E.22 (a) Four boats can be completed.
 (b) Five boats can be completed.
E.24 .227 hr
E.26 (a) 476.3
 (b) 429
 (c) 410.4
 (d) 369.3
E.28 1,106.4 days
E.30 58,320 hours
E.32 .877 or 88%

Business Analytics Module F

F.2 0, 0, 0, 0, 0, 0, 0, 2, 0, 2
F.4 Profits = 20, −15, 20, 17.50, 20; average equals $12.50.
F.6 At the end of 5 min, two checkouts are still busy and one is available.
F.8 Aver. no. of failures = 2.88 units/month
 7 units failed over each 3-month stretch
F.10 (a) 24
 (b) $36.70
 (c) $0.30
 (d) $6.10
 (e) 21
F.12 (a) 5 times
 (b) 6.95 times; yes
 (c) 7.16 heaters
F.14 Average = 7
F.16

Arrivals	Arrival Time	Service Time	Departure Time
1	11:01	3	11:04
2	11:04	2	11:06
3	11:06	2	11:08
4	11:07	1	11:09

F.18 During 4 hours, 7 customers balked.
 Taboo missed 105 minutes = $21.00/day or $504/month. Additional bed not justified.
F.20 Average weekly stockout cost = $20; Weekly holding cost = $2.30
F.22 First order, total demand during lead time = 31.
 No stockout.
 Second order, total demand during lead time = 42.
 One stockout.
F.24 Balance never drops below $400, she should be able to balance her account.

Online Tutorial 1

T1.2 5.45; 4.06
T1.4 (a) .2743
 (b) 0.5
T1.6 .1587; .2347; .1587
T1.8 (a) .0548
 (b) .6554
 (c) .6554
 (d) .2119

Online Tutorial 2

T2.2 (selected values)

Fraction Defective	Mean of Poisson	$P(x \leq 1)$
.01	.05	.999
.05	.25	.974
.10	.50	.910
.30	1.50	.558
.60	3.00	.199
1.00	5.00	.040

T2.4 The plan meets neither the producer's nor the consumer's requirement.

Online Tutorial 3

T3.2 (a) Max $3x_1 + 9x_2$

$$x_1 + 4x_2 + s_1 = 24$$
$$x_1 + 2x_2 + s_2 = 16$$

(b) See the steps in the tutorial.

(c) Second tableau:

c_j	Mix	x_1	x_2	s_1	s_2	Qty.
9	x_2	.25	1	.25	0	6
0	s_2	.50	0	−.50	1	4
	z_j	2.25	9	2.25	0	54
	$c_j - z_j$	.75	0	−2.25	0	

(d) $x_1 = 8$, $x_2 = 4$, Profit = $60

T3.4 Basis for 1st tableau:

$A_1 = 80$
$A_2 = 75$

Basis for 2nd tableau:

$A_1 = 55$
$X_1 = 25$

Basis for 3rd tableau:

$X_1 = 14$
$X_2 = 33$

Cost = $221 at optimal solution

T3.6 (a) x_1

(b) A_1

Online Tutorial 4

T4.2 Cost = $980; 1–A = 20; 1–B = 50; 2–C = 20; 2–Dummy = 30; 3–A = 20; 3–C = 40

T4.4 Total = 3,100 mi; Morgantown–Coaltown = 35; Youngstown–Coal Valley = 30; Youngstown–Coaltown = 5; Youngstown–Coal Junction = 25; Pittsburgh–Coaltown = 5; Pittsburgh–Coalsburg = 20

T4.6 (a) Using VAM, cost = $635; A–Y = 35; A–Z = 20; B–W = 10; B–X = 20; B–Y = 15; C–W = 30

(b) Using MODI, cost is also $635 (i.e., initial solution was optimal). An alternative optimal solution is A–X = 20; A–Y = 15; A–Z = 20; B–W = 10; B–Y = 35; C–W = 30

Online Tutorial 5

T5.2 (a) $I_{13} = 12$

(b) $I_{35} = 7$

(c) $I_{51} = 4$

T5.4 (a) Tour: 1–2–4–5–7–6–8–3–1; 37.9 mi

(b) Tour: 4–5–7–6–8–1–2–3–4; 30.2 mi

T5.6 (a) Vehicle 1: Tour 1–2–4–3–5–1 = $134

Vehicle 2: Tour 1–6–10–9–8–7–1 = $188

T5.8 The cost matrix is shown below:

	1	2	3	4	5	6	7	8
1	—	107.26	118.11	113.20	116.50	123.50	111.88	111.88
2		—	113.53	111.88	118.10	125.30	116.50	118.10
3			—	110.56	118.70	120.50	119.90	124.90
4				—	109.90	119.10	111.88	117.90
5					—	111.88	106.60	118.50
6						—	111.88	123.50
7							—	113.20
8								—

Bibliography

Chapter 1

Broedner, P., S. Kinkel, and G. Lay. "Productivity Effects of Outsourcing." *International Journal of Operations and Production Management* 29, no. 2 (2009): 127.

Hounshell, D. A. *From the American System to Mass Production 1800–1932: The Development of Manufacturing.* Baltimore: Johns Hopkins University Press, 1985.

Lewis, William W. *The Power of Productivity.* Chicago: University of Chicago Press, 2005.

Malone, T. W., R J. Laubacher, and T. Johns, "The Age of Hyperspecialization." *Harvard Business* 89, no. 7 (July–August 2011): 56–65.

Maroto, A., and L. Rubalcaba. "Services Productivity Revisited." *The Service Industries Journal* 28, no. 3 (April 2008): 337.

McLaughlin, Patrick. "Measuring Productivity." *Management Services* 58, no. 4 (Winter 2014): 31–37.

Sahay, B. S. "Multi-factor Productivity Measurement Model for Service Organization." *International Journal of Productivity and Performance Management* 54, no. 1–2 (2005): 7–23.

San, G., T. Huang, and L. Huang. "Does Labor Quality Matter on Productivity Growth?" *Total Quality Management and Business Excellence* 19, no. 10 (October 2008): 1043.

Sprague, Linda G. "Evolution of the Field of Operations Management." *Journal of Operations Management* 25, no. 2 (March 2007): 219–238.

Tangen, S. "Demystifying Productivity and Performance." *International Journal of Productivity and Performance Measurement* 54, no. 1–2 (2005): 34–47.

Taylor, F. W. *The Principles of Scientific Management.* New York: Harper & Brothers, 1911.

van Biema, Michael, and Bruce Greenwald. "Managing Our Way to Higher Service-Sector Productivity." *Harvard Business Review* 75, no. 4 (July–August 1997): 87–95.

Wren, Daniel A. *The Evolution of Management Thought.* New York: Wiley, 1994.

Chapter 2

Beckman, S. L., and D. B. Rosenfield. *Operations Strategy: Competing in the 21st Century.* New York: McGraw-Hill, 2008.

Bravard, J., and R. Morgan. *Smarter Outsourcing.* Upper Saddle River, NJ: Pearson, 2006.

Crotts, J. C., D. R. Dickson, and R. C. Ford. "Aligning Organizational Processes with Mission." *Academy of Management Executive* 19, no. 3 (August 2005): 54–68.

Flynn, B. B., R. G. Schroeder, and E. J. Flynn. "World Class Manufacturing." *Journal of Operations Management* 17, no. 3 (March 1999): 249–269.

Greenwald, Bruce C., and Judd Kahn. *Globalization: The Irrational Fear That Someone in China Will Take Your Job.* New York: Wiley, 2009.

Gordon, John Steel. *An Empire of Wealth: the Epic History of American Economic Power.* New York: HarperCollins, 2005.

Hirschheim, R., A. Heinzl, and J. Dibbern. *Information Systems Outsourcing.* Secaucus, NJ: Springer, 2009.

Lee, Hau L., and Chung-Yee Lee. *Building Supply Chain Excellence in Emerging Economies.* Secaucus, NJ: Springer, 2007.

Kaplan, Robert S., and David P. Norton. *Strategy Maps.* Boston: Harvard Business School Publishing, 2004.

Kathuria, R., M. P. Joshi, and S. Dellande. "International Growth Strategies of Service and Manufacturing Firms." *International Journal of Operations and Production Management* 28, no. 10 (2008): 968.

Midler, Paul. *Poorly Made in China: An Insider's Account of the Tactics Behind China's Production Game.* New York: Wiley, 2009.

Porter, Michael, and Nicolaj Siggelkow. "Contextuality within Activity Systems and Sustainability of Competitive Advantage." *Academy of Management Perspectives* 22, no. 2 (May 2008): 34–36.

Rothfeder, Jeffry. *Driving Honda: Inside the World's Most Innovative Car Company.* New York: Penguin Group, 2014.

Rudberg, Martin, and B. M. West. "Global Operations Strategy." *Omega* 36, no. 1 (February 2008): 91.

Skinner, Wickham. "Manufacturing Strategy: The Story of Its Evolution." *Journal of Operations Management* 25, no. 2 (March 2007): 328–334.

Slack, Nigel, and Mike Lewis. *Operation Strategy,* 3rd ed. Upper Saddle River, NJ: Prentice Hall, 2011.

Wolf, Martin. *Why Globalization Works.* London: Yale University Press, 2004.

Chapter 3

Balakrishnan, R., B. Render, and R. M. Stair. *Managerial Decision Modeling with Spreadsheets,* 3rd ed. Upper Saddle River, NJ: Prentice Hall, 2012.

Cleland, D. L., and L. R. Ireland. *Project Management,* 6th ed. New York: McGraw-Hill/Irwin, 2010.

Gray, C. L., and E. W. Larson. *Project Management with MS Project.* New York: McGraw-Hill/Irwin, 2008.

Helgadottir, Hilder. "The Ethical Dimension of Project Management." *International Journal of Project Management* 26, no. 7 (October 2008): 743.

Karlos, A., et al. "Foundations of Project Management." *International Journal of Project Management* 27, no. 1 (January 2009): 1.

Kerzner, H. *Project Management Case Studies,* 3rd ed. New York: Wiley, 2009.

Matta, N. F., and R. N. Ashkenas. "Why Good Projects Fail Anyway." *Harvard Business Review* 85, no. 5 (September 2003): 109–114.

Maylor, Harvey. *Project Management,* 5th ed. Upper Saddle River, NJ: Prentice Hall, 2011.

Meredith, J. R., and S. Mantel. *Project Management,* 8th ed. New York: Wiley, 2011.

Oates, David. "Understanding and Solving the Causes of Project Failure." *Knowledge Management Review* 9, no. 5 (May–June 2006): 5.

Render, B., R. M. Stair, and M. Hanna. *Quantitative Analysis for Management,* 11th ed. Upper Saddle River, NJ: Prentice Hall, 2012.

Verzuh, Eric. *The Fast Forward MBA in Project Management.* New York: Wiley, 2008.

Wysocki, R. K. *Effective Project Management,* 6th ed. New York: Wiley, 2012.

Chapter 4

Balakrishnan, R., B. Render, and R. M. Stair. *Managerial Decision Modeling with Spreadsheets,* 3rd ed. Upper Saddle River, NJ: Prentice Hall, 2012.

Berenson, Mark, Tim Krehbiel, and David Levine. *Basic Business Statistics,* 12th ed. Upper Saddle River, NJ: Prentice Hall, 2012.

Campbell, Omar. "Forecasting in Direct Selling Business: Tupperware's Experience." *The Journal of Business Forecasting* 27, no. 2 (Summer 2008): 18–19.

Diebold, F. X. *Elements of Forecasting,* 6th ed. Cincinnati: South-Western College Publishing, 2013.

Fildes, Robert, and Paul Goodwin. "Against Your Better Judgment? How Organizations Can Improve Their Use of Management Judgment in Forecasting." *Decision Sciences* 37, no. 6 (November–December 2007): 570–576.

Georgoff, D. M., and R. G. Murdick. "Manager's Guide to Forecasting." *Harvard Business Review* 64 (January–February 1986): 110–120.

Gilliland, M., and M. Leonard. "Forecasting Software—The Past and the Future." *The Journal of Business Forecasting* 25, no. 1 (Spring 2006): 33–36.

Hanke, J. E. and D. W. Wichern. *Business Forecasting*, 10th ed. Upper Saddle River, NJ: Prentice Hall, 2012.

Jain, Chaman L. "Benchmarking Forecasting Software and Systems." *The Journal of Business Forecasting* 26, no. 4 (Winter 2007/2008): 30–34.

Onkal, D., M. S. Gonul, and M. Lawrence. "Judgmental Adjustments of Previously Adjusted Forecasts." *Decision Sciences* 39, no. 2 (May 2008): 213–238.

Render, B., R. M. Stair, and M. Hanna. *Quantitative Analysis for Management*, 11th ed. Upper Saddle River, NJ: Prentice Hall, 2012.

Shah, Piyush. "Techniques to Support Better Forecasting." *APICS Magazine* (November/December 2008): 49–50.

Urs, Rajiv. "How to Use a Demand Planning System for Best Forecasting and Planning Results." *The Journal of Business Forecasting* 27, no. 2 (Summer 2008): 22–25.

Wilson, J. H., B. Keating, and J. Galt. *Business Forecasting,* 7th ed. New York: McGraw-Hill, 2012.

Yurklewicz, Jack. "Forecasting an Upward Trend." *OR/MS Today* (June 2012): 52–61.

Chapter 5

Alexy Oliver, P. Criscuelo, and A. Salter. "Managing Unsolicited Ideas for R&D." *California Management Review* 54, no. 3 (Spring 2012): 116–139.

Brown, Bruce, and S.D. Anthony; "How P&G Tripled Its Innovation Success Rate." *Harvard Business Review* 89, no. 6 (June 2011): 64–72.

Buckley, Peter J., and Roger Strange. "The Governance of the Global Factory: Location and Control of World Economic Activity." *Academy of Management Perspectives* 29, no. 2 (May 2015): 237–249.

Camevalli, J. A., and P. A. C. Miguel. "Review, Analysis, and Classification of the Literature on QFD." *International Journal of Production Economics* 114, no. 2 (August 2008): 737.

Ernst, David, and James Bamford. "Your Alliances Are too Stable." *Harvard Business Review* 83, no. 5 (June 2005): 133–141.

Gerwin, Donald. "Coordinating New Product Development in Strategic Alliances." *The Academy of Management Review* 29, no. 2 (April 2004): 241–257.

Gwynne, Peter. "Measuring R&D Productivity." *Research Technology Management* 58, no. 1 (Jan/Feb. 2015): 19–22.

Haines, Steven. *Managing Product Management.* New York; McGraw-Hill, 2012.

Krishnan, V., and Karl T. Ulrich. "Product Development Decisions: A Review of the Literature." *Management Science* 47, no. 1 (January 2001): 1–21.

Loch, C. H., and C. Terwiesch. "Rush and Be Wrong or Wait and Be Late?" *Production and Operations Management* 14, no. 3 (Fall 2005): 331–343.

Miguel, P. A. C., and J. A. Camevalli. "Benchmarking Practices of Quality Function Deployment." *Benchmarking* 15, no. 6 (2008): 657.

Phyper, J. D., and D. MacLean. *Good to Green: Managers' Business Risks and Opportunities in an Age of Environmental Awareness.* New York: Wiley, 2009.

Pisano, Gary P., and Roberto Verganti. "Which Kind of Collaboration Is Right for You?" *Harvard Business Review* 86, no. 12 (December 2008):78–86.

Reeves, Martin, and Mike Deimler. "Adaptability: The New Competitive Advantage." *Harvard Business Review* 90, no. 7 (July–August 2011): 135–141.

Saaksvuori, A., and A. Immonen. *Product Lifecycle Management.* Berlin: Springer-Verlag, 2004.

Seider, Warren D., et al. *Product and Process Design Principles,* 3rd. ed. New York: Wiley, 2008.

Ulrich, K., and S. Eppinger. *Product Design and Development*, 4th ed. New York: McGraw-Hill, 2008.

Supplement 5

Ambec, Stefan, and Paul Lanoie. "Does It Pay to Be Green? A Systematic Overview." *Academy of Management Perspectives* 22, no. 4 (November 2008): 13–20.

Banerjee, S. B. "Embedding Sustainability Across the Organization: A Critical Perspective." *Academy of Management, Learning & Education* 10, no. 4 (December 2011): 719–731.

Epstein, Marc J. *Making Sustainability Work.* San Francisco: Berrett-Koehler Publisher, 2008.

Haugh, Helen M., and A. Talwar. "How Do Corporations Embed Sustainability Across the Organization?" *Academy of Management, Learning & Education* 9, no. 3 (September 2010): 384–396.

Laszlo, Chris. *Sustainable Value.* Stanford, CA: Stanford University Press, 2008.

Laszlo, Chris, and N. Zhexembayeva. *Embedded Sustainability.* Stanford, CA: Stanford University Press, 2011.

Nidumolu, Ram, C. K. Prahalad, and M. R. Rangaswami. "Why Sustainability Is Now the Key Driver of Innovation." *Harvard Business Review* 87, no. 9 (September 2009): 56–64.

Stoner, J. A. F., and C. Wankel (Ed). *Global Sustainability Initiatives.* Charlotte, NC: Information Age Publishing, 2008.

Chapter 6

Besterfield, Dale H. *Quality Control*, 8th ed. Upper Saddle River, NJ: Prentice Hall, 2009.

Brown, Mark G. *Baldrige Award Winning Quality*, 19th ed. University Park, IL: Productivity Press, 2010.

Crosby, P. B. *Quality Is Still Free*. New York: McGraw-Hill, 1996.

Evans, J. R., and W. M. Lindsay. *Managing for Quality and Performance Excellence*, 8th ed. Mason, OH: Thomson-South-Western, 2012.

Feigenbaum, A. V. "Raising the Bar." *Quality Progress* 41, no. 7 (July 2008): 22–28.

Foster, Thomas. *Managing Quality,* 4th ed. Upper Saddle River, NJ: Pearson/Prentice Hall, 2010.

Gitlow, Howard S. *A Guide to Lean Six Sigma Management Skills.* University Park, IL: Productivity Press, 2009.

Gonzalez-Benito, J., and O. Gonzalez-Benito. "Operations Management Practices Linked to the Adoption of ISO 14001." *International Journal of Production Economics* 113, no. 1 (May 2008): 60.

Gray, John V., Gopesh Anand, and Aleda V. Roth. "The Influence of ISO 9000 Certification on Process Compliance." *Production and Operations Management* 24, no. 3 (March 2015): 369–382.

Gryna, F. M., R. C. H. Chua, and J. A. DeFeo. *Juran's Quality Planning and Analysis for Enterprise Quality*, 5th ed. New York: McGraw-Hill, 2007.

Mitra, Amit. *Fundamentals of Quality Control and Improvement.* New York: Wiley, 2009.

Pande, P. S., R. P. Neuman, R. R. Cavanagh. *What Is Design for Six Sigma?* New York: McGraw-Hill, 2005.

Petroski, Henry. *To Forgive Design: Understanding Failure.* Cambridge, MA: Belknap, 2012.

Schroeder, Roger G., et al. "Six Sigma: Definition and Underlying Theory." *Journal of Operations Management* 26, no. 4 (2008): 536–554.

Stewart, D. M. "Piecing Together Service Quality: A Framework for Robust Service." *Production and Operations Management* (Summer 2003): 246–265.

Summers, Donna. *Quality Management,* 2nd ed. Upper Saddle River, NJ: Prentice Hall, 2009.

Yan, Xinghao, Hui Zhao, and Kwei Tang. "Requirement or Promise? An Analysis of the First-Mover Advantage in Quality Contracting." *Production and Operations Management* 24, no. 6 (June 2015): 917–933.

Supplement 6

Bakir, S. T. "A Quality Control Chart for Work Performance Appraisal." *Quality Engineering* 17, no. 3 (2005): 429.

Besterfield, Dale H. *Quality Control*, 8th ed. Upper Saddle River, NJ: Prentice Hall, 2009.

Elg, M., J. Olsson, and J. J. Dahlgaard. "Implementing Statistical Process Control." *The International Journal of Quality and Reliability Management* 25, no. 6 (2008): 545.

Goetsch, David L., and Stanley B. Davis. *Quality Management*, 6th ed. Upper Saddle River, NJ: Prentice Hall, 2009.

Gryna, F. M., R. C. H. Chua, and J. A. DeFeo. *Juran's Quality Planning and Analysis*, 5th ed. New York: McGraw-Hill, 2007.

Lin, H., and G. Sheen. "Practical Implementation of the Capability Index C_{pk} Based on Control Chart Data." *Quality Engineering* 17, no. 3 (2005): 371.

Matthes, N., et al. "Statistical Process Control for Hospitals." *Quality Management in Health Care* 16, no. 3 (July–September 2007): 205.

Mitra, Amit. *Fundamentals of Quality Control and Improvement*, 3rd ed. New York: Wiley, 2008.

Montgomery, D. C., C. L. Jennings, and M. E. Pfund. *Managing, Controlling, and Improving Quality*. New York: Wiley, 2011.

Roth, H. P. "How SPC Can Help Cut Costs." *Journal of Corporate Accounting and Finance* 16, no. 3 (March–April 2005): 21–30.

Sower, V. E. *Essentials of Quality*. New York: Wiley, 2011.

Summers, Donna. *Quality Management*, 2nd ed. Upper Saddle River, NJ: Prentice Hall, 2009.

Chapter 7

Davenport, T. H. "The Coming Commoditization of Processes." *Harvard Business Review* 83, no. 6 (June 2005): 101–108.

Debo, L. G., L. B. Toktay, and L. N. Van Wassenhove. "Market Segmentation and Product Technology Selection for Remanufacturable Products." *Management Science* 51, no. 8 (August 2005): 1193–1205.

Duray, R., P. T. Ward, G. W. Milligan, and W. L. Berry. "Approaches to Mass Customization: Configurations and Empirical Validation." *Journal of Operations Management* 18, no. 6 (November 2000): 605–625.

Duray, R. "Mass Customization Origins: Mass or Custom Manufacturing." *International Journal of Operations and Production Management* 22, no. 3 (2002): 314–328.

Hall, Joseph M., and M. Eric Johnson. "When Should a Process Be Art, Not Science?" *Harvard Business Review* 87, no. 3 (March 2009): 58–65.

Hegde, V. G., et al. "Customization: Impact on Product and Process Performance." *Production and Operations Management* 14, no. 4 (Winter 2005): 388–399.

Inderfurth, Karl, I. M. Langella. "An Approach for Solving Disassembly-to-order Problems under Stochastic Yields." In *Logistik Management*. Heidelberg: Physica, 2004: 309–331.

Moultrie, James, and Anja M. Maier. "A Simplified Approach to Design for Assembly." *Journal of Engineering Design* 25, no. 1–3 (March 2014): 44–63.

Rugtusanatham, M. Johnny, and Fabrizio Salvador. "From Mass Production to Mass Customization." *Production and Operations Management* 17, no. 3 (May–June 2008): 385–396.

Swamidass, Paul M. *Innovations in Competitive Manufacturing*. Dordrecht, NL: Kluwer, 2000.

Welborn, Cliff. "Mass Customization." *OR/MS Today* (December 2007): 38–42.

Zhang, M., Y. Qi, and X. Zhao. "The Impact of Mass Customization Practices on Performance." *International Journal of Mass Customization* 4, no. 1–2 (2011): 44–66.

Zipkin, Paul. "The Limits of Mass Customization." *MIT Sloan Management Review* 40, no. 1 (Spring 2001): 81–88.

Supplement 7

Anderson, Edward James, and Shu-Jung Sunny Yang. "The Timing of Capacity Investment with Lead Times: When Do Firms Act in Unison?" *Production and Operations Management* 24, no. 1 (January 2015): 21–41.

Anupindi, Ravi, S. Deshmukh, and S. Chopra. *Managing Business Process Flows*, 2nd ed. Upper Saddle River, NJ: Prentice Hall (2007).

Bowers, John, et al. "Modeling Outpatient Capacity for a Diagnosis and Treatment Center." *Health Care Management Science* 8, no. 3 (August 2005): 205.

Chambers, Chester, Eli M. Snir, and Asad Ata. "The Use of Flexible Manufacturing Capacity in Pharmaceutical Product Introductions." *Decision Sciences* 40, no. 2 (May 2009): 243–268.

Chen, Wen-Chih, and C. Chien. "Evaluating Capacity Pooling Strategy in Semiconductor Manufacturing: A Productivity Perspective Study." *International Journal of Production Research* 49, no 12 (June 2011): 3635–3652.

Goldratt, Eliyaha. *The Choice*. Great Barrington, MA: North River Press (2009).

Goodale, John C., Rohit Verma, and Madeleine E. Pullman. "A Market Utility-Based Model for Capacity Scheduling in Mass Services." *Production and Operations Management* 12, no. 2 (Summer 2003): 165–185.

Gupta, M. C., and L. H. Boyd. "Theory of Constraints: A Theory for Operations Management." *International Journal of Operations Management* 28, no. 10 (2008): 991.

Jonsson, Patrik, and Stig-Arne Mattsson. "Use and Applicability of Capacity Planning Methods." *Production and Inventory Management Journal* (3rd/4th Quarter 2002): 89–95.

Lee, Eva K., et al. "Transforming Hospital Emergency Department Workflow and Patient Care." *Interfaces* 45, no. 1 (January–February 2015): 58–82.

Li, Shanling, and L. Wang. "Outsourcing and Capacity Planning in an Uncertain Global Environment." *European Journal of Operational Research* 207, no. 1 (November 2010): 131–141.

May, Jerrold H., W. E. Spangler, D. P. Strum, and L. G. Vargas. "The Surgical Scheduling Problem: Current Research and Future Opportunities." *Production & Operations Management* 20, no. 3 (May–June 2011): 392–405.

Mincsovics, G. Z., and N. P. Dellaert. "Workload-Dependent Capacity Control in Production-to-Order Systems." *IIE Transactions,* 41, no. 10 (October 2009): 853–865.

Roy, Anjan. "Strategic Positioning and Capacity Utilization: Factors in Planning for Profitable Growth in Banking." *Journal of Performance Management* 23, no. 3 (November 2010): 23.

Tanrisever, Fehmi, D. Morrice, and D. Morton. "Managing Capacity Flexibility in Make-to-Order Production Environments." *European Journal of Operational Research* 216, no. 2 (January 2012): 334–345.

Tibben-Lembke, Ronald S. "Theory of Constraints at UniCo." *International Journal of Production Research* 47, no. 7 (January 2009): 1815.

Watson, Kevin J., John H. Blackstone, and Stanley C. Gardiner. "The Evolution of a Management Philosophy: The Theory of Constraints." *Journal of Operations Management* 25, no. 2 (March 2007): 387–402.

Chapter 8

Ballou, Ronald H. *Business Logistics Management*, 5th ed. Upper Saddle River, NJ: Prentice Hall, 2004.

Bartness, A. D. "The Plant Location Puzzle." *Harvard Business Review* 72, no. 2 (March–April 1994).

Denton, B. "Decision Analysis, Location Models, and Scheduling Problems." *Interfaces* 30, no. 3 (May–June 2005): 262–263.

Drezner, Z. *Facility Location: Applications and Theory*. Berlin: Springer-Verlag, 2002.

Florida, R. *The Flight of the Creative Class: The New Global Competition for Talent.* New York: HarperCollins, 2005.

Klamroth, K. *Single Facility Location Problems*. Berlin: Springer-Verlag, 2002.

Kennedy, M. *Introducing Geographic Information Systems with ArcGIS*. New York: Wiley, 2006.

Mentzer, John T. "Seven Keys to Facility Location." *Supply Chain Management Review* 12, no. 5 (May 2008): 25.

Partovi, F. Y. "An Analytic Model for Locating Facilities Strategically." *Omega* 34, no. 1 (January 2006): 41.

Porter, Michael E., and Scott Stern. "Innovation: Location Matters." *MIT Sloan Management Review* (Summer 2001): 28–36.

Render, B., R. M. Stair, and M. Hanna. *Quantitative Analysis for Management*, 11th ed. Upper Saddle River, NJ: Prentice Hall, 2012.

Snyder, L. V. "Facility Location Under Uncertainty." *IIE Transactions* 38, no. 7 (July 2006): 547.

Tallman, Stephen, et al. "Knowledge, Clusters, and Competitive Advantage." *The Academy of Management Review* 29, no. 2 (April 2004): 258–271.

White, G. "Location, Location, Location." *Nation's Restaurant News* 42, no. 27 (July 14, 2008): S10–S11.

Chapter 9

Aghazadeh, S. M., S. Hafeznezami, L. Najjar, and Z. Hug. "The Influence of Work-Cells and Facility Layout on Manufacturing Efficiency." *Journal of Facilities Management* 9, no. 3 (2011): 213–224.

Birchfield, J. C., and J. Birchfield. *Design and Layout of Foodservice Facilities*, 3rd ed. New York, Wiley & Sons, 2007.

Francis, R. L., L. F. McGinnis, and J. A. White. *Facility Layout and Location*, 3rd ed. Upper Saddle River, NJ: Prentice Hall, 1998.

Heragu, S. S. *Facilities Design,* 3rd ed. New York: CRC Press, 2008.

Heyer, N., and U. Wemmerlöv. *Reorganizing the Factory: Competing through Cellular Manufacturing.* Portland, OR: Productivity Press, 2002.

Johnson, Alan. "Getting the Right Factory Layout." *Manufacturer's Monthly* (July 2008): 16.

Kator, C. "Crossdocking on the Rise." *Modern Materials Handling* 63, no. 6 (June 2008): 15.

Larson, S. "Extreme Makeover—OR Edition." *Nursing Management* (November 2005): 26.

Quillien, Jenny. *Clever Digs: How Workspaces Can Enable Thought.* Ames, Iowa: Culicidae Press, LLC., 2012.

Roodbergen, K. J., and I. F. A. Vis. "A Model for Warehouse Layout." *IIE Transactions* 38, no. 10 (October 2006): 799–811.

Stanowy, A. "Evolutionary Strategy for Manufacturing Cell Design." *Omega* 34, no. 1 (January 2006): 1.

Taghavi, A., and A. Murat. "A Heuristic Procedure for the Integrated Facility Layout Design and Flow Assignment Problem." *Computers & Industrial Engineering* 61, no. 1 (August 2011): 55–63.

Tompkins, James A. *Facility Planning*, 4th ed. New York: Wiley, 2009.

Upton, David. "What Really Makes Factories Flexible?" *Harvard Business Review* 73, no. 4 (July–August 1995): 74–84.

Zhao, T., and C. L. Tseng. "Flexible Facility Interior Layout." *The Journal of the Operational Research Society* 58, no. 6 (June 2007): 729–740.

Chapter 10

Aft, Larry, and Neil Schmeidler. "Work Measurement Practices." *Industrial Engineer* 35, no. 11 (November 2003): 44.

Barnes, R. M. *Motion and Time Study, Design and Measurement of Work*, 7th ed. New York: Wiley, 1980.

Bridger, R. S. *Introduction to Ergonomics*, 3rd ed. New York: CRC Press, 2008.

De Jong, A., K. De Ruyter, and J. Lemmink. "Service Climate in Self-Managing Teams." *The Journal of Management Studies* 42, no. 8 (December 2005): 1593.

Freivalds, Andris, and B. W. Niebel. *Methods, Standards, and Work Design*, 12th ed. New York: Irwin/McGraw-Hill, 2009.

Huselid, Mark A., Richard W. Beatty, and Brian E. Becker. "'A Players' or 'A Positions'? The Strategic Logic of Workforce Management." *Harvard Business Review* (December 2005): 110–117.

Konz, S., and Steven Johnson. *Work Design: Industrial Ergonomics*, 7th ed. Scottsdale, AZ: Holcomb Hathaway, 2007.

Muthusamy, S. K., J. V. Wheeler, and B. L. Simmons. "Self-Managing Work Teams." *Organization Development Journal* 23, no. 3 (Fall 2005): 53–66.

Pfeffer, Jeffrey. "Producing Sustainable Competitive Advantage Through the Effective Management of People." *Academy of Management Executive* 19, no. 4 (2005): 95.

Salvendy, G., ed. *Handbook of Human Factors and Ergonomics*, 3rd ed. New York: Wiley, 2006.

Shahrokh, Shahraki, and N. A. Bakar. "Relationship Between Human Factors Engineering and Productivity." *Interdisciplinary Journal of Contemporary Research in Business* 3, no. 3 (July 2011): 706–712.

Sonne, Michael, D. L. Villalta, and D. M. Andrews. "Development and Evaluation of an Office Ergonomic Risk Check List." *Applied Ergonomics* 43, no. 1 (January 2012): 98–100.

Tolo, B. "21st-Century Stopwatch." *Industrial Engineer* 37, no. 7 (July 2005): 34–37.

Village, Judy, Patrick W. Neumann. "Designing for Human Factors." *Industrial Engineer: IE* 46, no. 11 (November 2014): 36–41.

Walsh, Ellen. "Get Results with Workload Management." *Nursing Management* (October 2003): 16.

White, Catherine M. "Proactive Ergonomics." *Professional Safety* 60, no. 6 (June 2015): 69–73.

Chapter 11

Autry, Chad W., Thomas J. Goldsby, and John E. Bell. *Global Macrotrends and Their Impact on Supply Chain Management.* Upper Saddle River, NJ: FT Press, 2013.

Blackburn, Joseph, and Gary Scudder. "Supply Chain Strategies for Perishable Products." *Production and Operations Management* 18, no. 2 (March–April 2009): 129–137.

Boyer, Kenneth K., and G. Tomas M. Hult. "Extending the Supply Chain: Integrating Operations and Marketing in the Online Grocery Industry." *Journal of Operations Management* 23, no. 6 (September 2005): 642–661.

Chopra, Sunil, and Peter Meindl. *Supply Chain Management*, 4th ed. Upper Saddle River, NJ: Prentice Hall (2010).

Crandall, Richard E. "The Next Wave of Sourcing." *APICS* 24, no. 3 (May/June 2014): 26–28.

Crook, T. Russell, and James G. Combs. "Sources and Consequences of Bargaining Power in Supply Chains." *Journal of Operations Management* 25, no. 2 (March 2007): 546–555.

Hu, J., and C. L. Munson. "Speed versus Reliability Trade-offs in Supplier Selection." *International Journal Procurement Management* 1, no. 1/2 (2007): 238–259.

Kersten, Wolfgang, and Thorsten Blecker (eds.). *Managing Risk in Supply Chains*. Berlin: Erich Schmidt Verlag GmbH & Co. (2006).

Kreipl, Stephan, and Michael Pinedo. "Planning and Scheduling in Supply Chains." *Production and Operations Management* 13, no. 1 (Spring 2004): 77–92.

Linton, J. D., R. Klassen, and V. Jayaraman. "Sustainable Supply Chains: An Introduction." *Journal of Operations Management* 25, no. 6 (November, 2007): 1075–1082.

Monczka, R. M., R. B. Handfield, L. C. Gianipero, and J. L. Patterson. *Purchasing and Supply Chain Management*, 5th ed. Mason, OH: Cengage, 2012.

Munson, Chuck (ed.). *The Supply Chain Management Casebook: Comprehensive Coverage and Best Practices in SCM*. Upper Saddle River, NJ: FT Press, 2013.

Narayanan, Sriram, Ann S. Marucheck, and Robert B. Handfield. "Electronic Data Interchange: Research Review and Future Directions." *Decisions Sciences* 40, no. 1 (February 2009): 121–163.

Paine, Lincoln. *The Sea and Civilization.* New York: Knopf, 2013.

Pisano, Gary P., and Roberto Verganti. "Which Kind of Collaboration Is Right for You?" *Harvard Business Review* 86, no. 12 (December, 2008): 78–86.

Sinha, K. K., and E. J. Kohnke. "Health Care Supply Chain Design." *Decision Sciences* 40, no. 2 (May 2009): 197–212.

Stanley, L. L., and V. R. Singhal. "Service Quality Along the Supply Chain." *Journal of Operations Management* 19, no. 3 (May 2001): 287–306.

Wisner, Joel, K. Tan, and G. Keong Leong. *Principles of Supply Chain Management,* 4th ed., Mason, OH: Cengage, 2012.

Yang, Shilei, Charles L. Munson, Bintong Chen, and Chunming Shi. "Coordinated Contracts for Supply Chains that Market with Mail-In Rebates and Retailer Promotions." *Journal of the Operational Research Society* (2015), DOI: JORS.2014.127.

Supplement 11

Berger, Paul D., Arthur Gerstenfeld, and Amy Z. Zeng. "How Many Suppliers Are Best? A Decision-Analysis Approach." *Omega* 32, no. 1 (February 2004): 9–15.

Chopra, Sunil, and Peter Meindl. *Supply Chain Management,* 4th ed. Upper Saddle River, NJ: Prentice Hall, 2010.

Disney, Stephen M., and Marc R. Lambrecht. "On Replenishment Rules, Forecasting, and the Bullwhip Effect in Supply Chains." *Foundations and Trends in Technology, Information and Operations Management* 2, no. 1 (2007), 1–80.

Lee, Chieh, and Charles L. Munson. "A Predictive Global Sensitivity Analysis Approach to Monitoring and Modifying Operational Hedging Positions." *International Journal of Integrated Supply Management* 9, no. 3 (2015): 178–201.

Roodbergen, Kees Jan, Iris FA Vis, and G. Don Taylor Jr. "Simultaneous Determination of Warehouse Layout and Control Policies." *International Journal of Production Research* 53, no. 11 (2015): 3306–3326.

Wang, Phanich P., S. Kara, and B. Kayis. "Analysis of the Bullwhip Effect in Multi-product, Multi-stage Supply Chain Systems—A Simulation Approach." *International Journal of Production Research* 48, no. 15 (August 2010): 4501–4517.

Chapter 12

Abernathy, Frederick H., et al. "Control Your Inventory in a World of Lean Retailing." *Harvard Business Review* 78, no. 6 (November–December 2000): 169–176.

Arnold, J. R., S. N. Chapman, and L. M. Clive. *Introduction to Materials Management*, 6th ed. Upper Saddle River, NJ: Prentice Hall, 2008.

Baron, Opher, O. Derman, and D. Perry. "Shelf Space Management When Demand Depends on the Inventory Level." *Production and Operations Management* 20, no. 5 (September–October 2011): 714–726.

Burt, D. N., S. Petcavage, and R. Pinkerton. *Supply Management*, 8th ed. Burr Ridge, IL: Irwin/McGraw, 2010.

Chapman, Stephen. *Fundamentals of Production Planning and Control*. Upper Saddle River, NJ: Prentice Hall, 2006.

Chopra, Sunil, Gilles Reinhardt, and Maqbool Dada. "The Effect of Lead Time Uncertainty on Safety Stocks." *Decision Sciences* 35, no. 1 (Winter 2004): 1–24.

Doğru, Mustafa K., and Ulaş Özen. "Tactical Inventory Planning at Alcatel-Lucent's Repair and Exchange Services." *Interfaces* 45, no. 3 (May–June 2015): 228–242.

Geismar, H. N., M. Dawande, and C. Sriskandarajah. "Pool-Point Distribution of Zero-Inventory Products." *Production and Operations Management* 20, no. 5 (September–October 2011): 737–753.

Harris, Chris and Thomas Parker. "Portion Control." *APICS* 24, no. 5 (September/October 2014): 26–28.

Keren, Baruch. "The Single Period Inventory Model." *Omega* 37, no. 4 (August 2009): 801.

Lee, H., and O. Ozer. "Unlocking the Value of RFID." *Production and Operations Management* 16, no. 1 (2007): 40–64.

Liu, X., and Z. Lian. "Cost-effective Inventory Control in a Value-added Manufacturing System." *European Journal of Operational Research* 196, no. 2 (July 2009): 534.

McDonald, Stan C. *Materials Management*. New York: Wiley, 2009.

Munson, Charles L., and Jonathan Jackson. "Quantity Discounts: An Overview and Practical Guide for Buyers and Sellers." *Foundations and Trends in Technology, Information and Operations Management* 8, nos. 1–2 (2014): 1–130.

Render, B., R. M. Stair, and M. Hanna. *Quantitative Analysis for Management*, 11th ed. Upper Saddle River, NJ: Prentice Hall, 2012.

Rubin, Paul A., and W. C. Benton. "A Generalized Framework for Quantity Discount Pricing Schedules." *Decision Sciences* 34, no. 1 (Winter 2003): 173–188.

Sethi, Suresh P. "i3: Incomplete Inventory Models." *Decision Line* (October 2010): 16–19.

Stein, Andrew C. "Warehouse Measurement and Control." *APICS* 24, no. 3 (May/June 2014): 42–45.

Teunter, Ruud H., M. Z. Babai, and A. A. Syntetos. "ABC Classification: Service Levels and Inventory Cost." *Production and Operations Management* 19, no. 3 (May–June 2010): 343–352.

Vollmann, T. E., W. L. Berry, D. C. Whybark, and F. R. Jacobs. *Manufacturing Planning and Control for Supply Chain Management*, 5th ed. Burr Ridge, IL: Irwin/McGraw, 2005.

Witt, Clyde E. "Mobile Warehouse Supplies U.S. Marines in Iraq." *Material Handling Management* 60, no. 8 (August 2005): 24–25.

Chapter 13

APICS. *2011 Sales and Operations Planning Practices and Challenges*. Chicago: APICS, 2011.

Bilginer, Özlem, and Feryal Erhun. "Production and Sales Planning in Capacitated New Product Introductions." *Production and Operations Management* 24, no. 1 (January 2015): 42–53.

Buxey, G. "Aggregate Planning for Seasonal Demand." *International Journal of Operations & Production Management* 25, no. 11 (2005): 1083–1100.

Chen, Fangruo. "Salesforce Initiative, Market Information, and Production/Inventory Planning." *Management Science* 51, no. 1 (January 2005): 60–75.

Chen, Ming, and Zhi-Long Chen. "Recent Developments in Dynamic Pricing Research: Multiple Products, Competition, and Limited Demand Information." *Production and Operations Management* 24, no. 5 (May 2015): 704–731.

Jacobs, F. R., W. L. Berry, D. C. Whybark, and T. E. Vollmann. *Manufacturing Planning and Control for Supply Chain Management*, 6th ed. Burr Ridge, IL: Irwin, 2011.

Kin, S., and S. Yoo. "The Combined Manpower Planning Strategies by Aggregate Planning for the Service Division of Vending Machines." *Journal of the Operational Research Society* 62 (November 2011).

Kimes, S. E., and G. M. Thompson. "Restaurant Revenue Management at Chevy's." *Decision Sciences* 35, no. 3 (Summer 2004): 371–393.

Metters, R., K. King-Metters, M. Pullman, and S. Walton. *Successful Service Operations Management*. 2nd ed. Mason, OH: Thomson-South-Western, 2006.

Metters, Richard, et al. "The 'Killer Application' of Revenue Management: Harrah's Cherokee Casino and Hotel." *Interfaces* 38, no. 3 (May–June 2008): 161–178.

Mukhopadhyay, S., S. Samaddar, and G. Colville. "Improving Revenue Management Decision Making for Airlines." *Decision Science* 38, no. 2 (May 2007): 309–327.

Sillekens, Thomas, A. Koberstein, and L. Suhl, "Aggregate Production Planning in the Automotive Industry with Special Consideration of Workforce Flexibility." *International Journal of Production Research* 49, no. 17 (September 2011): 5055–5078.

Silver, E. A., D. F. Pyke, and R. Peterson. *Inventory Management and Production Planning and Scheduling*. New York: Wiley, 1998.

Chapter 14

Barba-Gutierrez, Y., B. Adenso-Diaz, and S. M. Gupta. "Lot Sizing in Reverse MRP for Scheduling Disassembly." *International Journal of Production Economics* 111, no. 2 (February 2008): 741.

Bell, Steve. "Time Fence Secrets." *APICS* 16, no. 4 (April 2006): 44–48.

Bolander, Steven, and Sam G. Taylor. "Scheduling Techniques: A Comparison of Logic." *Production and Inventory Management Journal* 41, no. 1 (1st Quarter 2000): 1–5.

Crandall, Richard E. "The Epic Life of ERP." *APICS* 16, no. 2 (February 2006): 17–19.

De Mathis J. J. "An Economic Lot-Sizing Technique: The Part-Period Algorithms." *IBM Systems Jounnal* 7 (1968): 30–38.

Diehl Gregory W., and A. J. Armstrong "Making MRP Work." *Industrial Engineer* 43, no. 11 (November 2011): 35–40.

Kanet, J., and V. Sridharan. "The Value of Using Scheduling Information in Planning Material Requirements." *Decision Sciences* 29, no. 2 (Spring 1998): 479–498.

Krupp, James A. G. "Integrating Kanban and MRP to Reduce Lead Time." *Production and Inventory Management Journal* 43, no. 3–4 (3rd/4th quarter 2002): 78–82.

Louly, Mohamed-Aly, and A. Dolgui. "Optimal Time Phasing and Periodicity for MRP with POQ Policy." *International Journal of Production Economics* 131, no. 1 (May 2011): 76.

Norris, G. *E-Business & ERP*. New York: Wiley, 2005.

O'Sullivan, Jill, and Gene Caiola. *Enterprise Resource Planning*, 2nd ed. New York: McGraw-Hill, 2008.

Segerstedt, A. "Master Production Scheduling and a Comparison of MRP and Cover-Time Planning." *International Journal of Production Research* 44, no. 18–19 (September 2006): 3585.

Steger-Jensen, Kenn, H. Hvolby, P. Nielsen, and I. Nielson. "Advanced Planning and Scheduling Technology." *Production Planning and Control* 22, no. 8 (December 2011): 800–808.

Summer, M. *Enterprise Resource Planning*. Upper Saddle River, NJ: Prentice Hall, 2005.

Tian, Feng, and Sean Xin Xu. "How do Enterprise Resource Planning Systems Affect Firm Risk? Post-Implementation Impact." *MIS Quarterly* 39, no. 1 (March 2015): 39–60.

Turbide, Dave. "New-Fashioned MRP." *APICS* 24, no. 3 (July/August 2015): 40–44.

Wagner, H. M., and T. M. Whitin. "Dynamic Version of the Economic Lot Size Model." *Management Science* 5, no. 1 (1958): 89–96.

Wu, Jen-Hur, et al. "Using Multiple Variables Decision-Making Analysis for ERP Selection." *International Journal of Manufacturing Technology and Management* 18, no. 2 (2009): 228.

Chapter 15

Baker, Kenneth A., and Dan Trietsch. *Principles of Sequencing and Scheduling.* New York: Wiley, 2009.

Cayirli, Tugba, and Emre Veral. "Outpatient Scheduling in Health Care: A Review of Literature." *Production and Operations Management* 12, no. 4 (Winter 2003): 519–549.

Chapman, Stephen. *Fundamentals of Production Planning and Control.* Upper Saddle River, NJ: Prentice Hall, 2006.

Deng, Honghui, Q. Wang, G. K. Leong, and S. X. Sun. "Usage of Opportunity Cost to Maximize Performance in Revenue Management." *Decision Sciences* 38, no. 4 (November 2008): 737–758.

Dietrich, Brenda, G. A. Paleologo, and L. Wynter. "Revenue Management in Business Services." *Production and Operations Management* 17, no. 4 (July–August 2008): 475–480.

Farmer, Adam, Jeffrey S. Smith, and Luke T. Miller. "Scheduling Umpire Crews for Professional Tennis Tournaments." *Interfaces* 37, no. 2 (March–April 2007): 187–196.

Kellogg, Deborah L., and Steven Walczak. "Nurse Scheduling." *Interfaces* 37, no. 4 (July–August 2007): 355–369.

Lopez, P., and F. Roubellat. *Production Scheduling.* New York: Wiley, 2008.

Mondschein, S. V., and G. Y. Weintraub. "Appointment Policies in Service Operations." *Production and Operations Management* 12, no. 2 (Summer 2003): 266–286.

Morton, Thomas E., and David W. Pentico. *Heuristic Scheduling Systems.* New York: Wiley, 1993.

Pinedo, M. *Scheduling: Theory, Algorithms, and Systems*, 2nd ed. Upper Saddle River, N.J.: Prentice Hall, 2002.

Plenert, Gerhard, and Bill Kirchmier. *Finite Capacity Scheduling.* New York: Wiley, 2000.

Render, B., R. M. Stair, and M. Hanna. *Quantitative Analysis for Management*, 11th ed. Upper Saddle River, NJ: Prentice Hall, 2012.

Robidoux, L., and P. Donnelly. "Automated Employee Scheduling." *Nursing Management* 42, no. 12 (December 2011): 41–43.

Veeraraghavan, S., and R. Vaidyanathan. "Measuring Seat Value in Stadiums and Theatres." *Production and Operations Management* 21, no. 1 (January–February 2012): 49–68.

Chapter 16

Black, I. T., and D. T. Phillips. "The Lean to Green Evolution." *Industrial Engineer* 42, no. 6 (June 2010): 46–51.

Flinchbauh, Jamie. *The Hitchhiker's Guide to Lean.* Dearborn, MI: Society of Manufacturing Engineers, 2006.

Graban, Mark. *Lean Hospitals.* 2nd ed. New York: CRC Press, 2012.

Hall, Robert W. "'Lean' and the Toyota Production System." *Target* 20, no. 3 (3rd Issue 2004): 22–27.

Keyte, Beau, and Drew Locher. *The Complete Lean Enterprise.* University Park, IL: Productivity Press, 2004.

Morgan, James M., and Jeffrey K. Liker. *The Toyota Product Development System.* New York: Productivity Press, 2007.

Nelson-Peterson, Dana L., and Carol J. Leppa, "Creating an Environment of Caring Using Lean Principles of the Virginia Mason Production System." *Journal of Nursing Administration* 37 (2007): 289.

Parks, Charles M. "The Bare Necessities of Lean." *Industrial Engineer* 35, no. 8 (August 2003): 39.

Radnor, Zoe J., M. Holweg, and J. Waring, "Lean in Healthcare: The Unfilled Promise?" *Social Science & Medicine* 74, no. 3 (February 2012): 364–371.

Sayre, Kim. "A Lean Introduction to Sustainability." *Industrial Engineer* 40, no. 9 (September 2008): 34.

Schonberger, Richard J. "Lean Extended." *Industrial Engineer* (December 2005): 26–31.

van Veen-Dirks, Paula. "Management Control and the Production Environment." *International Journal of Production Economics* 93 (January 8, 2005): 263.

Womack, James P., and Daniel T. Jones. "Lean Consumption." *Harvard Business Review* 83 (March 2005): 58–68.

Womack, James P., and Daniel T. Jones. *Lean Solutions: How Companies and Customers Can Create Value and Wealth Together.* New York: The Free Press, 2005.

Chapter 17

Ait-Kadi, D., J. B. Menge, and H. Kane. "Resource Assignment Model in Maintenance Activities Scheduling." *International Journal of Production Research* 49, no. 22 (November 2011): 6677–6689.

Bauer, Eric, X. Zhang, and D. A. Kimber. *Practical System Reliability.* New York: Wiley, 2009.

Blank, Ronald. *The Basics of Reliability*. University Park, IL: Productivity Press, 2004.

Finigen, Tim, and Jim Humphries. "Maintenance Gets Lean." *IE Industrial Systems* 38, no. 10 (October 2006): 26–31.

Phillippi, Brian, "3 Keys to Predictive Maintenance Success." *Flow Control* 21, no. 5 (May 2015): 7–8.

Rahman, Anisur, "Maintenance Contract Model for Complex Asset/Equipment." *International Journal of Reliability, Quality, & Safety Engineering* 21, no. 1 (February 2014): 1–11.

Stephens, M. P. *Productivity and Reliability-Based Maintenance Management.* Upper Saddle River, NJ: Prentice Hall, 2004.

Weil, Marty. "Beyond Preventive Maintenance." *APICS* 16, no. 4 (April 2006): 40–43.

Module A

Balakrishnan, R., B. Render, and R. M. Stair Jr. *Managerial Decision Modeling with Spreadsheets*, 3rd ed. Upper Saddle River, NJ: Prentice Hall, 2012.

Buchannan, Leigh, and Andrew O'Connell. "A Brief History of Decision Making." *Harvard Business Review* 84, no. 1 (January, 2006): 32–41.

Hammond, J. S., R. L. Kenney, and H. Raiffa. "The Hidden Traps in Decision Making." *Harvard Business Review* 84, no. 1 (January 2006): 118–126.

Keefer, Donald L. "Balancing Drug Safety and Efficacy for a Go/No-Go Decision." *Interfaces* 34, no. 2 (March–April 2004): 113–116.

Miller, C. C., and R. D. Ireland. "Intuition in Strategic Decision Making." *Academy of Management Executive* 19, no. 1 (February 2005): 19.

Parmigiani, G., and L. Inoue. *Decision Theory: Principles and Approaches.* New York: Wiley, 2010.

Raiffa, H., and R. Schlaifer. *Applied Statistical Decision Theory.* New York: Wiley, 2000.

Render, B., R. M. Stair Jr., and M. Hanna. *Quantitative Analysis for Management*, 11th ed. Upper Saddle River, NJ: Prentice Hall, 2012.

Module B

Anderson, Ross, et al. "Kidney Exchange and the Alliance for Paired Donation: Operations Research Changes the Way Kidneys Are Transplanted." *Interfaces* 45, no. 1 (January–February 2015), 26–42.

Balakrishman, R., B. Render, and R. M. Stair. *Managerial Decision Modeling with Spreadsheets*, 3rd ed. Upper Saddle River, NJ: Prentice Hall, 2012.

Denton, Brian T. "AusWest Timbers Uses an Optimization Model to Improve Its Manufacturing Process." *Interfaces* 38, no. 4 (July–August 2008): 341–344.

Duran, G., et al. "Scheduling the Chilean Soccer League by Integer Programming." *Interfaces* 37, no. 6 (November–December 2007): 539–555.

Harrod, Steven. "A Spreadsheet-Based, Matrix Formulation Linear Programming Lesson." *Decision Sciences Journal of Innovative Education* 7, no. 1 (January 2009): 249.

Martin, C. H. "Ohio University's College of Business Uses Integer Programming to Schedule Classes." *Interfaces* 34 (November–December 2004): 460–465.

Matthews, C. H. "Using Linear Programming to Minimize the Cost of Nurse Personnel." *Journal of Health Care Finance* (September 2005).

Pasupathy, K., and A. Medina-Borja. "Integrating Excel, Access, and Visual Basic to Deploy Performance Measurement and Evaluation at the American Red Cross." *Interfaces* 38, no. 4 (July–August 2008): 324–340.

Render, B., R. M. Stair, and Michael Hanna. *Quantitative Analysis for Management*, 11th ed. Upper Saddle River, NJ: Prentice Hall, 2012.

Sodhi, M. S., and S. Norri. "A Fast and Optimal Modeling Approach Applied to Crew Rostering at London Underground." *Annals of OR* 127 (March 2004): 259.

Taylor, Bernard. *Introduction to Management Science*, 10th ed. Upper Saddle River, NJ: Prentice Hall, 2011.

Tian, Zhili, Panos Kouvelis, and Charles L. Munson. "Understanding and Managing Product Line Complexity: Applying Sensitivity Analysis to a Large-Scale MILP Model to Price and Schedule New Customer Orders." *IIE Transactions* 47, no. 4 (2015), 307–328.

Module C

Balakrishnan, R., B. Render, and R. M. Stair. *Managerial Decision Modeling with Spreadsheets*, 3rd. ed. Upper Saddle River, NJ: Prentice Hall, 2012.

Drezner, Z. *Facility Location: A Survey of Applications and Methods*. Secaucus, NJ: Springer-Verlag, 1995.

Koksalan, M., and H. Sural. "Efes Beverage Group Makes Location and Distribution Decisions for Its Malt Plants." *Interfaces* 29 (March–April 1999): 89–103.

Ping, J., and K. F. Chu. "A Dual-Matrix Approach to the Transportation Problem." *Asia-Pacific Journal of Operations Research* 19 (May 2002): 35–46.

Render, B., R. M. Stair, and M. Hanna. *Quantitative Analysis for Management*, 11th ed. Upper Saddle River, NJ: Prentice Hall, 2012.

Schmenner, R. W. "Look Beyond the Obvious in Plant Location." *Harvard Business Review* 57, no. 1 (January–February 1979): 126–132.

Taylor, B. *Introduction to Management Science*, 10th ed., Upper Saddle River, NJ: Prentice Hall, 2011.

Module D

Balakrishnan, R., B. Render, and R. M. Stair. *Managerial Decision Modeling with Spreadsheets*, 3rd ed. Upper Saddle River, NJ: Prentice Hall, 2012.

Canonaco, P., et al. "A Queuing Network Model for the Management of Berth Crane Operations." *Computers & Operations Research* 35, no. 8 (August 2008): 2432.

Cochran, J. K., and K. Roche. "A Queueing-Based Decision Support Methodology to Estimate Hospital Inpatient Bed Demand." *Journal of the Operational Research Society* 59, no. 11 (November 2008): 1471–1483.

Gross, Donald, John F. Shortle, James M. Thompson, and Carl M. Harris. *Fundamentals of Queuing Theory*, 4th ed. New York: Wiley, 2008.

Parlar, M., and M. Sharafali. "Dynamic Allocation of Airline Check-In Counters: A Queueing Optimization Problem." *Management Science* 54, no. 8 (August 2008): 1410–1425.

Prabhu, N. U. *Foundations of Queuing Theory*. Dordecht, Netherlands: Kluwer Academic Publishers, 1997.

Render, B., R. M. Stair, and M. Hanna. *Quantitative Analysis for Management*, 11th ed. Upper Saddle River, NJ: Prentice Hall, 2012.

Stanford, D. A., E. Renouf, and V. C. McAlister. "Waiting for Liver Transplantation in Canada." *Health Care Management Science* 11, no. 2 (June 2008): 196–208.

Yan Kovic, N., and L. V. Green. "Identifying Good Nursing Levels: A Queuing Approach." *Operations Research* 59, no. 4 (July/August 2011): 942–955.

Module E

Boh, W. F., S. A. Slaughter, and J. A. Espinosa. "Learning from Experience in Software Development." *Management Science* 53, no. 8 (August 2007): 1315–1332.

Couto, J. P., and J. C. Teixeira. "Using a Linear Model for Learning Curve Effect on Highrise Floor Construction." *Construction Management & Economics* 23 (May 2005): 355.

McDonald, A., and L. Schrattenholzer. "Learning Curves and Technology Assessment." *International Journal of Technology Management* 23 (2002): 718.

Morrison, J. Bradley. "Putting the Learning Curve into Context." *Journal of Business Research* 61, no. 1 (November 2008): 1182.

Ngwenyama, O., A. Guergachi, and T. McLaren. "Using the Learning Curve to Maximize IT Productivity." *International Journal of Production Economics* 105, no. 2 (February 2007): 524.

Smunt, T. L., and C. A. Watts. "Improving Operations Planning with Learning Curves." *Journal of Operations Management* 21 (January 2003): 93.

Weston, M. *Learning Curves*. New York: Crown Publishing, 2000.

Module F

Balakrishnan, R., B. Render, and R. M. Stair. *Managerial Decision Modeling with Spreadsheets,* 3rd ed. Upper Saddle River, NJ: Prentice Hall, 2012.

Banks, Jerry, and Randall R. Gibson. "The ABC's of Simulation Practice." *Analytics* (Spring 2009): 16–23.

Banks, J., J. S. Carson, B. L. Nelson, and D. M. Nicol. *Discrete-Event System Simulation*, 5th ed. Upper Saddle River, NJ: Prentice Hall, 2010.

Huang, H. C., et al. "Sim Man—A Simulation Model for Workforce Capacity Planning." *Computers & Operations Research* 196, no. 3 (August 1, 2009): 1147.

Kelton, W. D., R. P. Sadowski, and N. B. Swets, *Simulation with Arena*, 5th ed. New York: McGraw-Hill, 2010.

Klassen, K., and R. Yoogalingam. "Improving Performance in Outpatient Appointment Services with a Simulation Optimization Approach." *Production and Operations Management* 18, no. 4 (2009): 447–458.

Render, B., R. M. Stair, and M. Hanna. *Quantitative Analysis for Management*, 11th ed. Upper Saddle River, NJ: Prentice Hall, 2012.

Rossetti, Manuel D. *Simulation Modeling and ARENA*. New York: Wiley, 2009.

Saltzman, Robert M., and Vijay Mehrotra. "A Call Center Uses Simulation to Drive Strategic Change." *Interfaces* 31, no. 3 (May–June 2001): 87–101.

Sud, V. P., et al. "Reducing Flight Delays Through Better Traffic Management." *Interfaces* 39, no. 1 (January/February 2009): 35–51.

Taylor, S. J .E., et al. "Simulation Modelling Is 50." *The Journal of the Operational Research Society* 60, no. S1 (May 2009): S69–S13.

Zhang, Aheng, and Xiaolan Xie. "Simulation-based Optimization for Surgery Appointment Scheduling of Multiple Operating Rooms." *IIE Transactions* 47, no. 9 (September 2015): 998–1012.